国际文化遗产保护文件
《实施世界遗产公约操作指南》选辑

（1997年、2005年、2015年）

西安市文物保护考古研究院
联合国教科文组织世界遗产中心
国际古迹遗址理事会
国际古迹遗址理事会西安国际保护中心
编译

文物出版社

图书在版编目（CIP）数据

国际文化遗产保护文件《实施世界遗产公约操作指南》
选辑：汉英对照 / 西安市文物保护考古研究院等编译
. -- 北京：文物出版社，2023.5
　　ISBN 978-7-5010-8003-8

　　Ⅰ.①国…　Ⅱ.①西…　Ⅲ.①文化遗产—保护—公约
—世界—汉、英　Ⅳ.① F591

　　中国国家版本馆 CIP 数据核字（2023）第 048645 号

国际文化遗产保护文件《实施世界遗产公约操作指南》选辑

编　　译：西安市文物保护考古研究院
　　　　　联合国教科文组织世界遗产中心
　　　　　国际古迹遗址理事会
　　　　　国际古迹遗址理事会西安国际保护中心

策划编辑：李　睿
责任编辑：吕　游
封面设计：王文娴
责任印制：王　芳

出版发行：文物出版社
社　　址：北京市东城区东直门内北小街 2 号楼
邮　　编：100007
网　　址：http://www.wenwu.com
经　　销：新华书店
印　　刷：宝蕾元仁浩（天津）印刷有限公司
开　　本：889mm×1194mm　1/16
印　　张：55.5
版　　次：2023 年 5 月第 1 版
印　　次：2023 年 5 月第 1 次印刷
书　　号：ISBN 978-7-5010-8003-8
定　　价：680.00 元（全二册）

国际文化遗产保护文件
《实施世界遗产公约操作指南》选辑

编委会

主　编：冯　健　姜　波　陶　亮

校　译：曹婼婧　孙　超　李同仙　周剑虹　李　燕

翻　译：（按姓氏拼音排列）

李同仙　李　丹　李丹丹　李尔吾　李娜宁

李文博　李　燕　李潇潇　巩　天　刘一思

石雪晨　徐　森　姚　逊　赵　戈　张竞秋

张　良　周剑虹　周晓晨　祝艺苗

目　录

◎ 2015

CONTENTS

◎ 2015

WHC-9712

February 1997

WHC-9712

1997年2月

联合国教科文组织
《实施〈保护世界文化与自然遗产公约〉操作指南》（1997）
The Operational Guidelines for
the Implementation of the World Heritage Convention

Table of Contents	目录

Ⅲ.ESTABLISHMENT OF THE LIST OF WORLD HERITAGE IN DANGER	**Ⅲ.设立《濒危世界遗产名录》**
A.Guidelines for the inclusion of properties in the List of World Heritage in Danger	A.遗产列入《濒危世界遗产名录》指南
B.Criteria for the inclusion of properties in the List of World Heritage in Danger	B.列入《濒危世界遗产名录》的标准
C.Procedure for the inclusion of properties in the List of World Heritage in Danger	C.列入《濒危世界遗产名录》的程序
Ⅳ. INTERNATIONAL ASSISTANCE	**Ⅳ.国际援助**
A.Different forms of assistance available under the World Heritage Fund	A.世界遗产基金提供的援助
(i)Preparatory assistance	（ⅰ）筹备性援助
(ii)Emergency assistance	（ⅱ）紧急援助
(iii)Training	（ⅲ）培训
(iv)Technical co-operation	（ⅳ）技术合作
(v)Assistance for promotional activities	（ⅴ）促进活动的援助
B.Deadlines for presentation of requests for international assistance for consideration by the Bureau and the Committee	B.提交国际援助的申请供主席团和委员会审议的截止日期
C.Order of priorities for the granting of international assistance	C.提供国际援助的优先次序
D.Agreement to be concluded with States receiving international assistance	D.与接受国际援助的国家签订协议
E.Implementation of projects	E.项目实施
F.Conditions for the granting of international assistance	F.提供国际援助的条件
Ⅴ.WORLD HERITAGE FUND	**Ⅴ.世界遗产基金**
Ⅵ. BALANCE BETWEEN THE CULTURAL AND THE NATURAL HERITAGE IN THE IMPLEMENTATION OF THE CONVENTION	**Ⅵ.在实施《公约》中保持文化和自然遗产平衡**
Ⅶ. OTHER MATTERS	**Ⅶ.其他事项**
A.Use of the World Heritage Emblem and the name,symbol or depiction of World Heritage sites	A.使用世界遗产标识和世界遗产地的名称、符号或描述

B.Production of plaques to commemorate the inclusion of properties in the World Heritage List

C.Rules of Procedure of the Committee

D.Meetings of the World Heritage Committee

E.Meetings of the Bureau of the World Heritage Committee

F.Participation of experts from developing countries

G.Publications of the World Heritage List

H.Action at the national level to promote a greater awareness of the activities undertaken under the Convention

Ⅰ.Links with other Conventions and Recommendations

B.制作遗产列入《世界遗产名录》的纪念牌

C.委员会议事规则

D.世界遗产委员会会议

E.世界遗产委员会执行局

F.来自发展中国家的专家参与

G.《世界遗产名录》出版物

H.在国家层面根据《公约》开展活动，提高对《公约》的认识

Ⅰ.与其他公约和建议的关联

INTRODUCTION

1.The cultural heritage and the natural heritage are among the priceless and irreplaceable possessions,not only of each nation,but of mankind as a whole.The loss, through deterioration or disappearance, of any of these most prized possessions constitutes an impoverishment of the heritage of all the peoples in the world.Parts of that heritage,because of their exceptional qualities,can be considered to be of outstanding universal value and as such worthy of special protection against the dangers which increasingly threaten them.

2.In an attempt to remedy this perilous situation and to ensure,as far as possible, the proper identification, protection, conservation and presentation of the world's irreplaceable heritage,the Member States of UNESCO adopted in 1972 the Convention concerning the Protection of the World Cultural and Natural Heritage, hereinafter referred to as "the Convention". The Convention complements heritage conservation programmes at the national level and provides for the establishment of a"World Heritage Committee"and a"World

引言

1.无论对各国还是对全人类而言，文化和自然遗产都是不可估价且无法替代的遗产。这些最珍贵的财富，一旦遭受破坏或消失，都是对世界各族人民遗产的一次浩劫。一些遗产具有独一无二的特性，因而认为其具有"突出普遍价值"，值得加以特殊的保护，以消除日益威胁遗产安全的各种危险。

2.为了尽可能保证对世界遗产的识别、保护、保存和展示，联合国教育、科学及文化组织成员国于1972年通过了《关于保护世界文化和自然遗产的公约》，以下简称《公约》。《公约》在国家层面补充了遗产保护方案，设立了世界遗产委员会和世界遗产基金，二者自1976年开始运行

Heritage Fund". Both the Committee and the Fund have been in operation since 1976.

3.The World Heritage Committee, hereinafter referred to as "the Committee", has four essential functions:

(i) to identify, on the basis of nominations submitted by States Parties, cultural and natural properties of outstanding universal value which are to be protected under the Convention and to list those properties on the "World Heritage List";

(ii)to monitor the state of conservation of properties inscribed on the World Heritage List,in liaison with the States Parties.

(iii)to decide in case of urgent need which properties included in the World Heritage List are to be inscribed on the "List of World Heritage in Danger" (only properties which require for their conservation major operations and for which assistance has been requested under the Convention can be considered);

(iv)to determine in what way and under what conditions the resources in the World Heritage Fund can most advantageously be used to assist States Parties, as far as possible, in the protection of their properties of outstanding universal value.

4.The Operational Guidelines which are set out below have been prepared for the purpose of informing States Parties to the Convention of the principles which guide the work of the Committee in establishing the World Heritage List and the List of World Heritage in Danger and in granting international assistance under the World Heritage Fund. These Guidelines also provide details on monitoring and other questions, mainly of a procedural nature, which relate to the implementation of the Convention.

5.The Committee is fully aware that its decisions must be based on considerations which are as objec-

3."世界遗产委员会"以下简称"委员会"，主要有四个基本功能；

（i）根据缔约国提交的申报，确定这些文化和自然遗产具有突出普遍价值，将其列入《世界遗产名录》以得到《公约》保护；

（ii）监督世界遗产名录上遗产的保护状况，与缔约国保存联络。

（iii）在紧急情况下把世界遗产名录》上的遗产列入《濒危世界遗产名录》。（只考虑那些按《公约》要求需进行重大保护行动、并申请紧急援助的遗产）；

（iv）决定有效利用世界遗产基金资源的具体方式和条件，尽可能协助缔约国保护其具有突出普遍价值的遗产。

4.制定如下《操作指南》的目的，是向公约缔约国提供指导委员会制定《世界遗产名录》和《世界濒危遗产名录》、以及通过世界遗产基金国际援助的原则。《操作指南》还详细说明了监测和其他问题，与执行《公约》有关的主要程序性问题。

5.委员会充分认识到，必须在尽可能客观、科学的考虑的基础上做出决定，必须彻底和负

tive and scientific as possible, and that any appraisal made on its behalf must be thoroughly and responsibly carried out. It recognizes that objective and well considered decisions depend upon:

- carefully prepared criteria,
- thorough procedures,
- evaluation by qualified experts and the use of expert referees.

The Operational Guidelines have been prepared with these objectives in mind.

I. ESTABLISHMENT OF THE WORLD HERITAGE LIST

A. General Principles

6.The Committee agreed that the following general principles would guide its work in establishing the World Heritage List:

(i) The Convention provides for the protection of those cultural and natural properties[①] deemed to be of outstanding universal value. It is not intended to provide for the protection of all properties of great interest, importance or value, but only for a select list of the most outstanding of these from an international viewpoint. The outstanding universal value of cultural and natural properties is defined by Articles 1 and 2 of the Convention. These definitions are interpreted by the Committee by using two sets of criteria: one set for cultural property and another set for natural property. The criteria and the conditions of authenticity or integrity adopted by the Committee for this purpose are set out in paragraphs 24 and 44 below.

(ii) The criteria for the inclusion of properties in the World Heritage List have been elaborated to

责任地执行代表委员会作出的任何评估。委员会认识到，客观和深思熟虑的决定取决于：

– 精心制定的标准；
– 完整的程序
– 有资质的专家评估和专家评审。

编写《操作指南》时必须考虑这些目标。

I. 设立《世界遗产名录》

A. 总则

6.委员会同意，下列一般原则将指导其制定《世界遗产名录》的工作：

（i）《公约》规定保护那些被认为具有突出普遍价值的文化和自然遗产。[①]《公约》并不是要保护所有有重大利益、重要或有价值的遗产，而是要从国际的角度选出最杰出的遗产，建立一个名录。《公约》第1条和第2条规定了文化和自然遗产的突出普遍价值。委员会用关于文化和自然遗产的两套标准来解释这些定义。委员会为此目的采用的真实性或完整性的标准和条件，见下文第24和44条。

（ii）制定了遗产列入《世界遗产名录》的标准，使委员会能够在评估遗产的内在价值时

---

①　Cf. definitions of « cultural heritage » and « natural heritage » in Articles 1 and 2 of the Convention are set out in paragraphs 23 and 43 below.

①　《公约》第1条和第2条对"文化遗产"和"自然遗产"的定义见下文第23和43段。

enable the Committee to act with full independence in evaluating the intrinsic merit of property, without regard to any other consideration (including the need for technical co-operation support).

(iii) Efforts will be made to maintain a reasonable balance between the numbers of cultural heritage and the natural heritage properties entered on the List.

(iv) Cultural and natural properties are included in the World Heritage List according to a gradual process and no formal limit is imposed either on the total number of properties included in the List or on the number of properties any individual State can submit at successive stages for inclusion therein.

(v) Inscriptions of sites shall be deferred until evidence of the full commitment of the nominating government, within its means, is demonstrated. Evidence would take the forms of relevant legislation, staffing, funding, and management plans, as described below in Paragraph 24 (b) (ii) for cultural properties, and in Paragraph 44 (b) (vi) for natural properties.

(vi) When a property has deteriorated to the extent that it has lost those characteristics which determined its inclusion in the World Heritage List, it should be placed on the World Heritage in Danger List, subsequently the procedure concerning the possible deletion from the List will be applied. This procedure is set out in paragraphs 46 to 54 below.

(vii) In view of the difficulty in handling the large numbers of cultural nominations now being received, however, the Committee invites States Parties to consider whether their cultural heritage is already well represented on the List and if so to slow down voluntarily their rate of submission of further nominations. This would help in making it possible for the List to become more universally representative. By the same token, the Committee calls on States Parties whose cultural heritage is not yet adequately represented on the List and who might need assistance in preparing nominations of

完全独立地行事，而不考虑任何其他因素（包括是否需要技术合作支持）。

（iii）尽力维持《世界遗产名录》内文化遗产与自然遗产的数目之间的合理平衡。

（iv）文化和自然遗产是逐步列入《世界遗产名录》的，对列入《世界遗产名录》的遗产总数、或任何国家申报《世界遗产名录》的遗产数量没有正式限制，各缔约国可连续在各个阶段提交申报。

（v）遗产的列入应推迟，直到有证据表明提交申报的政府在其力所能及的范围内作出了充分的承诺。将采取相关立法、人员配备、资金和管理计划的形式落实证据，如下文第24（b）（ii）条所述的文化遗产和第44条（b）（vi）所述的自然遗产。

（vi）当一项遗产衰退恶化失去其被列入《世界遗产名录》的特征时，将被列入《濒危世界遗产名录》，随后将适用可能从《名录》中删除的程序。这一程序见下文第46至54条。

（vii）然而，鉴于目前收到大量的难以处理的文化遗产申报，委员会请缔约国考虑其申报的文化遗产是否已在名录上得到充分体现，如果是，则自愿放慢提交进一步申报的速度。这将有助于使名录更具有普遍的代表性。同样，委员会呼吁那些文化遗产尚未在名录上得到充分代表、或在准备文化遗产申报方面可能需要援助的缔约国，向委员会寻求这种援助。

cultural properties to seek such assistance from the Committee.

B. Indications to States Parties concerning nominations to the List

7.The Committee requests each State Party to submit to it a tentative list of properties which it intends to nominate for inscription to the World Heritage List during the following five to ten years. This tentative list will constitute the "inventory" (provided for in Article 11 of the Convention) of the cultural and natural properties situated within the territory of each State Party and which it considers suitable for inclusion in the World Heritage List. The purpose of these tentative lists is to enable the Committee to evaluate within the widest possible context the "outstanding universal value" of each property nominated to the List. The Committee hopes that States Parties that have not yet submitted a tentative list will do so as early as possible. States Parties are reminded of the Committee's earlier decision not to consider cultural nominations unless such a list of cultural properties has been submitted.

8.In order to facilitate the work of all concerned, the Committee requests States Parties to submit their tentative lists in a standard format (see Annex 1) which provides for information under the following headings:

- the name of the property;
- the geographical location of the property;
- a brief description of the property;
- a justification of the "outstanding universal value" of the property in accordance with the criteria and conditions of authenticity or integrity set out in paragraphs 24 and 44 below, taking account of similar properties both inside and outside the boundaries of the State concerned.

Natural properties should be grouped according

B.关于缔约国申报《世界遗产名录》的说明

7.委员会请各缔约国向委员会提交一份《预备名录》，列出它打算在今后五至十年内列入《世界遗产名录》的遗产清单。《预备名录》是各缔约国认为位于领土内、并适合列入《世界遗产名录》的文化和自然遗产的"清单"（《公约》第11条规定）。这些《预备名录》的目的是使委员会能够在尽可能广泛的范围内评价列入清单的每一项遗产的"突出普遍价值"。委员会希望尚未提交《预备名录》的缔约国尽早提交。请缔约国注意委员会的早期决定，即除非提交了文化遗产清单，否则不审议文化遗产申报。

8.为了便利所有有关方面的工作，委员会请缔约国以标准格式（见附件1）提交它们的《预备名录》，规定提供下列标题下的资料：

– 遗产名称；
– 遗产的地理位置；
– 遗产的简要介绍；
– 根据下文第24和44条所述的真实性或完整性的标准和条件，说明遗产具有"突出的普遍价值"的理由，同时考虑到有关国家境内外的类似遗产。

自然遗产应按生物地理区域分类，文化遗

to biogeographical provinces and cultural properties should be grouped according to cultural periods or areas. The order in which the properties listed would be presented for inscription should also be indicated, if possible.

9.The fundamental principle stipulated in the Convention is that properties nominated must be of outstanding universal value and the properties nominated therefore should be carefully selected. The criteria and conditions of authenticity or integrity against which the Committee will evaluate properties are set out in paragraphs 24 and 44 below. Within a given geo-cultural region, it may be desirable for States Parties to make comparative assessments for the harmonization of tentative lists and nominations of cultural properties. Support for the organization of meetings for this purpose may be requested under the World Heritage Fund.

10.Each nomination should be presented in the form of a well-argued case. It should be sub-mitted on the appropriate form (see paragraph 64 below) and should provide all the information to demonstrate that the property nominated is truly of "outstanding universal value". Each nomination should be supported by all the necessary documen-tation, including suitable slides and maps and other material. With regard to cultural properties, States Parties are invited to attach to the nomination forms a brief analysis of references in world literature (e.g. reference works such as general or specialized encyclopaedias, histories of art or architecture, records of voyages and explorations, scientific reports, guidebooks, etc.) along with a comprehensive bibliography. With regard to newly-discovered properties, evidence of the attention which the discovery has received internationally would be equally helpful.

产应按文化时期或地区分类。如果可能的话，还应说明所列遗产的登记顺序。

9.《公约》规定的基本原则是，申报的遗产必须具有突出普遍价值，因此，应仔细选择申报的遗产。下文第24和44段列述了委员会评估遗产的真实性或完整性的标准和条件。在特定地理文化区域内，对缔约国的文化遗产《预备名录》和申报进行统一的比较评估，可请求世界遗产基金为组织此类会议提供援助。

10.每项申报都应以论证充分的形式提出，以适当的形式提交（见下文第64条），并应提供所有资料，以证明所申报的遗产确实具有"突出普遍价值"。每项申报都应得到所有必要文件的支持，包括适当的幻灯片、地图以及其他材料。关于文化遗产，请缔约国在申报表格中，附上对世界文学参考文献的简要分析（例如参考文献，如一般或专门的百科全书、艺术史或建筑史、航海和探险记录、科学报告、指南书、等）和综合的参考书目。对新发现的遗产，该遗产在国际上受到的关注也是同样有用的证据。

11.Under the management section of the nomination form States Parties should provide, in addition to the legal texts protecting the property being nominated, an explanation of the way in which these laws actually operate. Such an analysis is preferable to a mere enumeration or compilation of the legal texts themselves.

12.When nominating properties belonging to certain well-represented categories of cultural property the nominating State Party should provide a comparative evaluation of the property in relation to other properties of a similar type, as already required in paragraph 7 with regard to the tentative lists.

13.In certain cases it may be necessary for States Parties to consult the Secretariat and the specialized NGO concerned informally before submitting nomination forms. The Committee reminds States Parties that assistance for the purpose of preparing comprehensive and sound nominations is available to them at their request under the World Heritage Fund.

14.Participation of local people in the nomination process is essential to make them feel a shared responsibility with the State Party in the mainten-ance of the site.

15.In nominating properties to the List, States Parties are invited to keep in mind the desirability of achieving a reasonable balance between the numbers of cultural heritage and natural heritage properties included in the World Heritage List.

16.In cases where a cultural and/or natural property which fulfills the criteria adopted by the Committee extends beyond national borders the States Parties concerned are encouraged to submit a

11.对遗产申报表中的管理部分，缔约国除了提供有关保护申报遗产的法律文本外，还应解释这些法律的实际运作方式。这种分析比仅仅列举或汇编法律案文本身更可取。

12.在申报遗产属于某些代表性明确的文化遗产类别时，提交申报的缔约国应按照第7条关于《预备名录》的要求，将该遗产与其他类似遗产进行比较分析。

13.在某些情况下，缔约国在提交申报表格之前，可能需要非正式地与秘书处和相关专业非政府机构协商。委员会提醒缔约国，世界遗产基金可应缔约国的请求提供协助，以编制全面和合理的申遗文本。

14.当地民众参与申报过程至关重要，这使他们在维护该遗产地方面与缔约国共同承担责任。

15.请缔约国在申报列入《世界遗产名录》的遗产时，考虑合理平衡《世界遗产名录》中文化遗产和自然遗产的数目。

16.如果符合委员会通过的标准的文化和/或自然遗产超出某一缔约国国界，则鼓励有关缔约国提出联合申报。

joint nomination.

17.Whenever necessary for the proper conservation of a cultural or natural property nominated, an adequate "buffer zone" around a property should be provided and should be afforded the necessary protection. A buffer zone can be defined as an area surrounding the property which has restrictions placed on its use to give an added layer of protection; the area constituting the buffer zone should be determined in each case through technical studies. Details on the size, characteristics and authorized uses of a buffer zone, as well as a map indicating its precise boundaries, should be provided in the nomination file relating to the property in question.

18.In keeping with the spirit of the Convention, States Parties should as far as possible endeavour to include in their submissions properties which derive their outstanding universal value from a particularly significant combination of cultural and natural features.

19.States Parties may propose in a single nomination a series of cultural or natural properties in different geographical locations, provided that they are related because they belong to:

(i) the same historic cultural group or

(ii) the same type of property which is characteristic of the geographical zone

(iii) the same geomorphological formation, the same biogeographic province, or the same ecosystem type and provided that it is the series as such, and not its components taken individually, which is of outstanding universal value.

20.When a series of cultural or natural properties, as defined in paragraph 19 above, consists of properties situated in the territory of more than one State Party to the Convention, the States Parties concerned are encouraged to jointly submit a single nomination.

17. 为适当保护所申报的文化或自然遗产，必要时，应在遗产周围设立适当的"缓冲区"，并提供必要的保护。缓冲区可以定义为围绕遗产、对其使用加以限制、提供额外保护的区域；在任何情况下，应通过技术研究来确定缓冲区的面积。有关缓冲区的大小、特征和授权用途的详细资料，以及指明缓冲区精确边界的地图，应作为申遗文本的附件予以提供。

18. 根据《公约》的精神，缔约国应尽可能努力在其提交的材料中，列入那些因结合文化和自然特征，而具有特别重要的突出普遍价值的遗产。

19. 缔约国可在单一申报中提出一系列位于不同地理位置的、有相互关联的文化或自然遗产，因为它们属于：

（i）同一个文化群体

（ii）有同一地形特征的同类型的遗产

（iii）相同的地形地貌、相同的生物地理区、相同的生态系统类型，是整个遗产系列，而不是其单独的组成部分，具有突出普遍价值。

20. 如上文第19段所界定的一系列文化或自然遗产，由位于多个《公约》缔约国领土内的遗产点组成，则鼓励有关缔约国联合提出系列申报。

21.States Parties are encouraged to prepare plans for the management of each natural site nominated and for the safeguarding of each cultural property nominated. All information concerning these plans should be made available when technical co-operation is requested.

22.Where the intrinsic qualities of a property nominated are threatened by action of man and yet meet the criteria and the conditions of authenticity or integrity set out in paragraphs 24 and 44, an action plan outlining the corrective measures required should be submitted with the nomination file. Should the corrective measures submitted by the nominating State not be taken within the time proposed by the State, the property will be considered by the Committee for delisting in accordance with the procedure adopted by the Committee.

C. Criteria for the inclusion of cultural properties in the World Heritage List

23.The criteria for the inclusion of cultural properties in the World Heritage List should always be seen in relation to one another and should be considered in the context of the definition set out in Article 1 of the Convention which is reproduced below:

"monuments: architectural works, works of monumental sculpture and painting, elements or structures of an archaeological nature, inscriptions, cave dwellings and combinations of features, which are of outstanding universal value from the point of view of history, art or science;

-- groups of buildings: groups of separate or connected buildings which, because of their architecture, their homogeneity or their place in the landscape, are of outstanding universal value from the point of view of history, art or science;

--sites: works of man or the combined works of

21.鼓励缔约国为每一个申报的自然遗产制定管理规划，或为每一个申报的文化遗产点制定保护规划。在需要技术合作时，应提供有关这些计划的所有信息。

22.如果名录内的遗产的内在品质受到人为破坏的威胁，但又符合第24和44条所规定的真实性或完整性的标准和条件，则应随申报文件共同提交一份行动计划，概述所需纠正措施。如果申报国提交的纠正措施未在该国提议的时间内实施，委员会将按照委员会通过的程序，考虑是否将该遗产除名。

C.文化遗产列入《世界遗产名录》的标准

23.将文化遗产列入《世界遗产名录》的标准应始终相互关联，并应结合《公约》第1条中规定的定义加以考虑，该定义转载如下：

"建筑和构筑物：从历史、艺术或科学角度看具有突出普遍价值的建筑、纪念性雕塑和绘画、具有考古性质的构筑物或元素、铭文、洞窟以及综合体；

—— 建筑群：从历史、艺术或科学角度看在建筑整体性、分布均匀或与环境景色结合方面具有突出普遍价值的独立的或连接的建筑群；

—— 遗址：从历史、审美、人种学或人类学

nature and of man, and areas including archaeological sites which are of outstanding universal value from the historical, aesthetic, ethnological or anthropological points of view."

角度看具有突出普遍价值的人类作品或自然与人的共同作品及包括考古遗址的区域。"

24.A monument, group of buildings or site - as defined above - which is nominated for inclusion in the World Heritage List will be considered to be of outstanding universal value for the purpose of the Convention when the Committee finds that it meets one or more of the following criteria and the test of authenticity. Each property nominated should therefore:

24.一座纪念碑、一组建筑物或遗址 – 如上定义 – 如果委员会认为该申报遗产符合《世界遗产名录》以下一项或多项标准和真实性检验标准，将被视为具有突出普遍价值而列入《世界遗产名录》。因此，每个申报遗产都应：

(a) (i) represent a masterpiece of human creative genius; or

（a）（i）是体现人类创造精神的杰作；

(ii) exhibit an important interchange of human values, over a span of time or within a cultural area of the world, on developments in architecture or technology, monumental arts, town-planning or landscape design; or

（ii）体现一段时期内或世界某一文化区域内，人类价值观的重要交流，对建筑、技术、古迹艺术、城镇规划或景观设计的发展产生重大影响；

(iii) bear an unique or at least exceptional testimony to a cultural tradition or to a civilization which is living or which has disappeared; or

（iii）能为延续至今或业已消逝的文明或文化传统提供独特的或至少是特殊的见证；

(iv) be an outstanding example of a type of building or architectural or technological ensemble or landscape which illustrates (a) significant stage(s) in human history; or

（iv）是一种建筑、建筑学或整体技术、景观的杰出范例，展现人类历史上一个（或几个）重要阶段；

(v) be an outstanding example of a traditional human settlement or land-use which is representative of a culture (or cultures), especially when it has become vulnerable under the impact of irreversible change; or

（v）是传统人类居住地、土地使用或海洋开发的杰出范例，代表一种（或几种）文化，特别是当它面临不可逆变化的影响而变得易于损坏；

(vi) be directly or tangibly associated with events or living traditions, with ideas, or with beliefs, with artistic and literary works of outstanding universal significance (the Committee considers that this criterion should justify inclusion in the List only in exceptional circumstances and in conjunction with other criteria cultural or natural); and

（vi）与具有突出的普遍意义的事件、生活传统、观点、信仰、艺术或文学作品有直接或有形的联系。（委员会认为本标准最好与其他标准一起使用）；

(b) (i) meet the test of authenticity in design,

（b）（i）满足设计、材料、工艺或环境的真

material, workmanship or setting and in the case of cultural landscapes their distinctive character and components (the Committee stressed that reconstruction is only acceptable if it is carried out on the basis of complete and detailed documentation on the original and to no extent on conjecture).

(ii) have adequate legal and/or contractual and/or traditional protection and management mechanisms to ensure the conservation of the nominated cultural properties or cultural landscapes. The existence of protective legislation at the national, provincial or municipal level and/or a well-established contractual or traditional protection as well as of adequate management and/or planning control mechanisms is therefore essential and, as is clearly indicated in the following paragraph, must be stated clearly on the nomination form. Assurances of the effective implementation of these laws and/or contractual and/or traditional protection as well as of these management mechanisms are also expected. Furthermore, in order to preserve the integrity of cultural sites, particularly those open to large numbers of visitors, the State Party concerned should be able to provide evidence of suitable administrative arrangements to cover the management of the property, its conservation and its accessibility to the public.

25.Nominations of immovable property which are likely to become movable will not be considered.

26.With respect to groups of urban buildings, the Committee has furthermore adopted the following Guidelines concerning their inclusion in the World Heritage List.

27.Groups of urban buildings eligible for inclusion in the World Heritage List fall into three main categories, namely:

(i) towns which are no longer inhabited but

实性测试，以及，就文化景观而言，其独到之处和组成部分（委员会强调，只有在对原作的完整和详细记录的基础上进行重建，而不是根据推测进行重建，才是可以接受的）。

（ii）是否有足够的法律和/或合同和/或传统保护和管理机制，以确保申报的文化遗产或文化景观得到保护。现有保护法规，在国家、省或市层面有一个完善的合同、或传统的保护、以及足够的管理和/或规划控制机制是至关重要的，如下文所述，在申报表格必须清楚地说明。还应保证有效执行这些法律、和（或）合同保护、和（或）传统保护以及这些管理机制。此外，为了保护文化遗址的完整性，特别是那些向大量游客开放的文化遗址，有关缔约国应能够提供证据，证明其采取了适当的行政安排以保障对该遗址的管理、保护以及对公众的开放性。

25.不考虑申报有可能成为可移动文物的遗产。

26.关于城区建筑群，委员会还通过了下列关于将其列入《世界遗产名录》的准则。

27.符合列入《世界遗产名录》标准的城区建筑群包括三种类型，即：

（i）无人居住但提供了过去未被改变的考古

which provide unchanged archaeological evidence of the past; these generally satisfy the criterion of authenticity and their state of conservation can be relatively easily controlled;

(ii) historic towns which are still inhabited and which, by their very nature, have developed and will continue to develop under the influence of socio-economic and cultural change, a situation that renders the assessment of their authenticity more difficult and any conservation policy more problematical;

(iii) new towns of the twentieth century which paradoxically have something in common with both the aforementioned categories: while their original urban organization is clearly recognizable and their authenticity is undeniable, their future is unclear because their development is largely uncontrollable.

28. The evaluation of towns that are no longer inhabited does not raise any special difficulties other than those related to archaeological sites in general: the criteria which call for uniqueness or exemplary character have led to the choice of groups of buildings noteworthy for their purity of style, for the concentrations of monuments they contain and sometimes for their important historical associations. It is important for urban archaeological sites to be listed as integral units. A cluster of monuments or a small group of buildings is not adequate to suggest the multiple and complex functions of a city which has disappeared; remains of such a city should be preserved in their entirety together with their natural surroundings whenever possible.

29. In the case of inhabited historic towns the difficulties are numerous, largely owing to the fragility of their urban fabric (which has in many cases been seriously disrupted since the advent of the industrial era) and the runaway speed with which their surroundings have been urbanized. To qualify

证据的城镇，这些城镇一般符合真实性的评价标准且保护状况相对易于控制；

（ii）沿用至今的历史城镇，这些城镇在社会经济和文化的变化中不断发展并将持续发展，这种情况致使对它们真实性的评估更加困难，保护政策存在的问题也较多；

（iii）二十世纪的新镇，这类城镇与上述两种城镇都有相似之处：一方面它最初的城市组织结构仍清晰可见，其历史真实性不容置疑，另一方面它的未来是不明确的，因为它的发展基本是不可控的。

28. 对无人居住的城镇的评估除了有关的考古遗产的一般性问题，不会产生其他特殊困难：要求独特性或典范性的评价标准致使人们在选择建筑群时更关注其风格纯粹性，所含历史遗迹的集中程度，有时甚至包括与重要历史事件的关联性。列入时把城市里的文物古迹作为一个整体单位这一点很重要。几个纪念性建筑和建筑群不足以说明一个已消失城市复杂多样的功能，对于这种城市的遗迹，应尽可能地保留它们的完整性，包括它们周围的自然环境。

29. 评估尚有人居住的历史城镇困难较多，这在很大程度上是因为城市构造的脆弱性（其中大多数在工业时代到来后，发展被打乱）和其周围环境以近乎失控的速度不断被城市化。要想列入《世界遗产名录》，这些城镇的建筑价值应该得到认可，根据将文化遗产列入《世界

for inclusion, towns should compel recognition because of their architectural interest and should not be considered only on the intellectual grounds of the role they may have played in the past or their value as historical symbols under criterion (vi) for the inclusion of cultural properties in the World Heritage List (see paragraph 24 above). To be eligible for inclusion in the List, the spatial organization, structure, materials, forms and, where possible, functions of a group of buildings should essentially reflect the civilization or succession of civilizations which have prompted the nomination of the property. Four categories can be distinguished:

(i) Towns which are typical of a specific period or culture, which have been almostwholly preserved and which have remained largely unaffected by subsequent developments. Here the property to be listed is the entire town together with its surroundings, which must also be protected;

(ii) Towns that have evolved along characteristic lines and have preserved, sometimes in the midst of exceptional natural surroundings, spatial arrangements and structures that are typical of the successive stages in their history. Here the clearly defined historic part takes precedence over the contemporary environment;

(iii) "Historic centres" that cover exactly the same area as ancient towns and are now enclosed within modern cities. Here it is necessary to determine the precise limits of the property in its widest historical dimensions and to make appropriate provision for its immediate surroundings;

(iv) Sectors, areas or isolated units which, even in the residual state in which they have survived, provide coherent evidence of the character of a historic town which has disappeared. In such cases surviving areas and buildings should bear sufficient testimony to the former whole.

30.Historic centres and historic areas should

遗产名录》的标准（六），不应该仅仅依赖它们在历史中曾经的重要角色和作为历史象征的价值（参见前文第24条）。要达到列入《世界遗产名录》的要求，空间组织、结构、材料、形式，甚至建筑群的功能应从本质上反映遗产所在地区文明社会的文明和文明演进的过程。这类城镇可分为以下四类：

（ⅰ）突出代表了某一特定时期或文化的城镇，保存完整且未受到后续发展的影响。这种城镇将作为一个整体申报，其周围环境也要受到保护；

（ⅱ）城镇具有明显的演进脉络，有时在特殊的自然环境中保存了以后各个历史时期中的典型空间安排和结构的城镇。这种情况下，明确定义的历史城区比当代环境更具价值；

（ⅲ）古今城镇的分布区域几乎完全相同的"历史中心"，这种情况下，有必要在最宽泛的历史维度下，确定遗产范围并为它的周边环境制定适当的规定；

（ⅳ）城区、地域或一些孤立的城市空间单元，即使残破不堪，也为一个已消失的历史城镇的特征提供统一连贯的证明。这种情况下遗存空间和建筑蕴含的证据必须能充分见证原有整体地区。

30.只有当历史中心和历史区域包含了大量

be listed only where they contain a large number of ancient buildings of monumental importance which provide a direct indication of the characteristic features of a town of exceptional interest. Nominations of several isolated and unrelated buildings which allegedly represent, in themselves, a town whose urban fabric has ceased to be discernible, should not be encouraged.

31.However, nominations could be made regarding properties that occupy a limited space but have had a major influence on the history of town planning. In such cases, the nomination should make it clear that it is the monumental group that is to be listed and that the town is mentioned only incidentally as the place where the property is located. Similarly, if a building of clearly universal significance is located in severely degraded or insufficiently representative urban surroundings, it should, of course, be listed without any special reference to the town.

32.It is difficult to assess the quality of new towns of the twentieth century. History alone will tell which of them will best serve as examples of contemporary town planning. The examination of the files on these towns should be deferred, save under exceptional circumstances.

33.Under present conditions, preference should be given to the inclusion in the World Heritage List of small or medium-sized urban areas which are in a position to manage any potential growth, rather than the great metropolises, on which sufficiently complete information and documentation cannot readily be provided that would serve as a satisfactory basis for their inclusion in their entirety.

34.In view of the effects which the entry of a town in the World Heritage List could have on its future, such entries should be exceptional. Inclusion in the List

具有重大意义的古建筑，能直接显示一个具备极高价值的城镇的典型特征时，才可以被列入《世界遗产名录》。如只是若干孤立和毫无关联的建筑群，无法再现历史城市的原有格局，则不应申报。

31.可以申报空间有限但却对城镇规划的历史影响重大的遗产，这种情况下，需明确申报的是文物古迹，城镇只是作为其所在区域被提及。同样，如果一座具有明确的突出普遍价值的建筑坐落在已严重退化或不具有充分的代表性的城市环境中，则应被独立申报，不必专门提及城镇。

32.评定二十世纪新城镇的品质较困难。历史本身会说明哪座城镇最能代表当代城镇规划的典范。对这些城镇资料的审核可推后，某些特殊情况除外。

33.在现行条件下，《世界遗产名录》应优先选择能够控制发展的中小型城区而不是大都市，大城市也很难为其整体申报提供完整的信息和文献资料，作为满意的申报依据。

34.考虑到将一座城镇列入《世界遗产名录》对其未来发展的影响，应被视为特殊情况处理。申报列入《名录》意味着已经有相应的

implies that legislative and administrative measures have already been taken to ensure the protection of the group of buildings and its environment. Informed awareness on the part of the population concerned, without whose active participation any conservation scheme would be impractical, is also essential.

35.With respect to cultural landscapes, the Committee has furthermore adopted the following guidelines concerning their inclusion in the World Heritage List.

36.Cultural landscapes represent the "combined works of nature and of man" designated in Article 1 of the Convention. They are illustrative of the evolution of human society and settlement over time, under the influence of the physical constraints and/or opportunities presented by their natural environment and of successive social, economic and cultural forces, both external and internal.They should be selected on the basis both of their outstanding universal value and of their representativity in terms of a clearly defined geo-cultural region and also for their capacity to illustrate the essential and distinct cultural elements of such regions.

37.The term "cultural landscape" embraces a diversity of manifestations of the interaction between humankind and its natural environment.

38.Cultural landscapes often reflect specific techniques of sustainable land-use, considering the characteristics and limits of the natural environment they are established in, and a specific spiritual relation to nature. Protection of cultural landscapes can contribute to modern techniques of sustainable land-use and can maintain or enhance natural values in the landscape. The continued existence of traditional forms of land-use supports biological diversity in many regions of the world.

立法和行政手段确保对建筑群及其背景环境的保护。提高当地居民的保护意识也很重要，没有他们的积极参与，任何保护方案都是不切实际的。

35.关于将文化景观列入《世界遗产名录》，委员会进一步通过了以下指导方针。

36.《公约》第1条指出：文化景观属于文化遗产，代表着"自然与人的共同作品"。它们反映了因物质条件的限制或自然环境带来的机遇，在一系列社会、经济和文化因素的内外作用下，人类社会和定居地的历史沿革。应根据其突出的普遍价值和其在明确界定的地缘文化区域中的代表性，以及它们能够说明这些区域的基本和独特的文化因素来选择文化景观。

37."文化景观"一词包含了人类与其自然环境相互作用的多种表现形式。

38.文化景观往往反映可持续土地利用的具体技术，考虑到它们所处的自然环境的特点和环境限制，以及与自然的特定精神联系。保护文化景观可以促进可持续土地利用的现代技术，并可以保持或提高景观的自然价值。持续存在的传统的土地使用形式，支持了世界许多区域的生物多样性。因此，保护传统文化景观有助于保持生物多样性。

The protection of traditional cultural landscapes is therefore helpful in maintaining biological diversity.

39. Cultural landscapes fall into three main categories, namely:

(i) The most easily identifiable is the clearly defined landscape designed and created intentionally by man. This embraces garden and parkland landscapes constructed for aesthetic reasons which are often (but not always) associated with religious or other monumental buildings and ensembles.

(ii) The second category is the organically evolved landscape. This results from an initial social, economic, administrative, and/or religious imperative and has developed its present form by association with and in response to its natural environment. Such landscapes reflect that process of evolution in their form and component features. They fall into two sub-categories:

- a relict (or fossil) landscape is one in which an evolutionary process came to an end at some time in the past, either abruptly or over a period. Its significant distinguishing features are, however, still visible in material form.

- a continuing landscape is one which retains an active social role in contemporary society closely associated with the traditional way of life, and in which the evolutionary process is still in progress. At the same time it exhibits significant material evidence of its evolution over time.

(iii) The final category is the associative cultural landscape. The inclusion of such landscapes on the World Heritage List is justifiable by virtue of the powerful religious, artistic or cultural associations of the natural element rather than material cultural evidence, which may be insignificant or even absent.

40. The extent of a cultural landscape for inclusion on the World Heritage List is relative to its functionality and intelligibility. In any case,

39. 文化景观有三种主要的类型，即：

（i）最易识别的一类是明确定义的、人类刻意设计及创造的景观。其中包含出于美学原因建造的园林和公园景观，它们经常（但不总是）与宗教或其他纪念性建筑物或建筑群相结合。

（ii）第二类是有机演进的景观。它们产生于最初始的一种社会、经济、行政以及宗教需要，并通过与周围自然环境的联系或相适应而发展到目前的形式。这种景观反映了其形式和重要组成部分的进化过程。它们又可分为两类：

－残骸（或化石）景观，它代表过去某一时间内已经完成的进化过程，它的结束为突发性的和渐进式的。然而，它的显著特征在实物上仍清晰可见。

－另外一种是延续性景观，它在当今社会与传统生活方式的密切交融中持续扮演着一种积极的社会角色，演变过程仍在持续，同时，它也是历史演变发展的重要物证。

（iii）最后一种景观是关联性文化景观。将这一景观列入《世界遗产名录》是因为这类景观体现了强烈的与自然因素、宗教、艺术或文化的关联性，而不仅是实体的文化物证，后者对它来说并不重要，甚至是可以缺失的。

40. 文化景观列入《世界遗产名录》的范围，与它的功能和可理解性有关。在任何情况下，所选择的样本必须足够丰富，以充分代表其所

the sample selected must be substantial enough to adequately represent the totality of the cultural landscape that it illustrates. The possibility of designating long linear areas which represent culturally significant transport and communication networks should not be excluded.

41.The general criteria for conservation and management laid down in paragraph 24.(b).(ii) above are equally applicable to cultural landscapes. It is important that due attention be paid to the full range of values represented in the landscape, both cultural and natural. The nominations should be prepared in collaboration with and the full approval of local communities.

42.The existence of a category of "cultural landscape", included on the World Heritage List on the basis of the criteria set out in paragraph 24 above, does not exclude the possibility of sites of exceptional importance in relation to both cultural and natural criteria continuing to be included. In such cases, their outstanding universal significance must be justified under both sets of criteria.

D. Criteria for the inclusion of natural properties in the World Heritage List

43.In accordance with Article 2 of the Convention, the following is considered as "natural heritage": "natural features consisting of physical and biological formations or groups of such formations, which are of outstanding universal value from the aesthetic or scientific point of view; geological and physiographical formations and precisely delineated areas which constitute the habitat of threatened species of animals and plants of outstanding universal value from the point of view of science or conservation; natural sites or precisely delineated natural areas of outstanding universal value from the point of view of science,

说明的文化景观的整体。不应排除申报具有重要文化意义的运输和交流网络的线性区域的可能性。

41.上文第24（b）.（ii）条所述的保护及管理一般准则，同样适用于文化景观。重要的是，应充分注意景观中体现的各种价值，包括文化价值和自然价值。应与当地社区合作准备申报工作，并得到充分批准。

42. 依据上文第24条所列标准被列入《世界遗产名录》的"文化景观"类别，并不排除在文化和自然标准方面均具有特殊重要性的遗产后续被列入的可能性。在这种情况下，它们突出的普遍意义必须符合两套标准。

D. 自然遗产列入《世界遗产名录》的标准

43. 根据《公约》第2条，以下各项为"自然遗产"：从审美或科学角度看具有突出普遍价值的、由物理和生物结构或这类结构群组成的自然面貌；从科学或保护角度看具有突出普遍价值的地质和自然地理结构以及明确划为受威胁的动物和植物栖息地；从科学、保护或自然美角度看具有突出普遍价值的天然名胜或明确划分的自然区域。

conservation or natural beauty."

44.A natural heritage property - as defined above - which is submitted for inclusion in the World Heritage List will be considered to be of outstanding universal value for the purposes of the Convention when the Committee finds that it meets one or more of the following criteria and fulfills the conditions of integrity set out below. Sites nominated should therefore:

(a) (i) be outstanding examples representing major stages of earth's history, including the record of life, significant on-going geological processes in the development of land forms, or significant geomorphic or physiographic features; or

(ii) be outstanding examples representing significant on-going ecological and biological processes in the evolution and development of terrestrial, fresh water, coastal and marine ecosystems and communities of plants and animals; or

(iii) contain superlative natural phenomena or areas of exceptional natural beauty and aesthetic importance; or

(iv) contain the most important and significant natural habitats for in-situ conservation of biological diversity, including those containing threatened species of outstanding universal value from the point of view of science or conservation; and

(b) also fulfil the following conditions of integrity:

(i) The sites described in 44(a)(i) should contain all or most of the key interrelated and interdependent elements in their natural relationships; for example, an "ice age" area should include the snow field, the glacier itself and samples of cutting patterns, deposition and colonization (e.g. striations, moraines, pioneer stages of plant succession, etc.); in the case of volcanoes, the magmatic series should be complete and all or most of the varieties of effusive rocks and types of eruptions be represented.

44.自然遗产——如上定义——如果提交申报列入《世界遗产名录》，委员会认为其具有突出普遍价值，符合《公约》定义的下列一项或多项标准，并符合下列完整性条件。因此，提交申报的遗产应：

（a）（i）代表地球历史主要阶段的杰出案例，包括生命的记录、在地形发展过程中的重要地质过程，或重要的地貌或地貌特征；

（ii）成为代表陆地、淡水、沿海和海洋生态系统及动植物群落进化和发展的重要生态和生物过程的杰出案例；

（iii）包含最高级的自然现象或具有特别自然美和美学重要性的地区；

（iv）包含最重要及最有意义的自然生境，以便就地保存生物多样性，包括含有从科学或保育的角度来看具有突出普遍价值的濒危物种的生境；和

（b）同时满足以下真实性条件：

（i）依据44（a）（i）描述的遗产必须包括其自然关系中所有或大部分重要的相互联系、相互依存的因素。例如，"冰川期"遗址要满足完整性条件，则需包括雪地、冰河本体和凿面样本、沉积物和植物集群（例如，条痕、冰碛层及早期植物演替等）。如果是火山，则岩浆层必须完整，且能代表所有或大部分火山岩种类和喷发类型。

(ii) The sites described in 44(a)(ii) should have sufficient size and contain the necessary elements to demonstrate the key aspects of processes that are essential for the long-term conservation of the ecosystems and the biological diversity they contain; for example, an area of tropical rain forest should include a certain amount of variation in elevation above sea-level, changes in topography and soil types, patch systems and naturally regenerating patches; similarly a coral reef should include, for example, seagrass, mangrove or other adjacent ecosystems that regulate nutrient and sediment inputs into the reef.

(iii) The sites described in 44(a)(iii) should be of outstanding aesthetic value and include areas that are essential for maintaining the beauty of the site; for example, a site whose scenic values depend on a waterfall, should include adjacent catchment and downstream areas that are integrally linked to the maintenance of the aesthetic qualities of the site.

(iv) The sites described in paragraph 44(a)(iv) should contain habitats for maintaining the most diverse fauna and flora characteristic of the biographic province and ecosystems under consideration; for example, a tropical savannah should include a complete assemblage of co-evolved herbivores and plants; an island ecosystem should include habitats for maintaining endemic biota; a site containing wide-ranging species should be large enough to include the most critical habitats essential to ensure the survival of viable populations of those species; for an area containing migratory species, seasonal breeding and nesting sites, and migratory routes, wherever they are located, should be adequately protected; international conventions, e.g. the Convention of Wetlands of International Importance Especially as Waterfowl Habitat (Ramsar Convention), for ensuring the protection of habitats of migratory species of waterfowl, and other multi- and bilateral agreements could provide this assurance.

（ii）依据44（a）（ii）描述的遗产，必须具有足够的规模，且包含能够展示长期保护其内部生态系统和生物多样性的重要过程例如，热带雨林地区要满足完整性条件，需要有一定的海拔层次、多样的地形和土壤种类、群落系统和自然形成的群落；同样，珊瑚礁必须包括诸如海草、红树林和其他为珊瑚礁提供营养沉积物的临近生态系统。

（iii）依据第44（a）（iii）条描述的遗产，应具备突出的美学价值，且包括保持遗产美景所必须的关键地区。例如，某个遗产的景观价值在于瀑布，那么只有与维持遗产美景完整、关系密切的近处积水潭和下游地区也被涵盖在内，才能满足完整性条件。

（iv）依据44（a）（iv）描述的遗产，必须是对生物多样性保护至关重要的遗产。例如：热带草原需要具有完整的、共同进化的食草动物群和植物群；海岛生态系统则需要包括地方生态栖息地；包含多种物种的遗产范围必须足够大，能够包括确保这些物种生存的最重要的栖息地；如果某个地区有迁徙物种，则季节性的养育巢穴和迁徙路线，不管位于何处，都必须妥善保护。国际公约，例如，确保保护迁徙水禽物种的栖息地的《关于国际重要湿地特别是水禽栖息地的公约（拉姆萨尔公约）》，以及其他多边和双边协议，均可提供这方面的保证。

(v) The sites described in paragraph 44(a) should have a management plan. When a site does not have a management plan at the time when it is nominated for the consideration of the World Heritage Committee, the State Party concerned should indicate when such a plan will become available and how it proposes to mobilize the resources required for the preparation and implementation of the plan. The State Party should also provide other document(s) (e.g. operational plans) which will guide the management of the site until such time when a management plan is finalized.

(vi) A site described in paragraph 44(a) should have adequate long-term legislative, regulatory or institutional protection. The boundaries of that site should reflect the spatial requirements of habitats, species, processes or phenomena that provide the basis for its nomination for inscription on the World Heritage List. The boundaries should include sufficient areas immediately adjacent to the area of outstanding universal value in order to protect the site's heritage values from direct effects of human encroachment and impacts of resource use outside of the nominated area. The boundaries of the nominated site may coincide with one or more existing or proposed protected areas, such as national parks or biosphere reserves. While an existing or proposed protected area may contain several management zones, only some of those zones may satisfy criteria described in paragraph 44(a); other zones, although they may not meet the criteria set out in paragraph 44(a), may be essential for the management to ensure the integrity of the nominated site; for example, in the case of a biosphere reserve, only the core zone may meet the criteria and the conditions of integrity, although other zones, i.e. buffer and transitional zones, would be important for the conservation of the biosphere reserve in its totality.

(vii) Sites described in paragraph 44(a) should

（v）依据44（a）描述的遗产，必须有管理规划。如果遗产在向世界遗产委员会申报时还没有制定管理规划，相关缔约国应说明何时完成管理规划，以及如何调动必要资源编制和执行该规划。缔约国还应提供其他文件（例如工作计划），以便在管理规划定稿之前指导遗产地的管理工作。

（vi）依据44（a）描述的遗产，必须有长期、充分的立法、规范和机制，以确保遗产得到保护。划定的边界要反映其成为世界遗产基本条件的栖息地、物种、过程或现象的空间要求，能为其列入《世界遗产名录》提供依据。边界应包括与具有突出普遍价值紧邻的足够大的区域，以保护其遗产价值不因人类的直接侵蚀和该区域外的资源开发而受到损害。所申报遗产的边界可能会与一个或多个已存在或已建议的保护区重合，例如国家公园或自然保护区，生物圈保护区或历史保护区。虽然保护区可能包含几个管理带，但可能只有个别地带能达到44（a）所列的标准。其他区域，虽然可能不符合第44（a）条所列的标准，但对于确保管理申报遗产地的完整性，可能是必不可少的；例如，在生物圈保护区，可能只有核心区满足完整性的标准和条件，尽管其他区域，如缓冲区和过渡区，对整个生物圈保护区的保护也很重要。

（vii）依据44（a）描述的遗产，必须是对

be the most important sites for the conservation of biological diversity. Biological diversity, according to the new global Convention on Biological Diversity, means the variability among living organisms in terrestrial, marine and other aquatic ecosystems and the ecological complexes of which they are part and includes diversity within species, between species and of ecosystems. Only those sites which are the most biologically diverse are likely to meet criterion (iv) of paragraph 44 (a).

45.In principle, a site could be inscribed on the World Heritage List as long as it satisfies one of the four criteria and the relevant conditions of integrity. However, most inscribed sites have met two or more criteria. Nomination dossiers, IUCN evaluations and the final recommendations of the Committee on each inscribed site are available for consultation by States Parties which may wish to use such information as guides for identifying and elaborating nomination of sites within their own territories.

E. Procedure for the eventual deletion of properties from the World Heritage List

46.The Committee adopted the following procedure for the deletion of properties from the World Heritage List in cases:

(a) where the property has deteriorated to the extent that it has lost those characteristics which determined its inclusion in the World Heritage List; and

(b) where the intrinsic qualities of a World Heritage site were already threatened at the time of its nomination by action of man and where the necessary corrective measures as outlined by the State Party at the time, have not been taken within the time proposed.

47.When a property inscribed on the World

生物多样性保护至关重要的遗产。根据最新全球《生物多样性公约》，生物多样性是指陆地、海洋和其他水生生态系统中生物体之间的差异，以及它们所属的生态复合体，包括物种内部、物种之间和生态系统的多样性。只有那些生物多样性最丰富的场所才可能符合第44（a）（iv）条标准。

45.原则上，一处遗产只要符合四项标准中的一项以及完整性的相关条件，就可以列入《世界遗产名录》。然而，大多数列入《世界遗产名录》的遗产都符合两个或两个以上的标准。申遗文本、自然保护联盟的评价、和委员会对每一列入名录的地点的最后建议都可供各缔约国参阅，缔约国不妨利用这些资料作为指南，确定和准备本国境内遗产申报。

E. 从《世界遗产名录》中删除遗产的程序

46.在以下情况下，委员会采取下述步骤，将遗产从《世界遗产名录》中除名：

（a）遗产严重受损，丧失了其作为世界遗产的决定性特征；

（b）遗产在申报时便由于人为因素导致其内在特质受到威胁，而缔约国在规定时间内又没有采取必要的补救措施（见第116条）。

47.《世界遗产名录》内遗产严重受损，或

Heritage List has seriously deteriorated, or when the necessary corrective measures have not been taken within the time proposed, the State Party on whose territory the property is situated should so inform the Secretariat of the Committee.

48.When the Secretariat receives such information from a source other than the State Party concerned, it will, as far as possible, verify the source and the contents of the information in consultation with the State Party concerned and request its comments.

49.The Secretariat will request the competent advisory organization(s) (ICOMOS, IUCN or ICCROM) to forward comments on the information received.

50.The information received, together with the comments of the State Party and the advisory organization(s), will be brought to the attention of the Bureau of the Committee. The Bureau may take one of the following steps:

(a) it may decide that the property has not seriously deteriorated and that no further action should be taken;

(b) when the Bureau considers that the property has seriously deteriorated, but not to the extent that its restoration is impossible, it may recommend to the Committee that the property be maintained on the List, provided that the State Party takes the necessary measures to restore the property within a reasonable period of time. The Bureau may also recommend that technical co-operation be provided under the World Heritage Fund for work connected with the restoration of the property, proposing to the State Party to request such assistance, if it has not already been done;

(c) when there is evidence that the property has deteriorated to the point where it has irretrievably lost those characteristics which determined its

缔约国没有在限定的时间内采取必要的补救措施，此遗产所在缔约国应该把这种情况通知秘书处。

48.如果秘书处从缔约国之外的信息来源得到了这种信息，秘书处会与相关缔约国磋商，尽量核实信息来源与内容的可靠性，并且听取缔约国的意见。

49.秘书处将请咨询机构（国际古迹遗址理事会、世界自然保护联盟、国际文物保护与修复中心），评估所收到的信息。

50.所收到的信息，连同缔约国和相关咨询机构的意见，将提请委员会主席团注意。主席团可采取下列步骤之一：

（a）委员会认为该遗产未严重恶化，不应采取进一步行动；

（b）委员会主席团认为该遗产严重恶化，但未到不可恢复的地步，当主席团认为该遗产已严重变质，但未达到无法修复的程度时，可向委员会提出建议保留该遗产，但缔约国必须采取必要措施，在合理期限内恢复遗产。主席团还可建议利用世界遗产基金为遗产修复相关工作提供技术合作，如果缔约国尚未请求这种援助，建议缔约国在这种情况下，提出援助申请；

（c）如有证据表明遗产恶化，无可挽回地丧失当初其列入《世界遗产名录》的特征，主席团可建议委员会将该遗产遗产《世界遗产名

inclusion in the List, the Bureau may recommend that the Committee delete the property from the List; before any such recommendation is submitted to the Committee, the Secretariat will inform the State Party concerned of the Bureau's recommendation; any comments which the State Party may make with respect to the recommendation of the Bureau will be brought to the attention of the Committee, together with the Bureau's recommendation;

(d) when the information available is not sufficient to enable the Bureau to take one of the measures described in (a), (b) or (c) above, the Bureau may recommend to the Committee that the Secretariat be authorized to take the necessary action to ascertain, in consultation with the State Party concerned, the present condition of the property, the dangers to the property and the feasibility of adequately restoring the property, and to report to the Bureau on the results of its action; such measures may include the sending of a fact-finding mission or the consultation of specialists. In cases where emergency action is required, the Bureau may itself authorize the financing from the World Heritage Fund of the emergency assistance that is required.

51.The Committee will examine the recommendation of the Bureau and all the information available and will take a decision. Any such decision shall, in accordance with Article 13 (8) of the Convention, be taken by a majority of two-thirds of its members present and voting. The Committee shall not decide to delete any property unless the State Party has been consulted on the question.

52.The State Party shall be informed of the Committee's decision and public notice of this decision shall be immediately given by the Committee.

53.If the Committee's decision entails any

录》删除；在向委员会提交任何此类建议之前，秘书处将委员会的决定传达给缔约国。缔约国对主席团的建议的回应，将连同主席团的建议一并提请委员会注意。

（d）如现有资料不足以使主席团采取上文（a）、（b）或（c）项所述措施之一时，主席团可建议委员会授权秘书处采取必要行动，与有关缔约国协商，确定遗产的现状、面临的威胁和适当修复的可行性，并向主席团报告其行动的结果；这种措施可包括派遣现象调查团或与专家协商。在需要采取紧急行动时，主席团可自行授权世界遗产基金为缔约国提供所需的紧急援助资金。

51.委员会将审查主席团的建议以及所有可用信息，做出处理决定。根据《公约》第13（8）条的规定，委员会与会委员三分之二以上投票同意，该决定方能通过。在未就此事宜与缔约国协商之前，委员会不应做出把遗产除名的决定。

52.应将委员会的决定传达给缔约国，同时尽快将决定公布于世。

53.如果委员会的决定改变了目前的《世界

modification to the World Heritage List, this modification will be reflected in the next updated list that is published.

54.In adopting the above procedure, the Committee was particularly concerned that all possible measures should be taken to prevent the deletion of any property from the List and was ready to offer technical co-operation as far as possible to States Parties in this connection. Furthermore, the Committee wishes to draw the attention of States Parties to the stipulations of Article 4 of the Convention which reads as follows:

"Each State Party to this Convention recognizes that the duty of ensuring the identification, protection, conservation, presentation and transmission to future generations of the cultural and natural heritage referred to in Articles 1 and 2 and situated on its territory, belongs primarily to that State...".

55.In this connection, the Committee recommends that States Parties co-operate with the advisory bodies which have been asked by the Committee to carry out monitoring and reporting on its behalf on the progress of work undertaken for the preservation of properties inscribed on the World Heritage List.

56.The World Heritage Committee invites the States Parties to the Convention Concerning the Protection of the World Cultural and Natural Heritage to inform the Committee, through the UNESCO Secretariat, of their intention to undertake or to authorize in an area protected under the Convention major restorations or new constructions which may affect the World Heritage value of the property. Notice should be given as soon as possible (for instance, before drafting basic documents for specific projects) and before making any decisions that would be difficult to reverse, so that the Committee may assist in seeking appropriate

遗产名录》，变更内容将体现在下一期的《世界遗产名录》中。

54.在采用上述程序时，委员会特别关注的是，如何采取一切可能的措施，避免从《世界遗产名录》中删除任何遗产。因此，只要情况允许，委员会愿意向缔约国提供相关的技术合作。委员会希望各缔约国注意《公约》第4条的规定：

"本公约缔约国均认同，保证第1条和第2条中提及的、本国领土内的文化和自然遗产的确定、保护、保存、展示和传承后世主要是有关国家的责任……"

55.委员会建议缔约国与委员会指定的咨询机构合作，这些咨询机构受命代表委员会对列入《世界遗产名录》的遗产的保护工作进展，进行监督和汇报。

56.如《公约》缔约国将在受《公约》保护地区开展、或批准开展有可能影响到遗产突出普遍价值的大规模修复或建设工程，世界遗产委员会促请缔约国通过秘书处向委员会转达该意图。缔约国必须尽快（例如，在起草具体工程的基本文件之前）且在做出任何难以逆转的决定之前，发布通告，以便委员会及时帮助寻找合适的解决办法，保证继续维护遗产的突出普遍价值。

solutions to ensure that the world heritage value of the site is fully preserved.

F. Guidelines for the evaluation and examination of nominations

57.The evaluation of whether or not individual sites nominated by States Parties satisfy the criteria and the conditions of authenticity/integrity will be carried out by the International Council on Monuments and Sites (ICOMOS) for cultural properties and by the World Conservation Union (IUCN) for natural properties. In the case of nominations of cultural properties in the category of 'cultural landscapes', as appropriate, the evaluation will be carried out in consultation with the World Conservation Union (IUCN).

ICOMOS and IUCN present evaluation reports to the Bureau of the World Heritage Committee.

ICOMOS and IUCN, taking into account the decisions of the Bureau and additional information that might have been received from the nominating State Party, present a final evaluation report to the World Heritage Committee.

The report of the World Heritage Committee's session will include its decision, the criteria under which the nominated site has been inscribed, the justification of their application as well as any recommendation the Committee may wish to make on that occasion.

58.The World Heritage List should be as representative as possible of all cultural and natural properties which meet the Convention's requirement of outstanding universal value and the cultural and natural criteria and the conditions of authenticity or integrity adopted by the Committee (see paragraphs 24 to 44 above).

F. 评估和检查遗产申报的指导

57.由国际古迹遗址理事会和世界自然保护联盟评估申报遗产是否满足真实性／完整性的标准和条件。其中国际古迹遗址理事会负责评估文化遗产，世界自然保护联盟负责评估自然遗产。对于申报"文化景观"类别的文化遗产，将酌情与世界自然保护联盟协商进行评估。

国际古迹遗址理事会和世界自然保护联盟向委员会主席团呈递评估报告。

国际古迹遗址理事会和世界自然保护联盟在考虑到主席团的决定和申报缔约国提交的其他资料的情况下，向世界遗产委员会提交最终评估报告。

世界遗产委员会会议的报告将包括它的决定，符合入选标准的申报遗产、适用的理由以及委员会希望在该场合提出的任何建议。

58.《世界遗产名录》应尽可能代表符合《公约》关于具有突出普遍价值的要求、符合委员会通过的文化和自然标准、以及真实性或完整性条件的所有文化和自然遗产（见上文第24至44条）。

59.Each cultural property, including its state of preservation, should be evaluated relatively, that is, it should be compared with that of other property of the same type dating from the same period, both inside and outside the State Party's borders.

60.Each natural site should be evaluated relatively, that is, it should be compared with other sites of the same type, both inside and outside the State Party's borders, within a biogeographic province or migratory pattern.

61.Furthermore ICOMOS and IUCN should pay particular attention to the following points which relate to the evaluation and examination of nominations:

(a) both NGOs are encouraged to be as strict as possible in their evaluations;

(b) the manner of the professional evaluation carried out by ICOMOS and IUCN should be fully described when each nomination is presented;

(c) ICOMOS is requested to make comparative evaluations of properties belonging to the same type of cultural property;

(d) IUCN is requested to make comments and recommendations on the integrity and future management of each property recommended by the Bureau, during its presentation to the Committee;

(e) the NGO concerned is encouraged to present slides on the properties recommended for the World Heritage List during the preliminary discussions which take place prior to the examination of individual proposals for inscription on the List.

62.Representatives of a State Party, whether or not a member of the Committee, shall not speak to advocate the inclusion in the List of a property nominated by that State, but only to deal with a point of information in answer to a question.

59.每一项文化遗产包括保存状况，都应进行比较分析，即应将其与缔约国境内和境外同一时期的其他同类遗产进行比较。

60.每一项自然遗产都应进行比较分析，即应与缔约国境内和境外边界其他同类生物地理区、同类迁徙模式进行比较。

61.此外，国际古迹遗址理事会和世界自然保护联盟应特别注意评价和审查与申报遗产有关的下列各点：

（a）鼓励两个非政府机构尽可能严格评估；

（b）在评估每项申报时，应尽可能描述国际古迹遗址理事会和世界自然保护联盟使用的专业评估方法；

（c）要求国际古迹遗址理事会为申报的文化遗产提供与同类遗产的对比分析；

（d）要求世界自然保护联盟，向委员会介绍主席团为每一项遗产的完整性和今后的管理方面提出的评论和建议；

（e）我们鼓励有关非政府组织，在建议、审查遗产列入《世界遗产名录》的初步评估阶段，为其推荐列入《世界遗产名录》的遗产制作幻灯片进行介绍。

62.缔约国的代表，不论是否为委员会成员，均不得发言主张将其本国申报的遗产列入名录，而只能在回答问题时谈及相关信息。

63.The criteria for which a specific property is included in the World Heritage List will be set out by the Committee in its reports and publications, along with a clearly stated summary of the characteristics which justified the inclusion of the property which should be reflected in its future management.

63.委员会将在其报告和出版物中，列出将特定遗产列入《世界遗产名录》的标准，并明确说明列入该遗产的特征摘要，这些特征应反映在其未来的管理中。

G. Format and content of nominations

G.申报的格式和内容

64.The same form approved by the Committee is used for the submission of nominations of cultural and natural properties. Although it is recognized that all properties have specific characteristics, States Parties are encouraged to provide information and documentation on the following items①.

64.对文化和自然遗产的申报统一使用委员会批准的同一表格。虽然认识到所有遗产都有具体特点，但鼓励缔约国提供关于下列项目的资料和文件①。

    1.Identification of the Property

    a. Country (and State Party if different)

    b. State, Province or Region

    c. Name of Property

    d. Exact location on map and indication of geographical coordinates to the nearest second

    e. Maps and/or plans showing boundary of area proposed for inscription and of any buffer zone

    f. Area of site proposed for inscription (ha.) and proposed buffer zone (ha.) if any

    2.Justification for Inscription

    a. Statement of significance

    b. Possible comparative analysis (including state of conservation of similar sites)

    c. Authenticity/Integrity

    d. Criteria under which inscription is proposed (and justification for inscription under these criteria)

    3.Description

    a. Description of Property

    1.遗产的辨认

    a.国家（如果有不同的缔约国）；

    b. 州、省份或地区；

    c. 遗产名称；

    d.地图上的准确位置和精确到秒的地理坐标；

    e. 地图和平面图，显示申报遗产边界和缓冲区的范围；

    f.申报遗产和建议的缓冲区的面积（公顷）；

    2.列入理由

    a.价值声明

    b.比较分析（包括类似遗产的保护状况）

    c.真实性与完整性

    d.提议遗产列入所依据的标准（和根据这些标准的列入理由）

    3.遗产描述

    a.描述；

---

  ① This format was adopted by the Committee at its twentieth session in December 1996. The Committee decided to introduce this format for all nominations which shall be examined from 1st July 1998. For nominations that will be examined from 1st July 1997, use should be made of the existing form (which is available from the Secretariat as form Nº WHC.95/WS.1).

  ① 1996年12月委员会第二十次会议通过采用此表格，委员会决定自1998年7月1日起审查所有申报都使用此表格。而对于1997年7月1日前审查的申报，仍使用现有表格（可向秘书处索取表格NºWHC.95/WS.1）。

b. History and Development

c. Form and date of most recent records of site

d. Present state of conservation

e. Policies and programmes related to the presentation and promotion of the property

4.Management

a. Ownership

b. Legal status

c. Protective measures and means of implementing them

d. Agency/agencies with management authority

e. Level at which management is exercised (e.g., on site, regionally) and name and address of responsible person for contact purposes

f. Agreed plans related to property (e.g., regional, local plan, conservation plan, tourism development plan)

g. Sources and levels of finance

h. Sources of expertise and training in conservation and management techniques

i. Visitor facilities and statistics

j. Site management plan and statement of objectives (copy to be annexed)

k. Staffing levels (professional, technical, maintenance)

5.Factors Affecting the Site

a. Development Pressures (e.g., encroachment, adaptation, agriculture, mining)

b. Environmental Pressures (e.g., pollution, climate change)

c. Natural disasters and preparedness (earthquakes, floods, fires, etc.)

d. Visitor/tourism pressures

e. Number of inhabitants within site, buffer zone

f. Other

6.Monitoring

a. Key indicators for measuring state of conservation

b. Administrative arrangements for monitoring

b.历史沿革；

c.遗产地最近记录的形式和日期；

d.保护状况声明；

e.有关遗产介绍与宣传的政策及计划；

4.管理

a.所有权；

b.法律地位；

c.保护措施及执行手段；

d.管理机构；

e.执行管理者的级别（例如，现场，区域）和联系人的姓名和地址；

f.与遗产相关的、已通过的规划（比如，地区或地方规划、保护规划、旅游开发规划）；

g.资金来源和水平；

h.保护和管理技能的专业培训资源；

i.旅游参观基础设施；

j.遗产管理规划和目标说明（可作为附件）

k.人员配置水平（专业、技术、维修）

5.影响遗产的因素

a.开发压力（比如：侵占、改建、农业和采矿）；

b.环境压力（比如，污染、气候变化）；

c. 自然灾害和防灾情况（地震、洪水、火灾等）；

d. 游客和旅游压力

e. 遗产地内及缓冲区的居民人数；

f. 其他

6.监测

a.衡量保护状况的主要指标；

b. 遗产监测的行政安排；

property

  c. Results of previous reporting exercises

  7.Documentation

  a. Photographs, slides and, where available, films/viedos

  b. Copies of site management plans and extracts of other plans relevant to the site

  c. Bibliography

  d. Address where inventory, records and archives are held

  8.Signature on behalf of the State Party

  The Committee adopted at its twentieth session substantive Explanatory Notes to the above nomination form. These notes relate to each of the above headings and will be made available as an annex to the nomination form to the States Parties in order to provide guidance to those nominating properties for inclusion on the World Heritage List.

  H.Procedure and timetable for the processing of nominations

  65.The annual schedule set out below has been fixed for the receipt and processing of nominations to the World Heritage List. It should be emphasized, however, that the process of nominating properties to the World Heritage List is an ongoing one. Nominations to the List can be submitted at any time during the year. Those received by 1 July of a given year will be considered during the following year. Those received after 1 July of a given year can only be considered in the second subsequent year. Despite the inconvenience it may cause certain States Parties, the Committee has decided to bring forward the deadline for submission of nominations in order to ensure that all working documents can be made available to the Bureau as well as States members of the Committee no later than 6 weeks before the start of the sessions of the Bureau and the Committee. This will also enable the Committee

c. 前期实践报告的结果

7.文献

a.照片、幻灯片、可用视听影像材料

b.保护规划副本和其他遗产规划摘要

c. 参考书目

d. 清单、记录和档案的保存地址

8.缔约国代表签名

  委员会第二十届会议通过了对上述申报表格的实质的解释性说明。这些说明与上述每一个标题有关，将作为申报表格的附件提供给缔约国，以便为列入《世界遗产名录》的遗产申报提供指导。

H.处理申报的程序和时间表

  65.以下是接受和处理《世界遗产名录》申报的年度计划。然而，应该强调的是，申报《世界遗产名录》是一个持续的过程，可于年内任何时候提交申报。在当年7月1日之前收到的文件将在来年进行审议。在当年7月1日以后收到的申报只能在后年考虑。尽管这可能给某些缔约国带来不便，委员会决定设定每年提交遗产申报的截止日期，以确保相关缔约国可在委员会主席团会议开幕前至少6周，向委员会及主席团提交有效申报文件。这也将使委员会在其每年12月的年会上，了解到来年下一届会议上将审查的申报遗产的数目和性质。

at its annual December session to be made aware of the number and nature of nominations to be examined at its next session the following year.

1 July

Deadline for receipt by the Secretariat of nominations to be considered by the Committee the following year.

15 September

The Secretariat:

(1) registers each nomination and thoroughly verifies its contents and accompanying documentation. In the case of incomplete nominations, the Secretariat must immediately request the missing information from States Parties.

(2) transmits nominations, provided they are complete, to the appropriate international non-governmental organization (ICOMOS, IUCN or both), which: immediately examines each nomination to ascertain those cases in which additional information is required and takes the necessary steps, in co-operation with the Secretariat, to obtain the complementary data, and

By 1 April

The appropriate non-governmental organization undertakes a professional evaluation of each nomination according to the criteria adopted by the Committee. It transmits these evaluations to the Secretariat under three categories:

(a) properties which are recommended for inscription without reservation;

(b) properties which are not recommended for inscription;

(c) properties whose eligibility for inscription is not considered absolutely clear.

During April

The Secretariat checks the evaluations of the non-governmental organizations and ensures that States members of the Committee receive them by 1 May with available documentation.

7月1日

秘书处接受来年考虑的申报的截止日。

9月15日

秘书处将：

（1）秘书处对各项申报进行登记，检查提交申报的缔约国申报材料是否完整。如材料不完整，通知相关缔约国补齐所缺信息。

（2）秘书处将完整的申报材料转交相关国际性非政府机构进行评估（国际古迹遗址理事会，世界自然保护联盟），以便：立即审查每项申报，以确定哪些情况需要补充资料，并与秘书处合作，采取必要步骤，以取得补充资料，以及

至翌年4月1日

相关非政府机构根据委员会通过的标准，对每项申报进行专业评估。非政府机构转交秘书处秘书处的评估结果有三种：

a）建议无保留列入《世界遗产名录》的遗产；

b）建议不予列入《世界遗产名录》的遗产；

c）不确定是否适合列入《世界遗产名录》的遗产。

翌年4月

秘书处核查非政府机构的评估，并确保委员会成员国在5月1日前收到这些评估，以及相关文件。

June/July

The Bureau examines the nominations and makes its recommendations thereon to the Committee under the following four categories:

(a) properties which it recommends for inscription without reservation;

(b) properties which it does not recommend for inscription;

(c) properties that need to be referred back to the nominating State for further information or documentation;

(d) properties whose examination should be deferred on the ground that a more in-depth assessment or study is needed.

July-November

The report of the Bureau is transmitted by the Secretariat as soon as possible to all States Parties members of the Committee, as well as to all States Parties concerned. The Secretariat endeavours to obtain from the States Parties concerned the additional information requested on properties under category (c) above and transmits this information to ICOMOS, IUCN and States members of the Committee. If the requested information is not obtained by 1 October, the nomination will not be eligible for review by the Committee at its regular session in the same year. Nominations assigned to category (c) by the Bureau may not be examined except in the case that missing information at the time of the Bureau was factual. Nominations assigned to category (d) will not be examined by the Committee the same year.

December

The Committee examines the nominations on the basis of the Bureau's recommendations, together with any additional information provided by the States Parties concerned as well as the comments thereon of ICOMOS and IUCN. It classifies its decisions on nominated properties in the following three categories.

翌年6—7月

主席团审核申报，并向委员会提出下列四类建议：

（a）建议毫无保留地列入《名录》的遗产；

（b）建议不列入《名录》的遗产；

（c）建议发还申报缔约国，要求进一步补充信息材料的遗产；

（d）因需要更深入的评估或研究而建议推迟审核的遗产。

翌年7—11月

由秘书处尽快将委员会主席团的报告转递所有委员会成员国以及所有有关缔约国。秘书处敦促相关缔约国，尽快提供上文（c）要求进一步补充的遗产信息材料，并将这些资料转交给国际古迹遗址理事会、世界自然保护联盟和委员会成员国。如果在10月1日前未能得所要求的资料，该申报将失去在同年的委员会常会上接受审核的资格。主席团不审核（c）类的申报，但主席团认为遗漏的信息属于事实性错误的情况除外。主席团认定为（d）类申报也得不到同年的委员会常会上接受审核的资格。

12月

委员会根据主席团的建议，连同有关缔约国提供的任何补充资料，以及国际古迹遗址理事会和世界自然保护联盟对申报遗产的评估意见，审核这些申报。委员会对申报遗产的决定分为下列三类：

(a) properties which it inscribes on the World Heritage List;

(b) properties which it decides not to inscribe on the List;

(c) properties whose consideration is deferred.

January

The Secretariat forwards the report of the December session of the World Heritage Committee, which contains all the decisions taken by the Committee, to all States Parties.

66.In the event that a State Party wishes to nominate an extension to a property already inscribed on the World Heritage List, the same documentation should be provided and the same procedure shall apply as for new nominations, set out in paragraph 64 above. This provision will not apply for extensions which are simple modifications of these limits of the property in question: in this case, the request for modification of these limits is submitted directly to the Bureau which will examine in particular the relevant maps and plans. The Bureau can approve such modifications, or it may consider that the change is sufficiently important to constitute an extension of the property, in which case the procedure for new nominations will apply.

67.The normal deadlines for the submission and processing of nominations will not apply in the case of properties which, in the opinion of the Bureau, after consultation with the competent international non-governmental organization, would unquestionably meet the criteria for inclusion in the World Heritage List and which have suffered damage from disaster caused by natural events or by human activities. Such nominations will be processed on an emergency basis.

（a）决定列入《名录》的遗产；

（b）决定不列入《名录》的遗产；

（c）决定推迟审核的遗产

第三年1月

秘书处向所有缔约国传达包含世界遗产委员会所有决定的、12月会议的报告。

66.如某缔约国要求对已列入世界遗产名录的遗产边界进行扩展，应提供与上文第64条所述的、与新申报相同的文件和程序。本规定不适用于对遗产边界的细微调整：在这种情况下，这些修改边界的要求直接提交给主席团，主席团将特别审查相关的地图和规划。主席团或批准该申请，或认定边界修改过大，足以构成重大边界修改，在后一种情况下适用新申报程序。

67.提交和处理申报的正常期限，不适用于下列遗产：主席团在与相关国际非政府机构协商后认为，虽然遗产符合列入《世界遗产名录》的标准，但遭受了自然灾害或人类活动造成的破坏。此类申报将采用紧急申报程序。

II. MONITORING THE STATE OF CONSERVATION OF PROPERTIES INSCRIBED ON THE WORLD HERITAGE LIST

68.One of the essential functions of the Committee is to monitor the state of conservation of properties inscribed on the World Heritage List and to take action thereupon. In the following, a distinction will be made between systematic and reactive monitoring.

A. Systematic monitoring and reporting

69.Systematic monitoring and reporting is the continuous process of observing the conditions of World Heritage sites with periodic reporting on its state of conservation.

The objectives of systematic monitoring and reporting are:

World Heritage site: Improved site management, advanced planning, reduction of emergency and ad-hoc interventions, and reduction of costs through preventive conservation.

State Party: Improved World Heritage policies, advanced planning, improved site management and preventive conservation.

Region: Regional cooperation, regional World Heritage policies and activities better targeted to the specific needs of the region.

Committee/Secretariat: Better understanding of the conditions of the sites and of the needs on the site, national and regional levels. Improved policy and decision making.

70.It is the prime responsibility of the States Parties to put in place on-site monitoring arrangements as an integral component of day-to-day conservation and management of the sites. States Parties should do so in close collaboration with the site managers or the agency with management authority. It is necessary that every year the conditions of the site be recorded

II.《世界遗产名录》上遗产的保护状况监测

68.委员会的一项基本职能是监测列入《世界遗产名录》的遗产的保护状况，并就此采取行动。下面将分别说明系统性监测和反应性监测。

A.系统性监测和报告

69.系统性监测和报告是对世界遗产地状况的持续观察，并定期报告其保护状况。

系统性监测和报告的目标是：

世界遗产地：改进遗产管理，提前规划，减少紧急和临时性干预，通过预防性保护降低成本。

缔约国：完善世界遗产政策，提前规划，促进遗产管理和预防性保护。

区域：区域合作，更好地满足本区域内世界遗产政策和活动的具体需要。

委员会和秘书处：更好地了解遗产的状况以及国家、地区和遗产地各层面对遗产保护的需求。改进政策和决策。

70.缔约国的主要责任是安排现场监测，作为遗产地日常保护和管理的工作的组成部分。缔约国应与遗产地管理人员或具有管理权力的机构密切合作进行这项工作。遗产管理者或权威管理机构必须每年记录现场情况。

by the site manager or the agency with management authority.

71.The States Parties are invited to submit to the World Heritage Committee through the World Heritage Centre, every five years, a scientific report on the state of conservation of the World Heritage sites on their territories. To this end, the States Parties may request expert advice from the Secretariat or the advisory bodies. The Secretariat may also commission expert advice with the agreement of the States Parties.

72.To facilitate the work of the Committee and its Secretariat and to achieve greater regionalization and decentralization of World Heritage work, these reports will be examined separately by region as determined by the Committee. The World Heritage Centre will synthesize the national reports by regions. In doing so, full use will be made of the available expertise of the advisory bodies and other organizations.

73.The Committee will decide for which regions state of conservation reports should be presented to its forthcoming sessions. The States Parties concerned will be informed at least one year in advance so as to give them sufficient time to prepare the state of conservation reports.

74.The Secretariat will take the necessary measures for adequate World Heritage information collection and management, making full use, to the extent possible, of the information/documentation services of the advisory bodies and others.

B.Reactive monitoring

75.Reactive monitoring is the reporting by the World Heritage Centre, other sectors of UNESCO

71.缔约国每五年通过世界遗产中心,向世界遗产委员会提交一份关于其领土上世界遗产保护状况的科学报告。为此,缔约国可要求秘书处或咨询机构提供专家意见。经缔约国同意,秘书处也可委托专家提供咨询意见。

72.为便利委员会及其秘书处的工作,并实现世界遗产工作的区域化和分散化管理,委员会将按确定的区域分别审查这些报告。世界遗产中心将按区域汇总各国的报告。在这样做时,将充分利用各咨询机构和其他组织的现有专门知识。

73.委员会将决定向其即将召开的会议提交哪些区域的保护状况报告。并提前至少一年通知有关缔约国,使其有足够的时间编写保护状况报告。

74.秘书处将采取必要措施,充分收集和管理世界遗产资料,并尽可能充分利用咨询机构和其他机构提供的资料/文件服务。

B.反应性监测

75.反应性监测是指由秘书处、联合国教科文组织其他部门、咨询机构和主席团向委员会

and the advisory bodies to the Bureau and the Committee on the state of conservation of specific World Heritage sites that are under threat. To this end, the States Parties shall submit to the Committee through the World Heritage Centre, specific reports and impact studies each time exceptional circumstances occur or work is undertaken which may have an effect on the state of conservation of the site. Reactive monitoring is foreseen in the procedures for the eventual deletion of properties from the World Heritage List as set out in paras. 48-56. It is also foreseen in reference to properties inscribed, or to be inscribed, on the List of World Heritage in Danger as set out in paras 82-89.

III. ESTABLISHMENT OF THE LIST OF WORLD HERITAGE IN DANGER

A. Guidelines for the inclusion of properties in the List of World Heritage in Danger

76. In accordance with Article 11, paragraph 4, of the Convention, the Committee may include a property in the List of World Heritage in Danger when the following requirements are met:

(i) the property under consideration is on the World Heritage List;

(ii) the property is threatened by serious and specific danger;

(iii) major operations are necessary for the conservation of the property;

(iv) assistance under the Convention has been requested for the property; the Committee is of the view that its assistance in certain cases may most effectively be limited to messages of its concern, including the message sent by inclusion of a site on the List of World Heritage in Danger and that such assistance may be requested by any Committee member or the Secretariat.

递交的、有关具体濒危世界遗产保护状况的报告。为此，每当出现异常情况或开展可能影响遗产突出普遍价值及保护状况的活动时，缔约国都须向委员会递交具体报告和影响研究。反应性监测也涉及已列入《濒危世界遗产名录》的遗产如第48-56条所述。同时如第82-89条所述，反应性监测有助于预测已列入或即将列入《世界濒危遗产名录》的遗产点。

III. 设立《濒危世界遗产名录》

A. 列入《濒危世界遗产名录》的指导原则

76. 依照《公约》第11条第4条，当一项遗产满足以下要求时，委员会可将其列入《濒危世界遗产名录》。

（i）该遗产已列入《世界遗产名录》；

（ii）该遗产面临严重的、具体的危险；

（iii）该遗产的保护需要实施重大举措；

（iv）已依据《公约》为该遗产申请援助。委员会认为，在某些情况下对遗产表示关注并传递这一信息，可能是其所能够提供的最有效的援助手段。将遗产地列入《濒危世界遗产名录》就是这样一种信息。此类援助申请可能由委员会成员或秘书处提起。

B. Criteria for the inclusion of properties in the List of World Heritage in Danger

77.A World Heritage property - as defined in Articles 1 and 2 of the Convention - can be entered on the List of World Heritage in Danger by the Committee when it finds that the condition of the property corresponds to at least one of the criteria in either of the two cases described below.

78.In the case of cultural properties:

(i) ASCERTAINED DANGER - The property is faced with specific and proven imminent danger, such as:

(a) serious deterioration of materials;

(b) serious deterioration of structure and/or ornamental features;

(c) serious deterioration of architectural or town-planning coherence;

(d) serious deterioration of urban or rural space, or the natural environment;

(e) significant loss of historical authenticity;

(f) important loss of cultural significance.

(ii) POTENTIAL DANGER - The property is faced with threats which could have deleterious effects on its inherent characteristics. Such threats are, for example:

(a) modification of juridical status of the property diminishing the degree of its protection;

(b) lack of conservation policy;

(c) threatening effects of regional planning projects;

(d) threatening effects of town planning;

(e) outbreak or threat of armed conflict;

(f) gradual changes due to geological, climatic or other environmental factors.

79.In the case of natural properties:

(i) ASCERTAINED DANGER - The property is faced with specific and proven imminent danger,

B.列入《濒危世界遗产名录》的标准

77. 当委员会查明一项世界遗产（如《公约》第1和第2条所定义）符合以下两种情况中至少一种时，该遗产可被列入《濒危世界遗产名录》。

78.如属于文化遗产：

（i）已确知的危险 – 该遗产面临着具体的且确知即将来临的危险，例如：

（a）材料严重受损

（b）结构特征或装饰特色严重受损；

（c）建筑和城镇规划的统一性严重受损；

（4）城市或乡村空间，或自然环境严重受损；

（5）历史真实性严重丧失；

（6）文化意义严重丧失。

（ii）潜在的危险 – 该遗产面临可能会对其固有特性造成损害的威胁。此类威胁包括，如：

（a）该遗产法律地位的改变造成保护力度的削弱；

（b）缺乏保护政策；

（c）区域规划的威胁；

（d）城镇规划的威胁；

（e）武装冲突的爆发或威胁；

（f）地质、气候或其他环境因素导致的威胁。

79.如属于自然遗产：

（i）已确知的危险–该遗产面临着具体的且确知即将来临的危险，例如：

such as:

(a) A serious decline in the population of the endangered species or the other species of outstanding universal value which the property was legally established to protect, either by natural factors such as disease or by man-made factors such as poaching.

(b) Severe deterioration of the natural beauty or scientific value of the property, as by human settlement, construction of reservoirs which flood important parts of the property, industrial and agricultural development including use of pesticides and fertilizers, major public works, mining, pollution, logging, firewood collection, etc.

(c) Human encroachment on boundaries or in upstream areas which threaten the integrity of the property.

(ii) POTENTIAL DANGER - The property is faced with major threats which could have deleterious effects on its inherent characteristics. Such threats are, for example:

(a) a modification of the legal protective status of the area;

(b) planned resettlement or development projects within the property or so situated that the impacts threaten the property;

(c) outbreak or threat of armed conflict;

(d) the management plan is lacking or inadequate, or not fully implemented.

80. In addition, the factor or factors which are threatening the integrity of the property must be those which are amenable to correction by human action. In the case of cultural properties, both natural factors and man-made factors may be threatening, while in the case of natural properties, most threats will be man-made and only very rarely with a natural factor (such as an epidemic disease) be threatening to the integrity of the property. In some cases, the factors threatening the integrity of a property may be corrected by administrative or legislative action,

（a）作为确立该项遗产法定保护地位依据的濒危物种、或其他具有突出普遍价值的物种数量，由于自然因素（例如疾病）或人为因素（例如偷猎）锐减。

（b）遗产的自然美景和科学价值由于人类的定居、兴建的水库淹没遗产重要区域、工农业的发展（包括杀虫剂和农药的使用，大型公共工程、采矿、污染、采伐等）而遭受重大损害；

（c）人类活动对保护范围或上游区域的侵蚀，威胁遗产的完整性。

（ii）潜在的危险－该遗产面临可能会对其固有特性造成损害的威胁。此类威胁包括：

（a）该地区的法律保护地位发生变化

（b）在遗产范围内实施的，或虽在其范围外但足以波及和威胁到该遗产的移民或开发计划；

（c）武装冲突的爆发或威胁；

（d）管理规划或管理体系缺失、不完善或贯彻不彻底。

80. 另外，威胁遗产完整性的因素必须是人力可以补救的因素。对于文化遗产，自然因素和人为因素都可能构成威胁，而对于自然遗产来说，威胁其完整性的大多是人为因素，只有少数情况是由自然因素造成的（例如传染病）。某些情况下，对遗产完整性造成威胁的因素可通过行政或法律手段予以纠正，如取消某大型公共工程项目，加强法律地位。

such as the cancelling of a major public works project or the improvement of legal status.

81.The Committee may wish to bear in mind the following supplementary factors when considering the inclusion of a cultural or natural property in the List of World Heritage in Danger:

(a) Decisions which affect World Heritage properties are taken by Governments after balancing all factors. The advice of the World Heritage Committee can often be decisive if it can be given before the property becomes threatened.

(b) Particularly in the case of ascertained danger, the physical or cultural deteriorations to which a property has been subjected should be judged according to the intensity of its effects and analyzed case by case.

(c) Above all in the case of potential danger to a property, one should consider that:

- the threat should be appraised according to the normal evolution of the social and economic framework in which the property is situated;

- it is often impossible to assess certain threats - such as the threat of armed conflict - as to their effect on cultural or natural properties;

- some threats are not imminent in nature, but can only be anticipated, such as demographic growth.

(d) Finally, in its appraisal the Committee should take into account any cause of unknown or unexpected origin which endangers a cultural or natural property.

C. Procedure for the inclusion of properties in the List of World Heritage in Danger

82.When considering the inclusion of a property in the List of World Heritage in Danger, the Committee shall develop, and adopt, as far as possible, in consultation with the State Party concerned, a programme

81.审议是否将一项文化或自然遗产列入《濒危世界遗产名录》时，委员会可能要考虑到下列额外因素：

（a）政府是在权衡各种因素后才做出影响世界遗产的决定。世界遗产委员会如能在遗产遭到威胁之前给予建议的话，该建议往往具有决定性。

（b）尤其是对于已确知的危险，对遗产所遭受的物理和文化损害的判断应基于其影响程度，并应具体问题具体分析。

（c）对于潜在的危险必须首先考虑：

– 结合遗产所处的社会和经济环境的常规进程，对其所受到的威胁进行评估；

– 有些威胁对于文化和自然遗产的影响难以估量，例如武装冲突的威胁；

– 有些威胁在本质上不会立刻发生，而只能预见，例如人口的增长。

（d）最后，委员会在进行评估时应将所有未知或无法预料的，但可能危及文化或自然遗产的因素纳入考虑范围。

C.列入《濒危世界遗产名录》的程序

82.在考虑将一项遗产列入《濒危世界遗产名录》时，委员会应尽可能与相关缔约国磋商，确定或采纳将该遗产从濒危名录中移除的补救方案。

for corrective measures.

83.In order to develop the programme referred to in the previous paragraph, the Committee shall request the Secretariat to ascertain, as far as possible in cooperation with the State Party concerned, the present condition of the property, the dangers to the property and the feasibility of undertaking corrective measures. The Committee may further decide to send a mission of qualified observers from IUCN, ICOMOS, ICCROM or other organizations to visit the property, evaluate the nature and extent of the threats and propose the measures to be taken.

84.The information received, together with the comments as appropriate of the State Party and the advisory organization(s) shall be brought to the attention of the Committee by the Secretariat.

85.The Committee shall examine the information available and take a decision concerning the inscription of the property on the List of World Heritage in Danger. Any such decision shall be taken by a majority of two-thirds of the Committee members present and voting. The Committee will then define the programme of corrective action to be taken. This programme will be proposed to the State Party concerned for immediate implementation.

86.The State Party concerned shall be informed of the Committee's decision and public notice of the decision shall immediately be issued by the Committee, in accordance with Article 11.4 of the Convention.

87.The Committee shall allocate a specific, significant portion of the World Heritage Fund to financing of possible assistance to World Heritage properties inscribed on the List of World Heritage in Danger.

88.The Committee shall review at regular

83.为了制订前段所述补救方案，委员会应要求秘书处尽可能与相关缔约国合作，弄清遗产的现状，查明其面临的危险并探讨补救措施的可行性。此外委员会还可能决定派遣来自世界自然保护联盟、国际古迹遗址理事会、国际文物保护与修复研究中心的观察员前往遗产地地勘查，鉴定威胁的本质及程度，并针对补救措施提出建议。

84.获取的信息及相关缔约国和咨询机构的评论，将经秘书处送交委员会审阅。

85.委员会将审议现有信息，并就是否将该遗产列入《濒危世界遗产名录》做出决定。出席表决的委员会成员须以三分之二多数通过此类决定。之后委员会将确定补救方案，并建议相关缔约国立即执行。

86.依照《公约》第11条第4段，委员会应将决定通告相关缔约国，并随即就该项决定发表公告。

87.委员会将从世界遗产基金中特别划拨一笔相当数量的资金，为列入《濒危世界遗产名录》的遗产提供可能的援助。

88.委员会将定期对《濒危世界遗产名录》

intervals the state of property on the List of World Heritage in Danger. This review shall include such monitoring procedures and expert missions as might be determined necessary by the Committee.

89.On the basis of these regular reviews, the Committee shall decide, in consultation with the State Party concerned whether:

(i) additional measures are required to conserve the property;

(ii) to delete the property from the List of World Heritage in Danger if the property is no longer under threat;

(iii) to consider the deletion of the property from both the List of World Heritage in Danger and the World Heritage List if the property has deteriorated to the extent that it has lost those characteristics which determined its inclusion in the World Heritage List, in accordance with the procedure set out in paragraphs 46 to 56 above.

IV. INTERNATIONAL ASSISTANCE

A.Different forms of assistance available under the World Heritage Fund

(i)Preparatory assistance

90.Assistance is available to States Parties for the purpose of:

(a) preparing tentative lists of cultural and/or natural properties suitable for inclusion in the World Heritage List;

(b) organizing meetings for the harmonization of tentative lists within the same geo-cultural area;

(c) preparing nominations of cultural and natural properties to the World Heritage List; and

(d) preparing requests for technical cooperation,including requests relating to the organization of training courses.

上遗产的保护状况进行例行检查。检查的内容包括委员会可能认为必要的监测程序和专家考察。

89.在定期检查的基础上，委员会将与有关缔约国磋商，决定是否：

（i）该遗产需要额外的保护措施；

（ii）当该遗产不再面临威胁时，将其从《濒危世界遗产名录》中删除；

（iii）当该遗产由于严重受损而丧失列入《世界遗产名录》的特征时，依照第46-56条所列程序考虑将其同时从《世界遗产名录》和《濒危世界遗产名录》中删除。

IV.国际援助

A.世界遗产基金提供的援助

（i）筹备性援助

90.提供援助帮助缔约国：

（a）准备适合列入《世界遗产名录》的国家《预备名录》内的遗产；

（b）在同一地理文化区域内组织会议，综合协调各国的《预备名录》；

（c）准备申报列入《世界遗产名录》的、文化和自然遗产的申报文件；

（d）请求技术合作的申请，包括要求相关咨询机构的培训；

This type of assistance, known as"preparatory assistance", can take the form of consultant services, equipment or, in exceptional cases, financial grants. The budgetary ceiling for each preparatory assistance project is fixed at $15,000.

91.Requests for preparatory assistance should be forwarded to the Secretariat which will transmit them to the Chairperson, who will decide on the assistance to be granted. Request forms (reference WHC/5) can be obtained from the Secretariat.

(ii)Emergency assistance

92.States Parties may request emergency assistance for work in connection with cultural and natural properties included or suitable for inclusion in the World Heritage List and which have suffered severe damage due to sudden, unexpected phenomena (such as sudden land subsidence, serious fires or explosions, flooding) or are in imminent danger of severe damage caused by these phenomena. Emergency assistance does not concern cases of damage or deterioration that has been caused by gradual processes such as decay, pollution, erosion, etc. Such assistance may be made available for the following purposes:

(a)to prepare urgent nominations of properties for the World Heritage List inconformity with paragraph 65 of these Guidelines;

(b)to draw up an emergency plan to safeguard properties inscribed on or nominated to the World Heritage List;

(c) to undertake emergency measures for the safeguarding of a property inscribed on or nominated to the World Heritage List.

93.Requests for emergency assistance may be sent to the Secretariat at any time using Form WHC/5. The World Heritage Centre should consult to the extent possible relevant advisory bodies and then

这类援助称为"筹备性援助",可以采取咨询服务、设备或在特殊情况下提供财政补助的形式。每个筹备性援助项目的预算上限定为15,000美元。

91.筹备性援助的请求应提交秘书处,由秘书处转交主席,由主席决定给予何种援助。申请表格(参阅WHC/5)可向秘书处索取。

(ⅱ)紧急援助

92.缔约国可申请紧急援助,该援助用于《世界遗产名录》内或适合列入《世界遗产名录》遗产,由于突然、不可预料的现象(包括土地沉陷、大火、爆炸、洪水)遭受迫切威胁及重大损失。此类援助不用于由渐进的腐蚀、污染和侵蚀造成的遗产损害和蜕化。该援助可用于:

(a)根据本指南第65条紧急申报遗产列入《世界遗产名录》;

(b)为已列入《世界遗产名录》和准备申报的遗产制定紧急方案;

(c)为已列入《世界遗产名录》和准备申报的遗产采取紧急保护措施;

93.紧急援助的请求可在任何时间利用WHC/5的表格提交秘书处。世界遗产中心广泛咨询相关机构的意见并转交主席,主席有权批准50000美元以内的申请,主席团有权批准75000美元以内的

submit these requests to the Chairperson who has the authorization to approve emergency requests up to an amount of US$50,000 whereas the Bureau can approve requests up to an amount of US$75,000.

申请。

(iii) Training

（iii）培训援助

94.States Parties may request support for the training of specialised staff at all levels in the field of identification, protection, conservation, presentation and rehabilitation of the cultural and natural heritage. The training must be related to the implementation of the World Heritage Convention.

94.缔约国可申请培训援助，在世界遗产的识别、监测、保护、管理以及展示领域，培训各个级别的工作人员和专家。培训必须与《世界遗产公约》的执行有关。

95.Priority in training activities will be given to group training at the local or regional levels, particularly at national or regional centres in accordance with Article 23 of the Convention. The training of individual persons will be essentially limited to short term refresher programmes and exchanges of experience.

95.根据《公约》第23条，优先安排地方和地区级别，特别是国家或区域中心的培训活动。个体的培训以短期进修方案和交流经验为主。

96.Requests for the training of specialised staff at the national or regional level should contain the following information:

96.要求在国家或区域层面培训专门工作人员，应提供下列资料：

(a)details on the training course concerned (courses offered, level of instruction, teaching staff, number of students and country of origin, date, place and duration,etc.)and, when applicable, the functional responsibility of each participant with respect to a designated World Heritage site; priority should be given, if funds are not sufficient to satisfy all requests, to those concerning management or conservation personnel of inscribed properties;

（a）有关培训课程的详细信息（所提供的课程、教学水平、师资、学生人数及来源国、日期、地点及持续时间等），在适用的情况下，每个参与者对指定世界遗产地的职能责任；如果资金不足以满足所有要求，应优先考虑与名录内遗产管理和保护相关的人员；

(b)type of assistance requested (financial contribution to costs of training, provision of specialised teaching staff, provision of equipment, books and educational materials for training courses);

（b）所要求的援助类型（提供培训费、提供专门教学人员、为培训课程提供设备、书籍和教材）；

(c) approximate cost of support requested, including as appropriate tuition fees, daily subsistence

（c）提供援助预算，包括酌情收取学费、每日生活津贴、购买教材的拨款、往返培训中

allowance, allocation for purchase of educational material, travel costs to and from training centre,etc.

(d) other contributions: national financing, received or anticipated multilateral or bilateral contributions;

(e) for recurring training courses, an in-depth report of the results obtained in each previous session shall be submitted by the recipient government or organization. The report shall be forwarded to the appropriate advisory body for review and for its recommendations in connection with additional funding requests, as appropriate.

97.Requests for support for individual training courses should be submitted on the standard "Application for Fellowship" form used for all fellowships administered by UNESCO and which can be obtained from UNESCO National Commissions, UNESCO offices and the offices of the United Nations Development Programme in Member States, as well as from the Secretariat. Each request should be accompanied by a statement indicating the relationship of the proposed study plan to the implementation of the World Heritage Convention within the State Party submitting the request and by a commitment to submit a final technical report on the results obtained as a result of the training grant.

98.All requests for support for training activities should be transmitted to the Secretariat which will ensure that the information is complete and forward these requests along with an estimation of the costs to the Chairperson for his approval. In this regard the Chairperson can approve amounts up to $20,000. Requests for sums above this amount follow the same procedure for approval as for requests for technical cooperation set out in paragraphs 100-104.

心的旅费等。

（d）其他捐助：国家资助、已收到或预期受到的多边或双边捐助；

（e）对于循环举办的培训班，受援国政府或组织应当为每一次培训所取得的成果提交一份深入报告。该报告应提交适当的咨询机构审查，并酌情对申请预算外资金提供建议。

97.对个别培训课程的援助申请，应根据教科文组织管理的所有研究资金的使用标准，提交"研究金申请表"，该表格可从教科文组织国家委员会、教科文组织办事处和联合国开发计划署驻会员国办事处及本秘书处获得。每个申请都应附有一份声明，提交申请的缔约国应说明拟议的研究计划与实施《世界遗产公约》之间的关系，并承诺提交一份关于培训援助所获成果的最终技术报告。

98.所有申请培训援助的活动都应转交秘书处，秘书处将确保资料完整，并将这些申请连同预算转交主席核可。主席审核最高权限为20000美元。高于此金额以上的申请，按照第100-104条所述的申请技术合作援助的标准审核。

(iv) Technical co-operation

99.States Parties can request technical co-operation for work foreseen in safeguarding projects for properties included in the World Heritage List. This assistance can take the forms outlined in paragraph 22 of the Convention for World Heritage properties.

100.In order to make best use of the limited resources of the World Heritage Fund and because of the increasing number of cultural sites to be assisted, the Committee, while recognizing the importance of archaeological objects coming from sites inscribed on the World Heritage List, has decided not to accept requests which may be submitted for equipment for archaeological site museums whose function is the preservation of movables.

101.The following information should be provided in requests for technical co-operation:

(a)Details of property

- date of inscription in the World Heritage List,

- description of property and of dangers to property,

- legal status of property;

(b)Details of request

- scientific and technical information on the work to be undertaken,

- detailed description of equipment requested (notably make, type, voltage, etc.) and of required personnel (specialists and workmen), etc.,

- if appropriate, details on the "training" component of the project,

- schedule indicating when the project activities will take place;

(c)Cost of proposed activities

- paid nationally,

- requested under the Convention,

（iv）技术合作

99.缔约国为保护列入《世界遗产名录》遗产申请技术合作。这种援助可以采取《世界遗产公约》第22条所述的形式。

100.为了充分利用有限的世界遗产基金，并且由于需要援助的文化遗产越来越多，委员会虽然认识到《世界遗产名录》上遗产地的考古发掘很重要，但决定不接受为考古遗址博物馆提供设备的申请，因为博物馆的职能是保护可移动文物。

101.申请技术合作，需提供以下信息：

（a）遗产详情

– 列入《世界遗产名录》的时间；

– 遗产及遗产危险的描述；

– 遗产法律地位；

（b）具体申请

– 将进行的工作的科学和技术信息；

– 所需设备（特别是产地，型号，电压等）和人员（专家和操作工人）的详细说明

– 必要时，项目培训的详细详细；

– 项目进行的时间表

（c）计划的活动成本

– 国家承担的部分

–《公约》的要求

- other multilateral or bilateral contributions received or expected, indicating how each contribution will be used;

(d) National body responsible for the project and details of project administration;

(e) The Committee,wishing to establish a link between the monitoring of the state of conservation of World Heritage Sites and the granting of international assistance, has established as a requirement that requests for technical cooperation be accompanied by a state of conservation report of the property or site concerned.

102.The Secretariat, if necessary, will request the State Party concerned to provide further information. The Secretariat can also ask for expert advice from the appropriate organization (ICOMOS, IUCN, ICCROM).

103.The Bureau will consider the requests which are presented at its meetings and will make recommendations thereon to the Committee. The Secretariat will forward the Bureau's recommendation to all the States members of the Committee.

104.If the recommendation is positive, the Secretariat will proceed with all the preparatory work necessary for implementing the technical cooperation immediately after the Committee has decided to approve the project.

105.At the Committee meeting, the Committee will make a decision on each request for technical cooperation, and for emergency assistance and training beyond amounts authorized for approval by the Chairperson and Bureau, taking account of the Bureau's recommendation. Representatives of a States Party, whether or not a member of the Committee, shall not speak to advocate the approval of an assistance request submitted by that State, but

－已收到或预计收到的其他多边或双边捐助，说明每一捐助的用途；

（d）负责项目的国家机构和项目管理的细节；

（e）委员会希望在监测世界遗产点的保护状况与提供国际援助之间建立联系机制，要求缔约国，在申请技术合作时，应同时提交相关遗产或遗产点的保护状况报告。

102.必要时，秘书处会要求相关缔约国提交更多信息，秘书处也可以要求相关咨询机构（国际古迹遗址理事会、世界自然保护联盟、国际文物保护与修复研究中心）提供专家建议。

103.主席团会议将审议在其会议上提出的申请，并向委员会提出意见。秘书处将向所有委员会成员国转达主席团的意见。

104.如果建议是积极的，秘书处将在委员会决定审核该项目后，立即着手准备技术合作工作。

105.在委员会会议上，委员会根据主席团的建议，对高于主席和主席团批准权限的每一项技术合作申请、紧急援助申请和培训申请，作出决定。缔约国的代表，不论是否为委员会成员，均不得发言主张批准本国提出的援助申请，而只能在回答问题时谈及相关信息。将通知各缔约国委员会的决定，中心将着手执行已核准的项目。

only to deal with a point of information in answer to a question. The Committee's decisions will be forwarded to the States Parties and the Centre will proceed to implement approved projects.

106.The above schedule does not apply, however, to projects the cost of which does not exceed a ceiling of $30,000 for which the following simplified procedure will be applied.

(a) In the case of requests not exceeding $20,000, the Secretariat after examining the dossier and receiving the advice of ICCROM,ICOMOS or IUCN, as appropriate, will forward the request accompanied by all other relevant documents directly to the Chairperson, who is authorized to take decisions on the financing of such projects up to the total amount set aside for this purpose in the annual allocation from the World Heritage Fund, on the understanding that no more than 20 percent of the total annual assistance budget, including technical cooperation and training (but excluding emergency assistance and preparatory assistance, for which separate rules have been established) may be allocated by the Chairperson. The Chairperson is not authorized to approve requests submitted by his own country.

(b)The Bureau is authorized to approve requests up to a maximum of $30,000 except for requests from States members of the Bureau; in such cases, the Bureau can only make recommendations to the Committee.

(v) Assistance for promotional activities

107.(a) at the regional and international levels:
The Committee has agreed to support the holding of meetings which could:
- help to create interest in the Convention within the countries of a given region;
- create a greater awareness of the different issues related to the implementation of the Convention to

106.但是，上述计划不适用于总额不超过30000美元的项目，这些项目将适用下列简化程序。

（a）对低于20000美元的申请，秘书处在检查了文件并得到国际文物保护与修复研究中心、国际古迹遗址理事会和世界自然保护联盟的建议后，在适当情况下，将该申请连同所有其他相关文件直接转交给主席，主席有权处理此类项目的资金筹措，金额不超过世界遗产基金年度总额的20%，包括技术合作和培训申请（但不包括紧急援助申请和筹备性援助申请，此两项申请有各自的申请标准）。主席无权处理来自本国的申请。

（b）主席团有权处理最高30000美元的申请，但主席团成员国提出的申请除外；在这种情况下，主席团只能向委员会提出建议。

（v）促进活动的援助

107.（a）在地区和国际层面：
委员会同意资助举办下列会议：

－帮助在指定地区的国家内激发对《世界遗产公约》的兴趣；
－提高与实施《世界遗产公约》相关的不同议题的认识，推动更积极地参与《公约》的

promote more active involvement in its application;

- be a means of exchanging experiences;

- stimulate joint promotional activities.

(c) at the national level:

The Committee felt that requests concerning national activities for promoting the Convention could be considered only when they concern:

- meetings specifically organized to make the Convention better known or for the creation of national World Heritage associations, in accordance with Article 17 of the Convention;

- preparation of information material for the general promotion of the Convention and not for the promotion of a particular site.

The World Heritage Fund shall provide only small contributions towards national promotional activities on a selective basis and for a maximum amount of $5,000. However, requests for sums above this amount could exceptionally be approved for projects which are of special interest: the Chairperson's agreement would be required and the maximum amount approved would be $10,000.

B. Deadlines for presentation of requests for International Assistance for considerationby the Bureau and the Committee

108.All requests for international assistance which are to be examined by the Bureau, with the exception of requests for emergency assistance, should be submitted before 1 May and 1 September respectively for consideration by the following session of the Bureau. Large-scale requests (that is those exceeding US $30,000) will be forwarded, with the Bureau's recommendation, to the following session of the World Heritage Committee for decision-making.

C. Order of priorities for the granting of international

实施。

－经验交换的渠道；

－帮助开展联合教育。

（c）在国家层面：

关于促进《公约》的国家活动的申请，委员会只审议下列情况：

－组织召开特别会议，向公众宣传《公约》以便根据《世界遗产公约》第17条，创立国家世界遗产协会；

－为宣传《公约》准备新闻资料。本援助不用于某项特定遗产的宣传。

世界遗产基金仅有选择地为国家宣传活动提供少量捐款，最高限额为5000美元。但是，对于特别有意义的项目，可以破例，由主席审议批准的最高数额为10000美元。

B. 提交国际援助的申请供主席团和委员会审议的截止日期

108.除紧急援助申请外，需要主席团审查的所有国际援助申请，均应在5月1日至9月1日之前分别提出，供主席团下届会议审议。根据主席团的建议，提交大规模的申请（即超过30000美元的要求），将由下届世界遗产委员会会议作出决定。

C.提供国际援助的优先次序

assistance

109.Without prejudicing the provisions of the Convention, which shall always prevail, the Committee agreed on the following order of priorities with respect to the type of activities to be assisted under the Convention:

- emergency measures to save property included, or nominated for inclusion, in the World Heritage List (see paragraph 92 above);

- preparatory assistance for drawing up tentative lists of cultural and/or natural properties suitable for inclusion in the World Heritage List as well as nominations of types of properties underrepresented on the list and requests for technical co-operation;

- projects which are likely to have a multiplier effect ("seed money") because they:

· stimulate general interest in conservation;

· contribute to the advancement of scientific research;

· contribute to the training of specialized personnel;

· generate contributions from other sources.

110.The Committee also agreed that the following factors would in principle govern its decisions in granting assistance under the Convention:

(i) the urgency of the work and of the protective measures to be taken;

(ii) the legislative, administrative and financial commitment of the recipient State to protect and preserve the property;

(iii) the cost of the project;

(iv) the interest for, and exemplary value of, the project in respect of scientific research and the development of cost/effective conservation techniques;

(v) the educational value both for the training of local experts and for the general public;

(vi) the cultural and ecological benefits

109.在不影响《公约》的规定的情况下（《公约》的规定应始终优先），委员会根据《公约》应协助的活动的类型，商定了下列优先次序：

– 用于《世界遗产名录》内或适合列入《世界遗产名录》遗产的紧急援助（见前文第92条）；

– 筹备性，援助用于准备适合列入《世界遗产名录》的文化和/或自然遗产的预备名录、或《世界遗产名录》上代表性不足的各类遗产，或申请技术合作；

– 有倍增功效的项目（种子基金）：

·激发公众对遗产保护的兴趣；

·有利于科学进步；

·有助于培养专业人才；

·其他贡献。

110.委员会同意，根据《公约》，援助的决定原则上受以下因素的指导：

（ⅰ）工作和应采取的防护措施的紧迫性；

（ⅱ）受援国保护和保存遗产的立法、行政和财政承诺

（ⅲ）项目成本

（ⅳ）该项目在科学研究和发展成本/效益保护技术方面的效益和示范价值

（ⅴ）培训对当地专家和一般公众的教育价值；

（ⅵ）工程项目所带来的文化和生态效益

accruing from the project,and

(vii) the social and economic consequences.

111.Properties included in the World Heritage List are considered to be equal in value. A balance will be maintained between funds allocated to projects for the preservation of the cultural heritage on the one hand and projects for the conservation of the natural heritage on the other hand.

112.Requests for emergency, training and technical cooperation shall be referred,if deemed necessary by the Secretariat, to the appropriate advisory body (IUCN, ICOMOS, and/or ICCROM) for professional review and evaluation, and its recommendations shall be presented to the Bureau and the Committee for action.

D.Agreement to be concluded with States receiving international assistance

113.When technical co-operation on a large scale is granted to a State Party, an agreement will be concluded between the Committee and the State concerned in which will be set out:

(a) the scope and nature of the technical co-operation granted;

(b) the obligations of the Government, including the submission of mid-term and final financial and technical reports, which shall be referred,if deemed necessary by the Secretariat, to the appropriate advisory body (IUCN, ICOMOS, ICCROM) for review, and summaries of which shall be available to the Committee.

(c) the facilities, privileges and immunities to be applied by the Government to the Committee and/or UNESCO, to the property, funds and assets allocated to theproject as well as to the officials and other persons performing services on behalf of the Committee and/or UNESCO in connection with the project.

（vii）社会和经济效益。

111.列入《世界遗产名录》的遗产价值相等。因此，上述准则没有提及遗产的相对价值。分配给文化遗产保护项目和自然遗产保护项目的资金应保持平衡。

112.如果秘书处认为有必要，紧急援助，培训和技术合作的申请将提交相关咨询机构（世界自然保护联盟、国际古迹遗址理事会、国际文物保护与修复研究中心）进行专业审核和评估，评估意见交给主席团和委员会以便采取行动。

D. 与接受国际援助的国家签订协议

113.当委员会决定向某一缔约国提供大规模技术合作时，将与相关国家签订协议，其中将规定：

（a）技术援助的范围和特征；

（b）政府的义务，包括提交中期和最终财务和技术报告，秘书处认为必要时应将这些报告提交适当的咨询机构（世界自然保护联盟、国际古迹遗址理事会、国际文物保护与修复研究中心）审查，并应向委员会提供报告的摘要。

（c）政府对委员会和/或教科文组织给予适用的设施、特权和豁免。对分配给遗产地使用的资金和资产、以及代表委员会和/或教科文组织执行项目的有关官员和其他人员，提供服务。

114.The text of a standard agreement will be in conformity with UNESCO regulations.

115.The Committee decided to delegate authority to the Chairperson to sign such agreements on its behalf. In exceptional circumstances, or when necessary for practical purposes, the Chairperson may delegate authority to a member of the Secretariat whom he will designate.

E.Implementation of projects

116.In order to ensure the efficient implementation of a project for which technical co-operation has been granted under the World Heritage Fund, the Committee recommends that a single body - whether national, regional, local, public or private - should be entrusted with the responsibility of executing the project in the State Party concerned.

F. Conditions for the granting of international assistance

117.The conditions for and types of international assistance are established by Articles 19 to 26 of the World Heritage Convention. Establishing a parallel between the conditions of eligibility for the World Heritage Committee set out in Article 16 of the Convention, the Committee decided, at its thirteenth session (1989), that States who were in arrears of payment of their contributions to the World Heritage Fund would not be able to receive a grant of international assistance in the following calendar year, it being understood that this provision would not apply in case of emergency assistance and training as defined in these Guidelines. In making this decision, the Committee wished to emphasize the importance which it accorded to States Parties paying their entire contribution within the periods set out in Article 16 of the Convention.

114.标准的协议内容需符合教科文组织的条例。

115.委员会决定授权主席代表委员会签署协议。特殊情况下，或因实际情况，主席可委托秘书处成员作为代表，签署协议。

E. 项目实施

116. 为确保世界遗产基金援助的技术合作项目的有效实施，委员会建议，应委托单一机构－－不论是国家、区域、地方、公共或私营机构－－在相关缔约国负责执行该项目。

F.提供国际援助的条件

117.《世界遗产公约》第十九条至第二十六条规定了国际援助的条件和类型。根据《公约》第16条所规定的世界遗产委员会资格条件，委员会在其第十三届（1989年）会议上决定，拖欠向世界遗产基金缴纳会费的国家将无法在下一年获得国际援助赠款，需要理解的是，这一规定不适用于本准则所规定的紧急援助和培训。在作出这一决定时，根据《公约》第16条规定，委员会希望向缔约国强调，按时向世界遗产基金缴纳会费的重要性。

V. WORLD HERITAGE FUND

118.The Committee decided that contributions offered to the World Heritage Fund for international assistance campaigns and other UNESCO projects for any property inscribed on the World Heritage List shall be accepted and used as international assistance pursuant to Section V of the Convention, and in conformity with the modalities established for carrying out the campaign or project.

119.States Parties to the Convention who anticipate making contributions towards international assistance campaigns or other UNESCO projects for any property inscribed on the List are encouraged to make their contributions through the World Heritage Fund.

120.The financial regulations for the Fund are set out in document WHC/7.

VI. BALANCE BETWEEN THE CULTURAL AND THE NATURAL HERITAGE IN THE IMPLEMENTATION OF THE CONVENTION

121.In order to improve the balance between the cultural and natural heritage in the implementation of the Convention, the Committee has recommended that the following measures be taken:

(a) Preparatory assistance to States Parties should be granted on a priority basis for:

(i) the establishment of tentative lists of cultural and natural properties situated in their territories and suitable for inclusion in the World Heritage List;

(ii) the preparation of nominations of types of properties underrepresented in the World Heritage List.

(b) States Parties to the Convention should provide the Secretariat with the name and address of the governmental organization(s) primarily responsible

V. 世界遗产基金

118.委员会决定，根据《公约》第V部分的规定，在符合活动或项目开展的情况下，世界遗产基金收到的会费，应用于国际援助活动和其他联合国教科文组织《世界遗产名录》遗产保护项目。

119.鼓励缔约国通过世界遗产基金，为列入《名录》的任何遗产的国际援助活动或教科文组织其他项目提供捐助。

120.基金的财务管理条例见文件WHC/7。

VI. 在实施《公约》中保持文化和自然遗产的平衡

121.为了在实施《公约》中保持文化和自然遗产平衡，委员会建议采取以下措施：

（a）优先向这些缔约国提供筹备性援助：

（i）编制缔约国境内适合列入《世界遗产名录》的《预备名录》；

（ii）《世界遗产名录》中代表性不足的遗产类别的申报准备工作；

（b）《公约》缔约国应向秘书处提供主要负责文化和自然遗产的政府组织的名称和地址，以便秘书处及时寄送官方公函和其他文件。

for cultural and natural properties, so that copies of all official correspondence and documents can be sent by the Secretariat to these focal points as appropriate.

(c) States Parties to the Convention should convene at regular intervals at the national level a joint meeting of those persons responsible for natural and cultural heritage in order that they may discuss matters pertaining to the implementation of the Convention. This does not apply to States Parties where one single organization is dealing with both cultural and natural heritage.

(d) States Parties to the Convention should choose as their representatives persons qualified in the field of natural and cultural heritage, thus complying with Article 9, paragraph 3, of the Convention. States members of the Committee should communicate in advance to the Secretariat the names and status of their representatives.

(e) The Committee, deeply concerned with maintaining a balance in the number of experts from the natural and cultural fields represented on the Bureau, urges that every effort be made in future elections in order to ensure that:

(i) the chair is not held by persons with expertise in the same field, either cultural or natural, for more than two successive years;

(ii) at least two "cultural" and at least two "natural" experts are present at Bureau meetings to ensure balance and credibility in reviewing nominations to the World Heritage List.

(f) In accordance with Article 10.2 of the Convention and with Rule 7 of the Rules of Procedure, the Committee shall, at any time, invite to its meetings public or private bodies or individuals who would attend as observers and augment the expertise available to it. These observers shall be chosen with a view to a balanced participation between the natural and cultural heritage.

（c）《公约》缔约国应定期召开各国自然和文化遗产负责人联席会议，以便他们可以讨论与执行《公约》有关的事项。这不适用于由一个组织同时处理文化遗产和自然遗产的缔约国。

（d）根据《公约》第9条第3款规定，《公约》缔约国应选择在自然和文化遗产领域资深人士作为其代表，并事先将该代表的姓名和地位通知秘书处。

（e）委员会非常重视在主席团内保持自然和文化领域的专家代表人数平衡，促请在今后的选举中作出一切努力，以确保：

（i）连续两任主席不可为同一领域，不论是文化或自然领域的专家；

（ii）主席团会议中至少有两位"文化"和两位"自然"领域的专家，确保公平、诚信的审核世界遗产申报。

（f）按照《公约》第10.2条和《议事规则》第7条的规定，根据程序，委员会每次会议应邀请公共或私人机构或个人，以观察员的身份出席、并充分利用其专业知识。选择的观察员应着眼于自然遗产和文化遗产间的平衡参与。

VII. OTHER MATTERS

A.Use of the World Heritage Emblem and the name, symbol or depiction of World Heritage sites

122.At its second session,the Committee adopted the World Heritage Emblem which had been designed by Mr.Michel Olyff. This emblem symbolizes the interdependence of cultural and natural properties: the central square is a form created by man and the circle represents nature, the two being intimately linked. The emblem is round, like the world, but at the same time it is a symbol of protection. The Committee decided that the two versions proposed by the artist (see Annex 2) could be used, in any colour, depending on the use, the technical possibilities and considerations of an artistic nature. The emblem should always carry the text "World Heritage. Patrimoine Mondial". The space occupied by "Patrimonio Mundial" can be used for its translation into the national language of the country where the logo is to be used.

123.Properties included in the World Heritage List should be marked with the World Heritage emblem jointly with the UNESCO logo, which should, however, be placed in such a way that they do not visually impair the property in question.

124.States Parties to the Convention should take all possible measures to prevent the use of the emblem of the Convention and the use of the name of the Committee and the Convention in their respective countries by any group or for any purpose not explicitly recognized and approved by the Committee. The World Heritage emblem should, in particular, not be used for any commercial purposes unless specific authorization is obtained from the Committee.

VII. 其他事项

A. 对世界遗产标识、名称、符号或描述的正确使用

122.在世界遗产委员会第二届大会上采用了由米歇尔·奥利芙设计的遗产标识。该标识表现了文化与自然遗产之间的相互依存关系：代表大自然的圆形与代表人类创造的方形紧密相连。标识是圆形的，代表世界的形状，同时也是保护的象征。委员会决定根据具体的使用、技术水平和艺术考虑，两个版本的标识（见附件2）可采用任何颜色。标识上必须带有"world heritage.Patrimoine Mondial"（英语和法语的"世界遗产"）的字样。各国在使用该标识时，可用本国语言替代"Patrimonio Mundial（西语："世界遗产"）"字样。

123.列入《世界遗产名录》的遗产应标有该标识和联合国教科文组织标识，但要以不破坏遗产为前提。

124.缔约国政府应该采取一切可能的措施，防止未经委员会明确承认的任何组织或出于任何目的未经授权的使用该标识。除非得到委员会的授权，任何商业机构都不得直接在其产品上使用该标识，

125.The name, symbol or depiction of a World Heritage site, or of any element thereof, should not be used for commercial purposes unless written authorization has been obtained from the State concerned on the principles of using the said name, symbol or depiction, and unless the exact text or display has been approved by that State and, as far as possible, by the national authority specifically concerned with the protection of the site. Any such utilization should be in conformity with the reasons for which the property has been placed on the World Heritage List.

B.Production of plaques to commemorate the inclusion of properties in the World Heritage List

126.These plaques are designed to inform the public of the country concerned and foreign visitors, that the site visited has a particular value which has been recognized by the international community. In other words, the site is exceptional, of interest not only to one nation, but also to the whole world. However, these plaques have an additional function which is to inform the general public about the World Heritage Convention or at least about the World Heritage concept and the World Heritage List.

127.The Committee has adopted the following Guidelines for the production of these plaques:

- the plaque should be so placed that it can easily be seen by visitors, without disfiguring the site;

- the World Heritage symbol should appear on the plaque together with the UNESCO logo;

- the text should mention the site's exceptional universal value; in this regard it might be useful to give a short description of the site's outstanding characteristics. States may, if they wish, use the descriptions appearing in the various World Heritage publications or in the World Heritage exhibit, and

125.世界遗产的名称、标识、描述及其他元素，不得用于商业项目，除非获得有关国家关于使用该名称、符号或者描述的原则的书面授权，或确切的文字或展示已获得该国批准，并尽可能由专门负责保护该遗产点的国家当局批准。任何此类利用均应符合该遗产被列入《世界遗产名录》的原因。

B.制作标牌，纪念遗产列入《世界遗产名录》

126.设计的标牌，应向本国公众及外国游客说明该遗产具有特殊的价值且已得到国际社会的认可。换言之，该遗产无论对该国还是世界来说，都具有非同寻常的意义。此外，该标牌还有另外一个作用，即向公众介绍《世界遗产公约》，或者至少是世界遗产概念和《世界遗产名录》。

127.委员会就标牌的制作采用以下指导方针：

－标牌应放置在参观者容易看到的地方，但不能破坏遗产的美观；

－标牌上应带有世界遗产标识及联合国教科文组织徽标；

－标牌上的内容应体现遗产的突出普遍价值；考虑到这一点，内容中应对遗产的突出特点加以描述。如果愿意的话，缔约国政府可以使用各种世界遗产出版物或世界遗产展览对相关遗产的说明。这些内容可直接从秘书处获得。

which may be obtained from the Secretariat;

- the text should make reference to the World Heritage Convention and particularly to the World Heritage List and to the international recognition conferred by inscription on this List (however, it is not necessary to mention at which session of the Committee the site was inscribed);

- it may be appropriate to produce the text in several languages for sites which receive many foreign visitors.

128.The Committee proposed the following text as an example:

"(Name of site) has been inscribed upon the World Heritage List of the Convention concerning the Protection of the World Cultural and Natural Heritage. Inscription on this List confirms the exceptional universal value of a cultural or natural site which deserves protection for the benefit of all humanity."

This text could be then followed by a brief description of the site concerned.

C. Rules of Procedure of the Committee

129.The Rules of Procedure of the Committee, adopted by the Committee at its first session and amended at its second and third sessions, are to be found in document WHC/1.

D.Meetings of the World Heritage Committee

130.In years when the General Assembly of States Parties is held, the ordinary session of the World Heritage Committee will take place as soon as possible after the Assembly.

131.As provided for in Article 10.3 of the Convention and in accordance with Rules 20-21 of the Rules of Procedure, the Committee shall constitute sub-committees during its regular sessions to examine selected items of business referred to them with the

– 标牌上的内容应提及《保护世界文化和自然遗产公约》，尤其是《世界遗产名录》及国际社会对列入《名录》的遗产的承认（但无需指出是在委员会的哪届会议上通过的）。

– 如遗产有大量外国游客参观，标牌上的内容应使用多种语言。

128.委员会提供了下段文字作为范例：

"根据《保护世界文化和自然遗产公约》，（遗产名称）已经列入《世界遗产名录》。遗产列入《名录》说明该项文化或自然遗产具有突出普遍价值，对它的保护符合全人类的利益。"

在这段话的后面，可对该遗产进行简要介绍。

C.委员会议事规则

129.委员会议事规则由委员会第一届会议通过，并在第二和第三届会议上修正，见WHC/1号文件。

D. 委员会会议

130.在联合国教科文组织缔约国大会闭幕后，召开委员会会议。

131.根据《公约》第10.3条和议事规则20-21条，委员会在常会期间组织分组委员会，审查提交到委员会的事务项目，向全体委员会提出报告并提出行动建议。

object of reporting and making recommendations to the full Committee for action.

E.Meetings of the Bureau of the World Heritage Committee

132.The Bureau shall meet twice a year, once in June/July and a second time immediately preceding the Committee's regular session. The newly elected Bureau shall meet as necessary during the Committee's regular session.

F.Participation of experts from developing countries

133.In order to ensure a fair representation within the Committee of the various geographical and cultural areas, the Committee decided to include in its budget a sum intended to cover the cost of participation, in its sessions and sessions of its Bureau, of representatives of States members of the Committee which are on the list of least developed countries issued by the United Nations but only for persons who are experts in conservation of the cultural or natural heritage.

134.Requests for assistance to participate in the Bureau and Committee meetings should reach the Secretariat at least four weeks before the session concerned. These requests will be considered in the limit of resources available as decided by the Committee, in decreasing order of NGP of each State member of the Committee, and primarily for one representative from each State. In no event may the Fund finance more than two representatives by State, who must in this case be one expert in the natural and one in the cultural heritage field.

G.Publication of the World Heritage List

135.An up-to-date version of the World Heritage

E.委员会主席团会议

132. 主席团每年举行两次会议，第一次在6月/7月，第二次在委员会常会之前举行。新选出的主席团应视需要在委员会常会期间举行会议。

F.发展中国家的专家参与

133.为保证在委员会内不同地理和文化区域的公平代表性，委员会决定在其主席团各届会议预算中，包含来自联合国发布的、最不发达国家的参会专家的费用，仅限于文化和自然遗产保护方面的专家。

134.参加主席团和委员会会议的援助请求应至少在此届会议之前四个星期送达秘书处。这些请求将在委员会决定的可用资源限额内审议，按照每个委员会成员国的NGP递减顺序进行审议，一个国家审批一名代表的援助申请。如果基金资助了一个国家的两名代表时，他们必须是一名自然遗产专家和一名文化遗产领域的专家。

G.《世界遗产名录》出版物

135.应每年更新、发布一次《世界遗产名

List and the List of the World Heritage in Danger will be published every year.

136.The name of the States having nominated the properties inscribed on the World Heritage List will be presented in the published form of the List under the following heading:

"Contracting State having submitted the nomination of the property in accordance with the Convention".

H. Action at the national level to promote a greater awareness of the activities undertaken under the Convention

137.States Parties should promote the establishment and activities of associations concerned with the safeguarding of cultural and natural sites.

138.States Parties are reminded of Articles 17 and 27 of the Convention concerning the establishment of national, public and private foundations or associations whose purpose is to invite donations for the protection of the world heritage and the organization of educational and information programmes to strengthen appreciation and respect by their peoples of this heritage.

Ⅰ. Links with other Conventions and Recommendations

139.The World Heritage Committee has recognized the collective interest that would be advanced by closer coordination of its work with other international conservation instruments. These include the 1949 Geneva Convention, the 1954 Hague Convention, the 1970 UNESCO Convention, the Ramsar Convention, and CITES, as well as other regional conventions and future conventions that will pursue conservation objectives, as appropriate. The Committee will invite representatives of the intergovernmental bodies under related conventions

录》和《濒危世界遗产名录》。

136.申报《世界遗产名录》的缔约国的名称，应出现在公布的名单上，标题为：

"根据《公约》要求，提交申报的缔约国："

H.在国家层面根据《公约》开展的、提高对《公约》认识的活动

137.缔约国应促进建立与保护文化和自然遗址有关的协会并开展活动。

138.请缔约国根据《公约》第17条和第27条，建立国家、公共和私人基金会或协会，其目的是邀请捐款以保护世界遗产，并组织教育和信息方案，以加强其人民对世界遗产的欣赏和尊重。

Ⅰ.与其他公约和建议的联系

139.世界遗产委员会认识到，密切协调好与其他相关公约的关系受益匪浅。这些公约包括1949年的《日内瓦公约》，1954年的《海牙公约》，1970年的《联合国教科文组织公约》,《拉姆萨尔公约》、《濒危野生动植物物种国际贸易公约》，以及区域公约和未来以保护为目的的其他公约。委员会可能邀请相关公约的政府间组织的代表作为观察员，参加委员会的会议。同样，如受到其他政府间组织的邀请，委员会可能派遣代表作为观察员列席会议。秘书处将通过世界遗产中心，保证《世界遗产公约》和其

to attend its meetings as observers. Similarly, the Secretariat will appoint a representative to observe meetings of the other intergovernmental bodies upon receipt of an invitation. The Secretariat will ensure through the World Heritage Centre appropriate coordination and information-sharing between the Committee and other conventions, programmes and international organizations related to the conservation of cultural and natural heritage.

他公约、项目以及和保护文化和自然遗产有关的国际组织之间适当协调、信息共享工作。

Annex 1

MODEL FOR PRESENTING A TENTATIVE LIST

Name of country_____

List drawn up by_____

Date_____

NAME OF PROPERTY(①)

GEOGRAPHICAL LOCATION

DESCRIPTION

JUSTIFICATION OF "OUTSTANDING UNIVERSAL VALUE"

-Criteria met:

-Assurances of authenticity or integrity:

-Comparison with other similar properties:

*Please present, if possible, in the order to be nominated.

附件1

预备名录提交格式

国家名称_____

提交名录的机构_____

日期_____

遗产名称①

地理位置

描述

"突出普遍价值的理由"

– 符合标准

– 保证真实性或完整性

– 与其他类似遗产的比较分析：

请按顺序申报。

Annex 2/Annexe 2

EMBLEM

附件2

标识

The Operational Guidelines(in English and French), the text of the World Heritage Convention (in five languages), and other documents and information concerning World Heritage are available from the Secretariat:

UNESCO World Heritage Centre

7,place de Fontenoy

75352 Paris 07 SP

France

Tel:(33)1 45 68 18 76

Fax:(33)1 45 68 55 70

and on INTERNET:http://www.unesco.org

《操作指南》全文（英语和法语）、《世界遗产公约》全文（五种语言）及其他文件和相关信息，可向秘书处获取：

联合国教科文组织世界遗产中心

法国巴黎（7, place de Fontenoy

75352 Paris 07 SP

France）

电话：+33（0）1 4568 1276

传真：+33（0）1 4568 5570

线上：http://www.unesco.org

---

① Please present, if possible, in the order to be nominated.

① 请尽可能按照申报的顺序编制。

WHC. 05/2

2 February 2005

WHC. 05/2

2005年2月2日

实施保护世界文化与自然遗产公约的操作指南
Operational Guidelines for the Implementation of the World Heritage Convention

UNITED NATIONS EDUCATIONAL, SCIENTIFIC AND CULTURAL ORGANISATION

联合国教育、科学及文化组织

INTERGOVERNMENTAL COMMITTEE FOR THE PROTECTION OF THE WORLD CULTURAL AND NATURAL HERITAGE

保护世界文化与自然遗产的政府间委员会

WORLD HERITAGE CENTRE

世界遗产中心

The *Operational Guidelines* are periodically revised to reflect the decisions of the World Heritage Committee. Please verify that you are using the latest version of the *Operational Guidelines* by checking the date of the *Operational Guidelines* on the UNESCO World Heritage Centre Web address indicated below.

定期修订《操作指南》，体现世界遗产委员会的若干决定。请访问下面的教科文组织世界遗产中心网址，检查《操作指南》的日期，确认您使用的是最新版本。

The *Operational Guidelines* (in English and French), the text of the *World Heritage Convention* (in five languages), and other documents and information concerning World Heritage are available from the World Heritage Centre:

可从世界遗产中心获取《操作指南》（英文和法文）、《保护世界文化与自然遗产公约》全文（五种语言）、其他世界遗产相关的文书和信息：

UNESCO World Heritage Centre

7, place de Fontenoy

75352 Paris 07 SP

France

Tel　: +33 (0) 1 4568 1876

Fax　: +33 (0) 1 4568 5570

E-mail : wh-info@unesco.org

Links　: http://whc.unesco.org/

http://whc.unesco.org/en/guidelines
(English)

http://whc.unesco.org/fr/orientations
(French)

世界遗产中心

（法国巴黎：7, place de Fontenoy

75352 Paris 07 SP France）

电话　: +33（0）1 4568 1876

传真　: +33（0）1 4568 5570

E-mail : wh-info@unesco.org

链接　: http://whc.unesco.org/

http://whc.unesco.org/en/guidelines
（英文）

http://whc.unesco.org/fr/orientations
（法文）

Table of Contents

Chapter number

ACRONYMS AND ABBREVIATIONS

目录

章节

缩略语

Criteria for the inscription of properties on the List of World Heritage in Danger

列入《濒危世界遗产名录》的标准

Procedure for the inscription of properties on the List of World Heritage in Danger

列入《濒危世界遗产名录》的程序

Regular review of the state of conservation of properties on the List of World Heritage in Danger

对于《濒危世界遗产名录》上遗产保护状况的定期检查

Ⅳ.C　Procedure for the eventual deletion of properties from the World Heritage List

Ⅳ.C　《世界遗产名录》中遗产彻底除名的程序

Ⅴ.　PERIODIC REPORTING ON THE IMPLEMENTATION OF THE WORLD HERITAGE CONVENTION

Ⅴ.　有关《世界遗产公约》实施情况的《定期报告》

Ⅴ.A　Objectives

Ⅴ.A　目标

Ⅴ.B　Procedure and Format

Ⅴ.B.　程序和格式

Ⅴ.C　Evaluation and follow up

Ⅴ.C　评估和后续工作

Ⅵ.　ENCOURAGING SUPPORT FOR THE WORLD HERITAGE CONVENTION

Ⅵ.　鼓励对《世界遗产公约》的支持

Ⅴ.A　Objectives

Ⅵ.A　目标

Ⅵ.B　Capacity-building and research

Ⅵ.B　能力建设与研究

The Global Training Strategy

全球培训战略

National training strategies and regional co-operation

国家培训策略和区域性合作

Research

研究

International Assistance

国际援助

Ⅵ.C　Awareness-raising and education

Ⅵ.C　提高认识与教育

Awareness-raising

提高认识

Education

教育

International Assistance

国际援助

Ⅶ.　THE WORLD HERITAGE FUND AND INTERNATIONAL ASSISTANCE

Ⅶ.　世界遗产基金和国际援助

Ⅶ.A　The World Heritage Fund

Ⅶ.A　世界遗产基金

Ⅶ.B　Mobilization of other technical and financial resources and partnerships in support of the World Heritage Convention

Ⅶ.B　调动其他技术及财务资源，展开合作，支持《世界遗产公约》

Ⅶ.C　International Assistance

Ⅶ.C　国际援助

Ⅶ.D　Principles and priorities for International Assistance

Ⅶ.D　国际援助的原则和优先顺序

Ⅶ.E　Summary table

Ⅶ.E　总表

Ⅶ.F　Procedure and format

Ⅶ.F　程序和格式

Ⅶ.G　Evaluation and approval of International Assistance

Ⅶ.G　国际援助的评估和核准

8. International Assistance Request Form

9. Evaluation criteria of the Advisory Bodies for International Assistance requests

Select bibliography on World Heritage

8. 国际援助申请表

9. 专家咨询机构评估国际援助申请的标准

世界遗产相关的参考书目

ACRONYMS AND ABBREVIATIONS

缩略语

DoCoMoMo	International Committee for the Documentation and Conservation of Monuments and Sites of the Modern Movement	DoCoMoMo	国际现代主义建筑、保护与记录国际委员会
ICCROM	International Centre for the Study of the Preservation and Restoration of Cultural Property	ICCROM	国际文物保护与修复研究中心
ICOMOS	International Council on Monuments and Sites	ICOMOS	国际古迹遗址理事会
IFLA	International Federation of Landscape Architects	IFLA	国际景观设计师联合会
IUCN	World Conservation Union (formerly the International Union for Conservation of Nature and Natural Resources)	IUCN	世界保护自然联盟（前国际自然及自然资源保护联盟）
IUGS	International Union of Geological Sciences	IUGS	国际地质科学联合会
MAB	Man and the Biosphere programme of UNESCO	MAB	教科文组织人与生物圈方案
NGO	Non-governmental organization	NGO	非政府组织
TICCIH	International Committee for the Conservation of the Industrial Heritage	TICCIH	国际工业遗产保护委员会
UNEP	United Nations Environment Programme	UNEP	联合国环境规划署
UNEP-WCMC	World Conservation Monitoring Centre (UNEP)	UNEP–WCMC	世界保护监控中心（联合国环境规划署）
UNESCO	United Nations Educational, Scientific and Cultural Organization	UNESCO	联合国教育、科学及文化组织

Ⅰ. INTRODUCTION

Ⅰ.A The Operational Guidelines

1. The *Operational Guidelines for the Implementation of the World Heritage Convention* (hereinafter referred to as the *Operational Guidelines)* aim to facilitate the implementation of the *Convention concerning the Protection of the World Cultural and Natural Heritage* (hereinafter referred to as "the *World Heritage Convention"* or *"the Convention"*), by setting forth the procedure for:

a) the inscription of properties on the World Heritage List and the List of World Heritage in Danger;

b) the protection and conservation of World Heritage properties;

c) the granting of International Assistance under the World Heritage Fund; and

d) the mobilization of national and international support in favor of the *Convention*.

2. The *Operational Guidelines* are periodically revised to reflect the decisions of the World Heritage Committee.

The historical development of the Operational Guidelines is available at the following Web address: http://whc.unesco.org/en/guidel ineshistorical

3. The key users of the *Operational Guidelines* are:

a) the States Parties to the *World Heritage Convention*;

b) the Intergovernmental Committee for the Protection of the Cultural and Natural Heritage of Outstanding Universal Value, hereinafter referred to as "the World Heritage Committee" or "the Committee";

c) the UNESCO World Heritage Centre as

Ⅰ. 引言

Ⅰ.A《操作指南》

1.《实施保护世界文化与自然遗产公约的操作指南》（以下简称《操作指南》）的宗旨在于协助《保护世界文化和自然遗产公约》（以下简称《世界遗产公约》或《公约》）的实施，并为开展下列工作设置相应的程序：

a）将遗产列入《世界遗产名录》和《世界濒危遗产名录》

b）世界遗产的保护和保存

c）世界遗产基金项下提供的国际援助以及

d）调动国内和国际力量为《公约》提供支持。

2.《操作指南》将会定期修改，以反映世界遗产委员会的最新决策

《操作指南》的发展历程可参见以下网址：http://whc.unesco.org/en/guidelineshistorical

3.《操作指南》主要使用者：

a）《世界遗产公约》的缔约国；

b）保护具有突出的普遍价值的文化和自然遗产政府间委员会，以下简称"世界遗产委员会"或"委员会"；

c）世界遗产委员会秘书处，即联合国教育、

Secretariat to the World Heritage Committee, hereinafter referred to as "the Secretariat";

d) the Advisory Bodies to the World Heritage Committee ;

e) site managers, stakeholders and partners in the protection of World Heritage properties.

Ⅰ.B The *World Heritage Convention*

4. The cultural and natural heritage is among the priceless and irreplaceable assets, not only of each nation, but of humanity as a whole. The loss, through deterioration or disappearance, of any of these most prized assets constitutes an impoverishment of the heritage of all the peoples of the world. Parts of that heritage, because of their exceptional qualities, can be considered to be of "outstanding universal value" and as such worthy of special protection against the dangers which increasingly threaten them.

5. To ensure, as far as possible, the proper identification, protection, conservation and presentation of the world's heritage, the Member States of UNESCO adopted the *World Heritage Convention* in 1972. The *Convention* foresees the establishment of a "World Heritage Committee" and a "World Heritage Fund". Both the Committee and the Fund have been in operation since 1976.

6. Since the adoption of the *Convention* in 1972, the international community has embraced the concept of "sustainable development". The protection and conservation of the natural and cultural heritage are a significant contribution to sustainable development.

7. The *Convention* aims at the identification, protection, conservation, presentation and transmission to future generations of cultural and natural heritage of

科学及文化组织世界遗产中心，以下简称"秘书处"；

d）世界遗产委员会的咨询机构；

e）负责保护世界遗产的遗址管理人员、利益相关者和合作伙伴。

Ⅰ.B《世界遗产公约》

4. 无论对各国，还是对全人类而言，文化和自然遗产都是无可估价且无法替代的遗产。这些最珍贵的财富，一旦遭受任何破坏或消失，都是对世界各族人民遗产的一次浩劫。这些遗产的一部分，具有独一无二的特性，可以认为具有"突出的普遍价值"，因而需加以特殊的保护，以消除日益威胁这些遗产安全的各种危险。

5. 为了尽可能保证对世界遗产的确认、保护、保存和展示，联合国教育、科学及文化组织成员国于1972年通过了《世界遗产公约》。《公约》确认了世界遗产委员会和世界遗产基金的建立，二者自1976年开始运行。

6. 自从1972年通过《公约》以来，国际社会全面接受了"可持续发展"这一概念。而保护、保存自然和文化遗产就是对可持续发展的巨大贡献。

7.《公约》旨在确认、保护、保存、展示具有突出的普遍价值的文化和自然遗产，并将其代代相传。

outstanding universal value.

8. The criteria and conditions for the inscription of properties on the World Heritage List have been developed to evaluate the outstanding universal value of properties and to guide States Parties in the protection and management of World Heritage properties.

9. When a property inscribed on the World Heritage List is threatened by serious and specific dangers, the Committee considers placing it on the List of World Heritage in Danger. When the outstanding universal value of the property which justified its inscription on the World Heritage List is destroyed, the Committee considers deleting the property from the World Heritage List.

Ⅰ.C The States Parties to the *World Heritage Convention*

10. States are encouraged to become party to the *Convention*. Model instruments for ratification/acceptance and accession are included as Annex 1. The original signed version should be sent to the Director-General of UNESCO.

11. The list of States Parties to the *Convention* is available at the following Web address: http://whc.unesco.org/en/statesparties

12. States Parties to the *Convention* are encouraged to ensure the participation of a wide variety of stakeholders, including site managers, local and regional governments, local communities, non-governmental organizations (NGOs) and other interested parties and partners in the identification, nomination and protection of World Heritage properties.

13. States Parties to the *Convention* should provide the Secretariat with the names and addresses

8. 已规定了将遗产列入《世界遗产名录》的标准和条件，以评估遗产是否具有突出的普遍价值，并指导缔约国保护和管理世界遗产。

9. 当《世界遗产名录》上的某项遗产受到了严重的特殊的威胁时，委员会应该考虑将该遗产列入《濒危世界遗产名录》。当具有突出的普遍价值且已经列入《世界遗产名录》的遗产受到破坏时，委员会应该考虑将该遗产从《世界遗产名录》上删除。

Ⅰ.C《世界遗产公约》缔约国

10.鼓励各个国家加入《公约》，成为缔约国。附件1收录了批准/接受公约和正式加入公约的文书范本。签署后的文书原件应呈递联合国教育、科学及文化组织总干事。

11.《公约》各缔约国名单可参见以下网址：http://whc.unesco.org/en/statesparties

12.鼓励《公约》各缔约国保证各种利益相关者，包括遗址管理人、当地和地区政府、当地社区、非政府组织（NGO）、其他相关团体和合作伙伴，参与世界遗产的确认、申报和保护。

13.《公约》各缔约国应向秘书处提供作为实施国家《公约》协调中心的重要政府机构名称

of the governmental organization(s) primarily responsible as national focal point(s) for the implementation of the *Convention*, so that copies of all official correspondence and documents can be sent by the Secretariat to these national focal points as appropriate. A list of these addresses is available at the following Web address: http://whc.unesco.org/en/statespartiesfocalpoints

States Parties are encouraged to publicize this information nationally and ensure that it is up to date.

14. States Parties are encouraged to bring together their cultural and natural heritage experts at regular intervals to discuss the implementation of the *Convention*. States Parties may wish to involve representatives of the Advisory Bodies and other experts as appropriate.

15. While fully respecting the sovereignty of the States on whose territory the cultural and natural heritage is situated, States Parties to the *Convention* recognize the collective interest of the international community to cooperate in the protection of this heritage. States Parties to the *World Heritage Convention*, have the responsibility to:

Article 6(1) of the *World Heritage Convention*.

a) ensure the identification, nomination, protection, conservation, presentation, and transmission to future generations of the cultural and natural heritage found within their territory, and give help in these tasks to other States Parties that request it;

Article 4 and 6(2) of the *World Heritage Convention*.

b) adopt general policies to give the heritage a function in the life of the community;

和地址，以便秘书处把各种官方信函和文件送达该机构。这些机构的地址列表可参见以下网址：http://whc.unesco.org/en/statespartiesfocalpoints

鼓励《公约》各缔约国公开以上信息并保证不断更新。

14. 鼓励各缔约国召集本国文化和自然遗产专家，定期讨论《公约》的实施。各缔约国可以适当邀请咨询机构的代表和其他专家参加讨论。

15. 在充分尊重文化和自然遗产所在国主权的同时，《公约》各缔约国也应该认识到，合作开展遗产保护工作符合国际社会的共同利益。《世界遗产公约》各缔约国有责任做到以下几点：

《世界遗产公约》第6（1）条。

a）缔约国应该保证在本国境内文化和自然遗产的确认、申报、保护、保存、展出以及代代相传。并在其他国家提出请求时就以上事宜提供帮助；

《世界遗产公约》第4条和第6（2）条。

b）制定、通过旨在赋予文化和自然遗产合理功能，使其在社会生活中发挥一定作用的总体政策；

Article 5 of the *World Heritage Convention*.

《世界遗产公约》第5条。

c) integrate heritage protection into comprehensive planning programmes;

　c）并把遗产保护纳入全面规划方案；

d) establish services for the protection, conservation and presentation of the heritage;

　d）建立负责遗产保护、保存和展出事务的机构；

e) develop scientific and technical studies to identify actions that would counteract the dangers that threaten the heritage;

　e）开展科学和技术研究，找出实际方法消除对本国遗产的威胁；

f) take appropriate legal, scientific, technical, administrative and financial measures to protect the heritage;

　f）采取适当的法律、科学、技术、行政和财政措施来保护这类遗产；

g) foster the establishment or development of national or regional centres for training in the protection, conservation and presentation of the heritage and encourage scientific research in these fields;

　g）促进建立或发展有关保护、保存和展出文化和自然遗产的国家或地区培训中心，并鼓励这些领域的科学研究；

h) not take any deliberate measures that directly or indirectly damage their heritage or that of another State Party to the *Convention*;

　h）不得故意采取任何可能直接或间接损害本国或公约其他缔约国领土内遗产的措施；

Article 6(3) of the *World Heritage Convention*.

《世界遗产公约》第6（3）条。

i) submit to the World Heritage Committee an inventory of properties suitable for inscription on the World Heritage List (referred to as a Tentative List);

　i）应向世界遗产委员会递交一份关于本国领土内适于列入《世界遗产名录》的遗产清单（称为《预备名录》）；

Article 11(1) of the *World Heritage Convention*.

《世界遗产公约》第11（1）条。

j) make regular contributions to the World Heritage Fund, the amount of which is determined by the General Assembly of States Parties to the *Convention*;

　j）定期向世界遗产基金缴款，缴款额由公约缔约国大会决定；

Article 16(1) of the *World Heritage Convention*.

《世界遗产公约》第16（1）条。

k) consider and encourage the establishment of national, public and private foundations or associations to facilitate donations for the protection of World Heritage;

　k）考虑和鼓励设立国家、公立以及私立基金会或协会，促进保护世界遗产的募捐；

Article 17 of the *World Heritage Convention*.

　　《世界遗产公约》第17条。

l) give assistance to international fund-raising campaigns organized for the World Heritage Fund;

　　l）为世界遗产基金的国际募款运动给予援助；

Article 18 of the *World Heritage Convention*.

　　《世界遗产公约》第18条。

m) use educational and information programmes to strengthen appreciation and respect by their peoples of the cultural and natural heritage defined in Articles 1 and 2 of the *Convention*, and to keep the public informed of the dangers threatening this heritage;

　　m）通过教育和宣传计划，努力增强本国人民对本公约第1和2条中所确定的文化和自然遗产的赞赏和尊重，并使公众广泛了解这类遗产面临的威胁；

Article 27 of the *World Heritage Convention*.

　　《世界遗产公约》第27条。

(n) provide information to the World Heritage Committee on the implementation of the *World Heritage Convention* and state of conservation of properties; and

　　n）向世界遗产委员会递交报告，详述《世界遗产公约》的实施情况和这类遗产的保存状况；并且

Article 29 of the *World Heritage Convention*. Resolution adopted by the 11th General Assembly of States Parties (1997)

　　《世界遗产公约》第29条。1997年第十一届缔约国大会通过《决议》。

16. States Parties are encouraged to attend sessions of the World Heritage Committee and its subsidiary bodies.

　　16.鼓励各公约缔约国参加世界遗产委员会及其附属机构的各届会议。

Rule 8.1 of the *Rules of Procedure of the World Heritage Committee*.

　　《世界遗产委员会议事规则》第8.1条。

Ⅰ.D The General Assembly of States Parties to the *World Heritage Convention*

　　Ⅰ.D《世界遗产公约》缔约国大会

17. The General Assembly of States Parties to the *World Heritage Convention* meets during the sessions of the General Conference of UNESCO. The General Assembly manages its meetings according to its *Rules of Procedure*, available at the

　　17.大会在联合国教育、科学及文化组织大会常会期间召开。缔约国大会根据《议事规则》组织会议，相关内容可参见以下网址：http://whc.unesco.org/en/garules

following Web address: http://whc.unesco.org/en/garules

Article 8(1), of the *World Heritage Convention*, Rule 49 of the *Rules of Procedure of the World Heritage Committee*.

《世界遗产公约》第8（1）条，《世界遗产委员会议事规则》第49条。

18. The General Assembly determines the uniform percentage of contributions to the World Heritage Fund applicable to all States Parties and elects members to the World Heritage Committee. Both the General Assembly and General Conference of UNESCO receive a report from the World Heritage Committee on its activities.

18.大会确定适用于所有缔约国的统一缴款比例，并选举世界遗产委员会委员。缔约国大会和联合国教育、科学及文化组织大会都将收到世界遗产委员会关于各项活动的报告。

Articles 8(1), 16(1) and 29 of the *World Heritage Convention and* Rule 49 of the *Rules of Procedure of the World Heritage Committee.*

《世界遗产公约》第8（1）条、第16（1）条和第29条；《世界遗产委员会议事规则》第49条。

Ⅰ.E The World Heritage Committee

Ⅰ.E 世界遗产委员会

19. The World Heritage Committee is composed of 21 members and meets at least once a year (June/July). It establishes its Bureau, which meets during the sessions of the Committee as frequently as deemed necessary. The composition of the Committee and its Bureau is available at the following Web address: http://whc.unesco.org/en/committee

19.世界遗产委员会由二十一个成员国组成，每年的六月或者七月至少开一次会议。委员会设有主席团，通常在委员会常会期间召开会议。委员会及其主席团的组成可参见以下网址：http://whc.unesco.org/en/committee

The World Heritage Committee can be contacted through its Secretariat, the World Heritage Centre.

通过世界遗产中心，即世界遗产委员会秘书处，可以和委员会取得联系。

20. The Committee manages its meetings according to its *Rules of Procedure*, available at the following Web address: http://whc.unesco.org/committee

20.世界遗产委员会根据《议事规则》召开会议，可参见以下网址：http://whc.unesco.org/committee

21. The term of office of Committee members is six years but, in order to ensure equitable representation and rotation, States Parties are invited by the General Assembly to consider voluntarily

21.世界遗产委员会成员任期六年。然而，为了保证世界遗产委员会均衡的代表性和轮值制，大会向缔约国提出自愿考虑缩短任期从六年到四年，而且不鼓励连任。

reducing their term of office from six to four years and are discouraged from seeking consecutive terms of office.

Article 9(1) of the *World Heritage Convention*.

Article 8(2) of the *World Heritage Convention* and the Resolutions of the 7th (1989), 12th (1999) and 13th (2001) General Assembly of States Parties to the *World Heritage Convention*.

《世界遗产公约》第9（1）条

《世界遗产公约》第8（2）条和《世界遗产公约》缔约国第七届（1989年）、第十二届（1999年）及第十三届（2001年）大会决议。

22. A certain number of seats may be reserved for States Parties who do not have a property on the World Heritage List, upon decision of the Committee at the session that precedes the General Assembly.

22. 根据委员会在大会前一届会议期间所作的决定，为尚无遗产列入《世界遗产名录》的缔约国保留一定数量的席位。

Rule 14.1 of the *Rules of Procedure of the General Assembly of States Parties*.

《缔约国大会议事规则》第14.1条

23. Committee decisions are based on objective and scientific considerations, and any appraisal made on its behalf must be thoroughly and responsibly carried out. The Committee recognizes that such decisions depend upon:

a) carefully prepared documentation;

b) thorough and consistent procedures;

c) evaluation by qualified experts; and

d) if necessary, the use of expert referees.

23. 委员会的决定是出自客观和科学的考虑，为委员会进行的任何评估工作都应该本着彻底和负责的态度。委员会认识到这类决定取决于以下几个方面：

a）认真编撰的文献资料；

b）详尽、统一的程序；

c）资深专家的评估；以及

d）如有必要，使用专家仲裁。

24. The main functions of the Committee are, in co-operation with States Parties, to:

a) identify, on the basis of Tentative Lists and nominations submitted by States Parties, cultural and natural properties of outstanding universal value which are to be protected under the *Convention* and to inscribe those properties on the World Heritage List;

24. 委员会的主要职能是与缔约国合作开展下述工作：

a）根据缔约国递交的《预备名录》和申报文件，确认将在《公约》实施保护的、具有突出的普遍价值的、文化和自然遗产，并把这些遗产列入《世界遗产名录》；

Article 11(2) of the *World Heritage Convention*.

《世界遗产公约》第11（2）款。

b) examine the state of conservation of properties inscribed on the World Heritage List through

b）通过反应性监测（参见第Ⅳ章）和定期报告（参见第Ⅴ章）审查已经列入《世界遗产

processes of Reactive Monitoring (see Chapter IV) and Periodic Reporting (see Chapter V);

名录》的遗产保护状况；

Articles 11(7) and 29 of the *World Heritage Convention.*

《世界遗产公约》第11（7）条和第29条。

c) decide which properties inscribed on the World Heritage List are to be inscribed on, or removed from the List of World Heritage in Danger;

c）决定《世界遗产名录》中的哪些遗产应该列入《濒危世界遗产名录》或从中移除；

Article 11(4) and 11(5) of the *World Heritage Convention.*

《世界遗产公约》第11（4）条和第11（5）条。

d) decide whether a property should be deleted from the World Heritage List (see Chapter IV);

d）决定一项遗产是否应该从《世界遗产名录》上移除（参见第Ⅳ章）；

e) define the procedure by which requests for International Assistance are to be considered and carry out studies and consultations as necessary before coming to a decision (see Chapter VII);

e）制定关于国际援助申请的审议程序，在作出决定之前，进行必要的研究和磋商（参见第Ⅶ章）；

Article 21(1) and 21(3) of the *World Heritage Convention.*

《世界遗产公约》第21（1）条和第21（3）条。

f) determine how the resources of the World Heritage Fund can be used most advantageously to assist States Parties in the protection of their properties of outstanding universal value;

f）决定如何发挥世界遗产基金资源的最大优势，帮助缔约国保护他们具有突出的普遍价值的遗产；

Article 13(6) of the *World Heritage Convention.*

《世界遗产公约》第13（6）条。

g) seek ways to increase the World Heritage Fund;

g）设法增加世界遗产基金的资金；

h) submit a report on its activities every two years to the General Assembly of States Parties and to the UNESCO General Conference;

h）每两年向缔约国大会和联合国教育、科学及文化组织大会递交一份活动的报告；

Article 29(3) of the *World Heritage Convention* and Rule 49 of the Rules of procedure of the World Heritage Committee.

《世界遗产公约》第29（3）条和《世界遗产委员会议事规则》第49条。

i) review and evaluate periodically the implementation of the *Convention*;

i）定期审查和评估《公约》的实施情况；

j) revise and adopt the *Operational Guidelines.*

j）修改并通过《操作指南》。

25. In order to facilitate the implementation of the *Convention*, the Committee develops Strategic Objectives; they are periodically reviewed and revised to ensure that new threats placed on World Heritage are addressed effectively.

The first 'Strategic Orientations' adopted by the Committee in 1992 are contained in Annex II of document WHC- 92/ CONF.002/12

26. The current Strategic Objectives (also referred to as "the 4 Cs") are the following:

In 2002 the World Heritage Committee revised its Strategic Objectives. The *Budapest Declaration on World Heritage* (2002) is available at the following Web address: http://whc. unesco.org/en/budap estdeclaration

1. Strengthen the Credibility of the World Heritage List;

2. Ensure the effective Conservation of World Heritage Properties;

3. Promote the development of effective Capacity-building in States Parties;

4. Increase public awareness, involvement and support for World Heritage through Communication.

Ⅰ.F The Secretariat to the World Heritage Committee (World Heritage Centre)

UNESCO World Heritage Centre

7, place de Fontenoy

75352 Paris 07 SP

France

Tel: +33 (0) 1 4568 1571

Fax: +33 (0) 1 4568 5570

E-mail: wh-info@unesco.org

www: http://whc.unesco.org/

27. The World Heritage Committee is assisted by a Secretariat appointed by the Director-General of UNESCO. The function of the Secretariat is

---

25. 为了促进《公约》的实施，委员会制定了战略目标并对这些目标定期审查和修改，保证有效消除世界遗产面临的新威胁。

1992年委员会通过的第一份《战略方向》载列于文件WHC-92/CONF.002/12附件Ⅱ。

26. 目前的战略目标（简称为"4C"）是：

2002年世界遗产委员会修改了战略目标。《布达佩斯世界遗产宣言》（2002年）可参见以下网址：http://whc.unesco.org/en/budapestdeclaration

1. 增强《世界遗产名录》的可信性；

2. 保证世界遗产的有效保护；

3. 促进各缔约国有效的能力建设；

4. 通过宣传增强大众对世界遗产的认识、参与和支持。

Ⅰ.F 世界遗产委员会秘书处（世界遗产中心）

联合国教育、科学及文化组织世界遗产中心地址：

法国巴黎（7, place de Fontenoy

75352 Paris 07 SP

France）

电话：+33（0）1 4568 1571

传真：+33（0）1 4568 5570

电子邮箱：wh-info@unesco.org

网址：http://whc.unesco.org/

27. 由联合国教育、科学及文化组织总干事指定的秘书处协助世界遗产委员会工作。1992年创建了世界遗产中心，担负秘书处的职能，

currently assumed by the World Heritage Centre, established in 1992 specifically for this purpose. The Director-General designated the Director of the World Heritage Centre as Secretary to the Committee. The Secretariat assists and collaborates with the States Parties and the Advisory Bodies. The Secretariat works in close co-operation with other sectors and field offices of UNESCO.

联合国教科文组织总干事指派世界遗产中心主任为委员会的秘书。秘书处协助和协调缔约国和咨询机构的工作。秘书处还与联合国教科文组织的其他部门和外地办事处密切合作。

Article 14 of the *World Heritage Convention*.

Rule 43 of *Rules of Procedure of the World Heritage Committee*.

Circular Letter 16 of 21 October 2003

http://whc.unesco.org/circs/circ 03-16e.pdf

《世界遗产公约》第14条。

《世界遗产委员会议事规则》第43条。

2003年10月21日《通函16号》，可参见以下网址：

http://whc.unesco.org/circs/circ03-16e.pdf

28. The Secretariat's main tasks are:

a) the organization of the meetings of the General Assembly and the Committee;

28.秘书处主要任务包括：

ａ）组织缔约国大会和世界遗产委员会的会议；

Article 14.2 of the *World Heritage Convention*.

《世界遗产公约》第14.2条。

b) the implementation of decisions of the World Heritage Committee and resolutions of the General Assembly and reporting to them on their execution;

ｂ）执行世界遗产委员会的各项决定和联合国教科文组织大会的决议，并向委员会和大会汇报执行情况；

Article 14.2 of the *World Heritage Convention* and the *Budapest Declaration on World Heritage* (2002)

《世界遗产公约》第14.2条。《布达佩斯世界遗产宣言》（2002年）

c) the receipt, registration, checking the completeness, archiving and transmission to the relevant Advisory Bodies of nominations to the World Heritage List;

d) the co-ordination of studies and activities as part of the Global Strategy for a Representative, Balanced and Credible World Heritage List;

e) the organization of Periodic Reporting and co-ordination of Reactive Monitoring;

f) the co-ordination of International Assistance;

g) the mobilisation of extra-budgetary resources for the conservation and management of World

ｃ）接收、登记世界遗产申报文件，检查其完整性、存档并呈递到相关的咨询机构；

ｄ）协调各项研究和活动，作为加强《世界遗产名录》代表性、平衡性和可信性全球战略的一部分；

ｅ）组织定期报告和协调反应性监测；

ｆ）协调国际援助；

ｇ）调动预算外资金保护和管理世界遗产；

Heritage properties;

h) the assistance to States Parties in the implementation of the Committee's programmes and projects; and

i) the promotion of World Heritage and the *Convention* through the dissemination of information to States Parties, the Advisory Bodies and the general public.

29. These activities follow the decisions and Strategic Objectives of the Committee and the resolutions of the General Assembly of the States Parties and are conducted in close co-operation with the Advisory Bodies.

Ⅰ.G Advisory Bodies to the World Heritage Committee

30. The Advisory Bodies to the World Heritage Committee are ICCROM (the International Centre for the Study of the Preservation and Restoration of Cultural Property), ICOMOS (the International Council on Monuments and Sites), and IUCN - the World Conservation Union.

Article 8.3 of the *World Heritage Convention*

31. The roles of the Advisory Bodies are to:
a) advise on the implementation of the *World Heritage Convention* in the field of their expertise;

Article 13.7 of the *World Heritage Convention*.

b) assist the Secretariat, in the preparation of the Committee's documentation, the agenda of its meetings and the implementation of the Committee's decisions;

c) assist with the development and implementation of the Global Strategy for a Representative, Balanced and Credible World Heritage List, the Global Training Strategy, Periodic Reporting, and the strengthening

h）协助各缔约国实施委员会的方案和项目；以及

i）通过向缔约国、咨询机构和大众发布信息，促进世界遗产的保护和增强对《公约》的认识。

29.开展这些活动要服从于委员会的各项决定和战略目标、以及缔约国大会的各项决议，并与咨询机构密切合作。

Ⅰ.G 世界遗产委员会咨询机构

30.世界遗产委员会的咨询机构包括：ICCROM（国际文物保护和修复研究中心），ICOMOS（国际古迹遗址理事会）以及IUCN（世界自然保护联盟）

《世界遗产公约》第8.3条。

31.咨询机构的角色：
a）以本领域的专业知识指导《世界遗产公约》的实施；

《世界遗产公约》第13.7条。

b）协助秘书处准备委员会需要的文献资料，安排会议议程以及协助委员会实施各项决定；

c）协助制定和实施加强《世界遗产名录》代表性、平衡性和可信性全球战略和全球培训战略，定期报告以及加强世界遗产基金的有效使用；

of the effective use of the World Heritage Fund;

d) monitor the state of conservation of World Heritage properties and review requests for International Assistance;

Article 14.2 of the *World Heritage Convention*.

e) in the case of ICOMOS and IUCN evaluate properties nominated for inscription on the World Heritage List and present evaluation reports to the Committee; and

f) attend meetings of the World Heritage Committee and the Bureau in an advisory capacity.

Article 8.3 of the *World Heritage Convention*.

ICCROM

32. ICCROM (the International Centre for the Study of the Preservation and Restoration of Cultural Property) is an international intergovernmental organization with headquarters in Rome, Italy. Established by UNESCO in 1956, ICCROM's statutory functions are to carry out research, documentation, technical assistance, training and public awareness programmes to strengthen conservation of immovable and moveable cultural heritage.

ICCROM

Via di S. Michele, 13

I-00153 Rome, Italy

Tel : +39 06 585531

Fax: +39 06 5855 3349

Email: iccrom@iccrom.org

http://www.iccrom.org/

33. The specific role of ICCROM in relation to the *Convention* includes: being the priority partner in training for cultural heritage, monitoring the state of conservation of World Heritage cultural

d）监督世界遗产的保护状况并审查国际援助的申请；

《世界遗产公约》第14.2条。

e）国际古迹遗址理事会和世界自然保护联盟共同评估申请列入《世界遗产名录》的申报遗产并向委员会呈递评估报告；以及

f）以咨询者的身份，列席世界遗产委员会及其主席团会议。

《世界遗产公约》8.3条。

国际文物保护和修复研究中心

32. ICCROM，即国际文物保护和修复研究中心，是一个政府间组织，总部设在意大利的罗马。1956年联合国教科文组织创建了这个中心。根据规定，该中心的作用是进行调查研究，记录文献资料，提供技术援助、培训和推行增强公众意识的项目，加强对可移动和不可移动文化遗产的保护。

国际文物保护和修复研究中心地址：

意大利罗马（Via di S. Michele, 13

I-00153 Rome, Italy）

电话：+39 06 585531

传真：+39 06 5855 3349

电子邮箱：iccrom@iccrom.org

网址：http://www.iccrom.org/

33. 国际文物保护和修复研究中心和《公约》相关的特殊职责包括：文化遗产培训领域的重要合作伙伴，监督世界遗产文物保护状况，审查由缔约国提交的国际援助申请，以及为能

properties, reviewing requests for International Assistance submitted by States Parties, and providing input and support for capacity-building activities.

力建设活动出力献策和提供支持。

ICOMOS

34. ICOMOS (the International Council on Monuments and Sites) is a non-governmental organization with headquarters in Paris, France. Founded in 1965, its role is to promote the application of theory, methodology and scientific techniques to the conservation of the architectural and archaeological heritage. Its work is based on the principles of the 1964 International Charter on the Conservation and Restoration of Monuments and Sites (the Venice Charter).

ICOMOS

49-51, rue de la Fédération

75015 Paris, France

Tel: +33 (0)1 45 67 67 70

Fax: +33 (0)1 45 66 06 22

E-mail: secretariat@icomos.org

http://www.icomos.org/

35. The specific role of ICOMOS in relation to the *Convention* includes: evaluation of properties nominated for inscription on the World Heritage List, monitoring the state of conservation of World Heritage cultural properties, reviewing requests for International Assistance submitted by States Parties, and providing input and support for capacity-building activities.

IUCN

36. IUCN-The World Conservation Union (formely the International Union for the Conservation of Nature and Natural Resources) was founded in 1948

国际古迹遗址理事会

34. ICOMOS，即国际古迹遗址理事会，是一个非政府组织，总部在法国巴黎，创建于1965年。理事会的作用在于推广建筑和考古遗产保护理论、方法和科学技术的应用。理事会的工作以1964年《国际古迹遗址保护和修复宪章》（又称《威尼斯宪章》）的原则为基准。

国际古迹遗址理事会

法国巴黎（49–51, rue de la Fédération

75015 Paris, France）

电话：+33（0）1 45 67 67 70

传真：+33（0）1 45 66 06 22

电子邮箱：secretariat@icomos.org

网址：http://www.icomos.org/

35. 国际古迹遗址理事会和《公约》相关的特殊职责包括：评估申报世界遗产的项目，监督世界文化遗产保护状况，审查由缔约国提交的国际援助申请，以及为能力建设活动出力献策和提供支持。

世界保护自然联盟

36. IUCN，即世界保护自然联盟（前身是国际自然和自然资源保护联盟），创建于1948年，为各国政府、非政府组织和科学工作者在世界

and brings together national governments, NGOs, and scientists in a worldwide partnership. Its mission is to influence, encourage and assist societies throughout the world to conserve the integrity and diversity of nature and to ensure that any use of natural resources is equitable and ecologically sustainable. IUCN has its headquarters in Gland, Switzerland.

> IUCN - The World Conservation Union
> rue Mauverney 28
> CH-1196 Gland, Switzerland
> Tel: +41 22 999 0001
> Fax: +41 22 999 0010
> E-Mail: mail@hq.iucn.org
> http://www.iucn.org

37. The specific role of IUCN in relation to the *Convention* includes: evaluation of properties nominated for inscription on the World Heritage List, monitoring the state of conservation of World Heritage natural properties, reviewing requests for International Assistance submitted by States Parties, and providing input and support for capacity- building activities.

Ⅰ.H Other organizations

38. The Committee may call on other inter-national and non-governmental organizations with appropriate competence and expertise to assist in the implementation of the programmes and projects.

Ⅰ.I Partners in the protection of World Heritage

39. A partnership approach to nomination, management and monitoring provides a significant contribution to the protection of World Heritage properties and the implementation of the *Convention*.

40. Partners in the protection and conservation

范围的合作提供了机会。其使命在于影响、鼓励和协助世界各团体保护自然的完整性和多样化,并确保任何对自然资源的使用都是公正的、符合生态的可持续发展。世界保护自然联盟总部设在瑞士格朗德。

> IUCN——世界保护自然联盟
> 地址:瑞士格朗德(rue Mauverney 28
> CH–1196 Gland, Switzerland)
> 电话:+ 41 22 999 0001
> 传真:+41 22 999 0010
> 电子邮箱:mail@hq.iucn.org
> 网址:http://www.iucn.org

37.世界保护自然联盟和《公约》相关的特殊职责包括:评估申报世界遗产的项目,监督世界自然遗产保护状况,审查由缔约国提交的国际援助申请,以及为能力建设活动出力献策和提供支持。

Ⅰ.H 其他组织

38.委员会可能号召其他具有一定能力和专业技术的国际组织和非政府组织,协助各方案和项目的实施。

Ⅰ.I 保护世界遗产的合作伙伴

39.在申报、管理和监督工作中采用合作伙伴方式,有力地促进了世界遗产的保护和《公约》的实施。

40.保护和保存世界遗产的合作伙伴包括:

of World Heritage can be those individuals and other stakeholders, especially local communities, governmental, non-governmental and private organizations and owners who have an interest and involvement in the conservation and management of a World Heritage property.

Ⅰ.J Other Conventions, Recommendations and Programmes

41. The World Heritage Committee recognizes the benefits of closer co-ordination of its work with other UNESCO programmes and their relevant Conventions. For a list of relevant global conservation instruments, Conventions and programmes see paragraph 44.

42. The World Heritage Committee with the support of the Secretariat will ensure appropriate co-ordination and information-sharing between the *World Heritage Convention* and other Conventions, programmes and international organizations related to the conservation of cultural and natural heritage.

43. The Committee may invite representatives of the intergovernmental bodies under related Conventions to attend its meetings as observers. It may appoint a representative to observe meetings of the other intergovernmental bodies upon receipt of an invitation.

44. Selected global Conventions and programmes relating to the protection of cultural and natural heritage

UNESCO Conventions and Programmes

Convention for the Protection of Cultural Property in the Event of Armed Conflict (1954)

个人和其他利益相关者，尤其是对世界遗产的保存和管理感兴趣并参与其中的当地社区、政府组织、非政府组织和私人组织以及所有人。

Ⅰ.J 其他公约、建议和方案

41.世界遗产委员会认识到，密切协调好与教科文组织其他方案和相关公约是受益匪浅。参见第44条中相关全球保护文书、公约和方案。

42.在秘书处的支持下，世界遗产委员会将保证《世界遗产公约》和其他公约、方案以及和保护文化和自然遗产有关的国际组织之间适当协调工作，信息共享。

43.委员会可能邀请相关公约下政府间组织的代表，作为观察员，参加委员会的会议。如受到其他政府间组织的邀请，委员会可能派遣代表作为观察员列席会议。

44.与保护文化和自然遗产相关的部分全球公约和方案

联合国教育、科学及文化组织的其他公约和方案

《关于在武装冲突的情况下保护文化遗产的公约》（1954年）

Protocol I (1954)
Protocol II (1999)
http://www.unesco.org/culture/laws/hague/html_eng/page1.shtml

Convention on the Means of Prohibiting and Preventing the Illicit Import, Export and Transfer of Ownership of Cultural Property (1970)
http://www.unesco.org/culture/laws/1970/html_eng/page1.shtml

Convention concerning the Protection of the World Cultural and Natural Heritage (1972)
http://www.unesco.org/whc/world_he.htm

Convention on the Protection of the Underwater Cultural Heritage (2001)
http://www.unesco.org/culture/laws/underwater/html_eng/convention.shtml

Convention for the Safeguarding of the Intangible Cultural Heritage (2003)
http://unesdoc.unesco.org/images/0013/001325/132540e.pdf

Man and the Biosphere (MAB) Programme
http://www.unesco.org/mab/

Other Conventions

Convention on Wetlands of International Importance especially as Waterfowl Habitat (Ramsar) (1971)
http://www.ramsar.org/key_conv_e.htm

Convention on International Trade in Endangered Species of Wild Fauna and Flora (CITES) (1973)
http://www.cites.org/eng/disc/text.shtml

第一议定书（1954年）
第二议定书（1999年）
http://www.unesco.org/culture/laws/hague/html_eng/page1.shtml

《关于采取措施禁止并防止文化遗产非法进出口和所有权非法转让公约》（1970年）
http://www.unesco.org/culture/laws/1970/html_eng/page1.shtml

《保护世界文化和自然遗产公约》（1972年）
http://www.unesco.org/whc/world_he.htm

《保护水下文化遗产公约》（2001年）
http://www.unesco.org/culture/laws/underwater/html_eng/convention.shtml

《保护非物质文化遗产公约》（2003年）
http://unesdoc.unesco.org/images/0013/001325/132540e.pdf

"人类和生物圈"计划（MAB）
http://www.unesco.org/mab/

其他公约

《关于国际重要湿地特别是水禽栖息地的公约（卡姆萨尔公约）》（1971年）
http://www.ramsar.org/key_conv_e.htm

《濒危野生动植物种国际贸易公约》（CITES）（1973年）
http://www.cites.org/eng/disc/text.shtml

Convention on the Conservation of Migratory Species of Wild Animals (CMS) (1979)

http://www.unep-wcmc.org/cms/cms_conv.htm

United Nations Convention on the Law of the Sea (UNCLOS) (1982)

http://www.un.org/Depts/los/convention_agreements/texts/unclos/closindx.htm

Convention on Biological Diversity (1992)

http://www.biodiv.org/convention/articles.asp

UNIDROIT Convention on Stolen or Illegally Exported Cultural Objects (Rome, 1995)

http://www.unidroit.org/english/conventions/culturalproperty/c-cult.htm

United Nations Framework Convention on Climate Change (New York, 1992)

http://unfccc.int/essential_background/convention/background/items/1350.php

II. THE WORLD HERITAGE LIST

II.A Definition of World Heritage

Cultural and Natural Heritage

45. Cultural and natural heritage are defined in Articles 1 and 2 of the *World Heritage Convention*.

Article 1
For the purposes of this Convention, the following shall be considered as "cultural heritage";
- monuments: architectural works, works of monumental sculpture and painting, elements or structures of an archaeological nature, inscriptions, cave dwellings and combinations of features, which are of outstanding universal value from the point of

《养护野生迁徙动物物种保护公约》（CMS）（1979年）

http://www.unep-wcmc.org/cms/cms_conv.htm

《联合国海洋法公约》（UNCLOS）（1982年）

http://www.un.org/Depts/los/convention_agreements/texts/unclos/closindx.htm

《生物多样性公约》（1992年）

http://www.biodiv.org/convention/articles.asp

《国际统一私法协会关于被盗或非法出口文物的公约》（罗马，1995）

http://www.unidroit.org/english/conventions/culturalproperty/c-cult.htm

《联合国气候变化框架公约》（纽约，1992年）

http://unfccc.int/essential_background/convention/background/items/1350.php

II.《世界遗产名录》

II.A 世界遗产的定义

文化和自然遗产

45. 文化和自然遗产的定义见《世界遗产公约》第1条和第2条。

第1条
在本公约中，以下各项为"文化遗产"：

一文物：从历史、艺术或科学角度看，具有突出的普遍价值的建筑、碑雕和碑画、具有考古性质成份或结构、铭文、窟洞以及联合体；

view of history, art or science;

- groups of buildings: groups of separate or connected buildings which, because of their architecture, their homogeneity or their place in the landscape, are of outstanding universal value from the point of view of history, art or science;

- sites: works of man or the combined works of nature and of man, and areas including archaeological sites which are of outstanding universal value from the historical, aesthetic, ethnological or anthropological points of view.

Article 2

For the purposes of this Convention, the following shall be considered as "natural heritage":

-natural features consisting of physical and biological formations or groups of such formations, which are of outstanding universal value from the aesthetic or scientific point of view;

geological and physiographical formations and precisely delineated areas which constitute the habitat of threatened species of animals and plants of outstanding universal value from the point of view of science or conservation;

-natural sites or precisely delineated natural areas of outstanding universal value from the point of view of science, conservation or natural beauty.

Mixed Cultural and Natural Heritage

46. Properties shall be considered as "mixed cultural and natural heritage" if they satisfy a part or the whole of the definitions of both cultural and natural heritage laid out in Articles 1 and 2 of the *Convention.*

Cultural landscapes

47. Cultural landscapes are cultural properties and represent the "combined works of nature and

---

—建筑群：从历史、艺术或科学角度看，在建筑式样、分布均匀或与环境景色结合方面具有突出的普遍价值的独立的、或连接的建筑群；

—遗址：从历史、审美、人种学或人类学角度看，具有突出的普遍价值的人类工程或自然与人联合的工程以及考古地址等地方。

第2条

在本公约中，以下各项为"自然遗产"：.

—从审美或科学角度看，具有突出的普遍价值的由物质和生物结构或，这类结构群组成的自然面貌；

—从科学或保护角度看，具有突出的普遍价值的地质和自然地理结构以及明确划为受威胁的动物和植物生境区；

—从科学、保存或自然美角度看具有突出普遍价值的天然名胜或明确划分的自然区域。

文化和自然混合遗产

46.只有同时部分满足或完全满足《公约》第1条和第2条关于文化和自然遗产定义的遗产才能认为是"文化和自然混合遗产"。

文化景观

47.《公约》第1条就指出文化景观属于文化遗产，代表着"自然与人共同作品"。它们反

of man" designated in Article 1 of the *Convention*. They are illustrative of the evolution of human society and settlement over time, under the influence of the physical constraints and/or opportunities presented by their natural environment and of successive social, economic and cultural forces, both external and internal.

映了因物质条件的限制和/或自然环境带来的机遇，在一系列社会、经济和文化因素的内外作用下，人类社会和定居地的历史沿革。

Annex 3

附件3

Movable Heritage

可移动遗产

48. Nominations of immovable heritage which are likely to become movable will not be considered.

48. 对于可能发生迁移的不可移动遗产的申报将不作考虑。

Outstanding universal value

突出普遍价值

49. Outstanding universal value means cultural and/or natural significance which is so exceptional as to transcend national boundaries and to be of common importance for present and future generations of all humanity. As such, the permanent protection of this heritage is of the highest importance to the international community as a whole. The Committee defines the criteria for the inscription of properties on the World Heritage List.

49. 突出的普遍价值指文化和/或自然价值是如此罕见，超越了国家界限，对全人类的现在和未来均具有普遍的重要意义。因此，该项遗产的永久性保护对整个国际社会都具有至高的重要性。世界遗产委员会规定了遗产列入《世界遗产名录》的标准。

50. States Parties are invited to submit nominations of properties of cultural and/or natural value considered to be of "outstanding universal value" for inscription on the World Heritage List.

50. 邀请缔约国申报认为具有"突出普遍价值"的文化和/或自然遗产，以列入《世界遗产名录》。

51. At the time of inscription of a property on the World Heritage List, the Committee adopts a Statement of Outstanding Universal Value (see paragraph 154) which will be the key reference for the future effective protection and management of the property.

51. 遗产列入《世界遗产名录》时，世界遗产委员会会通过一个《突出普遍价值声明》(见第154段)，该声明将是以后遗产的有效保护与管理的重要援引文书。

52. The *Convention* is not intended to ensure the protection of all properties of great interest, importance or value, but only for a select list of the most

52. 该《公约》不是旨在保护所有具有重大意义或价值的遗产，而是只保护那些从国际观点看具有最突出价值的遗产。不应该认为某项具

outstanding of these from an international viewpoint. It is not to be assumed that a property of national and/or regional importance will automatically be inscribed on the World Heritage List.

53. Nominations presented to the Committee shall demonstrate the full commitment of the State Party to preserve the heritage concerned, within its means. Such commitment shall take the form of appropriate policy, legal, scientific, technical, administrative and financial measures adopted and proposed to protect the property and its outstanding universal value.

Ⅱ.B A Representative, Balanced and Credible World Heritage List

54. The Committee seeks to establish a representative, balanced and credible World Heritage List in conformity with the four Strategic Objectives adopted by the Committee at its 26th session (Budapest, 2002).

Budapest Declaration on World Heritage (2002) at http://whc.unesco.org/en/budapest declaration

The Global Strategy for a Representative, Balanced and Credible World Heritage List

55. The Global Strategy for a Representative, Balanced and Credible World Heritage List is designed to identify and fill the major gaps in the World Heritage List. It does this by encouraging more countries to become States Parties to the *Convention* and to develop Tentative Lists as defined in paragraph 62 and nominations of properties for inscription on the World Heritage List (see http://whc.unesco.org/en/globalstrategy)

The report of the Expert Meeting on the "Global Strategy"

有国家和/或区域重要性的遗产会自动列入《世界遗产名录》。

53.呈递给委员会的申报，应该表明该缔约国在其力所能及的范围内将全力以赴保存该项遗产。这种承诺应该体现在采纳和提出合适的政策、法律、科学、技术、管理和财政措施，保护该项遗产以及遗产的突出的普遍价值。

Ⅱ.B 具有代表性、平衡性和可信性的《世界遗产名录》

54.委员会根据第26届会议确定的四个战略目标，致力于构建一个具有代表性、平衡性和可信性的《世界遗产名录》。（布达佩斯，2002）

《布达佩斯世界遗产宣言》所在网址：http://whc.unesco.org/en/budapestdeclaration

构建具有代表性、平衡性、可信性的《世界遗产名录》的《全球战略》

55.构建具有代表性、平衡性、可信性的《世界遗产名录》的《全球战略》，旨在确定并填补《世界遗产名录》的主要空白。该战略鼓励更多的国家加入《保护世界文化与自然遗产公约》、按第62条的定义编撰《预备名录》、准备申请《世界遗产名录》的申报文件（详情请登陆：http://whc.unesco.org/en/globalstrategy）

关于"全球战略"的专家会议报告及构建具有代表性的

and thematic studies for a representative World Heritage List (20-22 June 1994) was adopted by the World Heritage Committee at its 18th session (Phuket, 1994).

The Global Strategy was initially developed with reference to cultural heritage. At the request of the World Heritage Committee, the Global Strategy was subsequently expanded to also include reference to natural heritage and combined cultural and natural heritage.

世界遗产名录的主题研究报告（1994年6月20–22日）在世界遗产委员会第18届大会通过。（福克，1994）

《全球战略》起初是为保护文化遗产提出的。应世界遗产委员会的要求，《全球战略》随后有所扩展，包括自然遗产和文化自然混合遗产。

56. States Parties and the Advisory Bodies are encouraged to participate in the implementation of the Global Strategy in co- operation with the Secretariat and other partners. Regional and thematic Global Strategy meetings and comparative and thematic studies are organized for this purpose. The results of these meetings and studies are available to assist States Parties in preparing Tentative Lists and nominations. The reports of the expert meetings and studies presented to the World Heritage Committee are available at the following Web address: http://whc.unesco.org/en/globalstrategy

56.鼓励各缔约国和咨询机构同秘书处及其他合作方合作，参与实施《全球战略》。为此，组织召开了区域及"全球战略"主题会议，并开展对比研究及主题研究。会议和研究成果将协助缔约国编撰《预备名录》和申报材料。可访问网站：http://whc.unesco.org/en/globalstrategy，查阅提交给世界遗产委员会的专家会议报告和研究报告。

57. All efforts should be made to maintain a reasonable balance between cultural and natural heritage on the World Heritage List.

57.要尽一切努力，保持《世界遗产名录》内文化和自然遗产的平衡。

58. No formal limit is imposed on the total number of properties to be inscribed on the World Heritage List.

58.《世界遗产名录》上的遗产总数没有正式限制。

Other measures

其他措施

59. To promote the establishment of a represent- ative, balanced and credible World Heritage List, States Parties are requested to consider whether their heritage is already well represented on the List and if so to slow down their rate of submission of further nominations by:

59.要构建具有代表性、平衡性、可信性的《世界遗产名录》，缔约国须考虑其遗产是否已在遗产名录上得到充分的代表，如果是，就要采取以下措施，放慢新申报的提交速度：

Resolution adopted by the 12th General Assembly of States Parties (1999).

缔约国第12届会议通过的决议（1999年）。

a) spacing voluntarily their nominations according to conditions that they will define, and/or;

b) proposing only properties falling into categories still under-represented, and/or;

c) linking each of their nominations with a nomination presented by a State Party whose heritage is under- represented; or

d) deciding, on a voluntary basis, to suspend the presentation of new nominations.

a）依据自身情况，自主增大申报间隔，和/或；

b）只申报名录内代表性不足的类别的遗产，和/或；

c）每次申报都同名录内代表性不足的缔约国的申报联系起来，或；

d）自主决定暂停提交新的申报。

60. States Parties whose heritage of outstanding universal value is under-represented on the World Heritage List are requested to:

a) give priority to the preparation of their Tentative Lists and nominations;

b) initiate and consolidate partnerships at the regional level based on the exchange of technical expertise;

c) encourage bilateral and multilateral co-operation so as to increase their expertise and the technical capacities of institutions in charge of the protection, safeguarding and management of their heritage; and,

d) participate, as much as possible, in the sessions of the World Heritage Committee.

60. 如果缔约国遗产具有突出的普遍价值，且在《世界遗产名录》上代表性不足，应：

a）优先考虑编撰《预备名录》和申报材料；

b）在所属区域内，寻求技术交流伙伴并巩固这种合作关系；

c）鼓励双边和多边合作以增强缔约国负责遗产保护、保存和管理机构的专业技能。

d）尽可能参加世界遗产委员会的各届会议。

Resolution adopted by the 12th General Assembly of States Parties (1999).

缔约国第12届会议通过的决议（1999年）。

61. The Committee has decided, on an experimental and transitory basis, to apply the following mechanism at its 30th session (2006):

61. 委员会决定，在第30届大会（2006年）上暂时试用以下机制：

Decisions 24 COM VI.2.3.3, 28 COM 13.1 and 7 EXT.COM 4B.1

第24 COM Ⅵ.2.3.3号决定、第28 COM 13.1号决定和第7EXT.COM 4B.1号决定

a) examine up to two complete nominations

a）最多审查同一个缔约国的两项完整申

per State Party, provided that at least one of such nominations concerns a natural property; and,

b) set at 45 the annual limit on the number of nominations it will review, inclusive of nominations deferred and referred by previous sessions of the Committee, extensions (except minor modifications of limits of the property), transboundary and serial nominations,

c) the following order of priorities will be applied:

i) nominations of properties submitted by States Parties with no properties inscribed on the List;

ii) nominations of properties from any State Party that illustrate un-represented or less represented categories of natural and cultural categories;

iii) other nominations;

iv) when applying this priority system, date of receipt of full and complete nominations by the Secretariat shall be used as secondary determining factor within the category where the number of nomination fixed by the Committee has been reached.

This decision will be re-examined at the Committee's 31st session (2007).

Ⅱ.C Tentative Lists

Procedure and Format

62. A Tentative List is an inventory of those properties situated on its territory which each State Party considers suitable for inscription on the World Heritage List. States Parties should therefore include, in their Tentative Lists, the names of those properties which they consider to be cultural and/or natural heritage of outstanding universal value and which they intend to nominate during the following years.

报，其中至少有一项与自然遗产有关；和

b）确定委员会每年审查的申报数目不超过45个，其中包括往届会议推迟审议的项目、再审项目、扩展项目（遗产边界的细微变动除外）、跨界项目和系列申报项目，

c）优先顺序如下所示：

ⅰ）尚无遗产列入名录的缔约国提交的遗产申报；

ⅱ）任一缔约国申报的、名录内没有或代表性不足的自然或文化遗产类别；

ⅲ）其他申报；

ⅳ）采用该优先顺序机制时，如果某领域内委员会所确定的申报名额已满，则秘书处收到完整申报材料的日期将被作为第二决定因素来考虑。

该决定将会在委员会第31届会议（2007年）上重新审议。

Ⅱ.C《预备名录》

程序和格式

62.《预备名录》是缔约国认为其境内具备列入世界遗产名录资格的遗产的详细目录，其中包括那些他们认为具有潜在突出普遍价值的遗产详情，以及今后几年内要申报的遗产。

Articles 1, 2 and 11(1) of the *World Heritage Convention.*

《保护世界文化与自然遗产公约》第1、2及11（1）条规定。

63. Nominations to the World Heritage List are not considered unless the nominated property has already been included on the State Party's Tentative List.

63. 如果缔约国提交的申报遗产未曾列入该国的《预备名录》，委员会将不予考虑。

Decision 24COM para. Ⅵ.2.3.2

第24COM　Ⅵ.2.3.2号决定

64. States Parties are encouraged to prepare their Tentative Lists with the participation of a wide variety of stakeholders, including site managers, local and regional governments, local communities, NGOs and other interested parties and partners.

64. 鼓励缔约国在各利益相关者、遗产地管理人员、当地和地区政府、社区、非政府组织以及其他相关机构广泛参与基础上，编制其《预备名录》。

65. States Parties shall submit Tentative Lists to the Secretariat, preferably at least one year prior to the submission of any nomination. States Parties are encouraged to re-examine and re-submit their Tentative List at least every ten years.

65. 缔约国应在遗产申报前至少一年将《预备名录》呈报至秘书处。委员会鼓励缔约国至少每十年重新审查或递交其《预备名录》。

66. States Parties are requested to submit their Tentative Lists in English or French using the standard format in Annex 2, containing the name of the properties, their geographical location, a brief description of the properties, and justification of their outstanding universal value.

66. 缔约国需要按照附件2所示的标准格式，递交英文或法语的《预备名录》，其中包括遗产名称、地理位置、简短描述以及其具有突出的普遍价值的声明。

67. The original duly signed version of the completed Tentative List shall be submitted by the State Party, to:

67. 缔约国应将已签名的完整《预备名录》原件递交至：

UNESCO World Heritage Centre

7, place de Fontenoy

75352 Paris 07 SP

France

Tel: +33 (0) 1 4568 1136

E-mail: wh-tentativelists@unesco.org

联合国教科文组织世界遗产中心

法国巴黎（7, place de

Fontenoy，Paris 07 SP，

France）

电话：+33（0）1 4568 1136

电邮：wh-tentativelists@unesco.org

68. If all information has been provided, the

68. 如果所有信息均已提供，秘书处会将

Tentative List will be registered by the Secretariat and transmitted to the relevant Advisory Bodies for information. A summary of all Tentative Lists is presented annually to the Committee. The Secretariat, in consultation with the States Parties concerned, updates its records, in particular by removing from the Tentative Lists the inscribed properties and nominated properties which were not inscribed.

《预备名录》登记并转呈给相关咨询机构。每年都要向委员会递交所有《预备名录》的概要。秘书处与相关缔约国协商，更新其记录，将《预备名录》上已纳入《世界遗产名录》和已拒绝的申报除名。

Decision 7 EXT.COM 4A

第7EXT.COM 4A 号决定

69. The Tentative Lists of States Parties are available at the following Web address: http://whc.unesco.org/en/tentativelists

69. 登录 http://whc.unesco.org/en/tentativelists，查阅缔约国《预备名录》

Decision 27 COM 8A

第27 COM 8A 号决定

Tentative Lists as a planning and evaluation tool

《预备名录》作为计划与评估工具

70. Tentative Lists are a useful and important planning tool for States Parties, the World Heritage Committee, the Secretariat, and the Advisory Bodies, as they provide an indication of future nominations.

70.《预备名录》提供未来遗产名录申报信息，是缔约国、世界遗产委员会、秘书处及咨询机构有用的重要计划工具。

71. States Parties are encouraged to consult the analyses of both the World Heritage List and Tentative Lists prepared at the request of the Committee by ICOMOS and IUCN to identify the gaps in the World Heritage List. These analyses could enable States Parties to compare themes, regions, geo-cultural groupings and bio-geographic provinces for prospective World Heritage properties.

71. 鼓励缔约国参考国际古迹遗址理事会（ICOMOS）和世界自然保护联盟（IUCN）应委员会要求准备的《世界遗产名录》和《预备名录》的分析报告，确定《世界遗产名录》内的空白。这些分析使缔约国能够通过比较主题、区域、地理文化群和生物地理区，确定未来的世界遗产。

Decision 24 COM para. Ⅵ.2.3.2(ii)
Documents WHC- 04/28.COM/13.B I and II
http://whc.unesco.org/archive/2 004/whc04-28com-13b1e.pdf

第24COM 号决定第Ⅵ.2.3.2（ii）段文书
WHC–04/28.COM/13.B 1 和2
请登陆：http://whc.unesco.org/archive/2004/whc04–28com-13b1e.pdf

and

和

http://whc.unesco.org/archive/2 004/whc04-28com-13b2e.pdf

http://whc.unesco.org/archive/2004/whc04–28com-13b2e.pdf

72. In addition, States Parties are encouraged to consult the specific thematic studies carried out by the Advisory Bodies (see paragraph 147). These studies are informed by a review of the Tentative Lists submitted by States Parties and by reports of meetings on the harmonization of Tentative Lists, as well as by other technical studies performed by the Advisory Bodies and qualified organizations and individuals. A list of those studies already completed is available at the following Web address: http://whc.unesco.org/en/globalstrategy

Thematic studies are different than the comparative analysis to be prepared by States Parties when nominating properties for inscription in the World Heritage List (see paragraph 132).

73. States Parties are encouraged to harmonize their Tentative Lists at regional and thematic levels. Harmonization of Tentative Lists is the process whereby States Parties, with the assistance of the Advisory Bodies, collectively assess their respective Tentative List to review gaps and identify common themes. The outcome of harmonization can result in improved Tentative Lists, new nominations from States Parties and co- operation amongst groups of States Parties in the preparation of nominations.

Assistance and Capacity-Building for States Parties in the preparation of Tentative Lists

74. To implement the Global Strategy, cooperative efforts in capacity-building and training may be necessary to assist States Parties to acquire and/or consolidate their expertise in the preparation, updating and harmonisation of their Tentative List and the preparation of nominations.

75. International Assistance may be requested

72.另外，鼓励缔约国参考由咨询机构开展的具体主题研究报告（见147段）。研讨内容参考了《预备名录》评估、《预备名录》协调会议报告、咨询机构以及其他具有资格的团体和个人的相关技术研究。已完成研究报告列表，详见：http://whc.unesco.org/en/globalstrategy

主题研究报告异于缔约国申报遗产列入《世界遗产名录》时编撰的比较分析（见第132段）。

73.鼓励缔约国在区域和主题级别协调《预备名录》。在这个过程中，缔约国在咨询机构的协助下，共同评估各自的《预备名录》，审查空白并确认相同主题。通过协调，《预备名录》得以改进，缔约国可以申报新遗产，且能与其他缔约国合作编撰申报材料。

缔约国编撰《预备名录》过程中的协助和能力建设

74.要实施《全球战略》，就有必要共同致力于协助缔约国进行能力建设和培训，获取和/或增强在编撰、更新和协调《预备名录》及准备申报材料的能力。

75.在编撰、更新和协调《预备名录》方

by States Parties for the purpose of preparing, updating and harmonizing Tentative Lists (see Chapter VII).

76. The Advisory Bodies and the Secretariat will use the opportunity of evaluation missions to hold regional training workshops to assist under-represented States in the methods of preparation of their Tentative List and nominations.

Decision 24COM Ⅵ.2.3.5(ii)

Ⅱ.D Criteria for the assessment of outstanding universal value

These criteria were formerly presented as two separate sets of criteria - criteria (i) - (vi) for cultural heritage and (i) - (iv) for natural heritage.
The 6th extraordinary session of the World Heritage Committee decided to merge the ten criteria (Decision 6 EXT. COM 5.1)

77. The Committee considers a property as having outstanding universal value (see paragraphs 49-53) if the property meets one or more of the following criteria. Nominated properties shall therefore :

(i) represent a masterpiece of human creative genius;

(ii) exhibit an important interchange of human values, over a span of time or within a cultural area of the world, on developments in architecture or technology, monumental arts, town-planning or landscape design;

(iii) bear a unique or at least exceptional testimony to a cultural tradition or to a civilization which is living or which has disappeared;

(iv) be an outstanding example of a type of building, architectural or technological ensemble or landscape which illustrates (a) significant stage(s) in human history;

面，缔约国可以请求国际援助（见第七章）。

76.咨询机构和秘书处可在考察评估期间，举办地区培训班，对名录中遗产代表性不足的国家，在准备预备名录和申报的方法上提供帮助。

第24COMⅥ.2.3.5号决定

Ⅱ.D 突出的普遍价值的评估标准

这些标准起初分为两组，标准（i）至（vi）适用于文化遗产，标准（i）至（iv）适用于自然遗产。

世界遗产委员会第6届特别会议决定将这十个标准合起来（第6EXT.COM 5.1号决定）

77.如果遗产符合下列一项或多项标准，委员会将会认为该遗产具有突出的普遍价值（见49–53段）。所申报遗产因而必须是：

（i）作为人类天才的创造力的杰作；

（ii）在一段时期内或世界某一文化区域内人类价值观的重要交流，对建筑、技术、古迹艺术、城镇规划或景观设计的发展产生过重大影响；

（iii）能为延续至今或已消逝的文明或文化传统提供独特的或至少是特殊的见证；

（iv）是一种建筑、建筑整体、技术整体及景观的杰出范例，展现历史上一个（或几个）重要阶段；

(v) be an outstanding example of a traditional human settlement, land-use, or sea-use which is representative of a culture (or cultures), or human interaction with the environment especially when it has become vulnerable under the impact of irreversible change;

(vi) be directly or tangibly associated with events or living traditions, with ideas, or with beliefs, with artistic and literary works of outstanding universal significance. (The Committee considers that this criterion should preferably be used in conjunction with other criteria) ;

(vii) contain superlative natural phenomena or areas of exceptional natural beauty and aesthetic importance;

(viii) be outstanding examples representing major stages of earth's history, including the record of life, significant on-going geological processes in the development of landforms, or significant geomorphic or physiographic features;

(ix) be outstanding examples representing significant on- going ecological and biological processes in the evolution and development of terrestrial, fresh water, coastal and marine ecosystems and communities of plants and animals;

(x) contain the most important and significant natural habitats for in-situ conservation of biological diversity, including those containing threatened species of outstanding universal value from the point of view of science or conservation.

78. To be deemed of outstanding universal value, a property must also meet the conditions of integrity and/or authenticity and must have an adequate protection and management system to ensure its safeguarding.

Ⅱ.E Integrity and/or authenticity

Authenticity

（v）是传统人类居住地、土地使用或海洋开发的杰出范例，代表一种（或几种）文化或者人类与环境的相互作用，特别当它面临不可逆变化的影响而变得脆弱；

（vi）与具有突出的普遍意义的事件、活传统、观点、信仰、艺术作品或文学作品有直接或有形的联系。（委员会认为本标准最好与其他标准一起使用）；

（vii）绝妙的自然现象或具有罕见自然美和美学价值的地区；

（viii）是地球演化史中重要阶段的突出例证，包括生命记载和地貌演变中的重要地质过程或显著的地质或地貌特征；

（ix）突出代表了陆地、淡水、海岸和海洋生物系统及动植物群落演变、发展的生态和生理过程；

（x）是生物多样性原地保护的最重要的自然栖息地，包括从科学和保护角度看，具有突出的普遍价值的濒危物种栖息地。

78. 只有具有完整性和/或真实性的特征，且有足够的保护和管理机制，确保遗产得到保护，遗产才能被视为具有突出的普遍价值。

Ⅱ.E 完整性和/或真实性

真实性

79. Properties nominated under criteria (i) to (vi) must meet the conditions of authenticity. Annex 4 which includes the Nara Document on Authenticity, provides a practical basis for examining the authenticity of such properties and is summarized below.

80. The ability to understand the value attributed to the heritage depends on the degree to which information sources about this value may be understood as credible or truthful. Knowledge and understanding of these sources of information, in relation to original and subsequent characteristics of the cultural heritage, and their meaning, are the requisite bases for assessing all aspects of authenticity.

81. Judgments about value attributed to cultural heritage, as well as the credibility of related information sources, may differ from culture to culture, and even within the same culture. The respect due to all cultures requires that cultural heritage must be considered and judged primarily within the cultural contexts to which it belongs.

82. Depending on the type of cultural heritage, and its cultural context, properties may be understood to meet the conditions of authenticity if their cultural value (as recognized in the nomination criteria proposed) are truthfully and credibly expressed through a variety of attributes including:
   • form and design;
   • materials and substance;
   • use and function;
   • traditions, techniques and management systems;
   • location and setting;
   • language, and other forms of intangible heritage;
   • spirit and feeling; and
   • other internal and external factors.

79. 依据标准（ⅰ）至（ⅵ）申报的遗产须具备真实性。附件4中包括了关于真实性规定的《奈良文件》，为评估遗产的真实性提供了操作基础，概要如下：

80. 理解遗产价值的能力，取决于关于该价值信息来源的真实度或可信度。对涉及文化遗产原始及后来特征的信息来源的认识和理解，是评价真实性各方面的必要基础。

81. 对于文化遗产价值和相关信息来源可信性的评价标准可能因文化而异，甚至同一种文化内也存在差异。出于对所有文化的尊重，文化遗产的审查和评估必须首先在其所在的文化背景中进行。

82. 依据文化遗产类别和其文化背景，如果遗产的文化价值（申报标准所认可的）之下列特征是真实可信的，则被认为具有真实性：
   • 外形和设计；
   • 材料和实体；
   • 用途和功能；
   • 传统，技术和管理体制；
   • 方位和位置；
   • 语言和其他形式的非物质遗产；
   • 精神和感觉；以及
   • 其他内外因素。

83. Attributes such as spirit and feeling do not lend themselves easily to practical applications of the conditions of authenticity, but nevertheless are important indicators of character and sense of place, for example, in communities maintaining tradition and cultural continuity.

84. The use of all these sources permits elaboration of the specific artistic, historic, social, and scientific dimensions of the cultural heritage being examined. "Information sources" are defined as all physical, written, oral, and figurative sources, which make it possible to know the nature, specificities, meaning, and history of the cultural heritage.

85. When the conditions of authenticity are considered in preparing a nomination for a property, the State Party should first identify all of the applicable significant attributes of authenticity. The statement of authenticity should assess the degree to which authenticity is present in, or expressed by, each of these significant attributes.

86. In relation to authenticity, the reconstruction of archaeological remains or historic buildings or districts is justifiable only in exceptional circumstances. Reconstruction is acceptable only on the basis of complete and detailed documentation and to no extent on conjecture.

Integrity

87. All properties nominated for inscription on the World Heritage List shall satisfy the conditions of integrity.

Decision 20 COM IX.13

88. Integrity is a measure of the wholeness and intactness of the natural and/or cultural heritage and

83.精神和感觉这样的特征在真实性评估中虽不易操作，却是评价一个地方特点和意义的重要指标，例如，在社区中保持传统和文化连续性。

84.利用所有这些信息使我们对相关文化遗产在艺术、历史、社会和科学等特定领域的研究更加深入。"信息来源"指所有物质的、书面的、口头和图形的信息，从而使理解文化遗产的性质、特性、意义和历史成为可能。

85.在考虑遗产申报的真实性时，缔约国首先要确认所有适用的真实性的重要载体。真实性声明应该评估真实性在每个载体特征上的体现程度。

86.在真实性问题上，考古遗址或历史建筑及街区的重建只有在个别情况才予以考虑。只有依据完整且详细的记载，不存在任何想象而进行的重建，才可以接受。

完整性

87.所有申报《世界遗产名录》的遗产必须满足完整性条件。

第20 COM IX.13号决定

88.完整性用来衡量自然和/或文化遗产及其特征的整体性和无缺憾性。因而，审查遗产

its attributes. Examining the conditions of integrity, therefore requires assessing the extent to which the property:

a) includes all elements necessary to express its outstanding universal value;

b) is of adequate size to ensure the complete representation of the features and processes which convey the property's significance;

c) suffers from adverse effects of development and/or neglect.

This should be presented in a statement of integrity.

89. For properties nominated under criteria (i) to (vi), the physical fabric of the property and/or its significant features should be in good condition, and the impact of deterioration processes controlled. A significant proportion of the elements necessary to convey the totality of the value conveyed by the property should be included. Relationships and dynamic functions present in cultural landscapes, historic towns or other living properties essential to their distinctive character should also be maintained.

Examples of the application of the conditions of integrity to properties nominated under criteria (i) - (vi) are under development.

90. For all properties nominated under criteria (vii) - (x), bio- physical processes and landform features should be relatively intact. However, it is recognized that no area is totally pristine and that all natural areas are in a dynamic state, and to some extent involve contact with people. Human activities, including those of traditional societies and local communities, often occur in natural areas. These activities may be consistent with the outstanding universal value of the area where they are ecologically sustainable.

完整性就要评估遗产满足以下特征的程度：

a）包括所有表现其突出的普遍价值的必要因素；

b）面积足够大，确保能完整地代表、体现遗产价值的特色和过程；

c）受到发展和/或缺乏维护的负面影响。

上述条件需要在完整性陈述中进行论述。

89.依据标准（i）至（vi）申报的遗产，其物理构造和/或重要特征都必须保存完好，且侵蚀退化过程得到控制。能表现遗产全部价值绝大部分必要因素也要包括在内。文化景观、历史名镇或其他活遗产中体现其显著特征的种种关系和动态功能也应予保存。

将完整性条件应用于依据标准（i）至（vi）的申报的遗产之例证正在开发。

90.所有依据标准（vii）至（x）申报的遗产，其生物物理过程和地貌特征应该相对完整。当然，由于任何区域都不可能是完全天然，且所有自然区域都在变动之中，某种程度上还会有人类的活动。在自然区域内，包括传统社会和当地社区在内的人类活动时有发生。如果对当地的生态并无损害，如果这些活动具有生态可持续性，也可以与自然区域的突出普遍价值一致。

91. In addition, for properties nominated under criteria (vii) to (x), a corresponding condition of integrity has been defined for each criterion.

92. Properties proposed under criterion (vii) should be of outstanding universal value and include areas that are essential for maintaining the beauty of the property. For example, a property whose scenic value depends on a waterfall, would meet the conditions of integrity if it includes adjacent catchment and downstream areas that are integrally linked to the maintenance of the aesthetic qualities of the property.

93. Properties proposed under criterion (viii) should contain all or most of the key interrelated and interdependent elements in their natural relationships. For example, an "ice age" area would meet the conditions of integrity if it includes the snow field, the glacier itself and samples of cutting patterns, deposition and colonization (e.g. striations, moraines, pioneer stages of plant succession, etc.); in the case of volcanoes, the magmatic series should be complete and all or most of the varieties of effusive rocks and types of eruptions be represented.

94. Properties proposed under criterion (ix) should have sufficient size and contain the necessary elements to demonstrate the key aspects of processes that are essential for the long term conservation of the ecosystems and the biological diversity they contain. For example, an area of tropical rain forest would meet the conditions of integrity if it includes a certain amount of variation in elevation above sea level, changes in topography and soil types, patch systems and naturally regenerating patches; similarly a coral reef should include, for example, seagrass, mangrove or other adjacent ecosystems that regulate nutrient and

91.另外，对于依据标准（vii）至（x）申报的遗产来说，每个标准又有一个相应的完整性条件。

92.依据标准（vii）申报的遗产应具备突出的普遍价值，且包括保持遗产美景的关键地区。例如，某个遗产的景观价值在于瀑布，那么只有把与维持遗产美景完整关系密切的临近的积水潭和下游地区也被涵盖在内，才能满足完整性条件。

93.依据标准（viii）申报的遗产必须包括其自然关系中所有或大部分重要的相互联系、相互依存的因素。例如，"冰川期"遗址要满足完整性条件，则需包括雪地、冰河本身和凿面样本、沉积物和植物集群（例如，条痕、冰碛层及早期植物演替等）。如果是火山，则岩浆层必须完整，且能代表所有或大部分的火山岩种类和喷发类型。

94.依据标准（ix）申报的遗产必须具有足够大小，且包含能够展示长期保护其内部生态系统和生物多样性的重要过程的必要因素。例如，热带雨林地区要满足完整性条件，需要有一定的海拔层次、多样的地形和土壤种类，群落系统和自然形成的群落；同样，珊瑚礁必须包括诸如海草、红树林和其他为珊瑚礁提供营养沉积物的邻近生态系统。

sediment inputs into the reef.

95. Properties proposed under criterion (x) should be the most important properties for the conservation of biological diversity. Only those properties which are the most biologically diverse and/or representative are likely to meet this criterion. The properties should contain habitats for maintaining the most diverse fauna and flora characteristic of the bio-geographic province and ecosystems under consideration. For example, a tropical savannah would meet the conditions of integrity if it includes a complete assemblage of co-evolved herbivores and plants; an island ecosystem should include habitats for maintaining endemic biota; a property containing wide ranging species should be large enough to include the most critical habitats essential to ensure the survival of viable populations of those species; for an area containing migratory species, seasonal breeding and nesting sites, and migratory routes, wherever they are located, should be adequately protected.

II .F Protection and management

96. Protection and management of World Heritage properties should ensure that the outstanding universal value, the conditions of integrity and/or authenticity at the time of inscription are maintained or enhanced in the future.

97. All properties inscribed on the World Heritage List must have adequate long-term legislative, regulatory, institutional and/or traditional protection and management to ensure their safeguarding. This protection should include adequately delineated boundaries. Similarly States Parties should demonstrate adequate protection at the national, regional, municipal, and/or traditional level for the nominated property. They should append appropriate

95.依据标准（x）申报的遗产必须在生物多样性保护方面具有至关重要的价值。只有最具生物多样性和/或代表性的申报遗产才有可能满足该标准。遗产必须包括某生物区或生态系统内最具多样性的动植物特征的栖息地。例如：要满足完整性条件，热带草原需要具有完整的、共同进化的草食动物群和植物群；海岛生态系统则需要包括地方生态栖息地；包含多种物种的遗产范围必须足够大，能够包括确保这些物种生存的最重要的栖息地；如果某个地区有迁徙物种，则季节性的养育巢穴和迁徙路线，不管位于何处，都必须妥善保护。

II .F 保护和管理

96.世界遗产的保护与管理须确保其在列入名录时所具有的突出的普遍价值以及完整性和/或真实性在之后得到保持或增强。

97.列入世界遗产名录的所有遗产必须有长期、充分的立法性、规范性、机制性的和/或传统保护及管理，以确保遗产得到保护。该保护必须包括充分描述的边界范畴。同样地，缔约国应该在国家、区域、城市和/或传统的各个级别上，对申报遗产予以足够力度的保护。申报文件上也需要附加明确说明保护措施的条款。

texts to the nomination with a clear explanation of the way this protection operates to protect the property.

Legislative, regulatory and contractual measures for protection

98. Legislative and regulatory measures at national and local levels should assure the survival of the property and its protection against development and change that might negatively impact the outstanding universal value, or the integrity and/or authenticity of the property. States Parties should also assure the full and effective implementation of such measures.

Boundaries for effective protection

99. The delineation of boundaries is an essential requirement in the establishment of effective protection of nominated properties. Boundaries should be drawn to ensure the full expression of the outstanding universal value and the integrity and/or authenticity of the property.

100. For properties nominated under criteria (i) - (vi), boundaries should be drawn to include all those areas and attributes which are a direct tangible expression of the outstanding universal value of the property, as well as those areas which in the light of future research possibilities offer potential to contribute to and enhance such understanding.

101. For properties nominated under criteria (vii) - (x), boundaries should reflect the spatial requirements of habitats, species, processes or phenomena that provide the basis for their inscription on the World Heritage List. The boundaries should include sufficient areas immediately adjacent to the area of outstanding universal value in order to protect the property's heritage values from direct

立法性、规范性和契约性的保护措施

98.国家和地方级的立法性、规范性措施应确保遗产的保护完好，使其突出的普遍性价值包括完整性和/或真实性不因社会经济发展及其他压力而受到负面影响。缔约国还需要保证这些措施得到切实有效的实施。

确保有效保护的边界

99.划定边界是对申报遗产进行有效保护的核心要求。划定的边界应确保遗产的突出的普遍价值及其完整性和/或真实性得到充分体现。

100.依据标准（i）至（vi）申报的遗产，划定边界需要包括所有有形的、能够直接体现遗产的突出普遍价值的区域和特征，以及在将来的研究中有可能加深这种理解的区域。

101.依据标准（vii）至（x）申报的遗产，划定边界要反映其成为世界遗产基本条件的栖息地、物种、过程或现象的空间要求。边界须包括与具有突出的普遍价值紧邻的足够大的区域，以保护其遗产价值不因人类的直接侵蚀和该区域外资源开发而受到损害。

effect of human encroachments and impacts of resource use outside of the nominated area.

102. The boundaries of the nominated property may coincide with one or more existing or proposed protected areas, such as national parks or nature reserves, biosphere reserves or protected historic districts. While such established areas for protection may contain several management zones, only some of those zones may satisfy criteria for inscription.

Buffer zones

103. Wherever necessary for the proper conservation of the property, an adequate buffer zone should be provided.

104. For the purposes of effective protection of the nominated property, a buffer zone is an area surrounding the nominated property which has complementary legal and/or customary restrictions placed on its use and development to give an added layer of protection to the property. This should include the immediate setting of the nominated property, important views and other areas or attributes that are functionally important as a support to the property and its protection. The area constituting the buffer zone should be determined in each case through appropriate mechanisms. Details on the size, characteristics and authorized uses of a buffer zone, as well as a map indicating the precise boundaries of the property and its buffer zone, should be provided in the nomination.

105. A clear explanation of how the buffer zone protects the property should also be provided.

106. Where no buffer zone is proposed, the nomination should include a statement as to why a buffer zone is not required.

102.所申报遗产的边界可能会与一个或多个已存或建议保护区重合，例如国家公园或自然保护区，生物圈保护区或历史文物保护区。虽然保护区可能包含几个管理带，可能只有个别地带能达到世界遗产的标准。

缓冲区

103.只要有必要，就应设立足够大的缓冲区以保护遗产。

104.缓冲区是为了有效保护申报遗产而划定设立的遗产周围区域，其使用和开发受到相关法律和/或习惯规定限制，以增加遗产的保护层。缓冲区包括申报遗产所在区域、重要景观，以及其他在功能上对遗产及其保护至关重要的区域或特征。缓冲区的构成区域应通过合适的机制来决定。申报时，需要提供有关缓冲区大小、特点、授权使用的详细信息以及一张精确标示边界和缓冲区的地图。

105.申报材料中还需明确描述缓冲区在保护申报遗产中的作用。

106.如果没有提议设定缓冲区，需要在申报材料中解释没有划定缓冲区的原因。

107. Although buffer zones are not normally part of the nominated property, any modifications to the buffer zone subsequent to inscription of a property on the World Heritage List should be approved by the World Heritage Committee.

Management systems

108. Each nominated property should have an appropriate management plan or other documented management system which should specify how the outstanding universal value of a property should be preserved, preferably through participatory means.

109. The purpose of a management system is to ensure the effective protection of the nominated property for present and future generations.

110. An effective management system depends on the type, characteristics and needs of the nominated property and its cultural and natural context. Management systems may vary according to different cultural perspectives, the resources available and other factors. They may incorporate traditional practices, existing urban or regional planning instruments, and other planning control mechanisms, both formal and informal.

111. In recognizing the diversity mentioned above, common elements of an effective management system could include:

a) a thorough shared understanding of the property by all stakeholders;

b) a cycle of planning, implementation, monitoring, evaluation and feedback;

c) the involvement of partners and stakeholders;

d) the allocation of necessary resources;

e) capacity-building; and

f) an accountable, transparent description of how the management system functions.

107.虽然缓冲区并非所申报的遗产的正式组成部分，但是《世界遗产名录》内遗产的缓冲区的任何变动，都需经世界遗产委员批准。

管理体制

108.每一个申报遗产都应有合适的管理规划或其他有文可依的管理体制，其中需要详细说明应如何采用多方参与的方式，保护遗产突出的普遍的价值。

109.管理体制旨在确保现在和将来对申报遗产进行有效的保护。

110.有效的管理体制的内容取决于申报遗产的类别、特点和需求及其文化和自然环境。由于文化视角、可用资源及其他因素的影响，管理体制也会有所差别。管理体制可能包含传统做法、现存的城市或地区设计方法和其他正式和非正式的计划控制机制。

111.考虑到上述多样性问题，有效管理体制需包括以下共同因素：

a）各利益相关者均透彻理解遗产价值；

b）规划、实施、监管、评估和反馈的循环机制；

c）合作者与各利益相关者的共同参与；

d）必要资源的配置；

e）能力建设；以及

f）管理体制运作的描述可信且透明。

112. Effective management involves a cycle of long-term and day-to-day actions to protect, conserve and present the nominated property.

113. Moreover, in the context of the implementation of the *Convention,* the World Heritage Committee has established a process of Reactive Monitoring (see Chapter IV) and a process of Periodic Reporting (see Chapter V).

114. In the case of serial properties, a management system or mechanisms for ensuring the co-ordinated management of the separate components are essential and should be documented in the nomination (see paragraphs 137-139).

115. In some circumstances, a management plan or other management system may not be in place at the time when a property is nominated for the consideration of the World Heritage Committee. The State Party concerned should then indicate when such a management plan or system would be put in place, and how it proposes to mobilize the resources required for the preparation and implementation of the new management plan or system. The State Party should also provide other document(s) (e.g. operational plans) which will guide the management of the site until such time when a management plan is finalized.

116. Where the intrinsic qualities of a property nominated are threatened by action of man and yet meet the criteria and the conditions of authenticity or integrity set out in paragraphs 78-95, an action plan outlining the corrective measures required should be submitted with the nomination file. Should the corrective measures submitted by the nominating State Party not be taken within the time proposed by the State Party, the property will be considered by the Committee for delisting in accordance with the procedure adopted by the Committee (see Chapter Ⅳ.C).

112.有效管理包括长期和日常对申报遗产的保护、保存和展示。

113.另外，为了实施《公约》，世界遗产委员会还建立了反应性监测程序（见第Ⅳ章）和《定期报告》机制（见第Ⅴ章）。

114.如果是系列遗产，须在申报材料中声明能确保各个组成部分协调管理的管理体制或机制（见137–139段）。

115.在某些情况下，管理规划或其他管理体制在该遗产向世界遗产委员会提出申报时还没有到位。相关缔约国则需要说明管理规划或体制何时能到位、以及如何调动准备和实施新的管理规划或体制的所需资源。缔约国还需要提供其他文件（例如，运作计划），在管理规划确定之前指导遗产的管理。

116.如果遗产的内在价值受到人类活动的威胁，且满足第78至95条规定的真实性或完整性的标准和条件，概述纠正措施的行动计划需要和申报材料一起提交。如果缔约国并未在拟定的时间内采取纠正措施，委员会将会考虑依据相关程序将该遗产从名录中删除。（见Ⅳ.C节）

117. States Parties are responsible for implementing effective management activities for a World Heritage property. State Parties should do so in close collaboration with property managers, the agency with management authority and other partners, and stakeholders in property management.

117.缔约国要对境内的世界遗产实施有效的管理。在管理过程中，缔约国要同其他参与方密切合作，其中包括遗产管理人员、管理权力机关和其他合作者及遗产管理的利益相关者。

118. The Committee recommends that States Parties include risk preparedness as an element in their World Heritage site management plans and training strategies.

118.委员会建议缔约国，将风险防范机制作为世界遗产管理计划和培训战略的组成部分。

Decision 28 COM 10B.4

第28COM10B.4号决定

Sustainable use

可持续利用

119. World Heritage properties may support a variety of ongoing and proposed uses that are ecologically and culturally sustainable. The State Party and partners must ensure that such sustainable use does not adversely impact the outstanding universal value, integrity and/or authenticity of the property. Furthermore, any uses should be ecologically and culturally sustainable. For some properties, human use would not be appropriate.

119.世界遗产存在多种现有的和潜在利用方式。缔约国和合作者必须确保这些可持续使用不会对遗产的突出的普遍价值，以及其完整性和/或真实性造成负面影响。另外，任何使用应该具有生态及文化可持续性。对于有些遗产来说，不宜承受人类活动。

III. PROCESS FOR THE INSCRIPTION OF PROPERTIES ON THE WORLD HERITAGE LIST

III. 列入《世界遗产名录》的程序

III.A Preparation of Nominations

III.A 编撰申报文件

120. The nomination document is the primary basis on which the Committee considers the inscription of the properties on the World Heritage List. All relevant information should be included in the nomination document and it should be cross-referenced to the source of information.

120.申报文件是委员会考虑是否将某项遗产列入《世界遗产名录》的重要基础。所有相关信息都应该包括在申报材料中，且其信息来源须是交叉引用的。

121. Annex 3 provides guidance to States Parties in preparing nominations of specific types of properties.

121.附件3为缔约国就具体类别遗产编撰申报文件提供指南。

122. Before States Parties begin to prepare a nomination of a property for inscription on the World Heritage List, they should become familiar with the nomination cycle, described in Paragraph 168.

122.缔约国在着手准备遗产申报前，应先熟悉第168段中描述的申报周期。

123. Participation of local people in the nomination process is essential to enable them to have a shared responsibility with the State Party in the maintenance of the property. States Parties are encouraged to prepare nominations with the participation of a wide variety of stakeholders, including site managers, local and regional governments, local communities, NGOs and other interested parties.

123.申报过程中当地群众的参与很必要，能使他们与缔约国共同承担保护遗产的责任。委员会鼓励多方参与编撰申报文件，其中包括遗产管理人员、当地和地区政府、当地社区、非政府组织和其他相关团体。

124. Preparatory Assistance, as described in Chapter Ⅶ.E, may be requested by States Parties for the preparation of nominations.

124.缔约国在编撰申报文件时，如第Ⅶ.E章节中所描述，可以申请"筹备性援助"。

125. States Parties are encouraged to contact the Secretariat, which can provide assistance throughout the nomination process.

125.鼓励缔约国同秘书处联系，秘书处能够在整个申报过程中提供帮助。

126. The Secretariat can also provide:

a) assistance in identifying appropriate maps and photographs and the national agencies from which these may be obtained;

b) examples of successful nominations, of management and legislative provisions;

c) guidance for nominating different types of properties, such as Cultural Landscapes, Towns, Canals, and Heritage Routes (see Annex 3)

d) guidance for nominating serial and transboundary properties (see paragraphs 134-139).

126.秘书处还能：

a）在确定合适的地图和照片以及从哪些部门取得这些资料方面提供帮助；

b）提供成功申报参考案例以及管理方法和立法条款；

c）为申报不同类别的遗产提供指导，例如文化景观、城镇、运河和遗产线路（见附件3）

d）为申报系列遗产和跨界遗产提供指导（见第134至139条）。

127. States Parties may submit draft nominations to the Secretariat for comment and review by 30 September of each year (see paragraph 168). This submission of a draft nomination is voluntary.

127.建议缔约国于每年的9月30日前（见168条），提交正式的申报文件的草案，以获得秘书处的意见和建议。该草案自愿提交。

128. Nominations may be submitted at any

128.任何时候都可以提交申报，但只有在二

time during the year, but only those nominations that are "complete" (see paragraph 132) and received by the Secretariat on or before 1 February will be considered for inscription on the World Heritage List by the World Heritage Committee during the following year. Only nominations of properties included in the State Party's Tentative List will be examined by the Committee (see paragraph 63).

月一日或之前递交到秘书处且完整的申报（见第132条），才会在次年被世界遗产委员审核，决定是否列入名录。委员会只审查已包含在缔约国《预备名录》内的遗产（见63条）。

Ⅲ.B Format and content of nominations

Ⅲ.B 申报文件的格式和内容

129. Nominations of properties for inscription on the World Heritage List should be prepared in accordance with the format set out in Annex 5.

129.《世界遗产名录》申报应依据附件5所示格式提交材料。

130. The format includes the following sections:
1. Identification of the Property
2. Description of the Property
3. Justification for Inscription
4. State of conservation and factors affecting the property
5. Protection and Management
6. Monitoring
7. Documentation
8. Contact Information of responsible authorities
9. Signature on behalf of the State Party(ies)

130.格式包括如下部分：
1. 遗产确认
2. 遗产描述
3. 列入理由
4. 保护状况和影响因素
5. 保护和管理
6. 监控
7. 文件
8. 负责当局的联系信息
9. 缔约国代表签名

131. Nominations to the World Heritage List are evaluated on content rather than on appearance.

131.《世界遗产名录》申报是重内容轻表象的。

132. For a nomination to be considered as "complete", the following requirements are to be met:
1. Identification of the Property
The boundaries of the property being proposed shall be clearly defined, unambiguously distinguishing between the nominated property and any buffer zone (when present) (see paragraphs 103-107). Maps shall be sufficiently detailed to determine precisely which area of land and/or water is nominated. Officially up-to-date published topographic maps of the State Party annotated

132."完整"申报需要满足下列要求：
1. 遗产确认
应清晰地定义申报遗产边界，清楚区分申报遗产和任何缓冲区（若存在）（见103-107段）之间的差异。地图应足够详细，能精确标出所申报的陆地和／或水域。若可能的话，应提供缔约国最新的官方地图，标注遗产边界。如果没有清晰的边界定义，申报会被认为是"不完整的"。

to show the property boundaries shall be provided if available. A nomination shall be considered "incomplete" if it does not include clearly defined boundaries.

2. Description of the Property

The Description of the property shall include the identification of the property, and an overview of its history and development. All component parts that are mapped shall be identified and described. In particular, where serial nominations are proposed, each of the component parts shall be clearly described.

The History and Development of the property shall describe how the property has reached its present form and the significant changes that it has undergone. This information shall provide the important facts needed to support and give substance to the argument that the property meets the criteria of outstanding universal value and conditions of integrity and/or authenticity.

3. Justification for Inscription

This section shall indicate the World Heritage criteria (see Paragraph 77) under which the property is proposed, together with a clearly stated argument for the use of each criterion. Based on the criteria, a proposed Statement of Outstanding Universal Value (see paragraphs 49-53and 155) of the property prepared by the State Party shall make clear why the property is considered to merit inscription on the World Heritage List. A comparative analysis of the property in relation to similar properties, whether or not on the World Heritage List, both at the national and international levels, shall also be provided. The comparative analysis shall explain the importance of the nominated property in its national and international context. Statements of integrity and/or authenticity shall be included and shall demonstrate how the property satisfies the conditions outlined in paragraphs 78-95.

The comparative analyses prepared by States Parties when nominating properties for inscription in the World Heritage List should not be confused with the thematic studies

2. 遗产描述

遗产描述应包括遗产确认和其历史及发展概述。应确认、描述所有的绘制在地图上的组成部分，如果是系列申报，应清晰描述每一组成部分。

在遗产的历史和发展中，应描述遗产是如何形成现在的状态以及所经历的重大变化。这些信息应包含所需的重要事实，证实遗产达到突出的普遍价值的标准，满足完整性和/或真实性声明的条件。

3. 申报理由

本部分应指出遗产申报依据的标准（见77条），且须明确说明依据此标准的原因。基于该标准，缔约国提交的遗产《突出普遍价值声明》（见49–53条及155条）应明确说明为什么该遗产值得列入《世界遗产名录》。应提供该遗产与类似遗产的比较分析，无论用于比较分析的类似遗产是否在《世界遗产名录》上，是国内还是国外遗产。比较分析应说明申报遗产在国内及国际上的重要性。完整性和/或真实性声明也应一并附上，且须显示该遗产如何满足78–95段所述的条件。

缔约国申报遗产时递交的比较分析不应和委员会顾问机构的主题研究相混淆（见下面的第148段）

prepared by the Advisory Bodies at the request of the Committee (paragraph 148 below)

Decision 7 EXT.COM 4A

4. State of conservation and factors affecting the property

This section shall include accurate information on the present state of conservation of the property (including information on its physical condition of the property and conservation measures in place). It shall also include a description of the factors affecting the property (including threats). Information provided in this section constitutes the baseline data which are necessary to monitor the state of conservation of the nominated property in the future.

5. Protection and management

Protection: Section 5 shall include the list of the legislative, regulatory, contractual, planning, institutional and/ or traditional measures most relevant to the protection of the property and provide a detailed analysis of the way in which this protection actually operates. Legislative, regulatory, contractual planning and/or institutional texts, or an abstract of the texts, shall also be attached in English or French.

Management: An appropriate management plan or other management system is essential and shall be provided in the nomination. Assurances of the effective implementation of the management plan or other management system are also expected.

A copy of the management plan or documentation of the management system shall be annexed to the nomination. If the management plan exists only in a language other than English or French, an English or French detailed description of its provisions shall be annexed.

A detailed analysis or explanation of the management plan or a documented management system shall be provided.

A nomination which does not include the above-mentioned documents is considered incomplete

第 7 EXT.COM 4A 号决定

4. 遗产保护状况和影响因素

本部分应包括目前遗产保护状况的准确信息（包括遗产的物理条件和到位的保护措施）。同时，也应包括影响遗产的因素描述（包括威胁）。本部分提供的基本数据信息是将来监控申报遗产保护状况必需的资料。

5. 保护和管理

保护：第五部分应包括与遗产保护最相关的立法、规章、契约、计划、机构和/或传统措施，并详尽分析实际保护措施的操作方法。立法、规章、契约计划和机构性文本或者文本摘要应以英文或法文附上。

管理：适宜的管理方案或其他管理体制很必要，应包括在申报文件中，并希望确保管理方案或其他管理体制有效执行。

管理方案或者管理体制文献的副本应附在申报文件后。如果管理方案为非英语或非法语，应附上英语或法语的条款详述。

应提供管理方案或者管理体系的详尽分析或者说明。

申报文件若不包括上述文献则被认为是不完整的，除非在管理方案完成之前，依据 115 段

unless other documents guiding the management of the property until the finalization of the management plan are provided as outlined in paragraph 115.

6. Monitoring

States Parties shall include the key indicators proposed to measure and assess the state of conservation of the property, the factors affecting it, conservation measures at the property, the periodicity of their examination, and the identity of the responsible authorities.

7. Documentation

All necessary documentation to substantiate the nomination shall be provided. In addition to what is indicated above, this shall include photographs, 35 mm slides, image inventory and photograph authorization form. The text of the nomination shall be transmitted in printed form as well as in electronic format (Diskette or CD-Rom).

8. Contact Information of responsible authorities

Detailed contact information of responsible authorities shall be provided.

9. Signature on behalf of the State Party

The nomination shall conclude with the original signature of the official empowered to sign it on behalf of the State Party.

10. Number of printed copies required

• Nominations of cultural properties (excluding cultural landscapes): 2 copies

• Nominations of natural properties: 3 copies

• Nominations of mixed properties and cultural landscapes: 4 copies

11. Paper and electronic format

Nominations shall be presented on A4-size paper (or "letter"); and in electronic format (diskette or CD-ROM). At least one paper copy shall be presented in a loose-leaf format to facilitate photocopying, rather than in a bound volume.

12. Sending

States Parties shall submit the nomination in English or French duly signed, to:

所述提交指导遗产管理的其他文书。

6. 监测

缔约国应在申报材料中提交衡量、评估遗产保护状况的关键指标、遗产影响因素、遗产保护措施、审查周期及负责机构名称。

7. 文件

应提供申报所需的所有文件。除了上述文件之外，还应包括照片，35mm幻灯片，图像清单，照片授权表。申报文本应以打印形式和电子文档提交（软盘或光盘）。

8. 负责当局的联系信息
应提供负责机构的详细联系信息。

9. 缔约国代表签名
申报材料结尾应有缔约国授权的官方原始签名。

10. 所需打印副本数量
• 文化遗产申报文件（不包括文化景观）：2个副本
• 自然遗产申报：3个副本
• 混合遗产和文化景观申报：4个副本

11. 纸质版和电子版文件
申报材料应是A4纸（或信纸），同时有电子版（软盘或光盘）。且至少一个副本应是活页形式，以便影印。

12. 寄送
缔约国应提交英语或法语申报材料，提交地址为：

UNESCO World Heritage Centre

7, place de Fontenoy 75352 Paris 07 SP

France

Tel: +33(0)1 4568 1136

Fax: +33(0)1 4568 5570

E-mail: wh-nominations@unesco.org

联合国教科文组织 世界遗产中心

法国巴黎（7, place de Fontenoy 75352 Paris 07 SP

France）

电话：+33（0）1 4568 1136

传真：+33（0）1 4568 5570

E-mail: wh-nominations@unesco.org

133. The Secretariat will retain all supporting documentation (maps, plans, photographic material, etc.) submitted with the nomination.

133.秘书处会保留和申报一起提交的所有相关资料（地图、规划、照片资料等）

III.C Requirements for the nomination of different types of properties

III.C 各类遗产申报的要求

Transboundary properties

跨境遗产

134. A nominated property may occur:

134.申报的遗产可能

Decision 7 EXT.COM 4A

第7EXT.COM 4A 号决定

a) on the territory of a single State Party, or

b) on the territory of all concerned States Parties having adjacent borders (transboundary property).

a）位于一个缔约国境内，或者

b）位于几个接壤的缔约国境内（跨境遗产）

135. Wherever possible, transboundary nominations should be prepared and submitted by States Parties jointly in conformity with Article 11.3 of the *Convention*. It is highly recommended that the States Parties concerned establish a joint management committee or similar body to oversee the management of the whole of a transboundary property.

135.跨境遗产的申报，应尽可能由几个缔约国遵照《公约》第11.3条共同准备和递交。大会强烈建议各相关缔约国建立联合管理委员会或类似组织监督该遗产的总体管理。

136. Extensions to an existing World Heritage property located in one State Party may be proposed to become transboundary properties.

136. 位于一个缔约国境内的现有世界遗产的扩展部分可以申请成为跨境遗产。

Serial properties

系列遗产

137. Serial properties will include component

137.系列遗产应包括几个相关组成部分，其

parts related because they belong to:

a) the same historico-cultural group;

b) the same type of property which is characteristic of the geographical zone;

c) the same geological, geomorphological formation, the same biogeographic province, or the same ecosystem type;

and provided it is the series as a whole-and not necessarily the individual parts of it-which are of outstanding universal value.

138. A serial nominated property may occur:

Decision 7 EXT.COM 4A

a) on the territory of a single State Party (serial national property); or

b) within the territory of different States Parties, which need not be contiguous and is nominated with the consent of all States Parties concerned (serial transnational property)

139. Serial nominations, whether from one State Party or multiple States, may be submitted for evaluation over several nomination cycles, provided that the first property nominated is of outstanding universal value in its own right. States Parties planning serial nominations phased over several nomination cycles are encouraged to inform the Committee of their intention in order to ensure better planning.

III.D Registration of nominations

140. On receipt of nominations from States Parties, the Secretariat will acknowledge receipt, check for completeness and register nominations. The Secretariat will forward complete nominations to the relevant Advisory Bodies for evaluation. The Secretariat will request any additional information from the State Party and when required by Advisory

属于

a）同一历史文化群体；

b）具有某一地域特征的同一类型的遗产；

c）同一地质、地形构造，同一生物地理亚区，或同类生态系统；

并且，系列遗产作为一个整体必须具有突出普遍价值

138.申报的系列遗产可能：

第7EXT.COM 4A号决定

a）位于一个缔约国境内（本国系列遗产）；

b）位于不同缔约国境内，不必相连，同时须经过所有相关缔约国同意，方可递交申报（跨国系列遗产）；

139. 如申报的第一项遗产本身具有突出的普遍价值，系列遗产（无论是由一国或是多国提起的）可历经数轮申报周期，递交申报文件并接受评估。计划在数轮周期中分阶段进行系列申报的缔约国可向委员会说明此意向，以确保计划更加完善。

III.D 申报的登记

140.收到各缔约国递交的申报文件后，秘书处将回执确认收到，核查材料是否完整，然后进行登记。秘书处将向相关咨询机构转交完整的申报文件，由咨询机构进行评估。经咨询机构提请，秘书处将向缔约国索要补充信息。登记的时间表和申报的受理过程在第168条中有详细说明。

Bodies. The timetable for registration and processing of nominations is detailed in paragraph 168.

141. The Secretariat establishes and submits at each Committee session a list of all nominations received, including the date of reception, an indication of their status "complete" or "incomplete", as well as the date at which they are considered as "complete" in conformity with paragraph 132.

Decisions 26 COM 14 and 28 COM 14B.57

142. A nomination passes through a cycle between the time of its submission and the decision by the World Heritage Committee. This cycle normally lasts one and a half years between submission in February of Year 1 and the decision of the Committee in June of Year 2.

Ⅲ.E. Evaluation of nominations by the Advisory Bodies

143. The Advisory Bodies will evaluate whether or not properties nominated by States Parties have outstanding universal value, meet the conditions of integrity and/or authenticity and meet the requirements of protection and management. The procedures and format of ICOMOS and IUCN evaluations are described in Annex 6.

144. Evaluations of cultural heritage nominations will be carried out by ICOMOS.

145. Evaluations of natural heritage nominations will be carried out by IUCN.

146. In the case of nominations of cultural properties in the category of 'cultural landscapes', as appropriate, the evaluation will be carried out by ICOMOS in consultation with IUCN. For mixed

141.秘书处在每届委员会会议时拟定并递交一份所有接收到的申报遗产清单，包括接收的日期，申报文件"完整"与否的陈述，以及按照第132条的要求将申报文件补充完整的日期。

第26 COM 14和28 COM 14B.57号决定

142.申报周期从递交之日起到世界遗产委员会做出决定之日结束。从每年二月缔约国递交申报材料至翌年六月委员会做出决定，通常历时一年半。

Ⅲ.E 咨询机构评估

143.咨询机构将评估各缔约国申报的遗产是否具有突出的普遍价值，是否符合完整性或真实性，以及是否能达到保护和管理的要求。国际古迹遗址理事会和世界保护自然联盟的评估程序和形式在附件6中有详细说明。

144.对文化遗产申报的评估将由国际古迹遗址理事会完成。

145.对自然遗产申报的评估将由世界自然保护联盟完成。

146.作为"文化景观"类申报的文化遗产，将由国际古迹遗址理事会与世界自然保护联盟磋商之后进行评估。对于混合遗产的评估将由国际古迹遗址理事会与世界自然保护联盟共同

properties, the evaluation will be carried out jointly by ICOMOS and IUCN.

147. As requested by the World Heritage Committee or as necessary, ICOMOS and IUCN will carry out thematic studies to evaluate proposed World Heritage properties in their regional, global or thematic context. These studies should be informed by a review of the Tentative Lists submitted by States Parties and by reports of meetings on the harmonization of Tentative Lists, as well as by other technical studies performed by the Advisory Bodies and qualified organizations and individuals. A list of those studies already completed may be found in section III of Annex 3, and on the Web addresses of the Advisory Bodies. These studies should not be confused with the comparative analysis to be prepared by States Parties in nominating properties for inscription on the World Heritage List (see paragraph 132).

ICOMOS:

http://www.icomos.org/studi es/

IUCN:

http://www.iucn.org/themes/ wcpa/pubs/Worldheritage.htm

148. The following principles must guide the evaluations and presentations of ICOMOS and IUCN. The evaluations and presentations should:

Decision 28 COM 14B.57.3

a) adhere to the *World Heritage Convention* and the relevant *Operational Guidelines* and any additional policies set out by the Committee in its decisions;

b) be objective, rigorous and scientific in their evaluations;

c) be conducted to a consistent standard of professionalism;

完成。

147. 如经世界遗产委员会要求或者在必要情况下，国际古迹遗址理事会与世界保护自然联盟将开展主题研究，将申报的世界遗产置于地区、全球或主题背景中进行评估。这些研究必须建立在审议各缔约国递交的预备名录、关于预备名录协调性的会议报告、以及由咨询机构或具备相关资质的组织或个人进行的其他技术研究的基础之上。已完成的相关研究列表见附件3第三节和咨询机构的网站。这些研究不得与缔约国在申报世界遗产时准备的"比较分析"相混淆（见第132条）。

国际古迹遗址理事会：

http://www.icomos.org/studies/

世界保护自然联盟：

http://www.iucn.org/themes/wcpa/pubs/Worldheritage.htm

148. 以下为国际古迹遗址理事会和世界自然保护联盟的评估与陈述所遵循的原则。评估与陈述必须：

第28 COM 14B.57.3号决定

a）遵守《世界遗产公约》和相关的《操作指南》以及委员会在决定中规定的其他政策；

b）做出客观、严谨和科学的评估；

c）依照一致的专业标准；

d) comply to standard format, both for evaluations and presentations, to be agreed with the Secretariat and include the name of the evaluator(s) who conducted the site visit;

d) indicate clearly and separately whether the property has outstanding universal value, meets the conditions of integrity and/or authenticity, a management plan/system and legislative protection;

f) evaluate each property systematically according to all relevant criteria, including its state of conservation, relatively, that is, by comparison with that of other properties of the same type, both inside and outside the State Party's territory;

g) include references to Committee decisions and requests concerning the nomination under consideration;

h) not take into account or include any information submitted by the State Party after 31 March in the year in which the nomination is considered. The State Party should be informed when information has arrived after the deadline and is not being taken into account in the evaluation. This deadline should be rigorously enforced; and

Decision 28 COM 14B.57.3

i) provide a justification for their views through a list of references (literature) consulted, as appropriate.

149. The Advisory Bodies are requested to forward to States Parties by 31 January of each year any final question or request for information that they may have after the examination of their evaluation.

Decision 7 EXT.COM 4B.1

150. The concerned States Parties are invited to send, at least two working days before the

---

d）遵从评估与报告的标准格式，在秘书处的认可下，列出所有参与评估过程的专家姓名，

e）清晰明确地指出申报遗产是否具有突出普遍价值，是否符合完整性和/或真实性的标准，是否拥有管理规划/系统和立法保护；

f）根据所有相关标准，对每处遗产进行系统地评估，并与缔约国境内或境外其他同类遗产的保护状况进行比较；

g）应注明所援引的、与被审议的申报项目相关的委员会决定和要求。

h）不考虑或计入缔约国于申报审议当年3月31日后递交的任何信息。同时应通知缔约国，因收到的信息已逾期，所以不被纳入考虑之列。必须严格遵守最后期限；

第28 COM 14B.57.3号决定

i）同时提供支持他们论点的参考书目（文献）。

149.咨询机构在审查其评估意见后，应在每年的1月31日以前向各缔约国进行最终征询或索要信息。

第7 EXT.COM 4B.1号决定

150.相关缔约国应邀在委员会大会开幕至少两个工作日前致信大会主席，附复印件寄致咨

opening of the session of the Committee, a letter to the Chairperson, with copies to the Advisory Bodies, detailing the factual errors they might have identified in the evaluation of their nomination made by the Advisory Bodies. This letter will be distributed in the working languages to the members of the Committee and may be read by the Chairperson following the presentation of the evaluation.

询机构，详细说明他们在咨询机构关于申报的评估意见中发现的事实性错误。此信将被翻译成工作语言，分发给委员会成员，也可在评估陈述之后由主席宣读。

Decision 7 EXT.COM 4B.1

第7 EXT.COM 4B.1 号决定

151. ICOMOS and IUCN make their recommendations under three categories:

a) properties which are recommended for inscription without reservation;

b) properties which are not recommended for inscription;

c) nominations which are recommended for referral or deferral.

151. 国际古迹遗址理事会和世界自然保护联盟的意见分三类：

a）建议无保留列入名录的遗产

b）建议不予列入名录的遗产

c）建议补充材料或重新申报的遗产

Ⅲ.F Withdrawal of nominations

Ⅲ.F 撤销申报

152. A State Party may withdraw a nomination it has submitted at any time prior to the Committee session at which it is scheduled to be examined. The State Party should inform the Secretariat in writing of its intention to withdraw the nomination. If the State Party so wishes it can resubmit a nomination for the property, which will be considered as a new nomination according to the procedures and timetable outlined in paragraph 168.

152. 缔约国可以在委员会召开会议审核申报之前任何时候撤销所递交的申报。但必须以书面形式向秘书处说明此意图。如某缔约国希望撤回申报，它可以重新递交一份遗产的申报。根据第168条所列程序和时间表，该申报将会被作为一项新申报。

Ⅲ.G Decision of the World Heritage Committee

Ⅲ.G 世界遗产委员会的决定

153. The World Heritage Committee decides whether a property should or should not be inscribed on the World Heritage List, referred or deferred.

153.世界遗产委员会决定一项遗产是否应被列入《世界遗产名录》、补充材料或重新申报。

Inscription

列入名录

154. When deciding to inscribe a property on the World Heritage List, the Committee, guided by the Advisory Bodies, adopts a Statement of Outstanding Universal Value for the property.

154.决定将遗产列入《世界遗产名录》时，在咨询机构的指导下，委员会将通过该遗产的《突出普遍价值声明》。

155. The Statement of Outstanding Universal Value should include a summary of the Committee's determination that the property has outstanding universal value, identifying the criteria under which the property was inscribed, including the assessments of the conditions of integrity or authenticity, and of the requirements for protection and management in force. The Statement of Outstanding Universal Value shall be the basis for the future protection and management of the property.

155.《突出普遍价值声明》应包括委员会关于该遗产具有的突出普遍价值的决定摘要，明确遗产列入名录所遵循的标准，包括对于完整性或真实性状况及实施保护和管理要求的评估。此声明将作为未来该遗产的保护和管理的基础。

156. At the time of inscription, the Committee may also make other recommendations concerning the protection and management of the World Heritage property.

156.列入名录时，委员会也可针对该世界遗产的保护和管理提出其他的建议。

157. The Statement of Outstanding Universal Value (including the criteria for which a specific property is inscribed on the World Heritage List) will be set out by the Committee in its reports and publications.

157.委员会将在其报告和出版物中公布《突出普遍价值声明》（包括将某具体遗产列入《世界遗产名录》的标准）。

Decision not to inscribe

决定不予列入

158. If the Committee decides that a property should not be inscribed on the World Heritage List, the nomination may not again be presented to the Committee except in exceptional circumstances. These exceptional circumstances may include new discoveries, new scientific information about the property, or different criteria not presented in the original nomination. In these cases, a new nomination shall be submitted.

158.如委员会决定某项遗产不予列入名录，除非在极特殊情况下，否则该申报不可重新向委员会提交。这些例外情况包括新发现、有关该遗产新的科学信息或者之前申报时未提出的不同标准。在上述情况下，允许提交新的申报。

Referral of Nominations

159. Nominations which the Committee decides to refer back to the State Party for additional information may be resubmitted to the following Committee session for examination. The additional information shall be submitted to the Secretariat by 1 February of the year in which examination by the Committee is desired. The Secretariat will immediately transmit it to the relevant Advisory Bodies for evaluation. A referred nomination which is not presented to the Committee within three years of the original Committee decision will be considered as a new nomination when it is resubmitted for examination, following the procedures and timetable outlined in paragraph 168.

Deferral of Nominations

160. The Committee may decide to defer a nomination for more in- depth assessment or study, or a substantial revision by the State Party. Should the State Party decide to resubmit the deferred nomination, it shall be resubmitted to the Secretariat by 1 February. These nominations will then be revaluated by the relevant Advisory Bodies during the course of the full year and a half evaluation cycle according to the procedures and timetable outlined in paragraph 168.

Ⅲ.H Nominations to be processed on an emergency basis

161. The normal timetable and definition of completeness for the submission and processing of nominations will not apply in the case of properties which, in the opinion of the relevant Advisory Bodies, would unquestionably meet the criteria for inscription on the World Heritage List and which have suffered damage or face serious and specific

需补充材料申报

159.委员会决定发还缔约国以补充相关信息的申报，可以在委员会下届会议上重新递交并接受审议。补充信息须在委员会拟定审议当年2月1日前呈交秘书处。秘书处将直接转交相关咨询机构进行评估。要求补报材料的申报如在原委员会决定下达三年内不曾提交委员会，再次递交审议时将被视为新申报，依据第168段所列程序及时间表进行。

重新申报

160.为了进行更深入的评估和研究，或便于缔约国对申报材料进行重大修改，委员会可能会做出重新申报的决定。如该缔约国决定重新申报，应于2月1日之前向秘书处提起。届时相关咨询机构将根据第168条所列程序和时间表，对这些申报重新进行周期为一年半的评估。

Ⅲ.H 紧急受理的申报

161.如果相关咨询机构认为某项遗产毫无疑问地拥有突出普遍价值，且因为自然或人为因素而受到损害或面临某种重大的危险，其申报材料的提交和受理不适用通常的时间表和关于材料完整性的定义。这类申报将被紧急受理，可能会被同时列入《世界遗产名录》和《濒危世界遗产名录》（见第177-191条）。

dangers from natural events or human activities. Such nominations will be processed on an emergency basis and may be inscribed simultaneously on the World Heritage List and on the List of World Heritage in Danger (see paragraphs 177-191).

162. The procedure for nominations to be processed on an emergency basis is as follows:

a) A State Party presents a nomination with the request for processing on an emergency basis. The State Party shall have already included, or immediately include, the property on its Tentative List.

b) The nomination shall:

i) describe and identify the property;

ii) justify its outstanding universal value according to the criteria;

iii) justify its integrity and/or authenticity;

iv) describe its protection and management system;

v) describe the nature of the emergency, including the nature and extent of the damage or danger and showing that immediate action by the Committee is necessary for the survival of the property.

c) The Secretariat immediately transmits the nomination to the relevant Advisory Bodies, requesting an assessment of its outstanding universal value, and of the nature of the emergency, damage and/or danger. A field visit may be necessary if the relevant Advisory Bodies consider it appropriate;

d) If the relevant Advisory Bodies determine that the property unquestionably meets the criteria for inscription, and that the requirements (see a) above) are satisfied, the examination of the nomination will be added to the agenda of the next session of the Committee.

e) When reviewing the nomination the Committee will also consider:

i) inscription on the List of World Heritage in Danger;

162.紧急受理申报的程序如下：

a）缔约国呈交申报材料并要求紧急受理。该缔约国此前已将该项遗产纳入《预备名录》，或者即刻将其纳入《预备名录》。

b）该项申报应：

i）描述遗产及精确界定遗产边界；

ii）根据标准论证其具有突出普遍价值；

iii）论证它的完整性和真实性；

iv）描述其保护和管理体制

v）描述情况的紧迫性，包括损害或危险的性质和程度，说明委员会即刻采取行动对该遗产的存续的必要性。

c）由秘书处直接将该申报转交相关咨询机构，要求对其具有的突出普遍价值以及对紧急情况、损害和/或危险的性质进行评估。如相关咨询机构认为恰当，须进行实地勘查。

d）如相关咨询机构判定该遗产毫无疑问地符合列入名录的标准，并满足上述条件，该项申报的审议将被列入委员会下一届会议议程。

e）审议该申报时，委员会将同时考虑：

i）列入濒危世界遗产名录；

ii) allocation of International Assistance to complete the nomination; and

iii) follow-up missions as necessary by the Secretariat and the relevant Advisory Bodies as soon as possible after inscription.

III.I Modifications to the boundaries, to the criteria used to justify inscription or to the name of a World Heritage property

Minor modifications to the boundaries

163. A minor modification is one which has not a significant impact on the extent of the property nor affects its outstanding universal value.

164. If a State Party wishes to request a minor modification to the boundaries of a property already on the World Heritage List, it shall submit this by 1 February to the Committee through the Secretariat, which will seek the advice of the relevant Advisory Bodies. The Committee can approve such modification, or it may consider that the modification to the boundary is sufficiently important to constitute an extension of the property, in which case the procedure for new nominations will apply.

Significant modifications to the boundaries

165. If a State Party wishes to significantly modify the boundary of a property already on the World Heritage List, the State Party shall submit this proposal as if it were a new nomination. This renomination shall be presented by 1 February and will be evaluated in the full year and a half cycle of evaluation according to the procedures and timetable outlined in paragraph 168. This provision applies to extensions, as well as reductions.

Modifications to the criteria used to justify

ii）提供国际援助，完成申报工作；

iii）列入名录后尽快由秘书处和相关咨询机构组织后续工作。

III.I 修改世界遗产的范围、原列入标准或名称

边界细微调整

163.边界的细微调整是指对遗产的范围及对其突出普遍价值影响不大的改动。

164.如某缔约国要求对已列入世界遗产名录的遗产边界进行轻微修改，该国可于2月1日以前通过秘书处向委员会递交申请。在征询相关咨询机构的意见之后，委员会或者批准该申请，或者认定边界修改过大，足以构成扩展项目，在后一种情况下适用新申报的程序。

边界重大修改

165.如某缔约国提出对已列入世界遗产名录的遗产边界进行重大修改，该缔约国应将其视为新申报并提交申请。新的申报材料应于2月1日以前递交，并根据第168条所列程序和时间表接受周期为一年半的评估。该规定同时适用于对遗产边界的扩展和缩小。

《世界遗产名录》所依据标准的变动

inscription on the World Heritage List

166. Where a State Party wishes to have the property inscribed under additional or different criteria other than those used for the original inscription, it shall submit this request as if it were a new nomination. This re-nomination shall be presented by 1 February and will be evaluated in the full year and a half cycle of evaluation according to the procedures and timetable outlined in paragraph 168. Properties recommended will only be evaluated under the new criteria and will remain on the World Heritage List even if unsuccessful in having additional criteria recognized.

Modification to the name of a World Heritage property

167. A State Party may request that the Committee authorize a modification to the name of a property already inscribed on the World Heritage List. A request for a modification to the name shall be received by the Secretariat at least 3 months prior to the meeting of the Committee.

166.当某缔约国希望增加、减少列入标准或选择不同于原列入标准的其他标准，将遗产列入名录，该国应将其视为新申报并提交申请。新的申报材料应于 2 月 1 日以前递交，并根据第168段所列程序和时间表接受周期为一年半的评估。所推荐遗产将只依照新的标准接受评估，即使最后对补充标准不予认定，该项遗产仍将保留在《世界遗产名录》上。

世界遗产名称的更改

167.缔约国可申请委员会批准对已列入世界遗产名录的遗产名称进行更改。更名申请应至少在委员会会议前三个月递交秘书处。

Ⅲ.J Timetable-overview

168. TIMETABLE	PROCEDURES
30 September (before Year 1)	Voluntary deadline for receipt of draft nominations from States Parties by the Secretariat.
15 November (before Year 1)	Secretariat to respond to the nominating State Party concerning the completeness of the draft nomination, and, if incomplete, to indicate the missing information required to make the nomination complete.
1 February Year 1	Deadline by which complete nominations must be received by the Secretariat to be transmitted to the relevant Advisory Bodies for evaluation. Nominations shall be received by 17h00 GMT, or, if the date falls on a weekend by 17h00 GMT the preceeding Friday. Nominations received after this date will be examined in a future cycle.
1 February-1 March Year 1	Registration, assessment of completeness and transmission to the relevant Advisory Bodies. The Secretariat registers each nomination, acknowledges receipt to the nominating State Party and inventories its contents. The Secretariat will inform the nominating State Party whether or not the nomination is complete. Nominations that are not complete (see paragraph 132) will not be transmitted to the relevant Advisory Bodies for evaluation. If a nomination is incomplete,

1 February-1 March Year 1	the State Party concerned will be advised of information required to complete the nomination by the deadline of 1 February of the following year in order for the nomination to be examined in a future cycle. Nominations that are complete are transmitted to the relevant Advisory Bodies for evaluation.
1 March Year 1	Deadline by which the Secretariat informs the State Party of the receipt of a Nomination, whether it is considered complete and whether it has been received by 1 February.
March Year 1-May Year 2	Evaluation by the Advisory Bodies
31 January Year 2	If necessary, the relevant Advisory Bodies may request States Parties to submit additional information during the evaluation and no later than 31 January Year 2.
31 March Year 2	Deadline by which additional information requested by the relevant Advisory Bodies shall be submitted by the State Party to them via the Secretariat. Additional information shall be submitted in the same number of copies and electronic formats as specified in Paragraph 132 to the Secretariat. To avoid confusing new and old texts, if the additional information submitted concerns changes to the main text of the nomination, the State Party shall submit these changes in an amended version of the original text. The changes shall be clearly identified. An electronic version (CD-ROM or diskette) of this new text shall accompany the paper version.
Six weeks prior to the annual World Heritage Committee session Year 2	The relevant Advisory Bodies deliver their evaluations and recommendations to the Secretariat for transmission to the World Heritage Committee as well as to States Parties.
At least two working days before the opening of the annual World Heritage Committee session Year 2	Correction of factual errors by States Parties The concerned States Parties can send, at least two working days before the opening of the session of the Committee, a letter to the Chairperson, with copies to the Advisory Bodies, detailing the factual errors they might have identified in the evaluation of their nomination made by the Advisory Bodies.
Annual session of the World Heritage Committee (June/July) Year 2	The Committee examines the nominations and makes its decisions.
Immediately following the annual session of the World Heritage Committee	Notification to the States Parties The Secretariat notifies all States Parties whose nominations have been examined by the Committee of the relevant decisions of the Committee. Following the decision of the World Heritage Committee to inscribe a property on the World Heritage List, the Secretariat writes to the State Party and site managers providing a map of the area inscribed and the Statement of Outstanding Universal Value (to include reference to the criteria met). The Secretariat publishes the updated World Heritage List every year following the annual session of the Committee. The name of the States Parties having nominated the properties inscribed on the World Heritage List are presented in the published form of the List under the following heading: "Contracting State having submitted the nomination of the property in accordance with the Convention".
In the month following the closure of the annual session of the World Heritage Committee	The Secretariat forwards the published report of all the decisions of the World Heritage Committee to all States Parties.

Ⅲ.J 时间表——总表

168. 时间表	程序
9 月 30 日（第一年以前）	秘书处收到各缔约国自愿提交申报材料草案的截止日期。
11 月 15 日（第一年以前）	秘书处就申报材料草稿完整与否答复相关缔约国，如不完整，注明要求补充的信息。
当年 2 月 1 日	秘书处收到完整的申报材料以便转交相关咨询机构评估的最后期限。 申报材料必须在格林威治时间 17 点以前到达，如当天为周末则必须在前一天即星期五的 17 点（格林威治时间）以前到达。 在此日期后收到的申报材料将进入下一轮周期审议。
当年 2 月 1 日—3 月 1 日	登记、评估完整性及转交相关咨询机构。 秘书处对各项申报进行登记，向提交申报的缔约国下发回执并将申报内容编目。秘书处将通知提交申报的缔约国申报材料是否完整。 不完整的申报材料（见第 132 条）不予转交相关咨询机构进行评估。如材料不完整，相关缔约国将被通知于翌年 2 月 1 日最后期限以前补齐所缺信息以便参与下一轮周期的审议。 完整的申报材料由秘书处转交相关咨询机构进行评估。
当年 3 月 1 日	秘书处告知各缔约国申报材料接收情况的最后期限，说明材料是否完整以及是否于 2 月 1 日以前收讫。
当年 3 月—翌年 5 月	咨询机构的评估
翌年 1 月 31 日	如有必要，相关咨询机构会要求缔约国在评估期间，最迟在翌年 1 月 31 日之前递交补充信息。
翌年 3 月 31 日	缔约国经秘书处向相关咨询机构转呈其要求的补充信息的最后期限。 应依照第 132 条中具体列出的数量准备复印件和电子版，向秘书处呈交补充信息。为了避免新旧文本的混淆，如所递交的补充信息中包含对申报材料主要内容的修改，缔约国应将修改部分作为原申报文件的修正版提交。修改的部分应清楚地标出。新文本除印刷版外还应附上电子版（光盘或软盘）。
翌年世界遗产委员会年会前六周	相关咨询机构向秘书处递送评估意见和建议，由秘书处转发给世界遗产委员会及各缔约国。
翌年世界遗产委员会年会开幕前至少两个工作日	缔约国更正事实性错误 相关缔约国可在委员会大会开幕前至少两个工作日致信大会主席，附寄致咨询机构的复印件，详细说明他们在咨询机构对于其申报材料的评估意见中发现的事实性错误。
翌年世界遗产委员会年会（6 月 /7 月）	委员会审议申报并做出决定
一俟世界遗产委员会年会结束	通知各缔约国 凡经委员会审议的申报，秘书处将通知该缔约国委员会的有关决定 在世界遗产委员会决定将某处遗产列入世界遗产名录之后，由秘书处书面通知该缔约国及遗址管理方，并提供列入名录区域的地图及突出普遍价值声明（注明适用标准） 每年委员会会议结束之后，秘书处随即公布最新的《世界遗产名录》 公布的名录将注明申报项目列入世界遗产名录的缔约国名称，标题为："根据《公约》递交遗产申报的缔约国"
世界遗产委员会年会闭幕后一个月	秘书处将世界遗产委员会全部决定报告公布并下发各缔约国。

IV. PROCESS FOR MONITORING THE STATE OF CONSERVATION OF WORLD HERITAGE PROPERTIES

IV. 对世界遗产保护状况的监测程序

IV.A Reactive Monitoring

IV.A 反应性监测

Definition of Reactive Monitoring

反应性监测的定义

169. Reactive Monitoring is the reporting by the Secretariat, other sectors of UNESCO and the Advisory Bodies to the Committee on the state of conservation of specific World Heritage properties that are under threat. To this end, the States Parties shall submit by 1 February to the Committee through the Secretariat, specific reports and impact studies each time exceptional circumstances occur or work is undertaken which may have an effect on the state of conservation of the property. Reactive Monitoring is also foreseen in reference to properties inscribed, or to be inscribed, on the List of World Heritage in Danger as set out in paragraphs 177-191. Reactive Monitoring is foreseen in the procedures for the eventual deletion of properties from the World Heritage List as set out in paragraphs 192-198.

169. 反应性监测是指由秘书处、联合国教科文组织其他部门和咨询机构，向委员会递交的、有关具体濒危世界遗产保护状况的报告。为此，每当出现异常情况或开展可能影响遗产保护状况的活动时，缔约国都须于2月1日以前经秘书处向委员会递交具体报告和影响调查。反应性监测也涉及已列入及待列入《濒危世界遗产名录》的遗产如第177–191条所述。同时如第192–198条所述，从《世界遗产名录》中彻底删除某些遗产之前须进行反应性监测。

Objective of Reactive Monitoring

反应性监测的目标

170. When adopting the process of Reactive Monitoring, the Committee was particularly concerned that all possible measures should be taken to prevent the deletion of any property from the List and was ready to offer technical co- operation as far as possible to States Parties in this connection.

170. 通过反应性监测程序时，委员会特别关注的是如何采取一切可能的措施，避免从世界遗产名录中剔除任何遗产。因此，只要情况允许，委员会愿意向缔约国提供相关的技术合作。

Article 4 of the *Convention*:

"Each State Party to this Convention recognizes that the duty of ensuring the identification, protection, conservation, presentation and transmission to future generations of the cultural and natural heritage referred to in Articles 1 and 2 and situated on its territory, belongs primarily to that State...".

《公约》第4条

"本公约缔约国均承认，保证第1条和第2条中提及的、本国领土内的文化和自然遗产的确定、保护、保存、展出和遗传后代，主要是有关国家的责任…"

171. The Committee recommends that States Parties co-operate with the Advisory Bodies which have been asked by the Committee to carry out monitoring and reporting on its behalf on the progress of work undertaken for the preservation of properties inscribed on the World Heritage List.

Information received from States Parties and/or other sources

172. The World Heritage Committee invites the States Parties to the *Convention* to inform the Committee, through the Secretariat, of their intention to undertake or to authorize in an area protected under the *Convention* major restorations or new constructions which may affect the outstanding universal value of the property. Notice should be given as soon as possible (for instance, before drafting basic documents for specific projects) and before making any decisions that would be difficult to reverse, so that the Committee may assist in seeking appropriate solutions to ensure that the outstanding universal value of the property is fully preserved.

173. The World Heritage Committee requests that reports of missions to review the state of conservation of the World Heritage properties include:

Decision 27 COM 7B.106.2

a) an indication of threats or significant improvement in the conservation of the property since the last report to the World Heritage Committee;

b) any follow-up to previous decisions of the World Heritage Committee on the state of conservation of the property;

c) information on any threat or damage to or loss of outstanding universal value, integrity and/or authenticity for which the property was inscribed on

171.委员会建议缔约国与委员会指定的咨询机构合作，这些咨询机构受命代表委员会，对列入世界遗产名录的遗产的保护工作进展进行监督和汇报。

来自缔约国和/或其他渠道的信息

172.如《公约》缔约国将在受《公约》保护地区，开展或批准开展可能影响到遗产突出的普遍价值的大规模修复或建设工程，且世界遗产委员会促请缔约国通过秘书处向委员会转达该意图。缔约国必须尽快（例如，在起草具体工程的基本文件之前）且在做出任何难以逆转的决定之前发布通告，以便委员会及时帮助寻找合适的解决办法，保证遗产的突出普遍价值得以维护。

173.世界遗产委员会要求检查世界遗产保护状况的工作报告必须包括：

第27 COM 7B.106.2号决定

a）说明自从世界遗产委员会收到上一份报告以来，遗产所面临的威胁或保护工作取得的重大进步。

b）世界遗产委员会此前关于遗产保护状况的决定的后续工作

c）有关遗产赖以列入《世界遗产名录》的突出普遍价值、完整性和/或真实性受到威胁、损害或减损的信息。

the World Heritage List.

174. When the Secretariat receives information that a property inscribed has seriously deteriorated, or that the necessary corrective measures have not been taken within the time proposed, from a source other than the State Party concerned, it will, as far as possible, verify the source and the contents of the information in consultation with the State Party concerned and request its comments.

Decision by the World Heritage Committee

175. The Secretariat will request the relevant Advisory Bodies to forward comments on the information received.

176. The information received, together with the comments of the State Party and the Advisory Bodies, will be brought to the attention of the Committee in the form of a state of conservation report for each property, which may take one or more of the following steps:

a) it may decide that the property has not seriously deteriorated and that no further action should be taken;

b) when the Committee considers that the property has seriously deteriorated, but not to the extent that its restoration is impossible, it may decide that the property be maintained on the List, provided that the State Party takes the necessary measures to restore the property within a reasonable period of time. The Committee may also decide that technical co- operation be provided under the World Heritage Fund for work connected with the restoration of the property, proposing to the State Party to request such assistance, if it has not already been done;

c) when the requirements and criteria set out in paragraphs 177-182 are met, the Committee may

174.一旦秘书处从相关缔约国以外的渠道获悉，已列入名录的遗产严重受损或在拟定期限内未采取必要的调整措施，秘书处将与有关缔约国磋商、证实消息来源和内容的真实性并要求该国对此做出解释。

世界遗产委员会的决定

175.秘书处将要求相关咨询机构评价获取的信息

176.将获取的信息与相关缔约国和咨询机构的评价一起，以遗产保护状况报告的形式呈交委员会审阅。委员会可采取以下一项或多项措施：

a）委员会可能认定该遗产未遭受严重损害，无须采取进一步行动；

b）当委员会认定该遗产确实遭受严重损害，但损害不至于不可修复，那么只要有关缔约国采取必要措施在合理时间期限之内对其进行修复，该遗产仍可保留在《世界遗产名录》上。同时委员会也可能决定启动世界遗产基金对遗产修复工作提供技术合作，并建议尚未提出类似要求的缔约国提起技术援助申请；

c）当满足第177–182段中所列要求与标准时，委员会可决定依照第183–189条所列程序，

decide to inscribe the property on the List of World Heritage in Danger according to the procedures set out in paragraphs 183-189;

d) when there is evidence that the property has deteriorated to the point where it has irretrievably lost those characteristics which determined its inscription on the List, the Committee may decide to delete the property from the List. Before any such action is taken, the Secretariat will inform the State Party concerned. Any comments which the State Party may make will be brought to the attention of the Committee;

e) when the information available is not sufficient to enable the Committee to take one of the measures described in a), b), c) or d) above, the Committee may decide that the Secretariat be authorized to take the necessary action to ascertain, in consultation with the State Party concerned, the present condition of the property, the dangers to the property and the feasibility of adequately restoring the property, and to report to the Committee on the results of its action; such measures may include the sending of a fact-finding or the consultation of specialists. In cases where emergency action is required, the Committee may authorize the financing from the World Heritage Fund of the Emergency Assistance that is required.

IV.B The List of World Heritage in Danger

Guidelines for the inscription of properties on the List of World Heritage in Danger

177. In accordance with Article 11, paragraph 4, of the *Convention*, the Committee may inscribe a property on the List of World Heritage in Danger when the following requirements are met:

a) the property under consideration is on the World Heritage List;

b) the property is threatened by serious and

将该遗产列入《濒危世界遗产名录》；

d）如证据表明，该遗产所受损害已使其不可挽回地失去了赖以列入《世界遗产名录》的诸项特征，委员会可能会做出将该遗产从《世界遗产名录》中剔除的决定。在采取任何措施之前，秘书处都将通知相关缔约国。该缔约国做出的任何评价都将上呈委员会；

d）当获取的信息不足以支持委员会采取上述a）、b）、c）、d）项中的任何一种措施时，委员会可能会决定授权秘书处采取必要手段，在与相关缔约国磋商的情况下，确定遗产当前状态、所面临的危险及充分修复该遗产的可行性，并向委员会报告行动结果；类似措施包括派遣人员实地调查或召集专家会谈。当需要采取紧急措施时，委员会可批准通过世界遗产基金的紧急援助筹措所需资金。

IV.B《濒危世界遗产名录》

列入《濒危世界遗产名录》的指导方针

177.依照《公约》第11条第4段，当一项遗产满足以下要求时，委员会可将其列入《濒危世界遗产名录》。

a）该遗产已列入《世界遗产名录》；

b）该遗产面临严重的、特殊的危险；

specific danger;

c) major operations are necessary for the conservation of the property;

d) assistance under the *Convention* has been requested for the property; the Committee is of the view that its assistance in certain cases may most effectively be limited to messages of its concern, including the message sent by inscription of a property on the List of World Heritage in Danger and that such assistance may be requested by any Committee member or the Secretariat.

Criteria for the inscription of properties on the List of World Heritage in Danger

178. A World Heritage property-as defined in Articles 1 and 2 of the *Convention*-can be inscribed on the List of World Heritage in Danger by the Committee when it finds that the condition of the property corresponds to at least one of the criteria in either of the two cases described below.

179. In the case of cultural properties:

a) ASCERTAINED DANGER - The property is faced with specific and proven imminent danger, such as:

i) serious deterioration of materials;

ii) serious deterioration of structure and/or ornamental features;

iii) serious deterioration of architectural or town-planning coherence;

iv) serious deterioration of urban or rural space, or the natural environment;

v) significant loss of historical authenticity;

vi) important loss of cultural significance.

b) POTENTIAL DANGER-The property is faced with threats which could have deleterious effects on its inherent characteristics. Such threats are, for example:

i) modification of juridical status of the property

c）该遗产的保护需要实施重大举措；

d）已申请依据公约为该遗产提供援助。委员会认为，在某些情况下对遗产表示关注并传递这一信息可能是其能够提供的最有效的援助手段。将遗产地列入《濒危世界遗产名录》就是这样一种信息。此类援助申请可能由委员会成员或秘书处提起。

列入《濒危世界遗产名录》的标准

178. 当委员会查明一项世界遗产（如公约第1和第2条所定义）符合以下两种情况中至少一项标准时，该遗产可被列入《濒危世界遗产名录》

179. 如属于文化遗产：

a）已确知的危险－该遗产面临着具体的且确知即将来临的危险，例如

i）材料严重受损；

ii）结构特征和/或装饰特色严重受损；

iii）建筑和城镇规划的统一性严重受损；

iv）城市或乡村空间，或自然环境严重受损；

v）历史真实性严重受损；

vi）文化意义严重受损。

b）潜在的危险－该遗产面临可能会对其固有特性造成损害的威胁。此类威胁包括：

i）该遗产法律地位的改变而引起保护力度

diminishing the degree of its protection;

ii) lack of conservation policy;

iii) threatening effects of regional planning projects;

iv) threatening effects of town planning;

v) outbreak or threat of armed conflict;

vi) gradual changes due to geological, climatic or other environmental factors.

180. In the case of natural properties:

a) ASCERTAINED DANGER-The property is faced with specific and proven imminent danger, such as:

i) A serious decline in the population of the endangered species or the other species of outstanding universal value for which the property was legally established to protect, either by natural factors such as disease or by man-made factors such as poaching.

ii) Severe deterioration of the natural beauty or scientific value of the property, as by human settlement, construction of reservoirs which flood important parts of the property, industrial and agricultural development including use of pesticides and fertilizers, major public works, mining, pollution, logging, firewood collection, etc.

iii) Human encroachment boundaries or in upstream areas which threaten the integrity of the property.

b) POTENTIAL DANGER-The property is faced with major threats which could have deleterious effects on its inherent characteristics. Such threats are, for example:

i) a modification of the legal protective status of the area;

ii) planned resettlement or development projects within the property or so situated that the impacts threaten the property;

iii) outbreak or threat of armed conflict;

的减弱；

ii）缺乏保护政策；

iii）地区规划项目的威胁；

iv）城镇规划的威胁；

v）武装冲突的爆发或威胁

vi）地质、气候或其他环境因素导致的渐进的变化

180. 如属于自然遗产：

a）已确知的危险－该遗产面临着具体的且确知即将来临的危险，例如

i）作为确立该项遗产法定保护地位依据的濒危物种或其他具有突出普遍价值的物种数量，由于自然因素（例如疾病）或人为因素（例如偷猎）锐减。

ii）遗产的自然美景和科学价值由于人类的定居、兴建的水库淹没遗产重要区域、工农业的发展（包括杀虫剂和农药的使用，大型公共工程，采矿，污染，采伐等）而遭受重大损害；

iii）人类活动对保护范围或上游区域的侵蚀，威胁遗产的完整性。

b）潜在的危险－该遗产面临可能会对其固有特性造成损害的威胁。此类威胁包括：

i）该地区的法律保护地位发生变化

ii）在遗产范围内实施的，或虽在其范围外但足以波及和威胁到该遗产的移民或开发计划；

iii）武装冲突的爆发或威胁；

iv)the management plan or management system is lacking or inadequate, or not fully implemented.

181. In addition, the factor or factors which are threatening the integrity of the property must be those which are amenable to correction by human action. In the case of cultural properties, both natural factors and man-made factors may be threatening, while in the case of natural properties, most threats will be man-made and only very rarely a natural factor (such as an epidemic disease) will threaten the integrity of the property. In some cases, the factors threatening the integrity of a property may be corrected by administrative or legislative action, such as the cancelling of a major public works project or the improvement of legal status.

182. The Committee may wish to bear in mind the following supplementary factors when considering the inclusion of a cultural or natural property in the List of World Heritage in Danger:

a) Decisions which affect World Heritage properties are taken by Governments after balancing all factors. The advice of the World Heritage Committee can often be decisive if it can be given before the property becomes threatened.

b) Particularly in the case of ascertained danger, the physical or cultural deteriorations to which a property has been subjected should be judged according to the intensity of its effects and analyzed case by case.

c) Above all in the case of potential danger to a property, one should consider that:

i)the threat should be appraised according to the normal evolution of the social and economic framework in which the property is situated;

ii)it is often impossible to assess certain threats-such as the threat of armed conflict-as to

iv）管理规划或管理系统缺失、不完善或贯彻不彻底。

181.另外，威胁遗产完整性的因素必须是人力可以补救的因素。对于文化遗产，自然因素和人为因素都可能成为威胁，而对于自然遗产来说，威胁其完整性的大多是人为因素，只有小部分是由自然因素造成的（例如传染病）。某些情况下，对遗产完整性造成威胁的因素可通过行政或法律手段予以纠正，如取消某大型公共工程项目，加强法律地位。

182.在审议是否将一项文化或自然遗产列入《濒危世界遗产名录》时，委员会可能要考虑到下列额外因素

a）政府往往是在权衡各种因素后才做出影响世界遗产的决定。因此世界遗产委员会如能在遗产遭到威胁之前给予建议的话，该建议往往具有决定性。

b）尤其是对于已确知的危险，对遗产所受的物质和文化损害的判断应基于其影响力度之上，并应具体问题具体分析。

c）对于潜在的危险必须首先考虑：

i）结合遗产所处的社会和经济环境的常规进程对其所受威胁进行评估；

ii）有些威胁对于文化和自然遗产的影响是难以估量的，例如武装冲突的威胁；

their effect on cultural or natural properties;

iii) some threats are not imminent in nature, but can only be anticipated, such as demographic growth.

d) Finally, in its appraisal the Committee should take into account any cause of unknown or unexpected origin which endangers a cultural or natural property.

Procedure for the inscription of properties on the List of World Heritage in Danger

183. When considering the inscription of a property on the List of World Heritage in Danger, the Committee shall develop, and adopt, as far as possible, in consultation with the State Party concerned, a programme for corrective measures.

184. In order to develop the programme of corrective measures referred to in the previous paragraph, the Committee shall request the Secretariat to ascertain, as far as possible in co- operation with the State Party concerned, the present condition of the property, the dangers to the property and the feasibility of undertaking corrective measures. The Committee may further decide to send a mission of qualified observers from the relevant Advisory Bodies or other organizations to visit the property, evaluate the nature and extent of the threats and propose the measures to be taken.

185. The information received, together with the comments as appropriate of the State Party and the relevant Advisory Bodies or other organizations, will be brought to the attention of the Committee by the Secretariat.

186. The Committee shall examine the information available and take a decision concerning the inscription of the property on the List of World

iii）有些威胁在本质上不会立刻发生，而只能预见，例如人口的增长。

d）最后，委员会在作评估时应将所有未知或无法预料的但可能危及文化或自然遗产的因素纳入考虑范围。

列入《濒危世界遗产名录》的程序

183.在考虑将一项遗产列入《濒危世界遗产名录》时，委员会应尽可能与相关缔约国磋商，制订或采纳一套补救方案。

184.为了制订前段所述补救方案，委员会应要求秘书处尽可能与相关缔约国合作，弄清遗产的现状，查明其面临的危险并探讨补救措施的可行性。此外委员会还可能决定派遣来自相关咨询机构或其他组织并具备相应资历的观察员前往实地勘查，鉴定威胁的本质及程度，并就补救措施提出建议。

185.获取的信息及相关缔约国和咨询机构或其他组织的评论将经秘书处送交委员会审阅。

186.委员会将审议现有信息，并针对是否将该遗产列入《濒危世界遗产名录》做出决定。出席表决的委员会成员须以三分之二多数通过

Heritage in Danger. Any such decision shall be taken by a majority of two-thirds of the Committee members present and voting. The Committee will then define the programme of corrective action to be taken. This programme will be proposed to the State Party concerned for immediate implementation.

187. The State Party concerned shall be informed of the Committee's decision and public notice of the decision shall immediately be issued by the Committee, in accordance with Article 11.4 of the *Convention*.

188. The Secretariat publishes the updated List of World Heritage in Danger in printed form and is also available at the following Web address: http://whc.unesco.org/en/danger

189. The Committee shall allocate a specific, significant portion of the World Heritage Fund to financing of possible assistance to World Heritage properties inscribed on the List of World Heritage in Danger.

Regular review of the state of conservation of properties on the List of World Heritage in Danger

190. The Committee shall review annually the state of conservation of properties on the List of World Heritage in Danger. This review shall include such monitoring procedures and expert missions as might be determined necessary by the Committee.

191. On the basis of these regular reviews, the Committee shall decide, in consultation with the State Party concerned, whether:
a) additional measures are required to conserve the property;
b) to delete the property from the List of World Heritage in Danger if the property is no longer

所有类似决定。之后委员会将确定补救方案，并建议相关缔约国立即执行。

187.依照《公约》第11条第4段，委员会应将决定通告相关缔约国，并随即就该项决定发表公告。

188.由秘书处印发最新的《濒危世界遗产名录》。同时也可在以下网站上获取最新的《濒危世界遗产名录》：http://whc.unesco.org/en/danger

189.委员会将从世界遗产基金中特别划拨一笔相当数量的资金，为列入《濒危世界遗产名录》的遗产提供可能的援助。

对于《濒危世界遗产名录》上遗产保护状况的定期检查

190.委员会每年将对《濒危世界遗产名录》上遗产的保护状况进行例行检查。检查的内容包括委员会可能认为必要的监测程序和专家考察。

191.在定期检查的基础上，委员会将与有关缔约国磋商，决定是否：

a）该遗产需要额外的保护措施；

b）当该遗产不再面临威胁时，将其从濒危世界遗产名录中删除；

under threat;

c) to consider the deletion of the property from both the List of World Heritage in Danger and the World Heritage List if the property has deteriorated to the extent that it has lost those characteristics which determined its inscription on the World Heritage List, in accordance with the procedure set out in paragraphs 192-198.

Ⅳ.C Procedure for the eventual deletion of properties from the World Heritage List

192. The Committee adopted the following procedure for the deletion of properties from the World Heritage List in cases:

a) where the property has deteriorated to the extent that it has lost those characteristics which determined its inclusion in the World Heritage List; and

b) where the intrinsic qualities of a World Heritage site were already threatened at the time of its nomination by action of man and where the necessary corrective measures as outlined by the State Party at the time, have not been taken within the time proposed (see paragraph 116).

193. When a property inscribed on the World Heritage List has seriously deteriorated, or when the necessary corrective measures have not been taken within the time proposed, the State Party on whose territory the property is situated should so inform the Secretariat.

194. When the Secretariat receives such information from a source other than the State Party concerned, it will, as far as possible, verify the source and the contents of the information in consultation with the State Party concerned and request its comments.

195. The Secretariat will request the relevant

c）当该遗产由于严重受损而丧失赖以列入世界遗产名录的特征时，考虑依照第192-198条所列程序，将其同时从《世界遗产名录》和《濒危世界遗产名录》中剔除。

Ⅳ.C《世界遗产名录》内遗产彻底除名的程序

192.在以下情况下，委员会采取以下步骤，把《世界遗产名录》内的遗产除名：

a）遗产严重受损，损坏了其作为世界遗产的决定性特征；

b）遗产在申报的时候便因为人为因素导致其内在特质受到威胁，而缔约国在规定时间内又没有采取必要的补救措施（见第116段）。

193.《世界遗产名录》内遗产因为严重受损，或者缔约国没有在限定的时间内采取必要的补救措施，此遗产所在缔约国应该把这种情况通知秘书处。

194.如果秘书处从缔约国之外的第三方得到了这种信息，秘书处会与相关缔约国磋商，尽量核实信息来源与内容的可靠性，并且听取他们的意见。

195.秘书处将要求相关咨询机构提交他们对

Advisory Bodies to forward comments on the information received.

所收到信息的意见。

196. The Committee will examine all the information available and will take a decision. Any such decision shall, in accordance with Article 13 (8) of the *Convention*, be taken by a majority of two-thirds of its members present and voting. The Committee shall not decide to delete any property unless the State Party has been consulted on the question.

196.委员会将审查所有可用信息，做出处理决定。根据《保护世界文化与自然遗产公约》第13（8）条的规定，委员会三分之二以上的委员到场并投票同意，该决定方能通过。在未就此事宜与缔约国协商之前，委员会不应做出把遗产除名的决定。

197. The State Party shall be informed of the Committee's decision and public notice of this decision shall be immediately given by the Committee.

197.应通知缔约国委员会的决定，同时尽快将决定公布于世。

198. If the Committee's decision entails any modification to the World Heritage List, this modification will be reflected in the next updated List that is published.

198.如果委员会的决定改变了目前的《世界遗产名录》，变更内容会体现在下一期的《世界文化遗产名录》中。

V. PERIODIC REPORTING ON THE IMPLEMENTATION OF THE *WORLD HERITAGE CONVENTION*

V.有关《世界遗产公约》实施的《定期报告》

V.A Objectives

V.A 目标

199. States Parties are requested to submit reports to the UNESCO General Conference through the World Heritage Committee on the legislative and administrative provisions they have adopted and other actions which they have taken for the application of the *Convention*, including the state of conservation of the World Heritage properties located on their territories.

199.要求缔约国经由世界遗产委员会将其通过的法律和行政条款以及实施《世界遗产公约》采取的其他行动报告提交教科文组织大会，其中包括其领土内世界遗产的保护状况。

Article 29 of the *World Heritage Convention* and Resolutions of the 11th session of the General Assembly of States Parties (1997) and the 29th session of the UNESCO General Conference.

《世界遗产公约》第29条，和缔约国第11届大会（1997年），以及联合国教科文组织第29届大会决议

200. States Parties may request expert advice from the Advisory Bodies and the Secretariat, which may also (with agreement of the States Parties concerned) commission further expert advice.

201. Periodic Reporting serves four main purposes:

a) to provide an assessment of the application of the *World Heritage Convention* by the State Party;

b) to provide an assessment as to whether the outstanding universal value of the properties inscribed on the World Heritage List is being maintained over time;

c) to provide up-dated information about the World Heritage properties to record the changing circumstances and state of conservation of the properties;

d) to provide a mechanism for regional co-operation and exchange of information and experiences between States Parties concerning the implementation of the *Convention* and World Heritage conservation.

202. Periodic Reporting is important for more effective long term conservation of the properties inscribed, as well as to strengthen the credibility of the implementation of the *Convention*.

V.B Procedure and Format

203. World Heritage Committee:

Decision 22 COM VI.7

a) adopted the Format and Explanatory Notes set out in Annex 7;

b) invited States Parties to submit periodic reports every six years;

c) decided to examine the States Parties' periodic reports region by region according to the following table:

200.缔约国也许会需要咨询机构和秘书处的专家意见，咨询机构和秘书处（在相关缔约国同意的前提下）会进一步寻求专家意见。

201.《定期报告》主要有以下四个目的：

a）评估缔约国《世界遗产公约》的执行情况；

b）评估《世界遗产名录》内遗产的突出的普遍价值是否得到长期的保持；

c）提供世界遗产的更新信息，记录遗产所处环境的变化以及遗产的保护状况；

d）就《世界遗产公约》实施及世界遗产保护事宜，为缔约国提供一种区域间合作以及信息分享、经验交流的机制。

202.《定期报告》不仅对更有效的长期保存遗产起到了重要的作用，而且提高了执行《世界遗产公约》的可信性。

V.B 程序和形式

203.世界遗产委员会：

第22 COM VI.7号决定

a）采用附录7中的形式和注解；

b）邀请成员国政府每六年提交一次《定期报告》；

c）决定按下表逐个区域地审查缔约国的定期报告：

Region	Examination of properties inscribed up to and including	Year of Examination by Committee
Arab States	1992	December 2000
Africa	1993	December 2001/July 2002
Asia and the Pacific	1994	June-July 2003
Latin America and the Caribbean	1995	June-July 2004
Europe and North America	1996/1997	June-July 2005/2006

地区	对名录上遗产的检查	委员会审查的年份
阿拉伯	1992 年	2000 年 12 月
非洲	1993 年	2001 年 12 月 /2002 年 7 月
亚太地区	1994 年	2003 年 6 月 –7 月
拉丁美洲和加勒比地区	1995 年	2004 年 6 月 –7 月
欧洲和北美洲	1996 年 /1997 年	2005 年 /2006 年 6 月 –7 月

d) requested the Secretariat, jointly with the Advisory Bodies, and making use of States Parties, competent institutions and expertise available within the region, to develop regional strategies for the periodic reporting process as per the timetable established under c) above.

204. The above-mentioned regional strategies should respond to specific characteristics of the regions and should promote co- ordination and synchronization between States Parties, particularly in the case of transboundary properties. The Secretariat will consult States Parties with regard to the development and implementation of those regional strategies.

205. After the first six-year cycle of periodic reports, each region will be assessed again in the same order as indicated in the table above. Following the first six-year cycle, there may be a pause for evaluation to assess and revise the periodic reporting mechanism before a new cycle is initiated.

d）要求秘书处与咨询机构合作，发挥缔约国、主管部门及当地专家的作用，根据上文 c）的时间表制定定期报告的区域性策略。

204. 上述的区域性策略应该体现当地的特征，并且能够促进缔约国间的合作与协调。这一点对于跨界遗产尤为重要。秘书处会就这些区域性策略的制定和执行事宜与缔约国磋商。

205. 为期六年的一轮定期报告周期结束后，会按上表标明的顺序对各区域进行评估。首个六年周期后，新周期开始前，会留出一段时间，评估和修正定期报告机制。

206. The Format for the periodic reports by the States Parties consists of two sections:

This Format was adopted by the Committee at its 22nd session (Kyoto 1998) and may be revised following the completion of the first cycle of Periodic Reporting in 2006. For this reason, the Format has not been revised.

a) Section I refers to the legislative and administrative provisions which the State Party has adopted and other actions which it has taken for the application of the *Convention*, together with details of the experience acquired in this field. This particularly concerns the general obligations defined in specific articles of the *Convention*.

b) Section II refers to the state of conservation of specific World Heritage properties located on the territory of the State Party concerned. This Section should be completed for each World Heritage property.

Explanatory Notes are provided with the Format in Annex 7.

207. In order to facilitate management of information, States Parties are requested to submit reports, in English or French, in electronic as well as in printed form to :

UNESCO World Heritage Centre

7, place de Fontenoy

75352 Paris 07 SP

France

Tél ： +33(0)1 45 68 15 71

Fax ： +33(0)1 45 68 55 70

Email ： wh-info@unesco.org

V.C Evaluation and Follow Up

208. The Secretariat consolidates national reports into Regional State of the World Heritage reports,

206.缔约国的定期报告主要包括以下两部分：

本格式在委员会的第22届大会上通过（1998年，京都）。2006年首个定期报告结束后，可能修订现有格式。为此，目前尚未对该格式做出任何修改。

a）第一部分包括缔约国为执行《公约》通过的法律和行政条款以及采取的其他行动，以及在这一领域获得的相关经验的详细内容。特别是与《保护世界文化与自然遗产公约》中具体条款所规定义务的相关情况。

b）第二部分阐述了在缔约国领土内特定世界遗产的保护状况。本部分应完整说明每个世界遗产的情况。

附录7中提供了格式注解。

207.为了便于信息管理，缔约国所提交的报告必须为英文或法文，并同时提交电子版本和纸印版本。提交地址如下：

联合国教科文组织世界遗产中心

法国巴黎（7, place de Fontenoy

75352 Paris 07 SP

France ）

电话 ： +33（0）1 45 68 15 71

传真 ： +33（0）1 45 68 55 70

Email ： wh-info@unesco.org

V.C 评估和后续工作

208.秘书处将各国报告整理、并写入"世界遗产区域性报告"。可获得"世界遗产区域性报

which are available in electronic format at the following Web address http://whc.unesco.org/en/publications and in paper version (series World Heritage Papers).

209. The World Heritage Committee carefully reviews issues raised in Periodic Reports and advises the States Parties of the regions concerned on matters arising from them.

210. The Committee requested the Secretariat with the Advisory Bodies, in consultation with the relevant States Parties, to develop long-term follow-up Regional Programmes structured according to its Strategic Objectives and to submit them for its consideration. These should accurately reflect the needs of World Heritage in the Region and facilitate the granting of International Assistance. The Committee also expressed its support to ensure direct links between the Strategic Objectives and the International Assistance.

VI. ENCOURAGING SUPPORT FOR *THE WORLD HERITAGE CONVENTION*

VI.A Objectives

Article 27 of the *World Heritage Convention*

211. The objectives are:

a) to enhance capacity-building and research;

b) to raise the general public's awareness, understanding and appreciation of the need to preserve cultural and natural heritage;

c) to enhance the function of World Heritage in the life of the community; and

Article 5(a) of the *World Heritage Convention*

d) to increase the participation of local and national populations in the protection and presentation of heritage.

告"的电子版：http://whc.unesco.org/en/publications 及文本（世界遗产系列文件）。

209.世界遗产委员会认真审查《定期报告》所述议题，并且针对不足之处，为相关区域的缔约国提出建议。

210.委员会要求秘书处、咨询机构与相关缔约国磋商，根据其《战略目标》制定长期"区域性计划"，并提交委员会审议。计划应该能够准确的反映当地世界遗产的需求，并且协助提供国际援助。委员会还表示，支持《战略目标》与国际援助之间的直接联系。

VI. 鼓励对《世界遗产公约》的支持

VI.A 目标

《世界遗产公约》第27条

211.目标如下：

a）加强能力建设与研究；

b）提高民众意识，使其逐渐理解并重视保护文化与自然遗产的重要性；

c）加强世界遗产在社会生活中的作用；

《世界遗产公约》第5（a）条

d）提高地方及全国民众参与保护、展现遗产的人数。

VI.B Capacity-building and research

VI.B 能力建设与研究

212. The Committee seeks to develop capacity-building within the States Parties in conformity with its Strategic Objectives.

212. 委员会根据"战略目标",致力于缔约国内的能力建设。

Budapest Declaration on World Heritage (2002)

《布达佩斯世界遗产宣言》(2002年)

The Global Training Strategy

全球培训策略

213. Recognizing the high level of skills and multidisciplinary approach necessary for the protection, conservation, and presentation of the World Heritage, the Committee has adopted a Global Training Strategy for World Cultural and Natural Heritage. The primary goal of the Global Training Strategy is to ensure that necessary skills are developed by a wide range of actors for better implementation of the *Convention*. In order to avoid overlap and effectively implement the Strategy, the Committee will ensure links to other initiatives such as the Global Strategy for a Representative, Balanced and Credible World Heritage List and Periodic Reporting. The Committee will annually review relevant training issues, assess training needs, review annual reports on training initiatives, and make recommendations for future training initiatives.

213.委员会认识到为了保护、保存、展出世界遗产,高技能以及多学科的方法是必不可少的,为此,委员会通过了"世界文化和自然遗产的全球培训策略"。"全球培训策略"的首要目标是确保多数参与者获得必要的技能,以便更好的实施《公约》。为了避免重复同时为了有效实施策略,委员会将确保与《构建具有代表性、平衡性、可信性的世界遗产名录的全球战略》、《定期报告》等工作之间的联系。委员会将每年评审相关培训议题、评估培训需求、审阅年度报告,并为进一步的培训提供建议。

Global Training Strategy for World Cultural and Natural Heritage adopted by the World Heritage Committee at its 25th session (Helsinki, Finland, 2001) (see ANNEX X of document WHC- 01/CONF.208/24).

"世界文化和自然遗产的全球培训策略"于世界遗产委员会第25届会议通过(芬兰赫尔辛基,2001年)(见文书WHC–01/CONF.208/24附件X).

National training strategies and regional co-operation

全国培训策略和区域性合作

214. States Parties are encouraged to ensure that their professionals and specialists at all levels are adequately trained. To this end, States Parties are encouraged to develop national training strategies

214.鼓励缔约国确保其各级专业人员和专家均训练有素。为此,鼓励缔约国制定全国培训策略,并把区域合作培训作为战略的一部分。

and include regional co-operation for training as part of their strategies.

Research

215. The Committee develops and coordinates international co-operation in the area of research needed for the effective implementation of the *Convention*. States Parties are also encouraged to make resources available to undertake research, since knowledge and understanding are fundamental to the identification, management, and monitoring of World Heritage properties.

International Assistance

216. Training and Research Assistance may be requested by States Parties from the World Heritage Fund (see Chapter VII).

VI.C Awareness-raising and education

Awareness-raising

217. States Parties are encouraged to raise awareness of the need to preserve World Heritage. In particular, they should ensure that World Heritage status is adequately marked and promoted on-site.

218. The Secretariat provides assistance to States Parties in developing activities aimed at raising public awareness of the *Convention* and informing the public of the dangers threatening World Heritage. The Secretariat advises States Parties regarding the preparation and implementation of on-site promotional and educational projects to be funded through International Assistance. The Advisory Bodies and appropriate State agencies may also be solicited to provide advice on such projects.

研究

215.委员会在有效实施《公约》所需的研究领域，展开并协调国际合作。既然知识和理解对于世界遗产的确认、管理和监测起着至关重要的作用，那么还鼓励缔约国提供开展研究所需资源。

国际援助

216.缔约国可向世界遗产基金申请培训和研究的援助（见第七章）。

VI.C 提高认识与教育

提高认识

217.鼓励缔约国提高对世界遗产保护需求的认识。尤其应确保在遗产地对世界遗产地位进行有效的标识和宣传。

218.秘书处向缔约国提供援助，开展活动，以提高公众对《公约》的认识，并告知公众世界遗产所面临的威胁。秘书处会针对如何筹划及开展"国际援助"资助的现场推广与教育项目，向缔约国提出建议。也会征求咨询机构和国家有关部门关于为此类活动的建议。

Education

219. The World Heritage Committee encourages and supports the development of educational materials, activities and programmes.

International Assistance

220. States Parties are encouraged to develop educational activities related to World Heritage with, wherever possible, the participation of schools, universities, museums and other local and national educational authorities.

Article 27.2 of the *World Heritage Convention*

221. The Secretariat, in co-operation with the UNESCO Education Sector and other partners, produces and publishes a World Heritage Educational Resource Kit, "World Heritage in Young Hands", for use in secondary schools around the world. The Kit is adaptable for use at other educational levels.

"World Heritage in Young Hands" is available at the following Web address http://whc.unesco.org/educatio n/index.htm

222. International Assistance may be requested by States Parties from the World Heritage Fund for the purpose of developing and implementing awareness-raising and educational activities or programmes (see Chapter VII).

VII. THE WORLD HERITAGE FUND AND INTERNATIONAL ASSISTANCE

VII.A The World Heritage Fund

223. The World Heritage Fund is a trust fund, established by the *Convention* in conformity with

教育

219.世界遗产委员会鼓励并支持编撰教育材料及开展和实施各种教育活动和方案。

国际援助

220.鼓励缔约国开展世界遗产相关教育活动，如果有可能，让中小学校、大学、博物馆以及其他地方或国家的教育机构参与其中。

《世界遗产公约》第27.2条

221.秘书处与联合国教科文组织教育部及其他伙伴合作，开发并出版世界遗产教育培训教材："世界遗产掌握在年轻人手中"。此教材供全世界的中学生使用。也可调整适用于其他教育水平的人群。

可访问：http://whc.unesco.org/education/index.htm查阅"世界遗产掌握在年轻人手中"

222.缔约国可向世界遗产基金申请国际援助，以提升遗产保护意识，开展教育活动与方案（见第七章）。

VII. 世界遗产基金和国际援助

VII.A 世界遗产基金

223.世界遗产基金是信托基金，是《公约》依据"联合国教科文组织财务条例"的规定建

the provisions of the Financial Regulations of UNESCO. The resources of the Fund consist of compulsory and voluntary contributions made by States Parties to the *Convention*, and any other resources authorized by the Fund's regulations.

立的。此基金由《公约》缔约国义务或者自愿的捐献及基金规章授权的其他来源组成。

Article 15 of the *World Heritage Convention.*

《世界遗产公约》第15条

224. The financial regulations for the Fund are set out in document WHC/7 available at the following Web address: http://whc.unesco.org/en/financialregulations

224.基金财务条例写进文书WHC/7内，可登录以下网址查阅：http://whc.unesco.org/en/financialregulations

Ⅶ.B Mobilization of other technical and financial resources and partnerships in support of the *World Heritage Convention*

Ⅶ.B 调动其他技术及财务资源，展开合作，支持《世界遗产公约》

225. To the extent possible, the World Heritage Fund should be used to mobilize additional funds for International Assistance from other sources.

225.应尽可能发挥世界遗产基金的作用，开发更多资金来源，支持国际援助。

226. The Committee decided that contributions offered to the World Heritage Fund for international assistance campaigns and other UNESCO projects for any property inscribed on the World Heritage List shall be accepted and used as international assistance pursuant to Section V of the *Convention*, and in conformity with the modalities established for carrying out the campaign or project.

226.委员会决定，根据《公约》第五部分的规定，在符合活动或项目开展的情况下，世界遗产基金收到的捐款应用于：国际援助活动和其他联合国教科文组织《世界遗产名录》遗产保护项目。

227. States Parties are invited to provide support to the *Convention* in addition to obligatory contributions paid to the World Heritage Fund. This voluntary support can be provided through additional contributions to the World Heritage Fund or direct financial and technical contributions to properties.

227.除了向世界遗产基金义务捐款之外，还鼓励缔约国为《公约》提供自愿支持。自愿支持包括向世界遗产基金提供额外捐款，或者直接对遗产提供财政或技术援助。

Article 15(3) of the *World Heritage Convention*

《世界遗产公约》第15（3）条

228. States Parties are encouraged to participate

228.鼓励缔约国参与联合国教科文组织发起

in international fund-raising campaigns launched by UNESCO and aimed at protecting World Heritage.

的旨在保护世界遗产的国际资金筹集活动。

229. States Parties and others who anticipate making contributions towards these campaigns or other UNESCO projects for World Heritage properties are encouraged to make their contributions through the World Heritage Fund.

229.委员会鼓励希望为上述国际资金筹募活动或联合国教科文组织其他的世界遗产保护项目提供支持的缔约国、其他组织或个人通过世界遗产基金捐款。

230. States Parties are encouraged to promote the establishment of national, public and private foundations or associations aimed at raising funds to support World Heritage conservation efforts.

230.鼓励缔约国创立国家、公共和私人基金或机构，用来筹资支持世界遗产保护。

Article 17 of the *World Heritage Convention*

《世界遗产公约》第17条

231. The Secretariat provides support in mobilizing financial and technical resources for World Heritage conservation. To this end, the Secretariat develops partnerships with public and private institutions in conformity with the Decisions and the Guidelines issued by the World Heritage Committee and UNESCO regulations.

231.秘书处支持调动财政或技术资源，保护世界遗产。为此，秘书处在遵守世界遗产委员会和联合国教科文组织相关指南和规定的前提下，与公共或私营机构建立伙伴关系。

232. The Secretariat should refer to the "Directives concerning UNESCO's co-operation with private extra-budgetary funding sources" and "Guidelines for mobilizing private funds and criteria for selecting potential partners" to govern external fund-raising in favour of the World Heritage Fund. These documents are available at the following Web address: http://whc.unesco.org/en/privatefunds

232.秘书处在为世界遗产基金展开外部筹资时，应该援引："联合国教科文组织与私人预算外集资相关的指示"以及"调动私人资金的指导方针和选择潜在合作伙伴的标准"。这些文件可以在以下网站获得：http://whc.unesco.org/en/privatefunds

"Directives concerning UNESCO's co-operation with private extra-budgetary funding sources" (Annex to the Decision 149 EX/Dec. 7.5) and "Guidelines for mobilizing private funds and criteria for selecting potential partners" (Annex to the Decision 156 EX/Dec. 9.4)

"联合国教科文组织与私人预算外集资相关的指示"（第149EX/Dec.7.5号决定的附录）和"调动私人资金的指导方针和选择潜在合作伙伴的标准"（第156EX/Dec.9.4.号决定的附录）

VII.C International Assistance

233. The *Convention* provides International Assistance to States Parties for the protection of the world cultural and natural heritage located on their territories and inscribed, or potentially suitable for inscription on the World Heritage List. International Assistance should be seen as supplementary to national efforts for the conservation and management of World Heritage and Tentative List properties when adequate resources cannot be secured at the national level.

See Articles 13 (1&2) and 19-26 of the *World Heritage Convention*.

234. International Assistance is primarily financed from the World Heritage Fund, established under the *World Heritage Convention*. The Committee determines International Assistance on a biennial basis.

Section IV of the *World Heritage Convention*

235. The World Heritage Committee co-ordinates and allocates types of International Assistance in response to State Party requests. These types of International Assistance, described in the summary table set out below, in order of priority are:
    a) Emergency assistance
    b) Preparatory assistance
    c) Training and research assistance
    d) Technical co-operation
    e) Assistance for education, information and awareness raising.

VII.D Principles and priorities for International Assistance

236. Priority is given to International Assistance

VII.C 国际援助

233.《公约》向各缔约国提供国际援助，保护其领土内、引入《世界遗产名录》的世界文化和自然遗产、以及符合名录要求的潜在世界遗产。当国家不能确保足够的资金时，国际援助辅助国家保护、管理世界遗产及《预备名录》内遗产。

见《世界遗产公约》第13条（1&2）和第19-26条

234.世界援助主要来源于世界遗产基金，世界遗产基金是依据《世界遗产公约》建立的。委员会每两年决定一次国际援助。

《世界遗产公约》第IV部分

235.世界遗产委员会应缔约国的请求，协商分配各种国际援助。国际援助有以下几种，按照优先性依次排列如下：

    a）紧急援助
    b）筹备性援助
    c）培训与研究援助
    d）技术合作
    e）教育、信息和意识提高援助。

VII.D 国际援助的原则和优先权

236.国际援助将优先给予那些《濒危世界遗

for properties inscribed on the List of World Heritage in Danger. The Committee created a specific budget line to ensure that a significant portion of assistance from the World Heritage Fund is allocated to properties inscribed on the List of World Heritage in Danger.

产名录》内遗产。委员会规定了具体的预算线，确保世界遗产基金相当一部分资金用来救援《濒危世界遗产名录》内的遗产。

Article 13(1) of the *World Heritage Convention.*

《世界遗产公约》第13（1）条

237. States Parties in arrears of payment of their compulsory or voluntary contributions to the World Heritage Fund are not eligible for international assistance, it being understood that this provision does not apply to requests for emergency assistance.

237. 拖欠世界遗产基金的义务或自愿捐款的缔约国，没有资格享受国际援助，但是这一条不适用于紧急援助。

Decision 13 COM Ⅻ.34

第13 COM Ⅻ.34号决定

238. To support its Strategic Objectives, the Committee also allocates International Assistance in conformity with the priorities set out by Regional Programmes. These Programmes are adopted as follow up to Periodic Reports and regularly reviewed by the Committee based on the needs of States Parties identified in Periodic Reports (see chapter V).

238. 为支持其战略目标，委员会也会根据"地区计划"的优先顺序分配国际援助，区域计划是《定期报告》的后续措施，委员会将根据《定期报告》中缔约国的需求定期评审区域计划（见第五章）。

Decisions 26 COM 17.2,
26 COM 20 and 26 COM 25.3

第26 COM 17.2号、
26 COM 20号和26 COM 25.3号决定

239. In addition to the priorities outlined in paragraphs 236-238 above, the following considerations govern the Committee's decisions in granting International Assistance:

a) the likelihood that the assistance will have a catalytic and multiplier effect ("seed money") and promote financial and technical contributions from other sources;

b) whether the International Assistance request is from a State Party which is a Least Developed Country or Low Income Country as defined by the

239. 委员会在分配国际援助时，除了按照上面236–238段所说的优先性顺序外，还会考虑以下因素：

a）带来催化和倍增效应的援助（"种子基金"），可能会吸引其他资金或技术贡献；

b）申请国际援助的国家，是否为联合国经济社会发展政策委员会所定义的最不发达国家或低收入国家；

United Nations Economic and Social Council's Committee for Development Policy;

c) the urgency of the protective measures to be taken at World Heritage properties;

d) whether the legislative, administrative and, wherever possible, financial commitment of the recipient State Party is available to the activity;

e) the impact of the activity on furthering the Strategic Objectives decided by the Committee;

Paragraph 26

f) the degree to which the activity responds to needs identified through the reactive monitoring process and/or the analysis of regional Periodic Reports;

Decision 20 COM XII

g) the exemplary value of the activity in respect to scientific research and the development of cost effective conservation techniques;

h) the cost of the activity and expected results; and

i) the educational value both for the training of experts and for the general public.

240. A balance will be maintained in the allocation of resources to activities for cultural and natural heritage. This balance is reviewed and decided upon on a regular basis by the Committee.

c）对世界遗产采取保护措施的紧急程度；

d）受益缔约国是否有法律、行政措施或者（在可能情况下）有承付款项，用来开展活动；

e）活动对于进一步达到委员会制定的"战略目标"的影响；

第26段

f）活动满足反应监测过程和/或《定期报告》地区分析所定需求的程度

第20 COM XII号决定

g）该活动对科学研究以及开发高效低成本的保护技术的示范价值；

h）该活动的成本和预期结果；

i）对专家培训和大众的教育价值。

240.平衡对文化与自然遗产的资源分配。委员会将定期检查这种平衡。

VII.E Summary Table

241.

Type of international assistance	Purpose	Budget ceilings	Deadline for submission of request	Authority for approval
Emergency Assistance	This assistance may be requested to address ascertained or potential threats facing properties included on the List of World Heritage in Danger and the World Heritage List which have suffered severe damage or are in imminent danger of severe damage due to sudden, unexpected phenomena. Such phenomena may include land subsidence, extensive fires, explosions, flooding or man-made disasters including war. This assistance does not concern cases of damage or deterioration caused by gradual processes of decay, pollution or erosion. It addresses emergency situations strictly relating to the conservation of a World Heritage property (see Decision 28 COM 10B 2.c). It may be made available, if necessary, to more than one World Heritage property in a single State Party (see Decision 6 EXT. COM 15.2). The budget ceilings relate to a single World Heritage property. The assistance may be requested to : (i) undertake emergency measures for the safeguarding of the property; (ii) draw up an emergency plan for the property.	Up to US$ 75,000 Over US$ 75,000	At any time 1 February	Chairperson of the Committee Committee
Preparatory assistance	This assistance may be requested to: (i) prepare or update national Tentative Lists of properties suitable for inscription on the World Heritage List; (ii) organize meetings for the harmonization of national Tentative Lists within the same geo- cultural area; (iii) prepare nominations of properties for inscription on the World Heritage List (this may include the preparation of a comparative analysis of the property in relation to other similar properties (see 3.c of Annex 5); (iv) prepare requests for training and research assistance and for technical co-operation for World Heritage properties. Requests by States Parties whose heritage in un-represented or under-represented in the World Heritage List will be given priority for preparatory assistance.	Up to US$ 30,000	At any time	Chairperson of the Committee

Type of international assistance	Purpose	Budget ceilings	Deadline for submission of request	Authority for approval
Training and Research assistance	This assistance may be requested for: (i)the training of staff and specialists at all levels in the fields of identification, monitoring, conservation, management and presentation of World Heritage, with an emphasis on group training; (ii)scientific research benefiting World Heritage properties; (iii)studies on the scientific and technical problems of conservation, management, and presentation of World Heritage properties. Note: Requests for support for individual training courses from UNESCO should be submitted on the standard "Aplication for fellowship" form available from the Secretariat.	Up to US$ 30,000 Over US$ 30,000	At any time 1 February	Chairperson of the Committee Committee
Technical co-operation	This assistance may be requested for: (i)provision of experts, technicians and skilled labour for the conservation, management, and presentation of properties inscribed on the List of World Heritage in Danger and the World Heritage List; (ii)supply of equipment which the State Party requires for the conservation, management, and presentation of properties inscribed on the List of World Heritage in Danger and the World Heritage List; (iii)low-interest or interest-free loans for undertaking activities for the conservation, management, and presentation of properties inscribed on the List of World Heritage in Danger and the World Heritage List, which may be repayable on a long-term basis.	Up to US$ 30,000 Over US$ 30,000	At any time 1 February	Chairperson of the Committee Committee
Assistance for education, information and awareness raising	This assistance may be requested: (i)At the regional and international levels for Programmes, activities and the holding of meetings that could: -help to create interest in the *Convention* within the countries of a given region; -create a greater awareness of the different issues related to the implementation of the *Convention* to promote more active involvement in its application; -be a means of exchanging experiences; -stimulate joint education, information and promotional programmes and activities, especially when they involve the participation of young people for the benefit of World Heritage conservation.	Up to US$ 5,000 Between US$ 5,000 and US$ 10,000	Any time Any time	Director of the World Heritage Centre Chairperson of the Committee

续表

Type of international assistance	Purpose	Budget ceilings	Deadline for submission of request	Authority for approval
Assistance for education, information and awareness raising	(ii)At the national level for: -meetings specifically organized to make the *Convention* better known, especially amongst young people, or for the creation of national World Heritage associations, in accordance with Article 17 of the *Convention*; -preparation and discussion of education and information material (such as brochures, publications, exhibitions, films, multimedia tools) for the general promotion of the *Convention* and the World Heritage List and not for the promotion of a particular property, and especially for young people.			

VII.E 总表

241.

国际援助种类	目的	最高预算额	提交请求的截止期限	核准机关
紧急援助	可以申请紧急援助来解决《濒危世界遗产名录》及《世界遗产名录》中面临确定及潜在威胁而遭受严重损坏的遗产，或由于突然、不可预料的现象遭受迫切威胁及重大损失的遗产。救援也可能用于处在意外环境中的遗产。这些不可预料的现象包括土地沉陷、大火、爆炸、洪水和诸如战争等的人为灾难。此类援助不可用于那些由渐进的腐蚀、污染和侵蚀造成的损害和蜕化。这些救助只用来救助那些严格与保护世界遗产有关的紧急情况（见第 28 COM 10B 2.c 号）。如果有可能的话，这些救助会用来援助同一缔约国的多处遗产（见第 6EXT.COM 15.2 号决定）。最高预算额适用单个世界遗产。 援助可用于： （i）采取紧急措施保护遗产； （ii）制定遗产的紧急方案。	最多 75000 美元 多于 75000 美元	任何时间 2 月 1 日	委员会主席
筹备性援助	援助可用于： （i）准备或更新适合列入《世界遗产名录》的国家《预备名录》内的遗产； （ii）在同一地理文化领域内组织会议，协商各国家《预备名录》；	最多 30000 美元	任何时间	委员会主席

续表

国际援助种类	目的	最高预算额	提交请求的截止期限	核准机关
筹备性援助	（iii）准备《世界遗产名录》的申报文件（其中可能包括准备遗产与其他类似遗产的比较分析）（见附录5的3c）； （iv）准备世界遗产保护所需培训和研究援助及技术合作的申请。 筹备性援助优先满足《世界遗产名录》内没有遗产或遗产代表性不足的缔约国的申请。			
培训和研究援助	援助可用于： （i）在世界遗产的确认、监测、保存、管理以及展示领域培训各个级别的工作人员和专家，培训以团体培训为主； （ii）对世界遗产有利的科学研究； （iii）致力于解决世界遗产保存、管理与展示问题的研究； 注释：如果向联合国教科文组织提出个人培训的请求，首先要填写由秘书处准备的"奖学金申请"表格。	最多30000美元 多于30000美元	任何时间 2月1日	委员会主席 委员会
技术合作	援助可用于： （i）对于列在《濒危世界遗产名录》和《世界遗产名录》上的遗产给予专家、技术支持，以保存、管理、展示遗产； （ii）缔约国为保存、管理、展示《濒危世界遗产名录》和《世界遗产名录》内遗产所需要的设备； （iii）为保存、管理、展示《濒危世界遗产名录》和《世界遗产名录》内遗产所需的低利率或零利率贷款，这些贷款可能是可长期偿还的。	最高30000美元 多于30000美元	任何时间 2月1日	委员会主席 委员会
教育、信息和意识提高援助	援助可用于： （i）用于地区和国际级别的计划、活动和会议： －帮助在国内或特定地区内激发对《世界遗产公约》的兴趣； －在执行《世界遗产公约》过程中提高对不同议题的认识，推动更多各方参与实施《公约》。 －经验交流的渠道； －帮助开展联合教育、信息、以及宣传活动，特别是有年轻人参加的世界遗产保护活动。 （ii）用于国家级别的会议： －组织特别会议，让《公约》得到更好的了解，特别是组织有年轻人参加的会议；根据《世界遗产公约》第17条，创立国家世界遗产协会；	最多5000美元 在5000美元和10000美元之间	任何时间 任何时间	世界遗产中心主任 委员会主席

国际援助种类	目的	最高预算额	提交请求的截止期限	核准机关
教育、信息和意识提高援助	– 为总的宣传《公约》和《世界遗产名录》，准备、讨论教育和信息资料（例如：宣传手册、出版物、展览会、电影、大众传媒工具），有年轻人参加尤为重要。本援助不用于某项特定遗产的宣传。			

Ⅶ.F Procedure and format

242. All States Parties submitting requests for international assistance are encouraged to consult the Secretariat and the Advisory Bodies during the conceptualization, planning and elaboration of each request. To facilitate States Parties, examples of successful international assistance requests may be provided upon request.

243. The application form for International Assistance is presented in Annex 8 and the types, amounts, deadlines for submission and the authorities responsible for approval are outlined in the summary table in Chapter Ⅶ.E.

244. The request should be submitted in English or French, duly signed and transmitted by the National Commission for UNESCO, the State Party Permanent Delegation to UNESCO and/or appropriate governmental Department or Ministry:

UNESCO World Heritage Centre

7, place de Fontenoy 75352 Paris 07 SP

France

Tel　：+33 (0) 1 4568 1276

Fax　：+33 (0) 1 4568 5570

E-mail：wh-intassistance@unesco.org

245. Requests for international assistance may

Ⅶ.F 程序和格式

242.鼓励所有申请国际援助的缔约国，在构想、计划和拟定申请期间，与秘书处和咨询机构进行磋商。为了协助缔约国申请国际援助，应缔约国的要求，委员会可提供国际援助的成功申请案例。

243.国际援助的申请表格可参阅附录8，第七.E章的总表概述了提交的种类、金额以及截止期限和核准批准机构。

244.用英语或者法语提出申请，联合国教科文组织国家委员会、联合国教科文组织缔约国常驻代表团和/或相关政府部门签字后按下列地址提交：

联合国教科文组织世界遗产中心

法国巴黎（7, place de Fontenoy

75352 Paris 07 SP France）

电话　：+33（0）1 4568 1276

传真　：+33（0）1 4568 5570

E-mail　：wh-intassistance@unesco.org

245.缔约国可用电子邮件申请国际援助，但

be submitted by electronic mail by the State Party but must be accompanied by an officially signed hard copy.

是必须同时提交一份正式签字的书面申请。

246. It is important that all information requested in this application form is provided. If appropriate or necessary, requests may be supplemented by additional information, reports, etc.

246.必须提供申请表中所要求填写的一切信息。在适当或必要的时候，可以随申请表附上相关信息、报告等。

Ⅶ.G Evaluation and approval of International Assistance requests

Ⅶ.G 国际援助的评估和核准

247. Provided that a request for assistance from a State Party is complete, the Secretariat, with the assistance of the Advisory Bodies, will process each request in a timely manner, as follows.

247.如果缔约国的国际援助申请信息完整，秘书处在咨询机构的帮助下，会通过以下方式及时处理每一份申请。

248. All requests for international assistance for cultural heritage are evaluated by ICOMOS and ICCROM.

248.所有文化遗产国际援助的申请，均由国际古迹遗址理事会和国际文物保护和修复研究中心评估。

Decision 13 COM Ⅻ.34

第13 COM Ⅻ.34号决定

249. All requests for international assistance for mixed heritage are evaluated by ICOMOS, ICCROM and IUCN.

249. 所有混合遗产国际援助的申请，均由国际古迹遗址理事会、国际文物保护和修复研究中心和世界保护自然联盟评估。

250. All requests for international assistance for natural heritage are evaluated by IUCN.

250.所有自然遗产国际援助的申请，均由世界保护自然联盟做出评估。

251. The evaluation criteria used by the Advisory Bodies are outlined in Annex 9.

251.咨询机构所使用的评估标准在附录9中列明。

252. All requests for the approval of the Chairperson can be submitted at anytime to the Secretariat and approved by the Chairperson after appropriate evaluation.

252.所有提交主席批准的申请都可以随时提交给秘书处，主席在做出适当的评估后会批准该申请。

253. The Chairperson is not authorized to approve requests submitted by his own country. These

253.主席不能批准来自本国的申请。委员会将审查这些申请。

will be examined by the Committee.

254. All requests for the approval of the Committee should be received by the Secretariat on or before 1 February. These requests are submitted to the Committee at its next session.

VII. H Contractual Arrangements

255. Agreements are established between UNESCO and the concerned State Party or its representative(s) for the implementation of the approved International Assistance requests in conformity with UNESCO regulations, following the work plan and budget breakdown described in the originally approved request.

VII.I Evaluation and follow-up of International Assistance

256. The monitoring and evaluation of the implementation of the International Assistance requests will take place within 12 months of the activities' completion. The results of these evaluations will be collated and maintained by the Secretariat in collaboration with the Advisory Bodies and examined by the Committee on a regular basis.

257. The Committee reviews the implementation, evaluation and follow-up of International Assistance in order to evaluate the International Assistance effectiveness and to redefine its priorities.

VIII. THE WORLD HERITAGE EMBLEM

VIII.A Preamble

258. At its second session (Washington, 1978), the Committee adopted the World Heritage Emblem which had been designed by Mr. Michel Olyff.

254.所有提交委员会审批的申请要在二月一日或之前交到秘书处。秘书处会在下届会议时将这些申请提交给委员会。

VII.H 合同安排

255.联合国教科文组织与相关缔约国政府或/及代表要达成协议：在使用国际援助的时候，必须要遵守联合国教科文组织规章，同时要与之前批准的申请中所描述的工作计划和预算明细保持一致。

VII.I 国际援助的评估和跟踪

256.在整个申请程序结束12个月之后，将开始对国际援助申请进行监测和评估。秘书处和咨询机构会对评估结果进行比较，委员会将对这些结果定期进行检查。

257.委员会将对国际援助的实施、评估和后续工作进行评论，以便评估国际援助的使用效力并重新定义国际援助的优先顺序。

VIII.世界遗产标志

VIII.A 前言

258.在世界遗产委员会第二届大会上（华盛顿，1978年），采用了由米歇尔·奥利芙设计的遗产标志。这个标志表现了文化与自然遗产之

This Emblem symbolizes the interdependence of cultural and natural properties: the central square is a form created by man and the circle represents nature, the two being intimately linked. The Emblem is round, like the world, but at the same time it is a symbol of protection. It symbolizes the *Convention*, signifies the adherence of States Parties to the *Convention*, and serves to identify properties inscribed in the World Heritage List. It is associated with public knowledge about the *Convention* and is the imprimatur of the *Convention*'s credibility and prestige. Above all, it is a representation of the universal values for which the *Convention* stands.

259. The Committee decided that the Emblem proposed by the artist could be used, in any colour or size, depending on the use, the technical possibilities and considerations of an artistic nature. The Emblem should always carry the text "WORLD HERITAGE. PATRIMOINE MONDIAL". The space occupied by "PATRIMONIO MUNDIAL" can be used for its translation into the national language of the country where the Emblem is to be used.

260. In order to ensure the Emblem benefits from as much visibility as possible while preventing improper uses, the Committee at its twenty-second session (Kyoto, 1998) adopted "Guidelines and Principles for the Use of the World Heritage Emblem" as set out in the following paragraphs.

261. Although there is no mention of the Emblem in the *Convention*, its use has been promoted by the Committee to identify properties protected by the *Convention* and inscribed on the World Heritage List since its adoption in 1978.

262. The World Heritage Committee is responsible for determining the use of the World Heritage Emblem and for making policy prescriptions

间的相互依存关系：代表大自然的圆形与代表人类创造的形状方形紧密相连。标志是圆形的，代表世界的，同时也是保护的象征。标志象征《公约》，代表缔约国将坚守《公约》，同时指明了列入《世界遗产名录》中的遗产。它与大众对《公约》的了解相互关联，是对《公约》可信度和威望的认可。总而言之，它是《公约》所代表的普世价值的集中体现。

259. 委员会决定，由该艺术家提交的标志，可用于任何颜色或任意尺寸的艺术品中，这主要取决于技术水平和艺术品的特性。但是标志上必须印有"world heritage（英语"世界遗产"）.Patrimoine Mondial"（法语"世界遗产"）的字样。但各国在使用该标志时，可用自己本国的语言来代替中间部分的"Patrimonio Mundial"（西语）字样。

260. 为了保证标志尽可能地引人注目，同时避免误用，委员会在第22届会议（京都，1998年）上通过了《世界遗产标志使用指南和原则》，内容在后续段落有所说明。

261. 尽管《公约》并未提到标志，但是自1978年采用该标志以来，委员会一直在推动使用该标志来标示受《公约》的保护的遗产以及列入《世界遗产名录》的遗产。

262. 世界遗产委员会负责决定世界遗产标志的使用，同时负责制定如何使用标志的政策规定。

regarding how it may be used.

263. As requested by the Committee at its 26th session (Budapest, 2002), the World Heritage Emblem, the "World Heritage" name and its derivatives are currently being registered under Article 6ter of the Paris Convention for the Protection of Industrial Property and are therefore protected.

Decision 26 COM 15

264. The Emblem also has fund-raising potential that can be used to enhance the marketing value of products with which it is associated. A balance is needed between the Emblem's use to further the aims of the *Convention* and optimize knowledge of the *Convention* worldwide and the need to prevent its abuse for inaccurate, inappropriate, and unauthorized commercial or other purposes.

265. The Guidelines and Principles for the Use of the Emblem and modalities for quality control should not become an obstacle to co-operation for promotional activities. Authorities responsible for reviewing and deciding on uses of the Emblem (see below) need parameters on which to base their decisions.

Ⅷ.B Applicability

266. The Guidelines and Principles proposed herein cover all proposed uses of the Emblem by:
    a. The World Heritage Centre;
    b. The UNESCO Publishing Office and other UNESCO offices;
    c. Agencies or National Commissions, responsible for implementing the *Convention* in each State Party;

263.按照委员会在其第26届大会（布达佩斯，2002年）上的要求，世界遗产标志、"世界遗产"名字本身，以及它所有的派生词都已根据《保护工业产权巴黎公约》第6条进行了注册，因此受到该《公约》的保护。

第26COM15号决定

264.标志还有筹集基金的潜力，可以用于提高相关产品的市场价值。在使用标志的过程中，要注意在以下两者之间保持平衡，即正确使用标志增进《公约》目标的实现，并在世界范围内最大限度地普及《公约》知识，但同时要避免不正确、不恰当、以及未经授权、出于商业或其他目的的滥用标志。

265.《世界遗产标志使用指南和原则》，以及质量控制的手段，不应成为就推广活动开展合作的障碍。负责审定标志使用的权威机构（见下文），在做出决定时需要有参照。

Ⅷ.B 适用性

266.本文所述的《指南和原则》涵盖了以下各方使用标志的所有可能情况：
    a.世界遗产中心
    b.联合国教科文组织公共信息部和其他联合国教科文机构
    c.各个缔约国负责实施《公约》的机构或国家委员会。

d. World Heritage properties;

e. Other contracting parties, especially those operating for predominantly commercial purposes.

VIII.C Responsibilities of States Parties

267. States Parties to the *Convention* should take all possible measures to prevent the use of the Emblem in their respective countries by any group or for any purpose not explicitly recognized by the Committee. States Parties are encouraged to make full use of national legislation including Trade Mark Laws.

VIII.D Increasing proper uses of the World Heritage Emblem

268. Properties inscribed on the World Heritage List should be marked with the emblem jointly with the UNESCO logo, which should, however, be placed in such a way that they do not visually impair the property in question.

Production of plaques to commemorate the inscription of properties on the World Heritage List

269. Once a property is inscribed on the World Heritage List, the State Party should place a plaque, whenever possible, to commemorate this inscription. These plaques are designed to inform the public of the country concerned and foreign visitors that the property visited has a particular value which has been recognized by the international community. In other words, the property is exceptional, of interest not only to one nation, but also to the whole world. However, these plaques have an additional function which is to inform the general public about the *World Heritage Convention* or at least about the World Heritage concept and the World Heritage List.

d. 世界遗产

e. 其他签约合作方，尤其是那些主要进行商业运营的机构。

VIII.C 缔约国的责任

267. 缔约国政府应该采取一切可能的措施，防止未经委员会明确承认的任何组织或出于任何目的未经授权的使用该标识。鼓励缔约国充分利用包括《商标法》在内的国家立法。

VIII.D 增加世界遗产标志的正确使用

268. 列入《世界遗产名录》的遗产应悬挂世界遗产标志和联合国教科文组织标识，但要以不破坏遗产为前提。

制作标牌，庆祝遗产列入《世界遗产名录》

269. 一旦遗产列入《世界遗产名录》，该缔约国将尽可能设立标牌来纪念这一事件。标牌应向本国公众及外国游客说明该遗产具有特殊的价值且已得到国际社会的认可。换言之，该遗产无论对该国还是世界来说，都具有非同寻常的意义。此外，该标牌还有另外一个作用，即向公众介绍《世界遗产公约》，或者至少是世界遗产概念和《世界遗产名录》。

270. The Committee has adopted the following Guidelines for the production of these plaques:

a) the plaque should be so placed that it can easily be seen by visitors, without disfiguring the property;

b) the World Heritage Emblem should appear on the plaque;

c) the text should mention the property's outstanding universal value; in this regard it might be useful to give a short description of the property's outstanding characteristics. States Parties may, if they wish, use the descriptions appearing in the various World Heritage publications or in the World Heritage exhibit, and which may be obtained from the Secretariat;

d) the text should make reference to the *World Heritage Convention* and particularly to the World Heritage List and to the international recognition conferred by inscription on this List (however, it is not necessary to mention at which session of the Committee the property was inscribed); it may be appropriate to produce the text in several languages for properties which receive many foreign visitors.

271. The Committee proposes the following text as an example:

"(Name of property) has been inscribed upon the World Heritage List of the *Convention concerning the Protection of the World Cultural and Natural Heritage*. Inscription on this List confirms the outstanding universal value of a cultural or natural property which deserves protection for the benefit of all humanity."

272. This text could be then followed by a brief description of the property concerned.

273. Furthermore, the national authorities should encourage World Heritage properties to make a broad use of the Emblem such as on their letterheads,

270.委员会对标牌的生产采用以下指导方针：

a）标牌应该挂放在容易被游客看到的地方，同时标牌不能破坏遗产的景观；

b）在标牌上应该带有世界遗产标志；

c）标牌上的内容应该能够体现遗产突出的普遍价值；考虑到这一点，内容中应该对遗产的突出特点加以描述。如果愿意的话，缔约国政府可以使用各种世界遗产出版物或世界遗产展览对相关遗产的说明。这些内容可直接从秘书处获得。

d）标牌上的内容应提及《保护世界文化和自然遗产公约》，尤其是《世界遗产名录》及国际社会对列入《名录》的遗产的承认（但无需指出是在委员会的哪届会议上通过的）。如遗产有大量外国游客参观，标牌上的内容应使用多种语言。

271.委员会提供了以下内容作为范例：

"根据《保护世界文化和自然遗产公约》，（遗产名称）列入《世界遗产名录》。遗产列入《名录》说明该项文化、自然遗产具有突出的普遍价值，对它的保护符合全人类的利益。"

272.在这段话的后面，可对该遗产进行简要介绍。

273.此外，国家政府应该鼓励世界遗产在诸如信笺抬头、宣传手册，以及员工的工作服等物体上，广泛使用世界遗产标识。

brochures and staff uniforms.

274. Third parties which have received the right to produce communication products related to the *World Heritage Convention* and World Heritage properties must give the Emblem proper visibility. They should avoid creating a different Emblem or logo for that particular product.

VIII.E Principles on the use of the World Heritage Emblem

275. The responsible authorities are henceforth requested to use the following principles in making decisions on the use of the Emblem:

a) The Emblem should be utilized for all projects substantially associated with the work of the *Convention*, including, to the maximum extent technically and legally possible, those already approved and adopted, in order to promote the *Convention*.

b) A decision to approve use of the Emblem should be linked strongly to the quality and content of the product with which it is to be associated, not on the volume of products to be marketed or the financial return expected. The main criterion for approval should be the educational, scientific, cultural, or artistic value of the proposed product related to World Heritage principles and values. Approval should not routinely be granted to place the Emblem on products that have no, or extremely little, educational value, such as cups, T-shirts, pins, and other tourist souvenirs. Exceptions to this policy will be considered for special events, such as meetings of the Committee and ceremonies at which plaques are unveiled.

c) Any decision with respect to authorizing the use of the Emblem must be completely unambiguous and in keeping with the explicit and implicit goals and values of the *World Heritage*

274.授权负责推广《保护世界文化和自然遗产公约》和世界遗产相关产品的第三方，应突出显示世界遗产标识，而且应避免在特定产品上使用不同的标识或徽标。

VIII.E 世界遗产标识的使用原则

275.有关权威机构在决定使用标识的过程中，应遵循以下原则：

a）标志应用于所有与《公约》的工作有密切关系的项目（包括在技术和法律许可的最大范围内，应用于那些已得到批准或已通过的项目上），以推广《公约》。

b）在决定是否授权使用标志时，应首先考虑相关产品的质量和内容，而非投入市场的产品数量或预期的经济回报。审核通过与否的主要标准是，所申请产品与世界遗产的原则与价值相关的教育、科学、文化和艺术价值。对于那些印上标志后没有教育意义的或是教育意义很小的产品，如茶杯、T恤、别针和其他旅游纪念品，不应予以批准。对于以上规定也有例外，例如委员会会议，标牌揭幕仪式。

c）所有涉及授权标志使用的决定都应该明确表述，同时必须与《保护世界文化和自然遗产公约》明确表示和隐含的目标和价值，保持一致。

Convention.

d) Except when authorized in accordance with these principles it is not legitimate for commercial entities to use the Emblem directly on their own material to show their support for World Heritage. The Committee recognizes, however, that any individual, organization, or company is free to publish or produce whatever they consider to be appropriate regarding World Heritage properties, but official authorization to do so under the World Heritage Emblem remains the exclusive prerogative of the Committee, to be exercised as prescribed in these Guidelines and Principles.

e) Use of the Emblem by other contracting parties should normally only be authorized when the proposed use deals directly with World Heritage properties. Such uses may be granted after approval by the national authorities of the countries concerned.

f) In cases where no specific World Heritage properties are involved or are not the principal focus of the proposed use, such as general seminars and/or workshops on scientific issues or conservation techniques, use may be granted only upon express approval in accordance with these Guidelines and Principles. Requests for such uses should specifically document the manner in which the proposed use is expected to enhance the work of the *Convention.*

g) Permission to use the Emblem should not be granted to travel agencies, airlines, or to any other type of business operating for predominantly commercial purposes, except under exceptional circumstances and when manifest benefit to the World Heritage generally or particular World Heritage properties can be demonstrated. Requests for such use should require approval in accordance with these Guidelines and Principles and the concurrence of the national authorities of countries specifically concerned.

d）除非依照这些原则得到授权，任何商业机构都不得直接在其产品上使用该标识，或以此表示对世界遗产的支持。虽然委员会承认，任何个人、组织或公司都可以自由出版或生产它们认为对世界遗产有利的产品，但委员会是唯一有权授予世界遗产标志使用权的官方机构，且它的授权必须遵守上述指南和原则。

e）只有当标志的使用与世界遗产直接相关时，其他签约合作方才能得到使用标志的授权。而且，申请机构只有在其所在国的主管当局批准后才能得到使用授权。

f）如果使用申请不涉及具体的世界遗产，或具体的世界遗产不是核心内容，例如一般性的学术研讨会和/或有关科学问题或保存技术的讨论会，那么标志的使用一定要根据上述指南和原则取得明确的批准。在使用标志的申请中，要明确体现标注的使用的方式，而且这种方式预计能够促进《公约》的工作。

g）通常标志的使用权不能授予旅行社、航空公司，除非在某些特殊情况以及世界遗产或特定的世界遗产项目能明确从中获益的情况下。这类使用申请需要与指南和原则保持一致，同时得到相关权威机构的批准。

The Secretariat is not to accept any advertising, travel, or other promotional considerations from travel agencies or other, similar companies in exchange or in lieu of financial remuneration for use of the Emblem.

h) When commercial benefits are anticipated, the Secretariat should ensure that the World Heritage Fund receives a fair share of the revenues and conclude a contract or other agreement that documents the nature of the understandings that govern the project and the arrangements for provision of income to the Fund. In all cases of commercial use, any staff time and related costs for personnel assigned by the Secretariat or other reviewers, as appropriate, to any initiative, beyond the nominal, must be fully covered by the party requesting authorization to use the Emblem.

National authorities are also called upon to ensure that their properties or the World Heritage Fund receive a fair share of the revenues and to document the nature of the understandings that govern the project and the distribution of any proceeds.

i) If sponsors are sought for manufacturing products whose distribution the Secretariat considers necessary, the choice of partner or partners should be consistent, at a minimum, with the criteria set forth in the "Directives concerning UNESCO's co-operation with private extra-budgetary funding sources" and "Guidelines for mobilizing private funds and criteria for selecting potential partners" and with such further fund-raising guidance as the Committee may prescribe. The necessity for such products should be clarified and justified in written presentations that will require approval in such manner as the Committee may prescribe.

"Directives concerning UNESCO's co-operation with private extra-budgetary funding sources" (Annex to the Decision 149 EX/Dec. 7.5) and "Guidelines for mobilizing private funds and criteria for selecting potential partners" (Annex to the

秘书处不接受旅行社或其他类似机构的任何广告、旅游或其他促销计划，以换取或代替使用标识的经济报酬的建议。

h）如果在标志的使用过程中产生了商业利益，秘书处应该确保世界遗产基金也从中分得部分收益。秘书处应该与相关方签订合同或其他协议，以确定协议的性质，管理项目和资金收益分配。对于所有将标志用于商业目的的情况，秘书处和其他审议者在批准使用标志申请的过程中所发生的、高于常规的、一切人力或物力的成本，都应该由提出申请方支付。

国家权威机构也要确保该国的遗产或者世界遗产基金，能够分得相应的收益，确定协议的性质，管理项目和资金的分配。

i）如果秘书处因需要制造产品进行分发而寻找赞助商，那么合作伙伴（或多个合作伙伴）的选择至少应与"有关联合国教科文组织与私人额外预算资金来源进行合作的方针"、"利用私人资金和选择潜在合作伙伴的指南"、以及其他委员会的资金筹措规定保持一致。对于生产这些商品的必要性，必须做出书面声明，并且得到委员会的批准。

"联合国教科文组织与私人预算外集资相关的指示"（附在第149EX/Dec.7.5号决定中）以及"调动私人资金的指导方针和选择潜在合作伙伴的标准"（附在第156EX/Dec.9.4号决定中）

Decision 156 EX/Dec. 9.4)

VIII.F Authorization procedure for the use of the World Heritage Emblem

VIII.F 使用世界遗产标志的授权程序

Simple agreement of the national authorities

国家权威机构的初步认定

276. National authorities may grant the use of the Emblem to a national entity, provided that the project, whether national or international, involves only World Heritage properties located on the same national territory. National authorities' decision should be guided by the Guidelines and Principles.

276.如果国家或国际项目只涉及本国的世界遗产，国家权威机构可授权国家实体使用标识。国家权威机构的决定应遵守相关指南和原则。

277. States Parties are invited to provide the Secretariat with the names and addresses of the authorities in charge of managing the use of the Emblem.

277.缔约国需要向秘书处提供负责管理标识使用的权威机构的名称和地址。

Circular letter dated 14 April 1999

http://whc.unesco.org/circs/circ 99-4e.pdf

1999年4月14日通函 http://whc.unesco.org/circs/circ99-4e.pdf

Agreement requiring quality control of content

要求对内容进行质量控制的协议

278. Any other request for authorization to use the Emblem should adopt the following procedure:

a) A request indicating the objective of the use of the Emblem, its duration and territorial validity, should be addressed to the Director of the World Heritage Centre.

b) The Director of the World Heritage Centre has the authority to grant the use of the Emblem in accordance with the Guidelines and Principles. For cases not covered, or not sufficiently covered, by the Guidelines and Principles, the Director refers the matter to the Chairperson who, in the most difficult cases, might wish to refer the matter to the Committee for final decision. A yearly report on the authorized uses of the Emblem will be submitted to the World Heritage Committee.

278.任何关于授权使用标识的申请都需遵循以下步骤：

a）申请应该说明使用标识的目的、使用时长及使用地域。该申请应提交世界遗产中心主任。

b）世界遗产中心主任有权根据指南和原则批准使用标识。遇到指南和原则尚未涉及或完全涵盖的情况，主任将申请提交主席，如果遇到很难处理的情况，主席会将该申请提交委员会做最后决定。有关授权使用标识的年度报告都将提交世界遗产委员会。

c) Authorization to use the Emblem in major products to be widely distributed over an undetermined period of time is conditional upon obtaining the manufacturer's commitment to consult with countries concerned and secure their endorsement of texts and images illustrating properties situated in their territory, at no cost to the Secretariat, together with the proof that this has been done. The text to be approved should be provided in either one of the official languages of the Committee or in the language of the country concerned. A draft model to be used by States Parties to authorize the use of the Emblem to third parties appears below.

Content Approval Form:

[Name of responsible national body], officially identified as the body responsible for approving the content of the texts and photos relating to the World Heritage properties located in the territory of [name of country], hereby confirms to [name of producer] that the text and the images that it has submitted for the [name of properties] World Heritage property(ies) are [approved] [approved subject to the following changes requested] [are not approved]

(delete whatever entry does not apply, and provide, as needed, a corrected copy of the text or a signed list of corrections).

Notes:

It is recommended that the initials of the responsible national official be affixed to each page of text.

The National Authorities are given one month from their acknowledged receipt in which to authorize the content, following which the producers may consider that the content has been tacitly approved, unless the responsible National Authorities request in writing a longer period.

Texts should be supplied to the National Authorities in one of the two official languages of the Committee, or in the official language (or in one of the official languages) of the country in which the

c）如授权在不确定的时期内在广泛行销的主要产品上使用标识，生产商承诺与相关缔约国协商，就有关其境内遗产的图片和文字取得其同意，同时生产商还应提供获取同意的证明，且秘书处不承担任何费用。报批的文书须以委员会规定的任意一种正式语言，或相关国家的语言书写。缔约方用于批准第三方使用标识的草拟范本，应按以下格式填写：

内容批准表：

作为负责批准有关该国[国家名称]世界遗产的图文的官方机构，[国家主管机构的名称]在此向[生产商名称]证实，它已提交的世界遗产[遗产名称]图文已[通过审批][如做出以下变更便可通过审批][未通过审批]。

（删除不适用的条目，并按需要提供文字或签名确认的变更文件的副本，含变更内容清单）。

注释：

建议在文本的每一页上都注明国家主管人员姓名的首字母。

自收到申请之日起一个月内，国家主管机构应该做出答复，批准文本内容。如果生产商未接到答复，可视为该内容已得到默许，除非该国家主管机构提出书面文件，需要延长批准时限。

提交给国家主管机构的申请所使用的语言应按照双方的需要，可为委员会的两种官方语言中的一种，或者是遗产所在国的官方语言（或是其中一种官方语言）。

properties are located, at the convenience of both parties.

d) After having examined the request and considered it as acceptable, the Secretariat may establish an agreement with the partner.

e) If the Director of the World Heritage Centre judges that a proposed use of the Emblem is not acceptable, the Secretariat informs the requesting party of the decision in writing.

Ⅷ.G Right of States Parties to exert quality control

279. Authorization to use the Emblem is inextricably linked to the requirement that the national authorities may exert quality control over the products with which it is associated.

a) The States Parties to the *Convention* are the only parties authorized to approve the content (images and text) of any distributed product appearing under the World Heritage Emblem with regard to the properties located in their territories.

b) States Parties that protect the Emblem legally must review these uses.

c) Other States Parties may elect to review proposed uses or refer such proposals to the Secretariat. States Parties are responsible for identifying an appropriate national authority and for informing the Secretariat whether they wish to review proposed uses or to identify uses that are inappropriate. The Secretariat maintains a list of responsible national authorities.

IX. INFORMATION SOURCES

IX.A Information archived by the Secretariat

280. The Secretariat maintains a database of all documents of the World Heritage Committee and the General Assembly of States Parties to the *World*

d）在审阅申请并且认为可批准后，秘书处应该与合作伙伴之间签订协议。

e）如果世界遗产中心主任没有批准标识的使用，秘书处会以书面形式通知申请方。

Ⅷ.G 缔约国政府有权进行质量控制

279.标志使用的授权与国家主管机构对相关产品实施的质量控制密切相关。

a）《公约》的缔约国是唯一有权批准行销带有世界遗产标识及其境内遗产内容（图文）的相关产品的机构。

b）合法保护标识的缔约国必须审查标识的使用情况。

c）其他缔约国也可决定审查所申请的使用方式，或者将提议提交给秘书处。缔约国政府负责指定相应的国家机构，并且通知秘书处他们是否希望审查所申请的使用方式，或明确指出使用方式不适当。秘书处持有国家主管机构清单。

IX. 信息来源

IX.A 秘书处存档的信息

280.秘书处将把所有与世界遗产委员会和《保护世界文化和自然遗产公约》缔约国大会的资料存入数据库。该数据库可以在以下网址得

Heritage Convention. This database is available at the following Web address: http://whc.unesco.org/en/statutorydoc

281. The Secretariat ensures that copies of Tentative Lists, World Heritage nominations, including copies of maps and relevant information received from States Parties are archived in hard copy and in electronic format where possible. The Secretariat also arranges for the archiving of relevant information relating to inscribed properties, including evaluations and other documents developed by the Advisory Bodies, any correspondence and reports received from States Parties (including Reactive Monitoring and Periodic Reports) and correspondence and material from the Secretariat and World Heritage Committee.

282. Archived material will be kept in a form appropriate to long-term storage. Provisions will be made for the storage of paper copies and electronic copies, as relevant. Provision will be made for copies to be provided to States Parties as requested.

283. Nominations of those properties inscribed on the World Heritage List by the Committee will be made available for consultation. States Parties are urged to place a copy of the nomination on their own Web addresses and inform the Secretariat of this action. States Parties preparing nominations may wish to use such information as guides for identifying and elaborating nomination of properties within their own territories.

284. Advisory Body evaluations for each nomination and the decision of the Committee concerning each nomination are available at the following Web address : http://whc.unesco.org/en/advisorybodies

IX.B Specific Information for World Heritage

到：http://whc.unesco.org/en/statutorydoc

281.秘书处将确保《预备名录》和世界遗产申报文件副本（包括地图和缔约国提交的相关信息副本）已通过硬拷贝形式存档，同时在可能的情况下保存电子版本。秘书处也安排对已列入《世界遗产名录》的遗产的相关信息进行存档，其中包括咨询机构发表的评估和其他文件、任一缔约国提交的信件和报告（包括反应性监测和定期报告），以及秘书处和世界遗产委员会发出的信件和材料。

282.存档材料的格式应适宜长期保存。将为供保存纸制和电子文件编列经费。所需的副本也将按要求提供给缔约国。

283.委员会将妥善保存列入《世界遗产名录》的遗产申报文件，方便查阅，并敦促缔约国将申报材料的副本发布在本国网站上，并且通知秘书处。其他预备申报的国家可以利用这些信息，确认和完善本国国境内遗产的申报材料。

284.咨询机构对于每一项申报的评估意见和委员会所做的决定，都可以在以下网站获取：http://whc.unesco.org/en/advisorybodies

IX.B 世界遗产委员会成员国和其他缔约国的详

Committee members and other States Parties

285. The Secretariat maintains two electronic mailing lists: one for Committee members (wh-committee@unesco.org) and one for all States Parties (wh-states@unesco.org). States Parties are requested to supply all appropriate email addresses for the establishment of these lists. These electronic mailing lists, which supplement but do not replace the traditional means of notifying States Parties, allow the Secretariat to communicate, in a timely manner, announcements about the availability of documents, changes to meeting schedules, and other issues relevant to Committee members and other States Parties.

286. Circular letters to the States Parties are available at the following Web address: http://whc.unesco.org/en/circularletters

Another Web address, linked to the public Web address through restricted access, is maintained by the Secretariat and contains specific information targeted at Committee members, other States Parties and Advisory Bodies.

287. The Secretariat maintains also a database of decisions of the Committee and resolutions of the General Assembly of States Parties. These are available at the following Web addres: http://whc.unesco.org/en/decisions

Decision 28 COM 9

IX.C Information and publications available to the public

288. The Secretariat provides access to information labelled as publicly available and copyright free on World Heritage properties and other relevant matters, wherever possible.

细信息

285.秘书处保存了两个电子邮件清单：一个是委员会成员联系方式（wh-committee@unesco.org），另一份是缔约国联系方式（wh-states@unesco.org）。缔约国必须提供所有相关邮箱地址，以供秘书处建立清单。电子邮件清单补充但不会取代传统的邮寄方式，但秘书处可通过电邮及时发表有关文件的适用性、会议计划的变更，以及其他与委员会成员和其他缔约国相关事宜的声明。

286.发给缔约国的函件可以在以下网址获得：http://whc.unesco.org/en/circularletters。

另外还可登录另一个网站链接到公共网址，但其权限受到严格限制。该网站由秘书处负责维护，包括针对委员会委员、缔约国和咨询机构的详细信息。

287.秘书处还在同时维护另外一个有关委员会决议、缔约国大会决议的数据库。这个信息库可以从以下网址登录：http://whc.unesco.org/en/decisions。

第28COM9号决议

IX.C 面向大众的信息和出版物

288.在可能的情况下，秘书处也提供标注为面向大众、且不受版权限制的、关于世界遗产和其他相关问题的信息。

289. Information on issues related to World Heritage is available at the Secretariat's Web address (http://whc.unesco.org), on the Web addresses of the Advisory Bodies and in libraries. A list of databases accessible on the web and links to relevant web addresses can be found in the Bibliography.

290. The Secretariat produces a wide variety of World Heritage publications, including the World Heritage List, the List of World Heritage in Danger, Brief Descriptions of World Heritage properties, World Heritage Papers series, newsletters, brochures and information kits. In addition, other information materials aimed specifically at experts and the general public are also developed. The list of World Heritage publications can be found in the Bibliography or at the following Web address: http://whc.unesco.org/en/publications.

These information materials are distributed to the public directly or through the national and international networks established by States Parties or by World Heritage partners.

289. 与世界遗产有关的信息，能够在秘书处网站（http://whc.unesco.org）、咨询机构网站和图书馆中获得。网上可以获得的数据库清单以及相关网站链接，也能在参考书目上找到。

290. 秘书处出版了大量有关世界遗产的出版物，包括《世界遗产名录》、《濒危世界遗产名录》、《世界遗产简要介绍》、《世界遗产论文》系列、简报、宣传册和信息工具包。此外，其他专门为专家和大众准备的信息也得到了发展。参考书目中列出了世界遗产出版物的名单，http://whc.unesco.org/en/publications。

这些信息资料将直接分发给大众，或者通过缔约国或世界遗产合作伙伴建立的国际网络，间接向大众公开。

附件
ANNEXES

ANNEXES 1

 MODEL INSTRUMENT OF RATIFICATION / ACCEPTANCE

附件 1

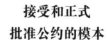 **接受和正式 批准公约的模本**

WHEREAS the Convention concerning the Protection of the World Cultural and Natural Heritage was adopted on 16 November 1972 by the General Conference of UNESCO at its seventeenth session;

NOW THEREFORE the Government of..........
....having considered the aforesaid *Convention*, hereby [*ratifies* the same and undertake faithfully to carry out

[*accepts*

the stipulations therein contained.

IN WITNESS WHEREOF, I have signed and sealed this instrument. Done at...............................
this...........................day of.........................20........ .

(Seal)　　　*Signature of Head of State,*
　　　　　　　Prime Minister or
　　　　　　　Minister of Foreign Affairs

- The model instrument of ratification / acceptance is available from the UNESCO World Heritage Centre and at the following Web address: http://whc.unesco.org/en/modelratification
- The original signed version of the completed form should be sent, preferably with an official translation in English or French, to: Director-General, UNESCO, 7 place de Fontenoy, 75352 Paris 07 SP, France

1972年11月16日的第17次联合国教科文组织大会上通过了《保护世界文化与自然遗产公约》。

因此，现在　　　　　　　政府已考虑

上述公约，并[同意　并将忠实地执行

[接受
上述公约。

特此证明，本人已在本文件上签字盖章。
20　　年　月　地点

（盖章）　　　国家首脑
　　　　　　　总理或
　　　　　　　外交部长的签字，

- 登录联合国教科文组织的世界遗产中心网站http://whc.unesco.org/en/modelratification 获得接受和正式批准的模板

- 填好的表格原件应发送至Director-General, UNESCO, 7 place de Fontenoy, 75352 Paris 07 SP, France，最好附有英文或法文的正式翻译件。

MODEL INSTRUMENT OF ACCESSION

正式批准的模板

WHEREAS the Convention concerning the Protection of the World Cultural and Natural Heritage was adopted on 16 November 1972 by the General Conference of UNESCO at its seventeenth session;

NOW THEREFORE the Government of...having considered the aforesaid *Convention*, hereby accedes the same and undertake faithfully to carry out the stipulations therein contained.

IN WITNESS WHEREOF, I have signed and sealed this instrument. Done at.................................this...........................day of..........................20....... .

(Seal)　　*Signature of Head of State,*
　　　　　Prime Minister or
　　　　　Minister of Foreign Affairs

- The model instrument of accession is available from the UNESCO World Heritage Centre and at the following Web address: http://whc.unesco.org/en/modelratification
- The original signed version of the completed form should be sent, preferably with an official translation in English or French, to: Director-General, UNESCO, 7 place de Fontenoy, 75352 Paris 07 SP, France

1972年11月16日的第17次联合国教科文组织大会上通过了《保护世界文化与自然遗产公约》。

现在本政府经考虑同意加入并忠实地执行上述公约。

特此证明，本人已在本文件上签字盖章。
20　　年　月　地点

（盖章）　　　　国家首脑
　　　　　　　　总理或
　　　　　　　　外交部长的签字，

- 登录联合国教科文组织的世界遗产中心网站http://whc.unesco.org/en/modelratification 获得此正式批准的模板
- 填好的表格原件应发送至Director-General, UNESCO, 7 place de Fontenoy, 75352 Paris 07 SP, France，最好附有英文或法文的正式翻译件。

ANNEXES 2

TENTATIVE LIST SUBMISSION FORMAT

附件 2

《预备名单》申报格式

STATE PARTY:　　DATE OF SUBMISSION:

Submission prepared by:

Name:　　　　　E-mail:

Address:　　　　Fax:

Institution:　　　Telephone:

NAME OF PROPERTY:

State, Province or Region:

Latitude and Longitude, or UTM coordinates:

DESCRIPTION:

JUSTIFICATION FOR OUTSTANDING UNIVERSAL VALUE

Criteria met [see Paragraph 77 of the *Operational Guidelines*]:

(Please tick the box corresponding to the proposed criteria and justify the use of each below)

(i) (ii) (iii) (iv) (v) (vi) (vii) (viii) (ix) (x)

Statements of authenticity and/or integrity [see Paragraphs 78-95 of the *Operational Guidelines*]:

Comparison with other similar properties:

• The Tentative List submission format is available from the UNESCO World Heritage Centre and at the following Web address: http://whc.unesco.org/en/tentativelists

• Further guidance on the preparation of Tentative Lists can be found in Paragraphs 62-67 of the *Operational Guidelines*.

• An example of a completed Tentative List

缔约国：　　　　　申报日期：

申报机构信息：

名称：　　　　　电子邮件：

地址：　　　　　传真：

机构：　　　　　电话：

申报遗产名称：

国家、省或地区：

经纬度，或 UTM 地理坐标：

描述：

突出的普遍价值声明

符合标准［参见《操作指南》第 77 段］：

（在符合标准的框里打钩，并针对提议的各条标准，提供相应理由）：

（i）（ii）（iii）（iv）（v）（vi）（vii）（viii）（ix）（x）

完整性和真实性声明[参见《操作指南》第 78–95 段]：

与其他类似遗产的比较分析：

• 登录联合国教科文组织的世界遗产中心网站 https://whc.unesco.org/en/convention/ 获取此《预备名单》提交格式；

•《操作指南》第 62–67 段中含有《预备名单》准备工作的详细指导。

• 登录 http://whc.unesco.org/en/tentativelists 网

submission format can be found at the following Web address: http://whc.unesco.org/en/tentativelists

- All Tentative Lists submitted by States Parties are available at the following Web address: http://whc.unesco.org/en/tentativelists
- The original signed version of the completed Tentative List submission format should be sent in English or French to: UNESCO World Heritage Centre, 7 place de Fontenoy, 75352 Paris 07 SP, France
- States Parties are encouraged to also submit this information in electronic format (diskette or CD-Rom) or by e-mail to wh-tentativelists@unesco.org

站可获得完整的《预备名录》提交格式样板。

- 登录网站http://whc.unesco.org/en/tentativelists可获得所有由缔约国提交的《预备名录》；

- 填好的《预备名录》原件应发送至Director-General, UNESCO, 7 place de Fontenoy, 75352 Paris 07 SP, France，最好附有英文或法文的正式翻译件。

- 鼓励缔约国同时提交电子版表格（磁盘或CD）或发送电子邮件至wh-tentativelists@unesco.org

ANNEXES 3

**GUIDELINES ON THE
INSCRIPTION OF
SPECIFIC TYPES
OF PROPERTIES
ON THE WORLD
HERITAGE LIST**①

附件 3

**特定类型遗产列入《世
界遗产名录》指南**①

INTRODUCTION

序言

1. This annex provides information on specific types of properties to guide States Parties in preparing nominations of properties for inscription on the World Heritage List. The following information constitutes guidelines that should be used in association with Chapter II of the *Operational Guidelines*, which contains the criteria for inscription of properties on the World Heritage List.

1.该附件提供了不同遗产类型的相关信息，以便指导缔约国申报遗产列入《世界遗产名录》的准备工作。下列信息可与《操作指南》第二章联合使用。该附件提供了不同遗产类型的相关信息，以便指导缔约国申报遗产列入《世界遗产名录》。下列信息包含遗产被列入《世界遗产名录》应满足的标准，可与《操作指南》第二章联合使用。

2. The Committee has endorsed the findings of expert meetings on the subject of cultural landscapes, towns, canals and routes (Part I, below).

2.该委员会已经批准了为文化景观、城镇、运河和文化线路而召开的专家会议所做的决议（参见下文第一部分）。

3. The reports of other expert meetings requested by the World Heritage Committee, in the framework of the Global Strategy for a representative, balanced and credible World Heritage List, are referred to in Part Ⅱ.

3.应世界遗产委员会要求，在具有代表性、均衡性和可信性《世界遗产名录》的全球战略大框架下的其他专家会议报告（参见第二部分）

4. Part III lists various comparative and thematic studies prepared by the Advisory Bodies.

4.第三部分列出了咨询机构完成的各种比较和主题研究。

I . CULTURAL LANDSCAPES, TOWNS, CANALS AND ROUTES

I . 文化景观、城镇、运河与文化线路

5. The World Heritage Committee has identified and defined several specific types of cultural and

5.世界遗产委员会已经识别并定义了几种特殊的文化与自然遗产类型，并制定具体的指

---

① The Committee may develop additional guidelines for other types of properties in future years.

① 将来，该委员会可能会为其他种类的遗产制定补充指南。

natural properties and has adopted specific guidelines to facilitate the evaluation of such properties when nominated for inscription on the World Heritage List. To date, these cover the following categories, although it is likely that others may be added in due course:

    a) Cultural Landscapes;
    b) Historic Towns and Town Centres;
    c) Heritage Canals;
    d) Heritage Routes.

CULTURAL LANDSCAPES[①]

Definition

6. Cultural landscapes are cultural properties and represent the "combined works of nature and of man" designated in Article 1 of the *Convention*. They are illustrative of the evolution of human society and settlement over time, under the influence of the physical constraints and/or opportunities presented by their natural environment and of successive social, economic and cultural forces, both external and internal.

7. They should be selected on the basis both of their outstanding universal value and of their representativity in terms of a clearly defined geo-cultural region and also for their capacity to illustrate the essential and distinct cultural elements of such regions.

8. The term "cultural landscape" embraces a diversity of manifestations of the interaction between

南以便对这些遗产申报列入《世界遗产名录》进行评估。目前为止，这些遗产包括以下种类，当然未来也可能有其他类型会被适时加入进来：

    a）文化景观；
    b）历史城镇和镇中心；
    c）遗产运河；
    d）遗产线路。

文化景观[①]

定义

6.文化景观属于文化遗产，正如《公约》第一条描述的，它们是"人类与大自然的共同杰作"。文化景观见证了人类社会和居住地在自然限制和/或自然环境的影响下，随着时间的推移而产生的进化，也展示了社会、经济和文化外部和内部的发展力量。

7.选择文化景观的依据，包括其突出的普遍价值、特定地理文化区域中的代表性，以及体现这些地区核心和特殊文化元素的能力。

8."文化景观"一词包含了人类与其所在的自然环境之间互动的多种表现。

[①]   This text was prepared by an Expert Group on Cultural Landscapes (La Petite Pierre, France, 24-26 October 1992) (see document *WHC-92/CONF.202/10/Add*). The text was subsequently approved for inclusion in the *Operational Guidelines* by the World Heritage Committee at its 16th session (Santa Fe 1992) (see document *WHC-92/CONF.002/12*).

[①]   本文件由一个文化景观专家组制定（法国的 La Petite Pierre，1992年10月24-26日）（见文件WHC-92/CONF.202/10/Add），随后世界遗产委员会在其第16次会议上（圣达菲，1992年）批准将该文件纳入《操作指南》中（见文件WHC-92/CONF.002/12.）

humankind and its natural environment.

9. Cultural landscapes often reflect specific techniques of sustainable land-use, considering the characteristics and limits of the natural environment they are established in, and a specific spiritual relation to nature. Protection of cultural landscapes can contribute to modern techniques of sustainable land-use and can maintain or enhance natural values in the landscape. The continued existence of traditional forms of land-use supports biological diversity in many regions of the world. The protection of traditional cultural landscapes is therefore helpful in maintaining biological diversity.

Definition and Categories

10. Cultural landscapes fall into three main categories, namely:

(i) The most easily identifiable is the clearly defined landscape designed and created intentionally by man. This embraces garden and parkland landscapes constructed for aesthetic reasons which are often (but not always) associated with religious or other monumental buildings and ensembles.

(ii) The second category is the organically evolved landscape. This results from an initial social, economic, administrative, and/or religious imperative and has developed its present form by association with and in response to its natural environment. Such landscapes reflect that process of evolution in their form and component features. They fall into two sub-categories:

- a relict (or fossil) landscape is one in which an evolutionary process came to an end at some time in the past, either abruptly or over a period. Its significant distinguishing features are, however, still visible in material form.

- a continuing landscape is one which retains an active social role in contemporary society

9.考虑到其所处自然环境的局限性和特点，文化景观通常能够反映可持续性土地利用的特殊技术，反映了与大自然特定的精神关系。保护文化景观有利于将可持续性的土地使用技术现代化，保持或提升景观的自然价值。传统土地使用形式的持续存在，支持了世界大多数地区的生物多样性，因此，对传统文化景观的保护也有益于保持生物多样性。

定义和种类

10.文化景观主要可以被分为以下三种：

（ⅰ）最易识别的一种是明确定义的人类刻意设计及创造的景观。其中包含出于美学原因建造的园林和公园景观，它们经常（但不总是）与宗教或其他纪念性建筑物或建筑群有关。

（ⅱ）第二种是有机演进的景观。它们产生于最初始的一种社会、经济、行政以及宗教需要，并通过与周围自然环境的相联系或相适应而发展到目前的形式。这种景观反映了其形式和重要组成部分的进化过程。它们又包括两种类型：

－残骸（或化石）景观，它代表过去某一时间内已经完成的进化过程，它的结束或为突发性的，或为渐进式的。然而，它的突出特色在于，显著特点在实物上仍清晰可见。

－另外一种是持续性景观，它在当今社会与传统的生活方式的密切交融中持续扮演着

closely associated with the traditional way of life, and in which the evolutionary process is still in progress. At the same time it exhibits significant material evidence of its evolution over time.

(iii) The final category is the associative cultural landscape. The inscription of such landscapes on the World Heritage List is justifiable by virtue of the powerful religious, artistic or cultural associations of the natural element rather than material cultural evidence, which may be insignificant or even absent.

Inscription of Cultural Landscapes on the World Heritage List

11. The extent of a cultural landscape for inscription on the World Heritage List is relative to its functionality and intelligibility. In any case, the sample selected must be substantial enough to adequately represent the totality of the cultural landscape that it illustrates. The possibility of designating long linear areas which represent culturally significant transport and communication networks should not be excluded.

12. General criteria for protection and management are equally applicable to cultural landscapes. It is important that due attention be paid to the full range of values represented in the landscape, both cultural and natural. The nominations should be prepared in collaboration with and the full approval of local communities.

13. The existence of a category of "cultural landscape", included on the World Heritage List on the basis of the criteria set out in Paragraph 77 of the *Operational Guidelines*, does not exclude the possibility of properties of exceptional importance in relation to both cultural and natural criteria continuing to be inscribed (see definition of mixed

一种积极的社会角色，演变过程仍在持续，而同时，它又是历史演变发展的物证。

（iii）最后一种景观是关联性文化景观。将这一景观列入《世界遗产名录》是因为这类景观体现了强烈的与自然因素、宗教、艺术或文化的关联，而不仅是实体的文化物证，后者对它来说并不重要，甚至是可以缺失的。

将文化景观列入《世界遗产名录》

11. 文化景观能否被列入《世界遗产名录》取决于它的功能性和可理解性。无论如何，备选的样品必须能够充分代表该种文化景观所要表达的全部内容的实质。不排除申报具有文化意义的，长距离的，代表交通和交流网络的线性区域的可能性。

12. 总的保护和管理标准同样适用于文化景观。应重视文化与自然景观所有方面的价值。申报应取得当地团体的同意并在与他们的协作下进行。

13. 现有的"文化景观"类别，根据《操作指南》的第77条标准已列入《世界遗产名录》的景观，并不排除继续吸收与文化自然均相关的重要遗产的可能性（参见第46条对综合遗产的定义）。在这种情况中，必须根据两套标准对其突出普遍价值进行评定。

properties as set out in Paragraph 46). In such cases, their outstanding universal value must be justified under both sets of criteria.

HISTORIC TOWNS AND TOWN CENTRES[①]

Definition and Categories

14. Groups of urban buildings eligible for inscription on the World Heritage List fall into three main categories, namely:

(i) towns which are no longer inhabited but which provide unchanged archaeological evidence of the past; these generally satisfy the criterion of authenticity and their state of conservation can be relatively easily controlled;

(ii) historic towns which are still inhabited and which, by their very nature, have developed and will continue to develop under the influence of socio-economic and cultural change, a situation that renders the assessment of their authenticity more difficult and any conservation policy more problematical;

(iii) new towns of the twentieth century which paradoxically have something in common with both the aforementioned categories: while their original urban organization is clearly recognizable and their authenticity is undeniable, their future is unclear because their development is largely uncontrollable.

Inscription of Historic Towns and Town Centres on the World Heritage List

15. The significance of Historic Towns and

历史城镇和城镇中心[①]

定义和种类

14.符合《世界遗产名录》申请条件的城区包括下列三种：

（ⅰ）无人居住但城镇原始考古证据保存完好的城镇，这些城镇一般符合真实性的评价标准且状态易于保留；

（ⅱ）沿用至今的历史城镇，这些城镇在社会经济和文化的变化中不断发展并将持续发展，这种情况致使对它们真实性的评估更加困难，保护政策存在的问题也较多；

（ⅲ）二十世纪的新镇，矛盾的是这类城镇与上述两种城镇都有相似之处：一方面它最初的城市组织结构仍清晰可见，其历史真实性不容置疑，另一方面它的未来是不明确的，因为它的发展极其不易控制。

将历史城镇和城镇中心列入《世界遗产名录》

15.通过下列因素可以检验历史城镇和城镇

[①]   This text was included in the January 1987 version of the *Operational Guidelines* following the discussion by the Committee at its 8th session (Buenos Aires, 1984) of the conclusions of the Meeting of Experts to Consult on Historic Towns which met in Paris from 5 to 7 September 1984 organized by ICOMOS.

[①]   本文本包含在该委员会历史名镇专家议事会第八次会议上（地点：布宜诺斯艾利斯）讨论的1987年1月版的《操作指南》中，会议地点在巴黎，时间是1984年9月5日至7日，由国际古迹遗址理事会组织。

Town Centres can be examined under the factors outlined below:

(i) Towns no longer inhabited

The evaluation of towns that are no longer inhabited does not raise any special difficulties other than those related to archaeological properties in general: the criteria which call for uniqueness or exemplary character have led to the choice of groups of buildings noteworthy for their purity of style, for the concentrations of monuments they contain and sometimes for their important historical associations. It is important for urban archaeological sites to be listed as integral units. A cluster of monuments or a small group of buildings is not adequate to suggest the multiple and complex functions of a city which has disappeared; remains of such a city should be preserved in their entirety together with their natural surroundings whenever possible.

(ii) Inhabited historic towns

In the case of inhabited historic towns the difficulties are numerous, largely owing to the fragility of their urban fabric (which has in many cases been seriously disrupted since the advent of the industrial era) and the runaway speed with which their surroundings have been urbanized. To qualify for inscription, towns should compel recognition because of their architectural interest and should not be considered only on the intellectual grounds of the role they may have played in the past or their value as historical symbols under criterion (vi) for the inscription of cultural properties on the World Heritage List (see Paragraph 77 (vi) of the *Operational Guidelines*). To be eligible for inscription in the List, the spatial organization, structure, materials, forms and, where possible, functions of a group of buildings should essentially reflect the civilization or succession of civilizations which have prompted the nomination of the property. Four categories can be distinguished:

中心的意义：

（i）无人居住的城镇

对无人居住的城镇的评估除了有关考古遗产的一般性问题，不会产生其他特殊问题，要求独特性或典范性的评价标准致使人们在选择建筑群时更关注其风格纯粹性，所含历史遗迹的集中程度，有时甚至包括与重要历史事件的关联性。列入时把城市里的文物古迹作为一个整体单位这一点很重要。几个纪念碑和建筑群不足以说明一个已消失城市复杂多样的功能，对于这样的城市的遗迹，应尽可能地保留它们的完整性，包括它们周围的自然环境。

（ii）尚有人居住的历史城镇

处理尚有人居住的历史城镇困难较多，很大程度上是因为其城市构造较脆弱（其中大部分在工业时代到来后发展被打乱），发展速度失控，周围的环境以近乎失控的速度不断被城市化。要想列入《世界遗产名录》，这些城镇的建筑价值应得到认可，而不应该仅仅依赖它们在历史中曾经的重要角色和作为历史象征的价值（将文化遗产列入《世界遗产名录》的标准（六））（参见《操作指南》第77（vi）段落内容）。为了达到该名录的要求，空间结构、构造、材料、形式、可能还包括建筑群的功能应从本质上反映遗产所在地区文明社会的文明化过程和演变。可分为以下四类；

a) Towns which are typical of a specific period or culture, which have been almost wholly preserved and which have remained largely unaffected by subsequent developments. Here the property to be listed is the entire town together with its surroundings, which must also be protected;

b) Towns that have evolved along characteristic lines and have preserved, sometimes in the midst of exceptional natural surroundings, spatial arrangements and structures that are typical of the successive stages in their history. Here the clearly defined historic part takes precedence over the contemporary environment;

c) "Historic centres" that cover exactly the same area as ancient towns and are now enclosed within modern cities. Here it is necessary to determine the precise limits of the property in its widest historical dimensions and to make appropriate provision for its immediate surroundings;

d) Sectors, areas or isolated units which, even in the residual state in which they have survived, provide coherent evidence of the character of a historic town which has disappeared. In such cases surviving areas and buildings should bear sufficient testimony to the former whole.

Historic centres and historic areas should be listed only where they contain a large number of ancient buildings of monumental importance which provide a direct indication of the characteristic features of a town of exceptional interest. Nominations of several isolated and unrelated buildings which allegedly represent, in themselves, a town whose urban fabric has ceased to be discernible, should not be encouraged.

However, nominations could be made regarding properties that occupy a limited space but have had

a）在某一特定时期或文化中具有代表性的城镇，保存完整且未受到后续开发的影响。这种城镇将作为一个整体被申报，其周围环境也要受到保护；

b）延续自身特征并保护了在历史时期交替中的典型空间安排和结构的城镇，有时它们位于特殊的自然环境中。这种情况下，明确定义的历史城区比当代环境更具价值；

c）"历史中心"与古镇的范围完全相同，今天它们被包围在现代城市中。这种情况下，有必要在最宽泛的历史维度下，确定遗产范围，并为它邻近的环境制定适当的规定；

d）城区、地域或一些孤立的城市空间，即使残破不堪，也为一个已消失的历史城镇提供一致的特征证明。这种情况下必须充分证实该遗存和建筑是原整体地区和建筑的一部分。

只有当历史中心和历史区域包含了大量的具有重大意义的古建筑，能直接显示一个具备极高价值的城镇的典型特征时，它们才应该被列入《世界遗产名录》。如只是若干孤立和毫无关联的建筑群，无法体现历史城市格局，则不应申报。

可以申报空间有限但却对城镇规划的历史影响重大的遗产，申报需明确归于文物古迹组，

a major influence on the history of town planning. In such cases, the nomination should make it clear that it is the monumental group that is to be listed and that the town is mentioned only incidentally as the place where the property is located. Similarly, if a building of clearly outstanding universal value is located in severely degraded or insufficiently representative urban surroundings, it should, of course, be listed without any special reference to the town.

(iii) New towns of the twentieth century

It is difficult to assess the quality of new towns of the twentieth century. History alone will tell which of them will best serve as examples of contemporary town planning. The examination of the files on these towns should be deferred, save under exceptional circumstances.

Under present conditions, preference should be given to the inscription in the World Heritage List of small or medium-sized urban areas which are in a position to manage any potential growth, rather than the great metropolises, on which sufficiently complete information and documentation cannot readily be provided that would serve as a satisfactory basis for their inscription in their entirety.

In view of the effects which the inscription of a town on the World Heritage List could have on its future, such entries should be exceptional. Inscription in the List implies that legislative and administrative measures have already been taken to ensure the protection of the group of buildings and its environment. Informed awareness on the part of the population concerned, without whose active participation any conservation scheme would be impractical, is also essential.

HERITAGE CANALS

16. The concept of "canals" is discussed in

该城镇只是作为其所在区域被提及。同样的，如果一座具有明确的突出普遍价值的建筑坐落在已严重退化或不具有充分的代表性的城市环境中，则应被独立申报，不必涉及城镇。

（iii）二十世纪的新城

评定二十世纪新城镇的品质比较困难。历史本身会体现哪座城镇最能代表当代城镇规划的典范。对这些城镇文献记录的核实可推后，除非某些特殊情况。

在现行条件下，《世界遗产名录》应优先选择能够控制发展的中小型城市地区，不像大城市很难提供完整的信息和文献资料，作为其整体申报的满意依据。

考虑到申报一座城镇进入《世界遗产名录》对其未来发展的影响，应被视为特殊情况处理。申报列入该名录意味着已经有相应的立法和行政手段确保对建筑群及其背景环境的保护。提高当地居民的保护意识也很重要，因为没有他们积极地参与，任何保护方案都是不切实际的。

传统运河

16. 关于传统运河的专家会议（加拿大，

detail in the Report of the Expert Meeting on Heritage Canals (Canada, September 1994).[1]

1994年9月）[1]报告中，对"运河"进行了详细的讨论。

Definition

定义

17. A canal is a human-engineered waterway. It may be of outstanding universal value from the point of view of history or technology, either intrinsically or as an exceptional example representative of this category of cultural property. The canal may be a monumental work, the defining feature of a linear cultural landscape, or an integral component of a complex cultural landscape.

17.运河是人类设计并兴建的水路。从历史或技术角度看，运河本质上或作为这种文化遗产种类的一个特例都可能具有突出的普遍价值。历史运河可以被看作，一个文物古迹，一种具有典型特征的线性文化景观，或是复杂的文化景观中的一个组成部分。

Inscription of Heritage Canals on the World Heritage List

将运河列入《世界遗产名录》中

18. Authenticity depends holistically upon values and the relationships between these values. One distinctive feature of the canal as a heritage element is its evolution over time. This is linked to how it was used during different periods and the associated technological changes the canal underwent. The extent of these changes may constitute a heritage element.

18.真实性整体上取决于价值和这些价值之间的关系。运河作为一种遗产要素的特征在于它动态的演变过程。这与它在不同时期的用途和它所经历过的技术改变相关。这些改变将可能组成重要的遗产要素。

19. The authenticity and historical interpretation of a canal encompass the connection between the real property (subject of the *Convention*), possible movable property (boats, temporary navigation items) and the associated structures (bridges, etc) and landscape.

19.一条运河的真实性和历史释义，包含真实的遗产（本公约主题）与可移动遗产（船只、临时航行设施）以及相关构造（桥等）和景观之间的关系。

20. The significance of canals can be examined under technological, economic, social, and landscape

20.可根据以下技术、经济、社会和景观因素测定运河的意义：

---

[1]　Expert meeting on "Heritage Canals" (Canada, 15-19 September 1994) (see document *WHC- 94/CONF.003/INF.10*) discussed by the World Heritage Committee at its 19th session (Berlin, Germany, 1995) (see document *WHC-95/CONF.203/16*).

[1]　世界遗产文员会第19次会议（德国柏林，1995年）（见文件*WHC-95/CONF.203/16*）上讨论了关于传统运河的专家会议（加拿大，1994年9月15-19日）（见文件*WHC-94/CONF.003/INF.10*）报告。

factors as outlined below:

(i) Technology

Canals can serve a variety of purposes: irrigation, navigation, defence, water-power, flood mitigation, land-drainage and water-supply. The following are areas of technology which may be of significance:

    a) The lining and waterproofing of the water channel;

    b) The engineering structures of the line with reference to comparative structural features in other areas of architecture and technology;

    c) The development of the sophistication of construction methods; and

    d) The transfer of technologies.

(ii) Economy

Canals contribute to the economy in a variety of ways, e.g. in terms of economic development and the conveyance of goods and people. Canals were the first man-made routes for the effective carriage of bulk cargoes. Canals played and continue to play a key role in economic development through their use for irrigation. The following factors are important:

    a) Nation building;

    b) Agricultural development;

    c) Industrial development;

    d) Generation of wealth;

    e) Development of engineering skills applied to other areas and industries; and

    f) Tourism.

(iii) Social Factors

The building of canals had, and their operation continues to have, social consequences:

    a) The redistribution of wealth with social and cultural results; and

    b) The movement of people and the interaction of cultural groups.

(iv) Landscape

Such large-scale engineering works had and continue to have an impact on the natural landscape.

（i）技术

运河服务目标众多，包括：灌溉、航运、防御、水力、泄洪、地面排水和给水。以下是比较重要的技术方面：

    a）水渠的衬砌和防水；

    b）该水道的工程结构，参考、比较了其他建筑和技术领域的结构特点；

    c）混合建造方法的发展；

    d）技术转移

（ii）经济

运河通过不同途径为经济做出贡献，如在经济发展和货物、人员运输方面。运河是最早的由人类开发的、用于有效地运输大批货物的路线。运河还通过发挥它的灌溉功能在经济发展中扮演了重要的角色。下列因素很重要：

    a）国家建筑；

    b）农业发展；

    c）工业发展；

    d）财富的聚集；

    e）应用在其他地区和行业中的工程技术；和

    f）旅游

（iii）社会因素

开凿运河及其持续使用具有社会影响：

    a）财富与社会和文化成果的再分配，和

    b）人口流动以及文化组群间的交互作用。

（iv）景观

如此大规模的工程曾经并将继续对自然景观造成影响。相关的工业活动和不断变换的定居

Related industrial activity and changing settlement patterns cause visible changes to landscape forms and patterns.

类型，使景观的形式和类型发生了显著的变化。

HERITAGE ROUTES

遗产线路

21. The concept of "routes" or cultural itineraries was discussed by the expert meeting on "Routes as a Part of our Cultural Heritage" (Madrid, Spain, November 1994).[1]

21.关于"将线路作为文化遗产的一部分"专家会议（1994年 西班牙 马德里）[1]上讨论了"线路"或文化线路的概念。

Definition

定义

22. The concept of heritage routes is shown to be a rich and fertile one, offering a privileged framework in which mutual understanding, a plural approach to history and a culture of peace can all operate.

22.遗产线路的概念丰富多彩，它提供了一种特殊构架，对相互理解、对待历史的多元态度与和平文化，都将起到一定作用。

23. A heritage route is composed of tangible elements of which the cultural significance comes from exchanges and a multi-dimensional dialogue across countries or regions, and that illustrate the interaction of movement, along the route, in space and time.

23.遗产线路由各种切实的要素组成，这些要素的文化意义来自于跨国界和跨地区的交流和多维对话，它们说明了在这条线路上展开的运动在时空上的交流互动。

Inscription of Heritage Routes on the World Heritage List

将遗产线路列入《世界遗产名录》

24. The following points should be considered when determining whether a heritage route is suitable for inscription on the World Heritage List:

(i) The requirement to hold outstanding universal value should be recalled.

(ii) The concept of heritage routes:

- is based on the dynamics of movement and

24. 在决定一条遗产线路是否具备被列入《世界遗产名录》的资格时，下列几点应予以考虑：

（i）重新考虑具有突出的普遍价值的相关要求。

（ii）遗产线路的概念

－基于动态的迁徙、思想的交流、空间和时

① Expert Meeting on "Routes as part of Our Cultural Heritage" (Madrid, 24-25 November 1994) (see document *WHC-94/CONF.003/INF.13*) discussed by the World Heritage Committee at its 19th session (Berlin, 1995) (see document *WHC-95/CONF.203/16*).

① 世界遗产文员会第19次会议（德国柏林，1995年）（见文件 *WHC-95/CONF.203/16*）上讨论了关于将线路作为文化遗产的一部分的专家会议（1994年11月24–25日 西班牙 马德里）报告（参见文件 *WHC-94/CONF.003/INF.13*）。

the idea of exchanges, with continuity in space and time;

- refers to a whole, where the route has a worth over and above the sum of the elements making it up and through which it gains its cultural significance;

- highlights exchange and dialogue between countries or between regions;

- is multi-dimensional, with different aspects developing and adding to its prime purpose which may be religious, commercial, administrative or otherwise.

(iii) A heritage route may be considered as a specific, dynamic type of cultural landscape, just as recent debates have led to their acceptance within the *Operational Guidelines*.

(iv) The identification of a heritage route is based on a collection of strengths and tangible elements, testimony to the significance of the route itself.

(v) The conditions of authenticity are to be applied on the grounds of its significance and other elements making up the heritage route. It will take into account the duration of the route, and perhaps how often it is used nowadays, as well as the legitimate wishes for development of peoples affected.

These points will be considered within the natural framework of the route and its intangible and symbolic dimensions.

II. REPORTS OF REGIONAL AND THEMATIC EXPERT MEETINGS

25. The World Heritage Committee, in the framework of the Global Strategy for a representative, balanced and credible World Heritage List has requested a number of regional and thematic expert meetings on different types of properties. The results of these meetings may guide States Parties

间上的连续性；

－涉及到一个整体，线路的整体价值要远远大于其各个组成要素价值之和，也因此获得其文化意义；

－强调国家间或地区间交流和对话；

－应是多维的，具有不同方面的发展，不断丰富和补充其主要用途，其中可能包括宗教、商业、行政管理或其他方面。

（iii）遗产线路可以被当作一种特殊的动态型文化景观，近期的争论使其被纳入《操作指南》。

（iv）对遗产线路的鉴定基于实力和有形要素的集合，要证实线路本身具有重大意义。

（v）真实性条件也将被应用在评定线路的重要性和其他组成要素方面。线路的使用期限也要考虑在内，可能还需考虑现在使用的频率和受其影响的人员对其发展的合理意愿。

以上几点需放在线路的自然构架及其无形的象征性层面考虑。

II. 地区和主题专家会议报告

25.在构建具有代表性、均衡性和可信性的《世界遗产名录》的全球战略构架中，世界遗产委员会要求就不同遗产举办一系列地区和主题专家会议。这些会议的结果将指导缔约国进行申报准备工作。登录下面网站可获得已呈递给世界遗产委员会的会议报告，网址：http://whc.

in preparing nominations. The reports of the expert meetings presented to the World Heritage Committee are available at the following Web address: http://whc.unesco.org/en/globalstrategy

III. THEMATIC AND COMPARATIVE STUDIES BY THE ADVISORY BODIES

26. To fulfil their obligations concerning evaluations of nominations of cultural and natural properties, the Advisory Bodies have undertaken comparative and thematic studies, often with partner organizations, in different subject areas in order to provide a context for their evaluations.

These reports, most of which are available on their respective Web addresses, include:

Earth's Geological History-A Contextual Framework for Assessment of World Heritage Fossil Site Nominations (September 1996)

International Canal Monuments List (1996)

http://www.icomos.org/studies/canals-toc.htm

World Heritage Bridges (1996)

http://www.icomos.org/studies/bridges.htm

A Global Overview of Forest Protected Areas on the World Heritage List (September 1997)

http://www.unep-wcmc.org/wh/reviews/forests/

A Global Overview of Wetland and Marine Protected Areas on the World Heritage List (September 1997)

http://www.unep-wcmc.org/wh/reviews/wetlands/

Human Use of World Heritage Natural Sites (September 1997)

http://www.unep-wcmc.org/wh/reviews/human/

Fossil Hominid Sites (1997)

http://www.icomos.org/studies/hominid.htm

The Urban Architectural Heritage of Latin America (1998)

http://www.icomos.org/studies/latin-towns.htm

Les Théâtres et les Amphithéâtres antiques (1999)

unesco.org/en/globalstrategy

III. 咨询机构的主题和比较研究

26. 为了履行评估文化与自然遗产申报的义务，咨询机构与合作伙伴组织一起，针对不同主题进行了各种比较研究和主题研究，目的是为他们的评估提供依据。

通过他们各自的网站可获得大部分相关报告，这些报告包括：

《地球的地质历史 -- 评估化石遗址世界遗产申报的关联框架》（1996年9月）

《国际运河遗产物名录》（1996年）

http://www.icomos.org/studies/canals-toc.htm

《世界遗产中的桥梁》（1996年）

http://www.icomos.org/studies/bridges.htm

《〈世界遗产名录〉中的全球森林保护区概览》（1997年9月）

http://www.unep-wcmc.org/wh/reviews/forests/

《〈世界遗产名录〉中的全球湿地和海洋保护区概览》（1997年9月）

http://www.unep-wcmc.org/wh/reviews/wetlands/

《人类对世界自然遗产的使用》（1997年9月）

http://www.unep-wcmc.org/wh/reviews/human/

《原始人类化石遗址》（1997年）

http://www.icomos.org/studies/hominid.htm

《拉丁美洲的城市建筑遗产》（1998年）

http://www.icomos.org/studies/latin-towns.htm

《古剧院和古剧场》（1999年）

http://www.icomos.org/studies/theatres.htm

Railways as World Heritage Sites (1999)

http://www.icomos.org/studies/railways.htm

A Global Overview of Protected Areas on the World Heritage List of Particular Importance for Biodiversity (November 2000)

http://www.unep-wcmc.org/wh/reviews/

Les villages ouvriers comme éléments du patrimoine de l'industrie (2001)

http://www.icomos.org/studies/villages-ouvriers.htm

A Global Strategy for Geological World Heritage (February 2002)

Rock-Art Sites of Southern Africa (2002)

http://www.icomos.org/studies/sarockart.htm

http://www.icomos.org/studies/theatres.htm

《铁路作为世界遗产》（1999 年）

http://www.icomos.org/studies/railways.htm

《〈世界遗产名录〉中具有特殊意义的全球生物多样性保护区概览》（2000年11月）

http://www.unep-wcmc.org/wh/reviews/

《作为工业遗产组成部分的工人村落》（2001年）

http://www.icomos.org/studies/villages-ouvriers.htm

《世界地质遗产的全球战略》（2002年2月）

《南非的岩石艺术遗址》（2002年）

http://www.icomos.org/studies/sarockart.htm

ANNEXES 4

AUTHENTICITY IN RELATION TO THE *WORLD HERITAGE CONVENTION*

附件 4

《保护世界文化与自然遗产公约》相关的真实性

INTRODUCTION

This Annex reproduces the Nara Document on Authenticity, drafted by the 45 participants to the Nara Conference on Authenticity in Relation to the *World Heritage Convention*, held at Nara, Japan, from 1-6 November 1994. The Nara Conference was organized in co-operation with UNESCO, ICCROM and ICOMOS.

The World Heritage Committee examined the report of the Nara meeting on Authenticity at its 18th session (Phuket, Thailand, 1994) (see document WHC-94/CONF.003/16).

Subsequent expert meetings have enriched the concept of authenticity in relation to the *World Heritage Convention* (see Bibliography of the *Operational Guidelines*).

I. THE NARA DOCUMENT ON AUTHENTICITY

Preamble

1. We, the experts assembled in Nara (Japan), wish to acknowledge the generous spirit and intellectual courage of the Japanese authorities in providing a timely forum in which we could challenge conventional thinking in the conservation field, and debate ways and means of broadening our horizons to bring greater respect for cultural and heritage diversity to conservation practice.

2. We also wish to acknowledge the value of the framework for discussion provided by the

前言

本附件再次使用了《奈良真实性文件》。1994年11月1日至6日，《世界遗产公约》相关真实性会议在日本奈良召开，与会的45位代表起草了《奈良真实性文件》。该奈良会议由联合国教科文组织、国际文化遗产保护与修复研究中心和国际古迹遗址理事会联合主办。

世界遗产委员会在其第18次会议（1994年泰国普吉岛）上，审核了奈良会议中关于真实性的报告（见文件WHC-94/CONF.003/16）。

后续的专家会议丰富了《保护世界文化与自然遗产公约》相关的真实性的概念（见《操作指南》的参考文献）。

I. 关于真实性的《奈良文件》

导言

1.作为参与奈良（日本）会与会专家，我们在此感谢日本当局的慷慨精神与学术勇气，为我们适时提供了此论坛，让我们能够挑战遗产保护领域的传统思想，讨论运用各种途径和方法扩大我们的视野，从而在保护实践中更大限度的尊重文化和遗产的多样性。

2.我们希望认可世界遗产委员会所提供的、以尊重所有社会的社会与文化价值的方式、在

World Heritage Committee's desire to apply the test of authenticity in ways which accord full respect to the social and cultural values of all societies, in examining the outstanding universal value of cultural properties proposed for the World Heritage List.

3. The Nara Document on Authenticity is conceived in the spirit of the Charter of Venice, 1964, and builds on it and extends it in response to the expanding scope of cultural heritage concerns and interests in our contemporary world.

4. In a world that is increasingly subject to the forces of globalization and homogenization, and in a world in which the search for cultural identity is sometimes pursued through aggressive nationalism and the suppression of the cultures of minorities, the essential contribution made by the consideration of authenticity in conservation practice is to clarify and illuminate the collective memory of humanity.

Cultural Diversity and Heritage Diversity

5. The diversity of cultures and heritage in our world is an irreplaceable source of spiritual and intellectual richness for all humankind. The protection and enhancement of cultural and heritage diversity in our world should be actively promoted as an essential aspect of human development.

6. Cultural heritage diversity exists in time and space, and demands respect for other cultures and all aspects of their belief systems. In cases where cultural values appear to be in conflict, respect for cultural diversity demands acknowledgment of the legitimacy of the cultural values of all parties.

7. All cultures and societies are rooted in the particular forms and means of tangible and

检验申报《世界遗产名录》的文化遗产的突出普遍性价值时，采用真实性检验标准提出的讨论构架的价值。

3.《奈良真实性文件》受到1964年的威尼斯宪法精神启发，在此基础上建立，并被延伸引用，以响应我们当代世界对文化遗产的关注与利益的范围的不断扩大。

4. 在一个日益受到全球化和同质化力量影响的世界里，在一个有时藉由带有侵略性的民族主义和压制少数民族文化以追求文化认同的世界里，真实性思考在保护实践中的重要的贡献是，澄清并阐明人类的集体记忆。

文化多样性和遗产多样性

5. 我们所处世界的文化和遗产的多样性，是所有人类丰富的精神和知识的不可替代的来源。对世界的文化和遗产的多样性的保护和加强，应得到积极的推动，使之成为人类发展的一个重要方面。

6. 文化遗产的多样性涉及时间和空间，需要对其他文化和它们所信仰的各个方面给予尊重。一旦文化价值发生了冲突，尊重文化多样性就需要承认所有成员的文化价值的合法性。

7. 所有的文化和社会都植根于特殊的形式和方法中，而有形的和无形的表达手段构成了

intangible expression which constitute their heritage, and these should be respected.

8. It is important to underline a fundamental principle of UNESCO, to the effect that the cultural heritage of each is the cultural heritage of all. Responsibility for cultural heritage and the management of it belongs, in the first place, to the cultural community that has generated it, and subsequently to that which cares for it. However, in addition to these responsibilities, adherence to the international charters and conventions developed for conservation of cultural heritage also obliges consideration of the principles and responsibilities flowing from them. Balancing their own requirements with those of other cultural communities is, for each community, highly desirable, provided achieving this balance does not undermine their fundamental cultural values.

Values and authenticity

9. Conservation of cultural heritage in all its forms and historical periods is rooted in the values attributed to the heritage. Our ability to understand these values depends, in part, on the degree to which information sources about these values may be understood as credible or truthful. Knowledge and understanding of these sources of information, in relation to original and subsequent characteristics of the cultural heritage, and their meaning, is a requisite basis for assessing all aspects of authenticity.

10. Authenticity, considered in this way and affirmed in the Charter of Venice, appears as the essential qualifying factor concerning values. The understanding of authenticity plays a fundamental role in all scientific studies of the cultural heritage, in conservation and restoration planning, as well as within the inscription procedures used for the World

它们的遗产并应得到充分地尊重。

8.强调每一种文化遗产都是所有人的文化遗产这一联合国教科文组织的基本原则是很重要的。文化遗产的责任和对它的管理权，首先应归属于产生这种文化遗产的文化社区，其次是关心它的社区。尽管如此，除了上述责任，遵守为保护文化遗产所制定的国际宪章和协定，同样是他们的原则与责任。对每个社区来说，平衡其自身与其他文化社区的要求，都是极重要的事，达到这种平衡并不会影响他们的基础文化价值。

价值与真实性

9.对所有历史阶段的所有形式的文化遗产的保护，源于遗产的属性价值。我们理解，这些价值的能力，部分取决于对这些价值的信息来源本身和其可信度的理解程度，与原始和后续的文化遗产特征有关，而它们是评定真实性的必备条件。

10.在《威尼斯宪章》中形成并确定的真实性，是价值评估的重要认证因素。对真实性的理解，在对文化遗产、对其保护和重建规划及《世界遗产公约》和其他文化遗产所进行的所有科学研究中，扮演着重要的角色。

Heritage Convention and other cultural heritage inventories.

11. All judgements about values attributed to cultural properties as well as the credibility of related information sources may differ from culture to culture, and even within the same culture. It is thus not possible to base judgements of values and authenticity within fixed criteria. On the contrary, the respect due to all cultures requires that heritage properties must be considered and judged within the cultural contexts to which they belong.

12. Therefore, it is of the highest importance and urgency that, within each culture, recognition be accorded to the specific nature of its heritage values and the credibility and truthfulness of related information sources.

13. Depending on the nature of the cultural heritage, its cultural context, and its evolution through time, authenticity judgements may be linked to the worth of a great variety of sources of information. Aspects of the sources may include form and design, materials and substance, use and function, traditions and techniques, location and setting, and spirit and feeling, and other internal and external factors. The use of these sources permits elaboration of the specific artistic, historic, social, and scientific dimensions of the cultural heritage being examined.

Appendix 1: Suggestions for follow-up (proposed by Herb Stovel)

1. Respect for cultural and heritage diversity requires conscious efforts to avoid imposing mechanistic formulae or standardized procedures in attempting to define or determine authenticity of particular monuments and sites.

11.不同文化间，甚至是相同文化中，对文化遗产所有价值的评估和相关信息来源可信度的评估都有所差异。因此，不可能将价值和真实性评估建立在固定标准上。相反，对所有文化的尊重、要求必须在遗产所属的文化环境中对其进行考虑和评定。

12.因此，这一点最重要也最迫切，那就是，在每一种文化中，必须依照其遗产价值的特殊本质、信息来源的可信度和真实性加以认定。

13.取决于文化遗产的本质、它的文化环境和它随着时间的演替，真实性的评估可能会与许多不同的信息来源的价值相关。资源方面包括形式和设计、材料与物质、用途与功能、传统与技术、位置与场合、精神与感情、以及其他内在和外在因素。对这些资源的使用，允许对文化遗产的特殊艺术性、历史性、社会性和科学性进行详细审核。

附录1：对后续跟踪的几点建议（由 Herb Stovel 提交）

1.对文化遗产多样性的尊重需要有意识的努力，避免在定义和决定其特定纪念物和遗址真实性时套用机械化公式和标准程序。

2. Efforts to determine authenticity in a manner respectful of cultures and heritage diversity requires approaches which encourage cultures to develop analytical processes and tools specific to their nature and needs. Such approaches may have several aspects in common:

- efforts to ensure assessment of authenticity involve multidisciplinary collaboration and the appropriate utilisation of all available expertise and knowledge;
- efforts to ensure attributed values are truly representative of a culture and the diversity of its interests, in particular monuments and sites;
- efforts to document clearly the particular nature of authenticity for monuments and sites as a practical guide to future treatment and monitoring;
- efforts to update authenticity assessments in light of changing values and circumstances.

3. Particularly important are efforts to ensure that attributed values are respected, and that their determination included efforts to build, as far as possible, a multidisciplinary and community consensus concerning these values.

4. Approaches should also build on and facilitate international co-operation among all those with an interest in conservation of cultural heritage, in order to improve global respect and understanding for the diverse expressions and values of each culture.

5. Continuation and extension of this dialogue to the various regions and cultures of the world is a prerequisite to increasing the practical value of consideration of authenticity in the conservation of the common heritage of humankind.

2.努力用一种尊重文化与遗产多样性的方法来决定真实性，要求采用能够鼓励不同文化根据其自身性质和需求，发展其分析过程和工具的方法。这些方法在下列方面有相似之处：

- 努力确保对真实性的评估中，涉及多学科合作和适当利用所有可用的专业技能和知识；

- 努力确保其价值能够真正代表一种文化和它的利益的多样性，特别是在纪念物和遗址上；

- 努力确保清晰的记录纪念物和遗址的真实性的特殊性质，将其作为将来治理和监测的实践指导；

- 在不断变换的价值和环境中努力更新真实性评估。

3.特别重要的是努力确保所有价值受到尊重，确保决策，包括尽可能就这些价值观念达成多学科和社区的共识。

4.建立多种途径并促进所有致力于文化遗产保护的组织之间的国际合作，从而促进对每种文化的不同表达和价值的尊重和理解。

5.将这种跨文化对话继续并扩展到全世界不同地区文化中，是提高人类共同遗产保护真实性意识的先决条件。

6. Increasing awareness within the public of this fundamental dimension of heritage is an absolute necessity in order to arrive at concrete measures for safeguarding the vestiges of the past. This means developing greater understanding of the values represented by the cultural properties themselves, as well as respecting the role such monuments and sites play in contemporary society.

Appendix 2: Definitions

Conservation: all efforts designed to understand cultural heritage, know its history and meaning, ensure its material safeguard and, as required, its presentation, restoration and enhancement. (Cultural heritage is understood to include monuments, groups of buildings and sites of cultural value as defined in Article 1 of the World Heritage Convention).

Information sources: all material, written, oral and figurative sources which make it possible to know the nature, specifications, meaning and history of the cultural heritage.

II. CHRONOLOGICAL BIBLIOGRAPHY-ON AUTHENTICITY

Publications which preceded the Nara meeting and which helped prepare the ground for the authenticity discussion which took place in Nara:

Larsen, Knut Einar, *A note on the authenticity of historic timber buildings with particular reference to Japan,* Occasional Papers for the World Heritage Convention, ICOMOS, December 1992.
Larsen, Knut Einar, *Authenticity and Reconstruction: Architectural Preservation in Japan,* Norwegian Institute of Technology, Vols. 1-2, 1993.

Preparatory meeting for the Nara Meeting,

6.为了获得保护过去遗迹的具体措施，提高公众对遗产的基本认识是十分必要的。这意味着，需要更大程度地理解文化遗产本身所代表的价值并尊重这些纪念物和遗址在当代社会中所扮演的角色。

附录2：定义

保护：所有努力都旨在理解文化遗产、了解其历史和含义、保证其物质安全，且根据要求，保证它的存在、修复和强化（通常人们所理解的文化遗产包括纪念碑、建筑群、和文化价值遗址，《世界遗产公约》第一条中已明确定义）。

信息来源：所有可以让人了解文化遗产的本质、规格、意义和历史的物质的、手写的、口头的和图像资源。

II. 按年代顺序排列的关于真实性的参考文献

早在奈良会议召开前出版的出版物和对奈良的真实性问题讨论的准备工作给予帮助的出版物包括：

《关于历史上著名木质建筑（尤指日本）的真实性的注解》，作者Larsen, Knut Einar,《世界遗产公约》的学术论文，国际古迹遗址理事会，1992年12月；
《真实性和重建：日本建筑的保护》作者Larsen, Knut Einar, 挪威科技大学第1-2卷，1993年。

1994年1月31日至2月1日在挪威的卑尔根

held in Bergen, Norway, 31 January - 1 February 1994:

Larsen, Knut Einar and Marstein, Nils (ed.), *Conference on authenticity in relation to the World Heritage Convention Preparatory workshop, Bergen, Norway, 31 January - 2 February 1994,* Tapir Forlag, Trondheim 1994.

The Nara meeting, 1-6 November 1994, Nara, Japan:

Larsen, Knut Einar with an editorial group (Jokilehto, Lemaire, Masuda, Marstein, Stovel), *Nara conference on authenticity in relation to the World Heritage Convention. Conférence de Nara sur l'authenticité dans le cadre de la Convention du Patrimoine Mondial.* Nara, Japan, 1-6 November 1994, Proceedings published by UNESCO-World Heritage Centre, Agency for Cultural Affairs of Japan, ICCROM and ICOMOS, 1994.

The Nara meeting brought together 45 experts from 26 countries and international organizations from around the world. Their papers are contained in the volume cited above, as is the Nara document prepared in a working group of 12 meeting participants and edited by Raymond Lemaire and Herb Stovel. This volume of Proceedings invites members of ICOMOS and others to extend the discussions of the Nara Document issues to other regions of the world.

Significant post-Nara regional meetings (as of January 2005):

Authenticity and Monitoring, October 17-22, 1995, Cesky Krumlov, Czech Republic, ICOMOS European Conference, 1995.

The European ICOMOS Conference of 17-22 October, 1995 which took place in Cesky Krumlov,

召开的奈良会议的预备会议：

《关于〈世界遗产公约〉真实性研究会的预备工作会议》，作者Larsen, Knut Einar 和 Marstein, Nils（ed.），1994年1月31日至2月1日挪威的卑尔根，特隆赫姆Tapir Forlag，1994年。

1994年11月1-6日日本奈良召开的奈良会议：

《关于〈世界遗产公约〉真实性的奈良会议》，（Conférence de Nara sur l'authenticité dans le cadre de la Convention du Patrimoine Mondial），作者Larsen, Knut Einar 为首的编辑组（包括Jokilehto, Lemaire, Masuda, Marstein, Stovel），1994年11月1-6日，日本奈良，1994年由联合国教科文组织世界遗产中心学报、日本文化部、国际文化遗产保护与修复研究中心和国际古迹遗址理事会刊登。

奈良会议召集了来自26个国家和国际组织的45名专家。专家的论文被包含在上述引用的会议论文中，由12个参会者组成的工作组准备的奈良文件，并由Raymond Lemaire 和 Herb Stovel 编辑完成。会议邀请国际古迹遗址理事会成员和其他有关专家一起，将对奈良文件问题相关讨论扩大到世界其他地区。

奈良会议后具有重大意义的地区性会议（截至2005年1月）：

《真实性及其监测，1995年10月17-22日》，捷克共和国契斯基库伦隆，欧洲国际古遗址理事会大会，1995年。

1995年10月17-22日的欧洲国际古遗址理事会在捷克共和国契斯基库伦隆召开。大会聚

Czech Republic brought together 18 European members of ICOMOS to present national views of the application of authenticity concepts from 14 countries. A synthesis of presentations affirmed the importance of authenticity within the analytical processes we apply to conservation problems as a means of assuring truthful, sincere and honest approaches to conservation problems, and gave emphasis to strengthening the notion of dynamic conservation in order to apply authenticity analysis appropriately to cultural landscapes and urban settings.

Interamerican symposium on authenticity in the conservation and management of the cultural heritage, US/ICOMOS, The Getty Conservation Institute, San Antonio, Texas 1996.

This Authenticity meeting which took place in San Antonio, Texas, USA in March 1996, brought together participants from ICOMOS national committees of North, Central and South America to debate the application of the concepts of Nara. The meeting adopted the *Declaration of San Antonio*, which discussed the relationship between authenticity and identity, history, materials, social value, dynamic and static sites, stewardship and economics, and contained recommendations extending "proofs" of authenticity to include *reflection of its true value, integrity, context, identity, use and function,* as well as recommendations pertinent to different typologies of sites.

Saouma-Forero, Galia, (edited by), *Authenticity and integrity in an African context: expert meeting, Great Zimbabwe*, Zimbabwe, 26-29 May 2000, UNESCO-World Heritage Centre, Paris 2001.

The Great Zimbabwe meeting organised by the World Heritage Centre (26-29 May 2000) focused attention on both authenticity and integrity in an African context. Eighteen speakers looked at issues arising in management of both cultural

集了18位国际古迹遗址理事会欧洲成员，提出了来自14个国家关于应用真实性概念的观点。这种综合阐述确认了真实性在处理保护问题中，作为保证信任、真诚和诚实的手段，在分析过程中的重要性，并强调加强动态保护的观念，以便在文化景观和城市遗产申报中恰当地应用真实性分析。

《美联关于文化遗产保护和管理中真实性的座谈会》，美国/国际古遗址理事会，美国德克萨斯州圣安东尼盖蒂保护研究所，1996年。

1996年3月在德克萨斯州圣安东尼召开的真实性会议、聚集了来自北美、中美和南美国际古遗址理事会国家委员会的参会者，共同商讨奈良概念的应用。该会议通过了《圣安东尼宣言》，该宣言讨论了真实性和身份认同、历史、材料、社会价值、动态和静态遗址、管理和经济学之间的关系，包含了扩充真实性"证据"的相关建议，包括真实价值、完整性、环境、特性、使用和功能的反映，以及对不同类型遗址的相关建议。

《非洲文化背景下保护遗产的真实性和完整性：大津巴布韦专家会议》，Saouma-Forero, Galia,（编辑），津巴布韦，2000年5月26—29日，2001年，巴黎联合国教科文组织世界遗产中心。

大津巴布韦会议由世界遗产中心召开（2000年5月26—29日），重点强调非洲遗产的真实性和完整性。18位发言人讨论了在文化与自然遗产管理中面临的问题。该会议后发表了上述论文，其中包含了参会人员提出的建议。这些建

and natural heritage properties. The meeting resulted in the publication cited above, which includes a set of recommendations coming from meeting participants. Among recommendations were suggestions to include *management systems, language, and other forms of intangible heritage* among attributes expressing authenticity, and an emphasis given to the place of local communities in the sustainable heritage management process.

Reconstruction discussions in the context of the *World Heritage Convention* (as of January 2005):

The Riga Charter on authenticity and historical reconstruction in relationship to cultural heritage adopted by regional conference, Riga, 24 October 2000, Latvian National Commission for UNESCO-World Heritage Centre, ICCROM.

Incerti Medici, Elena and Stovel, Herb, *Authenticity and historical reconstruction in relationship with cultural heritage, regional conference, Riga, Latvia, October 23-24 2000: summary report,* UNESCO-World Heritage Centre, Paris, ICCROM, Rome 2001.

Stovel, Herb, *The Riga Charter on authenticity and historical reconstruction in relationship to cultural heritage, Riga, Latvia, October 2000,* in *Conservation and management of archaeological sites,* Vol. 4, n. 4, 2001.

Alternatives to historical reconstruction in the World Heritage Cities, Tallinn, 16-18 May 2002, Tallinn Cultural Heritage Department, Estonia National Commission for UNESCO, Estonia National Heritage Board.

议包括将管理体系、语言和其他形式的无形遗产纳入真实性表达，并强调当地社区在可持续遗产管理过程中的作用。

《世界遗产公约》中关于重建问题的讨论（截止至2005年1月）：

里加地区会议通过的《关于文化遗产相关真实性和历史重建问题的里加宪章》，2000年10月24日，联合国教科文组织世界遗产中心拉脱维亚委员会，国际文化遗产保护与修复研究中心。

2000年10月23-24日拉脱维亚里加地区会议《关于文化遗产相关真实性和历史重建问题的会议总结报告》，起草人Incerti Medici, Elena和Stovel, Herb，2001年，巴黎联合国教科文组织世界遗产中心，罗马国际遗产理事会。

2000年10月拉脱维亚里加地区会议通过的《关于考古遗址保护和管理中的文化遗产相关真实性和历史重建问题的宪章》，起草人Stovel, Herb，2001年第4卷。

《避免世界遗产城市中历史建筑重建的选择》2002年5月16-18日，塔林文化遗产部，联合国教科文组织爱沙尼亚国家委员会，爱沙尼亚国家遗产部。

ANNEXES 5

FORMAT FOR THE NOMINATION OF PROPERTIES FOR INSCRIPTION ON THE WORLD HERITAGE LIST

附件 5

《世界遗产名录》遗产申报材料格式

This Format must be used for all nominations submitted after 2 February 2005

2005年2月2日后提交的所有申报材料均须遵循此格式

- The Nomination Format is available at the following Web address: http://whc.unesco.org/en/nominationform
- Further guidance on the preparation of nominations can be found in Section III of the *Operational Guidelines*
- The original signed version of the completed Nomination Format should be sent in English or French to

- 登录以下网址可获取本申报材料格式：http://whc.unesco.org/en/nominationform

- 有关申报材料编写的更多指导，请参见《操作指南》的第三部分

- 按完整申报格式编写的英文或法文原件，签字后发送至以下地址：

UNESCO World Heritage Centre

7, place de Fontenoy

75352 Paris 07 SP

France

Telephone: +33 (0) 1 4568 1571

Fax: +33 (0) 1 4568 5570

E-mail: wh-nominations@unesco.org

教科文组织世界遗产中心

法国巴黎（7, place de Fontenoy 75352 Paris 07 SP France）

电话：+33（0）1 4568 1571

传真：+33（0）1 4568 5570

电邮：wh-nominations@unesco.org

Executive Summary

执行摘要

This information, to be provided by the State Party, will be updated by the Secretariat following the decision by the World Heritage Committee. It will then be returned to the State Party confirming the basis on which the property is inscribed on the World Heritage List.

以下信息由缔约国提供，由秘书处根据世界遗产委员会的决定进行更新。之后会将其返还给缔约国，作为确认遗产列入《世界遗产名录》的依据。

State Party	
State, Province or Region	
Name of Property	
Geographical coordinates to the nearest second	
Textual description of the boundary(ies) of the nominated property	
A4 (or "letter") size map of the nominated property, showing boundaries and buffer zone (if present)	Attach A4 (or "letter") size map
Justification Statement of Outstanding Universal Value (text should clarify what is considered to be the outstanding universal value embodied by the nominated property)	
Criteria under which property is nominated (itemize criteria) (see Paragraph 77 of the Operational *Guidelines*)	
Name and contact information of official local institution/agency	Organization: Address: Tel: Fax: E-mail: Web address:

缔约国	
州、省份或地区	
遗产名称	
精确到秒的地理坐标	
申报遗产的保护范围的文字说明	
A4 纸大小（或"信纸"）的申报遗产地图，显示遗产保护范围和缓冲区（如果有）	附 A4 纸（或"信纸"）大小的地图
列入理由 《突出普遍价值声明》（正文应说明申报遗产所包含的突出普遍价值）	
遗产申报遵循的标准（列举标准）（见《操作指南》第 77 段）	
当地官方机关 / 机构的名称和联系信息	机构： 地址： 电话： 传真： 电邮： 网址：

Properties for inscription on the World Heritage List

Note: In preparing the nomination, States Parties should use this format but delete the explanatory notes.

NOMINATION FORMAT	EXPLANATORY NOTES
1. Identification of the Property	Together with Section 2, this is the most important section in the nomination. It must make clear to the Committee precisely where the property is located and how it is geographically defined. In the case of serial nominations, insert a table that shows the name of the component part, region (if different for different components), coordinates, area and buffer zone. Other fields could also be added (page reference or map number, etc.) that differentiate the several components.
1.a Country (and State Party if different)	
1.b State, Province or Region	
1.c Name of Property	This is the official name of the property that will appear in published material about World Heritage. It should be concise. Do not exceed 200 characters, including spaces and punctuation. In the case of serial nominations (see Paragraphs 137-140 of the *Operational Guidelines*), give a name for the ensemble (e.g., *Baroque Churches of the Philippines*). Do not include the name of the components of a serial nomination, which should be included in a table as part of 1.d and 1.f.
1.d Geographical coordinates to the nearest second	In this space provide the latitude and longitude coordinates (to the nearest second) or UTM coordinates (to the nearest 10 metres) of a point at the approximate centre of the nominated property. Do not use other coordinate systems. If in doubt, please consult the Secretariat.
	In the case of serial nominations, provide a table showing the name of each property, its region (or nearest town as appropriate), and the coordinates of its centre point. Coordinate format examples: N 45°06'05"　W 15°37'56" or UTM Zone 18 Easting: ^{5}45670　Northing: ^{45}86750
1.e Maps and plans, showing the boundaries of the nominated property and buffer zone	Annex to the nomination, and list below with scales and dates: (i) An original copy of a topographic map showing the property nominated, at the largest scale available which shows the entire property. The boundaries of the nominated property and buffer zone should be clearly marked. Either on this map, or an accompanying one, there should also be a record of the boundaries of zones of special legal protection from which the property benefits. Multiple maps may be necessary for serial nominations. Maps may be obtained from the addresses shown at the following Web address http://whc.unesco.org/en/mapagencies If topographic maps are not available at the appropriate scale, other maps may be substituted. All maps should be capable of being geo-referenced, with a minimum of three points on opposite sides of the maps with complete sets of coordinates. The maps, untrimmed, should show scale, orientation, projection, datum, property name and date. If possible, maps should be sent rolled and not folded.

续表

NOMINATION FORMAT	EXPLANATORY NOTES
	Geographic Information in digital form is encouraged if possible, suitable for incorporation into a GIS (Geographic Information System). In this case the delineation of the boundaries (nominated property and buffer zone) should be presented in vector form, prepared at the largest scale possible. The State Party is invited to contact the Secretariat for further information concerning this option. (ii) A Location Map showing the location of the property within the State Party, (iii) Plans and specially prepared maps of the property showing individual features are helpful and may also be annexed. To facilitate copying and presentation to the Advisory Bodies and the World Heritage Committee A4 (or "letter") size reduction and a digital image file of the principal maps should be included in the nomination text if possible. Where no buffer zone is proposed, the nomination must include a statement as to why a buffer zone is not required for the proper conservation of the nominated property.
1.f Area of nominated property (ha.) and proposed buffer zone (ha.) Area of nominated property: _____ha Buffer zone_____ha Total_____ha	In the case of serial nominations (see Paragraphs 137-140 of the *Operational Guidelines*), insert a table that shows the name of the component part, region (if different for different components), coordinates, area and buffer zone. The serial nomination table should also be used to show the size of the separate nominated areas and of the buffer zone(s).
2. Description	
2.a Description of Property	This section should begin with a description of the nominated property at the date of nomination. It should refer to all the significant features of the property. In the case of a cultural property this section will include a description of whatever elements make the property culturally significant. It could include a description of any building or buildings and their architectural style, date of construction, materials, etc. This section should also describe important aspects of the setting such as gardens, parks etc. For a rock art site, for example, the description should refer to the rock art as well as the surrounding landscapes. In the case of an historic town or district, it is not necessary to describe each individual building, but important public buildings should be described individually and an account should be given of the planning or layout of the area, its street pattern and so on. In the case of a natural property the account should deal with important physical attributes, geology, habitats, species and population size, and other significant ecological features and processes. Species lists should be provided where practicable, and the presence of threatened or endemic taxa should be highlighted. The extent and methods of exploitation of natural resources should be described. In the case of cultural landscapes, it will be necessary to produce a description under all the matters mentioned above. Special attention should be paid to the interaction of man and nature. The entire nominated property identified in section 1 (Identification of the Property) should be described. In the case of serial nominations (see Paragraphs 137-140 of the *Operational Guidelines*), each of the component parts should be separately described.

NOMINATION FORMAT	EXPLANATORY NOTES
2.b History and Development	Describe how the property has reached its present form and condition and the significant changes that it has undergone, including recent conservation history. This should include some account of construction phases in the case of monuments, sites, buildings or groups of buildings. Where there have been major changes, demolitions or rebuilding since completion they should also be described. In the case of a natural property, the account should cover significant events in history or pre- history that have affected the evolution of the property and give an account of its interaction with humankind. This will include changes in the use of the property and its natural resources for hunting, fishing or agriculture, or changes brought about by climatic change, floods, earthquake or other natural causes. Such information will also be required in the case of cultural landscapes, where all aspects of the history of human activity in the area needs to be covered.
3. Justification for Inscription	This section must make clear why the property is considered to be of "outstanding universal value". The whole of this section of the nomination should be written with careful reference to the criteria for inscription found in Paragraph 75 of the *Operational Guidelines*. It should not include detailed descriptive material about the property or its management, which are addressed in other sections, but should concentrate on why the property is important.
3.a Criteria under which inscription is proposed (and justification for inscription under these criteria)	See Paragraph 77 of the *Operational Guidelines*. Provide a separate justification for each criterion cited. State briefly how the property meets those criteria under which it has been nominated (where necessary, make reference to the "description" and "comparative analysis" sections below, but do not duplicate the text of these sections.).
3.b Proposed Statement of Outstanding Universal Value	Based on the criteria used above, the proposed Statement of Outstanding Universal Value should make clear why the property is considered to merit inscription on the World Heritage List (see Paragraphs 154-157 of the *Operational Guidelines*). It may be a unique survival of a particular building form or habitat or designed town. It may be a particularly fine or early or rich survival and it may bear witness to a vanished culture, way of life or eco-system. It may comprise assemblages of threatened endemic species, exceptional eco-systems, outstanding landscapes or other natural phenomena.
3.c Comparative analysis (including state of conservation of similar properties)	The property should be compared to similar properties, whether on the World Heritage List or not. The comparison should outline the similarities the nominated property has with other properties and the reasons that make the nominated property stand out. The comparative analysis should aim to explain the importance of the nominated property both in its national and international context (see Paragraph 132)
3.d Integrity and/or Authenticity	The statement of integrity and/or authenticity should demonstrate that the property fulfils the conditions of integrity and/or authenticity set out in Section Ⅱ.D of the *Operational Guidelines*, which describe these conditions in greater detail.

NOMINATION FORMAT	EXPLANATORY NOTES
	In the case of a cultural property it should also record whether repairs have been carried out using materials and methods traditional to the culture, in conformity with the Nara Document (1995) (see Annex 4). In the case of natural properties it should record any intrusions from exotic species of fauna or flora and any human activities that could compromise the integrity of the property.
4. State of Conservation and factors affecting the Property	
4.a Present state of conservation	The information presented in this section constitutes the base-line data necessary to monitor the state of conservation of the nominated property in the future. Information should be provided in this section on the physical condition of the property, any threats to the property and conservation measures at the property (see Paragraph 132) For example, in a historic town or area, buildings, monuments or other structures needing major or minor repair works, should be indicated as well as the scale and duration of any recent or forthcoming major repair projects. In the case of a natural property, data on species trends or the integrity of eco-systems should be provided. This is important because the nomination will be used in future years for purposes of comparison to trace changes in the condition of the property. For the indicators and statistical benchmarks used to monitor the state of conservation of the property see section 6 below.
4.b Factors affecting the property	This section should provide information on all the factors which are likely to affect or threaten a property. It should also describe any difficulties that may be encountered in addressing such problems. Not all the factors suggested in this section are appropriate for all properties. They are indicative and are intended to assist the State Party to identify the factors that are relevant to each specific property.
(i) Development Pressures (e.g., encroachment, adaptation, agriculture, mining)	Itemize types of development pressures affecting the property, e.g., pressure for demolition, rebuilding or new construction; the adaptation of existing buildings for new uses which would harm their authenticity or integrity; habitat modification or destruction following encroaching agriculture, forestry or grazing, or through poorly managed tourism or other uses; inappropriate or unsustainable natural resource exploitation; damage caused by mining; the introduction of exotic species likely to disrupt natural ecological processes, creating new centres of population on or near properties so as to harm them or their settings.
(ii) Environmental pressures (e.g., pollution, climate change, desertification)	List and summarize major sources of environmental deterioration affecting building fabric, flora and fauna.
(iii) Natural disasters and risk preparedness (earthquakes, floods, fires, etc.)	Itemize those disasters which present a foreseeable threat to the property and what steps have been taken to draw up contingency plans for dealing with them, whether by physical protection measures or staff training.

NOMINATION FORMAT	EXPLANATORY NOTES
(iv) Visitor/tourism pressures	Describe the "carrying capacity" of the property. Can it absorb the current or likely number of visitors without adverse effects? An indication should also be given of the steps taken to manage visitors and tourists. Possible forms of deterioration due to visitor pressure are: wear on stone, timber, grass or other ground surfaces; increases in heat or humidity levels; disturbances to species habitats; or disruption of traditional cultures or ways of life.
(v) Number of inhabitants within the property and the buffer zone Estimated population located within: Area of nominated property____ _____ Buffer zone_____ Total_____ Year_____	Give the best available statistics or estimate of the number of inhabitants living within the nominated property and any buffer zone. Indicate the year this estimate or count was made.
5. Protection and Management of the Property	This section of the nomination is intended to provide a clear picture of the legislative, regulatory, contractual, planning, institutional and/ or traditional measures (see Paragraphs 132 of the *Operational Guidelines*) and the management plan or other management system (Paragraphs of the *Operational Guidelines*) that is in place to protect and manage the property as required by the *World Heritage Convention*. It should deal with policy aspects, legal status and protective measures and with the practicalities of day-to-day administration and management.
5.a Ownership	Indicate the major categories of land ownership (including State, Provincial, private, community, traditional, customary and non-governmental ownership, etc.).
5.b Protective designation	List the relevant legal, regulatory, contractual, planning, institutional and/ or traditional status of the property: For example, national or provincial park; historic monument, protected area under national law or custom; or other designation. Provide the year of designation and the legislative act(s) under which the status is provided. If the document cannot be provided in English or French, an English or French executive summary should be provided highlighting the key provisions.
5.c Means of implementing protective measures.	Describe how the protection afforded by its legal, regulatory, contractual, planning, institutional and/ or traditional status indicated in section 5.b. actually works.
5.d Existing plans related to municipality and region in which the proposed property is located (e.g., regional or local plan, conservation plan, tourism development plan)	List the agreed plans which have been adopted with the date and agency responsible for preparation. The relevant provisions should be summarized in this section. A copy of the plan should be included as an attached document as indicated in section 7.b. If the plans exist only in a language other than English or French, an English or French executive summary should be provided highlighting the key provisions.

NOMINATION FORMAT	EXPLANATORY NOTES
5.e Property management plan or other management system	As noted in Paragraphs 132 of the *Operational Guidelines,* an appropriate management plan or other management system is essential and shall be provided in the nomination. Assurances of the effective implementation of the management plan or other management system are also expected. A copy of the management plan or documentation of the management system shall be annexed to the nomination, in English or French as indicated in section 7.b. If the management plan exists only in a language other than English or French, an English or French detailed description of its provisions shall be annexed. Give the title, date and author of management plans annexed to this nomination. A detailed analysis or explanation of the management plan or a documented management system shall be provided.
5.f Sources and levels of finance	Show the sources and level of funding which are available to the property on an annual basis. An estimate could also be given of the adequacy or otherwise of resources available, in particular identifying any gaps or deficiencies or any areas where assistance may be required.
5.g Sources of expertise and training in conservation and management techniques	Indicate the expertise and training which are available from national authorities or other organizations to the property.
5.h Visitor facilities and statistics	As well as providing any available statistics or estimates of visitor numbers or patterns over several years, this section could describe the facilities available on site for visitors, for example interpretation/explanation, whether by trails, guides, notices or publications; property museum, visitor or interpretation centre; overnight accommodation; restaurant or refreshment facilities; shops; car parking; lavatories; search and rescue.
5.i Policies and programmes related to the presentation and promotion of the property	This section refers to Articles 4 and 5 of the *Convention* regarding the presentation and transmission to future generations of the cultural and natural heritage. States Parties are encouraged to provide information on the policies and programmes for the presentation and promotion of the nominated property.
5.j Staffing levels (professional, technical, maintenance)	Indicate the skills and training which are available at the property.
6. Monitoring	This section of the nomination is intended to provide the evidence for the state of conservation of the property which can be reviewed and reported on regularly so as to give an indication of trends over time.
6.a Key indicators for measuring state of conservation	List in table form those key indicators that have been chosen as the measure of the state of conservation of the whole property (see section 4.a above). Indicate the periodicity of the review of these indicators and the location where the records are kept. They could be representative of an important aspect of the property and relate as closely as possible to the Statement of Outstanding Universal Value (see section 2.b above). Where possible they could be expressed numerically and where this is not possible they could be of a kind which can be repeated, for example by taking a photograph from the same point. Examples of good indicators are the:

NOMINATION FORMAT	EXPLANATORY NOTES
	(i) number of species, or population of a keystone species on a natural property; (ii) percentage of buildings requiring major repair in a historic town or district; (iii) number of years estimated to elapse before a major conservation programme is likely to be completed; (iv) stability or degree of movement in a particular building or element of a building; (v) rate at which encroachment of any kind on a property has increased or diminished.

Indicator	Periodicity	Location of Records

6.b Administrative arrangements for monitoring property	Give the name and contact information of the agency(ies) responsible for the monitoring referenced in 6.a.
6.c Results of previous reporting exercises	List, with a brief summary, earlier reports on the state of conservation of the property and provide extracts and references to published sources (for example, reports submitted in compliance with international agreements and programmes, e.g., Ramsar, MAB).
7. Documentation	This section of the nomination is the check-list of the documentation which shall be provided to make up a complete nomination.
7.a Photographs, slides, image inventory and authorization table and other audiovisual materials	States Parties shall provide a sufficient number of recent images (prints, slides and, where possible, electronic formats, videos and aerial photographs) to give a good general picture of the property. Slides shall be in 35mm format and electronic images in jpg format at a minimum of 300 dpi (dots per inch) resolution. If film material is provided, Beta SP format is recommended for quality assurances. This material shall be accompanied by the image inventory and photograph and audiovisual authorization form as set out below. At least one photograph that may be used on the public web page illustrating the property shall be included. States Parties are encouraged to grant to UNESCO, in written form and free of charge, the non exclusive cession of rights to diffuse, to communicate to the public, to publish, to reproduce, to exploit, in any form and on any support, including digital, all or part of the images provided and license these rights to third parties. The non exclusive cession of rights does not impinge upon intellectual property rights (rights of the photographer / director of the video or copyright owner if different) and that when the images are distributed by UNESCO a credit to the photographer / director of the video is always given, if clearly provided in the form. All possible profits deriving from such cession of rights will go to the World Heritage Fund.

IMAGE INVENTORY AND PHOTOGRAPH AND AUDIOVISUAL AUTHORIZATION FORM

Id. No	Format (slide/ print/ video)	Caption	Date of Photo (mo/yr)	Photographer/ Director of the video	Copyright owner (if different than photographer/ director of video)	Contact details of copyright owner (Name, address, tel/ fax, and e-mail)	Non exclusive cession of rights

NOMINATION FORMAT	EXPLANATORY NOTES
7.b Texts relating to protective designation, copies of property management plans or documented management systems and extracts of other plans relevant to the property	Attach the texts as indicated in sections 5.b, 5.d and 5.e above.
7.c Form and date of most recent records or inventory of property	Provide a straightforward statement giving the form and date of the most recent records or inventory of the property. Only records that are still available should be described.
7.d Address where inventory, records and archives are held	Give the name and address of the agencies holding inventory records (buildings, monuments, flora or fauna species).
7.e Bibliography	List the principal published references, using standard bibliographic format.
8. Contact Information of responsible authorities	This section of the nomination will allow the Secretariat to provide the property with current information about World Heritage news and other issues.
8.a Preparer Name: Title: Address: City, Province/State, Country: Tel: Fax: E-mail:	Provide the name, address and other contact information of the individual responsible for preparing the nomination. If an e-mail address cannot be provided, the information must include a fax number.
8.b Official Local Institution/ Agency	Provide the name of the agency, museum, institution, community or manager locally responsible for the management of the property. If the normal reporting institution is a national agency, please provide that contact information.

续表

NOMINATION FORMAT	EXPLANATORY NOTES
8.c Other Local Institutions	List the full name, address, telephone, fax and e-mail addresses of all museums, visitor centres and official tourism offices who should receive the free *World Heritage Newsletter* about events and issues related to World Heritage.
8.d Official Web address http:// Contact name: E-mail:	Please provide any existing official web addresses of the nominated property. Indicate if such web addresses are planned for the future with the contact name and e-mail address.
9. Signature on behalf of the State Party	The nomination should conclude with the signature of the official empowered to sign it on behalf of the State Party.

《世界遗产名录》的申报遗产

注：准备申报材料时，各缔约国应该使用本格式，但是把填报须知删掉。

申报材料格式	填报须知
1. 遗产的确认	本部分和下面的第 2 部分是申报材料中最重要的内容，必须向委员会精确说明遗产的位置，地理界限。如果是系列申报，插入一个表格，显示各组成部分的名称、所处地域（如果不同部分处于不同地域）、坐标、面积和缓冲区。也可列示其他表栏项目（页码说明或地图编号）以区别不同部分。
1.a 国家列出	
1.b 州、省份或地区	
1.c 遗产名称	是该遗产出现在世界遗产出版物上的正式名称，应该简洁，不超过 200 个字，包括空格和标点符号。如果是系列申报（见《操作指南》的第 137–140 条），为整体命名（比如，菲律宾巴洛克大教堂）。无需说明系列申报内各部分的名称，这些名称应该包括在 1.d 和 1.f 的表格内。
1.d 精确到秒的地理坐标	在此处提供申报遗产的中心纬度和经度坐标（精确到秒），或通用横轴墨卡托坐标（精确到 10 米）。不要用其他坐标体系。如有疑问，请咨询秘书处。 如果是系列申报，列表说明各遗产的名称、地域（或最近的城镇）、遗产中心点的坐标。坐标格式如下： 北纬 45°06'05"　西经 15°37'56"　或者 横轴墨卡托区 18　东：⁵45670 北：⁴⁵86750
1.e 地图和平面图，显示申报遗产和缓冲区的范围	附在申报材料后，标上比例和日期： （ⅰ）申报遗产的地形图原件，用尽可能最大的比例显示整个遗产。应明确标明申报遗产及缓冲区的范围。可在此图或另附地图上，标示有利于遗产保护的特殊法定保护区范围。系列申报可能需要多张地图。 登录以下网址，可获取地图：http://whc.unesco.org/en/mapagencies 如果不能用合适的比例绘制地形图，可以用其他地图代替。所有的地图都必须能够进行地理参照，地图上必须至少有三个点，点点相对，每个点都有完整的坐标。地图不能缩减，应该显示比例、方位、投影、数据、遗产名称和日期。如果可能，递送地图时应将其卷起，而不是折叠。

申报材料格式	填报须知
	如果可能，建议提供数字地理信息，便于纳入 GIS（地理信息系统）。在这种情况下，范围的划分（申报遗产和缓冲区）应以向量的形式提供，以尽可能大的比例编制。相关详情缔约国可联系秘书处。 （ii）一张位置图，显示该遗产在缔约国的位置。 （iii）展示遗产某项特征的平面图和特殊地图也很有用，可以随附于申报材料后面。 为了便于向咨询机构和世界遗产中心抄送和呈报，如果可能，A4 纸（或"信纸"）大小的缩图和主要地图的电子图像文件，应该包括在申报材料之中。 如果没有划分缓冲区，申报材料必须说明为什么申报遗产的适当保护不需要缓冲区。
1.f 申报遗产的面积（公顷）和提议的缓冲区（公顷） 申报遗产的面积：_____公顷 缓冲区_____公顷 共_____公顷	如果是 系列申报（见《操作指南》第 137-140 条），插入一张表格，显示组成部分的名称、所处地域（如果不同部分处于不同地域）、坐标、面积和缓冲区。 该系列申报表还应显示各个申报区及各缓冲区的大小。
2. 描述	
2.a 遗产描述	本部分首先描述申报时遗产的情况，应谈及该项遗产的各项显著特征。 如果是文化遗产，本部分应该描述该项遗产由于哪些因素而在文化方面具有了重要意义。可描述某个或多个建筑，其相应的建筑风格、建筑日期及所用材料等。还可以描述环境的重要因素，包括花园、公园等。比如，对某岩画遗址来说，描述内容应既包括岩画本身，还应包括其周围的景观。如果是历史名城或历史街区，没有必要描述各座建筑单体，但是应逐个描述重要的公共建筑，及该地区的规划和布局，街道格局，等等。 如果是自然遗产，应该说明重要的物理属性、地质情况、栖息地、物种及种群数量、其他重要的生态特征和进程。应尽可能提供物种列表，并突出濒危物种或地方特有的生物分类。应该描述自然资源开发的程度和方法。 如果是文化景观，有必要描述上文所提的各事项。应特别关注人与自然之间的关系。 应该描述第 1 部分（遗产的确认）说明的整个申报遗产。如果是系列申报（见《操作指南》第 137-140 条），应单独描述遗产的各组成部分。
2.b 历史沿革	描述该项遗产历史、说明其如何发展到今天的形式和状态，经历了什么样的重大变化，包括近期的保护状况。 如果是古迹、遗址、建筑或建筑群，应该描述其建筑阶段。如果在建成后曾有过重大的变化、拆除或重建事件，应对这些事件进行描述。 如果是自然遗产，应该描述史上或史前曾影响过该项遗产演化的重要事件，并描述该项遗产与人类之间的关系。包括遗产使用及用于狩猎、捕鱼或农业的自然资源发生的变化，以及天气变化、洪水、地震或其他自然现象带来的影响。 如果是自然景观，也要求提供这些信息，其中应包括这个地区人类活动史的所有方面。
3. 列入理由	这部分必须说明为什么认为遗产具有"突出普遍价值"。本部分遗产的描述应该严格参考《操作指南》第 75 条列出的列入标准。不应该包括详细的遗产描述性说明，和遗产管理情况说明，这些内容在其他部分提供，这部分应该着重说明遗产为什么重要。

申报材料格式	填报须知
3.a 提议遗产列入所依据的标准（和根据这些标准的列入理由）	（见《操作指南》第 77 条）。分别说明引用每个标准的理由。简述该项遗产如何满足申报标准，（如有必要，参考下文的"描述"和"比较分析"部分，但不是照抄这些部分的正文）。
3.b《突出普遍价值声明》	依据上面所用标准，《突出普遍价值声明》应该明确为什么该项遗产为有资格列入《世界遗产名录》（见《操作指南》第 154–157 条）。它可能是某个独特的建筑形式、栖息地或城镇的存续物，也可能极尽精妙、久远或丰富，见证了一种已消亡的文化、生活方式或生态系统。它可能包括特有濒危物种、独特的生态系统、突出的景观或其他自然现象。
3.c 比较分析（包括类似遗产的保护状况）	该项遗产应与类似遗产（无论是否列入《世界遗产名录》）相比。进行对比时应该罗列该项遗产与其他遗产之间的类似点，说明该项遗产之所以突出的原因。比较分析旨在解释申报遗产在本国及在国际上的重要性。（见第 132 条）
3.d 完整性和 / 或真实性	完整性和 / 或真实性的声明应证实该项遗产满足《操作指南》第Ⅱ.D 部分列出的完整性和 / 或真实性条件，《操作指南》详细描述了这些条件。如果是文化遗产，还应记录是否按照《奈良文件》（1995 年）（见附件四）的要求，使用符合文化传统的材料和方法进行了维修。如果是自然遗产，应该记录损害该项遗产完整性的、任何外来动植物物种的入侵及人类活动。
4. 保护状况和影响遗产的因素	
4.a 保护现状	本部分信息是在未来监测所申报遗产保护状况的基准数据。本部分内容应包括：该项遗产的自然条件、其面临的威胁和采取的保护措施（见第 132 条）。比如，应该指出历史城镇或区域内，建筑、古迹或其他建筑结构所需的大小修缮工作，以及近期主要修缮项目的规模和持续时间。如果是自然遗产，应该提供物种演化趋势或生态系统完整性的数据。这很重要，因为在未来几年，对比并跟踪遗产状态变化时会用到这些申报材料。至于监测遗产保护状况的指标和统计基准，请参见下文第 6 部分。
4.b 影响遗产的因素	本部分应说明可能影响或威胁遗产的所有因素。还应该说明在解决这些问题时会面临的困难。在此罗列的各项因素并非适用于所有遗产。它们只是标示性的，旨在协助缔约国确认与各自遗产相关的因素。
（ⅰ）开发压力（比如：侵占、改造、农业和采矿）	列举影响遗产的开发压力，比如，拆除、重建或新建项目的压力；因改变现有建筑用途而损害其真实性或完整性；由于侵占性农林牧活动、以及管理不善的旅游业、或其他原因而对栖息地造成改变和破坏；不当或非持续性自然资源开发；采矿带来的损害；引进可破坏自然生态进程的外来物种，在遗产内部或附近创建新的聚居中心，对遗产及其环境造成损害。
（ⅱ）环境压力（比如，污染、环境变化、沙化）	列出并总结影响建筑结构、动植物等环境恶化的主要根源
（ⅲ）自然灾害和防灾情况（地震、洪水、火灾等）	列举对遗产产生可预见威胁的那些灾害，采取了哪些步骤来制定应急方案以应对这些灾害，是否为此采取了物理保护措施，或开展了员工培训。
（ⅳ）旅游压力	描述遗产的"承载能力"。如何管理使其能接纳当前或一定数量参观者而不产生负面影响？应说明为管理参观者及旅游者而制定的措施。旅游压力带来的不良后果可能有：石质、木质、草地或其他类型地表的磨损；温度或湿度的增加；对物种栖息地的干扰；传统文化或生活方式的瓦解。

申报材料格式	填报须知
（ⅴ）遗产及缓冲区内的居民数量 以下区域内的估计人口： 申报遗产区＿＿＿＿＿＿＿ 缓冲区＿＿＿＿＿＿＿ 总计＿＿＿＿＿＿＿ 年份＿＿＿＿＿＿＿	提供申报遗产及缓冲区内居民人数的现有最准确数据或估计数。指出进行人数统计或估测的年份。
5. 遗产的保护与管理	本部分旨在清晰地说明法律、监管、合同、规划、机构和／或传统措施（见《操作指南》第132条）以及确立的管理规划或其他管理体系（见《操作指南》108–118条），以按照《世界遗产公约》的要求来保护、管理该项遗产。应该包括政策、法律地位和保护措施，以及日常管理的实际情况。
5.a 所有权	说明遗产范围内土地所有制类型（包括国家、省、私人、社区、传统、约定俗成和非政府所有权等）。
5.b 保护称号	列出遗产相关的法律、监管、合同、规划、制度和／或传统地位，比如，国家或省级公园；依据国家法律或习俗确立的历史古迹、保护区以及其他指定称号。 说明称号宣布及规定遗产地位的法律的年份。 如果文件所用语言并非英语或法语，应提供一份英语或法语的执行摘要，说明文件内容要点。
5.c 保护措施执行手段	描述第5.b.条所列法律、监管、合同、规划、制度和／或传统地位提供的保护如何实际生效。
5.d 申报遗产所在市或地区的现有规划（比如，地区或地方规划、保护、旅游开发规划）	列出通过的各种规划，标出制定日期和负责机构。其重要条款应在本部分概述。规划副本应作为附加文件（如第7.b.条所示）附后。 如果规划所用语言既非英语也非法语，应提供一份英语或法语的执行摘要，说明其内容要点。
5.e 遗产管理规划或其他管理制度	如《操作指南》第132条所示，一份适宜的管理规划或其他管理制度必不可少，应该收录在申报材料内。最好也能提供该管理规划或其他管理制度有效实施的保证。 如第7.b.条所示，英语或法语文本的管理规划或者管理制度文件应附在申报材料之后。 如果管理规划所用语言既非英语也非法语，应提供英语或法语的规划条款详述，附在申报材料之后。提供管理规划（附在申报材料后）的名称、日期和作者。 应提供该管理规划或成文管理制度的详细分析或说明。
5.f 资金来源和水平	说明遗产每年的资金来源和水平。还应该估计可用资金是否充足，特别要确认缺口、差额或其他需要援助的领域。
5.g 专业知识来源和保护与管理技术的培训	指出国家当局或其他组织提供的有关遗产的专业知识和培训。
5.h 旅游设施和统计资料	一方面提供最近几年参观人数和模式的有效数据或估计数，另一方面，描述现场的旅游设施，比如通过路径设置、导游人员、通知或公告进行展陈或解说；遗产博物馆，参观或展陈中心；住宿；餐馆或小吃店；商店；停车场；洗手间；搜寻和援救。

申报材料格式	填报须知
5.i 遗产展示和宣传相关的政策和方案	本部分援引《公约》的第 4 条和第 5 条，这两条阐述了文化及自然遗产的展示和传承事宜。鼓励缔约国提供申报遗产的展示和宣传政策及方案信息。
5.j 人员配置水平（专业、技术、维修）	说明可用于遗产保护的技术与培训。
6. 监测	本部分旨在提供说明遗产保护现状的证据，可用回访定期报告、审查等方式，以明确遗产的变化趋势。
6.a 衡量保护状况的主要指标	以表格形式列出用于衡量整个遗产保护状况的主要指标（见上文第 4.a 条）。指出审查这些指标的周期，以及记录保存地点。这些指标可代表遗产的某个重要方面，并尽可能地与《突出普遍价值声明》挂钩（见上文第 2.b 条）。如果可能，可用数字表示，不能用数字的话，以可重复的方式表现，比如，在同一地点拍照。有效指标的实例有： 自然遗产内物种种类或主要物种种群的数目； 历史城镇或历史街区内需要大规模修缮的建筑比例； 完成主要保护方案估计需要的时间； 某个建筑或建筑要素的稳定性或活动程度； 对遗产侵蚀的消长速度。

指标	周期	记录保存地点

6.b 监测遗产的行政安排	负责监测（如第 6.a 条所示）的机构名称和联系方式。
6.c 以前报告活动的结果	列出以前的遗产保护状况报告，并进行简要总结，提供报告摘要和参考文献（比如，根据国际协议和方案，如《拉姆萨湿地公约》，《人与生物圈计划》提交的报告）。
7. 文献	本部分列出了完备的申报材料所需的文献。
7.a 照片、幻灯片、图像清单和授权表及其他视听材料	缔约国应提供一定数量的近期图像（印制品、幻灯片，如果可能的话，还可提供电子格式、录像带和航摄照片），以便对该遗产有个清晰的整体印象。 幻灯片应为 35mm 格式，电子图像是 jpg 格式，其分辨率不应低于 300dpi（每英寸点数）。如果有录像带，建议用 Beta SP 格式，确保质量。这类材料应配有图像清单和照片，以及下文列出的视听材料授权表。 至少有一张照片可用于公共网页，说明该遗产应被列为世界遗产。 鼓励缔约国以书面形式，免费向教科文组织独家地转让传播、公示、出版、复制及利用（以各种方式，基于各种手段，包括数字形式）全部或部分图像的权利，并准予教科文组织把这些权利授予第三方。上述权利转让不得侵犯知识产权（摄影师 / 录像导演以及其他所有人的权利），另外，教科文组织在发行图像时，如果表格中有明确的说明，教科文组织一定会提供摄影师 / 录像导演的名单。 此类权利转让所产生的所有收益将纳入世界遗产基金。

续表

图像列表、照片、视听材料授权表

（i）编号	格式（幻灯片/印制品/录像）	图片说明	照片日期（年/月）	摄影师/录像导演	版权所有人（如果不是摄像师/导演）	版权所有人的详细联系信息（姓名、地址、电话/传真和电邮）	非排他性权利转让

申报材料格式	填报须知
7.b 与保护称号、遗产管理规划或成文管理制度相关的正文、其他遗产规划摘要	把上文第 5.b, 5.d 和 5.e 条所示文件正文附后。
7.c 遗产近期记录或列表的格式和日期	明确阐述遗产近期记录或列表的格式和日期。仅涉及手头现有的记录。
7.d 列表、记录和档案保存地址	提供保存列表记录（建筑、古迹、动植物种群）的机构名称和地址。
7.e 参考文献	列出主要的出版参考文献，用标准的参考文献格式。
8. 负责机构的联系方式	秘书处可通过该联系方式，把世界遗产的最新消息和其他相关事宜通知给遗产负责机构。
8.a 编纂人员 名字： 职称（头衔）： 地址： 国家、州/省、市： 电话： 传真： 电子邮件：	提供申报材料编纂人员的名称、地址和其他联系信息。如果没有电子邮箱，则联系信息中必须包括传真号码。
8.b 地方管理机关/机构	提供负责遗产管理的地方机构、博物馆、组织、社区或管理人员的名称。如果常规报告提供组织是国家机关，请提供该国家机关的联系方式。
8.c 其他地方机构	列出应接收免费《世界遗产时事通讯》（讨论关于世界遗产的事件和议题）的所有博物馆、参观中心和官方旅游办公室的全称、地址、电话、传真和电子邮件地址。
8.d 官方网站 http:// 联系人姓名： 电子邮件：	请提供申报遗产的现有官方网站。说明今后是否计划设立该类网站，并提供联系人姓名和电子邮件地址。
9. 代表缔约国签名	申报材料末尾应由缔约国的正式授权代表签字。

ANNEXES 6

EVALUATION PROCEDURES OF THE ADVISORY BODIES FOR NOMINATIONS

附件 6

咨询机构对申报材料的评估程序

This Annex includes:

A. THE ICOMOS PROCEDURE FOR THE EVALUATION OF CULTURAL PROPERTIES

B. THE IUCN PROCEDURE FOR THE EVALUATION OF NATURAL PROPERTIES

C. ADVISORY BODY COLLABORATION-PROCEDURE FOR THE EVALUATION OF CULTURAL AND NATURAL PROPERTIES AND OF CULTURAL LANDSCAPES

For further information please also refer to Paragraphs 143-151 of the *Operational Guidelines*.

A. THE ICOMOS PROCEDURE FOR THE EVALUATION OF CULTURAL PROPERTIES

1. In carrying out its evaluation of nominations of cultural properties ICOMOS (the International Council of Monuments and Sites) is guided by the *Operational Guidelines*; (see Paragraph 148).

2. The evaluation process (see Figure 1) involves consultation of the wide range of expertise represented by the membership of ICOMOS and its National and International Committees, as well as the many other specialist networks with which it is linked. Members are also sent on expert missions to carry out confidential on-site evaluations. This extensive consultation results in the preparation of detailed recommendations that are submitted to the World Heritage Committee at its annual meetings.

Choice of experts

3. There is a clearly defined annual procedure

本附件包括：

A.国际古迹遗址理事会的文化遗产评估程序

B.世界自然保护联盟的自然遗产评估程序

C.咨询机构对文化和自然遗产及文化景观的合作评估程序

如想了解更多信息，请参阅《操作指南》的第143–151条。

A.国际古迹遗址理事会的文化遗产评估程序

1.国际古迹遗址理事会遵循《操作指南》（见第148条）的指导来评估文化遗产的申报材料。

2.评估程序（见图1）包括向国际古迹遗址理事会会员及其国家和国际委员会，以及与之相联的许多其他专家网络咨询大量专业知识。国际古迹遗址理事会还将派出会员组成专家代表团，进行秘密的专家现场评估。经过这些广泛的咨询之后，会编纂详细的推荐意见，并提交给世界遗产委员会年度大会。

选择专家

3.申报遗产列入《世界遗产名录》有明确

for the submission of properties to the World Heritage List. Once new nominations have been checked for completeness by the UNESCO World Heritage Centre and the Advisory Bodies, the nomination dossiers are then delivered to ICOMOS, where they are handled by the ICOMOS World Heritage secretariat. The first action involved is the choice of the experts who are to be consulted. This involves two separate groups. First, there are those who can advise on the "outstanding universal value" of the nominated property. This is essentially a "library" exercise for specialist academics, and may sometimes involve non-ICOMOS members, in cases where there is no adequate expertise within the ICOMOS membership on a specific topic: an example is the occasional nomination of fossil hominid sites, where the services of palaeontologists are required.

4. The second group of experts are those with practical experience of the management, conservation, and authenticity aspects of individual properties, who are required to carry out site missions. The process of selecting these experts makes full use of the ICOMOS network. The advice of International Scientific Committees and individual members is sought, as is that of specialist bodies with whom ICOMOS has partnership agreements, such as The International Committee for the Conservation of the Industrial Heritage (TICCIH), the International Federation of Landscape Architects (IFLA), and the International Committee for the Documentation and Conservation of Monuments and Sites of the Modern Movement (DoCoMoMo).

Site missions

5. In selecting experts to carry out on-site evaluation missions, the policy of ICOMOS is wherever possible to choose someone from the

规定的年度程序。先由联合国教科文组织世界遗产中心和咨询机构检查申报材料是否完整，在这之后，申报材料提交给国际古迹遗址理事会，由国际古迹遗址理事会世界遗产秘书处接手处理。首要行动是选择咨询专家。这涉及到两个不同的群体。首先，需要可针对申报遗产的"突出普遍价值"提出意见的专家。这主要是专家学者的"图书馆"式运作，这一过程有时可能包括非国际古迹遗址理事会会员，因为有时候理事会的会员在某个领域的专业知识可能不够，比如：对古人类化石遗址申报时可能需要古生物学家的专业知识。

4.第二组专家是那些在单个遗产的管理、保护和真实性上具有实践经验，并且需要进行现场调研的专家。充分启用国际古迹遗址理事会的网络选择这些专家。国际古迹遗址理事会将征询国际科学委员会和单个会员，即与国际古迹遗址理事会签有伙伴协议的专家团体的建议。这些专家团体包括：国际产业遗产保护委员会（TICCIH），国际景观设计师联合会（IFLA），国际现代建筑文献组织（DoCoMoMo）等。

现场调研

5.在选择执行现场评估任务的专家时，国际古迹遗址理事会的政策是尽可能选择申报遗产所在地区的专家。这些专家必须有遗产管理

region in which the nominated property is located. Such experts are required to be experienced in heritage management and conservation: they are not necessarily high academic experts in the type of property. They are expected to be able to talk to site managers on a basis of professional equality and to make informed assessments of management plans, conservation practices, visitor handling, etc. They are provided with detailed briefings, which include copies of the relevant information from the dossiers. The dates and programmes of their visits are agreed in consultation with States Parties, who are requested to ensure that ICOMOS evaluation missions are given a low profile so far as the media are concerned. ICOMOS experts submit their reports in confidence to the Executive Committee on practical aspects of the properties concerned, and premature publicity can cause embarrassment both to ICOMOS and to the World Heritage Committee.

与保护的经验：没必要是该类遗产的资深学术专家。他们需要在专业平等的基础上与遗址管理人员进行专业交流，对管理规划、保护政策和参观处理等事宜进行评估。相关人员将向这些专家简要介绍情况，其中包括申报材料中相关信息的复印本。这些专家到访的日期和方案会与缔约国进行协商，以达成一致。理事会要求缔约国确保媒体对国际古迹遗址理事会的评估团保持低调。国际古迹遗址理事会专家把关于相关遗产的实际情况秘密上报给执行委员会，因为如果提前公示，会给国际古迹遗址理事会和世界遗产委员会带来麻烦。

World Heritage Panel

世界遗产评判小组

6. The two reports (cultural assessment and site mission report) that emerge from these consultations are received by the ICOMOS secretariat in Paris, and from them a draft evaluation is prepared. This contains a brief description and history of the property, summaries of its legislative protection, management, and state of conservation, comments on these aspects, and recommendations to the World Heritage Committee. Draft evaluations are then presented to a two or three-day meeting of the ICOMOS World Heritage Panel. The Panel comprises the members of the Executive Committee, who come from all parts of the world and who possess a wide range of skills and experience. The Executive Committee members are supplemented by experts in certain categories of heritage that figure on the annual list of nominations but which are not represented on the Committee.

6.通过这些咨询形成的两个报告（文化评估和现场调研报告），将提交给位于巴黎的国际古迹遗址理事会的秘书处，由秘书处负责制定评估草案，其中包括：遗产的简要描述和历史、立法保护、管理、保护状况的总结，对这些事宜的评论，以及对世界遗产委员会的建议。然后将评估草案提交给国际古迹遗址理事会世界遗产评判小组，届时它们将召开为期两天或三天的会议。评估小组包括执行委员会的委员，这些人来自世界各地，有着广博的技能和知识。除了执行委员会委员以外，还有某类遗产方面的专家。他们作为执行委员会的补充专家，参与申遗名单年度计划。

7. Each nominated property is the subject of a 10-15 minute illustrated presentation by a representative of ICOMOS, followed by discussion. Following the objective and exhaustive examination of the nominations, the collective recommendations of ICOMOS are prepared, and the evaluations are revised and printed, for presentation to the World Heritage Committee.

7.国际古迹遗址理事会的代表在就每个申报遗产进行 10-15分钟的陈述发言后，之后代表们将对此展开讨论。在对申报材料进行客观、详尽的审查之后，国际古迹遗址理事会将整理大家所提建议，修订并印制评估报告，以提交世界遗产委员会。

Firgure 1. SUMMARY OF ZCO,OS EVACUATZON PROCEDURE

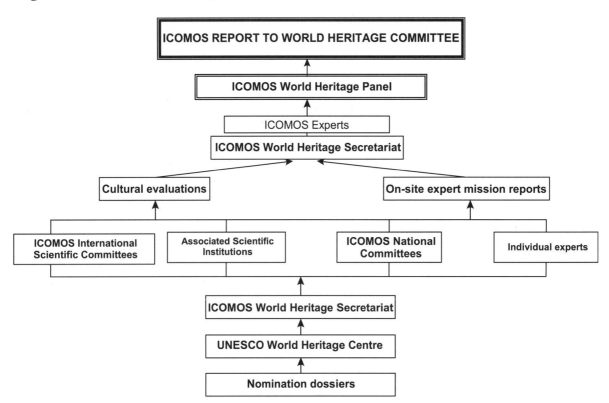

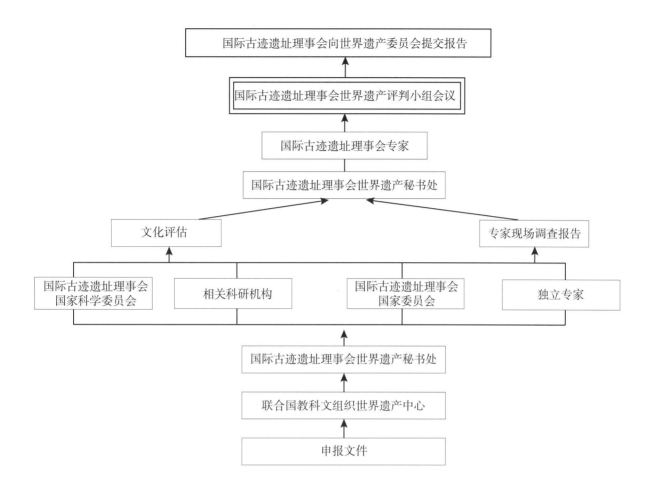

B. THE IUCN PROCEDURE FOR THE EVALUATION OF NATURAL PROPERTIES

8. In carrying out its evaluation of nominations of natural properties, IUCN (the World Conservation Union) is guided by the *Operational Guidelines* (see Paragraph 148). The evaluation process (see Figure 2) involves five steps:

(i) Data Assembly. Following receipt of the nomination dossier from the World Heritage Centre, a standardised data sheet is compiled on the property by the UNEP-World Conservation Monitoring Centre (UNEP-WCMC), using the Protected Area database, and verified with the State Party during the field inspection.

(ii) External Review. The nomination is normally sent for desk review to up to 15 experts knowledgeable about the property, primarily

B. 世界自然保护联盟的自然遗产评估程序

8. 世界自然保护联盟遵循《操作指南》（见第148条）的指导，评估自然遗产的申报材料。评估程序（见图2）包括五个步骤：

（i）搜集数据：在接到世界遗产中心递交的申报材料之后，联合国环境规划署的世界养护监测中心，会使用在现场调查时经缔约国确认过的保护区数据库，编制遗产的标准数据表。

（ii）外部评审：按常规，审核申报材料的评审专家最多为15名。这些专家应具备该项遗产的渊博知识，并且大部分是世界自然保护联

members of IUCN's specialist Commissions and networks.

(iii) Field Inspection. One or two IUCN experts visit each nominated property to clarify details about the area, to evaluate site management and to discuss the nomination with relevant authorities and stakeholders. IUCN experts, selected for their global perspective on conservation and natural history as well as their knowledge of the *Convention*, are usually members of the IUCN World Commission on Protected Areas' World Heritage Expert Network or are IUCN secretariat staff. (This field inspection is undertaken jointly with ICOMOS in certain situations - see Part C below)

(iv) Other sources of information. IUCN may also consult additional literature and receive comments from local NGOs and others.

(v) IUCN World Heritage Panel Review. The IUCN World Heritage Panel reviews all field inspection reports, reviewers' comments, the UNEP-WCMC data sheet and other background material before finalising the text of the IUCN evaluation report for each nominated property.

Each evaluation report presents a concise summary of the outstanding universal value of the property nominated, a comparison with other similar sites and a review of integrity and management issues. It concludes with the assessment of the applicability of the criteria, and a clear recommendation to the World Heritage Committee. The UNEP-WCMC data sheets are also made available to the World Heritage Committee.

The Udvardy biogeographic classification system

9. In the evaluations, IUCN uses Udvardy's "Biogeographical Provinces of the World" (1975) biogeographic classification system. This is a classification system for freshwater and terrestrial

盟专家委员会及网络的成员。

（iii）现场调查：每次申报遗产都会有一至两名世界自然保护联盟专家进行调查，以明确该区域的详细情况，评估遗址管理，与相关当局和利益相关方讨论申报情况。挑选世界自然保护联盟专家的标准，是其保护与自然历史的全球视角及对《公约》的知识。他们常常是世界自然保护联盟世界保护区委员会的世界遗产专家网络成员，或世界自然保护联盟秘书处的工作人员。（在某些情况下与国际古迹遗址理事会共同展开现场调查——见下文C部分）

（iv）其他信息来源：世界自然保护联盟也可参考其他文献，接受地方非政府组织及其他组织的意见和建议。

（v）世界自然保护联盟世界遗产评判小组的评审：世界自然保护联盟的每份遗产评估报告定稿以前，世界自然保护联盟世界遗产评判小组将会评审所有的现场调查报告、评审专家的意见、联合国环境规划署–世界养护监测中心数据表和其他背景材料。

每份评估报告包括：申报遗产突出普遍价值的简明摘要、与类似遗址的比较、审查完整性和管理议题。最后，评估报告会评估标准的适用性，并向世界遗产委员会提供明确的建议。联合国环境规划署–世界养护监测中心数据表也会提供给世界遗产委员会。

乌德瓦尔第（Udvardy）生物地理分类体系

9.评估时，世界自然保护联盟使用乌德瓦尔第（Udvardy）"世界生物地理区域"（1975年）的生物地理分类体系。该分类体系用于世界淡水和陆地区域，能对类似的生物地理区域做出预

areas of the world which enables predictions and assumptions to be made about similar biogeographical regions. The Udvardy system provides an objective means of comparing nominated properties with sites of similar climatic and ecological conditions.

10. It is stressed, however, that the Biogeographical Province concept is used as a basis for comparison only and does not imply that World Heritage properties are to be selected solely on this criterion. The guiding principle is that World Heritage properties must be of outstanding universal value.

Systems to identify priority areas for conservation

11. IUCN also uses systems which identify priority areas for conservation such as the Worldwide Fund for Nature's (WWF) Global Ecoregions, WWF/IUCN's Centres of Plant Diversity, Conservation International's Biodiversity Hotspots, and Birdlife International's Endemic Bird Areas and Important Bird Areas.

Systems to evaluate properties for earth science value

12. In evaluating properties which have been nominated for their geological value, IUCN consults with a range of specialised organisations such as the UNESCO Earth Sciences Division, the International Union of Speleology and the International Union of Geological Sciences (IUGS).

Relevant publications used in the evaluation process

13. The evaluation process is aided by the publication of some 20 reference volumes on the world's protected areas published by IUCN, UNEP, UNEP-WCMC, Birdlife International and other publishers. These include:

测。乌德瓦尔第（Udvardy）体系是用来比较具有类似天气与生态条件的申报遗产的客观手段。

10. 但是，需要强调的是，生态物理区域只是作为比较的基础，但不是选择世界遗产的唯一标准。一个指导性的原则是，世界遗产必须具有突出普遍价值。

确认优先保护区的体系

11. 世界自然保护联盟也使用确认优先保护区的体系，比如，世界自然基金会（WWF）全球生态区，世界自然保护联盟/世界自然基金会植物多样性中心、保护国际的生态多样性热点地区和国际特有鸟区和重要鸟区。

评估遗产地球科学价值的体系

12. 在对因地质价值而提出申报的遗产进行评估时，世界自然保护联盟会咨询一些专业组织，比如，联合国教科文组织的地球科学部、国际洞穴研究会和国际地质科学联合会。

评估时使用的相关出版物

13. 评估程序将参考世界自然保护联盟、联合国环境规划署、联合国环境规划署–世界养护监测中心、鸟类国际和其他出版机构出版的关于世界保护区的约20册参考书籍。包括：

(i) Reviews of Protected Area Systems in Oceania, Africa, and Asia;

(ii) The four volume directory of Protected Areas of the World;

(iii) The World Atlas of Coral Reefs;

(iv) The six volume Conservation Atlas series;

(v) The four volume "A Global Representative System of Marine Protected Areas";

(vi) The three volume Centres of Plant Diversity; and

(vii) Important Bird Areas and Endemic Bird Areas of the World

14. These documents together provide system-wide overviews which allow comparison of the conservation importance of protected areas throughout the world. With the development of the Global Strategy work for natural heritage, IUCN is increasingly using its "global overview" papers to identify gaps in natural World Heritage coverage and properties of World Heritage potential. These can be viewed on the IUCN website at http://iucn.org/themes/wcpa/wheritage/globalstrategy.htm

Evaluation of Cultural Landscapes (see also Annex 3)

15. IUCN has an interest in many cultural properties, especially those nominated as cultural landscapes. For that reason, it will on occasion participate in joint field inspections to nominated cultural landscapes with ICOMOS (see Part C below). IUCN's evaluation of such nominations is guided by an internal paper, "The Assessment of Natural Values in cultural landscapes", available on the IUCN web site at http://www.iucn.org/themes/wcpa/wheritage/culturallandscape.htm

16. In accordance with the natural qualities of certain cultural landscapes identified in Annex 3,

（ⅰ）大洋洲、非洲和亚洲保护区体系的评审；

（ⅱ）4册世界保护区的地址录；

（ⅲ）珊瑚礁世界地图；

（ⅳ）6册的保护地图系列；

（ⅴ）4册的"海洋保护区全球代表体系"；

（ⅵ）3册的植物多样性中心；和

（ⅶ）世界重要的鸟类栖息地和特种野鸟栖息地。

14.这些文件提供了系统的概览，因此，可用于比较全球保护区的保护重要性。随着自然遗产全球战略的演进，世界自然保护联盟越来越多地使用其"全球概览"来确认世界自然遗产覆盖面和世界遗产潜在的缺口。登录以下世界自然保护联盟的网址，可获取以上信息：http://iucn.org/themes/wcpa/wheritage/globalstrategy.htm

文化景观评估（另请见附件三）

15.世界自然保护联盟对很多文化遗产都感兴趣，特别是那些作为文化景观申报的遗产。因此，联盟偶尔会与国际古迹遗址理事会合作，对申报的文化景观进行现场考查（见下文的C部分）。世界自然保护联盟基于内部文件《文化景观内自然价值的评估》，对这些申报进行评估。登录以下网址，可查看该文件：http://www.iucn.org/themes/wcpa/wheritage/culturallandscape.htm

16.根据附件三第11段确认的某些文化景观的自然性质，世界自然保护联盟的评估主要涉

Paragraph 11, IUCN's evaluation is concerned with the following factors:

(i) Conservation of natural and semi-natural systems, and of wild species of fauna and flora

(ii) Conservation of biodiversity within farming systems;

(iii) Sustainable land use;

(iv) Enhancement of scenic beauty;

(v) Ex-situ collections;

(vi) Outstanding examples of humanity's inter-relationship with nature;

(vii) Historically significant discoveries

The following table sets each of the above list in the context of the categories of cultural landscapes in Annex 3, thereby indicating where each consideration is most likely to occur (the absence of a consideration does not mean that it will *never* occur, only that this is unlikely):

及以下几个因素：

（ⅰ）自然和半自然体系以及野生动植物物种的保护；

（ⅱ）耕种系统内生物多样性的保护；

（ⅲ）可持续性的水土使用；

（ⅳ）景色美感的提升；

（ⅴ）迁徙采集；

（ⅵ）人类与自然关系的典型事例；

（ⅶ）具有历史意义的发现。

下表把上文所提每个列表均放在附件三文化景观类型的背景之内，藉此指出哪个考虑最可能出现（没提到的考虑并不意味着永远不会出现，只是表明不太可能出现）：

Cultural Landscape type (see also Annex 3)	Natural considerations most likely to be relevant (see Paragraph 16 above)					
Designed landscape					(v)	
Organically evolving landscape-continuous	(i)	(ii)	(iii)	(iv)		
Organically evolving landscape-fossil	(i)				(vi)	
Associative landscape						(vii)

文化景观类型（另见附件三）	最相关的自然因素（见上文第 16 段）					
人为设计景观					（ⅴ）	
有机演变景观——持续性	（ⅰ）	（ⅱ）	（ⅲ）	（ⅳ）		
有机演变景观——化石	（ⅰ）				（ⅵ）	
关联性景观						（ⅶ）

C. ADVISORY BODY COLLABORATION-THE EVALUATION OF MIXED PROPERTIES AND OF CULTURAL LANDSCAPES

Mixed properties

17. Properties that are nominated as having both natural and cultural value entail a joint IUCN and ICOMOS mission to the nominated property. Following the mission, IUCN and ICOMOS prepare separate evaluation reports of the property under the relevant criteria (see A, Paragraph 5 and B, Paragraph 8 (iii) above).

Cultural Landscapes

18. Properties nominated as Cultural Landscapes are evaluated by ICOMOS under criteria (i)-(vi) (see Paragraph 77 of the *Operational Guidelines)*. IUCN is called upon by ICOMOS to review the natural values and the management of the nominated property. This has been the subject of an agreement between the Advisory Bodies. In some cases, a joint mission is required.

C.咨询机构的混合遗产和自然景观的的合作评估程序

混合遗产

17.申报具有自然价值和文化价值的遗产，需要世界自然保护联盟和国际古迹遗址理事会共同对该申报遗产进行现场调研。调研之后，世界自然保护联盟和国际古迹遗址理事会将根据相关标准，编制各自的遗产评估报告（见上文A第5和B，第8（iii））。

文化景观

18.作为文化景观申报的遗产，由国际古迹遗址理事会根据标准（i）–（vi）（见《操作指南》第77条）进行评估。国际古迹遗址理事会将邀请世界自然保护联盟，评审申报遗产的自然价值和管理。这是咨询机构达成协议的目标。在有些情况下，需要共同行动。

FIGURE 2: IUCN EVALUATION PROCEDURE

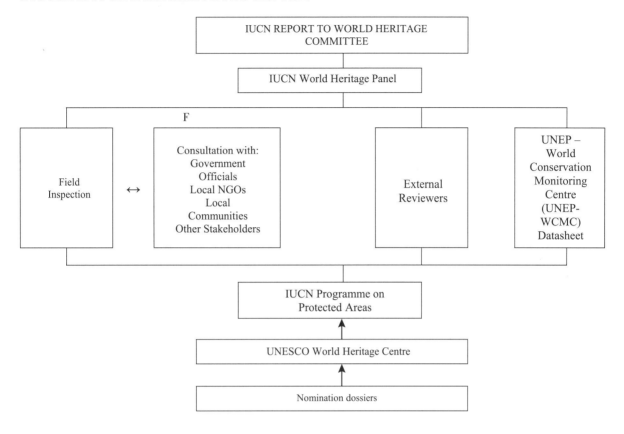

图2：世界自然保护联盟的评估程序

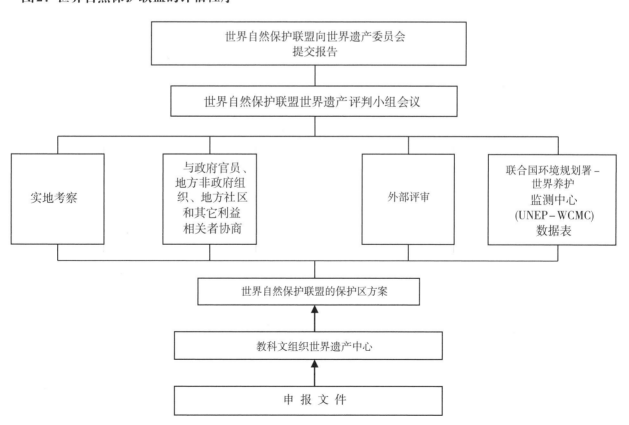

ANNEXES 7

FORMAT FOR THE PERIODIC REPORTING ON THE APPLICATION OF THE *WORLD HERITAGE CONVENTION*

附件 7

《世界遗产公约》实施的定期报告的格式

- The Format for Periodic Reporting is available at the following Web address: http://whc.unesco.org/en/periodicreporting
- Further guidance on Periodic Reporting can be found in Section V of the *Operational Guidelines*
- In order to facilitate management of information, States Parties are requested to submit reports, in English or French, in electronic as well as in printed form to :

UNESCO World Heritage Centre
7, place de Fontenoy
75352 Paris 07 SP
France
Telephone: +33 (0) 1 4568 1571
Fax: +33(0)1 4568 5570
E-mail through: http://whc.unesco.org/en/contacts

FORMAT PERIODIC REPORTING ON THE APPLICATION OF THE *WORLD HERITAGE CONVENTION*

General Requirements

- Information should be as precise and specific as possible. It should be quantified where possible and fully referenced.
- Information should be concise. In particular long historical accounts of sites and events which have taken place there should be

- 登录以下网址，可获取定期报告的格式：
http://whc.unesco.org/en/periodicreporting

- 定期报告的更多指导意见，请参见《操作指南》的第 V 部分

- 为了便于信息的管理，要求缔约国提交英语或法语报告，应同时提交报告的电子版本和印刷版本，提交地址如下：

联合国教科文组织世界遗产中心
法国巴黎（7, place de Fontenoy
75352 Paris 07 SP France）

电话：+33（0）1 4568 1571
传真：+33（0）1 4568 5570
电邮：http://whc.unesco.org/en/contacts

实施《世界遗产公约》的定期报告的格式

总要求

- 信息应该尽可能地精确、具体，应尽量量化，并提供完整的参考文献。

- 信息应该简洁。应该避免逐一叙述遗产地的漫长历史，以及相关事件。如果随时可从现有出版物找到这些信息时，更应避免

avoided, especially when they can be found in readily available published sources.

- Expressions of opinion should be supported by reference to the authority on which they are made and the verifiable facts which support them.
- Periodic reports should be completed on A4 paper (210mm x 297mm), with maps and plans a maximum of A3 paper (297mm x 420mm). States Parties are also encouraged to submit the full text of the periodic reports in electronic form.

SECTION I: APPLICATION OF THE *WORLD HERITAGE CONVENTION* BY THE STATE PARTY

States Parties are requested to give information on the legislative and administrative provisions which they have adopted and other action which they have taken for the application of this *Convention,* together with details of the experience acquired in this field (Article 29.1 of the *World Heritage Convention*).

Ⅰ.1 Introduction

(i) State Party

(ii) Year of ratification or acceptance of the *Convention*

(iii) Organization(s) or entity(ies) responsible for the preparation of the report

(iv) Date of the report

(v) Signature on behalf of the State Party

Ⅰ.2 Identification of cultural and natural heritage properties

This item refers in particular to Articles 3, 4 and 11 of the *Convention* regarding the

这样做。

- 观点陈述应得到当局的支持，并具备能够支持该观点的确切事实。

- 定期报告应用A4纸（210mm×297mm），地图和规划最大用A3纸（297mm×420mm）。也鼓励缔约国提交电子版的定期报告全文。

第Ⅰ部分：缔约国实施《世界遗产公约》的情况

要求缔约国提供为实施《公约》通过的法律和行政条款及其他举措，以及在此领域获得的具体经验（《世界遗产公约》第29.1条）。

Ⅰ.1 导言

（ⅰ）缔约国

（ⅱ）批准或接受《公约》的年份

（ⅲ）负责编制报告的组织或实体

（ⅳ）报告的日期

（ⅴ）缔约国代表签名

Ⅰ.2 文化和自然遗产确认

本条特别参阅《公约》的第3条、第4条和第11条，关于文化和自然遗产的确认，以及申

identification of cultural and natural heritage and the nomination of properties for inscription on the World Heritage List.

报列入《世界遗产名录》的遗产。

(i) National inventories

Inventories of cultural and natural heritage of national significance form the basis for the identification of possible World Heritage properties.

Indicate which institutions are in charge of the preparation and keeping up-to-date of these national inventories and if, and to what extent, inventories, lists and/or registers at the local, state and/or national level exist and have been completed.

（ⅰ）国家清单

国家级文化和自然遗产清单是确认潜在世界遗产的基础。

说明负责编制、更新国家清单的机构。是否存在地方、州和/或国家级的遗产清单、名单和/或登记簿，以及完成的比例。

(ii) Tentative List

Article 11 of the *Convention* refers to the submission by States Parties of inventories of property suitable for inscription on the World Heritage List. These tentative lists of cultural and natural properties should be prepared with reference to Paragraphs 62-69 and Annex 2 of the *Operational Guidelines*. States Parties should report on actions taken to implement the decision of the Committee at its twenty-fourth session (Cairns, December 2000) and the twelfth General Assembly of States Parties (UNESCO Headquarters, 1999) whereby tentative lists are to be used as a planning tool to reduce the imbalances in the World Heritage List.

Provide the date of submission of the Tentative List or any revision made since its submission. States Parties are also encouraged to provide a description of the process of preparation and revision of the Tentative List, e.g. has (have) any particular institution(s) been assigned the responsibility for identifying and delineating World Heritage properties, have local authorities and local population been involved in its preparation? If so,

（ⅱ）《预备名录》

《公约》第11条涉及缔约国提交适宜列入《世界遗产名录》的遗产的名单。应参阅《操作指南》第62-69条和附件二文化和自然遗产的预备名录。缔约国应该提交报告，说明委员会第24届会议（凯恩斯，2000年12月）、缔约国第十二届大会（联合国教科文组织总部，1999年）决议的实施情况。这些决议把预备名录作为规划工具，降低《世界遗产名录》上遗产分布的不均衡性。

提供《预备名录》提交的日期，及提交以后所做的任何修改信息。还鼓励缔约国描述《预备名录》的编制和修订过程，比如，是否委派某个（些）机构负责确认、描写世界遗产？当地机构和群众是否参与名录编制过程？如果是，提供相关的准确信息。

provide exact details.

(iii) Nominations

The periodic report should list properties that have been nominated for inscription on the World Heritage List. States Parties are encouraged to provide an analysis of the process by which these nominations are prepared, the collaboration and co-operation with local authorities and people, the motivation, obstacles and difficulties encountered in that process and perceived benefits and lessons learnt.

Ⅰ.3 Protection, conservation and presentation of the cultural and natural heritage

This item refers in particular to Articles 4 and 5 of the *Convention*, in which States Parties recognise their duty of ensuring the identification, protection, conservation, presentation and transmission to future generations of the cultural and natural World Heritage and that effective and active measures are taken to this effect. Additional guidance on States Parties obligations can be found in Paragraphs 10-16 of the *Operational Guidelines*.

Article 5 of the *Convention* specifies the following measures:

(i) General policy development

Provide information on the adoption of policies that aim to give the cultural and natural heritage a function in the life of the community. Provide information on the way the State Party or the relevant authorities has (have) taken steps to integrate the protection of World Heritage properties into comprehensive planning programmes. Areas where improvement would be desirable, and towards which the State Party is working should be indicated.

（iii）申报材料

定期报告应该列出申报列入《世界遗产名录》的遗产。鼓励缔约国对以下内容进行分析：申报材料的编制过程，与当地机构及群众的合作，编制过程中得到的动力、遇到的障碍和困难，以及得到的收益和经验。

Ⅰ.3 文化和自然遗产的保护与展示

本条特别参阅《公约》第4条、第5条，其中提到缔约国有责任确保本国领土内的文化和自然遗产的确认、保护、保存、展示和传承，并采取积极有效的措施履行这些责任。关于缔约国责任的更多指导，可参阅《操作指南》的第10–16条。

《公约》第5条明确了以下措施：

（i）总体政策制定

说明文化和自然遗产政策的通过情况，及其在社区生活中发挥的作用。阐述缔约国或相关机构把世界遗产的保护融入整体规划方案中的举措。应指出待改进之处的工作和缔约国的工作目标。

(ii) Status of services for protection, conservation and presentation

Provide information on any services within the territories of the State Party which have been set up or have been substantially improved since the previous periodic report, if applicable. Particular attention should be given to services aiming at the protection, conservation and presentation of the cultural and natural heritage, indicating the appropriate staff and the means to discharge their functions. Areas where improvement would be desirable, and towards which the State Party is working should be indicated.

(iii) Scientific and technical studies and research

Additional guidance on research can be found in Paragraph 215 of the *Operational Guidelines*.

List significant scientific and technical studies or research projects of a generic nature that would benefit World Heritage properties, initiated or completed since the last periodic report. Areas where improvement would be desirable, and towards which the State Party is working should be indicated.

Site specific scientific studies or research projects should be reported upon under Section Ⅱ.4 of this Format.

(iv) Measures for identification, protection, conservation, presentation and rehabilitation

Indicate appropriate legal and administrative measures that the State Party or relevant authorities have taken for the identification, protection, conservation, presentation and rehabilitation of cultural and natural heritage. Particular attention should be given to measures concerning visitor management and development in the region. The

（ⅱ）保护、展示服务的情况

提供自上次定期报告以后，缔约国内已确立或已得到大幅改进的服务（如适用）的信息。应特别关注旨在保护与展现文化和自然遗产的服务，说明履行这些功能的合适的人员配备和手段。应指出待改进的工作和缔约国的工作目标。

（ⅲ）科学和技术研究

有关研究的更多指导，请参阅《操作指南》的第215条。

列出自上一个定期报告提交以后，正在开展或完成的、有利于世界遗产的重大科学和技术项目。应指出待改进的工作和缔约国的工作目标。

应根据本格式第Ⅱ.4部分，报告遗产地的具体科学研究项目。

（ⅳ）确定、保护、保存、展出和修复利用的措施

指出缔约国或相关机构确定、保护、保存、展出和修复利用文化和自然遗产的法律和行政措施。应该特别关注本地区旅游管理和开发的措施。并鼓励缔约国说明，基于已有经验，是否有必要考虑进行相关政策和/或法规改革。也有必要说明，缔约国还签署和认可了哪些文化和自然遗产保护的国际公约。如签署了相关公

State Party is also encouraged to indicate if, on the basis of the experiences gained, policy and/or legal reform is considered necessary. It is also relevant to note which other international conventions for the protection of cultural or natural heritage have been signed or ratified by the State Party and if so, how the application of these different legal instruments is co-ordinated and integrated in national policies and planning.

Indicate relevant scientific, and technical measures that the State Party or relevant institutions within the State have taken for the identification, protection, conservation, presentation and rehabilitation of cultural and natural heritage.

Indicate relevant financial measures that the State Party or relevant authorities have taken for the identification, protection, conservation, presentation and rehabilitation of cultural and natural heritage.

Information on the presentation of the heritage can refer to publications, internet web-pages, films, stamps, postcards, books etc.

Areas where improvement would be desirable, and towards which the State Party is working should be indicated.

(v) Training

Additional guidance on training can be found in Paragraphs 213-214 of the *Operational Guidelines*.

Provide information on the training and educational strategies that have been implemented within the State Party for professional capacity building, as well as on the establishment or development of national or regional centres for training and education in the protection, conservation, and presentation of the cultural and natural heritage, and the degree to which such training has been integrated within existing university and educational systems.

Indicate the steps that the State Party has taken

约，在实施过程中，如何在国家政策和规划内协调与融合这些不同的法律文件。

说明缔约国及其相关机构采取了哪些重要的科学和技术措施，来确定、保护、保存、展出和修复利用文化和自然遗产。

说明缔约国及其相关机构采取了哪些相关财政措施，来确定、保护、保存、展出和修复利用文化和自然遗产。

遗产展示信息可包括出版物、互联网网页、影片、邮票、明信片、书籍等。

应指出待改进工作和缔约国的工作目标。

（ⅴ）培训

有关培训的更多指导，请参阅《操作指南》第213–214条。

提供缔约国内为促进专业能力建设而贯彻的培训和教育战略信息，提供为保护、保存和展出文化和自然遗产而建立的国家或地区培训和教育中心的成立或发展信息，以及这些培训与现有大学和教育体系的融合程度的信息。

说明缔约国为支持培训和教育活动，缔约

to encourage scientific research as a support to training and educational activities.

Areas where improvement would be desirable, and towards which the State Party is working should be indicated.

I .4 International co-operation and fund raising

This item refers particularly to Articles 4, 6, 17 and 18 of the *Convention.* Additional guidance on this issue can be found in Paragraphs 227-231 of the *Operational Guidelines.*

Provide information on the co-operation with other States Parties for the identification, protection, conservation and preservation of the World Heritage located on their territories.

Also indicate which measures have been taken to avoid damage directly or indirectly to the World Heritage on the territory of other States Parties.

Have national, public and private foundations or associations been established for, and has the State Party given assistance to, raising funds and donations for the protection of the World Heritage?

I .5 Education, information and awareness building

This item refers particularly to Articles 27 and 28 of the *Convention* on educational programmes. Additional guidance on these matters can be found in Chapter IX of the *Operational Guidelines.*

Indicate steps that the State Party has taken to raise the awareness of decision-makers, property owners, and the general public about the protection and conservation of cultural and natural heritage.

Provide information on education (primary, secondary and tertiary) and information programmes that have been undertaken or are planned to strengthen appreciation and respect by the population, to keep the public broadly informed of the dangers threatening the heritage and of activities

国采取的鼓励科学研究的措施。应指出待改进工作和缔约国的工作目标。

I .4 国际合作与资金筹集

本条特别参阅《公约》的第4、6、17 和18条。有关本议题的更多指导，请参阅《操作指南》第227–231条。

提供为其领土内世界遗产的确定、保护、保存事宜与其他缔约国开展合作的信息。

说明采取了哪些措施，来避免对其他缔约国领土内的世界遗产造成直接或间接的损害。

是否已建立国家、公共和私人基金或组织，以筹集世界遗产的保护资金，是否接受相关方的捐助？缔约国是否在这些方面给予了帮助？

I .5 教育、信息和意识的建立

本条特别参阅《公约》关于教育方案的27和28条。有关本事宜的更多指导，请参阅《操作指南》第九章。

说明缔约国为提升决策者、遗产所有者和社会大众关于文化和自然遗产的保护与保存上的意识而采取的措施。

说明已开展或规划中的教育（小学、中学和大学）和信息方案的基本情况，这些方案旨在加强群众欣赏和尊重遗产的能力，让公众了解遗产所面临的危险因素，及根据《公约》所采取的行动。指出缔约国是否参加了联合国教科文组织的特别项目"年轻人参与世界遗产的

carried out in pursuance of the *Convention*. Does the State Party participate in the UNESCO Special Project *Young People's Participation in World Heritage Preservation and Promotion*?

Information on sitespecific activities and programmes should be provided under item Ⅱ.4 concerning management, below.

Ⅰ.6 Conclusions and recommended action

The main conclusions under each of the items of Section I of the report should be summarized and tabulated together with the proposed action(s) to be taken, the agency(ies) responsible for taking the action(s) and the timeframe for its execution:

(i) Main conclusions

(ii) Proposed future action(s)

(iii) Responsible implementing agency(ies)

(iv) Timeframe for implementation

(v) Needs for international assistance

States Parties are also encouraged to provide in their first periodic report an analysis of the process by which they ratified the *Convention,* the motivation, obstacles and difficulties encountered in that process and perceived benefits and lessons learnt.

SECTION II: STATE OF CONSERVATION OF SPECIFIC WORLD HERITAGE PROPERTIES

The preparation of periodic state of conservation reports should involve those who are responsible for the day-to-day management of the property. For transboundary properties it is recommended that reports be prepared jointly by or in close collaboration between the agencies concerned.

The first periodic report should update the information provided in the original nomination dossier. Subsequent reports will then focus on any

保护与宣传"。

根据下文与管理相关的第 Ⅱ.4 部分，提供各遗产地具体活动与方案的信息。

Ⅰ.6 总结和建议采取的行动

应该总结本报告I部分内各条的主要结论，并将其与建议采纳的内容、负责采取行动的机构和执行时间表一起制成表格：

（ⅰ）主要结论

（ⅱ）建议采取的行动

（ⅲ）负责实施的机构

（ⅳ）执行时间表

（ⅴ）需要的国际援助

鼓励缔约国在首次定期报告中，提供加入《公约》的过程分析，实施过程中得到的动力、遇到的障碍和困难，以及得到的收益和经验。

第Ⅱ部分：世界遗产的具体保护状况

负责遗产日常管理的人员应参与编制保护状况的定期报告的工作。如果是跨国遗产，建议相关机构共同编制报告或在编制报告的过程中紧密合作。

首次定期报告应该更新原始申报材料内的信息。后续报告应着重说明自上一个报告提交后所发生的变化。

changes that may have occurred since the previous report was submitted.

This section of the periodic report follows, therefore, the format for the nomination dossier.

The state of properties included on the List of World Heritage in Danger are reviewed by the World Heritage Committee at regular intervals, in general once every year. This review concentrates on the specific factors and considerations that led to the inscription of the property on the List of World Heritage in Danger. It will still be necessary to prepare a complete periodic report on the state of conservation of these properties.

This section should be completed for each individual World Heritage property.

II.1 Introduction

(i) State Party
(ii) Name of the World Heritage property
(iii) Geographical coordinates to the nearest second
(iv) Date of inscription on the World Heritage List
(v) Organization(s) or entity(ies) responsible for the preparation of the report
(vi) Date of the report
(vii) Signature on behalf of the State Party

II.2 Statement of Outstanding Universal Value

At the time of inscription of a property on the World Heritage List, the World Heritage Committee indicates its outstanding universal value by deciding on the criteria for inscription. Please indicate the justification for inscription provided by the State Party, and the criteria under which the Committee inscribed the property on the World Heritage List.

In the view of the State Party, does the Statement of Outstanding Universal Value

定期报告的文本部分遵循申报材料的格式。

世界遗产中心定期对《濒危世界遗产名录》内的遗产进行审查，一般是每年一次。着重审查导致遗产列入《濒危世界遗产名录》的具体因素和观察意见。除此之外，仍有必要编制完整的定期报告，说明这些遗产的保护状况。

应为每个世界遗产完整编制保护状况定期报告。

II.1 引言

（i）缔约国
（ii）世界遗产的名称
（iii）精确到秒的地理坐标
（iv）列入《世界遗产名录》的日期
（v）负责编制报告的组织或机关
（vi）报告的日期
（vii）缔约国代表签名

II.2 "突出普遍价值声明"

遗产列入《世界遗产名录》时，世界遗产委员会通过确定其列入的标准，指出其突出的普遍价值。请说明缔约国提出的列入理由，以及委员会把该遗产列入《世界遗产名录》所遵循的标准。

按缔约国角度来看，"突出普遍价值声明"是否反映了该项遗产的突出普遍价值，或者是

adequately reflect the outstanding universal value of the property or is a re-submission necessary? This could be considered, for example, to recognise cultural values of a World Heritage property inscribed for its outstanding natural value, or vice-versa. This may become necessary either due to the substantive revision of the criteria by the World Heritage Committee or due to better identification or knowledge of specific outstanding universal value of the property.

Another issue that might be reviewed here is whether the delimitation of the World Heritage property, and its buffer zone if appropriate, is adequate to ensure the protection and conservation of the outstanding universal value embodied in it. A revision or extension of the boundaries might be considered in response to such a review.

If a Statement of Outstanding Universal Value is not available or incomplete, it will be necessary, in the first periodic report, for the State Party to propose such a statement. The Statement of Outstanding Universal Value should reflect the criterion (criteria) on the basis of which the Committee inscribed the property on the World Heritage List. It should also address questions such as: What does the property represent, what makes the property outstanding,

what are the specific values that distinguish the property, what is the relationship of the property with its setting, etc.? Such Statement of Outstanding Universal Value will be examined by the Advisory Body(ies) concerned and transmitted to the World Heritage Committee for approval, if appropriate.

II.3 Statement of authenticity and/or integrity

Under this item it is necessary to review whether the value on the basis of which the property was inscribed on the World Heritage List, and reflected in the Statement of Outstanding Universal

否有必要再次提交？对于因其突出的自然价值而列入《名录》的世界遗产，可考虑明确其文化价值，反之亦然。由于世界遗产委员会对标准进行了大量修改，或缔约国对遗产具体的突出的普遍价值有了更好的认识，这一做法变得极有必要。

此处审阅的另一个议题是世界遗产及其缓冲区的界定是否准确，是否足以确保遗产的突出的普遍价值得以保护与保存。评审之后，是否要考虑修改或扩大范围。

如果"突出普遍价值声明"不恰当或不完整，缔约国有必要在其首次定期报告中提出此类声明。"突出普遍价值声明"应该反映出委员会把该项遗产列入《世界遗产名录》所依据的标准，还应该回答以下问题：遗产代表的是什么，什么让该项遗产变得如此突出，是什么具体的价值使它区别于其他遗产，该项遗产与其环境有何关系？相关的咨询机构将会审查此类"突出普遍价值声明"，并提交世界遗产委员批准。

II.3 真实性和/或完整性声明

在本条中，有必要审查列入《世界遗产名录》的遗产所凭借的价值和前文 II.2 条"突出普遍价值声明"所反映的价值是否得以保持。

Value under item Ⅱ.2 above, are being maintained.

This should also include the issue of authenticity and/or integrity in relation to the property. What was the evaluation of the authenticity and/or integrity of the property at the time of inscription? What is the authenticity and/or integrity of the property at present?

Please note that a more detailed analysis of the conditions of the property is required under item Ⅱ.6 on the basis of key indicators for measuring its state of conservation.

Ⅱ.4 Management

Under this item, it is necessary to report on the implementation and effectiveness of protective legislation at the national, provincial or municipal level and/or contractual or traditional protection as well as of management and/or planning control for the property concerned, as well as on actions that are foreseen for the future, to preserve the value described in the Statement of Outstanding Universal Value under item Ⅱ.2. Additional guidance on this issue can be found in Section Ⅲ.D of the *Operational Guidelines*.

The State Party should also report on significant changes in the ownership, legal status and/or contractual or traditional protective measures, management arrangements and management plans as compared to the situation at the time of inscription or the previous periodic report. In such case, the State Party is requested to attach to the periodic report all relevant documentation, in particular legal texts, management plans and/or (annual) work plans for the management and maintenance of the property. Full name and address of the agency or person directly responsible for the property should also be provided.

The State Party could also provide an assessment of the human and financial resources that are available and required for the management of the

这些应该包括在遗产的真实性和/或完整性议题之中。遗产列入时，对其真实性和/或完整性的评估内容是什么？目前该项遗产的真实性和/或完整性又如何？

请注意：下面第Ⅱ.6条中要求基于衡量保护状况的关键指标，更详细的分析遗产情况。

Ⅱ.4 管理

根据本条，有必要报告国家、省或市级的相关保护法规，和/或合约或传统保护实践的实施情况及有效性，相关遗产管理和/或规划控制的实施情况和有效性，以及为保护第Ⅱ.2条下"突出普遍价值声明"内描述的价值而开展的行动。有关本议题的更多指导，请参阅《操作指南》第Ⅲ.D部分。

缔约国还应报告，与遗产列入时或上一个定期报告时相比，遗产所有权、法律地位和/或合约或传统保护措施、管理安排和管理规划上发生的重大变化。在这种情况下，要求缔约国在定期报告后附上所有的相关文件，特别是法律文本，管理规划和/或遗产管理和维护（年度）工作规划。还应提供直接负责遗产的机构或个人的全称和地址。

缔约国还可提供，对遗产管理所需的、可用的人力和财政资源、及工作人员培训需求的评估；

property, as well as an assessment of the training needs for its staff.

The State Party is also invited to provide information on scientific studies, research projects, education, information and awareness building activities directly related to the property and to comment on the degree to which heritage values of the property are effectively communicated to residents, visitors and the public. Matters that could be addressed are, among other things: is there a plaque at the property indicating that the property is a World Heritage property? Are there educational programmes for schools? Are there special events and exhibitions? What facilities, visitor centre, site museum, trails, guides, information material etc. are made available to visitors? What role does the World Heritage designation play in all these programmes and activities?

Furthermore, the State Party is invited to provide statistical information, if possible on an annual basis, on income, visitor numbers, staff and other items if appropriate.

On the basis of the review of the management of the property, the State Party may wish to consider if a substantive revision of the legislative and administrative provisions for the conservation of the property is required.

II.5 Factors affecting the property

Please comment on the degree to which the property is threatened by particular problems and risks. Factors that could be considered under this item are those that are listed in the nomination format, e.g. development pressure, environmental pressure, natural disasters and preparedness, visitor/tourism pressure, number of inhabitants.

Considering the importance of forward planning and risk preparedness, provide relevant information on operating methods that will make the State Party

描述与遗产直接相关的科研项目、教育、信息和意识提升活动，评论遗产价值在居民、参观者和公众中有效宣传的程度。此处应首要说明以下事宜：是否有标志、标牌表明该遗产地是世界遗产，是否有针对学校的教育方案，是否有特别活动和展览，参观者可使用哪些设施、游客中心、博物馆、参观线路、导游、信息资料等，世界遗产称谓在所有这些方案和活动中所发挥的作用如何。

如有可能，缔约国在此提供年收入、参观人数、工作人员和其他相关事项的信息。

根据遗产管理的评审结果，缔约国可能希望考虑是否要对遗产保护的法律和行政条款做一些重大的修改。

II.5 影响遗产的因素

请针对遗产受某些问题或风险的威胁程度做出评论。本条可考虑的因素是下列申报表格中的因素，例如，开发压力、环境压力、灾害预防、参观/旅游压力和居民人数。

考虑到远期规划和风险管理的重要性，需要缔约国提供应对危害其文化或自然遗产的各种危险因素所采取的措施的相关信息。危险因

capable of counteracting dangers that threaten or may endanger its cultural or natural heritage. Problems and risks to be considered could include earthquakes, floods, land-slides, vibrations, industrial pollution, vandalism, theft, looting, changes in the physical context of properties, mining, deforestation, poaching, as well as changes in land-use, agriculture, road building, construction activities, tourism. Areas where improvement would be desirable, and towards which the State Party is working should be indicated.

This item should provide up-to-date information on all factors which are likely to affect or threaten the property. It should also relate those threats to measures taken to deal with them.

An assessment should also be given if the impact of these factors on the property is increasing or decreasing and what actions to address them have been effectively taken or are planned for the future.

II.6 Monitoring

Whereas item II.3 of the periodic report provides an overall assessment of the maintenance of the outstanding universal value of the property, this item analyses in more detail the conditions of the property on the basis of key indicators for measuring its state of conservation.

If no indicators were identified at the time of inscription of the property on the World Heritage List, this should be done in the first periodic report. The preparation of a periodic report can also be an opportunity to evaluate the validity of earlier identified indicators and to revise them, if necessary.

Up-to-date information should be provided in respect to each of the key indicators. Care should be taken to ensure that this information is as accurate and reliable as possible, for example by carrying out observations in the same way, using similar equipment and methods at the same time of the year

素包括：地震、洪水、山崩、震动、工业污染、蓄意破坏、盗窃、掠夺、遗产物理环境的变化、采矿、滥伐森林、非法捕猎以及用地变化、农业、修路、建筑施工和旅游。应同时指出应对工作中待改进之处和缔约国的工作目标。

本条中应提供可能影响或威胁遗产的各种因素的更新信息。还应该把这些威胁因素与应对措施联系起来。

应评估上述因素对遗产的影响程度的变化，指出采取了哪些有效的应对措施和未来计划采取的措施。

II.6 监测

定期报告的第 II.3 条对遗产的普遍价值进行了全面的评估。本条将根据衡量保护现况的关键指标，更详细地分析遗产情况。

如果在遗产列入《世界遗产名录》时尚未确定指标，则应在首次定期报告中明确各项指标。编制定期报告也是评估以往使用指标的有效性的机会。必要时，应对指标作出修改。

提供每个关键指标的更新信息。注意尽可能地确保这些信息的准确度和可靠性，比如，使用同样的方式进行观察，在每年、每日的同一时间使用同样的设备和方法。

and day.

Indicate which partners if any are involved in monitoring and describe what improvement the State Party foresees or would consider desirable in improving the monitoring system.

In specific cases, the World Heritage Committee and/or its Bureau may have already examined the state of conservation of the property and made recommendations to the State Party, either at the time of inscription or afterwards. In such cases the State Party is requested to report on the actions that have been taken in response to the observations or recommendations made by the Bureau or Committee.

Ⅱ.7 Summary of conclusions and recommended actions

The main conclusions under each of the items of the state of conservation report, in particular, whether the outstanding universal value of the property are maintained, should be summarized and tabulated together with:

(i) Main conclusions regarding the state of the outstanding universal value of the property (see items Ⅱ.2. and Ⅱ.3. above)

(ii) Main conclusions regarding the management and factors affecting the property (see Items Ⅱ.4 and Ⅱ.5. above)

(iii) Proposed future action(s)

(iv) Responsible implementing agency(ies)

(v) Timeframe for implementation

(vi) Needs for international assistance

The State Party is also requested to indicate what experience the State Party has obtained that could be relevant to others dealing with similar problems or issues. Please provide names and contact details of organizations or specialists who could be contacted for this purpose.

指出哪些合作伙伴（如果有）也参与了监测工作，描述预见的改进，或利于改进监测体系的方法。

在某些情况下，世界遗产委员会和／或其理事会可能已检查过遗产的保护状况，并已在遗产列入时或列入后向缔约国提出了改进建议。在这种情况下，要求缔约国报告，为应对理事会或委员会提出建议而采取的相应措施。

Ⅱ.7 监测结果总结和建议采取的对策

应该总结保护状况报告内的各条主要结论，特别是遗产的突出的普遍价值是否得以保持，并把这些信息与以下内容一起编成表格：

（ⅰ）与遗产的突出的普遍价值状况相关的主要结论（见上文的第Ⅱ.2和Ⅱ.3条）

（ⅱ）涉及管理及影响遗产的因素的主要结论（见第Ⅱ.4和Ⅱ.5.条）

（ⅲ）建议采取的行动

（ⅳ）负责实施的机构

（ⅴ）实施时间表

（ⅵ）需要的国际援助

还要求缔约国说明保护管理中获得处理类似问题相关的经验，并提供与之相关的组织或专家的姓名和联系方式。

ANNEXES 8

INTERNATIONAL ASSISTANCE REQUEST FORM

附件 8

《国际援助申请表》

- The International Assistance request form is available at the following Web address: whc.unesco.org/en/intassistance
- Further guidance on International Assistance can be found in Section VII of the *Operational Guidelines*
- The original signed version of the completed International Assistance request form should be sent in English or French to:

UNESCO World Heritage Centre
7, place de Fontenoy 75352 Paris 07 SP
France
Telephone: +33(0)1 45 68 12 76
Fax: +33(0)1 45 68 55 70
E-mail: wh-intassistance@unesco.org

1. STATE PARTY＿＿＿＿＿＿＿＿＿＿
＿＿＿＿＿＿＿＿＿＿＿＿＿＿＿＿＿

2. TITLE OF ACTIVITY＿＿＿＿＿＿＿
＿＿＿＿＿＿＿＿＿＿＿＿＿＿＿＿＿
＿＿＿＿＿＿＿＿＿＿＿＿＿＿＿＿＿

3. THE ACTIVITY WILL BENEFIT A PROPERTY OR PROPERTIES:
　□ -inscribed on the List of World Heritage in Danger
　□ -inscribed on the List of World Heritage
　□ -nominated for inscription on the List of World Heritage (i.e. Tentative List)
　If any of the above, please indicate the name of the property(ies):

4. TYPE OF ACTIVITY (see summary table in

- 登录以下网址下载《国际援助申请表》：whc.unesco.org/intassistance
- 更多有关国际援助的详细指导说明。请参见《操作指南》的第七章
- 应将完整填写后的英文或法文版的国际援助申请表原件递交至：

联合国教科文组织世界遗产中心
地址：7, place de Fontenoy 75352 Paris 07 SP
France
电话：+33（0）1 45 68 12 76
传真：+33（0）1 45 68 55 70
电子邮箱：wh-intassistance@unesco.org

1. 缔约国＿＿＿＿＿＿＿＿＿＿＿＿＿
＿＿＿＿＿＿＿＿＿＿＿＿＿＿＿＿＿

2. 活动名称＿＿＿＿＿＿＿＿＿＿＿＿
＿＿＿＿＿＿＿＿＿＿＿＿＿＿＿＿＿
＿＿＿＿＿＿＿＿＿＿＿＿＿＿＿＿＿

3. 活动将有益于一项或多项遗产：
□ – 列入《濒危世界遗产名录》

□ – 列入《世界遗产名录》
□ – 申报列入《世界遗产名录》（例如：《预备名录》）
如果存有任何上述情况，请注明遗产名称：

4. 活动类型（有关详细内容，请参看《操

Paragraph 20 of this Application Form for details)

□ -Emergency Assistance

□ -Preparatory Assistance

□ -Training and Research Assistance

□ -Technical Co-operation

□ -Assistance for Education, Information and Awareness Raising

5. PREVIOUS CONTRIBUTIONS FROM THE WORLD HERITAGE FUND:

5.a If the activity is to benefit a World Heritage property or properties, have there been previous contributions from the World Heritage Fund benefiting this / these properties?

□ -yes　　　　　　□ -no

5.b Have similar or related activities been previously implemented within the State Party with contributions from the World Heritage Fund?

□ -yes　　　　　　□ -no

If yes to either 5.a or 5.b, indicate all previous contributions from the World Heritage Fund in the following format:

Type of international assistance	Year	Amount in US$	Title of activity

6. PLACE OF ACTIVITY:

Will the activity be held at a World Heritage property?

□ -yes　　　　　　□ -no

Will the activity include a field component?

□ -yes　　　　　　□ -no

If yes, where?_____

_____

作指南》第241条中的总结表格）。请选择一种活动类型。

□– 紧急援助

□– 筹备性援助

□– 培训与研究援助

□– 技术合作

□– 教育、信息和公众意识提升援助

5. 世界遗产基金以往的资助：

5.a 如果此项活动对于一项或多项世界遗产有益，那么世界遗产基金是否在此前曾出资资助过该项或该几项遗产？

□是　　　　　　□否

5.b 是否曾在缔约国内，利用世界遗产基金的资助，开展过类似或相关活动？

□是　　　　　　□否

如果5.a或5.b的答案为"是"，请在下表中对世界遗产基金之前的资助进行明确说明：

国际援助类型	年份	金额（美元）	活动名称

6. 活动地点：

此项活动是否会在一处世界遗产地举行？

□是　　　　　　□否

此项活动是否包括野外活动部分？

□是　　　　　　□否

如果答案为"是"，在哪里？_____

_____

7. DATES AND DURATION OF ACTIVITY
(foreseen or determined)

Dates:_____

_____

Duration:_____

_____

8. THE ACTIVITY IS
□ -local

□ -national

□ -sub-regional involving a few States Parties from a region

□ -regional involving most States Parties from a region

□ -international involving States Parties from different regions

If the activity is sub-regional, regional or international, please indicate the countries which will participate / benefit from the activity:

_____

_____

_____

_____

9. JUSTIFICATION FOR ACTIVITY
Indicate the problems or issues to be discussed/addressed. This description should justify the need for the activity and should provide indications on the degree of urgency of the activities to be undertaken where appropriate. If relevant, give details of ascertained or potential threat to the property(ies) concerned. Whenever possible support the justification with documentary evidence, such as reports, photographs, slides, maps, etc. Please list all documentation submitted.

If relevant, explain how the activity contributes to the implementation of:

(i) decisions of the World Heritage Committee;

(ii) recommendations of international expert missions undertaken at the request of the Committee,

7. 活动日期与持续时间（预计或确定）

日期：_____

_____

时长：_____

_____

8. 活动类型为：
□地方性活动

□国家性活动

□涉及某一区域少数几个缔约国的局部区域性活动

□涉及某一区域的多数缔约国在内的区域性活动

□涉及不同地区的众多缔约国在内的国际性活动

如果此项活动为局部区域性、区域性或国际性活动，请明确说明哪些国家将参加此项活动或哪些国家将从此项活动中收益：

_____

_____

_____

_____

9. 说明活动原因
指出活动中要解决/讨论的问题或事项。应能够证明活动的必要性并适当说明举行此项活动的紧迫程度。如涉及，应详细说明遗产面临的已知或潜在威胁。可能的话，提供各种形式的文献说明如报告、照片、幻灯片、地图册等，以展示活动的意义，并列出所有提交文件的清单。

解释此项活动将如何有益于实施：

（i）世界遗产委员会的决议；

（ii）委员会、主席或联合国教科文组织委派的国际专家工作组的建议；

Chairperson or UNESCO;

(iii) recommendations of the Advisory Bodies;

(iv) recommendations of UNESCO World Heritage Centre or other UNESCO Divisions;

(v) recommendations of management plans concerning the property;

(vi) guidelines elaborated from results of previous activities supported by the World Heritage Fund at the World Heritage property or State Party.

10. OJECTIVE(S) OF ACTIVITY(IES)

Clearly state the objectives of the activity proposed to be supported by the World Heritage Fund.

11. PROGRAMME AND WORK PLAN OF THE ACTIVITY(IES)

Describe the programme and work plan of the activity(ies) to be undertaken with specific reference to the objectives mentioned in Paragraph 10 above. For meetings and training activities, tentative programmes should be provided including the themes, issues and problems to be discussed.

12. TIMETABLE OF ACTIVITY(IES)

Provide a schedule (eg. bar-chart) covering the whole duration of the activity and giving the details such as:

(i) preparation of the activity;

(ii) duration of each action;

(iii) schedule for purchase of the equipment, if relevant;

(iv) dates on which certain funds are required to enable the successful completion of the activity(ies);

(v) evaluation following the implementation (mandatory).

13. PROFILES OF SPECIALISTS, TRAINERS, TECHNICIANS AND / OR SKILLED LABOUR, IF THE ACTIVITY FORESEES THE PARTICIPATION

（iii）专家咨询机构的建议；

（iv）联合国教科文组织世界遗产中心以及其他部门的建议；

（v）与遗产有关的管理规划建议；

（vi）世界遗产基金支持的在世界遗产地或缔约国举行的以往活动中制定出的指导方针。

10. 活动目的

详细说明申请世界遗产基金支持的活动的目的。

11. 活动方案与工作计划

围绕上面提及的活动目标描述活动方案与工作计划。对于会议或培训活动，应提供包括讨论主题等在内的临时方案。

12. 活动时间表

提供一份涵盖整个活动期的时间表（如条形图），包括以下细节：

（i）活动的准备工作；

（ii）各项行动时长；

（iii）如有需要，设备购置的时间安排；

（iv）为确保活动取得成功，所需资金的到位日期；

（v）结束后的评估（必须）。

13. 可能参加此项活动的专家、培训人员、技术人员和/或技工的简单介绍

OF SUCH PERSONS

Indicate the precise field of specialization and the work to be undertaken by each specialist as well as the duration required. The World Heritage Centre and the Advisory Bodies are available to recommend resource persons / trainers, should the State(s) Party(ies) concerned so request.

明确说明各个专家的专业领域及其承担的工作以及所需工作时间。如缔约国发出请求，世界遗产中心与专家咨询机构可以为活动推荐专家顾问/培训人员。

14. PROFILES OF TRAINEES / PARTICIPANTS, IF THE ACTIVITY FORESEES THE PARTICIPATION OF SUCH PERSONS

Indicate the target groups and beneficiaries of the activity, their professions, institutions, or field(s) of specialization.

14. 可能参加此项活动的受训人员/参与者的个人简介

指明活动的目标群体与受益人以及他们的职业、所属协会或专业领域。

15. EQUIPMENT

If provision of equipment is foreseen in the activity, provide a detailed list of the equipment to be purchased attaching copies of pro-forma invoices.

15. 设备

如果预测可能需要为活动提供设备，则需提供将采购的设备清单并附上估价单。

16. EXPECTED RESULTS, OUTCOME, FOLLOW-UP

Describe the expected results from the activity, especially with reference to the impact the activity will have to enhance the conservation, management and presentation of the World Heritage property(ies) concerned.

Describe the indicators and evidence which will demonstrate the impact the activity(ies) will have on the objectives mentioned in section 10 above.

Indicate the provisions made for reviewing the outcome of the activity at a national level, and any follow-up activities foreseen.

16. 预期结果、成果、后续实施

描述活动的预期成果，特别是活动对于促进该世界遗产保护、管理、展示等工作的促进作用。

描述活动将实现上述活动目标的指标和证据。

指明在国家范围内检验活动成果的规定，以及其他预期后续实施活动。

17. BUDGET

17.a Provide a detailed breakdown of costs in United States dollars of the individual elements within the following sections, including unit costs, if possible:

17. 预算

17.a 提供下列各项目的费用（以美元为单位），如可能，应包括单位成本：

(i) Organization (venue, office expenses such as photocopies, stationery, secretarial assistance, translation, interpretation, audio-visual arrangements)

(ii) Personnel and Consultancy Services (fees paid to international/national resource persons, indicating fee per day/week/month, etc.)

(iii) Travel (international, national or local travel)

(iv) Accommodation, Daily Subsistence Allowance (per day, etc.)

(v) Equipment (if relevant)

(vi) Reporting, evaluation, and publication (if the publication of the proceedings of the training exercise is foreseen, translation, editing, printing, layout, distribution, and communication costs, etc.)

(vii) Miscellaneous (visas, other costs).

（ⅰ）组织（活动地点、办公费用，如影印费、文具费、文秘助理费用、笔译费、口译费、影音设备费用）

（ⅱ）人员与咨询服务（支付给国际/国内学术顾问的费用等，每日/周/月的费用）

（ⅲ）差旅费（国际、国内或本地旅行）

（ⅳ）住宿、每日生活补助

（ⅴ）设备（如必要）

（ⅵ）报告、评估与出版发行（如果培训活动的活动过程将出版发行，则包括翻译费、编辑费、印刷费、排版费、发行费与通讯费等）

（ⅶ）其他杂费（签证及其他费用）。

EXAMPLE OF DETAILED BREAKDOWN OF COSTS:

Item	Detail US$	Subtotal US$
Organization • venue • office expenses • secretarial assistance • translation • simultaneous interpretation • audio-visual equipment • other	 US$____/day for____days=US$____ US$____/week for____weeks=US$____ US$____/page for____pages=US$____ US$____/hour for____hours=US$____ US$____/day for____days=US$____ US$____ US$____	US$____
Personnel / consultancy service • international expert for management • international expert for site management • national trainer • national coordinator • other	 US$____/week for weeks=US$____ US$____/week for weeks=US$____ US$____/week for weeks=US$____ US$____/week for weeks=US$____ US$____/week for weeks=US$____	US$__
Travel • international round trip (RT) airfare • domestic travel costs • other	 US$____/RT for____experts=US$ ____ US$____/bus/day for____days=US$____	US$____
Accommodation, Daily subsistence allowance • food • board	 US$____/day for____persons=US$____ US$____/day for____persons=US$____	US$____
Equipment	US$____/unit for____units=	US$____

Item	Detail US$	Subtotal US$
Reporting, evaluation and publication • reporting • evaluation • editing, layout • printing • distribution • other	US$____ US$____ US$____ US$____ US$____ US$____	US$____
Miscellaneous • visas	US$____for____participants=US$____	US$____

各项费用详细列表：

项目	具体金额（美元）	小计（美元）
组织 • 活动场所 • 办公费用 • 文秘助理费 • 笔译费 • 同声传译费 • 影音设备费 • 其他	每日___美元，共___日 = ___美元 每周___美元，共___周 = ___美元 每页___美元，共___页 = ___美元 每小时___美元，共___小时 = ___美元 每日___美元，共___日 = ___美元 ___美元 ___美元	___美元
人员 / 咨询服务 • 国际专家（专业领域） • 国内培训人员 • 国内协调人员 • 其他	每周___美元，共___周 = ___美元 每周___美元，共___周 = ___美元 每周___美元，共___周 = ___美元 每周___美元，共___周 = ___美元	___美元
差旅费 • 国际往返（RT）机票 • 国内旅行费用 • 其他	国际往返机票___美元，共___名专家 = ___美元 每辆大巴每日___美元，共___天 = ___美元	___美元
住宿、每日生活补助 • 餐饮 • 交通	每日___人___美元 = ___美元 每日___人___美元 = ___美元	___美元
设备	每台___美元，共___台 = ___美元	___美元
报告、评估与出版发行 • 报告 • 评估 • 编辑、排版 • 印刷 • 发行 • 其他	___美元 ___美元 ___美元 ___美元 ___美元 ___美元	___美元
其他杂费 签证	每人___美元，共___人 = ___美元	___美元
		___美元

17.b Indicate how the total estimated costs listed in Paragraph 17.a above will be met by contributions from:

(i) National agency(ies) in kind (specify in detail)

(ii) National agency(ies) in cash (specify)

(iii) Other bi/multi-lateral organizations, donors, etc (specify whether or not the resources are already available or being requested)

(iv) World Heritage Fund: Describe the reasons why the resources are insufficient at the national level.

18. AGENCY(IES) RESPONSIBLE FOR THE IMPLEMENTATION OF THE ACTIVITY

Please provide the name, title, address and all contact details of the person, agency(ies) who will be responsible for the implementation of the activity as well as those of any other participating agencies.

19. SIGNATURE ON BEHALF OF STATE PARTY

Full name_____

Title_____

_____

Date_____

17.b 指明上面列出的预估成本的资金来源：

（ⅰ）国内机构实物出资（详细说明）

（ⅱ）国内机构现金出资（详细说明）

（ⅲ）其他双边或多边组织、捐赠人等（详细说明资金来源是否已落实、可用、或仍在争取中）

（ⅳ）世界遗产基金：说明为何国内资金来源不够充足。

18. 负责开展活动的机构

请提供负责开展活动的人员或机构的姓名、名称、地址以及所有联系细节，以及其他参与活动的机构的详细信息。

19. 代表缔约国签字

全名_____

头衔_____

_____

日期_____

EVALUATION CRITERIA OF THE ADVISORY BODIES FOR INTERNATIONAL ASSISTANCE REQUESTS

 专家咨询机构评估国际援助申请的标准

This Annex is under preparation

本附件尚在准备

SELECT WORLD HERITAGE BIBLIOGRAPHY   **世界遗产相关的参考书目**

WORLD HERITAGE CENTRE DOCUMENTS DATABASE

http://whc.unesco.org/statutorydoc

The UNESCO World Heritage Centre "Official Records" searchable online document collection permits the retrieval of information contained in the reports of the World Heritage Committee and General Assembly of States Parties to the Convention

BASIC TEXTS

UNESCO, *Convention concerning the protection of the world cultural and natural heritage*, adopted by the General Conference at its seventeenth session, Paris, 16 November 1972, WHC-2001/WS/2
　http://whc.unesco.org/en/conventiontext

UNESCO, Intergovernmental Committee for the protection of the World Cultural and Natural Heritage, *Rules of Procedure*, WHC.2003/5.
　http://whc.unesco.org/en/committee

UNESCO, General Assembly of States Parties to the Convention concerning the protection of the World Cultural and Natural Heritage, *Rules of Procedure*, WHC-03/GA/1 Rev. 2 (as of 15 October 2003).
　http://whc.unesco.org/en/garules

UNESCO, Intergovernmental Committee for the protection of the World Cultural and Natural Heritage, *Financial Regulations for the World Heritage Fund*, Paris 1995 (WHC/7, August 1995).
　http://whc.unesco.org/en/committeerules

世界遗产中心文件数据库

网址 http://whc.unesco.org/statutorydoc

世界遗产中心在线检索文件集"官方数据"，允许对世界遗产委员会和缔约国大会报告中包含的信息进行检索。

基础文件

《联合国教科文组织保护世界文化与自然遗产公约》，1972年11月16日于巴黎举行的保护大会第七次会议上通过，WHC-2001/WS/2
　http://whc.unesco.org/en/conventiontext

联合国教科文组织保护世界文化与自然遗产政府间委员会，《程序规则》，WHC.2003/5.
　http://whc.unesco.org/en/committee

联合国教科文组织保护世界文化与自然遗产缔约国大会，《程序规则》，WHC-03/GA/1 Rev. 2（自2003年10月15日）.
　http://whc.unesco.org/en/garules

联合国教科文组织保护世界文化与自然遗产政府间委员会，《世界遗产基金财务规则》，巴黎1995年（WHC/1985年8月7日）.
　http://whc.unesco.org/en/committeerules

UNESCO, World Heritage Centre, *Properties inscribed on the World Heritage List*

http://whc.unesco.org/en/list

UNESCO, World Heritage Centre, *Brief Descriptions of the 754 properties inscribed on the World Heritage List.*

http://whc.unesco.org/briefdescriptions

Pressouyre, Léon, *The World Heritage Convention, twenty years later*, UNESCO, Paris 1993.

Batisse, Michel and Bolla, Gérard, *L'invention du "patrimoine mondial"*, Les Cahiers de l'Histoire, AAFU, Paris 2003.

STRATEGIC DOCUMENTS

World Heritage Committee, *Strategic Orientations*, in Annex II of the Report of the 16th Session of the World Heritage Committee, Santa Fe, United States of America 7-14 December 1992, Paris, December 1992 (WHC-92/CONF.002/12).

Report of the Expert Meeting on the "Global Strategy" and thematic studies for a representative World Heritage List (20-22 June 1994) (WHC-94/CONF.003/INF.6)

World Heritage Committee, *A Strategic Plan for World Heritage Documentation, Information and Education Activities*, Paris 1998 (WHC-98/CONF.203/15).

World Heritage Committee, *Global Training Strategy for World Cultural and Natural Heritage*, adopted by the World Heritage Committee at its 25th session in Helsinki, Finland, 11-16 December 2001 (see ANNEX X of WHC-01/CONF.208/24)

联合国教科文组织世界遗产中心,《世界遗产名录》

http://whc.unesco.org/en/list

联合国教科文组织世界遗产中心,《世界遗产名录754项遗产概述》。

http://whc.unesco.org/briefdescriptions

联合国教科文组织,《世界遗产公约二十年》,巴黎1993年,Pressouyre, Léon。

"世界遗产的诞生",历史手册,AAFU,巴黎2003年,Batisse, Michel与Bolla, Gérard。

战略性文件

世界遗产委员会《战略定位》,世界遗产委员会第16次会议报告附件2,美国圣达菲,1992年12月7日至14日,巴黎1992年12月（WHC-92/CONF.002/12）.

《世界遗产名录》的全球战略与主题研究专家会议报告（1994年6月20至22日）（WHC-94/CONF.003/INF.6）

世界遗产委员会,《世界遗产文件、信息与教育活动战略计划》,巴黎1998年（WHC-98/CONF.203/15）.

世界遗产委员会,《世界文化与自然遗产全球培训战略》,2001年11月11日至16日于芬兰赫尔辛基世界遗产委员会第25次会议通过（参见WHC-01/CONF.208/24附件10）

World Heritage Committee, *Budapest Declaration on World Heritage*, 2002
http://whc/unesco.org/en/budapestdeclaration

WORLD HERITAGE PAPER SERIES[1]

Pedersen, A., *Managing Tourism at World Heritage Sites: a Practical Manual for World Heritage site managers*, World Heritage Paper No. 1, UNESCO, World Heritage Centre, Paris 2002.

Investing in World Heritage: Past Achievements, Future Ambitions, World Heritage Paper No. 2, UNESCO, World Heritage Centre, Paris 2002.

Periodic Report Africa, World Heritage Report No. 3, UNESCO, World Heritage Centre, Paris 2003.

Hillary, A., Kokkonen, M. and Max, L., (edited by), *Proceedings of the World Heritage Marine Biodiversity Workshop, Hanoi, Viet Nam (February 25-March 1, 2002)*, World Heritage Paper No. 4, UNESCO, World Heritage Centre, Paris 2003.

Identification and Documentation of Modern Heritage, World Heritage Paper No. 5, UNESCO, World Heritage Centre, Paris 2003.

Fowler, P. J., (edited by), *World Heritage Cultural Landscapes 1992-2002*, World Heritage Paper No. 6, UNESCO, World Heritage Centre, Paris 2003.

Cultural Landscapes: the Challenges of Conservation, World Heritage Paper No. 7, UNESCO, World Heritage Centre, Paris 2003.

世界遗产委员会,《世界遗产布达佩斯宣言》, 2002年
http://whc/unesco.org/en/budapestdeclaration

世界遗产论文系列[1]

《世界遗产地旅游管理:世界遗产地管理人手册》,世界遗产论文集1,联合国教科文组织世界遗产中心,巴黎2002年,Pedersen, A.。

《投资世界遗产:过去的成果,未来的希望》世界遗产论文集2,联合国教科文组织世界遗产中心,巴黎2002年。

《非洲定期报告》,世界遗产报告3,联合国教科文组织世界遗产中心,巴黎2003年。

《世界遗产海洋生物多样性讨论会会议记录》,越南河内(2002年2月25日至3月1日),世界遗产论文4,联合国教科文组织世界遗产中心,巴黎2003年,Hillary, A., Kokkonen, M.与Max, L.(编辑)。

《现代遗产的确认与记录》,世界遗产论文5,联合国教科文组织世界遗产中心,巴黎2003年。

《1992–2002年世界遗产文化景观》,世界遗产论文6,联合国教科文组织世界遗产中心,巴黎2003年,Fowler, P. J.(编辑)。

《文化景观:遗产保护的挑战》,世界遗产论文7,联合国教科文组织世界遗产中心,巴黎2003年。

---

[1]　For online consultation: http://whc.unesco.org/publications
[1]　在线咨询: http://whc.unesco.org/publications

Mobilizing Young People for World Heritage, World Heritage Paper No. 8, UNESCO, World Heritage Centre, Paris 2003.

《动员年轻人保护世界遗产》，世界遗产论文8，联合国教科文组织世界遗产中心，巴黎2003年。

Partnerships for World Heritage Cities: Culture as a Vector for Sustainable Urban Development, World Heritage Paper No. 9, UNESCO, World Heritage Centre, Paris 2004.

《世界遗产城市合作：文化作为城市可持续发展之桥梁》，世界遗产论文9，联合国教科文组织世界遗产中心，巴黎2004年。

Monitoring World Heritage, World Heritage Paper No. 10, UNESCO, World Heritage Centre, Paris 2004.

《世界遗产监测》，世界遗产论文10，联合国教科文组织世界遗产中心，巴黎2004年。

Periodic Report and Regional Programme-Arab States-2000-2003, World Heritage Paper No. 11, UNESCO, World Heritage Centre, Paris 2004.

《2000-2003年定期报告与地区项目－阿拉伯国家》，世界遗产论文11，联合国教科文组织世界遗产中心，巴黎2004年。

The State of World Heritage in the Asia-Pacific Region-2003, World Heritage Paper No. 12, UNESCO, World Heritage Centre, Paris 2004.

《2003年亚太地区世界遗产状况》，世界遗产论文12，联合国教科文组织世界遗产中心，巴黎2004年。

Linking Universal and Local Values: Managing a Sustainable Future for World Heritage, World Heritage Paper No. 13, UNESCO, World Heritage Centre, Paris 2004.

《结合全球与地区价值观：管理世界遗产可持续发展的未来》，世界遗产论文13，联合国教科文组织世界遗产中心，巴黎2004年。

CULTURAL LANDSCAPES

文化景观

Von Droste, Bernd, Plachter, Harald, and Rössler, Mechtild (edited by), *Cultural Landscapes of Universal Value, Components of a Global Strategy*, Stuttgart New York 1995.

《一个全球战略的组成部分：具有普遍价值的文化景观》，Von Droste, Bernd, Plachter, Harald, 与 Rössler, Mechtild（编辑），斯图加特纽约1995年。

Rössler, Mechtild, and Saouma-Forero, Galia (edited by), *The World Heritage Convention and Cultural Landscapes in Africa Expert Meeting* (Tiwi, Kenya 9-14 March 1999), UNESCO, World Heritage Centre, Paris 2000.

《世界遗产公约与非洲文化景观专家会议》，Rössler, Mechtild, and Saouma-Forero, Galia（编辑），肯尼亚Tiwi1999年3月9日至14日），联合国教科文组织世界遗产中心，巴黎2000年。

Fowler, P. J., (edited by), *World Heritage*

《1992-2002年世界遗产文化景观》，世界遗

Cultural Landscapes 1992-2002, World Heritage Paper No. 6, UNESCO, World Heritage Centre, Paris 2003.

Cultural Landscapes: the Challenges of Conservation, World Heritage Paper No. 7, UNESCO, World Heritage Centre, Paris 2004.

GLOBAL STRATEGY FOR A BALANCED REPRESENTATIVE AND CREDIBLE WORLD HERITAGE LIST

Report of the Expert Meeting on the "Global Strategy" and Thematic Studies for a Representative World Heritage List (20-22 June 1994) (WHC-94/CONF.003/INF.6)

Report of the Expert Meeting on Evaluation of General Principles and Criteria for Nominations of Natural World Heritage sites (Parc national de la Vanoise, France, 22 - 24 March 1996) (WHC- 96/CONF.202/INF.9).

African Cultural Heritage and the World Heritage Convention, Fourth Global Strategy meeting (Porto- Novo, Benin, 16-19 September 1998), UNESCO 1998.

Von Droste, Bernd, and Rössler, Mechtild, and Titchen, Sarah (edited by), *Linking Nature and Culture, Report of the Global Strategy, Natural and Cultural Heritage Expert Meeting* (Theatre Institute, Amsterdam, The Netherlands 25-29 March 1998), (WHC-98/CONF.203/INF.7).

Saouma-Forero, Galia, (edited by), *Authenticity and Integrity in an African Context: Expert Meeting, Great Zimbabwe*, Zimbabwe, 26-29 May 2000, UNESCO - World Heritage Centre, Paris 2001.

产论文6，联合国教科文组织世界遗产中心，巴黎2004年，Fowler, P. J.（编辑）。

《文化景观：遗产保护的挑战》，《1992–2002年世界遗产文化景观》，世界遗产论文日，联合国教科文组织世界遗产中心，巴黎2004年。

有代表性、平衡性、可信性的《世界遗产名录》的全球战略：

《全球战略与具代表性的世界遗产名录主题研究专家会议报告》（1994年6月20–22日）（WHC–94/CONF.003/INF.6）

《世界自然遗产评价总则与申报标准专家会议报告》（法国Parc national de la Vanoise, 1996年3月22–24日）（WHC–96/CONF.202/INF.9）

《第四次全球战略会议：非洲文化遗产与世界遗产公约》，贝宁波多诺伏，1998年9月16–19日），联合国教科文组织1998年。

《联系自然与文化：自然与文化遗产专家会议全球战略报告》（荷兰阿姆斯特丹Theatre Institute，1998年3月25–29日），（WHC–98/CONF.203/INF.7），Von Droste, Bernd, Rössler, Mechtild, 与Titchen, Sarah（编辑）。

《非洲文化背景下的遗产真实性和完整性：专家会议》，津巴布韦大津巴布韦，2000年5月26–29日，联合国教科文组织世界遗产中心，巴黎2001年，Saouma–Forero, Galia（编辑）。

UNESCO Thematic Expert Meeting on Asia-Pacific Sacred Mountains (5-10 September 2001, Wakayama City, Japan), Final Report, UNESCO, World Heritage Centre, Agency for Cultural Affairs, Japan, Tokyo 2001.

Linking Universal and Local Values: Managing a Sustainable Future for World Heritage, Amsterdam, The Netherlands (22 - 24 May, 2003).
http://whc.unesco.org/archive/2003/Amsterdam_05_2003_en.pdf

MANAGEMENT GUIDELINES

Feilden, Bernard M., and Jokilehto, Jukka, *Management Guidelines for World Cultural Heritage Sites*, ICCROM, Rome 1993.

Stovel, Herb, *Risk Preparedness: a Management Manual for World Cultural Heritage*, ICCROM, Rome 1998.

Phillips, Adrian, (edited by), *Economic Values of Protected Areas-Guidelines for Protected Area Managers* (Task Force on Economic Benefits of protected Areas of the World Commission on Protected Areas (WCPA) of IUCN, in collaboration with the Economics Service Unit of IUCN), IUCN, The World Conservation Union, World Commission of Protected Areas (WCPA), Best Practice protected Area Guidelines Series No. 2, 1998.

Kelleher, G. and Philips, Adrian, (edited by), *Guidelines for Marine Protected Areas*, IUCN, World Commission on Protected Areas (WCPA), Best Practice Protected Area Guidelines Series No. 3, 1999.

Philips, Adrian, (edited by), *Evaluating Effectiveness - A Framework for Assessing the*

联合国教科文组织关于亚太圣山的主题专家会议（2001年9月5-10日，日本和歌山市），联合国教科文组织世界遗产中心，日本东京文化厅最终报告，2001年。

《结合全球与地区价值观：管理世界遗产可持续发展的未来》，荷兰阿姆斯特丹（2003年5月22-24日）。
http://whc.unesco.org/archive/2003/Amsterdam_05_2003_en.pdf

管理指南

《世界文化遗产管理指南》，ICCROM，罗马1993年，Feilden, Bernard M.，与Jokilehto, Jukka。

《灾害预防：世界文化遗产管理手册》，ICCROM, 罗马1998年，Stovel, Herb。

《保护区的经济价值—保护区管理者手册》，（国际自然与自然资源保护联合会（IUCN）世界保护区委员会任务对保护区的经济利益），与IUCN经济服务单元、世界自然保护联盟，与世界保护区委员会合作，保护区指南最佳惯例系列2，1998年，Phillips, Adrian（编辑）。

《海洋保护区指南》，IUCN、世界保护区委员会，保护区指南最佳惯例系列3，1999年，Kelleher, G. and Philips, Adrian（编辑）。

《评价实效性—保护区管理的评估框架》，ICUN、2001年世界自然保护联盟、世界保护

Management of Protected Areas, IUCN, The World Conservation Union 2001, World Commission of Protected Areas (WCPA), Best Practice Protected Area Guidelines Series No. 6, 2001.

Phillips, Adrian (edited by), *Transboundary Protected Areas for Peace and Co-operation (Based on the proceedings of workshops held in Bormio (1998) and Gland (2000)*, IUCN, The World Conservation Union, World Commission of Protected Areas (WCPA) Best Practice Protected Area Guidelines Series No. 7, 2001.

Philips, Adrian, *Management Guidelines for IUCN Category V Protected Areas, Protected Landscapes/Seascapes*, Cardiff University, IUCN, Cambridge 2002.

Thomas, Lee, and Middleton, Julie, and Philips, Adrian (edited by), *Guidelines for Management Planning of Protected Areas*, Cardiff University, IUCN, Cambridge 2003.

OTHER

World Heritage in Young Hands. To Know, Cherish and Act, an Educational Resource Kit for Teachers, UNESCO 2002.

World Heritage 2002. Shared Legacy, Common Responsibility, International Congress organized by UNESCO's World Heritage Centre and Regional Bureau for Science in Europe (ROSTE) with the support of the Italian Government on the occasion of the 30th anniversary of the *World Heritage Convention*, Cini Foundation, Island of San Giorgio Maggiore, Venice, Italy 14-16 November 2002, UNESCO, World Heritage Centre, Paris 2003.

区委员会保护区指南最佳惯例系列6，2001年，Philips, Adrian（编辑）。

《跨境保护区：和平与合作》（基于在Bormio（1998年）和Gland（2000年）举行的讨论会会议记录），世界自然保护联盟、世界保护区委员会保护区指南最佳实践系列7，2001年，Phillips, Adrian（编辑）。

《世界自然保护联盟第五类保护区管理指南》，保护区景观/海景，加的夫大学，IUCN，剑桥2002年，Philips, Adrian。

《保护区管理规划指南》，加的夫大学，IUCN，剑桥2003年，Thomas, Lee, 与Middleton, Julie, 和Philips, Adrian（编辑）。

其他

《教师用世界遗产教育教材：了解、珍惜与行动，世界遗产在青年手中》，联合国教科文组织2002年。

《2002年世界遗产，共享的遗产，共同的责任》，联合国教科文组织世界遗产中心与联合国教科文管理欧洲科学发展的威尼斯办事处组织的国际大会，在世界遗产公约30周年纪念日之际得到了意大利政府的支持，意大利威尼斯San Giorgio Maggiore岛Cini基金会，2002年11月14–16日，联合国教科文组织世界遗产中心，巴黎2003年。

WEB ADDRESSES

UNESCO
http://www.unesco.org
UNESCO World Heritage Centre
http://www.whc.unesco.org
ICCROM
http://www.iccrom.org
ICOMOS
http://www.icomos.org
UNESCO-ICOMOS Documentation Centre
http://www.international.icomos.org/centre_
documentation/index.html
IUCN
http://www.iucn.org
UNEP - World Conservation Monitoring
Centre, Protected Area Database
http://sea.unep-wcmc.org/wdbpa/
Documentation and Conservation of Monuments
and Sites of the Modern Movement (DOCOMOMO)
http://www.docomomo-us.org/
http://www.docomomo.nl
The International Committee for the Conservation
of the Industrial Heritage (TICCIH)
http://www.mnactec.com/TICCIH/
The International Federation of Landscape
Architects (IFLA)
Email: info@iflaonline.org
http://www.iflaonline.org/home.html

网站地址

联合国教科文组织（UNESCO）
http://www.unesco.org
联合国教科文组织世界遗产中心
http://www.whc.unesco.org
国际文化遗产保护与修复研究中心（ICCROM）
http://www.iccrom.org
国际古迹遗址理事会（ICOMOS）
http://www.icomos.org
UNESCO–ICOMOS文献中心
http://www.international.icomos.org/centre_
documentation/index.html
国际自然与自然资源保护联合会（IUCN）
http://www.iucn.org
联合国环境计划署世界养护监测中心管理
世界自然遗产数据库
http://sea.unep–wcmc.org/wdbpa/
国际现代主义建筑保护与文献组织
（DOCOMOMO）
http://www.docomomo–us.org/
http://www.docomomo.nl
国际工业遗产保护委员会（TICCIH）

http://www.mnactec.com/TICCIH/
国际景观建筑师联合会

电子邮件：info@iflaonline.org
http://www.iflaonline.org/home.html

WHC.15/01

8 July 2015

WHC.15/01

2015年7月8日

联合国教科文组织

《实施〈世界遗产公约〉操作指南》(2015)

The Operational Guidelines for
the Implementation of the World Heritage Convention

UNITED NATIONS EDUCATIONAL,
SCIENTIFIC AND CULTURAL ORGANISATION

联合国教育、科学及文化组织

INTERGOVERNMENTAL COMMITTEE
FOR THE PROTECTION OF THE WORLD
CULTURAL AND NATURAL HERITAGE

保护世界文化与自然遗产的政府间委员会

WORLD HERITAGE CENTRE

世界遗产中心

The *Operational Guidelines* are periodically revised to reflect the decisions of the World Heritage Committee. Please verify that you are using the latest version of the *Operational Guidelines* by checking the date of the *Operational Guidelines* on the UNESCO World Heritage Centre Web address indicated below.

定期修订《操作指南》，体现世界遗产委员会的若干决定。请访问下面的教科文组织世界遗产中心网址，检查《操作指南》的日期，确认您使用的是最新版本。

The *Operational Guidelines* (in English and French), the text of the *World Heritage Convention* (in five languages), and other documents and information concerning World Heritage are available

可从世界遗产中心获取《操作指南》(英文和法文）、《保护世界文化与自然遗产公约》全文（五种语言）、其他世界遗产相关的文书和信息：

from the World Heritage Centre:

UNESCO World Heritage Centre	世界遗产中心
7, place de Fontenoy	（法国巴黎：7, place de Fontenoy
75352 Paris 07 SP	75352 Paris 07 SP France）

France

Tel	:	+33 (0) 1 4568 1876
Fax	:	+33 (0) 1 4568 5570
E-mail	:	wh-info@unesco.org
Links	:	http://whc.unesco.org/
		http://whc.unesco.org/en/guidelines
		(English)
		http://whc.unesco.org/fr/orientations
		(French)

电话	:	+33（0）1 4568 1876
传真	:	+33（0）1 4568 5570
E-mail	:	wh-info@unesco.org
链接	:	http://whc.unesco.org/
		http://whc.unesco.org/en/guidelines
		（英文）
		http://whc.unesco.org/fr/orientations
		（法文）

Table of Contents　　　　　　　　**目录**

Chapter number　　　　　　　　**章节**

and Programmes

Ⅱ. THE WORLD HERITAGE LIST

Ⅱ.A Definition of World Heritage

Cultural and Natural Heritage

Mixed Cultural and Natural Heritage

Cultural landscapes

Movable Heritage

Outstanding Universal Value

Ⅱ.B A Representative, Balanced and Credible World Heritage List

The Global Strategy for a Representative, Balanced and Credible World Heritage List

Other measures

Ⅱ.C Tentative Lists

Procedure and Format

Tentative Lists as a planning and evaluation tool

Assistance and Capacity-Building for States Parties in the preparation of Tentative Lists

Ⅱ.D Criteria for the assessment of Outstanding Universal Value

Ⅱ.E Integrity and/or authenticity

Authenticity

Integrity

Ⅱ.F Protection and management

Legislative, regulatory and contractual measures for protection

Boundaries for effective protection

Buffer zones

Management systems

Sustainable use

Ⅲ. PROCESS FOR THE INSCRIPTION OF PROPERTIES ON THE WORLD HERITAGE LIST

Ⅲ.A Preparation of Nominations

Ⅲ.B Format and content of nominations

1. Identification of the Property

2. Description of the Property

3. Justification for Inscription

4. State of conservation and factors affecting the property

5. Protection and Management

Ⅱ.《世界遗产名录》

Ⅱ.A 世界遗产的定义

文化和自然遗产

文化和自然混合遗产

文化景观

可移动遗产

突出普遍价值

Ⅱ.B 具有代表性、平衡性和可信性的《世界遗产名录》

构建具有代表性、平衡性、可信性的《世界遗产名录》的《全球战略》

其他措施

Ⅱ.C 《预备名录》

程序和格式

《预备名录》作为规划与评估工具

缔约国编撰《预备名录》过程中提供的协助和能力建设

Ⅱ.D 突出普遍价值的评估标准

Ⅱ.E 完整性和/或真实性

真实性

完整性

Ⅱ.F 保护和管理·

立法、规范和契约性的保护措施

确保有效保护的边界

缓冲区

管理体制

可持续使用

Ⅲ.列入《世界遗产名录》的程序

Ⅲ.A 申报准备

Ⅲ.B 申报文件的格式和内容

1.遗产的辨认

2.遗产描述

3,列入理由

4.保护状况和影响因素

5.保护和管理

other sources

Evaluation procedures of the Advisory Bodies for nominations		咨询机构对提名材料的评估程序	
Format for the Periodic Reporting on the application of the World Heritage Convention		《世界遗产公约》实施的定期报告的格式	
International Assistance Request Form		国际援助申请表	
Evaluation criteria of the Advisory Bodies for International Assistance requests		专家咨询机构评估国际援助申请的标准	
Statement of Outstanding Universal Value		突出普遍价值声明	
Modifications to World Heritage properties		对世界遗产的修改	
Form for the submission of Factual Errors in the Advisory Bodies Evaluations		咨询机构提交事实性错误格式	
Format for the submission of State of Conservation Reports by the States Parties		缔约国提交保护状况声明格式	
Table of uses of the World Heritage Emblem		世界遗产标识使用表	
Select bibliography on World Heritage		世界遗产相关的参考书目	

ACRONYMS AND ABBREVIATIONS   缩略语

DoCoMoMo	International Committee for the Documentation and Conservation of Monuments and Sites of the Modern Movement	DoCoMoMo	国际现代主义建筑、保护与记录国际委员会
ICCROM	International Centre for the Study of the Preservation and Restoration of Cultural Property	ICCROM	国际文化遗产保护与修复研究中心
ICOMOS	International Council on Monuments and Sites	ICOMOS	国际古迹遗址理事会
IFLA	International Federation of Landscape Architects	IFLA	国际景观设计师联合会
IUCN	World Conservation Union (formerly the International Union for Conservation of Nature and Natural Resources)	IUCN	世界保护自然联盟（前国际自然及自然资源保护联盟）
IUGS	International Union of Geological Sciences	IUGS	国际地质科学联合会
MAB	Man and the Biosphere programme of UNESCO	MAB	教科文组织人与生物圈方案
NGO	Non-governmental organization	NGO	非政府组织
TICCIH	International Committee for the Con-	TICCIH	国际工业遗产保护委员会

	servation of the Industrial Heritage		
UNEP	United Nations Environment Programme	UNEP	联合国环境规划署
UNEP-WCMC	World Conservation Monitoring Centre (UNEP)	UNEP-WCMC	世界保护监控中心（联合国环境规划署）
UNESCO	United Nations Educational, Scientific and Cultural Organization	UNESCO	联合国教育、科学及文化组织

Ⅰ. INTRODUCTION

1. AThe *OperationalGuidelines*

1. The *Operational Guidelines for the Implementation of the World Heritage Convention* (hereinafter referred to as the *Operational Guidelines)* aim to facilitate the implementation of the *Convention concerning the Protection of the World Cultural and Natural Heritage* (hereinafter referred to as "the *World Heritage Convention»* or" the *Convention"*), by setting forth the procedurefor:

a) the inscription of properties on the World Heritage List and the List of World Heritage inDanger;

b) the protection and conservation of World Heritageproperties;

c) the granting of International Assistance under the World Heritage Fund;and

d) the mobilization of national and international support in favor of the*Convention.*

2. The *Operational Guidelines* are periodically revised to reflect the decisions of the World Heritage Committee.

3. The key users of the *Operational Guidelines* are:

a) the States Parties to the *World Heritage Convention*;

b) the Intergovernmental Committee for the Protection of the Cultural and Natural Heritage of

1. 引言

1. A《操作指南》

1.《实施《世界遗产公约》的操作指南》（以下简称《操作指南》）旨在促进《保护世界文化和自然遗产公约》（以下简称《世界遗产公约》或《公约》）的实施，并为开展下列工作设置相应的程序：

a）将遗产列入《世界遗产名录》和《濒危世界遗产名录》

b）世界遗产的保护和保存

c）世界遗产基金项下提供的国际援助

d）调动国家和国际力量，为《公约》提供支持

2.《操作指南》将会定期修改，以反映世界遗产委员会的最新决策。

3.《操作指南》主要使用者：

a）《世界遗产公约》的缔约国；

b）保护具有突出普遍价值的文化和自然遗产政府间委员会，以下简称"世界遗产委员会"

Outstanding Universal Value, hereinafter referred to as «the World Heritage Committee» or "the Committee";

c) the UNESCO World Heritage Centre as Secretariat to the World Heritage Committee, hereinafter referred to as "the Secretariat";

d) the Advisory Bodies to the World Heritage Committee;

e) site managers, stakeholders and partners in the protection of World Heritage properties.

1. B The *World Heritage Convention*

4.　The cultural and natural heritage is among the priceless and irreplaceable assets, not only of each nation, but of humanity as a whole. The loss, through deterioration or disappearance, of any of these most prized assets constitutes an impoverishment of the heritage of all the peoples of the world. Parts of that heritage, because of their exceptional qualities, can be considered to be of "Outstanding Universal Value" and as such worthy of special protection against the dangers which increasingly threaten them.

The historical development of the Operational Guidelines is available at the following Web address:

http://whc.unesco.org/en/guidelineshistorical

5.　To ensure, as far as possible, the proper identification, protection, conservation and presentation of the world's heritage, the Member States of UNESCO adopted the *World Heritage Convention* in 1972. The *Convention* foresees the establishment of a "World Heritage Committee" and a "World Heritage Fund". Both the Committee and the Fund have been in operation since 1976.

6.　Since the adoption of the *Convention* in 1972, the international community has embraced

---

或 "委员会";

c）世界遗产委员会秘书处，即联合国教育、科学及文化组织世界遗产中心，以下简称 "秘书处";

d）世界遗产委员会的咨询机构;

e）负责保护世界遗产的遗产地管理人员、利益相关方和合作伙伴。

1.B《世界遗产公约》

4. 无论对各国还是对全人类而言，文化和自然遗产都是不可估价且无法替代的财产。这些最珍贵的财富，一旦遭受任何破坏或消失，都是对世界各族人民遗产的一次浩劫。一些遗产具有独一无二的特性，可以认为其具有 "突出的普遍价值"，需加以特殊的保护，以消除日益威胁遗产安全的各种危险。

《操作指南》的发展历程可参见以下网址：

http://whc.unesco.org/en/guidelineshistorical

5. 为了尽可能保证对世界遗产的确认、保护、保存和展示，联合国教育、科学及文化组织成员国于 1972 年通过了《世界遗产公约》。《公约》确认了世界遗产委员会和世界遗产基金的建立，二者自 1976 年开始运行。

6. 自从 1972 年通过《公约》以来，国际社会全面接受了 "可持续发展" 这一概念。而保

the concept of «sustainable development». The protection and conservation of the natural and cultural heritage are a significant contribution to sustainable development.

7. The *Convention* aims at the identification, protection, conservation, presentation and transmission to future generations of cultural and natural heritage of Outstanding Universal Value.

8. The criteria and conditions for the inscription of properties on the World Heritage List have been developed to evaluate the Outstanding Universal Value of properties and to guide States Parties in the protection and management of World Heritage properties.

9. When a property inscribed on the World Heritage List is threatened by serious and specific dangers, the Committee considers placing it on the List of World Heritage in Danger. When the Outstanding Universal Value of the property which justified its inscription on the World Heritage List is destroyed, the Committee considers deleting the property from the World Heritage List.

1.C The States Parties to the *World Heritage Convention*

10. States are encouraged to become party to the *Convention*. Model instruments for ratification/acceptance and accession are included as Annex 1. The original signed version should be sent to the Director-General of UNESCO.

11. The list of States Parties to the *Convention* is available at the following Web address:http://whc.unesco.org/en/statesparties

12. States Parties to the *Convention* are encouraged to ensure the participation of a wide variety of stakeholders, including site managers, local and regional

护、保存自然和文化遗产就是对可持续发展的巨大贡献。

7.《公约》旨在确认、保护、保存、展示具有突出普遍价值的文化和自然遗产，并将其代代相传。

8. 已制定了遗产列入《世界遗产名录》的标准和条件，以评估遗产是否具有突出普遍价值，并指导缔约国保护和管理世界遗产。

9. 当《世界遗产名录》上的某项遗产受到了严重的特殊的威胁时，委员会将考虑把该遗产列入《濒危世界遗产名录》。当该遗产藉以列入《世界遗产名录》的突出普遍价值受到破坏时，委员会将考虑把该遗产从《世界遗产名录》上删除。

1.C《世界遗产公约》缔约国

10.鼓励各个国家加入《公约》，成为缔约国。附件1收录了批准/接受公约和正式加入公约的文书范本。签署后的文书原件应呈递联合国教育、科学及文化组织总干事。

11.《公约》各缔约国名单可参见以下网址：http：//whc.unesco.org/en/statesparties

12.鼓励《公约》缔约国保证各利益相关方，包括遗产管理者、当地和地区政府、当地社区、非政府组织（NGO）、其他相关团体和合

governments, local communities, non-governmental organizations (NGOs) and other interested parties and partners in the identification, nomination and protection of World Heritage properties.

作伙伴，参与世界遗产的确认、申报和保护。

13. States Parties to the *Convention* should provide the Secretariat with the names and addresses of the governmental organization(s) primarily responsible as national focal point(s) for the implementation of the *Convention*, so that copies of all official correspondence and documents can be sent by the Secretariat to these national focal points as appropriate. A list of these addresses is available at the following Web address:http://whc.unesco.org/en/statespartiesfocalpoints

13.《公约》各缔约国应向秘书处提供作为国家实施《公约》协调中心的政府机构的名称和地址，以便秘书处发放各种官方信函和文件。这些机构的地址列表可参见以下网址：http：//whc.unesco.org/en/statespartiesfocalpoints

14. States Parties are encouraged to bring together their cultural and natural heritage experts at regular intervals to discuss the implementation of the *Convention*. States Parties may wish to involve representatives of the Advisory Bodies and other experts as appropriate.

14. 鼓励《公约》各缔约国公开以上信息并保证不断更新。鼓励各缔约国召集本国文化和自然遗产专家定期讨论《公约》的实施。各缔约国可以适当邀请咨询机构的代表和其他专家参加讨论。

15. While fully respecting the sovereignty of the States on whose territory the cultural and natural heritage is situated, States Parties to the *Convention* recognize the collective interest of the international community to cooperate in the protection of this heritage. States Parties to the *World Heritage Convention*, have the responsibility to:

15. 在充分尊重文化和自然遗产所在国主权的同时，《公约》各缔约国也应该认识到，合作开展遗产保护工作符合国际社会的共同利益。《世界遗产公约》各缔约国有责任做到以下几点：

Article 6(1) of the *World HeritageConvention*.

《世界遗产公约》第6（1）条。

a) ensure the identification, nomination, protection, conservation, presentation, and transmission to future generations of the cultural and natural heritage found within their territory, and give help in these tasks to other States Parties that request it;

a）保证在本国境内文化和自然遗产的确认、申报、保护、保存、展示以及代代相传，并在其他国家提出请求时，针对以上事宜提供帮助；

Article 4 and 6(2) of the *World HeritageConvention*.

《世界遗产公约》第4条和第6（2）条。

b) adopt general policies to give the heritage a function in the life of the community;

Article 5 of the *World Heritage Convention*.

c) integrate heritage protection into comprehensive planning programmes;

d) establish services for the protection, conservation and presentation of the heritage;

e) develop scientific and technical studies to identify actions that would counteract the dangers that threaten the heritage;

f) take appropriate legal, scientific, technical, administrative and financial measures to protect the heritage;

g) foster the establishment or development of national or regional centres for training in the protection, conservation and presentation of the heritage and encourage scientific research in the sefields;

h) not take any deliberate measures that directly or indirectly damage their heritage or that of another State Party to the *Convention*;

Article 6(3) of the *World Heritage Convention*.

i) submit to the World Heritage Committee an inventory of properties suitable for inscription on the World Heritage List (referred to as a TentativeList);

Article 11(1) of the *World Heritage Convention*.

j) make regular contributions to the World Heritage Fund, the amount of which is determined by the General Assembly of States Parties to the *Convention*;

Article 16(1) of the *World Heritage Convention*.

b）制定、通过旨在赋予文化和自然遗产合理功能，使其在社会生活中发挥一定作用的总体政策；

《世界遗产公约》第5条。

c）将遗产保护纳入综合整体规划；

d）建立负责遗产保护、保存和展示事务的机构；

e）开展科学和技术研究，找出消除对本国遗产的威胁的方法；

f）采取适当的法律、科学、技术、行政和财政措施来保护遗产；

g）促进建立或发展有关保护、保存和展示文化和自然遗产的国家或地区培训中心，并鼓励这些领域的科学研究；

h）不得故意采取任何可能直接或间接损害本国或公约其他缔约国领土内遗产的措施；

《世界遗产公约》第6（3）条。

i）向世界遗产委员会递交一份关于本国领土内适于列入《世界遗产名录》的遗产清单（称为《预备名录》）；

《世界遗产公约》第11（1）条。

j）定期向世界遗产基金缴款，缴款额由公约缔约国大会决定；

《世界遗产公约》第16（1）条。

k) consider and encourage the establishment of national, public and private foundations or associations to facilitate donations for the protection of World Heritage;

Article 17 of the World Heritage Convention.

l) give assistance to international fund-raising campaigns organized for the World Heritage Fund;

Article 18 of the World Heritage Convention.

m) use educational and information programmes to strengthen appreciation and respect by their peoples of the cultural and natural heritage defined in Articles 1 and 2 of the *Convention*, and to keep the public informed of the dangers threatening this heritage;

Article 27 ofthe World Heritage Convention.

n) provide information to the World Heritage Committee on the implementation of the *World Heritage Convention* and state of conservation of properties; and

Article 29 of the World Heritage Convention. Resolution adopted by the 11th General Assembly of States Parties (1997)

16. States Parties are encouraged to attend sessions of the World Heritage Committee and its subsidiary bodies.

Rule8.1of the Rulesof Procedure of theWorld Heritage Committee.

1.D The General Assembly of States Parties to the *World Heritage Convention*

17. The General Assembly of States Parties to the *World Heritage Convention* meets during the sessions of the General Conference of UNESCO.

k）考虑和鼓励设立国家、公立以及私立基金会或协会，促进保护世界遗产的募捐；

《世界遗产公约》第17条。

l）对世界遗产基金的国际募款活动给予协助；

《世界遗产公约》第18条。

m）通过教育和宣传活动，努力加强本国人民对公约第1和2条中所确定的文化和自然遗产的理解和尊重，并使公众广泛了解遗产面临的威胁；

《世界遗产公约》第27条。

n）向世界遗产委员会递交报告，详述《世界遗产公约》的实施情况和这类遗产保护状况；

《世界遗产公约》第29条。
1997年第十一届缔约国大会通过《决议》。

16.鼓励本公约缔约国参加世界遗产委员会及其附属机构的各届会议。

《世界遗产委员会议事规则》第8.1条。

1.D《世界遗产公约》缔约国大会

17.大会在联合国教科文组织大会常会期间召开。缔约国大会根据《议事规则》组织会议，相关内容可参见以下网址：http：//whc.unesco.

The General Assembly manages its meetings according to its Rules of Procedure, available at the following Web address:http://whc.unesco.org/en/garules

org/en/garules

Article 8(1), of the *World Heritage Convention*, Rule 49 of the Rulesof Procedure of the World Heritage Committee.

《世界遗产公约》第8（1）条，
《世界遗产委员会议事规则》第49条。

18. The General Assembly determines the uniform percentage of contributions to the World Heritage Fund applicable to all States Parties and elects members to the World Heritage Committee. Both the General Assembly and General Conference of UNESCO receive a report from the World Heritage Committee on its activities.

18.大会确定适用于所有缔约国的统一缴款比例，并选举世界遗产委员会成员。缔约国大会和联合国教科文组织大会都将收到世界遗产委员会关于各项活动的报告。

Articles 8(1), 16(1) and 29 of the *World Heritage Convention* and Rule 49 of the Rules of Procedure of the World Heritage Committee.

《世界遗产公约》第8（1）条、第16（1）条和第29条；
《世界遗产委员会议事规则》第49条。

1.E The World Heritage Committee

1.E 世界遗产委员会

19. The World Heritage Committee is composed of 21 members and meets at least once a year (June/July). It establishes its Bureau, which meets during the sessions of the Committee as frequently as deemed necessary. The composition of the Committee and its Bureau is available at the following Webaddress:

http://whc.unesco.org/en/committeemembers

19.世界遗产委员会由二十一个成员国组成，每年至少召开一次会议（六月或七月）。委员会设有主席团，在委员会常会期间召集会议，会议次数根据实际需求确定。委员会及其主席团的组成可参见以下网址：http：//whc.unesco.org/en/committeemembers

The World Heritage Committee can be contacted through its Secretariat, the World Heritage Centre.

可以通过世界遗产中心，即世界遗产委员会秘书处，与委员会取得联系。

20. The Committee manages its meetings according to its Rules of Procedure, available at the following Web address:http://whc.unesco.org/committeerules

20.世界遗产委员会根据《议事规则》召开会议，可参见以下网址：http：//whc.unesco.org/committeerules

21. The term of office of Committee members is six years but, in order to ensure equitable representation

21.世界遗产委员会成员任期六年。然而，为了保证世界遗产委员会公正的代表性和轮值

and rotation, States Parties are invited by the General Assembly to consider voluntarily reducing their term of office from six to four years and are discouraged from seeking consecutive terms of office.

Article 9(1) of the *World Heritage Convention*.

Article 8(2) of the *World Heritage Convention* and the Resolutions of the 7th (1989), 12th (1999) and 13th (2001) General Assembly of States Parties to the *World Heritage Convention*.

22. A certain number of seats may be reserved for States Parties who do not have a property on the World Heritage List, upon decision of the Committee at the session that precedes the General Assembly.

Rule 14.1 of the Rules of Procedure of the General Assembly of States Parties.

23. Committee decisions are based on objective and scientific considerations, and any appraisal made on its behalf must be thoroughly and responsibly carried out. The Committee recognizes that such decisions depend upon:

a) carefully prepared documentation;
b) thorough and consistent procedures;
c) evaluation by qualified experts;and
d) if necessary, the use of exper treferees.

24. The main functions of the Committee are, in co-operation with States Parties, to:

a) identify, on the basis of Tentative Lists and nominations submitted by States Parties, cultural and natural properties of Outstanding Universal Value which are to be protected under the *Convention* and to inscribe those properties on the World Heritage List;

Article 11(2) of the *World Heritage Convention*.

b) examine the state of conservation of properties

制，大会建议缔约国自愿考虑将任期从六年缩短到四年，并不鼓励连任。

《世界遗产公约》第9（1）条
《世界遗产公约》第8（2）条和《世界遗产公约》缔约国第七届（1989年）、第十二届（1999年）及第十三届（2001年）大会决议。

22. 根据委员会在大会前一届会议中达成的决议，为尚无遗产列入《世界遗产名录》的缔约国保留一定数量的席位。

《缔约国大会议事规则》第14.1条

23. 委员会的决定基于客观和科学的考虑，为此进行的任何评估工作都应该得到彻底和负责的贯彻。委员会认识到这类决定取决于以下几个方面：

a）认真编撰的文献资料；
b）详尽、统一的程序；
c）资深专家的评估；
d）必要时，使用专家仲裁。

24. 委员会的主要职能是与缔约国合作开展下述工作：

a）根据缔约国递交的《预备名录》和申报文件，确认将按照《公约》实施保护的具有突出普遍价值的文化和自然遗产，并把这些遗产列入《世界遗产名录》；

《世界遗产公约》第11（2）款。

b）通过反应性监测（参见第四章）和定期

inscribed on the World Heritage List through processes of Reactive Monitoring (see Chapter IV) and Periodic Reporting (see Chapter V);

报告（参见第五章）审查已经列入《世界遗产名录》的遗产的保护状况；

Articles 11(7) and 29 of the *World Heritage Convention*.

《世界遗产公约》第 11（7）条和第 29 条。

c) decide which properties inscribed on the World Heritage List are to be inscribed on, or removed from the List of World Heritage in Danger;

c）决定《世界遗产名录》中的哪些遗产应该列入《濒危世界遗产名录》或从中移除；

Article 11(4) and 11(5) of the *World Heritage Convention*.

《世界遗产公约》第 11（4）条和第 11（5）条。

d) decide whether a property should be deleted from the World Heritage List (see Chapter IV);

d）决定是否应将一项遗产从《世界遗产名录》上移除（参见第四章）；

e) define the procedure by which requests for International Assistance are to be considered and carry out studies and consultations as necessary before coming to a decision (see Chapter VII);

e）制定关于国际援助申请的审议程序，在作出决定之前，进行必要的研究和磋商（参见第七章）；

Article 21(1) and 21(3) of the *World Heritage Convention*.

《世界遗产公约》第 21（1）条和第 21（3）条。

f) determine how the resources of the World Heritage Fund can be used most advantageously to assist States Parties in the protection of their properties of Outstanding Universal Value;

f）决定如何发挥世界遗产基金资源的最大优势，帮助缔约国保护具有突出普遍价值的遗产；

Article 13(6) of the *World Heritage Convention*.

《世界遗产公约》第 13（6）条。

g) seek ways to increase the World Heritage Fund;

g）设法增加世界遗产基金的资金；

h) submit a report on its activities every two years to the General Assembly of States Parties and to the UNESCO General Conference;

h）每两年向缔约国大会和联合国教科文组织大会递交一份活动报告；

Article 29(3) of the *World Heritage Convention* and Rule 49 of the *Rules of procedure of the World HeritageCommittee*.

《世界遗产公约》第 29（3）条和《世界遗产委员会议事规则》第 49 条。

i) review and evaluate periodically the implementation of the *Convention*;

i）定期审查并评估《公约》的实施情况；

j) revise and adopt the *Operational Guidelines*.

25. In order to facilitate the implementation of the *Convention*, the Committee develops Strategic Objectives; they are periodically reviewed and revised to define the goals and objectives of the Committee to ensure that new threats placed on World Heritage are addressed effectively.

The first 'Strategic Orientations' adopted by the Committee in 1992 are contained in Annex II of document WHC-92/CONF.002/12

26. The current Strategic Objectives (also referred to as "the 5 Cs") are the following:

1. Strengthen the Credibility of the World HeritageList;

2. Ensure the effective Conservation of World Heritage Properties;

3. Promote the development of effective Capacity-building in States Parties;

4. Increase public awareness, involvement and support for World Heritage through Communication.

5. Enhance the role of Communities in the implementation of the *World Heritage Convention*.

In 2002 the World Heritage Committee revised its Strategic Objectives. The *Budapest Declaration on World Heritage* (2002) is available at the following Web address:http://whc.unesco.org/en/budapestdeclaration

Decision 31 COM 13B

1.F The Secretariat to the World Heritage Committee (World HeritageCentre)

UNESCO World Heritage Centre 7, place de Fontenoy

75352 Paris 07 SP

France

Tel: +33 (0) 1 4568 1276

E-mail: wh–info@unesco.org

www: http://whc.unesco.org/

---

j）修改并通过《操作指南》。

25. 为了促进《公约》的实施，委员会制定了战略目标，并对这些目标定期审查和修改，确保有效应对世界遗产面临的新威胁。

1992 年委员会通过的第一份《战略方向》载列于文件 WHC-92/CONF.002/12 附件II。

26. 目前的战略目标（简称为"5C"）是：

1. 提高《世界遗产名录》的可信度；

2. 保证对世界遗产的有效保护；

3. 促进各缔约国有效的能力建设；

4. 通过宣传增强大众对世界遗产的认识、参与和支持；

5. 加强社区在实施《世界遗产公约》中的作用。

2002 年世界遗产委员会修改了战略目标。《布达佩斯世界遗产宣言》（2002 年）可参见以下网址：http: //whc.unesco.org/en/budapestdeclaration

第 31 COM13B 决定

1.F 世界遗产委员会秘书处（世界遗产中心）

联合国教科文组织世界遗产中心地址：

法国巴黎（7，placede Fontenoy 75352 Paris 07 SP France）

电话：+33（0）145681571

传真：+33（0）145685570

电子邮箱：wh–info@unesco.org

网址：http: //whc.unesco.org/

27. The World Heritage Committee is assisted by a Secretariat appointed by the Director-General of UNESCO. The function of the Secretariat is currently assumed by the World Heritage Centre, established in 1992 specifically for this purpose. The Director-General designated the Director of the World Heritage Centre as Secretary to the Committee. The Secretariat assists and collaborates with the States Parties and the Advisory Bodies.The Secretariat works in close co-operation with other sectors and field offices of UNESCO.

Article 14 of the *World Heritage Convention.*

Rule 43 of Rules of Procedure of the World Heritage Committee.

Circular Letter 16 of 21 October 2003

http://whc.unesco.org/circs/circ03–16e.pdf

28. The Secretariat's main tasksare:

a) the organization of the meetings of the General Assembly and the Committee;

Article 14.2 of the *World Heritage Convention.*

b) the implementation of decisions of the World Heritage Committee and resolutions of the General Assembly and reporting to them on their execution;

Article 14.2 of the *World Heritage Convention* and the *Budapest Declaration on World Heritage* (2002)

c) the receipt, registration, checking the completeness, archiving and transmission to the relevant Advisory Bodies of nominations to the World Heritage List;

Decision 39 COM 11

d) the co-ordination of studies and activities

---

27. 由联合国教科文组织总干事指定的秘书处协助世界遗产委员会工作。1992年创建了世界遗产中心，担负秘书处的职能，联合国教科文组织总干事指派世界遗产中心主任为委员会的秘书。秘书处协助和协调缔约国和咨询机构的工作。秘书处还与联合国教科文组织的其他部门和外地办事处密切合作。

《世界遗产公约》第14条。

《世界遗产委员会议事规则》第43条。

2003年10月21日《通函16号》，可参见以下网址：

http://whc.unesco.org/circs/circ03-16e.pdf

28. 秘书处主要任务包括：

a）组织缔约国大会和世界遗产委员会的会议；

《世界遗产公约》第14.2条。

b）执行世界遗产委员会的各项决定和联合国教科文组织大会的决议，并向委员会和大会汇报执行情况；

《布达佩斯世界遗产宣言》（2002年）

c）接收、登记世界遗产申报文件，检查其完整性、存档并呈递到相关的咨询机构；

第39 COM11决议.

d）协调各项研究和活动，作为加强《世界

as part of the Global Strategy for a Representative, Balanced and Credible World Heritage List;

　　e) the organization of PeriodicReporting;

　　f) co-ordination and conduct of Reactive Monitoring, including Reactive Monitoring missions ①, as well coordination of and participation in Advisory missions②, as appropriate;

　　g) the co-ordination of International Assistance;

遗产名录》代表性、平衡性和可信性全球战略的一部分；

　　e）组织定期报告；

　　f）协调并施行反应性监测。包括派遣反应性监测工作组①，并在适当条件下协调参与咨询机构工作组②的有关工作。

　　g）协调国际援助；

---

① Reactive Monitoring missions are part of the statutory reporting by the Secretariat and the Advisory Bodies to the World Heritage Committee on the state of conservation of specific properties that are under threat (see Paragraph 169). They are requested by the World Heritage Committee to ascertain, in consultation with the State Party concerned, the condition of the property, the dangers to the property and the feasibility of adequately restoring the property or to assess progress made in implementing such corrective measures, and include a reporting back to the Committee on the findings of the mission (see Paragraph 176.e). The terms of reference of Reactive Monitoring missions are proposed by the World Heritage Centre, in line with the decision adopted by the World Heritage Committee, and consolidated in consultation with the State Party and the relevant Advisory Body(ies).The costs of the Reactive Monitoring missions are borne by the World Heritage Fund.

① 反应性监测工作组负责对处在危险状况下的特定遗产的保护状况做出评估。评估结果将作为秘书处及相关咨询机构向世界遗产委员会所递交报告的一部分（见 169 条）。反应性监测评估工作组是应世界遗产委员的要求而派遣的，它将与相关缔约国就遗产的保护状况进行磋商，意在查明遗产可能遇到的危险，并研究适当修复该遗产的可行性。同时，它还将评估相关补救措施的实施情况，并将调查结果一并反馈给委员会（见 176 条 e 部分）。反应性监测工作组的相关任务由世界遗产中心指定，须遵守世界遗产委员会所采纳各项决定，并征求缔约国及相关咨询机构的同意。反应性监测工作组在考察期间的花费由世界遗产基金承担。

② Advisory missions are not part of the strict statutory and mandatory processes, as they are voluntarily initiated by States Parties and depend on the considerations and judgement of the States Parties requesting them. Advisory missions are to be understood as missions providing expert advice to a State Party on specific matters. They can concern provision of "upstream" support and advice on identification of sites, tentative lists or nomination of sites for inscription on the World Heritage List or alternatively, they can relate to the state of conservation of properties and provide advice in evaluating possible impact of a major development project on the Outstanding Universal Value of the property, advice in the preparation/revision of a management plan, or in the progress achieved in the implementation of specific mitigation measures, etc. The terms of reference of Advisory missions are proposed by the State Party itself, and consolidated in consultation with the World Heritage Centre and the relevant Advisory Bod(ies) or other organization. The entire costs of Advisory missions are borne by the State Party inviting the mission, except where the State Party is eligible for relevant International Assistance or funding from the new budget line for Advisory missions approved by Decision 38 COM 12.

② 咨询机构工作组不是严格的法定监测程序的一部分，而是缔约国主动发起，基于申请缔约国的考虑和判断。特别咨询工作组的任务旨在就特定事务为缔约国提供专家意见和建议。具体可以涉及针对遗产识别、预备名单、申遗项目等提供"上游"支持，或者与遗产的保护状况相关，评估周边的大规模建设对遗产的突出普遍性价值所产生的影响，对管理规划的制定和修订、相关缓解措施的实施进展等提出意见。咨询机构工作组的相关任务由缔约国自身所提出，并需征得世界遗产中心、相关咨询机构以及其他相关组织的同意。咨询机构工作组在考察期间的花费由邀请方缔约国负责（除非该缔约国满足相关国际援助的条件，或者符合 38COM12 号决议通过的咨询考察新预算部分经费补助的要求）。

h) the mobilisation of extra-budgetary resources for the conservation and management of World Heritage properties;

i) the assistance to States Parties in the implementation of the Committee's programmes and projects;and

j) the promotion of World Heritage and the *Convention* through the dissemination of information to States Parties, the Advisory Bodies and the general public.

29. These activities follow the decisions and Strategic Objectives of the Committee and the resolutions of the General Assembly of the States Parties and are conducted in close co-operation with the Advisory Bodies.

1.G Advisory Bodies to the World Heritage Committee

30. The Advisory Bodies to the World Heritage Committee are ICCROM (the International Centre for the Study of the Preservation and Restoration of Cultural Property), ICOMOS (the International Council on Monuments and Sites), and IUCN - the International Union for Conservation of Nature.

Article 8.3 of the *World Heritage Convention*

31. The roles of the Advisory Bodies are to:
a) advise on the implementation of the *World Heritage Convention* in the field of their expertise;

Article 13.7 of the *World Heritage Convention*.
Decision 39 COM11

b) assist the Secretariat, in the preparation of the Committee's documentation, the agenda of its meetings and the implementation of the Committee's decisions;

h）调动预算外资金保护和管理世界遗产；

i）协助各缔约国实施委员会的方案和项目；

j）通过向缔约国、咨询机构和公众发布信息，促进世界遗产的保护和增强对《公约》的认识。

29.开展这些活动要服从于委员会的各项决定和战略目标以及缔约国大会的各项决议，并与咨询机构密切合作。

1.G世界遗产委员会咨询机构

30.世界遗产委员会的咨询机构包括：ICCROM（国际文物保护和修复研究中心）、ICOMOS（国际古迹遗址理事会）以及IUCN（世界自然保护联盟）。

《世界遗产公约》第8.3条。

31.咨询机构的角色：
a）以本领域的专业知识指导《世界遗产公约》的实施；

《世界遗产公约》第13.7条。
第39 COM1311决定

b）协助秘书处准备委员会需要的文献资料，安排会议议程以及协助委员会实施各项决定；

c) assist with the development and implementation of the Global Strategy for a Representative, Balanced and Credible World Heritage List, the Global Training Strategy, Periodic Reporting, and the strengthening of the effective use of the World Heritage Fund;

d) monitor the state of conservation of World Heritage properties (including through Reactive Monitoring missions at the request of the Committee and Advisory missions at the invitation of the States Parties) and review requests for International Assistance;

Article 14.2 of the World Heritage Convention.

e) in the case of ICOMOS and IUCN evaluate properties nominated for inscription on the World Heritage List, in consultation and dialogue with nominating States Parties, and present evaluation reports to the Committee; and

f) attend meetings of the World Heritage Committee and the Bureau in an advisory capacity.

Article 8.3 of the World Heritage Convention.

ICCROM

32. ICCROM (the International Centre for the Study of the Preservation and Restoration of Cultural Property) is an international intergovernmental organization with headquarters in Rome, Italy. Established by UNESCO in 1956, ICCROM's statutory functions are to carry out research, documentation, technical assistance, training and public awareness programmes to strengthen conservation of immovable and moveable cultural heritage.

ICCROM

Via di S. Michele, 13 I–00153 Rome, Italy Tel : +39 06 585531

Fax: +39 06 58553349

c）协助制定和实施加强《世界遗产名录》代表性、平衡性和可信性全球战略、全球培训战略、定期报告，加强世界遗产基金的有效使用；

d）对世界遗产的保护状况进行监测（包括应委员会要求派出的反应性监测及应缔约国邀请开展的咨询考察）并审核国际援助申请；

《世界遗产公约》第14.2条。

e）国际古迹遗址理事会和世界自然联盟评估申请列入《世界遗产名录》的遗产时，与申报缔约国进行协商与对话，并向委员会呈递评估报告；

f）以咨询者的身份列席世界遗产委员会及其主席团会议。

《世界遗产公约》8.3条。

国际文物保护和修复研究中心

32. ICCROM，即国际文物保护和修复研究中心，是一个国际政府间组织，总部设在意大利的罗马，由联合国教科文组织于1956年创建，根据规定，该中心的作用是开展研究、记录，提供技术援助、培训和推行增强公众意识的项目，加强对可移动和不可移动文化遗产的保护。

国际文物保护和修复研究中心地址：

意大利罗马（ViadiS. Michele，13　I-00153Rome，Italy）

电话：+39 06 585531

Email: iccrom@iccrom.org

http://www.iccrom.org/

33. The specific role of ICCROM in relation to the *Convention* includes: being the priority partner in training for cultural heritage, monitoring the state of conservation of World Heritage cultural properties, reviewing requests for International Assistance submitted by States Parties, and providing input and support for capacity-building activities.

ICOMOS

34. ICOMOS (the International Council on Monuments and Sites) is a non- governmental organization with headquarters in Paris, France. Founded in 1965, its role is to promote the application of theory, methodology and scientific techniques to the conservation of the architectural and archaeological heritage. Its work is based on the principles of the 1964 International Charter on the Conservation and Restoration of Monuments and Sites (the Venice Charter).

35. The specific role of ICOMOS in relation to the *Convention* includes: evaluation of properties nominated for inscription on the World Heritage List, monitoring the state of conservation of World Heritage cultural properties, reviewing requests for International Assistance submitted by States Parties, and providing input and support for capacity-building activities.

ICOMOS

11 rue du S é minaire de Conflans

94220 Charenton–le–Pont France

Tel:+33(0)141941759

Fax:+33(0)148931916

传真：+39 06 5855 3349

电子邮箱：iccrom@iccrom.org

网址：http：//www.iccrom.org/

33.国际文物保护和修复研究中心和《公约》相关的特殊职责包括：文化遗产培训领域的重要合作伙伴、监督世界文化遗产保护状况、审查由缔约国提交的国际援助申请，以及为能力建设活动提供支持。

国际古迹遗址理事会

34.ICOMOS，即国际古迹遗址理事会，是一个非政府组织，总部在法国巴黎，创建于1965年。理事会的作用在于推广建筑和考古遗产保护理论、方法和科学技术的应用。理事会的工作以1964年《国际古迹遗址保护和修复宪章》（又称《威尼斯宪章》）的原则为基准。

35.国际古迹遗址理事会和《公约》相关的特殊职责包括：评估申报世界遗产的项目，监测世界文化遗产保护状况，审查由缔约国提交的国际援助申请，以及为能力建设活动出力献策和提供支持。

国际古迹遗址理事会法国巴黎（11ruedu Séminaire de Conflans

94220 Charenton-le-Pont France）

电话：+33（0）141941759

传真：+33（0）148931916

E–mail: secretariat@icomos.org

http://www.icomos.org/

IUCN

36. IUCN – The International Union for Conservation of Nature was founded in 1948 and brings together national governments, NGOs, and scientists in a worldwide partnership. Its mission is to influence, encourage and assist societies throughout the world to conserve the integrity and diversity of nature and to ensure that any use of natural resources is equitable and ecologically sustainable. IUCN has its headquarters in Gland, Switzerland.

37. The specific role of IUCN in relation to the *Convention* includes: evaluation of properties nominated for inscription on the World Heritage List, monitoring the state of conservation of World Heritage natural properties, reviewing requests for International Assistance submitted by States Parties, and providing input and support for capacity-building activities.

IUCN – The International Union for Conservation of Nature

rue Mauverney 28

CH–1196 Gland, Switzerland

Tel:+41229990001

Fax: +41 22 9990010

E–Mail: mail@hq.iucn.org

http://www.iucn.org

1.H Other organizations

38. The Committee may call on other inter-national and non-governmental organizations with appropriate competence and expertise to assist in the implementation of the programmes and projects, including for Reactive Monitoring missions.

世界自然保护联盟

36. IUCN，即世界自然保护联盟（前身是国际自然和自然资源保护联盟），创建于 1948 年，为各国政府、非政府组织和科学工作者在世界范围的合作提供了平台。其使命在于影响、鼓励和协助世界各团体保护自然的完整性和多样化，并确保任何对自然资源的使用都是公平的、并符合生态的可持续发展。世界自然保护联盟总部设在瑞士格朗德。

37. 世界自然保护联盟和《公约》相关的特殊职责包括：评估申报世界遗产的项目、监测世界自然遗产保护状况、审查由缔约国提交的国际援助申请，以及为能力建设活动出力献策并提供支持。

IUCN——世界自然保护联盟

地址：瑞士格兰德（rue Mauverney 28 CH-1196 Gland, Switzerland）

电话：+ 41 22 999 0001

传真：+41 22 999 0010

电子邮箱：mail@hq.iucn.org

网址：http://www.iucn.org

1.H 其他组织

38. 委员会可能号召其他具有一定能力和专业技术的国际组织和非政府组织协助各方案和项目的实施（包括反应性监测）。

Decision 39. COM. 11

第39COM11决议

1.I Partners in the protection of World Heritage

1.I 保护世界遗产的合作伙伴

39. A partnership approach to nomination, management and monitoring provides a significant contribution to the protection of World Heritage properties and the implementation of the *Convention*.

39.在申报、管理和监测工作中采用合作伙伴方式，有力地促进了世界遗产的保护和《公约》的实施。

40. Partners in the protection and conservation of World Heritage can be those individuals and other stakeholders, especially local communities, indigenous peoples, governmental, non-governmental and private organizations and owners who have an interest and involvement in the conservation and management of a World Heritage property.

40.保护和保存世界遗产的合作伙伴包括：个人和其他利益相关方，尤其是对世界遗产的保护和管理感兴趣并参与其中的当地社区、原住民族、政府组织、非政府组织和私人组织以及产权人。

The Declaration on the Rights of Indigenous Peoples (2007)

Decision 39 COM 11

联合国原住民权利宣言（2007）

第39COM11决议

1.J Other Conventions, Recommendations and Programmes

1.J 其他公约、建议和方案

41. The World Heritage Committee recognizes the benefits of closer co-ordination of its work with other UNESCO programmes and their relevant *Convention*s. For a list of relevant global conservation instruments, *Convention*s and programmes see paragraph 44.

41.世界遗产委员会认识到，密切协调好与教科文组织其他计划和相关公约的关系受益匪浅。下文第44条中列举了相关的全球文件、公约和方案。

42. The World Heritage Committee with the support of the Secretariat will ensure appropriate co-ordination and information-sharing between the *World Heritage Convention* and other Conventions, programmes and international organizations related to the conservation of cultural and natural heritage.

42.在秘书处的支持下，世界遗产委员会将保证《世界遗产公约》和保护文化和自然遗产有关的其他公约、项目以及国际组织之间适当协调工作，信息共享。

43. The Committee may invite representatives of the intergovernmental bodies under related

43.委员会可能邀请相关公约下政府间组织的代表作为观察员，参加委员会的会议。如受

*Convention*s to attend its meetings as observers. It may appoint a representative to observe meetings of the other intergovernmental bodies upon receipt of aninvitation.

到其他政府间组织的邀请，委员会可派遣代表作为观察员列席会议。

44. Selected global *Convention*s and programmes relating to the protection of cultural and natural heritage

44. 与保护文化和自然遗产相关的部分全球公约和方案

Decision 39 COM 11

第39COM11决议

UNESCO *Convention*s and Programmes
Convention for the Protection of Cultural Property in the Event of Armed Conflict (1954)
Protocol I (1954)
Protocol II (1999)
http://www.unesco.org/culture/laws/hague/html_eng/page1.shtml

联合国教科文组织公约和方案
《关于在武装冲突的情况下保护文化遗产的公约》(1954年)
第一议定书（1954年）
第二议定（1999年）
http：//www.unesco.org/culture/laws/hague/html_eng/page1.shtml

Convention on the Means of Prohibiting and Preventing the Illicit Import, Export and Transfer of Ownership of Cultural Property (1970) http://www.unes co.org/culture/laws/1970/html_eng/page1.shtml

《关于采取措施禁止并防止文化遗产非法进出口和所有权非法转让公约》
（1970 年）http：//www.unesco.org/culture/laws/1970/html_eng/page1.shtml

Convention concerning the Protection of the World Cultural and Natural Heritage (1972)
http://www.unesco.org/whc/world_he.htm

《保护世界文化和自然遗产公约》(1972 年)

http：//www.unesco.org/whc/world_he.htm

Convention on the Protection of the Underwater Cultural Heritage (2001)
http://www.unesco.org/culture/laws/underwater/html_eng/ *Convention*.shtml

《保护水下文化遗产公约》(2001 年)

http：//www.unesco.org/culture/laws/underwater/html_eng/convention.shtml

Convention for the Safeguarding of the Intangible Cultural Heritage (2003)
http://unesdoc.unesco.org/images/0013/001325/132540e.pdf

《保护非物质文化遗产公约》(2003年)

http：//unesdoc.unesco.org/images/0013/001325/132540e.pdf

Man and the Biosphere (MAB) Programme

"人类和生物圈"计划(MAB)

http://www.unesco.org/mab/

http：//www.unesco.org/mab/

Convention on the Protection and Promotion of the Diversity of Cultural Expressions 2005
http://unesdoc.unesco.org/images/0014/001429/142919e.pdf

《保护和促进文化表达多样性公约》（2005年）

http：//unesdoc.unesco.org/images/0014/001429/142919e.pdf

Other Conventions

其他公约

Convention on Wetlands of International Importance especially as Waterfowl Habitat (Ramsar) (1971)
http://www.ramsar.org/key_conv_e.htm

《关于国际重要湿地特别是水禽栖息地的公约（拉姆萨尔公约）》（1971年）

http：//www.ramsar.org/key_conv_e.htm

Convention on International Trade in Endangered Species of Wild Fauna and Flora (CITES) (1973)
http://www.cites.org/eng/disc/text.shtml

《濒危野生动植物物种国际贸易公约》（CITES）（1973年）

http：//www.cites.org/eng/disc/text.shtml

Convention on the Conservation of Migratory Species of Wild Animals (CMS) (1979)
http://www.unep-wcmc.org/cms/cms_conv.htm

《野生迁徙类动物物种保护公约》（CMS）（1979年）
http：//www.unep-wcmc.org/cms/cms_conv.htm

United Nations *Convention* on the Law of the Sea (UNCLOS) (1982)http://www.un.org/Depts/los/*Convention*_agreements/texts/unclos/closindx.htm

《联合国海洋法公约》（UNCLOS）（1982年）http：//www.un.org/Depts/los/convention_agreements/texts/unclos/closindx.htm

Convention on Biological Diversity (1992)
http://www.biodiv.org/ *Convention*/articles.asp

《生物多样性公约》（1992年）http：//www.biodiv.org/convention/articles.asp

UNIDROIT *Convention* on Stolen or Illegally Exported Cultural Objects (Rome, 1995)
http://www.unidroit.org/english/ *Convention*s/culturalproperty/c-cult.htm

《国际统一私法协会关于被盗或非法出口文物的公约》（罗马，1995）

http：//www.unidroit.org/english/conventions/culturalproperty/c-cult.htm

United Nations Framework Convention on Climate Change (New York, 1992)
http://unfccc.int/essential_background/*Convention*/background/items/1350.php

《联合国气候变化框架公约》（纽约，1992年）

http：//unfccc.int/essential_background/convention/background/items/1350.php

Ⅱ. THE WORLD HERITAGE LIST

Ⅱ.A Definition of World Heritage

Cultural and Natural Heritage

45. Cultural and natural heritage are defined in Articles 1 and 2 of the *World Heritage Convention*.

Article 1

For the purposes of this Convention, the following shall be considered as "cultural heritage";

- monuments: architectural works, works of monumental sculpture and painting, elements or structures of an archaeological nature, inscriptions, cave dwellings and combinations of features, which are of Outstanding Universal Value from the point of view of history, art or science;

- groups of buildings: groups of separate or connected buildings which, because of their architecture, their homogeneity or their place in the landscape, are of Outstanding Universal Value from the point of view of history, art or science;

- sites: works of man or the combined works of nature and of man, and areas including archaeological sites which are of Outstanding Universal Value from the historical, aesthetic, ethnological or anthropological points of view.

Article 2

For the purposes of this Convention, the following shall be considered as "natural heritage":

- natural features consisting of physical and biological formations or groups of such formations, which are of Outstanding Universal Value from the aesthetic or scientific point of view;

geological and physiographical formations and precisely delineated areas which constitute the habitat of threatened species of animals and plants of Outstanding Universal Value from the point of

Ⅱ.《世界遗产名录》

Ⅱ.A 世界遗产的定义

文化和自然遗产

45. 文化和自然遗产的定义见《世界遗产公约》第1条和第2条。

第1条

在本公约中，以下各项为"文化遗产"：

—文物：从历史、艺术或科学角度看，具有突出的普遍价值的建筑物、碑雕和碑画、具有考古性质成份或结构、铭文、窟洞以及联合体；

—建筑群：从历史、艺术或科学角度看在建筑式样、分布均匀或与环境景色结合方面具有突出的普遍价值的单立或连接的建筑群；

—遗址：从历史、审美、人种学或人类学角度看，具有突出的普遍价值的人类工程或自然与人联合工程以及考古遗址等地方。

第2条

在本公约中，以下各项为"自然遗产"：.

—从审美或科学角度看，具有突出的普遍价值的由物质和生物结构或这类结构群组成的自然面貌；

—从科学或保护角度看，具有突出的普遍价值的地质和自然地理结构以及明确划为受威胁的动物和植物栖息地；

view of science or conservation;

- natural sites or precisely delineated natural areas of Outstanding Universal Value from the point of view of science, conservation or natural beauty.

—从科学、保护或自然美角度看，具有突出普遍价值的天然名胜、或明确划分的自然区域。

Mixed Cultural and Natural Heritage

文化和自然混合遗产

46. Properties shall be considered as «mixed cultural and natural heritage» if they satisfy a part or the whole of the definitions of both cultural and natural heritage laid out in Articles 1and 2 of the *Convention*.

46. 只有同时部分满足或完全满足《公约》第1条和第2条关于文化和自然遗产定义的遗产，才能认为是"文化和自然混合遗产"。

Cultural landscapes

文化景观

47. Cultural landscapes are cultural properties and represent the "combined works of nature and of man" designated in Article 1 of the *Convention*. They are illustrative of the evolution of human society and settlement over time, under the influence of the physical constraints and/or opportunities presented by their natural environment and of successive social, economic and cultural forces, both external and internal.

47.《公约》第1条指出文化景观属于文化遗产，代表着"自然与人的共同作品"。它们反映了因物质条件的限制和／或自然环境带来的机遇，在一系列社会、经济和文化因素的内外作用下，人类社会和定居地的历史沿革。

Annex 3

见附件3

Movable Heritage

可移动遗产

48. Nominations of immovable heritage which are likely to become movable will not be considered.

48. 对于可能发生迁移的不可移动遗产的申报将不作考虑。

Outstanding Universal Value

突出普遍价值

49. Outstanding Universal Value means cultural and/or natural significance which is so exceptional as to transcend national boundaries and to be of common importance for present and future generations of all humanity. As such, the permanent protection of this heritage is of the

49. 突出普遍价值指罕见的、超越了国家界限的、对全人类的现在和未来均具有普遍的重要意义的文化和／或自然价值。因此，该项遗产的永久性保护，对整个国际社会都具有至高的重要性。世界遗产委员会规定了遗产列入《世界遗产名录》的标准。

highest importance to the international community as a whole. The Committee defines the criteria for the inscription of properties on the World Heritage List.

50. States Parties are invited to submit nominations of properties of cultural and/or natural value considered to be of "Outstanding Universal Value" for inscription on the World Heritage List.

51. At the time of inscription of a property on the World Heritage List, the Committee adopts a Statement of Outstanding Universal Value (see paragraph 154) which will be the key reference for the future effective protection and management of the property.

52. The *Convention* is not intended to ensure the protection of all properties of great interest, importance or value, but only for a select list of the most outstanding of these from an international viewpoint. It is not to be assumed that a property of national and/or regional importance will automatically be inscribed on the World Heritage List.

53. Nominations presented to the Committee shall demonstrate the full commitment of the State Party to preserve the heritage concerned, within its means. Such commitment shall take the form of appropriate policy, legal, scientific, technical, administrative and financial measures adopted and proposed to protect the property and its Outstanding Universal Value.

Ⅱ.B A Representative, Balanced and Credible World Heritage List

54. The Committee seeks to establish a representative, balanced and credible World Heritage List in conformity with the four Strategic Objectives

50. 邀请缔约国申报认为具有"突出普遍价值"的文化和 /或自然遗产，以列入《世界遗产名录》。

51. 遗产列入《世界遗产名录》时，世界遗产委员会会通过一个《突出普遍价值声明》（见第 154 段），该声明将是以后遗产有效保护与管理的重要参考文书。

52. 该《公约》不是旨在保护所有具有重大意义或价值的遗产，而是只保护那些从国际观点看具有最突出价值的遗产。不应该认为某项具有国家和/ 或区域重要性的遗产会自动列入《世界遗产名录》。

53. 呈递给委员会的申报文件，应该表明该缔约国在其力所能及的范围内将全力保存该项遗产。这种承诺应该体现在采纳和提出合适的政策、法律、科学、技术、管理和财政措施，保护该项遗产以及遗产的突出的普遍价值。

Ⅱ.B 具有代表性、平衡性和可信性的《世界遗产名录》

54. 委员会根据第 26 届会议确定的四个战略目标，致力于构建一个具有代表性、平衡性和可信性的《世界遗产名录》。（布达佩斯，2002 ）

adopted by the Committee at its 26th session (Budapest, 2002).

Budapest Declaration on World Heritage (2002) athttp://whc. unesco.org/en/budapestdeclaration

《布达佩斯世界遗产宣言》见：http：//whc.unesco.org/en/budapestdeclaration

The Global Strategy for a Representative, Balanced and Credible World Heritage List

构建具有代表性、平衡性、可信性的《世界遗产名录》的《全球战略》

55. The Global Strategy for a Representative, Balanced and Credible World Heritage List is designed to identify and fill the major gaps in the World Heritage List. It does this by encouraging more countries to become States Parties to the *Convention* and to develop Tentative Lists as defined in paragraph 62 and nominations of properties for inscription on the World Heritage List.

(see http://whc.unesco.org/en/globalstrategy)

55. 构建具有代表性、平衡性、可信性的《世界遗产名录》的《全球战略》，旨在确定并填补《世界遗产名录》的主要空白。该战略鼓励更多的国家加入《保护世界文化与自然遗产公约》，按第 62 条的定义编撰《预备名录》、准备《世界遗产名录》的申报文件。

（详见：http：//whc.unesco.org/en/globalstrategy）

The report of the Expert Meeting on the «Global Strategy» and thematic studies for a representative World Heritage List (20-22 June 1994) was adopted by the World Heritage Committee at its 18th session (Phuket, 1994).

关于"全球战略"的专家会议报告及构建具有代表性的世界遗产名录的主题研究报告（1994年6月20–22日）在世界遗产委员会第18届大会通过（福克，1994）。

The Global Strategy was initially developed with reference to cultural heritage. At the request of the World Heritage Committee, the Global Strategy was subsequently expanded to also include reference to natural heritage and combined cultural and natural heritage.

《全球战略》起初是为保护文化遗产提出的。应世界遗产委员会的要求，《全球战略》随后有所扩展，包括自然遗产和文化自然混合遗产。

56. States Parties and the Advisory Bodies are encouraged to participate in the implementation of the Global Strategy in co-operation with the Secretariat and other partners. Regional and thematic Global Strategy meetings and comparative and thematic studies are organized for this purpose. The results of these meetings and studies are available to assist States Parties in preparing Tentative Lists and nominations. The reports of the expert meetings and studies presented to the

56. 鼓励各缔约国和咨询团体、秘书处及其他合作方合作，参与实施《全球战略》。为此，组织召开了区域及"全球战略"主题会议，并开展对比研究及主题研究。会议和研究成果将有助于缔约国编撰《预备名录》和申报材料。可访问网站：http：//whc.unesco.org/en/globalstrategy，查阅提交给世界遗产委员会的专家会议报告和研究报告。

World Heritage Committee are available at the following Web address:http://whc.unesco.org/en/globalstrategy.

57. All efforts should be made to maintain a reasonable balance between cultural and natural heritage on the World Heritage List.

58. No formal limit is imposed on the total number of properties to be inscribed on the World Heritage List.

Other measures

59. To promote the establishment of a representative, balanced and credible World Heritage List, States Parties are requested to consider whether their heritage is already well represented on the List and if so to slow down their rate of submission of further nominations by:

Resolution adopted by the 12th General Assembly of States Parties (1999).

a) spacing voluntarily their nominations according to conditions that they will define, and/or;

b) proposing only properties falling into categories still under-represented, and/or;

c) linking each of their nominations with a nomination presented by a State Party whose heritage is under-represented; or

d) deciding, on a voluntary basis, to suspend the presentation of new nominations.

60. States Parties whose heritage of Outstanding Universal Value is under-represented on the World Heritage List are requested to:

Resolution adopted by the 12th General Assembly of States Parties (1999).

57. 应不遗余力地保持《世界遗产名录》内文化和自然遗产的合理平衡。

58. 《世界遗产名录》上的遗产总数没有正式限制。

其他措施

59. 要构建具有代表性、平衡性、可信性的《世界遗产名录》，缔约国须考虑其遗产是否已在遗产名录上得到充分的代表。如果是，就要采取以下措施，减缓新的申报：

缔约国第 12 届会议通过的决议（1999 年）。

a）依据自身情况，自主增大申报间隔，和 / 或；

b）只申报《世界遗产名录》内代表性不足的类别的遗产，和 / 或；

c）每次申报都与《世界遗产名录》内代表性不足的缔约国的申报联系起来，或；

d）自主决定暂停提交新的申报。

60. 如果缔约国的遗产具有突出普遍价值，且在《世界遗产名录》上代表性不足，应：

缔约国第 12 届会议通过的决议（1999 年）。

a) give priority to the preparation of their Tentative Lists and nominations;

b) initiate and consolidate partnerships at the regional level based on the exchange of technical expertise;

c) encourage bilateral and multilateral co-operation so as to increase their expertise and the technical capacities of institutions in charge of the protection, safeguarding and management of their heritage; and,

d) participate, as much as possible, in the sessions of the World Heritage Committee.

61. The Committee has decided to apply the following mechanism:

a) examine up to two complete nominations per State Party, provided that at least one of such nominations concerns a natural property or a cultural landscape and,

b) set at 45 the annual limit on the number of nominations it will review, inclusive of nominations deferred and referred by previous sessions of the Committee, extensions (except minor modifications of limits of the property), transboundary and serial nominations,

c) the following order of priorities will be applied in case the overall annual limit of 45 nominations is exceeded:

i) nominations of properties submitted by States Parties with no properties inscribed on the List;

ii) nominations of properties submitted by States Parties having up to 3 properties inscribed on the List,

iii) nominations of properties that have been previously excluded due to the annual limit of 45 nominations and the application of these priorities,

iv) nominations of properties for natural heritage,

v) nominations of properties for mixed heritage,

vi) nominations of transboundary/transnational

a）优先考虑编制《预备名录》和申报材料；

b）在所属区域内，寻求技术交流伙伴并巩固这种合作关系；

c）鼓励双边和多边合作以增强缔约国负责遗产保护、保存和管理机构的专业技能。

d）尽可能参加世界遗产委员会的各届会议。

61.委员会决定使用以下机制：

a）最多审查同一个缔约国的两项完整申报，其中至少有一项需与自然遗产或文化景观有关。

b）确定委员会每年审查的申报数目不超过45个，其中包括往届会议重报的项目、补报的项目、扩展项目（遗产边界的细微调整除外）、跨境项目和系列申报项目，

c）当申报项目超出每年限定的45个时，审查的优先顺序如下：

i）尚无遗产列入《世界遗产名录》的缔约国提交的遗产申报；

ii）仅有三项及以下遗产列入《世界遗产名录》的缔约国提交的遗产申报；

iii）由于每年申报数目限制未能处理的遗产申报；

iv）自然遗产申报；

v）混合遗产申报；

vi）跨境或跨国遗产申报；

properties,

vii)nominations from States Parties in Africa, the Pacific and the Caribbean,

> Decisions 24 COM Ⅵ.2.3.3,
> 28 COM 13.1and 7 EXT.COM4B.1
> 29 COM 18A 31 COM 10
> 35 COM 8B.61

viii) nominations of properties submitted by States Parties having ratified the *World Heritage Convention* during the last ten years,

ix) nominations of properties submitted by States Parties that have not submitted nominations for ten years ormore,

x) when applying this priority system, date of receipt of full and complete nominations by the World Heritage Centre shall be used as a secondary factor to determine the priority between those nominations that would not be designated by the previous points.

d) the States Parties co-authors of a transboundary or transnational serial nomination can choose, amongst themselves and with a common understanding, the State Party which will be bearing this nomination; and this nomination can be registered exclusively within the ceiling of the bearing State Party.

The impact of this decision will be evaluated at the Committee's 39th session (2015). This paragraph takes effect on 2 February 2012, in order to ensureas moothtransitionperiodforallStatesParties.

Ⅱ.C Tentative Lists

Procedure and Format

62. A Tentative List is an inventory of those properties situated on its territory which each State Party considers suitable for nomination to the

---

vii）非洲、太平洋和加勒比地区缔约国的遗产申报；

> 第24COM Ⅵ.2.3.3号决定、
> 第28COM13.1号决定、第7EXT.COM4B.1号决定、
> 第29 COM18A号决定以及第31 COM10决定

viii）最近十年加入《世界遗产公约》的缔约国的遗产申报；

ix）最近十年或十年以上时间没有提交过申报的缔约国的遗产申报；

x）采用该优先机制时，若使用上述条件均无法确定申报的优先顺序时，则世界遗产中心收到完整申报材料的日期，将被作为次要因素来决定它们的优先权；

d）联合编写跨境或跨国系列申报文本的缔约国，可以在达成共识的基础上决定提交申报的缔约国；该申报仅占用申报国的名额。

委员会第39届会议（2015年）评估该决定的影响。本段内容自2012年2月2日生效，以确保所有缔约国有一个平缓过渡期。

Ⅱ.C《预备名录》

程序和格式

62.《预备名录》是缔约国认为其境内具备列入世界遗产名录资格的遗产的详细目录，其中包括那些他们认为具有潜在突出普遍价值的

World Heritage List. States Parties should therefore include, in their Tentative Lists, details of those properties which they consider to be of potential Outstanding Universal Value and which they intend to nominate during the following years.

Articles 1,2 and 11(1) of the *World Heritage Convention.*
Decision 39 COM 11

63. Nominations to the World Heritage List are not considered unless the nominated property has already been included on the State Party's Tentative List.

Decision 24COM para. VI.2.3.2

64. States Parties are encouraged to prepare their Tentative Lists with the participation of a wide variety of stakeholders, including site managers, local and regional governments, local communities, NGOs and other interested parties and partners.

65. States Parties shall submit Tentative Lists to the Secretariat, at least one year prior to the submission of any nomination. States Parties are encouraged to re-examine and re-submit their Tentative List at least every ten years.

66. States Parties are requested to submit their Tentative Lists in English or French using the standard formats in Annex 2A and Annex 2B (for transnational and transboundary future nominations), containing the name of the properties, their geographical location, a brief description of the properties, and justification of their Outstanding Universal Value.

Decision 39. COM 11.

67. The original duly signed version of the completed Tentative List shall be submitted by the

遗产，以及今后几年内要申报的遗产详情。

《保护世界文化与自然遗产公约》第1、2及11（1）条规定。
第39 COM 11决定

63. 如果缔约国提交申报的遗产未曾列入该国的《预备名录》，委员会将不予考虑。

第24COM VI.2.3.2号决定

64. 鼓励缔约国在各利益相关者、遗产地管理人员、当地和地区政府、社区、非政府组织以及其他相关机构广泛参与基础上，编制其《预备名录》。

65. 建立相应机制，以鼓励不同合作伙伴和利益相关者参与和协调各种活动.委员会鼓励缔约国至少每十年重新审查和递交其《预备名录》。

66. 缔约国需要采用附件 2A 及附件 2B（用于未来跨国及跨境遗产的申报）所示的标准格式，递交英文或法语的《预备名录》，包括遗产名称、地理位置、简短描述以及其具有的突出普遍价值的陈述。

第39 COM. 11诀议.

67. 缔约国应将已签名的完整《预备名录》原件递交至：联合国教科文组织世界遗产中心

State Party,to: UNESCO World Heritage Centre 7, place de Fontenoy 75352 Paris 07 SP France:

Tel: +33 (0) 1 4568 1136

E-mail: wh-tentativelists@unesco.org

68. Upon reception of the Tentative Lists from the States Parties, the World Heritage Centre checks for compliance of the documentation with Annex 2. If the documentation is not considered in compliance with Annex 2, the World Heritage Centre refers it back to the State Party. When all information has been provided, the Tentative List is registered by the Secretariat and transmitted to the relevant Advisory Bodies for information. A summary of all Tentative Lists is presented annually to the Committee. The Secretariat, in consultation with the States Parties concerned, updates its records, in particular by removing from the Tentative Lists the inscribed properties and nominated properties which were not inscribed.

Decision 7 EXT.COM 4A

69. The Tentative Lists of States Parties are available at the following Web address: http://whc.unesco.org/en/tentativelists

Decision 27 COM 8A

Tentative Lists as a planning and evaluation tool

70. Tentative Lists are a useful and important planning tool for States Parties, the World Heritage Committee, the Secretariat, and the Advisory Bodies, as they provide an indication of future nominations.

71. Tentative Lists should be drawn selectively and on the basis of evidence that supports potential

法国巴黎（7，placede Fontenoy，Paris 07 SP）

电话：+33（0）1 4568 1136

电邮：wh-tentativelists@unesco.org

68. 收到缔约国提交的《预备名录》后，世界遗产中心将检查文件是否符合附件2的要求，如认为不符合，会将文件退回缔约国。如果所有信息均已提供，秘书处会将《预备名录》登记并转呈给相关咨询机构。每年都要向委员会递交所有《预备名录》的概要。秘书处与相关缔约国协商，更新其记录，将《预备名录》上已列入《世界遗产名录》和已否决列入的遗产移除。

第 7EXT.COM 4A 号决定

69. 登录 http://whc.unesco.org/en/tentativelists，查阅缔约国《预备名录》。

第 27COM8A 号决定

《预备名录》作为规划与评估工具

70.《预备名录》提供未来遗产名录申报信息，是对缔约国、世界遗产委员会、秘书处及咨询机构工作有帮助的重要规划工具。

71. 要有针对性的筛选《预备名单》，并以满足潜在的突出普遍性价值为基础。鼓励缔约

Outstanding Universal Value. States Parties are encouraged to consult the analyses of both the World Heritage List and Tentative Lists prepared at the request of the Committee by ICOMOS and IUCN to identify the gaps in the World Heritage List. These analyses could enable States Parties to compare themes, regions, geo-cultural groupings and bio-geographic provinces for prospective World Heritage properties. States Parties are encouraged to seek as early as possible upstream advice from the Advisory Bodiesduring the development of their Tentative Lists as appropriate.

Decision 24 COM para. Ⅵ.2.3.2(ii)
Decision 39 COM 11 Documents WHC- 04/28.COM/13.B I and IIhttp://whc.unesco.org/archive/2004/whc04-28com-13b1e.pdf and http://whc.unesco.org/archive/2004/whc04-28com-13b2e.pdf
Decision 39 COM 11

72. In addition, States Parties are encouraged to consult the specific thematic studies carried out by the Advisory Bodies (see paragraph 147). These studies are informed by a review of the Tentative Lists submitted by States Parties and by reports of meetings on the harmonization of Tentative Lists, as well as by other technical studies performed by the Advisory Bodies and qualified organizations and individuals. A list of those studies already completed is available at the following Web address: http://whc.unesco.org/en/globalstrategy

Thematic studies are different than the comparative analysis to be prepared by States Parties when nominating properties for inscription in the World Heritage List (see paragraph 132).

73. States Parties are encouraged to harmonize their Tentative Lists at regional and thematic levels. Harmonization of Tentative Lists is the process whereby States Parties, with the assistance of the

国参考国际古迹遗址理事会（ICOMOS）和世界自然保护联盟（IUCN）应委员会要求编制的《世界遗产名录》和《预备名录》分析报告，确定《世界遗产名录》上的缺项和空白。这些分析使缔约国能够通过比较主题、区域、地理文化群和生物地理区，来更好地确定未来的世界遗产。鼓励缔约国在编制准备《预备名录》过程中尽早地征求咨询机构的上游建议。

第24COM号决定第Ⅵ.2.3.2（ii）段文书
WHC-04/28.COM/13.B 1 和 2
详见：http://whc.unesco.org/archive/2004/whc04-13b1e.pdf 和 http://whc.unesco.org/archive/2004/ whc04-28com-13b2e.pdf

第39 COM 11诀议

72. 另外，鼓励缔约国参考由咨询机构完成的具体主题研究报告（见147条）。这些研究评估了缔约国提交的《预备名录》、参考了《预备名录》协调会议报告、咨询团体以及其他具有资格的团体和个人的相关技术研究。已完成的研究报告列表详见：http://whc.unesco.org/en/globalstrategy

主题研究报告异于缔约国申报遗产列入《世界遗产名录》时编撰的比较分析（见第132段）。

73. 鼓励缔约国在区域和主题上协调《预备名录》。在这个过程中，缔约国在咨询团体的协助下，共同评估各自的《预备名录》，审查缺项并确认相同主题。通过协调，《预备名录》将得

Advisory Bodies, collectively assess their respective Tentative List to review gaps and identify common themes. The outcome of harmonization can result in improved Tentative Lists, new nominations from States Parties and co-operation amongst groups of States Parties in the preparation of nominations.

以改进，缔约国也可以更好地申报新遗产，和与其他缔约国合作申报。

Assistance and Capacity-Building for States Parties in the preparation of Tentative Lists

缔约国编撰《预备名录》过程中提供的协助和能力建设

74. To implement the Global Strategy, cooperative efforts in capacity-building and training may be necessary to assist States Parties to acquire and/or consolidate their expertise in the preparation, updating and harmonisation of their Tentative List and the preparation of nominations.

74. 要实施《全球战略》，就有必要共同致力于协助缔约国进行能力建设和培训，获取和 / 或增强编制、更新和平衡《预备名录》及准备申报材料的能力。

75. International Assistance may be requested by States Parties for the purpose of preparing, updating and harmonizing Tentative Lists (see Chapter VII).

75. 在编制、更新和协调《预备名录》方面，缔约国可以请求国际援助（见第七章）。

76. The Advisory Bodies and the Secretariat will use the opportunity of evaluation missions to hold regional training workshops to assist under-represented States in the methods of preparation of their Tentative List and nominations.

76. 咨询机构和秘书处可在考察评估期间举办地区培训班，对《世界遗产名录》中遗产代表性不足的国家，在准备《预备名录》和申报方面提供帮助。

Decision 24COM VI.2.3.5(ii)

第 24COM VI.2.3.5 号决定

II.D Criteria for the assessment of Outstanding Universal Value

II.D 突出的普遍价值的评估标准

These criteria were formerly presented as two separate sets of criteria – criteria (i) – (vi) for cultural heritage and (i) – (iv) for natural heritage.
The 6th extraordinary session of the World Heritage Committee decided to merge the ten criteria (Decision 6 EXT.COM 5.1)

这些标准起初分为两组，标准（i）至（vi）适用于文化遗产，标准（i）至（iv）适用于自然遗产。

世界遗产委员会第 6 届特别会议决定将这十个标准合起来（第 6EXT.COM5.1 号决定）

77. The Committee considers a property as

77. 如果遗产符合下列一项或多项标准，委

having Outstanding Universal Value (see paragraphs 49-53) if the property meets one or more of the following criteria. Nominated properties shall therefore:

(i) represent a masterpiece of human creative genius;

(ii) exhibit an important interchange of human values, over a span of time or within a cultural area of the world, on developments in architecture or technology, monumental arts, town-planning or landscape design;

(iii) bear a unique or at least exceptional testimony to a cultural tradition or to a civilization which is living or which has disappeared;

(iv) be an outstanding example of a type of building, architectural or technological ensemble or landscape which illustrates (a) significant stage(s) in human history;

(v) be an outstanding example of a traditional human settlement, land-use, or sea-use which is representative of a culture (or cultures), or human interaction with the environment especially when it has become vulnerable under the impact of irreversible change;

(vi) be directly or tangibly associated with events or living traditions, with ideas, or with beliefs, with artistic and literary works of outstanding universal significance. (The Committee considers that this criterion should preferably be used in conjunction with other criteria);

(vii) contain superlative natural phenomena or areas of exceptional natural beauty and aesthetic importance;

(viii) be outstanding examples representing major stages of earth's history, including the record of life, significant on-going geological processes in the development of landforms, or significant geomorphic or physiographic features;

(ix) be outstanding examples representing significant on-going ecological and biological

员会将会认为该遗产具有突出的普遍价值（见49–53条）。所申报遗产因而必须是：

（i）作为人类天才的创造力的杰作；

（ii）在一段时期内或世界某一文化区域内人类价值观的重要交流，对建筑、技术、古迹艺术、城镇规划或景观设计的发展产生重大影响；

（iii）能为延续至今或业已消逝的文明或文化传统提供独特的或至少是特殊的见证；

（iv）是一种建筑、建筑或技术整体、或景观的杰出范例，展现人类历史上一个（或几个）重要阶段；

（v）是传统人类居住地、土地使用或海洋开发的杰出范例，代表一种（或几种）文化或人类与环境的相互作用，特别是当它面临不可逆变化的影响而变得脆弱；

（vi）与具有突出普遍意义的事件、活传统、观点、信仰、艺术或文学作品有直接或有形的联系。（委员会认为本标准最好与其他标准一起使用）；

（vii）绝妙的自然现象或具有罕见自然美和美学价值的地区；

（viii）是地球演化史中重要阶段的突出例证，包括生命记载和地貌演变中的重要地质过程或显著的地质或地貌特征；

（ix）突出代表了陆地、淡水、海岸和海洋生态系统及动植物群落演变、发展的生态和生

processes in the evolution and development of terrestrial, fresh water, coastal and marine ecosystems and communities of plants and animals;

(x) contain the most important and significant natural habitats for in-situ conservation of biological diversity, including those containing threatened species of Outstanding Universal Value from the point of view of science or conservation.

78. To be deemed of Outstanding Universal Value, a property must also meet the conditions of integrity and/or authenticity and must have an adequate protection and management system to ensure its safeguarding.

Ⅱ.E Integrity and/or authenticity

Authenticity

79. Properties nominated under criteria (i) to (vi) must meet the conditions of authenticity. Annex 4 which includes the Nara Document on Authenticity, provides a practical basis for examining the authenticity of such properties and is summarized below.

80. The ability to understand the value attributed to the heritage depends on the degree to which information sources about this value may be understood as credible or truthful. Knowledge and understanding of these sources of information, in relation to original and subsequent characteristics of the cultural heritage, and their meaning as accumulated over time, are the requisite bases for assessing all aspects of authenticity.

Decision 39 COM 11

81. Judgments about value attributed to cultural heritage, as well as the credibility of related

理过程；

（x）是生物多样性原址保护的最重要的自然栖息地，包括从科学和保护角度看，具有突出的普遍价值的濒危物种栖息地。

78. 只有同时具有完整性和 / 或真实性的特征，且有恰当的保护和管理机制确保遗产得到保护，遗产才能被视为具有突出普遍价值。

Ⅱ.E 完整性和 / 或真实性

真实性

79. 依据标准（ⅰ）至（ⅵ）申报的遗产须符合真实性的条件。附件 4 中包括了关于真实性的《奈良文件》，为评估相关遗产的真实性提供了操作基础，概要如下：

80. 理解遗产价值的能力，取决于该价值信息来源的真实度或可信度。对历史上积累的，涉及文化遗产原始及发展变化的特征的信息来源的认识和理解，及随时间积累形成的意义，是评价真实性各方面的必要基础。

第 39 COM 11 决议

81. 对于文化遗产价值和相关信息来源可信性的评价标准可因文化而异，甚至同一种文化

information sources, may differ from culture to culture, and even within the same culture. The respect due to all cultures requires that cultural heritage must be considered and judged primarily within the cultural contexts to which it belongs.

82. Depending on the type of cultural heritage, and its cultural context, properties may be understood to meet the conditions of authenticity if their cultural values (as recognized in the nomination criteria proposed) are truthfully and credibly expressed through a variety of attributes including:
- form and design;
- materials and substance;
- use and function;
- traditions, techniques and management systems;
- location and setting;
- language, and other forms of intangible heritage;
- spirit and feeling; and
- other internal and external factors.

83. Attributes such as spirit and feeling do not lend themselves easily to practical applications of the conditions of authenticity, but nevertheless are important indicators of character and sense of place, for example, in communities maintaining tradition and cultural continuity.

84. The use of all these sources permits elaboration of the specific artistic, historic, social, and scientific dimensions of the cultural heritage being examined. "Information sources" are defined as all physical, written, oral, and figurative sources, which make it possible to know the nature, specificities, meaning, and history of the cultural heritage.

85. When the conditions of authenticity are considered in preparing a nomination for a property, the State Party should first identify all of the applicable significant attributes of authenticity. The

内也存在差异。出于对所有文化的尊重，文化遗产的分析和判断，必须首先在其所在的文化背景中进行。

82. 依据文化遗产类别及其文化背景，如果遗产的文化价值（申报标准所认可的）的下列特征真实可信，则被认为具有真实性：

- 外形和设计；
- 材料和实质；
- 用途和功能；
- 传统，技术和管理体系；
- 位置和环境；
- 语言和其他形式的非物质遗产；
- 精神和感觉；
- 其他内外因素。

83. 精神和感觉这样的属性，在真实性评估中虽不易操作，却是评价一个遗产地特质和场所精神的重要指标，例如，在社区中保持传统和文化连续性。

84. 利用所有这些信息使我们对相关文化遗产在艺术、历史、社会和科学等特定领域的研究更加深入。"信息来源"指所有物质的、书面的、口头和图形的信息来源，从而使理解文化遗产的性质、特性、意义和历史成为可能。

85. 在考虑申报遗产的真实性时，缔约国首先要确认所有适用的真实性的重要载体。真实性声明应该评估真实性在每个载体特征上的体现程度。

statement of authenticity should assess the degree to which authenticity is present in, or expressed by, each of these significant attributes.

86. In relation to authenticity, the reconstruction of archaeological remains or historic buildings or districts is justifiable only in exceptional circumstances. Reconstruction is acceptable only on the basis of complete and detailed documentation and to no extent on conjecture.

Integrity

87. All properties nominated for inscription on the World Heritage List shall satisfy the conditions of integrity.

Decision 20 COM IX.13

88. Integrity is a measure of the wholeness and intactness of the natural and/or cultural heritage and its attributes. Examining the conditions of integrity, therefore requires assessing the extent to which the property:

a) includes all elements necessary to express its Outstanding Universal Value;

b) is of adequate size to ensure the complete representation of the features and processes which convey the property's significance;

c) suffers from adverse effects of development and/or neglect.

This should be presented in a statement of integrity.

89. For properties nominated under criteria (i) to (vi), the physical fabric of the property and/or its significant features should be in good condition, and the impact of deterioration processes controlled. A significant proportion of the elements necessary to convey the totality of the value conveyed by the

86. 在真实性问题上，只有在极个别情况下，才考虑重建考古遗址或历史建筑及街区。只有意见完整且详细的记载，不存在任何想象而进行的重建，才可以接受。

完整性

87. 所有申报列入《世界遗产名录》的遗产必须满足完整性条件。

第20COM IX.13号决定

88. 完整性用来衡量自然和/或文化遗产及其特征的整体性和无缺憾性。因而，审查遗产完整性需要评估遗产符合以下特征的程度：

a）包括所有表现其突出普遍价值的必要因素；

b）面积足够大，确保能完整地代表体现遗产价值的特色和过程；

c）受到发展的负面影响和/或缺乏维护。

上述条件需要在完整性陈述中进行论述。

89. 依据标准（i）至（vi）申报的遗产，其物理构造和/或重要特征都必须保存完好，且侵蚀退化过程的影响得到控制。能表现遗产全部价值的绝大部分必要因素也要包括在内。文化景观、历史村镇或其他活遗产中体现其显著特征的种种关系和动态功能也应予保存。

property should be included. Relationships and dynamic functions present in cultural landscapes, historic towns or other living properties essential to their distinctive character should also be maintained.

Examples of the application of the conditions of integrity to properties nominated under criteria (i) – (vi) are under development.

90. For all properties nominated under criteria (vii) - (x), bio-physical processes and landform features should be relatively intact. However, it is recognized that no area is totally pristine and that all natural areas are in a dynamic state, and to some extent involve contact with people. Human activities, including those of traditional societies and local communities, often occur in natural areas. These activities may be consistent with the Outstanding Universal Value of the area where they are ecologically sustainable.

91. In addition, for properties nominated under criteria (vii) to (x), a corresponding condition of integrity has been defined for each criterion.

92. Properties proposed under criterion (vii) should be of Outstanding Universal Value and include areas that are essential for maintaining the beauty of the property. For example, a property whose scenic value depends on a waterfall, would meet the conditions of integrity if it includes adjacent catchment and downstream areas that are integrally linked to the maintenance of the aesthetic qualities of the property.

93. Properties proposed under criterion (viii) should contain all or most of the key interrelated and interdependent elements in their natural relationships. For example, an "ice age" area would meet the conditions of integrity if it includes the snow field, the glacier itself and samples of cutting

将完整性条件应用于依据标准（i）至（vi）的申报的遗产之例证正在开发。

90. 所有依据标准（vii）至（x）申报的遗产，其生物物理过程和地貌特征应该相对完整。当然，由于任何区域都不可能完全保持天然，且所有自然区域都在变动之中，而且在某种程度上还会有人类的活动。在自然区域内，包括传统社会和当地社区在内的人类活动时有发生。如果这些活动具有生态可持续性，也可以同自然区域突出的普遍价值一致。

91. 另外，对于依据标准（vii）至（x）申报的遗产来说，每个标准又有一个相应的完整性条件。

92. 依据标准（vii）申报的遗产应具备突出的普遍价值，且包括保持遗产美景所必须的关键地区。例如，某个遗产的景观价值在于瀑布，那么只有与维持遗产美景完整关系密切的邻近的积水潭和下游地区也被涵盖在内，才能满足完整性条件。

93. 依据标准（viii）申报的遗产必须包括其自然关系中所有或大部分重要的相互联系、相互依存的因素。例如，"冰川期"遗址要满足完整性条件，则需包括雪地、冰河本身和凿面样本、沉积物和植物集群（例如，条痕、冰碛层及植物演替的先锋阶段等）。如果是火山，则岩

patterns, deposition and colonization (e.g. striations, moraines, pioneer stages of plant succession, etc.); in the case of volcanoes, the magmatic series should be complete and all or most of the varieties of effusive rocks and types of eruptions be represented.

94. Properties proposed under criterion (ix) should have sufficient size and contain the necessary elements to demonstrate the key aspects of processes that are essential for the long term conservation of the ecosystems and the biological diversity they contain. For example, an area of tropical rain forest would meet the conditions of integrity if it includes a certain amount of variation in elevation above sea level, changes in topography and soil types, patch systems and naturally regenerating patches; similarly a coral reef should include, for example, seagrass, mangrove or other adjacent ecosystems that regulate nutrient and sediment inputs into the reef.

95. Properties proposed under criterion (x) should be the most important properties for the conservation of biological diversity. Only those properties which are the most biologically diverse and/or representative are likely to meet this criterion. The properties should contain habitats for maintaining the most diverse fauna and flora characteristic of the bio-geographic province and ecosystems under consideration. For example, a tropical savannah would meet the conditions of integrity if it includes a complete assemblage of co-evolved herbivores and plants; an island ecosystem should include habitats for maintaining endemic biota; a property containing wide ranging species should be large enough to include the most critical habitats essential to ensure the survival of viable populations of those species; for an area containing migratory species, seasonal breeding and nesting sites, and migratory routes, wherever they are located, should be adequately protected.

浆层必须完整，且能代表所有或大部分火山岩种类和喷发类型。

94. 依据标准（ix）申报的遗产必须具有足够的规模，且包含能够展示长期保护其内部生态系统和生物多样性的重要过程的必要因素。例如，热带雨林地区要满足完整性条件，需要有一定的海拔层次、多样的地形和土壤种类、群落系统和自然形成的群落；同样，珊瑚礁必须包括诸如海草、红树林和其他为珊瑚礁提供营养沉积物的邻近生态系统。

95. 依据标准（x）申报的遗产必须是对生物多样性保护至关重要的遗产。只有最具生物多样性和／或代表性的申报遗产，才有可能满足该标准。遗产必须包括某生物区或生态系统内最具多样性的动植物特征的栖息地。例如：要满足完整性条件，热带草原需要具有完整的、共同进化的草食动物群和植物群；海岛生态系统则需要包括地方生态栖息地；包含多种物种的遗产必须足够大，能够包括确保这些物种生存的最重要的栖息地；如果某个地区有迁徙物种，则季节性的养育巢穴和迁徙路线，不管位于何处，都必须妥善保护。

Ⅱ.F Protection and management

96. Protection and management of World Heritage properties should ensure that their Outstanding Universal Value, including the conditions of integrity and/or authenticity at the time of inscription, are sustained or enhanced over time. A regular review of the general state of conservation of properties, and thus also their Outstanding Universal Value, shall be done within a framework of monitoring processes for World Heritage properties, as specified within the *Operational Guidelines*[①].

97. All properties inscribed on the World Heritage List must have adequate long-term legislative, regulatory, institutional and/or traditional protection and management to ensure their safeguarding. This protection should include adequately delineated boundaries. Similarly States Parties should demonstrate adequate protection at the national, regional, municipal, and/or traditional level for the nominated property. They should append appropriate texts to the nomination with a clear explanation of the way this protection operates to protect the property.

Legislative, regulatory and contractual measures for protection

98. Legislative and regulatory measures at national and local levels should assure the protection of the property from social, economic and other pressures or changes that might negatively impact the Outstanding Universal Value, including the integrity and/or authenticity of the property. States

Ⅱ.F 保护和管理

96. 世界遗产的保护与管理须确保其在列入《世界遗产名录》时所具有的突出的普遍价值以及完整性和／或真实性在之后得到保持或加强。为此，须按照《操作指南》中规定的，在世界遗产监测的总体框架下，定期对列入遗产及其突出普遍价值的保护状况进行定期审查[①]。

97. 列入《世界遗产名录》的所有遗产必须有长期、充分的立法、规范、机构的和／或传统的保护及管理，以确保遗产得到保护。保护必须包括充分的边界划定。同样，缔约国应该在国家、区域、城市和／或传统各个级别上对申报遗产予以足够力度的保护。申报文件上也需要附加明确说明解释具体保护措施。

立法、规范和契约性的保护措施

98. 国家和地方级的立法、规范措施应确保遗产的保护完好，使其突出的普遍性价值包括完整性和／或真实性，不因社会经济发展及其他压力而受到负面影响。缔约国还需要保证这些措施得到切实有效的实施。

---

① The processes of monitoring specified in the Operational Guidelines are Reactive Monitoring (see paragraphs 169-176) and Periodic Reporting (see paragraphs 199-210).

① 《操作指南》中具体规定的监测程序为反应性监测（见169-176条）和定期报告（199-210条）。

Parties should also assure the full and effective implementation of such measures.

Decision 39 COM 11

Boundaries for effective protection

99. The delineation of boundaries is an essential requirement in the establishment of effective protection of nominated properties. Boundaries should be drawn to incorporate all the attributes that convey the Outstanding Universal Value and to ensure the integrity and/or authenticity of the property.

Decision 39 COM 11

100. For properties nominated under criteria (i) - (vi), boundaries should be drawn to include all those areas and attributes which are a direct tangible expression of the Outstanding Universal Value of the property, as well as those areas which in the light of future research possibilities offer potential to contribute to and enhance such understanding.

101. For properties nominated under criteria (vii) - (x), boundaries should reflect the spatial requirements of habitats, species, processes or phenomena that provide the basis for their inscription on the World Heritage List. The boundaries should include sufficient areas immediately adjacent to the area of Outstanding Universal Value in order to protect the property's heritage values from direct effect of human encroachments and impacts of resource use outside of the nominated area.

102. The boundaries of the nominated property may coincide with one or more existing or proposed protected areas, such as national parks or nature reserves, biosphere reserves or protected cultural or historic districts or other areas and territories. While

第 39 COM 11决议

确保有效保护的边界

99.划定边界是对申报遗产进行有效保护的核心要求，划定的边界范围内应包含所有能够体现遗产突出普遍性价值的元素，并保证其完整性与（或）真实性不受破坏。

第 39 COM 11决议

100. 依据标准（ⅰ）至（ⅵ）申报的遗产，划定的边界需要包括所有有形的、能够直接体现遗产的突出普遍价值的区域和特征，以及在将来的研究中有可能加深这种理解的区域。

101. 依据标准（ⅶ）至（ⅹ）申报的遗产，划定的边界要反映其成为世界遗产基本条件的栖息地、物种、过程或现象的空间要求。边界须包括与具有突出的普遍价值紧邻的足够大的区域，以保护其遗产价值不因人类的直接侵蚀和该区域外资源开发而受到损害。

102. 所申报遗产的边界可能会与一个或多个现存或已建成的保护区重合，例如国家公园或自然保护区，生物圈保护区，文化或历史保护区、或者其他地区和区域。虽然保护区可能包含几个管理带，可能只有个别地带能达到世

such established areas for protection may contain several management zones, only some of those zones may satisfy requirements for inscription.

界遗产的要求。

Decision 39 COM 11

第 39 COM 11 决议

Buffer zones

缓冲区

103. Wherever necessary for the proper protection of the property, an adequate buffer zone should be provided.

103. 只要有必要，就应设立足够大的缓冲区以有效保护遗产。

104. For the purposes of effective protection of the nominated property, a buffer zone is an area surrounding the nominated property which has complementary legal and/or customary restrictions placed on its use and development to give an added layer of protection to the property. This should include the immediate setting of the nominated property, important views and other areas or attributes that are functionally important as a support to the property and its protection. The area constituting the buffer zone should be determined in each case through appropriate mechanisms. Details on the size, characteristics and authorized uses of a buffer zone, as well as a map indicating the precise boundaries of the property and its buffer zone, should be provided in the nomination.

104. 缓冲区是为了有效保护申报遗产而划定的遗产周围的区域，其使用和开发受到相关法律和 / 或习惯规定的限制，为遗产增加了保护层。缓冲区包括申报遗产直接所在的区域、重要景观，以及其他在功能上对遗产及其保护至关重要的区域或特征。缓冲区的构成区域应通过合适的机制来决定。申报时，需要提供有关缓冲区大小、特点、授权用途的详细信息，以及一张精确标示边界和缓冲区的地图。

105. A clear explanation of how the buffer zone protects the property should also be provided.

105. 申报材料中还需明确描述缓冲区在保护申报遗产中的作用。

106. Where no buffer zone is proposed, the nomination should include a statement as to why abuffer zone is not required.

106. 如果没有提议建立缓冲区，则申报材料需要解释没有划定缓冲区的原因。

107. Although buffer zones are not part of the nominated property, any modifications to or creation of buffer zones subsequent to inscription of a property on the World Heritage List should be

107. 虽然缓冲区并非所申报的遗产的正式组成部分，但是一旦列入《世界遗产名录》，对缓冲区的划定或任何变动，都需经世界遗产委员会按照边界微调的程序（详见 164 条和附件

approved by the World Heritage Committee using the procedure for a minor boundary modification (see paragraph 164 and Annex 11). The creation of buffer zones subsequent to inscription is normally considered to be a minor boundary modification[①].

1）批准。列入后新建的缓冲区设定通常被视作边界细微调整[①]。

Management systems

管理体制

108. Each nominated property should have an appropriate management plan or other documented management system which must specify how the Outstanding Universal Value of a property should be preserved, preferably through participatory means.

108. 每一处申报遗产都应有适宜的管理规划或其他有文可依的管理体制，其中需要详细说明将如何采取措施（最好是多方参与的方式）保护遗产突出的普遍价值。

109. The purpose of a management system is to ensure the effective protection of the nominated property for present and future generations.

109. 管理体制旨在确保现在和将来对申报遗产进行有效的保护。

110. An effective management system depends on the type, characteristics and needs of the nominated property and its cultural and natural context. Management systems may vary according to different cultural perspectives, the resources available and other factors. They may incorporate traditional practices, existing urban or regional planning instruments, and other planning control mechanisms, both formal and informal. Impact assessments for proposed interventions are essential for all World Heritage properties.

110. 有效的管理体制的内容取决于申报遗产的类别、特点、需求以及文化和自然环境。由于文化视角、可用资源及其他因素的影响，管理体制也会有所差别。管理体制可能包含传统做法、现行的城市或地区规划手段、和其他正式和非正式的规划控制机制。对所有提议的干预措施进行影响评估，是至关重要的工作。

111. 考虑到上述多样性问题，有效管理体制应包括以下共同因素：

111. In recognizing the diversity mentioned above, common elements of an effective management system could include:

Decision 39 COM 11

第39 COM 11决定

---

①　In case of transnational/transboundary properties any modification will need the agreement of all States Parties concerned.

①　涉及跨国/跨境世界遗产项目，任何调整修订均需得到所有相关缔约国的同意。

a) a thorough shared understanding of the property by all stakeholders, including the use of participatory planning and stakeholder consultation process;

b) a cycle of planning, implementation, monitoring, evaluation and feedback;

c) an assessment of the vulnerabilities of the property to social, economic, and other pressures and changes, as well as the monitoring of the impacts of trends and proposed interventions;

d) the development of mechanisms for the involvement and coordination of the various activities between different partners and stakeholders;

e) the allocation of necessary resources;

f) capacity-building; and

g) an accountable, transparent description of how the management system functions.

112. Effective management involves a cycle of short, medium and long-term actions to protect, conserve and present the nominated property. An integrated approach to planning and management is essential to guide the evolution of properties over time and to ensure maintenance of all aspects of their Outstanding Universal Value. This approach goes beyond the property to include any buffer zone(s), as well as the broader setting. The broader setting, may relate to the property's topography, natural and built environment, and other elements such as infrastructure, land use patterns, spatial organization, and visual relationships. It may also include related social and cultural practices, economic processes and other intangible dimensions of heritage such as perceptions and associations. Management of the broader setting is related to its role in supporting the Outstanding Universal Value.

Decision 39 COM 11

a）各利益方均透彻理解遗产价值（包括采用参与式规划和利益相关方咨询程序）；

b）规划、实施、监测、评估和反馈的循环机制；

c）评估遗产可能受到的来自社会、经济及其他方面的压力，监测时下各种趋势和干预活动对遗产的影响；

d）建立相应机制，以鼓励不同合作伙伴和利益相关方参与和协调各种活动；

e）必要的资源配置；

f）能力建设；

g）对管理体制运作的描述可信且透明。

112. 有效管理包括对申报遗产的保护、保存和展示的短、中、长期措施。规划管理采取整体综合的方式对指导遗产长期发展至关重要，也可确保其突出普遍价值的所有方面得以维持。这一综合视角不局限于遗产本身，而是包括所有缓冲区和更广泛的背景环境。更广泛的背景环境可以指该遗产的地形、自然环境与建造环境、以及其他元素例如基础设施建设、土地利用模式、空间组织、视觉关系等。它也可以是相关的社会与文化实践，经济发展进程，以及遗产的认知、关联等其他非物质层面。对更广泛的背景环境的管理起到了支持突出普遍价值的重要作用。

第39 COM 11决定

113. Moreover, in the context of the implementation of the *Convention*, the World Heritage Committee has established a process of Reactive Monitoring (see Chapter IV) and a process of Periodic Reporting (see Chapter V).

114. In the case of serial properties, a management system or mechanisms for ensuring the co-ordinated management of the separate components are essential and should be documented in the nomination (see paragraphs137-139).

115. [Deleted]

Decision 39 COM 11

116. Where the intrinsic qualities of a property nominated are threatened by human action and yet meet the criteria and the conditions of authenticity or integrity set out in paragraphs 78-95, an action plan outlining the corrective measures required should be submitted with the nomination file. Should the corrective measures submitted by the nominating State Party not be taken within the time proposed by the State Party, the property will be considered by the Committee for delisting in accordance with the procedure adopted by the Committee (see Chapter Ⅳ.C).

Decision 39 COM 11

117. States Parties are responsible for implementing effective management activities for a World Heritage property. State Parties should do so in close collaboration with property managers, the agency with management authority and other partners, and stakeholders in property management.

118. The Committee recommends that States Parties include risk preparedness as an element in their World Heritage site management plans and

113. 另外，为了实施《公约》，世界遗产委员会还建立了反应监测程序（见第四章）和《定期报告》机制（见第五章）。

114. 如果是系列遗产，须在申报材料中阐明能确保各个组成部分协调管理的管理体制或机制（见 137–139 条）。

115.［已删除］。

第 39 COM 11 决定

116. 如果遗产的内在品质由于人类活动而受到威胁，且满足第 78 至 95 条规定的真实性或完整性的标准和条件，概述纠正措施的行动计划需要和申报材料一起提交。如果缔约国并未在拟定的时间内采取纠正措施，委员会将会考虑依据相关程序将该遗产从名单上删除。（见四.C 节）

第 39 COM 11 决定

117. 缔约国要对境内的世界遗产实施有效的管理。在管理过程中，缔约国要同其他参与方密切合作，其中包括遗产管理人员、管理权力机关和其他合作者及遗产管理的利益相关者。

118. 委员会建议缔约国将风险防范机制作为其世界遗产管理规划和培训战略的组成部分。

training strategies.

Decision 28 COM 10B.4

第 28COM10B.4 号决定

Sustainable use

可持续使用

119. World Heritage properties may support a variety of ongoing and proposed uses that are ecologically and culturally sustainable and which may contribute to the quality of life of communities concerned. The State Party and its partners must ensure that such sustainable use or any other change does not impact adversely on the Outstanding Universal Value of the property. For some properties, human use would not be appropriate. Legislations, policies and strategies affecting World Heritage properties should ensure the protection of the Outstanding Universal Value, support the wider conservation of natural and cultural heritage, and promote and encourage the active participation of the communities and stakeholders concerned with the property as necessary conditions to its sustainable protection, conservation, management and presentation.

119. 世界遗产存在多种现有和潜在的利用方式，对其生态和文化可持续的利用可能提高所在社区的生活质量。缔约国和合作者必须确保这些可持续使用或任何其他的改变，不会对遗产的突出的普遍价值、完整性和 / 或真实性造成负面影响。对于有些遗产来说，人类不宜使用。世界遗产的相关立法、政策和策略措施都应确保其突出普遍价值的保护，支持对更大范围的自然和文化遗产的保护、促进和鼓励所在社区公众和所有利益相关方的积极参与，是遗产可持续保护、保存、管理、展示的必要条件。

Ⅲ. PROCESS FOR THE INSCRIPTION OF PROPERTIES ON THE WORLD HERITAGE LIST

Ⅲ. 列入《世界遗产名录》的程序

Ⅲ.A Preparation of Nominations

Ⅲ.A 申报准备

120. The nomination document is the primary basis on which the Committee considers the inscription of the properties on the World Heritage List. All relevant information should be included in the nomination document and it should be cross-referenced to the source of information.

120. 申报文件是委员会考虑是否将某项遗产列入《世界遗产名录》的首要基础。所有相关信息都应该包括在申报材料中，并注明信息的出处。

121. Annex 3 provides guidance to States Parties in preparing nominations of specific types of properties.

121. 附件 3 为缔约国对具体类别遗产的申报提供了指南。

122. Before States Parties begin to prepare a nomination of a property for inscription on the World Heritage List, they should become familiar with the nomination cycle, described in Paragraph 168. It is desirable to carry out initial preparatory work to establish that a property has the potential to justify Outstanding Universal Value, including integrity or authenticity, before the development of a full nomination dossier which could be expensive and time-consuming. Such preparatory work might include collection of available information on the property, thematic studies, scoping studies of the potential for demonstrating Outstanding Universal Value, including integrity or authenticity, or an initial comparative study of the property in its wider global or regional context, including an analysis in the context of the Gap Studies produced by the Advisory Bodies. This first phase of work will help to establish the feasibility of a possible nomination and avoid the use of resources on preparing nominations that may be unlikely to succeed. States Parties are encouraged to seek upstream advice[①] from the relevant Advisory Body(ies) for this first phase as well as to contact the World Heritage Centre at the earliest opportunity in considering nominations to seek information and guidance.

122. 缔约国在着手准备遗产申报前，应先熟悉第168条描述的申报周期。在提交耗时耗资的完整的申遗文本前，最好先开展初步的筹备工作，确认该遗产有潜力证明其拥有突出普遍价值，包括完整性和真实性。这类准备工作包括收集遗产的相关信息、主题研究、展示潜在突出普遍价值证明包括完整性与真实性范围界定研究、或关于遗产在更广泛的全球或区域背景下的初期比较分析，包括咨询机构以遗产空白研究为背景的分析。初期的筹备工作有助于在申报的早期阶段建立具有可行性的申遗战略，避免将资源用在不太可能申报成功的项目上。鼓励缔约国尽早征询相关咨询机构上游建议[①]，同时尽早和世界遗产中心联系，了解相关申报信息和指南。

---

① Upstream Processes: In relation to the nomination of sites for inscription on the World Heritage List, "Upstream processes" include advice, consultation and analysis that occur prior to the submission of a nomination and are aimed at reducing the number of nominations that experience significant problems during the evaluation process. The basic principle of the upstream processes is to enable the Advisory Bodies and the Secretariat to provide support directly to States Parties, throughout the whole process leading up to apossible World Heritage nomination.For the upstream support to beeffective, it should ideally be undertaken from the earliest stage in the nomination process, at the moment of the preparation or revision of the States Parties' Tentative Lists.

① 上游程序：在遗产申报录入名录时，上游程序包括在递交申报前的建议、咨询和分析，在评估程序中减少有重大问题的申报数量。上游程序的基本原则是使咨询机构和秘书处可以对缔约国提供直接支持，通过全部程序使申报可能实现。上游程序的有效性，理想情况下是在缔约国准备和修订预备名录的申遗初始阶段就开始运作。

Decision 34 COM 12 (III) Report of the Expert meeting on «Upstream Processes to Nominations: Creative Approaches in the Nomination Process» (Phuket: 2010)

Decision 36 COM 13.I Decision 39 COM 11

第34 COM 12（III）决议，专家会议报告:"申报中的上游程序：申报程序中的创意方法"（普吉岛，2010）

第36 COM 13.Ⅰ及第39 COM11决议

123. Participation in the nomination process of local communities, indigenous peoples, governmental, non-governmental and private organizations and other stakeholders is essential to enable them to have a shared responsibility with the State Party in the maintenance of the property. States Parties are encouraged to prepare nominations with the widest possible participation of stakeholders and to demonstrate, as appropriate, that the free, prior and informed consent of indigenous peoples has been obtained, through, inter alia making the nominations publicly available in appropriate languages and public consultations and hearings.

123. 申报过程中，本土社区、原住民、政府组织、非政府组织、私人机构以及其他利益相关方有效、广泛的参与都很重要，这使他们能够与缔约国共同承担保护遗产的责任。鼓励缔约国在申报准备中让利益相关方尽可能广泛参与，通过公共协商和听证会等形式，用适当的语言，公开申报信息，确保获得原住民自由、事先和知情的同意。

Decision 39 COM 11

第39 COM 11决定

124. Preparatory Assistance, as described in Chapter Ⅶ.E, may be requested by States Parties for the preparation of nominations.

124. 如第 七.E章节中所述，缔约国准备申报时可以申请"筹备性援助"。

125. States Parties are encouraged to contact the Secretariat, which can provide assistance throughout the nomination process.

125. 鼓励缔约国同秘书处联系，秘书处能够在整个申报过程中提供帮助。

126. The Secretariat can also provide:

a) assistance in identifying appropriate maps and photographs and the national agencies from which these may be obtained;

b) examples of successful nominations, of management and legislative provisions;

c) guidance for nominating different types of properties, such as Cultural Landscapes, Towns, Canals, and Heritage Routes (see Annex 3)

d) guidance for nominating serial and

126. 秘书处还能：

a）在确定合适的地图和照片以及从哪些国家机构部门取得这些资料方面提供帮助；

b）提供成功申报案例以及管理方法和立法条款上的参考范例；

c）为不同类别的遗产申报提供指导，例如文化景观、城镇、运河和遗产线路（见附件3）

d）为申报系列遗产和跨境遗产提供指导

transboundary properties (see paragraphs 134-139).

127. States Parties may submit draft nominations to the Secretariat for comment and review at any time during the year. However, States Parties are strongly encouraged to transmit to the Secretariat by 30 September of the preceding year (see paragraph 168) the draft nominations that they wish to submit by the 1 February deadline. This submission of a draft nomination should include maps showing the boundaries for the proposed site. Draft nominations could be submitted either in electronic format or in printed version (only in 1 copy without annexes except for maps). In both cases they should be accompanied by a cover letter.

Decision 37 COM 12.II

128. Nominations may be submitted at any time during the year, but only those nominations that are "complete" (see paragraph 132 and Annex 5) and received by the Secretariat on or before 1 February[①] will be considered for inscription on the World Heritage List by the World Heritage Committee during the following year. Only nominations of properties included in the State Party's Tentative List will be examined by the Committee (see paragraphs 63 and 65).

Decision 37 COM 12.II Decision 39 COM 11

Ⅲ.B Format and content of nominations

129. Nominations of properties for inscription on the World Heritage List should be prepared in

（见第 134 至 139 条）。

127. 缔约国可以在全年任何时间提交申报文本初稿至秘书处，听取意见，接受初审。但强烈鼓励缔约国，将其计划于 2 月 1 日截止日期前提交的申报文本的初稿，于前一年 9 月 30 日之前交到秘书处。初稿提交须包括显示申报遗产边界的地图。初稿提交可以是电子或纸质形式（除地图外，仅一个文件无需附件）。提交材料需要附有说明。

第 37 COM 12.II 决议

128. 全年任何时候都可以提交申报，但只有在二月一日[①]或之前递交到秘书处且"完整"的申报（见第 132 条及附件 5）才会被世界遗产委员审核，决定是否次年列入《世界遗产名录》。委员会只审查已包含在缔约国《预备名录》上的遗产（见第 63 和 65 条）。

第 37 COM 12.II 及第 39 COM 11 决议

Ⅲ.B 申报文件的格式和内容

129.《世界遗产名录》申报应依据附件 5 所示格式提交材料。

① If 1 February falls on a weekend, the nomination must be received by 17h00 GMT the preceding Friday.
① 如果 2 月 1 日是周末，申报必须在格林威治时间前一个周五 17:00 前收到。

accordance with the format set out in Annex 5.

130. The format includes the following sections:

1. Identification of the Property

2. Description of the Property

3. Justification for Inscription

4. State of conservation and factors affecting the property

5. Protection and Management

6. Monitoring

7. Documentation

8. Contact Information of responsible authorities

9. Signature on behalf of the State Party(ies)

131. Nominations to the World Heritage List are evaluated on content rather than on appearance.

132. For a nomination to be considered as "complete", the following requirements (see format in Annex 5) are to be met:

Decision 37 COM 12.II, Decision 39 COM 11

Executive Summary

An Executive Summary shall include essential information (see Annex 5) extracted from the main text of the nomination including a reduced size version of the map(s) indicating the boundaries of the nominated property and of the buffer zone (where appropriate) and the draft Statement of Outstanding Universal Value (the same text presented in Section 3.3 of the nomination).

1. Identification of the Property

The boundaries of the property being proposed shall be clearly defined, unambiguously distinguishing between the nominated property and any buffer zone (when present) (see paragraphs 103-107). Maps

130. 格式包括如下部分：

1. 遗产的辨认

2. 遗产描述

3. 列入理由

4. 保护状况和影响因素

5. 保护和管理

6. 监测

7. 文件

8. 负责机构的联系信息

9. 缔约国代表签名

131.《世界遗产名录》申报是重内容轻表象的。

132. "完整"申报需要满足下列要求（见附件 5 中的格式）：

第 37 COM 12.II 及第 39 COM 11 决定

执行概要

执行概要应包括从申报文本中摘录的所有重要信息。包括标明申报遗产和缓冲区的边界的合适的缩小版地图，以及《突出的普遍价值声明》草案（与申报文本的 3.3 部分内容一致）。

1. 遗产辨认

应清晰地定义申报遗产边界，清楚区分申报遗产和任何缓冲区（若存在）（见 103-107 条）的界限。地图应足够详细（见附件 5 中 1.e 部分的注释），能精确标出所申报的陆地和/或水域。

shall be sufficiently detailed (see Explanatory Note of section 1.e in Annex 5) to determine precisely which area of land and/or water is nominated. Officially up-to-date published topographic maps of the State Party annotated to show the property boundaries and any buffer zone (when present) shall be provided if available in printed version. A nomination shall be considered "incomplete" if it does not include clearly defined boundaries.

若有可能，应提供缔约国最新的官方出版的地形图，注清遗产边界。如果没有清晰的边界定义，申报会被认为"不完整"。

2. Description of the Property

The Description of the property shall include the identification of the property, and an overview of its history and development. All component parts that are mapped shall be identified and described. In particular, where serial nominations are proposed, each of the component parts shall be clearly described.

The History and Development of the property shall describe how the property has reached its present form and the significant changes that it has undergone. This information shall provide the important facts needed to support and give substance to the argument that the property meets the criteria of Outstanding Universal Value and conditions of integrity and/or authenticity.

2. 遗产描述

遗产描述应包括遗产辨认及其历史及发展概述。应确认、描述所有的绘制在地图上的组成部分，如果是系列申报，应清晰描述每一组成部分。

在遗产的历史和发展中应描述遗产是如何形成现在的状态以及所经历的重大变化。这些信息应包含所需的重要事实，以证实遗产达到突出普遍价值的标准，满足完整性和／或真实性的条件。

3. Justification for Inscription

This section must make clear why the property is considered to be of Outstanding Universal Value.

The text in sections from 3.1.a to 3.1.e should contain more detailed information to support the text of the proposed Statement of Outstanding Universal Value (section3.3).

3. 列入理由

此部分应该明示为什么该遗产具有突出的普遍性价值。

从 3.1a 到 3.1e 的文本应该包含更多具体的信息，以支持缔约国所提交的《突出的普遍性价值声明》(见 3.3)。

The comparative analyses prepared by States Parties when

缔约国申报遗产时提交的比较分析不可与委员会要求咨

nominating properties for inscription in the World Heritage List should not be confused with the thematic studies prepared by the Advisory Bodies at the request of the Committee (paragraph 148 below)

Decision 7 EXT.COM 4A

Section 3.1.b shall indicate the World Heritage criteria (see Paragraph 77) under which the property is proposed, together with a clearly stated argument for the use of each criterion. Statements of integrity and (when cultural criteria are proposed) of authenticity shall be included and shall demonstrate how the property satisfies the conditions outlined in paragraphs 78-95.

In section 3.2, a comparative analysis of the property in relation to similar properties, whether or not on the World Heritage List, both at the national and international levels, shall be provided. The comparative analysis shall explain the importance of the nominated property in its national and international context.

In section 3.3, a proposed Statement of Outstanding Universal Value (see paragraphs 49-53 and 155) of the property prepared by the State Party shall make clear why the property is considered to merit inscription on the World Heritage List.

The comparative analyses prepared by States Parties when nominating properties for inscription in the World Heritage List should not be confused with the thematic studies prepared by the Advisory Bodies at the request of the Committee (paragraph 148 below)

4. State of conservation and factors affecting the property

This section shall include accurate information on the present state of conservation of the property

询机构做的专题研究相混淆。（见下文 148.）

第 7 EXT.COM 4A 决定

3.1.b 应指出遗产申报依据的标准（见 77 条），且须明确说明依据此标准的原因。遗产的完整性与真实性（如果申报的是文化遗产）声明应该包含在内，且清楚地说明为什么该遗产满足 78 条到 95 条所列出的条件。

在 3.2 应提供该遗产与类似遗产的比较分析，无论类似遗产是否已被列入《世界遗产名录》，是国内还是国外。比较分析应说明申报遗产在国内及国际范围内的重要性。

3.3 是缔约国所提交的遗产《突出普遍性价值声明》（见 49 条到 53 条，以及 155 条）。这部分应清楚说明为什么该遗产值得列入《世界遗产名录》。

缔约国申报遗产时递交的比较分析不应和咨询机构应委员会要求编制的主题研究相混淆（见下面的第 148 段）第 7EXT.COM 4A 号决定

4. 保护状况和影响因素

本部分应包括目前遗产保护状况的准确信息（包括遗产的物理状况和现有的保护措施）。

(including information on its physical condition of the property and conservation measures in place). It shall also include a description of the factors affecting the property (including threats). Information provided in this section constitutes the baseline data which are necessary to monitor the state of conservation of the nominated property in the future.

5. Protection and management

Protection: Section 5 shall include the list of the legislative, regulatory, contractual, planning, institutional and/ or traditional measures most relevant to the protection of the property and provide a detailed analysis of the way in which this protection actually operates. Legislative, regulatory, contractual planning and/or institutional texts, or an abstract of the texts, shall also be attached in English or French.

Management: An appropriate management plan or other management system is essential and shall be provided in the nomination. Assurances of the effective implementation of the management plan or other management system are also expected. Sustainable development principles should be integrated into the management system.

A copy of the management plan or documentation of the management system shall be annexed to the nomination. If the management plan exists only in a language other than English or French, an English or French detailed description of its provisions shall be annexed.

A detailed analysis or explanation of the management plan or a documented management system shall be provided in Section 5.e of the nomination.

同时，也应包括影响遗产的因素描述（包括威胁）。本部分提供的信息是将来监测申报遗产保护状况必要的基础数据。

5. 保护和管理

保护：第五部分包括与遗产保护联系最为紧密的立法、规章、契约、规划、机构和／或传统措施，并详尽分析了实际保护措施的操作方法。立法、规章、契约、规划和机构性文本或者文本摘要，应以英文或法文附上。

管理：适宜的管理规划或其他管理体制很必要，应包括在申报文件中，并希望说明管理规划或其他管理体制可以确保得到有效执行。可持续发展原则应综合纳入管理体系。

管理规划或者管理体制文献的副本应附在申报文件后。如果管理规划为非英语或非法语，应附上英语或法语的条款详述。

应在申报文件的5.e部分提供管理规划或者管理体系的详尽分析或者说明。

A nomination which does not include the above-mentioned documents is considered incomplete unless other documents guiding the management of the property until the finalization of the management plan are provided.

申报文件若不包括上述文书则被认为不完整，除非在管理规划完成之前，提交了指导遗产管理的其他文书。

6. Monitoring

States Parties shall include the key indicators in place and/or proposed to measure and assess the state of conservation of the property, the factors affecting it, conservation measures at the property, the periodicity of their examination, and the identity of the responsible authorities.

6：监测

缔约国应在申报材料提供衡量、评估遗产保护状况的关键指标、其影响因素、遗产保护措施、审查周期及负责机构的名称。

7. Documentation

All documentation necessary to substantiate the nomination shall be provided. In addition to what is indicated above, this shall include a) images of a quality suitable for printing (digital photographs at 300 dpi minimum, and if essential, supplementary film, video or other audio visual material); and b) image/audiovisual inventory and authorization form (see Annex 5, point 7.a). The text of the nomination shall be transmitted in printed form as well as in electronic format (Word and/or PDF format preferred).

7. 文件

应提供申报所需的所有文件。除了上述文件之外，还应包括1）达到打印标准的照片（最低像素300dpi；如必要，补充电影、录像或其他视听材料）；2）图像清单以及授权表（见附件5，7a）。申报文本应以打印形式和电子文档提交（word或pdf文件为佳）。

8. Contact Information of responsible authorities

Detailed contact information of responsible authorities shall be provided.

8. 负责机构的联系信息

应提供负责机构的详细联系信息。

9. Signature on behalf of the State Party

The nomination shall conclude with the original signature of the official empowered to sign it on behalf of the State Party.

9. 缔约国代表签名

申报材料结尾应有缔约国授权的官方原始签名。

10. Number of printed copies required (including maps annexed)

10. 所需打印数量（包括地图附件）

Nominations of cultural and natural properties

= 文化与自然遗产申报文件（不包括文化景

(excluding cultural landscapes): 2 identical copies

Nominations of mixed properties and cultural landscapes: 3 identical copies

11. Paper and electronic format

Nominations shall be presented on A4-size paper and in electronic format (Word and/or PDF format).

12. Sending

States Parties shall submit the nomination in English or French duly signed,to:

UNESCO World Heritage Centre 7, place de Fontenoy 75352 Paris 07 SP France

Tel: +33 (0) 1 4568 1136

E-mail: wh-nominations@unesco.org

133. The Secretariat will retain all supporting documentation (maps, plans, photographic material, etc.) submitted with the nomination.

Ⅲ.C Requirements for the nomination of different types of properties

Transboundary properties

134. A nominated property may occur:

Decision 7 EXT.COM 4A

a) on the territory of a single State Party, or

b) on the territory of all concerned States Parties having adjacent borders (transboundary property).

135. Wherever possible, transboundary nominations should be prepared and submitted by States Parties jointly in conformity with Article 11.3 of the Convention. It is highly recommended

观）：2 份

混合遗产和文化景观申报：3 份

11. 文件和电子版

申报材料应使用 A4 纸张（或信纸），同时有电子版（word 和 / 或 pdf 格式）。

12. 寄送

缔约国应提交经签署的英语或法语申报材料，至：法国巴黎 联合国教科文组织 世界遗产中心

法国巴黎（7，placede Fontenoy 75352 Paris 07 SP）

电话：+33（0）1 4568 1136

E-mail：wh-nominations@unesco.org

133. 秘书处会保留和申报文本一起提交的所有相关资料（地图、规划、照片资料等）

Ⅲ.C 各类遗产申报的要求

跨境遗产

134. 申报的遗产可能：

第7EXT.COM 4A 号决定

a）位于一个缔约国境内；

b）位于几个接壤的缔约国境内（跨境遗产）。

135. 跨境遗产的申报，应尽可能由几个缔约国遵照大会公约第 11.3 条规定，共同准备和递交。大会强烈建议各相关缔约国建立联合管理委员会或类似组织，监督该遗产的总体管理。

that the States Parties concerned establish a joint management committee or similar body to oversee the management of the whole of a transboundary property.

136. Extensions to an existing World Heritage property located in one State Party may be proposed to become transboundary properties.

136. 位于一个缔约国境内的现有世界遗产的扩展部分可以申请成为跨境遗产。

Serial properties

系列遗产

137. Serial properties will include two or more component parts related by clearly defined links:

a) Component parts should reflect cultural, social or functional links over time that provide, where relevant, landscape, ecological, evolutionary or habitat connectivity.

b) Each component part should contribute to the Outstanding Universal Value of the property as a whole in asubstantial, scientific, readily defined and discernible way, and may include, inter alia, intangible attributes. The resulting Outstanding Universal Value should be easily understood and communicated.

c) Consistently, and in order toavoid an excessive fragmentation of component parts, the process of nomination of the property, including the selection of the component parts, should take fully into account the overall manageability and coherence of the property (see paragraph 114).

137. 系列遗产应包括两个或两个以上逻辑联系清晰的组成部分：

a）各组成部分应体现出因长期发展而来文化、社会或功能性关联的相互联系，进而形成景观、生态、空间演变或栖居地上的关联性；

b）每个组成部分都应对遗产整体的突出普遍价值有实质性、科学的、可清晰界定和辨识的贡献，亦可包含非物质载体。最终的突出普遍价值应该是容易理解和便于沟通的；

c）与此一致的，为避免各组成部分过度分裂，遗产申报的过程，包括对各组成部分的选择，应该充分考虑遗产整体的连贯和管理上的可行性（见第114条）。

and provided it is the series as a whole – and not necessarily the individual parts of it – which are of Outstanding Universal Value.

并且该系列作为一个整体（而非各组成部分）具有共同的突出普遍价值。

138. A serial nominated property may occur :

138. 申报的系列遗产可能：

Decision 7 EXT.COM 4A

第7 EXT.COM 4A决定

a) On the territory of a single State Party

a）位于一个缔约国境内（本国系列遗产）；

(Serial national property);or

b) within the territory of different States Parties, which need not be contiguous and is nominated with the consent of all States Parties concerned (serial transnationalproperty)

139. Serial nominations, whether from one State Party or multiple States, may be submitted for evaluation over several nomination cycles, provided that the first property nominated is of Outstanding Universal Value in its own right. States Parties planning serial nominations phased over several nomination cycles are encouraged to inform the Committee of their intention in order to ensure better planning.

Ⅲ.D Registration of nominations

140. On receipt of nominations from States Parties, the Secretariat will acknowledge receipt, check for completeness and register nominations. The Secretariat will forward complete nominations to the relevant Advisory Bodies for evaluation. The Secretariat will also make available the electronic format of the text of the nominations to the Members of the Committee on the World Heritage Centre's website. The Secretariat will request any additional information from the State Party and when required by Advisory Bodies. The timetable for registration and processing of nominations is detailed in paragraph 168.

Decision 39 COM 11

141. The Secretariat establishes and submits at each Committee session a list of all nominations received, including the date of reception, an indication of their status "complete" or "incomplete", as well as the date at which they are considered as "complete" in conformity with paragraph 132 and Annex5.

b）位于不同缔约国境内，不必相连，同时须经过所有相关缔约国同意进行申报（跨国系列遗产）。

139. 如申报的第一项遗产本身具有突出普遍价值，系列遗产（无论是由一国或是多国提起的）可历经数个申报周期，递交申报文件并接受评估。计划在数轮周期中分阶段进行系列申报的缔约国可向委员会说明此意向，以确保计划更加完善。

Ⅲ.D 申报登记

140. 收到各缔约国递交的申报文件后，秘书处将发送回执确认收到，核查材料是否完整，然后进行登记。秘书处将向相关咨询机构转交完整的申报文件，由咨询机构进行评估。秘书处也会将申报文本的电子版上传到世界遗产中心官网，以供委员会的各成员国参考。经咨询机构提请，秘书处将向缔约国索要补充信息。登记的时间表和申报的受理过程在第 168 条中有详细说明。

第 39 COM 11 决定

141. 秘书处在每届委员会会议时拟定并递交一份所有接收到的申报遗产名单，包括接收的日期，申报文件"完整"与否的陈述，以及按照第 132 条和附件 5 的要求申报文件被认为"完整"的日期。

Decisions 26 COM 14

Decision 28 COM 14B.57

Decision 39 COM 11

第26 COM 14和28 COM 14B.57及

第39 COM 11决议

142. A nomination passes through a cycle between the time of its submission and the decision by the World Heritage Committee. This cycle normally lasts one and a half years between submission in February of Year 1 and the decision of the Committee in June of Year 2.

142. 申报周期从递交之日起到世界遗产委员会做出决定之日结束。从每年二月缔约国递交申报材料至翌年六月委员会做出决定，通常历时一年半。

Ⅲ.Evaluation of nominations by the Advisory Bodies

Ⅲ.E. 咨询机构评估

143. The Advisory Bodies will evaluate whether or not properties nominated by States Parties have Outstanding Universal Value, meet the conditions of integrity and (when relevant) of authenticity and meet the requirements of protection and management. The procedures and format of ICOMOS and IUCN evaluations are described in Annex 6.

143. 咨询机构将评估各缔约国申报的遗产是否具有突出普遍价值，是否符合完整性或真实性（如果适用）的条件，以及是否能达到保护和管理的要求。国际古迹遗址理事会和世界自然保护联盟的评估程序和格式，在附件6中有详细说明。

Decision 39 COM 11

第39 COM 11号决议

144. Evaluations of cultural heritage nominations will be carried out by ICOMOS.

144. 对文化遗产申报的评估将由国际古迹遗址理事会完成。

145. Evaluations of natural heritage nominations will be carried out by IUCN.

145. 对自然遗产申报的评估将由世界自然保护联盟完成。

146. In the case of nominations of cultural properties in the category of 'cultural landscapes', as appropriate, the evaluation will be carried out by ICOMOS in consultation with IUCN. For mixed properties, the evaluation will be carried out jointly by ICOMOS and IUCN.

146. 作为"文化景观"类申报的文化遗产，将由国际古迹遗址理事会与世界自然保护联盟磋商之后进行评估。对于混合遗产的评估，将由国际古迹遗址理事会与世界自然保护联盟共同完成。

147. As requested by the World Heritage Committee or as necessary, ICOMOS and IUCN will carry out thematic studies to evaluate proposed World Heritage properties in their regional, global or

147. 如经世界遗产委员会要求或者在必要情况下，国际古迹遗址理事会与世界自然保护联盟将开展主题研究，将申报的世界遗产置于地区、全球或主题背景中进行评估。这些研究，

thematic context. These studies should be informed by a review of the Tentative Lists submitted by States Parties and by reports of meetings on the harmonization of Tentative Lists, as well as by other technical studies performed by the Advisory Bodies and qualified organizations and individuals. A list of those studies already completed may be found in section III of Annex 3, and on the Web addresses of the Advisory Bodies. These studies should not be confused with the comparative analysis to be prepared by States Parties in nominating properties for inscription on the World Heritage List (see paragraph 132).

ICOMOS:

http://www.icomos.org/studies/

IUCN:

http://www.iucn.org/themes/wcpa/pubs/worldheritage.htm

148. The following principles must guide the evaluations and presentations of ICOMOS and IUCN. The evaluations and presentations should:

Decision 28 COM 14B.57 Decision 30 COM 13
Decision 39 COM 11

a) adhere to the *World Heritage Convention* and the relevant *Operational Guidelines* and any additional policies set out by the Committee in its decisions;

b) be objective, rigorous and scientific including in considering all information provided to the Advisory Bodies regarding a nomination;

c) be conducted to a consistent standard of professionalism, equity and transparency throughout the evaluation process in consultation and dialogue with nominating States Parties;

d) comply to standard format, both for evaluations and presentations, to be agreed with the Secretariat and include names of all experts who

必须建立在对各缔约国递交的预备名录的审议，关于平衡预备名录的会议报告以及由咨询机构或具备相关资质的组织或个人进行的其他技术研究的基础之上。已完成的相关研究列表见附件 3 第三节和咨询机构的网站。这些研究不得与缔约国在申报世界遗产时准备的"比较分析"相混淆（见第 132 条）。

国际古迹遗址理事会：http：//www.icomos. org/studies/

世界自然保护联盟：http：//www.iucn.org/themes/wcpa/ pubs/ Worldheritage.htm

148. 以下为国际古迹遗址理事会和世界自然保护联盟的评估与陈述所遵循的原则。评估与陈述应：

第 28 COM 14B.57，第 30 COM 13 号及
第 39 COM 11 决议

a）遵守《世界遗产公约》及其《操作指南》，以及委员会在决定中规定的其他政策；

b）做到客观、严谨和科学，包括审查缔约国上交给咨询机构的有关申报的所有信息；

c）依照一致的专业标准；在评估过程中依照平等与透明的原则，与缔约国展开磋商与对话；

d）评估和陈述均须遵守标准格式，与秘书处一致，注明所有参与评估的专家的名字（提供保密意见的书面评估人员除外），另外在附件

participated in the evaluation process, except desk reviewers who provide confidential reviews, and, in an annex, a detailed breakdown of all costs and expenses related to the evaluation;

e) involve regional experts familiar with the subject;

f) indicate clearly and separately whether the property has Outstanding Universal Value, meets the conditions of integrity and/or authenticity, a management plan/system and legislative protection;

g) evaluate each property systematically according to all relevant criteria, including its state of conservation, relatively, that is, by comparison with that of other properties of the same type, both inside and outside the State Party's territory;

h) include references to Committee decisions and requests concerning the nomination under consideration;

i) not take into account or include any information submitted by the State Party after 28 February, in the year in which the nomination is considered. The State Party should be informed when information has arrived after the deadline and is not being taken into account in the evaluation. This deadline should be rigorously enforced; and

j) provide a justification for their views through a list of references (literature) consulted, as appropriate.

149. The Advisory Bodies are requested to forward to States Parties, with copy to the World Heritage Centre for distribution to the Chair of the World Heritage Committee, by 31 January of each year a short interim report outlining the status and any issues relevant to evaluations, and detailing any requests for supplementary information, in one of the two working languages of the *Convention*.

中应分类写清楚评估过程中所产生的花销;

e）让熟悉相关课题的地区专家参与进来;

f）清晰、明确地指出所申报遗产是否具有突出普遍价值，是否符合完整性和/或真实性的标准，是否拥有管理规划/系统和立法保护;

g）根据所有相关标准，对每处遗产（包括其保护状况），进行系统的比较性的评估，即需与缔约国境内或境外其他同类遗产进行比较;

h）应注明所援引的、与被审议的申报项目相关的委员会决定和要求;

i）不考虑或不计入缔约国于申报审议当年2月28日后递交的任何信息。同时应通知缔约国，因收到的信息已逾期，所以不纳入考虑之列。必须严格遵守最后期限;

j）同时提供支持他们论点的参考书目（文献）。

149. 咨询机构应在每年的1月31日以前，以一或两种公约要求的工作语言，向缔约国提供一份简短的评估报告，副本送世界遗产中心及委员会主席，报告应简要阐述遗产现状、以及其他与评估相关问题，详细说明需要补充的材料。

Decision 7 EXT.COM 4B.1 Decision 39 COM 11　　　　　第7 EXT.COM 4B.1及39 COM 11号决议

150. Letters from the concerned States Parties, submitted in the appropriate form in Annex 12, detailing the factual errors that might have been identified in the evaluation of their nomination made by the Advisory Bodies, must be received by the World Heritage Centre no later than 14 days before the opening of the session of the Committee with copies to the relevant Advisory Bodies. The letters shall be made available as an annex to the documents for the relevant agenda item, and no later than the first day of the Committee session. The World Heritage Centre and the Advisory Bodies may add their comments to the letters, in the relevant section of the form, before they are mad eavailable.

150. 相关缔约国应邀，在委员会大会开幕至少14天前，按附件12提供的格式，致信世界遗产中心，同时抄送咨询机构，详细说明咨询机构在评估其申报时可能发现的事实性错误。此信件作为相关文件的有效附件，最晚将在委员会会议前一天，按大会相应议程提交。世界遗产中心和咨询机构可在该信件发布前，在表格的相应部分加入他们的意见。

Decision 7 EXT.COM 4B.1 Decision 37 COM 12.II

第 7 EXT.COM 4B.1、37 COM 12.II 号决定

151. ICOMOS and IUCN make their recommendations under three categories:

a) properties which are recommended for inscription without reservation;

b) properties which are not recommended for inscription;

c) nominations which are recommended for referral or deferral.

151. 国际古迹遗址理事会和世界自然保护联盟的意见分三类：

ａ）建议无保留列入《世界遗产名录》的遗产；

ｂ）建议不予列入《世界遗产名录》的遗产；

ｃ）建议补充材料或重新申报《世界遗产名录》的遗产。

Ⅲ.F Withdrawal of nominations

Ⅲ.F 撤销申报

152. A State Party may withdraw a nomination it has submitted at any time prior to the Committee session at which it is scheduled to be examined. The State Party should inform the Secretariat in writing of its intention to withdraw the nomination. If the State Party so wishes it can resubmit a nomination for the property, which will be considered as a new nomination according to the procedures and timetable outlined in paragraph 168.

152. 缔约国可以在委员会召开会议审核申报之前任何时候，撤销所递交的申报，但必须以书面形式向秘书处说明意图。如某缔约国希望撤回申报，它可以重新递交一份遗产的申报，根据第 168 条所列程序和时间表，该申报将会被作为一项新申报。

Ⅲ..G Decision of the World Heritage Committee

Ⅲ..G 世界遗产委员会的决定

153. The World Heritage Committee decides whether a property should or should not be inscribed on the World Heritage List, referred or deferred.

153. 世界遗产委员会决定一项遗产是否应被列入《世界遗产名录》、或是要求补充材料或重新申报。

Inscription

列入名录

154. When deciding to inscribe a property on the World Heritage List, the Committee, guided by the Advisory Bodies, adopts a Statement of Outstanding Universal Value for the property.

154. 决定将遗产列入《世界遗产名录》时，在咨询机构的指导下，委员会将通过该遗产的《突出普遍价值声明》。

155. The Statement of Outstanding Universal Value should include a summary of the Committee's determination that the property has Outstanding Universal Value, identifying the criteria under which the property was inscribed, including the assessments of the conditions of integrity, and, for cultural and mixed properties, authenticity. It should also include a statement on the protection and management in force and the requirements for protection and management for the future. The Statement of Outstanding Universal Value shall be the basis for the future protection and management of the property.

155.《突出普遍价值声明》应包括委员会确定该遗产具有突出普遍价值的决定摘要，明确遗产列入《世界遗产名录》所遵循的标准，包括对于完整性或真实性（如果是文化遗产或混合遗产的话）状况的评估。还应该包括对现行保护管理情况及未来保护管理要求的说明。突出普遍价值声明将作为未来该遗产的保护和管理的基础。

Decision 39 COM 11

第 39 COM 11 号决定

Where necessary, the protection and management part of the Statement of Outstanding Universal Value may be updated by the World Heritage Committee, in consultation with the State Party and further to a review by the Advisory Bodies. Such updates could be made periodically further to the outcomes of Periodic reporting cycles, or at any Committee session, if required.

经与缔约国磋商，并在相关咨询机构的审核下，世界遗产委员会可以对遗产《突出的普遍价值声明》中的保护与管理部分进行必要的更新。更新可以在定期报告公布之后，或应要求于任一届委员会会议上执行。

The World Heritage Centre will automatically keep the Statements of Outstanding Universal Value

如果委员会决议变更遗产名称、微调遗产边界，或在相关咨询机构同意下修改任何事实

updated further to subsequent decisions taken by the Committee concerning a change of name of the property and change of surface further to minor boundary modifications and correct any factual errors as agreed with the relevant Advisory Bodies.

In the framework of the Gender Equality Priority of UNESCO, the use of gender-neutral language in the preparation of Statements of Outstanding Universal Value is encouraged.

156. At the time of inscription, the Committee may also make other recommendations concerning the protection and management of the World Heritage property.

157. The Statement of Outstanding Universal Value (including the criteria for which a specific property is inscribed on the World Heritage List) will be set out by the Committee in itsreports and publications.

Decision not to inscribe

158. If the Committee decides that a property should not be inscribed on the World Heritage List, the nomination may not again be presented to the Committee except in exceptional circumstances. These exceptional circumstances may include new discoveries, new scientific information about the property, or different criteria not presented in the original nomination. In these cases, a new nomination shall be submitted.

Referral of Nominations

159. Nominations which the Committee decides to refer back to the State Party for additional

性错误，则世界遗产中心将随之对《突出的普遍价值声明》自动更新。

在《联合国教科文组织性别平等条例》的框架下，委员会鼓励在《突出普遍价值声明》中使用性别中立语言。

156. 列入《世界遗产名录》时，委员会也可就该世界遗产的保护和管理提出其他的建议。

157. 委员会将在其报告和出版物中公布《突出的普遍价值声明》（包括将某具体遗产列入《世界遗产名录》的标准）。

决定不予列入

158. 如委员会决定某项遗产不予列入《世界遗产名录》，除非在极特殊情况下，否则该项申报不可重新向委员会提交。这些例外情况包括新发现、有关该遗产新的科学信息、或者之前申报时未提出的不同标准。在上述情况下，允许提交新的申报。

要求补充材料的申报

159. 委员会要求缔约国补充材料的申报，可以在下一次委员会会议上重新递交并接受审

information may be resubmitted to the following Committee session for examination. The additional information must be received by the Secretariat by 1 February[①] of the year in which examination by the Committee is desired. The Secretariat will immediately transmit it to the relevant Advisory Bodies for evaluation. A referred nomination which is not presented to the Committee within three years of the original Committee decision will be considered as a new nomination when it is resubmitted for examination, following the procedures and timetable outlined in paragraph 168. States Parties might seek advice from the relevant Advisory Body(ies) and/ or the World Heritage Centre to discuss how the recommendations of the Committee might be addressed.

议。补充信息须在委员会拟定审议当年 2 月 1 日前[①]呈交秘书处。秘书处将直接转交相关咨询机构进行评估。要求补报的申报材料如在原委员会决定下达三年内不曾提交委员会，再次递交审议时将被视为新申报，依据第 168 条所列程序及时间表进行。缔约国可以向相关咨询机构和（或）世界遗产中心征求意见，共同商议如何处理委员会提出的建议。

Decision 39 COM 11

第 39 COM 11 号决定

Deferral of Nominations

要求重新申报

160. The Committee may decide to defer a nomination for more in depth assessment or study, or a substantial revision by the State Party. Should the State Party decide to resubmit the deferred nomination in any subsequent year, it must be received by the Secretariat by 1 February[①]. These nominations will then be reevaluated evaluated again by the relevant Advisory Bodies during the course of the full year and a half evaluation cycle including an evaluation mission according to the procedures and timetable outlined in paragraph 168. States Parties are encouraged to seek advice from the relevant Advisory Body

160. 为了进行更深入的评估和研究，或便于缔约国对申报材料进行重大修改，委员会可能会做出要求缔约国重报的决定。如该缔约国决定在之后任一年重新递交申报，应于 2 月 1 日[①]之前提交至秘书处。届时相关咨询机构将根据第 168 条所列程序和时间表对这些申报重新进行周期为一年半的评估（包括派出现场评估专家）。委员会鼓励缔约国向相关咨询机构和（或）世界遗产中心征求意见，共同商议并处理委员会提出的建议。如有需要，缔约国可以考虑邀请咨询机构派出专家咨询考察。

---

① If 1 February falls on a weekend, the nomination must be received by 17h00 GMT the preceding Friday.

① 如 2 月 1 日恰为周末，申报材料需于之前周五格林威治时间 17 点前递交至秘书处。

② If 1 February falls on a weekend, the nomination must be received by 17h00 GMT the preceding Friday.

② 同上。

and/ or the World Heritage Centre to discuss how the recommendations of the Committee might be addressed. Where required, the State Parties may wish to consider inviting an Advisory mission.

Decision 39 COM 11

第 39 COM 11 决定

III.H Nominations to be processed on an emergency basis

III.H 紧急受理的申报

161. The normal timetable and definition of completeness for the submission and processing of nominations will not apply in the case of properties which would be in Danger, as a result of having suffered damage or facing serious and specific dangers from natural events or human activities, which would constitute an emergency situation for which an immediate decision by the Committee is necessary to ensure their safeguarding, and which, according to the report of the relevant Advisory Bodies, may unquestionably justify Outstanding Universal Value. Such nominations will be processed on an emergency basis and their examination is included in the agenda of the next Committee session. These properties may be inscribed on the World Heritage List. They shall, in that case, be simultaneously inscribed on the List of World Heritage in Danger (see paragraphs177-191).

161. 如果相关咨询机构认为某项遗产毫无疑问地拥有突出普遍价值，且因为自然或人为因素而受到损害或面临某种重大的危险，已经构成某种紧急状况，需要委员会迅速决定以确保它的保存，这种情况下，其申报材料的提交和受理不适用通常的时间表和关于材料完整性的定义。这类申报将被紧急受理，对它的审核将被纳入下届委员会会议议程。该遗产可能会被同时列入《世界遗产名录》和《濒危世界遗产名录》（见第 177–191 条）。

Decision 37 COM 12.II

第 37 COM 12.II 决定

162. The procedure for nominations to be processed on an emergency basis is as follows:

162. 紧急受理申报的程序如下：

Decisio37 COM 12.II

第 37 COM 12.II 决定

a) A State Party presents a nomination with the request for processing on an emergency basis. The State Party shall have already included, or immediately include, the property on its Tentative

a）缔约国呈交申报材料并要求紧急受理。该缔约国此前已将该项遗产列入《预备名录》，或立即将其纳入《预备名录》。

List.

b) The nomination shall:

i) describe the property and identify precisely its boundaries;

ii) justify its Outstanding Universal Value according to the criteria;

iii) justify its integrity and/or authenticity;

iv) describe its protection and management system;

v) describe the nature of the emergency, and the nature and extent of the damage or specific danger and showing that immediate action by the Committee is necessary to ensure the safeguarding of the property.

c) The Secretariat immediately transmits the nomination to the relevant Advisory Bodies, requesting an assessment of the qualities of the property which may justify its Outstanding Universal Value, of the nature of the danger and the urgency of a decision by the Committee. A field visit may be necessary if the relevant Advisory Bodies consider it appropriate and if the time allows.

d) When reviewing the nomination the Committee will also consider:

vi) allocation of International Assistance to complete the nomination; and

vi) follow-up missions as necessary by the Secretariat and the relevant Advisory Bodies as soon as possible after inscription to fulfil the Committee's recommendations.

Ⅲ.I Modifications to the boundaries, to the criteria used to justify inscription or to the name of a World Heritage property

Minor modifications to the boundaries

163. A minor modification is one which has not a significant impact on the extent of the property nor affects its Outstanding Universal Value.

b）该项申报应：

ⅰ）描述遗产及准确界定遗产边界；

ⅱ）根据标准论证其具有突出普遍价值；

ⅲ）论证该遗产的完整性和真实性；

ⅳ）描述其保护和管理体制

ⅴ）描述情况的紧迫性，损害或具体危险的性质和程度，说明委员会需即刻采取行动方可保证该遗产的存续。

c）由秘书处直接将该项申报转交相关咨询机构，要求对其具有的突出普遍价值以及对紧急情况、损害和／或危险的性质进行评估。如相关咨询机构认为恰当且时间允许，须进行实地勘查。

d）审议该申报时，委员会将同时考虑：

vi) 提供国际援助，完成申报工作；

vi) 列入《世界遗产名录》后尽快由秘书处和相关咨询机构组织后续工作。

Ⅲ.I 修改世界遗产的边界、原列入标准或名称

边界细微调整

163. 细微调整是指对遗产的范围和突出普遍价值影响不大的改动。

164. If a State Party wishes to request a minor modification to the boundaries of a property already on the World Heritage List, it must be prepared in compliance with the format of Annex 11 and must be received by 1 February[①] by the Committee through the Secretariat, which will seek the evaluation of the relevant Advisory Bodies on whether this can be considered a minor modification or not. The Secretariat shall then submit the Advisory Bodies' evaluation to the World Heritage Committee. The Committee may approve such a modification, or it may consider that the modification to the boundary is sufficiently significant as to constitute a significant boundary modification of the property, in which case the procedure for new nominations will apply.

164. 如某缔约国要求对已列入世界遗产名录的遗产边界进行细微调整，则必须依照附件11的格式准备相关材料，并于2月1日[①]以前通过秘书处向委员会递交申请。在征询相关咨询机构的意见之后，委员会或批准该申请，或认定边界修改过大，足以构成重大边界修改，在后一种情况下适用新申报程序。

Decision 39 COM 11

第39 COM 11决定

Significant modifications to the boundaries

边界重大修改

165. If a State Party wishes to significantly modify the boundary of a property already on the World Heritage List, the State Party shall submit this proposal as if it were a new nomination (including the requirement to be previously included on the Tentative List – see paragraph 63 and 65). This re-nomination shall be presented by 1 February[②] and will be evaluated in the full year and a half cycle of evaluation according to the procedures and timetable outlined in paragraph 168. This provision applies to extensions, as well as reductions.

165. 如某缔约国提出对已列入世界遗产名录的遗产边界进行重大修改，该缔约国应将其视为新申报并提交申请（包括事先纳入《预备名录》的要求—见63条及65条）。新的申报材料应于2月1日[②]以前递交，并根据第168条所列程序和时间表接受周期为一年半的评估。该规定同时适用于对遗产边界的扩大和缩小。

Decision 39 COM 11

第39 COM 11决定

---

① If 1 February falls on a weekend, the nomination must be received by 17h00 GMT the preceding Friday.

① 如2月1日恰为周末，申报材料需于格林威治时间前一个周五17点前递交至秘书处。

② If 1 February falls on a weekend, the nomination must be received by 17h00 GMT the preceding Friday.

② 如2月1日恰为周末，申报材料需于格林威治时间前一个周五17点前递交至秘书处。

Modifications to the criteria used to justify inscription on the World Heritage List

166. Where a State Party wishes to have the property inscribed under additional, fewer or different criteria other than those used for the original inscription, it shall submit this request as if it were a new nomination (including the requirement to be previously included on the Tentative List – see paragraph 63 and 65). This re-nomination must be received by 1 February[①] and will be evaluated in the full year and a half cycle of evaluation according to the procedures and timetable outlined in paragraph 168. Properties recommended will only be evaluated under the new criteria and will remain on the World Heritage List even if unsuccessful in having additional criteria recognized.

Decision 39 COM 11

Modification to the name of a World Heritage property

167. A State Party [②]may request that the Committee authorize a modification to the name of a property already inscribed on the World Heritage List. A request for a modification to the name shall be received by the Secretariat at least 3 months prior to the meeting of the Committee.

修改依据的《世界遗产名录》的标准

166. 当某缔约国希望增加、减少列入标准或选择不同于原列入标准的其他标准，将遗产列入名录，该国应将其视为新申报项目提交申请（包括事先纳入《预备名录》的要求—见63条及65条）。再次申报应于2月1日[①]以前递交，并根据第168条所列程序和时间表接受周期为一年半的评估。所推荐遗产将只依照新的标准接受评估，即使最后对补充标准不予认定，该项遗产仍将保留在《世界遗产名录》上。

第39 COM 11决定

世界遗产名称的修改

167.缔约国[②]可提请委员会批准对已列入世界遗产名录的遗产名称进行更改。更名申请应至少在委员会会议前三个月递交秘书处。

---

① If 1 February falls on a weekend, the nomination must be received by 17h00 GMT the preceding Friday.
① 如2月1日恰为周末，申报材料需于格林威治时间前一周的周五17点前递交至秘书处。
② In case of transnational/transboundary properties any modification will need the agreement of all States Parties concerned.
② 如果是跨境或跨界遗产，任何更改都要得到所有相关缔约国的同意。

Ⅲ.J Timetable –overview 168.

Timetable	Procedures
30 September (before Year 1)	Voluntary deadline for receipt of draf tnominations from States Parties by the Secretariat.
15 November (before Year 1)	Secretariat to respond to the nominating State Party concerning the completeness of the draft nomination, and, if incomplete, to indicate the missing information required to make the nomination complete.
1 February Year 1	Deadline by which complete nominations must be received by the Secretariat to be transmitted to the relevant Advisory Bodies for evaluation. Nominations shall be received by 17h00 GMT, or, if the date falls on a weekend by 17h00 GMT the preceeding Friday. Nominations received after this date will be examined in a future cycle.
1 February – 1 March Year 1	Registration, assessment of completeness and transmission to the relevant Advisory Bodies. The Secretariat registers each nomination, acknowledges receipt to the nominating State Party and inventories its contents. The Secretariat will inform the nominating StateParty whether or not the nomination is complete. Nominations that are not complete(see paragraph 132) will not be transmitted to the relevant Advisory Bodies for evaluation. If a nomination is incomplete, the State Party concerned will be advised of information required to complete the nomination by the deadline of 1 February of the following year in order for the nomination to be examined in a future cycle. Nominations that are completeare transmitted to the relevant Advisory Bodies for evaluation. The Secretariat will also make available the electronic format of the text of the nominations to the Members of the Committee on the World Heritage Centre's website.
1 March Year 1	Deadline by which the Secretariat informs the State Party of the receipt of a Nomination, whether it is considered complete and whether it has been received by 1 February.
March Year 1 – May Year 2	Evaluation by the Advisory Bodies
31 January Year 2	The Advisory Bodies are requested to forward to States Parties with copy to the World Heritage Centre for distribution to the Chair of the World Heritage Committee by 31 January of each year a short interim report outlining the status of and any issues relevant to evaluations, and detailing any requests for supplementary information, in one of the two working languages of the *Convention*. Deadline by which additional information requested by the relevant Advisory Bodies shall be submitted by the State Party to them via the Secretariat.
28 February Year 2	Additional information shall be submitted in the same number of copies and electronic formats as specified in Paragraph 132 to the Secretariat. To avoid confusing new and old texts, if the additional information submitted concerns changes to the main text of the nomination, the State Party shall submit these changes in an amended version of the original text. The changes shall be clearly identified. An electronic version (CD-ROM or diskette) of this new text shall accompany the paper version.

Timetable	Procedures
Six weeks prior to the annual World Heritage Committee session Year 2	The relevant Advisory Bodies deliver their evaluations and recommendations to the Secretariat for transmission to the World Heritage Committee as well as to States Parties.
At least 14 working days before theopening of the annual World Heritage Committee session Year 2	Correction of factual errors by States Parties The concerned States Parties can send, at least 14 working days before the opening of the session of the Committee, a letter to the Chairperson, with copies to the Advisory Bodies, detailing the factual errors they might have identified in the evaluation of their nomination made by the Advisory Bodies.
Annual session of the World Heritage Committee (June/July) Year 2	The Committee examines the nominations and makes its decisions.
Immediately following the annual session of the World Heritage Committee	Notification to the States Parties The Secretariat notifies all States Parties whose nominations have been examined by the Committee of the relevant decisions of the Committee. Following the decision of the World Heritage Committee to inscribea property on the World Heritage List, the Secretariat writes to the State Party and site managers providing a map of the area inscribed and the Statement of Outstanding Universal Value (to include reference to the criteria met).
Immediately following the annual session of the World Heritage Committee	The Secretariat publishes the updated World Heritage List every year following the annual session of the Committee. The name of the States Parties having nominated the properties inscribed on the World Heritage List are presented in the published form of the List under the following heading: "Contracting State having submitted the nomination of the property in accordance with the *Convention*».
In the month following the closure of the annual session of the World Heritage Committee	The Secretariat forwards the published report of all the decisions of the World Heritage Committee to all States Parties.

Ⅲ.J 时间表   总表 168.

时间表	程序
9 月 30 日（申报前一年）	各缔约国自愿向秘书处提交下年度申报材料初稿的截止期限。
11 月 15 日（申报前一年）	秘书处针对申报材料初稿完整与否答复相关缔约国，如不完整，注明要求补充的信息。
申报当年 2 月 1 日	秘书处收到完整的申报材料以便转交相关咨询机构评估的最后期限。 申报材料必须在格林威治时间 17 点以前送达，如当天为周末则必须在前一个星期五的 17 点（格林威治时间）以前送达。 在此日期后收到的申报材料将进入下一周期审议。
申报当年 2 月 1 日 – 3 月 1 日	登记、评估其完整性及转交相关咨询机构。 秘书处对各项申报进行登记，向提交申报的缔约国下发回执并将申报内容编目。秘书处将通知提交申报的缔约国申报材料是否完整。 不完整的申报材料（见第 132 条）不予转交相关咨询机构进行评估。如材料不完整，相关缔约国将被通知于翌年 2 月 1 日最后期限以前，补齐所缺信息以便参与下一周期的审议。 完整的申报材料由秘书处转交相关咨询机构进行评估。 秘书处将在世界遗产中心网站上，向委员会成员提供申报文件电子格式。

续表

时间表	程序
申报当年 3 月 1 日	秘书处告知各缔约国申报材料接收情况的最后期限，说明材料是否完整以及是否于 2 月 1 日以前收讫。
申报当年 3 月 – 申报翌年 5 月	咨询机构的评估。
申报翌年 1 月 31 日	咨询机构向缔约国进行征询，副本送世界遗产中心及委员会主席，在每年的 1 月 31 日以前，以一或两种公约要求的工作语言，提交简短的临时状况概要及与评估相关问题、需要补充的详细信息报告。 相关咨询机构要求缔约国补充的信息需在最后期限前通过秘书处提交。
申报翌年 2 月 28 日	向秘书处呈交的补充信息，应依照第 132 条中具体列出的数量准备复印件和电子版。为了避免新旧文本的混淆，如所递交的补充信息中包含对申报材料主要内容的修改，缔约国应将修改部分作为原申报文件的修正版提交，修改的部分应标示清楚。新文本除印刷版外还应附上电子版（光盘或软盘）。
申报翌年世界遗产委员会年会前 6 周	相关咨询机构向秘书处递送评估意见和建议，由秘书处转发给世界遗产委员会及各缔约国。
申报翌年世界遗产委员会年会开幕前至少 14 个工作日	缔约国更正事实性错误。 相关缔约国可在委员会大会开幕前至少 14 个工作日致信大会主席，副本送咨询机构，详细说明在咨询机构关于申报材料的评估意见中发现的事实性错误。
申报翌年（6 月 /7 月）世界遗产委员会年会	委员会审议申报材料并做出决定。
申报翌年世界遗产委员会年会结束	通知各缔约国。 凡经委员会审议的申报，秘书处将通知该缔约国有关委员会的相关决定。 在世界遗产委员会决定将某处遗产列入《世界遗产名录》之后，由秘书处书面通知该缔约国及遗产管理方，并提供列入名录区域的地图及《突出普遍价值声明》（注明适用标准）。
申报翌年世界遗产委员会年会结束	每年委员会会议结束之后，秘书处随即公布最新的《世界遗产名录》。 公布新的《世界遗产名录》，将注明申报项目列入《名录》的缔约国名称，标题为："缔约国根据《公约》递交遗产申报"。
世界遗产委员会年会闭幕后一个月内	秘书处将向各缔约国公告并报告世界遗产委员会全部决定。

IV. PROCESS FOR MONITORING THE STATE OF CONSERVATION OF WORLD HERITAGE PROPERTIES

IV. 世界遗产保护状况的监测程序

IV.A Reactive Monitoring

IV.A 反应性监测

Definition of Reactive Monitoring

反应性监测的定义

169. Reactive Monitoring is the reporting by the Secretariat, other sectors of UNESCO and the Advisory Bodies to the Committee on the state of

169. 反应性监测是指由秘书处、联合国教科文组织其他部门和咨询机构向委员会递交的有关具体濒危世界遗产保护状况的报告。为此，

conservation of specific World Heritage properties that are under threat. To this end, the States Parties shall submit specific reports and impact studies each time exceptional circumstances occur or work is undertaken which may have an impact on the Outstanding Universal Value of the property or its state of conservation. Reactive Monitoring is also foreseen in reference to properties inscribed, or to be inscribed, on the List of World Heritage in Danger as set out in paragraphs 177-191. Reactive Monitoring is also foreseen in the procedures for the eventual deletion of properties from the World Heritage List as set out inparagraphs 192-198.

每当出现异常情况或开展可能影响遗产的突出普遍性价值及其保护状况的活动时，缔约国须向委员会递交具体报告和影响调查。反应性监测也涉及已列入或待列入《濒危世界遗产名录》的遗产（如第 177-191 条所述）。同时，如第 192-198 条所述，从《世界遗产名录》中彻底删除某些遗产之前，也须进行反应性监测。

Decision 39 COM 11

第 39 COM 11 决定

These reports shall be submitted to the World Heritage Committee through the Secretariat, using the standard format in Annex 13, in English or French:

这些报告都应使用附件 13 中的标准格式（用英语或法语），经秘书处递交给世界遗产委员会：

a) by 1 December of the year preceding the examination of the property by the Committee, for the properties inscribed on the World Heritage List,

b) by 1 February of the year of examination of the property by the Committee, for the properties inscribed on the List of World Heritage in Danger, and for specific cases of utmosturgency.

a）在委员会审核申报列入《世界遗产名录》前一年的 12 月 1 日前提交。

b）在委员会审核申报列入《世界濒危遗产名录》及受理紧急申报前一年的 2 月 1 日前提交。

Objective of Reactive Monitoring

反应性监测的目标

170. When adopting the process of Reactive Monitoring, the Committee was particularly concerned that all possible measures should be taken to prevent the deletion of any property from the List and was ready to offer technical co-operation as far as possible to States Parties in this connection.

170. 实施反应性监测程序时，委员会特别关注的是如何采取一切可能的措施，避免从《世界遗产名录》中删除任何遗产。因此，只要情况允许，委员会愿意向缔约国提供相关的技术合作。

Article 4 of the Convention:

«Each State Party to this Convention recognizes that the duty of

《公约》第 4 条

"本公约缔约国均认同，保证第 1 条和第 2 条中提及的、

ensuring the identification, protection, conservation, presentation and transmission to future generations of the cultural and natural heritage referred to in Articles 1 and 2 and situated on its territory, belongs primarily to that State...».

本国领土内的文化和自然遗产的确定、保护、保存、展示和传承后世，主要是有关国家的责任…"

171. The Committee recommends that States Parties co-operate with the Advisory Bodies which have been asked by the Committee to carry out monitoring and reporting on its behalf on the progress of work undertaken for the preservation of properties inscribed on the World Heritage List.

171. 委员会建议缔约国与委员会指定的咨询机构合作，这些咨询机构受命代表委员会，对列入《世界遗产名录》的遗产的保护工作进展，进行监督和汇报。

Information received from States Parties and/or other sources

来自缔约国和/或其他渠道的信息

172. The World Heritage Committee invites the States Parties to the *Convention* to inform the Committee, through the Secretariat, of their intention to undertake or to authorize in an area protected under the *Convention* major restorations or new constructions which may affect the Outstanding Universal Value of the property. Notice should be given as soon as possible (for instance, before drafting basic documents for specific projects) and before making any decisions that would be difficult to reverse, so that the Committee may assist in seeking appropriate solutions to ensure that the Outstanding Universal Value of the property is full ypreserved.

172. 如《公约》缔约国，将在受《公约》保护地区开展或批准开展有可能影响到遗产突出的普遍价值的大规模修复或建设工程，世界遗产委员会促请缔约国通过秘书处向委员会转达该意图。缔约国必须尽快（例如，在起草具体工程的基本文件之前）且在做出任何难以逆转的决定之前 发布通告，以便委员会及时帮助寻找合适的解决办法，保证继续维护遗产的突出普遍价值。

173. The World Heritage Committee requests that reports of missions to review the state of conservation of the World Heritage properties include:

173. 世界遗产委员会要求检查世界遗产保护情况的工作报告，必须包括：

Decision 27 COM 7B.106

第27 COM 7B.106决定

a) an indication of threats or significant improvement in the conservation of the property since the last report to the World Heritage Committee;

a）说明自世界遗产委员会收到上一份报告以来，遗产所面临的威胁或保护工作取得的重大进步；

b) any follow-up to previous decisions of the World Heritage Committee on the state of conservation of the property;

c) information on any threat or damage to or loss of Outstanding Universal Value, integrity and/or authenticity for which the property was inscribed on the World Heritage List.

174. When the Secretariat receives information that a property inscribed has seriously deteriorated, or that the necessary corrective measures have not been taken within the time proposed, from a source other than the State Party concerned, it will, as far as possible, verify the source and the contents of the information in consultation with the State Party concerned and request its comments.

Decision by the World Heritage Committee

175. The Secretariat will request the relevant Advisory Bodies to forward comments on the information received.

176. The information received, together with the comments of the State Party and the Advisory Bodies, will be brought to the attention of the Committee in the form of a state of conservation report for each property, which may take one or more of the following steps:

Decision 39 COM 11

a) it may decide that the property has not seriously deteriorated and that no further action should betaken;

b) when the Committee considers that the property has seriously deteriorated, but not to the extent that its restoration is impossible, it may decide that the property be maintained on the List, provided that the State Party takes the necessary

b）世界遗产委员会此前关于遗产保护状况的决定的后续工作；

c）有关遗产赖以列入《世界遗产名录》的突出普遍价值、完整性和／或真实性受到威胁、破坏或减损的信息。

174. 一旦秘书处从相关缔约国以外的渠道获悉，已列入《名录》的遗产严重受损或在拟定期限内未采取必要的调整措施，秘书处将与有关缔约国磋商、证实消息来源和内容的真实性，并要求该国对此做出解释。

世界遗产委员会的决定

175. 秘书处将要求相关咨询机构对获取的信息给予评价。

176. 获取的信息与相关缔约国和咨询机构的评价一起，以遗产保护状况报告的形式呈交委员会审阅。委员会可采取以下一项或多项措施：

第39 COM 11决定

a）委员会可能认定该遗产未遭受严重损害，无须采取进一步行动；

b）当委员会认定该遗产确实遭受严重损害，但损害不至于不可修复，那么只要有关缔约国采取必要措施，在合理时间期限之内对其进行修复，该遗产仍可保留在《世界遗产名录》上。同时委员会也可能决定启动世界遗产基金

measures to restore the property within a reasonable period of time. The Committee may also decide that technical co-operation be provided under the World Heritage Fund for work connected with the restoration of the property, proposing to the State Party to request such assistance, if it has not already been done; in some circumstances States Parties may wish to invite an Advisory mission by the relevant Advisory Body(ies) or other organizations to seek advice on necessary measures to reverse deterioration and address threats.

c) when the requirements and criteria set out in paragraphs 177-182 are met, the Committee may decide to inscribe the property on the List of World Heritage in Danger according to the procedures set out in paragraphs 183-189;

d) when there is evidence that the property has deteriorated to the point where it has irretrievably lost those characteristics which determined its inscription on the List, the Committee may decide to delete the property from the List. Before any such action is taken, the Secretariat will inform the State Party concerned. Any comments which the State Party may make will be brought to the attention of the Committee;

e) when the information available is not sufficient to enable the Committee to take one of the measures described in a), b), c) or d) above, the Committee may decide that the Secretariat be authorized to take the necessary action to ascertain, in consultation with the State Party concerned, the present condition of the property, the dangers to the property and the feasibility of adequately restoring the property. Such measures may include the sending of a Reactive Monitoring mission or the consultation of specialists, or through an Advisory mission. The Secretariat shall report to the Committee on the results of its action. In case an emergency action is required, the Committee may authorize its financing from the World Heritage Fund through an emergency assistance request.

对遗产修复工作提供技术合作，并建议尚未提出类似要求的缔约国提起技术援助申请；在某些情况下，缔约国可能希望邀请相关的咨询机构或其他组织，派遣专家考察以征求相关意见，进而采取必要的措施，以扭转遗产恶化的局面并处理相应的威胁。

c）当满足第 177-182 条中所列要求与标准时，委员会可决定依照第 183-189 条所列程序，将该遗产列入《濒危遗产名录》；

d）如证据表明，该遗产所受损害已使其不可挽回地失去了赖以列入世界遗产名录的诸项特征，委员会可能会做出决定将该遗产从《世界遗产名录》中剔除。在采取任何措施之前，秘书处都将通知相关缔约国。该缔约国做出的任何回应都将上呈委员会；

e）当获取的信息不足以支持委员会采取上述 a）、b）、c）、d）项中的任何一种措施时，委员会可能会决定授权秘书处采取必要手段，在与相关缔约国磋商的情况下，确定遗产当前状态、所面临的危险及充分修复该遗产的可行性，类似措施包括派遣反应性监测工作组或咨询工作组，秘书处将会向委员会汇报上述行动的结果。当需要采取紧急措施时，委员会可批准通过世界遗产基金的紧急援助，筹措所需资金。

IV.B The List of World Heritage in Danger

IV.B《濒危世界遗产名录》

Guidelines for the inscription of properties on the List of World Heritage in Danger

列入《濒危世界遗产名录》的指南

177. In accordance with Article 11, paragraph 4, of the *Convention*, the Committee may inscribe a property on the List of World Heritage in Danger when the following requirements are met:

a) the property under consideration is on the World Heritage List;

b) the property is threatened by serious and specific danger;

c) major operations are necessary for the conservation of the property;

d) assistance under the *Convention* has been requested for the property; the Committee is of the view that its assistance in certain cases may most effectively be limited to messages of its concern, including the message sent by inscription of a property on the List of World Heritage in Danger and that such assistance may be requested by any Committee member or the Secretariat.

177. 依照《公约》第 11 条第 4 段，当一项遗产满足以下要求时，委员会可将其列入《濒危世界遗产名录》。

a）该遗产已列入《世界遗产名录》；

b）该遗产面临严重的、具体的危险；

c）该遗产的保护需要实施重大举措；

d）已申请依据《公约》为该遗产提供援助。委员会认为，在某些情况下，传递对该遗产关注的信息可能是最有效的援助手段。将遗产地列入《濒危世界遗产名录》就是这样一种信息。此类援助申请可能由委员会成员或秘书处提起。

Criteria for the inscription of properties on the List of World Heritage in Danger

列入《濒危世界遗产名录》的标准

178. A World Heritage property - as defined in Articles 1 and 2 of the *Convention* - can be inscribed on the List of World Heritage in Danger by the Committee when it finds that the condition of the property corresponds to at least one of the criteria in either of the two cases described below.

178. 当委员会查明一项世界遗产（如《公约》第 1 和第 2 条所定义）符合以下两种情况中至少一项时，该遗产可被列入《濒危世界遗产名录》。

179. In the case of cultural properties:

a) ASCERTAINED DANGER- The property is faced with specific and proven imminent danger, suchas:

i) serious deterioration of materials;

ii) serious deterioration of structure and/or

179. 如属于文化遗产：

a）已确知的危险——该遗产面临着具体的且确知即将来临的危险，例如

i）材料严重受损；

ii）结构特征和 /或装饰特色严重受损；

ornamental features;

iii) serious deterioration of architectural or town-planning coherence;

iv) serious deterioration of urban or rural space, or the natural environment;

v) significant loss of historical authenticity;

vi) important loss of cultural significance.

b) POTENTIAL DANGER–The property is faced with threats which could have deleterious effects on its inherent characteristics. Such threats are, for example:

i) modification of juridical status of the property diminishing the degree of its protection;

ii) lack of conservation policy;

iii) threatening effects of regional planning projects;

iv) threatening effects of town planning;

v) outbreak or threat of armed conflict;

vi) threatening impacts of climatic, geological or other environmental factors.

180. In the case of natural properties:

Decision 39 COM 11

c) ASCERTAINED DANGER–The property is faced with specific and proven imminent danger, suchas:

i) A serious decline in the population of the endangered species or the other species of Outstanding Universal Value for which the property was legally established to protect, either by natural factors such as disease or by human-made factors such as poaching.

ii) Severe deterioration of the natural beauty or scientific value of the property, as by human settlement, construction of reservoirs which flood important parts of the property, industrial and agricultural development including use of pesticides and fertilizers, major public works, mining, pollution, logging, firewood collection, etc.

iii）建筑和城镇规划的统一性严重受损；

iv）城市或乡村空间，或自然环境严重受损；

v）历史真实性严重丧失；

vi）文化意义严重丧失。

b）潜在的危险—该遗产面临可能会对其固有特性造成损害的威胁。此类威胁包括，如：

i）该遗产法律地位的改变引起的保护力度的削弱；

ii）缺乏保护政策；

iii）区域规划项目的威胁；

iv）城镇规划的威胁；

v）武装冲突的爆发或威胁，

vi）地质、气候或其他环境因素导致的威胁。

180. 如属于自然遗产：

第39 COM 11决定

c）已确知的危险—该遗产面临着具体的且确知即将来临的危险，例如

i）作为确立该项遗产法定保护地位依据的濒危物种、或其他具有突出普遍价值的物种数量，由于自然因素（例如疾病）或人为因素（例如偷猎）锐减。

ii）遗产的自然美景和科学价值由于人类的定居、兴建的水库淹没遗产重要区域、工农业的发展（包括杀虫剂和农药的使用，大型公共工程、采矿、污染、采伐、砍柴等）而遭受重大损害；

iii) Human encroachment on boundaries or in upstream areas which threaten the integrity of the property.

d) POTENTIAL DANGER–The property is faced with major threats which could have deleterious effects on its inherent characteristics. Such threats are, for example:

i) a modification of the legal protective status of the area;

ii) planned resettlement or development projects within the property or so situated that the impacts threaten the property;

iii) outbreak or threat of armedconflict;

iv) the management plan or management system is lacking or inadequate, or not fully implemented.

v) threatening impacts of climatic, geological or other environmental factors.

181. In addition, the threats and/or their detrimental impacts on the integrity of the property must be those which are amenable to correction by human action. In the case of cultural properties, both natural factors and human-made factors may be threatening, while in the case of natural properties, most threats will be human-made and only very rarely a natural factor (such as an epidemic disease) will threaten the integrity of the property. In some cases, the threats and/or their detrimental impacts on the integrity of the property may be corrected by administrative or legislative action, such as the cancelling of a major public works project or the improvement of legal status.

Decision 39 COM 11

182. The Committee may wish to bear in mind the following supplementary factors when considering the inclusion of a cultural or natural property in the List of World Heritage in Danger:

iii）人类活动对遗产或上游区域的侵蚀，威胁遗产的完整性。

d）潜在的危险—该遗产面临可能会对其固有特性造成损害的威胁。此类威胁包括：

i）该地区的法律保护地位发生变化

ii）在遗产范围内实施的，或虽在其范围外但足以波及和威胁到该遗产的移民或开发计划；

iii）武装冲突的爆发或威胁；

iv）管理规划或管理体系缺失、不完善或贯彻不彻底。

v）气候，地质或其他环境因素造成的威胁。

181. 另外，威胁遗产完整性的因素必须是人力可以补救的因素。对于文化遗产，自然因素和人为因素都可能构成威胁，而对于自然遗产来说，威胁其完整性的大多是人为因素，只有少数情况是由自然因素造成的（例如传染病）。某些情况下，对遗产完整性造成威胁的因素可通过行政或法律手段予以纠正，如取消某大型公共工程项目，加强法律地位。

第39 COM 11决定

182. 审议是否将一项文化或自然遗产列入《濒危世界遗产名录》时，委员会可能要考虑到下列额外因素：

a) Decisions which affect World Heritage properties are taken by Governments after balancing all factors. The advice of the World Heritage Committee can often be decisive if it can be given before the property becomes threatened.

b) Particularly in the case of ascertained danger, the physical or cultural deteriorations to which a property has been subjected should be judged according to the intensityof its effects and analyzed case by case.

c) Above all in the case of potential danger to a property, one should consider that:

i) the threat should be appraised according to the normal evolution of the social and economic framework in which the property is situated;

ii) it is often impossible to assess certain threats such as the threat of armed conflict as to their effect on cultural or naturalproperties;

iii) some threats are not imminent in nature, but can only be anticipated, such as demographic growth.

d) Finally, in its appraisal the Committee should take into account any cause of unknown or unexpected origin which endangers a cultural or natural property.

Procedure for the inscription of properties on the List of World Heritage in Danger

183. When considering the inscription of a property on the List of World Heritage in Danger, the Committee shall develop, and adopt, as far as possible, in consultation with the State Party concerned, a Desired state of conservation for the removal of the property from the List of World Heritage in Danger, and a programme for corrective measures.

184. In order to develop the programme of

a）政府是在权衡各种因素后才做出影响世界遗产的决定。世界遗产委员会如能在遗产遭到威胁之前给予建议的话，该建议往往具有决定权。

b）尤其是对于已确知的危险，对遗产所遭受的物理和文化损害的判断应基于其影响程度，并应具体问题具体分析。

c）对于潜在的危险必须首先考虑：

ⅰ）结合遗产所处的社会和经济环境的常规进程，对其所受到的威胁进行评估；

ⅱ）有些威胁对于文化和自然遗产的影响难以估量，例如武装冲突的威胁；

ⅲ)有些威胁在本质上不会立刻发生，而只能预见，例如人口的增长。

d）最后，委员会在进行评估时应将所有未知或无法预料的、但可能危及文化或自然遗产的因素纳入考虑范围。

列入《濒危世界遗产名录》的程序

183. 在考虑将一项遗产列入《濒危世界遗产名录》时，委员会应尽可能与相关缔约国磋商，确定或采纳将该遗产从《濒危名录》中移出的理想保护状况，和一套补救方案。

184. 为了制订前段所述补救方案，委员会

corrective measures referred to in the previous paragraph, the Committee shall request the Secretariat to ascertain, as far as possible in co-operation with the State Party concerned, the present condition of the property, the dangers to the property and the feasibility of undertaking corrective measures. The Committee may further decide to send a Reactive Monitoring mission from the relevant Advisory Bodies or other organizations to visit the property, evaluate the nature and extent of the threats and propose the measures to be taken. In some circumstances, the State Party may wish to invite an Advisory mission to provide advice and guidance.

应要求秘书处尽可能与相关缔约国合作，弄清遗产的现状，查明其面临的危险并探讨补救措施的可行性。此外委员会还可能决定派遣来自相关咨询机构或其他组织的反应性监测观察员，前往实地勘查，鉴定威胁的本质及程度，并根据补救措施提出建议。在某些情况下，缔约国可能希望邀请咨询机构的咨询专家进行实地考察并提供意见与指导。

Decision 39 COM 11

第39 COM 11决定

185. The information received, together with the comments as appropriate of the State Party and the relevant Advisory Bodies or other organizations, will be brought to the attention of the Committee by the Secretariat.

185. 获取的信息及相关缔约国和咨询机构或其他组织的评论，将经秘书处送交委员会审阅。

186. The Committee shall examine the information available and take a decision concerning the inscription of the property on the List of World Heritage in Danger. Any such decision shall be taken by a majority of two-thirds of the Committee members present and voting. The Committee will then define the programme of corrective action to be taken. This programme will be proposed to the State Party concerned for immediate implementation.

186. 委员会将审议现有信息，并针对是否将该遗产列入《濒危世界遗产名录》做出决定。出席表决的委员会成员须以三分之二多数通过类似决定。之后委员会将确定补救方案，并建议相关缔约国立即执行。

187. The State Party concerned shall be informed of the Committee's decision and public notice of the decision shall immediately be issued by the Committee, inaccordance with Article 11.4 of the *Convention*.

187. 依照《公约》第11条第4段，委员会应将决定通告相关缔约国，并随即就该项决定发表公告。

188. The Secretariat publishes the updated List

188. 由秘书处印发最新的《濒危世界遗产

of World Heritage in Danger in printed form and is also available at the following Web address: http://whc.unesco.org/en/danger

189. The Committee shall allocate a specific, significant portion of the World Heritage Fund to financing of possible assistance to World Heritage properties inscribed on the List of World Heritage in Danger.

Regular review of the state of conservation of properties on the List of World Heritage in Danger

190. The Committee shall review annually the state of conservation of properties on the List of World Heritage in Danger. This review shall include such monitoring procedures and expert missions as might be determined necessary by the Committee.

191. On the basis of these regular reviews, the Committee shall decide, in consultation with the State Party concerned, whether:

a) additional measures are required to conserve theproperty;

b) to delete the property from the List of World Heritage in Danger if the property is no longer under threat;

c) to consider the deletion of the property from both the List of World Heritage in Danger and the World Heritage List if the property has deteriorated to the extent that it has lost those characteristics which determined its inscription on the World Heritage List, in accordance with the procedure set out in paragraphs 192-198.

Ⅳ.C Procedure for the eventual deletion of properties from the World Heritage List

192. The Committee adopted the following procedure for the deletion of properties from the

名录》，同时电子版也可在以下网站上获取：http：//whc.unesco.org/en/danger

189. 委员会将从世界遗产基金中特别划拨一笔相当数量的资金，为列入《濒危世界遗产名录》的遗产提供可能的援助。

对于《濒危世界遗产名录》上遗产保护状况的定期检查

190. 委员会每年将对《濒危世界遗产名录》上遗产的保护状况进行例行检查。检查的内容包括委员会认为必要的监测程序和专家考察。

191. 在定期检查的基础上，委员会将与有关缔约国磋商，决定是否：

a）该遗产需要额外的保护措施；

b）当该遗产不再面临威胁时，将其从《濒危世界遗产名录》中删除；

c）当该遗产由于严重受损而丧失赖以列入《世界遗产名录》的特征时，考虑依照第 192-198 条所列程序，将其同时从《世界遗产名录》和《濒危世界遗产名录》中删除。

Ⅳ.C《世界遗产名录》中遗产彻底除名的程序

192. 在以下情况下，委员会采取下述步骤，将遗产从《世界遗产名录》中除名：

World Heritage Listincases:

Decision 39 COM 11   第39 COM 11决定

a) where the property has deteriorated to the extent that it has lost those characteristics which determined its inclusion in the World Heritage List; and

b) where the intrinsic qualities of a World Heritage site were already threatened at the time of its nomination by human action and where the necessary corrective measures as outlined by the State Party at the time, have not been taken within the time proposed (see paragraph116).

193. When a property inscribed on the World Heritage List has seriously deteriorated, or when the necessary corrective measures have not been taken within the time proposed, the State Party on whose territory the property is situated should so inform the Secretariat.

194. When the Secretariat receives such information from a source other than the State Party concerned, it will, as far as possible, verify the source and the contents of the information in consultation with the State Party concerned and request its comments.

195. The Secretariat will request the relevant Advisory Bodies to forward comments on the information received.

196. The Committee will examine all the information available and will take a decision. Any such decision shall, in accordance with Article 13 (8) of the *Convention*, be taken by a majority of two-thirds of its members present and voting. The Committee shall not decide to delete any property unless the State Party has been consulted on the question.

a）遗产严重受损，丧失了其作为世界遗产的决定性特征；

b）遗产在申报时便由于人为因素导致其内在特质受到威胁，而缔约国在规定时间内又没有采取必要的补救措施（见第116段）。

193.《世界遗产名录》内遗产严重受损，或缔约国没有在限定的时间内采取必要的补救措施，此遗产所在缔约国应该把这种情况通知秘书处。

194. 如果秘书处从缔约国之外的第三方得到了这种信息，秘书处会与相关缔约国磋商，尽量核实信息来源与内容的可靠性，并且听取缔约国的意见。

195. 秘书处将要求相关咨询机构提交对所收到信息的意见。

196. 委员会将审查所有可用信息，做出处理决定。根据《公约》第13（8）条的规定，委员会与会委员三分之二以上投票同意，该决定方能通过。在未就此事宜与缔约国协商之前，委员会不应做出把遗产除名的决定。

197. The State Party shall be informed of the Committee's decision and public notice of this decision shall be immediately given by the Committee.

198. If the Committee's decision entails any modification to the World Heritage List, this modification will be reflected in the next updated List that is published.

V. PERIODIC REPORTING ON THE IMPLEMENTATION OF THE *WORLD HERITAGE CONVENTION*

V.A Objectives

199. States Parties are requested to submit reports to the UNESCO General Conference through the World Heritage Committee on the legislative and administrative provisions they have adopted and other actions which they have taken for the application of the *Convention*, including the state of conservation of the World Heritage properties located on their territories.

Article 29 of the *World Heritage Convention* and Resolutions of the 11th session of the General Assembly of States Parties (1997) and the 29th session of the UNESCO General Conference.

200. States Parties may request expert advice from the Advisory Bodies and the Secretariat, which may also (with agreement of the States Parties concerned) commission further expert advice.

201. Periodic Reporting serves four main purposes:

a) to provide an assessment of the application of the *World Heritage Convention* by the State Party;

b) to provide an assessment as to whether the Outstanding Universal Value of the properties inscribed on the World Heritage List is being maintained

197. 应将委员会的决定传达给缔约国，同时尽快将决定公布于世。

198. 如果委员会的决定变更了目前的《世界遗产名录》，变更内容将体现在下一期的《世界遗产名录》中。

V. 有关《世界遗产公约》实施情况的《定期报告》

V.A 目标

199. 要求缔约国经由世界遗产委员会，将其通过的法律和行政条款以及实施《世界遗产公约》采取的其他行动报告，提交教科文组织大会，其中包括其领土内世界遗产的保护状况。

《世界遗产公约》第 29 条，缔约国第 11 届大会（1997年）以及联合国教科文组织第 29 届大会决议

200. 缔约国可能需要咨询机构和秘书处的专业意见，咨询机构和秘书处在缔约国同意的情况下也可寻求其他专业意见。

201.《定期报告》主要有以下四个目的：

a）评估缔约国《世界遗产公约》的执行情况；

b）评估《世界遗产名录》内遗产的突出普遍价值是否得到长期的保持；

over time;

c) to provide up-dated information about the World Heritage properties to record the changing circumstances and state of conservation of the properties;

d) to provide a mechanism for regional co-operation and exchange of information and experiences between States Parties concerning the implementation of the *Convention* and World Heritage conservation.

202. Periodic Reporting is important for more effective long term conservation of the properties inscribed, as well as to strengthen the credibility of the implementation of the *Convention*.

V.B Procedure and Format

203. World Heritage Committee:

Decision 22 COM Ⅵ.7

a) adopted the Format and Explanatory Notes set out in Annex 7;

b) invited States Parties to submit periodic reports every six years;

c) decided to examine the States Parties' periodic reports region by region according to the following table:

Region	Examination of properties inscribed up to and including	Year of Examination by Committee
Arab States	1992	December 2000
Africa	1993	December 2001/July 2002
Asia and the Pacific	1994	June-July 2003
Latin America and the Caribbean	1995	June-July2004
Europe and North America	1996/1997	June-July 2005/2006

c）提供世界遗产的相关更新信息，记录遗产所处环境和保护状况的变化；

d）针对《世界遗产公约》实施及世界遗产保护事宜，为缔约国提供一种区域间合作以及信息分享、经验交流的机制。

202.《定期报告》不仅对更有效的对遗产的长期保存起到了至关重要的作用，也提高了《世界遗产公约》实施的可信性。

V.B. 程序和格式

203. 世界遗产委员会：

第 22 COM Ⅵ.7 号决定

a）通过了附录 7 中的格式和相关注解；

b）邀请缔约国每六年提交一次《定期报告》；

c）决定按下表逐个区域地审查缔约国的定期报告：

地区	对《名录》中遗产的检查	委员会检查的年度
阿拉伯国家	1992 年	2000 年 12 月
非洲	1993 年	2001 年 12 月 /2002 年 7 月
亚太地区	1994 年	2003 年 6 月 -7 月
拉丁美洲和加勒比地区	1995 年	2004 年 6 月 -7 月
欧洲和北美洲	1996 年 /1997 年	2005 年 /2006 年 6 月 -7 月

d) requested the Secretariat, jointly with the Advisory Bodies, and making use of States Parties, competent institutions and expertise available within the region, to develop regional strategies for the periodic reporting process as per the timetable established under c) above.

204. The above-mentioned regional strategies should respond to specific characteristics of the regions and should promote co-ordination and synchronization between States Parties, particularly in the case of transboundary properties. The Secretariat will consult States Parties with regard to the development and implementation of those regional strategies.

205. After the first six-year cycle of periodic reports, each region will be assessed again in the same order as indicated in the table above. Following the first six-year cycle, there may be a pause for evaluation to assess and revise the periodic reporting mechanism before a new cycle is initiated.

206. The Format for the periodic reports by the States Parties consists of two sections:

This Format was adopted by the Committee at its 22nd session (Kyoto 1998) and may be revised following the completion of the first cycle of Periodic Reporting in 2006. For this reason, the Format has not been revised.

a) Section I refers to the legislative and administrative provisions which the State Party has adopted and other actions which it has taken for the application of the *Convention*, together with details of the experience acquired in this field. This particularly concerns the general obligations defined in specific articles of the *Convention*.

b) Section II refers to the state of conservation of specific World Heritage properties located on the

d）要求秘书处与咨询机构合作，发挥缔约国、主管部门及当地专家的作用，根据上文 c）段的时间表，制定定期报告的区域性策略。

204. 上述的区域性策略应该体现当地的特征，且能促进缔约国间的合作与协调。这一点对于跨界遗产尤为重要。秘书处会针对这些区域性策略的制定和执行事宜，与缔约国磋商。

205. 为期六年的定期报告周期结束后，会再按上表标明的顺序对各区域进行评估。首个六年周期后，新周期开始前，会留出一段时间对定期报告机制进行评估和修正。

206. 缔约国的定期报告主要包括以下两部分：

本格式在委员会的第 22 届大会上通过（1998年，京都）。2006 年首个定期报告结束后，可能修订现有格式。目前尚未对该格式做出任何修改。

a）第一部分包括缔约国为执行《公约》通过的法律和行政条款，采取的其他行动，以及在这一领域获得的相关经验的详细内容，特别是与《公约》中具体条款所规定义务的相关情况。

b）第二部分阐述在缔约国领土内特定世界遗产的保护状况。本部分应完整说明每处世界

territory of the State Party concerned. This Section should be completed for each World Heritage property.

Explanatory Notes are provided with the Format in Annex 7.

207. In order to facilitate management of information, States Parties are requested to submit reports, in English or French, in electronic as well as in printed form to:

UNESCO World Heritage Centre
7, place de Fontenoy 75352 Paris 07 SP
France
Tel:　　　+33 (0)1 45 68 1276
Email: wh-info@unesco.org

1.C Evaluation and Follow Up

208. The Secretariat consolidates national reports into Regional State of the World Heritage reports, which are available in electronic format at the following Web address http://whc.unesco.org/en/publications and in paper version (series World Heritage Papers).

209. The World Heritage Committee carefully reviews issues raised in Periodic Reports and advises the States Parties of the regions concerned on matters arising from them.

210. The Committee requested the Secretariat with the Advisory Bodies, in consultation with the relevant States Parties, to develop long-term follow-up Regional Programmes structured according to its Strategic Objectives and to submit them for its examination. These Programmes are adopted as follow up to Periodic Reports and regularly reviewed by the Committee based on the needs of States Parties identified in Periodic Reports. They should accurately reflect the needs of World Heritage in the Region and facilitate the granting of International Assistance.

遗产的情况。

附录 7 中提供了格式注解。

207. 为了便于信息管理，缔约国应同时提交电子版和打印版的报告，英文或法文均可。提交地址如下：

联合国教科文组织世界遗产中心法国巴黎
（7，place de Fontenoy 75352 Paris 07SP France）电话：+33（0）145681571
传真：+33（0）1 45 68 55 70
电子邮件：wh-info@unesco.org

Ⅴ.C 评估和后续工作

208. 秘书处将国家报告整理成《世界遗产区域性报告》。该《报告》有电子版（http://whc.unesco.org/en/publications）及纸质印刷版（世界遗产论文系列）。

209. 世界遗产委员会认真审查《定期报告》所述议题，并针对其中的问题为相关区域的缔约国提出建议。

210. 委员会要求秘书处、咨询机构与相关缔约国进行磋商，根据其《战略目标》制定长期《区域性计划》，并提交委员会审议。这些区域性计划是《定期报告》的后续跟踪活动，委员会应根据缔约国在《定期报告》中所确定的需要，定期进行审查。计划应能准确反映该区域世界遗产保护的需求，方便国际援助。委员会还表示，会确保《战略目标》与国际援助之间的直接联系。

The Committee also expressed its support to ensure direct links between the Strategic Objectives and the International Assistance.

Decision 36 COM 13.I

第 36 COM 13.I 决定

VI ENCOURAGING SUPPORT FOR THE *WORLD HERITAGE CONVENTION*

Ⅵ. 鼓励对《世界遗产公约》的支持

Ⅵ.A Objectives

Ⅵ.A 目标

Article 27 of the *World Heritage Convention*

《世界遗产公约》第27条

211. The objectives are:

a) to enhance capacity-building and research;

b) to raise the general public's awareness, understanding and appreciation of the need to preserve cultural and natural heritage;

c) to enhance the function of World Heritage in the life of the community; and

211. 目标如下：

a）加强能力建设与研究；

b）提高民众意识，使其逐渐理解并重视保护文化与自然遗产的重要性；

c）加强世界遗产在社会生活中的作用；

Article 5(a) of the *World HeritageConvention*

《世界遗产公约》第5（a）条

d) to increase the participation of local and national populations in the protection and presentation of heritage.

d）提高地方及全国民众对遗产保护与展示的参与。

Ⅵ.B Capacity–building and research

Ⅵ.B 能力建设与研究

212. The Committee seeks to develop capacity-building within the States Parties in conformity with its Strategic Objectives.

212. 委员会根据《战略目标》，致力于缔约国内的能力建设。

Budapest Declaration on World Heritage (2002)

《布达佩斯世界遗产宣言》（2002 年）

The Global Training Strategy

全球培训战略

213. Recognizing the high level of skills and multidisciplinary approach necessary for the protection, conservation, and presentation of the World

213. 委员会认识到，为了世界遗产的保护、保存和展示，高技能以及多学科的方法是必不可少的，为此，委员会通过了"世界文化和自

Heritage, the Committee has adopted a Global Training Strategy for World Cultural and Natural Heritage. The primary goal of the Global Training Strategy is to ensure that necessary skills are developed by a wide range of actors for better implementation of the *Convention*. In order to avoid overlap and effectively implement the Strategy, the Committee will ensure links to other initiatives such as the Global Strategy for a Representative, Balanced and Credible World Heritage List and Periodic Reporting. The Committee will annually review relevant training issues, assess training needs, review annual reports on training initiatives, and make recommendations for future training initiatives.

然遗产的全球培训战略"。"全球培训战略"的首要目标是确保相关领域工作者获得必要的技能，以便更好地实施《公约》。为了避免重复，同时有效实施该策略，委员会将确保其与《构建具有代表性、平衡性、可信性的〈世界遗产名录〉的全球战略》、"定期报告"等其他倡议工作之间的联系。委员会将每年评审相关培训议题、评估培训需求、审阅年度报告并为进一步的培训提供建议。

Global Training Strategy for World Cultural and Natural Heritage adopted by the World Heritage Committee at its 25th session (Helsinki, Finland, 2001) (see ANNEX X of document WHC- 01/CONF.208/24).

"世界文化和自然遗产的全球培训策略"于世界遗产委员会第 25 届会议通过（芬兰赫尔辛基，2001年）（见文书 WHC–01/CONF.208/24 附件Ｘ）.

National training strategies and regional co-operation

国家培训策略和区域性合作

214. States Parties are encouraged to ensure that their professionals and specialists at all levels are adequately trained. To this end, States Parties are encouraged to develop national training strategies and include regional cooperation for training as part of their strategies.

214. 鼓励缔约国确保其各级专业人员和专家均训练有素。为此，鼓励缔约国制定国家培训策略，并把区域合作培训作为战略的一部分。

Research

研究

215. The Committee develops and coordinates international co-operation in the area of research needed for the effective implementation of the *Convention*. States Parties are also encouraged to make resources available to undertake research, since knowledge and understanding are fundamental to the identification, management, and monitoring of World Heritage properties.

215. 委员会在有效实施《公约》所需的研究领域开展并协调国际合作。由于知识和理解对于世界遗产的确认、管理和监测起着至关重要的作用，还鼓励缔约国提供开展研究所需资源。

International Assistance

国际援助

216. Training and Research Assistance may be requested by States Parties from the World Heritage Fund (see Chapter VII).

216. 缔约国可向世界遗产基金申请培训和研究援助（见第七章）。

Ⅵ.C Awareness-raising and education

Ⅵ.C 提高认识与教育

Awareness-raising

提高认识

217. States Parties are encouraged to raise awareness of the need to preserve World Heritage. In particular, they should ensure that World Heritage status is adequately marked and promoted on-site.

217. 鼓励缔约国提高对世界遗产保护需求的认识，尤其应确保在遗产地对世界遗产地位进行有效的标识和宣传。

218. The Secretariat provides assistance to States Parties in developing activities aimed at raising public awareness of the *Convention* and informing the public of the dangers threatening World Heritage. The Secretariat advises States Parties regarding the preparation and implementation of on-site promotional and educational projects to be funded through International Assistance. The Advisory Bodies and appropriate State agencies may also be solicited to provide advice on such projects.

218. 秘书处向缔约国提供援助，开展活动，以提高公众对《公约》的认识，并告知公众世界遗产所面临的威胁。秘书处将针对如何筹划及开展"国际援助"资助的现场推广与教育项目向缔约国提出建议，也会征求咨询机构和国家，有关部门关于此类活动的建议。

Education

教育

219. The World Heritage Committee encourages and supports the development of educational materials, activities and programmes.

219. 世界遗产委员会鼓励并支持编撰教材，开展和实施各种教育活动和方案。

International Assistance

国际援助

220. States Parties are encouraged to develop educational activities related to World Heritage with, wherever possible, the participation of schools, universities, museums and other local and national educational authorities.

220. 鼓励缔约国开展世界遗产相关教育活动，如有可能，让中小学校、大学、博物馆以及其他地方或国家的教育机构参与其中。

Article 27.2 of the *World Heritage Convention*

《世界遗产公约》第 27.2 条

221. The Secretariat, in co-operation with the UNESCO Education Sector and other partners, produces and publishes a World Heritage Educational Resource Kit, "World Heritage in Young Hands", for use in secondary schools around the world. The Kit is adaptable for use at other educational levels.

«World Heritage in Young Hands» is available at the following Web address http://whc.unesco.org/education / index.htm

222. International Assistance may be requested by States Parties from the World Heritage Fund for the purpose of developing and implementing awareness-raising and educational activities or programmes (see Chapter VII).

VII THE WORLD HERITAGE FUND AND INTERNATIONAL ASSISTANCE

VII.A The World Heritage Fund

223. The World Heritage Fund is a trust fund, established by the *Convention* in conformity with the provisions of the Financial Regulations of UNESCO. The resources of the Fund consist of compulsory and voluntary contributions made by States Parties to the *Convention*, and any other resources authorized by the Fund's regulations.

Article 15 of the *World Heritage Convention*.

224. The financial regulations for the Fund are set out in document WHC/7 available at the following Web address: http://whc.unesco.org/en/financialregulations

VII.B Mobilization of other technical and financial resources and partnerships in support of the *World Heritage Convention*

221. 秘书处与联合国教科文组织教育部及其他伙伴合作，开发并出版世界遗产教育培训教材："世界遗产掌握在年轻人手中"。此教材供全世界的中学使用，也可调整后用于其他教育水平的人群。

可访问：http://whc.unesco.org/education/index.htm 查阅"世界遗产掌握在年轻人手中"

222. 缔约国可向世界遗产基金申请国际援助，以提升遗产保护意识，开展教育活动与方案（见第七章）。

VII. 世界遗产基金和国际援助

VII.A 世界遗产基金

223. 世界遗产基金是信托基金，是《公约》依据《联合国教科文组织财务条例》的规定建立的。此基金由《公约》缔约国义务或者自愿的捐献及基金规章授权的其他来源组成。

《世界遗产公约》第 15 条

224. 基金财务条例写进文书 WHC/7 内，可登录以下网址查阅：http://whc.unesco.org/en/financialregulations

VII.B. 调动其他技术及财务资源，展开合作，支持《世界遗产公约》

225. To the extent possible, the World Heritage Fund should be used to mobilize additional funds for International Assistance from other sources.

226. The Committee decided that contributions offered to the World Heritage Fund for international assistance campaigns and other UNESCO projects for any property inscribed on the World Heritage List shall be accepted and used as international assistance pursuant to Section V of the *Convention*, and in conformity with the modalities established for carrying out the campaign or project.

227. States Parties are invited to provide support to the *Convention* in addition to obligatory contributions paid to the World Heritage Fund. This voluntary support can be provided through additional contributions to the World Heritage Fund or direct financial and technical contributions to properties.

Article 15(3) of the *World Heritage Convention*

228. States Parties are encouraged to participate in international fund-raising campaigns launched by UNESCO and aimed at protecting World Heritage.

229. States Parties and others who anticipate making contributions towards these campaigns or other UNESCO projects for World Heritage properties are encouraged to make their contributions through the World Heritage Fund.

230. States Parties are encouraged to promote the establishment of national, public and private foundations or associations aimed at raising funds to support World Heritage conservation efforts.

Article 17 of the World Heritage Convention.

225．应尽可能发挥世界遗产基金的作用，开发更多资金来源，促进国际援助。

226．委员会决定，根据《公约》第 V 部分的规定，在符合活动或项目开展的情况下，世界遗产基金收到的捐款，应用于国际援助活动和其他联合国教科文组织《世界遗产名录》遗产保护项目。

227．除了向世界遗产基金义务捐款之外，还鼓励缔约国为《公约》提供自愿支持。自愿支持包括向世界遗产基金提供额外捐款，或者直接对遗产提供财政或技术援助。

《世界遗产公约》第 15（3）条

228．鼓励缔约国参与联合国教科文组织发起的、旨在保护世界遗产的国际资金筹募活动。

229．委员会鼓励那些希望为上述国际资金筹募活动或联合国教科文组织其他的世界遗产保护项目提供支持的缔约国、其他组织或个人，通过世界遗产基金捐款。

230．鼓励缔约国创立国家、公共和私人基金或机构，用来筹资支持世界遗产保护。

《世界遗产公约》第 17 条

231. The Secretariat provides support in mobilizing financial and technical resources for World Heritage conservation. To this end, the Secretariat develops partnerships with public and private institutions in conformity with the Decisions and the Guidelines issued by the World Heritage Committee and UNESCO regulations.

231. 秘书处支持调动财政或技术资源保护世界遗产。为此，秘书处在遵守世界遗产委员会和联合国教科文组织相关指南和规定的前提下，与公共或私人组织发展伙伴关系。

232. The Secretariat should refer to "UNESCO's "Comprehensive Partnership Strategy" to govern external fund-raising in favour of the World Heritage Fund. This document is available at the following Web address: http://en.unesco.org/partnerships.

232. 秘书处在为世界遗产基金进行外部筹资时，应该援引：联合国教科文组织的 "全面合作伙伴战略"。这份文件可以在以下网站获得：http：/ en.unesco.org/partnerships.

"Comprehensive Partnership Strategy" including "Separate strategies for engagement with individual categories of partners" 192 EX/5.INF

Decision 30 COM 13.13

"联合国教科文组织全面合作伙伴关系战略" 包括 "与特定合作伙伴约定的独立战略" 192 EX/5.INF

第 30 COM 13.13 号决定

VII.C International Assistance

VII .C 国际援助

233. The *Convention* provides International Assistance to States Parties for the protection of the world cultural and natural heritage located on their territories and inscribed, or potentially suitable for inscription on the World Heritage List. International Assistance should be seen as supplementary to national efforts for the conservation and management of World Heritage and Tentative List properties when adequate resources cannot be secured at the national level.

233.《公约》向各缔约国提供国际援助，以保护其领土内的世界文化和自然遗产、《世界遗产名录》内遗产以及符合《名录》要求的潜在世界遗产。当国家不能确保足够的资金时，国际援助将辅助该缔约国保护、管理世界遗产及《预备名录》内遗产。

See Articles 13 (1&2) and 19- 26 of the *World Heritage Convention*.

见《世界遗产公约》第 13 条（1&2）和第 19-26 条

234. International Assistance is primarily financed from the World Heritage Fund, established under the *World Heritage Convention*. The Committee determines the budget for International Assistance on a biennial basis.

234. 国际援助主要来自世界遗产基金，世界遗产基金是依据《世界遗产公约》建立的。委员会每两年决定一次国际援助的预算。

Section IV of the World Heritage Convention

《世界遗产公约》第四部分

235. The World Heritage Committee co-ordinates and allocates types of International Assistance in response to State Party requests. These types of International Assistance, described in the summary table set out below, in order of priority are:

235. 世界遗产委员会应缔约国的请求，协调分配各种国际援助。国际援助有以下几种，按照优先性依次排列如下：

Decision 30 COM 14A

Decision 36 COM 13.I

第 30 COM 14A 号决定

第 36 COM 13.I 号决定

a) Emergency assistance

b) Conservation and Management assistance (incorporating assistance for training and research, technical co-operation and promotion and education)

c) Preparatory assistance.

a）紧急援助

b）保护与管理援助（包括培训与研究援助、技术合作援助 以及宣传和教育援助）

c）筹备性援助

VII.D Principles and priorities for International Assistance

VII .D 国际援助的原则和优先顺序

236. Priority is given to International Assistance for properties inscribed on the List of World Heritage in Danger. The Committee created a specific budget line to ensure that a significant portion of assistance from the World Heritage Fund is allocated to properties inscribed on the List of World Heritage in Danger.

236. 国际援助将优先给予《濒危世界遗产名录》内的遗产。委员会规定了具体的预算线，确保世界遗产基金相当大的一部分资金，用来救援《濒危世界遗产名录》内的遗产。

Article 13(1) of the *World Heritage Convention*.

《世界遗产公约》第 13（1）条

237. States Parties in arrears of payment of their compulsory or voluntary contributions to the World Heritage Fund are not eligible for international assistance, it being understood that this provision does not apply to requests for emergency assistance.

237. 拖欠世界遗产基金的义务或自愿捐款的缔约国，没有资格享受国际援助，但是这一条不适用于紧急援助。

Decision 13 COM XII.34

第 13 COM XII.34 号决定

238. To support its Strategic Objectives, the Committee also allocates International Assistance in conformity with the priorities set out in its decisions and in the Regional Programmes it adopts as a

238. 为支持其战略目标，委员会也会根据其决议和作为《定期报告》后续措施的区域计划的优先顺序，分配国际援助（参见第 210 条）。

follow up to Periodic Reports (see para.210).

Decision 36 COM 13.I

239. In addition to the priorities outlined in paragraphs 236-238 above, the following considerations govern the Committee's decisions in granting International Assistance:

Decisions 26 COM 17.2,
Decision 26 COM 20 and Decision 26 COM 25.3

a) the likelihood that the assistance will have a catalytic and multiplier effect ("seed money") and promote financial and technical contributions from othersources;

b) when funds available are limited and a selection has to be made, preference is given to:

Decision 31 COM 18B

• a Least Developed Country or Low Income Economy as defined by the United Nations Economic and Social Council's Committee for Development Policy, or

• a Lower Middle Income Country as defined by the World Bank, or
• a Small Island Developing State (SIDS), or
• a StateParty in a post-conflict situation;

c) the urgency of the protective measures to be taken at World Heritage properties;

d) whether the legislative, administrative and, wherever possible, financial commitment of the recipient State Party is available to the activity;

e) the impact of the activity on furthering the Strategic Objectives decided by the Committee;

Paragraph 26 of *Operational Guidelines*

f) the degree to which the activity responds to

第36 COM 13.I号决定

239. 委员会在分配国际援助时，除按上述236— 238条规定的优先性顺序外，还会考虑以下因素：

第26 COM 17.2号、
第26 COM 20号和26 COM 25.3号决定

a）引起推动和倍增效应（"种子基金"）的援助，可能吸引其他资金或技术贡献；

b）由于资金有限，必须做出抉择时，将优先考虑符合下列条件的国家：

第31COM 18B号决定

•联合国经济社会发展政策委员会所定义的、最不发达国家或低收入国家；

•世界银行定义的、低水平中等收入国家；

•"小岛屿发展中国家"（SIDS）；
•冲突后缔约国；
c）对世界遗产采取保护措施的紧急程度；

d）受益缔约国是否有法律、行政支持或在可能情况下资金的支持，用来开展活动；

e）活动对于进一步达到委员会制定的"战略目标"的影响；

《操作指南》第26条

f）活动满足反应性监测过程和/或《定期

needs identified through the reactive monitoring process and/or the analysis of regional Periodic Reports;

Decision 20 COM XII

g) the exemplary value of the activity in respect to scientific research and the development of cost effective conservation techniques;

h) the cost of the activity and expected results; and

i) the educational value both for the training of experts and for the general public.

240. A balance will be maintained in the allocation of resources between cultural and natural heritage and between Conservation and Management and Preparatory Assistance. This balance is reviewed and decided upon on a regular basis by the Committee and during the second year of each biennium by the Chairperson or the World Heritage Committee.

65% of the total International Assistance budget is set aside for cultural properties and 35% for natural properties
Decision 31 COM 18B
Decision 36 COM 13.I
Decision 37 COM 13.II

VII.E SummaryTable

241.

Decision 36 COM 13.I
Decision 30 COM 13.13

报告》地区分析所定需求的程度

第 20 COM XII 号决定

g）该活动对科学研究以及开发高效低成本的保护技术的示范价值；

h）该活动的成本和预期结果；

i）对专业培训和大众的教育价值。

240. 为保持对文化与自然遗产的援助资源分配的平衡以及保护和管理与筹备援助之间的平衡，委员会将定期，及在世界遗产委员会主席两年任期的第二年对此平衡加以检查并作出相应决策。

国际援助总预算的 65% 用于文化遗产，35% 用于自然遗产
第 31 COM 18B 号
第 36 COM 13.I 号，
第 37 COM 13.II 号决定

VII.E 总 表

241.

第 36 COM 13.I 号决定
第 30 COM 13.13 号决定

Type of international assistance	Purpose	Budget ceilings per request	Deadline for submission of request	Authority for approval
Emergency Assistance	This assistance may be requested to address ascertained or potential threats facing properties included on the List of World Heritage in Danger and the World Heritage List which have suffered severe damage or are in imminent danger of severe damage due to sudden, unexpected phenomena. Such phenomena may include land subsidence,	Up to US$5,000	At anytime	Director of the World Heritage Centre

Type of international assistance	Purpose	Budget ceilings per request	Deadline for submission of request	Authority for approval
Emergency Assistance	extensive fires, explosions, flooding or human-made disasters including war. This assistance does not concern cases of damage or deterioration caused by gradual processes of decay, pollution or erosion. It addresses emergency situations strictly relating to the conservation of a World Heritage property (see Decision 28 COM 10B 2.c). It may be made available, if necessary, to more than one World Heritage property in a single State Party (see Decision 6 EXT. COM 15.2). The budget ceilings relate to a single World Heritage property. The assistance may be requested to : undertake emergency measures for the safeguarding of the property; draw up an emergency plan for the property.	Between US$ 5,001 and 75,000 Over US$ 75,000	At anytime At any time before the Committee	Chairperson of the Committee Committee
Preparatory assistance	This assistance may be requested to (in order of priority): (i) prepare or update national Tentative Lists of properties suitable for inscription on the World Heritage List; a commitment will be required from the State Party to nominate in priority on these lists sites recognized in approved thematic advice, such as the thematic studies prepared by the Advisory Bodies, as corresponding to gaps on the List; (ii) organize meetings for the harmonization of national Tentative Lists within the same geo-cultural area; (iii) prepare nominations of properties for inscription on the World Heritage List (including preparatory work such as collection of basic information, scoping studies of the potential for demonstration of Outstanding Universal Value, including integrity or authenticity, comparative studies of the property in relation to other similar properties (see 3.2 of Annex 5), including analysis in the context of the Gap Studies produced by the Advisory Bodies.Priority will be given to requests for sites recognized in approved thematic advice ascorresponding to gaps on the List and/or for sites where preliminary investigations have shown that further inquiries would be justified, especially in the case of States Parties whose heritage is un- represented or under represented on the World Heritage List;	Up to US$5,000 Between US$ 5,001 and 30,000	At anytime 31 October	Director of the World Heritage Centre Chairperson of the Committee

Type of international assistance	Purpose	Budget ceilings per request	Deadline for submission of request	Authority for approval
	(iv) prepare requests for Conservation & Management assistance for consideration by the World Heritage Committee.			
Conservation and Management Assistance (incorporating Training and Research assistance, Technical co-operation assistance and Promotion and education assistance)	This assistance may be requested for: (i) the training of staff and specialists at all levels in the fields of identification, monitoring, conservation, management and presentation of World Heritage, with an emphasis on group training;	Only for requests falling under items (i) to (vi):	Only for requests falling under items (i) to (vi):	Only for requests falling under items (i) to (vi)
	(ii) scientific research benefiting World Heritage properties; (iii) studies on the scientific and technical problems of conservation, management, and presentation of World Heritage properties.	Up to US$5,000	At any time	Director of the World Heritage Centre
	Note: Requests for support for individual training courses from UNESCO should be submitted on the standard "Application for fellowship" form available from the Secretariat.	Between US$ 5,001 and 30,000	31 October	Chairperson of the Committee
	(iv) provision of experts, technicians and skilled labour for the conservation, management, and presentation of properties inscribed on the List of World Heritage in Danger and the World Heritage List; (v) supply of equipment which the State Party requires for the conservation, management, and presentation of properties inscribed on the List of World Heritage in Danger and the World Heritage List;	Over US$ 30,000	31 October	Committee
	(vi) low-interest or interest-free loans for undertaking activities for the conservation, management, and presentation of properties inscribed on the List of World Heritage in Danger and the World Heritage List, which may be repayable on a long-term basis. (vii) At the regional and international levels for Programmes, activities and the holding of meetings that could: - help to create interest in the *Convention* within the countries of a given region;	Only for requests falling under items (vii) and(viii):	Only for requests falling under items (vii) and(viii):	Only for requests falling under items (vii) and (viii):

Type of international assistance	Purpose	Budget ceilings per request	Deadline for submission of request	Authority for approval
	- create a greater awareness of the different issues related to the implementation of the *Convention* to promote more active involvement in its application; - be a means of exchanging experiences; - stimulate joint education, information and promotional programmes and activities, (viii) At the national level for: - meetings specifically organized to make the Convention better known, especially amongst young people, or for the creation of national World Heritage associations, in accordance with Article 17 of the Convention; - preparation and discussion of education and information material (such as brochures, publications, exhibitions, films, multimedia tools) for the general promotion of the Convention and the World Heritage List and not for the promotion of a particular property, and especially for young people.	Up to US$5,000	At any time	Director of the World Heritage Centre

国际援助种类	目的	最高预算额	提交请求的截止期限	核准机关
紧急援助	该援助用于《濒危世界遗产名录》内遭受已确知及潜在威胁的遗产、及《世界遗产名录》内遭受严重损坏的遗产，或由于突然、不可预料的现象遭受迫切威胁及重大损失。这些不可预料的现象包括土地沉陷、大火、爆炸、洪水和战争等的人为灾难。此类援助不用于由渐进的腐蚀、污染和侵蚀造成的遗产损害和蜕化，只用于救助那些严格与保护世界遗产有关的紧急情况（见第 28 COM 10B 2.c 号）。如有需要，该援助可以拨付给同一缔约国的多处遗产（见第 6EXT.COM 15.2 号决定）。最高预算额为单项世界遗产的预算限额。 援助可用于： 1）采取紧急措施保护遗产； 2）为遗产制定紧急方案。	5000 美元 5001-75000 美元 75000 美元以上	随时 随时 委员会之前任何时间	世界遗产中心主任 委员会主席 委员会
筹备性援助	援助可用于（根据优先顺序）： 1）准备或更新适合列入《世界遗产名录》的国家《预备名录》内的遗产；要求缔约国做出承诺，根据已获得核准的主题建议（专家咨询机构准备的主题研究）按照优先顺序对这些遗产进行申报； 2）在同一地理文化区域内组织会议，综合协调各国的《预备名录》； 3）准备申报列入《世界遗产名录》遗产的申报文件（其中包括基本信息收集，对展示突出普遍价值的潜力（包括完整性或真实性）进行范围界	5000 美元 5001-30000 美元	随时 10 月 31 日	世界遗产中心主任 委员会主席

续表

国际援助种类	目的	最高预算额	提交请求的截止期限	核准机关
筹备性援助	定研究，以及与其他类似遗产的比较分析）（见附录5的3.2）；包括咨询机构提出的以填补空白为背景的分析。优先考虑经过主题研究后认为在名录中相应缺少的空白遗产类型，以及那些初步调查后认为应该进行进一步申请，特别是在《世界遗产名录》上没有遗产或遗产代表性不足的缔约国的申请。 4）准备向世界遗产委员会申请的保护和管理援助。			
保护与管理援助（包括培训和研究援助、技术合作援助以及宣传和教育援助）	要求援助： (i) 在世界遗产的识别、监测、保护、管理以及展示领域培训各个级别的工作人员和专家，以团体培训为主； (ii) 对世界遗产有利的科学研究；致力于解决世界遗产保护、管理与展示问题的研究； 注：如果针对个人培训课程向联合国教科文组织提出支持申请，应填写秘书处统一提供的"奖学金申请"表格。 (iv) 对于列在《濒危世界遗产名录》和《世界遗产名录》上的遗产给予专家、技术支持，以保护、管理、展示遗产； (v) 缔约国为保护、管理、展示《濒危世界遗产名录》和《世界遗产名录》内遗产所需要的设备； (vi) 为保护、管理、展示《濒危世界遗产名录》和《世界遗产名录》内遗产所需的低利率或零利率贷款，这些贷款可能是长期、可偿还的。 (vii) 用于地区和国际级别的计划、活动和会议： - 帮助在特定地区的国家内激发公众对《世界遗产公约》的兴趣； - 提高与实施《世界遗产公约》相关的不同议题的认识，推动更积极地参与《公约》的实施。 - 经验交换的渠道； - 帮助开展联合教育、信息、以及宣传活动，特别是让年轻人参加到世界遗产保护活动中来。 (viii) 在国家层面： - 为向公众，特别是年轻人宣传《公约》组织召开特别会议；根据《世界遗产公约》第17条，创立国家世界遗产协会； - 为宣传《公约》和《世界遗产名录》，准备、讨论教育和信息资料（例如：宣传手册、出版物、展览会、电影、大众传媒工具），有年轻人参加尤为重要。本援助不用于某项特定遗产的宣传。	仅限于第（i）至（vi）项： 5000美元 5001-30000美元 30000美元以上 仅限于第（vii）至（viii）项： 5000美元 5000-10000美元	仅限于第（i）至（vi）项： 随时 10月31日 10月31日 仅限于第（vii）至（viii）项： 随时 10月31日	仅限于第（i）至（vi）项： 世界遗产中心主任委员会主席 委员会 仅限于第（vii）至（viii）项： 世界遗产中心主任 委员会主席

Ⅶ.F Procedure and format

Ⅶ.F 程序和格式

242. All States Parties submitting requests for international assistance are encouraged to consult

242. 鼓励所有申请国际援助的缔约国在构想、计划和拟定申请期间，向秘书处和咨询

the Secretariat and the Advisory Bodies during the conceptualization, planning and elaboration of each request. To facilitate States Parties' work, examples of successful international assistance requests may be provided upon request.

机构进行咨询。为方便缔约国的工作，委员会可应缔约国的要求，提供国际援助的成功申请案例。

243. The application form for International Assistance is presented in Annex 8 and the types, amounts, deadlines for submission and the authorities responsible for approval are outlined in the summary table in Chapter VII.E.

243. 国际援助的申请表格可参阅附录 8，第七.E 章的总表概述了提交的种类、金额以及截止期限和核准批准机构。

244. The request should be submitted in English or French, duly signed and transmitted by the National Commission for UNESCO, the State Party Permanent Delegation to UNESCO and/or appropriate governmental Department or Ministry to the following address:

244. 用英语或法语提出申请，联合国教科文组织国家委员会、联合国教科文组织缔约国常驻代表团和 / 或相关政府部门签字后，按下列地址提交：

UNESCO World Heritage Centre
7, place de Fontenoy 75352 Paris 07 SP
France
Tel: +33 (0) 1 4568 12 76
E-mail: wh-intassistance@unesco.org

联合国教科文组织世界遗产中心
法国巴黎（7，place de Fontenoy 75352 Paris 07SP France）电话：+33（0）145681276
传真：+33（0）145685570
电邮：wh−intassistance@unesco.org

245. Requests for international assistance may be submitted by electronic mail by the State Party but must be accompanied by an officially signed hard copy or be filled-in using the online format on the World Heritage Centre's Website at the following address: http://whc.unesco.org

245. 缔约国可用电子邮件申请国际援助，但必须同时提交一份官方签字的书面申请，或使用世界遗产中心网站（http: //whc.unesco.org）提供的电子格式。

246. It is important that all information requested in this application form is provided. If appropriate or necessary, requests may be supplemented by additional information, reports, etc.

246. 必须提供申请表中所要求填写的一切信息。在适当或必要的时候，可以随申请表附上相关信息、报告等。

VII.G Evaluation and approval of International Assistance requests

VII .G 国际援助的评估和核准

247. Provided that a request for assistance from a State Party is complete, the Secretariat, with the assistance of the Advisory Bodies, for requests above US$5,000, will process each request in a timely manner, as follows.

247. 如果缔约国的国际援助申请信息完整，秘书处在咨询机构的帮助下，会通过以下方式及时处理每一份金额超过5000美元的申请。

248. All requests for international assistance for cultural heritage are evaluated by ICOMOS and ICCROM, except requests up to and including US$ 5,000.

248. 所有关于文化遗产的国际援助申请，均由国际古迹遗址理事会和国际文物保护与修复研究中心评估，申请金额低于（含）5000美元的除外。

Decision 13 COM XII.34

Decision 31 COM18B

第13 COM XII.34号决定

第31 COM18B号决定

249. All requests for international assistance for mixed heritage are evaluated by ICOMOS, ICCROM and IUCN, except requests up to and including US$ 5,000.

249. 所有关于混合遗产的国际援助申请，均由国际古迹遗址理事会、国际文物保护和修复研究中心和世界自然保护联盟评估，申请金额低于（含）5000美元的除外。

Decision 31 COM18B

第31 COM18B号决定

250. All requests for international assistance for natural heritage are evaluated by IUCN, except requests up to and including US$ 5,000.

250. 所有自然遗产国际援助的申请，均由世界自然保护联盟做出评估，申请金额低于（含）5000美元的除外。

Decision 31 COM18B

第31 COM18B号决定

251. The evaluation criteria used by the Advisory Bodies are outlined in Annex 9.

251. 咨询机构所使用的评估标准在附录9中列明。

Decision 31 COM 18B

第31COM18B号决定

252. All requests for International Assistance of more than US$ 5,000, except those of Emergency Assistance, are evaluated by a panel composed of representatives of the World Heritage Centre Regional Desks and the Advisory Bodies, and if possible, the Chairperson of the World Heritage Committee or, in observer capacity, a person designated by the Chairperson, meeting once or

252. 所有金额超过5000美元的国际援助申请，紧急援助除外，均需要进行小组评估，小组成员包括世界遗产中心区域代表，咨询机构代表，如有可能，包括世界遗产委员会主席或由主席任命的观察员。在主席和/或委员会作出决策前，每年召开一至两次小组会议。所有提交给主席批准的紧急援助申请都可以随时提交给秘书处。这些申请无需经小组审核，在征求咨

twice a year before action by the Chairperson and/or Committee. Requests for Emergency Assistance can be submitted at any time to the Secretariat and will be submitted to the Chairperson or to the Committee at its next session for decision after comments by the Advisory Bodies and without examination by the panel.

询机构意见后提交主席或下届委员会会议决定。

Decision 31 COM 18B

第 31 COM18B 号决定

253. The Chairperson is not authorized to approve requests submitted by his owncountry. These will be examined by the Committee.

253. 主席不能批准来自本国的申请，这些申请将由委员会进行审查。

254. All requests for Preparatory Assistance or Conservation and Management Assistance of more than US$ 5,000 should be received by the Secretariat on or before 31 October. Incomplete forms which do not come back duly completed by 30 November will be sent back to the States Parties for submission to a next cycle. Complete requests are examined by a first panel held in January during the meeting between the Secretariat and the Advisory Bodies. Requests for which the panel issues a positive or a negative recommendation will be submitted to the Chairperson/Committee for decision. A second panel may be held at least eight weeks before the Committee session for requests which were revised since the first panel. Requests sent back for a substantial revision will be examined by the panel depending on their date of receipt. Requests requiring only minor revision and no further examination by the panel must come back within the year when they were examined first; otherwise they will be sent again to a next panel.The chart detailing the submission process is attached in Annex 8.

254. 秘书处将于每年 10 月 31 日前受理所有金额超过 5000 美元的筹备援助或修复管理援助。申请未在 11 月 30 日补全表格内容的申请将退回缔约国，进入下一轮申请。完整的申请文件将于 1 月进行第一次小组讨论。无论小组给予正面或负面建议，均应提交给主席（委员会）决议。在委员会会议之前至少 8 个星期，应当举行第二次小组会议，审查第一次小组会议之后修订过的申请。发回重新进行重大修订的申请将视收到日期由小组会议进行审查。只需细微修订，无需小组会议进一步审查的申请必须在首次审查后一年内返回；否则将于下次小组会议重新提交。关于提交流程的详细图，请参见附录 8。

Decision 36 COM 13.

第 36 COM 13 号决议

VII.H ContractualArrangements

255. Agreements are established between UNESCO and the concerned State Party or its representative(s) for the implementation of the approved International Assistance requests in conformity with UNESCO regulations, following the work plan and budget breakdown described in the originally approved request.

VII.I Evaluation and follow-up of International Assistance

256. The monitoring and evaluation of the implemention of the International Assistance requests will take place within 3 months of the activities' completion. The results of these evaluations will be collated and maintained by the Secretariat in collaboration with the Advisory Bodies and examined by the Committee on aregular basis.

257. The Committee reviews the implementation, evaluation and follow-up of International Assistance in order to evaluate the International Assistance effectiveness and to redefine its priorities.

VIII THE WORLD HERITAGE EMBLEM

VIII.A Preamble

258. At its second session (Washington, 1978), the Committee adopted the World Heritage Emblem which had been designed by Mr. Michel Olyff. This Emblem symbolizes the interdependence of cultural and natural properties: the central square is a form created by man and the circle represents nature, the two being intimately linked. The Emblem is round, like the world, but at the same time it is a symbol of protection. It symbolizes the *Convention*, signifies the adherence of States Parties to the *Convention*, and serves to identify properties inscribed in the World

VII.H 合同安排

255. 联合国教科文组织与相关缔约国政府或／及代表要达成协议：在使用国际援助的时候，必须要遵守联合国教科文组织规章，同时要与之前批准的申请中所描述的工作计划和预算明细保持一致。

VII.I 国际援助的评估和后续跟踪

256. 在活动结束 3 个月之内，将开始对国际援助申请进行监测和评估。秘书处和咨询机构将整理、保存这些结果，委员会将对这些结果定期进行检查。

257. 委员会将对国际援助的实施、评估和后续工作进行审查，以便评估国际援助的使用效力并重新定义国际援助的优先顺序。

VIII. 世界遗产标识

VIII.A 前言

258. 在世界遗产委员会第二届大会上（华盛顿，1978 年），采用了由米歇尔·奥利芙设计的遗产标志。该标志表现了文化与自然遗产之间的相互依存关系：代表大自然的圆形与人类创造的形状方形紧密相连。标志是圆形的，代表世界的形状，同时也是保护的象征。标志象征《公约》，代表缔约国将遵守《公约》，同时指明了列入《世界遗产名录》中的遗产。它与大众对《公约》的了解相互关联，是对《公约》可信度和威望的认可。总而言之，它是《公约》所代表的普世价值的集中体现。

Heritage List. It is associated with public knowledge about the *Convention* and is the imprimatur of the *Convention*'s credibility and prestige. Above all, it is a representation of the universal values for which the *Convention* stands.

259. The Committee decided that the Emblem proposed by the artist could be used, in any colour or size, depending on the use, the technical possibilities and considerations of an artistic nature. The Emblem should always carry the text "WORLD HERITAGE. PATRIMOINE MONDIAL". The space occupied by "PATRIMONIO MUNDIAL" can be used for its translation into the national language of the country where the Emblem is to be used.

259. 委员会决定，根据具体的使用、技术水平和艺术考虑，该艺术家提交的标志可采用任何颜色或尺寸。标志上必须带有 "world heritage（英语"世界遗产"）.Patrimoine Mondial"（法语"世界遗产"）的字样。各国在使用该标志时，可用本国的语言来代替中间部分的 "Patrimonio Mundial"（西语）字样。

260. In order to ensure the Emblem benefits from as much visibility as possible while preventing improper uses, the Committee at its twenty-second session (Kyoto, 1998) adopted "Guidelines and Principles for the Use of the World Heritage Emblem" as set out in the following paragraphs. In addition, a "Table of Uses" (Annex 14) provides complementary guidance.

260. 为了保证标志尽可能地引人注目，同时避免误用，委员会在第 22 届会议（京都，1998 年）上通过了《世界遗产标识使用指南和原则》，内容在后续段落有所说明。另外，附件 14 中的使用表格将提供补充的指导说明。

Decision 39 COM 11

第 39 COM 11 号决定

261. Although there is no mention of the Emblem in the *Convention*, its use has been promoted by the Committee to identify properties protected by the *Convention* and inscribed on the World Heritage List since its adoption in 1978.

261. 尽管《公约》并未提到标志，自 1978 年采用该标志以来，委员会一直在推动使用该标志，来标示受《公约》的保护的遗产、以及列入《世界遗产名录》的遗产。

262. The World Heritage Committee is responsible for determining the use of the World Heritage Emblem and for making policy prescriptions regarding how it may be used. Since the adoption by the UNESCO General Conference in October 2007 of the *Directives concerning the Use of the Name, Acronym, Logo and Internet Domain Names of UNESCO*[①], it is strongly encouraged to use the World Heritage Emblem as part of a linked logo block accompanied by UNESCO's logo, whenever feasible. The use of the World Heritage Emblem alone remains however possible, in line with the present *Guidelines* and with the Table of Uses (Annex14).

Decision 39 COM 11

263. As requested by the Committee at its 26th session (Budapest, 2002), the World Heritage Emblem, with and without its surrounding text, has been notified and accepted on 21 May 2003 by the Paris Union Member states under Article 6th of the Paris *Convention* for the Protection of Industrial Property, adopted in 1883 and revised at Stockholm in 1967. Therefore UNESCO has recourse to Paris *Convention* Member States' domestic systems to prevent the use of the World Heritage Emblem where such use falsely suggests a connection with UNESCO, the *World Heritage Convention*, or any other abusive use.

Decision 26 COM 15

Decision 39 COM 11

262. 世界遗产委员会负责决定世界遗产标识的使用，同时负责制定如何使用标志的政策规定。2007年10月，联合国教科文组织大会审议通过了《联合国教科文组织相关名称、缩略语、标志及互联网域名使用指南》。[①]委员会鼓励在任何适当的情况下，将世界遗产的标志作为联合国教科文组织的延伸部分加以使用。世界遗产标志也可以以不同方式单独使用，需符合现行《操作指南》和《使用表》（见附件14）的要求。

第39 COM 11号决定

263. 按照委员会在第26届大会（布达佩斯，2002年）上的要求，世界遗产标识根据1883年通过的《保护工业产权巴黎公约》（1967年重新修订于斯德哥尔摩）第6款的规定，于2003年5月21日被《巴黎公约》成员国正式确认为受保护的标志（不论其是单独使用还是附加于其他项目之中）。因此，联合国教科文组织可以依靠《巴黎公约》成员国内部体系，防止世界遗产的标志被误用或滥用。

第26 COM 15号决定

第39 COM 11号决定

---

① The most recent version of the *Directives concerning the Use of the Name, Acronym, Logo and Internet Domain Names of UNESCO* is found in the annex to Resolution 86 of the 34th session of the General Conference (34 C/Resolution 86) or at http://unesdoc.unesco.org/images/0015/001560/156046e.pdf

最新版本的《关于使用国教科文组织名称、缩写、标志及互联网域名的方针》见34次大会第86号决议附件(34 C/Resolution 86)或登录http://unesdoc.unesco.org/images/0015/001560/156046e.pdf

264. The Emblem also has fund-raising potential that can be used to enhance the marketing value of products with which it is associated. A balance is needed between the Emblem's use to further the aims of the *Convention* and optimize knowledge of the *Convention* worldwide and the need to prevent its abuse for inaccurate, inappropriate, and unauthorized commercial or other purposes.

265. The Guidelines and Principles for the Use of the Emblem and modalities for quality control should not become an obstacle to co-operation for promotional activities. Authorities responsible for reviewing and deciding on uses of the Emblem may base their decisions on the parameters developed below and those contained in the Table of Uses (Annex 14).

Decision 39 COM 11

VIII.B Applicability

266. The Guidelines and Principles proposed herein cover all proposed uses of the Emblem by:

Decision 39 COM 11

a) The World Heritage Centre;

b) The UNESCO Division of Public Information and other UNESCO offices;

c) Agencies or National Commissions, responsible for implementing the *Convention* in each State Party;

d) World Heritage properties;

e) Other contracting parties, especially those operating for predominantly commercial purposes.

VIII.C Responsibilities of States Parties

267. States Parties to the *Convention* should take all possible measures to prevent the use of the

264. 该标志还具有筹集基金的潜力，可以用于提高相关产品的市场价值。在使用该标志的过程中，要注意在以下两者之间保持平衡，即正确使用标志促进《公约》目标的实现，并在世界范围内最大限度地普及《公约》知识，但同时要避免不正确、不恰当、以及未经授权、出于商业或其他目的滥用标志。

265.《世界遗产标识使用指南和原则》以及质量控制的手段，不应成为合作开展宣传活动的障碍。负责审定标志使用的权威机构可以依据附件14的《使用表》，在考虑多种因素发展变化的条件下做出它们的决定。

第39 COM 11号决定

VIII.B 适用性

266. 本文所述的《指南和原则》涵盖了以下各方使用标志的所有可能情况：

第39 COM 11号决定

a. 世界遗产中心

b. 联合国教科文组织公共信息部和联合国教科文组织其他机构

c. 各个缔约国负责实施《公约》的机构或国家委员会

d. 世界遗产

e. 其他签约合作方，尤其是主要进行商业运营的机构

VIII.C 缔约国的责任

267. 缔约国政府应该采取一切可能的措施，防止未经委员会明确承认的任何组织或出于未

Emblem in their respective countries by any group or for any purpose not explicitly recognized by the Committee. States Parties are encouraged to make full use of national legislation including Trade Mark Laws.

经授权的任何目的在本国内使用该标志。鼓励缔约国充分利用包括《商标法》在内的国家立法。

Ⅷ..D Increasing proper uses of the World Heritage Emblem

Ⅷ..D 增加对世界遗产标识的正确使用

268. Properties inscribed on the World Heritage List should be marked with the emblem jointly with the UNESCO logo, which should, however, be placed in such a way that they do not visually impair the property in question.

268. 列入《世界遗产名录》的遗产应标有该标志和联合国教科文组织标识，但要以不破坏遗产景观为前提。

Production of plaques to commemorate the inscription of properties on the World Heritage List

制作纪念遗产列入《《世界遗产名录》》的标牌

269. Once a property is inscribed on the World Heritage List, the State Party should place a plaque, whenever possible, to commemorate this inscription. These plaques are designed to inform the public of the country concerned and foreign visitors that the property visited has a particular value which has been recognized by the international community. In other words, the property is exceptional, of interest not only to one nation, but also to the whole world. However, these plaques have an additional function which is to inform the general public about the *World Heritage Convention* or at least about the World Heritage concept and the World Heritage List.

269. 一旦遗产列入《世界遗产名录》，该缔约国将尽可能附上标牌来纪念这一事件。标牌应向本国公众及外国游客说明该遗产具有特殊的价值且已得到国际社会的认可。换言之，该遗产无论对该国还是世界来说，都具有非同寻常的意义。此外，该标牌还有另外一个作用，即向公众介绍《世界遗产公约》，或者至少是世界遗产概念和《世界遗产名录》。

270. The Committee has adopted the following Guidelines for the production of these plaques:

a) the plaque should be so placed that it can easily be seen by visitors, without disfiguring the property;

b) the World Heritage Emblem should appear on the plaque;

270. 委员会就标牌的制作采用以下指导方针：

a）标牌应放置在参观者容易看到的地方，但不能破坏遗产的美观；

b）标牌上应带有世界遗产标识；

c) the text should mention the property's Outstanding Universal Value; in this regard it might be useful to give a short description of the property's outstanding characteristics. States Parties may, if they wish, use the descriptions appearing in the various World Heritage publications or in the World Heritage exhibit, and which may be obtained from the Secretariat;

d) the text should make reference to the *World Heritage Convention* and particularly to the World Heritage List and to the international recognition conferred by inscription on this List (however, it is not necessary to mention at which session of the Committee the property was inscribed); it may be appropriate to produce the text in several languages for properties which receive many foreign visitors.

271. The Committee proposes the following text as an example:

"(Name of property) has been inscribed upon the World Heritage List of the *Convention concerning the Protection of the World Cultural and Natural Heritage*. Inscription on this List confirms the Outstanding Universal Value of a cultural or natural property which deserves protection for the benefit of all humanity."

272. This text could be then followed by a brief description of the property concerned.

273. Furthermore, the national authorities should encourage World Heritage properties to make a broad use of the Emblem such as on their letterheads, brochures and staff uniforms.

274. Third parties which have received the right to produce communication products related to the *World Heritage Convention* and World Heritage properties must give the Emblem proper visibility.

c）标牌上的内容应体现遗产的突出普遍价值；考虑到这一点，内容中应对遗产的突出特点加以描述。如果愿意的话，缔约国政府可以使用各种世界遗产出版物或世界遗产展览对相关遗产的说明。这些内容可直接从秘书处获得。

d）标牌上的内容应提及《保护世界文化和自然遗产公约》，尤其是《世界遗产名录》及国际社会对列入《名录》的遗产的承认（但无需指出是在委员会的哪届会议上通过的）。如遗产有大量外国游客参观，标牌上的内容应使用多种语言。

271. 委员会提供了下段文字作为范例：

"根据《保护世界文化和自然遗产公约》，（遗产名称）列入《世界遗产名录》。遗产列入《名录》说明该项文化或自然遗产具有突出普遍价值，对它的保护符合全人类的利益。"

272. 在这段话的后面，可对该遗产进行简要介绍。

273. 此外，国家主管机构应该鼓励世界遗产在诸如信笺抬头、宣传手册，以及员工的工作服等物上广泛使用世界遗产标识。

274. 授权负责推广《保护世界文化和自然遗产公约》和世界遗产相关产品的第三方，应突出显示世界遗产标识，而且应避免在特定产品上使用不同的标志或标识。

They should avoid creating a different Emblem or logo for that particular product.

VIII..E Principles on the use of the World Heritage Emblem

275. The responsible authorities are henceforth requested to use the following principles in making decisions on the use of the Emblem:

Decision 39 COM 11

a) The Emblem should be utilized for all projects substantially associated with the work of the *Convention*, including, to the maximum extent technically and legally possible, those already approved and adopted, in order to promote the *Convention*.

b) A decision to approve use of the Emblem should be linked strongly to the quality and content of the product with which it is to be associated, not on the volume of products to be marketed or the financial return expected. The main criterion for approval should be the educational, scientific, cultural, or artistic value of the proposed product related to World Heritage principles and values. Approval should not routinely be granted to place the Emblem on products that have no, or extremely little, educational value, such as cups, T-shirts, pins, and other tourist souvenirs. Exceptions to this policy will be considered for special events, such as meetings of the Committee and ceremonies at which plaques are unveiled.

c) Any decision with respect to authorizing the use of the Emblem must be completely unambiguous and in keeping with the explicit and implicit goals and values of the *World Heritage Convention*.

d) Except when authorized in accordance with these principles it is not legitimate for commercial entities to use the Emblem directly on their own

VIII..E 世界遗产标识的使用原则

275. 有关权威机构在决定使用标识的过程中，应遵循以下原则：

第39 COM 11号决定

a）标志应用于所有与《公约》的工作密切相关的项目（包括在技术和法律许可的最大范围内，应用于已得到批准或已通过的项目上），以推广《公约》。

b）在决定是否授权使用标志时，应首先考虑相关产品的质量和内容，而非投入市场的产品数量或预期的经济回报。审核通过与否的主要标准是，所申请产品的教育、科学、文化和艺术价值与世界遗产的原则与价值相关。对于没有教育意义或教育意义很小的产品，如茶杯、T恤、别针，和其他旅游纪念品等等，应不予批准。以上规定的例外情况包括委员会会议、标牌揭幕仪式等。

c）所有涉及授权使用该标识的决定都应该非常明确，同时必须与《保护世界文化和自然遗产公约》明确表示和隐含的目标和价值保持一致。

d）除非依照这些原则得到授权，任何商业机构都不得直接在其产品上使用该标识，以此表示对世界遗产的支持。虽然委员会承认，任

material to show their support for World Heritage. The Committee recognizes, however, that any individual, organization, or company is free to publish or produce whatever they consider to be appropriate regarding World Heritage properties, but official authorization to do so under the World Heritage Emblem remains the exclusive prerogative of the Committee, to be exercised as prescribed in these Guidelines and Principles and in the Table of Uses.

e) Use of the Emblem by other contracting parties should normally only be authorized when the proposed use deals directly with World Heritage properties. Such uses may be granted after approval by the national authorities of the countries concerned.

f) In cases where no specific World Heritage properties are involved or are not the principal focus of the proposed use, such as general seminars and/ or workshops on scientific issues or conservation techniques, use may be granted only upon express approval in accordance with these Guidelines and Principles and with the Table of Uses. Requests for such uses should specifically document the manner in which the proposed use is expected to enhance the work of the *Convention*.

g) Permission to use the Emblem should not be granted to travel agencies, airlines, or to any other type of business operating for predominantly commercial purposes, except under exceptional circumstances and when manifest benefit to the World Heritage generally or particular World Heritage properties can be demonstrated. Requests for such use should require approval in accordance with these Guidelines and Principles and with the Table of Uses. Such requests should be approved by the national authorities concerned, and be defined within the framework of specific partnership agreements with UNESCO/World Heritage Centre.

何个人、组织或公司都可以自由出版或生产它们认为对世界遗产有利的产品，但委员会是唯一有权授予世界遗产标识使用权的官方机构，且其授权必须遵守上述指南和原则，以及《使用表》的要求。

e）只有当该标识的使用与世界遗产直接相关时，其他签约合作方才能得到使用该标志的授权。而且，申请机构只有在其所在国的主管机构批准后，才能得到使用授权。

f）如果标识的使用不涉及具体的世界遗产，或具体的世界遗产不是核心内容，例如一般性的学术研讨会和有关科学问题或保存技术的讨论会，必须要根据上述指南和原则及"使用表"得到明确批准。申请使用该标识时，要明确体现标识的使用的方式，而且这种方式预计能够促进《公约》的工作。

g）通常标识的使用权不能授予旅行社、航空公司或任何其他商业机构的商业用途，除非在某些特殊情况下，世界遗产或特定的世界遗产项目能明确从中获益。这类使用申请需遵循《指南和原则》和《使用表》并得到相关权威机构的批准。这类申请应得到相关国家当局的批准，并在与联合国教科文组织/世界遗产中心的具体合作伙伴协议的框架内加以界定。

The Secretariat is not to accept any advertising, travel, or other promotional considerations from travel agencies or other, similar companies in exchange or in lieu of financial remuneration for use of the Emblem.

"Comprehensive Partnership Strategy" including "Separate strategies for engagement with individual categories of partners" 192 EX/5.INF and PACT Strategy (Document WHC-13/37.COM/5D)

Decision 37 COM 5D

h) When commercial benefits are anticipated, the Secretariat should ensure that the World Heritage Fund receives a fair share of the revenues and conclude a contract or other agreement that documents the nature of the understandings that govern the project and the arrangements for provision of income to the Fund. In all cases of commercial use, any staff time and related costs for personnel assigned by the Secretariat or other reviewers, as appropriate, to any initiative, beyond the nominal, must be fully covered by the party requesting authorization to use the Emblem.

National authorities are also called upon to ensure that their properties or the World Heritage Fund receive a fair share of the revenues and to document the nature of the understandings that govern the project and the distribution of any proceeds.

i) If sponsors are sought for manufacturing products whose distribution the Secretariat considers necessary, the choice of partner or partners should be consistent, at a minimum, with the criteria set forth in the "Comprehensive Partnership Strategy" including "Separate strategies for engagement with individual categories or parners" 192 EX/5.INF and PACT Strategy (Document WHC-13/37.COM/5D) and with such further fund-raising guidance as the

秘书处不接受旅行社或其他类似机构的任何广告、旅游或其他促销计划，以换取或替代使用标识的经济报酬的建议。

"全面战略伙伴关系"包括"与个别类别合作伙伴接触的独立战略" 192 EX/5.INF and PACT 战略（文件WHC-13/37.COM/5D）

第 37 COM 5D 决定

h）如果在标识的使用过程中产生了商业利益，秘书处应该确保世界遗产基金也从中分得部分收益。秘书处应该与相关方签订合同或其他协议，以确定协议的性质、管理项目和收益分配。对于所有将标识用于商业目的的情况，秘书处和其他审议者，在批准使用标识申请的过程中所发生的、高于常规的、一切人力或物力的成本，都应该由提出申请方支付。

国家权威机构也要确保该国的遗产或者世界遗产基金能够得到相应的收益，确定协议性质、管理项目和收益分配。

i）如果秘书处因需要制作产品进行分发而寻找赞助商，合作伙伴(或多个合作伙伴）的选择至少应与"全面伙伴战略"，包括"独立合作伙伴的参与战略" 192 EX/5.INF、保护伙伴关系战略（文件 WHC-13/37.COM/5D）、及委员会规定的其他资金筹措标准一致。生产此类产品的必要性应以书面形式明确和证明，并以此得到委员会的批准。

Committee may prescribe. The necessity for such products should be clarified and justified in written presentations that will require approval in such manner as the Committee may prescribe.

j) The sale of goods or services bearing the name, acronym, logo and/or Internet domain name of UNESCO combined with the World Heritage Emblem chiefly for profit shall be regarded as "commercial use" for the purpose of the *Operational Guidelines*. Such use must be expressly authorized by the Director-General, under a specific contractual arrangement (definition adapted from 2007 UNESCO Logo Directives. Art Ⅲ.2.1.3).

VⅢ.F   Authorization procedure for the use of the World Heritage Emblem

Simple agreement of the national authorities

276. National authorities may grant the use of the Emblem to a national entity, provided that the project, whether national or international, involves only World Heritage properties located on the same national territory. National authorities' decision should be guided by the Guidelines and Principles and by the Table of Uses.

Decision 39 COM 11

277. States Parties are invited to provide the Secretariat with the names and addresses of the authorities in charge of managing the use of the Emblem.

Circular letter dated 14 April 1999.
http://whc.unesco.org/circs/circ99-4e.pdf

Agreement requiring quality control of content

278. Any other request for authorization to use

j）附有联合国教科文组织名称、缩略语、标志和网络域名，以及世界遗产标识的主要用于盈利的商品或服务项目，将被视为"商业使用"。如需使用这一标志，则必须在相关的条约签署后，经总干事核准（见 2007 年联合国教科文组织标志使用指南第 Ⅲ.2.1.3 款）。

VⅢ.F 使用世界遗产标识的授权程序

国家权威机构的初步认定

276. 如果国家或国际项目只涉及本国的世界遗产，国家权威机构可授权国家实体使用标识。国家权威机构的决定应遵守《指南和原则》以及《使用表》。

第 39 COM 11 号决定

277. 缔约国需要向秘书处提供负责管理标识使用的权威机构的名称和地址。

1999 年 4 月 14 日通函
http：//whc.unesco.org/circs/circ99- 4e.pdf

要求对内容进行质量控制的协议

278. 任何关于授权使用标志的申请都需遵

the Emblem should adopt the following procedure:

循以下步骤：

Decision 39 COM 11

第 39 COM 11 号决定

a) A request indicating the objective of the use of the Emblem, its duration and territorial validity, should be addressed to the Director of the World Heritage Centre.

b) The Director of the World Heritage Centre has the authority to grant the use of the Emblem in accordance with the Guidelines and Principles. For cases not covered, or not sufficiently covered, by the Guidelines and Principles and by the Table of Uses, the Director refers the matter to the Chairperson who, in the most difficult cases, might wish to refer the matter to the Committee for final decision. A yearly report on the authorized uses of the Emblem will be submitted to the World Heritage Committee.

c) Authorization to use the Emblem in major products to be widely distributed over an undetermined period of time is conditional upon obtaining the manufacturer's commitment to consult with countries concerned and secure their endorsement of texts and images illustrating properties situated in their territory, at no cost to the Secretariat, together with the proof that this has been done. The text to be approved should be provided in either one of the official languages of the Committee or in the language of the country concerned. A draft model to be used by States Parties to authorize the use of the Emblem to third parties appears below.

Content Approval Form:

[Name of responsible national body], officially identified as the body responsible for approving the content of the texts and photos relating to the World Heritage properties located in the territory of [name of country], hereby confirms to [name of producer] that the text and the images that it has submitted

a）申请应该说明使用标志的目的、使用时长及使用地域并提交给世界遗产中心主任。

b）世界遗产中心主任有权根据《指南和原则》批准使用标志。遇到《指南和原则》以及《使用表》尚未涉及或未完全涵盖的情况，主任应将申请提交给主席，如果是很难处理的情况，主席会将该申请提交委员会做最后决定。有关授权使用标识的年度报告应提交给世界遗产委员会。

c）如授权在不确定的时期内在广泛行销的主要产品上使用标识，生产商应承诺与相关国家协商，针对使用其境内遗产的图片和文字取得其同意，同时生产商还应提供获取同意的证明，且秘书处不承担任何费用。报批的文书须以委员会任意一种正式语言或相关国家的语言书写。缔约国用于批准第三方使用标志的草拟范本应按以下格式填写：

内容批准表：

作为负责批准有关 [国家名称] 世界遗产图文的官方机构，[国家主管机构的名称] 在此向 [生产商名称] 证实，它提交的世界遗产 [遗产名称] 图文已 [通过审批][如做出以下变更便可通过审批][未通过审批]。

for the [name of properties] World Heritage property(ies) are [approved] [approved subject to the following changes requested] [are not approved]

(delete whatever entry does not apply, and provide, as needed, a corrected copy of the text or a signed list of corrections).

（删除不适用的条目，并按需要提供文字的变更经签名的文件副本，含变更内容清单）。

Notes:

注释：

It is recommended that the initials of the responsible national official be affixed to each page of text.

The National Authorities are given one month from their acknowledged receipt in which to authorize the content, following which the producers may consider that the content has been tacitly approved, unless the responsible National Authorities request in writing a longer period.

Texts should be supplied to the National Authorities in one of the two official languages of the Committee, or in the official language (or in one of the official languages) of the country in which the properties are located, at the convenience of both parties.

建议在文本的每一页上都注明国家主管人员姓名的首字母。

自收到申请之日起一个月内，国家主管机构应该做出答复，批准文本内容。如未接到答复，生产商可视为该内容已得到默许，除非该国家主管机构提出书面申请，要求延长批准时限。

提交给国家主管机构的申请所使用的语言应按照双方的需要，可使用委员会的两种官方语言之一或遗产所在国的官方语言（或其中一种官方语言）。

d) After having examined the request and considered it as acceptable, the Secretariat may establish an agreement with the partner.

d）在审阅申请并认为可批准后，秘书处应该与合作伙伴签订协议。

e) If the Director of the World Heritage Centre judges that a proposed use of the Emblem is not acceptable, the Secretariat informs the requesting party of the decision in writing.

e）如果世界遗产中心主任没有批准标志的使用，秘书处会以书面形式通知申请方。

Ⅷ.G Right of States Parties to exert quality control

Ⅷ.G 缔约国政府有权进行质量控制

279. Authorization to use the Emblem is inextricably linked to the requirement that the national authorities may exert quality control over the products with which it is associated.

279. 标识使用的授权与国家主管机构对相关产品实施的质量控制密切相关。

a) The States Parties to the *Convention* are the only parties authorized to approve the content (images and text) of any distributed product

a）《公约》的缔约国是唯一有权批准带有世界遗产标识并与其境内遗产相关的分销产品内容（图片和文字）的机构。

appearing under the World Heritage Emblem with regard to the properties located in their territories.

b) States Parties that protect the Emblem legally must review these uses.

c) Other States Parties may elect to review proposed uses or refer such proposals to the Secretariat. States Parties are responsible for identifying an appropriate national authority and for informing the Secretariat whether they wish to review proposed uses or to identify uses that are inappropriate. The Secretariat maintains a list of responsible national authorities.

IX. INFORMATION SOURCES

IX.A Information archived by the Secretariat

280. The Secretariat maintains a database of all documents of the World Heritage Committee and the General Assembly of States Parties to the *World Heritage Convention*. This database is available at the following Web address: http: //whc.unesco.org/en/statutorydoc

281. The Secretariat ensures that copies of Tentative Lists, World Heritage nominations, including copies of maps and relevant information received from States Parties are archived in hard copy and in electronic format where possible. The Secretariat also arranges for the archiving of relevant information relating to inscribed properties, including evaluations and other documents developed by the Advisory Bodies, any correspondence and reports received from States Parties (including Reactive Monitoring and Periodic Reports) and correspondence and material from the Secretariat and World Heritage Committee.

282. Archived material will be kept in a form appropriate to long-term storage. Provisions will be made for the storage of paper copies and electronic

b）合法保护标志的缔约国必须审查标志的使用情况。

c）其他缔约国也可决定审查所申请的使用方式，或者将提议提交给秘书处。缔约国政府负责指定相应的国家机构，并通知秘书处是否希望审查所申请的使用方式，或明确指出使用方式不适当。秘书处持有国家主管机构清单。

IX. 信息来源

IX.A 秘书处存档的信息

280. 委员会将所有世界遗产委员会和《保护世界文化和自然遗产公约》缔约国大会的资料存入数据库。该数据库可在以下网址访问：http：//whc.unesco.org/en/statutorydoc

281. 秘书处将确保《预备名录》和世界遗产申报文件副本（包括地图和缔约国提交的相关信息副本）已通过硬拷贝形式存档，同时在可能的情况下保存电子版本。秘书处也安排对已列入《世界遗产名录》的遗产的相关信息进行存档，其中包括咨询机构发表的评估和其他文件、任何缔约国提交的信件和报告（包括反应性监测和定期报告），以及秘书处和世界遗产委员会发出的信件和材料。

282. 存档材料的格式应适宜长期保存。将为供保存纸制和电子文件编列经费。所需的副本也将按要求提供给缔约国。

copies, as relevant. Provision will be made for copies to be provided to States Parties as requested.

283. Nominations of those properties inscribed on the World Heritage List by the Committee will be made available for consultation. States Parties are urged to place a copy of the nomination on their own Web addresses and inform the Secretariat of this action. States Parties preparing nominations may wish to use such information as guides for identifying and elaborating nomination of properties within their own territories.

284. Advisory Body evaluations for each nomination and the decision of the Committee concerning each nomination are available at the following Web address: http://whc.unesco.org/en/advisorybodies

IX.B Specific Information for World Heritage Committee members and other States Parties

285. The Secretariat maintains two electronic mailing lists: one for Committee members (wh-committee@unesco.org) and one for all States Parties (wh- states@unesco.org). States Parties are requested to supply all appropriate email addresses for the establishment of these lists. These electronic mailing lists, which supplement but do not replace the traditional means of notifying States Parties, allow the Secretariat to communicate, in a timely manner, announcements about the availability of documents, changes to meeting schedules, and other issues relevant to Committee members and other States Parties.

286. Circular letters to the States Parties are available at the following Web address: http://whc.unesco.org/en/circularletters

Another Web address, linked to the public Web address through restricted access, is maintained by the Secretariat and contains specific information targeted at Committee members, other States Parties

283. 委员会将妥善保存列入《世界遗产名录》的遗产申报文件，方便查阅。敦促缔约国将申报材料的电子版发布在本国的网站上，并通知秘书处。其他筹备申报的国家可以利用这些信息确认并完善本国境内遗产的申报材料。

284. 咨询机构对于每一项申报的评估意见和委员会所做的决定，都可以在以下网站获取：http://whc.unesco.org/en/advisorybodies

IX.B 世界遗产委员会成员国和其他缔约国的详细信息

285. 秘书处保存了两份电子邮件清单：一份是委员会成员联系方式（wh-committee@unesco.org），另一份是缔约国联系方式（wh-states@unesco.org）。缔约国必须提供所有相关邮箱地址，以供秘书处建立清单。电子邮件清单是补充而不会取代传统的邮寄方式，但秘书处可通过电子邮件及时发表有关文件的适用性、会议计划的变更，以及其他与委员会成员和其他缔约国相关的事宜。

286. 发给缔约国的通函可以在以下网址获取：http://whc.unesco.org/en/circularletters。

还可登录另一个网站链接到公共网址，但其权限受到严格限制。该网站包括委员会委员、缔约国和咨询机构的详细信息，由秘书处负责维护。

and Advisory Bodies.

287. The Secretariat maintains also a database of decisions of the Committee and resolutions of the General Assembly of States Parties. These are available at the following Web addres: http://whc.unesco.org/en/decisions

287. 秘书处还同时维护另外一个有关委员会决议、缔约国大会决议的数据库。可通过以下网址登录：http：//whc.unesco.org/en/decisions。

Decision 28 COM 9

第28COM9号决议

IX.C Information and publications available to the public

IX.C. 向大众公开的信息和出版物

288. The Secretariat provides access to information labelled as publicly available and copyright free on World Heritage properties and other relevant matters, wherever possible.

288. 在可能的情况下，秘书处提供标注为面向公众且不受版权限制的、关于世界遗产和其他相关问题的信息。

289. Information on issues related to World Heritage is available at the Secretariat's Web address (http://whc.unesco.org), on the Web addresses of the Advisory Bodies and in libraries. A list of databases accessible on the web and links to relevant web addresses can be found in the Bibliography.

289. 与世界遗产有关的信息能在秘书处网站（http：//whc.unesco.org）、咨询机构网站和图书馆中获取。参考书目中提供了可在线访问的数据库清单以及相关网站链接。

290. The Secretariat produces a wide variety of World Heritage publications, including the World Heritage List, the List of World Heritage in Danger, Brief Descriptions of World Heritage properties, World Heritage Papersseries, newsletters, brochures and information kits. In addition, other information materials aimed specifically at experts and the general public are also developed. The list of World Heritage publications can be found in the Bibliography or at the following Web address:
http://whc.unesco.org/en/publications.

290 秘书处出版了大量有关世界遗产的出版物，包括《世界遗产名录》、《濒危世界遗产名录》、《世界遗产简要介绍》、《世界遗产论文》系列、简报宣传册和信息工具包。此外，其他专门为专家和大众准备的信息也得到了发展。参考书目中列出了世界遗产出版物的名单，也可通过以下网址获取：http：//whc.unesco.org/en/publications。

These information materials are distributed to the public directly or through the national and international networks established by States Parties or by World Heritage partners..

这些信息资料将直接分发给公众，或通过缔约国或世界遗产合作伙伴建立的国家或国际网络，向大众公开。

ANNEXES   附件

MODEL INSTRUMENT

OF RATIFICATION / ACCEPTANCE

WHEREAS the Convention concerning the Protection of the World Cultural and Natural Heritage was adopted on 16 November 1972 by the General Conference of UNESCO at its seventeenth session;

NOW THEREFORE the Government of.·· having considered the aforesaid Convention, hereby   [ratifies   the same and   undertake faithfully to carryout   [accepts   the stipulations therein contained.

IN WITNESS WHEREOF, I have signed and sealed this instrument.

Doneat·······························this··································day of····················20·········.

(Seal)   *Signature of Head of State,*

                                                           Prime Minister or

                                                           Minister of Foreign Affairs

附件1-1

 接受/正式批准《公约》的模本

1972年11月16日,联合国教科文组织第17届大会上通过了《保护世界文化与自然遗产公约》。

因此,现在
政府已考虑
上述公约,并 [同意 并将忠实地执行
[接受
上述公约中包含的各项规定。

特此证明,本人已在本文件上签字盖章。
20 年 月 地点

(盖章) 国家首脑,
总理或
外交部长的签字

登录联合国教科文组织世界遗产中心网站http://whc.unesco.org/en/modelratification获取接受和正式批准的模板

填好的表格原件应发送至Director-General, UNESCO, 7 place de Fontenoy, 75352 Paris 07 SP, France,最好附有英语或法语的正式翻译件。

Annex 1-2

Model Instrument Of Accession

WHEREAS the Convention concerning the Protection of the World Cultural and Natural Heritage was adopted on 16 November 1972 by the General Conference of UNESCO at its seventeenth session;

NOW THEREFORE the Government of .... having considered the aforesaid Convention, hereby accedes the same and undertake faithfully to carry out the stipulations therein contained.

IN WITNESS WHEREOF, I have signed and sealed this instrument.
Done at ....this ....day of ....20....... .
(Seal)　　　　　　　　　Signature of Head of State,
Prime Minister or
Minister of Foreign Affairs

The model instrument of accession is available from the UNESCO World Heritage Centre and at the following Web address: http://whc.unesco.org/en/modelratification

The original signed version of the completed form should be sent, preferably with an official translation in English or French, to: Director-General, UNESCO, 7 place de Fontenoy, 75352 Paris 07 SP, France

附件 1-2

 正式批准的模板

1972年11月16日，联合国教科文组织第17届大会通过了《保护世界文化与自然遗产公约》。

现在本政府经考虑同意加入并忠实地执行上述公约。

特此证明，本人已在本文件上签字盖章。
20　　　年　　　月　　地点

（盖章）　　　　　　　　　　　　　国家首脑

　　　　　　　　　　　　　　　　　总理或

　　　　　　　　　　　　　　　　　外交部长的签字，

登录联合国教科文组织的世界遗产中心网站http://whc.unesco.org/en/modelratification 获取此正式
批准的模板

填好的表格原件应发送至Director-General, UNESCO, 7 place de Fontenoy, 75352 Paris 07 SP,
France，最好附有英语或法语的正式翻译件。

Annex 2A

United Nations · World
Educational, Scientific and · Heritage
Cultural Organization · Convention

TENTATIVE LIST SUBMISSION FORMAT

STATE PARTY: DATE OF SUBMISSION:

Submission prepared by:

Name: E-mail:

Address: Fax:

Institution: Telephone:

NAME OF PROPERTY:

State, Province or Region:

Latitude and Longitude, or UTM coordinates

DESCRIPTION:

Justification of Outstanding Universal Value:

(Preliminary identification of the values of the property which merit inscription on the World Heritage List)

Criteria met [see Paragraph 77 of the Operational Guidelines]:

(i)	(ii)	(iii)	(iv)	(v)	(vi)	(vii)	(viii)	(ix)	(x)

(Please tick the box corresponding to the proposed criteria and justify the use of each below)

Statements of authenticity and/or integrity [see Paragraphs 78-95 of the Operational Guidelines]:

Comparison with other similar properties:

(The comparison should outline similarities with other properties on the World Heritage List or not, and the reasons that make the property stand out)

The Tentative List submission format is available from the UNESCO World Heritage Centre and at the following Web address: http://whc.unesco.org/en/tentativelists

Further guidance on the preparation of Tentative Lists can be found in Paragraphs 62-67 of the Operational Guidelines.

An example of a completed Tentative List submission format can be found at the following Web address: http://whc.unesco.org/en/tentativelists

All Tentative Lists submitted by States Parties are available at the following Web address: http://whc.unesco.org/en/tentativelists

The original signed version of the completed Tentative List submission format should be sent in English or French to: UNESCO World Heritage Centre, 7 place de Fontenoy, 75352 Paris 07 SP, France

States Parties are encouraged to also submit this information in electronic format (diskette or CD-Rom) or by e-mail to wh-tentativelists@unesco.org

附件2A

《预备名单》提交格式

缔约国：　　　　　　　提交日期：
提交准备机构：
名称：　　　　　　　　电子邮件：
地址：　　　　　　　　传真：
机构：　　　　　　　　电话：

遗产名称：

州、省份或地区：

经纬度或通用横轴墨卡托UTM坐标：

描述：

突出普遍价值申明：
（初步确认应列入《世界遗产名录》的遗产价值）

符合标准［参见《操作指南》第77条］：

(i)	(ii)	(iii)	(iv)	(v)	(vi)	(vii)	(viii)	(ix)	(x)

（请勾选与提议的标准相对应的文本框，并提供选择理由）

完整性和真实性声明［参见《操作指南》第78–95条］：

与其他类似遗产的比较分析：
（比较分析应体现出该遗产与《世界遗产名录》中遗产或其他遗产的相似性、以及该遗产卓尔不群的原因）

登录http://whc.unesco.org/en/tentativelists网站可获得完整的《预备名录》提交格式样板。

《操作指南》第62-67条中含有《预备名单》准备工作的详细指导。

完整的预备名录提交表格范例可在http://whc.unesco.org/en/tentativelists下载

缔约国提交的预备名录可在下列网站查询
http://whc.unesco.org/en/tentativelists

填好的《预备名录》原件应发送至Director-General, UNESCO, 7 place de Fontenoy, 75352 Paris 07 SP, France，最好附有英语或法语的正式翻译件。

鼓励缔约国同时提交电子版表格（磁盘或CD）或发送电子邮件至wh-tentativelists@unesco.org

Annex 2B

United Nations
Educational, Scientific and · Heritage
Cultural Organization · Convention

World

TENTATIVE LIST SUBMISSION FORMAT

FOR SERIAL TRANSNATIONAL AND TRANSBOUNDARY

FUTURE NOMINATIONS

STATE PARTY: DATE OF SUBMISSION:

Submission① prepared by:

Name: E-mail:

Title:

Address: Fax:

Institution: Telephone:

1.a Name of the transnational / transboundary future nomination②:
1.b Other States Parties participating:

1.c Name(s) of the national component part(s):
1.d State, Province or Region:
1.e Latitude and Longitude, or Universal Transverse Mercator (UTM) coordinates:

2.a Brief Description of the transnational / transboundary future nomination③:

2.b Description of the component part(s):

3.JUSTIFICATION FOR OUTSTANDING UNIVERSALVALUE④OF THE FUTURE NOMINATION AS A WHOLE

(Preliminary identification of the values of the future nomination as a whole which merit inscription on the World Heritage List)

(i)	(ii)	(iii)	(iv)	(v)	(vi)	(vii)	(viii)	(ix)	(x)

3.a Criteria met⑤[see Paragraph 77 of the Operational Guidelines]:

(Please tick the box corresponding to the proposed criteria and justify the use of each below)

3.b Statements of authenticity and/or integrity⑥:

---

① This submission will be valid only when all the States Parties indicated in Section 1.b have sent their submissions.

② The text provided in this section should be identical in all submissions of the States Parties involved in the presentation of the same transnational / transboundary future nomination.

③ In case of transnational/transboundary properties any modification will need the agreement of all States Parties concerned.

④ In case of transnational/transboundary properties any modification will need the agreement of all States Parties concerned.

⑤ In case of transnational/transboundary properties any modification will need the agreement of all States Parties concerned.

⑥ In case of transnational/transboundary properties any modification will need the agreement of all States Parties concerned.

3.c.1 Justification of the selection of the component part(s) in relation to the future nomination as a whole:

3.c.2 Comparison with other similar properties[①] :

(This comparison should outline the similarities with other properties inscribed or not on the World Heritage List, and the reasons for the exceptional character of the future nomination).

---

① In case of transnational/transboundary properties any modification will need the agreement of all States Parties concerned.

附件2B

系列跨国和跨境遗产申报

《预备名单》提交格式

缔约国：　　　　　　　　　　　　　　提交日期：

提交①准备机构：

名称：　　　　　　　　　　　　　　　　电子邮件：

地址：　　　　　　　　　　　　　　　　传真：

机构：　　　　　　　　　　　　　　　　电话：

1.a 未来申报跨国或跨境系列遗产名称②：

1.b 其他参与缔约国：

1.c 本国构成部分的名称：

1.d 州、省份或地区：

1.c 经纬度或通用横轴墨卡托UTM坐标：

2.a 跨国或跨境系列遗产申报的简介③：

2.b 各组成部分描述：

3. 申报遗产整体的突出普遍价值④声明

（对遗产整体赖以列入《世界遗产名单》的突出普遍价值的初步认定）

(i)	(ii)	(iii)	(iv)	(v)	(vi)	(vii)	(viii)	(ix)	(x).

3.a 符合标准⑤［参见《操作指南》第77条］：

(请勾选与提议的标准相对应的文本框，并提供选择理由)

3.b 完整性和真实性声明⑥［参见《操作指南》第78-95条］：

---

① 只有当1.b中涉及的所有缔约国都提交后，该提交方被认可。

② 本部分提交的文本与相关缔约国展示的跨境、跨界或未来申报完全一致。

③ 对跨境、跨界遗产的任何修改都需要全体相关缔约国的一致同意。

④ 对跨境、跨界遗产的任何修改都需要全体相关缔约国的一致同意。

⑤ 对跨境、跨界遗产的任何修改都需要全体相关缔约国的一致同意。

⑥ 对跨境、跨界遗产的任何修改都需要全体相关缔约国的一致同意。

3.c.1　对整体申报项目中各构成部分的选择加以解释：

3.c.2　与其他类似遗产的比较分析[①]：

（比较分析应体现出该遗产与《世界遗产名录》中遗产或其他遗产的相似性、以及该遗产卓尔不群的原因）

---

① 对跨境、跨界遗产的任何修改都需要全体相关缔约国的一致同意。

annex 3

GUIDELINES ON THE INSCRIPTION OF SPECIFIC TYPES OF PROPERTIES ON THE WORLD HERITAGE LIST①

The ICOMOS List of thematic studies is available at the following address:http://www.icomos.org/studies

The IUCN List of thematic studies is available at the following address: http://www.iucn.org/about/work/programmes/wcpa_worldheritage/wheritage_pub/

INTRODUCTION

1.This annex provides information on specific types of properties to guide States Parties in preparing nominations of properties for inscription on the World Heritage List. The following information constitutes guidelines that should be used in association with Chapter II of the *Operational Guidelines*, which contains the criteria for inscription of properties on the World Heritage List.

2.The Committee has endorsed the findings of expert meetings on the subject of cultural landscapes, towns, canals and routes (Part I, below).

3. The reports of other expert meetings requested by the World Heritage Committee, in the framework of the Global Strategy for a representative, balanced and credible World Heritage List, are referred to in Part II.

附件 3

特定类型遗产列入《世界遗产名录》指南①

ICOMOS 主题研究详细目录可见于：http：//www.icomos.org/studies

IUCN 主题研究详细目录可见于：http：//www.iucn.org/about/work/programmes/wcpa_world heritage/wheritage_pub/

序言

1. 该附件提供了特定类型遗产的相关信息，以便指导缔约国申报遗产列入《世界遗产名录》的准备工作。下列信息可与《操作指南》第二章联合使用，其中包含遗产列入《世界遗产名录》应满足的标准。

2. 委员会已经批准了针对文化景观、城镇、运河和文化线路召开的专家会议所做的决议（参见下文第一部分）。

3. 应世界遗产委员会要求的、在具代表性、平衡性和可信性《世界遗产名录》的全球战略大框架下的、其他专家会议报告，请参见第二部分。

---

① The Committee may develop additional guidelines for other types of properties in future years.

① 委员会未来可能会为其他类型遗产开发，附加指导。

4. Part III lists various comparative and thematic studies prepared by the Advisory Bodies.

Ⅰ. CULTURAL LANDSCAPES, TOWNS, CANALS AND ROUTES

5. The World Heritage Committee has identified and defined several specific types of cultural and natural properties and has adopted specific guidelines to facilitate the evaluation of such properties when nominated for inscription on the World Heritage List. To date, these cover the following categories, althoughit is likely that others may be added in due course:

    a) Cultural Landscapes;
    b) Historic Towns and Town Centres;
    c) Heritage Canals;
    d) Heritage Routes.

CULTURAL LANDSCAPES①

Definition

6. Cultural landscapes are cultural properties and represent the "combined works of nature and of man" designated in Article 1 of the *Convention*. They are illustrative of the evolution of human society and settlement over time, under the influence of the physical constraints and/or opportunities presented by their natural environment and of successive social, economic and cultural forces, both external and internal.

4. 第三部分列出了咨询机构完成的各种比较和主题研究。

Ⅰ. 文化景观、城镇、运河与文化线路

5. 世界遗产委员会已经识别并定义了几种特殊的文化与自然遗产类型，并制定了具体的指南，以便对这些遗产申报列入《世界遗产名录》进行评估。到目前为止，这些遗产包括以下种类，当然未来也可能会有其他类型被适时加入进来：

    a) 文化景观；
    b) 历史城镇和城镇中心；
    c) 遗产运河；
    d) 遗产线路。

文化景观①

定义

6. 文化景观属于文化遗产，正如《公约》第一条所述，它们是"人类与大自然的共同杰作"。文化景观见证了人类社会和居住地在自然限制和/或自然环境的影响下随着时间的推移而产生的进化，也展示了社会、经济和文化外部和内部的发展力量。

---

① This text was prepared by an Expert Group on Cultural Landscapes (La Petite Pierre, France, 24 -26 October 1992) (see document *WHC-92/CONF.202/10/Add*). The text was subsequently approved for inclusion in the *Operational Guidelines* by the World Heritage Committee at its 16th session (Santa Fe 1992) (see document *WHC- 92/CONF.002/12*).

① 本文件由文化景观专家组制定（法国的 LaPetitePierre，1992 年 10 月 24-26 日）（见文件 WHC-92/ CONF.202/10/Add），随后世界遗产委员会在其第 16 次会议上（圣达菲，1992 年）批准将该文件纳入《操作指南》中（见文件 WHC-92/CONF.002/12）。

7. They should be selected on the basis both of their Outstanding Universal Value and of their representativity in terms of a clearly defined geo-cultural region and also for their capacity to illustrate the essential and distinct cultural elements of such regions.

8. The term "cultural landscape" embraces a diversity of manifestations of the interaction between humankind and its natural environment.

9. Cultural landscapes often reflect specific techniques of sustainable land-use, considering the characteristics and limits of the natural environment they are established in, and a specific spiritual relation to nature. Protection of cultural landscapes can contribute to modern techniques of sustainable land-use and can maintain or enhance natural values in the landscape. The continued existence of traditional forms of land-use supports biological diversity in many regions of the world. The protection of traditional cultural landscapes is therefore helpful in maintaining biological diversity.

Definition and Categories

10. Cultural landscapes fall into three main categories, namely:

(i) The most easily identifiable is the clearly defined landscape designed and created intentionally by man. This embraces garden and parkland landscapes constructed for aesthetic reasons which are often (but not always) associated with religious or other monumental buildings and ensembles.

(ii) The second category is the organically evolved landscape. This results from an initial social, economic, administrative, and/or religious imperative and has developed its present form by association with and in response to its natural environment. Such landscapes reflect that process

7. 文化景观选择的依据包括其突出的普遍价值、在特定地理文化区域中的代表性，以及体现这些地区核心和独特文化元素的能力。

8. "文化景观"一词包含了人类与其所在的自然环境之间互动的多种表现。

9. 考虑到其所处自然环境的局限性和特点，文化景观通常能够反映可持续性土地利用的特殊技术，反映了与大自然特定的精神关系。保护文化景观有利于将可持续性土地使用技术现代化，保持或提升景观的自然价值。传统土地使用形式的持续存在支持了世界大多数地区的生物多样性，因此，对传统文化景观的保护也有益于保持生物多样性。

定义和种类

10. 文化景观主要可以被分为以下三类：

（i）最易识别的一种是明确定义的、人类刻意设计及创造的景观。其中包含出于美学原因建造的园林和公园景观，它们经常（但不总是）与宗教或其他纪念性建筑物或建筑群相结合。

（ii）第二种是有机演进的景观。它们产生于最初始的一种社会、经济、行政以及宗教需要，并通过与周围自然环境的相联系或相适应而发展到目前的形式。这种景观反映了其形式和重要组成部分的进化过程。它们又可分为两类：

of evolution in their form and component features. They fall into two sub-categories:

- a relict (or fossil) landscape is one in which an evolutionary process came to an end at some time in the past, either abruptly or over a period. Its significant distinguishing features are, however, still visible in material form.

- a continuing landscape is one which retains an active social role in contemporary society closely associated with the traditional way of life, and in which the evolutionary process is still in progress. At the same time it exhibits significant material evidence of its evolution overtime.

(iii) The final category is the associative cultural landscape. The inscription of such landscapes on the World Heritage List is justifiable by virtue of the powerful religious, artistic or cultural associations of the natural element rather than material cultural evidence, which may be insignificant or even absent.

Inscription of Cultural Landscapes on the World Heritage List

11. The extent of a cultural landscape for inscription on the World Heritage List is relative to its functionality and intelligibility. In any case, the sample selected must be substantial enough to adequately represent the totality of the cultural landscape that it illustrates. The possibility of designating long linear areas which represent culturally significant transport and communication networks should not be excluded.

12. General criteria for protection and management are equally applicable to cultural landscapes. It is important that due attention be paid to the full range of values represented in the landscape, both cultural and natural. The nominations should be prepared in collaboration with and the full approval of local communities.

– 残骸（或化石）景观，它代表过去某一时间内已经完成的进化过程，它的结束或为突发性或渐进式的。然而，它的显著特点在实物上仍清晰可见。

– 另外一种是持续性景观，它在当今社会与传统的生活方式的密切交融中持续扮演着一种积极的社会角色，演变过程仍在持续，而同时，它又是历史演变发展的重要物证。

（iii）最后一种景观是关联性文化景观。将这一景观列入《世界遗产名录》是因为这类景观体现了强烈的与自然因素、宗教、艺术或文化的关联，而不仅是实体的文化物证，后者对它来说并不重要，甚至是可以缺失的。

将文化景观列入《世界遗产名录》

11. 文化景观能否列入《世界遗产名录》取决于其功能性和可理解性。无论如何，被选的样品必须能够充分代表该种文化景观所要表达的全部内容的实质。不排除申报具有文化意义的、长距离的、代表交通和交流网络的、线性区域的可能性。

12. 总的保护和管理标准同样适用于文化景观。应重视景观所表现的包含文化与自然所有方面的价值。申报应取得当地社区的同意并在与他们的协作下进行。

13. The existence of a category of "cultural landscape", included on the World Heritage List on the basis of the criteria set out in Paragraph 77 of the *Operational Guidelines*, does not exclude the possibility of properties of exceptional importance in relation to both cultural and natural criteria continuing to be inscribed (see definition of mixed properties as set out in Paragraph 46). In such cases, their Outstanding Universal Value must be justified under both sets of criteria.

13. "文化景观"类别根据《操作指南》的第 77 条标准已列入《世界遗产名录》的景观，不排除继续吸收与文化和自然均相关的重要遗产的可能性（参见第 46 条落中对混合遗产的定义）。在这种情况下，必须根据两套标准对其突出的普遍价值进行评定。

HISTORIC TOWNS AND TOWN CENTRES[①]

Definition and Categories

14. Groups of urban buildings eligible for inscription on the World Heritage List fall into three main categories, namely:

(i) towns which are no longer inhabited but which provide unchanged archaeological evidence of the past; these generally satisfy the criterion of authenticity and their state of conservation can be relatively easily controlled;

(ii) historic towns which are still inhabited and which, by their very nature, have developed and will continue to develop under the influence of socio-economic and cultural change, a situation that renders the assessment of their authenticity more difficult and any conservation policy more problematical;

(iii) new towns of the twentieth century which paradoxically have something in common with both the aforementioned categories: while their original

历史城镇和城镇中心 [①]

定义和种类

14. 符合《世界遗产名录》申请条件的城区包括下列三种：

（ⅰ）无人居住但城镇原始考古证据保存完好的城镇，这些城镇一般符合真实性的评价标准且保护状况相对易于控制；

（ⅱ）沿用至今的历史城镇，这些城镇在社会经济和文化的变化中不断发展并将持续发展，这种情况致使对它们真实性的评估更加困难，保护政策存在的问题也较多；

（ⅲ）二十世纪的新镇，矛盾的是这类城镇与上述两种城镇都有相似之处：一方面它最初的城市组织结构仍清晰可见，其历史真实性不

---

① This text was in cluded in the January 1987 version of the *Operational Guidelines* following the discussion by the Committee at its 8th session (Buenos Aires, 1984) of the conclusions of the Meeting of Experts to Consult on Historic Towns which met in Paris from 5 to 7 September 1984 organized by ICOMOS.

① 本文本包含在委员会第八届会议（1984，布宜诺斯艾利斯）后出台的 1987 年 1 月版的《操作指南》中，这次会议讨论了 1984 年 9 月 5 日至 7 日在巴黎召开的历史名镇专家咨询会的结论，专家咨询会由国际古迹遗址理事会组织。

urban organization is clearly recognizable and their authenticity is undeniable, their future is unclear because their development is largely uncontrollable.

Inscription of Historic Towns and Town Centres on the World Heritage List

15. The significance of Historic Towns and Town Centres can be examined under the factors outlined below:

(i) Towns no longer inhabited

The evaluation of towns that are no longer inhabited does not raise any special difficulties other than those related to archaeological properties in general: the criteria which call for uniqueness or exemplary character have led to the choice of groups of buildings noteworthy for their purity of style, for the concentrations of monuments they contain and sometimes for their important historical associations. It is important for urban archaeological sites to be listed as integral units. A cluster of monuments or a small group of buildings is not adequate to suggest the multiple and complex functions of a city which has disappeared; remains of such a city should be preserved in their entirety together with their natural surroundings whenever possible.

(ii) Inhabited historic towns

In the case of inhabited historic towns the difficulties are numerous, largely owing to the fragility of their urban fabric (which has in many cases been seriously disrupted since the advent of the industrial era) and the runaway speed with which their surroundings have been urbanized. To qualify for inscription, towns should compel recognition because of their architectural interest and should not be considered only on the intellectual grounds of the role they may have played in the past or their value as historical symbols under criterion (vi) for the inscription of cultural properties on the World Heritage List (see Paragraph 77 (vi)

容置疑，另一方面它的未来是不明确的，因为它的发展基本是不可控的。

将历史城镇和城镇中心列入《世界遗产名录》

15. 历史城镇和城镇中心的价值，可以通过下列因素评估：

（i）无人居住的城镇

对无人居住的城镇的评估，除了有关考古遗产的一般性问题，不会产生其他特殊困难：要求独特性或典范性的评价标准，致使人们在选择建筑群时更关注其风格纯粹性，所含历史遗迹的集中程度，有时甚至包括与重要历史事件的关联性。列入时把城市里的文物古迹作为一个整体单位这一点很重要。几个纪念性建筑和建筑群不足以说明一个已消失城市复杂多样的功能，对于这种城市的遗迹，应尽可能地保留它们的完整性，包括它们周围的自然环境。

（ii）尚有人居住的历史城镇

评估尚有人居住的历史城镇困难较多，这在很大程度上是因为其城市构造的脆弱性（其中大多数在工业时代到来后发展被打乱），周围的环境以近乎失控的速度不断被城市化。要想列入《世界遗产名录》，这些城镇的建筑价值应该得到认可，而不应该仅仅依赖它们在历史中曾经的重要角色和作为历史象征的价值（将文化遗产列入《世界遗产名录》的标准（六））（参见《操作指南》第 77（vi）条内容）。要达到列入《世界遗产名录》的要求，空间组织、结构、材料、形式，甚至建筑群的功能，应从本质上反映遗产所在地区文明社会的文明和文明演进的过程。这类城镇可分为以下四类：

of the *Operational Guidelines*). To be eligible for inscription in the List, the spatial organization, structure, materials, forms and, where possible, functions of a group of buildings should essentially reflect the civilization or succession of civilizations which have prompted the nomination of the property. Four categories can be distinguished:

a) Towns which are typical of a specific period or culture, which have been almost wholly preserved and which have remained largely unaffected by subsequent developments. Here the property to be listed is the entire town together with its surroundings, which must also be protected;

b) Towns that have evolved along characteristic lines and have preserved, sometimes in the midst of exceptional natural surroundings, spatial arrangements and structures that are typical of the successive stages in their history. Here the clearly defined historic part takes precedence over the contemporary environment;

c) "Historic centres" that cover exactly the same area as ancient towns and are now enclosed within modern cities. Here it is necessary to determine the precise limits of the property in its widest historical dimensions and to make appropriate provision for its immediate surroundings;

d) Sectors, areas or isolated units which, even in the residual state in which they have survived, provide coherent evidence of the character of a historic town which has disappeared. In such cases surviving areas and buildings should bear sufficient testimony to the former whole.

Historic centres and historic areas should be listed only where they contain a large number of ancient buildings of monumental importance which provide a direct indication of the characteristic features of a town of exceptional interest. Nominations of several isolated and unrelated buildings which allegedly represent, in themselves, a town whose urban fabric has ceased to be discernible, should not been

a）突出代表了某一特定时期或文化的城镇，保存完整且未受到后续发展的影响。这种城镇将作为一个整体申报，其周围环境也要受到保护；

b）延续自身特征并时常在特殊的自然环境中保存了以后各个历史时期中的典型空间安排和结构的城镇。这种情况下，明确定义的历史城区比当代环境更具价值；

c）与原来古镇的范围完全相同，但今天身处在现代城市中的"历史中心"，这种情况下，有必要在最宽泛的历史维度下，确定遗产范围并为它的周边环境，制定适当的规定；

d）城区、地域或一些孤立的城市空间单元，即使残破不堪，也为一个已消失的历史城镇的特征提供统一连贯的证明。这种情况下必须充分证实，遗存空间和建筑足够见证原来整体地区。

只有当历史中心和历史区域包含了大量具有重大意义的古建筑，能直接显示一个具备极高价值的城镇的典型特征时，才可以被列入《世界遗产名录》。如只是若干孤立和毫无关联的建筑群，再无法体现历史城市的原有格局，则不应申报。

couraged.

However, nominations could be made regarding properties that occupy a limited space but have had a major influence on the history of town planning. In such cases, the nomination should make it clear that it is the monumental group that is to be listed and that the town is mentioned only incidentally as the place where the property is located. Similarly, if a building of clearly Outstanding Universal Value is located in severely degraded or insufficiently representative urban surroundings, it should, of course, be listed without any special reference to the town.

(iii) New towns of the twentieth century

It is difficult to assess the quality of new towns of the twentieth century. History alone will tell which of them will best serve as examples of contemporary town planning. The examination of the files on these towns should be deferred, save under exceptional circumstances.

Under present conditions, preference should be given to the inscription in the World Heritage List of small or medium-sized urban areas which are in a position to manage any potential growth, rather than the great metropolises, on which sufficiently complete information and documentation cannot readily be provided that would serve as a satisfactory basis for their inscription in their entirety.

In view of the effects which the inscription of a town on the World Heritage List could have on its future, such entries should be exceptional. Inscription in the List implies that legislative and administrative measures have already been taken to ensure the protection of the group of buildings and its environment. Informed awareness on the part of the population concerned, without whose active participation any conservation scheme would be

可以申报空间有限但却对城镇规划的历史影响重大的遗产，这种情况下，需明确申报的是文物古迹，城镇只是作为其所在区域被提及。同样，如果一座具有明确的突出普遍价值的建筑，坐落在已严重退化或不具有充分的代表性的城市环境中，则应被独立申报，不必专门提及城镇。

（iii）二十世纪的新城

评定二十世纪新城镇的质量比较困难。历史本身会体现哪座城镇最能代表当代城镇规划的典范。对这些城镇资料的审核可推后，某些特殊情况除外。

在现行条件下，《世界遗产名录》应优先选择能够控制发展的中小型城区而不是大都市，大城市也很难提供完整的信息和文献资料作为其整体申报的满意依据。

考虑到将一座城镇列入《世界遗产名录》对其未来发展的影响，应被视为特殊情况处理。申报列入《名录》意味着已经有相应的立法和行政手段确保对建筑群及其背景环境的保护。提高当地居民的保护意识也很重要，没有他们的积极参与，任何保护方案都是不切实际的。

impractical, is also essential.

HERITAGE CANALS

16. The concept of "canals" is discussed in detail in the Report of the Expert Meeting on Heritage Canals (Canada, September 1994)[1].

Definition

17. A canal is a human-engineered waterway. It may be of Outstanding Universal Value from the point of view of history or technology, either intrinsically or as an exceptional example representative of this category of cultural property. The canal may be a monumental work, the defining feature of a linear cultural landscape, or an integral component of a complex cultural landscape.

Inscription of Heritage Canals on the World Heritage List

18. Authenticity depends holistically upon values and the relationships between these values. One distinctive feature of the canal as a heritage element is its evolution over time. This is linked to how it was used during different periods and the associated technological changes the canal underwent. The extent of these changes may constitute a heritage element.

19. The authenticity and historical interpretation of a canal encompass the connection between the real property (subject of the *Convention*), possible movable property (boats, temporary navigation items) and the

遗产运河

16. 关于遗产运河的专家会议（加拿大，1994年9月）[1]报告中对"运河"这一概念进行了详细的讨论。

定义

17. 运河是人类兴建的水路。从历史或技术角度看，运河本质上或作为这种文化遗产类型的一个特例，都可能具有突出的普遍价值。历史运河可以被看作一个文物古迹，一种线性文化景观的决定性特征，或是一个复杂的文化景观中的一个组成部分。

将运河列入《世界遗产名录》

18. 真实性整体上取决于价值和这些价值之间的关系。运河作为一种遗产要素，其特征在于动态的演变过程。这与它在不同时期的用途和它所经历过的技术改变相关，这些改变可能构成重要的遗产要素。

19. 一条运河的真实性和历史阐释包含真实的遗产（本《公约》主题）、可能的可移动遗产（船只、临时航运设施）以及相关构造（桥等）和景观之间的关系。

---

[1]　Expert meeting on «Heritage Canals» (Canada, 15-19 September 1994) (see document *WHC-94/CONF.003/INF.10*) discussed by the World Heritage Committee at its 19th session (Berlin, Germany, 1995) (see document *WHC-95/CONF.203/16*).

[1]　世界遗产委员会第19届会议（德国柏林，1995年）（见文件WHC-95/CONF.203/16）上讨论的关于遗产运河的专家会议（加拿大，1994年9月15-19日）（见文件WHC-94/CONF.003/INF.10）报告。

associated structures (bridges, etc) and landscape.

20. The significance of canals can be examined under technological, economic, social, and landscape factors as outlined below:

(i) Technology

Canals can serve a variety of purposes: irrigation, navigation, defence, water-power, flood mitigation, land-drainage and water-supply. The following are areas of technology which may be of significance:

a) The lining and waterproofing of the water channel;

b) The engineering structures of the line with reference to comparative structural features in other areas of architecture and technology;

c) The development of the sophistication of construction methods; and

d) The transfer of technologies.

(ii) Economy

Canals contribute to the economy in a variety of ways, e.g. in terms of economic development and the conveyance of goods and people. Canals were the first man-made routes for the effective carriage of bulk cargoes. Canals played and continue to play a key role in economic development through their use for irrigation. The following factors are important:

a) National building;

b) Agricultural development;

c) Industrial development;

d) Generation of wealth;

e) Development of engineering skills applied to other areas and industries; and

f) Tourism.

(iii) Social Factors

The building of canals had, and their operation continues to have, social consequences:

e) The redistribution of wealth with social and cultural results; and

f) The movement of people and the interaction

20. 运河的意义可根据以下的技术、经济、社会和景观因素测定：

（i）技术

运河的用途众多，包括：灌溉、航运、防御、水力、泄洪、地面排水和给水。以下是比较重要的技术方面：

a）水渠的衬砌和防水；

b）该水道的工程结构，参考、比较了其他建筑和技术领域的结构特点；

c）综合建造方法的开发；

d）技术转让

（ii）经济

运河以多种形式为经济做出贡献，如在经济发展和货物和人员运输方面。运河是人类开发最早的、有效运输大批货物的线路。运河还通过发挥灌溉功能，在经济发展中扮演了和并将继续扮演重要的角色。下列因素很重要：

a）促进国民经济；

b）农业发展；

c）工业发展；

d）创造财富；

e）可应用于其他领域和产业中的工程技术的发展；

f）旅游

（iii）社会因素

开凿运河及其持续使用具有社会影响：

a）具有社会和文化效应的财富的再分配；

b）人口流动以及文化组群间的交互作用。

of cultural groups.

(iv) Landscape

Such large-scale engineering works had and continue to have an impact on the natural landscape. Related industrial activity and changing settlement patterns cause visible changes to landscape forms and patterns.

HERITAGE ROUTES

21. The concept of "routes" or cultural itineraries was discussed by the expert meeting on "Routes as a Part of our Cultural Heritage" (Madrid, Spain, November 1994)[①].

Definition

22. The concept of heritage routes is shown to be a rich and fertile one, offering a privileged framework in which mutual understanding, apluralap proach to history and a culture of peace can all operate.

23. A heritage route is composed of tangible elements of which the cultural significance comes from exchanges and a multi-dimensional dialogue across countries or regions, and that illustrate the interaction of movement, alongthe route, in space and time.

Inscription of Heritage Routes on the World Heritage List

24. The following points should be considered when determining whether a heritage route is suitable for inscription on the World HeritageList:

（iv）景观

如此规模的工程曾经并将继续对自然景观造成影响。相关的工业活动和不断变换的聚居形式，使景观的形式和格局发生了显著的变化。

遗产线路

21. "将线路作为文化遗产的一部分"专家会议（西班牙马德里，1994年12月）[①]上讨论了"线路"或文化线路的概念。

定义

22. 遗产线路的概念丰富多彩，它提供了一种有效的构架，使相互理解、多种历史观的共存及和平文化能在其中发挥作用。

23. 遗产线路由各种有形的要素构成，这些要素的文化意义来自于跨国界和跨地区的交流和多维对话，说明了沿这条线路上展开的运动在时空上的交流互动。

将遗产线路列入《世界遗产名录》

24. 在决定一条遗产线路是否具备列入《世界遗产名录》的资格时，下列几点应予以考虑：

---

① Expert Meeting on «Routes as part of Our Cultural Heritage» (Madrid, 24-25 November 1994) (see document *WHC-94/CONF.003/INF.13*) discussed by the World Heritage Committee at its 19th session (Berlin, 1995) (see document *WHC-95/CONF.203/16*).

① 世界遗产文员会第19次会议（德国柏林，1995年）（见文件 WHC-95/CONF.203/16）上讨论的关于将线路作为文化遗产的一部分的专家会议（西班牙马德里，1994年11月24-25日）报告（参见文件 WHC-94/CONF.003/INF.13）。

(i) The requirement to hold Outstanding Universal Value should be recalled.

(ii) The concept of heritager outes:

\- is based on the dynamics of movement and the idea of exchanges, with continuity in space and time;

\- refers to a whole, where the route has a worth over and above the sum of the elements making it up and through which it gains its cultural significance;

\- highlights exchange and dialogue between countries or between regions;

\- is multi-dimensional, with different aspects developing and adding to its prime purpose which may be religious, commercial, administrative or otherwise.

(iii) A heritage route may be considered as a specific, dynamic type of cultural landscape, just as recent debates have led to their acceptance within the *Operational Guidelines*.

(iv) The identification of a heritage route is based on a collection of strengths and tangible elements, testimony to the significance of the route itself.

(v) The conditions of authenticity are to be applied on the grounds of its significance and other elements making up the heritage route. It will take into account the duration of the route, and perhaps how often it is used nowadays, as well as the legitimate wishes for development of peoples affected.

These points will be considered within the natural framework of the route and its intangible and symbolic dimensions.

Ⅱ. REPORTS OF REGIONAL AND THEMATIC EXPERT MEETINGS

25. The World Heritage Committee, in the framework of the Global Strategy for a representative, balanced and credible World Heritage List has requested a number of regional and thematic expert

（ⅰ）重新考虑具有突出普遍价值的相关要求。

（ⅱ）遗产线路的概念

– 基于动态的迁徙、思想的、交流的概念、空间和时间上的连续性；

– 涉及一个整体，线路因此具备了比各组成要素的总和更多的价值，也因此获得了其文化意义；

– 强调国家间或地区间交流和对话；

– 应是多维的，不同方面的发展，不断丰富和补充其主要用途，可能是宗教的、商业、行政的或其他。

（ⅲ）遗产线路可被视为一种特殊的、动态的文化景观（近期这种争论使其被纳入《操作指南》）。

（ⅳ）对遗产线路的认定基于各种力量和有形要素的集合，以见证线路本身的重大意义。

（ⅴ）真实性条件也将基于线路的重要性和其他组成要素。线路的使用时间也要考虑在内，可能还需考虑其现今使用的频率和受其影响的族群对其发展的合理意愿。

以上几点需放在线路的自然框架及其无形的和象征性的层面考虑。

Ⅱ. 地区和主题专家会议报告

25. 在构建具有代表性、平衡性和可信性的《世界遗产名录》的全球战略构架中，世界遗产委员会要求根据不同遗产类型举行一系列地区和主题专家会议。这些会议的结果将指导缔约

meetings on different types of properties. The results of these meetings may guide States Parties in preparing nominations. The reports of the expert meetings presented to the World Heritage Committee are available at the following Web address:

　　http://whc.unesco.org/en/globalstrategy

Ⅲ. THEMATIC AND COMPARATIVE STUDIES BY THE ADVISORY BODIES

26. To fulfil their obligations concerning evaluations of nominations of cultural and natural properties, the Advisory Bodies have undertaken comparative and thematic studies, often with partner organizations, in different subject areas in order to provide a context for theire valuations.

These reports, most of which are available on their respective Web addresses, include:

Earth's Geological History - A Contextual Framework for Assessment of World Heritage Fossil Site Nominations (September 1996)

International Canal Monuments List (1996) http://www.icomos.org/studies/canals-toc.htm

World Heritage Bridges (1996)http://www. icomos.org/studies/bridges.htm

A Global Overview of Forest Protected Areas on the World Heritage List (September 1997)http:// www.unep-wcmc.org/wh/reviews/forests/

A Global Overview of Wetland and Marine Protected Areas on the World Heritage List (September 1997)http://www.unep-wcmc.org/wh/reviews/wetlands/

Human Use of World Heritage Natural Sites

国进行申报准备工作。可通过下列网址获取已呈递给世界遗产委员会的会议报告：http：//whc.unesco.org/en/globalstrategy

Ⅲ. 咨询团体的主题和比较研究

26. 为了履行评估文化与自然遗产申报的责任，咨询团体与合作伙伴组织，针对不同主题进行了各种比较研究和主题研究，旨在提供评估依据。

大部分相关报告可通过各有关网站获取，这些报告包括：

《地球地质史——评估化石遗址世界遗产申报的背景框架》（1996年9月）

《国际运河遗址名录》（1996年）http：//www.icomos.org/studies/canals-toc.htm

《世界遗产中的桥梁》（1996年）http：//www.icomos.org/studies/bridges.htm

《〈世界遗产名录〉中的全球森林保护区的概览》（1997年9月）http：//www.unep-wcmc.org/wh/reviews/forests/

《〈世界遗产名录〉中的全球湿地和海洋保护区的概览》（1997年9月）http：//www.unep-wcmc.org/wh/reviews/wetlands/

《人类对世界自然遗产的利用》（1997年 9

(September 1997)http://www.unep-wcmc.org/wh/reviews/human/

Fossil Hominid Sites (1997)http://www.icomos.org/studies/hominid.htm

The Urban Architectural Heritage of Latin America (1998)http://www.icomos.org/studies/latin-towns.htm

Les Théâtres et les Amphithéâtres antiques (1999) http://www.icomos.org/studies/theatres.htm

Railways as World Heritage Sites (1999)http://www.icomos.org/studies/railways.htm

A Global Overview of Protected Areas on the World Heritage List of Particular Importance for Biodiversity (November 2000)http://www.unep-wcmc.org/wh/reviews/

Les villages ouvriers comme éléments du patrimoine de l'industrie (2001)http://www.icomos.org/studies/villages-ouvriers.htm

A Global Strategy for Geological World Heritage (February 2002)

Rock-Art Sites of Southern Africa (2002)http://www.icomos.org/studies/sarockart.htm

月）http：//www.unep-wcmc.org/wh/reviews/human/

《原始人类化石遗址》（1997年）http：//www.icomos.org/studies/hominid.htm

《拉丁美洲的城市建筑遗产》（1998年）http://www.icomos.org/studies/latin-towns.htm

《古剧院和古剧场》（1999年）http：//www.icomos.org/studies/theatres.htm

《铁路作为世界遗产》（1999年）http：//www.icomos.org/studies/railways.htm

《〈世界遗产名录〉中对生物多样性具有特殊意义的保护区的全球概览》（2000年11月）http：//www.unep-wcmc.org/wh/reviews/

《作为工业遗产组成要素的村镇工厂》（2001年）http：//www.icomos.org/studies/villages-ouvriers.htm

《世界地质遗产的全球战略》（2002年2月）

《南非的岩石艺术遗址》（2002年）http：//www.icomos.org/studies/sarockart.htm

Annex 4

AUTHENTICITY IN RELATION TO THE WORLD HERITAGE CONVENTION

INTRODUCTION

This Annex reproduces the Nara Document on Authenticity, drafted by the 45 participants to the Nara Conference on Authenticity in Relation to the *World Heritage Convention*, held at Nara, Japan, from 1-6 November 1994. The Nara Conference was organized in co-operation with UNESCO, ICCROM and ICOMOS.

The World Heritage Committee examined the report of the Nara meeting on Authenticity at its 18th session (Phuket, Thailand, 1994) (see document WHC-94/CONF.003/16).

Subsequent expert meetings have enriched the concept of authenticity in relation to the *World Heritage Convention* (see Bibliography of the *Operational Guidelines*).

Ⅰ. THE NARA DOCUMENT ON AUTHENTICITY

Preamble

1. We, the experts assembled in Nara (Japan), wish to acknowledge the generous spirit and intellectual courage of the Japanese authorities in providing a timely forum in which we could challenge conventional thinking in the conservation field, and debate ways and means of broadening our horizons to bring greater respect for cultural and heritage diversity to conservation practice.

2. We also wish to acknowledge the value of the framework for discussion provided by the World Heritage Committee's desire to apply the test of authenticity in ways which accord full respect

附件 4

《保护世界文化与自然遗产公约》相关的真实性

前言

本附件使用了《奈良真实性文件》。1994 年 11 月 1 日至 6 日，《世界遗产公约》相关的真实性会议在日本奈良召开，与会的 45 位代表起草了《奈良真实性文件》。奈良会议由联合国教科文组织、国际文化遗产保护与修复研究中心和国际古迹遗址理事会联合主办。

世界遗产委员会第 18 届会议（泰国普吉岛，1994 年）上审核了奈良会议中关于真实性的报告（见文件 WHC-94/CONF.003/16）。

此后的专家会议丰富了《世界遗产公约》相关的真实性的概念（见《操作指南》的参考文献）。

Ⅰ.《奈良真实性文件》

导言

1. 作为参与奈良（日本）会与会专家，我们在此感谢日本当局的慷慨精神与学术勇气，为我们适时提供了此论坛，让我们能够挑战遗产保护领域的传统思想，讨论运用各种途径和方法扩大我们的视野，从而在保护实践中更大限度的尊重文化和遗产的多样性让我们能够挑战保护领域的传统思想，讨论运用各种途径和方法扩大我们的视野，从而在保护实践中更大限度的尊重文化和遗产的多样性。

2. 我们希望认可世界遗产委员会所提供的、以尊重所有社会的社会与文化价值的方式、在检验申报《世界遗产名录》的文化遗产的突出普遍性价值时，采用真实性检验标准提出的讨

to the social and cultural values of all societies, in examining the outstanding universal value of cultural properties proposed for the World Heritage List.

论构架的价值。

3. The Nara Document on Authenticity is conceived in the spirit of the Charter of Venice, 1964, and builds on it and extends it in response to the expanding scope of cultural heritage concerns and interests in our contemporary world.

3.《奈良真实性文件》受到1964年的威尼斯宪法精神启发，在此基础上建立，并被延伸引用，以响应我们当代世界对文化遗产的关注与利益的范围的不断扩大。

4. In a world that is increasingly subject to the forces of globalization and homogenization, and in a world in which the search for cultural identity is sometimes pursued through aggressive nationalism and the suppression of the cultures of minorities, the essential contribution made by the consideration of authenticity in conservation practice is to clarify and illuminate the collective memory of humanity.

4. 在一个日益受到全球化和同一化力量影响的世界里，在一个有时藉由带有侵略性的民族主义和压制少数民族文化以追求文化认同的世界里，真实性思考在保护实践中的重要的贡献是，澄清并阐明人类的集体记忆。

Cultural Diversity and Heritage Diversity

文化多样性和遗产多样性

5. The diversity of cultures and heritage in our world is an irreplaceable source of spiritual and intellectual richness for all humankind. The protection and enhancement of cultural and heritage diversity in our world should be actively promoted as an essential aspect of human development.

5. 我们所处世界的文化和遗产的多样性是所有人类丰富的精神和知识的不可替代的来源。对世界的文化和遗产的多样性的保护和加强应得到积极的推动，使之成为人类发展的一个重要方面。

6. Cultural heritage diversity exists in time and space, and demands respect for other cultures and all aspects of their belief systems. In cases where cultural values appear to be in conflict, respect for cultural diversity demands acknowledgment of the legitimacy of the cultural values of all parties.

6. 文化遗产的多样性涉及时间和空间，需要对其他文化和它们所信仰的各个方面给予尊重。一旦文化价值发生了冲突，尊重文化多样性就需要承认所有成员的文化价值的合法性。

7. All cultures and societies are rooted in the particular forms and means of tangible and intangible expression which constitute their heritage, and these should be respected.

7. 所有的文化和社会都植根于特殊的形式和方法中，而有形的和无形的表达手段构成了它们的遗产并应得到充分地尊重。

8. It is important to underline a fundamental principle of UNESCO, to the effect that the cultural heritage of each is the cultural heritage of all.Responsibility for cultural heritage and the management of it belongs, in the first place, to the cultural community that has generated it, and subsequently to that which cares for it. However, in addition to these responsibilities, adherence to the international charters and conventions developed for conservation of cultural heritage also obliges consideration of the principles and responsibilities flowing from them. Balancing their own requirements with those of other cultural communities is, for each community, highly desirable, provided achieving this balance does not undermine their fundamental cultural values.

Values and authenticity

9. Conservation of cultural heritage in all its forms and historical periods is rooted in the values attributed to the heritage. Our ability to understand these values depends, in part, on the degree to which information sources about these values may be understood as credible or truthful. Knowledge and understanding of these sources of information, in relation to original and subsequent characteristics of the cultural heritage, and their meaning, is a requisite basis for assessing all aspects of authenticity.

10. Authenticity, considered in this way and affirmed in the Charter of Venice, appears as the essential qualifying factor concerning values. The understanding of authenticity plays a fundamental role in all scientific studies of the cultural heritage, in conservation and restoration planning, as well as within the inscription procedures used for the World Heritage Convention and other cultural heritage inventories.

8. 强调每一种文化遗产都是所有人的文化遗产这一联合国教科文组织的基本原则是很重要的。文化遗产的责 任和对它的管理权，首先应归属于产生这种文化遗产的文化社区，其次是照看它的社区。尽管如此，除了这些责任，遵守为保护文化遗产所制定的国际宪章和协定，同样是他们的原则与责任。对每个社区来说，平衡其自身与其他文化社区的要求，都是一件极重要的事，达到这种平衡并不会影响他们的基础文化价值。

价值与真实性

9. 对所有历史阶段的所有形式的文化遗产的保护，源于遗产的属性价值。我们理解这些价值的能力，部分取决于对这些价值的信息来源本身和其可信度的理解程度。对这些与原始和后续的文化遗产特征有关的信息来源及其意义的认知与理解，是全面评定真实性的必备条件。

10. 在《威尼斯宪章》中形成并确定的真实性，是价值评估的重要质量因素。对真实性的理解，在对文化遗产、对其保护和重建规划及《世界遗产公约》和其他文化遗产所进行的所有科学研究中，扮演着重要的角色。

11. All judgements about values attributed to cultural properties as well as the credibility of related information sources may differ from culture to culture, and even within the same culture. It is thus not possible to base judgements of values and authenticity within fixed criteria. On the contrary, the respect due to all cultures requires that heritage properties must be considered and judged within the cultural contexts to which they belong.

11. 不同文化间，甚至是相同文化中，对文化遗产所有价值的评估和相关信息来源可信度的评估都有所差异。因此，不可能将价值和真实性评估建立在固定标准上。相反，对所有文化的尊重，要求必须在遗产所属的文化环境中对其进行考虑和评定。

12. Therefore, it is of the highest importance and urgency that, within each culture, recognition be accorded to the specific nature of its heritage values and the credibility and truthfulness of related information sources.

12. 因此，这一点最重要也最迫切，那就是，在每一种文化中，必须依照其遗产价值的特殊本质、信息来源的可信度和真实性加以认定。

13. Depending on the nature of the cultural heritage, its cultural context, and its evolution through time, authenticity judgements may be linked to the worth of a great variety of sources of information. Aspects of the sources may include form and design, materials and substance, use and function, traditions and techniques, location and setting, and spirit and feeling, and other internal and external factors. The use of these sources permits elaboration of the specific artistic, historic, social, and scientific dimensions of the cultural heritage being examined.

13. 取决于文化遗产的本质、它的文化环境和它随着时间的演替，真实性的评估可能会与许多不同的信息来源 的价值相关。资源方面包括形式和设计、材料与物质、用途与功能、传统与技术、位置与场合、精神与感情、以及其他内在和外在因素。对这些资源的使用，允许对文化遗产的特殊艺术性、历史性、社会性和科学性进行详细审核。

Appendix 1: Suggestions for follow-up (proposed by Herb Stovel)

附录1：对后续跟踪的几点建议（ 由 HerbStovel 提交 ）

1. Respect for cultural and heritage diversity requires conscious efforts to avoid imposing mechanistic formulae or standardized procedures in attempting to define or determine authenticity of particular monuments and sites.

1. 对文化遗产多样性的尊重需要有意识的努力，避免在定义和决定特定纪念物和遗址的真实性时套用机械化公式和标准程序。

2. Efforts to determine authenticity in a manner respectful of cultures and heritage diversity requires

2. 努力用一种尊重文化与遗产多样性的方法来决定真实性，要求采用能够鼓励不同文化

approaches which encourage cultures to develop analytical processes and tools specific to their nature and needs. Such approaches may have several aspects in common:

- efforts to ensure assessment of authenticity involve multidisciplinary collaboration and the appropriate utilisation of all available expertise and knowledge;

- efforts to ensure attributed values are truly representative of a culture and the diversity of its interests, in particular monuments and sites;

- efforts to document clearly the particular nature of authenticity for monuments and sites as a practical guide to future treatment and monitoring;

- efforts to update authenticity assessments in light of changing values and circumstances.

3. Particularly important are efforts to ensure that attributed values are respected, and that their determination included efforts to build, as far as possible, a multidisciplinary and community consensus concerning these values.

4. Approaches should also build on and facilitate international co-operation among all those with an interest in conservation of cultural heritage, in order to improve global respect and understanding for the diverse expressions and values of each culture.

5. Continuation and extension of this dialogue to the various regions and cultures of the world is a prerequisite to increasing the practical value of consideration of authenticity in the conservation of the common heritage of humankind.

6. Increasing awareness within the public of this fundamental dimension of heritage is an absolute necessity in order to arrive at concrete measures for safeguarding the vestiges of the past. This means

根据其自身性质和需求，发展其分析过程和工具的方法。这些方法在下列方面有相似之处：

- 努力确保对真实性的评估中，涉及多学科合作和适当利用所有可用的专业技能和知识；

- 努力确保其价值能够真正代表一种文化和它的利益的多样性，特别是在纪念物和遗址上；

- 努力确保清晰的记录纪念物和遗址的真实性的特殊性质，将其作为将来治理和监测的实践指导；

- 在不断变换的价值和环境中努力更新真实性评估。

3. 特别重要的是要努力确保所有价值能够受到尊重，特别重要的是努力确保所有价值受到尊重，确保决策包括尽可能针对这些价值观念达成多学科和社区的共识。

4. 建立多种途径并促进所有致力于文化遗产保护的组织之间的国际合作，从而促进全球对每种文化的不同表达和价值的尊重和理解。

5. 将这种跨文化对话继续并扩展到全世界不同的地区和文化中，是提高人类共同遗产保护真实性意识的先决条件。

6. 为了获得保护过去遗迹的具体措施，提高公众对遗产的基本的认识是十分必要的。这意味着，需要更大程度地理解文化遗产本身所代表的价值，并尊重这些纪念物和遗址在当代社会

developing greater understanding of the values represented by the cultural properties themselves, as well as respecting the role such monuments and sites play in contemporary society.

Appendix 2: Definitions

Conservation: all efforts designed to understand cultural heritage, know its history and meaning, ensure its material safeguard and, as required, its presentation, restoration and enhancement. (Cultural heritage is understood to include monuments, groups of buildings and sites of cultural value as defined in Article 1 of the World Heritage Convention).

Information sources: all material, written, oral and figurative sources which make it possible to know the nature, specifications, meaning and history of the cultural heritage.

II. CHRONOLOGICAL BIBLIOGRAPHY - ON AUTHENTICITY

Publications which preceded the Nara meeting and which helped prepare the ground for the authenticity discussion which took place in Nara:

Larsen, Knut Einar, *A note on the authenticity of historic timber buildings with particular reference to Japan,* Occasional Papers for the World Heritage Convention, ICOMOS, December 1992.

Larsen, Knut Einar, *Authenticity and Reconstruction: Architectural Preservation in Japan,* Norwegian Institute of Technology, Vols. 1-2, 1993.

Preparatory meeting for the Nara Meeting, held in Bergen, Norway, 31 January - 1 February 1994:

Larsen, Knut Einar and Marstein, Nils (ed.),

中所扮演的角色。

附录 2：定义

保护：所有努力都旨在理解文化遗产、了解其历史和含义、保证其物质安全，且根据要求，保证它的存在、修复和强化（通常人们所理解的文化遗产包括纪念碑、建筑群、和文化价值遗址，《世界遗产公约》第一条中已明确定义）。

信息来源：所有可以让人了解文化遗产的本质、规格、意义和历史的物质的、手写的、口头的和图像的资源。

II. 按年代顺序排列的关于真实性的参考文献

奈良会议召开前出版的出版物和有助于奈良的真实性讨论的出版物包括：

《关于木质历史建筑（尤指日本）的真实性的注解》，作者 Larsen，Knut Einar，《世界遗产公约》的学术论文，国际古迹遗址理事会，1992 年 12 月；

《真实性和重建：日本建筑的保护》作者 Larsen，Knut Einar，挪威科技大学第 1–2 卷，1993 年。

1994 年 1 月 31 日至 2 月 1 日在挪威卑尔根召开的奈良会议的预备会议：

《关于〈世界遗产公约〉中真实性研讨会

Conference on authenticity in relation to the World Heritage Convention Preparatory workshop, Bergen, Norway, 31 January - 2 February 1994, Tapir Forlag, Trondheim 1994.

The Nara meeting, 1-6 November 1994, Nara, Japan:

Larsen, Knut Einar with an editorial group (Jokilehto, Lemaire, Masuda, Marstein, Stovel), Nara conference on authenticity in relation to the World Heritage Convention. Conférence de Nara sur l'authenticité dans le cadre de la Convention du Patrimoine Mondial. Nara, Japan, 1-6 November 1994, Proceedings published by UNESCO - World Heritage Centre, Agency for Cultural Affairs of Japan, ICCROM and ICOMOS,1994.

The Nara meeting brought together 45 experts from 26 countries and international organizations from around the world.Their papers are contained in the volume cited above, as is the Nara document prepared in a working group of 12 meeting participants and edited by Raymond Lemaire and Herb Stovel. This volume of Proceedings invites members of ICOMOS and others to extend the discussions of the Nara Document issues to other regions of the world.

Significant post-Nara regional meetings (as of January 2005):

Authenticity and Monitoring, October 17-22, 1995, Cesky Krumlov, Czech Republic, ICOMOS European Conference, 1995.

The European ICOMOS Conference of 17-22 October, 1995 which took place in Cesky Krumlov, Czech Republic brought together 18 European members of ICOMOS to present national views of the application of authenticity concepts from

的预备工作会议》，作者 Larsen，Knut Einar 和 Marstein, Nils（ed.），1994 年 1 月 31 日至 2 月 1 日挪威卑尔根，特隆赫姆 Tapir Forlag，1994年。

1994 年 11 月 1-6 日在日本奈良召开的奈良会议：

《与〈世界遗产公约〉相关的奈良真实性会议》，（法语名：Conférencede Narasurl'authenticitédans lecadre de la Convention du Patrimoine Mondial），作者 Larsen 和 Knut Einar领导的编辑组（包括Jokilehto，Lemaire，Masuda，Marstein和 Stovel），日本奈良，1994年 11 月 1-6 日，会议论文集，联合国教科文组织世界遗产中心、日本文化部、国际文化遗产保护与修复研究中心和国际古迹遗址理事会，1994年。

奈良会议汇聚了来自 26 个国家和国际组织的 45 名专家。和由 12 个参会者组成的工作组准备的并由 Raymond Lemaire 和 Herb Stovel 编辑的奈良文件一样，这 45 名专家的论文也包含在上述引用的会议论文集中。该论文集邀请国际古迹遗址理事会成员和其他有关专家一起，将对奈良文件问题相关讨论扩大到世界其他地区。

奈良会议后具有重大意义的地区性会议（截至 2005 年 1 月 ）：

《真实性和遗产监测，1995 年 10 月 17-22 日》，捷克共和国契斯基库伦隆，国际古遗址理事会欧洲会议，1995 年。

1995 年 10 月 17-22 日，欧洲国际古遗址理事会欧洲会议在捷克共和国契斯基库伦隆召开。会议聚集了 18 位国际古迹遗址理事会欧洲成员，提出了来自 14 国的关于应用真实性概念的观点。这些综合阐述确认了真实性在申请保护问题中，

14 countries. A synthesis of presentations affirmed the importance of authenticity within the analytical processes we apply to conservation problems as a means of assuring truthful, sincere and honest approaches to conservation problems, and gave emphasis to strengthening the notion of dynamic conservation in order to apply authenticity analysis appropriately to cultural landscapes and urban settings.

Interamerican symposium on authenticity in the conservation and management of the cultural heritage, US/ICOMOS, The Getty Conservation Institute, San Antonio, Texas 1996.

This Authenticity meeting which took place in San Antonio, Texas, USA in March 1996, brought together participants from ICOMOS national committees of North, Central and South America to debate the application of the concepts of Nara. The meeting adopted the *Declaration of San Antonio*, which discussed the relationship between authenticity and identity, history, materials, social value, dynamic and static sites, stewardship and economics, and contained recommendations extending "proofs" of authenticity to include *reflection of its true value, integrity, context, identity, use and function,* as well as recommendations pertinent to different typologies of sites.

Saouma-Forero, Galia, (edited by), *Authenticity and integrity in an African context: expert meeting, Great Zimbabwe*, Zimbabwe, 26-29 May 2000, UNESCO - World Heritage Centre, Paris 2001.

The Great Zimbabwe meeting organised by the World Heritage Centre (26-29 May 2000) focused attention on both authenticity and integrity in an African context. Eighteen speakers looked at issues arising in management of both cultural and natural heritage properties. The meeting

作为保证信任、真诚和诚实的手段，在分析过程中的重要性，强调加强动态保护的观念，以便在文化景观和城市遗产申报中恰当地应用真实性分析。

《美联关于文化遗产保护和管理中真实性的研讨会》，美国/国际古遗址理事会，美国德克萨斯州圣安东尼，盖蒂保护研究所，1996年。

1996 年 3 月在德克萨斯州圣安东尼奥召开的真实性会议，汇聚了来自北美、中美和南美国际古遗址理事会国家委员会的参会者，共同商讨了奈良概念的应用。该会议通过了《圣安东尼奥宣言》，该宣言讨论了真实性和身份认同、历史、材料、社会价值、动态和静态遗产、管理和经济学之间的关系，包含了扩充真实性"证据"的相关建议，包括对真实价值、完整性、文脉环境、身份特性、使用和功能的反映，以及针对不同类型遗产的相关建议。

《非洲文化背景下遗产保护的真实性和完整性：大津巴布韦专家会议》，Saouma-Forero, Galia,（编辑），津巴布韦，2000 年 5 月 26-29 日，联合国教科文组织世界遗产中心，2001 年，巴黎。

大津巴布韦会议由世界遗产中心组织召开（2000 年 5 月 26-29 日），会议重点强调非洲遗产的真实性和完整性。18 位发言人讨论了文化与自然遗产管理面临的问题。该会议后发表了上述出版物，其中包含了参会人员提出的建议。这些建议包括将管理体系、语言和其他形式的

resulted in the publication cited above, which includes a set of recommendations coming from meeting participants. Among recommendations were suggestions to include *management systems, language, and other forms of intangible heritage* among attributes expressing authenticity, and an emphasis given to the place of local communities in the sustainable heritage management process.

Reconstruction discussions in the context of the *World Heritage Convention* (as of January 2005):

The Riga Charter on authenticity and historical reconstruction in relationship to cultural heritage adopted by regional conference, Riga, 24 October 2000, Latvian National Commission for UNESCO - World Heritage Centre, ICCROM.

Incerti Medici, Elena and Stovel, Herb, *Authenticity and historical reconstruction in relationship with cultural heritage, regional conference, Riga, Latvia, October 23-24 2000: summary report,* UNESCO - World Heritage Centre, Paris, ICCROM, Rome 2001.

Stovel, Herb, *The Riga Charter on authenticity and historical reconstruction in relationship to cultural heritage, Riga, Latvia, October 2000,* in *Conservation and management of archaeological sites,* Vol. 4, n. 4, 2001.

Alternatives to historical reconstruction in the World Heritage Cities, Tallinn, 16-18 May 2002, Tallinn Cultural Heritage Department, Estonia National Commission for UNESCO, Estonia National Heritage Board.

无形遗产纳入真实性表达，并强调当地社区在可持续遗产管理过程中的作用。

《世界遗产公约》中关于重建问题的讨论（截止至 2005 年 1 月）：

里加地区会议通过的《关于文化遗产相关真实性和历史重建问题的里加宪章》，2000年 10 月 24 日，联合国教科文组织世界遗产中心拉脱维亚委员会，国际文化遗产保护与修复研究中心。

2000年 10 月 23–24 日拉脱维亚里加地区会议《关于文化遗产相关真实性和历史重建问题的地区会议总结报告》，起草人 Incerti Medici, Elena 和 Stovel, Herb，2001年，巴黎联合国教科文组织世界遗产中心，罗马国际遗产理事会。

2000 年 10月拉脱维亚里加地区会议通过的《关于考古遗址保护和管理中的文化遗产相关真实性和历史重建问题的里加宪章》，起草人 Stovel，Herb，《考古遗址保护和管理》2001年第 4卷。

《避免世界遗产城市中历史建筑重建的选择》2002年 5月 16–18 日，塔林文化遗产部，联合国教科文组织爱沙尼亚国家委员会，爱沙尼亚国家遗产部。

FORMAT FOR THE NOMINATION OF PROPERTIES

FOR INSCRIPTION ON THE WORLD HERITAGE　LIST

This Format must be used for all nominations submitted after 2 February 2005

The Nomination Format is available at the following Web address:

http://whc.unesco.org/en/nominationform

Further guidance on the preparation of nominations can be found in Section III of the Operational Guidelines

The original signed version of the completed Nomination Format should be sent in English or French to

UNESCO World Heritage Centre

7, place de Fontenoy

75352 Paris 07 SP

France

Telephone: +33 (0) 1 4568 1571

Fax: +33 (0) 1 4568 5570

E-mail: wh-nominations@unesco.org

Executive Summary

This information, to be provided by the State Party, will be updated by the Secretariat following the decision by the World Heritage Committee. It will then be returned to the State Party confirming the basis on which the property is inscribed on the World Heritage List.

State Party	
State, Province or Region	
Name of Property	
Geographical coordinates to the nearest second	
Textual description of the boundary(ies) of the nominated property	A4 or A3 size map(s) of the nominated property, showing boundaries and buffer zone (if present) Attach A4 or A3 size map(s) which should be the reduced size version of the original copies of topographic or cadastral maps showing the nominated property and buffer zone (if present) at the largest scale available included or annexed to the nomination.
Criteria under which property is nominated (itemize criteria) (see Paragraph 77 of the Operational Guidelines)	

State Party	
Draft Statement of Outstanding Universal Value (text should clarify what is considered to be the Outstanding Universal Value embodied by the nominated property, approximately 1-2 page format)	According to the paragraph 155, the Statement of Outstanding Universal Value should be composed of: a. Brief synthesis b. Justification for Criteria c. Statement of Integrity (for all properties) d. Statement of authenticity for properties nominated under criteria (i) to (vi) e. Requirements for protection and management See format in Annex 10
Name and contact information of official local institution/agency	Organization: Address: Tel: Fax: E-mail: Web address:

Properties for inscription on the World Heritage List

Note: In preparing the nomination, States Parties should use this format but delete the explanatory notes.

NOMINATION Format	Explanatory NoteS
1. Identification of the Property	Together with Section 2, this is the most important section in the nomination. It must make clear to the Committee precisely where the property is located and how it is geographically defined. In the case of serial nominations, insert a table that shows the name of the component part, region (if different for different components), coordinates, area and buffer zone. Other fields could also be added (page reference or map number, etc.) that differentiate the several components.
1.a Country (and State Party if different)	
1.b State, Province or Region	
1.c Name of Property	This is the official name of the property that will appear in published material about World Heritage. It should be concise. Do not exceed 200 characters, including spaces and punctuation. In the case of serial nominated properties (see Paragraphs137-140 of the Operational Guidelines), give a name for the ensemble (e.g., Baroque Churches of the Philippines). Do not include the name of the components parts of a serial nominated properties, which should be included in a table as part of 1.d and 1.f.

续表

NOMINATION Format	Explanatory NoteS
1.d Geographical coordinates to the nearest second	In this space provide the latitude and longitude coordinates (to the nearest second) or UTM coordinates (to the nearest 10 metres) of a point at the approximate centre of the nominated property. Do not use other coordinate systems. If in doubt, please consult the Secretariat. In the case of serial nominated properties, provide a table showing the name of each component part, its region (or nearest town as appropriate), and the coordinates of its centre point. Coordinate format examples: N 45° 06' 05" W 15° 37' 56" or UTM Zone 18 Easting: 545670 　　　　　Northing: 4586750

Id n°	Name of the component part	Region(s) / District(s)	Coordinates of the Central Point	Map N°
001				
002				
003				
004				
Etc.				
Total area (in hectares)				

NOMINATION Format	Explanatory NoteS
1.e Maps and plans, showing the boundaries of the nominated property and buffer zone	Annex to the nomination, and list below with scales and dates: (i) Original copies of topographic maps showing the property nominated, at the largest scale available which shows the entire property. The boundaries of the nominated property and buffer zone should be clearly marked. The boundaries of zones of special legal protection from which the property benefits should be recorded on maps to be included under the protection and management section of the nomination text. Multiple maps may be necessary for serial nominations (see table in 1.d). The maps provided should be at the largest available and practical scale to allow the identification of topographic elements such as neighbouring settlements, buildings and routes in order to allow the clear assessment of the impact of any proposed development within, adjacent to, or on the boundary line. The choice of the adequate scale is essential to clearly show the boundaries of the proposed site and shall be in relation to the category of site that is proposed for inscription: cultural sites would require cadastral maps, while natural sites or cultural landscapes would require topographic maps (normally 1:25 000 to 1:50 000 scale). Utmost care is needed with the width of boundary lines on maps, as thick boundary lines may make the actual boundary of the property ambiguous. Maps may be obtained from the addresses shown at the following Web address http://whc.unesco.org/en/mapagencies.

NOMINATION Format	Explanatory NoteS
1.e Maps and plans, showing the boundaries of the nominated property and buffer zone	All maps should be capable of being geo-referenced, with a minimum of three points on opposite sides of the maps with complete sets of coordinates. The maps, untrimmed, should show scale, orientation, projection, datum, property name and date. If possible, maps should be sent rolled and not folded. Geographic Information in digital form is encouraged if possible, suitable for incorporation into a GIS (Geographic Information System). however, this may not substitute the submission of printed maps. In this case the delineation of the boundaries (nominated property and buffer zone) should be presented in vector form, prepared at the largest scale possible. The State Party is invited to contact the Secretariat for further information concerning this option. (ii) A Location Map showing the location of the property within the State Party, (iii) Plans and specially prepared maps of the property showing individual features are helpful and may also be annexed. To facilitate copying and presentation to the Advisory Bodies and the World Heritage Committee A4 (or "letter") size reduction and a digital image file of the principal maps should also be included in the nomination text if possible. Where no buffer zone is proposed, the nomination must include a statement as to why a buffer zone is not required for the proper protection of the nominated property.
1.f Area of nominated property (ha.) and proposed buffer zone (ha.) Area of nominated property: _____ ha Buffer zone _____ ha Total _____ ha	In the case of serial nominations (see Paragraphs 137-140 of the Operational Guidelines), insert a table that shows the name of the component part, region (if different for different components), coordinates, area and buffer zone. The serial nomination table should also be used to show the size of the separate nominated areas and of the buffer zone(s).
2. Description	This section should begin with a description of the nominated property at the date of nomination. It should refer to all the significant features of the property. In the case of a cultural property this section will include a description of whatever elements make the property culturally significant. It could include a description of any building or buildings and their architectural style, date of construction, materials, etc. This section should also describe important aspects of the setting such as gardens, parks etc. For a rock art site, for example, the description should refer to the rock art as well as the surrounding landscapes. In the case of an historic town or district, it is not necessary to describe each individual building, but important public buildings should be described individually and an account should be given of the planning or layout of the area, its street pattern and so on.

Explanatory NoteS	
2. Description	In the case of a natural property the account should deal with important physical attributes, geology, habitats, species and population size, and other significant ecological features and processes. Species lists should be provided where practicable, and the presence of threatened or endemic taxa should be highlighted. The extent and methods of exploitation of natural resources should be described.
2.a Description of Property	In the case of cultural landscapes, it will be necessary to produce a description under all the matters mentioned above. Special attention should be paid to the interaction of people and nature. The entire nominated property identified in section 1 (Identification of the Property) should be described. In the case of serial nominations (see Paragraphs 137-140 of the Operational Guidelines), each of the component parts should be separately described.
2.b History and Development	Describe how the property has reached its present form and condition and the significant changes that it has undergone, including recent conservation history. This should include some account of construction phases in the case of monuments, sites, buildings or groups of buildings. Where there have been major changes, demolitions or rebuilding since completion they should also be described. In the case of a natural property, the account should cover significant events in history or pre-history that have affected the evolution of the property and give an account of its interaction with humankind. This will include changes in the use of the property and its natural resources for hunting, fishing or agriculture, or changes brought about by climatic change, floods, earthquake or other natural causes. Such information will also be required in the case of cultural landscapes, where all aspects of the history of human activity in the area needs to be covered.
3. Justification for Inscription[①]	The justification should be set out under the following sections. This section must make clear why the property is considered to be of "Outstanding Universal Value". The whole of this section of the nomination should be written with careful reference to the requirements of the *Operational Guidelines*. It should not include detailed descriptive material about the property or its management, which are addressed in other sections, but should convey the key aspects that are relevant to the definition of the Outstanding Universal Value of the property.
3.1.a Brief synthesis	The brief synthesis should comprise (i) a summary of factual information and (ii) a summary of qualities. The summary of factual information sets out the geographical and historical context and the main features. The summary of qualities should present to decision-makers and the general public the potential Outstanding Universal Value that needs to be sustained, and should also include a summary of the attributes that convey its potential Outstanding Universal Value, and need to be protected, managed and monitored. The summary should relate to all stated criteria in order to justify the nomination. The brief synthesis thus encapsulates the whole rationale for the nomination and proposed inscription.

① See also paragraphs 132 and 133。

NOMINATION Format	Explanatory NoteS
3.1.b Criteria under which inscription is proposed (and justification for inscription under these criteria)	See Paragraph 77 of the *Operational Guidelines*. Provide a separate justification for each criterion cited. State briefly how the property meets those criteria under which it has been nominated (where necessary, make reference to the "description" and "comparative analysis" sections of the nomination, but do not duplicate the text of these sections) and describe for each criteri on the relevant attributes.
3.1. c Statement of Integrity	The statement of integrity should demonstrate that the property fulfils the conditions of integrity set out in Section Ⅱ.D of the *Operational Guidelines*, which describe these conditions in greater detail. The *Operational Guidelines* set out the need to assess the extent to which the property: • includes all elements necessary to express its Outstanding Universal Value; • is of adequate size to ensure the complete representation of the features and processes which convey the property's significance; • suffers from adverse effects of development and/or neglect (Paragraph 88). The *Operational Guidelines* provide specific guidance in relation to the various World Heritage criteria, which is important to understand (Paragraphs 89–95).
3.1.d Statement of Authenticity (for nominations made under criteria (i) to (vi)	The statement of authenticity should demonstrate that the property fulfils the conditions of authenticity set out in Section Ⅱ.D of the *Operational Guidelines*, which describe these conditions in greater detail. This section should summarise information that may be included in more detail in section 4 of the nomination (and possibly in other sections), and should not reproduce the level of detail included in those sections. Authenticity only applies to cultural properties and to the cultural aspects of 'mixed' properties. The *Operational Guidelines* state that 'properties may be understood to meet the conditions of authenticity if their cultural values (as recognized in the nomination criteria proposed) are truthfully and credibly expressed through a variety of attributes' (Paragraph 82). The *Operational Guidelines* suggest that the following types of attributes might be considered as conveying or expressing Outstanding Universal Value: • form and design; • materials and substance; • use and function; • traditions, techniques and management systems; • location and setting; • language and other forms of intangible heritage; • spirit and feeling; and • other internal/external factors.
3.1.e Protection and management requirements	This section should set out how the requirements for protection and management will be met, in order to ensure that the Outstanding Universal Value of the property is maintained over time. It should include both details of an overall framework for protection and management, and the identification of specific long term expectations for the protection of the property. This section should summarise information that may be included in more detail in section 5 of the nomination document (and also potentially in sections 4 and 6), and should not reproduce the level of detail included in those sections.

NOMINATION Format	Explanatory NoteS
3.1.e Protection and management requirements	The text in this section should first outline the framework for protection and management. This should include the necessary protection mechanisms, management systems and/or management plans (whether currently in place or in need of establishment) that will protect and conserve the attributes that carry Outstanding Universal Value, and address the threats to and vulnerabilities of the property. These could include the presence of strong and effective legal protection, a clearly documented management system, including relationships with key stakeholders or user groups, adequate staff and financial resources, key requirements for presentation (where relevant), and effective and responsive monitoring. Secondly this section needs to acknowledge any long-term challenges for the protection and management of the property and state how addressing these will be a long-term strategy. It will be relevant to refer to the most significant threats to the property, and to vulnerabilities and negative changes in authenticity and/or integrity that have been highlighted, and to set out how protection and management will address these vulnerabilities and threats and mitigate any adverse changes. As an official statement, recognised by the World Heritage Committee, this section of the Statement of Outstanding Universal Value should convey the most important commitments that the State Party is making for the long-term protection and management of the property.
3.2 Comparative Analysis	The property should be compared to similar properties, whether on the World Heritage List or not. The comparison should outline the similarities the nominated property has with other properties and the reasons that make the nominated property stand out. The comparative analysis should aim to explain the importance of the nominated property both in its national and international context (see Paragraph 132). The purpose of the comparative analysis is to show that there is room on the List using existing thematic studies and, in the case of serial properties, the justification for the selection of the component parts.
3.3 Proposed Statement of Outstanding Universal Value	A Statement of Outstanding Universal Value is the official statement adopted by the World Heritage Committee at the time of inscription of a property on the World Heritage List. When the World Heritage Committee agrees to inscribe a property on the World Heritage List, it also agrees on a Statement of Outstanding Universal Value that encapsulates why the property is considered to be of Outstanding Universal Value, how it satisfies the relevant criteria, the conditions of integrity and (for cultural properties) authenticity, and how it meets the requirements for protection and management in order to sustain Outstanding Universal Value in the long-term. Statements of Outstanding Universal Value should be concise and are set out in a standard format. They should help to raise awareness regarding the value of the property, guide the assessment of its state of conservation and inform protection and management. Once adopted by the Committee, the Statement of Outstanding Universal Value is displayed at the property and on the UNESCO World Heritage Centre's website. The main sections of a Statement of Outstanding Universal Value are the following: a)Brief synthesis b)Justification for Criteria c)Statement of Integrity (for all properties) d)Statement of authenticity for properties nominated under criteria (i) to (vi) e)Requirements for protection and management

NOMINATION Format	Explanatory NoteS
4. State of Conservation and factors affecting the Property	
4.a Present state of conservation	The information presented in this section constitutes the base-line data necessary to monitor the state of conservation of the nominated property in the future. Information should be provided in this section on the physical condition of the property, any threats to the Outstanding Universal Value of the property and conservation measures at the property (see Paragraph 132). For example, in a historic town or area, buildings, monuments or other structures needing major or minor repair works, should be indicated as well as the scale and duration of any recent or forthcoming major repair projects. In the case of a natural property, data on species trends or the integrity of eco-systems should be provided. This is important because the nomination will be used in future years for purposes of comparison to trace changes in the condition of the property. For the indicators and statistical benchmarks used to monitor the state of conservation of the property see section 6 below.
4.b Factors affecting the property	This section should provide information on all the factors which are likely to affect or threaten the Outstanding Universal Value of a property. It should also describe any difficulties that may be encountered in addressing such problems. Not all the factors suggested in this section are appropriate for all properties. They are indicative and are intended to assist the State Party to identify the factors that are relevant to each specific property.
(i) Development Pressures (e.g., encroachment, adaptation, agriculture, mining)	Itemize types of development pressures affecting the property, e.g., pressure for demolition, rebuilding or new construction; the adaptation of existing buildings for new uses which would harm their authenticity or integrity; habitat modification or destruction following encroaching agriculture, forestry or grazing, or through poorly managed tourism or other uses; inappropriate or unsustainable natural resource exploitation; damage caused by mining; the introduction of exotic species likely to disrupt natural ecological processes, creating new centres of population on or near properties so as to harm them or their settings.
(ii) Environmental pressures (e.g., pollution, climate change, desertification)	List and summarize major sources of environmental deterioration affecting building fabric, flora and fauna.
(iii) Natural disasters and risk preparedness (earthquakes, floods, fires, etc.)	Itemize those disasters which present a foreseeable threat to the property and what steps have been taken to draw up contingency plans for dealing with them, whether by physical protection measures or staff training.
(iv) Responsible visitation at World Heritage sites	Provide the status of visitation to the property (notably available baseline data; patterns of use, including concentrations of activity in parts of the property; and activities planned in the future). Describe projected levels of visitation due to inscription or other factors. Define the carrying-capacity of the property and how its management could be enhanced to meet the current or expected visitor numbers and related development pressure without adverse effects. Consider possible forms of deterioration of the property due to visitor pressure and behaviour including those affecting its intangible attributes.

NOMINATION Format	Explanatory NoteS
(v) Number of inhabitants within the property and the buffer zone Estimated population located within: Area of nominated property _____ Buffer zone _____ Total _____ Year _____	Give the best available statistics or estimate of the number of inhabitants living within the nominated property and any buffer zone. Indicate the year this estimate or count was made.
5. Protection and Management of the Property	This section of the nomination is intended to provide a clear picture of the legislative, regulatory, contractual, planning, institutional and/ or traditional measures (see Paragraph 132 of the Operational Guidelines) and the management plan or other management system (Paragraphs 108 to 118 of the Operational Guidelines) that is in place to protect and manage the property as required by the World Heritage Convention. It should deal with policy aspects, legal status and protective measures and with the practicalities of day-to-day administration and management.
5.a Ownership	Indicate the major categories of land ownership (including State, Provincial, private, community, traditional, customary and non-governmental ownership, etc.).
5.b Protective designation	List the relevant legal, regulatory, contractual, planning, institutional and/ or traditional status of the property: For example, national or provincial park; historic monument, protected area under national law or custom; or other designation. Provide the year of designation and the legislative act(s) under which the status is provided. If the document cannot be provided in English or French, an English or French executive summary should be provided highlighting the key provisions.
5.c Means of implementing protective measures.	Describe how the protection afforded by its legal, regulatory, contractual, planning, institutional and/ or traditional status indicated in section 5.b. actually works.
5.d Existing plans related to municipality and region in which the proposed property is located (e.g., regional or local plan, conservation plan, tourism development plan)	List the agreed plans which have been adopted with the date and agency responsible for preparation. The relevant provisions should be summarized in this section. A copy of the plan should be included as an attached document as indicated in section 7.b. If the plans exist only in a language other than English or French, an English or French executive summary should be provided highlighting the key provisions.
5.e Property management plan or other management system	As noted in Paragraphs 132 of the Operational Guidelines, an appropriate management plan or other management system is essential and shall be provided in the nomination. Assurances of the effective implementation of the management plan or other management system are also expected. Sustainable development principles should be integrated into the management system.

NOMINATION Format	Explanatory NoteS
5.e Property management plan or other management system	A copy of the management plan or documentation of the management system shall be annexed to the nomination, in English or French as indicated in section 7.b. If the management plan exists only in a language other than English or French, an English or French detailed description of its provisions shall be annexed. Give the title, date and author of management plans annexed to this nomination. A detailed analysis or explanation of the management plan or a documented management system shall be provided. A timetable for the implementation of the management plan is recommended.
5.f Sources and levels of finance	Show the sources and level of funding which are available to the property on an annual basis. An estimate could also be given of the adequacy or otherwise of resources available, in particular identifying any gaps or deficiencies or any areas where assistance may be required.
5.g Sources of expertise and training in conservation and management techniques	Indicate the expertise and training which are available from national authorities or other organizations to the property.
5.h Visitor facilities and infrastructure	The section should describe the inclusive facilities available on site for visitors and demonstrate that they are appropriate in relation to the protection and management requirements of the property. It should set out how the facilities and services will provide effective and inclusive presentation of the property to meet the needs of visitors, including in relation to the provision of safe and appropriate access to the property. The section should consider visitor facilities that may include interpretation/explanation (signage, trails, notices or publications, guides); museum/exhibition devoted to the property, visitor or interpretation centre; and/or potential use of digital technologies and services (overnight accommodation; restaurant; car parking; lavatories; search and rescue; etc.)
5.i Policies and programmes related to the presentation and promotion of the property	This section refers to Articles 4 and 5 of the Convention regarding the presentation and transmission to future generations of the cultural and natural heritage. States Parties are encouraged to provide information on the policies and programmes for the presentation and promotion of the nominated property.
5.j Staffing levels and expertise (professional, technical, maintenance)	Indicate the skills and qualifications available needed for the good management of the property, including in relation to visitation and future training needs.
6. Monitoring	This section of the nomination is intended to provide the evidence for the state of conservation of the property which can be reviewed and reported on regularly so as to give an indication of trends over time.
6.a Key indicators for measuring state of conservation	List in table form those key indicators that have been chosen as the measure of the state of conservation of the whole property (see section 4.a above). Indicate the periodicity of the review of these indicators and the location where the records are kept. They could be representative of an important aspect of the property and relate as closely as possible to the Statement of Outstanding Universal Value (see section 2.b above). Where possible they could be expressed numerically and where this is not possible they could be of a kind which can be repeated, for example by taking a photograph from the same point. Examples of good indicators are the:

NOMINATION Format	Explanatory NoteS
6.a Key indicators for measuring state of conservation	(i) number of species, or population of a keystone species on a natural property; (ii) percentage of buildings requiring major repair in a historic town or district; (iii) number of years estimated to elapse before a major conservation programme is likely to be completed; (iv) stability or degree of movement in a particular building or element of a building; (v) rate at which encroachment of any kind on a property has increased or diminished.
6.b Administrative arrangements for monitoring property	Give the name and contact information of the agency(ies) responsible for the monitoring referenced in 6.a.
6.c Results of previous reporting exercises	List, with a brief summary, earlier reports on the state of conservation of the property and provide extracts and references to published sources (for example, reports submitted in compliance with international agreements and programmes, e.g., Ramsar, MAB).

Indicator	Periodicity	Location of Records

NOMINATION FORMAT	EXPLANATORY NOTES
6.b Administrative arrangements for monitoring property	Give the name and contact information of the agency(ies) responsible for the monitoring referenced in 6.a.
6.c Results of previous reporting exercises	List, with a brief summary, earlier reports on the state of conservation of the property and provide extracts and references to published sources (for example, reports submitted in compliance with international agreements and programmes, e.g., Ramsar, MAB).
7. Documentation	This section of the nomination is the check-list of the documentation which shall be provided to make up a complete nomination.
7.a Photographs and audiovisual image inventory and authorization form	States Parties shall provide a sufficient number of recent images (prints, slides and, where possible, electronic formats, videos and aerial photographs) to give a good general picture of the property. Slides shall be in 35mm format and electronic images in jpg format at a minimum of 300 dpi (dots per inch) resolution. If film material is provided, Beta SP format is recommended for quality assurances. This material shall be accompanied by the image inventory and photograph and audiovisual authorization form as set out below.

续表

NOMINATION FORMAT	EXPLANATORY NOTES
7.a Photographs and audiovisual image inventory and authorization form	At least one photograph that may be used on the public web page illustrating the property shall be included. States Parties are encouraged to grant to UNESCO, in written form and free of charge, the non exclusive cession of rights to diffuse, to communicate to the public, to publish, to reproduce, to exploit, in any form and on any support, including digital, all or part of the images provided and license these rights to third parties. The non exclusive cession of rights does not impinge upon intellectual property rights (rights of the photographer / director of the video or copyright owner if different) and that when the images are distributed by UNESCO a credit to the photographer / director of the video is always given, if clearly provided in the form. All possible profits deriving from such cession of rights will go to the World Heritage Fund.

PHOTOGRAPHS AND AUDIOVISUAL IMAGE INVENTORY AND AUTHORIZATION FORM

Id. No	Format (slide/ print/ video)	Caption	Date of Photo (mo/ yr)	Photographer/ Director of the video	Copyright owner (if different than photographer/ director of video)	Contact details of copyright owner (Name, address, tel/fax, and e-mail)	Non exclusive cession of rights

NOMINATION FORMAT	EXPLANATORY NOTES
7.b Texts relating to protective designation, copies of property management plans or documented management systems and extracts of other plans relevant to the property	Attach the texts as indicated in sections 5.b, 5.d and 5.e above.
7.c Form and date of most recent records or inventory of property	Provide a straightforward statement giving the form and date of the most recent records or inventory of the property. Only records that are still available should be described.
7.d Address where inventory, records and archives are held	Give the name and address of the agencies holding inventory records (buildings, monuments, flora or fauna species).
7.e Bibliography	List the principal published references, using standard bibliographic format.

NOMINATION FORMAT	EXPLANATORY NOTES
8. Contact Information of responsible authorities	This section of the nomination will allow the Secretariat to provide the property with current information about World Heritage news and other issues.
8.a Preparer Name: Title: Address: City, Province/State, Country: Tel: Fax: E-mail:	Provide the name, address and other contact information of the individual responsible for preparing the nomination. If an e-mail address cannot be provided, the information must include a fax number.
8.b Official Local Institution/Agency	Provide the name of the agency, museum, institution, community or manager locally responsible for the management of the property. If the normal reporting institution is a national agency, please provide that contact information.
8.c Other Local Institutions	List the full name, address, telephone, fax and e-mail addresses of all museums, visitor centres and official tourism offices who should receive the free World Heritage Newsletter about events and issues related to World Heritage.
8.d Official Web address http:// Contact name: E-mail:	Please provide any existing official web addresses of the nominated property. Indicate if such web addresses are planned for the future with the contact name and e-mail address.
9. Signature on behalf of the State Party	The nomination should conclude with the signature of the official empowered to sign it on behalf of the State Party.

 《世界遗产名录》遗产申报材料格式

2005年2月2日后提交的所有申报材料均须遵循此格式

登录以下网址可获取本申报材料格式：http://whc.unesco.org/en/nominationform

有关申报材料编写的更多指导，请参见《操作指南》的第三部分

按完整申报格式编写，英语或法语原件，签字后寄送至以下地址：

联合国教科文组织世界遗产中心

法国巴黎(7, place de Fontenoy

75352 Paris 07 SP France)

电话：+33 (0) 1 4568 1571

传真：+33 (0) 1 4568 5570

电邮：wh–nominations@unesco.org

执行摘要

以下信息由缔约国提供，由秘书处根据世界遗产委员会的决定进行更新。之后将返还给缔约国，作为确认遗产列入《世界遗产名录》的依据。

缔约国	
州、省份或地区	
遗产名称	
精确到秒的地理坐标	
遗产申报保护范围的文字说明	
A4 纸（或"信纸"）大小的申报遗产地图，显示遗产保护范围和缓冲区（如果有）	附 A4 或 A3 纸大小原始地形或则给图的缩版图以尽可能大的规格，指明申报遗产边界和缓冲区（如有）的，作为申报文件的附件。
遗产申报符合的标准（列举标准）（见《操作指南》第 77 条）	
列入的理由《突出普遍价值声明》草案（正文应说明申报遗产所包含的突出普遍价值，约 1-2 页篇幅）	根据第 155 条，《突出普遍价值声明》应包含： 1）简要综述 2）符合标准的理由 3）完整性声明（适用所有遗产） 4）真实性声明（适用按照标准 i-vi 条申报的遗产） 5）保护和管理要求 见附件 10 中的格式

续表

缔约国	
当地官方机关、机构的名称和联系信息：	机构： 地址： 电话： 传真： 电邮： 网址：

申报列入《世界遗产名录》的遗产

注：准备申报材料时，各缔约国应该使用本格式，但应把填报须知删除。

申报材料格式	填报须知
1. 遗产的确认	本部分和下面的第 2 部分是申报材料中最重要的内容，必须向委员会准确说明遗产的位置和地理界限。 如果是系列申报，插入一个表格，说明各组成部分的名称、所处地域（如果不同部分处于不同地域）、坐标、面积和缓冲区。也可列示其他表栏项目（页码说明或地图编号）以区别不同部分。
1.a 国家（缔约国，如果不同）	
1.b 州、省份或地区	
1.c 遗产名称	是该遗产出现在世界遗产出版物上的正式名称，应简洁，不超过 200 个字符，包括空格和标点符号。 如果是系列申报（见《操作指南》的第137-139 条），为整体名称（比如，菲律宾巴洛克大教堂）。无需说明系列申报内各组成部分的名称，这些名称应该包括在 1.d 和 1.f 的表格内。
1.d 精确到秒的地理坐标	在此处提供申报遗产的中心纬度和经度坐标（精确到秒），或通用横轴墨卡托坐标（精确到 10 米）。不要用其他坐标体系。如有疑问，请咨询秘书处。 如果是系列申报，列表说明各遗产的名称、地域（或最近的城镇）、遗产中心点的坐标。 坐标格式如下： 北纬45° 06' 05" 西经15° 37' 56" 或者通用横轴墨卡托区 18 东：^{5}45670 　　　　　　　　　　北：^{45}86750

编号	组成部分名称	地区 / 城区	中心点坐标	地图编号
001				
002				
003				
……				
总面积（公顷）				

申报材料格式	填报须知
1.e 地图和平面图，显示申报遗产和缓冲区的范围	附在申报材料后，标上比例和日期： 用于申报遗产的地形图原件，尽可能用最大的比例显示整个遗产。应明确标明申报遗产及缓冲区的范围。可在此图或另附地图上，标示有利于遗产的保护的特殊法定保护区的范围。系列申报可能需要多种地图（见 1.d 中表格）。应尽可能提供最大比例的实用地图，以便清晰辨认如周边聚落、建筑和道路等地形要素，以便对遗产范围内、或邻近、或位于遗产边界上的开发计划，对遗产地的影响有清晰的评估。适当比例的地图必须包括清晰的遗产边界线，并与计划要申报的遗产类别相关：文化遗产应有地籍图，自然遗产或景观需要地形图（一般比例为 1:25 000 至 1:50 000） 对地图上的边界线条的宽度处理需极其谨慎，因为使用粗线可能会导致对遗产地边界的辨认模糊。 登录以下网址，可获取地图：http://whc.unesco.org/en/mapagencies 所有的地图都必须能够进行地理参照，地图上必须至少有三个点，点点相对，每个点都有完整的坐标。地图不能缩减，应该显示比例、方位、投影、数据、遗产名称和日期。如果可能，递送地图时应将其卷起，而不是折叠。 如果可能，建议提供数字地理信息，便于纳入 GIS（地理信息系统），尽管这些信息不能替代纸质地图。在这种情况下，范围的划分（申报遗产和缓冲区）应以向量形式提供，以尽可能大的比例编制。相关详情缔约国可联系秘书处。 (ii) 一张位置图，显示该遗产在缔约国的位置。 (iii) 展示遗产各项特征的平面图和特殊地图也很有帮助，可以随附于申报材料后面。 为了便于向咨询机构和世界遗产中心抄送和呈报，如果可能，A4 纸（或"信纸"）大小缩略图和主要地图的电子图像文件，应该包括在申报材料之中。 如果没有划分缓冲区，申报材料中必须说明对申报遗产的适当保护不需要缓冲区的原因。
1.f 申报遗产和建议的缓冲区的面积（公顷） 申报遗产的面积：_____ 公顷 缓冲区 _____ 公顷 共 _____ 公顷	如果是系列申报（见《操作指南》第 137-140 条），插入一张表格，显示组成部分的名称、所处地域（如果不同部分处于不同地域）、坐标、面积和缓冲区。 该系列申报表还应显示各个申报区及各缓冲区的大小。
2. 描述	
2.a 遗产描述	本部分首先描述申报时遗产的情况，应涉及该项遗产的各项显著特征。如果是文化遗产，本部分应描述使该项遗产在文化方面具有重要意义的任何因素。可描述某个或多个建筑，及其建筑风格、建筑日期及所用材料等。还可以描述重要环境因素，如花园、公园等。比如，对某岩画遗址来说，描述内容应既包括岩画，还应包括其周围的景观。如果是历史名城或历史街区，没有必要描述每座建筑单体，但是应逐个描述重要的公共建筑，及该地区的规划和布局，街巷格局等等。
	如果是自然遗产，应该说明重要的物理属性、地质情况、栖息地、物种及种群数量、其他重要的生态特征和进程。应尽可能提供物种列表，并突出濒危物种或地方特有的生物分类。应该描述自然资源开发的程度和方法。 如果是文化景观，有必要描述上文所提的各项内容。应特别关注人与自然之间的关系。 应该描述第 1 部分（遗产的确认）说明的整个申报遗产。如果是系列申报（见《操作指南》第 137-140 条），应单独描述遗产的各组成部分。

申报材料格式	填报须知
2.b 历史沿革	描述该项遗产形成和发展的历程及当下的形式和状态，经历了什么样的重大变化，包括近期的保护情况。 如果是古迹、遗址、建筑或建筑群，应该描述其发展变化的不同阶段。如果在建成后曾有过重大的变化、拆除或重建，应对这些事件进行描述。 如果是自然遗产，应该描述历史上或史前曾影响过该项遗产演化的重要事件，及该项遗产与人类之间的关系。包括遗产使用及用于狩猎、捕鱼或农业的自然资源发生的变化，以及天气变化、洪水、地震或其他自然现象带来的影响。 如果是文化景观，也要求提供这些信息，其中应包括这个地区人类活动史的所有方面。
3. 列入理由①	理由陈述应按照以下顺序。 这部分必须明确为什么认为遗产具有"突出普遍价值"。 本部分遗产的描述应该严格参考《操作指南》中的相关要求。不应该包括详细的描述性的遗产情况说明和遗产管理情况说明，这些内容在其他部分提供，这部分应该着重传达与遗产突出普遍价值相关的、各方面的关键信息。
3.1.a 简要综述	简要综述应包含 (1) 事实性信息概述（2）品质概述。事实性信息总结列出遗产地理和历史背景及主要特征。品质概述应向决策者和公众展示遗产需要被维持的潜在的突出普遍价值，也应包括体现其突出普遍价值、并因此需要得到妥善保护管理和监测的价值载体的概述。这部分应结合所有依据的标准以解释申报理由。因此简要概述是遗产申报和建议列入的全部原理阐述的浓缩。
3.1.b 提议遗产列入所依据的标准 (和根据这些标准的列入理由)	见《操作指南》第 77 条。 分别说明引用每个标准的理由。 简述该项遗产如何满足申报标准，(如有必要，参考"描述"和"比较分析"部分，但不是照抄这些部分的文字内容)，并描述符合每项标准的相关价值载体。
3.1.c 完整性声明	完整性声明应证实该项遗产满足《操作指南》第二 .D 部分列出的完整性条件，《操作指南》详细描述了这些条件。 《操作指南》列出了对遗产符合以下各项的程度进行评估的必要： - 包含表现遗产突出普遍价值所需的所有要素； - 规模范围足够大以确保传递遗产重要性的所有特征和过程的完整； - 因开发或废弃带来的负面影响（第 88 条）； 《操作指南》提供了对应不同世界遗产标准的具体指导，理解这一点很重要（89-95 条）。
3.1.d　真实性声明（适用于建议根据标准 i-vi 列入的遗产申报）	真实性的声明应证实该项遗产满足:《操作指南》第二 .D 部分列出的真实性条件，《操作指南》详细描述了这些条件。 这部分应简要总结申遗文本第四部分（也可能其他部分）详述的一些内容，但详略程度不应和其他章节重复。 真实性仅适用于文化遗产和混合遗产中的文化部分。 《操作指南》指出："如果遗产的文化价值（申报标准所认可的）是通过多个载体得到真实可信的表现，则被认为符合真实性条件"（见第 82 条）。

---

① 　见132-133条。

申报材料格式	填报须知
3.1.d 真实性声明（适用于建议以标准 i-vi 列入的遗产申报）	根据《操作指南》，以下类型载体可被认为传递或表现突出普遍价值： • 外形和设计 • 材料和质地 • 用途和功能 • 传统、技术和管理体系 • 环境和位置 • 语言和其他形式的非物质遗产 • 精神和感觉 • 其他内外因素
3.1.e 保护和管理要求	这部分应包含如何达到了保护管理的各项要求，从而确保遗产的突出普遍价值得到长期的维持。内容应包括对保护管理整体框架体系的详细描述，和对遗产管理长期、具体的目标的预期。 这部分应简要总结申遗文本第五部分（也可能在第四和第六部分）详述的一些内容，但详略程度不应和其他章节重复。 本部分文字应首先概述保护管理框架。其中包括保护遗产突出普遍价值载体、应对威胁和自身脆弱性的必要的保护机制、管理体系或管理规划（已存在或尚需制定）。具体包括健全有效的法律保护、记录明晰的管理体系，与主要利益相关方使用群体的必要沟通，足够的人员和财政资源，符合展示要求，有效而、有针对性的监测等。 此外，这部分需要写明遗产保护管理面临的长期挑战，以及应对这些挑战的长期战略。有必要提及对遗产最大的威胁因素、在其真实性和完整性中发现的脆弱性和负面变化，并列举出如何针对这些威胁实施保护管理措施，减小负面影响。 作为受世界遗产委员会认可的官方声明，突出普遍价值声明部分将重申缔约国为遗产的长期保护和管理所做出的最重要的承诺。
3.2 比较分析	该项遗产应与类似遗产（无论是否列入《世界遗产名录》）进行比较。比较时应该罗列该项遗产与其他遗产之间的类似点，说明该项遗产之所以突出的原因。比较分析旨在解释申报遗产在本国及在国际上的重要性。（见第 132 条）。 比较分析的目的在于，通过现有主题研究显示其列入名录的合理性，如果是系列遗产申报，则是对其构成部分的选择依据。
3.3 建议的《突出普遍价值声明》	《突出普遍价值声明》是世界遗产委员会在遗产列入名录时通过的官方声明。世界遗产委员会同意将某项遗产列入《世界遗产名录》，就意味着认可其声明中解释的为何该遗产被认为具有突出普遍价值，它如何符合了相关标准、完整性和（对文化遗产来说）真实性，以及它如何满足了确保突出普遍价值得以长期保存的保护管理条件。 《突出普遍价值声明》应力求简明，并遵循标准格式。应有助于提高对遗产价值的公众认识，指导现状评估和保护管理。一经委员会通过，该声明将在遗产地和联合国教科文世界遗产中心网站上公布。 《突出普遍价值声明》主要包含以下章节： 1）简要综述 2）对应标准的列入理由 3）完整性声明（所有遗产） 4）真实性声明（按照标准 i-vi 申报的遗产） 5）保护和管理要求

续表

申报材料格式	填报须知
4. 保护情况和影响遗产的因素	
4.a　保护现状	本部分信息是监测所申报遗产未来保护情况的基线数据。本部分内容应包括：该项遗产的自然条件、其突出普遍价值面临的威胁和采取的保护措施（见第 132 条）。 比如，应该指出历史城镇或区域内，建筑、古迹或其他构筑物所需的大小修缮工作，以及近期主要修缮项目的规模和持续时间。 如果是自然遗产，应该提供物种演化趋势或生态系统完整性的数据。这很重要，因为在未来几年，对比并跟踪遗产状态变化时会用到这些申报材料。 至于监测遗产保护情况的指标和统计基准，请参见下文第 6 部分。
4.b　影响遗产的因素	本部分应说明可能影响或威胁遗产突出普遍价值的所有因素。还应该说明在解决这些问题时会面临的困难。 在此罗列的各项因素并非适用于所有遗产。它们只是标示性的，旨在协助缔约国确认与各自遗产相关的因素。
(i) 开发压力（比如：侵占、改建、农业和采矿）	列举影响遗产的开发压力，比如，拆除、重建或新建项目的压力；因改变现有建筑用途而损害其真实性和完整性；由于农林牧活动的扩张、管理不善的旅游业或其他原因而对栖息地造成的改变和破坏；不当或非持续性自然资源开发；采矿带来的损害；引进可破坏自然生态进程的外来物种，在遗产内部或附近形成新的栖息中心，对遗产及其环境造成损害。
(ii) 环境压力（比如，污染、气候变化、沙化）	列出并总结影响建筑结构、动植物环境恶化的主要根源。
(iii) 自然灾害和防灾情况（地震、洪水、火灾等）	列举对遗产产生威胁的可预见的灾害，制定的应急方案中采取了哪些步骤来应对这些灾害，是否为此采取了物理保护措施，或开展了员工培训。
(iv) 对世界遗产地负责任的旅游参观	提供遗产地参观状况信息（尤其是现有的基线数据，使用格局，包括遗产地各部分活动分布以及未来规划的活动等）。 描述由于列入世界遗产名录或其他因素引发的、参观数量的变化。 描述遗产的"承载能力"，以及如何管理使其能接纳当前或预期游客量且应对开发压力而不产生负面影响。应考虑由于参观压力和游客行为可能导致的遗产劣化形式，包括影响其非物质特征的形式。
(v) 遗产及缓冲区内的居民数量 以下区域内的估计人口： 申报遗产区 _____ 缓冲区 _____ 总计 _____ 年份 _____	应提供申报遗产及缓冲区内居民人数的现有最准确数据或估计数。标明进行人数统计或估测的年份。
5. 遗产的保护与管理	本部分旨在清晰地说明法律、监管、契约、规划、机构或传统措施（见《操作指南》第 132 条）、以及已确立的管理规划或其他管理体系（见《操作指南》内的段落），按照《世界遗产公约》的要求保护、管理遗产。应该包括政策、法律地位和保护措施，以及日常管理的实际情况。

续表

申报材料格式	填报须知
5.a 所有权	说明遗产范围内土地所有制类型（包括国家、地方、私人、社区、传统、约定俗成和非政府所有权等）。
5.b 保护性称号	列出遗产相关的法律、监管、合同、规划、制度或传统地位，比如，国家或省级公园；依据国家法律或习俗确立的历史古迹、保护区以及其他指定称号。 说明指定称号宣布的年份及规定遗产地位的法律。 如果文件所用语言不是英语或法语，应提供一份英语或法语的执行摘要，说明文件内容要点。
5.c 保护措施执行手段	描述第 5.b. 条所列法律、监管、合同、规划、制度或传统地位提供的保护的具体生效方式。
5.d 申报遗产所在市或地区的现有规划（比如，地区或地方规划、保护、旅游开发规划）	列出通过的各种规划，标出制定日期和负责机构。其重要条款应在本部分概述。规划副本应作为附件（如第 7.b. 条所示）附后。 如果规划所用语言既非英语也非法语，应提供一份英语或法语的执行摘要，说明其内容要点。
5.e 遗产管理规划或其他管理制度	如《操作指南》第 132 条所示，一份适宜的管理规划或其他管理制度必不可少，应该收录在申报材料内。最好也能提供该管理规划或其他管理制度有效实施的保证。 如第 7.b. 条所示，英语或法语文本的管理规划或者管理制度文件，应附在申报材料之后。 如果管理规划所用语言既非英语也非法语，应提供英语或法语的规划条款详述，附在申报材料之后。提供管理规划（附在申报材料后）的名称、日期和编制机构或个人。 应提供该管理规划或成文管理制度的详细分析或说明。 建议提供管理规划实施时间表。
5.f 资金来源和水平	说明遗产每年的资金来源和水平。还应估计可用资金是否充足，特别要明确指出缺口、差额或其他需要援助的领域。
5.g 专业知识来源和保护与管理技术的培训	指出国家当局或其他组织提供的有关遗产的专业知识和培训。
5.h 旅游参观基础设施	本部分应描述遗产地现有的参观设施，并说明符合保护管理要求。应具体列出这些设施和服务如何能够为遗产地提供有效展示，满足游客需要，包括提供安全、适当的到达和进入遗产地的形式。本部分的考虑范围包括阐释与展示（指示牌、路径设置、通知公告或出版物、导游讲解等）；博物馆或现场展示，参观或展陈中心；利用可能的数码技术和其他服务（住宿、参观、停车、洗手间、救援等）
5.i 遗产展示和宣传相关的政策和方案	本部分援引《公约》的第 4 条和第 5 条，这两条阐述了文化及自然遗产的展示和传承事宜。鼓励缔约国提供申报遗产的展示和宣传政策及方案信息。
5.j 人员配置水平（专业、技术、维修）	说明良好的遗产管理所需的人员技能与资质，包括客流以及未来培训相关的需求。

续表

申报材料格式	填报须知
6. 监测	本部分旨在提供说明遗产保护现状的证据，可用回访、定期报告、审查等方式，以明确遗产的变化趋势。
6.a 衡量保护状况的主要指标	以表格形式列出用于衡量整个遗产保护情况的主要指标（见上文第4.a条）。指出审查这些指标的周期，以及记录保存地点。这些指标可代表遗产的某个重要方面，并尽可能地与《突出普遍价值声明》挂钩（见上文第2.b条）。如果可能，用数字表示，不能用数字的话，以可重复的方式表现，比如，在同一地点拍照。有效指标的实例有： （i）自然遗产内物种种类或主要物种种群的数目； （ii）历史城镇或历史街区内需要大规模修缮的建筑比例； （iii）完成主要保护方案估计需要的时间； （iv）某个建筑或建筑要素的稳定性或活动程度； （v）对遗产侵蚀的消长速度。

指标	周期	记录保存地点

6.b 遗产监测的行政安排	负责监测（如第6.a条所示）的机构名称和联系方式。
6.c 前期实践报告的结果	列出遗产保护状况的前期报告，并进行简要总结，提供报告摘要和参考文献（比如，根据国际协议和方案，如《拉姆萨湿地公约》,《人与生物圈计划》，提交的报告）。
7. 文献	本部分列出了完备的申报材料所需的文献。
7.a 照片、视听影像材料的清单和授权表	缔约国应提供一定数量的近期影像资料（印制品、幻灯片，如果可能的话，还可提供电子格式、录像和航拍照片），以便对该遗产有清晰的整体的印象。 幻灯片应为35mm格式，电子图像是jpg格式，其分辨率不应低于300dpi（每英寸点数）。如果有影像材料，为确保质量，建议使用Beta SP格式。 这类材料应配有影像清单和照片，以及下文列出的视听材料授权表。 至少有一张照片可用于公共网页，说明该遗产被列为世界遗产。 鼓励缔约国以书面形式，免费向教科文组织独家转让传播、公示、出版、复制及利用（以各种方式，基于各种手段，包括数字形式）全部或部分图像的权利，并准予教科文组织把这些权利授予第三方。 上述权利转让不得侵犯知识产权（摄影师、录像导演以及其他所有人的权利），另外，教科文组织在发行图像时，如果表格中有明确的说明，教科文组织一定会提供摄影师、录像导演的姓名。 此类权利转让所产生的收益将纳入世界遗产基金

照片、图像视听材料清单及授权表

编号	格式 (幻灯片 / 印制品 / 录像)	图片说明	照片日期 (年 / 月)	摄影师 / 录像导演	版权所有人 (如果不是摄像师 / 导演)	版权所有人的详细联系信息 (姓名、地址、电话 / 传真和电邮)	独家权利转让

申报材料格式	填报须知
7.b 与保护性称号、遗产管理规划或成文管理制度相关的正文、其他遗产规划摘要	把上文第 5.b, 5.d 和 5.e 条所示文件正文附后。
7.c 遗产近期记录或列表的格式和日期	明确阐述遗产近期记录或列表的格式和日期。仅涉及手头现有的记录。
7.d 列表、记录和档案的保存地址	提供保存这些记录 (建筑、古迹、动植物种群) 的机构名称和地址。
7.e 参考文献	列出主要的出版参考文献，用标准的参考文献格式。
8. 负责机构的联系方式	秘书处可通过该联系方式，把世界遗产的最新消息和其他相关事宜通知给该遗产负责机构。
8.a 编纂人员 名字： 职称 (头衔) ： 地址： 国家、州 / 省、市： 电话： 传真： 邮箱：	提供申报材料编纂人员的名称、地址和其他联系信息。如果没有电子邮箱，则联系信息中必须包括传真号码。
8.b 地方管理机构	提供负责遗产管理的地方机构、博物馆、组织、社区或管理人员的名称。如果常规报告的提供组织是国家机关，请提供该国家机关的联系方式。
8.c 其他地方机构	应列出接收免费《世界遗产时事通讯》(讨论关于世界遗产的事件和议题) 的所有博物馆、参观中心和官方旅游办公室的全称、地址、电话、传真和电子邮件地址。
8.d 官方网站 http:// 联系人姓名： 电子邮件：	请提供申报遗产的现有官方网站。说明今后是否计划设立该类网站，并提供联系人姓名和电子邮件地址。
9. 缔约国代表签名	申报材料末尾应由缔约国的正式授权代表签字。

Annex 6

EVALUATION PROCEDURES OF THE ADVISORY BODIES FOR NOMINATIONS

This Annex includes:

A. THE ICOMOS PROCEDURE FOR THE EVALUATION OF CULTURAL PROPERTIES

B. THE IUCN PROCEDURE FOR THE EVALUATION OF NATURAL PROPERTIES

C. ADVISORY BODY COLLABORATION - PROCEDURE FOR THE EVALUATION OF CULTURAL AND NATURAL PROPERTIES AND OF CULTURAL LANDSCAPES

For further information please also refer to Paragraphs 143-151 of the *Operational Guidelines*.

A. THE ICOMOS PROCEDURE FOR THE EVALUATION OF CULTURAL PROPERTIES

In carrying out its evaluation of nominations of cultural properties ICOMOS (the International Council of Monuments and Sites) is guided by the *Operational Guidelines*; (see Paragraph 148).

Once new nominations have been checked for completeness by the UNESCO World Heritage Centre, the nomination dossiers that are deemed as complete are delivered to ICOMOS, where they are handled by the ICOMOS World Heritage Unit. From this point, dialogue and consultation with the nominating States Parties may begin and will continue throughout the evaluation process. ICOMOS will use its best endeavours to allocate its available resources equitably, efficiently and effectively to maximise the opportunity for dialogue with all nominating States Parties.

附件 6

咨询机构对申报材料的评估程序

本附件包括：

A. 国际古迹遗址理事会的文化遗产评估程序

B. 世界自然保护联盟的自然遗产评估程序

C. 咨询机构对文化和自然遗产及文化景观的合作评估程序

了解更多信息，请参阅《操作指南》第 143–151 条。

A. 国际古迹遗址理事会的文化遗产评估程序

国际古迹遗址理事会遵循《操作指南》（见第 148 条）的指导，来评估文化遗产的申报材料。

在联合国教科文组织世界遗产中心确认申报材料完整后，缔约国的申报材料将被递送至国际古迹遗址理事会，由其下属的世界遗产处进行处理。从此时起，国际古迹遗址理事会与申报缔约国的对话与协商，并贯穿评估全过程。国际古迹遗址理事会将尽最大努力公正、高效地分配一切可用资源，最大程度地与各缔约国展开对话。

The ICOMOS evaluation process involves the following stages as illustrated in figure 1:

1. Requests for further information

When it has identified that further information or clarification of existing information is needed, ICOMOS starts a dialogue with States Parties in order to explore ways to meet the needs. This may involve letters, face-to-face meetings, teleconferences or other forms of communication as agreed between ICOMOS and the State Party concerned.

2. Desk Reviews

Each nomination is assessed by up to ten experts who are knowledgeable about the property in its geo-cultural context and who advise on the proposed "Outstanding Universal Value" of the nominated property. This is essentially a "library" exercise undertaken by specialist academics within the membership of ICOMOS, its National and International Committees, or by individuals within many other specialist networks or institutions with which it is linked.

3. On site missions

These are carried out by experts who have practical experience of the management, conservation, and authenticity aspects of individual properties. The process of selecting these experts makes full use of the ICOMOS network. The advice of International Scientific Committees and individual members is sought, as is that of specialist bodies with whom ICOMOS has partnership agreements, such as The International Committee for the Conservation of the Industrial Heritage (TICCIH), the International Federation of Landscape Architects (IFLA), and

国际古迹遗址理事会的评估流程包括以下几个阶段（见图1）：

1. 要求获取更多信息

当国际古迹遗址理事会需要更多信息，或者需要澄清已有信息时，它将与缔约国展开对话。双方的沟通方式包括信件交流、面对面会谈、电话会议或其他双方认可的交流方式。

2. 书面评估

每个申报材料都将由多名专家（最多十人）进行书面审核，他们深谙遗产的地缘文化，并将针对其"突出普遍性价值"提出建议。这纯粹是一个"图书馆式"的、专家学者的学术性活动，评估专家来自国际古迹遗址理事会、其下属的国家或国际委员会、或者与之相关的其他专家网络或机构。

3. 实地考察

对申报遗产的保护、管理及其真实性有实际经验的专家，将赴现场进行考察。专家的甄选过程将充分地利用国际古迹遗址理事会的专家网络。国际古迹遗址理事会将向国际科学委员会及个人会员、以及那些与该会有合作协定的专业机构征求建议。这些机构包括国际工业遗产保护委员会（TICCIH）、国际景观设计师联盟（IFLA）、以及国际现代建筑遗产保护和纪录委员会（DOCOMOMO）。

the International Committee for the Documentation and Conservation of Monuments and Sites of the Modern Movement (DoCoMoMo).

In selecting experts to carry out on-site missions, the policy of ICOMOS is wherever possible to choose someone from the region in which the nominated property is located. Such experts are required to be experienced in heritage management and conservation of the type of property concerned: they are not necessarily high academic experts. They are expected to be able to talk to site managers on a basis of professional equality and to make informed assessments of management plans, conservation practices, visitor handling, etc. They are provided with detailed briefings, which include copies of the relevant information from the dossiers. The dates and programmes of their visits are agreed in consultation with States Parties, who are requested to ensure that ICOMOS evaluation missions are given a low profile so far as the media are concerned. ICOMOS experts submit their reports in confidence on practical aspects of the properties concerned, and may also comment in their reports on other aspects of the nomination.

在选择执行现场考察的专家时，国际古迹遗址理事会的政策是，尽可能选择申报遗产所在地区的专家。这些专家必须具有遗产管理与保护的经验，但无需是该类遗产的资深学术专家。他们需要在专业、平等的基础上与遗址管理人员进行专业交流，对管理规划、保护政策和游客管理等事宜进行评估。相关人员将向这些专家简要介绍情况，其中包括申报材料中相关信息的复印本。这些专家到访的时间和日程会与缔约国进行协商，以达成一致。理事会要求缔约国确保媒体对国际古迹遗址理事会的评估团报道真实低调。国际古迹遗址理事会专家把关于遗产的实际问题如实上报，也可能会在报告中评论申报的其他方面。

3. bis Other sources of information

3. 另：其他信息资源

Other relevant institutions, such as UNESCO Chairs, universities and research institutes may also be consulted during the evaluation process, and listed, as appropriate, in the evaluation report.

也可在评估过程中咨询其他相关机构（例如联合国教科文组织主席团、大学及研究所等），并将参与机构的名单以适当形式列入《评估报告》。

4. Review by the ICOMOS Panel

4. 国际古迹遗址理事会评估工作组的审查

The ICOMOS World Heritage Panel comprises individual ICOMOS members who collectively represent all regions of the world and possess a wide range of relevant cultural heritage skills and experience. Some of these members serve on the

国际古迹遗址理事会评估工作组由其个人会员组成，代表世界不同区域，并掌握大量相关的文化遗产保护技术与经验。工作组的一些成员有固定的任期，另一些成员则根据需要检查的申报遗产的特点进行为期一年的工作。国

Panel for a fixed term while others are appointed for one year only according to the characteristics of the nominated properties to be examined. ICOMOS will include within its Panel membership some experts who have past experience as members of State Parties delegations, but who are no longer serving as members of the World Heritage Committee. These experts will serve in a personal and professional capacity.

The Panel meets twice, first in December and then in March. At the first meeting, the Panel evaluates each nomination, based on the reports of Desk experts and of the site missions.

The Panel aims to reach its recommendations on nominations by consensus.

The first Panel may come to final collective recommendations on some nominations while for others further dialogue with States Parties may be agreed related to the need for more information or the need for adjustments to the approach of the nomination. In cases where the Panel has concluded that the nomination has no potential to justify Outstanding Universal Value, ICOMOS will contact States Parties at this stage. A short interim report for each nomination, in one of the two working languages of the Convention, outlining the status and any issues relevant to the evaluation process, and any further requests for supplementary information, will be provided in January to the nominating States Parties and copied to the World Heritage Centre for distribution to the Chair of the World Heritage Committee.

The second Panel undertakes further evaluation of nominations for which a recommendation has not yet been reached based on the receipt of further information or the outcome of dialogue

际古迹遗址理事会评估工作组有些专家，是前缔约国代表，但如今已不再是世界遗产委员会委员。这些专家将以个人身份和自己的专业能力，参与工作组的审查工作。

工作组将在十二月和来年三月分别会谈一次。在第一次的会谈中，工作组将依据书面评估报告及实地考察报告对遗产进行评估。

工作组将力图在审核会上对遗产申报项目达成共识。

第一次评估工作组会议将对部分申报形成集体意见，同时建议另外部分申报，需要与相关缔约国协商，以提供更多信息或调整申报方法。如果评估工作组得出的结论是申报无法满足突出的普遍性价值，则国际古迹遗址理事会将及时联系相关缔约国。每项申报都要用公约要求的一或两种工作语言，编制一个简短的中期报告，重点描述遗产现状及其他与评估过程相关的议题，并提出相应要求以获取补充信息并抄送世界遗产中心和世界遗产委员会主席团。这份报告将在一月份提交给申报缔约国，并抄送世界遗产中心和世界遗产委员会主席团。

评估工作组将根据收到的补充信息和与缔约国协商的成果，召集第二次会议，对未达成共识的申报进行进一步评估，进而达成共识。第二次会议后所有最终评估将送交世界遗产中

with States Parties. The Panel then agrees the remaining collective recommendations. Following the second Panel meeting, the text of all evaluations is finalised and sent to the World Heritage Centre for distribution to States Parties. The names and qualifications of the members of the Panel are then provided to the World Heritage Centre and published on the ICOMOS website.

The ICOMOS evaluations provide an assessment of Outstanding Universal Value, including the applicability of the criteria and the requirements of integrity and authenticity, assessment of the adequacy of legislative protection, management, and the state of conservation, and finally draft recommendations to the World Heritage Committee with respect to inscription.

心以便于分送至缔约国。第二次工作组会议后，汇总所有的评估报告，发送至世界遗产中心并分发给各缔约国。工作组成员的姓名与资历将提供给世界遗产中心，并公布于国际古迹遗址理事会的官方网站上。

国际古迹遗址理事会将评估申报遗产的突出普遍价值、适用的标准、完整性真实性要求，还将评估遗产地是否有充分的立法保护、管理，并分析保护状况，最终形成建议草案提供给世界遗产委员会。

EvaluationproceduresoftheAdvisoryBodiesfornominations　　　*Annex6*

Figure 1 SUMMARY OF ICOMOS EVALUATION PROCEDURES

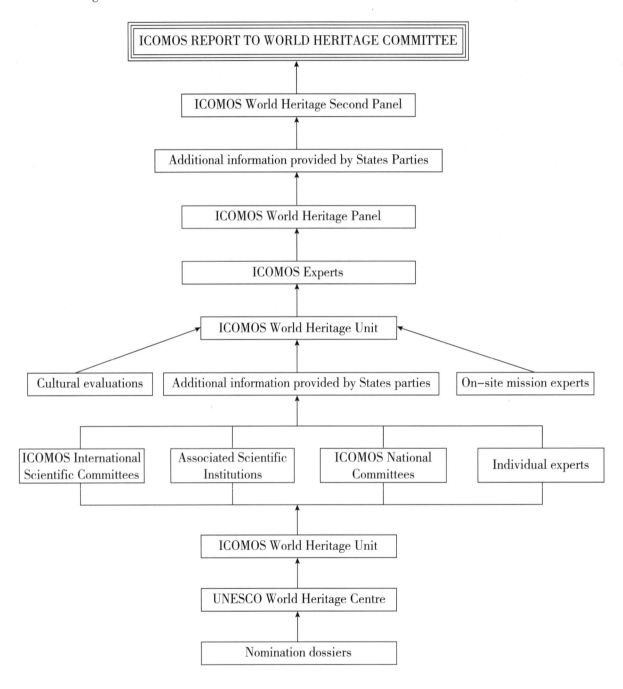

附件6

图1　国际古迹遗址理事会评估程序

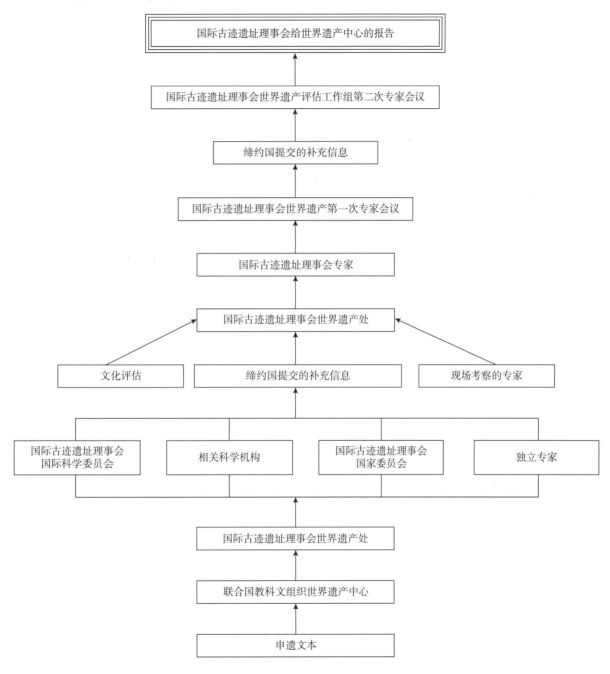

B. THE IUCN PROCEDURE FOR THE EVALUATION OF NATURAL PROPERTIES

1. In carrying out its evaluation of nominations of natural properties, IUCN (the International Union for Conservation of Nature) is guided by the *Operational Guidelines* (see Paragraph 148). The evaluation process (see Figure 2) involves five elements:

(i) Data Assembly.Following receipt of the nomination dossier from the World Heritage Centre, a standardised analysis is compiled on the property using the World Database on Protected Areas and other IUCN global databases and thematic studies. This may include comparative analyses on biodiversity values undertaken in partnership with the UNEP World Conservation Monitoring Centre (UNEP-WCMC). Key findings of data analysis are the subject of dialogue with the State Party during the evaluation mission, and at other stages of the process.

(ii) External Review. The nomination is sent for desk review to independent experts knowledgeable about the property and/or the values that are the subject of the nomination, who are primarily members of IUCN's specialist Commissions and networks, or expert members of partner organisations of IUCN. The documents used to guide IUCN desk reviews are publicly available on the IUCN website: www.iucn.org/worldheritage.

(iii) Evaluation mission to the property. One or two appropriately qualified IUCN experts visit each nominated property to clarify details about the area, to evaluate site management and to discuss the nomination with relevant authorities and stakeholders. IUCN experts, selected for their global perspective on conservation and natural history as well as their knowledge of the Convention, are usually experienced members of the IUCN World Commission on Protected Areas. (This field

B. 世界自然保护联盟的自然遗产评估程序

1. 世界自然保护联盟遵循《操作指南》（见第148条）的指导对自然遗产的申报材料进行评估。评估程序（见图2）包括五个步骤：

（ⅰ）搜集数据：接到世界遗产中心递交的申报材料之后，将使用世界保护区数据库、其他世界自然保护联盟全球资料库和主题研究，进行标准化分析。这可能包括与联合国环境规划署世界保护监测中心合作开展的生物多样性价值比较分析。数据分析所获得的重要成果将成为评估过程及其他阶段与缔约国进行对话的主题。

（ⅱ）外部评审：申报材料将提交给独立专家进行案头评审。这些专家应具备世界遗产和／或该项遗产价值的渊博知识，并且大部分是世界自然保护联盟专家委员会及网络的成员，或世界自然保护联盟合作伙伴组织的专家成员。可登录世界自然保护联盟网站 www.iucn.org/worldheritage 获取世界自然保护联盟案头评审的指导文件。

（ⅲ）遗产现场评估考察：选派一至两名有合格资质的世界自然保护联盟专家，对每一处申报遗产进行考察，以明确该区域的详细情况，评估遗址管理，与相关当局和利益相关方讨论申报情况。挑选世界自然保护联盟专家的标准，是其保护与自然历史的全球视角及对《公约》的了解。这些专家通常是世界自然保护联盟保护区遗产专家（在某些情况下与国际古迹遗址理事会共同展开现场调查——见下文C部分）。可登录世界自然保护联盟网站 www.iucn.

inspection is undertaken jointly with ICOMOS in certain situations - see Part C below). The format of IUCN field evalution mission reports is publicly available on the IUCN website: www.iucn.org/worldheritage.

(iv) Other sources of information. IUCN also consults additional literature and may receive comments from local NGOs, communities, indigenous peoples and other interested parties in the nomination. Where relevant IUCN will also coordinate with other international conservation instruments such as the Ramsar Convention, the Man and Biosphere Programme and the Global Geoparks Network, and will consult with universities and research institutes as appropriate.

(v) IUCN World Heritage Panel Review. The IUCN World Heritage Panel is established by the Director General of IUCN to provide high quality and independent technical and scientific advice to IUCN on its work as an Advisory Body to the World Heritage Committee and strategic advice to IUCN's work on World Heritage throughout the IUCN Programme. Specific Tasks of the World Heritage Panel are to conduct a rigorous evaluation of all nominations of natural and mixed properties to the World Heritage List, leading to a panel recommendation on the IUCN position in relation to each new nomination, in line with the requirements established in the Operational Guidelines of the World Heritage Convention. The Panel also provides comment where relevant to ICOMOS in relation to nominations of cultural landscapes to the World Heritage List. The Panel normally meets at least twice in the evaluation process, once in December (year 1) and a second meeting in March/April (year 2);

The members of the Panel comprise senior IUCN staff, IUCN Commission members and external experts selected for their high level of experience

org/worldheritage获取现场评估考察报告格式。

（iv）其他信息来源：世界自然保护联盟也可参考其他文献，接受地方非政府组织、社区、当地土著居民及其他遗产申报利益相关方的意见和建议。世界自然保护联盟也会使用其他国际保护工具如《拉姆萨尔湿地公约》、（联合国教科文组织）人与生物圈计划、世界地质公园网络，并酌情咨询大学及研究机构的意见。

（v）世界自然保护联盟世界遗产评审小组：世界自然保护联盟世界遗产评审小组由世界自然保护联盟总干事设立，作为世界自然保护联盟世界遗产委员会咨询机构，向世界遗产自然联盟提供高质、独立的技术和科学建议、及向世界遗产自然联盟的保护项目提供战略性建议。世界自然保护联盟世界遗产评审小组的特别任务是，按照《世界遗产公约操作指南》的要求，对所有申报列入《世界遗产名录》的自然和混合遗产进行严格的评估，以世界自然保护联盟的立场为每项新的申报提供意见。如申报遗产为文化景观，则世界自然保护联盟世界遗产评审小组将与对申报遗产与文化相关的部分提供建议的国际古迹遗址理事会评估工作组协商。通常，世界遗产评审小组在每个评估过程中至少开两次会，一次在12月（第一年），一次在来年3月或四月（第二年）。

世界遗产小组由资深世界自然保护联盟成员、世界自然保护联盟委员会成员和外部专家构成，其入选标准是应具备高水平的经验、公

and recognised leading expertise and knowledge relevant to IUCN's work on World Heritage, including a balance of particular thematic and/or regional perspectives. It includes some experts who have past experience as members of State Party delegations, but are not current serving members of the World Heritage Committee. These experts will serve in a personal and professional capacity. The IUCN World Heritage Panel reviews all field evaluation reports (and normally hears direct feedback from the mission team), reviewers' comments, the UNEP-WCMC and other analyses and all other background material before finalising the text of the IUCN evaluation report foreach nominated property. The membership, terms of reference and working methods of the IUCN World Heritage Panel are publicly available on the IUCN website, and are provided to the World Heritage Committee.

Each evaluation report presents a concise summary of the proposed Outstanding Universal Value of the property nominated, a global comparative analysis with other similar sites (including both World Heritage properties and other protected areas) and a review of integrity and management issues. It concludes with the assessment of the applicability of the criteria, and a clear recommendation to the World Heritage Committee. The names of all experts involved in the evaluation process are included in the final evaluation report, except in the case of reviewers who have provided confidential reviews.

IUCN undertakes dialogue with the nominating States Party/ies at all stages of the nomination process. IUCN will use its best endeavours to allocate its available resources equitably, efficiently and effectively, to maximise the opportunities for dialogue with all nominating States Parties. Dialogue starts early in the evaluation process and intensifies after the meeting of the IUCN World Heritage Panel in December, and includes the

认的业内领先的专业知识和技能，能胜任世界自然保护联盟所承担的世界遗产相关工作，同时应具有独特的主题和／或区域视角。某些世界遗产小组专家可能曾是缔约国代表团成员，但目前不再服务于世界遗产委员会。这些专家具有一定的个人及专业能力。世界自然保护联盟在每份遗产评估报告定稿以前，世界自然保护联盟世界遗产专家小组将评审所有的现场评估考察报告（通常也听取现场评估小组的直接反馈意见）、译审专家意见、联合国环境规划署世界养护监测中心、其他资料及所有背景材料分析。可登录世界自然保护联盟网站获取世界自然保护联盟世界遗产小组的成员、审查范围及工作方法相关资料，这些同时也提供给世界遗产委员会。

每份评估报告包括申报遗产突出普遍价值的简明摘要、与世界上类似遗址（包括世界遗产及其他保护区）的对比分析、审查完整性和管理问题以及评估标准的适用性，并向世界遗产委员会提供明确建议。参与整个评估过程的专家姓名也会包含在评估报告终稿中，提供机密审核意见的专家除外。

世界自然保护联盟负责在申报过程各个阶段与提出申报的缔约国保持对话。世界自然保护联盟将尽最大可能实现可用资源的公平、有效和高效分配，并尽量创造机会与申报缔约国加强对话和沟通。评估一旦开始也意味着对话的开始，世界自然保护联盟世界遗产小组十二月份会议之后将展开更多对话，包括：

following:

i)　Prior to the evaluation mission, IUCN may request additional information on questions in the nomination document that require clarification, and will always contact the State Party to prepare for the evaluationmission.

ii)　During the evaluation mission the IUCN mission team is able to undertake in-depth discussions on site with representatives of the State Party and with stakeholders.

iii) After the evaluation mission, IUCN may discuss issues that have been identified by the mission team, and request further information from the State Party as required.

iv) After IUCN's first World Heritage Panel meeting, normally held in December, IUCN will discuss issues raised by the Panel, and request further information from the State Party as required. A short interim report outlining the status, and any issues relevant to the evaluation, and detailing any requests for supplementary information, in one of the two working languages of the Convention, is sent to the nominating State Party/ies, a nd copied to the World Heritage Centre, for transmission to the Chairperson of the World Heritage Committee. Dialogue and consultation takes place either through teleconference and/or face-to-face meetings, as mutually agreed.

IUCN takes into account in its evaluation all information that is officially submitted by the State Party in writing to the World Heritage Centre by the specified deadline (see paragraph 148 of the Operational Guidelines). However, at all of the above stages any stakeholder in the nomination is also at liberty to contact IUCN to provide

ⅰ）现场评估考察正式开始之前，世界自然保护联盟可能要求缔约国为申报文件中需要阐明的问题提供补充信息，且将时刻与缔约国的保持联系，为现场评估考察做准备。

ⅱ）在现场评估考察过程中，世界自然保护联盟现场考察小组将在现场与缔约国代表及利益相关方代表，展开深入讨论。

ⅲ）现场评估考察结束后，世界自然保护联盟将讨论评审小组确认的事项，并要求缔约国按要求提供更多的信息。

ⅳ）世界自然保护联盟首次世界遗产小组会议通常于十二月份召开，之后世界自然保护联盟将讨论世界遗产小组提出的问题，并要求缔约国按需求提供更多信息。用一或两种公约要求的工作语言准备一个简短的中期报告，简述进展状况、评估相关事项、需要补充信息的详细要求，发送给申报缔约国，复件同时发给世界遗产中心，由其交由世界遗产委员会。将依照双方协商确认的方式开展对话和咨询，如电话会议、碰头会等。

世界自然保护联盟将考虑、评估所有缔约国在截止日期前正式提交给世界遗产中心书面资料（见操作指南第148条）。然而，在评估任何阶段，申报遗产利益相关方可按其需求自由与世界自然保护联盟取得联系、提供相关信息资料。

information if they wish.

IUCN also always considers fully all past decisions of the World Heritage Committee relevant to the nomination, such as in cases of nominations that have been previously referred or deferred by the Committee, or where the Committee has taken any position in relation to issues of policy.

世界自然保护联盟将充分考虑世界遗产委员会过去对遗产申报的所有决定，例如委员会曾决定的补充材料后申报或重新申报的遗产，或委员会在某些政策问题上有特殊立场。

In the case of renominations, extensions and boundary modifications to an existing World Heritage property, IUCN also considers all matters regarding the state of conservation of that property that have been previously reported to the World Heritage Committee. IUCN may also consider bringing to the attention of the Committee, through the state of conservation reporting process, any significant matters regarding the state of conservation of that property, when such are identified for the first time during the evaluation process.

如申报遗产为重新申报、对现有世界遗产进行扩展、或边界调整，世界自然保护联盟将考虑所有与该遗产保护状况相关的、曾报告给世界遗产委员会的事项。世界自然保护联盟也将通过保护状况报告程序提请委员会注意，在评估过程中首次发现的、与保护状况相关的任何重大事项。

Biogeographic classification systems as a basis for comparison

生物地理分类体系作为比较基础

2. In the evaluations, IUCN uses biogeographic classification systems such as Udvardy's "Biogeographical Provinces of the World" (1975) and the more recent terrestrial, freshwater and marine ecoregions of the world as a central element of its approach to the global comparative analysis. These systems provide an objective means of comparing nominated properties with sites of similar climatic and ecological conditions.

2. 评估时，世界自然保护联盟将使用乌德瓦尔第（Udvardy"）世界生物地理区域（1975年）的生物地理分类体系、以及世界最新的陆地、淡水和海洋生态区，作为其全球比较分析方法的核心要素。这些体系是把那些申报遗产与具有类似天气与生态条件的遗产，进行对比分析的客观手段。

3. It is stressed, however, that these biogeographical classification systems are used as a measure for comparison only and do not imply that World Heritage properties are to be selected solely on this basis, nor that the representation of all such classification systems is the basis for the selection process. The guiding principle is that World Heritage properties must be of Outstanding

3. 但需要强调的是，生态地理学分类系统仅是比较的手段，既不意味着这是选择世界遗产的唯一标准，也不意味着，这些分类系统的代表性是选择的基础。一个指导性的原则是 世界遗产必须具有突出普遍价值。

Universal Value.

Systems to identify priority areas for conservation

4. IUCN also uses systems which identify priority areas for conservation such as the World Wide Fund for Nature's (WWF) Global 200 Ecoregions, WWF/IUCN's Centres of Plant Diversity, Conservation International's Biodiversity Hotspots and High-Biodiversity Wilderness Areas, Birdlife International's Endemic Bird Areas and Important Bird Areas, and other Key Biodiversity Areas such as Alliance for Zero Extinction sites. These systems provide additional information on the significance of the nominated properties for biodiversity conservation; however it is not assumed that all such sites should be included on the World Heritage List. The guiding principle is that World Heritage properties must be of Outstanding Universal Value.

Systems to evaluate properties for earth science value

5. In evaluating properties which have been nominated for their geological value, IUCN consults with a range of specialised organisations such as the UNESCO Earth Sciences Division, International Association of Geomorphologists, the International Union of Speleology and the International Union of Geological Sciences(IUGS).

Additional reference publications used in the evaluation process

6. The evaluation process also includes consideration of key reference publications on the world's protected areas published by IUCN and a range of international conservation organisations. These documents together provide system-wide overviews which allow comparison of the conservation importance of protected areas throughout the world. IUCN has also undertaken a range

确认优先保护区的体系

4. 世界自然保护联盟同时使用确认优先保护区的体系，比如，世界自然基金会（WWF）全球 200 强生态区、世界自然基金会 / 世界自然保护联盟植物多样性中心、保护国际的生态多样性热点地区、高密度生物多样性自然保护区、国际特有鸟类区和重要鸟类区，以及其他重要生物多样性区域，如零灭绝联盟等。这些体系提供了关于申报遗产对生物多样性保护的重要性的更多信息，但是并不意味着要将所有这些遗址列入世界遗产名录。一个指导性的原则是世界遗产必须具有突出普遍价值。

评估遗产地球科学价值的体系

5. 在对因地质价值而提出申报的遗产进行评估时，世界自然保护联盟会咨询一些专业组织，比如联合国教科文组织的地球科学部、国际地貌学家协会、国际洞穴研究会和国际地质科学联盟的意见。

评估时使用的相关出版物

6. 评估程序将参考世界自然保护联盟以及其他一些国际保护机构出版的、关于世界保护区的主要参考书籍，这便于对全球保护区的保护重要性进行比较。世界自然保护联盟同时开展了大量主题研究，来确认自然世界遗产的覆盖面以及潜在的缺口。登录以下世界自然保护联盟的网址 http：//iucn.org/themes/wcpa/

of thematic studies to identify gaps in natural World Heritage coverage and properties of World Heritage potential. These can be viewed on the IUCN website at www.iucn.org/worldheritage.

wheritage/globalstrategy.htm 可获取以上信息。

IUCN also draws upon references specific to the nominated properties in order to gain insights into site values and conservation issues.

世界自然保护联盟还引用特别针对申报遗产的相关资料，以获得对遗址价值和保护事项更多的见解。

Evaluation of Cultural Landscapes (see also Annex 3)

文化景观评估（ 另请见附件三 ）

7. IUCN has an interest in many cultural properties, especially those nominated as cultural landscapes. For that reason, it will on occasion participate in joint field inspections to nominated cultural landscapes with ICOMOS (see Part C below).

7. 世界自然保护联盟对很多文化遗产都感兴趣，特别是作为文化景观申报的遗产。因此，联盟有时会与国际古迹遗址理事会合作，对申报的文化景观进行现场考察（ 见下文的 C 部分 ）。

8. In accordance with the natural qualities of certain cultural landscapes identified in Annex 3, Paragraph 11, IUCN's evaluation is concerned with the following factors:

(i) Conservation of natural and semi-natural systems, and of wild species of fauna and flora

(ii) Conservation of biodiversity within sustainable use systems (farming, traditional fisheries, forestry);

(iii) Sustainable land and wateruse;

(iv) Enhancement of scenic beauty;

(v) Ex-situ collections, such as botanic gardens or arboreta;

(vi) Outstanding examples of humanity's inter-relationship with nature;

(vii) Historically significant discoveries

8. 根据附件 3 第 11 段确认的某些文化景观遗产的自然特性，世界自然保护联盟的评估主要涉及以下几个因素：

（ⅰ）自然、半自然体系以及野生动植物物种的保护；

（ⅱ）可持续利用系统（农业、传统渔业、林业）内的生物多样性的保护；

（ⅲ）可持续的水土使用；

（ⅳ）景色美感的提升；

（ⅴ）迁地采集，如植物园或植物园等；

（ⅵ）人类与自然关系的杰出范例；

（ⅶ）具有重大历史意义的发现。

The following table sets each of the above list in the context of the categories of cultural landscapes in Annex 3, thereby indicating where each consideration is most likely to occur (the absence of a consideration does not mean that it will *never* occur, only that this is unlikely):

下表把上文所提每个列表均放在附件 3 文化景观类型的背景之内，藉此指出哪项内容最可能出现（ 没提到的内容并不意味着永远不会出现，只是可能性不太大 ）：

附件 6-2

Cultural Landscape type (see also Annex 3)	Natural considerations most likely to be relevant (see Paragraph 16 above)						
Designed landscape					(v)		
Organically evolving landscape - continuous	(i)	(ii)	(iii)	(iv)			
Organically evolving landscape - fossil	(i)					(vi)	
Associative landscape							(vii)

文化景观类型（另见附件 3）	最可能相关的自然内容（见上文第 16 段）						
人工设计的景观					（ⅴ）		
有机演变的景观——持续	（ⅰ）	（ⅱ）	（ⅲ）	（ⅳ）			
有机演变的景观——化石	（ⅰ）					（ⅵ）	
关联性景观							（ⅶ）

FIGURE 2: SUMMARY OF IUCN EVALUATION PROCEDURE

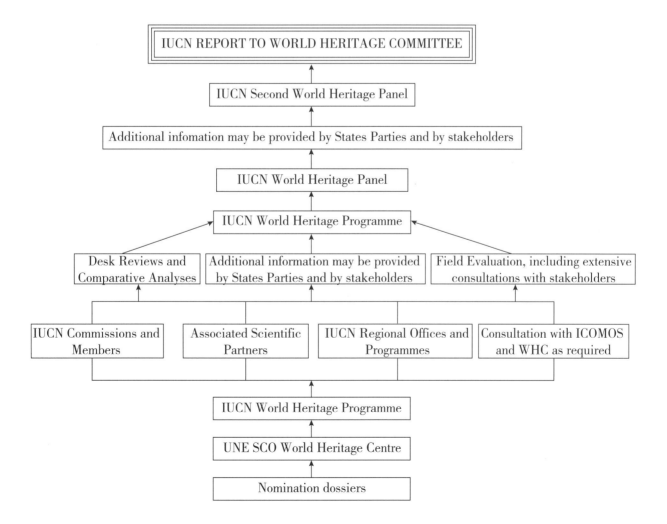

图2　世界自然保护联盟评估程序概要

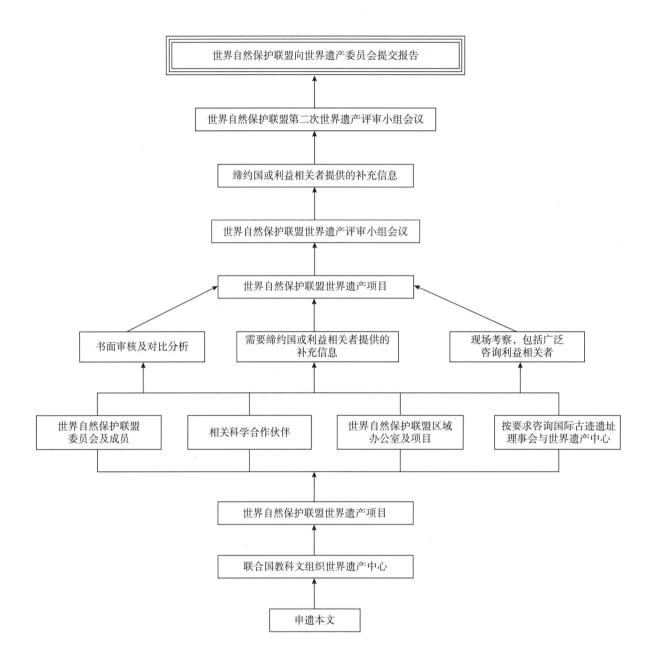

C. ADVISORY BODY COLLABORATION

Nominations of mixed properties

1. Properties that are nominated under both natural and cultural criteria entail a joint IUCN and ICOMOS mission to the nominated property. Following the mission, IUCN and ICOMOS prepare separate evaluation reports of the property under the relevant criteria (see above), and harmonise and coordinate their evaluations to the extent possible.

Cultural Landscapes

2. Properties nominated as Cultural Landscapes are evaluated by ICOMOS under criteria (i) - (vi) (see Paragraph 77 of the *Operational Guidelines)*. IUCN may provide advice when relevant on the natural values and the conservation and management of the nominated property, and addresses any questions that are raised by ICOMOS. Insome cases, a joint mission is required.

Linkages between nature and culture

3. As most properties nominated to the World Heritage List include aspects of management related to the interaction of nature and culture, IUCN and ICOMOS, to the extent possible, discuss any such interactions during their evaluationp rocesses.

C. 咨询机构的合作

混合遗产申报

1. 按照自然价值和文化价值双重标准申报的遗产，需要世界自然保护联盟和国际古迹遗址理事会共同对该遗产申报进行现场评估考察。考察之后，世界自然保护联盟和国际古迹遗址理事会将根据相关标准（见上文）编制独立的遗产评估报告，并尽最大可能协调和整合其评估报告。

文化景观

2. 作为文化景观申报的遗产，由国际古迹遗址理事会根据标准（i）–（vi）（见《操作指南》第77条）进行评估。由世界自然保护联盟对该申报遗产自然价值及其保护和管理提供相关评估意见，并解决国际古迹遗址理事会提出的问题。在有些情况下，需要共同行动。

自然和文化的联系

3. 由于大部分申请列入世界遗产名录的遗产都包括对自然与文化交互作用的管理，世界自然保护联盟和国际古迹遗址理事会将尽最大可能在其评估过程中地讨论这些交互作用。

Annex 7

Format for the periodic reporting on the application of the _World Heritage Convention_

• The Format for Periodic Reporting is available at the following Web address: http://whc.unesco.org/en/periodicreporting

• Further guidance on Periodic Reporting can be found in Section V of the _Operational Guidelines_

• In order to facilitate management of information, States Parties are requested to submit reports, in English or French, in electronic as well as in printed form to:

UNESCO World Heritage Centre 7, place de Fontenoy 75352 Paris 07 SP

France

Telephone: +33 (0) 1 4568 1571

Fax: +33 (0) 1 4568 5570

E-mail through: http://whc.unesco.org/en/contacts

FORMAT PERIODIC REPORTING ON THE APPLICATION OF THE _WORLD HERITAGE CONVENTION_

General Requirements

• Information should be as precise and specific as possible. It should be quantified where possible and fully referenced.

• Information should be concise. In particular long historical accounts of sites and events which have taken place there should be avoided, especially when they can be found in readily available published sources.

• Expressions of opinion should be supported by reference to the authority on which they are

---

附件7

《世界遗产公约》实施的定期报告的格式

• 登录以下网址，可获取定期报告的格式：http：//whc.unesco.org/en/periodicreporting

• 定期报告的更多指导意见，请参见《操作指南》的第 V 部分

• 为了便于信息的管理，要求缔约国提交英语或法语报告，应同时提交报告的电子版本和印刷版本，提交地址如下：

联合国教科文组织世界遗产中心法国巴黎（7，place de Fontenoy 75352 Paris 07 SP France）

电话：+33（0）1 4568 1571

　　传真：+33（0）1 4568 5570

电邮：http：//whc.unesco.org/en/contacts

实施《世界遗产公约》的定期报告的格式

总体要求

• 信息应该尽可能地精确、具体，应尽量量化，并提供完整的参考文献。

• 信息应该简洁。应该避免逐一叙述遗产地的漫长历史和相关事件。如果可随时从现有出版物找到这些信息，更应避免这样做。

• 观点陈述应得到当局的支持，并具备能够支持该观点的确切事实。

made and the verifiable facts which support them.

• Periodic reports should be completed on A4 paper (210mm x 297mm), with maps and plans a maximum of A3 paper (297mm x 420mm). States Parties are also encouraged to submit the full text of the periodic reports in electronic form.

•定期报告应用 A4 纸（210mmx297mm），地图和规划最大用 A3 纸（297mmx420mm）。也鼓励缔约国提交电子版的定期报告全文。

SECTION I:
APPLICATION OF THE *WORLD HERITAGE CONVENTION* BY THE STATE PARTY

第I部分：
缔约国实施《世界遗产公约》的情况

States Parties are requested to give information on the legislative and administrative provisions which they have adopted and other action which they have taken for the application of this *Convention,* together with details of the experience acquired in this field (Article 29.1 of the *World Heritage Convention*).

要求缔约国提供为实施《公约》通过的法律和行政条款及其他举措，以及在该领域获得的具体经验（《世界遗产公约》第 29.1 条）。

1.1 Introduction

1.1 导言

    (i) StateParty
    (ii) Year of ratification or acceptance of the *Convention*
    (iii) Organization(s) or entity(ies) responsible for the preparation of the report
    (iv) Date of the report
    (v) Signature on behalf of the State Party

    （ⅰ）缔约国
    （ⅱ）批准或接受《公约》的年份
    （ⅲ）负责编制报告的组织或实体
    （ⅳ）报告日期
    （ⅴ）缔约国代表签名

1.2 Identification of cultural and natural heritage properties

1.2 文化和自然遗产确认

This item refers in particular to Articles 3, 4 and 11 of the *Convention* regarding the identification of cultural and natural heritage and the nomination of properties for inscription on the World Heritage List.
    (i) National inventories

本条特别参阅《公约》的第 3 条、第 4 条和第 11 条关于文化和自然遗产的确认以及遗产申报列入《世界遗产名录》的内容。

    （ⅰ）国家清单

Inventories of cultural and natural heritage of national significance form the basis for the

国家级文化和自然遗产清单，是确认潜在世界遗产的基础。

identification of possible World Heritage properties.

Indicate which institutions are in charge of the preparation and keeping up-to-date of these national inventories and if, and to what extent, inventories, lists and/or registers at the local, state and/or national level exist and have been completed.

(ii) Tentative List

Article 11 of the *Convention* refers to the submission by States Parties of inventories of property suitable for inscription on the World Heritage List. These tentative lists of cultural and natural properties should be prepared with reference to Paragraphs 62-69 and Annex 2 of the *Operational Guidelines*. States Parties should report on actions taken to implement the decision of the Committee at its twenty-fourth session (Cairns, December 2000) and the twelfth General Assembly of States Parties (UNESCO Headquarters, 1999) whereby tentative lists are to be used as a planning tool to reduce the imbalances in the World Heritage List.

Provide the date of submission of the Tentative List or any revision made since its submission. States Parties are also encouraged to provide a description of the process of preparation and revision of the Tentative List, e.g. has (have) any particular institution(s) been assigned the responsibility for identifying and delineating World Heritage properties, have local authorities and local population been involved in its preparation? If so, provide exact details.

(iii) Nominations

The periodic report should list properties that have been nominated for inscription on the World Heritage List. States Parties are encouraged to provide

说明负责编制、更新国家清单的机构。是否存在地方、州和 / 或国家级的遗产清单、名单和 / 或登记簿，以及完成的情况。

（ii）《预备名录》

《公约》第 11 条涉及缔约国提交适宜列入《世界遗产名录》的遗产的名单。文化和自然遗产的《预备名录》应参阅《操作指南》第 62-69 条和附件 2。缔约国应该提交报告，说明委员会第 24 届会议（凯恩斯，2000 年 12 月）、缔约国第十二届大会（联合国教科文组织总部，1999 年）决议的实施情况。这些决议把预备名录作为规划工具，降低《世界遗产名录》上遗产分布的不均衡性。

提供《预备名录》提交的日期，及提交以后所做的任何修改信息。同时鼓励缔约国描述《预备名录》的编制和修订过程，比如，是否委派某个（些）机构负责确认、界定世界遗产？当地机构和群众是否参与名录编制过程？如果是，提供准确细节。

（iii）申报材料

定期报告应该列出申报列入《世界遗产名录》的遗产。鼓励缔约国对以下内容进行分析：申报材料的编制过程、与当地机构及群众的合

an analysis of the process by which these nominations are prepared, the collaboration and co-operation with local authorities and people, the motivation, obstacles and difficulties encountered in that process and perceived benefits and lessons learnt.

作、编制过程中得到的动力、遇到的障碍和困难，以及得到的经验和教训。

1.3 Protection, conservation and presentation of the cultural and natural heritage

1.3 文化和自然遗产的保护、保存与展示

This item refers in particular to Articles 4 and 5 of the *Convention*, in which States Parties recognise their duty of ensuring the identification, protection, conservation, presentation and transmission to future generations of the cultural and natural World Heritage and that effective and active measures are taken to this effect. Additional guidance on States Parties obligations can be found in Paragraphs 10-16 of the *Operational Guidelines*.

本条特别参阅《公约》第 4 条、第 5 条，其中提到的、缔约国有责任确保本国领土内的文化和自然遗产的确定、保护、保存、展示和传承，并采取积极有效的措施履行这些责任。更多关于缔约国责任的指导，可参阅《操作指南》的第 10–16 条。

Article 5 of the *Convention* specifies the following measures:

《公约》第 5 条明确了以下措施：

(i) General policy development

（i）总体政策制定

Provide information on the adoption of policies that aim to give the cultural and natural heritage a function in the life of the community. Provide information on the way the State Party or the relevant authorities has (have) taken steps to integrate the protection of World Heritage properties into comprehensive planning programmes. Areas where improvement would be desirable, and towards which the State Party is working should be indicated.

说明关于文化和自然遗产在社会生活中发挥作用的政策的通过情况。阐述缔约国或相关机构把世界遗产的保护融入整体规划方案中的举措。应指出待改进的工作和缔约国的工作目标。

(ii) Status of services for protection, conservation and presentation

（ii）保护、展示服务的情况

Provide information on any services within the territories of the State Party which have been set

提供自上次定期报告以后，缔约国内已确立或已大幅改善的服务（如适用）的信息。应

up or have been substantially improved since the previous periodic report, if applicable. Particular attention should be given to services aiming at the protection, conservation and presentation of the cultural and natural heritage, indicating the appropriate staff and the means to discharge their functions. Areas where improvement would be desirable, and towards which the State Party is working should be indicated.

特别关注旨在保护与展示文化和自然遗产的服务，说明履行这些功能的合适的人员配备和手段。应指出待改进的工作和缔约国的工作目标。

(iii) Scientific and technical studies and research

（iii）科学和技术研究

Additional guidance on research can be found in Paragraph 215 of the *Operational Guidelines*.

有关研究的更多指导，请参阅《操作指南》的第 215 条。

List significant scientific and technical studies or research projects of a generic nature that would benefit World Heritage properties, initiated or completed since the last periodic report. Areas where improvement would be desirable, and towards which the State Party is working should be indicated.

列出自上一个定期报告提交以后，正在开展或业已完成的、有利于世界遗产的重大科学和技术项目。应指出待改进的工作和缔约国的工作目标。

Site specific scientific studies or research projects should be reported upon under Section Ⅱ.4 of this Format.

应根据本格式第 Ⅱ.4 部分，报告遗产地的具体科学研究项目。

(iv) Measures for identification, protection, conservation, presentation and rehabilitation

（iv）确定、保护、保存、展示和修复、利用的措施

Indicate appropriate legal and administrative measures that the State Party or relevant authorities have taken for the identification, protection, conservation, presentation and rehabilitation of cultural and natural heritage. Particular attention should be given to measures concerning visitor management and development in the region. The State Party is also encouraged to indicate if, on the basis of the experiences gained, policy and/or legal reform is considered necessary. It is also relevant to note which other international conventions for the

指出缔约国或相关机构确定、保护、保存、展示和修复利用文化和自然遗产的法律和行政措施。应该特别关注本地区旅游管理和开发的措施。同时鼓励缔约国说明，基于已有经验，是否有必要考虑进行相关政策和 / 或法规改革。也有必要说明，缔约国还签署和认可了哪些文化和自然遗产保护的国际公约。如签署了相关公约，在实施过程中，是如何在国家政策和规划内协调与融合。

protection of cultural or natural heritage have been signed or ratified by the State Party and if so, how the application of these different legal instruments is co-ordinated and integrated in national policies and planning.

Indicate relevant scientific, and technical measures that the State Party or relevant institutions within the State have taken for the identification, protection, conservation, presentation and rehabilitation of cultural and natural heritage.

说明缔约国及其相关机构采取了哪些重要的科学和技术措施，来确定、保护、保存、展出和修复、利用文化和自然遗产。

Indicate relevant financial measures that the State Party or relevant authorities have taken for the identification, protection, conservation, presentation and rehabilitation of cultural and natural heritage.

说明缔约国及其相关机构采取了哪些相关财政措施，来确定、保护、保存、展出和修复、利用文化和自然遗产。

Information on the presentation of the heritage can refer to publications, internet web-pages, films, stamps, postcards, books etc.

遗产展示信息可包括出版物、互联网网页、影片、邮票、明信片、书籍等。

Areas where improvement would be desirable, and towards which the State Party is working should be indicated.

应指出待改进的工作和缔约国的工作目标。

(v) Training

（ⅴ）培训

Additional guidance on training can be found in Paragraphs 213-214 of the *Operational Guidelines*.

更多有关培训的指导，请参阅《操作指南》第 213–214 条。

Provide information on the training and educational strategies that have been implemented within the State Party for professional capacity building, as well as on the establishment or development of national or regional centres for training and education in the protection, conservation, and presentation of the cultural and natural heritage, and the degree to which such training has been integrated within existing university and educational systems.

提供缔约国在国内为促进专业能力建设执行的培训和教育战略的信息，提供为保护、保存和展出文化和自然遗产而建立的国家或地区培训和教育中心及其发展的信息，以及这些培训与现有大学和教育体系的融合程度的信息。

Indicate the steps that the State Party has taken to

说明为支持培训和教育活动，缔约国采取

encourage scientific research as a support to training and educational activities.

的鼓励科学研究的措施。

Areas where improvement would be desirable, and towards which the State Party is working should be indicated.

应指出待改进的工作和缔约国的工作目标。

1.4 International co-operation and fund raising

1.4 国际合作与资金筹集

This item refers particularly to Articles 4, 6, 17 and 18 of the *Convention*. Additional guidance on this issue can be found in Paragraphs 227-231 of the *Operational Guidelines*.

本条特别参阅《公约》的第 4、6、17 和 18 条。有关本议题的更多指导，请参阅《操作指南》第 227-231 条。

Provide information on the co-operation with other States Parties for the identification, protection, conservation and preservation of the World Heritage located on their territories.

提供为其领土内世界遗产的确定、保护、保存事宜与其他缔约国开展合作的信息。

Also indicate which measures have been taken to avoid damage directly or indirectly to the World Heritage on the territory of other States Parties.

说明采取了哪些措施，来避免对其他缔约国领土内的世界遗产造成直接或间接的损害。

Have national, public and private foundations or associations been established for, and has the State Party given assistance to, raising funds and donations for the protection of the World Heritage?

是否为筹集和募捐世界遗产的保护资金建立了国家、公共和私人基金或组织？缔约国是否在这些方面给予了帮助？

1.5 Education, information and awareness building

1.5 教育、信息和公众意识的提升

This item refers particularly to Articles 27 and 28 of the *Convention* on educational programmes. Additional guidance on these matters can be found in Chapter IX of the *Operational Guidelines*.

本条特别参阅《公约》关于教育方案的 27 和 28 条。有关本事宜的更多指导，请参阅《操作指南》第九章。

Indicate steps that the State Party has taken to raise the awareness of decision-makers, property owners, and the general public about the protection and conservation of cultural and natural heritage.

说明为提升决策者、遗产所有者和社会大众关于文化和自然遗产的保护与保存的意识，缔约国所采取的措施。

Provide information on education (primary, secondary and tertiary) and information programmes that have been undertaken or are planned to strengthen appreciation and respect by the population, to keep the public broadly informed of the dangers threatening the heritage and of activities carried out in pursuance of the *Convention*. Does the State Party participate in the UNESCO Special Project *Young People's Participation in World Heritage Preservation and Promotion*?

Information on site-specific activities and programmes should be provided under item Ⅱ.4 concerning management, below.

1.6 Conclusions and recommendedaction

The main conclusions under each of the items of Section I of the report should be summarized and tabulated together with the proposed action(s) to be taken, the agency(ies) responsible for taking the action(s) and the timeframe for its execution:

    i)   Mainconclusions
    ii) Proposed futureaction(s)
    iii) Responsible implementing agency(ies)
    iv) Timeframe for implementation
    v) Needs for international assistance

States Parties are also encouraged to provide in their first periodic report an analysis of the process by which they ratified the *Convention,* the motivation, obstacles and difficulties encountered in that process and perceived benefits and lessons learnt.

说明已开展或规划中的教育（小学、中学和大学）和信息方案的基本情况，这些方案旨在加强群众欣赏和尊重遗产的能力，让公众了解遗产所面临的危险因素，及根据《公约》所采取的行动。指出缔约国是否参加了联合国教科文组织的特别项目"年轻人参与世界遗产的保护与宣传"。

根据下文与管理相关的第二.4 部分，提供各遗产地具体活动与方案的信息。

1.6 总结和建议采取的行动

应该总结本报告 I 部分内各条的主要结论，并与建议采取的行动、负责实施的机构和执行时间表一起制成表格：

（i）主要结论
（ii）建议采取的行动
（iii）负责实施的机构
（iv）执行时间表
（v）国际援助需求

鼓励缔约国在首次定期报告中，提供加入《公约》的过程分析，在该过程中得到的动力、遇到的障碍和困难，以及得到的经验和教训。

SECTION II:
STATE OF CONSERVATION OF SPECIFIC
WORLD HERITAGE PROPERTIES

The preparation of periodic state of conservation reports should involve those who are responsible for the day-to-day management of the property. For transboundary properties it is recommended that reports be prepared jointly by or in close collaboration between the agencies concerned.

The first periodic report should update the information provided in the original nomination dossier. Subsequent reports will then focus on any changes that may have occurred since the previous report was submitted.

This section of the periodic report follows, therefore, the format for the nomination dossier.

The state of properties included on the List of World Heritage in Danger are reviewed by the World Heritage Committee at regular intervals, in general once every year. This review concentrates on the specific factors and considerations that led to the inscription of the property on the List of World Heritage in Danger. It will still be necessary to prepare a complete periodic report on the state of conservation of these properties.

This section should be completed for each individual World Heritage property.

II.1 Introduction

　i) StateParty
　ii) Name of the World Heritage property
　iii) Geographical coordinates to the nearest second
　iv) Date of inscription on the World Heritage List
　v) Organization(s) or entity(ies) responsible for

第 II 部分:
具体世界遗产的保护现状

负责遗产日常管理的人员应参与编制保护状况定期报告的工作。如果是跨国遗产，建议相关机构共同编制报告或在编制报告的过程中紧密合作。

首次定期报告应更新原始申报材料内的信息。后续报告应着重说明上一个报告提交后所发生的变化。

定期报告的文本部分应遵循申报材料的格式。

世界遗产中心定期对《濒危世界遗产名录》内的遗产进行审查，一般是每年一次。着重审查导致遗产列入《濒危世界遗产名录》的具体原因和观察意见。除此之外，仍有必要编制完整的定期报告，说明遗产的保护状况。

应为每项世界遗产完整编制保护状况定期报告。

II.1 引言

　（i）缔约国
　（ii）世界遗产名称
　（iii）精确到秒的地理坐标
　（iv）列入《世界遗产名录》日期
　（v）编制报告的组织或机构

the preparation of the report

    vi) Date of the report

    vii)Signature on behalf of the State Party

Ⅱ.2 Statement of Outstanding UniversalValue

At the time of inscription of a property on the World Heritage List, the World Heritage Committee indicates its Outstanding Universal Value by deciding on the criteria for inscription. Please indicate the justification for inscription provided by the State Party, and the criteria under which the Committee inscribed the property on the World Heritage List.

In the view of the State Party, does the Statement of Outstanding Universal Value adequately reflect the Outstanding Universal Value of the property or is a re-submission necessary? This could be considered, for example, to recognise cultural values of a World Heritage property inscribed for its outstanding natural value, or vice-versa. This may become necessary either due to the substantive revision of the criteria by the World Heritage Committee or due to better identification or knowledge of specific Outstanding Universal Value of the property.

Another issue that might be reviewed here is whether the delimitation of the World Heritage property, and its buffer zone if appropriate, is adequate to ensure the protection and conservation of the Outstanding Universal Value embodied in it. A revision or extension of the boundaries might be considered in response to such a review.

If a Statement of Outstanding Universal Value is not available or incomplete, it will be necessary, in the first periodic report, for the State Party to propose such a statement. The Statement of Outstanding Universal Value should reflect the criterion (criteria) on the basis of which the Committee inscribed the property on the

（ⅵ）报告日期

（ⅶ）缔约国代表签名

Ⅱ.2 "突出普遍价值声明"

遗产列入《世界遗产名录》时，世界遗产委员会通过确定其列入的标准，指出其突出普遍价值。请说明缔约国提出的列入理由，以及委员会把该遗产列入《世界遗产名录》所遵循的标准。

从缔约国的角度来看，《突出的普遍价值声明》是否反映了该项遗产突出普遍价值，或者是否有必要再次提交？对于因其突出的自然价值而列入《名录》的世界遗产，可考虑明确其文化价值，反之亦然。由于世界遗产委员会对标准进行了大量修改，或缔约国对遗产具体的突出普遍价值有了更好的认识，这一做法变得极有必要。

此处审阅的另一个议题是世界遗产及其缓冲区的界定是否准确，是否足以确保遗产的突出普遍价值得以保护与保存。评审之后，是否要考虑修改或扩大范围。

如果《突出普遍价值声明》不恰当或不完整，缔约国有必要在其首次定期报告中提出该声明。《突出普遍价值声明》应该反映出委员会把该项遗产列入《世界遗产名录》所依据的标准，还应该回答以下问题：遗产代表的是什么，什么让该项遗产变得如此突出，是什么具

World Heritage List. It should also address questions such as: What does the property represent, what makes the property outstanding, what are the specific values that distinguish the property, what is the relationship of the property with its setting, etc.? Such Statement of Outstanding Universal Value will be examined by the Advisory Body(ies) concerned and transmitted to the World Heritage Committee for approval, if appropriate.

体的价值使它区别于其他遗产，该项遗产与其环境有何关系？相关的咨询机构将会审查此类"突出的普遍价值声明"，并提交世界遗产委员批准。

Ⅱ.3 Statement of authenticity and/or integrity

Ⅱ.3 真实性和/或完整性声明

Under this item it is necessary to review whether the value on the basis of which the property was inscribed on the World Heritage List, and reflected in the Statement of Outstanding Universal Value under item Ⅱ.2 above, are being maintained.

在本条中，有必要审查列入《世界遗产名录》的遗产所凭借的和二.2条"突出普遍价值声明"所反映的价值是否得以保持。

This should also include the issue of authenticity and/or integrity in relation to the property. What was the evaluation of the authenticity and/or integrity of the property at the time of inscription? What is the authenticity and/or integrity of the property at present?

这些应该包括在遗产的真实性和/或完整性议题之中。遗产列入时，对其真实性和/或完整性的评估内容是什么？目前该项遗产的真实性和/或完整性如何？

Please note that a more detailed analysis of the conditions of the property is required under item Ⅱ.6 on the basis of key indicators for measuring its state of conservation.

请注意：下面第二.6条中要求基于衡量保护状况的关键指标，更详细的分析遗产情况。

Ⅱ.4 Management

Ⅱ.4 管理

Under this item, it is necessary to report on the implementation and effectiveness of protective legislation at the national, provincial or municipal level and/or contractual or traditional protection as well as of management and/or planning control for the property concerned, as well as on actions that are foreseen for the future, to preserve the value described in the Statement of Outstanding Universal Value under item Ⅱ.2. Additional guidance on

根据本条，有必要报告国家、省或市级的相关保护法规，和/或合约或传统保护实践的实施情况及有效性，相关遗产管理和/或规划控制的实施情况和有效性，以及为保护第二.2条下"突出普遍价值声明"描述的价值而开展的行动。有关本议题的更多指导，请参阅《操作指南》第三.D部分。

this issue can be found in Section Ⅲ.D of the *Operational Guidelines*.

The State Party should also report on significant changes in the ownership, legal status and/or contractual or traditional protective measures, management arrangements and management plans as compared to the situation at the time of inscription or the previous periodic report. In such case, the State Party is requested to attach to the periodic report all relevant documentation, in particular legal texts, management plans and/or (annual) work plans for the management and maintenance of the property. Full name and address of the agency or person directly responsible for the property should also be provided.

The State Party could also provide an assessment of the human and financial resources that are available and required for the management of the property, as well as an assessment of the training needs for its staff.

The State Party is also invited to provide information on scientific studies, research projects, education, information and awareness building activities directly related to the property and to comment on the degree to which heritage values of the property are effectively communicated to residents, visitors and the public. Matters that could be addressed are, among other things: is there a plaque at the property indicating that the property is a World Heritage property? Are there educational programmes for schools? Are there special events and exhibitions? What facilities, visitor centre, site museum, trails, guides, information material etc. are made available to visitors? What role does the World Heritage designation play in all these programmes and activities?

Furthermore, the State Party is invited to provide statistical information, if possible on an

缔约国还应报告，与遗产列入时或上一个定期报告时相比，遗产在所有权、法律地位和／或合约或传统保护措施、管理安排和管理规划上发生的重大变化。在这种情况下，要求缔约国在定期报告后附上所有的相关文件，特别是法律文本、管理规划和／或遗产管理和维护（年度）工作规划。还应提供直接负责遗产管理的机构或个人的全称和地址。

缔约国还可提供对遗产管理所需的、可用人力和财政资源及工作人员培训需求的评估；

描述与遗产直接相关的科研项目、教育、信息和意识提升活动，评论遗产价值在居民、参观者和公众中有效宣传的程度。此处应主要说明以下事宜：是否有标志、标牌表明该遗产地是世界遗产，是否有针对学校的教育方案，是否有特别活动和展览，参观者可使用哪些设施、游客中心、博物馆、参观线路、导游、信息资料等，世界遗产称谓在所有这些方案和活动中所发挥的作用如何。

如有可能，缔约国还应在此提供年收入、参观人数、工作人员和其他相关事项的统计

annual basis, on income, visitor numbers, staff and other items if appropriate.

信息。

On the basis of the review of the management of the property, the State Party may wish to consider if a substantive revision of the legislative and administrative provisions for the conservation of the property is required.

根据遗产管理的评审结果，缔约国可能希望考虑，是否要对遗产保护的法律和行政条款做一些重大的修改。

II.5 Factors affecting the property

II.5 影响遗产的因素

Please comment on the degree to which the property is threatened by particular problems and risks. Factors that could be considered under this item are those that are listed in the nomination format, e.g. development pressure, environmental pressure, natural disasters and preparedness, visitor/tourism pressure, number of inhabitants.

请针对遗产受某些问题或风险的威胁程度做出评论。本条可考虑的因素是下列申报表格中的因素，如开发压力、环境压力、灾害预防、参观/旅游压力和居民人数。

Considering the importance of forward planning and risk preparedness, provide relevant information on operating methods that will make the State Party capable of counteracting dangers that threaten or may endanger its cultural or natural heritage. Problems and risks to be considered could include earthquakes, floods, land-slides, vibrations, industrial pollution, vandalism, theft, looting, changes in the physical context of properties, mining, deforestation, poaching, as well as changes in land-use, agriculture, road building, construction activities, tourism. Areas where improvement would be desirable, and towards which the State Party is working should be indicated.

考虑到远期规划和风险管理的重要性，需要缔约国提供应对危害其文化或自然遗产的各种危险因素所采取的措施的相关信息。危险因素包括：地震、洪水、山崩、震动、工业污染、蓄意破坏、盗窃、掠夺、遗产物理环境的变化、采矿、滥伐森林、非法捕猎以及用地变化、农业、修路、建筑施工和旅游。应同时指出应对工作中待改进之处和缔约国的工作目标。

This item should provide up-to-date information on all factors which are likely to affect or threaten the property. It should also relate those threats to measures taken to deal with them.

本条中应提供更新可能影响或威胁遗产的各种因素的信息，同时将这些威胁因素与应对措施联系起来。

An assessment should also be given if the impact of these factors on the property is increasing

应评估上述因素对遗产的影响程度的变化，指出采取了哪些有效的应对措施和未来计划采

or decreasing and what actions to address them have been effectively taken or are planned for the future.

取的措施。

Ⅱ.6 Monitoring

Ⅱ.6 监测

Whereas item Ⅱ.3 of the periodic report provides an overall assessment of the maintenance of the Outstanding Universal Value of the property, this item analyses in more detail the conditions of the property on the basis of key indicators for measuring its state of conservation.

定期报告的第二.3条对遗产的突出普遍价值进行了全面的评估。在本条中，应根据衡量保护状况的关键指标更详细地分析遗产情况。

If no indicators were identified at the time of inscription of the property on the World Heritage List, this should be done in the first periodic report. The preparation of a periodic report can also be an opportunity to evaluate the validity of earlier identified indicators and to revise them, if necessary.

如果在遗产列入《世界遗产名录》时尚未确定指标，则应在首次定期报告中明确各项指标。编制定期报告也应评估以往使用指标的有效性。必要时，应对指标作出修改。

Up-to-date information should be provided in respect to each of the key indicators. Care should be taken to ensure that this information is as accurate and reliable as possible, for example by carrying out observations in the same way, using similar equipment and methods at the same time of the year and day.

提供每个关键指标的最新信息。注意尽可能地确保这些信息的准确度和可靠性，比如，使用同样的方式进行观察，在每年、每日的同一时间，使用同样的设备和方法。

Indicate which partners if any are involved in monitoring and describe what improvement the State Party foresees or would consider desirable in improving the monitoring system.

指出哪些合作伙伴（ 如果有 ）参与了监测工作，描述预见到的改善，或利于改进监测体系的方法。

In specific cases, the World Heritage Committee and/or its Bureau may have already examined the state of conservation of the property and made recommendations to the State Party, either at the time of inscription or afterwards. In such cases the State Party is requested to report on the actions that have been taken in response to the observations or recommendations made by the Bureau or

在某些情况，世界遗产委员会和 /或其理事会可能已检查过遗产的保护状况，并在遗产列入时或列入后向缔约国提出了改进的建议。在这种情况下，要求缔约国报告为应对理事会或委员会提出建议而采取的相应措施。

Committee.

Ⅱ.7 Summary of conclusions and recommended actions

The main conclusions under each of the items of the state of conservation report, in particular, whether the Outstanding Universal Value of the property are maintained, should be summarized and tabulated together with:

i) Main conclusions regarding the state of the Outstanding Universal Value of the property (see items Ⅱ.2. and Ⅱ.3.above)

ii) Main conclusions regarding the management and factors affecting the property (see Items Ⅱ.4 and Ⅱ.5. above)

iii) Proposed future action(s)

iv) Responsible implementing agency(ies)

v) Timeframe for implementation

vi) Needs for international assistance

The State Party is also requested to indicate what experience the State Party has obtained that could be relevant to others dealing with similar problems or issues. Please provide names and contact details of organizations or specialists who could be contacted for this purpose.

Ⅱ.7 监测结果总结和建议采取的行动

应该总结保护状况报告内的各条主要结论，特别是遗产的突出的普遍价值是否得以保持，并把这些信息与以下内容一起编成表格：

（ⅰ）与遗产的突出的普遍价值状况相关的主要结论（见上文的第Ⅱ.2和Ⅱ.3条）

（ⅱ）涉及管理及影响遗产的因素的主要结论（见第Ⅱ.4和Ⅱ.5.条）

（ⅲ）建议采取的行动

（ⅳ）负责实施的机构

（ⅴ）实施时间表

（ⅵ）国际援助需求

还要求缔约国说明保护管理中获得的、处理此类问题相关的经验，并提供与之相关的组织或专家的姓名和联系方式。

Annex 8
INTERNATION ASSZSTANCE REQUEST FORM

• The International Assistance request form is available at the following Web address: http://whc.unesco.org/en/intassistance , and can be filled at the same address.

• Further guidance on International Assistance can be found in Section VII of the *Operational Guidelines*

• See attached Explanatory Notes on completing this Request form

• The original signed version of the completed International Assistance request form should be sent in English or French to:

UNESCO World Heritage Centre
7, place de Fontenoy 75352 Paris 07 SP
France
Telephone: +33 (0)1 45 68 12 76
Fax: +33 (0)1 45 68 55 70
E-mail: wh-intassistance@unesco.org

1. STATEPARTY

_____
_____

2. TITLE OFPROJECT

_____
_____

3. TYPE OFASSISTANCE

附件 8
《国际援助申请表》

·登录以下网址下载《国际援助申请表》：http：//whc.unesco.org/en/intassistance

·更多有关国际援助的指导说明，请参阅《操作指南》的第七章。

·参见所附的申请表填报须知。

·应将完整填写的英文或法文的国际援助申请表原件递交至：

联合国教科文组织世界遗产中心地址：
7, place de Fontenoy 75352 Paris 07 SP
France
电话：+33（0）1 45 68 12 76
传真：+33（0）1 45 68 55 70
电子邮箱：wh-intassistance@unesco.org

1. 缔约国

_____
_____

2. 项目名称

_____
_____

3. 援助类型

	Emergency Assistance	*Preparatory Assistance*	*Conservation and management*
Culture			
Nature			
Mixed			

	紧急援助	筹备性援助	保护与管理
文化			
自然			
混合			

4. PROJECT LOCATION:

a)　Will the project be implemented at a World Heritage property?

□ -yes　　□ -no

If yes, give the name of the property

_____

_____

b)　Will the project include a field component?

□ -yes　　□ - no

If yes, where and how?

_____

_____

c)　If the project is being implemented at a World Heritage property, indicate whether it will also benefit other World Heritage properties, and if so, which ones and how?

5. TIMEFRAME FOR THE IMPLEMENTATION OF THE PROJECT (indicate whether estimated or fixed)

Dates:_____

_____

Duration:_____

_____

6. THE PROJECT IS:

□ -local

□ -national

□ - sub-regional involving a few States Parties from a region

□ - regional involving most States Parties from a region

□ - international involving States Parties from different regions

4. 项目地点：

a）该项目是否会在一处世界遗产地实施？

□ 是 □ 否

如果答案为"是"，提供遗产名称：

_____

_____

b）该项目是否包括野外活动部分？

□ 是 □ 否

如果答案为"是"，提供地点和方式：

_____

_____

c）如果该项目在世界遗产地实施，请说明其他世界遗产是否也能受益。如果是，请说明受益的遗产以及具体受益方式？

5. 项目实施时间表（请说明是预计或确切时间表）

日期：_____

_____

时长：_____

_____

6. 项目类型为：

□ 地方性活动

□ 国家性活动

□ 涉及某一区域少数几个缔约国的次区域性活动

□ 涉及某一区域的多数缔约国的区域性活动

□ 涉及不同地区的众多缔约国的国际性活动

If the project is national, sub-regional, regional or international, please indicate the countries/ properties which will participate/benefit from the project:

_____
_____
_____
_____
_____
_____
_____

如果该项目为次区域性、区域性或国际性活动，请明确说明哪些国家或遗产将参加该项目，以及哪些遗产将从该项目中收益：

_____
_____
_____
_____
_____
_____
_____

7. JUSTIFICATION OF THEPROJECT

a) Explain why this project isneeded
(for Emergency Assistance, please fill in item 8 below instead).

_____
_____
_____
_____

7. 项目原因

a）说明需实施该项目的理由（如申请紧急援助，请省略此项，填写第八项）

_____
_____
_____
_____

b) List all supporting documents submitted, if applicable.

_____
_____
_____
_____

b）如有可能，请列举已提交的、能支持项目实施理由的文件

_____
_____
_____
_____

8. FOR EMERGENCY ASSISTANCE ONLY

a) Describe the actual or potential threat/ danger affecting the property

_____
_____
_____

8. 仅限紧急援助申请

a）描述遗产面临的已知或潜在威胁

_____
_____
_____

b) Indicate how it might affect the property's Outstanding Universal Value

_____

_____

_____

_____

c) Explain how the proposed project will address the threat/danger

_____

_____

_____

_____

9. OBJECTIVES OF THE PROJECT

Clearly set out the specific objectives of the project

10. EXPECTED RESULTS

a) Clearly state the results expected from the project

_____

_____

_____

_____

b) Define the indicators and means of verification which can be used to assess the achievements of these results:

Expected Results	Indicators	Means of verification

11. WORKPLAN
(including specific activities and timetable)

b）指出这种威胁对遗产突出的普遍价值的影响

_____

_____

_____

_____

c）解释该项目消除这种威胁或危险的方法

_____

_____

_____

_____

9. 项目目标

详细说明该项目的具体目标。

10. 预期结果

a）清晰说明项目的预期结果

_____

_____

_____

_____

b）定义能够评估预期结果的指标和验证方法

预期结果	指标	验证方法

Ⅱ. 项目计划
（包括具体活动和时间表）

Activities	Timeframe (in months)					
Activity						
Activity						
Activity						
Activity						

活动	时间表（月份）					
活动						
活动						
活动						
活动						

12. EVALUATION AND REPORTING

(to be submitted to the World Heritage Centre within three months after the project is completed)

13. PROFILES OF SPECIALISTS, TRAINERS, TECHNICIANS AND/OR SKILLED LABOUR, IF THE PROJECT FORESEES THE PARTICIPATION OF SUCH PEOPLE (if the identity of the specialists, trainers, technicians, and/or skilled labourers is already known, please state their names and include a brief CV if possible)

14. KEY TARGET AUDIENCES, INCLUDING PROFILES OF TRAINEES / PARTICIPANTS, IF THE PROJECT FORESEES THE PARTICIPATION OF SUCH PEOPLE

15. BUDGET BREAKDOWN

a) Provide, in the following table (in United States dollars), a detailed breakdown of costs of the individual elements of the project including, if possible, unit costs and show how these will be shared between the different funding sources.

12. 评估与报告

（应在项目结束三个月之内提交给世界遗产中心）

13. 可能参加此项活动的专家、培训人员、技术人员和 / 或技工的简介（如果已知上述人员身份，请陈述其姓名。如有可能，应提供个人简历）

14. 项目主要受众（包括受训人员和参与者的简介）

15. 详细预算

a）请在下表中（以美元为单位）提供项目各个组成部分所需的详细预算。如有可能，提供单位成本，并展示不同资金来源分担这些费用的情况。

Items (choose items as applicable to the project)	Detail US$ (for applicable items)	State Party Funds US$	Amount requested to the World Heritage Fund US$	Other sources US$	Total US$
Organization • venue • officeexpenses • secretarial assistance • translation • simultaneous interpretation • audio-visual equipment • other	US$____/dayfor____days=US$____ US$____ US$ /dayfor____days-US$____ US$____/pagefor____pages = US$ US$____/hourfor____hours = US$ US$____/dayfor____days=US$____ US$____				
Personnel / consultancy service (fees) • internationalexpert • nationalexpert • coordinator • other	US$____/ week for____weeks = US$ _ US$____/ week for____weeks = US$ _ US$____/ week for____weeks = US$ _ US$____/ week for____weeks = US$ _				
Travel • international travelcost • domestic travelcosts • other	US$____ US$____ US$____				
Daily subsistence allowance • accommodation • board	US$____/dayfor____persons=US$____ US$____/dayfor____persons =US$____				
Equipment • …… • ……	US$____/unitfor____units = US$____/unitfor____units=				
Evaluation, Reporting and Publication • evaluation • reporting • editing,layout • printing • distribution • other	US$____ US$____ US$____ US$____ US$____ US$____				
Miscellaneous • visas • other	US$____for____participants=US$____ US$____				
TOTAL					

项目 （选择适用的项目）	具体金额（美元） （选择适用的项目）	缔约国 资金 （美元）	向世界遗 产基金申 请数额 （美元）	其他资金 来源 （美元）	小计 （美元）
组织 活动场所 办公费用 文秘协理费 笔译费 同声传译费 影音设备费 其他	每天＿＿美元，共＿＿天 =＿＿美元 ＿＿美元 每天＿＿美元，共＿＿天 =＿＿美元 每页＿＿美元，共＿＿页 =＿＿美元 每小时＿＿美元，共＿＿小时 =＿＿ 美元 每天＿＿美元，共＿＿天 =＿＿美元 ＿＿美元				美元
人员／咨询服务 国际专家 国内专家 协调人员 其他	每周＿＿美元，共＿＿周 =＿＿美元 每周＿＿美元，共＿＿周 =＿＿美元 每周＿＿美元，共＿＿周 =＿＿美元 每周＿＿美元，共＿＿周 =＿＿美元				美元
差旅费 国际旅行费用 国内旅行费用 其他	＿＿美元 ＿＿美元 ＿＿美元				美元
每日生活补助 餐饮 住宿	每日＿＿人＿＿美元 =＿＿美元 每日＿＿人＿＿美元 =＿＿美元				美元
设备 …… ……	每台＿＿美元，共＿＿台 =＿＿美元 每台＿＿美元，共＿＿台 =＿＿美元				美元
评估、报告与出版发行 评估 报告 编辑、排版 印刷 发行 其他	＿＿美元 ＿＿美元 ＿＿美元 ＿＿美元 ＿＿美元 ＿＿美元				美元
其他杂费 签证 其他费用	共＿＿参加人员＿＿美元 =＿＿美元 ＿＿美元				美元
合计					美元

b) Specify whether or not resources from the State Party or other sources are already available or when they are likely to become available.

_____

_____

b）指明是否已经或可能从缔约国或其他渠道获取资源

_____

_____

16. IN KIND CONTRIBUTIONS FROM THE STATE PARTY AND OTHER AGENCIES

a) National agency(ies)

_____

_____

16. 缔约国或其他机构的实物捐赠

a）国家机构

_____

_____

b) Other bi/multi-lateral organizations, donors, etc

_____

_____

b）其他双边 / 多边组织、捐赠机构等

_____

_____

17. AGENCY(IES) RESPONSIBLE FOR THE IMPLEMENTATION OF THE PROJECT

_____

_____

17. 负责项目实施的机构

_____

_____

18. SIGNATURE ON BEHALF OF STATE PARTY

Fullname

_____

Title

_____

Date

_____

18. 缔约国代表签字

全名

_____

头衔

_____

日期

_____

19. ANNEXES

_____(number of annexes attached to therequest)

19. 附件

_____（附件编号）

EXPLANATORY NOTES

填报须知

	INTERNATIONAL ASSISTANCE APPLICATION FORM	EXPLANATORY NOTES
1.	STATE PARTY	Name of the State Party presenting the International Assistance request
2.	TITLE OF THE PROJECT	
3.	TYPE OF ASSISTANCE	See Paragraph 241 of the *Operational Guidelines* for details. Indicate the type of assistance you are requesting, as well as the type of heritage covered by the project. Please, tick only one box in the table. For example: Training project on rock paintings:

Section 3 form table:

	Emergency Assistance	Preparatory Assistance	Conservation and Management*
Culture			
Nature			
Mixed			

* Please note that « Conservation and Management » now includes the previous categories :
Training, Research Assistance
Technical Cooperation
Assistance for education, information and awareness raising

Explanatory notes example tables:

	Emergency Assistance	Preparatory Assistance	Conservation and Management
Culture			X
Nature			
Mixed			

Preparation of a nomination file for a mixed property:

	Emergency Assistance	Preparatory Assistance	Conservation and Management
Culture			
Nature			
Mixed		X	

Emergency assistance request following a tropical storm which affected a protected forest area:

	Emergency Assistance	Preparatory Assistance	Conservation and Management
Culture			
Nature	X		
Mixed			

	INTERNATIONAL ASSISTANCE APPLICATION FORM	EXPLANATORY NOTES
4.	PROJECT LOCATION Will the project be implemented at a World Heritage property? -yes ☐ -no If yes, give the name of the property Will the project include a field component? -yes ☐ - no If yes, where andhow? If the project is being implemented at a World Heritage property, indicate whether it will also benefit other World Heritage properties, and if so which ones and how?	

5.	TIMEFRAME FOR THE IMPLEMENTATION OF THE PROJECT (indicate whether estimated or fixed)	Indicate the proposed starting date for the project as well as its duration.
6.	THE PROJECT IS: local national sub-regional involving a few States Parties from a region regional involving most States Parties from a region international involving States Parties from different regions If the project is national, sub-regional, regional or international, please indicate the countries/properties which will participate/benefit from the project.）	If other countries benefit from the project, please state whether their support for the project has been obtained. Also note if a transboundary property is involved.
7.	JUSTIFICATION OF THE PROJECT a)　　Explain why the project isneeded (for Emergency Assistance, please fill in item 8 below instead)	decisions of the World Heritage Committee; recommendations of international expert missions undertaken at the request of the Committee, Chairperson or UNESCO; recommendations of the Advisory Bodies; recommendations of UNESCO World Heritage Centre or other UNESCO Divisions; management plans for the property; recommendations from previous activities supported by the World Heritage Fund. Clearly indicate which documents you are referring to (World Heritage Committee's decision number, Mission dates,etc…）
	b) List all supporting documents submitted, if applicable.	Whenever possible, support the justification with documentary evidence, such as reports, photographs, slides, maps, etc...
8	FOR EMERGENCY ASSISTANCE ONLY	
	a) Describe the actual or potential threat/danger affecting the property	Emergency Assistance funds will not be automatically granted after a major disaster has occurred. This type of assistance will be provided only in cases when an imminent danger related to a natural or human-made disaster is threatening the overall Outstanding Universal Value of a World Heritage property and its authenticity and/or integrity, to prevent or at least significantly mitigate its possible negative impact on the property. Emergency Assistance may also be provided to assess whether or not imminent danger is present, for example as a result of a major disaster. When, on the contrary, due to a disaster, a certain loss of heritage has already take nplace, but there is no more imminent threat or risk that needs to be addressed as a matter of urgency, other forms of assistance would appear to be more appropriate (e.g. conservation and management assistance).

	b) Indicate how it might affect the property's Outstanding Universal Value	In establishing priorities for granting Emergency Assistance, consideration will be given to whether the threat/danger to be addressed has the potential, if not mitigated, to affect the Outstanding Universal Value of the World Heritage property and its authenticity.
	c) Explain how the proposed project will address the threat/danger	Proposals for funding under the Emergency Assistance programme should set out how the scope of the project and its activities willassess the threat/danger to the World Heritage property and show how it will be effectively mitigated.
9	OBJECTIVE(S) OF THE PROJECT Clearly set out the specific objectives of the project	What are the objectives you want to achieve through the implementation of this particular project?
10	EXPECTED RESULTS	
	a) Clearly state the results expectedfrom the projectproposed.	The expected results should be concrete and measurable. Each expected result will be measured by a set of indicators (see Paragraph 10b).
	b) Define the indicators and means of verification which can be used to assess the achievements of these results: 	Expected Results	Indicators	Means of verification
				Indicators are used to measure the results achieved and to determine the progress towards the objective of the project. They are based on the expected results defined in Paragraph 10, and will serve as the base for the evaluation of the project after its completion. These indicators should be objective, measurable and expressed in quantifiable terms such as numeric values, or percentages. For example: Preparatory Assistance *Objective:* To prepare a complete nomination file for submission to the World Heritage Centre. | Expected Results	Indicators	Means of Verification
The completed nomination file submitted to the World Heritage Centre by 1 February 20xx.	•Nomination submitted by the deadline	•Postal record of sending the file •Report from the WHC/POL to the State Party
The completed management plan to be submitted along with the nomination file	•Management plan submitted by the deadline	•Postal record of sending the file •Report from the WHC/POL to the State Party	

Expected Results	Indicators	Means of Verification
The nomination file is judged complete by the World Heritage Centre and Advisory Bodies	●Successful examination by the World Heritage Centre and Advisory Bodies for completeness	●Letter from the World Heritage Centre to the State Party informing them the file is considered complete

Emergency Assistance

Objective:
To stabilize the structure of a building that has just been damaged due to flooding or an earthquake.

Expected Results	Indicators	Means of Verification
The structure of the building would have been stabilized	●Emergency structural problems identified ●Plans for emergency works finalized ●Temporary stabilization measures carried out	●Report of a structural engineer on the emergency state of the structure ●Costed proposal for emergency works to be carried out ●Final report of the stabilization work implemented
Plans for further conservation work would have been developed for future implementation	●Overall structural analysis carried out ●Costed plans for further necessary conservation work prepared	●Report of a structural engineer on the overall state of conservation of the structure ●Costed proposal for necessary conservation works to be carried out

10	b)	Conservation and Management Assistance
		Objective: To improve management at a property inscribed on the World Heritage List with special attention to community involvement

续表

10	b)		Expected Results	Indicators	Means of Verification
			An integrated management plan for the property	● Setting up of a management planning team for the development of the management plan with participants from the necessary sectors including the local community ● Completion of a Statement of Outstanding Universal Value for the property ● Analysis of the conservation and management problems affecting the property ● Existence of clear objectives and strategies for achieving them	● Monthly reports of the management planning team meetings ● Discussion papers produced by team members of each of the key issues faced in the management of the property ● Final management plan document
			A management committee including some members of the local community	●Appointment of members of the management committee including at least two members of the local community At least 3 regular monthly meetings of the Management Committee	●Statutes and rules of procedure for the Management Committee approved by appropriate authorities ● Monthly reports of the Management Committee
			Management plan approved with appropriate legal status	●Approval by the local government authority	●Decree placed in the "National Gazette" establishing the management plan as a local regulation.

11	WORK PLAN (including specific activities and timetable)	Describe the work plan of the activity(ies) to be undertaken with specific reference to the expected results mentioned in Paragraph 10 above. Indicate dates, duration of each activity. For meetings and training activities, tentative programmes should be provided including the themes, issues and problems to be discussed.

WORK PLAN table (left cell):

Activities	Timeframe (in months)				
Activity					
Activity					
Activity					
Activity					

Right cell continued:

For example:

For Expected Result No. 1:

Activities	Timeframe (in months)							
Activity								
Activity								
Activity								
Activity								

For Expected Result No. 2:

Activities	Timeframe (in months)							
Activity								
Activity								
Activity								
Activity								

| 12 | EVALUATION AND REPORTING (to be submitted to the World Heritage Centre within three months after the implementation of the project is completed) | Final Report: The final report should be prepared by the authority/person in charge of the implementation of the project. The final report should be structured according to the expected results defined in Paragraph 10.

Evaluation: The evaluation should focus on the results achieved and their impact on (for example): - the inscription of a property on the World Heritage List following a preparatory assistance, - the Periodic Report and the State of conservation, - the removal of a property from the List of World Heritage in danger following an emergency assistance, - the implementation of the World Heritage Convention, including its Strategic Objectives ("4Cs") and other strategies (e.g. Global Strategy, …), - the national and/or local institutions, - the capacity building of local staff, - the awareness raising of the general public, - the participants to the project, - attracting other resources, - etc…

Indicate who will be responsible for the evaluation of the project. |
|---|---|---|

13	PROFILES OF SPECIALISTS, TRAINERS, TECHNICIANS AND/OR SKILLED LABOUR, IF THE PROJECT FORESEES THE PARTICIPATION OF SUCH PEOPLE (if the identity of the specialists, trainers, technicians, and/or skilled labourers is already known, please state their names and include a brief CV if possible)	Indicate the precise field of specialization and the work to be undertaken by each specialist as well as the duration required. The World Heritage Centre and the Advisory Bodies are available to recommend resource persons / trainers, should the State(s) Party(ies) concerned so request. Please include the names of any specialists, if already known, who will be taking part in the project and send a short CV if possible as an annex to the request form.
14	KEY TARGET AUDIENCES, INCLUDING PROFILES OF TRAINEES / PARTICIPANTS, IF THE PROJECT FORESEES THE PARTICIPATION OF SUCH PEOPLE	Indicate the target groups and beneficiaries of the project, their professions, institutions, or field(s) of specialization.
15	BUDGET BREAKDOWN	
	a) Provide, in the following table (in United States dollars), a detailed breakdown of costs of the individual elements of the project including, if possible, unit costs and show how these will be shared between the different funding sources:	Indicate in the table the breakdown of all expenses related to the project, also indicating the cost-sharing between the various donors (State Party, World Heritage Fund, others).
	(i) Organization	Items within this section could include the cost of a venue, office expenses, secretarial assistance, translation, simultaneous interpretation, audio-visual equipment, or other organizational costs necessary for the successful implementation of the project.
	(ii) Personnel and Consultancy Services	Items within this section could include the cost of international experts, national experts, a local or international coordinator, or other personnel necessary for the successful implementation of the project.
	(iii) Travel	Items within this section could include the cost of international or domestic travel necessary for the successful implementation of the project.
	(iv) Daily Subsistence Allowance	Items within this section could include the cost of accommodation, meals, and incidentals necessary for the successful implementation of the project.
	(v) Equipment	Items within this section could include any equipment necessary for the successful implementation of the project.
	(vi) Evaluation, Reporting and Publication	Items within this section could include the cost of evaluation, reporting, editing and layout, printing, distribution, and other costs necessary for the successful implementation of the project.
	(vii) Miscellaneous	Items within this section could include the cost of visas or other small costs that are necessary for the successful implementation of the project.

续表

	b) Specify whether or not resources from the State Party or other sources are already available or when they are likely to become available	If the resources are not already available, indicate whether they will be before the beginning of the project.
16	IN KIND CONTRIBUTIONS FROM THE STATE PARTY AND OTHER AGENCIES	
	a) National agency(ies)	Specify in detail
	b) Other bi/multilateral organizations, donors, etc	Specify in detail
17	AGENCY(IES) RESPONSIBLE FOR THE IMPLEMENTATION OF THE PROJECT	Please provide the name, title, address and all contact details of the person/agency(ies) who will be responsible for the implementation of the project as well as those of any other participating agencies. Please, indicate whether the legislative and administrative commitment of the State Party is available for the project (see Paragraph 239d of the *Operational Guidelines*).
18	SIGNATURE ON BEHALF OF STATE PARTY	Full name Title Date
19	ANNEXES	In this section, list the number of annexes attached to the request and titles of each annex.

	国际援助申请格式	填报须知
1	缔约国	提出国际援助申请的缔约国名称
2	项目名称	
3	援助类型 （表格）紧急援助／预备援助／保护与管理* 文化 自然 混合 * 请注意，保护与管理一项现包括之前下列类别： 培训与研究援助 技术合作援助 教育、信息与意识提升援助	具体内容请参见《操作指南》第241条。 应指明所申请援助类型以及该项目涉及的遗产类型。仅选择表格中的一项内容，如： 岩画培训项目 （表格）紧急援助／预备援助／保护与管理 文化 —— —— X 自然 混合 编制混合遗产的申报文件 （表格）紧急援助／预备援助／保护与管理 文化 自然 混合 —— X —— ＿＿＿由于热带风暴影响了保护林区而申请紧急援助 （表格）紧急援助／预备援助／保护与管理 文化 自然 X —— —— 混合
4	项目地点 该项目是否会在一处世界遗产地实施？ 是□ 否 如果答案为"是"，提供遗产名称： 该项目是否包括野外活动部分？ 是□ 否 如果答案为"是"，提供地点和方式： 如果该项目在世界遗产地实施，请说明其他世界遗产是否也能受益。如果是，请说明受益遗产以及具体受益方式?	
5	项目时间表（请说明是预计或确切时间表）	说明项目计划开始的日期及持续时间。
6	项目类型为： 地方性活动 国家性活动 涉及某一区域少数几个缔约国的次区域性活动 涉及某一区域的多数缔约国的区域性活动 涉及不同地区的众多缔约国的国际性活动 如果该项目为国家性次区域性、区域性或国际性活动，请明确说明哪些国家将参加该项目以及哪些遗产将从该项目中获益。	如果其他国家也能从中受益，说明是否已经获得它们对项目的支持。 同时说明是否涉及跨境遗产。

	国际援助申请格式	填报须知
7	项目原因	
	a）说明需实施该项目的理由（如申请紧急援助，请省略此项，填写第八项）	阐明将要讨论或解决的问题。应尽量说明举办这些活动的紧迫程度。 如有涉及，应详细描述遗产面对的已知或潜在威胁，篇幅不超过两页。 解释此项活动将如何有益于实施： 世界遗产委员会的决议； 委员会、主席或联合国教科文组织委派的国际专家工作组的建议； 咨询机构的建议； 联合国教科文组织世界遗产中心以及其他部门的建议； 与遗产有关的管理规划建议； 世界遗产基金支持的、在世界遗产地或缔约国举行的、以往活动中制定出的指导方针。 应明确指出所参考的文件（世界遗产委员会的决定号码、代表团日期等等）
	b）如有可能，请列举已提交的能支持项目实施理由的文件	如有可能，提供各种形式文献说明如报告、照片、幻灯片、地图册等。
8	紧急援助申请	
	a）描述遗产面对的已知或潜在的威胁或危险	并非发生了重大灾难就会自动拨付紧急救助基金。只有当自然或人为灾难对世界遗产的突出普遍价值、真实性和／或完整性带来紧急威胁时，才会提供这种援助，用以避免或大幅降低可能对遗产造成的负面影响。 紧急援助也可用来评估重大灾难等是否带来了紧急威胁。 如果灾难已经给遗产带来了一定损失，但目前没有需要紧急处理的威胁或危险，申请其他类型的援助更为恰当（如保护与管理援助）。
	b）指出这种威胁对遗产的突出普遍价值的影响	在决定给予紧急援助时，应考虑该威胁／危险如果得不到缓解，是否有可能影响世界遗产的突出普遍价值、完整性和／或真实性。
	c）解释该项目消除这种威胁或危险的方法	申请紧急援助时，应阐明项目及其范围，评估世界遗产面临的威胁／危险的方式，以及有效缓解该威胁／危险的方法。
9	项目目标 清晰说明该项目的具体目标	希望通过实施该项目达成什么目标？
10	预期结果	
	a）清晰说明该项目的预期结果	预期结果应该具体且可衡量。每个预期结果都需要通过一组指标来衡量（见10b条）。
	b）定义能够评估预期结果的指标和验证方法 | 预期结果	指标	验证方法 | |---|---|---| | | | | | | | |	指标用于衡量取得的成果并判断项目目标的进展。这些指标基于第10条定义的预计结果，并将作为项目完成后评估的基础。 指标应客观、可衡量，以数值或百分比等量化的方式表示。 例如： 筹备性援助 目标：编制完整的申报文件提交给世界遗产中心

续表

国际援助申请格式	填报须知
b）定义能够评估预期结果的指标和验证方法 	预期结果	指标	验证方法
---	---	---
				<table>...</table>

预期结果表（填报须知）：

预期结果	指标	验证方法
于20xx年2月1日前向世界遗产中心提交完整的申报文件	在截至日期前提交申报文件	- 提交文件的邮政记录 - 世界遗产中心、政策及法律咨询部门给缔约国的报告
同时提交完整的管理规划	在截至日期前提交管理规划	- 提交文件的邮政记录 - 世界遗产中心、政策及法律咨询部门给缔约国的报告
世界遗产中心及咨询机构判定申报文件完整	世界遗产中心及咨询机构判定申报文件完整	- 世界遗产中心发给缔约国、通知缔约国文件完整的信件

紧急援助
目标：对因洪水或地震受损的建筑物结构进行加固

预期结果	指标	验证方法
稳定建筑物结构	- 确定紧急的结构问题 - 制定紧急工作计划 - 实施临时稳定措施	- 结构工程师关于结构紧急情况的报告 - 包含所需紧急工作预算的报告 - 稳定工作实施的最终报告
制定未来保护工作计划	- 完成全面的结构分析 - 制定包含未来所需保护工作预算价格的计划	- 结构工程师关于结构整体保护情况的报告 - 包含未来所需保护工作预算的报告

保护与管理援助
目标：改善世界遗产的管理，尤其注重社区参与

续表

国际援助申请格式	填报须知

	预期结果	指标	验证方法
	制定遗产管理综合规划	- 成立管理规划编制团队，成员包括当地社区等各相关领域的人员 - 编制完成遗产的《突出普遍价值声明》 - 分析影响遗产的保护与管理的问题 - 拥有清晰的目标以及实现目标的策略	- 项目规划团队会议的月报 - 团队成员编制的关于遗产管理中各关键问题的讨论文件 - 管理规划文件定稿
	成立包括当地社区人员在内的管理委员会	- 指定管理委员会成员，其中至少两名成员来自当地社区 - 至少召开三次管理委员会月度会议	- 管理委员会的法律法规被相关机构批准 - 管理委员会的月报
	管理规划获得适当的法律地位	- 获当地政府机构批准	- 国家公报刊载政令，确立该管理规划为当地法规

11	项目计划 （包括具体活动和时间表） 	活动	时间表（月份）					
活动						
活动						
活动						
活动								描述活动的计划，标明上文第 10 条中的预期结果。说明每一项活动的日期及持续时间。如果是会议、培训活动，应提供主题、议题等内容。如： 旨在取得第一项预期结果的活动： （时间表 月份） 旨在取得第二项预期结果的活动： （时间表 月份）

	国际援助申请格式	填报须知
12	评估与报告 （应在项目完成三个月内提交给世界遗产中心）	总结报告： 总结报告应由项目实施负责人编写，报告结构应遵循第 10 条中的预期结果。 评估： 评估应主要针对所取得的成果及产生的影响，如对下列内容的影响： 申请预备援助后，遗产列入《世界遗产名录》 定期报告及保护情况 申请紧急援助后，遗产从《濒危世界遗产名录》中删除 -《世界遗产公约》及其战略目标（4C）和其他战略（如全球战略）实施的情况 国家和 / 或当地机构 当地人员的能力建设 大众的意识提升 项目参与者 吸引其他资源，等 指定项目评估负责人。
13	可能参加此项活动的专家、培训人员、技术人员和 / 或技工的简介 （如果已知上述人员身份，请提供其姓名。如有可能，应提供个人简历）	明确说明各个专家的专业领域、承担的工作以及所需工作时间。如缔约国发出请求，世界遗产中心与专家咨询机构可以为活动推荐专家顾问 / 培训人员。 请提供已确定参加该项目的专家的姓名。如有可能，将其简历以附件形式与申请表一并提交。
14	项目主要受众（包括受训人员和参与者的简介）	说明项目的目标群体与受益人以及他们的职业、所属机构或专业领域。
15	详细预算	
	a）提供下列各项目的费用（以美元为单位），如可能，应包括单位成本以及不同资金来源分担这些成本的情况：	请在表中提供项目全部费用的详细预算，并说明不同资金来源（缔约国、世界遗产基金会、其他）分担这些费用的情况。
	（ⅰ）组织	该项包括活动地点、办公费用，如影印费、文具费、文秘协理费用、笔译费、口译费、影音设备费用以及项目实施所需的其他必要的组织费用。
	（ⅱ）人员与咨询服务	该项包括支付给国际、国内专家、协调人员费用以及项目实施所需的其他人员费用。
	（ⅲ）差旅费	该项包括项目实施所需的国际或国内旅行费用。
	（ⅳ）每日生活补助	该项包括项目实施所需的住宿、餐饮等相关费用。
	（ⅴ）设备	该项包括项目实施所需的设备费用。
	（ⅵ）评估、报告与出版	该项包括项目实施所需的评估、报告、编辑、排版、印刷、发行等费用。
	（ⅶ）其他杂费	该项包括项目实施所需的签证费等小额费用。
	b）详细说明缔约国或其他来源的资源是否已到位或在争取中	如果资源目前仍未到位，说明在项目实施时是否可以到位。

	国际援助申请格式	填报须知
16	缔约国或其他机构的实物捐赠	
	a）国家机构捐赠	请详细说明。
	b）其他双边或多变组织、捐赠机构等	请详细说明。
17	负责项目实施的机构	请提供负责项目实施的人员或机构的姓名、职位、地址、详细联系信息，以及其他参与机构的详细信息。请说明缔约国是否对该项目提供了立法或行政方面的支持（见《操作指南》第239d条）。
18	缔约国代表签字	姓名：职位：日期：
19	附件	列出援助申请附件的编号及名称。

Process of submission for International Assistance requests for Conservation & Management Assistance and Preparatory Assistance above US$ 5,000

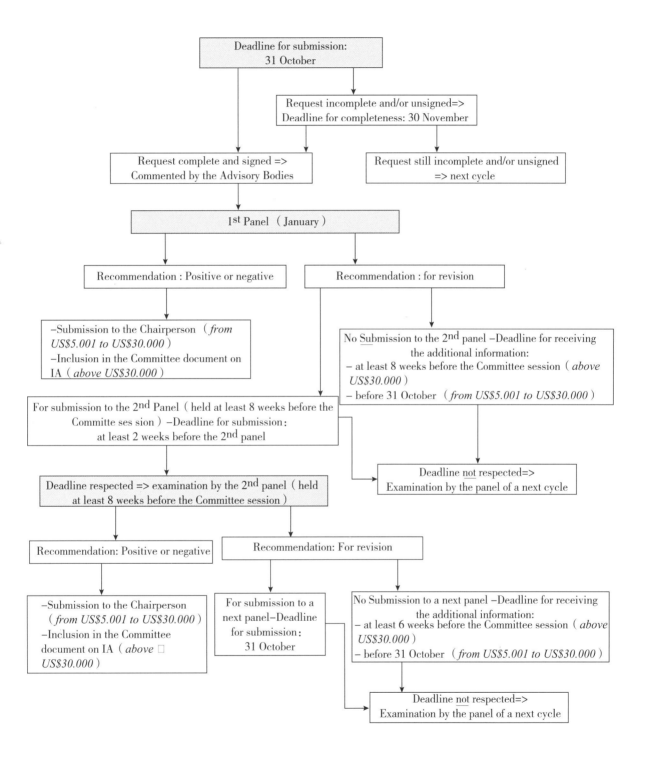

5000美元以上保护和管理国际援助及筹备性援助申请程序

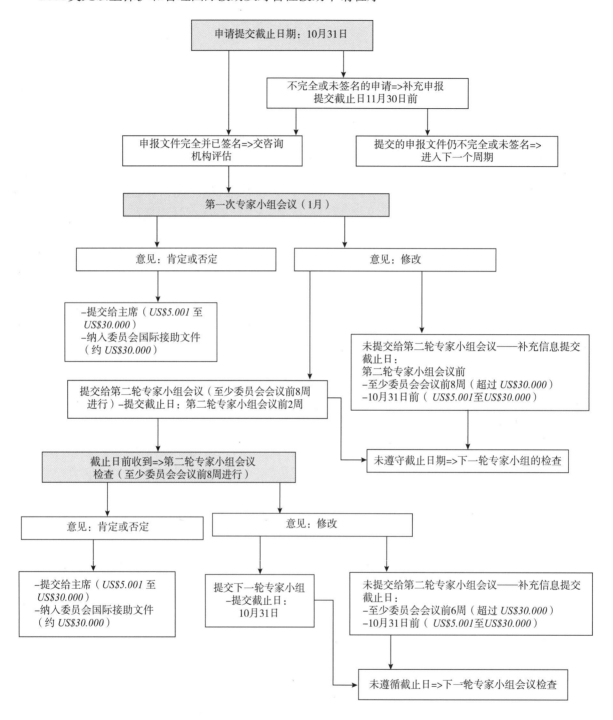

Annex 9

EVALUATION CRITERIA OF THE ADVISORY BODIES FOR INTERNATIONAL ASSISTANCE REQUESTS

The following considerations are to be taken into account by the Advisory Bodies, World Heritage Centre, and the relevant Decision-maker (the Chairperson of the World Heritage Committee, the World Heritage Committee or the Director of the World Heritage Centre) when assessing International Assistance requests.

These items do not constitute a checklist, and not every item will be applicable to every International Assistance Request. Rather the appropriate items are to be considered together in an integrated manner in making balanced judgments concerning the appropriateness of allocating the limited financial support available through the World Heritage Fund.

A. Eligibility requirements

1. Is the State Party in arrears for payment of its cont ribution to the World Heritage Fund?

2. Is the request coming from an authorized organization/institution of the State Party?

B. Priority considerations

3. Is the request from a State Party on the list of the Least Developed Countries (LDCs), Low Income Economies (LIEs), Small Island Developing States (SIDS) or post-conflictcountries?

4. Is the property on the List of World Heritage in Danger?

附件 9

专家咨询机构评估国际援助申请的标准

咨询机构、世界遗产中心以及相关决策方（世界遗产委员会主席、世界遗产委员会或世界遗产中心主任）对国际援助申请进行评估时，将考虑下列因素。

这些内容并非全部考虑因素，也不一定适用于每一份《国际援助申请》。确切地说，在考虑合理分配世界遗产基金提供的有限资金时，需要通盘考察全部适合的项目，方可做出均衡判断。

A. 资格要求

1. 缔约国是否拖欠给世界遗产基金支付的捐款？

2. 申请是否由缔约国授权的组织或机构提交？

B. 优先考虑因素

3. 申请援助的缔约国是否为最不发达国家、低收入国家、低水平中等收入国家、小岛屿发展中国家或冲突后国家？

4. 遗产是否列入了《濒危世界遗产名录》？

5. Does the request further one or more of the Strategic Objectives of the World Heritage Committee (Credibility, Conservation, Capacity building, and Communication)?

6. Does the request respond to needs identified through the Periodic Reporting process at the property and/or regional levels?

7. Is the request linked to a regional or sub-regional capacity building programme?

8. Is there a capacity building aspect to the activity (no matter what type of assistance sought)?

9. Will the lessons learned from the activity provide benefits tothe larger World Heritage system?

C. Considerations linked to the specific content of the proposed activity

10. Are the objectives of the request clearly stated and achievable?

11. Is there a clear work plan for achieving the results, including a timeline for its implementation? Is the work plan reasonable?

12. Does the agency/organization responsible for implementing the proposal have the capacity to do so, and is there a responsible person identified for ongoing contacts?

13. Are the professionals proposed to be used (whether national or international) qualified to carry out the work being requested? Are there clear terms of reference for them, including adequate period of their involvement?

14. Is the involvement of all relevant parties

5. 援助申请是否能推动世界遗产委员会一项或多项战略目标（可信性、保护、能力建设与宣传）?

6. 援助申请是否满足定期报告过程中定位的遗产和／或地区的需求?

7. 援助申请是否涉及地区或次区域能力建设计划?

8. 活动（援助类型不限）是否涉及能力建设?

9. 活动经验是否对更大范围的世界遗产系统有益?

C. 与活动内容相关的考虑因素

10. 援助申请的目的是否清晰、可行?

11. 是否具有针对结果的、清晰的工作计划（包括项目实施的时间表）? 工作计划是否合理?

12. 负责项目实施的机构或组织是否具备实施能力? 有没有目前可以联系的负责人?

13. 申请援助的工作所提议聘请的（国内或国际）专家是否合格? 他们的职权范围以及参与时间是否清晰明了?

14. 提议中是否考虑到了所有相关方的参与

taken into account in the proposal (for example stakeholders, other institutions,etc.)?

15. Are the technical requirements clearly expressed and are they reasonable?

16. Is there a clear plan for reporting the results and for continued monitoring, including appropriate indicators for success?

17. Is there a commitment of the State Party for appropriate follow-up after the activity is completed?

D. Budgetary / Financial considerations

18. Is theover all budget reasonable for the work that is proposed to be carried out?

19. Is the budget detailed sufficiently to ensure that the unit costs are reasonable and in line with local costs and/or UNESCO norms and rules as appropriate?

20. Does the request act as a catalyst (multiplier) for other funding (are other sources of funding, either cash or in-kind clearly specified)?

E. Considerations for specific types of International Assistance

a) Emergency Assistance Requests

21. Does the threat or disaster covered by the request conform to the definition of an emergency within the *Operational Guidelines* (unexpected phenomena)?

22. Can the proposed intervention be carried out with reasonable safety for those involved with its implementation?

（如利益相关方、其他机构等）?

15. 是否明确表达了技术要求？这些要求是否合理？

16. 是否具备关于结果报告、后续监测以及相关指标的清晰计划？

17. 缔约国是否承诺，活动完成后采取适当的后续措施？

D. 预算 /财政考虑因素

18. 建议开展的工作的总体预算是否合理?

19. 预算是否足够详细？能否确保合理的单位成本？单位成本是否与本地成本相一致，并符合联合国教科文组织的规范和规则？

20. 援助申请能否催化（倍增效应）其他资金（是否清晰说明其他的资金来源现金或实物性质）?

E. 特定类型国际援助的注意事项

a）紧急援助申请

21. 申请中提到的威胁或灾难是否符合《操作指南》中定义的紧急情况（意外现象）?

22. 建议采用的干预措施能否在保证相关人员安全的情况下实施？

23. Does the intervention respond to the most critical issues related to the protection/conservation of the property?

b) Preparatory Assistance Requests
For requests for preparation of nomination files

24. Is the property on the State Party's Tentative List?

25. Does the State Party already have properties inscribed on the World Heritage List? If yes, how many?

26. Is the type of property proposed for World Heritage listing un-represented or under-represented in the World Heritage List?

27. Is sufficient attention paid to necessary elements, such as the preparation of the management plan, comparative analysis, Statement of Outstanding Universal Value, mapping, etc.?

28. Is sufficient attention given to community involvement?

For requests for preparation of Tentative Lists

29. Is the process designed to include all the necessary stakeholders and points of view?

30. Are both natural and cultural heritage professionals proposed to be involved?

31. Is the State Party new to the *World Heritage Convention*?

32. If the request is for harmonization of Tentative Lists, are representatives from all the necessary States Parties in the region or sub-region involved?

23. 干预措施是否解决了遗产保护或保存中最重要的问题？

b）筹备性援助申请
编制申报文件申请

24. 遗产是否已列入缔约国的《预备名录》？

25. 缔约国是否有列入《世界遗产名录》遗产？如果有，具体数量是多少？

26. 所申报的遗产类型是否在《世界遗产名录》没有代表或代表性不足？

27. 对编制管理规划、比较分析、《突出普遍价值声明》、地图等必要因素的关注是否充分？

28. 对社区参与的关注是否充分？

编制《预备名录》申请

29. 该过程是否包括所有必要的利益相关方，是否体现了不同观点？

30. 文化遗产专家和自然遗产专家是否均有参与？

31. 缔约国是否为新加入《世界遗产公约》的国家？

32. 如果申请的目的是协商《预备名录》，该地区或次区域所有缔约国是否均有代表参加？

For requests for preparation of other types of assistance

筹备申请其他类型援助

33. If the request is for the preparation of a request for other assistance, is the need for the eventual request well documented?

33. 如果申请的目的是筹备申请其他类型的援助，最终的申请需求是否有充足的文件记录？

c) *Conservation and Management Assistance Requests*

c）保护与管理援助申请

For requests for conservation work or the preparation of a management plan

保护工作或编制管理规划申请

34. Is the property on the World HeritageList?

34. 该遗产是否已列入《世界遗产名录》？

35. Is the work being proposed apriority for protecting or safeguarding the property?

35. 所提议的工作是否在保护遗产方面应优先开展？

36. Does the work being proposed conform to best practice?

36. 所提议的工作是否是最好的方法？

For requests for training activities

培训活动

37. Is it clearly related to the implementation of the *World Heritage Convention*?

37. 是否与实施《世界遗产公约》明确相关？

38. Does it take place on a World Heritage property or involve a visit/case study of a World Heritage property?

38. 是否在世界遗产地举办，是否涉及参观世界遗产或案例研究？

39. Does it involve those responsible for conservation at a World Heritage property as trainees or resource persons?

39. 负责世界遗产保护的人员是否为培训对象或邀请他们分享经验？

40. Does it respond to well-defined training needs?

40. 是否针对明确的培训要求？

41. Are the training methods appropriate to ensure that the learning objectives will be met?

41. 培训方法能否保证实现培训目标？

42. Does it strengthen a local and/or regional

42. 能否加强当地或地区的培训机构的实力？

trainingi nstitution?

43. Is it linked with practical applications in the field?

43. 是否与实际应用相关?

44. Is there a provision for disseminating results and related training materials to other organizations in the World Heritag esystem?

44. 是否规定将培训成果及相关培训教材扩大到世界遗产系统中的其他组织?

For requests related to scientific research

科学研究

45. Can it be demonstrated that the subject matter is of a priority nature for better protection and safeguarding of World Heritage properties?

45. 能否证明该主题对改善世界遗产保护具有更重要的意义?

46. Can it be demonstrated that the results will be concrete and applicable widely within the World Heritage system?

46. 能否证明研究成果将非常具体,并可以广泛应用到世界遗产系统当中?

For requests for educational or awareness activities

教育或意识提升

47. Will it help make the *World Heritage Convention* better known or create a stronger interest in it amongst the target audience?

47. 能否提高《世界遗产公约》的知名度或提高公众对《世界遗产公约》的兴趣?

48. Will it create a greater awareness of the different issues related to the implementation of the *World Heritage Convention*?

48. 能否提高人们对实施《世界遗产公约》相关事项的意识?

49. Will it promote more involvement in *World Heritage Convention* related activities?

49. 能否推动更多人参与《世界遗产公约》相关的活动?

50. Will it be a means of exchanging experiences or stimulate joint educational and information programmes, especially amongst school children?

50. 能否成为经验交流的工具或促成教育或信息计划方面的合作,尤其是学生之间的交流或合作?

51. Will it produce appropriate awareness materials for the promotion of the *World Heritage Convention* for use by the target audience?

51. 能否为公众提供合适的、作为宣传《世界遗产公约》、提升意识的材料?

Annex 10

STATEMENT OF OUTSTANDING UNIVERSAL VALUE

Format of a Statement of Outstanding Universal Value, and of a retrospective Statement of Outstanding Universal Value.

The retrospective Statement of Outstanding Universal Value should be submitted either in English or in French. An electronic version (Word or .pdf format) should also be submitted.

A Statement of Outstanding Universal Value should respect the following format (2 A4 pages max):

a) Brief synthesis

b) Justification for Criteria

c) Statement of integrity (for allsites)

d) Statement of Authenticity (for sites under criteriai-vi)

e) Requirements for protection and management

Deadline

1 February^① of the year preceding the one in which the approval of the Committee is requested.

附件 10

《突出普遍价值声明》

《突出普遍价值声明》，以及《回顾性突出普遍价值声明》的格式。

回顾性突出普遍价值声明应以英文或法文提交，同时提交电子版（word 或 pdf 格式）。

《突出普遍价值声明》应遵循以下格式（A4 纸不超过两页）：

1）简要综述

2）符合标准的列入理由

3）完整性声明（所有遗产）

4）真实性声明（按照标准 i–vi 列入的遗产）

5）保护和管理要求

截止日期

要求委员会批准的年份前一年的 2 月 1 日 ^①

---

① If 1 February falls on a weekend, the nomination must be received by 17h00 GMT the preceding Friday

① 26.如果2月1日是周末，申报文件必须于格林威治时间前一个周五下午17:00前送达

Annex 11
MODIFICATIONS TO WORLD HERITAGE PROPERTIES

附件 11
对世界遗产的修改

MINOR MODIFICATIONS TO THE BOUNDARIES OF WORLD HERITAGE PROPERTIES

世界遗产边界的细微调整

Boundary modifications should serve better identification of World Heritage properties and enhance protection of their Outstanding Universal Value.

遗产边界的轻微的变动应更有利于识别世界遗产并加强遗产突出普遍价值的保护。

A proposal for a minor boundary modification, submitted by the State Party concerned, is subject to the review of the relevant Advisory Body(ies) and to the approval of the World Heritage Committee.

缔约国提出的关于边界细微调整的提议，由相关咨询机构进行审核，最终提交世界遗产委员会批准。

A proposal for a minor boundary modification can be approved, not approved, or referred by the World Heritage Committee.

世界遗产委员会可以批准、不批准或要求补充提交关于边界细微调整的提议。

Documentation requested

要求的文件材料：

1) Area of the property (in hectares): please indicate a) the area of the property as inscribedand b) the area of the property as proposed to be modified (or the area of the proposed buffer zone). (Note that reductions can be considered as minor modifications only under exceptional circumstances).

1）遗产面积（公顷）：请说明 a）列入遗产的面积和 b）提议修改的遗产面积（或提议的缓冲区面积）。（注意：只有在极个别情况下才会将面积缩小视作细微调整。）

2) Description of the modification: please provide a written description of the proposed change to the boundary of the property (or a written description of the proposed buffer zone).

2）修改描述：请提供关于遗产边界变动的书面说明（或关于提议的缓冲区的书面说明）。

3) Justification for the modification: please provide a brief summary of the reasons why the boundaries of the property should be modified (or why a buffer zone is needed), with particular emphasis on how such modification will improve

3）修改理由：请简要说明遗产边界变动的原因（或需要设立缓冲区的原因），应重点说明所提议的变动将如何改善遗产保存和 / 或保护。

the conservation and/or protection of the property.

4) Contribution to the maintenance of the Outstanding Universal Value: please indicate how the proposed change (or the proposed buffer zone) will contribute to the maintenance of the Outstanding Universal Value of the property.

5) Implications for legal protection: please indicate the implications of the proposed change for the legal protection of the property. In the case of a proposed addition, or of the creation of a buffer zone, please provide information on the legal protection in place for the area to be added and a copy of relevant laws and regulations.

6) Implications for management arrangements: please indicate the implications of the proposed change for the management arrangements of the property. In the case of a proposed addition, or of the creation of a buffer zone, please provide information on the management arrangements in place for the area to be added.

7) Maps: please submit two maps, one clearly showing both delimitations of the property (original and proposed revision) and the other showing only the proposed revision. In the case of the creation of a buffer zone, please submit a map showing both the inscribed property and the proposed buffer zone.

Please make sure that the maps:
- are either topographic or cadastral;
- are presented at a scale which is appropriate to the size in hectares of the property and sufficient to clearly show the detail of the current boundary and the proposed changes (and, in any case, the largest available and practical scale);
- have the title and the legend/key in English or French (if this is not possible, please attach a

4）促进突出普遍价值的保持：请说明所提议的变动（或提议设立的缓冲区）将以何种方式促进遗产突出普遍价值的保持。

5）对法律保护的影响：请说明所提议变动对遗产所受法律保护的影响。如果提议扩大遗产范围或设立缓冲区，请提供针对新增部分已经到位的、法律保护信息以及相关法律法规的副本。

6）对管理安排的影响：请说明所提议变动对遗产管理安排的影响。如果提议扩大遗产范围或设立缓冲区，请提供针对新增部分已经到位的管理安排。

7）地图：请提供两张地图，其中一张应清晰地显示遗产的两个边界（原边界和提议修改的边界），另一张仅显示所提议修改的边界。如果是提议设立缓冲区，请提交一张既包括列入遗产也包括所提议设立的缓冲区的地图。

请确认地图：
– 是地形图或测绘图；
– 以公顷为单位使用恰当的比例，能够清楚地显示现有边界及所提议修改的细节（以及最大可用比例和实际比例）；

– 使用英文或法文的标题、图例／符号（如不是，请附翻译件）；

translation);

- mark the boundaries of the property (current and proposed revision) through a clearly visible line that can be distinguished from other features on the maps;

- bear a clearly labeled coordinate grid (or coordinateticks);

- clearly refer (in the title and in the legend) to the boundary of the World Heritage property (and to the buffer zone of the World Heritage property, if applicable). Please clearly distinguish the boundary of theWorld Heritage property from any other protected area boundaries.

8) Additional information: In the case of a proposed addition, please submit some photographs of the area to be added that provide information on its key values and conditions of authenticity/integrity.

Any other relevant document can be submitted such as thematic maps (e.g. vegetation maps), summaries of scientific information concerning the values of the area to be added (e.g. species lists), and supporting bibliographies.

The above-mentioned documentation should be submitted in English or French in two identical copies (three for mixed properties). An electronic version (the maps in formats such as .jpg, .tif, .pdf) should also besubmitted.

Deadline

1 February[①] of the year in which the approval of the Committee is requested.

－ 使用清晰的线条标示遗产边界（现边界和提议修改的边界），从而与地图上的其他部分区分开来；

－ 带有清晰标记的坐标网（或坐标标记）；

－（在标题和图例中）清晰地指明世界遗产的边界（以及世界遗产的缓冲区，如适用）。请将世界遗产的边界与其他保护区的边界清晰地区分开。

8）补充信息：如果提议扩大遗产面积，请提交有关增加面积的图片，用于说明其核心价值以及真实性／完整性条件。

此外可以提交任何其他相关文件，例如专题地图（如植被图）、关于待增加地区价值的科学信息总结（如物种名录）以及参考书目。

上述文件应使用英语或法语提交，一式两份（混合遗产一式三份），同时还应提交电子版（地图格式为 .jpg，.tif，.pdf）.

截止日期

要求委员会批准的年份的 2 月 1 日。

---

① If 1 February falls on a weekend, the nomination must be received by 17h00 GMT the preceding Friday
① 如果2月1日是周末，申报文件必须于格林威治时间前一个周五下午17:00前送达

Annex 12

FORM FOR THE SUBMISSION OF

FACTUAL ERRORS IN

THE ADVISORY BODIES EVALUATIONS

(*in compliance with Paragraph 150 of the Operational Guidelines*)

STATE(S) PARTY(IES):

EVALUATION OF THE NOMINATION OF THE SITE:

RELEVANT ADVISORY BODY'S EVALUATION [①] **:**

Page, column, line of the Advisory Body Evaluation	Sentence including the factual error (the factual error should be highlighted in bold)	Proposed correction by the State Party	Comment (if any) by the Advisory Body and/or the World Heritage Centre

---

① For nominations of mixed sites, if there are errors in both the Evaluations of the Advisory Bodies, separate forms should be submitted for each Advisory Body indicating which Advisory Body's Evaluation each submission is referring to.

附件12

咨询机构评估中事实性错误提交表格

（对应《操作指南》正文第150条）

缔约国：

对申报遗产的评估

相关咨询机构的评估①：

所在咨询机构评估报告页码、列、行	包含事实性错误的句子（事实性错误应字体加粗）	缔约国建议的更正	咨询机构和／或世界遗产中心反馈意见（如有）

---

① 在申报混合遗产过程中，如果两个咨询机构的评估都发现有事实性错误，则分别向两个咨询机构提交表格，并写明所递交的对象。

• The Factual Errors submission form, as well as an example of such a completed form, are available from the UNESCO World Heritage Centre and at the following Web address: http://whc.unesco.org/en/factualerrors.

• Further guidance on the submission of Factual Errors can be found in Paragraph 150 of the *Operational Guidelines*.

• States Parties are requested to immediately submit this information in electronic format or by e-mail to wh-nominations@unesco.org.

The original signed version of the completed Factual Errors submission form should be received in English or French by the UNESCO World Heritage Centre, at the following address: 7 place de Fontenoy, 75352 Paris 07 SP, France, no later than 14 days before the opening of the session of the Committee.

• 事实性错误例表及一份填写完整的范本，见世界遗产中心网站：http:// whc.unesco.org/en/factualerrors.

• 有关事实性错误提交的更多指导信息，见《操作指南》正文第 150 条

• 缔约国需立即将该信息以电子形式提交或发电子邮件至 wh-nominations@unesco.org.

最晚于委员会大会开幕 14 天前，联合国教科文组织世界遗产中心必须收到填写完整并签字的事实性错误表格英文或法文版原件，邮寄至如下地址：7 place de Fontenoy, 75352 Paris 07 SP, France

Annex 13

FORMAT FOR THE SUBMISSION OF STATE OF CONSEVETION REPORTS BY THE STATES PARTIES

(in compliance with Paragraph 169 of the Operational Guidelines)

Name of World Heritage property (State(s) Party (ies)) (Identification number)

1. Executive Summary of the report

[Note: each of the sections described below should be summarized. The maximum length of the executive summary is 1 page.]

2. Response to the Decision of the World Heritage Committee

[Note: The State(s) Party(ies) is/are requested to address the most recent Decision of the World Heritage Committee for this property, paragraph by paragraph.]

If the property is inscribed on the List of World Heritage in Danger Please also provide detailed information on the following:

a) Progress achieved in implementing the corrective measures adopted by the World Heritage Committee

[Note: please address each corrective measure individually, providing factual information, including exact dates, figures, etc.]

If needed, please describe the success factors or difficulties in implementing each of the corrective measures identified

b) Is the timeframe for implementing the corrective measures suitable? If not, please propose an alternative timeframe and an explanation why this alternative timeframe is required.

附件 13

缔约国保护状态报告提交格式

（对应《操作指南》正文第 169 条）

（缔约国）世界遗产名称（认定编号）

1. 报告的执行摘要

【注意：应对下述每一章节进行概述。执行摘要最长篇幅：1 页。】

2. 对世界遗产委员会决议的回应

【注意：缔约国应逐段回应世界遗产委员会对该世界遗产的最新决定。】

如果该世界遗产被列入《濒危世界遗产名录》，缔约国还应提供以下详细信息：

a）在实施世界遗产委员会已通过的整改措施方面所取得的进展

【注意：请分别描述每一个整改措施的实施进展，包括确切日期、数据等事实信息。】

如有需要，可描述每一整改措施实施过程中的成功因素或困难要素。

b）实施这些整改措施所制定的时间表是否恰当？如果该时间表并不恰当，请提供其他时间表议，并解释为何需要这个时间表。

c) Progress achieved towards the Desired state of conservation for the removal of the property from the List of World Heritage in Danger (DSOCR)

3. Other current conservation issues identified by the State(s) Party(ies) which may have an impact on the property's Outstanding Universal Value

[Note: this includes conservation issues which are not mentioned in the Decision of the World Heritage Committee or in any information request from the World Heritage Centre]

4. In conformity with Paragraph 172 of the *Operational Guidelines*, describe any potential major restorations, alterations and/or new construction(s) intended within the property, the buffer zone(s) and/ or corridors or other areas, where such developments may affect the Outstanding Universal Value of the property, including authenticity andintegrity.

5. Public access to the state of conservation report
[Note: this report will be uploaded for public access on the World Heritage Centre's State of conservation Information System (http://whc.unesco.org/en/soc). Should your State Party request that the full report should not be uploaded, only the 1-page executive summary provided in point (1.) above will be uploaded for public access].

6. Signature of the Authority

c）描述为了达到预期的、将该遗产从《濒危世界遗产名录》中移除的理想保护状况，而取得的进展。

3. 缔约国确认的可能会影响遗产突出普遍价值的其他现有保护问题

（注意：包括世界遗产委员会决定或世界遗产中心要求提供的、任何资料中未提及的保护问题。）

4. 依照《操作指南》第172条规定，描述在该世界遗产内部、缓冲区和/或廊道或其他区域内任何可能的重大修复、改变和/或新建筑，这些开发可能会影响遗产的突出普遍价值真实性和完整性。

5. 公众获取对遗产保护状况报告
【注意：遗产保护状况报告将上传至世界遗产中心遗产保护状况信息系统（http：//whc.unesco.org/en/soc）。如果缔约国要求不上传报告全文，则仅按第一条要求上传一页执行摘要，供公众获取。】

6. 缔约国当局签署

Annex 14

TABLE OF USES OF THE WORLD HERITAGE EMBLE

This table was prepared on the basis of Chapter VIII of the *Operational Guidelines* of the World Heritage Convention and *the Directives Concerning the Use of the Name, Acronym, Logo and Internet Domain Names of UNESCO* (Resolution 34C/86).

Reminder concerning the authority and delegation of authority for the use of the World Heritage Emblem according to Chapter VIII of the *Operational Guidelines*:

Para. 262:

"The World Heritage Committee is responsible fordetermining the use of the World Heritage Emblem and for making policy prescriptions regarding how it may be used."

Para. 276:

"National authorities may grant the use of the Emblem to a national entity, provided that the project, whether national or international, involves only World Heritage properties located on the same national territory. National authorities' decision should be guided by the Guidelines and Principles."

Para. 278:

Any other request must be adressed to the Director of the World Heritage Centre, who has the authority to grant the use of the Emblem in accordance with the Guidelines and Principles.

For cases not covered, or not sufficiently covered, by the Guidelines and Principles and by the Table of

附件 14

世界遗产标识使用表格

本使用格基于世界遗产公约《操作指南》第八章及《联合国教科文组织名称、首字母缩略词、标识及互联网域名的决定》（决议34C/86）中的规定而制定。

管理《操作指南》第八章关于使用定世界遗产标识的权威机构及其授权代表的提示：

第262条：

"世界遗产委员会负责决定世界遗产标识的使用，同时负责制定如何使用标志的政策规定。"

第276条：

"如果国家或国际项目只涉及本国的世界遗产，国家权威机构可授权国家实体使用标识。国家权威机构的决定应遵守《指南和原则》以及《使用表》。"

第278条：

其他相关申请由世界遗产中心主任处理——他有权根据《指南和原则》批准使用标识。

遇到《指南和原则》及"使用表"尚未涉及或未完全涵盖的情况，主任应将申请提交给

Uses, the Director refers the matter to the Chairperson who, in the most difficult cases, might wish to refer the matter to the Committee for final decision.

Reminder concerning the use of the linked logo and of the stand aloneEmblem: Para. 262:

Since the adoption by the UNESCO General Conference in October 2007 of the *Directives concerning the Use of the Name, Acronym, Logo and InternetDomain Names of UNESCO*, it is strongly encouraged to use the World Heritage Emblem as part of a linked logo block accompanied by UNESCO's logo, whenever feasible. The use of the World Heritage Emblem alone remains however possible, in line with the present Guidelines and with the Table of Uses (Annex 14 of the Guidelines).

Reminder concerning the graphic charter:

The graphic charter of the UNESCO logo is available here: http://www.unesco.org/new/en/name-and-logo/graphics/

According to the Preamble of Chapter VIII of the *Operational Guidelines*, the stand alone World Heritage Emblem can be used in any colour or size.

The logos are provided by the authorizing entities (as detailed in the following table) in digital format which cannot be modified by the users in any way.

It is obligatory to submit the draft layout of the intended use to the authorizing entity for validation before production.

主席，如果是很难处理的情况，主席会将该申请提交委员会做最后决定。

第262条有关使用标识链接及独立标识的提示

2007年10月，联合国教科文组织大会审议通过了《联合国教科文组织相关名称、缩略语、标志及网域名称使用指南》。委员会鼓励在任何适当的情况下，将世界遗产的标志作为联合国教科文组织的延伸部分加以使用。世界遗产标志也可以不同方式单独使用，需符合现行《操作指南》和《使用表》（见附件14）的要求。

提示：关于使用标识的授权

可登录 http：//www.unesco.org/new/en/name-and-logo/graphics/ 查找使用联合国教科文组织标识的授权。

根据《操作指南》第八章前言，可以用任何颜色或尺寸使用独一无二的世界遗产标识。

这些标识由授权机构（见下文表格详述内容）以电子形式提供，使用者不得进行任何方式的改变。

必须将用于特定用途的布局设计草案提交给授权机构进行确认后方可生产。

Definition of commercial use:

The sale of goods or services bearing the name, acronym, logo and/or Internet domain name of UNESCO combined with the World Heritage Emblem chiefly for profit shall be regarded as "commercial use" for the purpose of the Operational Guidelines. Such use must be expressly authorized by the Director-General, under a specific contractual arrangement (definition adapted from UNESCO Logo Directives 2007. Art Ⅲ.2.1.3)

商业使用的定义：

以营利为目，销售带有联合国教科文组织名称、首字母缩略词、标识及联合互联网域名及世界遗产标识的商品或服务，被《操作指南》认定为"商业用途"。此类用途必须根据具体的合同安排，由总干事明确授权（定义摘自联合国教科文组织标识方针，2007年.第Ⅲ.2.1.3)。

WORLD HERITAGE CENTRE

Uses and purposes	Uses		Authorization		Graphic illustrations
	Type of Logo the WHC can use	Use of the Logo by the WHC is authorized by	WHC can authorize the Logo for	Type of Logo the WHC can authorize	Logo to be used and/or authorized by the WHC
World Heritage Centre - WHC (for international content) 1) Publications 2) Communication materials 3) Website, social media, apps, etc. 4) Working documents 5) Communication products (such as T-shirts, bags, umbrellas), for special events 6) Stationery	UNESCO/World Heritage Convention logo	Statutory use	State Party hosting a Committee	UNESCO/World Heritage Convention logo	
1) Publications 2) Communication materials 3) Website, social media, apps, etc. 4) Working documents 5) Communication products (such as T-shirts, bags, umbrellas), for special events 6) Stationery	UNESCO/World Heritage Centre logo	Statutory use			

Uses and purposes	Uses		Authorization		Graphic illustrations
	Type of Logo the WHC can use	Use of the Logo by the WHC is authorized by	WHC can authorize the Logo for	Type of Logo the WHC can authorize	
World Heritage Centre (continued)					Logo to be used and/or authorized by the WHC
1) Publications 2) Communication materials 3) Website, social media, apps,etc. 4) Small-size communication products (such as pens, key-rings etc), for specia levents 5) Stationery	World Heritage Emblem	Statutory use	World Heritage Site Management Authority State Party hosting a Committee	World Heritage Emblem	
Committee session	UNESCO/World Heritage logo + «XXth/st/rd/nd World Heritage Committee session»	Statutory use	State Party hosting a Committee	UNESCO/World Heritage logo + «XXth/st/rd/nd World Heritage Committee session»	
Partnership with external entities (private and public sector)	UNESCO/World Heritage Centre logo with text "With the support of", "In cooperation with", or "In partnership with"	Statutory use	Entities in the framework of contractual arrangements	UNESCO/World Heritage Centre logo with text "With the support of", "In cooperation with", or "In partnership with"	
	UNESCO/ WorldHeritage Centre or Conventionlogo +'Partner' slogo and/or text			UNESCO/ WorldHeritage Centre or Conventionlogo +Partner's logo and/or text	

世界遗产中心

用途及目的	用途 世界遗产中心可使用的标识类型	授权 授权世界遗产中心使用标识的主体	图解说明 世界遗产中心可使用的标识类型	可得到世界遗产中心授权使用标识的主体	世界遗产中心可使用和/或授权的标识
世界遗产中心 WHC（国际使用）					
1) 出版物 2) 传播材料 3) 网站、社交媒体及应用软件等 4) 工作文档 5) 特殊事件中用于宣传的产品（如 T 恤、袋子、雨伞等） 6) 文具	联合国教科文组织/世界遗产中心标识	依法使用	联合国教科文组织/世界遗产中心标识	组织举办委员会会议的缔约国	联合国教科文组织标识 + 世界遗产中心标识（World Heritage Centre / United Nations Educational, Scientific and Cultural Organization）
1) 出版物 2) 传播材料 3) 网站、社交媒体及应用软件等 4) 工作文档 5) 特殊事件中用于宣传的产品（如 T 恤、袋子、雨伞等） 6) 文具	联合国教科文组织/世界遗产中心标识	依法使用			联合国教科文组织标识 + 世界遗产中心标识（World Heritage Centre / United Nations Educational, Scientific and Cultural Organization）
1) 出版物 2) 传播材料 3) 网站、社交媒体及应用软件等 4) 特殊事件中小型宣传的产品（如钢笔、钥匙圈等） 5) 文具	世界遗产中心标识	依法使用	世界遗产标识	世界遗产遗址管理当局 组织举办委员会会议的缔约国	世界遗产标识 or 世界遗产标识
委员会大会	联合国教科文组织/世界遗产标识 +"第 xx 届世界遗产委员会大会"	依法使用	联合国教科文组织/"世界遗产标识 +"第 xx 届世界遗产委员会大会""	组织举办委员会会议的缔约国	联合国教科文组织标识 + 世界遗产标识（29th session of the World Heritage Committee / United Nations Educational, Scientific and Cultural Organization）

续表

用途及目的	用途		授权		图解说明
	授权世界遗产中心使用标识的主体	世界遗产中心可使用的标识类型	可得到世界遗产中心授权使用标识的主体	世界遗产中心可授权的标识类型	
世界遗产中心（国际使用）WHC					世界遗产中心可使用和/或授权的标识　世界遗产中心标识
与外部实体机构（私人领域或公共领域）合作	依法使用	联合国教科文组织/世界遗产标识+文字"用于支持…"、"与…"或"与…协调"	合同安排框架内的实体机构	联合国教科文组织/世界遗产标识+文字"用于支持…"、"与…"或"与…合作"	
		联合国教科文组织/世界遗产公约标识和/或世界遗产中心或合作伙伴标识+或文字		联合国教科文组织/世界遗产公约标识和/或世界遗产中心或合作伙伴标识+或文字	

NATIONAL COMMISSIONS OR AGENCIES

Uses and purposes	Uses		Authorization		Graphic illustrations
	Type of Logo the NatCom can use	Use of the Logo by the NatCom is authorized by	NatCom can authorize the use of the Logo for	Type of Logo the NatCom can authorize	Logo to be used and/or authorized by the NatCom
1 - National Commission (for national content)					
1) Non-commercial publications 2) Communication materials 3) Website, social media, apps, etc. 4) Communication products such as T-shirts, bags, umbrellas (non-merchandising, exceptionally for special events) 5) Stationery	UNESCO/World Heritage logo with text "World Heritage in… [Country name]"	Statutory use	Local government authorities and site managing authorities.	UNESCO/World Heritage logo with text «World Heritage in +country»	
1) Website, social media, apps, etc. when space is limited 2) Communication products as a graphic element or when space is limited 3) Stationery 4) Any other applicable case according to the *Operational Guidelines*	World Heritage Emblem	Statutory use	World Heritage site management authority	World Heritage Emblem	

Uses and purposes	Uses	Use of the Logo by the NatCom is authorized by	Authorization	Type of Logo the NatCom can authorize	Graphic illustrations
1 - National Commission (continued)	Type of Logo the NatCom can use		NatCom can authorize the use of the Logo for	Type of Logo the NatCom can authorize	Logo to be used and/or authorized by the NatCom
Road signs, highway signs	Choice of the logo according to the kind of sign and its location: UNESCO/World Heritage logo in full or simplified with site's name underneath	Statutory use	World Heritage site management authority	UNESCO/World Heritage logo in full or simplified with site's name underneath	Text under the name of the site is optional. Possibility to replace "inscribed on the World Heritage List in" by "World Heritage since"
	World Heritage Emblem	Statutory use	World Heritage site management authority	World Heritage Emblem	
Commercial use	UNESCO/World Heritage logo with text "World Heritage in... [Country name]"	Director-General of UNESCO			
	World Heritage Emblem	Statutory use	National entity	World Heritage Emblem	

Uses and purposes	Uses		Authorization		Graphic illustrations
1 - National Commission (continued)	Type of Logo the NatCom can use	Use of the Logo by the NatCom is authorized by	NatCom can authorize the use of the Logo for	Type of Logo the NatCom can authorize	Logo to be used and/or authorized by the NatCom
Committee session	UNESCO/World Heritage + «XXth/st/rd/nd World Heritage Committee Session»	World Heritage Centre	Organizing authority	UNESCO/World Heritage + «XXth/st/rd/nd World Heritage Committee session»	
Patronage for World Heritage related one-off events (ex: conferences, publications or audio-visual production activity on national or local level)			Organizing entities	UNESCO/World Heritage logo with text "Under the patronage of the National Commission of xxx for UNESCO"	
World Heritage related partnership with national organisations			National organisation having established a partnership with the National Commission	UNESCO/World Heritage logo with text "With the support of the xxx National Commission for UNESCO", or "In cooperation with the xxx National Commission for UNESCO", or "In partnership with the xxx National Commission for UNESCO"	

Uses and purposes	Uses	Authorization		Graphic illustrations
	Type of Logo the agency can use	Use of the Logo by the agency is authorized by	Agency can authorize the use of the Logo to	Type of Logo the agency can authorize	Logo to be used and/or authorised by the agency
2 - Agency -designated national authority (for national content)					
1) Non-commercial publications 2) Communication materials 3) Website, social media, apps, etc. 4) Communication products (such as T-shirts, bags, umbrellas) non-merchandising, for special events 5) Stationery	UNESCO/World Heritage logo with text "World Heritage in... [Country name]"	National Commission or World Heritage Centre			
1) Non-commercial publications 2) Communication materials 3) Website, social media, apps,etc. whenspaceis limited 4) Communication products (such as T-shirts, bags, umbrellas) non-merchandising, for specialevents 5) Stationery	World Heritage Emblem	Statutory use	World Heritage site management authority	World Heritage Emblem	

Uses and purposes	Uses		Authorization		Graphic illustrations
	Type of Logo the agency can use	Use of the Logo by the agency is authorized by	Agency can authorize the use of the Logo to	Type of Logo the agency can authorize	
2 - Agency - designated national authority (continued)					Logo to be used and/or authorised by the agency
Road signs, highway signs	Choice of the logo according to the kind of sign and its location: UNESCO/World Heritage logo in full or simplified with site's name underneath	National Commission or World Heritage Centre	World Heritage site management authority	UNESCO/World Heritage logo in full or simplified with site's name underneath	Text under the name of the site is optional. Possibility to replace "inscribed on the World Heritage List in" by "World Heritage since"
	World Heritage Emblem	Statutory use	World Heritage site management authority	World Heritage Emblem	
Commercial use	UNESCO/World Heritage logo with text "World Heritage in... [Country name]"	Director-General of UNESCO			
	World Heritage Emblem	Statutory use			

国家委员会或机构

用途及目的	用途	授权国家委员会使用标识的主体（授权）	可得到国家委员会授权使用标识的主体	国家委员会可授权的标识类型	图解说明
1- 国家委员会（国内使用）	国家委员会可使用的标识类型			国家委员会可授权的标识类型	国家委员会可使用和/或授权的标识
1）非商业用途出版物 2）传播材料 3）网站、社交媒体及应用软件等 4）特殊事件中用于宣传的产品（如T恤、袋子、雨伞等）5）文具	联合国教科文组织/世界遗产标识+"…[国家名称]的世界遗产"	依法使用	当地政府机构或遗址管理当局	联合国教科文组织/世界遗产标识+"…[国家名称]的世界遗产"	
1）非商业用途出版 2）传播材料 3）网站、社会媒体、应用程序 4）依照操作指南用案例	世界遗产标识	依法使用	世界遗产遗址管理当局	世界遗产标识	
公路标志、高速公路标志	依据标志类型及其位置选择适当的联合国教科文组织/世界遗产标识整体，或在标识下方简单标注遗址地名称	法定使用	世界遗产遗址管理当局	联合国教科文组织/世界遗产标识整体或在标识下方简单标注遗址地名称	
	世界遗产标识	法定使用	世界遗产遗址管理当局	世界遗产标识	可自行确定遗址地下方的文字 有可能使用自××年"成为世界遗产"来代替"××年列入世界遗产名录"

续表

用途及目的	用途	授权		国家委员会可授权的标识类型	图解说明
1-国家委员会（国内使用）	国家委员会可使用的标识类型	授权国家委员会使用标识的主体	可得到国家委员会授权使用标识的主体	国家委员会可授权的标识类型	国家委员会可使用和/或授权的标识
商业使用	联合国教科文组织/世界遗产标识+"…[国家名称]的世界遗产"	联合国教科文组织总干事			
	世界遗产标识	依法使用	国家实体	世界遗产标识	
委员会大会	联合国教科文组织/世界遗产+"第xx届世界遗产委员会大会"	世界遗产中心	主办方当局	联合国教科文组织/世界遗产标识+"第xx届世界遗产委员会大会"	
对世界遗产一次性活动的赞助（如大会、出版物或国家或地方的影音制作活动）			主办方当局	联合国教科文组织/世界遗产标识+文字"得到xxx国家委员会对联合国教科文组织的资助"	
世界遗产与国家组织的合作			已与国家委员会建立合作关系的国家组织	联合国教科文组织/世界遗产标识+国家委员会对联合国教科文组织的支持"，或"与联合国教科文组织xxx国家委员会协作"，或"得到xxx国家教科文组织的支持"，或"与联合国教科文组织xxx国家委员会合作"	

续表

用途及目的	用途	授权代理机构使用标识的主体	可得到代理机构授权使用标识的主体	代理机构可使用的标识类型	图解说明
2-代理机构-国家当局指定（国内使用）	代理机构可使用的标识类型			代理机构可使用的标识类型	代理机构可使用和／或授权的标识
1）非商业用途出版物 2）传播材料 3）网站 4）特殊事件中用于宣传的非商品化产品（如T恤、袋子、雨伞等） 5）文具	联合国教科文组织／世界遗产标识＋"…［国家名称］的世界遗产"	国家委员会或世界遗产中心			World Heritage in Switzerland — United Nations Educational, Scientific and Cultural Organization
1）非商业用途出版物 2）交流材料 3）网站、社会媒体、应用程序等 4）交流产品（如T恤、包、伞）为特别活动生产 5）文具　等非商业用途	世界遗产标识	法定使用	世界遗产遗址管理当局	世界遗产标识	or
公路标志，高速公路标志	依据标志类型及其位置选择适当的标识：联合国教科文组织／世界遗产标识整体，或在标识下方简单标注遗址地名称	国家委员会或世界遗产中心	世界遗产遗址管理当局	联合国教科文组织／世界遗产标识整体，或在标识下方简单标注遗址地名称	United Nations Educational, Scientific and Cultural Organization — Black Bay, Western Australia Inscribed on the World Heritage List in 1981 — Structure Annexe and Associated sites Inscribed on the World Heritage List in 1980 可自行确定遗址地名称下方的文字有可能使用"第××年成为世界遗产"来代替"××年列入世界遗产名录"

用途及目的	用途	授权	代理机构可授权的标识类型	可得到代理机构授权使用标识的主体	图解说明
2- 代理机构 - 指定国家当局（国内使用）	代理机构可使用的标识类型	授权代理机构使用标识的主体	世界遗产标识		代理机构可使用和/或授权的标识（UNESCO／世界遗产标识；or；"World Heritage in Switzerland"；"United Nations Educational, Scientific and Cultural Organization"）
公路标志，高速公路标志	世界遗产标识	法定使用		世界遗产遗址管理当局	
商业使用	联合国教科文组织/世界遗产标识＋"…[国家名称]的世界遗产"；世界遗产标识	联合国教科文组织总干事；法定使用			

WORLD HERITAGE SITE MANAGEMENT AUTHORITY

Uses and purposes	Uses		Authorization		Graphic illustrations
	Type of Logo the WH site can use	Use of the Logo by the WH site is authorized by	WH Site can authorize the Logo for	Type of Logo the WH Site can authorize	
World Heritage site management authority (for site-related content) 1) Non-commercial publications 2) Communication materials 3) Website, social media, apps,etc. 4) Communication products (such as T- shirts, bags, umbrellas) non-merchandising, for specialevents 5) Stationery 6) Plaque, flag,banner	UNESCO/World Heritage site-specific logo	National Commission or World Heritage Centre			Logo to be used and/or authorized by the WH site Possibility to replace "Inscribed on the World Heritage List in" by "World Heritage since"
1) Non-commercial publications 2) Communication materials 3) Website, social media, apps, etc. when space is limited 4) Communication products (T-shirts, bags, umbrellas, key- rings, pens etc.) non-merchandising, for special events 5) Plaque, flag, banner	World Heritage Emblem	National Commission or agency or World Heritage Centre			

Uses and purposes	Uses		Authorization		Graphic illustrations
	Type of Logo the WH site can use	Use of the Logo by the WH site is authorized by	WH site can authorize the Logo for	Type of Logo the WH site can authorize	Logo to be used and/or authorized by the WH site
World Heritage site Management Authority (continued)					
Road signs, highway signs	Choice of the logo according to the kind of sign and its location: UNESCO/World Heritage logo in full or simplified with site's name underneath	National Commission or World Heritage Centre			Text under the name of the site is optional. Possibility to replace «inscribed on the World Heritage List in» by "World Heritage since"
	World Heritage Emblem	National Commission or World Heritage Centre			

Uses and purposes		Uses	Authorization		Graphic illustrations
	Type of Logo the WH site can use	Use of the Logo by the WH site is authorized by	WH site can authorize the Logo for	Type of Logo the WH site can authorize	
World Heritage site Management Authority (continued)					Logo to be used and/or authorized by the WH site
Commercial use	UNESCO/ World Heritage site-specific logo	Director-General of UNESCO			Possibility to replace: "inscribed on the World Heritage List in" by "World Heritage since"
	World Heritage Emblem	National Commission			

世界遗产管理机构

用途及目的	用途	世界遗产遗址使用地使用标识的主体	授权（可得到世界遗产遗址地授权使用标识的主体）	世界遗产遗址地可授权的标识类型	图解说明（世界遗产遗址地可使用和/或授权使用的标识）
世界遗产遗址管理当局（用于遗址相关内容）	世界遗产遗址地可使用用的标识类型				
1）非商业用途出版物 2）传播材料 3）网站、社交媒体及应用软件等 4）特殊事件中用于宣传的非商品化产品（如T恤、袋子、雨伞等） 5）文具 6）匾、旗帜或横幅标语	联合国教科文组织／世界遗产遗址地专用标识	国家委员会或世界遗产中心			有可能使用"自××成为世界遗产"来代替"××年列入世界遗产名录"
1）非商业用途出版物 2）传播材料 3）网站、社交媒体及应用软件等如空间有限 4）特殊事件中用于宣传的非商品化产品（如T恤、袋子、雨伞钥匙圈、钢笔等） 5）匾、旗帜或横幅标语	世界遗产标识	国家委员会或代理机构或世界遗产中心			
公路标志，高速公路标志	依据标志类型及其位置选择适当的标识：联合国教科文组织／世界遗产标识整体，或在标识下方简单标注遗址地名称	国家委员会或世界遗产中心			可自行确定遗址地名称下方的文字有可能使用"××年成为世界遗产"来代替"××年列入世界遗产名录"

用途及目的	用途		授权		图解说明
	世界遗产遗址地可使用的标识类型	世界遗产遗址地使用标识的主体	可得到世界遗产遗址地授权使用标识的主体	世界遗产遗址地授权的标识类型	世界遗产遗址地可使用和／或授权的标识
世界遗产遗址管理当局（用于遗址相关内容）	世界遗产标识	国家委员会或世界遗产中心			
公路标志，高速公路标志	联合国教科文组织／世界遗产遗址地专用标识	联合国教科文组织总干事			
商业用途	世界遗产标识	国家委员会			

Specific case: serial sites or very large sites including several/various elements/monuments/places

Uses and purposes	Uses		Authorization		Graphic illustrations
World Heritage site management authority (continued)	Type of Logo the WH site can use	Use of the Logo by the WH site is authorized by	WH site can authorize the Logo for	Type of Logo the WH site can authorize	Logo to be used and/or authorized by the WH site
1) Non-commercial publications 2) Communication materials 3) Website, social media, apps, etc. 4) Communication products (T-shirts, bags, umbrellas, key-rings, pens etc.) non-merchandising, for special events 5) Stationery 6) Plaque, flag, banner	UNESCO/World Heritage site-specific logo, preceded by the mention "Xxxx [name of the element/monument/place], part of"	National Commission or World Heritage Centre			Xxxx part of

特别案例：系列遗产或包括数个或不同要素或纪念物或地方的超大型遗产

用途及目的	使用		授权		图形图例
世界遗产管理当局（续）	世界遗产点可使用的标识类型	世界遗产点使用标识的授权	世界遗产点可授权的标识	世界遗产点可授权的标识类型	世界遗产点可使用的标识类型
1）非商业出版物 2）交流材料 3）网站，社会媒体，应用程序等 4）交流产品（如T恤，包，伞）等非商业用途，为特别活动生产 5）文具 6）匾额，旗帜，横幅	联合国教科文组织或世界遗产+"xxxx（要素或纪念物或地方）部分"	国家委员会或世界遗产中心			"xxxx部分"

WORLD HERITAGE ADVISORY BODIES

Uses and purposes	Uses		Authorization		Graphic illustrations
Advisory Bodies	Type of Logo the Advisory Bodies can use	Use of the Logo by Advisory Bodies is authorized by	Advisory Bodies can authorize the Logo for	Type of Logo the Advisory Bodiescan authorize	Logo to be used by the Advisory Bodies
1) Non-commercial publications 2) Non-commercial communication materials 3) Website 4) Non-commercial stationery	UNESCO/World Heritage Convention logo	World Heritage Centre			UNESCO United Nations Educational, Scientific and Cultural Organization · World Heritage · Convention
1) Publications 2) Communication materials 3) Website 4) Stationery	World Heritage Emblem	World Heritage Centre			[World Heritage emblem] or [World Heritage emblem]

PATRONAGE

Uses and purposes	Uses	Authorization		Type of Logo Director-General can authorize	Graphic illustrations
Patronage		UNESCO Director-General can authorize	Organizing authorities		Logo to be authorized
One-off activities (conferences, exhibitions, festivals, publications or audio-visual productions)				UNESCO/World Heritage logo with text "Under the patronage of"	Under the patronage of UNESCO United Nations Educational, Scientific and Cultural Organization · World Heritage ·

世界遗产咨询机构

用途及目的	用途	授权	图解说明
咨询机构	咨询机构可使用的标识类型	咨询机构使用标识的主体 / 咨询机构可授权的标识类型 / 可得到咨询机构授权使用标识的主体	咨询机构可使用和 / 或授权的标识
1）非商业用途出版物 2）非商业用途传播材料 3）网站 4）非商业用途文具	联合国教科文组织 / 世界遗产公约标识	世界遗产中心	[United Nations Educational, Scientific and Cultural Organization — World Heritage Convention 标识]
1）出版物 2）传播材料 3）网站 4）文具	世界遗产标识	世界遗产中心	[标识] or [标识]

赞助

用途及目的	用途	授权	图解说明
赞助	联合国教科文组织总干事可授权的标识类型	联合国教科文组织总干事 / 组织当局	待授权的标识
一次性活动（会议，展览，节日出版物或视听产品）	联合国教科文组织标识 / 世界遗产标识 + 文本 "得到…的赞助"		[Under the patronage of — United Nations Educational, Scientific and Cultural Organization — World Heritage 标识]

Select world heritage Bibliography　　　世界遗产相关的参考书目

World Heritage Centre Documents Database
　　http://whc.unesco.org/en/documents/

世界遗产中心文件数据库
　　http：//whc.unesco.org/en/documents/

The UNESCO World Heritage Centre «Official Records» searchable online document collection permits the retrieval of information contained in the reports of the World Heritage Committee and General Assembly of States Parties to the Convention

联合国教科文组织世界遗产中心在线检索文件集"官方数据"，允许对世界遗产委员会和缔约国大会《公约》报告中的信息，进行检索。

BASIC TEXTS　　　　　　　　　　　基础文件

UNESCO. 1972. *Convention concerning the Protection of the World Cultural and Natural Heritage.* (World Heritage Convention).
　　http://whc.unesco.org/en/conventiontext

《联合国教科文组织保护世界文化与自然遗产公约》（世界遗产公约），1972 年，联合国教科文组织。
　　http：//whc.unesco.org/en/conventiontext

UNESCO General Assembly of States Parties to the Convention concerning the Protection of the World Cultural and Natural Heritage. 2014. *Rules of Procedure.* WHC-14/GA/1 Rev. 4 (as of 14 November 2014) http://whc.unesco.org/en/ga/

联合国教科文组织保护世界文化与自然遗产公约缔约国大会，2014年，《议事规则》，WHC– 14/GA/1Rev.4（截至 2014 年 11 月 14 日）
　　http：//whc.unesco.org/en/ga/

UNESCO Intergovernmental Committee for the Protection of the World Cultural and Natural Heritage. 1995. *Financial Regulations for the World Heritage Fund*, Paris. (WHC/7, August 1995).
　　http://whc.unesco.org/en/committeerules

联合国教科文组织保护世界文化与自然遗产政府间委员会，1995年，《世界遗产基金财务规则》，巴黎（WHC/7，1995年8月）
　　http：//whc.unesco.org/en/committeerules

UNESCO Intergovernmental Committee for the Protection of the World Cultural and Natural Heritage. 2013.*Rules of Procedure*, WHC-2013/5
　　http://whc.unesco.org/en/committee

联合国教科文组织保护世界文化与自然遗产政府间委员会，2013 年，《议事规则》，WHC.2013/5.
　　http：//whc.unesco.org/en/committee

UNESCO World Heritage Centre. 2005. *Basic Texts of the 1972 World Heritage Convention* (2005 Edition). Paris, UNESCO.
　　http://whc.unesco.org/en/basictexts/

联合国教科文组织世界遗产中心，2005年，《1972 年世界遗产公约基础文件》（2005 年版本），巴黎，联合国教科文组织。
　　http：//whc.unesco.org/en/basictexts/

UNESCO World Heritage Centre. *Properties inscribed on the World Heritage List.*

http://whc.unesco.org/en/list

联合国教科文组织世界遗产中心,《世界遗产名录》

http：//whc.unesco.org/en/list

UNESCO World Heritage Centre. *Tentative Lists.*

http://whc.unesco.org/en/tentativelists/

联合国教科文组织世界遗产中心,《预备名录》。

http：//whc.unesco.org/en/tentativelists/

STRATEGIC DOCUMENTS

战略性文件

UNESCO World Heritage Committee. 1992. *Strategic Orientations.* in Annex II of the Report of the 16th session of the World Heritage Committee (Santa Fe, 1992) (WHC-92/CONF.002/12).

http://whc.unesco.org/en/documents/940

联合国教科文组织世界遗产委员会, 1992 年,《战略定位》, 见世界遗产委员会第 16 次大会报告附件 II (1992 年, 圣达非) (WHC-92/CONF.002/12)。

http：//whc.unesco.org/archive/1992/whc-92-conf002-12e.pdf

UNESCO World Heritage Committee. 1994. *Report of the Expert Meeting on the «Global Strategy» and thematic studies for a representative World Heritage List* (20-22 June 1994) (WHC-94/CONF.003/INF.6)

http://whc.unesco.org/archive/global94.htm

联合国教科文组织世界遗产委员会, 1994 年,《< 世界遗产名录 > 的全球战略与主题研究专家会议报告》(1994 年 6 月 20 至 22 日) (WHC-94/CONF.003/INF.6)

http：//whc.unesco.org/archive/global94.htm

UNESCO World Heritage Committee. 1994. *Nara Document on Authenticity.* http://whc.unesco.org/archive/nara94.htm

联合国教科文组织世界遗产委员会, 1994 年,《奈良真实性文件》。http：//whc.unesco.org/archive/nara94.htm

UNESCO World Heritage Committee. 1996. *Report of the Expert Meeting on Evaluation of General Principles and Criteria for Nominations of Natural World Heritage sites.* (WHC-96/CONF.202/INF.9).

http://whc.unesco.org/archive/1996/whc-96-conf202-inf9e.htm

联合国教科文组织世界遗产委员会, 1996 年,《申报世界自然遗产遗址地一般评估原则和标准专家会议报告》(WHC-96/CONF.202/INF.9)。

http：//whc.unesco.org/archive/1996/whc-96-conf202-inf9e.htm

UNESCO World Heritage Committee. 2001. Global Training Strategy for World Cultural and Natural Heritage, adopted by the World Heritage Committee at its 25th session (Annex X of WHC-

联合国教科文组织世界遗产委员会 , 2001 年,《世界文化与自然遗产全球培训战略》, 于芬兰赫尔辛基世界遗产委员会第 25 次会议通过 (参见 WHC-01/CONF.208/24 附件 X-《全球培

01/CONF.208/24)- Update of the Global Training Strategy (Doc WHC-09/33.COM/10B).

http://whc.unesco.org/archive/2001/whc-01-conf208-24e.pdf

http://whc.unesco.org/archive/2009/whc09-33com-10Be.pdf

UNESCO World Heritage Committee. 2002. *Budapest Declaration on World Heritage.* (Doc WHC-02/CONF.202/5).

http://whc/unesco.org/en/budapestdeclaration

UNESCO World Heritage Committee. 2004. *Evaluation of the Global Strategy for a representative, balanced and credible World Heritage List* (1994-2004). (Doc WHC-04/28.COM/13)

http://whc.unesco.org/archive/2004/whc04-28com-13e.pdf

UNESCO World Heritage Comittee. 2005. *Vienna Memorandum on World Heritage and Contemporary Architecture – Managing the Historic Urban Landscape.* (Doc WHC-05/15.GA/INF.7).

http://whc.unesco.org/archive/2005/whc05-15ga-inf7e.pdf

UNESCO World Heritage Committee. 2007. *Strategy for Reducing Risks from Disasters at World Heritage Properties.* (Doc WHC-07/31.COM/7.2)

http://whc.unesco.org/archive/2007/whc07-31com-72e.pdf

UNESCO World Heritage Committee. 2007. *The "fifth C" for "Communities".* (Doc WHC-07/31.COM/13B).

http://whc.unesco.org/archive/2007/whc07-31com-13be.pdf

训战略》的更新（DocWHC- 09/33.COM/10B））。

http：//whc.unesco.org/archive/2001/whc-01-conf208-24e.pdf

http：//whc.unesco.org/archive/2009/whc09-33com-10Be.pdf

联合国教科文组织世界遗产委员会，2002年，《世界遗产布达佩斯宣言》，（DocWHC-02/CONF.202/5）

http：//whc/unesco.org/en/budapestdeclaration

联合国教科文组织世界遗产委员会，2004年，《建构具有代表性、均衡性、可信性〈世界遗产名录〉的全球战略评估（1994-2004年）》（DocWHC-04/28.COM/13）

http：//whc.unesco.org/archive/2004/whc04-28com-13e.pdf

联合国教科文组织世界遗产委员会，2005年，《维也纳世界遗产和当代建筑备忘录 – 管理城市历史景观》,（Doc WHC-05/15.GA/INF.7）

http：//whc.unesco.org/archive/2005/whc05-15ga-inf7e.pdf

联合国教科文组织世界遗产委员会，2007年，《世界遗产减少灾害风险策略》（DocWHC-07/31.COM/7.2）

http：//whc.unesco.org/archive/2007/whc07-31com-72e.pdf

联合国教科文组织世界遗产委员会，2007年，《"社区"的"五 C"战略》（DocWHC-07/31.COM/13B）.

http：//whc.unesco.org/archive/2007/whc07-31com-13be.pdf

UNESCO World Heritage Centre. 2008. *Policy Document on the Impacts of Climate Change on World Heritage Properties.* Paris, UNESCO World Heritage Centre.

http://whc.unesco.org/uploads/activities/documents/activity-397-2.pdf

联合国教科文组织世界遗产中心，2008 年，《气候变化对世界遗产影响的政策文件》，巴黎，联合国教科文组织世界遗产中心.

http：//whc.unesco.org/uploads/activities/documents/activity-397-2.pdf

UNESCO World Heritage Committee. 2010. *Reflection on the Trends of the State of Conservation.* (Doc WHC-10/34.COM/7C).

http://whc.unesco.org/archive/2010/whc10-34com-7Ce.pdf

联合国教科文组织世界遗产委员会，2010 年，《保护状况趋势的反思》，（Doc WHC-10/34.COM/7C）. http：//whc.unesco.org/archive/2010/whc10-34com-7Ce.pdf

UNESCO World Heritage Committee. 2011. *World Heritage Convention and Sustainable Development.*(Doc WHC-11/35.COM/5E).

http://whc.unesco.org/archive/2011/whc11-35com-5Ee.pdf

联合国教科文组织世界遗产委员会，2011 年，《世界遗产公约及可持续发展》（DocWHC-11/35.COM/5E）. http：//whc.unesco.org/archive/2011/whc11-35com-5Ee.pdf

UNESCO World Heritage Committee. 2011. *Presentation and adoption of the World Heritage strategy for capacity building.* (Doc WHC-11/35.COM/9B).

http://whc.unesco.org/archive/2011/whc11-35com-9Be.pdf

联合国教科文组织世界遗产委员会，2011 年，《展示和通过世界遗产能力建设战略》（DocWHC-11/35.COM/9B）.

http：//whc.unesco.org/archive/2011/whc11-35com-9Be.pdf

UNESCO World Heritage Committee. 2012. *World Heritage Tourism Programme.* (Doc WHC-12/36.COM/5E).

http://whc.unesco.org/archive/2012/whc12-36com-5E-en.pdf

联合国教科文组织世界遗产委员会，2012 年，《世界遗产旅游项目》，（DocWHC-12/36.COM/5E）.

http：//whc.unesco.org/archive/2012/whc12-36com-5E-en.pdf

UNESCO World Heritage Committee. 2013. *Revised Partnerships for Conservation (PACT) Initiative Strategy.* (Doc WHC-13/37.COM/5D).

http://whc.unesco.org/archive/2013/whc13-37com-5D-en.pdf

联合国教科文组织世界遗产委员会，2013 年，《修订保护合作伙伴关系战略倡住》（DocWHC-13/37.COM/5D）.

http：//whc.unesco.org/archive/2013/whc13-37com-5D-en.pdf

WORLD HERITAGE RESOURCE MANUALS
http://whc.unesco.org/en/resourcemanuals/

世界遗产资源手册
http：//whc.unesco.org/en/resourcemanuals/

UNESCO, ICCROM, ICOMOS and IUCN. 2010. *Managing Disaster Risks for World Heritage. Paris, UNESCO World Heritage Centre.*

　　http://whc.unesco.org/en/managing-disaster-risks/

联合国教科文组织、国际文物保护与修复研究中心、国际古迹遗址理事会和世界自然保护联盟，2010年。

《世界遗产灾害风险管理》。巴黎，联合国教科文组织世界遗产中心。http://whc.unesco.org/uploads/activities/documents/activity–630–1.pdf

UNESCO, ICCROM, ICOMOS and IUCN. 2011. *Preparing World Heritage Nominations. (Second edition).* Paris, UNESCO World Heritage Centre.

　　http://whc.unesco.org/en/preparing-world-heritage-nominations/

联合国教科文组织、国际文物保护与修复研究中心、国际古迹遗址理事会和世界自然保护联盟，2011 年，《世界遗产申报准备手册》（版本 2），巴黎，联合国教科文组织世界遗产中心。

　　http：//whc.unesco.org/en/activities/643/

UNESCO, ICCROM, ICOMOS and IUCN. 2012. *Managing Natural World Heritage.* Paris, UNESCO World HeritageCentre.

　　http://whc.unesco.org/en/managing-natural-world-heritage/

联合国教科文组织、国际文物保护与修复研究中心、国际古迹遗址理事会和世界自然保护联盟，2012年。《世界自然遗产管理手册》，巴黎，联合国教科文组织世界遗产中心。

　　http：//whc.unesco.org/uploads/activities/documents/activity–703–1.pdf

UNESCO, ICCROM, ICOMOS and IUCN. 2013. *Managing Cultural World Heritage.* Paris, UNESCO World Heritage Centre.

　　http://whc.unesco.org/en/managing-cultural-world-heritage/

联合国教科文组织、国际文物保护与修复研究中心、国际古迹遗址理事会和世界自然保护联盟，2013年。《世界文化遗产管理手册》，巴黎，联合国教科文组织世界遗产中心。

　　http：//whc.unesco.org/uploads/activities/documents/activity–827–1.pdf

WORLD HERITAGE REVIEW
http://whc.unesco.org/en/review/

世界遗产评论
http：//whc.unesco.org/en/review/

World Heritage is a quarterly review produced in English, French and Spanish by the UNESCO World Heritage Centre, featuring in-depth articles on world heritage-related issues and inscribed sites. 76 issues published since 1996.

《世界遗产》是联合国教科文组织世界遗产中心刊发的世界遗产评论季度期刊，使用英语、法语和西班牙发行，内容包括对世界遗产相关事项进行深入评论的文章。至 1996年已刊发76期。

WORLD HERITAGE PAPER SERIES
http://whc.unesco.org/en/series/

世界遗产文件系列
http：//whc.unesco.org/en/series/

UNESCO World Heritage Centre. 2002. *Managing Tourism at World Heritage Sites: a Practical Manual for World Heritage Site Managers*. Paris, UNESCO World Heritage Centre. (World Heritage Manual 1.)

　　http://whc.unesco.org/en/series/1/

UNESCO World Heritage Centre. 2002. *Investing in World Heritage: past achievements, future ambitions*. Paris, UNESCO World Heritage Centre. (World Heritage Papers 2.)

　　http://whc.unesco.org/en/series/2/

UNESCO World Heritage Centre. 2003. *Periodic Report Africa*. Paris, UNESCO World Heritage Centre. (World Heritage Reports 3.)

　　http://whc.unesco.org/en/series/3/

Hillary, A., Kokkonen, M. and Max, L. (eds). 2003. *Proceedings of the World Heritage Marine Biodiversity Workshop*. Paris, UNESCO World Heritage Centre. (World Heritage Papers 4.)

　　http://whc.unesco.org/en/series/4/

UNESCO World Heritage Centre. 2003. *Identification and Documentation of Modern Heritage*. Paris, UNESCO World Heritage Centre. (World Heritage Papers 5.)

　　http://whc.unesco.org/en/series/5/

Fowler, P. J., (ed.), *World Heritage Cultural Landscapes* 1992-2002. Paris, UNESCO World Heritage Centre. (World Heritage Papers 6.)

　　http://whc.unesco.org/en/series/6/

UNESCO World Heritage Centre. 2003. *Cultural Landscapes: the Challenges of Conservation*. Paris, UNESCO World Heritage Centre. (World Heritage Papers 7.)

　　http://whc.unesco.org/en/series/7/

联合国教科文组织世界遗产中心，2002年。《管理世界遗产地的旅游：世界遗产遗址地管理人实用手册》，巴黎，联合国教科文组织世界遗产中心。（世界遗产指南1）

　　http://whc.unesco.org/en/series/1/

联合国教科文组织世界遗产中心，2002年。《世界遗产投资：历史成果及未来目标》，巴黎，联合国教科文组织世界遗产中心。（世界遗产论文2）

　　http://whc.unesco.org/en/series/2/

联合国教科文组织世界遗产中心，2003年，《非洲定期报告》，巴黎，联合国教科文组织世界遗产中心。（世界遗产论文3）

　　http://whc.unesco.org/en/series/3/

Hillary, A., Kokkonen, M., Max, L.（eds），2003年，《世界遗产海洋生物多样性研讨会》，巴黎，联合国教科文组织世界遗产中心.（世界遗产论文4）

　　http://whc.unesco.org/en/series/4/

联合国教科文组织世界遗产中心，2003年，《现代遗产确认和文档编制》，巴黎，联合国教科文组织世界遗产中心，（世界遗产论文5）

　　http://whc.unesco.org/en/series/5/

Fowler, P. J.,（ed.），《世界遗产文化景观1992–2002年》，巴黎，联合国教科文组织世界遗产中心。（世界遗产论文6.）

　　http://whc.unesco.org/en/series/6/

联合国教科文组织世界遗产中心，2003年，《文化景观：遗产保护面临的挑战》，巴黎，联合国教科文组织世界遗产中心。（世界遗产论文7）

　　http://whc.unesco.org/en/series/7/

UNESCO World Heritage Centre. 2003. *Mobilizing Young People for World Heritage*. Paris, UNESCO World Heritage Centre. (World Heritage Papers 8.)

http://whc.unesco.org/en/series/8/

联合国教科文组织世界遗产中心，2003 年，《调动青年人服务世界遗产》，巴黎，联合国教科文组织世界遗产中心 .（世界遗产论文 8.）

http：//whc.unesco.org/en/series/8/

UNESCO World Heritage Centre. 2004. *Partnerships for World Heritage Cities: Culture as a Vector for Sustainable Urban Development*. Paris, UNESCO World Heritage Centre. (World Heritage Papers 9.)

http://whc.unesco.org/en/series/9/

联合国教科文组织世界遗产中心，2004年，《世界遗产城市合作：文化作为城市可持续发展的向量》，巴黎，联合国教科文组织世界遗产中心，（世界遗产论文 9）

http：//whc.unesco.org/en/series/9/

Stovel, H. (ed). 2004. *Monitoring World Heritage*, Paris, UNESCO World Heritage Centre. (World Heritage Papers 10.)

http://whc.unesco.org/en/series/10/

Stovel，H.（ed），2004年，《监测世界遗产》，巴黎，联合国教科文组织世界遗产中心，（世界遗产论文 10）

http：//whc.unesco.org/en/series/10/

UNESCO World Heritage Centre. 2004. *Periodic Report and Regional Programme Arab States 2000-2003*. Paris, UNESCO World Heritage Centre. (World Heritage Reports 11.)

http://whc.unesco.org/en/series/11/

联合国教科文组织世界遗产中心，2004 年，《2000–2003 年阿拉伯国家区域项目定期报告》，巴黎，联合国教科文组织世界遗产中心，（世界遗产论文11）

http：//whc.unesco.org/en/series/11/

UNESCO World Heritage Centre. 2004. *The State of World Heritage in the Asia-Pacific Region 2003*. Paris, UNESCO World Heritage Centre. (World Heritage Papers 12.)

http://whc.unesco.org/en/series/12/

联合国教科文组织世界遗产中心，2004 年，《2003 年亚太地区世界遗产状况》，巴黎，联合国教科文组织世界遗产中心，（世界遗产论文 12）

http：//whc.unesco.org/en/series/12/

de Merode, E., Smeets, R. and Westrik, C. 2004. *Linking Universal and Local Values: Managing a Sustainable Future for World Heritage*. Paris, UNESCO World Heritage Centre. (World Heritage Papers 13.)

http://whc.unesco.org/en/series/13/

de Merode，E.Smeets，R. 和 Westrik，C，2004 年，《全球和地区价值观的结合：实现世界遗产可持续发展的未来》，巴黎，联合国教科文组织世界遗产中心，（世界遗产论文 13）

http：//whc.unesco.org/en/series/13/

UNESCO World Heritage Centre. 2005. *Caribbean Archaeology and World Heritage Convention*. Paris, UNESCO World Heritage

联合国教科文组织世界遗产中心，2005 年，《加勒比考古及世界遗产公约》，巴黎，联合国教科文组织世界遗产中心，（世界遗产论文 14）

Centre. (World Heritage Papers 14.)

　　http://whc.unesco.org/en/series/14/

　　UNESCO World Heritage Centre. 2005. *Caribbean Wooden Treasures*. Paris, UNESCO World Heritage Centre. (World Heritage Papers 15.)

　　http://whc.unesco.org/en/series/15/

　　UNESCO World Heritage Centre. 2005. *World Heritage at the Vth IUCN World Parks Congress*. Paris, UNESCO World Heritage Centre. (World Heritage Reports 16.)

　　http://whc.unesco.org/en/series/16/

　　UNESCO World Heritage Centre. 2005. *Promoting and Preserving Congolese Heritage*. Paris, UNESCO World Heritage Centre. (World Heritage Papers 17.)

　　http://whc.unesco.org/en/series/17/

　　UNESCO World Heritage Centre. 2006. *Periodic Report 2004- Latin America and the Caribbean*. Paris, UNESCO World Heritage Centre. (World Heritage Papers 18.)

　　http://whc.unesco.org/en/series/18/

　　UNESCO World Heritage Centre. 2006. *American Fortifications and the World Heritage Convention*. Paris, UNESCO World Heritage Centre. (World Heritage Papers 19.)

　　http://whc.unesco.org/en/series/19/

　　UNESCO World Heritage Centre. 2006. *Periodic Report and Action Plan, Europe 2005-2006*. Paris, UNESCO World Heritage Centre. (World Heritage Reports 20.)

　　http://whc.unesco.org/en/series/20/

　　UNESCO World Heritage Centre. 2007. *World Heritage Forests - Leveraging Conservation at the*

联合国教科文组织世界遗产中心，2005 年，《加勒比木制珍品》，巴黎，联合国教科文组织世界遗产中心，（世界遗产论文15）

　　http：//whc.unesco.org/en/series/15/

联合国教科文组织世界遗产中心，2005 年，《第五届国际自然保护联盟世界公园大会之世界遗产》，巴黎，联合国教科文组织世界遗产中心，（世界遗产论文 16）

　　http：//whc.unesco.org/en/series/16/

联合国教科文组织世界遗产中心，2005年，《推广和保护刚果遗产》，巴黎，联合国教科文组织世界遗产中心，（世界遗产论文 17）

　　http：//whc.unesco.org/en/series/17/

联合国教科文组织世界遗产中心，2006年，《2004年定期报告 – 拉丁美洲及加勒比地区》，巴黎，联合国教科文组织世界遗产中心，（世界遗产论文 18）

　　http：//whc.unesco.org/en/series/18/

联合国教科文组织世界遗产中心，2006年，《美国防御工事及世界遗产公约》，巴黎，联合国教科文组织世界遗产中心，（世界遗产论文 19）

　　http：//whc.unesco.org/en/series/19/

联合国教科文组织世界遗产中心，2006 年，《2005–2006 年欧洲定期报告和行动规划》，巴黎，联合国教科文组织世界遗产中心，（世界遗产论文 20）

　　http：//whc.unesco.org/en/series/20/

联合国教科文组织世界遗产中心，2007年，《森林世界遗产 – 景观层面的利用保护》，巴

Landscape Level. Paris, UNESCO World Heritage Centre. (World Heritage Reports 21.)http://whc.unesco.org/en/series/21/

UNESCO World Heritage Centre. 2007. *Climate Change and World Heritage*. Paris, UNESCO World Heritage Centre. (World Heritage Reports 22.)

http://whc.unesco.org/en/series/22/

Hockings M., James R., Stolton S., Dudley N., Mathur V., Makombo J., Courrau J. and Parrish J. 2008.

Enhancing our Heritage Toolkit. Assessing management effectiveness of Natural World Heritage sites. Paris, UNESCO World Heritage Centre. (World Heritage Papers 23.)

http://whc.unesco.org/en/series/23/

UNESCO World Heritage Centre. 2008. *Rock Art in the Caribbean*. Paris, UNESCO World Heritage Centre. (World Heritage Papers 24.)

http://whc.unesco.org/en/series/24/

Martin O, and Piatti G. (eds). 2009. *World Heritage and Buffer Zones, International Expert Meeting on World Heritage and Buffer Zones*, Davos, Switzerland, 11–14 March 2008. Paris, UNESCO World Heritage Centre. (World Heritage Papers 25.)

http://whc.unesco.org/en/series/25/

Mitchell N., Rössler M. and Tricaud P-M. (authors/eds). 2009. *World Heritage Cultural Landscapes: A handbook for Conservation and Management*. Paris, UNESCO World Heritage Centre. (World Heritage Papers 26.)

http://whc.unesco.org/en/series/26/

UNESCO World Heritage Centre. 2010.

黎，联合国教科文组织世界遗产中心，（世界遗产论文 21）

http：//whc.unesco.org/en/series/21/

联合国教科文组织世界遗产中心，2007年，《气候变化和世界遗产》，巴黎，联合国教科文组织世界遗产中心，（世界遗产论文 22）

http：//whc.unesco.org/en/series/22/

Hockings M.，James R.，Stolton S.，Dudley，N.，Mathur V.，Makombo J.，Courrau J. 和 Parrish J，

2008 年，《优化遗产工具箱，评估世界自然遗产遗址的管理有效性》，巴黎，联合国教科文组织世界遗产中心，（世界遗产论文23）

http：//whc.unesco.org/en/series/23/

联合国教科文组织世界遗产中心，2008 年，《加勒比地区的岩石艺术》，巴黎，联合国教科文组织世界遗产中心，（世界遗产论文 24）

http：//whc.unesco.org/en/series/24/

Martin O.，Piatti G.（eds），2009 年，《世界遗产和缓冲区》，瑞士达沃斯世界遗产和缓冲区国际专家会议，2008 年 3 月 11 - 14 日，巴黎，联合国教科文组织世界遗产中心（世界遗产论文 25）

http：//whc.unesco.org/en/series/25/

Mitchell N.，Rössler M.，Tricaud P-M.（作者，编辑），2009年，《世界遗产文化景观：保护及管理手册》，巴黎，联合国教科文组织世界遗产中心，（世界遗产论文 26.）

http：//whc.unesco.org/en/series/26/

联合国教科文组织世界遗产中心，2010年，

Managing Historic Cities. Paris, UNESCO World Heritage Centre. (World Heritage Papers 27.)
http://whc.unesco.org/en/series/27/

UNESCO World Heritage Centre. 2011. *Navigating the Future of Marine World Heritage*. Paris, UNESCO World Heritage Centre. (World Heritage Papers 28.)
http://whc.unesco.org/en/series/28/

UNESCO World Heritage Centre. 2011. *Human Evolution: Adaptations, Dispersals and Social Developments (HEADS)*. Paris, UNESCO World Heritage Centre. (World Heritage Papers 29.)
http://whc.unesco.org/en/series/29/

UNESCO World Heritage Centre. 2011. *Adapting to Change: the State of Conservation of World Heritage Forests in 2011*. Paris, UNESCO World Heritage Centre. (World Heritage Papers 30.)
http://whc.unesco.org/en/series/30/

Albert M.-T., Richon M., Viñals M.J. and Witcomb A. (eds). 2012. *Community development through World Heritage*. Paris, UNESCO World Heritage Centre. (World Heritage Papers 31.)
http://whc.unesco.org/en/series/31/

Church, J., Gabrié, C., Macharia, D., Obura, D. 2012. *Assessing Marine World Heritage from an Ecosystem Perspective*. Paris, UNESCO World Heritage Centre. (World Heritage Papers 32.)
http://whc.unesco.org/en/series/32/

UNESCO World Heritage Centre. 2012. HEADS 2: *Human Origin Sites and the World Heritage Convention in Africa*. Paris, UNESCO World Heritage Centre. (World Heritage Papers 33.)
http://whc.unesco.org/en/series/33/

《管理历史城市》，巴黎，联合国世界遗产中心，（世界遗产论文 27）
http：//whc.unesco.org/en/series/27/

联合国教科文组织世界遗产中心，2011年，《引领海洋世界遗产走向未来》，巴黎，联合国教科文组织世界遗产中心，（世界遗产论文 28）
http：//whc.unesco.org/en/series/28/

联合国教科文组织世界遗产中心，2011年，《人类进化：适应、分散及社会发展（HEADS）》，巴黎，联合国教科文组织世界遗产中心，（世界遗产论文 29）
http：//whc.unesco.org/en/series/29/

联合国教科文组织世界遗产中心，2011 年，《适应改变：2011 年世界遗产森林的保护状况》，巴黎，联合国教科文组织世界遗产中心，（世界遗产论文 30）
http：//whc.unesco.org/en/series/30/

Albert M.-T.，Richon M.，Viñals M.J. 和 Witcomb A.（eds），2012年，《通过世界遗产推动社区发展》，巴黎，联合国教科文组织世界遗产中心，（世界遗产论文 31）
http：//whc.unesco.org/en/series/31/

Church，J.，Gabrié，C.，Macharia，D.，Obura，D. 2012 年，《从生态系统视角评估海洋世界遗产》，巴黎，联合国教科文组织世界遗产中心，（世界遗产论文 32）
http：//whc.unesco.org/en/series/32/

联合国教科文组织世界遗产中心，2012年，《HEADS 2：人类起源遗址地和世界遗产公约在非洲》，巴黎，联合国教科文组织世界遗产中心，（世界遗产论文 33）
http：//whc.unesco.org/en/series/33/

UNESCO World Heritage Centre. 2012. *World Heritage in a Sea of Islands - Pacific 2009 Programme*. Paris, UNESCO World Heritage Centre. (World Heritage Papers 34.)

http://whc.unesco.org/en/series/34/

Dingwall P., Kawakami K., Weise K. 2012. *Understanding World Heritage in Asia and the Pacific - The Second Cycle of Periodic Reporting 2010-2012*. Paris, UNESCO World Heritage Centre. (World Heritage Papers 35.)

http://whc.unesco.org/en/series/35/

Joffroy T., Eloundou L. (eds.). 2013. *Earthern Architecture in Today's World*. Paris, UNESCO World Heritage Centre. (World Heritage Papers 36.)

http://whc.unesco.org/en/series/36/

Falzon, C., Perry, J. 2014. *Climate Change Adaptation for Natural World Heritage Sites*. Paris, UNESCO World Heritage Centre. (World Heritage Papers 37.)

http://whc.unesco.org/en/series/37/

UNESCO World Heritage Centre. 2014. *Safeguarding Precious Resources for Island Communities*. Paris, UNESCO World Heritage Centre. (World Heritage Papers 38.)

http://whc.unesco.org/en/series/38/

UNESCO World Heritage Centre. 2014. *HEADS 3: Human Origin Sites and the World Heritage Convention in Asia*. Paris, UNESCO World Heritage Centre. (World Heritage Papers 39.)

http://whc.unesco.org/en/series/39/

Brown, J., Hay-Edie, T. 2014. *Engaging Local Communities in Stewardship of World Heritage*. Paris, UNESCO World Heritage Centre. (World Heritage Papers 40.)

http://whc.unesco.org/en/series/40/

联合国教科文组织世界遗产中心，2012年，《群岛世界遗产 – 太平洋2009年项目》，巴黎，联合国教科文组织世界遗产中心，（世界遗产论文34）

http：//whc.unesco.org/en/series/34/

Dingwall P.，Kawakami K.，Weise K，2012年，《理解亚太地区世界遗产 – 2010-2012年第二轮定期报告》，巴黎，联合国教科文组织世界遗产中心，（世界遗产论文35）

http：//whc.unesco.org/en/series/35/

Joffroy T.，Eloundou L.（编辑），2013年，《当今世界的土建筑》，巴黎，联合国教科文组织世界遗产中心，（世界遗产论文36）

http：//whc.unesco.org/en/series/36/

Falzon，C.，Perry，J，2014年，《世界自然遗产对气候变化的适应》，巴黎，联合国教科文组织世界遗产中心，（世界遗产论文37）

http：//whc.unesco.org/en/series/37/

联合国教科文组织世界遗产中心，2014年，《保护珍贵岛屿社区资源》，巴黎，联合国教科文组织世界遗产中心，（世界遗产论文38）

http：//whc.unesco.org/en/series/38/

联合国教科文组织世界遗产中心2014年，《HEADS3：人类起源遗址地和世界遗产公约在非洲》，巴黎，联合国教科文组织世界遗产中心，（世界遗产论文39）

http：//whc.unesco.org/en/series/39/

Brown，J.，Hay-Edie，T. 2014年，《提升当地社区对世界遗产的管理》，巴黎，联合国教科文组织世界遗产中心，（世界遗产论文40）

http：//whc.unesco.org/en/series/40/

GENERAL AND THEMATIC REFERENCES

Badman T., Bomhard B. and Dingwall P. 2008. *World Heritage Nominations for Natural Properties: A Resource Manual for Practitioners*. Gland, Switzerland, IUCN.

Batisse M., Bolla G. 2005. *The Invention of World Heritage*. Paris, UNESCO.

Cameron, C. 2005. *Background Paper for the Special Expert Meeting of the World Heritage Convention: The Concept of Outstanding Universal Value*. Kazan, Republic of Tatarstan, Russian Federation.
http://whc.unesco.org/archive/2005/whc05-29com-inf09Ae.pdf

Cameron C., Rössler M. 2013. Many Voices, One Vision: The Early Years of the World Heritage Convention. Farnham, Ashgate.

Galla A. (ed.). 2012. *World Heritage – Benefits Beyond Borders*. Paris/Cambridge, UNESCO Publishing/Cambridge University Press.

Feilden B.M. and Jokilehto J. 1993. *Management Guidelines for World Cultural Heritage Sites*. (First edition). Rome, ICCROM.

Francioni, F. (ed). 2008. The 1972 *World Heritage Convention: A Commentary*. Oxford Commentaries on International Law, UK.

ICOMOS. 1965. International Charter for the Conservation and Restoration of Monuments and Sites (The Venice Charter 1964). Paris, ICOMOS.
http://www.icomos.org/venice_charter.html

ICOMOS. 2004. ICOMOS Analysis of the

一般引用及主题引用

Badman T., Bomhard B. 和 Dingwall P, 2008年,《申报世界自然遗产:实践者资源手册》,瑞士格兰德,世界自然保护联盟

Batisse M., Bolla G. 2005 年,《世界遗产的发明》,巴黎,联合国教科文组织

Cameron, C.2005年,《世界遗产公约特别专家会议背景文件:突出普遍价值的概念》,俄罗斯联邦鞑靼斯坦共和国,喀山
http://whc.unesco.org/archive/2005/whc05-29com-inf09Ae.pdf

Cameron C., Rössler M, 2013 年,《不同声音一个愿景:早期的世界遗产公约》,Farnham, Ashgate.

Galla A.(ed.).2012年,《世界遗产 – 跨国界优势》,巴黎/剑桥,联合国教科文组织出版社/剑桥大学出版社

Feilden B.M. 和 Jokilehto J, 1993 年,《世界文化遗产地管理指南》(第一版),罗马,国际文物与修复保护研究中心

Francioni F.(ed), 2008 年《1972 年世界遗产公约:评论》,牛津国际法律评论,英国

国际古迹遗址理事会,1965年《国际古迹保护与修复宪章》(威尼斯宪章1964年),巴黎,国际古迹遗址理事会
http://www.icomos.org/venice_charter.html

国际古迹遗址理事会,2004年,《国际古迹

World Heritage List and Tentative Lists and Follow-Up Action Plan. Paris, ICOMOS.

ICOMOS. 2005. *The World Heritage List: Filling the Gaps – An Action Plan for the Future.* Paris, ICOMOS.

http://www.international.icomos.org/world_heritage/gaps.pdf

ICOMOS. 2005. *Xi'an Declaration on the Conservation of the Setting of Heritage Structures, Sites and Areas.*

http://www.international.icomos.org/charters/xian-declaration.pdf

ICOMOS. 2008. *Compendium on Standards for the Inscription of Cultural Properties to the World Heritage List.*

http://whc.unesco.org/en/sessions/32COM/documents/

ICOMOS. 2011. *Guidance on Heritage Impact Assessments for Cultural World Heritage Properties.* Paris, ICOMOS.

http://openarchive.icomos.org/266/1/ICOMOS_Heritage_Impact_Assessment_2010.pdf

ICOMOS technical and thematic studies

http://www.icomos.org/en/documentation-center

IUCN. 2006. *Enhancing the IUCN Evaluation Process of World Heritage Nominations: A Contribution to Achieving a Credible and Balanced World Heritage List.*

https://portals.iucn.org/library/efiles/documents/2006-059.pdf

IUCN. 2006. *The World Heritage List: Guidance and Future Priorities for Identifying Natural Heritage of Potential Outstanding Universal Value.*

遗址理事会世界遗产名录、预备名录及后续行动规划分析》，巴黎，国际古迹遗址理事会

国际古迹遗址理事会，2005年，《世界遗产名录：填补空白–未来行动规划》，巴黎，国际古迹遗址理事会.

http：//www.international.icomos.org/world_heritage/gaps.pdf

国际古迹遗址理事会，2005年，《西安宣言——保护历史建筑、古遗址和历史地区的环境》

http：//www.international.icomos.org/charters/xian–declaration.pdf

国际古迹遗址理事会，2008年，《文化遗产列入世界遗产名录标准刚要》

http：//whc.unesco.org/en/sessions/32COM/documents/

国际古迹遗址理事会，2011年，《世界文化遗产影响评估指南》，巴黎，国际古迹遗址理事会

http：//openarchive.icomos.org/266/1/ICOMOS_Heritage_Impact_Assessment_2010.pdf

国际古迹遗址理事会技术及主题研究

http：//www.icomos.org/en/documentation-center

世界自然保护联盟，2006年，《强化世界自然保护联盟对申报世界遗产的评估程序：促进建立可信的、平衡的世界遗产名录》

https：//portals.iucn.org/library/efiles/documents/2006–059.pdf

世界自然保护联盟，2006年，《世界遗产名录：未来重点确认有潜在突出普遍价值的自然遗产指南》

http://cmsdata.iucn.org/downloads/ouv2006_english.pdf

IUCN. 2008. *Outstanding Universal Value – Standards for Natural World Heritage, A Compendium on Standards for Inscriptions of Natural Properties on the World Heritage List.* http://cmsdata.iucn.org/downloads/ouv_compendium_english.pdf

IUCN Technical and Thematic Studies:
http://www.iucn.org/knowledge/publications_doc/

Pressouyre, L. 1993. *The World Heritage Convention, twenty years later.* UNESCO, Paris.
http://whc.unesco.org/en/280/?id=564&

Stovel, H. 1998. *Risk Preparedness: A Management Manual for World Cultural Heritage.* Rome, ICCROM.http://www.iccrom.org/pdf/ICCROM_17_RiskPreparedness_en.pdf

UNESCO World Heritage Centre. Education Kit. 2002. *World Heritage in Young Hands.* Paris, UNESCO World Heritage Centre.
http://whc.unesco.org/en/educationkit/

UNESCO World Heritage Centre. 2003. *World Heritage 2002 - Shared Legacy, Common Responsibility.* Paris, UNESCO World Heritage Centre.
http://whc.unesco.org/en/activities/563/

UNESCO World Heritage Centre. 2007. *World Heritage – Challenges for the Millenium.* Paris, UNESCO World Heritage Centre.
http://whc.unesco.org/en/challenges-for-the-Millennium/

UNESCO World Heritage Centre. 2007. *Case

http：// cmsdata.iucn.org/downloads/ouv2006_english.pdf

世界自然保护联盟，2008年，《突出普遍价值－世界自然遗产标准，世界自然遗产列入世界遗产名录标准刚要》
http：//cmsdata.iucn.org/downloads/ouv_compendium_english.pdf

世界自然保护联盟技术及主题研究：
http：//www.iucn.org/knowledge/publications_doc/

Pressouyre，L.1993年，《世界遗产公约：二十年之后》，联合国教科文组织，巴黎
http：//whc.unesco.org/en/280/? id=564&

Stovel，H.1998年，《风险准备：世界文化遗产管理手册》，罗马，国际文物与修复保护研究中心 http：//www.iccrom.org/pdf/ICCROM_17_RiskPreparedness_en.pdf

联合国教科文组织世界遗产中心，教育工具箱，2002年，《世界遗产在年轻人手中》，巴黎，联合国教科文组织世界遗产中心
http：//whc.unesco.org/en/educationkit/

联合国教科文组织世界遗产中心，2003年，《世界遗产2002年 － 共有遗产和共同责任》，巴黎，联合国教科文组织世界遗产中心
http：//whc.unesco.org/en/activities/563/

联合国教科文组织世界遗产中心，2007年，《世界遗产 － 千年挑战》，巴黎，联合国教科文组织世界遗产中心
http：//whc.unesco.org/en/challenges-for-the-Millennium/

联合国教科文组织世界遗产中心，2007年，

Studies on Climate Change and World Heritage. Paris, UNESCO World Heritage Centre.

http://whc.unesco.org/en/activities/473/

UNESCO World Heritage Centre. 2012. *African World Heritage – A Remarkable Diversity.* Paris, UNESCO World Heritage Centre.

UNESCO World Heritage Centre. 2013. *Celebrating 40 years of the World Heritage Convention.* Paris, UNESCO World Heritage Centre.

http://whc.unesco.org/en/celebrating-40-years

UNESCO World Heritage Centre. 2013. *Report of the 40th Anniversary of the World Heritage Convention.* Paris, UNESCO World Heritage Centre.
http://whc.unesco.org/en/report-40th-Anniversary

UNESCO World Heritage Centre. *Patrimonito's World Heritage Adventures.* Paris, UNESCO World HeritageCentre.

http://whc.unesco.org/en/patrimonito/

von Droste B., Plachter H. and Rössler M. (eds.). 1995. *Cultural Landscapes of Universal Value: Components of a Global Strategy*, Jena (Germany), Fischer Verlag.

von Droste, B., Rössler, M. and Titchen, S. (eds.). 1999. *Linking Nature and Culture*, Report of the Global Strategy Natural and Cultural Heritage Expert Meeting, 25-29 March 1998, Amsterdam, The Netherlands, UNESCO/ Ministry for Foreign Affairs/Ministry for Education, Science, and Culture, The Hague.http://whc.unesco.org/archive/amsterdam98.pdf

World Commission on Protected Areas

《气候变化与世界遗产案例研究》，巴黎，联合国教科文组织世界遗产中心

http：//whc.unesco.org/en/activities/473/

联合国教科文组织世界遗产中心，2012年，《非洲世界遗产 – 显著多样性》，巴黎，联合国教科文组织世界遗产中心

联合国教科文组织世界遗产中心，2013 年，《庆祝世界遗产公约 40 周年》，巴黎，联合国教科文组织世界遗产中心

http：//whc.unesco.org/en/celebrating-40-years

联合国教科文组织世界遗产中心，2013 年，《世界遗产公约 40 周年报告》，巴黎，联合国教科文组织世界遗产中心，

http：//whc.unesco.org/en/report-40th-Anniversary

联合国教科文组织世界遗产中心，《世界遗产青年保护者世界遗产探险》，巴黎，联合国教科文组织世界遗产中心

http：//whc.unesco.org/en/patrimonito/

von Droste B.，Plachter H. 和 Rössler M.（编辑），1995年，《文化景观的：普遍价值全球战略的组成部分》，耶拿（德国），菲舍尔出版社

von Droste，B.，Rössler，M. 和 Titchen，S.（编辑），1999年，《连接自然与文化：世界自然遗产与文化遗产专家会议全球战略报告》，1998 年 3 月 25-29 日，荷兰阿姆斯特丹，联合国教科文组织/外交部/教育、科学和文化部，海牙

http：//whc.unesco.org/archive/amsterdam98.pdf

保护区世界委员会（WCPA）最佳实践指南

(WCPA) Best Practice Guidelines

www.iucn.org/about/union/commissions/wcpa/wcpa_puball/wcpa_bpg/

- *National System Planning for Protected Areas,1998*
- *Economic Values of Protected Areas: Guidelines for Protected Area Managers,1998*
- *Guidelines for Marine Protected Areas,1999*
- *Indigenous and Traditional Peoples and Protected Areas,2000*
- *Financing Protected Areas: Guidelines for Protected Area Managers,2000*
- *Transboundary Protected Areas for Peace and Co-operation,2001*
- *Sustainable Tourism in Protected Areas: Guidelines for Planning and Management,2002*
- *Management Guidelines for IUCN Category V Protected Areas: Protected Landscapes/Seascapes, 2002*
- *Guidelines for Management Planning of Protected Areas,2003*
- *Indigenous and Local Communities and Protected Areas: Towards Equity and Enhanced Conservation,2004*
- *Forests and Protected Areas: Guidance on the use of the IUCN protected area management categories,2006*
- *Sustainable Financing of Protected Areas: A global review of challenges and options,2006*
- *Evaluating Effectiveness: A Framework for Assessing Management Effectiveness of Protected Areas, 2006*
- *Identification and Gap Analysis of Key Biodiversity Areas,2007*
- *Sacred Natural Sites: Guidelines for Protected Area Managers,2008*

WEB ADDRESSES
UNESCO
http://www.unesco.org

www.iucn.org/about/union/commissions/wcpa/wcpa_puball/wcpa_bpg/

《国家保护区系统规划》，1998 年
《保护区的经济价值：保护区管理人员指南》，1998 年
《海洋保护区指南》，1999 年
《本土传统居民及保护区》，2000 年

《资助保护区：保护区管理人员指南》，2000 年
《跨境保护区的和平及合作》，2001 年

《保护区可持续发展：规划及管理指南》，2002 年
《世界自然保护联盟第五类保护区：受保护的景观／海景》，2002 年

《保护区管理规划指南》，2003 年

《本土传统居民及保护区：实现均衡的、强化保护》，2004 年

《森林和保护区：世界自然保护联盟保护区管理类别使用指南》，2006 年

《为保护区提供可持续资质：挑战及选择全球视角》，2006 年
《有效性评估：保护区管理有效性评估框架》，2006 年

《确认主要生物多样化区域及差距分析》，2007 年
《神圣的自然遗产遗址地：保护区管理人员指南》，2008 年

网址
联合国教科文组织
http：//www.unesco.org

UNESCO World Heritage Centre
http://whc.unesco.org

联合国教科文组织世界遗产中心
http：//whc.unesco.org

UNESCO World Heritage Centre publications
http://whc.unesco.org/en/publications/
UNESCO World Heritage Review
http://whc.unesco.org/en/review/

联合国教科文组织世界遗产中心出版物
http：//whc.unesco.org/en/publications/
联合国教科文组织世界遗产回顾
http：//whc.unesco.org/en/review/

UNESCO World Heritage Map
http://whc.unesco.org/en/map/

联合国教科文组织世界遗产地图
http：//whc.unesco.org/en/map/

ICCROM
http://www.iccrom.org

国际文物与修复保护研究中心
http：//www.iccrom.org

ICCROM publications
http://www.archivalplatform.org/resources/
entry/iccrom_publications/

国际文物保护与修复研究中心出版物
http：//www.archivalplatform.org/resources/
entry/iccrom_publications/

ICOMOS
http://www.icomos.org

国际古迹遗址理事会
http：//www.icomos.org

ICOMOS publications
http://www.icomos.org/en/documentation-
center

国际古迹遗址理事会出版物
http：//www.icomos.org/en/documentation-
center

IUCN
http://www.iucn.org

世界自然保护联盟
http：//www.iucn.org

IUCN publications
http://www.iucn.org/knowledge/publications_
doc/

世界自然保护联盟出版物
http：//www.iucn.org/knowledge/publications_
doc/

World Commission on Protected Areas (WCPA)
Best Practice Guidelines
www.iucn.org/about/union/commissions/wcpa/
wcpa_puball/wcpa_bpg/

保护区世界委员会（WCPA）最佳实践指南

www.iucn.org/about/union/commissions/wcpa/
wcpa_puball/wcpa_bpg/

国际文化遗产保护文件

《实施世界遗产公约操作指南》选辑

（2021 年）

西安市文物保护考古研究院
联合国教科文组织世界遗产中心
国际古迹遗址理事会
国际古迹遗址理事会西安国际保护中心
编译

文物出版社

目　录

◎ 2021

CONTENTS

© 2021

WHC.21/01
31 July 2021

实施《世界遗产公约》操作指南
Operational Guidelines for the Implementation of the *World Heritage Convention*

UNITED NATIONS EDUCATIONAL, SCIE-NTIFIC AND CULTURAL ORGANIZA-TION

联合国教育、科学及文化组织

INTERGOVERNMENTAL COMMITTEE FOR THE PROTECTION OF THE WORLD CULTURAL AND NATURAL HERITAGE

保护世界文化与自然遗产政府间委员会

United Nations Educational, Scientific and Cultural Organization

World Heritage Convention

WORLD HERITAGE CENTRE

世界遗产中心

The *Operational Guidelines* are periodically revised to reflect the decisions of the World Heritage Committee. Please verify that you are using the latest version of the *Operational Guidelines* by checking the date of the *Operational Guidelines* on the UNESCO World Heritage Centre website indicated below.

会定期修订《操作指南》，以反映世界遗产委员会的最新决定。请通过联合国教科文组织下列网址，检查《操作指南》的日期，确认您所使用的是最新版本。

The *Operational Guidelines* (in English and French), the text of the *World Heritage Convention* (in five languages), and other documents and information concerning World Heritage are available from the World Heritage Centre:

UNESCO World Heritage Centre

7, place de Fontenoy

75352 Paris 07 SP

France

Contact: https://whc.unesco.org/en/world-heritage-centre

Links: https://whc.unesco.org/

https://whc.unesco.org/en/guidelines *(English)*

https://whc.unesco.org/fr/orientations *(French)*

可从世界遗产中心获取《操作指南》（英文和法文）、《保护世界文化与自然遗产公约》全文（五种语言）、其他世界遗产相关的文献和信息：

联合国教科文组织世界遗产中心（法国巴黎：

7，placede Fontenoy

75352 Paris 07 SP

France）

联系方式：https://whc.unesco.org/en/world–heritage–centre

链接：http://whc.unesco.org/

http://whc.unesco. org/en/guidelines（英文）

http://whc.unesco.org/fr/orientations（法文）

Table of Contents   Chapter number

目录

Annex 15: Upstream Process Request Format　　　　附录 15：上游程序申请格式

SELECT WORLD HERITAGE BIBLIOGRAPHY　　　　**选择世界遗产相关的参考书目**

ACRONYMS AND ABBREVIATIONS　　　　**缩略语**

DoCoMoMo　International Committee for the Documentation and Conservation of Monuments and Sites of the Modern Movement　　　　DoCoMoMo　国际现代主义建筑保护与记录国际委员会

ICCROM　International Centre for the Study of the Preservation and Restoration of Cultural Property　　　　ICCROM　国际文物保护与修复研究中心

ICOMOS　International Council on Monuments and Sites　　　　ICOMOS　国际古迹遗址理事会

IFLA　International Federation of Landscape Architects　　　　IFLA　国际景观建筑师联合会

IUCN　International Union for Conservation of Nature and Natural Resources　　　　IUCN　世界自然保护联盟（前国际自然及自然资源保护联盟）

IUGS　International Union of Geological Sciences　　　　IUGS　国际地质科学联合会

MAB　Man and the Biosphere Programme of UNESCO　　　　MAB　教科文组织人与生物圈计划

NGO　Non-governmental organization　　　　NGO　非政府组织

TICCIH　International Committee for the Conservation of the Industrial Heritage　　　　TICCIH　国际工业遗产保护委员会

UNEP　United Nations Environment Programme　　　　UNEP　联合国环境规划署

UNEP-WCMC　World Conservation Monitoring Centre (UNEP)　　　　UNEP–WCMC　世界保护监测中心（联合国环境规划署）

UNESCO　United Nations Educational, Scientific　　　　UNESCO　联合国教育、科学及文化组织

and Cultural Organization

Ⅰ. INTRODUCTION

Ⅰ.A　The *Operational Guidelines*

1. The *Operational Guidelines for the Imple-men-tation of the World Heritage Convention* (herein-after referred to as the *Operational Guidelines)* aim to facilitate the implementation of the *Convention concerning the Protection of the World Cultural and Natural Heritage* (hereinafter referred to as "the *World Heritage Convention*" or "the *Convention*"), by setting forth the procedures for:

a) the inscription of properties on the World Heritage List and the List of World Heritage in Danger;

b) the protection and conservation of World Heritage properties;

c) the granting of International Assistance under the World Heritage Fund; and

d) the mobilization of national and international support in favor of the *Convention*.

2. The *Operational Guidelines* are periodically revised to reflect the decisions of the World Heritage Committee.

The historical development of the *Operational Guidelines* is available at: https://whc.unesco.org/en/guidelines/

3. The key users of the *Operational Guidelines* are:

a) the States Parties to the *World Heritage Convention*;

b) the Intergovernmental Committee for the Protection of the Cultural and Natural Heritage of Outstanding Universal Value, hereinafter referred to as "the World Heritage Committee" or "the

Ⅰ. 引言

Ⅰ.A　《操作指南》

1.《实施《世界遗产公约》的操作指南》（以下简称《操作指南》）旨在促进《保护世界文化和自然遗产公约》（以下简称《世界遗产公约》或《公约》）的实施，并为开展下列工作设置相应的程序：

a）将遗产列入《世界遗产名录》和《濒危世界遗产名录》；

b）世界遗产的保护和保存；

c）世界遗产基金项下提供的国际援助；

d）调动国家和国际力量，为《公约》提供支持；

2.《操作指南》将会定期修改，以反映世界遗产委员会的最新决策。

《操作指南》的发展历程可参见以下网址：http://whc.unesco.org/en/ guidelineshistorical

3.《操作指南》主要使用者：

a)《世界遗产公约》的缔约国；

b) 保护具有突出的普遍价值的文化和自然遗产政府间委员会，以下简称"世界遗产委员会"或"委员会"；

Committee";

c) the UNESCO World Heritage Centre as Secretariat to the World Heritage Committee, hereinafter referred to as "the Secretariat";

d) the Advisory Bodies to the World Heritage Committee;

e) site managers, stakeholders and partners in the protection of World Heritage properties.

I.B   The *World Heritage Convention*

4. The cultural and natural heritage is among the priceless and irreplaceable assets, not only of each nation, but of humanity as a whole. The loss, through deterioration or disappearance, of any of these most prized assets constitutes an impoverishment of the heritage of all the peoples of the world. Parts of this heritage, because of their exceptional qualities, can be considered to be of "Outstanding Universal Value" and as such worthy of special protection against the dangers which increasingly threaten them.

5. To ensure, as far as possible, the proper identi-fication, protection, conservation and presentation of the world's heritage, the Member States of UNESCO adopted the *World Heritage Convention* in 1972. The *Convention* foresees the establishment of a "World Heritage Committee" and a "World Heritage Fund". Both the Committee and the Fund have been in operation since 1976.

6. Since the adoption of the *Convention* in 1972, the international community has embraced the concept of "sustainable development". The protection and conservation of the natural and cultural heritage constitute a significant contribution to sustainable development.

7. The *Convention* aims at the identification,

c) 世界遗产委员会秘书处，即联合国教育、科学及文化组织世界遗产中心，以下简称"秘书处"；

d) 世界遗产委员会的咨询机构；

e) 负责保护世界遗产的遗产地管理人员、利益相关方和合作伙伴。

I.B   《世界遗产公约》

4. 无论对各国还是对全人类而言，文化和自然遗产都是不可估价且无法替代的财产。这些最珍贵的财富，一旦遭受任何破坏或消失，都是对世界各族人民遗产的一次浩劫。一些遗产具有独一无二的特性，可以认为其具有"突出的普遍价值"，需加以特殊的保护，以消除日益威胁遗产安全的各种危险。

5. 为了尽可能保证对世界遗产的认定、保护、保存和展示，联合国教育、科学及文化组织成员国于 1972 年通过了《世界遗产公约》。《公约》确认了世界遗产委员会和世界遗产基金的建立，二者自 1976 年开始运行。

6. 自从 1972 年通过《公约》以来，国际社会全面接受了"可持续发展"这一概念。而保护、保存自然和文化遗产就是对可持续发展的巨大贡献。

7.《公约》旨在确认、保护、保存、展示具

prot-ection, conservation, presentation and trans-mission to future generations of cultural and natural heritage of Outstanding Universal Value.

8. The criteria and conditions for the inscription of properties on the World Heritage List have been developed to evaluate the Outstanding Universal Value of properties and to guide States Parties in the protection and management of World Heritage properties.

9. When a property inscribed on the World Heritage List is threatened by serious and specific dangers, the Committee considers placing it on the List of World Heritage in Danger. When the Outstanding Universal Value of the property which justified its inscription on the World Heritage List is lost, the Committee considers deleting the property from the World Heritage List.

Ⅰ. C　The States Parties to the *World Heritage Convention*

10. States are encouraged to become party to the *Convention*. Model instruments for ratification/acceptance and accession are included as Annex 1. The original signed version should be sent to the Director-General of UNESCO.

11. The list of States Parties to the *Convention* is available at: https://whc.unesco.org/en/statesparties

12. States Parties to the *Convention* are en-couraged to adopt a human-rights based approach, and ensure gender-balanced participation of a wide variety of stakeholders and rights-holders, including site managers, local and regional governments, local communities, indigenous peoples, non-governmental organizations (NGOs) and other

有突出的普遍价值的文化和自然遗产，并将其代代相传。

8. 已制定了遗产列入《世界遗产名录》的标准和条件，以评估遗产是否具有突出的普遍价值，并指导缔约国保护和管理世界遗产。

9. 当《世界遗产名录》上的某项遗产受到了严重的特殊的威胁时，委员会将考虑把该遗产列入《濒危世界遗产名录》。当该遗产藉以列入《世界遗产名录》的突出普遍价值受到破坏时，委员会将考虑把该遗产从《世界遗产名录》上移除。

Ⅰ. C　《世界遗产公约》缔约国

10. 鼓励各国加入《公约》，成为缔约国。附件 1 收录了批准 / 接受公约和正式加入公约的文献范本。签署后的文献原件应呈递联合国教育、科学及文化组织总干事。

11.《公约》各缔约国名单可参见以下网址：http://whc.unesco.org/en/statesparties

12. 鼓励《公约》缔约国采用基于人权和性别平等的方式，保证各利益相关方和产权人，包括遗产管理者、当地和地区政府、当地社区、原住民、非政府组织（NGO）、其他相关团体和合作伙伴，参与世界遗产的认定、申报和保护。

interested parties and partners in the identification, nomination, management and protection processes of World Heritage properties.

Decision 43 COM 11A

13. States Parties to the *Convention* should provide the Secretariat with the names and contact details of the governmental organization(s) primarily responsible as national focal point(s) for the implementation of the *Convention*, so that copies of all official correspondence and documents can be sent by the Secretariat to these national focal points as appropriate.

Decision 43 COM 11A

14. States Parties are encouraged to bring together their cultural and natural heritage experts at regular intervals to discuss the implementation of the *Convention*. States Parties may wish to involve representatives of the Advisory Bodies and other experts and partners as appropriate.

Decision 43 COM 11A

14bis. States Parties are encouraged to mainstream into their programmes and activities related to the *World Heritage Convention* the principles of the relevant policies adopted by the World Her-itage Committee, the General Assembly of States Parties to the *Convention* and the UNESCO Gove-rning Bodies, such as the Policy Document for the Integration of a Sustainable Development Perspective into the Processes of the *World Heritage Convention* and the UNESCO policy on engaging with indigenous peoples, as well as other related policies and documents, including the 2030 Agenda for Sustainable Development and international human rights standards.

第 43.COM.11A 号决议

13.《公约》各缔约国应向秘书处提供作为国家实施《公约》协调中心的政府机构的名称和详细联系方式，以便秘书处发放各种官方信函和文件。

第 43.COM.11A 号决议

14. 鼓励各缔约国召集本国文化和自然遗产专家定期讨论《公约》的实施。各缔约国可以适当邀请咨询机构的代表和其他专家参加讨论。

第 43.COM.11A 号决议

14 补充. 鼓励缔约国将世界遗产委员会、《世界遗产公约》缔约国大会、联合国教科文组织管理机构通过的相关政策原则，例如，《将可持续发展愿景融入世界遗产公约进程的政策》，联合国教科文组织关于融入原住民的政策文件、以及其他相关文件中，包括《2030 年可持续发展议程》和国际人权标准等，纳入到其与《世界遗产公约》相关的方案和活动中，形成主流。

15. While fully respecting the sovereignty of the States on whose territory the cultural and natural heritage is situated, States Parties to the *Convention* recognize the collective interest of the international community to cooperate in the protection of this heritage. States Parties to the *World Heritage Convention*, have the responsibility to:

15. 在充分尊重文化和自然遗产所在国主权的同时，《公约》各缔约国也应该认识到，合作开展遗产保护工作符合国际社会的共同利益。《世界遗产公约》各缔约国有责任做到以下几点：

Article 6(1) of the *World Heritage Convention*.
Decision 43 COM 11A

《世界遗产公约》第 6（1）条。
第 43.COM.11A 号决议

a) ensure the identification, nomination, protection, conservation, presentation, and transmission to future generations of the cultural and natural heritage found within their territory, and give help in these tasks to other States Parties that request it;

a）保证在本国境内文化和自然遗产的确认、申报、保护、保存、展示以及代代相传，并在其他国家提出请求时，针对以上事宜提供帮助；

Article 4 and 6(2) of the *World Heritage Convention*.

《世界遗产公约》第 4 条和第 6（2）条。

b) adopt general policies to give the heritage a function in the life of the community;

b）制定、通过旨在赋予文化和自然遗产合理功能，使其在社会生活中发挥一定作用的总体政策；

Article 5 of the *World Heritage Convention*.

《世界遗产公约》第 5 条。

c) integrate heritage protection into comprehensive planning programmes and coordination mechanisms, giving consideration in particular to the resilience of socio-ecological systems of properties;

c) 将遗产保护纳入综合规划方案和协调机制中，特别需要考虑到遗产的社会生态系统的复原力；

d) establish services for the protection, conservation and presentation of the heritage;

d) 建立负责遗产保护、保存和展示事务的机构；

e) develop scientific and technical studies to identify actions that would counteract the dangers that threaten the heritage;

e) 开展科学和技术研究，找出消除对本国遗产的威胁的方法；

f) take appropriate legal, scientific, technical, administrative and financial measures to protect the heritage;

f) 采取适当的法律、科学、技术、行政和财政措施来保护遗产；

g) foster the establishment or development of national or regional centres for training in the protec-

g) 促进建立或发展有关保护、保存和展示文化和自然遗产的国家或地区培训中心，并鼓

tion, conservation and presentation of the heritage and encourage scientific research in these fields;

h) not take any deliberate measures that directly or indirectly damage their heritage or that of another State Party to the *Convention*;

Article 6(3) of the *World Heritage Convention*.

i) submit to the World Heritage Committee an inventory of properties suitable for inscription on the World Heritage List (referred to as a Tentative List);

Article 11(1) of the *World Heritage Convention*.

j) make regular contributions to the World Heritage Fund, the amount of which is determined by the General Assembly of States Parties to the *Convention*;

Article 16(1) of the *World Heritage Convention*.

k) consider and encourage the establishment of national, public and private foundations or associations to facilitate donations for the protection of World Heritage;

Article 17 of the *World Heritage Convention*.

l) give assistance to international fundraising campaigns organized for the World Heritage Fund;

Article 18 of the *World Heritage Convention*.

m) use educational and information programmes to strengthen appreciation and respect by their peoples of the cultural and natural heritage defined in Articles 1 and 2 of the *Convention*, and to keep the public informed of the dangers threatening this heritage;

励这些领域的科学研究；

h）不得故意采取任何可能直接或间接损害本国或公约其他缔约国领土内遗产的措施；

《世界遗产公约》第6（3）条

i）向世界遗产委员会递交一份关于本国领土内适于列入《世界遗产名录》的遗产清单（称为《预备名录》）；

《世界遗产公约》第11（1）条

j）定期向世界遗产基金缴款，缴款额由公约缔约国大会决定；

《世界遗产公约》第16（1）条

k）考虑和鼓励设立国家、公立以及私立基金会或协会，促进保护世界遗产的募捐；

《世界遗产公约》第17条。

l）对世界遗产基金的国际募款活动给予协助；

《世界遗产公约》第18条。

m）通过教育和宣传活动努力加强本国人民对公约第1和2条中所确定的文化和自然遗产的理解和尊重，并使公众广泛了解遗产面临的威胁；

Article 27 of the *World Heritage Convention*.

《世界遗产公约》第 27 条。

n) provide information to the World Heritage Committee on the implementation of the *World Heritage Convention* and the state of conservation of properties; and

ｎ）向世界遗产委员会递交报告，详述《世界遗产公约》的实施情况和这类遗产保护状况；

Article 29 of the *World Heritage Convention*. Resolution adopted by the 11th General Assembly of States Parties (1997)

《世界遗产公约》第 29 条。

1997 年第十一届缔约国大会通过《决议》。

o) contribute to and comply with the sustainable development objectives, including gender equality, in the World Heritage processes and in their heritage conservation and management systems.

ｏ）在世界遗产进程及其遗产保护和管理系统中，促进实现并遵守包括性别平等在内的可持续发展目标。

16. States Parties are encouraged to attend sessions of the World Heritage Committee and its subsidiary bodies.

16. 鼓励本公约缔约国参加世界遗产委员会及其附属机构的各届会议。

Rule 8.1 of the Rules of Procedure of the World Heritage Committee.

《世界遗产委员会议事规则》第 8.1 条。

Ⅰ.D 《世界遗产公约》缔约国大会

Ⅰ.D　The General Assembly of States Parties to the *World Heritage Convention*

17. The General Assembly of States Parties to the *World Heritage Convention* meets during the sessions of the General Conference of UNESCO. The General Assembly manages its meetings according to its Rules of Procedure, available at: https://whc.unesco.org/en/ga

17. 大会在联合国教科文组织大会常会期间召开。缔约国大会根据《议事规则》组织会议，相关内容可参见以下网址：https://whc.unesco.org/en/ga

Article 8(1), of the *World Heritage Convention*, Rule 49 of the Rules of Procedure of the World Heritage Committee.

《世界遗产公约》第 8（1）条，《世界遗产委员会议事规则》第 49 条。

18. The General Assembly determines the uniform percentage of contributions to the World Heritage Fund applicable to all States Parties and elects members to the World Heritage Committee. Both the General Assembly and General Confer-

18. 大会确定适用于所有缔约国的统一缴款比例，并选举世界遗产委员会成员。缔约国大会和联合国教科文组织大会都将收到世界遗产委员会关于各项活动的报告。

ence of UNESCO receive a report from the World Heritage Committee on its activities.

Articles 8(1), 16(1) and 29 of the *World Heritage Convention* and Rule 49 of the Rules of Procedure of the World Heritage Committee.

《世界遗产公约》第 8（1）条、第 16（1）条和第 29 条；《世界遗产委员会议事规则》第 49 条。

Ⅰ.E   The World Heritage Committee

Ⅰ.E   世界遗产委员会

19. The World Heritage Committee is composed of 21 members and meets at least once a year (June/July). It establishes its Bureau, which meets during the sessions of the Committee as frequently as deemed necessary. The composition of the Committee and its Bureau is available at: https://whc.unesco.org/en/committee

19. 世界遗产委员会由二十一个成员国组成，每年至少召开一次会议（六月或七月）。委员会设有主席团，在委员会常会期间召开会议，会议次数根据实际需求确定。委员会及其主席团的组成可参见以下网址：https://whc.unesco.org/en/committee

The World Heritage Committee can be contacted through its Secretariat, the World Heritage Centre.

可以通过世界遗产中心，即世界遗产委员会秘书处，与委员会取得联系。

20. The Committee manages its meetings according to its Rules of Procedure, available at: https://whc.unesco.org/en/committee

20. 世界遗产委员会根据《议事规则》召开会议，可参见以下网址：https://whc.unesco.org/en/committee

21. The term of office of Committee members is six years but, in order to ensure equitable representation and rotation, States Parties are invited by the General Assembly to consider voluntarily reducing their term of office from six to four years and are discouraged from seeking consecutive terms of office.

21. 世界遗产委员会成员任期六年。然而，为了保证世界遗产委员会公正的代表性和轮值制，大会建议缔约国自愿考虑将任期从六年缩短到四年，并不鼓励连任。

Article 8(2) of the *World Heritage Convention* and the Resolutions of the 7th (1989), 12th (1999) and 13th (2001) General Assembly of States Parties to the *World Heritage Convention*.
Article 9(1) of the *World Heritage Convention*.

《世界遗产公约》第 9（1）条
《世界遗产公约》第 8（2）条和《世界遗产公约》缔约国第七届（1989 年）、第十二届（1999 年）及第十三届（2001 年）大会决议。
《世界遗产公约》第 1（12）款。

22. At each election, due consideration shall be given to the election of at least one State Party

22. 每次选举时，应适当考虑选举出至少一个从未担任过世界遗产委员会成员的缔约国。

which has never served as a Member of the World Heritage Committee.

Rule 14.1 of the Rules of Procedure of the General Assembly of States Parties.

Decision 43 COM 11A

《缔约国大会议事规则》第 14.1 条

第 43.COM.11A 号决议

23. Committee decisions are based on objective and scientific considerations, and any appraisal made on its behalf must be thoroughly and responsibly carried out. The Committee recognizes that such decisions depend upon:

a) carefully prepared documentation;
b) thorough and consistent procedures;
c) evaluation by qualified experts; and
d) if necessary, the use of expert referees.

23. 委员会的决定基于客观和科学的考虑，为此进行的任何评估工作都应该得到彻底和负责的贯彻。委员会认识到这类决定取决于以下几个方面：

a) 认真编撰的文献资料；
b) 详尽、统一的程序；
c) 资深专家的评估；
d) 必要时，使用专家仲裁。

24. The main functions of the Committee are, in cooperation with States Parties, to:

a) identify, on the basis of Tentative Lists and nominations submitted by States Parties, cultural and natural properties of Outstanding Universal Value which are to be protected under the *Convention* and to inscribe those properties on the World Heritage List;

24. 委员会的主要职能是与缔约国合作开展下述工作：

a）根据缔约国递交的《预备名录》和申报文件，确认将按照《公约》实施保护的具有突出的普遍价值的文化和自然遗产，并将这些遗产列入《世界遗产名录》；

Articles 11(2) and 11(7) of the *World Heritage Convention*.

《世界遗产公约》第 1（12）款。

b) examine the state of conservation of properties inscribed on the World Heritage List through processes of Reactive Monitoring (see Chapter IV) and Periodic Reporting (see Chapter V);

b）通过反应性监测（参见第四章）和定期报告（参见第五章）审查已经列入《世界遗产名录》的遗产的保护状况；

Article 29 of the *World Heritage Convention*.

《世界遗产公约》第 11（7）条和第 29 条。

c) decide which properties inscribed on the World Heritage List are to be inscribed on, or

c）决定《世界遗产名录》中的哪些遗产应该列入《濒危世界遗产名录》或从中移除；

removed from the List of World Heritage in Danger;

Article 11(4) and 11(5) of the
World Heritage Convention.

《世界遗产公约》第 11（4）条和第 11（5）条。

d) decide whether a property should be deleted from the World Heritage List (see Chapter Ⅳ);

e) define the procedure by which requests for International Assistance are to be considered and carry out studies and consultations as necessary before coming to a decision (see Chapter Ⅶ);

d）决定是否应将一项遗产从《世界遗产名录》上移除（参见第四章）；

e）制定关于国际援助申请的审议程序，在作出决定前，进行必要的研究和磋商（参见第七章）；

Article 21(1) and 21(3) of the
World Heritage Convention.

《世界遗产公约》第 21（1）条和第 21（3）条。
《世界遗产公约》第 13（6）条。

f) determine how the resources of the World Heritage Fund can be used most advantageously to assist States Parties in the protection of their properties of Outstanding Universal Value;

f）决定发挥世界遗产基金资源的最大优势，帮助缔约国保护具有突出普遍价值的遗产；

Article 13(6) of the *World Heritage Convention.*

《世界遗产公约》第 13（6）条。

g) seek ways to increase the World Heritage Fund;

h) submit a report on its activities every two years to the General Assembly of States Parties and to the UNESCO General Conference;

g）设法增加世界遗产基金的资金；

h）每两年向缔约国大会和联合国教科文组织大会递交一份活动报告；

Article 29(3) of the *World Heritage Convention* and Rule 49 of the *Rules of procedure of the World Heritage Committee.*

《世界遗产公约》第 29（3）条和《世界遗产委员会议事规则》第 49 条。

i) review and evaluate periodically the implementation of the *Convention*;

j) revise and adopt the *Operational Guidelines.*

i）定期审查并评估《公约》的实施情况；

j）修改并通过《操作指南》。

25. In order to facilitate the implementation of the *Convention*, the Committee develops Strategic Objectives; they are periodically reviewed and revised to define the goals and objectives of the Committee to ensure that new threats placed on World Heritage

25. 为了促进《公约》的实施，委员会制定了战略目标，并对这些目标定期审查和修改，确保有效应对世界遗产面临的新威胁。

are addressed effectively.

The first 'Strategic Orientations' adopted by the Committee in 1992 are contained in Annex Ⅱ of document WHC-92/CONF.002/12

1992 年委员会通过的第一份《战略方向》载列于文件 WHC-92/CONF.002/12 附件Ⅱ。

26. The current Strategic Objectives (also referred to as "the 5 Cs") are the following:

26. 目前的战略目标（简称为"5C"）是：

In 2002 the World Heritage Committee revised its Strategic Objectives. The *Budapest Declaration on World Heritage* (2002) is available at the following Web address: https://whc.unesco.org/en/budap estdeclaration

2002 年世界遗产委员会修改了战略目标。《布达佩斯世界遗产宣言》（2002 年）可参见以下网址：http://whc.unesco.org/en/budapestdeclaration

1. Strengthen the Credibility of the World Heritage List;

2. Ensure the effective Conservation of World Heritage Properties;

3. Promote the development of effective Capacity building in States Parties;

4. Increase public awareness, involvement and support for World Heritage through Commun-ica-tion;

5. Enhance the role of Communities in the implementation of the *World Heritage Conven-tion.*

1. 提高《世界遗产名录》的可信度；

2. 保证对世界遗产的有效保护；

3. 促进各缔约国有效的能力建设；

4. 通过沟通，宣传以增强大众对世界遗产的认识、参与和支持；

5. 加强社区在实施《世界遗产公约》中的作用。

Decision 31 COM 13B

第 31 COM13B 决议

Ⅰ.F The Secretariat to the World Heritage Committee (World Heritage Centre)

Ⅰ.F 世界遗产委员会秘书处（世界遗产中心）

UNESCO World Heritage Centre 7, place de Fontenoy 75352 Paris 07 SP
France https://whc.unesco.org/

联合国教科文组织世界遗产中心地址：法国巴黎（7, placede Fontenoy 75352 Paris 07 SP France）
电话：+33（0）145681571
传真：+33（0）1 4568 5570
电子邮箱：wh-info@unesco.org 网址：http://whc.unesco.org/

27. The World Heritage Committee is assisted by a Secretariat appointed by the Director-General

27. 由联合国教科文组织总干事指定的秘书处协助世界遗产委员会工作。1992 年创建了世

of UNESCO. The function of the Secretariat is currently assumed by the World Heritage Centre, established in 1992 specifically for this purpose. The Director-General designated the Director of the World Heritage Centre as Secretary to the Committee. The Secretariat assists and collaborates with the States Parties and the Advisory Bodies. The Secretariat works in close cooperation with other sectors and field offices of UNESCO.

界遗产中心，担负秘书处的职能。联合国教科文组织总干事指派世界遗产中心主任为委员会的秘书。秘书处协助和协调缔约国和咨询机构的工作。秘书处还与联合国教科文组织的其他部门和外地办事处密切合作。

Article 14 of the *World Heritage Convention*.

Rule 43 of Rules of Procedure of the World Heritage Committee.

Circular Letter 16 of 21 October 2003

https://whc.unesco.org/circs/circ 03-16e.pdf

《世界遗产公约》第 14 条。

《世界遗产委员会议事规则》第 43 条。

2003 年 10 月 21 日《通函 16 号》，可参见以下网址：

http://whc.unesco.org/circs/circ03-16e.pdf

28. The Secretariat's main tasks are:

28. 秘书处主要任务包括：

a) the organization of the meetings of the General Assembly and the Committee;

a）组织缔约国大会和世界遗产委员会的会议；

Decision 39 COM 11

Decision 43 COM 11A

Article 14(2) of the *World Heritage Convention*.

第 39 COM 11 号决议

第 43.COM.11A 号决议

《世界遗产公约》第 14.2 条。

b) the implementation of decisions of the World Heritage Committee and resolutions of the General Assembly and reporting on their execution;

b）执行世界遗产委员会的各项决定和联合国教科文组织大会的决议，并向委员会和大会汇报执行情况；

Article 14(2) of the *World Heritage Convention* and the *Budapest Declaration on World Heritage* (2002)

《世界遗产公约》第 14.2 条。

《布达佩斯世界遗产宣言》（2002 年）

c) the receipt, registration, checking the completeness, archiving and transmission to the relevant Advisory Bodies of nominations to the World Heritage List;

c）接收、登记世界遗产申报文件，检查其完整性、存档并呈递到相关的咨询机构；

d) the co-ordination of studies and activities as part of the Global Strategy for a Representative, Balanced and Credible World Heritage List;

d）协调各项研究和活动，作为加强《世界遗产名录》代表性、平衡性和 可信性全球战略的一部分；

e) the organization of Periodic Reporting;

e）组织定期报告；

f) coordination and conduct of Reactive Monitoring, including Reactive Monitoring missions [1], as well coordination of and participation in Advisory missions [2], as appropriate;

g) the coordination of International Assistance;

h) the mobilization of extra-budgetary resources for the conservation and management of World Heritage properties;

i) the assistance to States Parties in the implementation of the Committee's programmes and

f) 协调并执行反应性监测。包括派遣反应性监测工作组[1]，并在适当条件下协调参与咨询机构工作组[2]的有关工作。

g) 协调国际援助；

h) 调动预算外资金保护和管理世界遗产；

i) 协助各缔约国实施委员会的方案和项目；

---

[1] Reactive Monitoring missions are part of the statutory reporting by the Secretariat and the Advisory Bodies to the World Heritage Committee on the state of conservation of specific properties that are under threat (see Paragraph 169). They are requested by the World Heritage Committee to ascertain, in consultation with the State Party concerned, the condition of the property, the dangers to the property and the feasibility of adequately restoring the property or to assess progress made in implementing such corrective measures, and include a reporting back to the Committee on the findings of the mission (see Paragraph 176.e). The terms of reference of Reactive Monitoring missions are proposed by the World Heritage Centre, in line with the decision adopted by the World Heritage Committee, and consolidated in consultation with the State Party and the relevant Advisory Body(ies). Experts for such missions shall not be nationals of the country where the property is located. It is however encouraged that, where possible, they be from the same region as the property. The costs of the Reactive Monitoring missions are borne by the World Heritage Fund.

[1] 反应性监测工作组负责对处在危险状况下的特定遗产的保护状况做出评估。评估结果将作为秘书处及相关咨询机构向世界遗产委员会所递交报告的一部分（见 169 段）。反应性监测评估工作组是应世界遗产委员的要求而派遣的，它将与相关缔约国针对遗产的保护状况进行磋商，意在查明遗产可能遇到的危险，并研究适当修复该遗产的可行性。同时，它还将评估相关补救措施的实施情况，并将调查结果一并反馈给委员会（见 176 段 e 部分）。反应性监测工作组的相关任务由世界遗产中心指定，须遵守世界遗产委员会所采纳各项决定，并征求缔约国及相关咨询机构的同意。承担这类任务的专家不得是遗产所在地的公民。但是，如有可能，鼓励这些专家来自于遗产地所属同一地区。反应性监测工作组在考察期间的花费由世界遗产基金承担。

[2] Advisory missions are not part *stricto sensu* of the statutory and mandatory processes, as they are voluntarily initiated by States Parties and depend on the considerations and judgement of the States Parties requesting them. Advisory missions are to be understood as missions providing expert advice to a State Party on specific matters. They can concern provision of "upstream" support and advice on identification of sites, Tentative Lists or nomination of sites for inscription on the World Heritage List or alternatively, they can relate to the state of conservation of properties and provide advice in evaluating possible impact of a major development project on the Outstanding Universal Value of the property, advice in the preparation/revision of a management plan, or in the progress achieved in the implementation of specific mitigation measures, etc. The terms of reference of Advisory missions are proposed by the State Party itself, and consolidated in consultation with the World Heritage Centre and the relevant Advisory Bod(ies), other organization(s) or experts. Experts for such missions shall not be nationals of the country where the property is located. It is however encouraged that, where possible, they be from the same region as the property. The entire costs of Advisory missions are borne by the State Party inviting the mission, except where the State Party is eligible for relevant International Assistance or funding from the new budget line for Advisory missions approved by Decision 38 COM 12.

[2] 咨询机构工作组不是严格的法定监测程序的一部分，而是缔约国主动发起，基于申请针对国的考虑和判断。咨询工作组的特别任务旨在根据特定事务为缔约国提供专家意见和建议。具体可以涉及针对遗产识别、预备名单、申遗项目等提供"上游"支持，或者与遗产的保护状况相关，评估周边的大规模建设对遗产的突出普遍性价值所产生的影响，对管理规划的制定和修订、相关缓解措施的实施进展等提出意见。咨询机构工作组的相关任务由缔约国自己提出，并需征得世界遗产中心、相关咨询机构、其他相关组织、以及专家的同意。承担这类任务的专家不得是遗产所在地的公民。但是，如有可能，鼓励这些专家来自于遗产地所属同一区域。咨询机构工作组在考察期间的花费由邀请国负责（除非该缔约国满足相关国际援助的条件，或者符合 38COM 12 号决议通过的咨询考察新预算部分经费补助的要求）。

projects; and

j) the promotion of World Heritage and the *Convention* through the dissemination of information to States Parties, the Advisory Bodies and the general public.

29. These activities follow the decisions and Strategic Objectives of the Committee and the resolutions of the General Assembly of the States Parties and are conducted in close cooperation with the Advisory Bodies.

I.G　The Advisory Bodies to the World Heritage Committee

30. The Advisory Bodies to the World Heritage Committee are ICCROM (the International Centre for the Study of the Preservation and Restoration of Cultural Property), ICOMOS (the International Council on Monuments and Sites), and IUCN (the International Union for Conservation of Nature).

Article 8(3) of the *World Heritage Convention*

31. The roles of the Advisory Bodies are to:

a) advise on the implementation of the *World Heritage Convention* in the field of their expertise;

Article 13(7) of the *World Heritage Convention.*
Decision 39 COM 11

b) assist the Secretariat, in the preparation of the Committee's documentation, the agenda of its meetings and the implementation of the Committee's decisions;

c) assist with the development and implementation of the Global Strategy for a Representative, Balanced and Credible World Heritage List, the World Heritage Capacity Building Strategy, Period-

---

j) 通过向缔约国、咨询机构和公众发布信息，促进世界遗产的保护和增强对《公约》的认识。

29. 开展这些活动要服从于委员会的各项决定和战略目标以及缔约国大会的各项决议，并与咨询机构密切合作。

I.G　世界遗产委员会咨询机构

30. 世界遗产委员会的咨询机构包括：ICCROM（国际文物保护和修复研究中心）、ICOMOS（国际古迹遗址理事会）以及 IUCN（世界自然保护联盟）

《世界遗产公约》第8.3条。

31. 咨询机构的角色：

a) 以本领域的专业知识指导《世界遗产公约》的实施；

第 39 COM11 号决议
《世界遗产公约》第13.7条。

b) 协助秘书处准备委员会需要的文献资料，安排会议议程以及协助委员会实施各项决定；

c) 协助制定和实施《世界遗产名录》代表性、平衡性和可信性全球战略、世界遗产能力建设战略、定期报告，并加强世界遗产基金的有效使用；

ic Reporting, and the strengthening of the effective use of the World Heritage Fund;

d) monitor the state of conservation of World Heritage properties (including through Reactive Monitoring missions at the request of the Committee and Advisory missions at the invitation of the States Parties) and review requests for International Assistance;

Article 14(2) of the *World Heritage Convention.*

e) in the case of ICOMOS and IUCN, evaluate properties nominated for inscription on the World Heritage List, in consultation and dialogue with nominating States Parties, and present evaluation reports to the Committee; and

f) attend meetings of the World Heritage Committee and the Bureau in an advisory capacity.

Article 8(3) of the *World Heritage Convention.*

ICCROM

32. ICCROM (the International Centre for the Study of the Preservation and Restoration of Cultural Property) is an international intergovernmental organization with headquarters in Rome, Italy. Established by UNESCO in 1956, ICCROM's statutory functions are to carry out research, documentation, technical assistance, training and public awareness programmes to strengthen conservation of immovable and moveable cultural heritage.

ICCROM Via di S. Michele, 13 I-00153 Rome, Italy

Tel: +39 06 585531
Fax: +39 06 5855 3349
Email: iccrom@iccrom.org
http://www.iccrom.org/

d）对世界遗产的保护状况进行监测（包括应委员会要求派出的反应性监测及应缔约国邀请开展的咨询考察）并审核国际援助申请；

《世界遗产公约》第 14.2 条。

e）国际古迹遗址理事会和世界自然联盟，在评估申请列入《世界遗产名录》的遗产时，与申报缔约国进行协商与对话，并向委员会呈递评估报告；

f）以咨询者的身份列席世界遗产委员会及其主席团会议。

《世界遗产公约》8.3 条。

国际文物保护和修复研究中心

32. ICCROM，即国际文物保护和修复研究中心，是一个国际政府间组织，总部设在意大利的罗马，由联合国教科文组织于 1956 年创建，根据规定，该中心的作用是开展研究、记录，提供技术援助、培训和推行增强公众意识的项目，加强对可移动和不可移动文化遗产的保护。

国际文物保护和修复研究中心地址：意大利罗马（Viadi S.Michele，13I-00153Rome，Italy）

电话：+39 06 585531
传真：+39 06 5855 3349
电子邮箱：iccrom@iccrom.org
网址：http://www.iccrom.org/

33. The specific role of ICCROM in relation to the *Convention* includes: being the priority partner in training for cultural heritage, monitoring the state of conservation of World Heritage cultural properties, reviewing requests for International Assistance submitted by States Parties, and providing input and support for capacity building activities.

33. 国际文物保护和修复研究中心和《公约》相关的特殊职责包括：文化遗产培训领域的重要合作伙伴、监督世界文化遗产保护状况、审查由缔约国提交的国际援助申请，以及为能力建设活动提供支持。

ICOMOS

国际古迹遗址理事会

34. ICOMOS (the International Council on Monuments and Sites) is a non- governmental organization with headquarters in Charenton-le-Pont, France. Founded in 1965, its role is to promote the application of theory, methodology and scientific techniques to the conservation of the architectural and archaeological heritage. Its work is based on the principles of the 1964 International Charter on the Conservation and Restoration of Monuments and Sites (the Venice Charter).

34. ICOMOS，即国际古迹遗址理事会，是一个非政府组织，总部在法国沙朗通桥，创建于 1965 年。理事会的作用在于推广建筑和考古遗产保护理论、方法和科学技术的应用。理事会的工作以 1964 年《国际古迹遗址保护和修复宪章》（又称《威尼斯宪章》）的原则为基准。

ICOMOS

11 rue du Séminaire de Conflans

94220 Charenton-le-Pont France

Tel: +33 (0)1 41 94 17 59

Fax: +33 (0)1 48 93 19 16

E-mail: secretariat@icomos.org

http://www.icomos.org/

国际古迹遗址理事会法国巴黎（11 rue du Séminaire de Conflans

94220Charenton-le-Pont France）

电话：+33（0）141941759

传真：+33（0）148931916

电子邮箱：secretariat@icomos.org

网址：http://www.icomos.org/

35. The specific role of ICOMOS in relation to the *Convention* includes: evaluation of properties nominated for inscription on the World Heritage List, monitoring the state of conservation of World Heritage cultural properties, reviewing requests for International Assistance submitted by States Parties, and providing input and support for capacity building activities.

35. 国际古迹遗址理事会和《公约》相关的特殊职责包括：评估申报世界遗产的项目，监测世界文化遗产保护状况，审查由缔约国提交的国际援助申请，以及为能力建设活动出力献策和提供支持。

IUCN

世界自然保护联盟

36. IUCN – The International Union for Conservation of Nature was founded in 1948 and brings together national governments, NGOs, and scientists in a worldwide partnership. IUCN has its headquarters in Gland, Switzerland. Its mission is to influence, encourage and assist societies throughout the world to conserve the integrity and diversity of nature and to ensure that any use of natural resources is equitable and ecologically sustainable.

IUCN - The International Union for Conservation of Nature

rue Mauverney 28

CH-1196 Gland, Switzerland

Tel: + 41 22 999 0001

Fax: +41 22 999 0010

E-Mail: mail@hq.iucn.org

http://www.iucn.org

37. The specific role of IUCN in relation to the *Convention* includes: evaluation of properties nominated for inscription on the World Heritage List, monitoring the state of conservation of World Heritage natural properties, reviewing requests for International Assistance submitted by States Parties, and providing input and support for capacity building activities.

Ⅰ.H　Other organizations

38. The Committee may call on other international and non-governmental organizations with appropriate competence and expertise to assist in the implementation of its programmes and projects, including for Reactive Monitoring missions.

Decision 39 COM 11

Ⅰ.I　Partners in the protection of World Heritage

39. A partnership approach, underpinned by

36. IUCN，即世界自然保护联盟（前身是国际自然和自然资源保护联盟），创建于1948年，为各国政府、非政府组织和科学工作者在世界范围的合作提供了平台。世界自然保护联盟总部设在瑞士格兰德。其使命在于影响、鼓励和协助世界各团体，保护自然的完整性和多样化，并确保任何对自然资源的使用都是公平的、并符合生态的可持续发展。

IUCN——世界自然保护联盟

地址：瑞士格兰德（rue Mauverney 28 CH-1196 Gland, Switzerland）

电话：+41229990001

传真：+41229990010

电子邮箱：mail@hq.iucn.org 网址：

http://www.iucn.org

37. 世界自然保护联盟和《公约》相关的特殊职责包括：评估申报世界遗产的项目、监测世界自然遗产保护状况、审查由缔约国提交的国际援助申请，以及为能力建设活动出力献策并提供支持。

Ⅰ.H　其他组织

38. 委员会可能号召其他具有一定能力和专业技术的国际组织和非政府组织，协助各方案和项目的实施（包括反应性监测）。

第39 COM11号决议

Ⅰ.I　保护世界遗产的合作伙伴

39. 在遗产申报、管理和监测中，采取以

inclusive, transparent and accountable decision-making, to nomination, management and monitoring provides a significant contribution to the protection of World Heritage properties and the implementation of the *Convention*.

Decision 43 COM 11A

40. Partners in the protection and conservation of World Heritage can be those individuals and other stakeholders, especially local communities, indigenous peoples, governmental, non-governmental and private organizations and owners who have an interest and involvement in the conservation and management of a World Heritage property.

United Nations Declaration on the Rights of Indigenous
Peoples (2007)
Decision 39 COM 11

Ⅰ.J   Other Conventions, Recommendations and Programmes

41. The World Heritage Committee recognizes the benefits of closer coordination of its work with other UNESCO programmes and their relevant conventions. (For a list of relevant global conservation instruments, conventions and programmes see paragraph 44.)

42. The World Heritage Committee with the support of the Secretariat will ensure appropriate coordination and information-sharing between the *World Heritage Convention* and other conventions, programmes and international organizations related to the conservation of cultural and natural heritage.

43. The Committee may invite representatives of the intergovernmental bodies under related conventions to attend its meetings as observers. It

包容、透明和负责任的决策为基础的合作方法，将为保护世界遗产和实施《公约》做出重要的贡献。

第 43.COM.11A 号决议

40. 保护和保存世界遗产的合作伙伴包括：个人和其他利益相关方，尤其是对世界遗产的保护和管理感关趣并参与其中的当地社区、原住民族、政府组织、非政府组织和私人组织以及产权人。

《联合国原住民权利宣言》（2007 年）

第 39 COM11 号决议

Ⅰ.J   其他公约、建议和方案

41. 世界遗产委员会认识到，密切协调好与教科文组织其他计划和相关公约的关系，受益匪浅。第 44 条列举了有关的国际性保护文件、公约和方案。

42. 在秘书处的支持下，世界遗产委员会将保证《世界遗产公约》和保护文化和自然遗产有关的其他公约、项目以及国际组织之间适当协调工作，信息共享。

43. 委员会可邀请相关公约下政府间组织的代表，作为观察员参加委员会的会议。如受到其他政府间组织的邀请，委员会亦可派遣代表

may appoint a representative to observe meetings of the other intergovernmental bodies upon receipt of an invitation.

作为观察员列席会议。

44.Selected global conventions and programmes relating to the protection of cultural and natural heritage

44. 与保护文化和自然遗产相关的部分全球公约和方案

UNESCO conventions and programmes

联合国教科文组织公约和方案

Convention for the Protection of Cultural Property in the Event of Armed Conflict (1954)

《关于在武装冲突的情况下保护文化遗产的公约》（1954 年）

Protocol I (1954)

第一议定书（1954 年）

Protocol Ⅱ (1999)

第二议定书（1999 年）

http://www.unesco.org/new/en/culture/themes/armed-conflict-and-heritage/convention-and-protocols/

http://www.unesco.org/new/en/culture/themes/armed-conflict-and-heritage/convention-and-protocols/

Convention on the Means of Prohibiting and Preventing the Illicit Import, Export and Transfer of Ownership of Cultural Property (1970) http://www.unesco.org/new/en/culture/themes/illicit-trafficking-of-cultural-property/1970- convention

《关于采取措施禁止并防止文化遗产非法进出口和所有权非法转让公约》（1970 年 http://www.unesco.org/new/en/culture/themes/illicit-trafficking-of-cultural-property/1970-convention

Convention concerning the Protection of the World Cultural and Natural Heritage (1972) https://whc.unesco.org/en/conventiontext

《保护世界文化和自然遗产公约》（1972 年）

https://whc.unesco.org/en/conventiontext

Convention on the Protection of the Underwater Cultural Heritage (2001) https://unesdoc.unesco.org/ark:/48223/pf0000126065

《保护水下文化遗产公约》（2001 年）

https://unesdoc.unesco.org/ark：/48223/pf0000126065

Convention for the Safeguarding of the Intangible Cultural Heritage (2003) https://unesdoc.unesco.org/ark:/48223/pf0000132540

《保护非物质文化遗产公约》（2003 年）

https://unesdoc.unesco.org/ark：/48223/pf0000132540

Convention on the Protection and Promotion of the Diversity of Cultural Expressions (2005)
https://unesdoc.unesco.org/ark:/48223/pf0000 142919

《保护和促进文化表达多样性公约》（2005 年）
https://unesdoc.unesco.org/ark：/48223/ pf0000 0142919

Man and the Biosphere (MAB) Programme
http://www.unesco.org/new/en/natural-sciences/environment/ecological-sciences/man-and-biosphere-programme/

"人类和生物圈"计划（MAB）
http://www.unesco.org/mab/

International Geoscience and Geoparks Programme (IGGP)
http://www.unesco.org/new/en/natural-sciences/environment/earth-sciences/international-geoscience-and-geoparks-programme/

国际地球科学和地质公园计划（IGGP）

http://www.unesco.org/new/en/natural-science/environment/earth-sciences/international geos cience-and-geoparks-programme/

International Hydrological Programme (IHP)
https://en.unesco.org/themes/water-security/hydrology

国际水文计划（IHP）
https://en.unesco.org/themes/water-security/hydrology

Other conventions

其他公约

International Whaling Commission (IWC) (1946) https://iwc.int

国际捕鲸委员会（IWC）（1946 年）https://iwc.int

International Plant Protection Convention (IPPC) (1951) https://www.ippc.int

国际植物保护公约（IPPC）（1951 年）https://www.ippc.int

Convention on Wetlands of International Importance especially as Waterfowl Habitat (Ramsar) (1971) http://www.ramsar.org

《关于国际重要湿地特别是水禽栖息地的公约（拉姆萨尔公约）》（1971 年 http://www.ramsar.org

Convention on International Trade in Endangered Species of Wild Fauna and Flora (CITES) (1973) http://www.cites.org

《濒危野生动植物种国际贸易公约》（CITES）（1973 年）http://www.cites.org

Convention on the Conservation of Migratory Species of Wild Animals (CMS) (1979) http://www.cms.int

《野生迁徙类动物物种保护公约》（CMS）（1979 年）http://www.cms.int

United Nations Convention on the Law of the Sea (UNCLOS) (1982)

https://www.un.org/Depts/los/convention_agreements/convention_overview_convention.htm

Convention on Biological Diversity (1992) http://www.cbd.int

UNIDROIT Convention on Stolen or Illegally Exported Cultural Objects (Rome, 1995)

https://www.unidroit.org/cultural-property#Convention1995

United Nations Framework Convention on Climate Change (New York, 1992) http://unfccc.int

International Treaty on Plant Genetic Resources for Food and Agriculture (2001) http://www.fao.org/plant-treaty/en/

II. Definition of World Heritage

II.A　Cultural and Natural Heritage

45. Cultural and natural heritage are defined in Articles 1 and 2 of the *World Heritage Convention.*

Article 1

For the purposes of this Convention, the following shall be considered as "cultural heritage";

- monuments: architectural works, works of monumental sculpture and painting, elements or structures of an archaeological nature, inscriptions, cave dwellings and combinations of features, which are of Outstanding Universal Value from the point of view of history, art or science;

《联合国海洋法公约》（UNCLOS）（1982 年）

https://www.un.org/Depts/los/convention_agreements/ convention_overview_convention.htm

《生物多样性公约》（1992 年）http://www.cbd.int

《国际统一私法协会关于被盗或非法出口文物的公约》（罗马，1995 年）

https://www.unidroit.org/cultural-property#Convention1995

《联合国气候变化框架公约》（纽约，1992 年）http://unfccc.int

《粮食和农业植物遗传资源国际条约》（2001 年）http://www.fao.org/plant-treaty/en/

II.《世界遗产名录》

II.A　世界遗产的定义
文化和自然遗产
45. 文化和自然遗产的定义见《世界遗产公约》第 1 条和第 2 条。

第 1 条

在本公约中，以下各项为"文化遗产"：

一文物：从历史、艺术或科学角度看，具有突出的普遍价值的建筑物、碑雕和碑画、具有考古性质成份或结构、铭文、窟洞以及联合体；

- groups of buildings: groups of separate or connected buildings which, because of their architecture, their homogeneity or their place in the landscape, are of Outstanding Universal Value from the point of view of history, art or science;

- sites: works of man or the combined works of nature and of man, and areas including archaeological sites which are of Outstanding Universal Value from the historical, aesthetic, ethnological or anthropological points of view.

Article 2

For the purposes of this Convention, the following shall be considered as "natural heritage":

- natural features consisting of physical and biological formations or groups of such formations, which are of Outstanding Universal Value from the aesthetic or scientific point of view;

- geological and physiographical formations and precisely delineated areas which constitute the habitat of threatened species of animals and plants of Outstanding Universal Value from the point of view of science or conservation;

- natural sites or precisely delineated natural areas of Outstanding Universal Value from the point of view of science, conservation or natural beauty.

Mixed Cultural and Natural Heritage

46. Properties shall be considered as "mixed cultural and natural heritage" if they satisfy a part or whole of the definitions of both cultural and natural heritage laid out in Articles 1 and 2 of the *Convention*.

—建筑群：从历史、艺术或科学角度看，在建筑式样、分布均匀或与环境景色结合方面具有突出的普遍价值的单立或连接的建筑群；

—遗址：从历史、审美、人种学或人类学角度看具有突出的普遍价值的人类工程或自然与人，联合工程以及考古遗址等地方。

第 2 条

在本公约中，以下各项为"自然遗产"：

—从审美或科学角度看，具有突出的普遍价值的、由物质和生物结构或这类结构群组成的自然面貌；

—从科学或保护角度看，具有突出的普遍价值的地质和自然地理结构，以及明确划为受威胁的动物和植物栖息地；

—从科学、保护或自然美角度看，具有突出普遍价值的天然名胜、或明确划分的自然区域。

文化和自然混合遗产

46. 只有同时部分满足或完全满足《公约》第 1 条和第 2 条关于文化和自然遗产定义的遗产，才能认为是"文化和自然混合遗产"。

Cultural landscapes

文化景观

Definition

定义

47. Cultural landscapes inscribed on the World Heritage List are cultural properties and represent the "combined works of nature and of man" designated in Article 1 of the Convention. They are illustrative of the evolution of human society and settlement over time, under the influence of the physical constraints and/or opportunities presented by their natural environment and of successive social, economic and cultural forces, both external and internal.

47.《公约》第 1 条指出，列入《世界遗产名录》的文化景观属于文化遗产，代表着"自然与人的共同作品"。它们反映了因物质条件的限制或自然环境带来的机遇，在一系列社会、经济和文化因素的内外作用下，人类社会和定居地的历史沿革。

They should be selected on the basis both of their Outstanding Universal Value and of their representativity in terms of a clearly defined geo-cultural region. They should be selected also for their capacity to illustrate the essential and distinct cultural elements of such regions.

应根据其突出普遍价值和其在明确界定的地缘文化区域中的代表性来选择文化景观，同时也要关注它们展现这些区域的基本和独特的文化因素的能力。

The term "cultural landscape" embraces a diversity of manifestations of the interaction between humankind and the natural environment.

"文化景观"一词包含了人类与自然环境相互作用的多种表现形式。

Cultural landscapes often reflect specific techniques of sustainable land use, considering the characteristics and limits of the natural environment they are established in, and may reflect a specific spiritual relationship to nature. Protection of cultural landscapes can contribute to current techniques of sustainable land use and can maintain or enhance natural values in the landscape. The continued existence of traditional forms of land use supports biological diversity in many regions of the world. The protection of traditional cultural landscapes is therefore helpful in maintaining biological diversity.

文化景观往往反映了可持续土地利用的具体技术，同时考虑到它们所处的自然环境的特点和局限性，并可能反映与自然的特定精神关系。保护文化景观有助于维护现有的可持续利用土地的技术，同时保持或提高景观的自然价值。现存的传统土地利用形式，支持了世界许多区域的生物多样性。因此，保护传统文化景观有助于保持生物多样性。

Types

类型

47bis. Cultural landscapes fall into three main types, namely:

1) The most easily identifiable is the clearly defined landscape designed and created intentionally by people. This embraces garden and parkland landscapes constructed for aesthetic reasons which are often (but not always) associated with religious or other monumental buildings and ensembles.

2) The second type is the organically evolved landscape. This results from an initial social, economic, administrative, and/or religious imperative and has developed its present form by association with and in response to its natural environment. Such landscapes reflect that process of evolution in their form and component features. They fall into two sub-types:

a) a relict (or fossil) landscape is one in which an evolutionary process came to an end at some time in the past, either abruptly or over a period. Its significant distinguishing features are, however, still visible in material form;

b) a continuing landscape is one which retains an active social role in contemporary society closely associated with the traditional way of life, and in which the evolutionary process is still in progress. At the same time it exhibits significant material evidence of its evolution over time;

3) The final type is the associative cultural landscape. The inscription of such landscapes on the World Heritage List is justifiable by virtue of the powerful religious, artistic or cultural associations of the natural element rather than material cultural evidence, which may be insignificant or even absent.

47 补充 . 文化景观有三种主要类型，即：

1）最容易识别的是人们有意设计和创造的、明确定义的景观。包括因审美而建造的花园和公园景观，建造这类景观往往 (但并不总是) 与宗教或其他纪念性建筑和建筑群有关。

2）第二类是有机演化类景观，这源于最初的社会、经济、行政和宗教的需要，并通过与自然环境的联系和响应而发展成目前的形式。这类景观在其形式和组成特征上反映了进化的过程。它们分为两种子类型：

a）遗迹 (或化石) 景观，是指进化过程突然终止、或延续一段时间后终止在过去某个时间点的景观。它的显著特征在物质形式上仍然清晰呈现；

b）延续性景观是一个在当代社会仍保持活跃的社会角色，与传统的生活方式密切相关，其进化过程仍在进行中。同时，景观展示了景观随时间演变的重要物质证据；

3）最后一种类型是关联性文化景观。将这些景观列入《世界遗产名录》，是因为这些景观的自然元素与强大的宗教伦理、艺术或文化联系起来，而不是微不足道甚至缺失的物质文化证据。

Inscription of Cultural Landscapes on the World Heritage List

47ter. The extent of a cultural landscape for inscription on the World Heritage List is relative to its functionality and intelligibility. In any case, the sample selected must be substantial enough to represent adequately the totality of the cultural landscape that it illustrates. The possibility of designating long linear areas which represent culturally significant transport and communication networks should not be excluded.

General criteria for protection and management are equally applicable to cultural landscapes. It is important that due attention be paid to the full range of values represented in the landscape, both cultural and natural. The nominations should be prepared in collaboration with and the full approval of local communities.

The existence of a category of "cultural landscape", included on the World Heritage List on the basis of the criteria set out in Paragraph 77 of the *Operational Guidelines*, does not exclude the possibility of properties of exceptional importance in relation to both cultural and natural criteria continuing to be inscribed (see definition of mixed properties as set out in Paragraph 46). In such cases, their Outstanding Universal Value must be justified under both cultural and natural criteria (see Paragraph 77).

Movable Heritage

48. Nominations of immovable heritage which are likely to become movable will not be considered.

文化景观入选《世界遗产名录》

47 再补充／入选.《世界遗产名录》的文化景观的范围与其功能性和可理解性有关。在任何情况下，所选择的样本必须足够丰富，以充分代表它所说明的文化景观的整体。不应排除指定具有文化意义的、交通和沟通网络的、长途线性区域，作为文化景观的可能性。

保护和管理的一般标准同样适用于文化景观。重要的是，充分关注景观中所体现的各种价值，包括文化和自然价值。准备申报工作应与当地社区合作，并得到当地社区的充分认可。

根据《操作指南》第 77 条标准被列入《世界遗产名录》的"文化景观"遗产类别的存在，并不排除将与文化和自然标准有关的、具有特殊重要性的遗产继续被列入名录的可能性（见《操作指南》46 条《混合遗产的定义》）。在这种情况下，它们突出普遍价值必须根据文化和自然两套标准来证明其合理性（《操作指南》见第 77 段）。

可移动遗产

48. 对于可能发生迁移的不可移动遗产的申报，将不作考虑。

Outstanding Universal Value

突出普遍价值

49. Outstanding Universal Value means cultural and/or natural significance which is so exceptional as to transcend national boundaries and to be of common importance for present and future generations of all humanity. As such, the permanent protection of this heritage is of the highest importance to the international community as a whole. The Committee defines the criteria for the inscription of properties on the World Heritage List.

49. 突出普遍价值指罕见的、超越了国家界限的、对全人类的现在和未来均具有普遍的重要意义的文化和／或自然价值。因此，该项遗产的永久性保护，对整个国际社会都具有至高的重要性。世界遗产委员会规定了遗产列入《世界遗产名录》的标准。

50. States Parties are invited to submit nominations of properties of cultural and/or natural value considered to be of "Outstanding Universal Value" for inscription on the World Heritage List.

50. 邀请缔约国申报其认为具有"突出的普遍价值"的文化和／或自然遗产，以列入《世界遗产名录》。

51. At the time of inscription of a property on the World Heritage List, the Committee adopts a Statement of Outstanding Universal Value (see paragraph 154) which will be the key reference for the future effective protection and management of the property.

51. 遗产列入《世界遗产名录》时，世界遗产委员会会通过一个《突出普遍价值声明》（见第 154 段），该声明将是以后遗产有效保护与管理的重要参考文献。

52. The *Convention* is not intended to ensure the protection of all properties of great interest, importance or value, but only for a select list of the most outstanding of these from an international viewpoint. It is not to be assumed that a property of national and/or regional importance will automatically be inscribed on the World Heritage List.

52. 该《公约》不是旨在保护所有具有重大意义或价值的遗产，而是只保护那些从国际观点看具有最突出价值的遗产。不应该认为某项具有国家和／或区域重要性的遗产会自动列入《世界遗产名录》。

53. Nominations presented to the Committee shall demonstrate the full commitment of the State Party to preserve the heritage concerned, within its means. Such commitment shall take the form of appropriate policy, legal, scientific, technical, administrative and financial measures adopted and proposed to protect the property and its Outstanding Universal Value.

53. 呈递给委员会的申报文件，应该表明该缔约国在其力所能及的范围内将全力保存该项遗产。这种承诺应该体现在采纳和提出合适的政策、法律、科学、技术、管理和财政措施，保护该项遗产以及遗产的突出的普遍价值。

Ⅱ.B　A Representative, Balanced and Credible World Heritage List

54. The Committee seeks to establish a representative, balanced and credible World Heritage List in conformity with the four Strategic Objectives it adopted at its 26th session (Budapest, 2002).

Budapest Declaration on World Heritage (2002) at https://whc.unesco.org/en/budap estdeclaration

The Global Strategy for a Representative, Balanced and Credible World Heritage List

55.The Global Strategy for a Representative, Balanced and Credible World Heritage List is designed to identify and fill the major gaps in the World Heritage List. It does this by encouraging more countries to become States Parties to the *Convention* and to develop Tentative Lists as defined in paragraph 62 and nominations of properties for inscription on the World Heritage List (see https://whc.unesco.org/en/globalstrategy).

The report of the Expert Meeting on the "Global Strategy" and thematic studies for a representative World Heritage List (20-22 June 1994) was adopted by the World Heritage Committee at its 18th session (Phuket, 1994).

56. States Parties and the Advisory Bodies are encouraged to participate in the implementation of the Global Strategy in cooperation with the Secretariat and other partners. Regional and thematic Global Strategy meetings and comparative and thematic studies are organized for this purpose. The results of these meetings and studies are available to assist States Parties in preparing Tentative Lists and nominations. The reports of the expert meetings and studies presented to the World Heritage

Ⅱ.B　具有代表性、平衡性和可信性的《世界遗产名录》

54. 委员会根据第 26 届会议确定的四个战略目标，致力于构建一个具有代表性、平衡性和可信性的《世界遗产名录》。（布达佩斯，2002）

《布达佩斯世界遗产宣言》

见：http://whc.unesco.org/en/budapestdeclaration

构建具有代表性、平衡性、可信性的《世界遗产名录》的《全球战略》

55. 构建具有代表性、平衡性、可信性的《世界遗产名录》的《全球战略》，旨在确定并填补《世界遗产名录》的主要空白。该战略鼓励更多的国家加入《保护世界文化与自然遗产公约》、按第 62 条的定义编撰《预备名录》、准备《世界遗产名录》的申报文件。

（详见：http://whc.unesco.org/en/globalstrategy）

关于"全球战略"的专家会议报告及构建具有代表性的世界遗产名录的主题研究报告（1994 年 6 月 20-22 日），在世界遗产委员会第 18 届大会通过。（福克，1994 年）

56. 鼓励各缔约国和咨询团体、秘书处及其他合作方合作，参与实施《全球战略》。为此，组织召开了区域及"全球战略"主题会议，并开展对比研究及主题研究。会议和研究成果将有助于缔约国编撰《预备名录》和申报材料。可访问网站：http://whc.unesco.org/en/globalstrategy，查阅提交给世界遗产委员会的专家会议报告和研究报告。

Committee are available at: https://whc.unesco.org/en/globalstrategy.

The Global Strategy was initially developed with reference to cultural heritage. At the request of the World Heritage Committee, the Global Strategy was subsequently expanded to also include reference to natural heritage and combined cultural and natural heritage.

《全球战略》起初是为保护文化遗产提出的。应世界遗产委员会的要求,《全球战略》随后有所扩展,包括自然遗产和文化自然混合遗产。

57. All efforts should be made to maintain a reasonable balance between cultural and natural heritage on the World Heritage List.

57. 应不遗余力地保持《世界遗产名录》内文化和自然遗产的合理平衡。

58. No formal limit is imposed on the total number of properties to be inscribed on the World Heritage List.

58.《世界遗产名录》上的遗产总数没有正式限制。

Other measures

其他措施

59. To promote the establishment of a representative, balanced and credible World Heritage List, States Parties are requested to consider whether their heritage is already well represented on the List and if so, to slow down their rate of submission of further nominations by:

59. 要构建具有代表性、平衡性、可信性的《世界遗产名录》,缔约国须考虑其遗产是否已在遗产名录上得到充分的代表。如果是,就要采取以下措施,减缓新的申报:

Resolution adopted by the 12th General Assembly of States Parties (1999).

缔约国第 12 届会议通过的决议（1999 年）。

a) spacing voluntarily their nominations according to conditions that they will define, and/or;

a) 依据自身情况,自主增大申报间隔,和 / 或;

b) proposing only properties falling into categories still under-represented, and/or;

b) 只申报《世界遗产名录》内代表性不足的类别的遗产,和 / 或;

c) linking each of their nominations with a nomination presented by a State Party whose heritage is under-represented; or

c) 每次申报都与《世界遗产名录》内代表性不足的缔约国的申报联系起来或;

d) deciding, on a voluntary basis, to suspend the presentation of new nominations.

d) 自主决定暂停提交新的申报。

60. States Parties whose heritage of Outstanding Universal Value is under- represented on the

60. 如果缔约国的遗产具有突出普遍价值,且在《世界遗产名录》上代表性不足,应:

World Heritage List are requested to:

Resolution adopted by the 12th General Assembly of States Parties (1999).

a) give priority to the preparation of their Tentative Lists and nominations;

b) initiate and consolidate partnerships at the regional level based on the exchange of technical expertise;

c) encourage bilateral and multilateral cooperation so as to increase their expertise and the technical capacities of institutions in charge of the protection, safeguarding and management of their heritage; and,

d) participate, as much as possible, in the sessions of the World Heritage Committee.

60bis. The Committee has decided to apply the following annual limits and system of prioritization concerning Preliminary Assessments (see Section Ⅲ):

a) Advisory Bodies will review up to one complete Preliminary Assessment request per State Party;

b) set at 35 the annual limit on the number of Preliminary Assessment requests to be reviewed by Advisory Bodies;

c) should the number of Preliminary Assessment requests exceed 35, the order of priorities applied will be the same as set in paragraph 61.c);

d) the States Parties co-authors of a future transboundary or transnational serial nomination can choose, amongst themselves and with a common understanding, the State Party which will be submitting the Preliminary Assessment request; and this Preliminary Assessment request can be

缔约国第 12 届会议通过的决议（1999 年）。

a) 优先考虑编制《预备名录》和申报材料；

b) 在所属区域内，寻求技术交流伙伴并巩固这种合作关系；

c) 鼓励双边和多边合作以增强缔约国负责遗产保护、保存和管理机构的专业技能。

d) 尽可能参加世界遗产委员会的各届会议。

60 补充 . 委员会决定对初步评估实行下列年度限额和优先次序制度（见第三章）：

a）咨询机构将对每个缔约国最多一份完整的初步评估请求进行审查；

b）设定每年由咨询机构审查的初步评核申请数目的上限为 35 宗；

c）如初步评核申请数目超过 35 宗，申请的优先次序等同第 61.c）条所定优先次序；

d）未来共同申报跨境或跨国系列遗产的缔约国，可以在达成共识的情况下，选择一个缔约国提交初步评估的申请，这个初步评估申请仅在承担该申请的缔约国的上限内进行登记。

registered exclusively within the ceiling of the bearing State Party.

61. The Committee has decided to apply the following mechanism concerning examination of nominations:

Decision 24 COM VI.2.3.3,

Decision 28 COM 13.1 and

7 EXT.COM 4B.1

Decision 29 COM 18A

Decision 31 COM 10

Decision 35 COM 8B.61

Decision 40 COM 11

Decision 43 COM 11A

a) examine one complete nomination per State Party,

b) set at 35 the annual limit on the number of nominations it will review, inclusive of nominations deferred and referred by previous sessions of the Committee, extensions (except minor modifications of limits of the property), transboundary and serial nominations,

c) the following order of priorities will be applied in case the overall annual limit of 35 nominations is exceeded:

i) nominations of properties submitted by States Parties with no properties inscribed on the List,

ii) nominations of properties submitted by States Parties having up to 3 properties inscribed on the List,

iii) resubmitted referred nominations that were not transmitted to the relevant Advisory Bodies for evaluation further to the application of paragraph 61.b)[①],

61. 委员会决定检查申报时使用以下机制：

决议条款：第 24 COM VI.2.3.3 决议

第 28 COM 13.1 决议和

第 7 EXT.COM 4B.1 决议

第 29 COM 18A 决议

第 31 COM 10 决议

第 35 COM 8B.61 决议

第 40 COM 11 决议

第 43 COM 11A 决议

a）最多审议每个缔约国提交的一项完整申报，

b）确定委员会每年审查的申报数目不超过 35 个，其中包括往届会议审议确定重报的项目和补报的项目，扩展项目（遗产边界细微调整除外）、跨境和系列申报项目，

c）当申报项目超出每年限定的 35 个时，审查的优先顺序如下：

i）尚无遗产列入《世界遗产名录》的缔约国提交的遗产申报；

ii）仅有三项及以下遗产列入《世界遗产名录》的缔约国提交的遗产申报；

iii）按照第 61 段 . b）项规定[①]未能转交专业咨询机构评估的之前的补报项目再度提交；

---

① This provision also applies in case the resubmitted referred nomination is received in the third year following the referral decision.

① 本条款也适用于原补报项目于补报决议通过后第三年再次提交。

iv) nominations of properties that have been previously excluded due to the annual limit of 35 nominations and the application of these priorities,

v) nominations of properties submitted in the 5th year following the report by the Advisory Bodies on the related Preliminary Assessment (see Paragraph 122.g),

vi) nominations of properties for natural heritage,

vii) nominations of properties for mixed heritage,

viii) nominations of transboundary/transnational properties,

ix) nominations from States Parties in Africa, the Pacific and the Caribbean,

x) nominations of properties submitted by States Parties having ratified the *World Heritage Convention* during the last twenty years,

xi) nominations of properties submitted by States Parties that have not submitted nominations for five years or more,

xii) nominations of States Parties, former Members of the Committee, who accepted on a voluntary basis not to have a nomination reviewed by the Committee during their mandate. This priority will be applied for 4 years after the end of their mandate on the Committee,

xiii) when applying this priority system, date of receipt of full and complete nominations by the World Heritage Centre shall be used as a secondary factor to determine the priority between those nominations that would not be designated by the previous points.

d) the States Parties co-authors of a transboundary or transnational serial nomination can choose, amongst themselves and with a common understanding, the State Party which will be bearing this nomination; and this nomination can be registered exclusively within the ceiling of the bearing

iv）由于每年 35 项的申报限额和优先审查机制而未能处理的以往的遗产申报；

v）在咨询委员会提交初步评估报告后第 5 年内提交的遗产申报（见第 122.g 条），

vi）自然遗产申报；

vii）混合遗产申报；

viii）跨境或跨国遗产申报；

ix）非洲、太平洋和加勒比地区缔约国的遗产申报；

x）最近二十年加入《世界遗产公约》的缔约国的遗产申报；

xi）最近五年或五年以上时间没有提交过申报项目的缔约国的遗产申报；

xii）在其任期内自愿放弃申报的前委员国的遗产申报，这一优先机制将于该缔约国在委员会任期结束后的四年间生效；

xiii）采用上述优先机制时，世界遗产中心收到完整申报材料的日期，将被用作次要决定要素，来确定上述各条都无法确定的申报项目的优先顺序。

d）联合编写跨境或跨国系列申报文本的缔约国，可以在达成共识的基础上决定提交申报的缔约国；该申报仅占用此申报国的限额。

State Party.

This decision will be implemented on a trial basis for 4 years and takes effect on 2 February 2018, in order to ensure a smooth transition period for all States Parties. The impact of this decision will be evaluated at the Committee's 46th session (2022).

Ⅱ.C   Tentative Lists

Procedure and Format

62. A Tentative List is an inventory of those sites situated on its territory which each State Party considers suitable for nomination to the World Heritage List. States Parties should therefore include, in their Tentative Lists, details of those sites which they consider to be of potential Outstanding Universal Value and which they intend to nominate during the following years.

> Articles 1, 2 and 11(1) of the
> *World Heritage Convention.*
> Decision 39 COM 11

63. A nomination dossier will not be considered complete unless the nominated property has already been included on the State Party's Tentative List and has undergone a Preliminary Assessment.

> Decision 24 COM para.Ⅵ.2.3.2

64. States Parties are encouraged to prepare their Tentative Lists with the full, effective and gender-balanced participation of a wide variety of stakeholders and rights-holders, including site managers, local and regional governments, local communities, indigenous peoples, NGOs and other interested parties and partners. In the case

该条决议将实施 4 年的试用期，并于 2018 年 2 月 2 日开始生效，以确保所有缔约国享有平缓过渡期。该决议实施的影响将在 2022 年第 46 届大会上评估。

Ⅱ.C   《预备名录》

程序和格式

62.《预备名录》是缔约国认为其境内符合申报世界遗产条件的遗产的详细目录，缔约国应在《预备名录》中列出该国未来几年内要申报的，具有潜在的突出的普遍价值的文化和 / 或自然遗产的详细信息。

> 《保护世界文化与自然遗产公约》第 1、2 及 11（1）条规定。第 39 COM11 号决议

63. 如果缔约国提交申报的遗产未曾列入该国的《预备名录》并得到初步评估，该申遗文本将被视为不完整文件。

> 第 24COM Ⅵ.2.3.2 号决议

64. 鼓励缔约国在各利益相关方和产权持有者，在充分、有效、性别平等和广泛参与的基础上，编制其《预备名录》，并让遗产地管理人员、当地和地区政府、社区、原住民、非政府组织以及其他相关机构广泛参与编制过程。如果遗产对原住民的土地、领土或资源造成影响，缔约国应通过原住民代表机构，与相关原住民

of sites affecting the lands, territories or resources of indigenous peoples, States Parties shall consult and cooperate in good faith with the indigenous peoples concerned through their own representative institutions in order to obtain their free, prior and informed consent before including the sites on their Tentative List.

进行协商和诚信合作，以便在事先征得原住民自愿、知情的同意后，将遗产列入预备名录。

Decision 43 COM 11A

第 43.COM.11A 号决议

65. States Parties shall submit Tentative Lists to the Secretariat, at least one year prior to the submission of a Preliminary Assessment request to the Secretariat for review by the Advisory Bodies. States Parties are encouraged to re- examine and re-submit their Tentative List at least every ten years.

65. 缔约国应至少在向秘书处提交初步评估申请以供咨询机构审查的前一年，将《预备名录》呈报至秘书处。委员会鼓励缔约国至少每十年重新审查和递交《预备名录》。

66. States Parties are requested to submit their Tentative Lists in English or French using the standard formats in Annex 2A and Annex 2B (for transnational and transboundary future nominations), containing the name of the sites, their geographical location, a brief description of the sites, and justification of their potential Outstanding Universal Value.

66. 缔约国需要采用附件 2A 和 2B（未来跨国、跨境遗产申报）所示的标准格式，递交英语或法语的《预备名录》，包括遗产名称、地理位置、简短描述以及其具有突出的普遍价值声明。

Decision 39 COM 11

第 39 COM11 号决议

67. The original duly signed version of the completed Tentative List shall be submitted by the State Party, to: UNESCO World Heritage Centre 7, place de Fontenoy 75352 Paris 07 SP France

Tel: +33 (0) 1 4568 1104

E-mail: wh-tentativelists@unesco.org

67. 缔约国应将已签名的完整《预备名录》原件递交至：联合国教科文组织世界遗产中心法国巴黎（7，place de Fontenoy，Paris 07 SP）

电话：+33（0）1 4568 1136

电邮：wh–tentativelists@unesco.org

68. Upon reception of the Tentative Lists from the States Parties, the World Heritage Centre checks for compliance of the documentation with Annex 2. If the documentation is not considered

68. 收到缔约国提交的《预备名录》后，世界遗产中心将检查文件是否符合附件 2 的要求，如认为不符合，会将文件退回缔约国。如果所有信息均已提供，秘书处会将《预备名录》登

in compliance with Annex 2, the World Heritage Centre refers it back to the State Party. When all information has been provided, the Tentative List is registered by the Secretariat and transmitted to the relevant Advisory Bodies for information. A summary of all Tentative Lists is presented annually to the Committee. The Secretariat, in consultation with the States Parties concerned, updates its records, in particular by removing from the Tentative Lists the inscribed properties and nominated properties which were not inscribed.

记并转呈相关咨询机构。每年都要向委员会递交所有《预备名录》的概要。秘书处与相关缔约国协商后，更新其记录，将《预备名录》上已列入《世界遗产名录》和已否决列入的遗产移除。

Decision 7 EXT.COM 4A

第 7EXT.COM4A 号决议

The Tentative Lists of States Parties are published by the World Heritage Centre on its website and/or in working documents in order to ensure transparency, access to information and to facilitate harmonization of Tentative Lists at regional and thematic levels.

缔约国提交的《预备名录》将由世界遗产中心发布在其官网上和 / 或工作文件中，以确保信息公开透明，并有助于促进《预备名录》在地区间和特定主题方面的和谐。

Decision 41 COM 11

第 41 COM11 号决议

The sole responsibility for the content of each Tentative List lies with the State Party concerned. The publication of the Tentative Lists does not imply the expression of any opinion whatsoever of the World Heritage Committee or of the World Heritage Centre or of the Secretariat of UNESCO concerning the legal status of any country, territory, city or area or of its boundaries.

各国预备名录的内容由涉及的缔约国全权负责。《预备名录》的公开发表不意味着世界遗产委员会或世界遗产中心或联合国教科文秘书处就任何国家、领土、城市或地区或其边边界的任何意见和立场。

69. The Tentative Lists of States Parties are available at: https://whc.unesco.org/en/tentativelists

69. 登录 http://whc.unesco.org/en/tentativelists，查阅缔约国《预备名录》

Decision 27 COM 8A

第 27COM 8A 号决议

Tentative Lists as a planning and evaluation tool

《预备名录》作为规划与评估工具

70. Tentative Lists are a useful and important planning tool for States Parties, the World Heritage Committee, the Secretariat, and the Advisory Bodies, as they provide an indication of future nominations.

71. Tentative Lists should be established selectively and on the basis of evidence that supports potential Outstanding Universal Value. States Parties are encouraged to consult the analyses of both the World Heritage List and Tentative Lists prepared at the request of the Committee by ICOMOS and IUCN to identify the gaps in the World Heritage List. These analyses could enable States Parties to compare themes, regions, geo-cultural groupings and bio-geographic provinces for prospective World Heritage properties. States Parties are encouraged to seek as early as possible upstream advice from the Advisory Bodies during the development of their Tentative Lists as appropriate.

> Decision 24 COM para. Ⅵ.2.3.2(ii)
>
> Decision 39 COM 11
>
> Documents WHC-04/28.COM/13.B I and Ⅱ
>
> https://whc.unesco.org/document/5297 (ICOMOS) and
>
> https://whc.unesco.org/document/5298 (IUCN)

72. In addition, States Parties are encouraged to consult the specific thematic studies carried out by the Advisory Bodies (see paragraph 147). These studies are informed by a review of the Tentative Lists submitted by States Parties and by reports of meetings on the harmonization of Tentative Lists, as well as by other technical studies performed by the Advisory Bodies and qualified organizations and individuals. A list of studies already completed is available at: https://whc.unesco.org/en/globalstrategy

> Thematic studies are different than the comparative analysis to be prepared by States Parties when nominating properties

70.《预备名录》提供未来遗产名录申报信息，是对缔约国、世界遗产委员会秘书处及咨询机构工作有帮助的重要规划工具。

71.《预备名录》要进行有针对性的确立，并以满足潜在的突出普遍性价值为基础。鼓励缔约国参考国际古迹遗址理事会（ICOMOS）和世界自然保护联盟（IUCN）应委员会要求编制的《世界遗产名录》和《预备名录》分析报告，确定《世界遗产名录》上的缺项和空白。这些分析使缔约国能够通过比较主题、区域、地理文化群和生物地理区，来更好地确定未来的世界遗产。鼓励缔约国在编制准备《预备名录》过程中，尽早地征求咨询机构的上游意见。

> 第 24COM 号决议第Ⅵ.2.3.2（ⅱ）段文件
>
> 第 39 COM11 号决议
>
> WHC-04/28.COM/13.B1 和 2
>
> 详见: http://whc.unesco.org/archive/2004/whc04-28com-13b1e.pdf
>
> 和 http://whc.unesco.org/archive/2004/whc04-28com-13b2e.pdf

72. 另外，鼓励缔约国参考由咨询机构完成的具体主题研究报告（见 147 条）。这些研究评估了缔约国提交的《预备名录》、参考了《预备名录》协调会议报告、咨询团体以及其他具有资格的团体和个人的相关技术研究。已完成的研究报告列表详见: http://whc.unesco.org/en/globalstrategy

> 主题研究报告不同于缔约国申报遗产列入《世界遗产名录》时编撰的比较分析（见第 132 段）。

for inscription in the World Heritage List(see paragraph 132).

73. States Parties are encouraged to harmonize their Tentative Lists at regional and thematic levels. Harmonization of Tentative Lists is the process whereby States Parties, with the assistance of the Advisory Bodies, collectively assess their respective Tentative List to review gaps and identify common themes. The harmonization has considerable potential to generate fruitful dialogue between States Parties and different cultural communities, promoting respect for common heritage and cultural diversity and can result in improved Tentative Lists, new nominations from States Parties and cooperation amongst groups of States Parties in the preparation of nominations.

Decision 43 COM 11A

Assistance and Capacity Building for States Parties in the preparation of Tentative Lists

74. To implement the Global Strategy, cooperative efforts in capacity building and training for diverse groups of beneficiaries may be necessary to assist States Parties in acquiring and/or consolidating expertise in the preparation, updating and harmonization of their Tentative List and the preparation of nominations.

Decision 43 COM 11A

75. International Assistance may be requested by States Parties for the purpose of preparing, updating and harmonizing Tentative Lists (see Chapter Ⅶ). This can include use of the Upstream Process (see Paragraph 121).

76. The Advisory Bodies and the Secretariat will use the opportunity of evaluation missions to hold regional training workshops to assist under-

73. 鼓励缔约国在区域和主题上协调《预备名录》。在这个过程中，缔约国在咨询机构的协助下，共同评估各自的《预备名录》，审查缺项并确认相同主题。协调机制能够促成缔约国和不同文化社区之间产生富有成效的对话；提升对共同遗产和文化多样性的尊重；改进缔约国的《预备名录》、新申请项目和促进缔约国在申报筹备时与各方之间的合作。

第 43.COM.11A 号决议

缔约国编撰《预备名录》过程中提供的协助和能力建设

74. 为了实施《全球战略》，可能需要在能力建设和培训不同受益群体方面进行合作，以协助缔约国在筹备工作中巩固专业知识，更新和平衡《预备名录》及申报准备。

第 43.COM.11A 号决议

75. 在编制、更新和协调《预备名录》方面，缔约国可以请求国际援助（见第七章）。也包括使用上游程序（见第 121 条）。

76. 咨询机构和秘书处可在考察评估期间举办地区培训班，为《世界遗产名录》中遗产代表性不足的国家，在准备《预备名录》和申报

represented States in the methods of preparation of their Tentative List and nominations.

方面提供帮助。

Decision 24 COM Ⅵ.2.3.5(ii)

第 24COM Ⅵ.2.3.5 号决议

Ⅱ. D　Criteria for the assessment of Outstanding Universal Value

Ⅱ. D　突出的普遍价值的评估标准

77. The Committee considers a property as having Outstanding Universal Value (see paragraphs 49-53) if the property meets one or more of the following criteria. Nominated properties shall therefore:

77. 如果遗产符合下列一项或多项标准，委员会将会认为该遗产具有突出的普遍价值（见 49–53 条）。所申报遗产因而必须是：

These criteria were formerly presented as two separate sets of criteria - criteria (i) - (vi) for cultural heritage and (i) - (iv) for natural heritage.
The 6th extraordinary session of the World Heritage Committee decided to merge the ten criteria (Decision 6 EXT. COM 5.1)

这些标准起初分为两组，标 准（ⅰ）至（ⅵ）适用于文化遗产，标准（ⅰ）至（ⅳ）适用于自然遗产。世界遗产委员会第 6 届特别会议决定将这十个标准合起来（第 6EXT. COM5.1 号决议）

(i) represent a masterpiece of human creative genius;

(ⅰ) 作为人类天才的创造力的杰作；

(ii) exhibit an important interchange of human values, over a span of time or within a cultural area of the world, on developments in architecture or technology, monumental arts, town planning or landscape design;

(ⅱ) 在一段时期内或世界某一文化区域内人类价值观的重要交流，对建 筑、技术、古迹艺术、城镇规划或景观设计的发展产生重大影响；

(iii) bear a unique or at least exceptional testimony to a cultural tradition or to a civilization which is living or which has disappeared;

(ⅲ) 能为延续至今或业已消逝的文明或文化传统提供独特的或至少是特 殊的见证；

(iv) be an outstanding example of a type of building, architectural or technological ensemble or landscape which illustrates (a) significant stage(s) in human history;

(ⅳ) 是一种建筑、建筑或技术整体、或景观的杰出范例，展现人类历史上一个（或几个）重要阶段；

(v) be an outstanding example of a traditional human settlement, land-use, or sea-use which is representative of a culture (or cultures), or human interaction with the environment especially when

(ⅴ) 是传统人类居住地、土地使用或海洋开发的杰出范例，代表一种（或 几种）文化或人类与环境的相互作用，特别是当它面临不可逆变化的影响而变得脆弱；

it has become vulnerable under the impact of irreversible change;

(vi) be directly or tangibly associated with events or living traditions, with ideas, or with beliefs, with artistic and literary works of outstanding universal significance. (The Committee considers that this criterion should preferably be used in conjunction with other criteria);

(vii) contain superlative natural phenomena or areas of exceptional natural beauty and aesthetic importance;

(viii) be outstanding examples representing major stages of earth's history, including the record of life, significant on-going geological processes in the development of landforms, or significant geomorphic or physiographic features;

(ix) be outstanding examples representing significant on-going ecological and biological processes in the evolution and development of terrestrial, fresh water, coastal and marine ecosystems and communities of plants and animals;

(x) contain the most important and significant natural habitats for in-situ conservation of biological diversity, including those containing threatened species of Outstanding Universal Value from the point of view of science or conservation.

78. To be deemed of Outstanding Universal Value, a property must also meet the conditions of integrity and/or authenticity and must have an adequate protection and management system to ensure its safeguarding.

Ⅱ.E Authenticity and/or integrity

Authenticity

79. Properties nominated under criteria (i) to (vi) must meet the conditions of authenticity. Annex 4, which includes the Nara Document on Authenticity,

(vi) 与具有突出普遍意义的事件、活传统、观点、信仰、艺术或文学作品有直接或有形的联系。（委员会认为本标准最好与其他标准一起使用）；

(vii) 绝妙的自然现象或具有罕见自然美和美学价值的地区；

(viii) 是地球演化史中重要阶段的突出例证，包括生命记载和地貌演变中的重要地质过程或显著的地质或地貌特征；

(ix) 突出代表了陆地、淡水、海岸和海洋生态系统及动植物群落演变、发展的生态和生理过程；

(x) 是生物多样性原址保护的最重要的自然栖息地，包括从科学和保护角度看，具有突出的普遍价值的濒危物种栖息地。

78. 只有同时具有完整性和／或真实性的特征，且有恰当的保护和管理机制确保遗产得到保护，遗产才能被视为具有突出普遍价值。

Ⅱ.E 真实性和／或完整性

真实性

79. 依据标准（ⅰ）至（ⅵ）申报的遗产须符合真实性的条件。附件4中包括了关于真实性的《奈良文件》，为评估相关遗产的真实性提供

provides a practical basis for examining the authenticity of such properties and is summarized below.

了操作基础，概要如下：

80. The ability to understand the value attributed to the heritage depends on the degree to which information sources about this value may be understood as credible or truthful. Knowledge and understanding of these sources of information, in relation to original and subsequent characteristics of the cultural heritage, and their meaning as accumulated over time, are the requisite bases for assessing all aspects of authenticity.

80. 理解遗产价值的能力，取决于该价值信息来源的真实度或可信度。对历史上积累的，涉及文化遗产原始及发展变化的特征的信息来源的认识和理解，及随时间积累形成的意义，是评价真实性各方面的必要基础。

Decision 39 COM 11

第 39 COM 11 号决议

81. Judgments about value attributed to cultural heritage, as well as the credibility of related information sources, may differ from culture to culture, and even within the same culture. The respect due to all cultures requires that cultural heritage must be considered and judged primarily within the cultural contexts to which it belongs.

81. 对于文化遗产价值和相关信息来源可信性的评价标准可因文化而异，甚至同一种文化内也存在差异。出于对所有文化的尊重，文化遗产的分析和判断，必须首先在其所在的文化背景中进行。

82. Depending on the type of cultural heritage, and its cultural context, properties may be understood to meet the conditions of authenticity if their cultural values (as recognized in the nomination criteria proposed) are truthfully and credibly expressed through a variety of attributes including:

82. 依据文化遗产类别及其文化背景，如果遗产的文化价值（申报标准所认可的）的下列特征真实可信，则被认为具有真实性：

- form and design;
- materials and substance;
- use and function;
- traditions, techniques and management systems;
- location and setting;
- language, and other forms of intangible heritage;
- spirit and feeling; and
- other internal and external factors.

- 外形和设计；
- 材料和实质；
- 用途和功能；
- 传统，技术和管理体系；
- 位置和环境；
- 语言和其他形式的非物质遗产；
- 精神和感觉；
- 其他内外因素。

83. Attributes such as spirit and feeling do not lend themselves easily to practical applications of the conditions of authenticity, but nevertheless are important indicators of character and sense of place, for example, in communities maintaining tradition and cultural continuity.

83. 精神和感觉这样的属性，在真实性评估中虽不易操作，却是评价一个遗产地特质和场所精神的重要指标，例如，在社区中保持传统和文化连续性。

84. The use of all these sources permits elaboration of the specific artistic, historic, social, and scientific dimensions of the cultural heritage being examined. "Information sources" are defined as all physical, written, oral, and figurative sources, which make it possible to know the nature, specificities, meaning, and history of the cultural heritage.

84. 利用所有这些信息使我们对相关文化遗产在艺术、历史、社会和科学等特定领域的研究更加深入。"信息来源"指所有物质的、书面的、口头和图形的信息来源，从而使理解文化遗产的性质、特性、意义和历史成为可能。

85. When the conditions of authenticity are considered in preparing a nomination for a property, the State Party should first identify all of the applicable significant attributes of authenticity. The statement of authenticity should assess the degree to which authenticity is present in, or expressed by, each of these significant attributes.

85. 在考虑申报遗产的真实性时，缔约国首先要确认所有适用的真实性的重要载体。真实性声明应该评估真实性在每个载体特征上的体现程度。

86. In relation to authenticity, the reconstruction of archaeological remains or historic buildings or districts is justifiable only in exceptional circumstances. Reconstruction is acceptable only on the basis of complete and detailed documentation and to no extent on conjecture.

86. 在真实性问题上，只有在极个别情况下，才会考虑重建考古遗址或历史建筑及街区。只有依据完整且详细的记载，不存在任何想象而进行的重建，才可以接受。

Integrity

完整性

87. All properties nominated for inscription on the World Heritage List shall satisfy the conditions of integrity.

87. 所有申报列入《世界遗产名录》的遗产必须满足完整性条件。

Decision 20 COM IX.13

第 20COMIX.13 号决议

88. Integrity is a measure of the wholeness and intactness of the natural and/or cultural heritage and its

88. 完整性用来衡量自然和 / 或文化遗产及其特征的整体性和无缺憾性。因而，审查遗产

attributes. Examining the conditions of integrity, therefore requires assessing the extent to which the property:

a) includes all elements necessary to express its Outstanding Universal Value;

b) is of adequate size to ensure the complete representation of the features and processes which convey the property's significance;

c) suffers from adverse effects of development and/or neglect. This should be presented in a statement of integrity.

89. For properties nominated under criteria (i) to (vi), the physical fabric of the property and/or its significant features should be in good condition, and the impact of deterioration processes controlled. A significant proportion of the elements necessary to convey the totality of the value conveyed by the property should be included. Relationships and dynamic functions present in cultural landscapes, historic towns or other living properties essential to their distinctive character should also be maintained.

Examples of the application of the conditions of integrity to properties nominated under criteria (i) - (vi) are under development.

90. For all properties nominated under criteria (vii) - (x), bio-physical processes and landform features should be relatively intact. However, it is recognized that no area is totally pristine and that all natural areas are in a dynamic state, and to some extent involve contact with people. Biological diversity and cultural diversity can be closely linked and interdependent and human activities, including those of traditional societies, local communities and indigenous peoples, often occur in natural areas. These activities may be consistent with the Outstanding Universal Value of the area where they are ecologically sustainable.

完整性需要评估遗产符合以下特征的程度：

a) 包括所有表现其突出普遍价值的必要因素；

b) 面积足够大，确保能完整地代表体现遗产价值的特色和过程；

c) 受到发展的负面影响和／或缺乏维护。上述条件需要在完整性陈述中进行论述。

89. 依据标准（i）至（vi）申报的遗产，其物理构造和／或重要特征都必须保存完好，且侵蚀退化过程的影响得到控制。能表现遗产全部价值的绝大部分必要因素也要包括在内。文化景观、历史村镇或其他活遗产中体现其显著特征的种种关系和动态功能也应予保存。

将完整性条件应用于依据标准（i）至（vi）的申报的遗产之例证正在开发。

90. 所有依据标准（vii）至（x）申报的遗产，其生物物理过程和地貌特征应该相对完整。当然，由于任何区域都不可能完全保持天然，且所有自然区域都在变动之中，而且在某种程度上还会有人类的活动。在自然区域内，包括传统社会和当地社区在内的人类活动时有发生。生物多样性和文化多样性可与人类活动密切联系，相互依存，例如传统社会、地方社区和原住民的活动等往往发生在自然区域。如果这些活动具有生态可持续性，也可以与同自然区域的突出普遍价值一致。

91. In addition, for properties nominated under criteria (vii) to (x), a corresponding condition of integrity has been defined for each criterion.

92. Properties proposed under criterion (vii) should be of Outstanding Universal Value and include areas that are essential for maintaining the beauty of the property. For example, a property whose scenic value depends on a waterfall, would meet the conditions of integrity if it includes adjacent catchment and downstream areas that are integrally linked to the maintenance of the aesthetic qualities of the property.

93. Properties proposed under criterion (viii) should contain all or most of the key interrelated and interdependent elements in their natural relationships. For example, an "ice age" area would meet the conditions of integrity if it includes the snow field, the glacier itself and samples of cutting patterns, deposition and colonization (e.g. striations, moraines, pioneer stages of plant succession, etc.); in the case of volcanoes, the magmatic series should be complete and all or most of the varieties of effusive rocks and types of eruptions be represented.

94. Properties proposed under criterion (ix) should have sufficient size and contain the necessary elements to demonstrate the key aspects of processes that are essential for the long term conservation of the ecosystems and the biological diversity they contain. For example, an area of tropical rain forest would meet the conditions of integrity if it includes a certain amount of variation in elevation above sea level, changes in topography and soil types, patch systems and naturally regenerating patches; similarly a coral reef should include, for example, seagrass, mangrove or other adjacent ecosystems that regulate nutrient and

91. 另外，对于依据标准（vii）至（x）申报的遗产来说，每个标准又有一个相应的完整性条件。

92. 依据标准（vii）申报的遗产应具备突出的普遍价值，且包括保持遗产美景所必须的关键地区。例如，某个遗产的景观价值在于瀑布，那么只有与维持遗产美景完整关系密切的邻近的积水潭和下游地区也被涵盖在内，才能满足完整性条件。

93. 依据标准（viii）申报的遗产必须包括其自然关系中所有或大部分重要的相互联系、相互依存的因素。例如，"冰川期"遗址要满足完整性条件，则需包括雪地、冰河本身和凿面样本、沉积物和植物集群（例如，条痕、冰碛层及植物演替的先锋阶段等）。如果是火山，则岩浆层必须完整，且能代表所有或大部分火山岩种类和喷发类型。

94. 依据标准（ix）申报的遗产必须具有足够的规模，且包含能够展示长期保护其内部生态系统和生物多样性的重要过程的必要因素。例如，热带雨林地区要满足完整性条件，需要有一定的海拔层次、多样的地形和土壤种类、群落系统和自然形成的群落；同样，珊瑚礁必须包括诸如海草、红树林和其他为珊瑚礁提供营养沉积物的邻近生态系统。

sediment inputs into the reef.

95. Properties proposed under criterion (x) should be the most important properties for the conservation of biological diversity. Only those properties which are the most biologically diverse and/or representative are likely to meet this criterion. The properties should contain habitats for maintaining the most diverse fauna and flora characteristic of the biogeographic province and ecosystems under consideration. For example, a tropical savannah would meet the conditions of integrity if it includes a complete assemblage of co-evolved herbivores and plants; an island ecosystem should include habitats for maintaining endemic biota; a property containing wide ranging species should be large enough to include the most critical habitats essential to ensure the survival of viable populations of those species; for an area containing migratory species, seasonal breeding and nesting sites, and migratory routes, wherever they are located, should be adequately protected.

95. 依据标准（x）申报的遗产必须是对生物多样性保护至关重要的遗产。只有最具生物多样性和／或代表性的申报遗产才有可能满足该标准。遗产必须包括某生物区或生态系统内最具多样性的动植物特征的栖息地。例如：要满足完整性条件，热带草原需要具有完整的、共同进化的草食动物群和植物群；海岛生态系统则需要包括地方生态栖息地；包含多种物种的遗产必须足够大，能够包括确保这些物种生存的最重要的栖息地；如果某个地区有迁徙物种，则季节性的养育巢穴和迁徙路线，不管位于何处，都必须妥善保护。

II.F Protection and management

96. Protection and management of World Heritage properties should ensure that their Outstanding Universal Value, including the conditions of integrity and/or authenticity at the time of inscription, are sustained or enhanced over time. A regular review of the general state of conservation of properties, and thus also their Outstanding Universal Value, shall be done within a framework of monitoring processes for World Heritage properties, as specified within the *Operational Guidelines*[1].

II.F 保护和管理

96. 世界遗产的保护与管理须确保其在列入《世界遗产名录》时所具有的突出的普遍价值以及完整性和／或真实性在之后得到保持或加强。为此，须按照《操作指南》规定，在世界遗产监测的总体框架下，定期对列入遗产及其突出普遍价值的保护状况进行审查[1]。

---

[1] The processes of monitoring specified in the *Operational Guidelines* are Reactive Monitoring (see paragraphs 169-176) and Periodic Reporting (see paragraphs 199-210).

[1] 《操作指南》中具体规定的监测程序为反应性监测（见169–176条）和定期报告（199–210条）

97. All properties inscribed on the World Heritage List must have adequate long- term legislative, regulatory, institutional and/or traditional protection and management to ensure their safeguarding. This protection should include adequately delineated boundaries. Similarly States Parties should demonstrate adequate protection at the national, regional, municipal, and/or traditional level for the nominated property. They should append appropriate texts to the nomination with a clear explanation of the way this protection operates to protect the nominated property. Information on protection and management should also be included at the stage of the Preliminary Assessment.

Legislative, regulatory and contractual protection measures

98. Legislative and regulatory measures at national and local levels should assure the protection of the property from social, economic and other pressures or changes that might negatively impact the Outstanding Universal Value, including the integrity and/or authenticity of the property. States Parties should also assure the full and effective implementation of such measures.

Decision 39 COM 11

Boundaries for effective protection

99. The delineation of boundaries is an essential requirement in the establishment of effective protection of nominated properties. Boundaries should be drawn to incorporate all the attributes that convey the Outstanding Universal Value and to ensure the integrity and/or authenticity of the property.

97. 列入《世界遗产名录》的所有遗产必须有长期、充分的立法、规范、机构的和／或传统的保护及管理，以确保遗产得到保护。保护必须包括充分的边界划定。同样，缔约国应该在国家、区域、城市和／或传统各个级别上对申报遗产予以足够力度的保护。申报文件上也需要附加明确说明，解释具体保护措施。初步评估阶段也应当包括保护和管理信息。

立法、规范和契约性的保护措施

98. 国家和地方级的立法、规范措施应确保遗产的保护完好，使其突出的普遍性价值包括完整性和／或真实性，不因社会经济发展及其他压力而受到负面影响。缔约国还需要保证这些措施得到切实有效的实施。

第 39 COM11 号决议

确保有效保护的边界

99. 划定边界是对申报遗产进行有效保护的核心要求，划定的边界范围内应包含所有能够体现遗产突出普遍性价值的元素，并保证其完整性与（或）真实性不受破坏。

100. For properties nominated under criteria (i) - (vi), boundaries should be drawn to include all those areas and attributes which are a direct tangible expression of the Outstanding Universal Value of the property, as well as those areas which, in the light of future research possibilities, offer potential to contribute to and enhance such understanding.

101. For properties nominated under criteria (vii) - (x), boundaries should reflect the spatial requirements of habitats, species, processes or phenomena that provide the basis for their inscription on the World Heritage List. The boundaries should include sufficient areas immediately adjacent to the area of Outstanding Universal Value in order to protect the property's heritage values from direct effects of human encroachments and impacts of resource use outside of the nominated area.

102. The boundaries of the nominated property may coincide with one or more existing or proposed protected areas, such as national parks or nature reserves, biosphere reserves or protected cultural or historic districts or other areas and territories. While such established areas for protection may contain several management zones, only some of those zones may satisfy requirements for inscription.

Decision 39 COM 11

Buffer zones

103. Wherever necessary for the proper protection of the property, an adequate buffer zone should be provided.

104. For the purposes of effective protection of the nominated property, a buffer zone is an area surrounding the nominated property which has

100. 依据标准（i）至（vi）申报的遗产，划定的边界需要包括所有有形的、能够直接体现遗产的突出普遍价值的区域和特征，以及在将来的研究中有可能加深这种理解的区域。

101. 依据标准（vii）至（x）申报的遗产，划定的边界要反映其成为世界遗产基本条件的栖息地、物种、过程或现象的空间要求。边界须包括与具有突出的普遍价值紧邻的足够大的区域，以保护其遗产价值不因人类的直接侵蚀和该区域外资源开发而受到损害。

102. 所申报遗产的边界可能会与一个或多个现存或已建成的保护区重合，例如国家公园或自然保护区，生物圈保护区，文化或历史保护区、或者其他地区和区域。保护区可能包含几个管理带，但可能只有个别地带能达到世界遗产的要求。

第 39 COM11 号决议

缓冲区

103. 只要有必要，就应设立足够大的缓冲区以有效保护遗产。

104. 缓冲区是为了有效保护申报遗产而划定的遗产周围的区域，其使用和开发受到相关法律和 / 或习惯规定的限制，为遗产增加了保护

complementary legal and/or customary restrictions placed on its use and development in order to give an added layer of protection to the property. This should include the immediate setting of the nominated property, important views and other areas or attributes that are functionally important as a support to the property and its protection. The area constituting the buffer zone should be determined in each case through appropriate mechanisms. Details on the size, characteristics and authorized uses of a buffer zone, as well as a map indicating the precise boundaries of the property and its buffer zone, should be provided in the nomination.

105. A clear explanation of how the buffer zone protects the property should also be provided.

106. Where no buffer zone is proposed, the nomination should include a statement as to why a buffer zone is not required.

107. Although buffer zones are not part of the nominated property, any modifications to or creation of buffer zones subsequent to inscription of a property on the World Heritage List should be approved by the World Heritage Committee using the procedure for a minor boundary modification (see paragraph 164 and Annex 11). The creation of buffer zones subsequent to inscription is normally considered to be a minor boundary modification[①].

Management systems

108. Each nominated property should have an appropriate management plan or other documented management system which must specify how the

层。缓冲区包括申报遗产直接所在的区域、重要景观，以及其他在功能上对遗产及其保护至关重要的区域或特征。缓冲区的构成区域应通过合适的机制来决定。申报时，需要提供有关缓冲区大小、特点、授权用途的详细信息，以及一张精确标示边界和缓冲区的地图。

105. 申报材料中还需明确描述缓冲区在保护申报遗产中的作用。

106. 如果没有提议建立缓冲区，则申报材料需要解释没有规划缓冲区的原因。

107. 虽然缓冲区并非所申报的遗产的正式组成部分，但是一旦列入《世界遗产名录》，对缓冲区的划定或任何变动，都需经世界遗产委员会按照边界微调的程序（详见164条和附件1）批准。列入后新建缓冲区通常被视作边界微调[①]。

管理体制

108. 每一处申报遗产都应有适宜的管理规划或其他有文可依的管理体制，其中需要详细说明将如何采取措施（最好是多方参与的方式）

---

①　With regards to transnational/transboundary properties, any modification will need the agreement of all States Parties concerned.

①　涉及跨国/跨境世界遗产项目，任何调整修订均需得到所有相关缔约国的同意。

Outstanding Universal Value of a property should be preserved, preferably through participatory means.

保护遗产突出的普遍价值。

109. The purpose of a management system is to ensure the effective protection of the nominated property for present and future generations.

109. 管理体制旨在确保现在和将来对申报遗产进行有效的保护。

110. An effective management system depends on the type, characteristics and needs of the nominated property and its cultural and natural context. Management systems may vary according to different cultural perspectives, the resources available and other factors. They may incorporate traditional practices, existing urban or regional planning instruments, and other planning control mechanisms, both formal and informal. Impact assessments for proposed interventions are essential for all World Heritage properties.

110. 有效的管理体制的内容取决于申报遗产的类别、特点、需求以及文化和自然环境。由于文化视角、可用资源及其他因素的影响，管理体制也会有所差别。管理体制可能包含传统做法、现行的城市或地区规划手段、和其他正式和非正式的规划控制机制。对所有提议的干预措施进行影响评估，对世界遗产而言是至关重要的工作。

111. In recognizing the diversity mentioned above, common elements of an effective management system could include:

111. 考虑到上述多样性问题，有效管理体制应包括以下共同因素：

Decision 39 COM 11

Decision 43 COM 11A

第 39 COM 11 号决议

第 43.COM.11A 号决议

a) a thorough shared understanding of the property, its universal, national and local values and its socio-ecological context by all stakeholders, including local communities and indigenous peoples;

b) a respect for diversity, equity, gender equality and human rights and the use of inclusive and participatory planning and stakeholder consultation processes;

c) a cycle of planning, implementation, monitoring, evaluation and feedback;

d) an assessment of the vulnerabilities of the property to social, economic, environmental and other pressures and changes, including disasters and climate change, as well as the monitoring of the

a) 包括当地社区和原住民在内的所有利益相关方对遗产及其普世的、国家的和地方的价值、遗迹、社会生态背景的深入的、共同的理解；

b) 尊重多样性、公平、性别平等和人权，在制定规划以及和利益相关方协商进程时使用包容性和参与性原则；

c) 规划、实施、监测、评估和反馈的循环机制；

d) 评估遗产可能受到的来自社会、经济及其他方面的压力，如灾难和气候变化，监测时下各种趋势和干预活动对遗产的影响；

impacts of trends and proposed interventions;

e) the development of mechanisms for the involvement and coordination of the various activities between different partners and stakeholders;

f) the allocation of necessary resources;

g) capacity building;

h) an accountable, transparent description of how the management system functions.

112. Effective management involves a cycle of short, medium and long-term actions to protect, conserve and present the nominated property. An integrated approach to planning and management is essential to guide the evolution of properties over time and to ensure maintenance of all aspects of their Outstanding Universal Value. This approach goes beyond the property to include any buffer zone(s), as well as the wider setting. The wider setting may relate to the property's topography, natural and built environment, and other elements such as infrastructure, land use patterns, spatial organization, and visual relationships. It may also include related social and cultural practices, economic processes and other intangible dimensions of heritage such as perceptions and associations. Management of the wider setting is related to its role in supporting the Outstanding Universal Value. Its effective management may also contribute to sustainable development, through harnessing the reciprocal benefits for heritage and society.

Decision 39 COM 11

Decision 43 COM 11A

113. Moreover, in the context of the implementation of the *Convention*, the World Heritage Committee has established a process of Reactive Monitoring (see Chapter IV) and a process of Periodic Reporting (see Chapter V).

e) 建立相应机制，以有效吸纳并协调各类合作伙伴与利益相关方的活动；

f) 必要的资源配置；

g) 能力建设；

h) 对管理体制运作的描述可信且透明。

112. 有效管理包括对申报遗产的保护、保存和展示的短、中、长期措施。规划管理采取整体综合的方式对指导遗产长期发展至关重要，也可确保其突出普遍价值的所有方面得以维持。这一综合视角不局限于遗产本身，并包括所有缓冲区和更广泛的背景环境。更广泛的背景环境可以指该遗产的地形、自然环境与建造环境、以及其他元素（例如基础设施建设、土地利用模式空间组织、视觉关系等）。它也可以是相关社会与文化实践，经济进程以及遗产的认知、关联等其他非物质层面因素。对更广泛的背景环境的管理起到了支持突出普遍价值的重要作用。有效管理也意味着对可持续发展做出贡献，达到遗产和社会的互惠互利。

第 39 COM11 号决议

第 43.COM.11A 号决议

113. 另外，为了实施《公约》，世界遗产委员会还建立了反应监测程序（见第四章）和《定期报告》机制（见第五章）。

114. In the case of serial properties, whether national or transnational, a management system or mechanisms for ensuring the coordinated management of the separate components are essential and should be documented in the nomination (see Paragraphs 137-139).

115. [Deleted]

Decision 39 COM 11

116. Where the intrinsic qualities of a nominated site are threatened by human action and yet meet the criteria and the conditions of authenticity or integrity set out in paragraphs 78-95, an action plan outlining the corrective measures required should be submitted with the nomination file. Should the corrective measures submitted by the nominating State Party not be taken within the time proposed by the State Party, the property will be considered by the Committee for delisting in accordance with the procedure adopted by the Committee (see Chapter Ⅳ.C).

Decision 39 COM 11

117. States Parties are responsible for implementing effective management activities for a World Heritage property. States Parties should do so in close collaboration with property managers, the agency with management authority and other partners, local communities and indigenous peoples, rights-holders and stakeholders in property management, by developing, when appropriate, equitable governance arrangements, collaborative management systems and redress mechanisms.

Decision 43 COM 11A

118. The Committee recommends that States

114. 如果是系列遗产，无论是本国的还是跨国的，应在申报材料中阐明能确保各个组成部分协调管理的管理体制或机制（见 137–139 段）。

115. 本条移除。

第 39 COM11 号决议

116. 如果遗产的内在价值受到人类活动的威胁，且满足第 78 至 95 段规定的真实性或完整性的标准和条件，概述纠正措施的行动计划需要和申报材料一起提交。如果缔约国并未在拟定的时间内采取纠正措施，委员会将会考虑依据相关程序将该遗产以名单上移除。（见四 .C 节）

第 39 COM11 号决议

117. 缔约国要对境内的世界遗产实施有效的管理。在管理过程中，缔约国应与遗产管理人员、具有管理权力的机构和其他伙伴、地方社区和原住民、产权持有人和遗产管理方面的利益相关者密切合作，酌情制订公平的治理安排、合作管理体系和补救机制。

第 43.COM.11A 号决议

118. 委员会建议缔约国将灾害、气候变化

Parties include disaster, climate change and other risk preparedness as an element in their World Heritage site management plans and training strategies.

Decision 43 COM 11A

118bis. Notwithstanding Paragraphs 179 and 180 of the *Operational Guidelines*, States Parties shall ensure that Environmental Impact Assessments, Heritage Impact Assessments, and/or Strategic Environmental Assessments be carried out as a pre-requisite for development projects and activities that are planned for implementation within or around a World Heritage property. These assessments should serve to identify development alternatives, as well as both potential positive and negative impacts on the Outstanding Universal Value of the property and to recommend mitigation measures against degradation or other negative impacts on the cultural or natural heritage within the property or its wider setting. This will ensure the long-term safeguarding of the Outstanding Universal Value, and the strengthening of heritage resilience to disasters and climate change.

Decision 43 COM 11A

Sustainable use

119. World Heritage properties may sustain biological and cultural diversity and provide ecosystem services and other benefits, which may contribute to environmental and cultural sustainability. Properties may support a variety of ongoing and proposed uses that are ecologically and culturally sustainable and which may enhance the quality of life and well-being of communities concerned. The State Party and its partners must ensure their use is equitable and fully respects the Outstanding Universal Value of the property. For some properties, human

和其他风险防范作为其世界遗产管理规划和培训战略的组成部分。

第 28COM 10B.4 号决议第 43.COM.11A 号决议

118 补充.《操作指南》第 179 段和 180 段规定，如缔约国计划在世界遗产范围内或其周围开展预先规划的开发项目和活动，作为先决条件，应确保进行环境影响评估、遗产影响评估和 / 或战略环境评估。这些评估应有助于确定开发方式、明确对遗产突出普遍价值可能产生的积极和消极影响，并建议采取相关措施，减少该遗产地或其更广泛环境内的文化或自然遗产产生退化的情况，或减轻对其造成的其他消极影响。这将确保遗产地的突出普遍价值得到长期保护，并加强遗产抵御灾害和气候变化的能力。

第 43.COM.11A 号决议

可持续使用

119. 世界遗产可维持生物和文化多样性，提供生态系统服务及其他益处，这可能有助于环境和文化的可持续性。世界遗产可支持各种正在或计划采用的使用方式，以支持生态和文化的可持续性，这有助于提高相关社区的生活质量和幸福程度。缔约国和合作者必须确保这些可持续使用或任何其他的改变不会对遗产的突出的普遍价值、完整性和 / 或真实性造成负面影响。对于有些遗产来说，不宜承受人类活动。世界遗产的相关立法、政策和策略措施都应确保其突出普遍价值的保护，支持对更大范围的

use would not be appropriate. Legislation, policies and strategies affecting World Heritage properties should ensure the protection of the Outstanding Universal Value, support the wider conservation of natural and cultural heritage, and promote and encourage the effective, inclusive and equitable participation of the communities, indigenous peoples and other stakeholders concerned with the property as necessary conditions to its sustainable protection, conservation, management and presentation.

Decision 43 COM 11A

III. PROCESS FOR THE INSCRIPTION OF PROPERTIES ON THE WORLD HERITAGE LIST

The Process for the inscription of properties on the World Heritage List starts with the inclusion of a site on the Tentative List (see Section II.C), then there are two phases in the preparation of a nomination, the Preliminary Assessment and the full nomination dossier.

III.A　Preparation of Nominations

120. Before States Parties begin to prepare a nomination of a site for inscription on the World Heritage List (i.e. before submission of a Preliminary Assessment request and completion of that Assessment), they should become familiar with the nomination cycle (including the requirement for a completed Preliminary Assessment), described in Paragraph 168. It is desirable to carry out initial preparatory work to establish that a site has the potential to justify Outstanding Universal Value, including integrity and/or authenticity, at the earliest stage, possibly well before the development of a full nomination (including a Preliminary Assessment)

自然和文化遗产的保护、促进和鼓励所在社区公众和所有利益相关方的有效、包容性强和公正的参与，是遗产可持续保护、保存、管理、展示的必要条件。

第 43.COM.11A 号决议

III. 列入《世界遗产名录》的程序

遗产列入《世界遗产名录》的程序始于《预备名录》(见第二章 C)，然后是申报准备的两个阶段：初步评估和准备完整的申遗文本。

III.A　申报准备

120. 在缔约国准备申报遗产列入《世界遗产名录》(比如在提交初步评估申请并完成该项评估) 前，应先熟悉第 168 条描述的申报周期 (包括完成初步评估申请)。在提交耗时耗资的完整的申遗文本前，先开展初步的筹备工作，确认该遗产有潜力证明其拥有突出普遍价值，包括完整性和真实性。这类准备工作包括收集遗产的相关信息、主题研究、展示潜在突出普遍价值证明包括完整性与真实性范围界定研究、或关于遗产在更广泛的全球或区域背景下的初期比较分析，包括咨询机构以遗产空白研究为背景的分析。初期的筹备工作有助于在申报的早期阶段建立可行性申遗战略，避免将

which could be expensive and time-consuming. Such preparatory work might include the collection of available information on the site, thematic studies, scoping studies on the potential for demonstrating Outstanding Universal Value, including integrity and/or authenticity, or an initial comparative study of the site in its regional or wider global context, including an analysis in the context of the Gap Studies produced by the Advisory Bodies. This work will help to establish the feasibility of a possible nomination and avoid the use of resources in the preparation of nominations that may be unlikely to succeed. States Parties are encouraged to seek upstream advice from the relevant Advisory Body(ies) as well as to contact the World Heritage Centre at the earliest opportunity to seek information and guidance. Before the submission of nominations, States Parties are also encouraged to avoid, through constructive dialogue, as much as feasible, potential issues which may concern other States Parties.

资源用在不太可能申报成功的项目上。鼓励缔约国尽早征询相关咨询机构上游建议，同时尽早和世界遗产中心联系，了解相关申报信息和指南。在提交申报之前，还鼓励缔约国尽可能通过建设性对话，避免可能涉及其他缔约国等潜在问题。

Decision 34 COM 12 (Ⅲ) Report of the Expert meeting on Upstream Processes to Nominations: Creative Approaches in the Nomination Process" (Phuket: 2010)
Decision 36 COM 13.I
Decision 39 COM 11
Decision 43 COM 11A

第34COM 12（Ⅲ）号决议关于"上游程序：世界遗产申报的创新举措"的专家会议报告（普吉岛：2010 年）

第 36 COM 13.I 号决议
第 39 COM 11 号决议
第 43 COM 11A 号决议

Upstream Process

121. In relation to the nomination of sites for inscription on the World Heritage List, the voluntary "Upstream Process" comprises advice, consultation and analysis that occurs prior to the Preliminary Assessment and the preparation of a nomination dossier and is aimed at reducing the number of nominations that experience significant problems during the evaluation process. The basic principle of the Upstream Process is to enable the Advisory Bodies and the World Heritage Centre to

上游程序

121. 关于申报列入《世界遗产名录》的遗产，自愿的"上游程序"包括在初步评估和编制申遗文本之前提供的建议、咨询和分析，旨在在评估过程中减少申报可能遇到重大问题的项目。上游程序的基本原则是，在缔约国编制世界遗产申遗文本时，咨询机构和世界遗产中心能够在整个过程中直接向缔约国提供指导和能力建设。为了获得有效的上游支持，应在申报的最初阶段，即在准备和修订缔约国的《预备名录》时，就开始提供上游支持。上游程序

provide guidance and capacity building directly to States Parties, throughout the whole process leading up to the preparation of a possible World Heritage nomination. For the upstream support to be effective, it should be undertaken from the earliest stage in the nomination process, at the moment of the preparation or revision of the States Parties' Tentative Lists. The Upstream Process can also take place after a site is included on the State Party's Tentative List (see Paragraphs 62-76), but before any Preliminary Assessment request is submitted.

也可以在遗产列入缔约国《预备名录》后、提交初步评估申请之前开始（见 62—67 条）。

The UpstreamProcess advice may be desk based, but could involve a site visit and/or holding a workshop.

上游程序建议可能是案头研究，但可能包括现场考察和举办研讨会。

The purpose of the advice given in the context of a nomination is limited to providing guidance on the technical merit of the nomination and the technical framework needed, in order to offer the State(s) Party(ies) the essential tools that enable it(them) to assess the feasibility and/or actions necessary to prepare a possible nomination.

为申报提供咨询意见的目的，仅限于指导申报的技术水平和提供技术框架，以便向各缔约国提供基本工具，使其在在准备申报时评估可行性和／或采取必要行动。

The Upstream Process advice provided regarding a site will not prejudge the results of any future Preliminary Assessment.

有关申报的上游程序建议，不得预判任何初步评估的结果。

Requests for the Upstream Process shall be submitted by the annual deadline of 31 March, using the official format (Annex 15 of the *Operational Guidelines*). Should the number of requests exceed the capacity, then the prioritization system as per Paragraph 61.c) will be applied.

上游程序申请应使用正式格式（见《操作指南》附件 5）在每年的 3 月 31 日前提交。如果申请数量超出年度限额，将依据第 61.C）的优先次序评估。

Preliminary Assessment

初步评估

122. The Preliminary Assessment is a mandatory desk-based process for all sites that may be nominated

122. 初步评估是应相关缔约国的申请进行的，是针对所有可能申报列入《世界遗产名录》

to the World Heritage List and is undertaken following a request by the relevant State(s) Party(ies). Information included in the Preliminary Assessment request should build on the information provided in the Tentative List and also on any Upstream Process advice and/or Preparatory Assistance and its outcome must be provided at least one year before a full nomination dossier can be submitted by the State(s) Party(ies).

In particular:

a) The Preliminary Assessment provides States Parties with an opportunity for enhanced dialogue with the Advisory Bodies, and it will help to establish the feasibility of a potential nomination and avoid the use of resources in the preparation of nominations that may be unlikely to succeed.

b) The Preliminary Assessment provides guidance on the potential of a site to justify Outstanding Universal Value, including integrity and/or authenticity, and, if information is provided, on the requirements for protection and management. The decision to prepare a full nomination dossier, regardless of the outcome of the Preliminary Assessment, will rest with the concerned State(s) Party(ies).

c) States Parties shall submit their Preliminary Assessment request to the World Heritage Centre according to the timetable set in paragraph 168, and using the standard format provided in Annex 3. The request shall be submitted in English or French, in paper and electronic formats (Word and/or PDF format) and in the required number of printed copies (same as for nomination dossiers): 2 identical copies for cultural and natural sites, and 3 identical copies for mixed sites and cultural landscapes.

d) On receipt of Preliminary Assessment requests from States Parties, the Secretariat will acknowledge receipt, check for completeness

的遗产地的、强制性案头评估程序。初步评估申请中包括的信息应以《预备名录》中提供的信息以及任何上游程序建议和 / 或筹备性援助为基础。必须在缔约国提交完整申遗文本至少一年前，提供初步评估的结论。

特别是：

a）初步评估为缔约国提供了加强与咨询机构对话的机会，有助于确定申报的可行性，并避免将资源用于不太可能成功的申报。

b）初步评估为证明遗产的潜在突出普遍价值、包括完整性和 / 或真实性、以及（如果提供了信息）对保护和管理的要求提供指导。无论初步评估结果如何，均应由有关缔约国决定是否准备一份完整的申遗文本。

c）缔约国应按照第 168 段规定的时间表和附件 3 规定的标准格式，向世界遗产中心提交其初步评估申请。申请书应以英文或法文、以纸质和电子格式 (Word 和 / 或 PDF 格式) 以及规定数量的印刷副本 (与申报文件相同) 提交：文化和自然遗产需要两份，混合遗产和文化景观需要三份副本。

d）在收到缔约国提出的初步评估申请后，秘书处将确认收到，检查其完整性 (按照附件 3 规定) 并进行登记。秘书处将按照第 168 段时间

(in compliance with Annex 3) and register them. The Secretariat will forward, according to the timetable set in paragraph 168, complete Preliminary Assessment requests to the relevant Advisory Body(ies) for desk review. If necessary, the Advisory Body(ies) will request any additional information from the State(s) Party(ies), which should be submitted to the Secretariat. From the commencement of the Preliminary Assessment, the Advisory Body(ies) will initiate a dialogue with the concerned State(s) Party(ies) to establish a point of contact and agree on the process of exchange. States Parties are encouraged to appoint a technical focal point to ensure that dialogue is effective throughout the process, and to ensure that the conclusions of the Preliminary Assessment are communicated to the relevant stakeholders.

e) The Preliminary Assessment will be undertaken by ICOMOS and IUCN on a joint basis whenever relevant, and will be an independent desk review, which will include consultation with expert reviewers. No mission to the site will be undertaken (see Annex 6). Based on available information, the conclusions of the assessment will include an indication of whether the site may have potential to justify Outstanding Universal Value. If so, specific guidance and advice, in the form of recommendations, will be provided to assist the State(s) Party(ies) in the development of the nomination dossier. The Preliminary Assessment Report by the Advisory Bodies shall be provided to the State(s) Party(ies) via the Secretariat in one of the two working languages of the *Convention*.

f) The Preliminary Assessment Report by the Advisory Bodies is relevant for up to 5 years. A new Preliminary Assessment is required if a nomination is not submitted by 1 February on the fifth year following the transmission of the Report to the concerned State(s) Party(ies).

g) A State Party may withdraw a Preliminary

表的规定,将初步评估要求提交有关咨询机构进行案头审查。如有必要,咨询机构将通过秘书处要求缔约国提供任何补充资料。从初步评价开始,咨询机构开始与有关缔约国进行对话,并建立联络点以便对交流进程达成协议。鼓励缔约国任命一个技术协调中心,以确保在整个过程中有效对话,并确保将初步评估的结论传达给相关利益相关方。

e)初步评估将由国际古迹遗址理事会和世界自然保护联盟联合实施,分别进行独立的案头审查,包括与专业审查人员协商。不派遣现场考察(见附件6)。根据现有的信息,评估的结论将包括证明该遗产是否具有潜在突出的普遍价值。如有,将以建议的形式提供具体指导和意见,以协助缔约国编制申遗文本。咨询机构的初步评估报告,应通过秘书处以《公约》两种工作语言之一提供给缔约国。

f)咨询机构的初步评估报告的有效期最长为5年。如果提交报告后第五年的2月1日之前,相关缔约国未提交申报,则需要进行新的初步评估。

g)缔约国可随时撤回初步评估申请。在此

Assessment request it has submitted, at any time. In such circumstances, any further consideration of a possible nomination will need to be subject to a new request for a Preliminary Assessment.

h) At each session of the World Heritage Committee, the Secretariat will provide a list of Preliminary Assessments requests received and those undertaken, but will not indicate the guidance given by the Advisory Bodies to the concerned State(s) Party(ies) in a completed Preliminary Assessment. However, once a nomination is submitted, the related Preliminary Assessment Report shall be annexed to it.

i) Both Upstream Process and Preliminary Assessment imply guidance at an early stage, prior to the preparation of a nomination, however they are different mechanisms. The Upstream Process is not mandatory. The Preliminary Assessment is a mandatory phase possibly allowing access to the preparation of a nomination dossier. Within an Upstream Process a visit to the site may be possible, while the Preliminary Assessment is carried out exclusively on the basis of a desk review. The Upstream Process may provide general advice, in relation to revision of a Tentative List, while the Preliminary Assessment is undertaken on a single site (whether serial or not) already included on a State Party's Tentative List. While in general [①] the costs of Upstream Process requests are borne by the requesting State(s) Party(ies), the costs of Preliminary Assessments, being part of the nomination process, are included in the related evaluation process (see also Paragraph 168bis). In terms of sequence, Upstream Process advice should precede the Preliminary Assessment.

Participation in the nomination process

情况下，对任何可能进一步考虑的申报，都需要申请新的初步评估。

h）在每届世界遗产委员会的会议上，秘书处将提供一份收到的和已完成的初步评估申请的清单，但不必说明咨询机构在完成的初步评估中向相关缔约国提供的指导。但是，一旦提交申报，应附上相关的初步评估报告。

i）上游程序和初步评估都是在准备申报的早期阶段进行指导，但它们是不同的机制。上游程序不是强制性的，初步评估是准备申遗文本的强制性过程。在上游程序中，可以进行实地考察，而初步评估则完全是在案头审查的基础上进行的。上游程序可为修订《预备名录》提供一般性建议，而初步评估则针对已列入缔约国《预备名录》的单个遗产（不论是否系列申报）。一般而言[①]，上游程序申请的费用由申请国承担，初步评估的费用作为申报过程的一部分，包括在相关的评估过程中（另见第168条补充）。就顺序而言，上游程序建议应早于初步评估。

参与申报程序

---

① States Parties exempted: see Decision 41 COM 9A paragraph 14
① 缔约国的豁免：见第41 com 9A决定第14段。

123. Effective and inclusive participation in the nomination process of local communities, indigenous peoples, governmental, non-governmental and private organizations and other stakeholders is essential to enable them to have a shared responsibility with the State Party in the maintenance of the property. States Parties are encouraged to ensure that Preliminary Assessment requests involve appropriate stakeholders and rights-holders engagement. They are also encouraged to prepare nominations with the widest possible participation of stakeholders and shall demonstrate, as appropriate, that the free, prior and informed consent of indigenous peoples has been obtained, through, inter alia, making the nominations publicly available in appropriate languages and public consultations and hearings. Where appropriate, States Parties are also encouraged to consult potentially concerned States Parties, including neighbouring States Parties, to promote consensus, collaboration and to celebrate cultural diversity.

Decision 39 COM 11

Decision 43 COM 11A

Preparatory Assistance for the preparation of nominations

124. Preparatory Assistance, as described in Chapter Ⅶ.E, may be requested by States Parties for the preparation of nominations, and in evaluating such requests consideration will be given to the outcome of Preliminary Assessments.

Secretariat assistance throughout the nomination process

125. States Parties are encouraged to contact the Secretariat, which can provide assistance

123. 申报过程中，本土社区、原住民、政府组织、非政府组织、私人机构以及其他利益相关方有效、广泛的参与都很重要，这使他们能够与缔约国共同承担保护遗产的责任。鼓励缔约国在初步评估申请阶段让利益相关方和产权人尽可能广泛参与，鼓励通过公共协商和听证会等形式，用适当的语言，公开申报信息，确保获得原住民自愿、事先和知情的同意。在适当情况下，还鼓励缔约国与潜在的有关缔约国，包括邻国协商，以促进协商一致、合作和颂扬文化多样性。

第 39 COM 11 号决议

第 43.COM.11A 号决议

在准备申报过程中申请筹备性援助

124. 如第七.E 章节中所述，缔约国准备申报时可以申请"筹备性援助"。在评估此类申请时，将考虑初步评估的结果。

秘书处在整个准备申报过程中提供帮助

125. 鼓励缔约国同秘书处联系，秘书处能够在整个申报过程中提供帮助。

throughout the nomination process.

126. The Secretariat can also provide:

a) guidance on mapping and cartographic requirements;

b) examples of successful nominations, of management and legislative provisions;

c) guidance for nominating different types/ categories of sites;

d) guidance for nominating serial and trans-boundary sites (see Paragraphs 134-139).

Deadlines for the submission of draft nominations and nomination dossiers

127. States Parties may submit draft nomination dossiers to the Secretariat for comment and review at any time during the year. However, States Parties are strongly encouraged to transmit to the Secretariat by 30 September of the preceding year (see Paragraph 168), the draft nomination dossiers that they wish to submit by the 1 February deadline. This submission of a draft nomination dossiers should include maps showing the boundaries for the proposed site. Draft nomination dossiers could be submitted either in electronic format or in printed version (only in 1 copy without annexes except for maps). In both cases they should be accompanied by a cover letter.

Decision 37 COM 12. II

128. Nomination dossiers may be submitted at any time during the year, but only those nomination dossiers that are "complete" (see paragraph 132 and Annex 5) and received by the Secretariat on or before 1 February[①] will be considered for inscription

126. 秘书处还能：

a) 在确定合适的地图和照片这些资料方面提供帮助；

b) 提供成功申报案例以及管理方法和立法条款上的参考范例；

c) 为不同类别的遗产申报提供指导，

d) 为申报系列遗产和跨境遗产提供指导（见第 134 至 139 段）。

提交申报文件草案及申遗文本的最后期限

127. 缔约国可以在全年任何时间提交申报文本初稿至秘书处，听取意见，接受初审。但强烈鼓励缔约国，将其计划于 2 月 1 日截止日期前提交的申报文本的初稿，于前一年 9 月 30 日之前交到秘书处。初稿提交须包括显示申报遗产边界的地图。初稿提交可以是电子或纸质形式（除地图外，仅一个文件无需附件）。提交材料需要附有说明。

第 37COM12. II 号决议

128. 任何时候都可以提交申报，但只有在 2 月 1 日[①]或之前递交到秘书处且"完整"的申报（见第 132 条及附件 5）才会被世界遗产委员审核，决定是否次年列入《世界遗产名录》。委员会只审查已包含在缔约国《预备名录》上、已

---

① If 1 February falls on a weekend, the nomination dossier must be received by 17h00 GMT the preceding Friday.

① 如 2 月 1 日恰为周末，申报材料需于格林威治时间前一个周五 17 点前递交至秘书处。

on the World Heritage List by the World Heritage Committee during the following year. Only nomination dossiers of sites included in the State Party's Tentative List and which have undergone a complete Preliminary Assessment will be examined by the Committee (see Paragraphs 63, 65 and 122).

经完成初步评估的遗产（见 63、65. 及 122 条）。

Decision 37 COM 12. II

Decision 39 COM 11

第 37COM12. II 号决议

第 39 COM11 号决议

III. B　Format and content of nomination dossiers

III. B　申报文件的格式和内容

129. The nomination dossier is the primary basis on which the Committee considers the inscription of properties on the World Heritage List. All relevant information should be included in the nomination dossier and it should be cross-referenced to the source of information. Nomination dossiers of properties for inscription on the World Heritage List should be prepared in accordance with the format set out in Annex 5.

129. 申遗文本是委员会考虑列入世界遗产名录的主要依据。所有相关信息应包括在申遗文本中，并应与信息来源相互参照。《世界遗产名录》申报应依据附件 5 所示格式提交材料。

130. The format includes the following sections:

130. 格式包括如下部分：

1. Identification of the nominated property
2. Description of the nominated property
3. Justification for Inscription
4. State of conservation and factors affecting the nominated property
5. Protection and Management
6. Monitoring
7. Documentation
8. Contact Information of responsible authorities
9. Signature on behalf of the State Party(ies)

1. 遗产的辨认
2. 申报遗产描述
3. 列入理由
4. 申报遗产的保护状况和影响因素
5. 保护和管理
6. 监测
7. 文件
8. 负责机构的联系信息
9. 缔约国代表签名

131. Nomination dossiers to the World Heritage List are evaluated on content rather than on appearance of the dossier or the quantity of

131.《世界遗产名录》申报评估的重点是内容，不是封面和附件的数量。

annexes.

132. For a nomination dossier to be considered as "complete", the following requirements (see format in Annex 5) are to be met:

Decision 37 COM 12. Ⅱ

Decision 39 COM 11

Decision 43 COM 11A

Executive Summary

An Executive Summary shall include essential information (see Annex 5) extracted from the main text of the nomination dossier including a reduced size version of the map(s) indicating the boundaries of the nominated property and of the buffer zone (where appropriate) and the draft Statement of Outstanding Universal Value (the same text presented in Section 3.3 of the main text of the nomination dossier).

1. Identification of the nominated property

The boundaries of the nominated property shall be clearly defined, unambiguously distinguishing between the nominated property and any buffer zone (when present) (see Paragraphs 103-107). Maps shall be sufficiently detailed to determine precisely which area of land and/or water is nominated. Officially up-to-date published topographic maps of the State Party annotated to show the nominated property boundaries and any buffer zone (when present) shall be provided if available in printed version. A nomination dossier shall be considered "incomplete" if it does not include clearly defined boundaries.

2. Description of the nominated property

The Description of the nominated property

132. "完整" 申报需要满足下列要求（见包括每一部分的解释性说明的附件 5 的格式，及第 128 条）。

第 37COM12. Ⅱ 号决议

第 39 COM 11 号决议

第 43.COM.11A 号决议

执行摘要

执行摘要应包括从申报文本中摘录的所有重要信息。包括一份标明申报遗产和缓冲区（如适用）的边界的、合适的、缩小版地图，以及一份《突出的普遍价值声明》草案（与申报文本 3.3 部分内容一致）。

1. 遗产辨认

应清晰地定义申报遗产边界，清楚区分申报遗产和任何缓冲区（若存在）（见 103-107 条）的界限。地图应足够详细，能精确标出所申报的陆地和 / 或水域。若有可能，应提供缔约国最新的官方出版的地形图，注清遗产边界。如果没有清晰的边界定义，申报会被认为 "不完整"。

2. 遗产描述

遗产描述应包括遗产辨认及其历史及发展概

shall include the identification of the nominated property and an overview of its history and development. All component parts that are mapped shall be identified and described. In particular, where serial properties are nominated, each of the component parts shall be clearly described.

The History and Development of the nominated property shall describe how the nominated property has reached its present form and the significant changes that it has undergone. This information shall provide the important facts needed to support and give substance to the argument that the nominated property meets the criteria of Outstanding Universal Value and conditions of integrity and/or authenticity.

3. Justification for inscription

This section must make clear why the nominated property is considered to be of Outstanding Universal Value.

The comparative analyses prepared by States Parties when nominating properties for inscription in the World Heritage List should not be confused with the thematic studies prepared by the Advisory Bodies at the request of the Committee (paragraph 148 below)

Decision 7 EXT.COM 4A

The text in sections from 3.1.a to 3.1.e should contain more detailed information to support the text of the proposed Statement of Outstanding Universal Value (section 3.3).

Section 3.1.b shall indicate the World Heritage criteria (see Paragraph 77) under which the nominated property is proposed, together with a clearly stated argument for the use of each criterion. Statements of integrity and (when cultural criteria

述。应确认、描述所有的绘制在地图上的组成部分，如果是系列申报，应清晰描述每一组成部分。

在遗产的历史和发展中应描述遗产是如何形成现在的状态以及所经历的重大变化。这些信息应包含所需的重要事实，以证实遗产达到突出普遍价值的标准，满足完整性和／或真实性的条件。

3. 列入理由

此部分应该明示为什么该遗产具有突出的普遍性价值。

缔约国申报遗产时递交的比较分析不应和咨询机构应委员会要求编制的主题研究相混淆（见下面的第148条）第7EXT.COM4A号决议

从3.1a到3.1e的文本应该包含更多具体的信息，以支持缔约国所提交的《突出的普遍性价值声明》（见3.3）。

3.1.b应指出遗产申报依据的标准（见77条），且须明确说明依据此标准的原因。遗产的完整性与真实性（如果申报的是文化遗产）声明应该包含在内，且清楚地说明为什么该遗产满足78条到95条所列出的条件。

are proposed) of authenticity shall be included and shall demonstrate how the nominated property satisfies the conditions outlined in Paragraphs 78-95.

In section 3.2, a comparative analysis of the nominated property in relation to similar properties, whether or not on the World Heritage List, both at the national and international levels, shall be provided. The comparative analysis shall explain the importance of the nominated property in its national and international context.

In section 3.3, a proposed Statement of Outstanding Universal Value (see Paragraphs 49–53 and 155) of the nominated property prepared by the State Party shall make clear why the property is considered to merit inscription on the World Heritage List.

4. State of conservation and factors affecting the nominated property

This section shall include accurate information on the present state of conservation of the nominated property (including information on its physical condition of the property and conservation measures in place). It shall also include a description of the factors affecting the nominated property (including threats). Information provided in this section constitutes the baseline data which are necessary to monitor the state of conservation of the nominated property in the future.

5. Protection and management

Protection: Section 5 shall include the list of the legislative, regulatory, contractual, planning, institutional and/or traditional measures most relevant to the protection of the nominated property and

3.2 应提供该遗产与类似遗产的比较分析，无论类似遗产是否已被列入《世界遗产名录》，是国内还是国外。比较分析应说明申报遗产在国内及国际范围内的重要性。

3.3 是缔约国所提交的遗产《突出的普遍性价值》（见 49 条到 53 条，以及 155 条）。这部分应清楚说明为什么该遗产有资格列入《世界遗产名录》。

4. 保护状况和影响因素

本部分应包括目前遗产保护状况的准确信息（包括遗产的物理状况和现有的保护措施）。同时，也应包括影响遗产的因素描述（包括威胁）。本部分提供的信息是将来监测申报遗产保护状况必要的基础数据。

5. 保护和管理

保护：第五部分包括与遗产保护联系最为紧密的立法、规章、契约、规划、机构和 / 或传统措施，并详尽分析了实际保护措施的操作方法。立法、规章、契约、规划和机构性文本或

provide a detailed analysis of the way in which this protection actually operates. Legislative, regulatory, contractual planning and/or institutional texts, or an abstract of the texts, shall also be attached in English or French.

者文本摘要，应以英文或法文附上。

Management: An appropriate management plan or other management system is essential and shall be provided in the nomination dossier. Assurances of the effective implementation of the management plan or other management system are also expected. Sustainable development principles should be integrated into the management system, for all types of natural, cultural and mixed nominated properties, including their buffer zones and wider setting.

管理：适宜的管理规划或其他管理体制很必要，应包括在申报文件中，并希望说明管理规划或其他管理体制可以确保得到有效执行。应将可持续发展原则纳入管理体系，适用于所有类型的自然遗产、文化遗产和混合遗产，包括其缓冲区及更广泛的周边区域。

A copy of the management plan or documentation of the management system shall be annexed to the nomination dossier. If the management plan exists only in a language other than English or French, an English or French detailed description of its provisions shall be annexed.

管理规划或者管理体制文献的副本应附在申报文件后。如果管理规划为非英语或非法语，应附上英语或法语的条款详述。

A detailed analysis or explanation of the management plan or a documented management system shall be provided in Section 5.e of the nomination dossier.

应在申报文件的 5.e 部分提供管理规划或者管理体系的详尽分析或者说明。

A nomination dossier which does not include the above-mentioned documents is considered incomplete unless other documents guiding the management of the nominated property until the finalization of the management plan are provided.

申报文件若不包括上述文书则被认为不完整，除非在管理规划完成之前提交了指导遗产管理的其他文书。

6. Monitoring

6. 监测

States Parties shall include the key indicators in place and/or proposed to measure and assess the state of conservation of the nominated property, the factors affecting it, conservation measures at

缔约国应在申报材料提供衡量、评估申报遗产保护状况的关键指标、其影响因素、遗产保护措施、审查周期及负责机构的名称。

the nominated property, the periodicity of their examination, and the identity of the responsible authorities.

7. Documentation

All documentation necessary to substantiate the nomination dossier shall be provided. In addition to what is indicated above, this shall include a) images of a quality suitable for printing (digital photographs at 300 dpi minimum, and if essential, supplementary film, video or other audio visual material); and b) image/audiovisual inventory and authorization form (see Annex 5, point 7.a). The main text of the nomination dossier shall be transmitted in printed form as well as in electronic format (Word and/or PDF format preferred).

8. Contact information of responsible authorities

Detailed contact information of responsible authorities shall be provided.

9. Signature on behalf of the State Party

The main text of the nomination dossier shall conclude with the original signature of the official empowered to sign it on behalf of the State Party.

10. Number of printed copies required (including annexed maps)

Nomination dossiers of cultural and natural properties (excluding cultural landscapes): 2 identical copies

Nomination dossiers of mixed properties and

7. 文件

应提供申报所需的所有文件。除了上述文件之外，还应包括 1）达到打印标准的照片（最低像素 300dpi；如必要，补充电影、录像或其他视听材料）；2）图像清单以及授权表（见附件 5，7a）。申报文本应以打印形式和电子文档提交（word 或 pdf 文件为佳）。

8. 负责机构的联系信息

应提供负责机构的详细联系信息。

9. 缔约国代表签名

申报材料结尾应有缔约国授权的官方原始签名。

10. 所需打印数量（包括地图附件）

文化与自然遗产申报文件（不包括文化景观）：2 份

混合遗产和文化景观申报：3 份

cultural landscapes: 3 identical copies

11. Paper and electronic formats

Nomination dossiers shall be presented on A4-size paper and in electronic format (Word and/or PDF format). A nomination dossier shall not be considered submitted until its paper format is received by the Secretariat.

12. Sending

States Parties shall submit the nomination dossiers in English or French duly signed, to:
UNESCO World Heritage Centre
7, place de Fontenoy 75352 Paris 07 SP
France
Tel: +33 (0) 1 4568 1104
E-mail: wh-nominations@unesco.org

133. The Secretariat will retain all supporting documentation (maps, plans, photographic material, etc.) submitted with the nomination dossier.

Ⅲ. C　Requirements for nomination of different types of nominated properties

Nominated transboundary properties

134. A nominated property may be located:

Decision 7 EXT.COM 4A

a) on the territory of a single State Party, or
b) on the territory of all concerned States Parties having adjacent borders (nominated transboundary property).

135. Wherever possible, nomination dossiers

---

11. 纸质版和电子版文件

申报材料应使用 A4 纸张（或信纸），同时提供电子版（word 和 / 或 pdf 格式）。秘书处只认可收到的纸质版申遗文本。

12. 寄送

缔约国应提交经正式签署的英语或法语申报材料，至：法国巴黎联合国教科文组织世界遗产中心
（ 7，place de Fontenoy 75352 Paris 07 SP ）

电话：+33（0）145681104
E-mail：wh-nominations@unesco.org

133. 秘书处会保留和申遗文本一起提交的所有相关资料（地图、规划、照片资料等）。

Ⅲ. C　各类遗产申报的要求

跨境遗产

134. 申报的遗产可能：

第 7EXT.COM4A 号决议

a) 位于一个缔约国境内；
b) 位于几个接壤的缔约国境内（跨境遗产）。

135. 跨境遗产的申报文件，应尽可能由几

of transboundary sites should be prepared (see Annex 2B) and submitted by States Parties jointly in conformity with Article 11.3 of the *Convention*. The States Parties concerned shall establish a joint management committee or similar body to oversee the management of the whole nominated transboundary property.

136. Extensions to an existing World Heritage property located in one State Party may be proposed to become a transboundary property, with the consent of the State Party on the territory of which the existing World Heritage property is located.

Nominated serial properties

137. Nominated serial property includes two or more component parts related by clearly defined links:

a) Component parts should reflect cultural, social or functional links over time that provide, where relevant, landscape, ecological, evolutionary or habitat connectivity.

b) Each component part should contribute to the Outstanding Universal Value of the nominated property as a whole in a substantial, scientific, readily defined and discernible way, and may include, inter alia, intangible attributes. The resulting Outstanding Universal Value should be easily understood and communicated.

c) Consistently, and in order to avoid an excessive fragmentation of component parts, the process of nomination of the property, including the selection of the component parts, should take fully into account the overall manageability and coherence of the nominated property (see Paragraph 114).

and provided the series as a whole – and not

个缔约国遵照大会公约第 11.3 条规定, 共同准备（见附见 2B）和递交。大会强烈建议各相关缔约国建立联合管理委员会或类似组织, 监督该遗产的总体管理。

136. 在得到现有世界遗产所在缔约国同意的情况下, 位于该缔约国境内的现有世界遗产的扩展部分, 可以申请成为跨境遗产。

系列遗产

137. 系列遗产应包括两个或两个以上逻辑关系清晰的组成部分:

a）各组成部分应体现出文化、社会或功能性长期发展而来的相互联系, 进而形成景观、生态、空间演变或栖居地上的关联性;

b）每个组成部分都应对申报遗产整体的突出普遍价值有实质性、科学的、可清晰界定和辨识的贡献, 亦可包含非物质载体。最终的突出普遍价值应该是容易理解和便于沟通的;

c）与此一致的, 为避免各组成部分过度分裂, 遗产申报的过程, 包括对各组成部分的选择, 应该充分考虑遗产整体的连贯性和管理上的可行性（见第 114 条）, 并且该系列作为一个整体（不必是其各组成部分）必须具有突出普遍价值。

necessarily its individual component parts–is of Outstanding Universal Value.

138. A serial nominated property may occur:

Decision 7 EXT.COM 4A

a) on the territory of a single State Party (nominated serial national property); or

b) within the territory of different States Parties, which need not be contiguous and is nominated with the consent of all States Parties concerned (nominated serial transnational property).

138bis. The States Parties concerned shall establish a joint management committee or similar body to oversee the management of the whole of a nominated serial transnational property (see Paragraph 114). Extension to an existing World Heritage property located in one State Party may be proposed to become a transnational property, with the consent of the State Party on the territory of which the existing World Heritage property is located.

139. States Parties planning a group of transnational serial nomination dossiers linked by the same unifying cultural and/or natural concept and phased over different cycles are encouraged to prepare an agreed nomination strategy before their official submission, in order to inform the Committee of their intentions and to ensure better planning. In such cases, the nomination strategy should be discussed at the Preliminary Assessment stage and annexed to the subsequent nomination dossiers.

Decision 41 COM 8B.50

III . D　Registration of nomination dossiers

138. 申报的系列遗产可能

第 7EXT.COM4A 号决议

a) 位于一个缔约国境内（申报本国系列遗产）；

b) 位于不同缔约国境内，不必相连，同时须经过所有相关缔约国同意进行申报（申报跨国系列遗产）。

138 补充 . 相关缔约国应设立一个联合管理委员会或类似机构，监督跨国系列遗产的整体管理 (见第 114 条)。在得到现有世界遗产所在缔约国同意的情况下，可建议将位于一个缔约国境内的现有世界遗产的扩展部分，申请成为跨境遗产。

139. 如果缔约国计划申报由同一文化和 / 或自然概念相联系的系列遗产，建议缔约国在正式提交申报前，商讨申遗战略，按不同周期、分阶段编制跨国系列申遗文本，以便向委员会说明其意图，并确保进行更好的规划。在这种情况下，应在初步评估阶段就讨论申遗战略，并将初步评估结果作为附件与申遗文本一同提交。

第 41 COM 8B.50 号决议

III . D　申报登记

140. On receipt of nomination dossiers from States Parties, the Secretariat will acknowledge receipt, check for completeness and register them. The Secretariat will forward complete nomination dossiers to the relevant Advisory Bodies for evaluation. The Secretariat will also make available the electronic format of the main text of the nomination dossiers to the Members of the Committee on the World Heritage Centre's website. If necessary, the Advisory Bodies will request additional information from the State(s) Party(ies), which will be submitted to and registered by the World Heritage Centre. The timetable for registration and processing of nomination dossiers is detailed in Paragraph 168.

Decision 39 COM 11

141. The Secretariat establishes and submits at each Committee session a list of all nomination dossiers received, including the date of reception, an indication of their status "complete" or "incomplete", as well as the date at which they are considered as "complete" in conformity with paragraphs 128, 132 and Annex 5.

Decisions 26 COM 14

Decision 28 COM 14B.57

Decision 39 COM 11

142. A nomination dossier passes through a cycle between the time of its submission and the decision by the World Heritage Committee. This cycle normally lasts one and a half years between submission in February of Year 1 and the decision of the Committee in June/July of Year 2.

Ⅲ. E   Evaluation of nomination dossiers by the Advisory Bodies

140. 收到各缔约国递交的申报文件后,秘书处将并发送回执确认收到,核查材料是否完整,然后进行注册登记。秘书处将向相关咨询机构转交完整的申报文件,由咨询机构进行评估。秘书处也会将申报文本的电子版上传到世界遗产中心官网,以供委员会的各成员国参考。必要时,咨询机构将向缔约国索要补充信息并提交世界遗产中心注册。登记的时间表和申报的受理过程在第 168 段中有详细说明。

第 39 COM11 号决议

141. 秘书处在每届委员会会议时拟定并递交所有接收到的申报遗产名单,包括接收的日期,申报文件"完整"与否的陈述,以及按照第 128、132 段和附件 5 的要求、申报文件被认为"完整"的日期。

第 26COM14 和 28COM

14B.57 号决议

第 39 COM11 号决议

142. 申报周期从递交之日起到世界遗产委员会做出决定之日结束。从每年二月缔约国递交申报材料至翌年六月委员会做出决定,通常历时一年半。

Ⅲ. E   咨询机构评估

143. The Advisory Bodies will evaluate whether or not properties nominated by States Parties have Outstanding Universal Value, meet the conditions of integrity and (when relevant) of authenticity and meet the requirements of protection and management. The procedures and format of ICOMOS and IUCN evaluations are described in Annex 6.

Decision 39 COM 11

144. Evaluations of cultural heritage nomination dossiers will be carried out by ICOMOS.

145. Evaluations of natural heritage nomination dossiers will be carried out by IUCN.

146. In the case of nomination dossiers of cultural properties in the category of "cultural landscapes", the evaluation will be carried out by ICOMOS in consultation with IUCN, as appropriate. For mixed properties, the evaluation will be carried out jointly by ICOMOS and IUCN.

147. As requested by the World Heritage Committee or as necessary, ICOMOS and IUCN will carry out thematic studies to evaluate potential nominated properties in their regional, global or thematic context. These studies should be informed by a review of the Tentative Lists submitted by States Parties and by reports of meetings on the harmonization of Tentative Lists, as well as by other technical studies performed by the Advisory Bodies and qualified organizations and individuals. A list of those studies already completed may be found on the Web addresses of the Advisory Bodies. These studies should not be confused with the comparative analysis to be prepared by States Parties in nominating properties for inscription on the World Heritage List (see Paragraph 132).

143. 咨询机构将评估各缔约国申报的遗产是否具有突出普遍价值，是否符合完整性或真实性（如果适用）的条件，以及是否能达到保护和管理的要求。国际古迹遗址理事会和世界自然保护联盟的评估程序和格式，在附件 6 中有详细说明。

第 39 COM11 号决议

144. 对文化遗产申报文件的评估将由国际古迹遗址理事会完成。

145. 对自然遗产申报文本的评估将由世界自然保护联盟完成。

146. 作为"文化景观"类申报的文化遗产，将由国际古迹遗址理事会与世界自然保护联盟磋商之后进行评估。对于混合遗产的评估，酌情，将由国际古迹遗址理事会与世界自然保护联盟共同完成。

147. 如经世界遗产委员会要求或者在必要情况下，国际古迹遗址理事会与世界自然保护联盟将开展主题研究，将申报的世界遗产置于地区、全球或主题背景中进行评估。这些研究，必须建立在对各缔约国递交的预备名录的审议、关于平衡预备名录的会议报告、以及由咨询机构或具备相关资质的组织或个人进行的其他技术研究的基础之上。已完成的相关研究列表见咨询机构的网站。这些研究不得与缔约国在申报世界遗产时准备的"比较分析"相混淆（见第 132 条）。

148. The following principles must guide the evaluations and presentations of ICOMOS and IUCN. The evaluations and presentations should:

Decision 28 COM 14B.57

Decision 30 COM 13

Decision 39 COM 11

a) adhere to the *World Heritage Convention* and the relevant *Operational Guidelines* and any additional policies set out by the Committee in its decisions;

b) be objective, rigorous and scientific including in considering all information provided to the Advisory Bodies regarding a nomination;

c) be conducted to a consistent standard of professionalism, equity and transparency throughout the evaluation process in consultation and dialogue with nominating States Parties;

d) comply to standard format, both for evaluations and presentations, to be agreed with the Secretariat and include the names of all experts who participated in the evaluation process, except desk reviewers who provide confidential reviews, and, in an annex, a detailed breakdown of all costs and expenses related to the evaluation;

e) involve regional experts familiar with the subject;

f) indicate clearly and separately whether the property has Outstanding Universal Value, meets the conditions of integrity and/or authenticity, a management plan/system and legislative protection;

g) evaluate each property systematically according to all relevant criteria, including its state of conservation, relatively, that is, by comparison with that of other properties of the same type, both inside and outside the State Party's territory;

h) consider previous Upstream Process advice, if provided, and the outcome of the Preliminary Assessment and include references to Committee

148. 以下为国际古迹遗址理事会和世界自然保护联盟的评估与陈述所遵循的原则。评估与陈述应：

第 28COM14B.57.3 号决议

第 30 COM13.13 号决议

第 39 COM11 号决议

a) 遵守《世界遗产公约》及其《操作指南》，以及委员会在决定中规定的其他政策；

b) 做到客观、严谨和科学，包括审查缔约国上交给咨询机构的有关申报的所有信息；

c) 依照一致的专业标准；在评估过程中依照平等与透明的原则与缔约国展开磋商与对话；

d) 评估和陈述均须遵守标准格式，与秘书处一致，注明所有参与评估的专家的名字（提供书面保密意见的专家除外），另外在附件中应分类写清楚评估过程中所产生的花销；

e) 让熟悉相关课题的地区专家参与进来；

f) 清晰分明地指出所申报遗产是否具有突出普遍价值，是否符合完整性和 / 或真实性的标准，是否拥有管理规划 / 系统和立法保护；

g) 根据所有相关标准，对每处遗产（包括其保护状况），进行系统的比较评估，即需与缔约国境内或境外其他同类遗产进行比较；

h) 考虑早期的上游程序建议（如有）以及初步评估结果；参考与被审议的申报项目相关的委员会决定和要求；

decisions and requests concerning the nomination under consideration;

i) not take into account or include any information submitted by the State Party after 28 February, in the year in which the nomination is considered. The State Party should be informed when information has arrived after the deadline and is not being taken into account in the evaluation. This deadline should be rigorously enforced; and

j) provide a justification for their views through a list of references (literature) consulted, as appropriate.

149. The Advisory Bodies are requested to forward to States Parties, with copy to the World Heritage Centre for distribution to the Chair of the World Heritage Committee, by 31 January of each year, a short interim report outlining the status and any issues relevant to evaluations, and detailing any requests for supplementary information, in one of the two working languages of the *Convention*.

Decision 7 EXT.COM 4B.1

Decision 39 COM 11

150. Letters from the concerned States Parties, submitted in the appropriate form in Annex 12, detailing the factual errors that might have been identified in the evaluation of their nomination made by the Advisory Bodies, must be received by the World Heritage Centre no later than 14 days before the opening of the session of the Committee with copies to the relevant Advisory Bodies. The letters shall be made available as an annex to the documents for the relevant agenda item, and no later than the first day of the Committee session. The World Heritage Centre and the Advisory Bodies may add their comments to the letters, in the relevant section of the form, before they are made available.

i）不考虑缔约国于申报审议当年 2 月 28 日后递交的任何信息。同时应通知缔约国，因收到的信息已逾期，所以不纳入考虑之列。必须严格遵守最后期限；

j）同时提供支持他们论点的参考书目（文献）。

149. 咨询机构应在每年 1 月 31 日以前向各缔约国递送一份简短的中期报告。报告应简要阐述遗产的现状，以及其他与评估相关的议题，并且以《公约》规定的两种工作语言的任一种详列缔约国需要补交的信息。该报告也将附送至世界遗产中心，以供遗产委员会主席参考。

第 7 EXT.COM 4B.1 号决议

第 39 COM 11 号决议

150. 相关缔约国应邀，在委员会大会开幕至少 14 天前，按照附件 12 中提供的格式致信大会主席，同时抄送咨询机构，详细说明他们在咨询机构关于申报的评估意见中发现的事实性错误。这些信件将于最晚大会开始前 1 天作为相关文件的附件，在相应的大会议程项目中提供。世界遗产中心和咨询机构可以于信件发布前，在表格的相应部分加入他们的评论。

Decision 7 EXT.COM 4B.1

Decision 37 COM 12. Ⅱ

第 7 EXT.COM 4B.1 号决议

第 37 COM 12. Ⅱ 号决议

151. ICOMOS and IUCN make their recom-mendations under three categories:

a) properties which are recommended for inscription without reservation;

b) properties which are not recommended for inscription;

c) nominations which are recommended for referral or deferral.

151. 国际古迹遗址理事会和世界自然保护联盟的意见分三类：

a）建议无保留列入《世界遗产名录》的遗产；

b）建议不予列入《世界遗产名录》的遗产；

c）建议补报或重报《世界遗产名录》的遗产。

Ⅲ. F　Withdrawal of nominations

Ⅲ. F　撤销申报

152. A State Party may withdraw a nomination it has submitted at any time prior to the Committee session at which it is scheduled to be examined. The State Party should inform the Secretariat in writing of its intention to withdraw the nomination. If the State Party so wishes it can resubmit a nomination for the site, which will be considered as a new nomination according to the procedures and timetable outlined in paragraph 168.

152. 缔约国，可以在委员会召开会议审核申报之前任何时候撤销所递交的申报，但必须以书面形式向秘书处说明意图。如某缔约国希望撤回申报，它可以重新递交一份遗产的申报，根据第 168 条所列程序和时间表，该申报将会被作为一项新申报。

152bis. In the case of transnational/trans-boundary nominations, if one or more nominating State(s) Party(ies) inform the Secretariat in writing of its/their intention to withdraw all the component parts or the whole area of the site situated on its/their territory(ies), the Secretariat shall immediately notify all the other nominating State(s) Party(ies) and the nomination process for the site in its entirety shall be considered concluded. If the State(s) Party(ies) so wish it/they can resubmit a nomination for the site, which will be considered as a new nomination according to the procedures and timetable outlined in Paragraph 168.

152 补充．在跨国 / 跨界申报的情况下，如一个或多个申报缔约国以书面通知秘书处，打算撤销申报位于其领土上的该系列遗产的所有组成部分或整个遗产，秘书处应立即通知所有其他申报缔约国，并应认为该遗产的整个申报程序已终结。如果缔约国又希望重新提交对遗产的申报，将设为新的申报，按照第 168 段所述的程序和时间表提交申请。

Ⅲ. G　Decision of the World Heritage Committee

Ⅲ. G　世界遗产委员会的决定

153. The World Heritage Committee decides whether a property should or should not be inscribed on the World Heritage List, referred or deferred.

Inscription

154. When deciding to inscribe a property on the World Heritage List, the Committee, guided by the Advisory Bodies, adopts a Statement of Outstanding Universal Value for the property.

155. The Statement of Outstanding Universal Value should include a summary of the Committee's determination that the property has Outstanding Universal Value, identifying the criteria under which the property was inscribed, including the assessments of the conditions of integrity, and, for cultural and mixed properties, authenticity. It should also include a statement on the protection and management in force and the requirements for protection and management for the future. The Statement of Outstanding Universal Value shall be the basis for the future protection and management of the property.

Decision 39 COM 11

Where necessary, the protection and management part of the Statement of Outstanding Universal Value may be updated by the World Heritage Committee, in consultation with the State Party and further to a review by the Advisory Bodies. Such updates could be made periodically further to the outcomes of Periodic Reporting cycles, or at any Committee session, if required.

The World Heritage Centre will automatically keep the Statements of Outstanding Universal Value

153. 世界遗产委员会决定一项遗产是否应被列入《世界遗产名录》、或是要求补报或重报。

列入名录

154. 决定将遗产列入《世界遗产名录》时，在咨询机构的指导下，委员会将通过该遗产的《突出普遍价值声明》。

155.《突出普遍价值声明》应包括委员会确定该遗产具有突出普遍价值的决定摘要，明确遗产列入《世界遗产名录》所遵循的标准，包括对于完整性或真实性（如果是文化遗产或混合遗产的话）状况的评估。还应该包括对现行保护管理情况及未来保护管理要求的说明。突出普遍价值声明将作为未来该遗产的保护和管理的基础。

第 39 COM11 号决议

经与缔约国磋商，并在相关咨询机构的审核下，世界遗产委员会可以对遗产《突出的普遍价值声明》中的保护与管理部分进行必要的更新。更新可以在定期报告公布之后，或应要求于任一届委员会会议上执行。

如果委员会决议变更遗产名称、微调遗产边界，或在相关咨询机构同意下修改任何事实

updated further to subsequent decisions taken by the Committee concerning a change of name of the property and change of surface further to minor boundary modifications and correct any factual errors as agreed with the relevant Advisory Bodies.

In the framework of the Gender Equality Priority of UNESCO, the use of gender-neutral language in the preparation of Statements of Outstanding Universal Value is encouraged.

156. At the time of inscription, the Committee may also make other recommendations concerning the protection and management of the World Heritage property.

157. The Statement of Outstanding Universal Value (including the criteria for which a specific property is inscribed on the World Heritage List) will be set out by the Committee in its reports and publications.

Decision not to inscribe

158. If the Committee decides that a property should not be inscribed on the World Heritage List, the nomination may not be presented to the Committee again except in exceptional circumstances. These exceptional circumstances may include new discoveries, new scientific information about the property, or different criteria not presented in the original nomination. In these cases, a new nomination shall be submitted.

Referral of Nominations

159. Nominations which the Committee decides to refer back to the State Party for additional information may be resubmitted to the following Committee session for examination. Referral

性错误，则世界遗产中心将随后对《突出普遍价值声明》自动更新。

在《联合国教科文组织性别平等条例》的框架下，委员会鼓励在《突出普遍价值声明》中使用性别中立语言。

156. 列入《世界遗产名录》时，委员会也可针对该世界遗产的保护和管理提出其他的建议。

157. 委员会将在其报告和出版物中公布《突出普遍价值声明》（包括某具体遗产列入《世界遗产名录》的标准）。

决定不予列入

158. 如委员会决定某项遗产不予列入《世界遗产名录》，除非在极特殊情况下，否则该项申报不可重新向委员会提交。这些例外情况包括新发现、有关该遗产新的科学信息、或者之前申报时未提出的不同标准。在上述情况下，允许提交新的申报。

要求补报

159. 委员会要求缔约国补充材料的申报，可以在下一次委员会会议上重新递交补充并接受审议。补充材料是指在确定申报遗产的突出普遍价值时，按要求需要提供的附加信息，只

means that the requested additional information is necessary to determine the Outstanding Universal Value of the nominated property, which only occurs at the time a property is inscribed on the World Heritage List (see Paragraph 154). The referral procedure does not involve a mission to the site by the Advisory Body(ies) and it shall not involve change to criteria nor substantial change of area(s)/component(s) from those proposed in the original nomination dossier. In the referral procedure there is no submission of a new nomination dossier and the additional information that reactivates the referred nomination must be received by the Secretariat by 1 February[①] of the year in which examination by the Committee is desired. The Secretariat will immediately transmit it to the relevant Advisory Bodies for evaluation. A referred nomination which is not presented to the Committee within three years of the original Committee decision will be considered as a new nomination when it is resubmitted for examination, following the procedures and timetable outlined in paragraph 168. States Parties might seek advice from the relevant Advisory Body(ies) and/or the World Heritage Centre to discuss how the recommendations of the Committee might be addressed.

Decision 39 COM 11

Deferral of Nominations

160. The Committee may decide to defer a nomination for more in-depth assessment or study, or a substantial revision by the State Party. Should the State Party decide to resubmit the deferred nomination in any subsequent year, it must be received by the Secretariat by 1 February. This resubmission

有在遗产被列入世界遗产名录时才会出现这种情况（见第 154 条）。补充材料程序不涉及咨询机构派遣的现场考察，不涉及改变标准，也不涉及改变与原申遗文本中建议的、各地区 / 组成部分实际数量。在补充资料的程序中，不需要提交新的申遗文本，且补充信息须在委员会拟定审议当年的 2 月 1 日前[①]呈交秘书处。秘书处将直接转交相关咨询机构进行评估。要求补充材料的申报如在原委员会决定下达三年内不曾提交委员会，再次递交审议时将被视为新申报，依据第 168 条所列程序及时间表进行。缔约国可以向相关咨询机构和世界遗产中心征求意见，共同商议如何处理委员会提出的建议。

第 39 COM11 号决议

要求重报

160. 为了进行更深入的评估和研究，或便于缔约国对申报材料进行重大修改，委员会可能会做出要求缔约国重新申报的决定。如果该缔约国决定之后任一年重新递交申报，应于 2 月 1 日之前提交秘书处。除非委员会另有决定，本次重新提交不需要接受初步评估。届时相关

---

① If 1 February falls on a weekend, the nomination dossier must be received by 17h00 GMT the preceding Friday.

① 如 2 月 1 日恰为周末，申报材料需于格林威治时间，前一个周五 17 点前递交至秘书处。

shall not be subject to Preliminary Assessment, unless the Committee decides otherwise. These nominations will then be reevaluated (evaluated again) by the relevant Advisory Bodies during the course of the full year and a half evaluation cycle including an evaluation mission according to the procedures and timetable outlined in paragraph 168. States Parties are encouraged to seek advice from the relevant Advisory Body and/or the World Heritage Centre to discuss how the recommendations of the Committee might be addressed. Where required, the States Parties may wish to consider inviting an Advisory mission.

Decision 39 COM 11

Ⅲ. H　Nomination dossiers to be processed on an emergency basis

161. The normal timetable and definition of completeness for the submission and processing of nomination dossiers will not apply in the case of properties which would be in Danger, as a result of having suffered damage or facing serious and specific dangers from natural events or human activities, which would constitute an emergency situation for which an immediate decision by the Committee is necessary to ensure their safeguarding, and which, according to the report of the relevant Advisory Bodies, may unquestionably justify Outstanding Universal Value. Such nominations will be processed on an emergency basis and their examination is included in the agenda of the next Committee session. These properties may be inscribed on the World Heritage List. They shall, in that case, be simultaneously inscribed on the List of World Heritage in Danger (see Paragraphs 177-191).

Decision 37 COM 12.Ⅱ

咨询机构将根据第 168 条所列程序和时间表，对这些申报重新进行周期为一年半的评估。（包括派出现场评估专家）。委员会鼓励缔约国向相关咨询机构和世界遗产中心征求意见，共同商议并处理委员会提出的建议。必要时，缔约国可以考虑邀请咨询机构派出专家咨询考察。

第 39 COM11 号决议

Ⅲ. H　紧急受理的申报

161. 如某项遗产在相关咨询机构看来毫无疑问地拥有突出普遍价值，且因为自然或人为因素而受到损害或面临某种重大的危险，已经构成某种紧急状况，需要委员会迅速决定以确保它的保存，这种情况下，其申报材料的提交和受理不适用通常的时间表和关于材料完整性的定义。这类申报将被紧急受理，对它的审核将被纳入下届委员会会议议程。该遗产可能会被同时列入《世界遗产名录》和《濒危世界遗产名录》（见第 177–191 条）。

第 37COM12.Ⅱ 号决议

162. The procedure for nomination dossiers to be processed on an emergency basis is as follows:

Decision 37 COM 12.II

a) A State Party presents a nomination dossier with the request for processing on an emergency basis. The State Party shall have already included, or immediately include, the site on its Tentative List.

b) The nomination dossier shall:

i) describe the nominated property and identify precisely its boundaries;

ii) justify its Outstanding Universal Value according to the criteria;

iii) justify its integrity and/or authenticity;

iv) describe its protection and management system;

v) describe the nature of the emergency, and the nature and extent of the damage or specific danger and show that immediate action by the Committee is necessary to ensure the safeguarding of the nominated property.

c) The Secretariat immediately transmits the nomination dossier to the relevant Advisory Bodies, requesting an assessment of the qualities of the nominated property which may justify its Outstanding Universal Value, of the nature of the danger and the urgency of a decision by the Committee. A field visit may be necessary if the relevant Advisory Bodies consider it appropriate and if the time allows.

d) When reviewing the nomination dossier, the Committee will also consider:

vi) allocation of International Assistance to complete the nomination dossier; and

vii) follow-up missions as necessary by the

162. 紧急受理申报的程序如下：

第 37COM12.II 号决议

a) 缔约国呈交申报文本并要求紧急受理。该缔约国此前已将该项遗产列入《预备名录》，或立即将其纳入《预备名录》。

b) 该项申报应

i) 描述遗产及准确界定遗产边界；

ii) 根据标准论证其具有突出的普遍价值；

iii) 论证该遗产的完整性和真实性；
iv) 描述其保护和管理体制

v) 描述情况的紧迫性，损害或具体危险的性质和程度，说明委员会需即刻采取行动方可保证该遗产的存续。

c) 由秘书处直接将该项申报转交相关咨询机构，要求对其具有的突出普遍价值以及对紧急情况、损害和 / 或危险的性质进行评估。如相关咨询机构认为恰当且时间允许，须进行实地勘查。

d) 审议该申报时，委员会将同时考虑：

vi) 提供国际援助以完成申报工作；

vii)列入《世界遗产名录》后，由秘书处和

Secretariat and the relevant Advisory Bodies as soon as possible after inscription to fulfil the Committee's recommendations.

相关咨询机构尽快组织后续工作。

III.I   Modifications to the boundaries, to the criteria used to justify inscription or to the name of a World Heritage property

III.I   修改世界遗产的边界、原列入标准或名称

Minor modifications to the boundaries

边界细微调整

163. A minor modification is one which does not have a significant impact on the extent of the property nor affects its Outstanding Universal Value.

163. 微调是指既对遗产的范围不产生重大影响，又不影响其突出普遍价值的改动。

164. If a State Party wishes to request a minor modification to the boundaries of a property already on the World Heritage List, it must be prepared in compliance with the format of Annex¹¹ and must be received by 1 February^① by the Committee through the Secretariat, which will seek the evaluation of the relevant Advisory Bodies on whether this can be considered a minor modification or not. The Secretariat shall then submit the Advisory Bodies' evaluation to the World Heritage Committee. The Committee may approve such a modification, or it may consider that the modification to the boundary is sufficiently significant as to constitute a significant boundary modification of the property, in which case the procedure for new nominations will apply.

164. 如某缔约国要求对已列入世界遗产名录的遗产边界进行细微调整，则必须依照附件11的格式准备相关材料，并于2月1日^①以前通过秘书处向委员会递交申请。在征询相关咨询机构的意见之后，委员会或批准该申请，或认定边界修改过大，足以构成重大边界修改，在后一种情况下适用新申报程序。

Decision 39 COM 11

第39 COM11号决议

Significant modifications to the boundaries

边界重大修改

---

① If 1 February falls on a weekend, the nomination dossier must be received by 17h00 GMT the preceding Friday.

① 如2月1日恰为周末，申报材料需于格林威治时间前一周的周五17点前递交至秘书处。

165. If a State Party wishes to significantly modify the boundaries of a property already on the World Heritage List, the State Party shall submit this proposal as if it was a new nomination, including the requirement to be previously included on the Tentative List (see Paragraphs 63 and 65), and having undergone a Preliminary Assessment (see Paragraph 122). The requirement to undergo a Preliminary Assessment shall be disregarded when the Committee explicitly encourages in a decision a significant boundary modification not involving modifications to the criteria. This nomination dossier shall be presented by 1 February [1] and will be evaluated in the full year and a half cycle of evaluation according to the procedures and timetable outlined in Paragraph 168. This provision applies to extensions, as well as reductions.

Decision 39 COM 11

Modifications to the criteria used to justify inscription on the World Heritage List

166. Where a State Party wishes to have the property inscribed under additional, fewer or different criteria other than those used for the original inscription, it shall submit this request as if it was a new nomination, including the requirement to be previously included on the Tentative List (see Paragraphs 63 and 65), and having undergone a Preliminary Assessment (see Paragraph 122). This nomination must be received by 1 February [2] and will be evaluated in the full year and a half cycle of evaluation according to the procedures and timetable outlined in Paragraph 168. Properties recommended will only be evaluated under the new

165. 如某缔约国提出对已列入世界遗产名录的遗产边界进行重大修改，该缔约国应将其视为新申报并提交申请（包括事先纳入《预备名录》的要求－见63条及65条）并经过初步评估（见122段）。如果委员会在决定中明确鼓励对边界进行重大修改而不涉及对标准的修改，则无须申请初步评估。新的申报材料应于2月1日[1]以前递交，并根据第168条所列程序和时间表接受周期为一年半的评估。该规定同时适用于对遗产边界的扩大和缩小。

第39 COM11号决议

《世界遗产名录》所依据列入标准的修改

166. 当某缔约国希望增加、减少列入标准或选择不同于原列入标准的其他标准，将遗产列入名录，该国应将其视为新申报项目提交申请（包括事先纳入《预备名录》的要求—见63条及65条）。并经过初步评估（见122条）。再次申报应于2月1日12[2]以前递交，并根据第168段所列程序和时间表接受周期为一年半的评估。所推荐遗产将只依照新的标准接受评估，即使最后对补充标准不予认定，该项遗产仍将保留在《世界遗产名录》上。

---

[1]　If 1 February falls on a weekend, the nomination dossier must be received by 17h00 GMT the preceding Friday.
[1]　如2月1日恰为周末，申报材料需于格林威治时间，前一个周五17点前递交至秘书处。
[2]　If 1 February falls on a weekend, the nomination dossier must be received by 17h00 GMT the preceding Friday.
[2]　如2月1日恰为周末，申报材料需于格林威治时间，前一个周五17点前递交至秘书处。

criteria and will remain on the World Heritage List even if unsuccessful in having additional criteria recognized.

Decision 39 COM 11

第 39 COM11 号决议

Modification to the name of a World Heritage property

世界遗产名称的修改

167. A State Party ① may request that the Committee authorize a modification to the name of a property already inscribed on the World Heritage List. A request for a modification to the name along with a short justification shall be received by the Secretariat at least 3 months prior to the meeting of the Committee.

167. 缔约国①可提请委员会批准对已列入世界遗产名录的遗产名称进行更改。更名申请应至少在委员会会议三个月前随附一份简短说明递交秘书处。

Ⅲ. J   Timetable – overview

Ⅲ. J   时间表 —— 总表

168. Preliminary Assessment Phase

168. 初步评估阶段

Decision 39 COM 11

第 39COM11 号决议

---

①   In case of transnational/transboundary properties, any modification will need the agreement of all States Parties concerned.

①   如涉及对跨国 / 跨境遗产的任何修改，则需所有相关缔约国同意。

Timetable	Procedures
15 September (Year 1)	Deadline by which complete Preliminary Assessment requests must be received in printed format by the Secretariat to be transmitted to the relevant Advisory Bodies for review (see Paragraph 122.c). Preliminary Assessment requests shall be received by 17h00 GMT, or, if the date falls on a weekend by 17h00 GMT the preceding Friday. Preliminary Assessment requests received after this date will be examined in a future cycle.
15 October (Year 1)	Deadline by which the Secretariat acknowledges receipt of a Preliminary Assessment request and informs the State Party whether it is considered complete. Preliminary Assessment requests that are not complete (see Annex 3) will not be transmitted to the relevant Advisory Body(ies) for review. If a Preliminary Assessment request is incomplete, the State Party concerned will be advised of information required to complete it by the deadline of 15 September of the following year. Preliminary Assessment requests that are complete are transmitted to the relevant Advisory Body(ies) for assessment.
October (Year 1) - September (Year 2)	Desk review by the Advisory Body(ies). If necessary, the Advisory Body(ies) will request any additional information from the State(s) Party(ies), which should be submitted to the Secretariat.
1 October (Year 2)	The relevant Advisory Bodies deliver their assessments to the Secretariat for transmission to the concerned States Parties.

[The years concerning the Preliminary Assessment Phase and the Nomination Dossier Phase are not consecutive. A minimum of 12 months shall occur between reception of the Preliminary Assessment outcome and the submission of the related Nomination Dossier.]

Nomination Dossier Phase

30 September (before Year 1)	Voluntary deadline for receipt of draft nomination dossiers from States Parties by the Secretariat.
15 November (before Year 1)	Secretariat to respond to the nominating State Party with comments and review of the draft nomination dossier indicating missing information required and corrections to make.
1 February Year 1	Deadline by which complete nomination dossiers must be received in printed format by the Secretariat to be transmitted to the relevant Advisory Bodies for evaluation (see Paragraph 132). Nomination dossiers shall be received by 17h00 GMT, or, if the date falls on a weekend by 17h00 GMT the preceding Friday. Nomination dossiers received after this date will be examined in a future cycle.
1 February – 1 March Year 1	Registration, assessment of completeness and transmission to the relevant Advisory Bodies. The Secretariat registers each nomination dossier, acknowledges receipt to the nominating State Party and inventories its contents. The Secretariat will inform the nominating State Party whether or not the nomination dossier is complete. Nomination dossiers that are not complete (see paragraph 132) will not be transmitted to the relevant Advisory Bodies for evaluation. If a nomination dossier is incomplete, the State Party concerned will be advised of information required to complete the nomination dossier by the deadline of 1 February of the following year in order for the nomination dossier to be examined in a future cycle. Nomination dossiers that are complete are transmitted to the relevant Advisory Bodies for evaluation. The Secretariat will also make available the electronic format of the text of the nomination dossiers to the Members of the Committee on the World Heritage Centre's website.
1 March Year 1	Deadline by which the Secretariat informs the State Party of the receipt of a nomination dossier, whether it is considered complete and whether it has been received by 1 February.

Timetable	Procedures
March Year 1 – May Year 2	Evaluation by the Advisory Bodies
31 January Year 2	The Advisory Bodies are requested to forward to States Parties, with copy to the World Heritage Centre for distribution to the Chair of the World Heritage Committee, by 31 January of Year 2 a short interim report outlining the status of and any issues relevant to evaluations, and detailing any requests for supplementary information, in one of the two working languages of the *Convention*.
28 February Year 2	Deadline by which additional information requested by the relevant Advisory Bodies shall be submitted by the State Party to them via the Secretariat. Additional information shall be submitted in the same number of copies and electronic formats as specified in Paragraph 132 to the Secretariat. To avoid confusing new and old texts, if the additional information submitted concerns changes to the main text of the nomination dossier, the State Party shall submit these changes in an amended version of the original text. The changes shall be clearly identified. An electronic version of this new text shall accompany the paper version.
Six weeks prior to the annual World Heritage Committee session Year 2	The relevant Advisory Bodies deliver their evaluations and recommendations to the Secretariat for transmission to the World Heritage Committee as well as to States Parties.
At least 14 days before the opening of the annual World Heritage Committee session Year 2	Correction of factual errors by States Parties. The concerned States Parties can send, at least 14 days before the opening of the session of the Committee, a letter to the Chairperson, with copies to the Advisory Bodies, detailing the factual errors they might have identified in the evaluation of their nomination dossier made by the Advisory Bodies.
Annual session of the World Heritage Committee (June/July) Year 2	The Committee examines the nomination dossiers and makes its decisions.
Immediately following the annual session of the World Heritage Committee	Notification to the States Parties The Secretariat notifies all States Parties whose nomination dossiers have been examined by the Committee of the relevant decisions of the Committee. Following the decision of the World Heritage Committee to inscribe a property on the World Heritage List, the Secretariat writes to the State Party and site managers providing a map of the area inscribed and the Statement of Outstanding Universal Value.
Immediately following the annual session of the World Heritage Committee	The Secretariat publishes the updated World Heritage List every year following the annual session of the Committee. The name of the States Parties having nominated the properties inscribed on the World Heritage List are presented in the published form of the List under the following heading: "Contracting State having submitted the nomination of the property in accordance with the *Convention*".
In the month following the closure of the annual session of the World Heritage Committee	The Secretariat forwards the published report of all the decisions of the World Heritage Committee to all States Parties.

时间表	程序
（第一年） 9 月 15 日以前	秘书处接受完整的纸质版初步评估申请以便转交相关咨询机构评估的最后期限（见 122.C 段）。 秘书处需于格林威治时间 17 点前收到初步评估申请，如果赶上周末，应在格林威治时间前一个周五 17 点前收到。 最后期限后收到的初步评估申请，将进入下一个周期审议。
（第一年） 10 月 15 日以前	秘书处确认收到初步评估申请、并通知缔约国该申请是否完整的最后期限。 不完整的初步评估申请（见附件 3）不得转交相关咨询机构评估，如果初步评估申请不完整，告知相关缔约国需要补充的材料，在来年 9 月 15 日最后期限前交到秘书处。 完整的初步评估申请将转交相关咨询机构进行评估。
第一年 10 月至 第二年九月	咨询机构案头审核，必要时，咨询机构经由秘书处向相关缔约国索要补充资料。
第二年 10 月 1 日	相关咨询机构将评估意见送秘书处传达各相关缔约国。

[初步评估阶段和准备申遗文本阶段的年份没有连续性。从收到初步评估结果到提交相关申遗文本之间，最少应有 12 个月的间隔。]

申遗文本阶段

时间表	程序
9 月 30 日 （申报前一年）	秘书处收到各缔约国自愿提交申报材料草案的截止日期。
11 月 15 日 （申报前一年）	秘书处针对申报材料草案完整与否，答复相关缔约国，如不完整，注明要求补充和更正的信息。
申报当年 2 月 1 日	秘书处收到完整的申报材料以便转交相关咨询机构评估的最后期限。 申报材料必须在椨林威治时间 17 点以前到达，如当天为周末则必须在林威治时间前一个星期五的 17 点以前到达。 在此日期后收到的申报材料将进入下一轮周期审议。
申报当年 2 月 1 日—3 月 1 日	登记、评估完整性及转交相关咨询机构。 秘书处对各项申报进行登记，向提交申报的缔约国下发回执并将申报内容编目。 秘书处将通知提交申报的缔约国申报材料是否完整。 不完整的申报材料（见第 132 条）不予转交相关咨询机构进行评估。如材料不完整，相关缔约国将被通知于翌年 2 月 1 日最后期限以前，补齐所缺信息以便参与下一轮周期的审议。 完整的申报材料由秘书处转交相关咨询机构进行评估。 秘书处也会将申报文本的电子版上传到世界遗产中心官网，以供委员会的各成员国参考。
申报当年 3 月 1 日	秘书处告知各缔约国申报材料接收情况的最后期限，说明材料是否完整以及是否于 2 月 1 日以前收讫。
申报当年 3 月—申报翌年 5 月	咨询机构的评估
申报翌年 1 月 31 日	咨询机构应在第二年 1 月 31 日以前向各缔约国递送一份简短的中期报告。报告应简要阐述遗产的现状，以及其他与评估相关的议题，并且以《公约》规定的两种工作语言的任意一种详列缔约国需要补交的信息。该报告也将附送至世界遗产中心，以供遗产委员会主席参考。

续表

时间表	程序
翌年 2 月 28 日	缔约国经秘书处向相关咨询机构转呈其要求的补充信息的最后期限。 向秘书处呈交的补充信息应依照第 132 条中具体列出的数量准备复印件和电子版。为了避免新旧文本的混淆，如所递交的补充信息中包含对申报材料主要内容的修改，缔约国应将修改部分作为原申报文件的修正版提交，修改的部分应标示清楚。新文本除印刷版外还应附上电子版（CD 光盘，或者 USB 闪存盘）。
翌年世界遗产委员会年会的六周前	相关咨询机构向秘书处递送评估意见和建议，由秘书处转发给世界遗产委员会及各缔约国。
翌年世界遗产委员会年会开幕前至少 14 个工作日	缔约国更正事实性错误 相关缔约国可在委员会大会开幕前至少 14 个工作日，致信大会主席，附件送咨询机构，详细说明在咨询机构关于申报材料的评估意见中发现的事实性错误。
（6 月/7 月）翌年世界遗产委员会年会	委员会审议申报材料并做出决定
一俟世界遗产委员会年会结束	通知各缔约国 凡经委员会审议的申报，秘书处将通知该缔约国有关委员会的相关决定。在世界遗产委员会决定将某处遗产列入《世界遗产名录》之后，由秘书处书面通知该缔约国及遗产管理者，并提供列入名录区域的地图及《突出普遍价值声明》（注明适用标准）
一俟世界遗产委员会年会结束	每年委员会会议结束之后，秘书处随即公布最新的《世界遗产名录》 公布的《世界遗产名录》将注明申报项目列入《名录》的缔约国名称，标题为"根据《公约》递交遗产申报的缔约国"
世界遗产委员会年会闭幕后一个月内	秘书处将世界遗产委员会全部决定的公布报告下发各缔约国。

Ⅲ.K　Financing of evaluation of nominations

Ⅲ.K　筹集申报评估的经费

168bis. States Parties submitting new nomination dossiers are expected to make voluntary contributions towards funding evaluation of nominations by the Advisory Bodies, taking into account the average costs of evaluations as indicated by the Secretariat in the document related to the World Heritage Fund presented at each Committee session. The same principle applies to the submission of Preliminary Assessment requests. The modalities are as follows:

168 补充. 希望提交新申遗文本的缔约国自愿捐款，以资助咨询机构对申报遗产进行评估，同时还应考虑秘书处在每届委员会会议上提出的与世界遗产基金有关文件中所列的平均评估费用。该原则同样适用于提交初步评估申请。方式如下：

Decision 43 COM 11A

Decision 43 COM 14

第 43.COM.11A 号决议

第 43.COM.14 号决议

a) The contributions shall be made to a dedicated sub-account of the World Heritage Fund;

b) No contributions would be expected from Least Developed Countries or Low-Income Economies (as defined by the United Nations Economic and Social Council's Committee for Development Policy), Lower Middle-Income Countries as defined by the World Bank, Small Island Developing States and States Parties in conflict or post-conflict situations;

c) The contributions are expected to be made after the Preliminary Assessment or the nomination dossier enters the evaluation cycle upon a positive outcome of the completeness check;

d) This mechanism shall not impact the objective evaluation of sites by the Advisory Bodies, nor the order of priority as defined in the *Operational Guidelines* to be used when handling nominations.

IV. PROCESS FOR MONITORING THE STATE OF CONSERVATION OF WORLD HERITAGE PROPERTIES

IV. A　Reactive Monitoring

Definition of Reactive Monitoring

169. Reactive Monitoring is the reporting by the Secretariat, other sectors of UNESCO and the Advisory Bodies to the Committee on the state of conservation of specific World Heritage properties that are under threat. To this end, the States Parties shall submit specific reports and impact studies each time exceptional circumstances occur or work is undertaken which may have an impact on the Outstanding Universal Value of the property or its state of conservation.

a) 捐款应存入世界遗产基金的专用分帐户；

b) 最不发达国家或低收入经济体（依照联合国经济及社会理事会发展政策 委员会的定义）、世界银行所定义的中低收入国家、小岛屿发展中国家、以及正处于冲突中或冲突后政局的缔约国，将无需捐款；

c) 在申报遗产地完成初步评估及申遗文本的完整性检查、并得出积极结果，进入评审周期后，将进行捐款；

d) 这一机制不应影响咨询机构对申报遗产的客观评价，也不应影响依据《操作指南》规定的优先次序。

IV. 世界遗产保护状况的监测程序

IV. A　反应性监测

反应性监测的定义

169. 反应性监测是指由秘书处、联合国教科文组织其他部门和咨询机构，向委员会递交的有关具体濒危世界遗产保护状况的报告。为此，每当出现异常情况或开展可能影响遗产的突出普遍性价值及其保护状况的活动时，缔约国须向委员会递交具体报告和影响调查。

Reactive Monitoring is also foreseen in reference to properties inscribed, or to be inscribed, on the List of World Heritage in Danger as set out in paragraphs 177-191. Reactive Monitoring is also foreseen in the procedures for the eventual deletion of properties from the World Heritage List as set out in paragraphs 192-198.

反应性监测也涉及已列入或待列入《濒危世界遗产名录》的遗产（如第 177–191 段所述）。同时，如第 192–198 段所述，从《世界遗产名录》中彻底移除某些遗产之前也须进行反应性监测。

These reports shall be submitted to the World Heritage Committee through the Secretariat, using the standard format in Annex 13, in English or French:

这些报告都应使用附件 13 中的标准格式（用英语或法语），经秘书处递交给世界遗产委员会：

a) by 1 December of the year preceding the examination of the property by the Committee, for the properties inscribed on the World Heritage List,

a) 在委员会审核申报列入《世界遗产名录》前一年的 12 月 1 日前提交。

b) by 1 February of the year of examination of the property by the Committee, for the properties inscribed on the List of World Heritage in Danger, and for specific cases of utmost urgency.

b) 在委员会审核申报列入《世界濒危遗产名录》及受理紧急申报前一年的 2 月 1 日前。

Objective of Reactive Monitoring

反应性监测的目标

170. When adopting the process of Reactive Monitoring, the Committee was particularly concerned that all possible measures should be taken to prevent the deletion of any property from the List and was ready to offer technical cooperation as far as possible to States Parties in this connection.

170. 实施反应性监测程序时，委员会特别关注的是如何采取一切可能的措施，避免从《世界遗产名录》中移除任何遗产。因此，只要情况允许，委员会愿意向缔约国提供相关的技术合作。

Article 4 of the Convention:
"Each State Party to this Convention recognizes that the duty of ensuring the identification, protection, conservation, presentation and transmission to future generations of the cultural and natural heritage referred to in Articles 1 and 2 and situated on its territory, belongs primarily to that State...".

《公约》第 4 条
"本公约缔约国均认同，保证第 1 条和第 2 条中提及的、本国领土内的文化和自然遗产的确定、保护、保存、展示和传承后世，主要是有关国家的责任……"

171. The Committee recommends that States Parties cooperate with the Advisory Bodies which

171. 委员会建议缔约国与委员会指定的咨询机构合作，这些咨询机构受命代表委员会，

have been asked by the Committee to carry out monitoring and reporting on its behalf on the progress of work undertaken for the preservation of properties inscribed on the World Heritage List.

对列入《世界遗产名录》的遗产的保护工作进展，进行监督和汇报。

Information received from States Parties and/or other sources

来自缔约国和／或其他渠道的信息

172. The World Heritage Committee invites the States Parties to the *Convention* to inform the Committee, through the Secretariat, of their intention to undertake or to authorize in an area protected under the *Convention* major restorations or new constructions which may affect the Outstanding Universal Value of the property. Notice should be given as soon as possible (for instance, before drafting basic documents for specific projects) and before making any decisions that would be difficult to reverse, so that the Committee may assist in seeking appropriate solutions to ensure that the Outstanding Universal Value of the property is fully preserved.

172. 如《公约》缔约国，将在受《公约》保护地区开展或批准开展有可能影响到遗产突出的普遍价值的大规模修复或建设工程，世界遗产委员会促请缔约国通过秘书处向委员会转达该意图。缔约国必须尽快（例如，在起草具体工程的基本文件之前）且在做出任何难以逆转的决定之前，发布通告，以便委员会及时帮助寻找合适的解决办法，保证维护遗产的突出普遍价值继续得以维护。

Decision 27 COM 7B.106

第27COM7B.106.2号决议

173. The World Heritage Committee requests that reports of missions to review the state of conservation of the World Heritage properties include:

173. 世界遗产委员会要求检查世界遗产保护情况的工作报告，必须包括：

a) an indication of threats or significant improvement in the conservation of the property since the last report to the World Heritage Committee;

a) 说明自世界遗产委员会收到上一份报告以来，遗产所面临的威胁或保护工作取得的重大进步；

b) any follow-up to previous decisions of the World Heritage Committee on the state of conservation of the property;

b) 世界遗产委员会此前关于遗产保护状况的决定的后续工作；

c) information on any threat or damage to or loss of Outstanding Universal Value, integrity and/or authenticity for which the property was inscribed on the World Heritage List.

c) 有关遗产赖以列入《世界遗产名录》的突出普遍价值、完整性和／或真实性受到威胁、破坏或减损的信息。

174. When the Secretariat receives information that a property inscribed has seriously deteriorated, or that the necessary corrective measures have not been taken within the time proposed, from a source other than the State Party concerned, it will, as far as possible, verify the source and the contents of the information in consultation with the State Party concerned and request its comments.

174. 一旦秘书处从相关缔约国以外的渠道获悉，已列入《名录》的遗产严重受损、或在拟定期限内未采取必要的调整措施，秘书处将与有关缔约国磋商、证实消息来源和内容的真实性，并要求该国对此做出解释。

Decision by the World Heritage Committee

世界遗产委员会的决定

175. The Secretariat will request the relevant Advisory Bodies to forward comments on the information received.

175. 秘书处将要求相关咨询机构对获取的信息给予评价。

176. The information received, together with the comments of the State Party and the Advisory Bodies, will be brought to the attention of the Committee in the form of a state of conservation report for each property, which may take one or more of the following steps:

176. 把获取的信息与相关缔约国和咨询机构的评价一起，以遗产保护状况报告的形式，呈交委员会审阅。委员会可采取以下一项或多项措施：

Decision 39 COM 11
Decision 43 COM 11A

第 39 COM 11 号决议
第 43.COM.11A 号决议

a) it may decide that the property has not seriously deteriorated and that no further action should be taken;

b) when the Committee considers that the property has seriously deteriorated, but not to the extent that its restoration is impossible, it may decide that the property be maintained on the List, provided that the State Party takes the necessary measures to restore the property within a reasonable period of time. The Committee may also decide that technical cooperation be provided under the World Heritage Fund for work connected with the restoration of the property, proposing to the State Party to request such assistance, if it has not already been done; in some circumstances States Parties

a) 委员会可能认定该遗产未遭受严重损害，无须采取进一步行动；

b) 当委员会认定该遗产遭受严重损害，但损害不至于不可修复，那么只要有关缔约国采取必要措施，在合理时间期限之内对其进行修复，该遗产仍可在《世界遗产名录》上保留。同时委员会也可决定启动世界遗产基金对遗产修复工作提供技术合作，并建议尚未提出类似要求的缔约国提出技术援助申请；在某些情况下，缔约国可能希望邀请相关的咨询机构或其他组织，派遣专家考察以征求相关意见，进而采取必要的措施扭转遗产恶化的局面并处理相应的威胁。

may wish to invite an Advisory mission by the relevant Advisory Body(ies) or other organization(s) or expert(s) to seek advice on necessary measures to reverse deterioration and address threats;

c) when the requirements and criteria set out in Paragraphs 177-182 are met, the Committee may decide to inscribe the property on the List of World Heritage in Danger according to the procedures set out in Paragraphs 183-189;

d) when there is evidence that the property has deteriorated to the point where it has irretrievably lost those characteristics which determined its inscription on the List, the Committee may decide to delete the property from the List. Before any such action is taken, the Secretariat will inform the State Party concerned. Any comments which the State Party may make will be brought to the attention of the Committee;

e) when the information available is not sufficient to enable the Committee to take one of the measures described in a), b), c) or d) above, the Committee may decide that the Secretariat be authorized to take the necessary action to ascertain, in consultation with the State Party concerned, the present condition of the property, the dangers to the property and the feasibility of adequately restoring the property. Such measures may include the sending of a Reactive Monitoring mission or the consultation of specialists, or through an Advisory mission. The Secretariat shall report to the Committee on the results of its action. In case an emergency action is required, the Committee may authorize its financing from the World Heritage Fund through an emergency assistance request.

c) 当满足第 177–182 条中所列要求与标准时，委员会可决定依照第 183–189 条所列程序，将该遗产列入《濒危遗产名录》；

d) 如证据表明，该遗产所受损害，已使其不可挽回地失去了赖以列入世界遗产名录的诸项特征，委员会可能会做出将该遗产以《世界遗产名录中剔除决定。在采取任何措施之前，秘书处都将通知相关缔约国。该缔约国做出的任何回应，都将上呈委员会；

e) 当获取的信息不足以支持委员会采取上述 a），b），c），d）项中的任何一种措施时，委员会可能会决定授权秘书处采取必要手段，在与相关缔约国磋商的情况下，确定遗产当前状态、所面临的危险及充分修复该遗产的可行性，类似措施包括派遣反应性监测工作组、专家磋商或派遣咨询工作组，秘书处将会向委员会汇报上述行动的结果。当需要采取紧急措施时，委员会可批准通过世界遗产基金的紧急援助，筹措所需资金。

Ⅳ. B　The List of World Heritage in Danger

Ⅳ. B　《濒危世界遗产名录》

Guidelines for the inscription of properties on the List of World Heritage in Danger

列入《濒危世界遗产名录》的指导原则

177. In accordance with Article 11, paragraph 4, of the *Convention*, the Committee may inscribe a property on the List of World Heritage in Danger when the following requirements are met:

a) the property under consideration is on the World Heritage List;

b) the property is threatened by serious and specific danger;

c) major operations are necessary for the conservation of the property;

d) assistance under the *Convention* has been requested for the property; the Committee is of the view that its assistance in certain cases may most effectively be limited to messages of its concern, including the message sent by inscription of a property on the List of World Heritage in Danger and that such assistance may be requested by any Committee member or the Secretariat.

Criteria for the inscription of properties on the List of World Heritage in Danger

178. A World Heritage property-as defined in Articles 1 and 2 of the *Convention*-can be inscribed on the List of World Heritage in Danger by the Committee when it finds that the condition of the property corresponds to at least one of the criteria in either of the two cases described below.

179. In the case of cultural properties:

a) ASCERTAINED DANGER - The property is faced with specific and proven imminent danger, such as:

i) serious deterioration of materials;

ii) serious deterioration of structure and/or ornamental features;

iii) serious deterioration of architectural or

177. 依照《公约》第 11 条第 4 段，当一项遗产满足以下要求时，委员会可将其列入《濒危世界遗产名录》。

a) 该遗产已列入《世界遗产名录》；

b) 该遗产面临严重的、具体的危险；

c) 该遗产的保护需要实施重大举措；

d) 依据《公约》，已申请为该遗产提供援助。委员会认为，在某些情况下传递对该遗产关注的信息，可能是最有效的援助手段。将遗产地列入《濒危世界遗产名录》就是这样一种信息。此类援助申请可能由委员会成员或秘书处提起。

列入《濒危世界遗产名录》的标准

178. 当委员会查明一项世界遗产（如《公约》第 1 和第 2 条所定义）符合以下两种情况中至少一项时，该遗产可被列入《濒危世界遗产名录》。

179. 如属于文化遗产：

a) 已确知的危险 – 该遗产面临着具体的，且确知即将来临的危险，例如

i) 材料严重受损；

ii) 结构特征和 / 或装饰特色严重受损；

iii) 建筑和城镇规划的统一性严重受损；

town-planning coherence;

iv) serious deterioration of urban or rural space, or the natural environment;

v) significant loss of historical authenticity;

vi) important loss of cultural significance.

b) POTENTIAL DANGER - The property is faced with threats which could have deleterious effects on its inherent characteristics. Such threats are, for example:

i) modification of juridical status of the property diminishing the degree of its protection;

ii) lack of conservation policy;

iii) threatening effects of regional planning projects;

iv) threatening effects of town planning;

v) outbreak or threat of armed conflict;

vi) threatening impacts of climatic, geological or other environmental factors.

180. In the case of natural properties:

Decision 39 COM 11

a) ASCERTAINED DANGER-The property is faced with specific and proven imminent danger, such as:

i) A serious decline in the population of the endangered species or the other species of Outstanding Universal Value for which the property was legally established to protect, either by natural factors such as disease or by human-made factors such as poaching.

ii) Severe deterioration of the natural beauty or scientific value of the property, as by human settlement, construction of reservoirs which flood important parts of the property, industrial and agricultural development including use of pesticides and fertilizers, major public works, mining,

iv) 城市或乡村空间，或自然环境严重受损；

v) 历史真实性严重丧失；

vi) 文化意义严重丧失。

b) 潜在的危险 – 该遗产面临的威胁可能会对其固有特性造成损害。此类威胁包括，如：

i) 该遗产法律地位的改变，造成保护力度的削弱；

ii) 缺乏保护政策；

iii) 区域规划项目的威胁；

iv) 城镇规划的威胁；

v) 武装冲突的爆发或威胁

vi) 地质、气候或其他环境因素导致的威胁

180. 如属于自然遗产：

第 39 COM11 号决议

a) 已确知的危险 – 该遗产面临着具体的且确知即将来临的危险，例如：

i) 作为确立该项遗产法定保护地位依据的濒危物种或其他具有突出普遍价值的物种数量，由于自然因素（例如疾病）或人为因素（例如偷猎）锐减。

ii) 遗产的自然美景和科学价值，由于人类的定居、修建的水库淹没遗产重要区域、工农业的发展（包括杀虫剂和农药的使用，大型公共工程、采矿、污染、采伐、砍柴等）而遭受重大损害；

pollution, logging, firewood collection, etc.

iii) Human encroachment on boundaries or in upstream areas which threaten the integrity of the property.

b) POTENTIAL DANGER-The property is faced with major threats which could have deleterious effects on its inherent characteristics. Such threats are, for example:

i) a modification of the legal protective status of the area;

ii) planned resettlement or development projects within the property or so situated that the impacts threaten the property;

iii) outbreak or threat of armed conflict;

iv) the management plan or management system is lacking or inadequate, or not fully implemented.

v) threatening impacts of climatic, geological or other environmental factors.

181. In addition, the threats and/or their detrimental impacts on the integrity of the property must be those which are amenable to correction by human action. In the case of cultural properties, both natural factors and human-made factors may be threatening, while in the case of natural properties, most threats will be human-made and only very rarely a natural factor (such as an epidemic disease) will threaten the integrity of the property. In some cases, the threats and/or their detrimental impacts on the integrity of the property may be corrected by administrative or legislative action, such as the cancelling of a major public works project or the improvement of legal status.

Decision 39 COM 11

182. The Committee may wish to bear in mind the following supplementary factors when

iii) 人类活动对保护范围或上游区域的侵蚀，威胁遗产的完整性。

b) 潜在的危险该 – 遗产面临的威胁可能会对其固有特性造成损害。此类威胁包括：

i) 该地区的法律保护地位发生变化

ii) 在遗产范围内实施的，或虽在其范围外但足以波及和威胁到该遗产的移民或开发计划；

iii) 武装冲突的爆发或威胁；

iv) 管理规划或管理体系缺失、不完善或贯彻不彻底。

Ⅴ）气候，地质或其他环境因素造成的威胁

181. 另外，威胁、影响遗产完整性的因素必须是人力可以补救的因素。对于文化遗产，自然因素和人为因素都可能构成威胁，而对于自然遗产来说，威胁其完整性的大多是人为因素，只有少数情况是由自然因素造成的（例如传染病）。某些情况下，对遗产完整性造成威胁的因素可通过行政或法律手段予以纠正，如取消某大型公共工程项目，加强法律地位。

第 39 COM11 号决议

182. 审议是否将一项文化或自然遗产列入《濒危世界遗产名录》时，委员会可能要考虑到

considering the inclusion of a cultural or natural property in the List of World Heritage in Danger:

a) Decisions which affect World Heritage properties are taken by Governments after balancing all factors. The advice of the World Heritage Committee can often be decisive if it can be given before the property becomes threatened.

b) Particularly in the case of ascertained danger, the physical or cultural deteriorations to which a property has been subjected should be judged according to the intensity of its effects and analyzed case by case.

c) Above all, in the case of potential danger to a property, one should consider that:

i) the threat should be appraised according to the normal evolution of the social and economic framework in which the property is situated;

ii) it is often impossible to assess certain threats such as the threat of armed conflict as to their effect on cultural or natural properties;

iii) some threats are not imminent in nature, but can only be anticipated, such as demographic growth.

d) Finally, in its appraisal, the Committee should take into account any cause of unknown or unexpected origin which endangers a cultural or natural property.

Procedure for the inscription of properties on the List of World Heritage in Danger

183. When considering the inscription of a property on the List of World Heritage in Danger, the Committee shall develop, and adopt, as far as possible, in consultation with the State Party concerned, a "Desired state of conservation for the

下列额外因素：

a) 政府是在权衡各种因素后，才做出影响世界遗产的决定。世界遗产委员会如能在遗产遭到威胁之前给予建议的话，该建议往往具有决定权。

b) 尤其是对于已确知的危险，对遗产所遭受的物理和文化损害的判断，应基于其影响程度，并应具体问题具体分析。

c) 对于潜在的危险必须首先考虑：

i) 结合遗产所处的社会和经济环境的常规进程，对其所受到的威胁进行评估；

ii) 有些威胁对于文化和自然遗产的影响难以估量，例如武装冲突的威胁；

iii) 有些威胁在本质上不会立刻发生，而只能预见，例如人口的增长。

d) 最后，委员会在进行评估时，应将所有未知或无法预料的但、可能危及文化或自然遗产的因素，纳入考虑范围。

列入《濒危世界遗产名录》的程序

183. 在考虑将一项遗产列入《濒危世界遗产名录》同时，委员会应尽可能与相关缔约国磋商，确定或采纳将该遗产从《濒危名录》中移出的理想保护状况，和一套补救方案。

removal of the property from the List of World Heritage in Danger", and a programme for corrective measures.

184. In order to develop the programme of corrective measures referred to in the previous paragraph, the Committee shall request the Secretariat to ascertain, as far as possible in cooperation with the State Party concerned, the present condition of the property, the dangers to the property and the feasibility of undertaking corrective measures. The Committee may further decide to send a Reactive Monitoring mission from the relevant Advisory Bodies or other organizations to visit the property, evaluate the nature and extent of the threats and propose the measures to be taken. In some circumstances, the State Party may wish to invite an Advisory mission to provide advice and guidance.

184. 为了制订前段所述补救方案，委员会应要求秘书处尽可能与相关缔约国合作，弄清遗产的现状，查明其面临的危险并探讨补救措施的可行性。此外委员会还可能决定派遣来自相关咨询机构或其他组织的反应性监测观察员，前往实地勘查，鉴定威胁的本质及程度，并根据补救措施提出建议。在某些情况下，缔约国可能希望邀请咨询机构的咨询专家进行实地考察并提供意见与指导。

Decision 39 COM 11

第 39 COM11 号决议

185. The information received, together with the comments as appropriate of the State Party and the relevant Advisory Bodies or other organizations, will be brought to the attention of the Committee by the Secretariat.

185. 获取的信息及相关缔约国和咨询机构或其他组织的评论，将经秘书处送交委员会审阅。

186. The Committee shall examine the information available and take a decision concerning the inscription of the property on the List of World Heritage in Danger. Any such decision shall be taken by a majority of two-thirds of the Committee members present and voting. The Committee will then define the programme of corrective action to be taken. This programme will be proposed to the State Party concerned for immediate implementation.

186. 委员会将审议现有信息，并针对是否将该遗产列入《濒危世界遗产名录》做出决定。出席表决的委员会成员须以三分之二多数通过类似决定。之后委员会将确定补救方案，并建议相关缔约国立即执行。

187. The State Party concerned shall be informed of the Committee's decision and public notice of the decision shall immediately be issued by the

187. 依照《公约》第 11 条第 4 段，委员会应将决定通告相关缔约国，并随即就该项决定发表公告。

Committee, in accordance with Article 11.4 of the *Convention*.

188. The Secretariat publishes the updated List of World Heritage in Danger in printed form and is also available at: https://whc.unesco.org/en/danger

189. The Committee shall allocate a specific, significant portion of the World Heritage Fund to financing of possible assistance to World Heritage properties inscribed on the List of World Heritage in Danger.

Regular review of the state of conservation of properties on the List of World Heritage in Danger

190. The Committee shall review annually the state of conservation of properties on the List of World Heritage in Danger. This review shall include such monitoring procedures and expert missions as might be determined necessary by the Committee.

191. On the basis of these regular reviews, the Committee shall decide, in consultation with the State Party concerned, whether:

a) additional measures are required to conserve the property;

b) to delete the property from the List of World Heritage in Danger if the property is no longer under threat;

c) to consider the deletion of the property from both the List of World Heritage in Danger and the World Heritage List if the property has deteriorated to the extent that it has lost those characteristics which determined its inscription on the World Heritage List, in accordance with the procedure set out in paragraphs 192-198.

Ⅳ．C　Procedure for the eventual deletion of

188. 由秘书处印发最新的《濒危世界遗产名录》，同时电子版也可在以下网站上获取：http://whc.unesco.org/en/danger

189. 委员会将从世界遗产基金中特别划拨一笔相当数量的资金，为列入《濒危世界遗产名录》的遗产提供可能的援助。

对于《濒危世界遗产名录》上遗产保护状况的定期检查

190. 委员会每年将对《濒危世界遗产名录》上遗产的保护状况进行例行检查。检查的内容包括委员会认为必要的监测程序和专家考察。

191. 在定期检查的基础上，委员会将与有关缔约国磋商，决定是否：

a) 该遗产需要额外的保护措施；

b) 当该遗产不再面临威胁时，将其从《濒危世界遗产名录》中移除；

c) 当该遗产由于严重受损而丧失赖以列入《世界遗产名录》的特征时，考虑依照第192–198条所列程序，将其同时从《世界遗产名录》和《濒危世界遗产名录》中移除。

IV.C　将遗产从《世界遗产名录》中彻底除名

properties from the World Heritage List

192. The Committee adopted the following procedure for the deletion of properties from the World Heritage List in cases:

Decision 39 COM 11

a) where the property has deteriorated to the extent that it has lost those characteristics which determined its inclusion in the World Heritage List; and

b) where the intrinsic qualities of a World Heritage property were already threatened at the time of its nomination by human action and where the necessary corrective measures as outlined by the State Party at the time, have not been taken within the time proposed (see paragraph 116).

193. When a property inscribed on the World Heritage List has seriously deteriorated, or when the necessary corrective measures have not been taken within the time proposed, the State Party on whose territory the property is situated should so inform the Secretariat.

194. When the Secretariat receives such information from a source other than the State Party concerned, it will, as far as possible, verify the source and the contents of the information in consultation with the State Party concerned and request its comments.

195. The Secretariat will request the relevant Advisory Bodies to forward comments on the information received.

196. The Committee will examine all the information available and will take a decision. Any such decision shall, in accordance with Article 13

的程序

192. 在以下情况下，委员会采取下述步骤，将遗产从《世界遗产名录》中除名：

第 39 COM11 号决议

a) 遗产严重受损，丧失了其作为世界遗产的决定性特征；

b) 遗产在申报时便由于人为因素导致其内在特质受到威胁，而缔约国在规定时间内又没有采取必要的补救措施（见第 116 条）。

193.《世界遗产名录》内遗产严重受损，或缔约国没有在限定的时间内采取必要的补救措施，此遗产所在缔约国应该将这种情况通知秘书处。

194. 如果秘书处从缔约国之外的第三方得到了这种信息，秘书处会与相关缔约国磋商，尽量核实信息来源与内容的可靠性，并且听取缔约国的意见。

195. 秘书处将要求相关咨询机构提交对所收到信息的意见。

196. 委员会将审查所有可用信息，做出处理决定。根据《公约》第 13（8）条的规定，委员会与会委员三分之二以上投票同意，该决定

(8) of the *Convention*, be taken by a majority of two-thirds of its members present and voting. The Committee shall not decide to delete any property unless the State Party has been consulted on the question.

197. The State Party shall be informed of the Committee's decision and public notice of this decision shall be immediately given by the Committee.

198. If the Committee's decision entails any modification to the World Heritage List, this modification will be reflected in the next updated List that is published.

V. PERIODIC REPORTING ON THE IMPLEMENTATION OF THE *WORLD HERITAGE CONVENTION*

V.A   Objectives

199. States Parties are requested to submit reports to the UNESCO General Conference through the World Heritage Committee, on the legislative and administrative provisions they have adopted and other actions which they have taken for the application of the *Convention*, including the state of conservation of the World Heritage properties located on their territories.

Article 29 of the *World Heritage Convention* and Resolutions of the 11th session of the General Assembly of States Parties (1997) and the 29th session of the UNESCO General Conference.

200. Periodic Reporting is a self-reporting process and should be led as far as possible by the States Parties in each region. The Secretariat coordinates and facilitates the Periodic Reporting Process at the global level. States Parties may

方能通过。在未就此事宜与缔约国协商之前，委员会不应做出将遗产除名的决定。

197. 应将委员会的决定传达给缔约国，同时尽快将决定公布于世。

198. 如果委员会的决定变更了目前的《世界遗产名录》，变更内容将体现在下一期的《世界遗产名录》中。

V. 有关《世界遗产公约》实施情况的《定期报告》

V.A   目标

199. 要求缔约国经由世界遗产委员会，将其通过的法律和行政条款以及实施《世界遗产公约》采取的其他行动报告，提交教科文组织大会，其中包括其领土内世界遗产的保护状况。

《世界遗产公约》第29条，缔约国第11届大会（1997年）以及联合国教科文组织第29届大会决议

200. 定期报告是一个自我报告过程，应尽可能由各区域的缔约国主导。秘书处负责在全球层面协调和促进定期报告的进程。缔约国可能需要咨询机构和秘书处的专业意见，咨询机构和秘书处在缔约国同意的情况下，也可寻求

request expert advice from the Advisory Bodies and the Secretariat, which may also (with agreement of the States Parties concerned) commission further expert advice.

其他专业意见。

Decision 41 COM 11

第 41COM11 号决议

201. Periodic Reporting serves four main purposes:

a) to provide an assessment of the application of the *World Heritage Convention* by the State Party;

b) to provide an assessment as to whether the Outstanding Universal Value of the properties inscribed on the World Heritage List is being maintained over time;

c) to provide up-dated information about the World Heritage properties to record the changing circumstances and state of conservation of the properties;

d) to provide a mechanism for regional cooperation and exchange of information and experiences between States Parties concerning the implementation of the *Convention* and World Heritage conservation.

202. Periodic Reporting is important for more effective long term conservation of the properties inscribed, as well as to strengthen the credibility of the implementation of the *Convention*. It is also an important tool for assessing the implementation by States Parties and World Heritage properties of policies adopted by the World Heritage Committee and the General Assembly.

201.《定期报告》主要有以下四个目的：

a) 评估缔约国《世界遗产公约》的执行情况；

b) 评估《世界遗产名录》内遗产的突出的普遍价值是否得到长期的保持；

c) 提供世界遗产的相关更新信息，记录遗产所处环境和保护状况的变化；

d) 针对《世界遗产公约》实施及世界遗产保护事宜，为缔约国提供一种区域间合作以及信息分享、经验交流的机制。

202.《定期报告》不仅对遗产更有效的长期保存起到了至关重要的作用，也提高了《世界遗产公约》实施的可信性。这同样是一个评估缔约国和世界遗产地执行世界遗产委员会和缔约国大会决定的重要工具。

Decision 41 COM 11

第 41COM11 号决议

V. B   Procedure and Format

V. B   程序和格式

203. Every six years, States Parties submit

203. 每 6 年，缔约国提交一次《定期报告》

periodic reports for examination by the World Heritage Committee. During the six-year Periodic Reporting cycle, States Parties report region by region in the following order:

Decision 22 COM Ⅵ.7

Decision 41 COM 11

- Arab States
- Africa
- Asia and the Pacific
- Latin America and the Caribbean
- Europe and North America

204. The sixth year of each cycle is a period for reflection and evaluation. This pause allows the Periodic Reporting mechanism to be assessed and revised as appropriate before a new cycle is initiated. The World Heritage Committee may also decide to use the reflection to initiate the development and publication of a Global World Heritage Report.

Decision 41 COM 11

205. At appropriate intervals, and whenever deemed necessary, the World Heritage Committee adopts and revises Monitoring Indicators and an Analytical Framework for Periodic Reporting.

205bis. The Periodic Reporting process is used as an opportunity for regional exchange and cooperation and to enhance active coordination and synchronization between States Parties, particularly in the case of transboundary and transnational properties.

Decision 41 COM 11

206. The Periodic Reporting questionnaire is an online tool to be completed by the respective

供世界遗产委员会审查。在 6 年的周期内，缔约国按下表逐个区域报告；

第 22 COM Ⅵ.7 号决议

第 41 COM11 号决议

- 阿拉伯国家
- 非洲
- 亚太地区
- 拉丁美洲和加勒比地区
- 欧洲和北美洲

204. 每个周期的第六年是反思和评估阶段。新周期开始前，利用这个阶段对定期报告机制进行评估和修正。世界遗产委员会也决定利用这个反思机会，公开发布和出版一份全球世界遗产报告。

第 41 COM 11 号决议

205. 世界遗产委员会将在适当的时间间隔，并在必要时，通过并修订定期报告的监测指标和分析框架。

205 补充：定期报告过程也为地区交流和合作、加强缔约国间、特别是跨境跨国遗产间的协调和统一，提供了机会。

第 41 COM11 号决议

206. 定期报告问卷是线上工具，在恰当时由各国国家协调中心和遗产地管理人员根

National Focal Points and Site Managers of the World Heritage properties, as appropriate.

The format of this questionnaire was reviewed further to the second cycle of Periodic Reporting and was adopted by the World Heritage Committee at its 41st session (Krakow, 2017).

Decision 41 COM 10A

据情况完成。

本问卷格式在第二轮定期报告后进一步修订，在世界遗产委员会第41届会议上通过（克拉科夫，2017年）。

第41 COM 10A 号决议

a) Section I refers to the legislative and administrative provisions which the State Party has adopted and other actions which it has taken for the application of the *Convention*, together with details of the experience acquired in this field. This particularly concerns the general obligations defined in specific articles of the *Convention*.

b) Section II refers to the state of conservation of specific World Heritage properties located on the territory of the State Party concerned. This Section should be completed for each World Heritage property.

a）第一部分包括缔约国执行《公约》及其他行动时所采取的法律和行政条款，以及在这一领域获得的相关经验的详细内容，特别是与《公约》中具体条款所规定义务的相关情况。

b) 第二部分阐述在缔约国领土内特定世界遗产的保护状况。本部分应完整说明每处世界遗产的情况。

206bis. The Periodic Reporting format may be reviewed following each cycle of Periodic Reporting. An outline of the format is contained in Annex 7 to the *Operational Guidelines*.

Decision 41 COM 11

206 补充：定期报告格式在每一个定期报告周期后会被修订。格式大纲包含在《操作指南》附件7中。

第41 COM11 号决议

207. In order to facilitate management and analysis of information, States Parties are requested to submit reports, in English or French, using the online tool provided on the website of the World Heritage Centre. The online tool of the full questionnaire can be accessed here: https://whc.unesco.org/en/periodicreporting/

Decision 41 COM 11

207. 为了便于信息管理，缔约国应提交电子版报告，英文或法文均可。完整的在线报告可通过以下网址获得：https://whc.unesco.org/en/periodicreporting/

第41 COM11 号决议

V.C   Evaluation and Follow Up

V.C   评估和后续工作

208. The Secretariat and the Advisory Bodies facilitate the States Parties to consolidate national reports into Regional State of the World Heritage reports, which are available in electronic format at https://whc.unesco.org/en/publications and in paper version (World Heritage Paper series).

Decision 41 COM 11

209. The World Heritage Committee carefully reviews issues raised in Periodic Reports and advises the States Parties of the regions concerned on matters arising from them.

210. States Parties, working in partnership with the Secretariat and the Advisory Bodies, develop long-term regional follow-up programmes structured according to the Committee's Strategic Objectives and submit them for examination. These programmes are adopted as follow-up to Periodic Reports and regularly reviewed by the Committee based on the needs of States Parties identified in Periodic Reports. They should accurately reflect the needs of World Heritage in the region and facilitate the granting of International Assistance.

Decision 36 COM 13.I
Decision 41 COM 11

VI. ENCOURAGING SUPPORT FOR THE WORLD HERITAGE CONVENTION

VI. A　Objectives

Article 27 of the *World Heritage Convention*

211. The objectives are:

208. 秘书处将国家报告整理成《世界遗产区域性报告》。该《报告》有电子版（http://whc.unesco.org/en/publications）及打印版（世界遗产论文系列）。

第 41 COM11 号决议

209. 世界遗产委员会认真审查《定期报告》所述议题，并针对其中的问题为相关区域的缔约国提出建议。

210. 缔约国与秘书处、咨询机构进行磋商，根据其《战略目标》制定长期《区域性计划》，并提交委员会审议。这计划是定期报告的后续行动，由委员会根据定期报告中确定的、缔约国的需要进行定期审查。该《计划》应该能准确地反映当地世界遗产的需求，并协助提供国际援助。

第 36 COM13.I 号决议
第 41 COM11 号决议

VI. 鼓励对《世界遗产公约》的支持

VI.A 目标

《世界遗产公约》第 27 条

211. 目标如下：

Decision 43 COM 11A

a) to enhance capacity building and research;

b) to raise the general public's awareness, understanding and appreciation of the need to preserve cultural and natural heritage;

c) to enhance the function of World Heritage in the life of the community; and

Article 5(a) of the *World Heritage Convention*

d) to increase equitable, inclusive and effective participation of local and national populations, including indigenous peoples, in the protection and presentation of heritage.

VI. B　Capacity building and research

212. The Committee seeks to develop capacity building within the States Parties in conformity with its Strategic Objectives and the World Heritage Capacity Building Strategy adopted by the Committee.

Budapest Declaration on World Heritage (2002)

Decision 43 COM 11A

The World Heritage Capacity Building Strategy

213. Recognizing the high level of skills and multidisciplinary approach necessary for the protection, conservation, and presentation of the World Heritage, the Committee has adopted the World Heritage Capacity Building Strategy. The definition of capacity building identifies three broad areas where capacities reside and for which audiences for capacity building need targeting: practitioners, institutions, and communities and networks. The World Heritage Capacity Building Strategy provides a framework of action, and orients actors at the

第 43.COM.11A 号决议

a）加强能力建设与研究；

b）提高民众意识，使其逐渐理解并重视保护文化与自然遗产的重要性；

c）加强世界遗产在社会生活中的作用；

《世界遗产公约》第 5（a）条

d）提高地方及全国民众，包括原住民，对遗产保护与展示的公正的、包容性强的、有效的参与。

VI. B　能力建设与研究

212. 委员会根据《战略目标》，致力于缔约国内的能力建设。

《布达佩斯世界遗产宣言》（2002 年）

第 43.COM.11A 号决议

世界遗产能力建设战略

213. 由于认识到保护、保存和展示世界遗产需要高水平的技能和多学科的方法，世界遗产委员会通过了世界遗产能力建设战略。在能力建设的定义中，确定了需要开展能力建设的三个广泛领域以及能力建设的目标群体：从业者、机构、社区和网络。世界遗产能力建设战略提供了一个行动框架，并引导国际、区域或国家各级的行动者，在开展各自能力建设活动的同时，制定区域和国家能力建设战略。许多行动者都可以采取这些行动，他们目前正在提供或可能提供有利于世界遗产的能力建设活动。能

international, regional, or national levels to create regional and national capacity building strategies in addition to individual capacity building activities. The actions can be taken up by the many actors who currently provide or could provide capacity building activities for the benefit of World Heritage. The primary goal of the Capacity Building Strategy is to ensure that necessary skills are developed by a wide range of actors for better implementation of the *Convention*. In order to avoid overlap and effectively implement the Strategy, the Committee will ensure links to other initiatives such as the Global Strategy for a Representative, Balanced and Credible World Heritage List and Periodic Reporting. The Committee will annually review relevant capacity building issues, assess capacity building needs, review annual reports on capacity building initiatives, and make recommendations for future capacity building initiatives.

World Heritage Capacity Building Strategy adopted by the World Heritage Committee at its 35th session (UNESCO, 2011) (see Document WHC- 11/35.COM/9B).

Decision 43 COM 11A

National capacity building strategies and regional co-operation

214. States Parties are encouraged to ensure that there is a gender-balanced representation of their professionals and specialists at all levels and that they are adequately trained. To this end, States Parties are encouraged to develop national capacity building strategies and include regional cooperation for training as part of their strategies. Development of such regional and national strategies can be assisted by the Advisory Bodies and the various UNESCO Category 2 Centres related to World Heritage, taking into consideration the World Heritage Capacity Building Strategy.

力建设战略的主要目标是确保大部分的行动者都能开发出必要的技能，以便更好地执行《世界遗产公约》。为了避免重复，以便有效执行战略，世界遗产委员会将确保与其他倡议行动的联系，例如具有代表性、平衡的和可信的《世界遗产名录》全球战略和《定期报告》。世界遗产委员会每年将会审议相关能力建设问题、评估能力建设需求、审议能力建设活动年度报告，并对未来能力建设活动提出建议。

世界遗产能力建设战略于世界遗产委员会第 35 届会议通过（联合国教科文组织，2011 年）（见文件 WHC11/35.COM/9B）。

第 43 COM 11A 号决议

国家能力建设战略和区域性合作

214. 鼓励缔约国确保其各级专业人员和专家均训练有素。为此，鼓励缔约国制定国家能力建设策略，开展区域合作培训是战略的一部分。咨询机构和联合国教科文组织与各世界遗产二类中心可以协助制定这种区域战略和国家战略，同时还应考虑到世界遗产能力建设战略。

Decision 43 COM 11A

214bis. States Parties are encouraged to develop educational and capacity building programmes that harness the reciprocal benefits of the *Convention* for heritage and society. The programmes may be based on innovation and local entrepreneurship, and aimed in particular at medium/small/micro scale levels, to promote sustainable and inclusive economic benefits for local communities and indigenous peoples and to identify and promote opportunities for public and private investment in sustainable development projects, including those that promote use of local materials and resources and foster local cultural and creative industries and safeguarding intangible heritage associated with World Heritage properties.

Decision 43 COM 11A

Research

215. The Committee develops and coordinates international cooperation in the area of research needed for the effective implementation of the *Convention*. States Parties are also encouraged to make resources available to undertake research, since knowledge and understanding are fundamental to the identification, management, and monitoring of World Heritage properties. States Parties are encouraged to support scientific studies and research methodologies, including traditional and indigenous knowledge held by local communities and indigenous peoples, with all necessary consent. Such studies and research are aimed at demonstrating the contribution that the conservation and management of World Heritage properties, their buffer zones and wider setting make to sustainable development, such as in conflict prevention and resolution,

第 43.COM.11A 号决议

214 补充．鼓励缔约国制定教育和能力建设方案，以便充分利用《世界遗产公约》，为遗产和整个社会带来的互惠利益。项目应以创新和地方企业精神为基础，并特别针对中 / 小 / 微各个级别，以促进地方社区和原住民的可持续和全部的经济利益，并确认和增加社会和个人对可持续发展项目的投资机会，包括促进使用当地材料和资源、培育地方文化和创意产业、保护与世界遗产相关的非物质遗产项目等。

第 43.COM.11A 号决议

研究

215. 委员会在有效实施《公约》所需的研究领域开展并协调国际合作。由于知识和理解对于世界遗产的确认、管理和监测至关重要，因此还鼓励缔约国提供开展研究所需资源。鼓励缔约国在征得所有同意的情况下，支持各种科学研究活动及研究方法，包括地方社区和原住民所掌握的传统知识和当地民族知识等。这种研究和调查活动旨在展示世界遗产地、缓冲区及更广泛的周边区域，在促进可持续发展中所起到的重要作用，例如在预防和解决冲突方面，包括在适当时，利用社区内可能存在的传统方式，解决争端。

including, where relevant, by drawing on traditional ways of dispute resolution that may exist within communities.

Decision 43 COM 11A

第 43.COM.11A 号决议

International Assistance

国际援助

216. Training and Research Assistance may be requested by States Parties from the World Heritage Fund (see Chapter VII).

216. 缔约国可向世界遗产基金申请培训和研究援助（见第七章）。

VI. C　Awareness-raising and education

VI.C 提高认识与教育

Awareness-raising

提高认识

217. States Parties are encouraged to raise awareness of the need to preserve World Heritage in their own countries. In particular, they should ensure that World Heritage status is adequately marked and promoted on-site.

217. 鼓励缔约国在本国内提高对世界遗产保护需求的认识，尤其应确保在遗产地，对世界遗产的地位进行有效的标识和宣传。

218. The Secretariat provides assistance to States Parties in developing activities aimed at raising public awareness of the *Convention* and informing the public of the dangers threatening World Heritage. The Secretariat advises States Parties regarding the preparation and implementation of on-site promotional and educational projects to be funded through International Assistance. The Advisory Bodies and appropriate State agencies may also be solicited to provide advice on such projects.

218. 秘书处向缔约国提供援助，开展活动，以提高公众对《公约》的认识，并告知公众世界遗产所面临的威胁。秘书处将对如何筹划及开展"国际援助"资助的现场推广与教育项目，向缔约国提出建议，也会征求咨询机构和国家有关部门关于此类活动的建议。

Education

教育

219. The World Heritage Committee encourages and supports the development of educational materials, activities and programmes.

219. 世界遗产委员会鼓励并支持编撰教材，开展和实施各种教育活动和方案。

International Assistance

220. States Parties are encouraged to develop quality educational activities related to World Heritage through a variety of learning environments tailored to each audience with, wherever possible, the participation of schools, universities, museums and other local and national educational authorities.

Article 27(1) of the *World Heritage Convention*
Decision 43 COM 11A

221. The Secretariat, in cooperation with the UNESCO Education Sector and other partners, produces and publishes a World Heritage Educational Resource Kit, "World Heritage in Young Hands", for use in secondary schools around the world. The Kit is adaptable for use at other educational levels.

"World Heritage in Young Hands" is available at https://whc.unesco.org/en/whed ucation/

222. International Assistance may be requested by States Parties from the World Heritage Fund for the purpose of developing and implementing awareness-raising and educational activities or programmes (see Chapter Ⅶ).

Ⅶ. THE WORLD HERITAGE FUND AND INTERNATIONAL ASSISTANCE

Ⅶ. A   The World Heritage Fund

223. The World Heritage Fund is a trust fund, established by the *Convention* in conformity with the provisions of the Financial Regulations of UNESCO. The resources of the Fund consist of compulsory and voluntary contributions made by States Parties to the *Convention*, and any other resources authorized by the Fund's regulations.

国际援助

220. 鼓励缔约国通过设立多种类的、对公众有益的学习环境，开展高质量的世界遗产相关教育活动，如有可能，让中小学校、大学、博物馆、以及其他地方或国家的教育机构参与其中。

《世界遗产公约》第 27（1）条
第 43.COM.11A 号决议

221. 秘书处与联合国教科文组织教育部及其他伙伴合作，开发并出版世界遗产教育培训教材："世界遗产掌握在年轻人手中"。此教材供全世界的中学使用，也可调整后用于其他教育水平的人群。

可访问：http://whc.unesco.org/education/index.htm 查阅"世界遗产掌握在年轻人手中"

222. 缔约国可向世界遗产基金申请国际援助，以提升遗产保护意识，开展教育活动与方案（见第Ⅶ章）。

Ⅶ. 世界遗产基金和国际援助

Ⅶ. A   世界遗产基金

223. 世界遗产基金是信托基金，是《公约》依据《联合国教科文组织财务条例》的规定建立的。此基金由《公约》缔约国义务或者自愿的捐献、及基金规章授权的其他来源组成。

Article 15 of the *World Heritage Convention*

《世界遗产公约》第 15 条

224. The financial regulations for the Fund are set out in document WHC/7 available at https://whc.unesco.org/en/financialregulations

224. 基金财务条例见文献 WHC/7，可登录以下网址查阅：http://whc.unesco.org/en/financialregulations

Ⅶ. B　Mobilization of other technical and financial resources and partnerships in support of the *World Heritage Convention*

VII.B　调动其他技术及财务资源，展开合作，支持《世界遗产公约》

225. To the extent possible, the World Heritage Fund should be used to mobilize additional funds for International Assistance from other sources.

225. 应尽可能发挥世界遗产基金的作用，开发更多资金来源，促进国际援助。

226. The Committee decided that contributions offered to the World Heritage Fund for international assistance campaigns and other UNESCO projects for any property inscribed on the World Heritage List shall be accepted and used as International Assistance pursuant to Section V of the *Convention*, and in conformity with the modalities established for carrying out the campaign or project.

226. 委员会决定，根据《公约》第五部分的规定，在符合活动或项目开展的情况下，世界遗产基金收到的捐款，应用于国际援助活动和其他联合国教科文组织《世界遗产名录》遗产保护项目。

227. States Parties are invited to provide support to the *Convention* in addition to obligatory contributions paid to the World Heritage Fund. This voluntary support can be provided through additional contributions to the World Heritage Fund or direct financial and technical contributions to properties.

227. 除了向世界遗产基金义务捐款之外，还鼓励缔约国为《公约》提供自愿支持。自愿支持包括向世界遗产基金提供额外捐款，或者直接对遗产提供财政或技术援助。

Article 15(3) of the *World Heritage Convention*

《世界遗产公约》第 15（3）条

228. States Parties are encouraged to participate in international fundraising campaigns launched by UNESCO and aimed at protecting World Heritage.

228. 鼓励缔约国参与联合国教科文组织发起的、旨在保护世界遗产的国际资金筹募活动。

229. States Parties and others who anticipate making contributions towards these campaigns or

229. 委员会鼓励那些希望为上述国际资金筹募活动或联合国教科文组织其他的世界遗产

other UNESCO projects for World Heritage properties are encouraged to make their contributions through the World Heritage Fund.

230. States Parties are encouraged to promote the establishment of national, public and private foundations or associations aimed at raising funds to support World Heritage conservation efforts.

Article 17 of the *World Heritage Convention*

231. The Secretariat provides support in mobilizing financial and technical resources for World Heritage conservation and actively engages in resource mobilization, including through developing partnerships with public and private institutions in conformity with the decisions and the strategies adopted by the World Heritage Committee and UNESCO regulations.

"Comprehensive Partnership Strategy" including "Separate strategies for engagement with individual categories of partners" 192 EX/5.INF
Decision 43 COM 11A

232. The Secretariat should refer to UNESCO's "Comprehensive Partnership Strategy" to govern external fundraising in favour of the World Heritage Fund. This document is available at http://en.unesco.org/partnerships

Decision 39 COM 11

Ⅶ.C　International Assistance

233. The *Convention* provides International Assistance to States Parties for the protection of the world cultural and natural heritage located on their territories and inscribed, or potentially suitable for inscription on the World Heritage List. International

保护项目提供支持的缔约国、其他组织或个人，通过世界遗产基金捐款。

230.鼓励缔约国创立国家、公共和私人基金或机构，用来筹资支持世界遗产保护。

《世界遗产公约》第 17 条

231.秘书处根据世界遗产委员会的决定和战略，以及联合国教科文组织的条例，动员为世界遗产的保护提供财政和技术资源方面的支持，并积极调动各类资源，包括与公共和私营领域构建伙伴关系等。

"全面合作伙伴战略"包括"不同合作伙伴的参与战略"
192 EX/5.INF
第 43.COM.11A 号决议

232.秘书处在为世界遗产基金进行外部筹资时，应该援引：联合国教科文组织的"全面合作伙伴战略"。这份文件可以在以下网站获得：http:/ en.unesco.org/partnerships.

第 39 COM11 号决议

Ⅶ.C　**国际援助**

233.《公约》向各缔约国提供国际援助，以保护其领土内的世界文化和自然遗产、《世界遗产名录》内遗产以及符合《名录》要求的潜在世界遗产。当国家不能确保足够的资金时，国际援助将辅助该缔约国保护、管理世界遗产及

Assistance should be seen as supplementary to national efforts for the conservation and management of World Heritage and Tentative List properties when adequate resources cannot be secured at the national level.

See Articles 13 (1)(2) and Articles 19-26 of the *World Heritage Convention*

234. International Assistance is primarily financed from the World Heritage Fund, established under the *World Heritage Convention*. The Committee determines the budget for International Assistance on a biennial basis.

Section IV of the *World Heritage Convention*

235. The World Heritage Committee coordinates and allocates types of International Assistance in response to State Party requests. These types of International Assistance, described in the summary table set out below, in order of priority are:

a) Emergency assistance;
b) Conservation and Management assistance (incorporating assistance for training and research, technical cooperation and promotion and education);
c) Preparatory assistance.

Decision 30 COM 14A
Decision 36 COM 13.I

Ⅶ. D   Principles and priorities for International Assistance

236. Priority is given to International Assistance for properties inscribed on the List of World Heritage in Danger. The Committee created a specific budget line to ensure that a significant portion of assistance

《预备名录》内遗产。

见《世界遗产公约》第 13 条（1&2）和第 19-26 条

234. 国际援助主要来自世界遗产基金，世界遗产基金是依据《世界遗产公约》建立的。委员会每两年决定一次国际援助的预算。

《世界遗产公约》第 IV 部分

235. 世界遗产委员会应缔约国的请求，协调分配各种国际援助。国际援助有以下几种，按照优先性依次排列如下：

a) 紧急援助
b) 保护与管理援助（包括培训与研究援助、技术合作援助以及宣传和教育援助）

c) 筹备性援助

第 30COM14A 号决议
第 36COM13.I 号决议

VII. D   国际援助的原则和优先顺序

236. 国际援助将优先给予《濒危世界遗产名录》内的遗产。委员会规定了具体的预算线，确保世界遗产基金相当大的一部分资金用来救援《濒危世界遗产中名录》内的遗产。

from the World Heritage Fund is allocated to properties inscribed on the List of World Heritage in Danger.

Article 13(1) of the *World Heritage Convention*

237. States Parties in arrears of payment of their compulsory or voluntary contributions to the World Heritage Fund are not eligible for International Assistance, it being understood that this provision does not apply to requests for emergency assistance.

Decision 13 COM XII.34

238. To support its Strategic Objectives, the Committee also allocates International Assistance in conformity with the priorities set out in its decisions and in the Regional Programmes it adopts as a follow-up to Periodic Reports (see para. 210).

Decision 26 COM 17.2

Decision 26 COM 20

Decision 26 COM 25.3

Decision 36 COM 13.I

239. In addition to the priorities outlined in paragraphs 236-238 above, the following considerations govern the decisions of the Committee in granting International Assistance:

Decision 43 COM 11A

a) the likelihood that the assistance will have a catalytic and multiplier effect ("seed money") and promote financial and technical contributions from other sources;

b) when funds available are limited and a selection has to be made, preference is given to:

Decision 31 COM 18B

《世界遗产公约》第 13（1）条

237. 拖欠世界遗产基金的义务或自愿捐款的缔约国、没有资格享受国际援助，但是这一条不适用于紧急援助。

第 13COMXII.34 号决议

238. 为支持其战略目标，委员会也会根据其决议和作为《定期报告》后续措施的区域计划的优先顺序，分配国际援助（参见第 210 段）。

第 26 COM17.2 号、

26COM20 号和

26COM25.3 号决议

第 36 COM13.I 号决议

239. 委员会在分配国际援助时，除按上述 236 — 238 段规定的优先性顺序外，还会考虑以下因素：

第 43.COM.11A 号决议

a）带来催化和倍增效应（"种子基金"），可能会吸引其他资金或技术贡献的；

b) 由于资金有限，必须做出抉择时，将优先考虑符合下列条件的国家：

第 31COM 18B 号决议

● a Least Developed Country or Low Income Economy as defined by the United Nations Economic and Social Council's Committee for Development Policy, or

● a Lower Middle Income Country as defined by the World Bank, or

● a Small Island Developing State (SIDS), or

● a State Party in a post-conflict situation;

c) the urgency of the protective measures to be taken at World Heritage properties;

d) whether the legislative, administrative and, wherever possible, financial commitment of the recipient State Party is available to the activity;

e) the impact of the activity on furthering the Strategic Objectives or on the implementation of policies adopted by the Committee, such as the Policy Document for the Integration of a Sustainable Development Perspective into the Processes of the World Heritage Convention or the Policy Document on the Impact of Climate Change on World Heritage properties;

Paragraph 26 of *Operational Guidelines*

f) the degree to which the activity responds to needs identified through the reactive monitoring process and/or the analysis of regional Periodic Reports;

Decision 20 COM XII

g) the exemplary value of the activity in respect to scientific research and the development of cost-effective conservation techniques;

h) the cost of the activity and expected results;

i) the educational value both for the training of experts and for the general public; and

● 联合国经济社会发展政策委员会所定义的、最不发达国家或低收入国家；

● 世界银行定义的低水平中等收入国家；

● 小岛屿发展中国家；
● 冲突后的缔约国；

c）对世界遗产采取保护措施的紧急程度；

d）受益缔约国是否有法律、行政支持或在可能情况下资金的支持，用来开展活动；

e）考虑活动对进一步实施战略目标或实施世界遗产委员会政策造成的影响，例如，《将可持续发展愿景融入世界遗产公约进程的政策》或《关于气候变化对世界遗产影响的政策文件》。

第 26 段

f）活动满足反应监测过程和 / 或《定期报告》地区分析确定需求的程度

第 20COMXII 号决议

g）该活动对科学研究以及开发高效低成本的保护技术的示范价值；

h) 该活动的成本和预期结果；

i) 对专业培训和大众的教育价值。

j) the inclusive nature of the activity, in particular as concerns gender equality and the involvement of local communities and indigenous peoples.

65% of the total International Assistance budget is set aside for cultural properties and 35% for natural properties

Decision 31 COM 18B

Decision 36 COM 13.I

Decision 37 COM 12. II

240. A balance will be maintained in the allocation of resources between cultural and natural heritage and between Conservation and Management and Preparatory Assistance. This balance is reviewed and decided upon on a regular basis by the Committee and during the second year of each biennium by the Chairperson or the World Heritage Committee.

j) 活动的包容性，特别是在性别平等、地方社区和原住民参与方面。

国际援助总预算的 65% 用于文化遗产，

35% 用于自然遗产

第 31COM18B 号决议

第 36COM13.I 号决议

第 37 COM12. II 号决议

240. 为保持对文化与自然遗产的援助资源分配的平衡，以及保护和管理与筹备援助之间的平衡，委员会将定期，及在世界遗产委员会主席两年任期的第二年，对此平衡加以检查并作出相应决策。

VII. E　Summary Table

241.

Decision 36 COM 13.I

Decision 30 COM 13.13

Decision 43 COM 11A

Type of international assistance	Purpose	Budget ceilings per request	Deadline for submission of request	Authority for approval
	This assistance may be requested to address ascertained or potential threats facing properties included on the List of World Heritage in Danger and the World Heritage List which have suffered severe damage or are in imminent danger of severe damage due to sudden, unexpected phenomena. Such phenomena may include land subsidence, extensive fires, explosions, flooding or human-made disasters including war. This assistance does not concern cases of damage or deterioration caused by gradual processes of decay, pollution or erosion. It addresses emergency situations strictly relating to the conservation of	Up to US$ 5,000	At any time	Director of the World Heritage Centre
Emergency Assistance	a World Heritage property (see Decision 28 COM 10B 2.c). It may be made available, if necessary, to more than one World Heritage property in a single State Party [(see Decision 6 EXT. COM 15.2). The budget ceilings relate to a single World Heritage property. The assistance may be requested to : (i) undertake emergency measures for the safeguarding of the property; (ii) draw up an emergency plan for the property.]	Between US$ 5,001 and 75,000	At any time	Chairperson of the Committee
	This assistance may be requested to (in order of priority): (i) prepare or update national Tentative Lists of properties suitable for inscription on the World Heritage List; a commitment will be required from the State Party to nominate in priority on these lists sites recognized in approved thematic advice, such as the thematic studies prepared by the Advisory Bodies, as corresponding to gaps on the List; (ii) organize meetings for the harmonization of national Tentative Lists within the same geo-cultural area;	Up to US$ 5,000	At any time	Director of the World Heritage Centre
Preparatory assistance	(iii) prepare nominations of properties for inscription on the World Heritage List, including preparatory work such as collection of basic information, scoping studies of the potential for demonstration of Outstanding Universal Value, including integrity or authenticity, comparative studies of the property in relation to other similar properties (see 3.2 of Annex 5), including analysis in the context of the Gap Studies produced by the Advisory Bodies. Priority will be given to requests for sites recognized in approved thematic advice as corresponding to gaps on the List and/or for sites where preliminary investigations have shown that further inquiries would be justified, especially in the case of States Parties whose heritage is unrepresented or under-represented on the World Heritage List; (iv) prepare requests for Conservation & Management assistance for consideration by the World Heritage Committee.	Between US$ 5,001 and 30,000	31 October	Chairperson of the Committee

续表

Type of international assistance	Purpose	Budget ceilings per request	Deadline for submission of request	Authority for approval
Conservation and Management Assistance (incorporating Training and Research assistance, Technical co-operation assistance and Promotion and education assistance)	This assistance may be requested for: (i) the training of staff and specialists at all levels in the fields of identification, monitoring, conservation, management and presentation of World Heritage, with an emphasis on group training; (ii) scientific research benefiting World Heritage properties or studies on the scientific and technical problems of conservation, management, and presentation of World Heritage properties; (iii) establishment/revision of national policies or legal frameworks on heritage preservation benefitting World Heritage properties; Note: Requests for support for individual training courses from UNESCO should be submitted on the standard "Application for fellowship" form available from the Secretariat. (iv) provision of experts, technicians and skilled labour for the conservation, management and presentation of properties inscribed on the List of World Heritage in Danger and the World Heritage List; (v) supply of equipment which the State Party requires for the conservation, management, and presentation of properties inscribed on the List of World Heritage in Danger and the World Heritage List; (vi) low-interest or interest-free loans for undertaking activities for the conservation, management, and presentation of properties inscribed on the List of World Heritage in Danger and the World Heritage List, which may be repayable on a long-term basis; (vii) At the regional and international levels for programmes, activities and the holding of meetings that could: - help to create interest in the Convention within the countries of a given region; - create a greater awareness of the different issues related to the implementation of the Convention to promote more active involvement in its application; - be a means of exchanging experiences; - stimulate joint education, information and promotional programmes and activities, especially when they involve the participation of young people in World Heritage conservation activities;	Only for requests falling under items (i) to (vi):	Only for requests falling under items (i) to (vi):	Only for requests falling under items (i) to (vi):
		Up to US$ 5,000	At any time	Director of the World Heritage Centre
		Between US$ 5,001 and 30,000	31 October	Chairperson of the Committee
		Over US$ 30,000	31 October	Committee
		Only for requests falling under items (vii) and (viii):	Only for requests falling under items (vii) and (viii):	Only for requests falling under items (vii) and (viii):
		Up to US$ 5,000	At any time	Director of the World Heritage Centre
		Between US$ 5,001 and 10,000	31 October	Chairperson of the Committee

续表

Type of international assistance	Purpose	Budget ceilings per request	Deadline for submission of request	Authority for approval
	(viii) At the national level for: - meetings specifically organized to make the *Convention* better known, especially amongst young people, or for the creation of national World Heritage associations, in accordance with Article 17 of the *Convention*; - the preparation and discussion of education and information material (such as brochures, publications, exhibitions, films, multimedia tools) for the general promotion of the *Convention* and the World Heritage List and not for the promotion of a particular property, and especially for young people.			

VII.E　总表

241.

第 30COM13.13 号决议

第 36COM13.I 号决议

第 43.COM.11A 号决议

国际援助种类	目的	最高预算额	提交请求的截止期限	核准机关
紧急援助	可以申请紧急援助来解决列入《濒危世界遗产名录》和《世界遗产名录》中，面临已确定或潜在威胁遗产，或由于突发、不可预料的现象而遭受迫切威胁及重大损失的遗产。这些不可预料的现象包括土地沉陷、大火、爆炸、洪水和战争等的人为灾难。此类援助不用于由新进的腐蚀、污染和侵蚀造成的遗产损害和蜕化，只用于救助那些与保护世界遗产有关的紧急情况（见第 28 COM 10B 2.c 号）。如有需要，该援助可以拨付给同一缔约国的多处遗产（见第 6 ext.COM 15.2 号）。 最高预算额为单项世界遗产的预算限额。 援助可用于： （i）采取紧急措施保护遗产； （ii）为遗产制定紧急方案。	5000 美元	随时	世界遗产中心主任
		5001－75000 美元	随时	委员会主席

续表

国际援助种类	目的	最高预算额	提交请求的截止期限	核准机关
筹备性援助	援助可用于（根据优先顺序）： (i) 准备或更新列入《世界遗产名录》的国家《预备名录》；缔约国将要求被做出承诺，根据已获核准的主题建议（专家咨询机构序优先顺序对这些遗产进行申报）； (ii) 在同一地理文化区域内组织会议，综合协调各国家《预备名录》； (iii) 准备申报实性的突出普遍价值列入《世界遗产名录》遗产的潜力的特定范围下所展开的分析，与名录的对比分析。应当优先考虑在获得核准的主题建议中所提到的（或）遗址空缺相关的，经初步调查显示其需要进一步调查的缔约国的援助。（参见附录 5 的附录 3.2），包括专家真实性的突出普遍价值列入《世界遗产名录》的主题建议中所提到的，与名录和（或）遗址《世界遗产名录》申请，尤其是在《世界遗产名录》中尚没有代表或代表性不足的缔约国。 (iv) 准备向世界遗产委员会申请保护和管理的援助。	5000 美元	随时	世界遗产中心主任
		5001–30000 美元	10月31日	委员会主席
保护与管理援助（包括培训和研究援助，技术合作援助，以及宣传和教育援助）	要求援助： (i) 在世界遗产的识别、监测、保护、管理以及展示领域培训各个级别的工作人员和专家，以团体培训为主； (ii) 对世界遗产有利的科学研究；建立或修订有利于世界遗产保护的国家遗产保护政策或法律框架； (iii) 致力于解决世界遗产保护、管理与展示问题的研究。 注：如果对个人培训课程向联合国教科文组织提出支持申请，应填写秘书处统一提供的"奖学金申请"表格。 (iv) 对于列入《濒危世界遗产名录》和《世界遗产名录》上的遗产给予专家、技术支持，以保护、以保护、管理、展示遗产； (v) 缔约国为保护、管理、展示《濒危世界遗产名录》和《世界遗产名录》内遗产所需要的设备； (vi) 为保护、管理、展示《濒危世界遗产名录》和《世界遗产名录》内遗产所需的低利率或零利率贷款，这些贷款可能是长期、可偿还的； (vii) 用于地区和国际级别的《世界遗产公约》的实施、活动和会议。 - 帮助在特定地区或国家内，激发公众对《世界遗产公约》的兴趣； - 提高与实施《世界遗产名录》相关的不同问题的认识，推动各方更积极地参与《公约》的实施。 - 经验交换的渠道； - 帮助开展联合教育、信息，以及宣传的渠道； (viii) 在国家层面： - 为向公众、特别是年轻人宣传《公约》，组织召开特别会议；根据《世界遗产公约》第 17 条，创立国家世界遗产协会； - 准备教育和信息资料以宣传《公约》和《世界遗产名录》，（例如：宣传手册、出版物、展览会、讨论世界遗产的会议、电影、大众传媒工具），有年轻人参加的尤为重要。本援助不用于某项特定遗产的宣传。	仅限于第(i)至(vi)项：	仅限于第(i)至(vi)项：	仅限于第(i)至(vi)项：
		5000 美元	随时	世界遗产中心主任
		5001–30000 美元	10月31日	委员会主席
		30000 美元以上	10月31日	委员会
		仅限于第(vii)至(viii)项：	仅限于第(vii)至(viii)项：	仅限于第(vii)至(viii)项：
		5000 美元	随时	世界遗产中心主任
		5000–10000 美元	10月31日	委员会主席

VII. F　Procedure and format

242. All States Parties submitting requests for international assistance are encouraged to consult the Secretariat and the Advisory Bodies during the conceptualization, planning and elaboration of each request. To facilitate States Parties' work, examples of successful international assistance requests may be provided upon request.

243. The application form for International Assistance is presented in Annex 8 and the types, amounts, deadlines for submission and the authorities responsible for approval are outlined in the summary table in Chapter VII.E.

244. The request should be submitted in English or French, duly signed and transmitted by the National Commission for UNESCO, the State Party Permanent Delegation to UNESCO and/or appropriate governmental Department or Ministry to the following address:
UNESCO World Heritage Centre
7, place de Fontenoy
75352 Paris 07 SP
France
Tel: +33 (0) 1 4568 1104
E-mail: wh-intassistance@unesco.org

245. Requests for international assistance may be submitted by electronic mail by the State Party or by filling the online format on the World Heritage Centre's website at: https://whc.unesco.org; they must be accompanied by an officially signed copy.

Decision 43 COM 11A

246. It is important that all information requested in this application form is provided. If appropriate or necessary, requests may be supple-

VII.F　程序和格式

242. 鼓励所有申请国际援助的缔约国在构想、计划和拟定申请期间，向秘书处和咨询机构进行咨询。为方便缔约国的工作，委员会可应缔约国的要求，提供国际援助的成功申请案例。

243. 国际援助的申请表格可参阅附录 8，第 VII.E 章的总表概述了提交的种类、金额以及截止期限和核准批准机构。

244. 用英语或法语提交申请，联合国教科文组织国家委员会、联合国教科文组织缔约国常驻代表团和 / 或相关政府部门签字后，按下列地址提交：

联合国教科文组织世界遗产中心
法国巴黎
（7，placedeFontenoy
75352Paris 07 SP
France）
电话：+33（0）145681276
电邮：wh-intassistance@unesco.org

245. 缔约国可使用世界遗产中心网站（http://whc.unesco.org）提供的电子格式，用电子邮件申请国际援助，但必须同时提交一份官方签字的书面申请。

第 43.COM.11A 号决议

246. 必须提供申请表中所要求填写的一切信息。在适当或必要的时候，可以随申请表附上相关信息、报告等。

mented by additional information, reports, etc.

VII.G Assessment of International Assistance requests

247. Provided they are complete, all requests are assessed by the Secretariat irrespective of the amount requested. In addition, requests with a budget above US$ 30,000 are assessed as follows:

Decision 43 COM 11A

a) By ICOMOS for requests for cultural heritage (all types of assistance) and ICCROM (all types of assistance except Preparatory assistance);

b) By IUCN for requests for natural heritage;

c) By ICOMOS and IUCN for requests for mixed heritage (all types of assistance) and ICCROM (all types of assistance except Preparatory assistance).

The Secretariat processes requests for Emergency assistance within up to 10 working days.

Whenever necessary, the Secretariat may consult the Advisory Bodies, for the assessment of requests with a budget under US$ 30,000.

ICOMOS, IUCN and ICCROM will be consulted on all requests which specifically demand the involvement of one or more Advisory Bodies in the respective project.

248.[Deleted]

Decision 43 COM 11A

249.[Deleted]

Decision 43 COM 11A

VII. G 国际援助的评定

247. 只要这些申请是完整的，那么不论申请的数额多少，秘书处都会加以评定。此外，预算超过 30,000 美元的请求将按如下要求进行评定：

第 43.COM.11A 号决议

a) 由国际古迹遗址理事会（所有类型的援助）及国际文物保护与修复研究中心评定关于文化遗产的申请（除筹备性援助外所有类型的援助）；

b) 由世界自然保护联盟评定关于自然遗产的申请；

由国际古迹遗址理事会和世界自然保护联盟评定关于混合遗产（所有类型的援助）的申请；由国际文物保护与修复研究中心评定关于混合遗产（除筹备性援助外所有类型的援助）的申请。

秘书处将在最多 10 个工作日内处理紧急援助申请。

必要时，秘书处可与咨询机构协商，以评定预算不足 30,000 美元的申请

如果申请中特别要求一个或多个咨询机构的参与，将与国际古迹遗址理事会、世界自然保护联盟和国际文化文物保护与修复研究中心进行协商。

248. [已删除]

第 43.COM.11A 号决议

249. [已删除]

第 43.COM.11A 号决议

250.[Deleted]

Decision 43 COM 11A

251. The criteria used for the assessment of international assistance requests are outlined in Annex 9.

Decision 31 COM 18B
Decision 43 COM 11A

252. A panel composed of representatives of the World Heritage Centre Regional Desks and the Advisory Bodies, and if possible, the Chairperson of the World Heritage Committee or, in observer capacity, a person designated by the Chairperson, meets once or twice a year to examine the International Assistance requests of more than US$ 5,000, except those for Emergency Assistance, and to make recommendations to the Chairperson and/or the Committee.

Decision 31 COM 18B
Decision 36 COM 13.I
Decision 43 COM 11A

253. The Chairperson is not authorized to approve requests submitted by his/her own country. These will be examined by the Committee.

254. All requests for Preparatory Assistance or Conservation and Management Assistance of more than US$ 5,000 should be received by the Secretariat on or before 31 October. Incomplete forms which do not come back duly completed by 30 November will be sent back to the States Parties for submission to a next cycle. Complete requests are examined by a first panel held in January. Requests for which the panel issues a positive or a negative recommendation will be submitted to the Chairperson/Committee for decision. A second panel may be held at least eight weeks before the Committee session for requests which were revised since the first

250. [已删除]

第 43.COM.11A 号决议

251. 咨询机构所使用的评估标准在附录 9 中列明。

第 31 COM 18B 号决议
第 43.COM.11A 号决议

252. 由世界遗产中心区域办事处和咨询机构代表组成的评定小组，将每年召开一次或两次会议，审查除紧急援助外超过 5000 美元的国际援助申请，并向主席和 / 或委员会提出建议。如有可能，该评定小组还将包括世界遗产委员会主席，或者，由主席指定的以观察员身份参会的人员。

第 31 COM18B 号决议
第 36 COM13.I 号决议
第 43.COM.11A 号决议

253. 主席不能批准来自本国的申请，这些申请将由委员会进行审查。

254. 所有超出 5000 美元的预备援助或保护和管理援助申请，应在 10 月 31 日或之前交到秘书处。在 11 月 30 日之前未重新完整填写的表格将被发回给缔约国，等待下一轮重新提交。材料完整的申请将在 1 月举行的第一次会议上审查。无论是小组给予的是正面或负面建议，均应提交给主席（委员会）决议。在委员会会议之前至少 8 个星期，应当举行第二次小组会议，审查第一次小组会议之后修订过的申请。发回重新进行重大修订的申请将视收到日期由小组会议进行审查。只需细微修订，无需小组会议进一步审查的申请必须在首次审查后一年内返回；

panel. Requests sent back for a substantial revision will be examined by the panel depending on their date of receipt. Requests requiring only minor revision and no further examination by the panel must come back within the year when they were examined first; otherwise they will be sent again to a next panel. The chart detailing the submission process is attached in Annex 8.

否则将于下次小组会议重新提交。关于提交的详细流程图，请参见附录8。

Decision 36 COM 13.I

Decision 43 COM 11A

第 36 COM13.I 号决议

第 43.COM.11A 号决议

VII.H   Contractual Arrangements

VII. H   合同安排

255. Agreements are established between UNESCO and the concerned State Party or its representative(s) for the implementation of the approved International Assistance requests in conformity with UNESCO regulations, following the work plan and budget breakdown described in the originally approved request.

联合国教科文组织与相关缔约国政府或／及代表要达成协议：在使用国际援助的时候，必须要遵守联合国教科文组织规章，同时要与之前批准的申请中所描述的工作计划和预算明细保持一致。

VII. I   Evaluation and follow-up of International Assistance

VII. I   国际援助的评估和后续跟踪

256. The monitoring and evaluation of the implementation of the International Assistance requests will take place within 3 months of the activities' completion. The results of these evaluations will be collated and maintained by the Secretariat in collaboration with the Advisory Bodies and examined by the Committee on a regular basis.

256. 在活动结束 3 个月之内，将开始对国际援助申请进行监测和评估。秘书处和咨询机构将整理、保存这些结果，委员会将对这些结果定期进行检查。

257. The Committee reviews the implementation, evaluation and follow-up of International Assistance in order to evaluate the International Assistance effectiveness and to redefine its priorities.

257. 委员会将对国际援助的实施、评估和后续工作进行审查，以便评估国际援助的使用效力并重新定义国际援助的优先顺序。

VIII. THE WORLD HERITAGE EMBLEM

VIII. 世界遗产标识

VIII. A   Preamble

VIII. A   前言

258. At its second session (Washington, 1978), the Committee adopted the World Heritage Emblem which had been designed by Mr. Michel Olyff. This Emblem symbolizes the interdependence of cultural and natural properties: the central square is a form created by humans and the circle represents nature, the two being intimately linked. The Emblem is round, like the world, but at the same time it is a symbol of protection. It symbolizes the *Convention*, signifies the adherence of States Parties to the *Convention*, and serves to identify properties inscribed in the World Heritage List. It is associated with public knowledge about the *Convention* and is the imprimatur of the *Convention*'s credibility and prestige. Above all, it is a representation of the universal values for which the *Convention* stands.

258. 在世界遗产委员会第二届大会上（华盛顿，1978 年），采用了由米歇尔·奥利芙设计的遗产标志。该标志表现了文化与自然遗产之间的相互依存关系：代表大自然的圆形与代表人类创造的方形紧密相连。标志是圆形的，代表世界的形状，同时也是保护的象征。标志象征《公约》，代表缔约国将遵守《公约》，同时指明了列入《世界遗产名录》中的遗产。它与大众对《公约》的了解相互关联，是对《公约》可信度和威望的认可。总而言之，它是《公约》所代表的突出普遍价值的集中体现。

Decision 43 COM 11A

第 43.COM.11A 号决议

259. The Committee decided that the Emblem proposed by the artist could be used, in any colour or size, depending on the use, the technical possibilities and considerations of an artistic nature. The Emblem should always carry the text "WORLD HERITAGE. PATRIMOINE MONDIAL". The space occupied by "PATRIMONIO MUNDIAL" can be used for its translation into the national language of the country where the Emblem is to be used.

259. 委员会决定，根据具体的使用、技术水平和艺术考虑，该艺术家提交的标志可采用任何颜色或尺寸。标志上必须带有"worldheritage（英语"世界遗产"）.Patrimoine Mondial"（法语"世界遗产"）的字样。各国在使用该标志时，可用本国的语言来代替中是部分的"Patrimonio Mundial"（西语）字样。

260. In order to ensure the Emblem benefits from as much visibility as possible while preventing improper uses, the Committee at its twenty-second session (Kyoto, 1998) adopted "Guidelines and Principles for the Use of the World Heritage Emblem" as set out in the following paragraphs. In addition, a "Table of Uses"

260. 为了保证标志尽可能地引人注目，同时避免误用，委员会在第 22 届会议（京都，1998 年）上通过了《世界遗产标识使用指南和原则》内容在后续段落有所说明。另外，附件 14 中的使用表格将提供补充的指导说明。

(Annex 14) provides complementary guidance.

261. Although there is no mention of the Emblem in the *Convention*, its use has been promoted by the Committee to identify properties protected by the *Convention* and inscribed on the World Heritage List since its adoption in 1978.

Decision 39 COM 11

262. The World Heritage Committee is responsible for determining the use of the World Heritage Emblem and for making policy prescriptions regarding how it may be used. Since the adoption by the UNESCO General Conference in October 2007 of the *Directives concerning the Use of the Name, Acronym, Logo and Internet Domain Names of UNESCO* ①, it is strongly encouraged to use the World Heritage Emblem as part of a linked logo block accompanied by UNESCO's logo, whenever feasible. The use of the World Heritage Emblem alone remains however possible, in line with the present Guidelines and with the Table of Uses (Annex 14).

Decision 39 COM 11

263. As requested by the Committee at its 26th session (Budapest, 2002), the World Heritage Emblem, with and without its surrounding text, has been notified and accepted on 21 May 2003 by the Paris Union Member states under Article 6ter of the Paris *Convention* for the Protection of Industrial Property, adopted in 1883 and revised at Stockholm in 1967. Therefore UNESCO has recourse to Paris Convention

261. 尽管《公约》并未提到标志，自 1978 年采用该标志以来，委员会一直在推动使用该标志，来标示受《公约》的保护的遗产、以及列入《世界遗产名录》的遗产。

第 39 COM11 号决议

262. 世界遗产委员会负责决定世界遗产标识的使用，同时负责制定如何使用标志的政策规定。2007 年 10 月，联合国教科文组织大会审议通过了《联合国教科文组织相关名称、缩略语、标志及网域名称使用指南》①。极力鼓励在可行的情况下同时使用世界遗产标识和联合国教科文组织标识。世界遗产标志也可以不同方式单独使用，需符合现行《操作指南》和《使用表》（见附件 14）的要求。

第 39 COM11 号决议

263. 按照委员会在第 26 届大会（布达佩斯，2002 年）上的要求，世界遗产标识根据 1883 年通过的《保护工业产权巴黎公约》（1967 年重新修订于斯德哥尔摩）第 6 款的规定，于 2003 年 5 月 21 日被《巴黎公约》成员国正式确认为受保护的标志（不论其是单独使用还是附加于其他项目之中）。因此，联合国教科文组织可以依靠《巴黎公约》成员国内部体系，防止世界遗

---

①　The most recent version of the *Directives concerning the Use of the Name, Acronym, Logo and Internet Domain Names of UNESCO* is found in the annex to Resolution 86 of the 34th session of the General Conference (34 C/Resolution 86) or at http://unesdoc.unesco.org/images/0015/001560/156046e.pdf

①　最新版本参见第 34 届大会第 86 条决议附件（34C/Resolution86）或 http://unesdoc.unesco.org/images/0015/001560/156046e.pdf

Member States' domestic systems to prevent the use of the World Heritage Emblem where such use falsely suggests a connection with UNESCO, the *World Heritage Convention*, or any other abusive use.

产的标志被误用或滥用。

Decision 26 COM 15
Decision 39 COM 11

第 26COM15 号决议
第 39 COM11 号决议

264. The Emblem also has fund-raising potential that can be used to enhance the marketing value of products with which it is associated. A balance is needed between the Emblem's use to further the aims of the *Convention* and optimize knowledge of the *Convention* worldwide and the need to prevent its abuse for inaccurate, inappropriate, and unauthorized commercial or other purposes.

264.该标志还具有筹集基金的潜力，可以用于提高相关产品的市场价值。在使用该标志的过程中，要注意在以下两者之间保持平衡，即正确使用标志促进《公约》目标的实现，并在世界范围内最大限度地普及《公约》知识，但同时要避免不正确、不恰当、以及未经授权、出于商业或其他目的滥用标志。

265. The Guidelines and Principles for the Use of the Emblem and modalities for quality control should not become an obstacle to cooperation for promotional activities. Authorities responsible for reviewing and deciding on uses of the Emblem may base their decisions on the parameters developed below and those contained in the Table of Uses (Annex 14).

265.《世界遗产标识使用指南和原则》以及质量控制的手段，不应成为合作开展宣传活动的障碍。负责审定标志使用的权威机构，可以依据附件 14 的《使用表》，在考虑多种因素发展变化的条件下做出它们的决定。

Decision 39 COM 11

第 39 COM11 号决议

VIII. B　Applicability

266. The Guidelines and Principles proposed herein cover all proposed uses of the Emblem by:

VIII. B　适用性

266.本文所述的《指南和原则》涵盖了以下各方使用标志的所有可能情况：

Decision 39 COM 11

第 39 COM11 号决议

a) The World Heritage Centre;

b) The UNESCO Division of Public Information and other UNESCO offices;

c) Agencies or National Commissions, responsible for implementing the *Convention* in each State Party;

d) World Heritage properties;

a. 世界遗产中心；

b. 联合国教科文组织公共信息部和联合国教科文组织其他机构；

c. 各个缔约国负责实施《公约》的机构或国家委员会；

d. 世界遗产；

e) Other contracting parties, especially those operating for predominantly commercial purposes.

e. 其他签约合作方，尤其是主要进行商业运营的机构。

VIII. C   Responsibilities of States Parties

VIII. C   缔约国的责任

267. States Parties to the *Convention* should take all possible measures to prevent the use of the Emblem in their respective countries by any group or for any purpose not explicitly recognized by the Committee. States Parties are encouraged to make full use of national legislation including Trade Mark Laws.

267. 缔约国政府应该采取一切可能的措施，防止未经委员会明确承认的任何组织或出于未经授权的任何目的使用该标志。鼓励缔约国充分利用包括《商标法》在内的国家立法。

VIII. D   Increasing proper uses of the World Heritage Emblem

VIII. D   加强对世界遗产标识的正确使用

268. Properties inscribed on the World Heritage List should be marked with the emblem jointly with the UNESCO logo, which should, however, be placed in such a way that they do not visually impair the property in question.

268. 列入《世界遗产名录》的遗产应标有该标志和联合国教科文组织标识，但要以不破坏遗产为前提。

Production of plaques to commemorate the inscription of properties on the World Heritage List

制作纪念遗产列入《世界遗产名录》的标牌

269. Once a property is inscribed on the World Heritage List, the State Party should place a plaque, whenever possible, to commemorate this inscription. These plaques are designed to inform the public of the country concerned and foreign visitors that the property visited has a particular value which has been recognized by the international community. In other words, the property is exceptional, of interest not only to one nation, but also to the whole world. However, these plaques have an additional function which is to inform the general public about the *World Heritage Convention,* or at least about the World Heritage concept and the World Heritage List.

269. 一旦遗产列入《世界遗产名录》，该缔约国将尽可能附上标牌来纪念这一事件。标牌应向本国公众及外国游客说明，该遗产具有特殊的价值且已得到国际社会的认可。换言之，该遗产无论对该国还是世界来说，都具有非同寻常的意义。此外，该标牌还有另外一个作用，即向公众介绍《世界遗产公约》，或者至少是介绍世界遗产概念和《世界遗产名录》。

270. The Committee has adopted the following Guidelines for the production of these plaques:

270. 委员会就标牌的制作采用以下指导方针：

a) the plaque should be so placed that it can easily be seen by visitors, without disfiguring the property;

b) the World Heritage Emblem should appear on the plaque;

c) the text should mention the property's Outstanding Universal Value; in this regard it might be useful to give a short description of the property's outstanding characteristics. States Parties may, if they wish, use the descriptions appearing in the various World Heritage publications or in the World Heritage exhibit, and which may be obtained from the Secretariat;

d) the text should make reference to the *World Heritage Convention* and particularly to the World Heritage List and to the international recognition conferred by inscription on this List (however, it is not necessary to mention at which session of the Committee the property was inscribed); it may be appropriate to produce the text in several languages for properties which receive many foreign visitors.

271. The Committee proposes the following text as an example:

"(Name of property) has been inscribed upon the World Heritage List of the *Convention concerning the Protection of the World Cultural and Natural Heritage*. Inscription on this List confirms the Outstanding Universal Value of a cultural or natural property which deserves protection for the benefit of all humanity."

272. This text could be then followed by a brief description of the property concerned.

273. Furthermore, the national authorities should encourage World Heritage properties to make a broad use of the Emblem such as on their letterheads, brochures and staff uniforms.

274. Third parties which have received the

a) 标牌应放置在参观者容易看到的地方，但不能破坏遗产的美观；

b) 标牌上应带有世界遗产标识；

c) 标牌上的内容应体现遗产突出的普遍价值；考虑到这一点，内容中应对遗产的突出特点加以描述。如果愿意的话，缔约国政府可以使用各种世界遗产出版物或世界遗产展览对相关遗产的说明。这些内容可直接从秘书处获得。

d) 标牌上的内容应提及《保护世界文化和自然遗产公约》，尤其是《世界遗产名录》及国际社会对列入《名录》的遗产的承认（但无需指出是在委员会的哪届会议上通过的）。如遗产有大量外国游客参观，标牌上的内容应使用多种语言。

271. 委员会提供了下段文字作为范例：

"根据《保护世界文化和自然遗产公约》，（遗产名称）列入《世界遗产名录》。遗产列入《名录》说明该项文化或自然遗产具有突出的普遍价值，对它的保护符合全人类的利益。"

272. 在这段话的后面，可对该遗产进行简要介绍。

273. 此外，国家主管机构应该鼓励世界遗产在诸如信笺抬头、宣传手册，以及员工的工作服等物品上广泛使用世界遗产标识。

274. 授权负责推广《保护世界文化和自然

right to produce communication products related to the *World Heritage Convention* and World Heritage properties must give the Emblem proper visibility. They should avoid creating a different Emblem or logo for that particular product.

Ⅷ. E　Principles on the use of the World Heritage Emblem

275. The responsible authorities are henceforth requested to use the following principles in making decisions on the use of the Emblem:

Decision 39 COM 11

a) The Emblem should be utilized for all projects substantially associated with the work of the *Convention*, including, to the maximum extent technically and legally possible, those already approved and adopted, in order to promote the *Convention*.

b) A decision to approve use of the Emblem should be linked strongly to the quality and content of the product with which it is to be associated, not on the volume of products to be marketed or the financial return expected. The main criterion for approval should be the educational, scientific, cultural, or artistic value of the proposed product related to World Heritage principles and values. Approval should not routinely be granted to place the Emblem on products that have no, or extremely little, educational value, such as cups, T-shirts, pins, and other tourist souvenirs. Exceptions to this policy will be considered for special events, such as meetings of the Committee and ceremonies at which plaques are unveiled.

c) Any decision with respect to authorizing the use of the Emblem must be completely unambiguous and in keeping with the explicit and implicit goals and values of the *World Heritage Convention*.

d) Except when authorized in accordance with these principles, it is not legitimate for commercial

遗产公约》和世界遗产相关产品的第三方　应突出显示世界遗产标识，而且应避免在特定产品上使用自创的、不同的标志或标识。

Ⅷ. E　世界遗产标识的使用原则

275. 有关权威机构在决定使用标志的过程中，应遵循以下原则：

第 39 COM11 号决议

a) 标志应用于所有与《公约》的工作密切相关的项目（包括在技术和法律许可的最大范围内，应用于已得到批准或已通过的项目上），以推广《公约》。

b) 在决定是否授权使用标志时，应首先考虑相关产品的质量和内容，而非投入市场的产品数量或预期的经济回报。审核通过与否的主要标准是，所申请产品的教育、科学、文化和艺术价值与世界遗产的原则与价值相关。对于没有教育意义或教育意义很小的产品，如茶杯、T 恤、别针，和其他旅游纪念品等等，应不予批准。以上规定的例外情况包括委员会会议、标牌揭幕仪式等。

c) 所有涉及授权使用该标志的决定都应该非常明确，同时必须与《保护世界文化和自然遗产公约》明确表示和隐含的目标和价值，保持一致。

d) 除非依照这些原则得到授权，任何商业

entities to use the Emblem directly on their own material to show their support for World Heritage. The Committee recognizes, however, that any individual, organization, or company is free to publish or produce whatever they consider to be appropriate regarding World Heritage properties, but official authorization to do so under the World Heritage Emblem remains the exclusive prerogative of the Committee, to be exercised as prescribed in these Guidelines and Principles and in the Table of Uses.

e) Use of the Emblem by other contracting parties should normally only be authorized when the proposed use deals directly with World Heritage properties. Such uses may be granted after approval by the national authorities of the countries concerned.

f) In cases where no specific World Heritage properties are involved or are not the principal focus of the proposed use, such as general seminars and/or workshops on scientific issues or conservation techniques, use may be granted only upon express approval in accordance with these Guidelines and Principles and with the Table of Uses. Requests for such uses should specifically document the manner in which the proposed use is expected to enhance the work of the *Convention*.

g) Permission to use the Emblem should not be granted to travel agencies, airlines, or to any other type of business operating for predominantly commercial purposes, except under exceptional circumstances and when manifest benefit to the World Heritage generally or particular World Heritage properties can be demonstrated. Requests for such use should require approval in accordance with these Guidelines and Principles and with the Table of Uses. Such requests should be approved by the national authorities concerned, and be defined within the framework of specific partnership agreements with UNESCO/World Heritage Centre.

The Secretariat is not to accept any advertising, travel, or other promotional considerations

机构都不得直接在其产品上使用该标志，以此表示对世界遗产的支持。虽然委员会承认，任何个人、组织或公司都可以自由出版或生产它们认为对世界遗产有利的产品，但委员会是唯一有权授予世界遗产标识使用权的官方机构，且其授权必须遵守上述指南和原则，以及《使用表》。

e) 只有当该标志的使用与世界遗产直接相关时，其他签约合作方才能得到使用该标志的授权。而且，申请机构只有在其所在国的主管机构批准后，才能得到使用授权。

f) 如果标志的使用不涉及具体的世界遗产，或具体的世界遗产不是核心内容，例如一般性的学术研讨会和／或有关科学问题或保存技术的讨论会，必须要根据上述指南和原则以及《使用表》，得到明确批准。申请使用该标志时，要明确体现标注的使用的方式，而且这种方式预计能够促进《公约》的工作。

g）通常标志的使用权不能授予旅行社、航空公司或任何其他商业机构的商业用途，除非在某些特殊情况下，世界遗产或特定的世界遗产项目能明确从中获益。这类使用申请需遵循《指南和原则》以及《使用表》并得到相关权威机构的批准。这些要求应得到国家官方的同意，并在联合国教科文组织／世界遗产中心特别合作伙伴协议的框架内加以界定。

秘书处不接受旅行社或其他类似机构的任何广告、旅游或其他促销计划，以换取或替代

from travel agencies or other, similar companies in exchange or in lieu of financial remuneration for use of the Emblem.

> "Comprehensive Partnership Strategy" including "Separate strategies for engagement with individual categories of partners" 192 EX/5.INF and PACT Strategy (Document WHC-13/37.COM/5D)
>
> Decision 37 COM 5D

h) When commercial benefits are anticipated, the Secretariat should ensure that the World Heritage Fund receives a fair share of the revenues and conclude a contract or other agreement that documents the nature of the understandings that govern the project and the arrangements for provision of income to the Fund. In all cases of commercial use, any staff time and related costs for personnel assigned by the Secretariat or other reviewers, as appropriate, to any initiative, beyond the nominal, must be fully covered by the party requesting authorization to use the Emblem.

National authorities are also called upon to ensure that their properties or the World Heritage Fund receive a fair share of the revenues and to document the nature of the understandings that govern the project and the distribution of any proceeds.

i) If sponsors are sought for manufacturing products whose distribution the Secretariat considers necessary, the choice of partner or partners should be consistent, at a minimum, with the criteria set forth in the "Comprehensive Partnership Strategy" including "Separate strategies for engagement with individual categories or partners" 192 EX/5.INF and PACT Strategy (Document WHC-13/37.COM/5D) and with such further fund-raising guidance as the Committee may prescribe. The necessity for such products should be clarified and justified in written presentations that will require approval in such manner as the Committee may prescribe.

j) The sale of goods or services bearing the

使用标识的经济报酬的建议。

> "独立合作伙伴参与战略"的"综合合作伙伴战略"192EX/5. INF 以及保护伙伴关系战略（见文件 WHC-13/37.COM/5D ）
>
> 第 37COM5D 号决议

h) 如果在标志的使用过程中产生了商业利益，秘书处应该确保世界遗产基金也从中分得部分收益。秘书处应该与相关方签订合同或其他协议，以确定协议的性质、管理项目和收益分配。对于所有将标志用于商业目的的情况，秘书处和其他审议者在批准使用标志申请的过程中所发生的、高于常规的、一切人力或物力的成本，都应该由提出申请方支付。

国家权威机构也要确保该国的遗产或者世界遗产基金能够得到相应的收益，确定协议性质、管理项目和收益分配。

i) 如果秘书处因需要制作产品进行分发而寻找赞助商，合作伙伴（或多个合作伙伴）的选择至少应与"全面伙伴战略"，包括"独立合作伙伴的参与战略"192 EX/5.INF、保护伙伴关系战略（文件 WHC-13/37.COM/5D)、及委员会规定的其他资金筹措标准一致。生产这类产品的必要性应在书面陈述中加以明确和说明，需要以委员会规定的方式予以批准。

j) 附有联合国教科文组织名称、缩略语、标

name, acronym, logo and/or Internet domain name of UNESCO combined with the World Heritage Emblem chiefly for profit shall be regarded as "commercial use" for the purpose of the *Operational Guidelines*. Such use must be expressly authorized by the Director-General, under a specific contractual arrangement (definition adapted from 2007 UNESCO Logo Directives. Art Ⅲ.2.1.3).

Ⅷ. F　Authorization procedure for the use of the World Heritage Emblem

Simple agreement of the national authorities

276. National authorities may grant the use of the Emblem to a national entity, provided that the project, whether national or international, involves only World Heritage properties located on the same national territory. National authorities' decision should be guided by the Guidelines and Principles and by the Table of Uses.

Decision 39 COM 11

277. States Parties are invited to provide the Secretariat with the names and addresses of the authorities in charge of managing the use of the Emblem.

Circular letter dated 14 April 1999.

https://whc.unesco.org/circs/circ 99-4e.pdf

Agreement requiring quality control of content

278. Any other request for authorization to use the Emblem should adopt the following procedure:

Decision 39 COM 11

a) A request indicating the objective of the use of the Emblem, its duration and territorial validity, should be addressed to the Director of the World

志和网络域名，以及世界遗产标识的、主要用于盈利的商品或服务项目，将被视为"商业使用"。如需使用这一标志，则必须在相关的条约签署后，经总干事核准。（见 2007 年联合国教科文组织标志使用指南第 Ⅲ.2.1.3 款）

Ⅷ. F　使用世界遗产标识的授权程序

国家权威机构的初步认定

276. 如果国家或国际项目只涉及本国的世界遗产，国家权威机构可授权国家实体使用标志。国家权威机构的决定应遵守《指南和原则》以及《使用表》。

第 39 COM11 号决议

277. 缔约国需要向秘书处提供负责管理标志使用的权威机构的名称和地址。

1999 年 4 月 14 日通函

http://whc.unesco.org/circs/circ99- 4e.pdf

要求对内容进行质量控制的协议

278. 任何关于授权使用标志的申请都需遵循以下步骤：

第 39 COM11 号决议

a) 申请应该说明使用标志的目的、使用时长及使用地域、并提交给世界遗产中心主任。

Heritage Centre.

b) The Director of the World Heritage Centre has the authority to grant the use of the Emblem in accordance with the Guidelines and Principles. For cases not covered, or not sufficiently covered, by the Guidelines and Principles and by the Table of Uses, the Director refers the matter to the Chairperson who, in the most difficult cases, might wish to refer the matter to the Committee for final decision. A yearly report on the authorized uses of the Emblem will be submitted to the World Heritage Committee.

c) Authorization to use the Emblem in major products to be widely distributed over an undetermined period of time is conditional upon obtaining the manufacturer's commitment to consult with countries concerned and secure their endorsement of texts and images illustrating properties situated in their territory, at no cost to the Secretariat, together with the proof that this has been done. The text to be approved should be provided in either one of the official languages of the Committee or in the language of the country concerned. A draft model to be used by States Parties to authorize the use of the Emblem to third parties appears below.

Content Approval Form:

[Name of responsible national body], officially identified as the body responsible for approving the content of the texts and photos relating to the World Heritage properties located in the territory of [name of country], hereby confirms to [name of producer] that the text and the images that it has submitted for the [name of property(ies)] World Heritage property(ies) are [approved] [approved subject to the following changes requested] [are not approved]

(delete whatever entry does not apply, and provide, as needed, a corrected copy of the text or a signed list of corrections).

b) 世界遗产中心主任有权根据《指南和原则》批准使用标志。遇到《指南和原则》以及《使用表》尚未涉及或未完全涵盖的情况，主任应将申请提交给主席，如果是很难处理的情况，主席会将该申请提交委员会做最后决定。有关授权使用标志的年度报告，应提交给世界遗产委员会。

c) 如授权在不确定的时期内在广泛行销的主要产品上使用标志，生产商应承诺与相关国家协商，针对使用有关其境内遗产的图片和文字取得其同意，同时生产商还应提供获取同意的证明，且秘书处不承担任何费用。报批的文献须以委员会任意一种正式语言或相关国家的语言书写。缔约国用于批准第三方使用标志的草拟范本。应按以下格式填写：

内容批准表：

作为负责批准使用［国家名称］世界遗产图文的官方机构，［国家主管机构的名称］在此向［生产商名称］证实，它提交的世界遗产［遗产名称］图文已［通过审批］［如做出以下变更便可通过审批］［未通过审批］。

（删除不适用的条目，并按需要提供文字变更后经签名的副本变更内容清单）。

Notes:

It is recommended that the initials of the responsible national official be affixed to each page of text.

The National Authorities are given one month from their acknowledged receipt in which to authorize the content, following which the producers may consider that the content has been tacitly approved, unless the responsible National Authorities request in writing a longer period.

Texts should be supplied to the National Authorities in one of the two official languages of the Committee, or in the official language (or in one of the official languages) of the country in which the properties are located, at the convenience of both parties.

d) After having examined the request and considered it as acceptable, the Secretariat may establish an agreement with the partner.

e) If the Director of the World Heritage Centre judges that a proposed use of the Emblem is not acceptable, the Secretariat informs the requesting party of the decision in writing.

Ⅷ. G　Right of States Parties to exert quality control

279. Authorization to use the Emblem is inextricably linked to the requirement that the national authorities may exert quality control over the products with which it is associated.

a) The States Parties to the *Convention* are the only parties authorized to approve the content (images and text) of any distributed product appearing under the World Heritage Emblem with regard to the properties located in their territories.

b) States Parties that protect the Emblem

注释：

建议在文本的每一页上都注明国家主管人员姓名的首字母。

自收到申请之日起一个月内，国家主管机构应该做出答复，批准文本内容。如未接到答复，生产商可视为该内容已得到默许，除非该国家主管机构书面要求延长批准时限。

提交给国家主管机构的申请所使用的语言，应按照双方的需要，可使用委员会的两种官方语言之一或遗产所在国的官方语言（或其中一种官方语言）。

d) 在审阅申请并认为可批准后，秘书处应该与合作伙伴签订协议。

e) 如果世界遗产中心主任没有批准标志的使用，秘书处会以书面形式通知申请方。

VIII. G　缔约国政府有权进行质量控制

279. 国家主管机构对授权使用标志的相关产品实施密切的质量控制。

a)《公约》的缔约国是唯一有权批准在其境内行销带有世界遗产标志、并与遗产内容（图文）相关的产品的机构。

b) 合法保护标志的缔约国必须审查标志的

legally must review these uses.

　　c) Other States Parties may elect to review proposed uses or refer such proposals to the Secretariat. States Parties are responsible for identifying an appropriate national authority and for informing the Secretariat whether they wish to review proposed uses or to identify uses that are inappropriate. The Secretariat maintains a list of responsible national authorities.

IX. INFORMATION SOURCES

IX. A　Information archived by the Secretariat

　　280. The Secretariat maintains a database of all documents of the World Heritage Committee and the General Assembly of States Parties to the *World Heritage Convention*. This database is available at: https://whc.unesco.org/en/documents.

　　281. The Secretariat ensures that copies of Tentative Lists submissions, Preliminary Assessment requests, World Heritage nominations, including copies of maps and relevant information received from States Parties are archived in hard copy and in electronic format where possible. The Secretariat also arranges for the archiving of relevant information relating to inscribed properties, including evaluations and other documents developed by the Advisory Bodies, any correspondence and reports received from States Parties (including Reactive Monitoring and Periodic Reports) and correspondence and material from the Secretariat and World Heritage Committee.

　　282. Archived material will be kept in a form appropriate to long-term storage. Provisions will be made for the storage of paper copies and electronic copies, as relevant. Provision will be made for copies to be provided to States Parties as requested.

　　283. Nomination dossiers of those properties

使用情况。

　　c) 其他缔约国也可决定审查所申请的使用方式，或者将提议提交给秘书处。缔约国政府负责指定相应的国家机构，并通知秘书处是否希望审查所申请的使用方式，或明确指出使用方式不适当。秘书处持有国家主管机构清单。

IX. 信息来源

IX. A　秘书处存档的信息

　　280. 委员会将所有世界遗产委员会和《保护世界文化和自然遗产公约》缔约国大会的资料存入数据库。该数据库可在以下网址访问：https://whc.unesco.org/en/documents

　　281. 秘书处将确保《预备名录》意见书、初步评估申请、和世界遗产申报文件副本（包括地图和缔约国提交的相关信息副本）已通过硬拷贝形式存档，同时在可能的情况下保存电子版本。秘书处也安排对已列入《世界遗产名录》的遗产的相关信息进行存档，其中包括咨询机构发表的评估和其他文件、任何缔约国提交的信件和报告（包括反应性监测和定期报告），以及秘书处和世界遗产委员会发出的信件和材料。

　　282. 存档材料应以适合长期储存的形式保存。将为储存纸张副本和电子副本编列经费，按要求向缔约国提供副本。

　　283. 委员会将妥善保存列入《世界遗产名

inscribed on the World Heritage List by the Committee will be made available for consultation. States Parties are urged to upload a copy of the nomination on their own websites and inform the Secretariat of this action. States Parties preparing nominations may wish to use such information as guides for identifying and elaborating nomination of properties within their own territories.

录》的遗产申报文件，方便查阅。敦促缔约国将申报材料的电子版发布在本国的网站上，并通知秘书处。其他筹备申报的国家可以利用这些信息，确认并完善本国境内遗产的申报材料。

284. Advisory Body evaluations and Committee decisions concerning each inscribed property are available on the World Heritage Centre's website on the page dedicated to each property of the World Heritage List. For the sites not inscribed on the List, the Advisory Body evaluation is available on the World Heritage Centre's website on the page dedicated to the Committee session when the nomination was examined.

284. 咨询机构的评估和委员会关于每个列入遗产的相关决定，都可在世界遗产中心网站上获取。关于每个未列入《世界遗产目录》遗产的评估结果，也可在世界遗产中心网站上查到，网址即审议申报文件时专为委员会会议制作的网页。

Decision 43 COM 11A

第 43.COM.11A 号决议

IX. B Specific Information for World Heritage Committee members and other States Parties

IX. B 世界遗产委员会成员国和其他缔约国的详细信息

285. The Secretariat maintains two electronic mailing lists: one for Committee members (wh-committee@unesco.org) and one for all States Parties (wh- states@unesco.org). States Parties are requested to supply all appropriate email addresses for the establishment of these lists. These electronic mailing lists, which supplement but do not replace the traditional means of notifying States Parties, allow the Secretariat to communicate, in a timely manner, announcements about the availability of documents, changes to meeting schedules, and other issues relevant to Committee members and other States Parties.

285. 秘书处保存了两份电子邮件清单：一份是委员会成员联系方式（wh-committee@unesco.org），另一份是缔约国联系方式（wh-states@unesco.org）。缔约国必须提供所有相关邮箱地址，以供秘书处建立清单。电子邮件清单是补充而不会取代传统的邮寄方式，但秘书处可通过电子邮件、及时发表有关文件适用性、会议计划的变更，以及其他与委员会成员和缔约国相关的事宜。

286. Specific information targeted at Committee members, other States Parties and Advisory Bodies is available on the World Heritage Centre's website (https://whc.unesco.org) with restricted access.

286. 有关委员会委员、缔约国和咨询机构的详细信息，可在世界文化遗产中心官方网站（https://whc.unesco.org）获取，但有访问权限限制。

Decision 43 COM 11A

287. The Secretariat also maintains a database of decisions of the Committee and resolutions of the General Assembly of States Parties. These are available at: https://whc.unesco.org/en/decisions

Decision 28 COM 9

IX.C　Information and publications available to the public

288. The Secretariat provides access to information labelled as publicly available and copyright free on World Heritage properties and other relevant matters, wherever possible.

289. Information on issues related to World Heritage is available on the Secretariat's website (https://whc.unesco.org), on the websites of the Advisory Bodies and in libraries. A list of online databases and links to relevant webpages can be found in the Bibliography.

290. The Secretariat produces a wide variety of World Heritage publications, including the World Heritage List, the List of World Heritage in Danger, Brief Descriptions of World Heritage properties, World Heritage Paper series, newsletters, brochures and information kits. In addition, other information materials aimed specifically at experts and the general public are also developed. The list of World Heritage publications can be found in the Bibliography or at: https://whc.unesco.org/en/publications

These information materials are distributed to the public directly or through the national and international networks established by States Parties or by World Heritage partners.

第 43.COM.11A 号决议

287. 秘书处还同时维护另外一个有关委员会决议、缔约国大会决议的数据库。可通过以下网址登录：http://whc.unesco.org/en/decisions。

第 28COM9 号决议

IX. C　向大众公开的信息和出版物

288. 在可能的情况下，秘书处提供标注为面向公众且不受版权限制的，关于世界遗产和其他相关问题的信息。

289. 与世界遗产有关的信息能在秘书处网站（http://whc.unesco.org）、咨询机构网站和图书馆中获取。参考书目中提供了可在线访问的数据库清单以及相关网站链接。

290. 秘书处出版了大量有关世界遗产的出版物，包括《世界遗产名录》、《濒危世界遗产名录》、《世界遗产简要介绍》、《世界遗产论文》系列、简报、宣传册和信息工具包。此外，其他专门为专家和大众准备的信息也得到了发展。参考书目中列出了世界遗产出版物的名单，也可通过以下网址获取：http://whc.unesco.org/en/publications。

这些信息资料将直接分发给公众，或通过缔约国或世界遗产合作伙伴建立的国家或国际网络，向大众公开。

附 件
ANNEXES

MODEL INSTRUMENT

United Nations   World

Educational, Scientific and   Heritage   **OF RATIFICATION / ACCEPTANCE**

Cultural Organization   Convention

WHEREAS the Convention concerning the Protection of the World Cultural and Natural Heritage was adopted on 16 November 1972 by the General Conference of UNESCO at its seventeenth session;

NOW THEREFORE the Government of _____ having considered the aforesaid Convention, hereby [ratifies the same and undertake faithfully to carry out

[accepts

the stipulations therein contained.

IN WITNESS WHEREOF, I have signed and sealed this instrument.

Done at _____ this _____ day of _____ 20 _____ .

(Seal)

Signature of Head of State,

Prime Minister or

Minister of Foreign Affairs

● The model instrument of ratification / acceptance is available from the UNESCO World Heritage Centre and at: https://whc.unesco.org/en/convention/

● The original signed version of the completed form should be sent, preferably with an official translation in English or French, to: Director-General, UNESCO, 7 place de Fontenoy, 75352 Paris 07 SP, France

附件 1   接受 / 正式批准《公约》的模本

1972 年 11 月 16 日，联合国教科文组织第 17 届大会上通过了《保护世界文化与自然遗产公约》。

因此，现在_____政府已考虑
上述公约，并   [同意   并将忠实地执行
                   [接受上述公约中包含的各项规定。

特此证明，本人已在本文件上签字盖章。

20____年____月____地点

（盖章）   国家首脑，
                                                       总理或
                                                  外交部长的签字

● 登录联合国教科文组织世界遗产中心网站 http://whc.unesco.org/en/modelratification 获取接受和正式批准的模板

● 填好的表格原件应发送至 Director-General，UNESCO，7 place de Fontenoy，75352 Paris 07 SP，France，最好附有英文或法文的正式翻译件。

United Nations	World
Educational, Scientific and	Heritage
Cultural Organization	Convention

MODEL INSTRUMENT OF ACCESSION

WHEREAS the Convention concerning the Protection of the World Cultural and Natural Heritage was adopted on 16 November 1972 by the General Conference of UNESCO at its seventeenth session;

NOW THEREFORE the Government of _____ having considered the aforesaid *Convention*, hereby accedes the same and undertake faithfully to carry out the stipulations therein contained.

IN WITNESS WHEREOF, I have signed and sealed this instrument.

Done at _____ this _____ day of _____ 20 _____.

(Seal)   *Signature of Head of State,*

Prime Minister or

Minister of Foreign Affairs

- The model instrument of accession is available from the UNESCO World Heritage Centre and at: https://whc.unesco.org/en/convention/

- The original signed version of the completed form should be sent, preferably with an official translation in English or French, to: Director-General, UNESCO, 7 place de Fontenoy, 75352 Paris 07 SP, France

正式批准的模板

1972 年 11 月 16 日，联合国教科文组织第 17 届大会通过了《保护世界文化与自然遗产公约》。现在本政府经考虑同意加入并忠实地执行上述公约。

特此证明，本人已在本文件上签字盖章。

20___年___月___地点

（盖章）
国家首脑，
总理或
外交部长的签字

● 登录联合国教科文组织的世界遗产中心网站 https://whc.unesco.org/en/convention/ 获取此正式批准的模板

● 填好的表格原件应发送至 Director-General，UNESCO，7 place de Fontenoy，75352 Paris 07 SP，France，最好附有英文或法文的正式翻译件。

United Nations
Educational, Scientific and
Cultural Organization

World
Heritage
Convention

TENTATIVE LIST SUBMISSION FORMAT

STATE PARTY:

DATE OF SUBMISSION:

Submission prepared by:

Name:

E-mail:

Address:

Fax:

Institution:

Telephone:

Name of Property:

State, Province or Region:

Latitude and Longitude, or UTM coordinates:

DESCRIPTION:

Justification of Outstanding Universal Value:

(Preliminary identification of the values of the property which merit inscription on the World Heritage List)

Criteria met [see Paragraph 77 of the *Operational Guidelines*]:

(Please tick the box corresponding to the proposed criteria and justify the use of each below)

(i)	(ii)	(iii)	(iv)	(v)	(vi)	(vii)	(viii)	(ix)	(x)

Statements of authenticity and/or integrity [see Paragraphs 78-95 of the *Operational Guidelines*]:

Comparison with other similar properties:

(The comparison should outline similarities with other properties on the World Heritage List or not, and the reasons that make the property stand out)

● The Tentative List submission format is available from the UNESCO World Heritage Centre and at: https://whc.unesco.org/en/tentativelists

● Further guidance on the preparation of Tentative Lists can be found in Paragraphs 62-67 of the *Operational Guidelines*.

● An example of a completed Tentative List submission format can be found at: https://whc.unesco.org/en/tentativelists

● All Tentative Lists submitted by States Parties are available at: https://whc.unesco.org/en/tentativelists

● The original signed version of the completed Tentative List submission format should be sent in English or French to: UNESCO World Heritage Centre, 7 place de Fontenoy, 75352 Paris 07 SP, France

● States Parties are encouraged to also submit this information in electronic format (USB Flash Drive or CD-Rom) or by e-mail to wh-tentativelists@unesco.org

附件 2A 《预备名录》提交格式

締约国：　　　　　　　　　　　　　　提交日期：
提交准备机构：
名称：　　　　　　　　　　　　　　　　电子邮件：
地址：　　　　　　　　　　　　　　　　传真：
机构：　　　　　　　　　　　　　　　　电话：

> 遗产名称：

> 州、省份或地区：

> 经纬度或通用横轴墨卡托坐标：

描述：

突出的普遍价值申明
（初步确认应列入《世界遗产名录》的遗产价值）

符合标准 [参见《操作指南》第 77 段]：
（ 请勾选与提议的标准相对应的文本框，并给出选择理由 ）

| (i) | (ii) | (iii) | (iv) | (v) | (vi) | (vii) | (viii) | (ix) | (x) |

完整性和真实性声明 [参见《操作指南》第 78-95 段]：
与其他类似遗产的比较分析：
（比较分析应体现出该遗产与《世界遗产名录》中遗产或其他遗产的相似性、以及该遗产卓尔不群的原因）

● 登录联合国教科文组织的世界遗产中心网站 https://whc.unesco.org/en/convention/ 获取此《预备名单》提交格式；

● 《操作指南》第 62–67 段中含有《预备名录》准备工作的详细指导。

● 登录 http://whc.unesco.org/en/tentativelists 网站可获得完整的《预备名录》提交格式样板。

● 登录网站 http://whc.unesco.org/en/tentativelists 可获得所有由缔约国提交的《预备名录》；

● 填好的《预备名录》原件应发送至 Director–General，UNESCO，7 place de Fontenoy，75352 Paris 07 SP，France，最好附有英文或法文的正式翻译件。

● 鼓励缔约国同时提交电子版表格（磁盘或 CD）或发送电子邮件至 wh–tentativelists@unesco.org

United Nations
Educational, Scientific and
Cultural Organization

World
Heritage
Convention

TENTATIVE LIST SUBMISSION FORMAT
FOR FUTURE TRANSNATIONAL AND TRANSBOUNDARY NOMINATIONS

STATE PARTY: DATE OF SUBMISSION:

Submission[①] prepared by:

Name: E-mail:

Title:

Address: Fax:

Institution: Telephone:

Name of the transnational/transboundary future nomination[②] :

Other States Parties participating:

Name(s) of the national component part(s):

State, Province or Region:

Latitude and Longitude, or Universal Transverse Mercator (UTM) coordinates:

---

2. a　Brief Description of the transnational/transboundary future nomination[③] :

2. b　Description of the component part(s):

3. JUSTIFICATION FOR OUTSTANDING UNIVERSAL VALUE [④] OF THE FUTURE NOMINA-
TION AS A WHOLE:

(Preliminary identification of the values of the future nomination as a whole which merit inscription
on the World Heritage List)

---

① This submission will be valid only when all the States Parties indicated in Section 1.b have sent their submissions.

② The text provided in this section should be identical in all submissions of the States Parties involved in the presentation of the same transnational / transboundary future nomination.

③ In case of transnational/transboundary properties any modification will need the agreement of all States Parties
concerned.

④ In case of transnational/transboundary properties any modification will need the agreement of all States Parties
concerned.

3.a　Criteria met[①] [see Paragraph 77 of the *Operational Guidelines*]:

(Please tick the box corresponding to the proposed criteria and justify the use of each below)

(i)　(ii)　(iii)　(iv)　(v)　(vi)　(vii)　(viii)　(ix)　(x)

3.b　Statements of authenticity and/or integrity [see Paragraphs 79-95 of the *Operational Guidelines*]:

3.c.1　Justification of the selection of the component part(s) in relation to the future nomination as a whole:

3.c.2　Comparison with other similar properties[②]:

(This comparison should outline the similarities with other properties inscribed or not on the World Heritage List, and the reasons for the exceptional character of the future nomination).

---

①　In case of transnational/transboundary properties any modification will need the agreement of all States Parties concerned.

②　In case of transnational/transboundary properties any modification will need the agreement of all States Parties concerned.

附件 2B　未来申报跨国、跨境遗产的《预备名录》提交格式

缔约国：　　　　　　　　　　　　　　　提交日期：

提交^① 准备机构：

名称：　　　　　　　　　　　　　　　　电子邮件：

地址：　　　　　　　　　　　　　　　　传真：

机构：　　　　　　　　　　　　　　　　电话：

1.a 未来申报跨国 / 境遗产名称^②：

1.b 其他参与缔约国：

1.c 本国构成部分的名称：

1.d 州、省份或地区：

1.e 经纬度或通用横轴墨卡托坐标：

2.a　跨国 / 境遗产申报的简介^③：

2.b　各组成部分描述：

3. 申报遗产整体的突出普遍价值^④ 声明

（对遗产整体赖以列入《世界遗产名录》的突出普遍价值的初步认定）

3.a 符合标准^⑤ [参见《操作指南》第 77 条]：

（请勾选与提议的标准相对应的文本框，并给出选择理由）

| (i) | (ii) | (iii) | (iv) | (v) | (vi) | (vii) | (viii) | (ix) | (x) |

---

① 必须 1.b 中提到的所有缔约国都提交申请的情况下，本提交材料才生效。
② 此处填写内容，与参与该跨国 / 境遗产申报的缔约国提交的所有申请，必须一致。
③ 对跨国 / 境系列遗产申报项目的任何修改，需征得所有相关缔约国的同意。
④ 对跨国 / 境系列遗产申报项目的任何修改，需征得所有相关缔约国的同意。
⑤ 对跨国 / 境系列遗产申报项目的任何修改，需征得所有相关缔约国的同意。

3.b 完整性和真实性声明 [参见《操作指南》第 78–95 条]：

3.c1 对整体申报项目中各构成部分的选择加以解释：

3.c2 与其他类似遗产的比较分析 [①]：
（比较分析应体现出该遗产与《世界遗产名录》中遗产或其他遗产的相似性，以及该遗产卓尔不群的原因）

---

① 对跨国 / 境系列遗产申报项目的任何修改，需征得所有相关缔约国的同意。

United Nations
Educational, Scientific and
Cultural Organization

World
Heritage
Convention

REQUEST FORMAT FOR A PRELIMINARY ASSESSMENT OF A POTENTIAL NOMINATION TO THE WORLD HERITAGE LIST

(in compliance with Paragraph 122 of the *Operational Guidelines*)

- The Request Format for a Preliminary Assessment of a Potential Nomination to the World Heritage List is available at the following Web address: https://whc.unesco.org/en/nominations
- Further guidance on the preparation of the Preliminary Assessment Request Format can be found in Section Ⅲ of the *Operational Guidelines*
- The original signed version of the completed Preliminary Assessment Request Format should be sent in English or French to:

UNESCO World Heritage Centre
7, place de Fontenoy 75352 Paris 07 SP
France
Telephone: +33 (0) 1 4568 11 04

- States Parties must also submit this information in electronic format (USB Key or by e-mail to wh-nominations@unesco.org)

附件 3　潜在遗产列入《世界遗产名录》的初步评估申请格式
（参照《操作指南》第 122 段）

- 潜在遗产列入《世界遗产名录》的初步评估申请格式可登录：https://whc.unesco.org/en/nominations 获取。
- 潜在遗产列入《世界遗产名录》的初步评估申请的更多指导，见《操作指南》第三部分。
- 以英文或法文填好并签字的初步评估申请原件，应发送至：

联合国教科文组织世界遗产中心：法国巴黎

7, place de Fontenoy 75352 Paris 07 SP

电话：+33 (0) 1 4568 11 04

- 缔约国应同时提交该文件的电子版（通过 U 盘或电子邮件）发送至 wh-nominations@unesco.org：

Note: In preparing the request for Preliminary Assessment, States Parties should use this format but delete the explanatory notes.

PRELIMINARY ASSESSMENT RE-QUEST FORMAT	EXPLANATORY NOTES
1. IDENTIFICATION OF THE POTENTIAL NOMINATED PROPERTY	
1.a Country (and State Party if different)	
1.b State, Province or Region	
1.c Name of potential nominated property	Do not to punctuation. exceed 200 characters, including spaces and
1.d Latitude and Longitude coordinates	In this space provide the latitude and longitude coordinates of a point at the approximate centre of the potential nominated property. In the case of potential serial nominated property, provide a table showing the name of each component part, its region and the coordinates of its centre point.
1.e Map showing the features/attributes of the potential nominated property	Provide as a minimum a simple map with a scale and legend to show where the potential nominated property is situated and another map showing where its potential main heritage features and attributes are located. Where more detailed maps (including GIS shapefiles) are available these are welcome and should be included. If proposals for boundaries and buffer zones exist, also provide maps of these.
1.f Name and date of submission of the potential nominated property on the Tentative List of the relevant State(s) Party(ies) as registered by the Secretariat	Indicate precisely the title of the Tentative List entry to which the potential nominated property relates.
1.g Has the potential nominated property received funds from the International Assistance mechanism?	If so, briefly explain the scope of the International Assistance provided, specify the date and include any documentation on the advice provided by the Advisory Bodies.
1.h Has the potential nominated property received advice through Upstream Process mechanism?	If so, briefly explain the scope of the advice provided, specify the date and include any documentation on the advice provided by the Advisory Bodies.
1.i International designations	Indicate if the potential nominated property, as a whole or part of it, is internationally recognized as significant under other global conventions and programmes relating to the protection of cultural and natural heritage (see Paragraph 44). Maximum word length: 500 words
2. DESCRIPTION OF THE POTENTIAL NOMINATED PROPERTY	

PRELIMINARY ASSESSMENT RE-QUEST FORMAT	EXPLANATORY NOTES
2.a Summary description and history of the potential nominated property	Provide a brief description of the potential nominated property, including its main heritage features/attributes and relevant geographic characteristics (see Explanatory Notes of Section 2.a of Annex 5). Provide a brief description of the history of the potential nominated property, including significant events and development of its main heritage features/attributes. Maximum word length: 3000 words
2.b Status of the research and historical documentation related to the nominated property	Provide a brief description of the extent of documentation and relevant research available on the potential nominated property, including the following elements: when it has begun, what are the major sources, if published/unpublished, whether major research is ongoing, potential identified gaps in the knowledge including the language in which this information is available. Provide at least one reference that provides a good description of the heritage values of the potential nominated property. Maximum word length: 500 words
2.c Settings of the potential nominated property	Bearing in mind that attributes and features that convey the potential Outstanding Universal Value should be located within the nominated property, describe the immediate and wider settings (see Paragraphs 104, 112 and 118bis) of the potential nominated property and how they support the potential Outstanding Universal Value (including any particular relationship in terms of the values and attributes in the potential nominated property). Maximum word length: 500 words

3. SIGNIFICANCE OF THE POTENTIAL NOMINATED PROPERTY

3.1.a Global significance of the potential nominated property	Explain the reasons for which this potential nominated property could be considered globally significant within the context of the *World Heritage Convention*. Maximum word length: 500 words

3.1.b Which World Heritage criteria could be relevant to justify the potential Outstanding Universal Value of the potential nominated property? [see Paragraph 77 of the *Operational Guidelines*]:

| (i) | (ii) | (iii) | (iv) | (v) | (vi) | (vii) | (viii) | (ix) | (x) |

(Tick the box corresponding to the proposed criteria and provide a brief explanation to justify the use of each, not exceeding 100 words per selected criteria.)

3.2. Nomination Strategy

3.2.a Are you considering a potential serial nomination? Yes/No	If yes, provide an explanation and a rationale for the serial approach. Maximum word length: 500 words
3.2.b Are you considering a potential transboundary or transnational nomination? Yes/No	If yes, provide information on whether a nomination strategy has been planned and what will be the proposed approach. Maximum word length: 500 words

PRELIMINARY ASSESSMENT RE-QUEST FORMAT	EXPLANATORY NOTES
3.2.c Are you considering nominating the area as a Cultural Landscape? Yes/No	If yes, provide an explanation and a rationale for the approach (see Paragraphs 47, 47bis and 47ter of the Operational Guidelines). Maximum word length: 500 words
4. INTEGRITY	
4.a Inclusion of attributes in the potential nominated property	Describe the main attributes/elements which would be included within the boundaries of the potential nominated property, in order to fully understand and express its potential Outstanding Universal Value. Are there any important features or attributes that have been compromised or lost from the area, such as heavily modified ecosystems, extinct species etc.? If so, provide details. For potential serial nominated properties, explain how the proposed component parts contribute to the potential Outstanding Universal Value of the site as a whole. Maximum word length: 750 words
4.b Conservation status of the attributes, and factors affecting the potential nominated property	Provide information on the condition of the attributes of the potential nominated property, including where relevant physical fabric, processes and associations. Does the potential nominated property suffer from any actual or potential adverse effects of development and/or neglect? How have such factors been addressed in order to remove/reduce their negative impact? Maximum word length: 750 words
5. AUTHENTICITY [for potential properties proposed under criteria (i) to (vi) only]	
5.a Attributes and Information sources	Describe how each of the relevant attributes convey truthfully and credibly the values expressed in the proposed criteria (see paragraphs 79 to 86). Maximum word length: 750 words
5.b Changes to the relevant attributes	Describe what type or degree of change to the relevant attributes has occurred that may reduce their ability to convey potential Outstanding Universal Value. Maximum word length: 750 words
6. FRAMEWORK FOR COMPARATIVE ANALYSIS	
6.a Approach proposed to comparative analysis	Outline the main factors that you consider need to be taken into account in order to develop a relevant comparative analysis in relation to the potential Outstanding Universal Value of the potential nominated property. In this section outline briefly the main elements of the comparative framework that you think need to be adopted (such as the biogeographic or the geo-cultural context, or the particular type of natural or cultural phenomenon that the potential nominated property represents). Maximum word length: 1500 words

续表

PRELIMINARY ASSESSMENT REQUEST FORMAT	EXPLANATORY NOTES
6.b Comparison with other similar properties or sites	List the most relevant comparable areas, which have been considered concerning the potential nominated property (including which properties on the World Heritage List, on Tentative Lists, or more widely are the most relevant comparable sites). Describe briefly how the potential nominated property would differ from properties already inscribed on the World Heritage List, or sites included on the Tentative Lists or other sites. Maximum word length: 1000 words
6.c Selection of component parts for potential serial nominated properties	In the case of potential serial nominated properties, provide details of the approach used to select their component parts and the rationale for the selection. Maximum word length: 500 words
6.d Gaps and underrepresented heritage on the World Heritage List	Identify whether the potential nominated property addresses a particular gap or underrepresented area or theme on the World Heritage List and how it would contribute to achieving a more balanced and representative World Heritage List. Indicate if the potential nominated property is mentioned in the thematic studies of the Advisory Bodies. Maximum 500 words.
7. PROTECTION AND MANAGEMENT	
7.a Protection status	Describe the current legislative and regulatory measures at national and local level. Describe any protection measures that apply to the immediate and wider settings of the potential nominated property. Maximum word length: 500 words
7.b Management status	In case a management system is in place, or is envisaged, for the conservation of the potential nominated property, provide a brief description of its organization, priorities, conservation measures and the adequacy of resources (capacity and financial) available. In case the potential nominated property already has a management plan, or other documented management system, attach a copy of the most recent version. In the case of potential serial nominated properties, provide information on whether an overall management framework for all components parts is already in place or envisaged. Maximum word length: 500 words
7.c Engagement of indigenous peoples and local communities	If the potential nominated property might affect the lands, territories or resources of indigenous peoples and/or local communities, explain how they are represented, and in how far they have participated in the preparation of the Tentative List and the Preliminary Assessment request (see paragraphs 64 and 123). Demonstrate, as appropriate, that the free, prior and informed consent of indigenous peoples has been obtained, through, inter alia, making the planned nomination publicly available in appropriate languages and public consultations and hearings. Maximum word length: 500 words

续表

PRELIMINARY ASSESSMENT RE-QUEST FORMAT	EXPLANATORY NOTES
7.d Additional key questions and issues	Describe any issues or difficulties, which have been identified to date in considering a possible World Heritage nomination, or any specific area(s) where advice is required in considering the potential nominated property. Maximum word length: 500 words
8. CONTACT INFORMATION OF RESPONSIBLE AUTHORITIES	
8. Name and contact information of official local institution/agency/organization	Institution/Agency/Organization: Address: Tel: E-mail: Web address:
9. SIGNATURE	
9. Signature on behalf of the State Party	The Preliminary Assessment request should conclude with the signature of the official empowered to sign it on behalf of the State Party.

注意：缔约国可使用下表填写初步评估申请，删除填报须知部分。

初步评估申请格式	填报须知
1. 识别潜在申报遗产	
1.a 国家（如果有不同的及缔约国列出）	
1.b 州，省份，地区	
1.c 潜在申报遗产的名称	包括空格和标点符号不得超过 200 字符
1.d 经纬度坐标	提供潜在申报遗产的中心点的纬度和经度坐标 如果是系列申报，列表说明各遗产的名称、地域（或最近的城镇）、遗产中心点的坐标。
1.e 显示潜在申报遗产特征和属性的地图	至少提供一张标有比例尺和图例的简单地图，显示潜在申报遗产的位置，以及一张主要显示遗产特征和属性的地图。 如有包含数字地理信息的地图 (GIS 形式的文件) 同样欢迎提供应提供详细标明了潜在申报遗产及缓冲区的范围的地图。
1.f 秘书处登记的、已在相关缔约国预备名录上的、潜在申报遗产的名称和提交日期	准确标明已列入缔约国《预备名录》的、潜在申报遗产的名称。
1.g 潜在申报遗产是否得到国际援助体系的资金支持？	如果是，请简要说明所提供的国际援助的范围，具体日期，包括咨询机构提供咨询意见的任何文件。

续表

初步评估申请格式	填报须知
1.h 潜在申报遗产是否得到上游程序建议？	如果是，请简要说明所提供建议的范围，具体日期，包括咨询机构提供咨询意见的任何文件。
1.i 国际称号	说明潜在申报遗产作为一个整体或组成部分，是否在其他有关全球性文化和自然遗产保护公约和项目中，得到公认的全球性重要意义（见 44 段）。最多不超过 500 字词。
2. 潜在申报遗产描述	
2.a 简要描述潜在申报遗产及其历史	简要描述潜在申报遗产，包括主要遗产特征和属性，相关地理特征。（见附件 5 填报须知的 2.a） 简要描述潜在申报遗产的历史，包括重大事件和主要遗产特征和属性。 最多不超过 3000 字词。
2.b 与潜在申报遗产相关的研究状况及历史文献	简要描述潜在申报遗产相关的历史文献范围及研究状况，包括下列因素：开始时间，主要来源，是否公开发表，是否正在进行的重大研究，是否有潜在的认知缺陷包括提供可用信息的语言。最少提供一份参考资料，可对潜在申报遗产做出良好描述。 最长不超过 500 字词。
2.c 潜在申报遗产的环境	牢记，能传递潜在突出普遍价值的特征和属性必须位于申报遗产内，说明潜在申报遗产的直接和广泛的环境（见 104，112 及 118 补充段）及其如何支持遗产的潜在突出普遍价值（包括与潜在申报遗产价值和属性相关的特殊关系） 最多不超过 500 字词。
3. 潜在申报遗产的意义	
3.1.a 潜在申报遗产的全球意义	在《世界遗产公约》背景下，解释认为该潜在申报遗产具有全球意义的原因。最多不超过 500 字词。
3.1.b 哪些标准可以证明潜在申报遗产具有潜在的突出普遍价值？（见《操作指南》77 段） 　　　　(i)　(ii)　(iii)　(iv)　(v)　(vi)　(vii)　(viii)　(ix)　(x) （在每项符合标准的对应方框内打勾，并附上使用每个标准的理由，每项选择标准最多不超过 100 字词。）	
3.2. 申遗策略	
3.2.a 是否考虑系列申报的可能性？是 / 否	如果是，说明考虑系列申报的原因。 最多不超过 500 字词 .
3.2.b 是否考虑跨国跨境申报的可能性？是 / 否	如果是，说明是否已计划相应的申报策略及建议的方法。 最多不超过 500 字词。
3.2.c 是否考虑申报文化景观的可能性？是 / 否	如果是，说明考虑申报文化景观的原因（（见《操作指南》47，47 补充及 47 再补充段））。 最多不超过 500 字词。
4. 完整性	
4.a 潜在申报遗产包含的属性	描述潜在申报遗产的主要属性 / 要素，以充分理解和表达其潜在的突出普遍价值。 该地区是否有任何重要的特征或属性被破坏或丢失，例如严重改变的生态系统、灭绝的物种等？如果有，请提供详细信息。 对于潜在的系列申报属性，解释其，建议的遗产组成作为一个整体的系列遗产组成部分，如何为潜在的突出普遍价值做出贡献。 最多不超过 750 字词。

初步评估申请格式	填报须知
4.b 遗产属性的保存状态，以及影响潜在申报遗产的因素	提供有关潜在申报遗产属性保护状况的信息，包括相关的物理结构、工艺流程和关联。 潜在的申报遗产是否因发展及 / 或疏忽，而受到任何实际或潜在的不利影响？如何处理这些因素以消除 / 减少其负面影响？ 最多不超过 750 字词。
5. 真实性（仅适用于符合标准 (i) 至 (vi) 的遗产）	
5.a 属性和信息来源	描述每一个相关属性，如何真实和可信地表达拟议标准中所表达的价值（见第 79 至 86 段）。 最多不超过 750 字词。
5.b 相关属性的变化	描述相关属性发生了何种类型或程度的变化，可能会降低其传达潜在突出普遍价值的能力。 最多不超过 750 字词。
6. 比较分析框架	
6.a 提出的比较分析的方法	概述您认为需要考虑的主要因素，以便对潜在申报遗产的突出普遍价值进行相关的比较分析。 在本节中，简要概述您认为需要采用的比较框架的主要元素（例如生物地理或地理文化背景，或潜在申报遗产所代表的、特定类型的自然或文化现象）。 最多不超过 1500 字词。
6.b 与其他类似遗产或遗址的比较	列出与潜在申报遗产最相关的可比较地区（包括《世界遗产名录》、《预备名录》上的遗产或更广泛的最相关可比较的遗产）。 简要描述潜在申报遗产与已列入《世界遗产名录》、《预备名录》或其他名录的遗产有何不同。 最多不超过 1000 字词。
6.c 选择潜在申报系列遗产的组成部分	在潜在申报系列遗产的情况下，提供用于选择其组成部分的方法的细节和选择的理由。 最多不超过 500 字词。
6.d 填报《世界遗产名录》上空白或代表性不足	确定候选遗产是否填补了《世界遗产名录》的某个空白或代表性不足的领域或主题，以及它将如何促进《世界遗产名录》的平衡性和代表性。 说明咨询机构的专题研究中是否提到该潜在申报遗产。 最多不超过 500 字词。
7. 保护和管理	
7.a 保护状况	说明国家和地方层面现行的立法和监管措施。 描述任何适用于潜在申报遗产的直接和更广泛环境的保护措施。 最多不超过 500 字词。
7.b 管理状况	如果已经建立或计划建立保护申报遗产的管理制度，则应简要说明其组织、优先次序、保护措施和现有资源（能力和财政）是否充足。 如果潜在申报遗产已经有管理计划或其他档案管理系统，请附上最新版本的副本。 在潜在的系列申报的情况下，提供信息，说明所有组成部分的总体管理框架是否已经就位或设想中。 最多不超过 500 字词。

续表

初步评估申请格式	填报须知
7.c 原住民和当地社区的参与	如果潜在申报遗产可能对原住民的土地、领土或资源造成影响，解释它们是如何表现的，以及原住民在多大程度上参与了预备名录和初步评估申请的编制（见第 64 和 123 段）。 在适当情况下，需酌情证明，已通过公共协商和听证会等形式，用适当的语言文字，公开申报信息，从而事先征得了原住民自愿、知情的同意。 最多不超过 500 字词。
7.d 其他关键问题和问题	描述到目前为止，在考虑世界遗产申报时发现的任何问题或困难，或在考虑潜在申报遗产时，需要咨询专业建议的特定领域。 最多不超过 500 字词。
8. 主管部门联系方式	
8. 当地官方机关、机构、组织的名称和联系信息	当地官方机关、机构、组织： 地址： 电话： 电邮： 网址：
9. 签名	
9. 缔约国代表签名	初步评估申请应有缔约国授权的官方代表签字。

United Nations
Educational, Scientific and
Cultural Organization

World
Heritage
Convention

AUTHENTICITY IN RELATION TO THE *WORLD HERITAGE CONVENTION*

INTRODUCTION

This Annex reproduces the Nara Document on Authenticity, drafted by the 45 participants to the Nara Conference on Authenticity in Relation to the *World Heritage Convention*, held at Nara, Japan, from 1- 6 November 1994. The Nara Conference was organized in cooperation with UNESCO, ICCROM and ICOMOS.

The World Heritage Committee examined the report of the Nara meeting on Authenticity at its 18th session (Phuket, Thailand, 1994) (see document WHC-94/CONF.003/16).

Subsequent expert meetings have enriched the concept of authenticity in relation to the *World Heritage Convention* (see Bibliography of the *Operational Guidelines*).

Ⅰ. THE NARA DOCUMENT ON AUTHENTICITY

Preamble

1. We, the experts assembled in Nara (Japan), wish to acknowledge the generous spirit and intellectual courage of the Japanese authorities in providing a timely forum in which we could challenge conventional thinking in the conservation field, and debate ways and means of broadening our

附件 4　《保护世界文化与自然遗产公约》相关的真实性

前言

本附件再次使用了《奈良真实性文件》。1994年11月1日至6日，《世界遗产公约》相关的奈良真实性会议在日本奈良召开，与会的45位代表起草了《奈良真实性文件》。奈良会议由联合国教科文组织、国际文化遗产保护与修复研究中心和国际古迹遗址理事会联合主办。

世界遗产委员会第18届会议（泰国普吉岛，1994年）上审核了奈良会议中关于真实性的报告（见文件WHC–94/CONF.003/16）。

此后的专家会议丰富了《世界遗产公约》相关的真实性的概念（见《操作指南》的参考文献）。

Ⅰ.《奈良真实性文件》导言

导言

1. 作为参与奈良（日本）会议与会专家，我们在此感谢日本当局的慷慨精神与学术勇气，为我们适时提供了此论坛，让我们能够挑战遗产保护领域的传统思想，讨论运用各种途径和方法扩大我们的视野，从而在保护实践中更大限度的尊重文化和遗产的多样性。

horizons to bring greater respect for cultural and heritage diversity to conservation practice.

2. We also wish to acknowledge the value of the framework for discussion provided by the World Heritage Committee's desire to apply the test of authenticity in ways which accord full respect to the social and cultural values of all societies, in examining the outstanding universal value of cultural properties proposed for the World Heritage List.

3. The Nara Document on Authenticity is conceived in the spirit of the Charter of Venice, 1964, and builds on it and extends it in response to the expanding scope of cultural heritage concerns and interests in our contemporary world.

4. In a world that is increasingly subject to the forces of globalization and homogenization, and in a world in which the search for cultural identity is sometimes pursued through aggressive nationalism and the suppression of the cultures of minorities, the essential contribution made by the consideration of authenticity in conservation practice is to clarify and illuminate the collective memory of humanity.

Cultural Diversity and Heritage Diversity

5. The diversity of cultures and heritage in our world is an irreplaceable source of spiritual and intellectual richness for all humankind. The protection and enhancement of cultural and heritage diversity in our world should be actively promoted as an essential aspect of human development.

6. Cultural heritage diversity exists in time and space, and demands respect for other cultures and all aspects of their belief systems. In cases where cultural values appear to be in conflict, respect for

2. 我们希望认可世界遗产委员会所提供的、以尊重所有社会的社会与文化价值的方式、在检验申报《世界遗产名录》的文化遗产的突出普遍性价值时，采用真实性检验标准提出的讨论构架的价值。

3.《奈良真实性文件》受到 1964 年的威尼斯宪法精神启发，在此基础上建立，并被延伸引用，以响应我们当代世界对文化遗产的关注与利益的范围的不断扩大。

4. 在一个日益受到全球化和同一化力量影响的世界里，在一个有时藉由带有侵略性的民族主义和压制少数民族文化以追求文化认同的世界里，真实性思考在保护实践中的重要的贡献是，澄清并阐明人类的集体记忆。

文化多样性和遗产多样性

5. 我们所处世界的文化和遗产的多样性，是所有人类丰富的精神和知识的不可替代的来源。对世界的文化和遗产的多样性的保护和加强应得到积极的推动，使之成为人类发展的一个重要方面。

6. 文化遗产的多样性涉及时间和空间，需要对其他文化和它们所信仰的各个方面给予尊重。一旦文化价值发生了冲突，尊重文化多样性需要承认所有成员的文化价值的合法性 。

cultural diversity demands acknowledgment of the legitimacy of the cultural values of all parties.

7. All cultures and societies are rooted in the particular forms and means of tangible and intangible expression which constitute their heritage, and these should be respected.

8. It is important to underline a fundamental principle of UNESCO, to the effect that the cultural heritage of each is the cultural heritage of all. Responsibility for cultural heritage and the management of it belongs, in the first place, to the cultural community that has generated it, and subsequently to that which cares for it. However, in addition to these responsibilities, adherence to the international charters and conventions developed for conservation of cultural heritage also obliges consideration of the principles and responsibilities flowing from them. Balancing their own requirements with those of other cultural communities is, for each community, highly desirable, provided achieving this balance does not undermine their fundamental cultural values.

Values and authenticity

9. Conservation of cultural heritage in all its forms and historical periods is rooted in the values attributed to the heritage. Our ability to understand these values depends, in part, on the degree to which information sources about these values may be understood as credible or truthful. Knowledge and understanding of these sources of information, in relation to original and subsequent characteristics of the cultural heritage, and their meaning, is a requisite basis for assessing all aspects of authenticity.

10. Authenticity, considered in this way and affirmed in the Charter of Venice, appears as the

7. 所有的文化和社会都植根于特殊的形式和方法中，而有形的和无形的表达手段构成了它们的遗产并应得到充分地尊重。

8. 强调每一种文化遗产都是所有人的文化遗产这一联合国教科文组织的基本原则，是很重要的。文化遗产的责任和对它的管理权首先应归属于产生这种文化遗产的文化社区，其次是照看它的社区。尽管如此，除了这些责任，遵守保护文化遗产所制定的国际宪章和协定，同样是他们的原则与责任。对每个社区来说，平衡其自身与其他文化社区的要求都是一件极度重要的事，达到这种平衡并不会对他们的基础文化价值造成影响。

价值与真实性

9. 对所有历史阶段的所有形式的文化遗产的保护，源于遗产的属性价值。我们理解这些价值的能力，部分取决于对这些价值的信息来源本身和其可信度的理解程度。对这些与原始和后续的文化遗产特征有关的信息来源及其意义的认知与理解是全面评定真实性的必备条件。

10. 在《威尼斯宪章》中形成，并确定的真实性，是价值评估的重要质量因素。对真实性

essential qualifying factor concerning values. The understanding of authenticity plays a fundamental role in all scientific studies of the cultural heritage, in conservation and restoration planning, as well as within the inscription procedures used for the World Heritage Convention and other cultural heritage inventories.

的理解在对文化遗产、对其保护和重建规划及《世界遗产公约》和其他文化遗产所进行的所有科学研究中，扮演着重要的角色。

11. All judgements about values attributed to cultural properties as well as the credibility of related information sources may differ from culture to culture, and even within the same culture. It is thus not possible to base judgements of values and authenticity within fixed criteria. On the contrary, the respect due to all cultures requires that heritage properties must be considered and judged within the cultural contexts to which they belong.

11. 不同文化间，甚至是相同文化中，对文化遗产所有价值的评估和相关信息来源可信度的评估，都有所差异。因此，不可能将价值和真实性评估建立在固定标准上。相反，对所有文化的尊重，要求必须在遗产所属的文化环境中对其进行考虑和评定。

12. Therefore, it is of the highest importance and urgency that, within each culture, recognition be accorded to the specific nature of its heritage values and the credibility and truthfulness of related information sources.

12. 因此，这一点最重要也最迫切，那就是，在每一种文化中，必须依照其遗产价值的特殊本质、信息来源的可信度和真实性，加以认定。

13. Depending on the nature of the cultural heritage, its cultural context, and its evolution through time, authenticity judgements may be linked to the worth of a great variety of sources of information. Aspects of the sources may include form and design, materials and substance, use and function, traditions and techniques, location and setting, and spirit and feeling, and other internal and external factors. The use of these sources permits elaboration of the specific artistic, historic, social, and scientific dimensions of the cultural heritage being examined.

13. 取决于文化遗产的本质、它的文化环境和它随着时间的演替，真实性的评估可能会与许多不同的信息来源的价值相关。资源方面包括形式和设计、材料与物质、用途与功能、传统与技术、位置与场合、精神与感情、以及其他内在和外在因素。对这些资源的使用，允许对文化遗产的特殊艺术性、历史性、社会性和科学性进行详细审核。

Appendix 1: Suggestions for follow-up

附录1：对后续跟踪的几点建议

1. Respect for cultural and heritage diver-

1. 对文化遗产多样性的尊重需要有意识的

sity requires conscious efforts to avoid imposing mechanistic formulae or standardized procedures in attempting to define or determine authenticity of particular monuments and sites.

2. Efforts to determine authenticity in a manner respectful of cultures and heritage diversity requires approaches which encourage cultures to develop analytical processes and tools specific to their nature and needs. Such approaches may have several aspects in common:

- efforts to ensure assessment of authenticity involve multidisciplinary collaboration and the appropriate utilisation of all available expertise and knowledge;
- efforts to ensure attributed values are truly representative of a culture and the diversity of its interests, in particular monuments and sites;
- efforts to document clearly the particular nature of authenticity for monuments and sites as a practical guide to future treatment and monitoring;
- efforts to update authenticity assessments in light of changing values and circumstances.

3. Particularly important are efforts to ensure that attributed values are respected, and that their determination included efforts to build, as far as possible, a multidisciplinary and community consensus concerning these values.

4. Approaches should also build on and facilitate international co-operation among all those with an interest in conservation of cultural heritage, in order to improve global respect and understanding for the diverse expressions and values of each culture.

5. Continuation and extension of this dialogue to the various regions and cultures of the world is

努力，避免使用在定义和决定特定纪念物和遗址时，套用机械化公式和标准程序。

2. 努力用一种尊重文化与遗产多样性的方法来决定真实性，要求采用能够鼓励不同文化根据其自身性质和需求，发展其分析过程和工具的方法。这些方法在下列方面有相似之处：

– 努力确保对真实性的评估，涉及不同领域间的合作，恰当利用所有可用专门技术和知识；

– 努力确保其价值能够真正代表一种文化和它的利益的多样性，特别是在纪念物和遗址上；

– 努力确保清晰的记录纪念物和遗址的真实性的特殊性质，将其作为将来处理和监测的实践指导；

– 在不断变换的价值和环境中，努力更新真实性评估。

3. 特别重要的是努力确保所有价值受到尊重，确保决策，包括尽可能根据这些价值观念达成多学科和社区的共识。

4. 建立多种途径，并促进所有致力于文化遗产保护的组织之间的国际合作，从而促进对全球每种文化的不同表达和价值的尊重和理解。

5. 将这种跨文化对话继续并扩展到全世界不同的地区和文化中，是提高人类共同遗产保

a prerequisite to increasing the practical value of consideration of authenticity in the conservation of the common heritage of humankind.

6. Increasing awareness within the public of this fundamental dimension of heritage is an absolute necessity in order to arrive at concrete measures for safeguarding the vestiges of the past. This means developing greater understanding of the values represented by the cultural properties themselves, as well as respecting the role such monuments and sites play in contemporary society.

Appendix 2: Definitions

Conservation: all efforts designed to understand cultural heritage, know its history and meaning, ensure its material safeguard and, as required, its presentation, restoration and enhancement. (Cultural heritage is understood to include monuments, groups of buildings and sites of cultural value as defined in Article 1 of the World Heritage Convention).

Information sources: all material, written, oral and figurative sources which make it possible to know the nature, specifications, meaning and history of the cultural heritage.

Ⅱ. CHRONOLOGICAL BIBLIOGRAPHY - ON AUTHENTICITY

Publications which preceded the Nara meeting and which helped prepare the ground for the authenticity discussion which took place in Nara:

Larsen, Knut Einar, *A note on the authenticity of historic timber buildings with particular reference to Japan,*

Occasional Papers for the World Heritage

护真实性意识的先决条件。

6. 为了获得保护过去遗迹的具体措施，提高公众对遗产的基本认识是十分必要的。这意味着，需要更大程度地理解文化遗产本身所代表的价值，并尊重这些纪念物和遗址在当代社会中所扮演的角色。

附录 2：定义

保护：所有努力都旨在理解文化遗产、了解其历史和含义、保证其物质安全，且根据要求，保证它的存在、修复和强化（通常人们所理解的文化遗产包括纪念碑、建筑群、和文化价值遗址，《世界遗产公约》第一条中已明确定义）。

信息来源：所有可以让人了解文化遗产的本质、规格、意义和历史的物质的、手写的、口头的和图像的资源。

Ⅱ. 按年代顺序排列的关于真实性的参考文献

奈良会议召开前出版的出版物和有助于奈良的真实性讨论的出版物包括：

《关于历史上木质建筑（尤指日本）的真实性的注解》，作者 Larsen, Knut Einar，《世界遗产公约》的学术论文，国际古迹遗址理事会，1992 年 12 月；

Convention, ICOMOS, December 1992.

Larsen, Knut Einar, *Authenticity and Reconstruction: Architectural Preservation in Japan,* Norwegian Institute of Technology, Vols. 1-2, 1993.

Preparatory meeting for the Nara Meeting, held in Bergen, Norway, 31 January - 1 February 1994:

Larsen, Knut Einar and Marstein, Nils (ed.), *Conference on authenticity in relation to the World Heritage Convention Preparatory workshop,* Bergen, Norway, 31 January - 2 February 1994, Tapir Forlag, Trondheim 1994.

The Nara meeting, 1-6 November 1994, Nara, Japan:

Larsen, Knut Einar with an editorial group (Jokilehto, Lemaire, Masuda, Marstein, Stovel), *Nara conference on authenticity in relation to the World Heritage Convention. Conférence de Nara sur l'authenticité dans le cadre de la Convention du Patrimoine Mondial.* Nara, Japan, 1-6 November 1994, Proceedings published by UNESCO - World Heritage Centre, Agency for Cultural Affairs of Japan, ICCROM and ICOMOS, 1994.

The Nara meeting brought together 45 experts from 26 countries and international organizations from around the world. Their papers are contained in the volume cited above, as is the Nara document prepared in a working group of 12 meeting participants and edited by Raymond Lemaire and Herb Stovel. This volume of Proceedings invites members of ICOMOS and others to extend the discussions of the Nara Document issues to other regions of the world.

《真实性和重建：日本建筑的保护》作者 Larsen，KnutEinar，挪威科技大学第 1-2 卷，1993 年。

1994 年 1 月 31 日至 2 月 1 日在挪威卑尔根召开的奈良会议的预备会议：

《关于〈世界遗产公约〉中真实性研讨会的预备工作会议》，作者 Larsen，KnutEinar 和 Marstein，Nils（ed.），1994 年 1 月 31 日至 2 月 1 日挪威卑尔根，特隆赫姆 Tapir Forlag，1994 年。

1994 年 11 月 1-6 日在日本奈良召开的奈良会议：

《关于〈世界遗产公约〉真实性的奈良会议》，（法语名：Conférence de Naras url'authenticité dansle cadre de la Convention du Patrimoine Mondial），作者 Larsen 和 Knut Einar 领导的编辑组（包括 Jokilehto，Lemaire，Masuda，Marstein 和 Stovel），日本奈良，1994 年 11 月 1-6 日，会议论文集，联合国教科文组织世界遗产中心、日本文化部、国际文化遗产保护与修复研究中心和国际古迹遗址理事会，1994 年。

奈良会议召集了来自 26 个国家和国际组织的 45 名专家。专家的论文被包含在上述引用的会议论文中，由 12 个参会者组成的工作组准备的奈良文件，并由 Raymond Lemaire 和 Herb Stovel 编辑完成。会议邀请国际古迹遗址理事会成员和其他有关专家一起，将对奈良文件问题相关讨论扩大到世界其他地区。

Significant post-Nara regional meetings (as of January 2005):

Authenticity and Monitoring, October 17-22, 1995, Cesky Krumlov, Czech Republic, ICOMOS European Conference, 1995.

The European ICOMOS Conference of 17-22 October, 1995 which took place in Cesky Krumlov, Czech Republic brought together 18 European members of ICOMOS to present national views of the application of authenticity concepts from 14 countries. A synthesis of presentations affirmed the importance of authenticity within the analytical processes we apply to conservation problems as a means of assuring truthful, sincere and honest approaches to conservation problems, and gave emphasis to strengthening the notion of dynamic conservation in order to apply authenticity analysis appropriately to cultural landscapes and urban settings.

Interamerican symposium on authenticity in the conservation and management of the cultural heritage, US/ICOMOS, The Getty Conservation Institute, San Antonio, Texas 1996.

This Authenticity meeting which took place in San Antonio, Texas, USA in March 1996, brought together participants from ICOMOS national committees of North, Central and South America to debate the application of the concepts of Nara. The meeting adopted the *Declaration of San Antonio,* which discussed the relationship between authenticity and identity, history, materials, social value, dynamic and static sites, stewardship and economics, and contained recommendations extending "proofs" of authenticity to include *reflection of its true value, integrity, context, identity, use and function,* as well as recommendations pertinent to

奈良会议后具有重大意义的地区性会议（截至 2005 年 1 月）：

《真实性和遗产监测，1995 年 10 月 17-22 日》，捷克共和国契斯基库伦隆，国际古遗址理事会欧洲会议，1995 年。

1995 年 10 月 17-22 日，欧洲国际古遗址理事会欧洲会议在捷克共和国契斯基库伦隆召开。会议聚集了 18 位国际古迹遗址理事会欧洲成员，提出了来自 14 国的关于应用真实性概念的观点。这些综合阐述确认了真实性在处理保护问题中，作为保证信任、真诚和诚实的手段，在分析过程中的重要性，强调加强动态保护的观念，以便在文化景观和城市遗产申报中恰当地应用真实性分析。

《美洲关于文化遗产保护和管理中真实性的研讨会》，美国 / 国际古遗址理事会，美国德兖萨斯州圣安东尼，盖蒂保护研究所，1996 年。

1996 年 3 月在德克萨斯州圣安东尼奥召开的真实性会议汇聚了来自北美、中美和南美国际古遗址理事会国家委员会的参会者，共同商讨了奈良概念的应用。该会议通过了《圣安东尼奥宣言》，该宣言讨论了真实性和身份认同、历史、材料、社会价值、动态和静态遗产、管理和经济学之间的关系，包含了扩充真实性"证据"的相关建议，包括对真实价值、完整性、环境、特性、使用和功能的反映，以及针对不同类型遗产的相关建议。

different typologies of sites.

Saouma-Forero, Galia, (edited by), *Authenticity and integrity in an African context: expert meeting, Great Zimbabwe*, Zimbabwe, 26-29 May 2000, UNESCO - World Heritage Centre, Paris 2001.

The Great Zimbabwe meeting organised by the World Heritage Centre (26-29 May 2000) focused attention on both authenticity and integrity in an African context. Eighteen speakers looked at issues arising in management of both cultural and natural heritage properties. The meeting resulted in the publication cited above, which includes a set of recommendations coming from meeting participants. Among recommendations were suggestions to include *management systems, language, and other forms of intangible heritage* among attributes expressing authenticity, and an emphasis given to the place of local communities in the sustainable heritage management process.

Reconstruction discussions in the context of the *World Heritage Convention* (as of January 2005):

The Riga Charter on authenticity and historical reconstruction in relationship to cultural heritage adopted by regional conference, Riga, 24 October 2000, Latvian National Commission for UNESCO - World Heritage Centre, ICCROM.

Incerti Medici, Elena and Stovel, Herb, *Authenticity and historical reconstruction in relationship with cultural heritage, regional conference, Riga, Latvia, October 23-24 2000: summary report*, UNESCO - World Heritage Centre, Paris, ICCROM, Rome 2001.

《非洲文化背景下遗产保护的真实性和完整性：大津巴布韦专家会议》，Saouma-Forero, Galia,（编辑），津巴布韦，2000 年 5 月 26-29 日，联合国教科文组织世界遗产中心，2001 年，巴黎。

大津巴布韦会议由世界遗产中心组织召开（2000 年 5 月 26-29 日），会议重点强调非洲遗产的真实性和完整性。18 位发言人讨论了文化与自然遗产管理面临的问题。该会议后发表了上述出版物，其中包含了参会人员提出的建议。这些建议包括将管理体系、语言和其他形式的无形遗产纳入真实性表达，并强调当地社区在可持续遗产管理过程中的作用。

《世界遗产公约》中关于重建问题的讨论（截止至 2005 年 1 月）：

里加地区会议通过的《关于文化遗产相关真实性和历史重建问题的里加宪章》，2000 年 10 月 24 日，联合国教科文组织世界遗产中心拉脱维亚委员会，国际文化遗产保护与修复研究中心。

2000 年 10 月 23-24 日拉脱维亚里加地区会议《关于文化遗产相关真实性和历史重建问题的地区会议总结报告》，起草人 Incerti Medici, Elena 和 Stovel, Herb，2001 年，巴黎联合国教科文组织世界遗产中心，国际文化遗产保护与修复研究中心。

Stovel, Herb, *The Riga Charter on authenticity and historical reconstruction in relationship to cultural heritage, Riga, Latvia, October 2000*, in *Conservation and management of archaeological sites,* Vol. 4, n. 4, 2001.

Alternatives to historical reconstruction in the World Heritage Cities, Tallinn, 16-18 May 2002, Tallinn Cultural Heritage Department, Estonia National Commission for UNESCO, Estonia National Heritage Board.

2000 年 10 月拉脱维亚里加地区会议通过的《关于考古遗址保护和管理中的文化遗产相关真实性和历史重建问题的里加宪章》，起草人 Stovel，Herb，《考古遗址保护和管理》2001 年第 4 卷。

《避免世界遗产城市中历史建筑重建的选择》2002 年 5 月 16–18 日，塔林文化遗产部，联合国教科文组织爱沙尼亚国家委员会，爱沙尼亚国家遗产部。

United Nations
Educational, Scientific and
Cultural Organization

World
Heritage
Convention

FORMAT FOR THE NOMINATION OF PROPERTIES FOR INSCRIPTION ON THE WORLD HERITAGE LIST

This Format must be used for all nomination dossiers

- The Nomination Format is available at https://whc.unesco.org/en/nominations/
- Further guidance on the preparation of nomination dossiers can be found in Section Ⅲ of the *Operational Guidelines*
- The original signed version of the completed Nomination Format should be sent in English or French to UNESCO World Heritage Centre

7, place de Fontenoy 75352 Paris 07 SP

France

Telephone: +33 (0) 1 4568 1104

E-mail: wh-nominations@unesco.org

Executive Summary

This information, to be provided by the State Party, will be updated by the Secretariat following the decision by the World Heritage Committee. It will then be returned to the State Party confirming the basis on which the property is inscribed on the World Heritage List.

State Party	
State, Province or Region	
Name of nominated property	
Geographical coordinates to the nearest second	
Textual description of the boundary(ies) of the nominated property	
A4 or A3 size map(s) of the nominated property, showing boundaries and buffer zone (if present)	Attach A4 or A3 size map(s) which should be the reduced size version of the original copies of topographic or cadastral maps showing the nominated property and buffer zone (if present) at the largest scale available included or annexed to the nomination.

Criteria under which property is nominated (itemize criteria) (see Paragraph 77 of the *Operational Guidelines*)	
Cultural Landscape	Indicate whether the property is nominated as a cultural landscape (YES) or (NO) (see Paragraphs 47, 47bis and 47ter)
Draft Statement of Outstanding Universal Value (text should clarify what is considered to be the Outstanding Universal Value embodied by the nominated property, approximately 1-2 page format)	According to the paragraph 155, the Statement of Outstanding Universal Value should be composed of: Brief synthesis Justification for Criteria Statement of Integrity (for all properties) Statement of authenticity for properties nominated under criteria (i) to (vi) Requirements for protection and management See format in Annex 10
Name and contact information of official local institution/agency/organization	Institution/Agency/Organization: Address: Tel: Fax: E-mail: Web address:

Properties for inscription on the World Heritage List

Note: In preparing the nomination dossier, States Parties should use this format but delete the explanatory notes.

NOMINATION FORMAT	EXPLANATORY NOTES
1. Identification of the nominated property	Together with Sections 2 and 3, this is the most important section in the nomination. It must make clear to the Committee precisely where the nominated property is located and how it is geographically defined. In the case of serial nominated properties, insert a table that shows the name of the component part, region (if different for different components), coordinates, area and buffer zone. Other fields could also be added (page reference or map number, etc.) that differentiate the several components.
1.a Country (and State Party if different)	
1.b State, Province or Region	
1.c Name of nominated property	This is the official name of the nominated property that will appear in published material about World Heritage. It should be concise. Do not exceed 200 characters, including spaces and punctuation. In the case of serial nominated properties (see Paragraphs 137-139 of the *Operational Guidelines*), give a name for the ensemble (e.g., *Baroque Churches of the Philippines*). Do not include the name of the component parts of a serial nominated property, which should be included in a table as part of 1.d and 1.f.

NOMINATION FORMAT	EXPLANATORY NOTES
1.d　Geographical coordinates to the nearest second	In this space provide the latitude and longitude coordinates (to the nearest second) or UTM coordinates (to the nearest 10 metres) of a point at the approximate centre of the nominated property. Do not use other coordinate systems. If in doubt, please consult the Secretariat. In the case of serial nominated properties, provide a table showing the name of each component part, its region (or nearest town as appropriate), and the coordinates of its centre point. Coordinate format examples: N 45° 06' 05" W 15° 37' 56" or UTM Zone 18 Easting: 545670 　　　　　　　Northing: 4586750

Id n°	Name of the component part	Region (s) / District (s)	Coordinates of the central point	Area of nominated component part (ha)	Area of the Buffer Zone (ha)	Map N°
001						
002						
003						
004						
Etc.						
Total area (in hectares)				ha	ha	

NOMINATION FORMAT	EXPLANATORY NOTES
1.e Maps and plans, showing the boundaries of the nominated property and buffer zone	Annex to the nomination, and list below with scales and dates: (i)Original copies of topographic maps showing the property nominated, at the largest scale available which shows the entire nominated property. The boundaries of the nominated property and buffer zone should be clearly marked. The boundaries of zones of special legal protection from which the nominated property benefits should be recorded on maps to be included under the protection and management section of the nomination text. Multiple maps may be necessary for serial nominated properties (see table in 1.d). The maps provided should be at the largest available and practical scale to allow the identification of topographic elements such as neighbouring settlements, buildings and routes in order to allow the clear assessment of the impact of any proposed development within, adjacent to, or on the boundary line. The choice of the adequate scale is essential to clearly show the boundaries of the nominated property and shall be in relation to the category of site that is proposed for inscription: cultural sites would require cadastral maps, while natural sites or cultural landscapes would require topographic maps (normally 1:25 000 to 1:50 000 scale). Utmost care is needed with the width of boundary lines on maps, as thick boundary lines may make the actual boundary of the nominated property ambiguous.

NOMINATION FORMAT	EXPLANATORY NOTES
1.e Maps and plans, showing the boundaries of the nominated property and buffer zone	All maps should be capable of being geo-referenced, with a minimum of three points on opposite sides of the maps with complete sets of coordinates. The maps, untrimmed, should show scale, orientation, projection, datum, nominated property name and date. If possible, maps should be sent rolled and not folded. Geographic Information in digital form is encouraged if possible, suitable for incorporation into a GIS (Geographic Information System), however, this may not substitute the submission of printed maps. In this case the delineation of the boundaries (nominated property and buffer zone) should be presented in vector form, prepared at the largest scale possible. The State Party is invited to contact the Secretariat for further information concerning this option. A Location Map showing the location of the nominated property within the State Party, Plans and specially prepared maps of the nominated property showing individual features are helpful and may also be annexed. To facilitate copying and presentation to the Advisory Bodies and the World Heritage Committee A4 (or "letter") size reduction and a digital image file of the principal maps should also be included in the main text of the nomination dossier if possible. Where no buffer zone is proposed, the main text of the nomination dossier must include a statement as to why a buffer zone is not required for the proper protection of the nominated property.
1.f Area of nominated property (ha.) and proposed buffer zone (ha.) Area of nominated property: _____ ha Buffer zone _____ ha Total _____ ha	In the case of serial nominated properties (see Paragraphs 137-139 of the *Operational Guidelines*), insert a table that shows the name of the component part, region (if different for different components), coordinates, area of each component part and buffer zone. The serial nominated properties table should also be used to show the size of each component part separately and of the buffer zone(s).
2. Description	
2.a Description of nominated property [This section should not exceed 16,000 words (about 50 A4 pages) for a single site nomination or 24,000 words (about 75 A4 pages) for a serial site nomination]	This section should begin with a description of the nominated property at the date of nomination. It should refer to all the significant features of the nominated property. In the case of a cultural nominated property this section will include a description of whatever elements make the nominated property culturally significant. It could include a description of any building or buildings and their architectural style, date of construction, materials, etc. This section should also describe important aspects of the setting such as gardens, parks etc. For a rock art site, for example, the description should refer to the rock art as well as the surrounding landscapes. In the case of an historic town or district, it is not necessary to describe each individual building, but important public buildings should be described individually and an account should be given of the planning or layout of the area, its street pattern and so on. In the case of a natural nominated property this section should deal with important physical attributes, geology, habitats, species and population size, and other significant ecological features and processes. Species lists should be provided where practicable, and the presence of threatened or endemic taxa should be highlighted. The extent and methods of the use of natural resources should be described. In the case of cultural landscapes, it will be necessary to produce a description under all the matters mentioned above. Special attention should be paid to the interaction of people and nature. The entire nominated property identified in section 1 (Identification of the Nominated Property) should be described. In the case of serial nominated properties (see Paragraphs 137-139 of the *Operational Guidelines*), each of the component parts should be separately described.

NOMINATION FORMAT	EXPLANATORY NOTES
2.a Description of nominated property [This section should not ex-ceed 16,000 words (about 50 A4 pages) for a single site nomination or 24,000 words (about 75 A4 pages) for a seri-al site nomination]	This section should contain a list and short description of the main attributes. Nominated properties are required to demonstrate their potential Outstand-ing Universal Value through their attributes. Attributes convey the potential Outstanding Universal Value and enable an understanding of that value. These attributes will be the focus of protection and management actions, and institutional arrangements, and their spatial distribution and respective pro-tection requirements will inform the boundary of the property. Attributes can be physical qualities or fabric, but can also include processes, associated with a property, that impact on physical qualities, such as natural or agricultural processes, social arrangements or cultural practices that have shaped distinctive landscapes. For natural properties they can be specific landscape features, areas of habitat, flagship species, aspects relating to en-vironmental quality (such as intactness, high/pristine environmental quality), scale and naturalness of habitats, and size and viability of wildlife popula-tions.
2.b History and Development [This section should not ex-ceed 6,400 words (about 20 A4 pages)]	The History and Development of the nominated property shall describe how the nominated property has reached its present form and the significant changes that it has undergone. This information shall provide the important facts needed to support and give substance to the argument that the nominat-ed property meets the criteria of Outstanding Universal Value and conditions of integrity and/or authenticity.
3. Justification for Inscription [①]	The justification should be set out under the following sections. This section must make clear why the nominated property is considered to be of "Outstanding Universal Value". The whole of this section of the nomination should be written with careful reference to the requirements of the *Operational Guidelines*. It should not include detailed descriptive material about the nominated property or its management, which are addressed in other sections, but should convey the key aspects that are relevant to the definition of the Outstanding Universal Value of the nominated property.
3.1.a Brief synthesis	The brief synthesis should comprise (i) a summary of factual information and (ii) a summary of qualities. The summary of factual information sets out the geographical and historical context and the main features. The summary of qualities should present to de-cision-makers and the general public the potential Outstanding Universal Value that needs to be sustained, and should also include a summary of the attributes that convey its potential Outstanding Universal Value, and need to be protected, managed and monitored. The summary should relate to all stated criteria in order to justify the nomination. The brief synthesis thus encapsulates the whole ratio-nale for the nomination and proposed inscription.
3.1.b Criteria under which in-scription is proposed (and jus-tification for inscription under these criteria)	See Paragraph 77 of the *Operational Guidelines.* Provide a separate justification for each criterion cited. State briefly how the property meets those criteria under which it has been nominated (where necessary, make reference to the "description" and "com-parative analysis" sections of the nomination, but do not duplicate the text of these sections) and describe for each criterion the relevant attributes.

① See also paragraphs 132 and 133.

NOMINATION FORMAT	EXPLANATORY NOTES
3.1.c Statement of Integrity	The statement of integrity should demonstrate that the nominated property fulfils the conditions of integrity set out in Section Ⅱ.D of the *Operational Guidelines*, which describe these conditions in greater detail. The *Operational Guidelines* set out the need to assess the extent to which the nominated property: ● includes all elements necessary to express its Outstanding Universal Value; ● is of adequate size to ensure the complete representation of the features and processes which convey the property's significance; ● suffers from adverse effects of development and/or neglect (Paragraph 88). The *Operational Guidelines* provide specific guidance in relation to the various World Heritage criteria, which is important to understand (Paragraphs 89–95).
3.1.d Statement of Authenticity (for nominations made under criteria (i) to (vi))	The statement of authenticity should demonstrate that the nominated property fulfils the conditions of authenticity set out in Section Ⅱ.D of the *Operational Guidelines*, which describe these conditions in greater detail. This section should summarise information that may be included in more detail in section 4 of the nomination (and possibly in other sections), and should not reproduce the level of detail included in those sections. Authenticity only applies to cultural properties and to the cultural aspects of 'mixed' properties. The *Operational Guidelines* state that 'properties may be understood to meet the conditions of authenticity if their cultural values (as recognized in the nomination criteria proposed) are truthfully and credibly expressed through a variety of attributes' (Paragraph 82). The *Operational Guidelines* suggest that the following types of attributes might be considered as conveying or expressing Outstanding Universal Value: ● form and design; ● materials and substance; ● use and function; ● traditions, techniques and management systems; ● location and setting; ● language and other forms of intangible heritage; ● spirit and feeling; and ● other internal/external factors.
3.1.e Protection and management requirements	This section should summarise information that may be included in more detail in section 5 of the nomination dossier (and also potentially in sections 4 and 6), and should not reproduce the level of detail included in those sections. This section should set out how the requirements for protection and management will be met, in order to ensure that the Outstanding Universal Value of the nominated property is maintained over time. It should include both details of an overall framework for protection and management, and the identification of specific long-term expectations for the protection of the nominated property. The text in this section should first provide an overview of the protection and management system. This should include the necessary protection mechanisms, management systems and/or management plans (whether currently in place or in need of establishment) that will protect and conserve the attributes that carry Outstanding Universal Value, and address the threats to and vulnerabilities of the nominated property. These could include the presence of strong and effective legal protection, a clearly documented management system, including relationships with key stakeholders or user groups, adequate staff and financial resources, key requirements for presentation (where relevant), and effective and responsive monitoring.

NOMINATION FORMAT	EXPLANATORY NOTES
3.1.e Protection and management requirements	Secondly this section needs to acknowledge any long-term challenges for the protection and management of the nominated property and state how addressing these will be a long-term strategy. It will be relevant to refer to the most significant threats to the nominated property, and to vulnerabilities and negative changes in authenticity and/or integrity that have been highlighted, and to set out how protection and management will address these vulnerabilities and threats and mitigate any adverse changes. As an official statement, recognised by the World Heritage Committee, this section of the Statement of Outstanding Universal Value should convey the most important commitments that the State Party is making for the long-term protection and management of the nominated property.
3.2 Comparative Analysis	The nominated property should be compared to similar properties, whether on the World Heritage List or not. The comparison should outline the similarities the nominated property has with other properties and the reasons that make the nominated property stand out. The comparative analysis should aim to explain the importance of the nominated property both in its national and international context (see Paragraph 132). Comparisons should be made with properties expressing the same values as the nominated property, and within a defined geo-cultural area (cultural properties) or globally (natural properties). The combination of values and attributes on which the comparative analysis is based must match the key aspects that are relevant to the definition of the Outstanding Universal Value of the nominated property conveyed in the rest of section 3. The purpose of the comparative analysis is to show that there is room on the List using existing thematic studies and the gap analysis. In the case of serial nominated properties, text needs to set out the rationale for choosing the component parts, in terms of comparing them with other similar component parts and justifying the choice made. The comparative analysis must conclude by drawing conclusions.
3.3 Draft Statement of Outstanding Universal Value (see annex 10)	A Statement of Outstanding Universal Value is the official statement adopted by the World Heritage Committee at the time of inscription of a property on the World Heritage List. When the World Heritage Committee agrees to inscribe a property on the World Heritage List, it also agrees on a Statement of Outstanding Universal Value that encapsulates why the property is considered to be of Outstanding Universal Value, how it satisfies the relevant criteria, the conditions of integrity and (for cultural properties) authenticity, and how it meets the requirements for protection and management in order to sustain Outstanding Universal Value in the long-term. Statements of Outstanding Universal Value should be concise and are set out in a standard format. They should help to raise awareness regarding the value of the property, guide the assessment of its state of conservation and inform protection and management. Once adopted by the Committee, the Statement of Outstanding Universal Value is displayed at the property and on the UNESCO World Heritage Centre's website. The main sections of a Statement of Outstanding Universal Value are the following: Brief synthesis Justification for Criteria Statement of Integrity (for all properties) Statement of authenticity for properties nominated under criteria (i) to (vi) Requirements for protection and management

NOMINATION FORMAT	EXPLANATORY NOTES
4. State of Conservation and factors affecting the nominated property	
4.a Present state of conservation	The information presented in this section constitutes the base-line data necessary to monitor the state of conservation of the nominated property in the future. Information should be provided in this section on the physical condition of the nominated property, any threats to the potential Outstanding Universal Value of the nominated property and conservation measures in place (see Paragraph 132). The state of conservation of the attributes as identified in section 2.a and 3.1.a. should be described, including attributes which have been lost or whose condition is compromised. For example, in a historic town or area, buildings, monuments or other structures needing major or minor repair works, should be indicated as well as the scale and duration of any recent or forthcoming major repair projects. In the case of a natural nominated property, data on species trends or the integrity of eco-systems should be provided. This is important because the nomination will be used in future years for purposes of comparison to trace changes in the condition of the property. For the indicators and statistical benchmarks used to monitor the state of conservation of the property see section 6 below.
4.b Factors affecting the nominated property	This section should firstly provide information on all the factors which are likely to affect or threaten the Outstanding Universal Value of a nominated property. Secondly, it should describe the proposed management response to those factors that may negatively affect the nominated property. A list of factors that may be relevant is available at https://whc.unesco.org/en/factors/
4.b (i) Development pressures and management response	Describe development pressures affecting the nominated property and the management response to avert impacts on the nominated property's authenticity and/or integrity from factors such as: Buildings and Development (e.g. housing, commercial development, including tourism); Transportation infrastructure (e.g. ground transport, air transport); Utilities or service infrastructure (e.g. renewable and/or non- renewable energy facilities); Biological resource use/modification (e.g. fishing, agriculture, forestry); - Physical resource extraction (e.g. mining, quarrying, oil and gas, water extraction). For more details on these factors, see https://whc.unesco.org/en/factors/
4.b (ii) Environmental pressures, natural disasters and risk preparedness	List and summarize major factors of environmental deterioration and foreseeable natural disasters, such as: Local conditions affecting physical fabric (e.g. wind, humidity, temperature, dust); Invasive/alien species or hyper-abundant species (e.g. translocated species, hyper-abundant species, invasive/alien terrestrial, freshwater and/or marine species); Pollution (e.g. marine, surface and/or ground water pollution); Climate change and severe weather events (e.g. storms, flooding, desertification); Sudden ecological or geological events (e.g. volcanic eruptions, earthquakes, tsunami/tidal wave). For more details on these factors, see https://whc.unesco.org/en/factors/ As applicable, include information on contingency plans.

NOMINATION FORMAT	EXPLANATORY NOTES
4.b (iii) Visitation, other human activities and sustainable use	Provide the status of visitation to the nominated property (notably available baseline data; patterns of use, including concentrations of activity in parts of the nominated property; and activities planned in the future). Describe projected levels of visitation due to inscription or other factors. Define the carrying-capacity of the nominated property and how its management could be enhanced to meet the current or expected visitor numbers and related development pressure without adverse effects. Consider possible forms of deterioration of the nominated property due to visitor pressure and behaviour including those affecting its intangible attributes. Further factors that may be considered as applicable include: Social/cultural uses of heritage (e.g. Ritual/spiritual/religious and associative uses, uses by Indigenous Peoples, changes in traditional ways of life and knowledge system); Other human activities (e.g. illegal activities, deliberate destruction of heritage, war). For more details on these factors, see https://whc.unesco.org/en/factors/
5. Protection and Management of the nominated property	This section of the main text of the nomination dossier is intended to provide a clear picture of the legislative, regulatory, contractual, planning, institutional and/ or traditional measures (see Paragraph 132 of the Operational Guidelines) and the management plan or other management system (Paragraphs 108 to 118 of the Operational Guidelines) that is in place to protect and manage the nominated property as required by the World Heritage Convention. It should deal with policy aspects, legal status and protective measures and with the practicalities of day-to-day administration and management.
5.a Stakeholders	Identify stakeholders, including owners, inhabitants, indigenous peoples and local communities, governmental, non-governmental and private stakeholders and rights-holders, as applicable.
5.a (i) Ownership and inhabitants	Indicate the major categories of land ownership (including State, Provincial, private, community, traditional, customary and non-governmental ownership, etc.), and give the best available statistics or estimate of the number of inhabitants living within the nominated property and any buffer zone(s). Indicate the year this estimate or count was made. Estimated population located within The nominated property____ Year____ The buffer zone____ Year____
5.a (ii) Indigenous Peoples	If the nominated property might affect the lands, territories or resources of indigenous peoples, demonstrate whether their free, prior and informed consent to the nomination has been obtained, through, inter alia, making the nomination publicly available in appropriate languages and public consultations and hearings (Paragraph 123). Demonstrate the extent of consultation and collaboration with indigenous peoples, as applicable, in the management of the nominated property (Paragraphs 111 and 117).
5.a (iii) Participation	Demonstrate the extent of participation in the nomination process of stakeholders and right-holders through, inter alia, making the nomination publicly available in appropriate languages and through public consultations and hearings. Equally demonstrate the extent of consultation and collaboration with stakeholders and right-holders in the management of the nominated property (see Paragraphs 12, 119, 123 and 211).

NOMINATION FORMAT	EXPLANATORY NOTES
5.b Protective designation	List the relevant legal, regulatory, contractual, planning, institutional and/ or traditional status of the nominated property: For example, national or provincial park; historic monument, protected area under national law or custom; or other designation. Provide the year of designation and the legislative act(s) under which the status is provided. If the document cannot be provided in English or French, an English or French executive summary should be provided highlighting the key provisions.
5.c Means of implementing protective measures	Describe how the protection afforded by its legal, regulatory, contractual, planning, institutional and/ or traditional status indicated in section 5.b. actually works.
5.d Existing plans related to municipality and region in which the nominated property is located (e.g., regional or local plan, conservation plan, tourism development plan)	List the agreed plans which have been adopted with the date and agency responsible for preparation. The relevant provisions should be summarized in this section. A copy of the plan should be included as an attached document as indicated in section 7.b. If the plans exist only in a language other than English or French, an English or French executive summary should be provided highlighting the key provisions.
5.e Property management plan or other management system	As noted in Paragraphs 132 of the *Operational Guidelines*, an appropriate management plan or other management system is essential and shall be provided in the nomination. Assurances of the effective implementation of the management plan or other management system are also expected. Sustainable development principles should be integrated into the management system. A copy of the management plan or documentation of the management system shall be annexed to the nomination, in English or French as indicated in section 7.b. If the management plan exists only in a language other than English or French, an English or French detailed description of its provisions shall be annexed. Give the title, date and author of management plans annexed to this nomination. A detailed analysis or explanation of the management plan or a documented management system shall be provided. A timetable for the implementation of the management plan is recommended.
5.f Sources and levels of finance	Show the sources and level of funding which are available to the nominated property on an annual basis. An estimate could also be given of the adequacy or otherwise of resources available, in particular identifying any gaps or deficiencies or any areas where assistance may be required.
5.g Sources of expertise and training in conservation and management techniques	Indicate the expertise and training which are available from national authorities or other organizations to the nominated property.
5.h Visitor facilities and infrastructure	The section should describe the inclusive facilities available on site for visitors and demonstrate that they are appropriate in relation to the protection and management requirements of the nominated property. It should set out how the facilities and services will provide effective and inclusive presentation of the nominated property to meet the needs of visitors, including in relation to the provision of safe and appropriate access to the site. The section should consider visitor facilities that may include interpretation/explanation (signage, trails, notices or publications, guides); museum/exhibition devoted to the nominated property, visitor or interpretation centre; and/or potential use of digital technologies and services (overnight accommodation; restaurant; car parking; lavatories; search and rescue; etc.).

续表

NOMINATION FORMAT	EXPLANATORY NOTES
5.i Policies and programmes related to the presentation and promotion of the nominated property	This section refers to Articles 4 and 5 of the *Convention* regarding the presentation and transmission to future generations of the cultural and natural heritage. States Parties are encouraged to provide information on the policies and programmes for the presentation and promotion of the nominated property.
5.j Staffing levels and expertise (professional, technical, maintenance)	Indicate the skills and qualifications available needed for the good management of the nominated property, including in relation to visitation and future training needs.
6. Monitoring	This section of the nomination is intended to provide the evidence for the state of conservation of the nominated property which can be reviewed and reported on regularly so as to give an indication of trends over time.
6.a Key indicators for measuring state of conservation	List in table form those key indicators that have been chosen as the measure of the state of conservation of the whole nominated property (see section 4.a above). Indicate the periodicity of the review of these indicators and the location where the records are kept. They could be representative of an important aspect of the nominated property and relate as closely as possible to the Statement of Outstanding Universal Value. Where possible they could be expressed numerically and where this is not possible they could be of a kind which can be repeated, for example by taking a photograph from the same point. Examples of good indicators are the: (i) number of species, or population of a keystone species on a natural property; (ii) percentage of buildings requiring major repair in a historic town or district; (iii) number of years estimated to elapse before a major conservation programme is likely to be completed; (iv) stability or degree of movement in a particular building or element of a building; (v) rate at which encroachment of any kind on a property has increased or diminished.

Indicator	Periodicity	Location of Records

NOMINATION FORMAT	EXPLANATORY NOTES
6.b Administrative arrangements for monitoring property	Give the name and contact information of the agency(ies) responsible for the monitoring referenced in 6.a.
6.c Results of previous reporting exercises	List, with a brief summary, earlier reports on the state of conservation of the nominated property and provide extracts and references to published sources (for example, reports submitted in compliance with international agreements and programmes, e.g., Ramsar, MAB).

续表

NOMINATION FORMAT	EXPLANATORY NOTES
7. Documentation	This section of the nomination is the check-list of the documentation which shall be provided to make up a complete nomination.
7.a Photographs and audiovisual image inventory and authorization form	States Parties shall provide a sufficient number of recent images (prints, slides and, where possible, electronic formats, videos and aerial photographs) to give a good general picture of the nominated property. Slides shall be in 35mm format and electronic images in jpg format at a minimum of 300 dpi (dots per inch) resolution. If film material is provided, Beta SP format is recommended for quality assurances. This material shall be accompanied by the image inventory and photograph and audiovisual authorization form as set out below. At least ten photographs that may be used on the public web page illustrating the nominated property shall be included. States Parties are encouraged to grant to UNESCO, in written form and free of charge, the non exclusive cession of rights to diffuse, to communicate to the public, to publish, to reproduce, to exploit, in any form and on any support, including digital, all or part of the images provided and license these rights to third parties. The non exclusive cession of rights does not impinge upon intellectual property rights (rights of the photographer / director of the video or copyright owner if different) and that when the images are distributed by UNESCO a credit to the photographer / director of the video is always given, if clearly provided in the form. All possible profits deriving from such cession of rights will go to the World Heritage Fund.

PHOTOGRAPHS AND AUDIOVISUAL IMAGE INVENTORY AND AUTHORIZATION FORM

Id. No	Format (slide/ print/ video)	Caption	Date of Photo (mo/yr)	Photographer/ Director of the video	Copyright owner (if different than photographer/ director of video)	Contact details of copyright owner (Name, address, tel/fax, and e-mail)	Non exclusive cession of rights [(Yes/ No -see Annex 5, Section 7a, of the *Operational Guidelines*)]

NOMINATION FORMAT	EXPLANATORY NOTES
7.b Texts relating to protective designation, copies of property management plans or documented management systems and extracts of other plans relevant to the nominated property	Attach the texts as indicated in sections 5.b, 5.d and 5.e above.

续表

NOMINATION FORMAT	EXPLANATORY NOTES
7.c Form and date of most recent records or inventory of the nominated property	Provide a straightforward statement giving the form and date of the most recent records or inventory of the nominated property. Only records that are still available should be described.
7.d Address where inventory, records and archives are held	Give the name and address of the agencies holding inventory records (buildings, monuments, flora or fauna species).
7.e Bibliography	List the principal published references, using standard bibliographic format.
8. Contact Information of responsible authorities	This section of the nomination will allow the Secretariat to provide the property with current information about World Heritage news and other issues.
8.a Preparer Name: Title: Address: City, Province/State, Country: Tel: Fax: E-mail:	Provide the name, address and other contact information of the individual responsible for preparing the nomination, including an e-mail address.
8.b Official Local Institution/Agency	Provide the name of the agency, museum, institution, community or manager locally responsible for the management of the nominated property. If the normal reporting institution is a national agency, provide that contact information.
8.c Other Local Institutions	List the full name, address, telephone, fax and e-mail addresses of all museums, visitor centres and official tourism offices who should receive the free *World Heritage Newsletter* about events and issues related to World Heritage.
8.d Official Website http:// Contact name: E-mail:	Provide any existing official website of the nominated property. Indicate if such websites are planned for the future with the contact name and e-mail address.
9. Signature on behalf of the State Party	The nomination should conclude with the signature of the official empowered to sign it on behalf of the State Party.

附件 5 提交《世界遗产名录》遗产申报材料格式

提交所有申遗文本均须遵循此格式

- 登录以下网址可获取本申报材料格式：http://whc.unesco.org/en/nominationform
- 有关申报材料编写的更多指导请参见《操作指南》的第三部分
- 按完整申报格式编写的英文或法文原件签字后发送至以下地址：

联合国教科文组织世界遗产中心

法国巴黎（7，place de Fontenoy 75352 Paris 07 SP France）

电话：+33（0）1 4568 1136

电邮：wh–nominations@unesco.org

执行摘要

以下信息由缔约国提供，由秘书处根据世界遗产委员会的决定进行更新。之后将返还给缔约国，作为确认遗产列入《世界遗产名录》的依据。

缔约国	
州、省份或地区	
遗产名称	
精确到秒的地理坐标	
遗产申报保护范围的文字说明	
A4 或 A3 纸大小的申报遗产地图，显示遗产保护范围和缓冲区（如果有）	附 A4 或 A3 纸大小的缩小版遗产地形图或测绘图。该图应以尽可能大的规模囊括遗产区及缓冲区（如果存在），并将其包含在申报文本或附件中。
遗产申报遵循的标准（列举标准）（见《操作指南》第 77 段）	
文化景观	说明遗产是否作为文化景观申报（是）或（否）（见 47，47 补充及 47 再补充）
《突出的普遍价值声明》草案	根据第 155 条，《突出普遍价值声明》应包含：
（正文应说明申报遗产所包含的突出普遍价值，约 1–2 页篇幅）	1）简要综述 2）符合标准的理由 3）完整性声明（适用所有遗产） 4）真实性声明（适用按照标准 i–vi 条申报的遗产） 5）保护和管理要求 见附件 10 中的格式
当地官方机构的名称和联系方式	机构： 地址： 电话： 传真： 电邮： 网址：

申报列入《世界遗产名录》的遗产

注：准备申报材料时，各缔约国应该使用本格式，但应将填报须知删掉。

申报材料格式	填报须知
1. 遗产的辨认	本部分和下面的第 2 部分是申报材料中最重要的内容，必须向委员会准确说明遗产的位置和地理界限。如果是系列申报，插入一个表格，说明各组成部分的名称、所处地域 (如果不同部分处于不同地域)、坐标、面积和缓冲区。也可列示其他表栏项目 (页码说明或地图编号) 以区别不同部分。
1.a 国家如果有不同的缔约国	
1.b 州、省份或地区	
1.c 申报遗产名称	为该遗产出现在世界遗产出版物上的正式名称，应该简洁，不超过 200 个字符，包括空格和标点符号。如果是系列申报 (见《操作指南》的第 137–139 段)，为整体命名 (比如，菲律宾巴洛克大教堂)。无需说明系列申报内各部分的名称，这些名称应该包括在 1.d 和 1.f 的表格内。
1.d 精确到秒的地理坐标	在此处提供申报遗产的中心纬度和经度坐标 (精确到秒)，或通用横轴墨卡托坐标 (精确到 10 米) 不要用其他坐标体系。如有疑问，请咨询秘书处。 如果是系列申报，列表说明各遗产的名称、地域 (或最近的城镇)、遗产中心点的坐标。坐标格式如下： 北纬 45° 06' 05"　　西经 15° 37' 56" 或者 UTM 区 18　　东：^{5}45670 北：^{45}86750

编号	组成部分名称	地区 / 城区	中心点坐标	申报部分面积（公顷）	缓冲区面积（ha）	地图编号
001						
002						
003						
……						
总面积（公顷）					公顷	公顷

申报材料格式	填报须知
1.e 地图和平面图，显示申报遗产和缓冲区的范围	附在申报材料后，标上比例和日期： (i) 申报遗产的地形图原件，尽可能用最大的比例显示整个遗产。应明确标明申报遗产及缓冲区的范围。可在此图或其他地图上标示有利于遗产保护的特殊法定保护区范围。系列申报可能需要多张地图 (见 1.d 中表格)。提供的地图比例应尽可能大和实用，以清晰辨认如周边聚落、建筑和道路等地形要素，以对遗产范围内、或邻近、或位于遗产边界上的开发计划对遗产地的影响，有清晰的评估。 适当比例的地图必须包括清晰的遗产边界线并与计划要申报的遗产类别相关：文化遗产应有地籍图，自然遗产或文化景观需要地形图 (一般比例为 1∶25000 至 1∶50000) 对地图上的边界线条的宽度需谨慎处理，因为使用粗线条或会导致对遗产地边界的辨认模糊。 登录以下网址，可获取地图：http://whc.unesco.org/en/mapagencies

续表

申报材料格式	填报须知
1.e 地图和平面图，显示申报遗产和缓冲区的范围	如果没有合适比例的地形图，可以用其他地图代替。所有的地图都必须能够进行地理参照，地图上必须至少有三个点，点点相对，每个点都有完整的坐标。地图不能缩减，应该显示比例、方位、投影、数据、遗产名称和日期。如果可能，递送地图时应将其卷起，而不是折叠。 如果可能，建议提供数字地理信息，便于纳入 GIS（地理信息系统）。在这种情况下，范围的划分（申报遗产和缓冲区）应以向量的形式提供，以尽可能大的比例编制。相关详情缔约国可联系秘书处。 (ii) 一张位置图，显示该遗产在缔约国的位置。 (iii) 展示遗产各项特征的平面图和特殊地图也很有帮助，可以随附于申报材料后面。 为了便于向咨询机构和世界遗产中心抄送和呈报，如果可能，A4 纸（或"信纸"）大小的缩图和主要地图的电子图像文件，应该包括在申报材料之中。 如果没有划分缓冲区，申报材料必须说明为什么申报遗产的适当保护不需要缓冲区。
1.f 申报遗产和提议的缓冲区的面积（公顷） 申报遗产的面积：＿＿公顷 缓冲区＿＿＿＿公顷 共 ＿＿＿＿＿＿公顷	如果是系列申报（见《操作指南》第 137-140 条），插入一张表格，显示组成部分的名称、所处地域（如果不同部分处于不同地域）、坐标、面积和缓冲区该系列申报表还应显示各个申报区域及其缓冲区的大小。
2. 描述	
2.a 遗产描述 [本部分如为独立遗产申报，不超过 16000 字词（A4 纸 约 50 页 ），如为系列申报不超过 24000 字词（A4 纸 约 75 页 ）。]	本部分首先描述申报时遗产的情况，应涉及该项遗产的各项显著特征。如果是文化遗产，本部分应该描述使该项遗产在文化方面具有重要意义的任何因素。可描述某个或多个建筑，其建筑风格、建筑日期及所用材料等。还可以描述重要环境因素，如花园、公园等。比如，对某岩画遗址来说，描述内容既应包括岩画本身，还应包括其周围的景观。如果是历史名城或历史街区，没有必要描述每座建筑单体，但是应逐个描述重要的公共建筑，及该地区的规划和布局，街巷格局等等。 如果是自然遗产，应该说明重要的物理属性、地质情况、栖息地、物种及种群数量、其他重要的生态特征和进程。应尽可能提供物种列表，并突出濒危物种或地方特有的生物分类。应该描述自然资源开发的程度和方法。 如果是文化景观，有必要描述上文所提的各项内容。应特别关注人与自然之间的关系。 应该描述第 1 部分 (遗产的辨认) 说明的整个申报遗产。如果是系列申报 (见《操作指南》第 137-139 段)，应单独描述遗产的各组成部分。 此次应插入一个清单显示主要特征及其简短说明。 申报遗产需要通过特征来展示其潜在的突出的普遍价值。 特征既传达了潜在的突出普遍价值，又能使人们能够理解这种价值。这些特征将是保护和管理行动的重点，也是制度安排、它们的空间分布和各自的保护要求、遗产边界等信息的重点。特征可以是物理特性或构造，但也可以是包括与属性相关的、影响物理特性的过程，如形成了独特的景观的自然或农业过程，社会安排或文化实践。就自然遗产而言，可以是特定的景观特征、栖息地的面积、主要物种、与环境质量有关的方面 (如完整性、高品质 / 原始环境质量)、栖息地的规模和自然性，以及野生动物种群的规模和生存能力。
2.b 历史沿革 [此处不超过 6400 字词（A4 约 20 页)]	描述该项遗产的发展和历史，说明其如何发展到今天的形式和状态，经历了什么样的重大变化。 应提供所需的重要事实，作为支持申报遗产符合突出普遍价值的标准、满足完整性和真实性的条件的论据。

续表

申报材料格式	填报须知
3. 列入理由①	理由陈述应按照以下顺序。 这部分必须明确，为什么认为遗产具有"突出的普遍价值"。 本部分遗产的描述应该严格参考《操作指南》中的相关要求。不应该包括详细的、描述性遗产情况说明和遗产的管理情况说明，这些内容在其他部分提供，这部分应该着重传达与遗产突出普遍价值相关的各方面关键信息。
3.1.a 简要综述	简要综述应包含 (1) 事实性信息概述；(2) 品质概述。事实性信息总结列出遗产地理和历史背景及主要特征。品质概述应向决策者和公众展示遗产需要被维持的潜在的突出普遍价值，也应包括体现其突出普遍价值、并因此需要得到妥善保护管理和监测的价值载体的概述。这部分应结合所有依据的标准以解释申报理由。因此简要概述是遗产申报和建议列入的全部原理阐述的浓缩。
3.1.b 提议遗产列入所依据的标准（和根据这些标准的列入理由）	见《操作指南》第 77 条。 分别说明引用每个标准的理由。 简述该项遗产如何满足申报标准，（如有必要，参考"描述"和"比较分析部分，但不是照抄这些部分的文字内容），并描述符合每项标准的相关价值载体。
3.1.c 完整性声明	完整性声明应证实该项遗产满足《操作指南》第 Ⅱ.D 部分列出的完整性条件，《操作指南》详细描述了这些条件。 《操作指南》列出了对遗产符合以下各项的程度进行评估的必要： – 包含表现遗产突出普遍价值所需的所有要素 – 规模范围足够大，以确保完全传递遗产重要性的所有特征和过程 – 遭受开发和 / 或废弃带来的负面影响（第 88 条） 《操作指南》提供了对应不同世界遗产标准的具体指导，理解这一点很重要（89–95 条）
3.1.d 真实性声明（适用于建议根据标准 i–vi 列入的遗产申报）	真实性声明应证实该项遗产满足《操作指南》第二.D 部分列出的真实性条件，《操作指南》详细描述了这些条件。 这部分应简要总结申遗文本第四部分（也可能其他部分）详述的一些内容，但详略程度不应和其他章节重复。 真实性仅适用于文化遗产和混合遗产中的文化部分。 《操作指南》指出："如果遗产的文化价值（申报标准所认可的）通过多个载体得到真实可信的表现，则被认为符合真实性条件"（见第 82 段）。 根据《操作指南》，以下类型载体可被认为传递或表现突出普遍价值： – 外形和设计 – 材料和质地 – 用途和功能 – 传统、技术和管理体系 – 环境和位置 – 语言和其他形式的非物质遗产 – 精神和感觉 – 其他内外因素
3.1.e 保护和管理要求	这部分应简要总结申报文本第五部分（也可能在第四和第六部分）详述的一些内容，但详略程度不应和其他章节重复。 这部分应包含如何达到了保护管理的各项要求，从而确保遗产的突出普遍价值得到长期的维持。内容应包括对保护管理整体框架体系的详细描述，和对遗产管理长期具体的目标的明确。 本部分文字应首先概述保护管理框架。其中包括保护遗产突出普遍价值载体和应对威胁和自身脆弱性的必要的保护机制、管理体系和 / 或管理规划（已存在或尚需制定）。具体包括健全有效的法律保护、记录明晰的管理体系，与主要利益相关方使用群体的必要沟通，足够的人员和财政资源，符合展示要求，有效和有针对性的监测等。

---

① 见第 132 和 133 条。

申报材料格式	填报须知
3.1.e 保护和管理要求	此外，这部分需要告知遗产保护管理面临的任何长期挑战以及应对这些挑战的长期战略。有必要提到对遗产最大的威胁因素，其真实性和 / 或完整性中发现的脆弱性和负面变化，并列出保护管理措施将如何针对这些威胁，减小负面影响。 作为受世界遗产委员会认可的官方声明，突出普遍价值声明部分将重申缔约国为遗产的长期保护和管理所做出的最重要的承诺。
3.2 比较分析	该项遗产应与类似遗产 (无论是否列入《世界遗产名录》) 进行比较。比较时应该概述该项遗产与其他遗产之间的类似点，说明该项遗产之所以突出的原因。比较分析旨在解释申报遗产在本国及在国际上的重要性。(见第 132 条) 用来进行比较分析的遗产，应该与申报遗产具有相同价值、处于相同的地理文化区域内（文化遗产）或全球范围（自然遗产）。比较分析所依据的价值和属性，必须符合相关申报遗产的突出普遍价值定义、第 3 节其余部分所传达关键内容。 比较分析的目的在于通过现有专题研究和差距分析主题研究，确定名录的空白，显示其列入名录的合理性。 在申报系列遗产的情况下，文本需要阐述选择各组成部分的理由，将它们与其他类似组成部分进行比较以证明选择的合理性。 比较分析必须得出结论。
3.3《突出普遍价值声明》草案（见附件 10）	《突出普遍价值声明》是世界遗产委员会在遗产列入名录时通过的官方声明。世界遗产委员会同意将某项遗产列入《世界遗产名录》，就意味着认可其声明集中解释了为何该遗产被认为具有突出普遍价值，它如何符合了相关标准、完整性和（对文化遗产来说）真实性，以及它满足了确保突出普遍价值得以长期保存的保护管理条件。 《突出普遍价值声明》应力求简明，并遵循标准格式。应有助于提高对遗产价值的公众认识，指导现状评估和保护管理。一经委员会通过，该声明将在遗产地和联合国教科文世界遗产中心网站上公布。 《突出普遍价值声明》主要包含以下章节： 1）简要综述 2）符合标准的理由 3）完整性声明（所有遗产） 4）真实性声明（按照标准 i–vi 申报的遗产） 5）保护和管理要求
4. 保护情况和影响遗产的因素	
4.a 保护现状	本部分信息是在未来监测所申报遗产保护情况的基线数据。本部分内容应包括：该项遗产的自然条件、其突出的普遍价值面临的威胁和采取的保护措施（见第 132 条）。应描述第 2.a 和 3.1.a. 定义的保护状况的特征，包括已经消失或正在变坏的。 比如，应该指出历史城镇或区域内的建筑、古迹或其他构筑物所需的大小修缮工作，以及近期主要修缮项目的规模和持续时间。 如果是自然遗产申报，应该提供物种演化趋势或生态系统完整性的数据。这很重要，因为在未来几年，对比并跟踪遗产状态变化时，会用到这些申报材料。 至于监测遗产保护情况的指标和统计基准，请参见下文第 6 部分。
4.b 影响申报遗产的因素	本部分应说明可能影响或威胁遗产突出普遍价值的所有因素。还应该说明在解决这些问题时会面临的困难。相关因素的清单可登录：https://whc.unesco.org/en/factors/

申报材料格式	填报须知
(i) 开发压力及管理应对	列举影响申报遗产的开发压力，以及对下列影响申报遗产的真实性和 / 或完整性的因素，管理层的应对措施： – 建设和开发（例如，住宅，商业开发，旅游开发）； – 交通设施（例如：地面运输，空中运输）； – 公共设施和服务设施（可再生及 / 或不可再生能源设施）； 生物资源的利用 / 改造（例如渔业、农业、林业） – 资源开采（如采矿、采石、石油和天然气、水开采）。 有关这些因素的更多详细信息，请参见 https://whc.unesco.org/en/factors/ ）
(ii) 环境压力，自然灾害及风险防范	列出和总结环境恶化的主要因素和可预见的自然灾害，如 – 影响物理结构的当地条件（如风、湿度、温度、灰尘）； – 入侵 / 外来物种或超丰富物种（例如迁移物种、泛滥物种、入侵 / 外来陆地、淡水和 / 或海洋物种） – 污染（例如海洋、地表和 / 或地下水污染）； – 气候变化和严重天气事件（如风暴、洪水、荒漠化）； – 突发的生态或地质事件（例如火山爆发、地震、海啸 / 海啸） 有关这些因素的更多详细信息，请参见 https://whc.unesco.org/en/factors/ 如适用，提供关于应急计划的信息。
(iii) 旅游，其他人类活动和可持续利用	提供遗产地参观情况的信息（尤其是现有的基线数据；遗产地的使用格局包括各部分活动的分布情况等；以及未来规划的活动等）。预测列入世界遗产名录或其他因素带来的参观人数水平的变化。确定遗产的"承载力"，以及如何改善管理，使其能够接纳当前或预期的参观者、应对开发压力而不产生负面影响。考虑由于游客的压力和行为（包括那些影响其无形属性的行为）而可能导致申报遗产恶化的形式。可考虑的其他适用因素包括： – 遗产的社会 / 文化用途（例如仪式 / 精神 / 宗教等综合用途、原住民的使用、传统生活方式和知识系统的改变）； – 其他人类活动（如非法活动、蓄意破坏遗产、战争等） 相关因素的详细信息，可登录：https://whc.unesco.org/en/factors/
5. 申报遗产的保护管理	申遗文本正文的这一节旨在明晰对立法、监管、合同、规划、根据《世界遗产公约》的要求，为保护和管理申报遗产而采取的方法和 / 或传统措施（见《操作指南》第 132 条）以及管理计划或其他管理制度（《操作指南》第 108 至 118 条）。它应涉及政策方面、法律地位和保护措施以及日常行政和管理的实际情况。
5.a 利益相关者	确定利益相关者，包括业主、居民、原住民和当地社区、政府、非政府和私人利益相关者和持有人（如适用）。
(i) 所有权和居民	说明土地所有权的主要类别（包括国家所有权、省所有权、私人所有权、社区所有权、传统所有权、习惯所有权和非政府所有权等），并统计居住在申报遗产和任何缓冲区内的居民人数，提供现有的最佳统计数字或估计数。 说明作出这项统计或计算的年份。 区域内的估计人口： 申报遗产区＿＿＿＿＿＿　年份＿＿＿＿＿＿＿＿ 缓冲区＿＿＿＿＿＿　年份＿＿＿＿＿＿＿＿
(ii) 原住民	如果申报遗产可能影响原住民的土地、领土或资源，说明是否已通过适当语言公开信息、并进行公众磋商和听证会(第 123 条)，使申报已获得他们自愿、事先和知情地同意。说明在适当情况下与原住民在申报遗产的管理方面进行协商和合作的程度（第 111 和 117 条）。

续表

申报材料格式	填报须知
(iii) 参与	通过以适当语言公开信息以及通过公众磋商和听证会，展示利益相关者和权利持有人参与申报过程的程度。 同样说明在管理申报遗产方面与利益相关者和权利人的协商和合作的程度（见第 12、119、123 和 211 条）。
5.b 保护地位	列出遗产相关的法律、法规、契约、规划、制度和 / 或传统地位，比如，国家或省级公园；依据国家法律或习俗确立的历史古迹、保护区以及其他保护身份。 说明保护身份宣布及规定遗产地位的法律文件的年份。 如果文件所用语言不是英语或法语，应提供一份英语或法语的执行摘要，说明文件内容要点。
5.c 保护措施执行手段	描述第 5.b. 条所列法律、法规、契约、规划、制度和 / 或传统地位提供的保护的具体生效方式。
5.d 申报遗产所在市或地区的现有规划（比如，地区或地方规划、保护、旅游开发规划）	列出通过的各种规划，标出制定日期和负责机构。其重要条款应在本部分概述。规划副本应作为附件（如第 7.b. 条所示）附后。 如果规划所用语言既非英语也非法语，应提供一份英语或法语的执行摘要，说明其内容要点。
5.e 遗产管理规划或其他管理制度	如《操作指南》第 132 条所示，一份适宜的管理规划或其他管理制度必不可少，应该收录在申报材料内。最好也能提供该管理规划或其他管理制度有效实施的保证。可持续发展的原则也应纳入管理体系中。 如第 7.b. 条所示，英语或法语文本的管理规划或者管理制度文件应附在申报材料之后。 如果管理规划所用语言既非英语也非法语，应提供英语或法语的规划条款详述，附在申报材料之后。提供管理规划（附在申报材料后）的名称、日期和作者。 应提供该管理规划或成文管理制度的详细分析或说明。 建议提供管理规划实施时间表。
5.f 资金来源和水平	说明遗产每年的资金来源和水平。还应该估计可用资金是否充足，特别要确认缺口、差额或其他需要援助的领域。
5.g 专业知识来源和保护与管理技术的培训	指出国家当局或其他组织提供的、有关遗产的专业知识和培训。
5.h 旅游基础设施	本部分应描述遗产地现有参观设施，并说明符合保护管理要求。应具体列出这些设施和服务如何能够为遗产地提供有效展示，满足游客需要，包括提供安全、适当的到达和进入遗产地的形式。本部分的考虑范围包括阐释与说明（指示牌、路径设置、通知公告或出版物、导游讲解等）；博物馆 / 展览，参观或展陈中心；和 / 或利用数码技术的可能性和其他服务（住宿、餐饮、停车、洗手间、救援等）
5.i 遗产展示和宣传相关的政策和方案	本部分援引《公约》的第 4 条和第 5 条，这两条阐述了文化及自然遗产的展示和传承事宜。鼓励缔约国提供申报遗产的展示和宣传政策及方案信息。
5.j 人员和专业配置（专业、技术、维修）	说明良好的遗产地管理者所需的技能和资质，包括与参观有关的人员，以及未来培训的需求。
6. 监测	申遗文本的本部分，旨在提供证据，证明该申报遗产的保护状况，以便定期审查和报告，显示遗产随时间发生变化的趋势。

申报材料格式	填报须知
6.a 衡量保护状况的主要指标	以表格形式列出用于衡量整个遗产保护情况的主要指标 (见上文第 4.a 条)。指出审查这些指标的周期，以及记录保存地点。这些指标可代表遗产的某个重要方面，并尽可能地与《突出普遍价值声明》挂钩 (见上文第 2.b 条)。如果可能，用数字标示，不能用数字的话，以可重复的方式表现，比如，在同一地点拍照。有效指标的实例有： (i) 自然遗产内物种种类或主要物种种群的数目； (ii) 历史城镇或历史街区内需要大规模修缮的建筑的比例； (iii) 估计完成主要保护方案需要的时间； (iv) 某个建筑或建筑要素的稳定性或活动程度； (v) 对遗产侵蚀的消长速度。
6.b 监测遗产的行政安排	负责监测 (如第 6.a 条所示) 的机构名称和联系方式。
6.c 以前报告实践的结果	列出以前的遗产保护状况报告，并进行简要总结，提供报告摘要和参考文献 (比如，根据国际协议和方案，如《拉姆萨湿地公约》,《人与生物圈计划》提交的报告)。
7. 文献	本部分列出了完备的申报材料所需的文献。
7.a 照片、视听影像清单和授权表	缔约国应提供充足的近期影像 (照片、幻灯片，如果可能的话，还可提供电子格式、录像和航拍照片)，以便对该遗产有个清晰的整体印象。 幻灯片应为 35mm 格式，电子图像是 jpg 格式，其分辨率不应低于 300dpi (每英寸点数)。如果有影像材料，为确保质量，建议使用 Beta SP 格式。 这类材料应配有影像清单和照片，以及下文列出的视听材料授权表。 至少有一张照片可用于公共网页，说明该遗产应被列为世界遗产。 鼓励缔约国以书面形式，免费向教科文组织非排他性地转让传播、公示、出版、复制及利用 (以各种方式，基于各种手段，包括数字形式) 全部或部分图像的权利，并准予教科文组织将这些权利授予第三方。 上述权利转让不得侵犯知识产权 (摄影师 / 录像导演以及其他所有人的权利)，另外，教科文组织在发行图像时，如果表格中有明确的说明，教科文组织一定会提供摄影师 / 录像导演的姓名。 此类权利转让所产生的所有收益将纳入世界遗产基金。

指标	周期	记录保存地点

照片、图像视听材料清单及授权表

(i) 编号	格式（幻灯片 / 印制品 / 录像）	图片说明	照片日期（年 / 月）	摄影师 / 录像导演	版权所有人（如果不是摄像师 / 导演）	版权所有人的详细联系信息（姓名、地址、电话 / 传真和电邮）	非排他性权利转让（是 / 否—见《操作指南》附件 5 第 7a 条）

申报材料格式	填报须知
7.b 与保护地位、遗产管理规划或成文管理制度相关的正式文件、其他遗产规划摘要	将上文第 5.b，5.d 和 5.e 条所示文件的正文附后。
7.c 遗产近期记录或列表的格式和日期	明确阐述遗产近期记录或列表的格式和日期。仅涉及手头现有的记录。
7.d 记录和档案保存地址	提供保存列表记录（建筑、古迹、动植物种群）的机构名称和地址。
7.e 参考文献	列出主要的出版参考文献，用标准的参考文献格式。
8. 负责机构的联系方式	秘书处可通过该联系方式，将世界遗产的最新消息和其他相关事宜通知给遗产负责机构。
8.a 编纂人员 名字： 职称（头衔）：___ 地址： 国家、州 / 省、市：___ 电话： 传真： 电子邮件：___	提供申报材料编纂人员的名称、地址、电子邮箱和其他联系信息。
8.b 地方官方机关 / 机构	提供负责遗产管理的地方机构、博物馆、组织、社区或管理人员的名称。如果常规报告提供组织是国家机关，请提供该国家机关的联系方式。
8.c 其他地方机构	列出应接收免费《世界遗产时事通讯》（讨论关于世界遗产的事件和议题）的所有博物馆、游客中心和官方旅游办公室的全称、地址、电话、传真和电子邮件地址。
8.d 官方网站 http:// 联系人姓名： 电子邮件：	请提供申报遗产的现有官方网站。说明今后是否计划设立该类网站，并提供联系人姓名和电子邮件地址。
9. 缔约国代表签名	申报材料末尾应由缔约国的正式授权代表签字。

United Nations
Educational, Scientific and
Cultural Organization

World
Heritage
Convention

PROCEDURES OF THE ADVISORY BODIES FOR PRELIMINARY ASSESSMENTS AND THE EVALUATION OF NOMINATIONS

This Annex includes:

A. THE JOINT ICOMOS/IUCN PROCEDURE FOR PRELIMINARY ASSESSMENT OF POTENTIAL NOMINATED PROPERTIES
B. THE ICOMOS PROCEDURE FOR THE EVALUATION OF CULTURAL PROPERTIES
C. THE IUCN PROCEDURE FOR THE EVALUATION OF NATURAL PROPERTIES
D. ADVISORY BODY COLLABORATION PROCEDURE FOR THE EVALUATION OF CULTURAL AND NATURAL PROPERTIES AND OF CULTURAL LANDSCAPES

For further information please also refer to Paragraphs 122, 143-151 of the *Operational Guidelines*.

A. THE JOINT ICOMOS/IUCN PROCEDURE FOR PRELIMINARY ASSESSMENT OF POTENTIAL NOMINATED PROPERTIES

The below paragraphs outline agreed procedures of ICOMOS and IUCN to undertake Preliminary Assessments of potential nominated properties (Preliminary Assessments), based on requests (Preliminary Assessment requests) made by the relevant State(s) Party(ies).

附件6　咨询机构对申报材料的初步评估及评估程序

本附件包括：

A. 国际古迹遗址理事会和世界自然保护联盟联合对潜在申报遗产的初步评估程序

B. 国际古迹遗址理事会的文化遗产评估程序

C. 世界自然保护联盟的自然遗产评估程序

D. 咨询机构对文化和自然遗产及文化景观的合作评估程序

了解更多信息，请参阅《操作指南》第143-151条。

A. 国际古迹遗址理事会和世界自然保护联盟联合对潜在申报遗产的初步评估程序

以下各段概述了国际古迹遗址理事会和世界自然保护联盟商定的、对相关缔约国提出的潜在申报遗产评估申请(初步评估)的程序。

In undertaking Preliminary Assessments, ICOMOS (the International Council of Monuments and Sites) and IUCN (International Union for Conservation of Nature) are guided by the *Operational Guidelines* (see Paragraph 122).

Preliminary Assessments will be undertaken by ICOMOS and IUCN on a joint basis whenever relevant, and will be an independent desk review, which will include consultation with expert reviewers.

Once Preliminary Assessment requests from States Parties have been checked for completeness by the UNESCO World Heritage Centre, the requests that are deemed as complete are delivered to ICOMOS and IUCN. From this point, dialogue and consultation with the relevant States Parties may begin and will continue throughout the assessment process.

Preliminary Assessments aim to both support efficient work to develop successful nominations, and to avoid situations where nominations that are unlikely to be successful proceed further.

The ICOMOS/IUCN assessment process involves the following stages:

1. Data Assembly

Following receipt of the Preliminary Assessment requests from the World Heritage Centre, a standardised analysis is compiled on the potential nominated property using ICOMOS and IUCN thematic studies, ICOMOS Filling the gaps study, the World Database on Protected Areas and other IUCN global databases as relevant. This may include additional literature and advice provided concerning the potential nominated property, or concerning

在进行初步评估时，国际古迹遗址理事会和世界自然保护联盟以《操作指南》(见第 122 条) 为指导。

初步评估将由国际古迹遗址理事会和世界自然保护联盟联合进行，但分别进行独立的书面审查，其中将包括与专家审查人员协商。

联合国教科文组织世界遗产中心将检查缔约国的初步评估请求的完整性，并将完整的请求提交给国际古迹遗址理事会和世界自然保护联盟。从这一点起，将在整个评估过程中继续保持与相关缔约国的对话和协商。

初步评估的目的是既支持有效的工作，获得成功的申报，又避免为不太可能成功的申报付出更多。

国际古迹遗址理事会和的世界自然保护联盟的评估过程涉及以下几个阶段：

1. 收集数据

在收到世界遗产中心的初步评估请求后，我们利用国际古迹遗址理事会和的世界自然保护联盟专题研究、国际古迹遗址理事会填补空白研究、世界保护区数据库和世界自然保护联盟其他相关的全球数据库，对潜在申报遗产进行标准化分析。这部分工作可能包括国际援助和上游程序机制提供的、关于潜在申报遗产或预备名录的参考文献和咨询意见。

Tentative Lists, through the International Assistance and Upstream process mechanisms.

2. Exchange with States Parties

The Advisory Bodies will review the requests received, check the information provided and wherever necessary, will request additional information from the State(s) Party(ies), which should be submitted to the Secretariat. This may involve letters, face-to face meetings, teleconferences or other forms of communication as agreed between the Advisory Body(ies) and the State(s) Party(ies) concerned. In all assessments there will be dialogue between the Advisory Bodies and the concerned State(s) Party(ies) to agree on the process of exchange, and to ensure full and effective feedback of conclusions.

3. Desk Reviews

Preliminary Assessments are conducted exclusively on a desk review basis, focused in particular on the potential justification of Outstanding Universal Value, and related questions of authenticity and integrity. They do not focus in depth on protection and management issues of the potential nominated properties unless major issues have become evident at this early stage of analysis. There is no possibility for any field mission to take place in the framework of a Preliminary Assessment.

Each Preliminary Assessment involves the input of a range of experts who are knowledgeable about the site in its geo-cultural and ecological context and who advise on the potential of the site to justify Outstanding Universal Value and to achieve the development of a robust World Heritage nomination dossier.

2. 与缔约国交流

咨询机构将审查收到的申请，检查提供的信息，必要时，要求缔约国经由秘书处提供更多的信息。交流可能包括信函、面对面会谈、电话会议或咨询机构与有关缔约国之间商定的其他通信形式。在所有评估中，咨询机构和相缔约国之间将进行对话，商定交流进程，并确保对结论作出充分和有效的反馈。

3. 书面评估

初步评估只在书面评估的基础上进行，特别关注证明潜在突出普遍价值，以及真实性和完整性的相关问题。除非在分析的早期阶段已明显发现重大问题，否则它们不会深入探讨潜在申报遗产的保护和管理问题。在初步评估的框架内不可能进行任何现场考察。

每项初步评估都需要一系列专家的参与，这些专家了解该遗址的地理、文化和生态背景，并根据该遗址的潜力提出建议，以证明其突出普遍价值，并制定一份完善的世界遗产申报材料。

The experts are specialists identified within the membership of ICOMOS, its National and International Scientific Committees, and within IUCN Commissions and Members and IUCN Regional Offices. Experts may also be identified by ICOMOS and IUCN within other specialist networks or institutions, universities and research institutes.

这些专家是从国际古迹遗址理事会各国家和国际科学委员会、世界自然保护联盟委员会和成员以及世界自然保护联盟区域办事处的成员中选择的专家。专家也可由国际古迹遗址理事会和世界自然保护联盟从其他专家网络或机构、大学和研究机构中选择。

The assessment may include consultation with local NGOs, communities, indigenous peoples and other interested parties in the potential nominated property and/or coordination with other international conservation instruments.

评估包括与申报遗产地的当地非政府组织、社区、原住民和其他利益相关者协商和／或与其他国际保护文件协调。

4. Review by the ICOMOS/IUCN Panel for Preliminary Assessment of Potential Nominated Properties

4. 国际古迹遗址理事会和世界自然保护联盟联合小组审查潜在申报遗产的初步评估

The joint ICOMOS/IUCN Panel comprises individuals appointed by ICOMOS and IUCN from their networks who collectively possess a wide range of relevant cultural and natural heritage skills and experience, having regard to gender and regional balance. Some of these members serve on the Panel for a fixed term while others are appointed for one year only according to the characteristics of the potential nominated properties to be examined in a particular year.

国际古迹遗址理事会和世界自然保护联盟联合评估小组成员，在考虑到性别和区域平衡的情况下，由国际古迹遗址理事会和世界自然保护联盟从其网络中，选拔拥有广泛的相关文化和自然遗产技能和经验的专家担任。这些成员有的任期固定，而有的则根据当年申报遗产的特点任期一年。

The Panel meets once annually in May and considers each Preliminary Assessment. The Panel aims to reach its conclusions by consensus. If there is a need for further clarification in relation to detailed questions from the Panel, further exchange with relevant State(s) Party(ies) is organized following the Panel meeting. Any questions from the Panel can only be on points of details necessary and agreed by the Panel to complete the evaluation of the Preliminary Assessment.

评估小组每年五月举行一次会议，审议每份初步评审。小组的目标是得出协商一致的结论。如果需要对小组专家提出的详细问题作进一步澄清，则需在专家组会议后组织相关缔约国进行进一步交流。评估小组提出的任何问题，只能涉及必要的细节问题，并经评估小组同意以完成初步评估。

The Preliminary Assessment Report provides an assessment, to a standard format, on whether the site has the potential to justify Outstanding Universal Value, including an assessment of the proposed nomination strategy, considerations on authenticity (for cultural sites) and integrity, the framework for comparative analysis and protection and management issues. Conclusions of the report will inform whether or not the site might have the potential to justify Outstanding Universal Value and to achieve the development of a robust World Heritage nomination, and if so, under what conditions; or whether further exploratory work is needed before it can be determined whether or not the site may have potential to justify Outstanding Universal Value, or to achieve the development of a robust World Heritage nomination. The formats for Preliminary Assessment Reports, together with any other relevant information on review formats and working methods are made publicly available by ICOMOS and IUCN via their websites.

5. Delivery of the Preliminary Assessment Reports

Following the Panel meeting, the Preliminary Assessment Reports are finalised and sent to the World Heritage Centre for distribution to State(s) Party(ies) that has requested the Preliminary Assessment. The Preliminary Assessment Report shall be provided in one of the two working languages of the *Convention*. The names and qualifications of the members of the ICOMOS/IUCN Preliminary Assessment Panel are then published on the ICOMOS and IUCN web sites.

As a desk exercise, all advice provided is subject to consideration through a full evaluation, including an evaluation mission, should a nomination be submitted.

初步评估报告以标准格式，评估该遗产点是否有潜力证明其具有突出普遍价值，评估包括拟定的申报策略、对真实性（文化遗产）和完整性的考虑，比较分析框架以及保护和管理问题。报告的结论将告知，该遗产是否有潜力证明其突出普遍价值，从而实现强有力的世界遗产申报，如果有，需要具备哪些条件；或是否需要进一步的探索工作，才能确定该遗址有潜力证明其具有突出普遍价值，并获得世界遗产申报资格。国际古迹遗址理事会和世界自然保护联盟通过其网站公开了初步评估报告的格式，以及关于审查格式和工作方法的其他相关信息。

5. 递交初步评估报告

小组会议结束后，完成初步评估报告并送往世界遗产中心，发还给要求进行初步评估的缔约国。应以《公约》两种工作语言之一提供初步评估报告。国际古迹遗址理事会和世界自然保护联盟初步评估小组成员的姓名和资格，将在国际古迹遗址理事会和世界自然保护联盟网站上公布。

作为书面工作，如果提出申报，所提供的所有咨询意见都要经过全面评价，包括评估团的审议。

The relevant final Preliminary Assessment Reports will be made available to the ICOMOS and IUCN World Heritage Panels should a potential nominated property that has been assessed become the subject of a full Advisory Body evaluation in future nomination processes.

如果完成评估的潜在申报遗产在未来的申报过程中，成为咨询机构全面评估的对象，将向国际古迹遗址理事会和世界自然保护联盟世界遗产小组提供相关的最终初步评估报告。

B. THE ICOMOS PROCEDURE FOR THE EVALUATION OF CULTURAL PROPERTIES

B. 国际古迹遗址理事会的文化遗产评估程序

In carrying out its evaluation of nominations of cultural properties ICOMOS (the International Council of Monuments and Sites) is guided by the *Operational Guidelines*; (see Paragraph 148).

国际古迹遗址理事会遵循《操作指南》（见第 148 条）指导来评估文化遗产的申报材料。

Once new nominations have been checked for completeness by the UNESCO World Heritage Centre, the nomination dossiers that are deemed as complete are delivered to ICOMOS, where they are handled by the ICOMOS World Heritage Unit. From this point, dialogue and consultation with the nominating States Parties may begin and will continue throughout the evaluation process. ICOMOS will use its best endeavours to allocate its available resources equitably, efficiently and effectively to maximise the opportunity for dialogue with all nominating States Parties.

一旦联合国教科文组织世界遗产中心认为一个新的申报是完整的，该完整的申报文件将递交到国际古迹遗址理事会世界遗产处。随后国际古迹遗址理事会与申报国的对话及讨论将贯穿整个评估过程。国际古迹遗址理事会将尽最大努力，公平、有效、高效的分配现有资源，与所有申遗的缔约国最大限度的进行对话。

The ICOMOS evaluation process involves the following stages as illustrated in figure 1:

国际古迹遗址理事会的评估流程包括以下几个阶段（见图 1）：

1. Requests for further information

1. 要求获取更多信息

When it has identified that further information or clarification of existing information is needed, ICOMOS starts a dialogue with States Parties in order to explore ways to meet the needs. This may involve letters, face-to-face meetings, teleconferences or other forms of communication as agreed between ICOMOS and the State Party concerned.

当国际古迹遗址理事会需要更多信息，或者需要澄清已有信息时，它将与缔约国展开对话。双方的沟通方式包括信件交流、面对面会谈、电话会议或其他双方认可的交流方式。

2. Desk Reviews

Each nomination is assessed by up to ten experts who are knowledgeable about the property in its geo-cultural context and who advise on the proposed "Outstanding Universal Value" of the nominated property. This is essentially a "library" exercise undertaken by specialist academics within the membership of ICOMOS, its National and International Committees, or by individuals within many other specialist networks or institutions with which it is linked.

3. On site missions

These are carried out by experts who have practical experience of the management, conservation, and authenticity aspects of individual properties. The process of selecting these experts makes full use of the ICOMOS network. The advice of International Scientific Committees and individual members is sought, as is that of specialist bodies with whom ICOMOS has partnership agreements, such as The International Committee for the Conservation of the Industrial Heritage (TICCIH), the International Federation of Landscape Architects (IFLA), and the International Committee for the Documentation and Conservation of Monuments and Sites of the Modern Movement (DoCoMoMo).

In selecting experts to carry out on-site missions, the policy of ICOMOS is wherever possible to choose someone from the region in which the nominated property is located. Such experts are required to be experienced in heritage management and conservation of the type of property concerned: they are not necessarily high academic experts. They are expected to be able to talk to site managers on a basis of professional equality and

2. 书面评估

每个申报材料都将由多名专家（最多十人）进行书面审核，他们深谙遗产的地缘文化，并将针对其"突出普遍性价值"提出建议。这是一个纯粹的"图书馆式"的专家学者的学术性活动，评估专家来自国际古迹遗址理事会、其下属国家或国际委员会、或者与之相关的其他专家网络或机构。

3. 实地考察

对申报遗产的保护、管理及其真实性有实际经验的专家将赴现场进行考察。专家的甄选过程将充分地利用国际古迹遗址理事会的专家网络。国际古迹遗址理事会将向国际科学委员会及个人会员征求意见，或是向那些与该会有合作协定的专业机构征求建议。这些机构包括国际工业遗产保护委员会（TICCIH）、国际景观设计师联盟（IFLA）、以及国际现代建筑遗产保护和纪录委员会（DOCOMOMO）。

国际古迹遗址理事会将尽可能以申报遗产所在地区内，挑选专家实施实地考察。此类专家必须对遗产管理及此类型遗产的保护有丰富的经验（他们不一定是高层次的学术专家）。他们应在专业平等的基础上与遗产管理者进行交谈，并对遗产地的管理规划、保护政策及游客管控等方面做出有根据的评估。申报缔约国相关工作人员将向这些专家简要介绍情况，其中包括申报文本中相关信息。会与缔约国协商确

to make informed assessments of management plans, conservation practices, visitor handling, etc. They are provided with detailed briefings, which include copies of the relevant information from the dossiers. The dates and programmes of their visits are agreed in consultation with States Parties, who are requested to ensure that ICOMOS evaluation missions are given a low profile so far as the media are concerned. ICOMOS experts submit their reports in confidence on practical aspects of the properties concerned, and may also comment in their reports on other aspects of the nomination.

定这些专家到访的时间和日程。理事会要求缔约国确保媒体对国际古迹遗址理事会的现场评估保持低调。国际古迹遗址理事会考察专家将以保密形式提交针对遗产现实情况的评估报告，也可以在报告中对申报遗产的其他方面进行评价。

3bis. Other sources of information

Other relevant institutions, such as UNESCO Chairs, universities and research institutes may also be consulted during the evaluation process, and listed, as appropriate, in the evaluation report.

3. 补充 . 其他信息资源

也可在评估过程中咨询其他相关机构（例如联合国教科文组织主席团、大学及研究所等），并将参与机构的名单以适当形式列入《评估报告》。

4. Review by the ICOMOS Panel

The ICOMOS World Heritage Panel comprises individual ICOMOS members who collectively represent all regions of the world and possess a wide range of relevant cultural heritage skills and experience. Some of these members serve on the Panel for a fixed term while others are appointed for one year only according to the characteristics of the nominated properties to be examined. ICOMOS will include within its Panel membership some experts who have past experience as members of States Parties delegations, but who are no longer serving as members of the World Heritage Committee. These experts will serve in a personal and professional capacity.

4. 国际古迹遗址理事会评估工作组的审查

国际古迹遗址理事会世界遗产专家小组，由国际古迹遗址理事会中能代表世界各个地区、并拥有相关文化遗产技巧和经历的特别会员组成。部分成员定期为专家小组工作，另一些则根据需要检查的申报遗产的特点，进行为期一年的工作。国际古迹遗址理事会专家小组成员包括有经验的、但不再是世界遗产委员会委员的缔约国代表。这些专家以个人身份和专业能力进行工作。

The Panel meets twice, first in December and then in March. At the first meeting, the Panel evaluates each nomination, based on the reports of

工作组将在十二月和来年三月分别会谈一次。在第一次的会谈中，工作组将依据书面评估报告及实地考察报告对遗产进行评估。

Desk experts and of the site missions.

The Panel aims to reach its recommendations on nominations by consensus.

The first Panel may come to final collective recommendations on some nominations while for others further dialogue with States Parties may be agreed related to the need for more information or the need for adjustments to the approach of the nomination. In cases where the Panel has concluded that the nomination has no potential to justify Outstanding Universal Value, ICOMOS will contact States Parties at this stage. A short interim report for each nomination, in one of the two working lan-guages of the Convention, outlining the status and any issues relevant to the evaluation process, and any further requests for supplementary information, will be provided in January to the nominating States Parties and copied to the World Heritage Centre for distribution to the Chair of the World Heritage Committee.

The second Panel undertakes further evalua-tion of nominations for which a recommendation has not yet been reached based on the receipt of further information or the outcome of dialogue with States Parties. The Panel then agrees the remaining collective recommendations. Following the second Panel meeting, the text of all evaluations is finalised and sent to the World Heritage Centre for distribu-tion to States Parties. The names and qualifications of the members of the Panel are then provided to the World Heritage Centre and published on the ICOMOS web site.

The ICOMOS evaluations provide an assess-ment of Outstanding Universal Value, including the applicability of the criteria and the requirements of integrity and authenticity, assessment of the

工作组将力图在审核会上针对遗产申报项目达成一致的建议。

第一次会议将对部分申报形成集体意见，另外部分申报需要与相关缔约国协商以提供更多信息或需要调整申报方法。如果会议认为申报不具备潜在的突出普遍价值，国际古迹遗址理事会将与缔约国联系。每项申报都要用公约要求的两种工作语言之一，编制一个简短的临时报告，简要描述遗产状况及与评估程序相关的问题、及要求进一步补充的信息，于1月交给提出申报的缔约国，并将副本交世界遗产中心以抄送给世界遗产委员会主席。

第二次会议将根据收到的更多信息和与缔约国协商的结果，对未达成共识的申报进行进一步评估。进而达成共识。第二次会议后，所有最终评估将送交世界遗产中心以便于分送至缔约国。参会人员的姓名、资质将提交给世界遗产中心，并在国际古迹遗址理事会网站上公布。

国际古迹遗址理事会将评估、认定申报遗产是否具有突出的普遍性价值，包括其所满足的标准及其完整性与真实性状况。它还将评估遗产地是否具有充分的立法保护与管理，并分

adequacy of legislative protection, management, and the state of conservation, and finally draft recommendations to the World Heritage Committee with respect to inscription.

析其保护状况。最终形成建议草案，提供给世界遗产委员会。

Figure 1: SUMMARY OF ICOMOS EVALUATION PROCEDURES

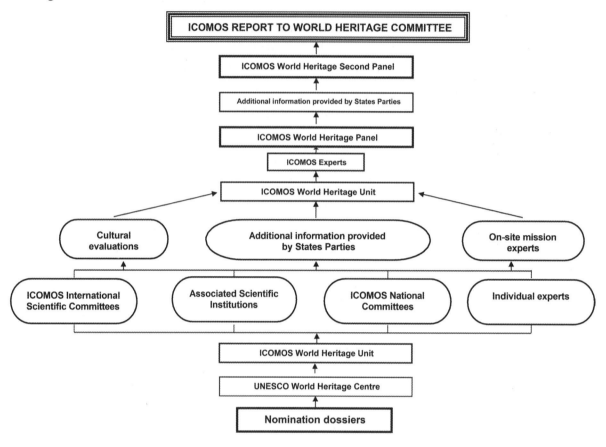

C. THE IUCN PROCEDURE FOR THE EVALUATION OF NATURAL PROPERTIES

1. In carrying out its evaluation of nominations of natural properties, IUCN (the International Union for Conservation of Nature) is guided by the *Operational Guidelines* (see Paragraph 148). The evaluation process (see Figure 2) involves five elements:

(i) Data Assembly.
Following receipt of the nomination dossier from the World Heritage Centre, a standardised analysis is compiled on the property using the

C. 世界自然保护联盟的自然遗产评估程序

1. 世界自然保护联盟遵循《操作指南》（见第 148 条）的指导对自然遗产的申报材料进行评估。评估程序（见图 2）包括五个步骤：

（i）搜集数据：
接到世界遗产中心递交的申报材料之后，将使用保护区数据库、其他世界自然保护联盟全球资料库和主题研究进行标准化分析。这可

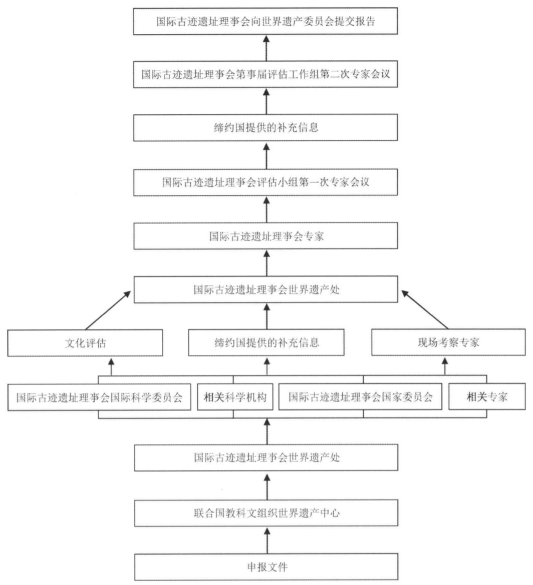

图1：国际古迹遗址理事会评估程序

World Database on Protected Areas and other IUCN global databases and thematic studies. This may include comparative analyses on biodiversity values undertaken in partnership with the UNEP World Conservation Monitoring Centre (UNEP-WCMC). Key findings of data analysis are the subject of dialogue with the State Party during the evaluation mission, and at other stages of the process.

(ii) External Review.

The nomination is sent for desk review to independent experts knowledgeable about the

能包括与联合国环境规划署世界保护监测中心合作开展的生物多样性价值比较分析。数据分析所获得的重要成果将成为评估过程及其他阶段与缔约国进行对话的主题内容。

（ii）外部评审：

申报材料将提交给独立专家进行书面评审。这些专家应具备世界遗产和 / 或该项遗产价值的

property and/or the values that are the subject of the nomination, who are primarily members of IUCN's specialist Commissions and networks, or expert members of partner organisations of IUCN. The documents used to guide IUCN desk reviews are publicly available on the IUCN website: www.iucn.org/worldheritage.

(iii) Evaluation mission to the property.

One or two appropriately qualified IUCN experts visit each nominated property to clarify details about the area, to evaluate site management and to discuss the nomination with relevant authorities and stakeholders. IUCN experts, selected for their global perspective on conservation and natural history as well as their knowledge of the Convention, are usually experienced members of the IUCN World Commission on Protected Areas. (This field inspection is undertaken jointly with ICOMOS in certain situations - see Part C below). The format of IUCN field evaluation mission reports is publicly available on the IUCN website: www.iucn.org/worldheritage.

(iv) Other sources of information.

IUCN also consults additional literature and may receive comments from local NGOs, communities, indigenous peoples and other interested parties in the nomination. Where relevant IUCN will also coordinate with other international conservation instruments such as the Ramsar Convention, the Man and Biosphere Programme and the Global Geoparks Network, and will consult with universities and research institutes as appropriate.

(v) IUCN World Heritage Panel Review.

The IUCN World Heritage Panel is established by the Director General of IUCN to provide high quality and independent technical and scientific advice to IUCN on its work as an Advisory Body to the World Heritage Committee and strategic advice

渊博知识，并且大部分是世界自然保护联盟专家委员会及网络的成员，或世界自然保护联盟合作伙伴组织的专家成员。可登录世界自然保护联盟网站 www.iucn.org/worldheritage 获取世界自然保护联盟书面评审的指导文件。

（iii）遗产现场评估考察：

一至两名世界自然保护联盟专家对每一处申报遗产进行考察，以明确该区域的详细情况，评估遗址管理，与相关当局和利益相关方讨论申报情况。挑选世界自然保护联盟专家的标准是其保护与自然历史的全球视角及对《公约》的了解。这些专家通常是世界自然保护联盟保护区遗产专家。（在某些情况下与国际古迹遗址理事会共同展开现场调查——见下文 C 部分）。可登录世界自然保护联盟网站 www.iucn.org/worldheritage 获取现场评估考察报告。

（iv）其他信息来源：

世界自然保护联盟也可参考其他文献，接受地方非政府组织、社区、当地土著居民及其他遗产申报利益相关团体的意见和建议。世界自然保护联盟也会使用《拉姆萨尔湿地公约》、（联合国教科文组织）人与生物圈计划、世界地质公园网络等国际保护工具，并酌情咨询大学及研究机构的意见。

（v）世界自然保护联盟世界遗产评审小组：

世界自然保护联盟世界遗产评审小组由世界自然保护联盟总干事设立，作为世界自然保护联盟世界遗产委员会咨询机构，向世界自然保护联盟提供高质、独立的技术和科学建议、及向世界自然联盟的保护项目提供战略性建议。

to IUCN's work on World Heritage throughout the IUCN Programme. Specific Tasks of the World Heritage Panel are to conduct a rigorous evaluation of all nominations of natural and mixed properties to the World Heritage List, leading to a panel recommendation on the IUCN position in relation to each new nomination, in line with the requirements established in the Operational Guidelines of the World Heritage Convention. The Panel also provides comment where relevant to ICOMOS in relation to nominations of cultural landscapes to the World Heritage List. The Panel normally meets at least twice in the evaluation process, once in December (year 1) and a second meeting in March/April (year 2).

The members of the Panel comprise senior IUCN staff, IUCN Commission members and external experts selected for their high level of experience and recognised leading expertise and knowledge relevant to IUCN's work on World Heritage, including a balance of particular thematic and/or regional perspectives. It includes some experts who have past experience as members of State Party delegations, but are not current serving members of the World Heritage Committee. These experts will serve in a personal and professional capacity. The IUCN World Heritage Panel reviews all field evaluation reports (and normally hears direct feedback from the mission team), reviewers' comments, the UNEP-WCMC and other analyses and all other background material before finalising the text of the IUCN evaluation report for each nominated property. The membership, terms of reference and working methods of the IUCN World Heritage Panel are publicly available on the IUCN website, and are provided to the World Heritage Committee.

Each evaluation report presents a concise

世界自然保护联盟世界遗产评审小组的特别任务是，按照《世界遗产公约操作指南》的要求，对所有申报列入《世界遗产名录》的自然和混合遗产进行严格的评估，以世界自然保护联盟的立场为每项新的申报提供意见。如申报遗产为文化景观，则世界自然保护联盟世界遗产评审小组将与国际古迹遗址理事会评估工作组协商提供相关建议。通常，世界遗产评审小组在每个评估过程中至少开两次会，一次在12月（第一年），一次在来年三月或四月（第二年）。

（注：对于文化景观，主导方是ICOMOS，提供建议的是IUCN）

世界遗产小组由资深世界自然保护联盟成员、世界自然保护联盟委员会成员和外部专家构成，其入选标准是应具备高水平的经验、公认的业内领先的专业知识和技能，能胜任世界自然保护联盟所承担的世界遗产相关工作，同时应具有独特的主题和/或区域视角。某些世界遗产小组专家可能曾是缔约国代表团成员，但目前不再服务于世界遗产委员会。这些专家具有一定的个人及专业能力。在每份世界自然保护联盟的遗产评估报告定稿以前，世界自然保护联盟世界遗产专家小组将评审所有的现场评估考察报告（通常也听取现场评估小组的直接反馈意见）、评审专家的意见、联合国环境规划署世界保护监测中心、分析其他资料及所有背景材料。可登录世界自然保护联盟网站获取世界自然保护联盟世界遗产小组的成员、职权范围及工作方法，这些同时也提供给世界遗产委员会。

每份评估报告包括申报遗产突出普遍价值

summary of the proposed Outstanding Universal Value of the property nominated, a global comparative analysis with other similar sites (including both World Heritage properties and other protected areas) and a review of integrity and management issues. It concludes with the assessment of the applicability of the criteria, and a clear recommendation to the World Heritage Committee. The names of all experts involved in the evaluation process are included in the final evaluation report, except in the case of reviewers who have provided confidential reviews.

IUCN undertakes dialogue with the nominating States Party/ies at all stages of the nomination process. IUCN will use its best endeavours to allocate its available resources equitably, efficiently and effectively, to maximise the opportunities for dialogue with all nominating States Parties. Dialogue starts early in the evaluation process and intensifies after the meeting of the IUCN World Heritage Panel in December, and includes the following:

i) Prior to the evaluation mission, IUCN may request additional information on questions in the nomination document that require clarification, and will always contact the State Party to prepare for the evaluation mission.

ii) During the evaluation mission the IUCN mission team is able to undertake in-depth discussions on site with representatives of the State Party and with stakeholders.

iii) After the evaluation mission, IUCN may discuss issues that have been identified by the mission team, and request further information from the State Party as required.

的简明摘要、与世界上类似遗址（包括世界遗产及其他保护区）的对比分析、审查完整性和管理议题的评论。最后，评估报告会评估标准的适用性，并向世界遗产委员会提供明确建议。参与整个评估过程的专家姓名将出现在最终在评估报告中，提供机密评论的评论人员除外。

世界自然保护联盟负责在申报过程的各个阶段，与提出申报的缔约国保持对话。世界自然保护联盟将尽最大可能实现可用资源的公平、有效和高效分配，并尽量创造机会与申报缔约国加强对话和沟通。评估一旦开始也意味着对话的开始，世界自然保护联盟世界遗产小组十二月份会议之后将展开更多对话，包括：

i) 现场评估考察正式开始之前，世界自然保护联盟可能要求缔约国为申报文件中需要阐明的问题提供附加信息，且将时刻保持与缔约国的联系，为现场评估考察做准备。

ii) 在现场评估考察过程中，世界自然保护联盟现场考察小组将在现场与缔约国代表及利益相关方代表展开深入讨论。

iii) 现场评估考察结束后，世界自然保护联盟将讨论评审小组确认的事项，并要求缔约国按要求提供更多的信息。

iv) After IUCN's first World Heritage Panel meeting, normally held in December, IUCN will discuss issues raised by the Panel, and request further information from the State Party as required. A short interim report outlining the status, and any issues relevant to the evaluation, and detailing any requests for supplementary information, in one of the two working languages of the Convention, is sent to the nominating State Party/ies, an d copied t o t h e World Heritage Centre, for transmission to the Chairperson of the World Heritage Committee. Dialogue and consultation takes place either through teleconference and/or face-to-face meetings, as mutually agreed.

IUCN takes into account in its evaluation all information that is officially submitted by the State Party in writing to the World Heritage Centre by the specified deadline (see paragraph 148 of the *Operational Guidelines*). However, at all of the above stages any stakeholder in the nomination is also at liberty to contact IUCN to provide information if they wish.

IUCN also always considers fully all past decisions of the World Heritage Committee relevant to the nomination, such as in cases of nominations that have been previously referred or deferred by the Committee, or where the Committee has taken any position in relation to issues of policy.

In the case of renominations, extensions and boundary modifications to an existing World Heritage property, IUCN also considers all matters regarding the state of conservation of that property that have been previously reported to the World Heritage Committee. IUCN may also consider bringing to the attention of the Committee, through the state of conservation reporting process, any significant matters regarding the state of conservation of that property, when such are identified for the first time during the evaluation process.

iv) 通常在 12 月世界自然保护联盟举行第一次专家会议后，世界自然保护联盟将讨论专家会议提出的问题，并要求缔约国按要求提供更多的信息。用两种公约要求的工作语言之一准备一个简短的临时报告，概述状况、与评估相关的问题、需要补充信息的详细要求，送达申报缔约国同时副本送世界遗产中心以递交世界遗产委员会主席。对话或商谈按约定可以通过电话会议或面对面会议进行。

世界自然保护联盟将考虑、评估所有缔约国在最后期限期前正式提交给世界遗产中心书面资料（见操作指南第 148 段）。然而，在评估任何阶段，申报遗产利益相关方可按其需求自由与世界自然保护联盟取得联系、提供相关信息资料。

世界自然保护联盟将充分考虑世界遗产委员会过去对遗产申报的所有决定，例如委员会曾决定的补充材料或重新申报的遗产，或委员会在某些政策问题上有特殊立场。

如申报遗产为重新申报、对现有世界遗产进行扩展、或边界调整，世界自然保护联盟将考虑所有与该遗产保护状况相关的、曾报告给世界遗产委员会的事项。世界自然保护联盟也将通过保护状况报告程序提请委员会注意，在评估过程中首次发现的、与保护状况相关的任何重大事项。

Biogeographic classification systems as a basis for comparison

生物地理学分类体系作为比较基础

2. In the evaluations, IUCN uses biogeographic classification systems such as Udvardy's "Biogeographical Provinces of the World" (1975) and the more recent terrestrial, freshwater and marine ecoregions of the world as a central element of its approach to the global comparative analysis. These systems provide an objective means of comparing nominated properties with sites of similar climatic and ecological conditions.

2. 评估时，世界自然保护联盟将使用之德瓦尔第（Udvardy）"世界生物地理区域"（1975年）的生物地理分类体系、以及最新的陆地、淡水和海洋世界生态区作为其对比分析方法的核心要素。这些体系是把那些具有类似天气与生态条件的申报遗产进行对比分析的客观手段。

3. It is stressed, however, that these biogeographical classification systems are used as a measure for comparison only and do not imply that World Heritage properties are to be selected solely on this basis, nor that the representation of all such classification systems is the basis for the selection process. The guiding principle is that World Heritage properties must be of Outstanding Universal Value.

3. 但需要强调的是，生态物理学分类系统仅是比较的手段，并不意味着这是选择世界遗产的唯一标准，也不意味着，表现出这一分类系统是选择的基础。一个指导性的原则是世界遗产必须具有突出的普遍价值。

Systems to identify priority areas for conservation

确认优先保护区的体系

4. IUCN also uses systems which identify priority areas for conservation such as the World Wide Fund for Nature's (WWF) Global 200 Ecoregions, WWF/IUCN's Centres of Plant Diversity, Conservation International's Biodiversity Hotspots and High-Biodiversity Wilderness Areas, Birdlife International's Endemic Bird Areas and Important Bird Areas, and other Key Biodiversity Areas such as Alliance for Zero Extinction sites. These systems provide additional information on the significance of the nominated properties for biodiversity conservation; however it is not assumed that all such sites should be included on the World Heritage List. The guiding principle is that World Heritage properties must be of Outstanding Universal Value.

4. 世界自然保护联盟同时使用确认优先保护区的体系，比如，世界自然基金会（WWF）全球200强生态区、世界自然基金会/世界自然保护联盟植物多样性中心、保护国际的生态多样性热点地区、高密度生物多样性自然保护区、国际特有鸟类区和重要鸟类区，以及其他重要生物多样性区域，如零灭绝联盟等。这些体系提供了更多信息，以认识到这些申报遗产对保护生物多样性的重要性；但是并不意味着要将所有这些遗址列入世界遗产名录。一个指导性的原则是，世界遗产必须具有突出普遍价值。

Systems to evaluate properties for earth science

评估遗产地球科学价值的体系

value

5. In evaluating properties which have been nominated for their geological value, IUCN consults with a range of specialised organisations such as the UNESCO Earth Sciences Division, International Association of Geomorphologists, the International Union of Speleology and the International Union of Geological Sciences (IUGS).

Additional reference publications used in the evaluation process

6. The evaluation process also includes consideration of key reference publications on the world's protected areas published by IUCN and a range of international conservation organisations. These documents together provide system-wide overviews which allow comparison of the conservation importance of protected areas throughout the world. IUCN has also undertaken a range of thematic studies to identify gaps in natural World Heritage coverage and properties of World Heritage potential. These can be viewed on the IUCN website at www.iucn.org/worldheritage.

IUCN also draws upon references specific to the nominated properties in order to gain insights into site values and conservation issues.

Evaluation of Cultural Landscapes (see also paragraphs 47-47ter)

7. IUCN has an interest in many cultural properties, especially those nominated as cultural landscapes. For that reason, it will on occasion participate in joint field inspections to nominated cultural landscapes with ICOMOS (see Part D below).

8. In accordance with the natural qualities of certain cultural landscapes, IUCN's evaluation is

5. 在对因地质价值而提出申报的遗产进行申报时，世界自然保护联盟会咨询一些专业组织，比如联合国教科文组织的地球科学部、国际地貌学家协会、国际洞穴研究会和国际地质科学联盟。

评估时使用的相关出版物

6. 评估程序将参考世界自然保护联盟以及其他一些国际保护机构出版的、关于世界保护区的主要参考书籍，这便于对全球保护区的保护重要性进行比较。世界自然保护联盟同时开展了大量主题研究来确认自然世界遗产的覆盖面以及潜在的缺口。登录以下世界自然保护联盟的网址 http://iucn.org/themes/wcpa/wheritage/globalstrategy.htm 可获取以上信息。

世界自然保护联盟还引用特别针对申报遗产的相关资料，以获得对遗址价值和保护事项更多的见解。

文化景观评估（另请见 47–47 ter）

7. 世界自然保护联盟对很多文化遗产都感兴趣，特别是作为文化景观申报的遗产。因此，联盟有时会与国际古迹遗址理事会合作，对申报的文化景观进行现场考察（见下文的 D 部分）。

8. 根据某些文化景观遗产的自然特性，世界自然保护联盟的评估主要涉及以下几个因素：

concerned with the following factors:

(i) Conservation of natural and semi-natural systems, and of wild species of fauna and flora

(ii) Conservation of biodiversity within sustainable use systems (farming, traditional fisheries, forestry);

(iii) Sustainable land and water use;

(iv) Enhancement of scenic beauty;

(v) Ex-situ collections, such as botanic gardens or arboreta;

(vi) Outstanding examples of humanity's inter-relationship with nature;

(vii) Historically significant discoveries

The following table sets each of the above list in the context of the categories of cultural landscapes, thereby indicating where each consideration is most likely to occur (the absence of a consideration does not mean that it will *never* occur, only that this is unlikely):

D. ADVISORY BODY COLLABORATION

(i) 自然、半自然体系以及野生动植物的保护；

(ii) 可持续利用系统（农业、传统渔业、林业）内的生物多样性的保护；

(iii) 可持续的水土使用；

(iv) 景色美感的提升；

(v) 异地移植，如植物园或植物园等；

(vi) 人类与自然关系的杰出范例；

(vii) 具有重大历史意义的发现。

下表把上文所提每个列表均放在附件 3 文化景观类型的背景之内，藉此指出哪项内容最可能出现（没提到的内容并不意味着永远不会出现，只是可能性不太大）：

D. 咨询机构的合作

Cultural Landscape type	Natural considerations most likely to be relevant (see Paragraph 16 above)						
Designed landscape					(v)		
Organically evolving landscape - continuous	(i)	(ii)	(iii)	(iv)			
Organically evolving landscape - fossil	(i)					(vi)	
Associative landscape							(vii)

文化景观类型（另见附件 3）	最可能相关的自然内容（见上文第 16 段）						
人工设计的景观					（ⅴ）		
有机演变的景观——持续	（ⅰ）	（ⅱ）	（ⅲ）	（ⅳ）			
有机演变的景观——化石	（ⅰ）					（ⅵ）	
关联性景观							（ⅶ）

FIGURE 2: SUMMARY OF IUCN EVALUATION PROCEDURE

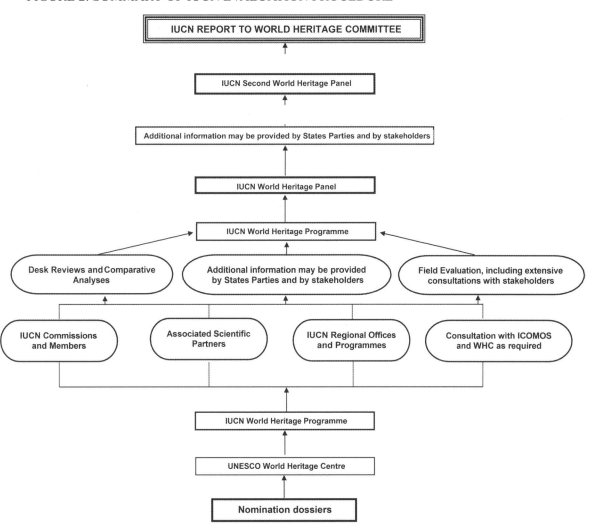

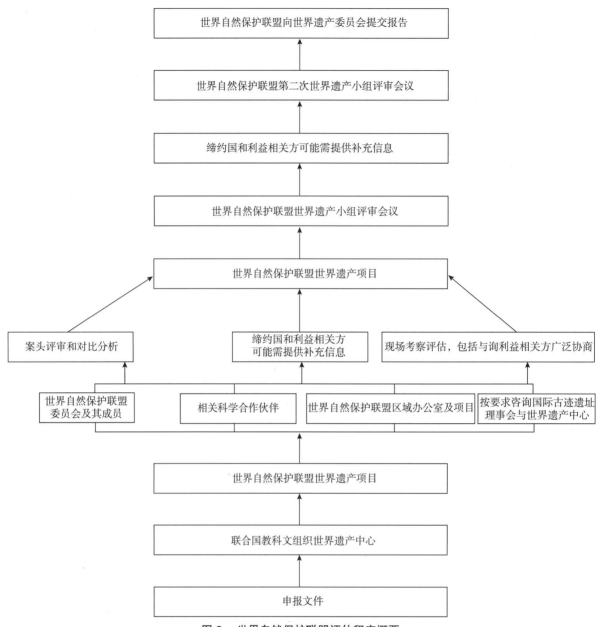

图 2：世界自然保护联盟评估程序概要

Nominations of mixed properties

混合遗产申报

1. Properties that are nominated under both natural and cultural criteria entail a joint IUCN and ICOMOS mission to the nominated property. Following the mission, IUCN and ICOMOS prepare separate evaluation reports of the property under the relevant criteria (see above), and harmonise and coordinate their evaluations to the extent possible.

1. 按照自然价值和文化价值双重标准申报的遗产，需要世界自然保护联盟和国际古迹遗址理事会共同对该遗产申报进行现场评估考察。考察之后，世界自然保护联盟和国际古迹遗址理事会将根据相关标准（见上文）编制独立的遗产评估报告，并尽最大可能协调和整合其评估报告。

Cultural Landscapes

2. Properties nominated as Cultural Landscapes are evaluated by ICOMOS under criteria (i) - (vi) (see Paragraph 77 of the *Operational Guidelines)*. IUCN may provide advice when relevant on the natural values and the conservation and management of the nominated property, and addresses any questions that are raised by ICOMOS. In some cases, a joint mission is required.

Linkages between nature and culture

3. As most properties nominated to the World Heritage List include aspects of management related to the interaction of nature and culture, IUCN and ICOMOS, to the extent possible, discuss any such interactions during their evaluation processes.

文化景观

2. 作为文化景观申报的遗产由国际古迹遗址理事会根据标准（i）-（vi）（见《操作指南》第 77 条）进行评估。世界自然保护联盟将针对申报遗产自然价值及其保护和管理相关方面提供建议，并解决国际古迹遗址理事会提出的问题。在有些情况下，需要共同行动。

自然遗产和文化景观的联系

3. 由于大部分申请列入世界遗产名录的遗产都包括对自然与文化交互作用的管理，世界自然保护联盟和国际古迹遗址理事会将在其评估过程中尽最大可能地讨论这些交互作用。

United Nations
Educational, Scientific and
Cultural Organization

World
Heritage
Convention

FORMAT FOR PERIODIC REPORTING ON THE APPLICATION OF THE *WORLD HERITAGE CONVENTION*

- The Format for Periodic Reporting is available at https://whc.unesco.org/en/periodicreporting

- Further guidance on Periodic Reporting can be found in Section V of the *Operational Guidelines*

- In order to facilitate management of information, States Parties are requested to submit reports, in English or French, in electronic as well as in printed form to:

UNESCO World Heritage Centre
7, place de Fontenoy 75352 Paris 07 SP
France
E-mail through: https://whc.unesco.org/en/contacts

FORMAT

PERIODIC REPORTING ON THE APPLICATION OF THE *WORLD HERITAGE CONVENTION*

This Annex presents an outline of the Periodic Reporting questionnaire. The full questionnaire can be accessed at https://whc.unesco.org/en/periodicreporting/.

General Requirements

- Information should be as precise, specific and concise as possible. It should be quantified where possible and fully referenced. Opportunities

附件 7　实施《世界遗产公约》定期报告的格式

- 登录以下网址，可获取定期报告的格式：http://whc.unesco.org/en/periodicreporting

- 定期报告的更多指导意见，请参见《操作指南》的第五部分

- 为了便于信息的管理，要求缔约国提交英语或法语报告，应同时提交报告的电子版本和印刷版本，提交地址如下：

联合国教科文组织世界遗产中心法国巴黎
（7，placede Fontenoy 75352 Paris 07 SP France）
电邮：http://whc.unesco.org/en/contacts

实施《世界遗产公约》的定期报告的格式

本附件是定期报告调查问卷的大纲。完整的问卷可以登录 https://whc.unesco.org/en/periodicreporting/ 查找。

基本要求

- 信息应尽可能精确、具体和简明。在可能的情况下，应将其量化并标注好所有参考的内容。每一章都可以进行评论。

for comment are provided in each chapter.

• Expressions of opinion should be supported by reference to the authority on which they are made and the verifiable facts which support them.

SECTION I: APPLICATION OF THE *WORLD HERITAGE CONVENTION* BY THE STATE PARTY

Section I requests that the State Party provide information or validate existing information on the legislative and administrative provisions which they have adopted and other actions which they have taken for the application of this *Convention*, together with details of the experience acquired in this field (Article 29.1 of the *World Heritage Convention*).

1. INTRODUCTION

Chapter 1 lists the name of the State Party and the year of ratification or acceptance of the *Convention* and seeks information on the groups and institutions involved in the preparation of Section I of the report.

2. SYNERGIES WITH OTHER CONVENTIONS, PROGRAMMES AND RECOMMENDATIONS FOR THE CONSERVATION OF THE NATURAL AND CULTURAL HERITAGE

Chapter 2 aims to gather information on existing and potential synergies between Multilateral Environmental Agreements, as well as other UNESCO conventions, programmes, and recommendations. The State Party is also invited to provide information on the extent to which it has implemented relevant policies adopted by the World Heritage Committee.

3. TENTATIVE LIST

Chapter 3 aims to gather information on the

• 所表达的意见应以相关权威意见作为参考、有可验证的事实加以支持。

第 I 部分：缔约国实施《世界遗产公约》的情况

要求缔约国提供资料或证明其通过的现有立法和行政规定已经有效实施，及缔约国为实施本公约而采取的其他行动和在这一领域取得的经验的细节（《世界遗产公约》第 29.1 条）。

1. 简介

第 1 章列出缔约国的名称及其批准或接受《公约》的年份，并要求缔约国提供编写报告第 I 部分的团体和机构的资料。

2. 为保护自然和文化遗产而与其他公约、项目和建议的协同合作

第 2 章收集下述信息：有关多边环境协定以及联合国教科文组织其他公约、项目和建议之间现有及潜在的协同合作资料。还邀请缔约国提供资料，说明其在多大程度上实施了世界遗产委员会通过的有关政策。

3. 预备名录

第 3 章收集下述信息：预备名录的拟定过

process of preparing the tentative list, the tools and guidance used, potential synergies with other conventions of properties on the tentative list as well as the sustainability of the process in line with the World Heritage and Sustainable Development Policy (2015).

程、所使用的工具和指南、与预备名录所列遗产相关的其他公约之间的潜在协同合作，以及符合"世界遗产和可持续发展政策"（2015 年）实现进程的可持续性。

4. NOMINATIONS

4. 申报

Chapter 4 aims to gather information on the process of nominating properties for inscription on the World Heritage List, the tools and guidance used, as well as the sustainability of the process in line with the World Heritage and Sustainable Development Policy (2015).

第 4 章收集下述信息：申报遗产列入《世界遗产名录》的过程、所使用的工具和指南，以及符合"世界遗产和可持续发展政策"（2015 年）实现进程的可持续性。

5. GENERAL POLICY DEVELOPMENT

5. 总体政策制定

Chapter 5 aims to gather information on the legal framework for the protection, conservation and presentation of the cultural and/or natural heritage and its effectiveness.

第 5 章收集下述信息：保护、保存和展示文化和 / 或自然遗产的法律架构及其有效性资料。

6. INVENTORIES/LISTS/REGISTERS OF CULTURAL AND NATURAL HERITAGE

6. 文化和自然遗产详细目录 / 清单 / 登记造册

Chapter 6 aims to gather information on the status of inventories/lists/registers of cultural and natural heritage of national significance and the processes used to compile them.

第 6 章收集下述信息：具有国家重要性的文化和自然遗产的详细目录 / 清单 / 登记造册的现状，以及编制这些详细目录 / 清单 / 登记造册的程序。

7. STATUS OF SERVICES FOR PROTECTION, CONSERVATION AND PRESENTATION

7. 保护、保存及展示服务的状况

Chapter 7 aims to gather information on services within the territories of the State Party for the identification, protection, conservation and presentation of the cultural and natural heritage and on cooperation between the stakeholders involved.

第 7 章收集下述信息：缔约国境内为识别、保护、保存和展示文化和自然遗产而提供的服务、以及与利益相关者合作的资料。

8. FINANCIAL STATUS AND HUMAN

8. 财务状况和人力资源

RESOURCES

Chapter 8 aims to gather information on the availability and adequacy of financial resources for the conservation and protection of cultural and natural heritage.

第 8 章收集下述信息：为保存和保护文化和自然遗产所需的财政资源是否可用、是否充足。

9. CAPACITY DEVELOPMENT

9. 能力建设

Chapter 9 aims to gather information on capacity building in heritage conservation, protection, presentation and management, in line with World Heritage Capacity Building Strategy (2011).

第 9 章收集下述信息：根据"世界遗产能力建设战略"（2011 年），关于遗产保存、保护、展示和管理方面的能力建设信息。

10. POLICY AND RESOURCING OF WORLD HERITAGE PROPERTIES

10. 世界遗产的政策和资源

Chapter 10 aims to gather information on specific legislation, policies and measures for the protection, conservation, presentation and management of World Heritage.

第 10 章收集下述信息：保护、保存、介绍和管理世界遗产的具体法律、政策和措施的资料。

11. INTERNATIONAL COOPERATION AND FUNDRAISING

11. 国际合作与资金筹集

Chapter 11 aims to gather information on the cooperation with other States Parties in the field of cultural and natural heritage.

第 11 章收集下述信息：同其他缔约国在文化和自然遗产领域进行合作的资料。

12. EDUCATION, INFORMATION AND AWARENESS BUILDING

12. 教育、信息和意识树立

Chapter 12 aims to gather information on steps taken to raise the awareness of decision-makers, property owners and the general public, and in particular the youth, about the protection and conservation of cultural and natural heritage.

第 12 章收集下述信息：为提高决策制定者、遗产所有人和公众特别是青少年，保护和保存文化和自然遗产的意识而采取的措施。

13. CONCLUSIONS AND RECOMMENDED ACTIONS

13. 结论和建议采取的行动

Chapter 13 automatically generates the main conclusions under each of the items of Section I based on the answers provided in the questionnaire. States Parties should also provide information about the actions they have taken regarding their implementation of the *World Heritage Convention*.

第 13 章根据调查问卷所获得的答案，得出本报告第 I 部分内各章节的主要结论，缔约国还应提供相关资料，说明其在实施《公约》方面所采取的行动。

14. GOOD PRACTICES IN THE IMPLEME-NTA-TION OF THE *WORLD HERITAGE CONV-EN-TION*

14. 实施《世界遗产公约》的良好范例

Chapter 14 offers the opportunity to provide an example of a good practice in World Heritage protection, identification, conservation or management implemented at national level.

第 14 章提供在国家层面实施世界遗产保护、识别、保存或管理的良好范例。

15. ASSESSMENT OF THE PERIODIC REPORTING EXERCISE

15. 定期报告工作的评估

Chapter 15 assesses the format, content and process of the Periodic Reporting exercise, including the degree to which it meets the objectives of Periodic Reporting, how the data generated is used and the training and guidance available to respondents.

第 15 章评估定期报告工作的格式、内容和过程，包括它在多大程度上符合定期报告的目标、如何使用所产生的数据、以及如何向调查对象提供培训和指导。

SECTION II: STATE OF CONSERVATION OF SPECIFIC WORLD HERITAGE PROPERTIES

第 II 部分：具体世界遗产的保护状况

Section II gathers information on the implementation of the *Convention* at site-level and must be completed for each individual World Heritage property. The preparation of this report should involve those who are responsible for the day-to-day management of the property. For transboundary properties, it is recommended that reports be prepared jointly by or with close collaboration between the agencies concerned.

第 II 部分收集世界遗产地现场实施《公约》的情况，每一项世界遗产都必须参与。负责遗产日常管理的人员应参与本报告的编制。如果是跨境遗产，建议相关机构共同编制报告或在编制报告的过程中紧密合作。

1. WORLD HERITAGE PROPERTY DATA

1. 世界遗产数据

Chapter 1 requires that information be provided

第 1 章提供有关遗产的基本数据（名称、

or existing information validated with regards to the basic data of the property (name, year of inscription, geographic coordinates, maps, social media presence), and also gathers information on the organizations or entities involved in the preparation of Section I of the report.

列入年份、地理坐标、地图、社交媒体）信息或经过验证的现有信息，并收集参与编写报告第I部分的组织或机构信息。

2. OTHER CONVENTIONS/PROGRAMMES UNDER WHICH THE WORLD HERITAGE PROPERTY IS PROTECTED

2. 其他保护世界遗产的公约 / 项目

Chapter 2 gathers information relating to synergies with other conventions and programmes (UNESCO and others) relevant to the property and on the extent of cooperation and integration existing between these conventions and programmes (where applicable).

第 2 章收集下述信息：与世界遗产相关的其他公约和项目（联合国教科文组织和其他组织）的协同合作，以及这些公约和项目之间现有的合作和一体化程度（如适用）。

3. STATEMENT OF OUTSTANDING UNIVERSAL VALUE AND DEFINING OF ATTRIBUTES

3. 突出普遍价值声明和属性的定义

Chapter 3 gathers information on the attributes of Outstanding Universal Value (OUV), their current condition and the trend in that condition since the last cycle of Periodic Reporting.

第 3 章收集下述信息：突出普遍价值（OUV）的属性、它们的当前状况、以及自上一个定期报告周期以来该状况的发展趋势。

4. FACTORS AFFECTING THE PROPERTY

4. 影响遗产的因素

Chapter 4 gathers information on the range of factors that are currently affecting or have strong potential to affect the property, both positively and negatively.

第 4 章收集下述信息：目前正在影响或有很大可能对世界遗产造成影响的一系列因素，包括积极和消极两个方面。

5. PROTECTION AND MANAGEMENT OF THE PROPERTY

5. 遗产的保护和管理

Chapter 5 gathers information on practical issues of management, and the effectiveness of protection, management and monitoring of the property and its Outstanding Universal Value.

第 5 章收集下述信息：遗产管理中出现的实际问题、对遗产及其突出普遍价值加以保护、管理和监测的有效性。

6. FINANCIAL AND HUMAN RESOURCES

Chapter 6 gathers information on the sources of funding available, the adequacy of budget for management needs, as well as the availability of human resources and levels of capacity building at the property.

7. SCIENTIFIC STUDIES AND RESEARCH PROJECTS

Chapter 7 gathers information on the adequacy of available knowledge (both scientific and traditional) regarding the values and attributes of the World Heritage property and the existence of research programmes directed towards management needs and/or the improvement of the understanding of the Outstanding Universal Value.

8. EDUCATION, INFORMATION AND AWARENESS BUILDING

Chapter 8 gathers information on the existence and effectiveness of heritage education and awareness programmes at the property as well as general services dedicated to education, information, interpretation and awareness building.

9. VISITOR MANAGEMENT

Chapter 9 gathers information on tourism activities and visitor management at the property.

10. MONITORING

Chapter 10 gathers information on the existence of monitoring programmes and indicators for the property as well as on the implementation of property related Committee Decisions (where

6. 财务及人力资源

第 6 章收集下述信息：现有资金来源、预算能否充分满足管理需要、可用的人力资源、以及遗产能力建设的水平。

7. 科学研究和科研项目

第 7 章收集下述信息：现有关于世界遗产价值及其属性的知识（包括科学知识和传统知识）是否充分、以及针对管理需要和 / 或增进对世界遗产突出普遍价值了解的研究项目情况。

8. 教育、信息和意识树立

第 8 章收集下述信息：遗产教育和意识提升项目的情况及其有效性、以及致力于遗产教育、信息、阐释和意识树立的服务。

9. 游客管理

第 9 章收集下述信息：遗产地的旅游活动和游客管理情况。

10. 监测

第 10 章收集下述信息：遗产监测项目及指标情况、以及与遗产有关的、委员会决定的实施情况（如适用）。

applicable).

11. IDENTIFICATION OF PRIORITY MANAGEMENT NEEDS

Chapter 11 automatically lists all the management needs requiring further action which have been highlighted in this Section of the Periodic Report.

12. SUMMARY AND CONCLUSIONS

Chapter 12 highlights the most important positive and negative factors (up to ten of each) which have been highlighted in this Section of the Periodic Report.

13. IMPACT OF WORLD HERITAGE STATUS

Chapter 13 gathers information regarding the impact of World Heritage status in relation to various topics, with a particular focus on the World Heritage and Sustainable Development Policy (2015).

14. GOOD PRACTICES IN THE IMPLEMENTATION OF THE *WORLD HERITAGE CONVENTION*

Chapter 14 offers the opportunity to provide an example of a good practice in World Heritage protection, identification, conservation and preservation implemented at the property level.

15. ASSESSMENT OF THE PERIODIC REPORTING EXERCISE

Chapter 15 assesses the format, content and process of the Periodic Reporting exercise, including how the data generated is used and the training and guidance available to respondents.

11. 确定优先管理需求

第 11 章列出定期报告部分所强调的、需采取进一步行动的所有管理需求。

12. 总结与结论

第 12 章强调定期报告部分所指出的、最重要的积极因素和消极因素（各因素均不超过十个）。

13. 世界遗产现状的影响

第 13 章收集下述信息：世界遗产现状对不同主题的影响情况，特别关注"世界遗产与可持续发展政策"（2015 年）。

14. 实施《世界遗产公约》的良好范例

第 14 章提供一个基于遗产地本身，在实施世界遗产的保护、识别、保存和管理方面的良好范例。

15. 定期报告工作的评估

第 15 章评估定期报告工作的格式、内容和过程，包括如何使用所产生的数据、以及如何向调查对象提供培训和指导。

United Nations	World
Educational, Scientific and	Heritage
Cultural Organization	Convention

INTERNATIONAL ASSISTANCE REQUEST FORM

- The International Assistance request form is available at: https://whc.unesco.org/en/intassistance and can be filled out online.
- Further guidance on International Assistance can be found in Section Ⅶ of the *Operational Guidelines*
- See attached Explanatory Notes on completing this Request form
- The original signed version of the completed International Assistance request form should be sent in English or French to:

UNESCO World Heritage Centre

7, place de Fontenoy 75352 Paris 07 SP

France

E-mail: wh-intassistance@unesco.org

1. STATE PARTY

2. TITLE OF PROJECT

3. TYPE OF ASSISTANCE

	Emergency Assistance	*Preparatory Assistance*	*Conservation and management*
Culture			
Nature			
Mixed			

4. PROJECT LOCATION:

a) Will the project be implemented at a World Heritage property?

☐ - yes　　☐ - no

附件 8 《国际援助申请表》

- 登录以下网址下载并在线填写《国际援助申请表》：http://whc.unesco.org/en/intassistance

- 更多有关国际援助的指导说明，请参阅《操作指南》的第七节。

- 参见所附的申请表填报须知。
- 应将完整填写的英文或法文的国际援助申请表原件递交至：

联合国教科文组织世界遗产中心

地址：7，place de Fontenoy 75352 Paris 07 SP France

电子邮箱：wh-intassistance@unesco.org

1. 缔约国

_____

2. 项目名称

_____

_____

_____

_____

3. 援助类型

	紧急援助	筹备性援助	保护与管理
文化			
自然			
混合			

4. 项目地点：

a）该项目是否会在一处世界遗产地实施？

□ 是 □ 否

If yes, give the name of the property

_____

_____

b) Will the project include a field component?

☐ - yes   ☐ - no If yes, where and how?

_____

_____

c) If the project is being implemented at a World Heritage property, indicate whether it will also benefit other World Heritage properties, and if so, which ones and how?

_____

_____

5. TIMEFRAME FOR THE IMPLEMENTATION OF THE PROJECT (indicate whether estimated or fixed)

Dates: _____

Duration: _____

6. THE PROJECT IS:

☐ - local

☐ - national

☐ - sub-regional involving a few States Parties from a region

☐ - regional involving most States Parties from a region

☐ - international involving States Parties from different regions

If the project is national, sub-regional, regional or international, please indicate the countries/properties which will participate/benefit from the project:

_____

_____

_____

7. JUSTIFICATION OF THE PROJECT

a) Explain why this project is needed

(for Emergency Assistance, please fill in item 8 below instead).

_____

_____

_____

_____

_____

如果答案为"是"，提供遗产名称：

_____

b）该项目是否包括野外活动部分？ □ 是 □ 否
如果答案为"是"，提供地点和方式：

_____

_____

c）如果该项目在世界遗产地实施，请说明其他世界遗产是否也能受益。如果是，请说明受益的遗产以及具体受益方式？

_____

_____

5. 项目实施时间表（请说明是预计或确切时间表）

日期：_____

持续时间：_____

6. 项目类型为：
□地方性活动
□国家性活动
□涉及某一区域少数几个缔约国的次区域性活动
□涉及某一区域的多数缔约国的区域性活动
□涉及不同地区的众多缔约国的国际性活动
如果该项目为次区域性、区域性或国际性活动，请明确说明哪些国家或遗产将参加该项目活动，以及哪些遗产将从该项目中收益：

_____

_____

_____

7. 项目原因
a）说明需实施该项目的理由
（如申请紧急援助，请省略此项，填写第八项）

_____

_____

_____

_____

b) List all supporting documents submitted, if applicable.

_____

_____

_____

_____

8. FOR EMERGENCY ASSISTANCE ONLY

a) Describe the actual or potential threat/danger affecting the property

_____

_____

b) Indicate how it might affect the property's Outstanding Universal Value

_____

_____

c) Explain how the proposed project will address the threat/danger

_____

_____

9. OBJECTIVES OF THE PROJECT

Clearly set out the specific objectives of the project

10. EXPECTED RESULTS

a) Clearly state the results expected from the project

_____

_____

b) Define the indicators and means of verification which can be used to assess the achievements of these results:

Expected Results	Indicators	Means of verification

11. WORK PLAN (including specific activities and timetable)

Activities	Timeframe (in months)					
Activity						
Activity						
Activity						
Activity						

b）如有可能，请列举已提交的、能支持项目实施的理由的文件

_____

_____

_____

_____

8. 紧急援助申请
a）描述遗产面临的已知或潜在威胁

_____

_____

b）指出这种威胁对遗产的突出普遍价值的影响

_____

_____

c）解释该项目消除这种威胁或危险的方法

_____

_____

9. 项目目标
详细说明该项目的具体目标。

10. 预期结果
a）清晰说明项目的预期结果

_____

_____

b）说明能够评估预期结果的指标和验证方法

预期结果	指标	验证方法

11. 项目计划（包括具体活动和时间表）

活动	时间表（月份）					
活动						
活动						
活动						
活动						

12. EVALUATION AND REPORTING

(to be submitted to the World Heritage Centre within three months after the project is completed)

13. PROFILES OF SPECIALISTS, TRAINERS, TECHNICIANS AND/OR SKILLED LABOUR, IF THE PROJECT FORESEES THE PARTICIPATION OF SUCH PEOPLE

(if the identity of the specialists, trainers, technicians, and/or skilled labourers is already known, please state their names and include a brief CV if possible)

14. KEY TARGET AUDIENCES, INCLUDING PROFILES OF TRAINEES / PARTICIPANTS, IF THE PROJECT FORESEES THE PARTICIPATION OF SUCH PEOPLE

15. BUDGET BREAKDOWN

a) Provide, in the following table (in United States dollars), a detailed breakdown of costs of the individual elements of the project including, if possible, unit costs and show how these will be shared between the different funding sources.

Items (choose items as applicable to the project)	Detail US$ (for applicable items)	State Party Funds US$	Amount requested to the World Heritage Fund US$	Other sources US$	Total US$
Organization • venue • office expenses • secretarial assistance • translation • simultaneous interpret-ation • audiovisual equipment • other	US$ /day for　days = US$__ US$__ US$ /day for　days - US$__ US$ /page for　pages = US$__ US$ /hour for　hours = US$__ US$ /day for　days = US$__ US$__				
Personnel / consultancy service (fees) • international expert • national expert • coordinator • other	US$ / week for__weeks = US$ _ US$ / week for__weeks = US$ _ US$ / week for__weeks = US$ _ US$ / week for__-weeks = US$ _				
Travel • international travel cost • domestic travel costs • other	US$__ US$__ US$__				
Daily subsistence allowance • accommodation • board	US$__ / day for__persons = US$__ US$__ / day for__persons = US$__				

12. 评估与报告

（应在项目结束三个月之内提交给世界遗产中心）

13. 可能参加此项活动的专家、培训人员、技术人员和 / 或技工的简介

（如果已知上述人员身份，请陈述其姓名。如有可能，应提供个人简历）

_____

_____

14. 项目主要受众（包括受训人员和参与者的简介）

_____

_____

15. 详细预算

a）请在下表中（以美元为单位）提供项目各个组成部分所需的详细预算。如有可能，提供单位成本，并展示不同资金来源分担这些费用的情况。

项目 （选择适用的项目）	具体金额（美元） （选择适用的项目）	缔约国资金（美元）	向世界遗产基金申请数额（美元）	其他资金来源（美元）	小计（美元）
组织 ● 活动场所 ● 办公费用 ● 文秘协理费 ● 笔译费 ● 同声传译费 ● 影音设备费 ● 其他	每天____美元，共___天 = ____美元 ____美元 每天____美元，共___天 = ____美元 每页____美元，共___页 = ____美元 每小时____美元，共___小时 = ____美元 每天____美元，共___天 = ____美元 ____美元				____美元
人员 / 咨询服务 ● 国际专家 ● 国内专家 ● 协调人员 ● 其他	每周____美元，共___周 = ____美元 每周____美元，共___周 = ____美元 每周____美元，共___周 = ____美元 每周____美元，共___周 = ____美元				____美元
差旅费 ● 国际旅行费用 ● 国内旅行费用 ● 其他	____美元 ____美元 ____美元				____美元
每日生活补助 ● 餐饮 ● 住宿	每日___人____美元 = ____美元 每日___人____美元 = ____美元				____美元
设备 ● …… ● ……	每台___美元，共___台 = ____美元 每台___美元，共___台 = ____美元				____美元

Items (choose items as applicable to the project)	Detail US$ (for applicable items)	State Party Funds US$	Amount requested to the World Heritage Fund US$	Other sources US$	Total US$
Equipment ● …… ● ……	US$ / unit for units US$ / unit for units=				
Evaluation, Reporting and Publication ● evaluation ● reporting ● editing, layout ● printing ● distribution ● other	US$__ US$__ US$__ US$__ US$__ US$__				
Miscellaneous ● visas ● other	US$__ for __ participants = US$__ US$__				
TOTAL					

b) Specify whether or not resources from the State Party or other sources are already available or when they are likely to become available.

_____

_____

16. IN KIND CONTRIBUTIONS FROM THE STATE PARTY AND OTHER AGENCIES

a) National agency(ies)

_____

_____

b) Other bi/multi-lateral organizations, donors, etc

_____

_____

17. AGENCY(IES) RESPONSIBLE FOR THE IMPLEMENTATION OF THE PROJECT

_____

_____

18. SIGNATURE ON BEHALF OF STATE PARTY

Full name _____

Title _____

Date _____

19. ANNEXES

_____ (number of annexes attached to the request)

续表

项目 （选择适用的项目）	具体金额（美元） （选择适用的项目）	缔约国资金（美元）	向世界遗产基金申请数额（美元）	其他资金来源（美元）	小计（美元）
评估、报告与出版发行 ● 评估 ● 报告 ● 编辑、排版 ● 印刷 ● 发行 ● 其他	＿＿＿美元 ＿＿＿美元 ＿＿＿美元 ＿＿＿美元 ＿＿＿美元 ＿＿＿美元				＿＿＿美元
其他杂费 ● 签证 ● 其他费用	每人＿＿＿美元，共＿＿＿人参加＝＿＿＿美元 每人＿＿＿美元，共＿＿＿人参加＝＿＿＿美元				＿＿＿美元
合计					＿＿＿美元

b）指明是否已经或可能从缔约国或其他渠道获取资源

_____

_____

16. 缔约国或其他机构的实物捐赠

a）国家机构

_____

b）其他双边／多边组织、捐赠人等

_____

17. 负责项目实施的机构

_____

18. 缔约国代表签字

全名＿＿＿＿＿＿＿＿＿＿＿＿＿＿＿＿＿＿＿＿＿＿＿＿

头衔＿＿＿＿＿＿＿＿＿＿＿＿＿＿＿＿＿＿＿＿＿＿＿＿

日期＿＿＿＿＿＿＿＿＿＿＿＿＿＿＿＿＿＿＿＿＿＿＿＿

19. 附件

（附件编号）

EXPLANATORY NOTES

<table>
<tr><th></th><th>INTERNATIONAL ASSISTANCE APPLICATION FORM</th><th>EXPLANATORY NOTES</th></tr>
<tr><td>1.</td><td>STATE PARTY</td><td>Name of the State Party presenting the International Assistance request</td></tr>
<tr><td>2.</td><td>TITLE OF THE PROJECT</td><td></td></tr>
<tr><td>3.</td><td>TYPE OF ASSISTANCE
<table>
<tr><th></th><th>Emergency Assistance</th><th>Preparatory Assistance</th><th>Conservation and Management*</th></tr>
<tr><td>Culture</td><td></td><td></td><td></td></tr>
<tr><td>Nature</td><td></td><td></td><td></td></tr>
<tr><td>Mixed</td><td></td><td></td><td></td></tr>
</table>
* Please note that "Conservation and Management" now includes the previous categories :
-Training, Research Assistance
-Technical Cooperation
-Assistance for education, information and awareness raising</td>
<td>See Paragraph 241 of the Operational Guidelines for details.

Indicate the type of assistance you are requesting, as well as the type of heritage covered by the project.

Please, tick only one box in the table. For example:

-Training project on rock paintings:
<table>
<tr><th></th><th>Emergency Assistance</th><th>Preparatory Assistance</th><th>Conservation and Management</th></tr>
<tr><td>Culture</td><td></td><td></td><td>X</td></tr>
<tr><td>Nature</td><td></td><td></td><td></td></tr>
<tr><td>Mixed</td><td></td><td></td><td></td></tr>
</table>
-Preparation of a nomination file for a mixed property:
<table>
<tr><th></th><th>Emergency Assistance</th><th>Preparatory Assistance</th><th>Conservation and Management</th></tr>
<tr><td>Culture</td><td></td><td></td><td></td></tr>
<tr><td>Nature</td><td></td><td></td><td></td></tr>
<tr><td>Mixed</td><td></td><td>X</td><td></td></tr>
</table>
-Emergency assistance request following a tropical storm which affected a protected forest area:
<table>
<tr><th></th><th>Emergency Assistance</th><th>Preparatory Assistance</th><th>Conservation and Management</th></tr>
<tr><td>Culture</td><td></td><td></td><td></td></tr>
<tr><td>Nature</td><td>X</td><td></td><td></td></tr>
<tr><td>Mixed</td><td></td><td></td><td></td></tr>
</table></td></tr>
<tr><td>4.</td><td>PROJECT LOCATION</td><td></td></tr>
</table>

续表

	INTERNATIONAL ASSISTANCE APPLICATION FORM	*EXPLANATORY NOTES*
	a) Will the project be implemented at a World Heritage property? 　☐ - yes　　☐ - no 　If yes, give the name of the property b) Will the project include a field component? 　☐ - yes　　☐ - no 　If yes, where and how? e) If the project is being implemented at a World Heritage property, indicate whether it will also benefit other World Heritage properties, and if so which ones and how?	
5.	TIMEFRAME FOR THE IMPLEMENTATION OF THE PROJECT (indicate whether estimated or fixed)	Indicate the proposed starting date for the project as well as its duration.
6.	THE PROJECT IS: ☐ local ☐ national ☐ sub-regional involving a few States Parties from a region ☐ regional involving most States Parties from a region ☐ international involving States Parties from different regions If the project is national, sub-regional, regional or international, please indicate the countries/properties which will participate/benefit from the project.	If other countries benefit from the project, please state whether their support for the project has been obtained. Also note if a transboundary property is involved.
7.	JUSTIFICATION OF THE PROJECT	
	a) Explain why the project is needed (for Emergency Assistance, please fill in item 8 below instead)	Set out the problems or issues to be discussed/addressed. This should include, where appropriate, the degree of urgency of the activities to be undertaken where appropriate. If relevant, give details, in no more than 2 pages, of ascertained or potential threat to the property(ies). Explain how the project contributes to the implementation of: decisions of the World Heritage Committee; recommendations of international expert missions undertaken at the request of the Committee, Chairperson or UNESCO; recommendations of the Advisory Bodies; recommendations of UNESCO World Heritage Centre or other UNESCO Divisions; management plans for the property; recommendations from previous activities supported by the World Heritage Fund. Clearly indicate which documents you are referring to (World Heritage Committee's decision number, Mission dates, etc...)

续表

	INTERNATIONAL ASSISTANCE APPLICATION FORM	EXPLANATORY NOTES
	b) List all supporting documents submitted, if applicable.	Whenever possible, support the justification with documentary evidence, such as reports, photographs, slides, maps, etc...
8.	FOR EMERGENCY ASSISTANCE ONLY	
	a) Describe the actual or potential threat/danger affecting the property	Emergency Assistance funds will not be automatically granted after a major disaster has occurred. This type of assistance will be provided only in cases when an imminent danger related to a natural or human-made disaster is threatening the overall Outstanding Universal Value of a World Heritage property and its authenticity and/or integrity, to prevent or at least significantly mitigate its possible negative impact on the property. Emergency Assistance may also be provided to assess whether or not imminent danger is present, for example as a result of a major disaster. When, on the contrary, due to a disaster, a certain loss of heritage has already taken place, but there is no more imminent threat or risk that needs to be addressed as a matter of urgency, other forms of assistance would appear to be more appropriate (e.g. conservation and management assistance).
	b) Indicate how it might affect the property's Outstanding Universal Value	In establishing priorities for granting Emergency Assistance, consideration will be given to whether the threat/danger to be addressed has the potential, if not mitigated, to affect the Outstanding Universal Value of the World Heritage property and its authenticity and/or integrity.
	c) Explain how the proposed project will address the threat/danger	Proposals for funding under the Emergency Assistance programme should set out how the scope of the project and its activities will assess the threat/danger to the World Heritage property and show how it will be effectively mitigated.
9.	OBJECTIVE(S) OF THE PROJECT Clearly set out the specific objectives of the project	What are the objectives you want to achieve through the implementation of this particular project?
10.	EXPECTED RESULTS	
	a) Clearly state the results expected from the project proposed.	The expected results should be concrete and measurable. Each expected result will be measured by a set of indicators (see Paragraph 10b).

INTERNATIONAL ASSISTANCE APPLICATION FORM	EXPLANATORY NOTES
b) Define the indicators and means of verification which can be used to assess the achievements of these results:	Indicators are used to measure the results achieved and to determine the progress towards the objective of the project. They are based on the expected results defined in Paragraph 10, and will serve as the base for the evaluation of the project after its completion.

b) Define the indicators and means of verification which can be used to assess the achievements of these results:

Expected Results	Indicators	Means of Verification

Indicators are used to measure the results achieved and to determine the progress towards the objective of the project. They are based on the expected results defined in Paragraph 10, and will serve as the base for the evaluation of the project after its completion.

These indicators should be objective, measurable and expressed in quantifiable terms such as numeric values, or percentages.

For example:

Preparatory Assistance

Objective:

To prepare a complete nomination file for submission to the World Heritage Centre.

Expected Results	Indicators	Means of Verification
The completed nomination file submitted to the World Heritage Centre by 1 February 20xx.	• Nomination submitted by the deadline	• Postal record of sending the file Report from WHC to the State Party
The completed management plan to be submitted along with the nomination file	• Management plan submitted by the deadline	• Postal record of sending the file Report from WHC to the State Party
The nomination file is judged complete by the World Heritage Centre and Advisory Bodies	• Successful examination by the World Heritage Centre and Advisory Bodies for completeness	• Letter from the World Heritage Centre to the State Party informing them the file is considered complete

Emergency Assistance

Objective:

To stabilize the structure of a building that has just been damaged due to flooding or an earthquake.

INTERNATIONAL ASSISTANCE APPLICATION FORM	EXPLANATORY NOTES

Expected Results	Indicators	Means of Verification
The structure of the building would have been stabilized	• Emergency structural problems Identified • Plans for emergency works finalized • Temporary stabilization measures carried out	• Report of a structural engineer on the emergency state of the structure • Costed proposal for emergency works to be carried out • Final report of the stabilization work implemented
Plans for further conservation work would have been developed for future implementation	• Overall structural analysis carried out • Costed plans for further necessary conservation work prepared	• Report of a structural engineer on the overall state of conservation of the structure • Costed proposal for necessary conservation works to be carried out

Conservation and Management Assistance

Objective:

To improve management at a property inscribed on the World Heritage List with special attention to community involvement

续表

INTERNATIONAL ASSISTANCE APPLICATION FORM	EXPLANATORY NOTES		
	Expected Results	Indicators	Means of Verification
	An integrated management plan for the property	• Setting up of a management planning team for the development of the manage-ment plan with participants from the necessary sec-tors including the local community • Completion of a Statement of Outstanding Uni-versal Value for the property • Analysis of the conservation and management pro-blems affecting the property • Existence of clear objectives and strategies for achieving them	• Monthly reports of the mana ge-ment planning team meetings • Discussion pa-pers produced by team mem-bers of each of the key issues faced in the man-agement of the property • Final man-agement plan document
	A management committee in-cluding some members of the local commu-nity	• Appointment of members of the management com-mittee including at least two mem-bers of the local community • At least 3 regu-lar monthly me-etings of the Man-agement Com-mittee	• Statutes and rules of procedure for the Manage-ment Committee approved by appropriate au-thorities • Monthly re-ports of the Man-agement Com-mittee
	Management plan approved with appropri-ate legal status	• Approval by the local government authority	• Decree placed in the "National Gazette" estab-lishing the ma-nagement plan as a local reg-ulation.

INTERNATIONAL ASSISTANCE APPLICATION FORM	*EXPLANATORY NOTES*
11. **WORK PLAN** (including specific activities and timetable) | Activities	Timeframe (in months)
---	---	---	---	---	---
Activity					
Activity					
Activity					
Activity							Describe the work plan of the activity(ies) to be undertaken with specific reference to the expected results mentioned in Paragraph 10 above. Indicate dates, duration of each activity. For meetings and training activities, tentative programmes should be provided including the themes, issues and problems to be discussed. For example: *For Expected Result No. 1:* | Activities	Timeframe (in months)
Activity	
Activity	
Activity	
Activity		 *For Expected Result No. 2:* 	Activities	Timeframe (in months)
Activity	
Activity	
Activity	
Activity		
12. **EVALUATION AND REPORTING** (to be submitted to the World Heritage Centre within three months after the implementation of the project is completed)	Final Report: The final report should be prepared by the authority/person in charge of the implementation of the project. The final report should be structured according to the expected results defined in Paragraph 10. Evaluation: The evaluation should focus on the results achieved and their impact on (for example): - the inscription of a property on the World Heritage List following a preparatory assistance, -the Periodic Report and the State of conservation, -the removal of a property from the List of World Heritage in danger following an emergency assistance, -the implementation of the *World Heritage Convention*, including its Strategic Objectives ("5Cs") and other strategies (e.g. Global Strategy, …), -the national and/or local institutions, -the capacity building of local staff, -the awareness raising of the general public, -the participants to the project, -attracting other resources, -etc… Indicate who will be responsible for the evaluation of the project.

	INTERNATIONAL ASSISTANCE APPLICATION FORM	EXPLANATORY NOTES
13.	PROFILES OF SPECIALISTS, TRAINERS, TECHNICIANS AND/OR SKILLED LABOUR, IF THE PROJECT FORESEES THE PARTICIPATION OF SUCH PEOPLE (if the identity of the specialists, trainers, technicians, and/or skilled labourers is already known, please state their names and include a brief CV if possible)	Indicate the precise field of specialization and the work to be undertaken by each specialist as well as the duration required. The World Heritage Centre and the Advisory Bodies are available to recommend resource persons / trainers, should the State(s) Party(ies) concerned so request. Please include the names of any specialists, if already known, who will be taking part in the project and send a short CV if possible as an annex to the request form.
14.	KEY TARGET AUDIENCES, INCLUDING PROFILES OF TRAINEES / PARTICIPANTS, IF THE PROJECT FORESEES THE PARTICIPATION OF SUCH PEOPLE	Indicate the target groups and beneficiaries of the project, their professions, institutions, or field(s) of specialization.
15.	BUDGET BREAKDOWN	
	a) Provide, in the following table (in United States dollars), a detailed breakdown of costs of the individual elements of the project including, if possible, unit costs and show how these will be shared between the different funding sources:	Indicate in the table the breakdown of all expenses related to the project, also indicating the cost-sharing between the various donors (State Party, World Heritage Fund, others).
	(i) Organization	Items within this section could include the cost of a venue, office expenses, secretarial assistance, translation, simultaneous interpretation, audio-visual equipment, or other organizational costs necessary for the successful implementation of the project.
	(ii) Personnel and Consultancy Services	Items within this section could include the cost of international experts, national experts, a local or international coordinator, or other personnel necessary for the successful implementation of the project.
	(iii) Travel	Items within this section could include the cost of international or domestic travel necessary for the successful implementation of the project.
	(iv) Daily Subsistence Allowance	Items within this section could include the cost of accommodation, meals, and incidentals necessary for the successful implementation of the project.
	(v) Equipment	Items within this section could include any equipment necessary for the successful implementation of the project.
	(vi) Evaluation, Reporting and Publication	Items within this section could include the cost of evaluation, reporting, editing and layout, printing, distribution, and other costs necessary for the successful implementation of the project.
	(vii) Miscellaneous	Items within this section could include the cost of visas or other small costs that are necessary for the successful implementation of the project.

续表

	INTERNATIONAL ASSISTANCE APPLICATION FORM	EXPLANATORY NOTES
	b) Specify whether or not resources from the State Party or other sources are already available or when they are likely to become available	If the resources are not already available, indicate whether they will be before the beginning of the project.
16.	IN KIND CONTRIBUTIONS FROM THE STATE PARTY AND OTHER AGENCIES	
	a) National agency(ies)	Specify in detail
	b) Other bi/multi-lateral organizations, donors, etc	Specify in detail
17.	AGENCY(IES) RESPONSIBLE FOR THE IMPLEMENTATION OF THE PROJECT	Please provide the name, title, address and all contact details of the person/agency(ies) who will be responsible for the implementation of the project as well as those of any other participating agencies. Please, indicate whether the legislative and administrative commitment of the State Party is available for the project (see Paragraph 239d of the *Operational Guidelines*).
18.	SIGNATURE ON BEHALF OF STATE PARTY	Full name Title Date
19.	ANNEXES	In this section, list the number of annexes attached to the request and titles of each annex.

填报须知

	国际援助申请格式	填报须知
1	缔约国	提出国际援助申请的缔约国名称
2	项目名称	
3	援助类型 表格见下方 * 请注意，保护与管理一项现包括之前下列类别： – 培训与研究援助 - 技术合作援助 - 教育、信息与意识提升援助	具体内容请参见《操作指南》第 241 段。 应指明所申请的援助类型以及该项目涉及的遗产类型。仅选择表格中的一项内容，如： – 岩画培训项目 表格见下方 编制混合遗产的申报文件 表格见下方 由于热带风暴影响了保护林区而申请紧急援助 表格见下方
4	项目地点	

援助类型（申请格式栏）

	紧急援助	预备援助	保护与管理 *
文化			
自然			
混合			

岩画培训项目

	紧急援助	筹备性援助	保护与管理
文化			X
自然			
混合			

编制混合遗产的申报文件

	紧急援助	筹备性援助	保护与管理
文化			
自然			
混合		X	

由于热带风暴影响了保护林区而申请紧急援助

	紧急援助	筹备性援助	保护与管理
文化			
自然	X		
混合			

	国际援助申请格式	填报须知
	a）该项目是否会在一处世界遗产地实施？ □是　　□否 如果答案为"是"，提供遗产名称： b）该项目是否包括野外活动部分？ □是　　□否 如果答案为"是"，提供地点和方式： c）如果该项目在世界遗产地实施，请说明其他世界遗产是否也能受益。如果是，请说明受益遗产以及具体受益方式？	
5	项目时间表（请说明是预计或确切时间表）	说明项目计划开始的日期及持续时间。
6	□项目类型为： □地方性活动 □国家性活动 □涉及某一区域少数几个缔约国的次区域性活动 □涉及某一区域的多数缔约国的区域性活动 □涉及不同地区的众多缔约国的国际性活动 如果该项目为次区域性、区域性或国际性活动，请明确说明哪些国家或遗产将参加该项目活动，以及哪些遗产将从该项目中收益。	如果其他国家也能以中受益，说明是否已经获得它们对项目的支持。 同时说明是否涉及跨境遗产。
7	项目原因	
	a）说明需实施该项目的理由（如申请紧急援助，请省略此项，填写第八项）	阐明将要讨论或解决的问题。应尽量说明举办这些活动的紧迫程度。 如有涉及，应详细描述遗产面对的已知或潜在威胁，篇幅不超过两页。 解释此项活动将如何有益于实施： － 世界遗产委员会的决议； － 委员会、主席或联合国教科文组织委派的国际专家工作组的建议； － 咨询机构的建议； － 联合国教科文组织世界遗产中心以及其他部门的建议； － 与遗产有关的管理规划建议； － 世界遗产基金支持的在世界遗产地或缔约国举行的、以往活动中制定出的指导方针。 应明确指出所引用的参考文件（世界遗产委员会的决定号码、代表团日期等等）

	国际援助申请格式	填报须知
	b）如有可能，请列举已提交的能支持项目实施理由的文件	如有可能，提供各种形式文献说明如报告、照片、幻灯片、地图册等。
8	紧急援助申请	
	a）描述遗产面对的已知或潜在的威胁或危险	并非发生了重大灾难就会自动拨付紧急救助基金。只有当自然或人为灾难对世界遗产的突出的普遍价值、真实性和／或完整性带来紧急威胁时，才会提供这种援助，用以避免或大幅降低可能对遗产造成的负面影响。 紧急援助也可用来评估重大灾难等是否带来了紧急威胁。 如果灾难已经给遗产带来了一定损失，但目前没有需要紧急处理的威胁或危险，申请其他类型的援助更为恰当（如保护与管理援助）。
	b）指出这种威胁对遗产突出普遍价值的影响	在决定给予紧急援助时，应考虑该威胁／危险如果得不到缓解是否有可能影响世界遗产突出普遍价值、完整性和／或真实性。
	c）解释该项目消除这种威胁或危险的方法	申请紧急援助时，应阐明项目及其范围评估世界遗产面临的威胁／危险的方式，以及有效缓解该威胁／危险的方法。
9	项目目标 清晰说明该项目的具体目标	希望通过实施该项目达成什么目标？
10	预期结果	
	a）清晰说明该项目的预期结果	预期结果应该具体且可衡量。每个预期结果都需要通过一组指标来衡量（见 10b 段）。

国际援助申请格式	填报须知
b）定义能够评估预期结果的指标和验证方法 	预期结果	指标	验证方法
---	---	---
				指标用于衡量取得的成果并判断项目目标的进展。这些指标基于第 10 段定义的预计结果，并将作为项目完成后评估的基础。 指标应客观、可衡量，以数值或百分比等量化的方式表示。例如： **筹备性援助** | 预期结果	指标	验证方法
---	---	---
于 20XX 年 2 月 1 日前向世界遗产中心提交完整的申报文件	在截至日期前提交申报文件	– 提交文件的邮政记录 – 世界遗产中心给缔约国的回执
同时提交完整的管理规划	在截至日期前提交管理规划	– 提交文件的邮政记录 – 世界遗产中心给缔约国的回执
世界遗产中心及咨询机构判定申报文件完整	世界遗产中心及咨询机构判定申报文件完整	– 世界遗产中心发回执给缔约国，通知缔约国文件完整的信件	 **紧急援助** 目标：对因洪水或地震受损的建筑物结构进行加固 	预期结果	指标	验证方法
---	---	---
加固建筑物的结构	– 确定紧急出现的结构问题 – 制定紧急工作计划 – 实施临时稳定措施	– 结构工程师关于结构紧急情况的报告 – 包含所需紧急工作预算的报告 – 加固工作实施的最终报告
制定未来保护修复的工作计划	– 完成全面的结构分析 – 制定包含未来所需保护修复工作预算的计划	– 结构工程师关于结构整体保护状况的报告 – 包含未来所需保护工作预算的报告	 **保护与管理援助** 目标：改善世界遗产的管理，尤其注重社区参与

国际援助申请格式	填报须知
	<table><tr><td>预期结果</td><td>指标</td><td>验证方法</td></tr><tr><td>制定综合的遗产管理规划</td><td>– 成立管理规划编制团队，成员包括当地社区等各相关领域的人员 – 编制完成遗产的《突出普遍价值声明》 – 分析影响遗产的保护与管理的问题 – 拥有清晰的目标及实现目标的策略</td><td>– 项目规划团队会议的月报 – 团队成员编制的关于遗产管理中各关键问题的讨论文件 – 管理规划文件定稿</td></tr><tr><td>成立包括当地社区人员的管理委员会</td><td>– 指定管理委员会成员，其中至少两名成员来自当地社区 – 每月至少召开三次管理委员会会议</td><td>– 管理委员会的规章制度被相关机构批准 – 管理委员会的月报</td></tr><tr><td>管理规划获得适当的法律地位</td><td>– 获当地政府机构批准</td><td>– 国家公报刊载政令，确立该管理规划为当地法规</td></tr></table>

国际援助申请格式	填报须知
11　项目计划（包括具体活动和时间表） _(活动/时间表（月份）表格)_	描述活动的计划，标明上文第 10 段中的预期结果。说明每一项活动的日期及持续时间。如果是会议、培训活动，应提供主题议题等内容。如： 旨在取得第一项预期结果的活动： _(活动/时间表（月份）甘特图表格)_ 旨在取得第二项预期结果的活动： _(活动/时间表（月份）甘特图表格)_
12　评估与报告 （应在项目完成三个月内提交给世界遗产中心）	总结报告： 总结报告应由项目实施负责人编写，报告结构应遵循第 10 段中的预期结果。 评估： 评估应主要针对所取得的成果及产生的影响，如对下列内容的影响： – 申请筹备援助后，遗产列入《世界遗产名录》 – 定期报告及保护情况 – 申请紧急援助后，遗产从《濒危世界遗产名录》中移除 –《世界遗产公约》及其战略目标（5Cs）和其他战略（如全球战略）实施的情况 – 国家和 / 或当地机构 – 当地人员的能力建设 – 大众的意识提升 – 项目参与者 – 吸引其他资源，等 指定项目评估负责人。

续表

	国际援助申请格式	填报须知
13	可能参加此项活动的专家、培训人员、技术人员和 / 或技工的简介 （如果已知上述人员身份，请提供其姓名。如有可能，应提供个人简历）	明确说明各个专家的专业领域、承担的工作以及所需工作时间。如缔约国发出请求，世界遗产中心与专家咨询机构可以为活动推荐专家顾问 / 培训人员。 请提供任何已确定参加该项目的专家的姓名。如有可能，将其简历以附件形式与申请表一并提交。
14	项目主要受众（包括受训人员和参与者的简介）	说明项目的目标群体与受益人以及他们的职业、所属机构或专业领域。
15	详细预算	
	a) 提供下列各项目的费用（以美元为单位），如可能，应包括单位成本以及不同资金来源分担这些成本的情况：	请在表中提供项目全部费用的详细预算，并说明不同资金来源（缔约国、世界遗产基金会、其他）分担这些费用的情况。
	(i) 组织	该项包括活动地点、办公费用，如影印费、文具费、秘书协助费用、笔译费、口译费、影音设备费用以及项目实施所需的其他必要的组织费用。
	(ii) 人员与咨询服务	该项包括支付给国际、国内专家、协调人员费用以及项目实施所需的其他人员费用。
	(iii) 差旅费	该项包括项目实施所需的国际或国内旅行费用。
	(iv) 每日生活补助	该项包括项目实施所需的住宿、餐饮等相关费用。
	(v) 设备	该项包括项目实施所需的设备费用。
	(vi) 评估、报告与出版	该项包括项目实施所需的评估、报告、编辑、排版、印刷、发行等费用。
	(vii) 其他杂费	该项包括项目实施所需的签证费等小额费用。
	b）详细说明缔约国或其他来源的资源是否已到位或在争取中	如果资源目前尚未到位，说明在项目实施时是否可以到位。
16	缔约国或其他机构的实物捐赠	
	a）国家机构	请详细说明。
	b）其他双边或多变组织、捐赠者等	请详细说明。
17	负责项目实施的机构	请提供负责项目实施的人员或机构的姓名、职位、地址、详细联系信息以及其他参与机构的详细信息。 请说明缔约国是否对该项目提供了立法或行政方面的支持（见《操作指南》第 239d 条）。
18	缔约国代表签字	姓名： 职位： 日期：
19	附件	列出援助申请附件的编号及名称。

Process of submission for International Assistance requests for Conservation & Management Assistance and Preparatory Assistance above US$5,000

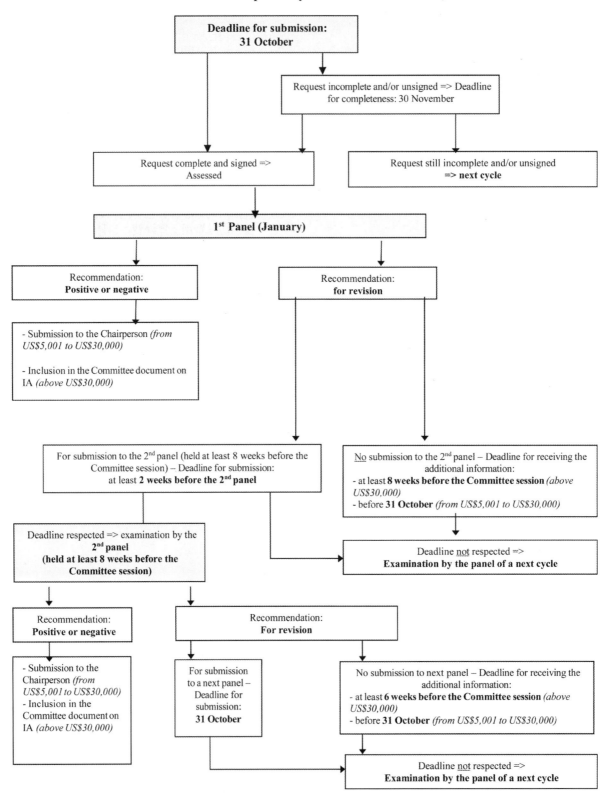

5000 美元以上保护和管理国际援助及筹备援助申请流程

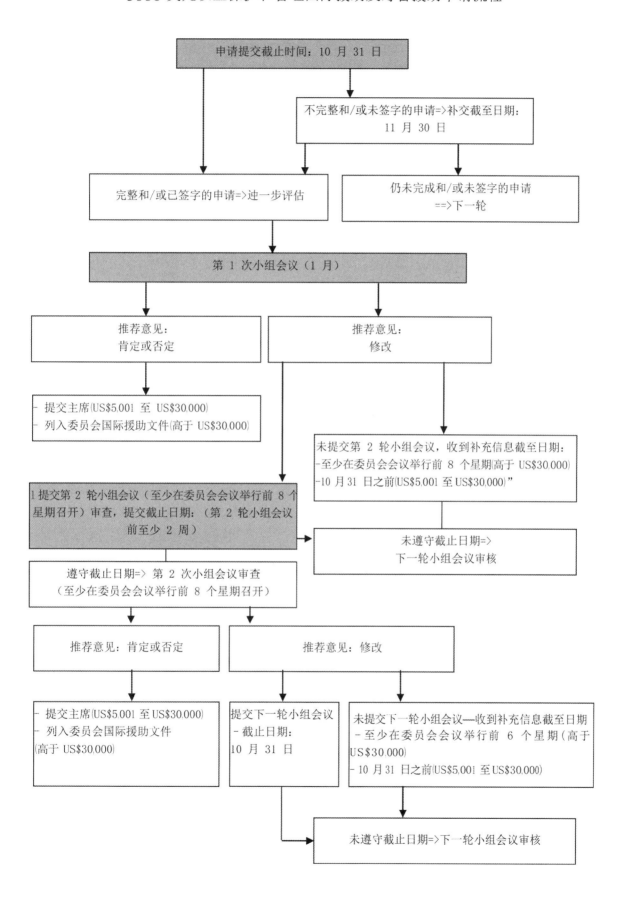

United Nations
Educational, Scientific and
Cultural Organization

World
Heritage
Convention

EVALUATION CRITERIA
FOR INTERNATIONAL ASSISTANCE
REQUESTS

The following considerations are to be taken into account by the Advisory Bodies, World Heritage Centre, and the relevant Decision-maker (the Chairperson of the World Heritage Committee, the World Heritage Committee or the Director of the World Heritage Centre) when assessing International Assistance requests.

These items do not constitute a checklist, and not every item will be applicable to every International Assistance Request. Rather the appropriate items are to be considered together in an integrated manner in making balanced judgments concerning the appropriateness of allocating the limited financial support available through the World Heritage Fund.

A. Eligibility

1. Is the State Party in arrears for payment of its contribution to the World Heritage Fund?

2. Is the request coming from an authorized organization/institution of the State Party?

B. Priority considerations

3.Is the request from a State Party on the list of the Least Developed Countries (LDCs), Low In-

附件 9   评估国际援助申请的标准

咨询机构、世界遗产中心以及相关决策方（世界遗产委员会主席、世界遗产委员会或世界遗产中心主任）对国际援助申请进行评估时，将考虑下列因素。

这些内容并非全部考虑因素，也不一定适用于每一份《国际援助申请》。确切地说，在考察将有限的资金通过世界遗产基金进行拨付是否合适时，需要对全部适当的因素进行通盘考虑，做出均衡判断。

A. 资格

1. 缔约国是否拖欠给世界遗产基金缴纳的捐款?

2. 申请是否由缔约国授权的组织或机构提交?

B. 优先考虑因素

3. 申请援助的缔约国是否为最不发达国家、低收入国家、低水平中等收入国家、小岛屿发

come Economies (LIEs), Small Island Developing States (SIDS) or post-conflict countries?

展中国家或冲突后国家？

4. Is the property on the List of World Heritage in Danger?

4. 遗产是否列入了《濒危世界遗产名录》？

5. Does the request further one or more of the Strategic Objectives of the World Heritage Committee (Credibility, Conservation, Capacity building, and Communication)?

5. 援助申请是否能推动世界遗产委员会实现一项或多项战略目标（可信性、保护、能力建设与宣传）？

6. Does the request respond to needs identified through the Periodic Reporting process at the property and/or regional levels?

6. 援助申请是否满足定期报告过程中定位的遗产和 / 或地区需求？

7. Is the request linked to a regional or sub-regional capacity building programme?

7. 援助申请是否与地区或次地区能力建设计划有关？

8. Is there a capacity building aspect to the activity (no matter what type of assistance sought)?

8. 活动（援助类型不限）是否涉及能力建设？

9. Will the lessons learned from the activity provide benefits to the larger World Heritage system?

9. 活动经验是否对更大范围的世界遗产系统有益？

C. Considerations linked to the specific content of the proposed activity

C. 与活动内容相关的考虑因素

10.Are the objectives of the request clearly stated and achievable?

10. 援助申请的目的是否清晰且切实可行？

11. Is there a clear work plan for achieving the results, including a timeline for its implementation? Is the work plan reasonable?

11. 是否具有针对结果的清晰的工作计划（包括项目实施的时间表）？工作计划是否合理？

12.Does the agency/organization responsible for implementing the proposal have the capacity to do so, and is there a responsible person identified for ongoing contacts?

12. 负责项目实施的机构或组织是否具备实施能力？目前有没有可以联系的负责人？

13. Are the professionals proposed to be used (whether national or international) qualified to carry out the work being requested? Are there clear terms of reference for them, including adequate period of their involvement?

14. Is the involvement of all relevant parties taken into account in the proposal (for example stakeholders, other institutions, etc.)?

15. Are the technical requirements clearly expressed and are they reasonable?

16. Is there a clear plan for reporting the results and for continued monitoring, including appropriate indicators for success?

17. Is there a commitment of the State Party for appropriate follow-up after the activity is completed?

D. Budgetary / Financial considerations

18. Is the overall budget reasonable for the work that is proposed to be carried out?

19. Is the budget detailed sufficiently to ensure that the unit costs are reasonable and in line with local costs and/or UNESCO norms and rules as appropriate?

20. Does the request act as a catalyst (multiplier) for other funding (are other sources of funding, either cash or in-kind clearly specified)?

E. Considerations for specific types of International Assistance

a) *Emergency Assistance Requests*

13. 申请援助的工作提议聘请的（国内或国际）专家是否合格？他们的职权范围以及参与时间是否清晰明了？

14. 提议中是否考虑到了所有相关方的参与（如利益相关方、其他机构等）？

15. 是否明确表达了技术要求？这些要求是否合理？

16. 是否具备关于结果报告、后续监测以及相关指标的清晰计划？

17. 缔约国是否承诺活动完成后采取适当的后续措施？

D. 预算 / 财政考虑因素

18. 建议开展的工作的总体预算是否合理？

19. 预算是否足够详细？能否确保合理的单位成本？单位成本是否与本地成本相一致，按照联合国教科文组织的规范和规则，是否合适？

20. 援助申请是否能够推动（倍增效应）其他资金（如有，说明其他现金或实物性质的资金来源）？

E. 特定类型国际援助的考虑因素

a) 紧急援助申请

21. Does the threat or disaster covered by the request conform to the definition of an emergency within the *Operational Guidelines* (unexpected phenomena)?

21. 申请中提到的威胁或灾难是否符合《操作指南》中定义的紧急情况（意外的现象）？

22. Can the proposed intervention be carried out with reasonable safety for those involved with its implementation?

22. 建议采用的干预措施能否在保证相关人员安全的情况下实施？

23. Does the intervention respond to the most critical issues related to the protection/conservation of the property?

23. 干预措施是否针对遗产保护或保存中最重要的问题？

b) *Preparatory Assistance Requests*

b) 筹备性援助的申请

For requests for preparation of nomination files

编制申报文件的申请

24. Is the property on the State Party's Tentative List?

24. 遗产是否已列入缔约国的《预备名录》？

25. Does the State Party already have properties inscribed on the World Heritage List? If yes, how many?

25. 缔约国是否有列入《世界遗产名录》遗产？如果有，具体数量是多少？

26. Is the type of property proposed for World Heritage listing un-represented or under-represented in the World Heritage List?

26.《世界遗产名录》中是否没有所申报类型的遗产或数量很少？

27. Is sufficient attention paid to necessary elements, such as the preparation of the management plan, comparative analysis, Statement of Outstanding Universal Value, mapping, etc.?

27. 对编制管理规划、比较分析、《突出普遍价值声明》、地图等必要因素的关注是否充分？

28. Is sufficient attention given to community involvement?

28. 对社区参与的关注是否充分？

For requests for preparation of Tentative Lists

编写《预备名录》

29. Is the process designed to include all the

29.该过程是否包括所有必要的利益相关方，

necessary stakeholders and points of view?

是否体现了不同观点？

30. Are both natural and cultural heritage professionals proposed to be involved?

30. 文化遗产专家和自然遗产专家是否都应参与？

31. Is the State Party new to the *World Heritage Convention*?

31. 缔约国是否为新加入《世界遗产公约》的国家？

32. If the request is for harmonization of Tentative Lists, are representatives from all the necessary States Parties in the region or sub-region involved?

32. 如果申请的目的是协商《预备名录》，该地区或次地区所有缔约国是否均有代表参加？

For requests for preparation of other types of assistance

筹备申请其他类型援助

33. If the request is for the preparation of a request for other assistance, is the need for the eventual request well documented?

33. 如果申请的目的是筹备申请其他类型的援助，最终的申请需求是否有充足的文件记录？

c) *Conservation and Management Assistance Requests*

c) 保护与管理援助

For requests for conservation work or the preparation of a management plan

保护工作或编制管理规划的申请

34. Is the property on the World Heritage List?

34. 该遗产是否已列入《世界遗产名录》？

35. Is the work being proposed a priority for protecting or safeguarding the property?

35. 所提议的工作是否在保护遗产方面应优先开展？

36. Does the work being proposed conform to best practice?

36. 所提议的工作是否是最好的方法？

For requests for training activities

培训活动

37. Is it clearly related to the implementation of the *World Heritage Convention*?

37. 是否与实施《世界遗产公约》明确相关？

38. Does it take place on a World Heritage

38. 是否在世界遗产地举办，是否涉及参观

property or involve a visit/case study of a World Heritage property?

世界遗产或世界遗产案例研究？

39. Does it involve those responsible for conservation at a World Heritage property as trainees or resource persons?

39. 负责世界遗产保护的人员是否为培训对象或邀请他们分享经验？

40. Does it respond to well-defined training needs?

40. 是否针对已明确定义的培训要求？

41. Are the training methods appropriate to ensure that the learning objectives will be met?

41. 培训方法是否恰当？能否保证实现培训目标？

42. Does it strengthen a local and/or regional training institution?

42. 能否改善当地或地区的培训习惯？

43. Is it linked with practical applications in the field?

43. 是否与实际应用相关？

44. Is there a provision for disseminating results and related training materials to other organizations in the World Heritage system?

44. 是否规定将培训成果及相关培训教材扩大到世界遗产系统中的其他组织？

For requests related to scientific research

科学研究

45. Can it be demonstrated that the subject matter is of a priority nature for better protection and safeguarding of World Heritage properties?

45. 能否证明该主题对改善世界遗产保护具有更重要的意义？

46. Can it be demonstrated that the results will be concrete and applicable widely within the World Heritage system?

46. 能否证明研究成果将非常具体并可以广泛应用到世界遗产系统当中？

For requests for educational or awareness activities

教育或意识提升

47. Will it help make the *World Heritage Convention* better known or create a stronger interest in it amongst the target audience?

47. 能否提高《世界遗产公约》的知名度或提高公众对《世界遗产公约》的关趣？

48. Will it create a greater awareness of the different issues related to the implementation of the *World Heritage Convention*?

49. Will it promote more involvement in *World Heritage Convention* related activities?

50. Will it be a means of exchanging experiences or stimulate joint educational and information programmes, especially amongst school children?

51. Will it produce appropriate awareness materials for the promotion of the *World Heritage Convention*

48. 能否提高人们对实施《世界遗产公约》相关事项的意识？

49. 能否推动更多人参与《世界遗产公约》相关的活动？

50. 能否成为经验交流的工具或促成教育和信息计划方面的合作，尤其是学生之间的交流或合作？

51. 能否为公众提供合适的、作为宣传《世界遗产公约》的、提升意识的材料？

United Nations
Educational, Scientific and
Cultural Organization

World
Heritage
Convention

STATEMENT OF OUTSTANDING UNIVERSAL VALUE

Format of a Statement of Outstanding Universal Value, and of a retrospective Statement of Outstanding Universal Value.

The retrospective Statement of Outstanding Universal Value should be submitted either in English or in French. An electronic version (Word or .pdf format) should also be submitted.

A Statement of Outstanding Universal Value should respect the following format (2 A4 pages max):

a) Brief synthesis
b) Justification for Criteria
c) Statement of integrity (for all sites)
d) Statement of Authenticity (for sites under criteria i-vi)
e) Requirements for protection and management

Deadline

1 February [1] of the year preceding the one in which the approval of the Committee is requested.

附件 10　《突出普遍价值声明》

《突出普遍价值声明》，以及《回顾性突出普遍价值声明》的格式。

回顾性突出普遍价值声明应以英文或法文提交，同时提交电子版（word 或 pdf 格式）。

《突出普遍价值声明》应遵循以下格式（A4纸不超过两页）：

1）简要综述
2）按标准给出列入理由
3）完整性声明（所有遗产）
4）真实性声明（按照标准 i–vi 列入的遗产）

5）保护和管理要求

截止日期

委员会批准当年之前一年的 2 月 1 日 [1]

---

① If 1 February falls on a weekend, the nomination dossier must be received by 17h00 GMT the preceding Friday

① 如 2 月 1 日恰逢周末，申报文件必须在前一个周五 17：00（格林威治时间）之前收悉。

United Nations
Educational, Scientific and
Cultural Organization

World
Heritage
Convention

MODIFICATIONS
TO WORLD HERITAGE PROPERTIES

附件 11　对世界遗产的修改

MINOR MODIFICATIONS TO THE BOUNDAR-
IES OF WORLD HERITAGE PROPERTIES

世界遗产边界的细微调整

Boundary modifications should serve better identification of World Heritage properties and enhance protection of their Outstanding Universal Value.

遗产边界的修改应有利于更好地识别世界遗产，加强对世界遗产突出普遍价值的保护。

A proposal for a minor boundary modification, submitted by the State Party concerned, is subject to the review of the relevant Advisory Body(ies) and to the approval of the World Heritage Committee.

缔约国提出的关于边界细微调整的提议由相关咨询机构进行审核，最终提交世界遗产委员会批准。

A proposal for a minor boundary modification can be approved, not approved, or referred by the World Heritage Committee.

世界遗产委员会可以批准、不批准或要求补充提交关于边界细微调整的提议。

Documentation requested

所需文件

1) Area of the property (in hectares): please indicate a) the area of the property as inscribed and b) the area of the property as proposed to be modified (or the area of the proposed buffer zone). (Note that reductions can be considered as minor modifications only under exceptional circumstances).

1) 遗产面积（公顷）：请说明 a）列入遗产的面积和 b）提议修改的遗产面积（或提议修改的缓冲区面积）。（注意：只有在极个别情况下才会将面积缩小视作细微调整。）

2) Description of the modification: please provide a written description of the proposed change to the boundary of the property (or a written

2) 修改描述：请提供关于遗产边界变动的书面说明（或关于提议的修改缓冲区的书面说明）。

description of the proposed buffer zone).

3) Justification for the modification: please provide a brief summary of the reasons why the boundaries of the property should be modified (or why a buffer zone is needed), with particular emphasis on how such modification will improve the conservation and/or protection of the property.

4) Contribution to the maintenance of the Outstanding Universal Value: please indicate how the proposed change (or the proposed buffer zone) will contribute to the maintenance of the Outstanding Universal Value of the property.

5) Implications for legal protection: please indicate the implications of the proposed change for the legal protection of the property. In the case of a proposed addition, or of the creation of a buffer zone, please provide information on the legal protection in place for the area to be added and a copy of relevant laws and regulations.

6) Implications for management arrangements: please indicate the implications of the proposed change for the management arrangements of the property. In the case of a proposed addition, or of the creation of a buffer zone, please provide information on the management arrangements in place for the area to be added.

7) Maps: please submit two maps, one clearly showing both delimitations of the property (original and proposed revision) and the other showing only the proposed revision. In the case of the creation of a buffer zone, please submit a map showing both the inscribed property and the proposed buffer zone.

Please make sure that the maps:

3) 修改理由：请简要说明遗产边界变动的原因（或需要设立缓冲区的原因），应重点说明所提议的变动将如何能够改善遗产保存和／或保护。

4) 促进突出普遍价值的保持：请说明所提议的变动（或提议的缓冲区）将以何种方式促进遗产突出普遍价值的保持。

5) 对法律保护的影响：请说明所提议变动对遗产所受法律保护的影响。如果提议扩大遗产或缓冲区范围，请提供针对新增部分已经到位的法律保护信息以及相关法律法规的副本。

6) 对管理安排的影响：请说明所提议变动对遗产管理安排的影响。如果提议扩大遗产缓冲区或范围，请提供针对新增部分的已经到位的管理安排。

7) 地图：请提供两张地图，其中一张应清晰地显示遗产的两个边界（原边界和提议修改的边界），另一张仅显示所提议修改的边界。如果是提议修改缓冲区，请提交一张既包括列入遗产也包括所提议修改的缓冲区的地图。

请确认地图：

- are either topographic or cadastral;

- are presented at a scale which is appropriate to the size in hectares of the property and sufficient to clearly show the detail of the current boundary and the proposed changes (and, in any case, the largest available and practical scale);

- have the title and the legend/key in English or French (if this is not possible, please attach a translation);

- mark the boundaries of the property (current and proposed revision) through a clearly visible line that can be distinguished from other features on the maps;

- bear a clearly labeled coordinate grid (or coordinate ticks);

- clearly refer (in the title and in the legend) to the boundary of the World Heritage property (and to the buffer zone of the World Heritage property, if applicable). Please clearly distinguish the boundary of the World Heritage property from any other protected area boundaries.

8) Additional information: In the case of a proposed addition, please submit some photographs of the area to be added that provide information on its key values and conditions of authenticity/ integrity.

Any other relevant document can be submitted such as thematic maps (e.g. vegetation maps), summaries of scientific information concerning the values of the area to be added (e.g. species lists), and supporting bibliographies.

The above-mentioned documentation should be submitted in English or French in two identical copies (three for mixed properties). An electronic version (the maps in formats such as .jpg, .tif, .pdf) should also be submitted.

– 是地形图或地籍图；

– 以公顷为单位所使用的比例尺恰当，能够清楚地显示现有边界及所提议修改的细节（以及最大可用且实际的比例尺）；

– 使用英文或法文的标题、图例 / 符号（如不是，请附翻译件）；

– 使用清晰的线条标示遗产边界（现边界和提议修改的边界），从而与地图上的其他部分区分开来；

– 带有清晰标记的坐标网（或坐标标记）；

–（在标题和图例中）清晰地指明世界遗产的边界（以及世界遗产的缓冲区，如适用）。请将世界遗产的边界与其他保护区的边界清晰地区分开。

8) 补充信息：如果提议扩大遗产面积，请提交有关待增加面积的图片，用于说明其核心价值以及真实性 / 完整性条件。

此外可以提交任何其他相关文件，例如专题地图（如植被图）、关于待增加地区价值的科学信息总结（如物种名录）以及参考书目。

上述文件应使用英语或法语提交，一式两份（混合遗产一式三份），同时还应提交电子版（地图格式为 .jpg，.tif，.pdf）。

Deadline

1 February[1] of the year in which the approval
of the Committee is requested.

截止日期

要求委员会批准的年份的 2 月 1 日[1]。

---

[1]　If 1 February falls on a weekend, the nomination dossier must be received by 17h00 GMT the preceding Friday

[1]　如果2月1日恰逢周末，申报文件必须在此前的周五17：00（格林威治时间）之前收悉。

United Nations
Educational, Scientific and
Cultural Organization

World
Heritage
Convention

FORM FOR THE SUBMISSION OF FACTUAL ERRORS IN
THE ADVISORY BODIES EVALUATIONS

(in compliance with Paragraph 150 of the *Operational Guidelines*)

STATE (S) PARTY (IES):

EVALUATION OF THE NOMINATION OF THE SITE:

RELEVANT ADVISORY BODY'S EVALUATION[①] :

Page, column, line of the Advisory Body Evaluation	Sentence including the factual error (the factual error should be highlighted in bold)	Proposed correction by the State Party	Comment (if any) by the Advisory Body and/or the World Heritage Centre

- The Factual Errors submission form, as well as an example of such a completed form, are available from the UNESCO World Heritage Centre and at https://whc.unesco.org/en/factualerrors.
- Further guidance on the submission of Factual Errors can be found in Paragraph 150 of the *Operational Guidelines*.

---

① For nominations of mixed sites, if there are errors in both the Evaluations of the Advisory Bodies, separate forms should be submitted for each Advisory Body indicating which Advisory Body's Evaluation each submission is referring to.

● States Parties are requested to immediately submit this information in electronic format or by e-mail to wh-nominations@unesco.org.

The original signed version of the completed Factual Errors submission form should be received in English or French by the UNESCO World Heritage Centre, at the following address: 7 place de Fontenoy, 75352 Paris 07 SP, France, no later than 14 days before the opening of the session of the Committee.

附件 12　咨询机构评估中事实性错误提交表格
（对应《操作指南》正文第 150 条）

缔约国：

遗产申报评估：

相关咨询机构评估①：

所在咨询机构评估报告页码、列、行	包含事实性错误的句子（事实性错误应字体加粗）	缔约国建议的更正	咨询机构和 / 或世界遗产中心反馈意见（如有）

- 登录网址 https://whc.unesco.org/en/factualerrors 可下载事实性错误提交表格，以及一份填写完整的范本。
- 有关事实性错误提交的更多指导信息，见《操作指南》正文第 150 条
- 缔约国需立即将该信息以电子形式提交或发电子邮件至 wh–nominations@unesco.org.

必须最晚于委员会大会开幕 14 天前，联合国教科文组织世界遗产中心收到填写完整并签字的、事实性错误提交表格的英文或法文版原件，邮寄地址如下：7 place de Fontenoy，75352 Paris 07 SP，France

---

① 在申报混合遗产过程中，如果两个咨询机构的评估都发现有事实性错误，则需分别向给两个咨询机构提交表格，并写明所递交的对象。

United Nations
Educational, Scientific and
Cultural Organization

World
Heritage
Convention

FORMAT FOR THE SUBMISSION OF STATE OF CONSERVATION REPORTS BY THE STATES PARTIES

(in compliance with Paragraph 169 of the *Operational Guidelines*)

Name of World Heritage property (State(s) Party(ies)) (Identification number)

1. Executive Summary of the report

[Note: each of the sections described below should be summarized. The maximum length of the executive summary is 1 page.]

2. Response to the Decision of the World Heritage Committee

[Note: The State(s) Party(ies) is/are requested to address the most recent Decision of the World Heritage Committee for this property, paragraph by paragraph.]

If the property is inscribed on the List of World Heritage in Danger Please also provide detailed information on the following:

a) Progress achieved in implementing the corrective measures adopted by the World Heritage Committee

[Note: please address each corrective measure individually, providing factual information, including exact dates, figures, etc.]

If needed, please describe the success factors

附件 13　缔约国保护状态报告提交格式

（对应《操作指南》正文第 169 条）

（缔约国）世界遗产名称（认定编号）

1. 报告的执行摘要

【注意：应对下述每一章节进行概述。执行摘要最长篇幅：1 页。】

2. 对世界遗产委员会决议的回应

【注意：缔约国应逐段回应世界遗产委员会对该世界遗产的最新决定。】

如果该世界遗产被列入《濒危世界遗产名录》，缔约国还应提供以下详细信息：

a) 在实施世界遗产委员会已通过的整改措施方面所取得的进展

【注意：请分别描述每一个整改措施的实施进展，包括确切日期、数据等事实信息。】

如有需要，可描述每一项整改措施实施过

or difficulties in implementing each of the corrective measures identified

b) Is the timeframe for implementing the corrective measures suitable? If not, please propose an alternative timeframe and an explanation why this alternative timeframe is required.

c) Progress achieved towards the Desired state of conservation for the removal of the property from the List of World Heritage in Danger (DSOCR)

3. Other current conservation issues identified by the State(s) Party(ies) which may have an impact on the property's Outstanding Universal Value

[Note: this includes conservation issues which are not mentioned in the Decision of the World Heritage Committee or in any information request from the World Heritage Centre]

4. In conformity with Paragraph 172 of the *Operational Guidelines*, describe any potential major restorations, alterations and/or new construction(s) intended within the property, the buffer zone(s) and/or corridors or other areas, where such developments may affect the Outstanding Universal Value of the property, including authenticity and integrity.

5. Public access to the state of conservation report

[Note: this report will be uploaded for public access on the World Heritage Centre's State of conservation Information System (https://whc. unesco.org/en/soc). Should your State Party request that the full report should not be uploaded, only the 1-page executive summary provided in point (1.) above will be uploaded for public access].

6. Signature of the Authority

程中的成功因素或困难要素。

b) 实施这些整改措施所制定的时间表是否恰当？如果该时间表并不恰当，请提供其他建议，并解释为何需要这个新的时间表。

c) 为将世界遗产从《濒危世界遗产名录》中除名应达到一定的保护状况，请描述目前已取得的进展。

3. 缔约国确认的可能会影响遗产突出普遍价值的其他现有保护问题

【注意：包括世界遗产委员会决定中，或世界遗产委员会所要求的信息中未提及的保护问题】

4. 依照《操作指南》第 172 条规定，描述在该世界遗产内部、缓冲区和 / 或廊道或其他区域内，任何可能的重大修复、改变和 / 或新建筑，这些开发可能会影响遗产的突出普遍价值真实性和完整性等。

5. 公众对获取遗产保护状况的报告

【注意：遗产保护状况报告将上传至世界遗产中心遗产保护状况信息系统（https://whc. unesco.org/en/soc）。（如果缔约国要求不上传报告全文，则仅按第一条要求上传一页执行摘要，供公众获取。】

6. 缔约国当局签署

United Nations
Educational, Scientific and
Cultural Organization

World
Heritage
Convention

TABLE OF USES
OF THE WORLD HERITAGE EMBLEM

This table was prepared on the basis of Chapter VIII of the *Operational Guidelines* of the World Heritage Convention and *the Directives Concerning the Use of the Name, Acronym, Logo and Internet Domain Names of UNESCO* (Resolution 34C/86).

Reminder concerning the authority and delegation of authority for the use of the World Heritage Emblem according to Chapter VIII of the *Operational Guidelines*:

Para. 262:

"The World Heritage Committee is responsible for determining the use of the World Heritage Emblem and for making policy prescriptions regarding how it may be used."

Para. 276:

"National authorities may grant the use of the Emblem to a national entity, provided that the project, whether national or international, involves only World Heritage properties located on the same national territory. National authorities' decision should be guided by the Guidelines and Principles."

Para. 278:

Any other request must be addressed to the

附件 14　世界遗产标识使用表格

本表格基于世界遗产公约《操作指南》第八章及《关于使用联合国教科文组织名称、首字母缩略词、标识及互联网域名的决定》（决议 34C/86 ）中的规定而制定。

提示－有关《操作指南》第八章关于使用世界遗产标识的管理机构及其授权代表：

第 262 条：

"世界遗产委员会负责决定世界遗产标识的使用，同时负责制定如何使用标志的政策规定。"

第 276 条：

"如果国家或国际项目只涉及本国的世界遗产，国家权威机构可授权国家实体使用标识。国家权威机构的决定应遵守《指南和原则》"。

第 278 条：

其他相关申请由世界遗产中心主任处理 --

Director of the World Heritage Centre, who has the authority to grant the use of the Emblem in accordance with the Guidelines and Principles.

For cases not covered, or not sufficiently covered, by the Guidelines and Principles and by the Table of Uses, the Director refers the matter to the Chairperson who, in the most difficult cases, might wish to refer the matter to the Committee for final decision.

Reminder concerning the use of the linked logo and of the stand alone Emblem: Para. 262:

Since the adoption by the UNESCO General Conference in October 2007 of the *Directives concerning the Use of the Name, Acronym, Logo and Internet Domain Names of UNESCO*, it is strongly encouraged to use the World Heritage Emblem as part of a linked logo block accompanied by UNESCO's logo, whenever feasible. The use of the World Heritage Emblem alone remains however possible, in line with the present Guidelines and with the Table of Uses (Annex 14 of the Guidelines).

Reminder concerning the graphic charter:

The graphic charter of the UNESCO logo is available here: http://www.unesco.org/new/en/name-and-logo/graphics/

According to the Preamble of Chapter VIII of the *Operational Guidelines*, the stand alone World Heritage Emblem can be used in any colour or size.

The logos are provided by the authorizing entities (as detailed in the following table) in digital format which cannot be modified by the users in any way.

他有权根据《指南和原则》批准使用标识。

遇到《指南和原则》及"使用表"尚未涉及或未完全涵盖的情况，主任应将申请提交给主席，如果是很难处理的情况，主席会将该申请提交委员会做最后决定。

第 262 条有关使用标识链接及独立标识的提示

2007 年 10 月，联合国教科文组织大会审议通过了《联合国教科文组织相关名称、缩略语、标志及网域名称使用指南》。委员会鼓励在任何适当的情况下，将世界遗产的标志作为联合国教科文组织的延伸部分加以使用。世界遗产标志也可以不同方式单独使用，需符合现行《操作指南》和《使用表》（见附件 14）的要求。

提示 – 有关使用标识的授权：

可登录 http://www.unesco.org/new/en/name–and–logo/graphics/ 查找使用联合国教科文组织标识的授权。

根据《操作指南》第八章序文，可以用任何颜色或尺寸使用独一无二的世界遗产标识。

这些标识由授权机构（见下文表格详述内容）以电子形式提供，使用者不得进行任何方式的改变。

It is obligatory to submit the draft layout of the intended use to the authorizing entity for validation before production.

Definition of commercial use:

The sale of goods or services bearing the name, acronym, logo and/or Internet domain name of UNESCO combined with the World Heritage Emblem chiefly for profit shall be regarded as "commercial use" for the purpose of the Operational Guidelines. *Such use must be expressly authorized by the Director-General, under a specific contractual arrangement* (definition adapted from UNESCO Logo Directives 2007. Art Ⅲ.2.1.3)

必须将用于特定用途的布局设计草案提交给授权实体进行确认后方可生产。

商业使用的定义：

以营利为目，销售带有联合国教科文组织名称、首字母缩略词、标识及联合互联网域名及世界遗产标识的商品或服务，被《操作指南》认定为"商业用途"。此类用途必须根据具体的合同安排，由总干事明确授权（定义摘自联合国教科文组织标识方针，2007 年 . 第Ⅲ.2.1.3)。

WORLD HERITAGE CENTRE

Uses and purposes	Uses		Authorization		Graphic illustrations
World Heritage Centre - WHC (for international content)	Type of Logo the WHC can use	Use of the Logo by the WHC is authorized by	WHC can authorize the Logo for	Type of Logo the WHC can authorize	Logo to be used and/or authorized by the WHC
1) Publications 2) Communication materials 3) Website, social media, apps, etc. 4) Working documents 5) Communication products (such as T-shirts, bags, umbrellas), for special events 6) Stationery	UNESCO/World Heritage Convention logo	Statutory use	State Party hosting a Committee	UNESCO/World Heritage Convention logo	World Heritage Convention / United Nations Educational, Scientific and Cultural Organization
1) Publications 2) Communication materials 3) Website, social media, apps, etc. 4) Working documents 5) Communication products (such as T-shirts, bags, umbrellas), for special events 6) Stationery	UNESCO/World Heritage Centre logo	Statutory use			United Nations Educational, Scientific and Cultural Organization / World Heritage Centre
1) Publications 2) Communication materials 3) Website, social media, apps, etc. 4) Small-size communication products (such as pens, key-rings etc), for special events 5) Stationery	World Heritage Emblem	Statutory use	1) World Heritage Site Management Authority 2) State Party hosting a Committee	World Heritage Emblem	or
Committee session	UNESCO/World Heritage logo + "XXth/st/rd/nd World Heritage Committee session"	Statutory use	State Party hosting a Committee	UNESCO/World Heritage logo + "XXth/st/rd/nd World Heritage Committee session"	United Nations Educational, Scientific and Cultural Organization / 39th session of the World Heritage Committee

Uses and purposes	Uses	Authorization	Graphic illustrations
Partnership with external entities (private and public sector)	Statutory use		
	UNESCO/World Heritage Centre logo with text "With the support of", "In cooperation with", or "In partnership with"	Entities in the framework of contractual arrangements	
		UNESCO/World Heritage Centre logo with text "With the support of", "In cooperation with", or "In partnership with"	
	UNESCO/World Heritage Centre or Convention logo + Partner's logo and/or text	UNESCO/World Heritage Centre or Convention logo+Partner's logo and/or text	

世界遗产中心

用途及目的	世界遗产中心可使用的标识类型	授权世界遗产中心使用标识的主体	可得到世界遗产中心授权使用标识的主体	世界遗产中心可授权的标识类型	图解说明
世界遗产中心 WHC（国际使用）					世界遗产中心可使用和／或授权的标识
1）出版物 2）传播材料 3）网站，社交媒体及应用软件等 4）工作文档 5）特殊事件中用于宣传的产品（如T恤，袋子，雨伞等） 6）文具	联合国教科文组织／世界遗产中心标识	依法使用	组织举办会议的缔约国	联合国教科文组织／世界遗产中心标识	
1）出版物 2）传播材料 3）网站，社交媒体及应用软件等 4）工作文档 5）特殊事件中用于宣传的产品（如T恤，袋子，雨伞等） 6）文具	联合国教科文组织／世界遗产中心标识	依法使用			
1）出版物 2）传播材料 3）网站，社交媒体及应用软件等 4）特殊事件中小型宣传的产品（如钢笔，钥匙圈等） 5）文具	世界遗产中心标识	依法使用	1）世界遗产遗址管理当局 2）组织举办委员会会议的缔约国	世界遗产标识	
委员会大会	联合国教科文组织／世界遗产标识＋"第xx届世界遗产委员会大会"	依法使用	组织举办会议的缔约国	联合国教科文组织／世界遗产标识＋"第xx届世界遗产委员会大会"	

续表

用途及目的	用途	授权	图解说明
与外部实体机构（私人领域或公共领域）合作	联合国教科文组织/世界遗产标识+文本"用于支持…"、"与…合作"、或"与…协调"	联合国教科文组织/世界遗产标识+文本"与…用于支持…"、"与…协作"或"与…合作"；合同安排框架内的实体机构	UNESCO United Nations Educational, Scientific and Cultural Organization / World Heritage Centre —— In partnership with；UNESCO United Nations Educational, Scientific and Cultural Organization / World Heritage Centre —— With the support of
	依法使用	联合国教科文组织/世界遗产中心或世界遗产公约标识和/合作伙伴标识和/或文本	联合国教科文组织/世界遗产中心或世界遗产公约标识+合作伙伴标识和/或文本；UNESCO United Nations Educational, Scientific and Cultural Organization / World Heritage Centre

NATIONAL COMMISSIONS OR AGENCIES

Uses and purposes	Uses		Authorization		Graphic illustrations
1 - National Commission (for national content)	Type of Logo the NatCom can use	Use of the Logo by the NatCom is authorized by	NatCom can authorize the use of the Logo for	Type of Logo the Nat-Com can authorize	Logo to be used and/ or authorized by the NatCom
1) Non-commercial publications 2) Communication materials 3) Website, social media, apps, etc. 4) Communication products such as T-shirts, bags, umbrellas (non-merchandising, exceptionally for special events) 5) Stationery	UNESCO/World Heritage logo with text "World Heritage in... [Country name]"	Statutory use	Local government authorities and site managing authorities.	UNESCO/World Heritage logo with text "World Heritage in +country"	(UNESCO / World Heritage logo: United Nations Educational, Scientific and Cultural Organization · World Heritage in · Switzerland)
1) Website, social media, apps, etc. when space is limited 2) Communication products as a graphic element or when space is limited 3) Stationery 4) Any other applicable case according to the Operational Guidelines	World Heritage Emblem	Statutory use	World Heritage site management authority	World Heritage Emblem	(World Heritage Emblem)
Road signs, highway signs	Choice of the logo according to the kind of sign and its location: UNESCO/World Heritage logo in full or simplified with site's name underneath	Statutory use	World Heritage site management authority	UNESCO/World Heritage logo in full or simplified with site's name underneath	(UNESCO / World Heritage logos: United Nations Educational, Scientific and Cultural Organization · Shark Bay, Western Australia inscribed on the World Heritage List in 1991; Stonehenge, Avebury and Associated sites inscribed on the World Heritage List in 1986) Text under the name of the site is optional. Possibility to replace "inscribed on the World Heritage List in" by "World Heritage since"
	World Heritage Emblem	Statutory use	World Heritage site management authority	World Heritage Emblem	(World Heritage Emblem)

续表

Uses and purposes	Uses		Authorization		Graphic illustrations
	Type of Logo the NatCom can use	Use of the Logo by the NatCom is authorized by	NatCom can authorize the use of the Logo for	Type of Logo the NatCom can authorize	Logo to be used and/ or authorized by the NatCom
1 - National Commission (for national content)	UNESCO/World Heritage logo with text "World Heritage in... [Country name]"	Director-General of UNESCO			[logo]
Commercial use	World Heritage Emblem	Statutory use	National entity	World Heritage Emblem	[logo]
Committee session	UNESCO/World Heritage + "XXth/st/rd/nd World Heritage Committee Session"	World Heritage Centre	Organizing authority	UNESCO/World Heritage+ "XXth/st/rd/nd World Heritage Committee session"	[logo]
Patronage for World Heritage related one-off events (ex: conferences, publications or audio-visual production activity on national or local level)			Organizing entities	UNESCO/World Heritage logo with text "Under the patronage of the National Commission of xxx for UNESCO"	[logo]
World Heritage related partnership with national Organisations			National organisation having established a partnership with the National Commission	UNESCO/World Heritage logo with text "With the support of the xxx National Commission for UNESCO", or "In cooperation with the xxx National Commission for UNESCO", or "In partnership with the xxx National Commission for UNESCO"	[logo]

续表

Uses and purposes	Uses		Authorization		Graphic illustrations
	Type of Logo the agency can use	Use of the Logo by the agency is authorized by	Agency can authorize the use of the Logo to	Type of Logo the agency can authorize	Logo to be used and/or authorised by the agency
2 - Agency - designated national authority (for national content)					
1) Non-commercial publications 2) Communication materials 3) Website, social media, apps, etc. 4) Communication products (such as T-shirts, bags, umbrellas) non-merchandising, for special events 5) Stationery	UNESCO/World Heritage logo with text "World Heritage in... [Country name]"	National Commission or World Heritage Centre			
1) Non-commercial publications 2) Communication materials 3) Website, social media, apps, etc. 4) Communication products (such as T-shirts, bags, umbrellas) non-merchandising, for special events 5) Stationery	World Heritage Emblem	Statutory use	World Heritage site management authority	World Heritage Emblem	
Road signs, highway signs	Choice of the logo according to the kind of sign and its location: UNESCO/World Heritage logo in full or simplified with site's name underneath	National Commission or World Heritage Centre	World Heritage site management authority	UNESCO/World Heritage logo in full or simplified with site's name underneath	Text under the name of the site is optional. Possibility to replace "inscribed on the World Heritage List in" by "World Heritage since"
	World Heritage Emblem	Statutory use	World Heritage site management authority	World Heritage Emblem	

续表

Uses and purposes	Uses		Authorization	Graphic illustrations
Commercial use	UNESCO/World Heritage logo with text "World Heritage in... [Country name]"	Director-General of UNESCO		United Nations Educational, Scientific and Cultural Organization / World Heritage in Switzerland
	World Heritage Emblem	Statutory use		or

国家委员会或机构

用途及目的	用途		授权		图解说明
	国家委员会可使用的标识类型	授权国家委员会使用标识的主体	可得到国家委员会授权使用标识的主体	国家委员会可授权的标识类型	国家委员会可使用和/或授权的标识
1- 国家委员会（国内使用） 1）非商业用途出版物 2）传播材料 3）网站、社交媒体及应用软件等 4）特殊事件中用于宣传的产品（如T恤、袋子、雨伞等） 5）文具	联合国教科文组织/世界遗产标识+"…[国家名称]的世界遗产"	依法使用	当地政府机构或遗址管理当局	联合国教科文组织/世界遗产标识+"…[国家名称]的世界遗产"	
1）非商业用途出版物，如会间空间所有 2）作为图形元素或适当空间有限时传播的产品 3）文具 4）符合《操作指南》规定的其他适用情况	世界遗产标识	依法使用	世界遗产遗址管理当局	世界遗产标识	
	依据标志类型及其位置选择适当的标识：联合国教科文组织/世界遗产标识整体，或在标识下方简单标注遗址地名称	依法使用	世界遗产遗址管理当局	联合国教科文组织/世界遗产标识整体，或在标识下方简单标注遗址地名称	可自行确定遗址地下方的文字，有可能为世界遗产"来代替"××年成为世界遗产"/"××年列入世界遗产名录"
公路标志，高速公路标志	世界遗产标识	依法使用	世界遗产遗址管理当局	世界遗产标识	

续表

用途及目的	用途		授权		图解说明
商业使用	联合国教科文组织/世界遗产标识 + "…[国家名称]的世界遗产"	联合国教科文组织总干事			
	世界遗产标识	依法使用	国家实体	世界遗产标识	
委员会大会	联合国教科文组织/世界遗产 + "第xxx届世界遗产委员会大会"	世界遗产中心	主办方当局	联合国教科文组织/世界遗产标识/世界遗产 + "第xx届世界遗产委员会大会"	
对世界遗产一次性活动的赞助（如大会，出版物或国家或地方的影音制作活动）			主办方当局	联合国教科文组织标识/世界遗产标识/世界遗产 + 文字"得到xxx国家教科文组织文委员会对联合国教科文组织的资助"	
世界遗产与国家组织的合作			已与国家委员会建立合作关系的国家组织	联合国教科文组织标识/世界遗产 + 文字"得到xxx国家教科文组织委员会对联合国教科文组织的支持"，或"与联合国教科文组织xxx国家委员会协作"，或"与联合国教科文组织xxx国家委员会合作"	
2－代理机构－指定国家当局（国内使用）	代理机构可使用的标识类型	授权代理机构使用用标识的主体	可得到代理机构授权使用标识的主体	代理机构可授权的标识类型	代理机构可使用和/或授权的标识

续表

用途及目的	用途		授权	图解说明
1）非商业用途出版物 2）传播材料 3）网站、社交媒体及应用软件等 4）特殊事件中用于宣传的非商品化产品（如T恤、袋子、雨伞等） 5）文具	联合国教科文组织/世界遗产标识+文字"…[国家名称]的世界遗产"	国家委员会或世界遗产中心		
1）非商业用途出版物 2）传播材料 3）网站、社交媒体及应用软件等如空间有限 4）特殊事件中用于宣传的非商品化产品（如T恤、袋子、雨伞等） 5）文具	世界遗产标识	依法使用	世界遗产遗址管理当局	
公路标志，高速公路标志	依据标志类型及其位置选择适当的标识：联合国教科文组织/世界遗产标识整体或世界遗产标识整体或在标识下方简单，标注遗址地名称	国家委员会或世界遗产中心	联合国教科文组织/世界遗产标识整体，或在标识下方简单标注遗址地名称	可自行确定遗址地名称下方的文字有可能使用"自××年成为世界遗产"来代替/列入世界遗产名录
	世界遗产标识	依法使用	世界遗产遗址管理当局	
商业使用	联合国教科文组织/世界遗产标识+"…[国家名称]的世界遗产"	联合国教科文组织总干事	世界遗产标识	
	世界遗产标识	依法使用	世界遗产标识	

WORLD HERITAGE SITE MANAGEMENT AUTHORITY

Uses and purposes	Uses		Authorization		Graphic illustrations
World Heritage site management authority (for site-related content)	Type of Logo the WH site can use	Use of the Logo by the WH site is authorized by	WH Site can authorize the Logo for	Type of Logo the WH Site can authorize	Logo to be used and/or authorized by the WH site
1) Non-commercial publications 2) Communication materials 3) Website, social media, apps, etc. 4) Communication products (such as T-shirts, bags, umbrellas) non-merchandising, for special events 5) Stationery 6) Plaque, flag, banner	UNESCO/World Heritage site specific logo	National Commission or World Heritage Centre			Possibility to replace "Inscribed on the World Heritage List in" by "World Heritage since"
1) Non-commercial publications 2) Communication materials 3) Website, social media, apps, etc. when space is limited 4) Communication products (T-shirts, bags, umbrellas, key-rings, pens etc.) non-merchandising, for special events 5) Plaque, flag, banner	World Heritage Emblem	National Commission or agency or World Heritage Centre			or
Road signs, highway signs	Choice of the logo according to the kind of sign and its location: UNESCO/ World Heritage logo in full or simplified with site's name underneath	National Commission or World Heritage Centre			Text under the name of the site is optional. Possibility to replace "inscribed on the World Heritage List in" by "World Heritage since"

Uses and purposes	Uses		Authorization		Graphic illustrations
	Type of Logo the WH site can use	Use of the Logo by the WH site is authorized by	WH site can authorize the Logo for	Type of Logo the WH site can authorize	Logo to be used and/or authorized by the WH site
World Heritage site Management Authority (continued)	World Heritage Emblem	National Commission or World Heritage Centre			
	UNESCO/World Heritage site-specific logo	Director-General of UNESCO			Possibility to replace: "inscribed on the World Heritage List in" by "World Heritage since"
Commercial use	World Heritage Emblem	National Commission			

世界遗产管理机构

用途及目的 世界遗产遗址地管理当局（用于遗址地相关内容）	用途		授权		图解说明 世界遗产遗址地可使用和／或授权的标识
	世界遗产遗址地可使用的标识类型	世界遗产遗址地使用标识的主体	可得到世界遗产遗址地授权使用标识的主体	世界遗产遗址地可授权的标识类型	
1) 非商业用途出版物 2) 传播材料 3) 网站、社交媒体及应用软件等 4) 特殊事件中用于宣传的非商品化产品（如T恤、袋子、雨伞等） 5) 文具 6) 匾、旗帜或横幅标语	联合国教科文组织／世界遗产遗址地专用标识	国家委员会或世界遗产中心			有可能使用"自××年成为世界遗产之后"来代替"××年列入世界遗产名录"
1) 非商业用途出版物 2) 传播材料 3) 网站、社交媒体及应用软件等如空间有限 4) 特殊事件中用于宣传的非商品化产品（如T恤、袋子、雨伞钥匙圈、钢笔等） 5) 匾、旗帜或横幅标语	世界遗产标识	国家委员会或代理机构或世界遗产中心			or
公路标志、高速公路标志	依据标志类型及其位置选择适当的标识：联合国教科文组织／世界遗产标识，或在标识下方简单标注遗址地名称	国家委员会或世界遗产中心			可自行确定遗址地名称下方的文字有可能使用"自××年成为世界遗产之后"来代替"××年列入世界遗产名录"
	世界遗产标识	国家委员会或世界遗产中心			or

续表

用途及目的	使用		授权	图形图例
	世界遗产点可使用的标识类型	世界遗产点使用标识的授权	世界遗产点可授权的标识	世界遗产点可授权的标识类型
世界遗产管理当局（与遗产相关内容）	联合国教科文组织/世界遗产遗址地专用标识	联合国教科文组织总干事	世界遗产点可授权的标识类型	世界遗产点可使用的标识类型
商业使用	世界遗产标识	国家委员会		

Specific case: serial sites or very large sites including several/various elements/monuments/places

Uses and purposes	Uses		Authorization		Graphic illustrations
	Type of Logo the WH site can use	Use of the Logo by the WH site is authorized by	WH site can authorize the Logo for	Type of Logo the WH site can authorize	Logo to be used and/or authorized by the WH site
World Heritage site management authority (continued) 1) Non-commercial publications 2) Communication materials 3) Website, social media, apps, etc. 4) Communication products (T-shirts, bags, umbrellas, key-rings, pens etc.) non-merchandising, for special events 5) Stationery 6) Plaque, flag, banner	UNESCO/World Heritage site-specific logo, preceded by the mention "Xxxx [name of the element/monument/place], part of"	National Commission or World Heritage Centre			Xxxx part of

特殊情况：系列遗产或超大型，包含多个、不同要素或纪念物和地方的遗产

用途及目的	使用		授权		图形图例
	世界遗产点可使用的标识类型	世界遗产点使用标识的授权	世界遗产点可授权的标识	世界遗产点可授权的标识类型	世界遗产点可使用的标识类型
世界遗产管理当局（与遗产相关内容） 1）非商业用途出版物 2）传播材料 3）网站、社交媒体及应用软件等 4）特殊事件中用于宣传的非商品化产品（如T恤、袋子、雨伞等） 5）文具 6）匾、旗帜或横幅标语	联合国教科文组织/世界遗产遗址地专用标识，前边应提及"…的xxxx[元素/古迹/地方]部分"	国家委员会或世界遗产中心			×××× 的一部分

WORLD HERITAGE ADVISORY BODIES

Uses and purposes	Uses		Authorization		Graphic illustrations
Advisory Bodies	Type of Logo the Advisory Bodies can use	Use of the Logo by Advisory Bodies is authorized by	Advisory Bodies can authorize the Logo for	Type of Logo the Advisory Bodies can authorize	Logo to be used by the Advisory Bodies
1)Non-commercial publications 2)Non-commercial communication materials 3)Website 4)Non-commercial stationery	UNESCO/World Heritage Convention logo	World Heritage Centre			
1) Publications 2) Communication materials 3) Website 4) Stationery	World Heritage Emblem	World Heritage Centre			

世界遗产咨询机构

用途及目的	用途		授权		图解说明
咨询机构	咨询机构可使用的标识类型	咨询机构使用标识的主体	可得到咨询机构授权使用标识的主体	咨询机构可授权的标识类型	咨询机构可使用和／或授权的标识
1）非商业用途出版物 2）非商业用途传播材料 3）网站 4）非商业用途文具	联合国教科文组织／世界遗产公约标识	世界遗产中心			
1）出版物 2）传播材料 3）网站 4）文具	世界遗产标识	世界遗产中心			

PATRONAGE

Uses and purposes	Uses	Authorization		Graphic illustrations
		UNESCO Director-General can authorize	Type of Logo Director-General can authorize	
Patronage	One-off activities (conferences, exhibitions, festivals, publications or audio-visual productions)	Organizing authorities	UNESCO/World Heritage logo with text "Under the patronage of"	Logo to be authorized

赞助

用途及目的	用途	授权		图解说明
		联合国教科文组织总干事可授权	联合国教科文组织可授权的标识类型	
赞助	一次性活动（会议，展览，节日出版物或视听所产品）	组织当局	联合国教科文组织标识/世界遗产标识＋文本"得到…的赞助"	待授权的标识

United Nations
Educational, Scientific and
Cultural Organization

World
Heritage
Convention

UPSTREAM PROCESS REQUEST FORMAT

1. State (s) Party(ies)

2. Object of the advice requested from the World Heritage Centre or the Advisory Bodies
(Please tick the corresponding box)

☐ Development, revision or harmonization of Tentative List(s)
☐ Potential future nomination – If applicable, name of the site(s)

3. Brief description of the site (summary of factual information and qualities of the site, if applicable)

4. Expected time frame for the realization of the Upstream Process

5. Would a site visit be necessary?
☐ Yes   ☐ No

6. Availability of funds to implement the request

(Please indicate how you intend to cover the costs related to the implementation of the Upstream Process request. Please also indicate whether you plan to apply for assistance from the World Heritage Fund, if eligible (International Assistance mechanism or Advisory Missions budget line), or from another funding source).

附件 15 上游程序申请格式

1. 缔约国

2. 要求世界遗产中心或咨询机构提供意见的目的（请在相应方格内打"√"号）

☐修订或协调预备名录

☐未来可能的申报—如适用，遗产地的名称

3. 遗产地简介（如适用，请简要说明遗产的实际信息和特质）

4. 实现上游程序的预期时间表

5. 是否有必要现场调研？
☐是   ☐否

6. 是否有资金来执行该申请？

（请说明打算如何支付实施上游程序申请的相关费用。是否计划向世界遗产基金申请援助如符合（国际援助机制或咨询任务预算线），或者申请其他资金来源）。

7. Any additional information you may wish to provide

7. 您可能希望提供的其他信息

8. Contact information of the responsible authorities (name, title, e-mail, telephone)

8. 责任机关的联系方式（名称、职称、邮箱、电话）

9. Signature on behalf of the State(s) Party(ies)

9. 缔约国签章

The original signed version of the completed Upstream Process request form should be sent in English or French to:
UNESCO World Heritage Centre
7, place de Fontenoy 75352 Paris 07 SP
France
Telephone: +33 (0)1 4568 1104
E-mail: wh-upstream@unesco.org

已签署的上游程序申请表格正本须以英文或法文寄送至：

联合国教科文组织世界遗产中心
7，place de Fontenoy 75352 Paris 07 SP
法国
电话：+33（0）145681136E-
电子邮件：wh-upstream@unesco.org

United Nations
Educational, Scientific and
Cultural Organization

World
Heritage
Convention

SELECT WORLD HERITAGE BIBLIOGRA-PHY
WORLD HERITAGE CENTRE DOCUMENTS DATABASE

https://whc.unesco.org/en/documents/

The UNESCO World Heritage Centre "Official Records" searchable online document collection permits the retrieval of information contained in the reports of the World Heritage Committee and General Assembly of States Parties to the Convention.

BASIC TEXTS

UNESCO. 1972. *Convention concerning the Protection of the World Cultural and Natural Heritage.* (World Heritage Convention).

https://whc.unesco.org/en/conventiontext

UNESCO General Assembly of States Parties to the Convention concerning the Protection of the World Cultural and Natural Heritage. 2014. *Rules of Procedure.* WHC-14/GA/1 Rev. 4 (as of 14 November 2014)

https://whc.unesco.org/en/ga/

UNESCO Intergovernmental Committee for the Protection of the World Cultural and Natural Heritage. 1995. *Financial Regulations for the World Heritage Fund*, Paris. (WHC/7, August 1995).

https://whc.unesco.org/en/financialregulations/

UNESCO Intergovernmental Committee for

选择世界遗产相关的参考书目
世界遗产中心文件数据库

http://whc.unesco.org/en/documents/

联合国教科文组织世界遗产中心在线检索文件集"官方数据"，允许对世界遗产委员会和缔约国大会《公约》报告中的信息进行检索。

基础文件

《联合国教科文组织保护世界文化与自然遗产公约》（世界遗产公约），1972 年，联合国教科文组织。

http://whc.unesco.org/en/conventiontext

联合国教科文组织保护世界文化与自然遗产公约缔约国大会，2014 年，《议事规则》，WHC–14/GA/1Rev.4（截至 2014 年 11 月 14 日）

http://whc.unesco.org/en/ga/

联合国教科文组织保护世界文化与自然遗产政府间委员会，1995 年，《世界遗产基金财务规则》，巴黎（WHC/7，1995 年 8 月）

http://whc.unesco.org/en/committeerules

联合国教科文组织保护世界文化与自然遗

the Protection of the World Cultural and Natural Heritage. 2013. *Rules of Procedure*, WHC-2013/5

https://whc.unesco.org/en/committee

UNESCO World Heritage Centre. 2017. *Basic Texts of the 1972 World Heritage Convention* (2017 Edition). Paris, UNESCO.

https://whc.unesco.org/en/basictexts/

UNESCO World Heritage Centre. *Properties inscribed on the World Heritage List.*

https://whc.unesco.org/en/list

UNESCO World Heritage Centre. *Tentative Lists.*

https://whc.unesco.org/en/tentativelists/

STRATEGIC DOCUMENTS

UNESCO World Heritage Committee. 1992. *Strategic Orientations*. in Annex II of the Report of the 16th session of the World Heritage Committee (Santa Fe, 1992) (WHC-92/CONF.002/12).

https://whc.unesco.org/en/documents/940

UNESCO World Heritage Committee. 1994. *Report of the Expert Meeting on the "Global Strategy" and thematic studies for a representative World Heritage List* (20-22 June 1994) (WHC-94/CONF.003/INF.6)

https://whc.unesco.org/archive/global94.htm

UNESCO World Heritage Committee. 1994. *Nara Document on Authenticity.*

https://whc.unesco.org/archive/nara94.htm

UNESCO World Heritage Committee. 1996. *Report of the Expert Meeting on Evaluation of General Principles and Criteria for Nominations of Natural World Heritage sites*. (WHC-96/CONF.202/

产政府间委员会，2013 年，《议事规则》，WHC.2013/5.

http://whc.unesco.org/en/committee

联合国教科文组织世界遗产中心，2005 年，《1972 年世界遗产公约基础文件》（2005 年版本），巴黎，联合国教科文组织。

http://whc.unesco.org/en/activities/562/

联合国教科文组织世界遗产中心，《世界遗产名录》

http://whc.unesco.org/en/list

联合国教科文组织世界遗产中心，《预备名录》。

http://whc.unesco.org/en/tentativelists/

战略性文件

联合国教科文组织世界遗产委员会，1992 年，《战略定位》，见世界遗产委员会第 16 次大会报告附件 II（1992 年，圣达非）（WHC-92/CONF.002/12）。

http://whc.unesco.org/archive/1992/whc-92-conf002-12e.pdf

联合国教科文组织世界遗产委员会，1994 年，《〈世界遗产名录〉的全球战略与主题研究专家会议报告》（1994 年 6 月 20 至 22 日）（WHC-94/CONF.003/INF.6）

http://whc.unesco.org/archive/global94.htm

联合国教科文组织世界遗产委员会，1994 年，《奈良真实性文件》。

http://whc.unesco.org/archive/nara94.htm

联合国教科文组织世界遗产委员会，1996 年，《申报世界自然遗产遗址地一般评估原则和标准专家会议报告》（WHC-96/CONF.202/INF.9）.

INF.9).

https://whc.unesco.org/archive/1996/whc-96-conf202-inf9e.htm

UNESCO World Heritage Committee. 2001. Global Training Strategy for World Cultural and Natural Heritage, adopted by the World Heritage Committee at its 25th session (Annex X of WHC-01/CONF.208/24)- Update of the Global Training Strategy (Doc WHC-09/33.COM/10B). https://whc.unesco.org/archive/2001/whc-01-conf208-24e.pdf

https://whc.unesco.org/archive/2009/whc09-33com-10Be.pdf - See update in 2011

UNESCO World Heritage Committee. 2002. *Budapest Declaration on World Heritage.* (Doc WHC-02/CONF.202/5).

https://whc.unesco.org/en/decisions/1217/ - See update in 2007. T*he "fifth C" for "Communities".*

UNESCO World Heritage Committee. 2004. *Evaluation of the Global Strategy for a representative, balanced and credible World Heritage List* (1994-2004). (Doc WHC-04/28.COM/13)

https://whc.unesco.org/archive/2004/whc04-28com-13e.pdf

UNESCO World Heritage Committee. 2005. *Vienna Memorandum on World Heritage and Contemporary Architecture – Managing the Historic Urban Landscape.* (Doc WHC-05/15.GA/INF.7).

https://whc.unesco.org/archive/2005/whc05-15ga-inf7e.pdf

UNESCO World Heritage Committee. 2007. *Strategy for Reducing Risks from Disasters at World Heritage Properties.* (Doc WHC-07/31.COM/7.2)

https://whc.unesco.org/archive/2007/whc07-31com-72e.pdf

http://whc.unesco.org/archive/1996/whc-96-conf202-inf9e.htm

联合国教科文组织世界遗产委员会，2001年，《世界文化与自然遗产全球培训战略》，于芬兰赫尔辛基世界遗产委员会第25次会议通过（参见 WHC-01/CONF.208/24 附件 X-《全球培训战略》的更新（DocWHC-09/33.COM/10B））。

http://whc.unesco.org/archive/2001/whc-01-conf208-24e.pdfhttp://whc.unesco.org/archive/2009/whc09-33com-10Be.pdf- 见 2011 年的更新

联合国教科文组织世界遗产委员会，2002年，《世界遗产布达佩斯宣言》，（DocWHC-02/CONF.202/5）

https://whc.unesco.org/en/decisions/1217/- 见 2017 年更新的《"社区"的"五C战略"》

联合国教科文组织世界遗产委员会，2004年，《建构具有代表性、均衡性、可信性〈世界遗产名录〉的全球战略评估（1994-2004年）》（DocWHC-04/28.COM/13）

http://whc.unesco.org/archive/2004/whc04-28com-13e.pdf

联合国教科文组织世界遗产委员会，2005年，《维也纳世界遗产和当代建筑备忘录 - 管理城市历史景观》,（DocWHC-05/15.GA/INF.7）

http://whc.unesco.org/archive/2005/whc05-15ga-inf7e.pdf

联合国教科文组织世界遗产委员会，2007年，《世界遗产减少灾害风险减缓策略》（DocWHC-07/31.COM/7.2）

http://whc.unesco.org/archive/ 2007/whc07-31com-72e.pdf

UNESCO World Heritage Committee. 2007. *The "fifth C" for "Communities"*. (Doc WHC-07/31.COM/13B).

https://whc.unesco.org/archive/2007/whc07-31com-13be.pdf

UNESCO World Heritage Centre. 2008. *Policy Document on the Impacts of Climate Change on World Heritage Properties*. Paris, UNESCO World Heritage Centre.

https://whc.unesco.org/uploads/activities/documents/activity-397-2.pdf

UNESCO World Heritage Committee. 2010. *Reflection on the Trends of the State of Conservation*. (Doc WHC-10/34.COM/7C).

https://whc.unesco.org/archive/2010/whc10-34com-7Ce.pdf

UNESCO World Heritage Committee. 2011. *Presentation and adoption of the World Heritage strategy for capacity building*. (Doc WHC-11/35.COM/9B).

https://whc.unesco.org/archive/2011/whc11-35com-9Be.pdf

UNESCO World Heritage Committee. 2013. *Revised Partnerships for Conservation (PACT) Initiative Strategy*. (Doc WHC-13/37.COM/5D).

https://whc.unesco.org/archive/2013/whc13-37com-5D-en.pdf

UNESCO General Assembly of States Parties to the Convention concerning the Protection of the World Cultural and Natural Heritage. 2015. *World Heritage and Sustainable Development*. Resolution 20 GA 13. (Doc WHC-15/20.GA/15).

https://whc.unesco.org/archive/2015/whc15-20ga-13-en.pdf

联合国教科文组织世界遗产委员会，2007 年，《"社区"的"五 C 战略"》（DocWHC-07/31.COM/13B）．

http://whc.unesco.org/archive/2007/whc07-31com-13be.pdf

联合国教科文组织世界遗产中心，2008 年，《气候变化对世界遗产影响的政策文件》，巴黎，联合国教科文组织世界遗产中心．

http://whc.unesco.org/uploads/activities/documents/activity-397-2.pdf

联合国教科文组织世界遗产委员会，2010 年，《保护状况趋势的反思》，（DocWHC-10/34.COM/7C）．

http://whc.unesco.org/archive/2010/whc10-34com-7Ce.pdf

联合国教科文组织世界遗产委员会，2011 年，《展示和通过世界遗产能力建设战略》（DocWHC-11/35.COM/9B）．

http://whc.unesco.org/archive/ 2011/whc11-35com-9Be.pdf

联合国教科文组织世界遗产委员会，2013 年，《修订保护合作伙伴关系战略倡议》（Doc WHC-13/37.COM/5D）．

http://whc.unesco.org/archive/2013/whc13-37com-5D-en.pdf

联合国教科文组织世界遗产委员会，2015 年，《世界遗产及可持续发展》决议 20GA13.（Doc WHC-15/20.GA/15）．

https://whc.unesco.org/archive/2015/whc15-20ga-13-en.pdf

WORLD HERITAGE THEMATIC PRO-
GRAMMES

世界遗产主题项目研究

World Heritage Cities Programme. 2001.
https://whc.unesco.org/archive/2001/whc-01-
conf208-19e.pdf

世界遗产城市项目，2001 年，
https://whc. unesco. org/archive/2001/whc–01–
conf208–19e.pdf

World Heritage Sustainable Tourism Programme. 2012.
https://whc.unesco.org/archive/2012/whc12-
36com-5E-en.pdf

世界遗产可持续旅游项目，2012 年，

https://whc.unesco.org/archive/2012/whc12–
36com–5E–en.pdf

Small Island Developing States Programme.
2005.
https://whc.unesco.org/archive/2005/whc05-
29com-05e.pdf. p14

小岛屿发展中国家项目，2005 年，

https://whc.unesco.org/archive/2005/whc05–
29com–05e.pdf.p14

World Heritage Marine Programme. 2005.
https://whc.unesco.org/archive/2005/whc05-
29com-05e.pdf. p16

世界遗产海洋项目，2005 年，
https://whc.unesco.org/archive/2005/whc05–
29com–05e.pdf.p16

Thematic Initiative on Astronomy and World
Heritage. 2005.
https://whc.unesco.org/archive/2005/whc05-
29com-05e.pdf. p18

世界遗产天文主题项目，2005 年，

https://whc.unesco.org/archive/2005/whc05–
29com–05e.pdf.p18

Initiative on Heritage of Religious Interest.
2011.
https://whc.unesco.org/archive/2011/whc11-
35com-5Ae.pdf

世界遗产宗教主题项目，2011 年，

https://whc.unesco.org/archive/2011/whc11–
35com–5Ae.pdf

World Heritage Earthen Architecture
Programme (WHEAP). 2007.
https://whc.unesco.org/archive/2007/whc07-
31com-21Ce.pdf

世界遗产土遗址项目（WHEAP），2007 年，

https://whc.unesco.org/archive/2007/whc07–
31com–21Ce.pdf

WORLD HERITAGE RESOURCE MANUALS
https://whc.unesco.org/en/resourcemanuals/

世界遗产资源手册
http://whc.unesco.org/en/resourcemanuals/

UNESCO, ICCROM, ICOMOS and IUCN. 2010. *Managing Disaster Risks for World Heritage. Paris, UNESCO World Heritage Centre.*

https://whc.unesco.org/en/managing-disaster-risks/

UNESCO, ICCROM, ICOMOS and IUCN. 2011. *Preparing World Heritage Nominations. (Second edition).* Paris, UNESCO World Heritage Centre.

https://whc.unesco.org/en/preparing-world-heritage-nominations/

UNESCO, ICCROM, ICOMOS and IUCN. 2012. *Managing Natural World Heritage.* Paris, UNESCO World Heritage Centre.

https://whc.unesco.org/en/managing-natural-world-heritage/

UNESCO, ICCROM, ICOMOS and IUCN. 2013. *Managing Cultural World Heritage.* Paris, UNESCO World Heritage Centre.

https://whc.unesco.org/en/managing-cultural-world-heritage/

WORLD HERITAGE REVIEW

https://whc.unesco.org/en/review/

World Heritage is a quarterly review produced in English, French and Spanish by the UNESCO World Heritage Centre, featuring in-depth articles on world heritage-related issues and inscribed sites. 93 issues published since 1996.

WORLD HERITAGE PAPER SERIES

https://whc.unesco.org/en/series/

联合国教科文组织、国际文物保护与修复研究中心、国际古迹遗址理事会和世界自然保护联盟，2010年。《世界遗产灾害风险管理》。巴黎，联合国教科文组织世界遗产中心。

https://whc.unesco.org/en/managing-disaster-risks/

联合国教科文组织、国际文物保护与修复研究中心、国际古迹遗址理事会和世界自然保护联盟，2011年，《世界遗产申报准备手册》（第2版），巴黎，联合国教科文组织世界遗产中心。

https://whc.unesco.org/en/preparing-world-heritage-nominations/

联合国教科文组织、国际文物保护与修复研究中心、国际古迹遗址理事会和世界自然保护联盟，2012年。《世界自然遗产管理手册》，巴黎，联合国教科文组织世界遗产中心。

https://whc.unesco.org/en/managing-natural-world-heritage/

联合国教科文组织、国际文物保护与修复研究中心、国际古迹遗址理事会和世界自然保护联盟，2013年。《世界文化遗产管理手册》，巴黎，联合国教科文组织世界遗产中心。

https://whc.unesco.org/en/managing-cultural-world-heritage/

世界遗产评论

http://whc.unesco.org/en/review/

《世界遗产》是联合国教科文组织世界遗产中心刊发的世界遗产评论季度期刊，使用英语、法语和西班牙发行，内容包括对世界遗产相关事项进行深入评论的文章。至1996年已刊发93期。

世界遗产文件系列

http://whc.unesco.org/en/series/

UNESCO World Heritage Centre. 2002. *Managing Tourism at World Heritage Sites: a Practical Manual for World Heritage Site Managers*. Paris, UNESCO World Heritage Centre. (World Heritage Manual 1.)

https://whc.unesco.org/en/series/1/

联合国教科文组织世界遗产中心，2002 年。《世界遗产地的旅游管理：世界遗产遗址地管理人实用手册》，巴黎，联合国教科文组织世界遗产中心（世界遗产指南 1）。

http://whc.unesco.org/en/series/1/

UNESCO World Heritage Centre. 2002. *Investing in World Heritage: past achievements, future ambitions*. Paris, UNESCO World Heritage Centre. (World Heritage Papers 2.)

https://whc.unesco.org/en/series/2/

联合国教科文组织世界遗产中心，2002 年。《世界遗产投资：历史成果及未来目标》，巴黎，联合国教科文组织世界遗产中心（世界遗产论文 2）。

http://whc.unesco.org/en/series/2/

UNESCO World Heritage Centre. 2003. *Periodic Report Africa*. Paris, UNESCO World Heritage Centre. (World Heritage Reports 3.)

https://whc.unesco.org/en/series/3/

联合国教科文组织世界遗产中心，2003 年，《非洲定期报告》，巴黎，联合国教科文组织世界遗产中心（世界遗产论文 3）。

http://whc.unesco. org/en/series/3/

Hillary, A., Kokkonen, M. and Max, L. (eds). 2003. *Proceedings of the World Heritage Marine Biodiversity Workshop*. Paris, UNESCO World Heritage Centre. (World Heritage Papers 4.)

https://whc.unesco.org/en/series/4/

Hillary A.，Kokkonen M.，Max L.（编辑），2003 年，《世界遗产海洋生物多样性研讨会论文集》，巴黎，联合国教科文组织世界遗产中心（世界遗产论文 4）。

http://whc.unesco.org/en/series/4/

UNESCO World Heritage Centre. 2003. *Identification and Documentation of Modern Heritage*. Paris, UNESCO World Heritage Centre. (World Heritage Papers 5.)

https://whc.unesco.org/en/series/5/

联合国教科文组织世界遗产中心，2003 年，《现代遗产确认和文档编制》，巴黎，联合国教科文组织世界遗产中心（世界遗产论文 5）。

http://whc.unesco.org/en/series/5/

Fowler, P. J., (ed.), *World Heritage Cultural Landscapes* 1992-2002. Paris, UNESCO World Heritage Centre. (World Heritage Papers 6.)

https://whc.unesco.org/en/series/6/

Fowler，P.J.，（ed.），《世界遗产文化景观 1992–2002 年》，巴黎，联合国教科文组织世界遗产中心（世界遗产论文 6）。

http://whc.unesco.org/en/series/6/

UNESCO World Heritage Centre. 2003. *Cultural Landscapes: the Challenges of Conservation*. Paris, UNESCO World Heritage Centre. (World Heritage Papers 7.)

https://whc.unesco.org/en/series/7/

联合国教科文组织世界遗产中心，2003 年，《文化景观：遗产保护面临的挑战》，巴黎，联合国教科文组织世界遗产中心（世界遗产论文 7）。

http://whc.unesco.org/en/series/7/

UNESCO World Heritage Centre. 2003. *Mobilizing Young People for World Heritage*. Paris, UNESCO World Heritage Centre. (World Heritage Papers 8.)

https://whc.unesco.org/en/series/8/

联合国教科文组织世界遗产中心，2003 年，《调动青年人服务世界遗产》，巴黎，联合国教科文组织世界遗产中心（世界遗产论文 8）。

http://whc.unesco.org/en/series/8/

UNESCO World Heritage Centre. 2004. *Partnerships for World Heritage Cities: Culture as a Vector for Sustainable Urban Development*. Paris, UNESCO World Heritage Centre. (World Heritage Papers 9.)

https://whc.unesco.org/en/series/9/

联合国教科文组织世界遗产中心，2004 年，《世界遗产城市合作：文化作为城市可持续发展的向量》巴黎，联合国教科文组织世界遗产中心（世界遗产论文 9）。

http://whc.unesco.org/en/series/9/

Stovel H. (ed). 2004. *Monitoring World Heritage*, Paris, UNESCO, World Heritage Centre. (World Heritage Papers 10.)

https://whc.unesco.org/en/series/10/

Stovel，H.（编辑），2004 年，《世界遗产监测》，巴黎，联合国教科文组织世界遗产中心（世界遗产论文 10）。

http://whc.unesco.org/en/series/10/

UNESCO World Heritage Centre. 2004. *Periodic Report and Regional Programme Arab States 2000-2003*. Paris, UNESCO World Heritage Centre. (World Heritage Reports 11.)

https://whc.unesco.org/en/series/11/

联合国教科文组织世界遗产中心，2004 年，《2000–2003 年阿拉伯国家区域项目定期报告》，巴黎，联合 国教科文组织世界遗产中心（世界遗产论文 11）。

http://whc.unesco.org/en/series/11/

UNESCO World Heritage Centre. 2004. *The State of World Heritage in the Asia-Pacific Region 2003*. Paris, UNESCO World Heritage Centre. (World Heritage Papers 12.)

https://whc.unesco.org/en/series/12/

联合国教科文组织世界遗产中心，2004 年，《2003 年亚太地区世界遗产状况》，巴黎，联合国教科文组织世界遗产中心（世界遗产论文 12）。

http://whc.unesco.org/en/series/12/

de Merode, E., Smeets, R. and Westrik, C. 2004. *Linking Universal and Local Values: Managing a Sustainable Future for World Heritage*. Paris, UNESCO World Heritage Centre. (World Heritage Papers 13.)

https://whc.unesco.org/en/series/13/

deMerode，E.Smeets，R. 和 Westrik，C，2004 年，《全球和地区价值观的结合：实现世界遗产可持续发展的未来》，巴黎，联合国教科文组织世界遗产中心（世界遗产论文 13）。

http://whc.unesco.org/en/series/13/

UNESCO World Heritage Centre. 2005. *Caribbean Archaeology and World Heritage Con-*

联合国教科文组织世界遗产中心，2005 年，《加勒比海地亚考古及世界遗产公约》，巴黎，

vention. Paris, UNESCO World Heritage Centre. (World Heritage Papers 14.)

https://whc.unesco.org/en/series/14/

UNESCO World Heritage Centre. 2005. *Caribbean Wooden Treasures*. Paris, UNESCO World Heritage Centre. (World Heritage Papers 15.)

https://whc.unesco.org/en/series/15/

UNESCO World Heritage Centre. 2005. *World Heritage at the Vth IUCN World Parks Congress*. Paris, UNESCO World Heritage Centre. (World Heritage Reports 16.)

https://whc.unesco.org/en/series/16/

UNESCO World Heritage Centre. 2005. *Promoting and Preserving Congolese Heritage*. Paris, UNESCO World Heritage Centre. (World Heritage Papers 17.)

https://whc.unesco.org/en/series/17/

UNESCO World Heritage Centre. 2006. *Periodic Report 2004- Latin America and the Caribbean*. Paris, UNESCO World Heritage Centre. (World Heritage Papers 18.)

https://whc.unesco.org/en/series/18/

UNESCO World Heritage Centre. 2006. *American Fortifications and the World Heritage Convention*. Paris, UNESCO World Heritage Centre. (World Heritage Papers 19.)

https://whc.unesco.org/en/series/19/

UNESCO World Heritage Centre. 2006. *Periodic Report and Action Plan, Europe 2005-2006*. Paris, UNESCO World Heritage Centre. (World Heritage Reports 20.)

https://whc.unesco.org/en/series/20/

UNESCO World Heritage Centre. 2007. *World*

联合国教科文组织世界遗产中心（世界遗产论文 14 ）。

http://whc.unesco.org/en/series/14/

联合国教科文组织世界遗产中心，2005 年，《加勒比木制珍品》，巴黎，联合国教科文组织世界遗产中心（世界遗产论文 15 ）。

http://whc.unesco.org/en/series/15/

联合国教科文组织世界遗产中心，2005 年，《第五届国际自然保护联盟世界公园大会之世界遗产》，巴黎，联合国教科文组织世界遗产中心（世界遗产论文 16 ）。

http://whc.unesco.org/en/series/16/

联合国教科文组织世界遗产中心，2005 年，《推广和保护刚果遗产》，巴黎，联合国教科文组织世界遗产中心（世界遗产论文 17 ）。

http://whc.unesco.org/en/series/17/

联合国教科文组织世界遗产中心，2006 年，《2004 年定期报告 – 拉丁美洲及加勒比地区》，巴黎，联合国教科文组织世界遗产中心（世界遗产论文 18 ）。

http://whc.unesco.org/en/series/18/

联合国教科文组织世界遗产中心，2006 年，《美国防御工事及世界遗产公约》，巴黎，联合国教科文组织世界遗产中心（世界遗产论文 19 ）。

http://whc.unesco.org/en/series/19/

联合国教科文组织世界遗产中心，2006 年，《2005–2006 年定期报告和欧洲行动规划》，巴黎，联合国教科文组织世界遗产中心（世界遗产论文 20 ）。

http://whc.unesco.org/en/series/20/

联合国教科文组织世界遗产中心，2007 年，

Heritage Forests - Leveraging Conservation at the Landscape Level. Paris, UNESCO World Heritage Centre. (World Heritage Reports 21.)

https://whc.unesco.org/en/series/21/

UNESCO World Heritage Centre. 2007. *Climate Change and World Heritage.* Paris, UNESCO World Heritage Centre. (World Heritage Reports 22.)

https://whc.unesco.org/en/series/22/

Hockings M., James R., Stolton S., Dudley N., Mathur V., Makombo J., Courrau J. and Parrish J. 2008. *Enhancing our Heritage Toolkit. Assessing management effectiveness of Natural World Heritage sites.* Paris, UNESCO World Heritage Centre. (World Heritage Papers 23.)

https://whc.unesco.org/en/series/23/

UNESCO World Heritage Centre. 2008. *Rock Art in the Caribbean.* Paris, UNESCO World Heritage Centre. (World Heritage Papers 24.)

https://whc.unesco.org/en/series/24/

Martin O. and Piatti G. (eds). 2009. *World Heritage and Buffer Zones, International Expert Meeting on World Heritage and Buffer Zones*, Davos, Switzerland, 11–14 March 2008. Paris, UNESCO World Heritage Centre. (World Heritage Papers 25.)

https://whc.unesco.org/en/series/25/

Mitchell N., Rössler M. and Tricaud P-M. (authors/eds). 2009. *World Heritage Cultural Landscapes: A handbook for Conservation and Management.* Paris, UNESCO World Heritage Centre. (World Heritage Papers 26.)

https://whc.unesco.org/en/series/26/

UNESCO World Heritage Centre. 2010.

《森林世界遗产 – 景观层面的利用保护》，巴黎，联合国教科文组织世界遗产中心（世界遗产论文 21 ）。

http://whc.unesco.org/en/series/21/

联合国教科文组织世界遗产中心，2007 年，《气候变化和世界遗产》，巴黎，联合国教科文组织世界遗产中心（世界遗产论文 22 ）。

http://whc.unesco.org/en/series/22/

Hockings M.， James R.， Stolton S.， Dudley N.， Mathur V.， Makombo J.， Courrau J. 和 Parrish J，2008 年，《优化遗产工具箱，评估世界自然遗产遗址的管理有效性》，巴黎，联合国教科文组织世界遗产中心（世界遗产论文 23 ）。

http://whc.unesco.org/en/series/23/

联合国教科文组织世界遗产中心，2008 年，《加勒比地区的岩石艺术》，巴黎，联合国教科文组织世界遗产中心（ 世界遗产论文 24 ）。

http://whc.unesco.org/en/series/24/

Martin O.， Piatti G.（编辑），2009 年，《世界遗产和缓冲区，瑞士达沃斯世界遗产和缓冲区国际专家会议》，2008 年 3 月 11 – 14 日，巴黎，联合国教科文组织世界遗产中心（世界遗产论文 25 ）。

http://whc.unesco.org/en/series/25/

Mitchell N.， Rössler M.， Tricaud P-M.（作者，编辑），2009 年，《世界遗产文化景观：保护及管理手册》，巴黎，联合国教科文组织世界遗产中心（世界遗产论文 26 ）。

http://whc.unesco.org/en/series/26/

联合国教科文组织世界遗产中心，2010 年，

Managing Historic Cities. Paris, UNESCO World Heritage Centre. (World Heritage Papers 27.)

https://whc.unesco.org/en/series/27/

UNESCO World Heritage Centre. 2011. *Navigating the Future of Marine World Heritage.* Paris, UNESCO World Heritage Centre. (World Heritage Papers 28.)

https://whc.unesco.org/en/series/28/

UNESCO World Heritage Centre. 2011. *Human Evolution: Adaptations, Dispersals and Social Developments (HEADS)*. Paris, UNESCO World Heritage Centre. (World Heritage Papers 29.)

https://whc.unesco.org/en/series/29/

UNESCO World Heritage Centre. 2011. *Adapting to Change: the State of Conservation of World Heritage Forests in 2011*. Paris, UNESCO World Heritage Centre. (World Heritage Papers 30.)

https://whc.unesco.org/en/series/30/

Albert M.-T., Richon M., Viñals M.J. and Witcomb A. (eds). 2012. *Community development through World Heritage*. Paris, UNESCO World Heritage Centre. (World Heritage Papers 31.)

https://whc.unesco.org/en/series/31/

Church J., Gabrié C., Macharia D., Obura D. 2012. *Assessing Marine World Heritage from an Ecosystem Perspective*. Paris, UNESCO World Heritage Centre. (World Heritage Papers 32.)

https://whc.unesco.org/en/series/32/

UNESCO World Heritage Centre. 2012. HEADS 2: *Human Origin Sites and the World Heritage Convention in Africa*. Paris, UNESCO World Heritage Centre. (World Heritage Papers 33.)

https://whc.unesco.org/en/series/33/

《管理历史城市》，巴黎，联合国世界遗产中心（世界遗产论文 27）。

http://whc.unesco.org/en/series/27/

联合国教科文组织世界遗产中心，2011 年，《引领海洋世界遗产走向未来》，巴黎，联合国教科文组织世界遗产中心（世界遗产论文 28）。

http://whc.unesco.org/en/series/28/

联合国教科文组织世界遗产中心，2011 年，《人类进化：适应、分散及社会发展（HEADS）》，巴黎，联合国教科文组织世界遗产中心（世界遗产论文 29）。

http://whc.unesco.org/en/series/29/

联合国教科文组织世界遗产中心，2011 年，《适应改变：2011 年世界遗产森林的保护状况》，巴黎，联合国教科文组织世界遗产中心（世界遗产论文 30）。

http://whc.unesco.org/en/series/30/

Albert M.-T.，Richon M.，Viñals M.J. 和 Witcomb A.（编辑），2012 年，《通过世界遗产推动社区发展》，巴黎，联合国教科文组织世界遗产中心（世界遗产论文 31）。

http://whc.unesco.org/en/series/31/

Church J.，Gabrié C.，Macharia D.，Obura D. 2012 年，《从生态系统视角评估海洋世界遗产》，巴黎，联合国教科文组织世界遗产中心（世界遗产论文 32）。

http://whc.unesco.org/en/series/32/

联合国教科文组织世界遗产中心，2012 年，《HEADS2：人类起源遗址地和世界遗产公约在非洲》，巴黎，联合国教科文组织世界遗产中心（世界遗产论文 33）。

http://whc.unesco.org/en/series/33/

UNESCO World Heritage Centre. 2012. *World Heritage in a Sea of Islands - Pacific 2009 Programme*. Paris, UNESCO World Heritage Centre. (World Heritage Papers 34.)

https://whc.unesco.org/en/series/34/

Dingwall, P., Kawakami, K., Weise, K. 2012. *Understanding World Heritage in Asia and the Pacific - The Second Cycle of Periodic Reporting 2010-2012*. Paris, UNESCO World Heritage Centre. (World Heritage Papers 35.)

https://whc.unesco.org/en/series/35/

Joffroy T., Eloundou L. (eds.). 2013. *Earthern Architecture in Today's World*. Paris, UNESCO World Heritage Centre. (World Heritage Papers 36.)

https://whc.unesco.org/en/series/36/

Falzon, C., Perry, J. 2014. *Climate Change Adaptation for Natural World Heritage Sites*. Paris, UNESCO World Heritage Centre. (World Heritage Papers 37.)

https://whc.unesco.org/en/series/37/

UNESCO World Heritage Centre. 2014. *Safeguarding Precious Resources for Island Communities*. Paris, UNESCO World Heritage Centre. (World Heritage Papers 38.)

https://whc.unesco.org/en/series/38/

UNESCO World Heritage Centre. 2014. *HEADS 3: Human Origin Sites and the World Heritage Convention in Asia*. Paris, UNESCO World Heritage Centre. (World Heritage Papers 39.)

https://whc.unesco.org/en/series/39/

Brown, J., Hay-Edie, T. 2014. *Engaging Local Communities in Stewardship of World Heritage*. Paris, UNESCO World Heritage Centre. (World Heritage Papers 40.)

联合国教科文组织世界遗产中心，2012 年，《海岛世界遗产 – 太平洋 2009 年项目》，巴黎，联合国教科文组织世界遗产中心（世界遗产论文 34）。

http://whc.unesco.org/en/series/34/

Dingwall，P.，Kawakami，K.，Weise，K，2012 年，《理解亚太地区世界遗产 –2010–2012 年第二轮定期报告》，巴黎，联合国教科文组织世界遗产中心（世界遗产论文 35）。

http://whc.unesco.org/en/series/35/

Joffroy T.，Eloundou L.（编辑.），2013 年，《当今世界的土建筑》，巴黎，联合国教科文组织世界遗产中心（世界遗产论文 36）。

http://whc.unesco.org/en/series/36/

Falzon，C.，Perry，J，2014 年，《世界自然遗产对气候变化的适应》，巴黎，联合国教科文组织世界遗产中心（世界遗产论文 37）。

http://whc.unesco.org/en/series/37/

联合国教科文组织世界遗产中心，2014 年，《保护珍贵岛屿社区资源》，巴黎，联合国教科文组织世界遗产中心（世界遗产论文 38）。

http://whc.unesco.org/en/series/38/

联合国教科文组织世界遗产中心 2014 年，《HEADS3：人类起源遗址地和世界遗产公约在非洲》，巴黎，联合国教科文组织世界遗产中心（世界遗产论文 39）。

http://whc.unesco.org/en/series/39/

Brown，J.，Hay-Edie，T.2014 年，《吸引当地社区对世界遗产的管理》，巴黎，联合国教科文组织世界遗产中心（世界遗产论文 40）。

https://whc.unesco.org/en/series/40/

http://whc.unesco.org/en/series/40/

UNESCO World Heritage Centre. 2015. *HEADS 4: Human Origin Sites and the World Heritage Convention in Eurasia.* Paris, UNESCO World Heritage Centre (World Heritage Papers 41)

https://whc.unesco.org/en/series/41/

联合国教科文组织世界遗产中心。HEADS 4:《人类起源地点和欧亚大陆世界遗产公约》巴黎，联合国教科文组织世界遗产中心 41)。

https://whc.unesco.org/en/series/41/

UNESCO World Heritage Centre. 2015. *HEADS 5: Human Origin Sites and the World Heritage Convention in the Americas.* Paris, UNESCO World Heritage Centre (World Heritage Papers 42)

https://whc.unesco.org/en/series/42/

联合国教科文组织世界遗产中心。HEADS 5:《人类起源遗址和美洲世界遗产公约》。巴黎，联合国教科文组织世界遗产中心 (世界遗产论文 42)。

https://whc.unesco.org/en/series/42/

UNESCO World Heritage Centre. 2016. *Understanding World Heritage in Europe and North America Final Report on the Second Cycle of Periodic Reporting, 2012-2015,* Paris, UNESCO World Heritage Centre (World Heritage Papers 43)

https://whc.unesco.org/en/series/43/

联合国教科文组织世界遗产中心。《第二轮定期报告终稿：了解欧洲和北美世界遗产》，2012–2015，巴黎，联合国教科文组织世界遗产中心（世界遗产论文 43)。

https://whc.unesco.org/en/series/43/

Freestone, J., Laffoley, D., Douvere, F., Badman, T. 2016. *World Heritage in the High Seas: An Idea Whose Time Has Come.* Paris, UNESCO World Heritage Centre (World Heritage Papers 44)

https://whc.unesco.org/en/series/44/

Freestone, J., Laffoley, D., Douvere, F., Badman, T. 2016 年,《公海中的世界遗产：一个成熟理念》。巴黎，联合国教科文组织世界遗产中心（世界遗产论文 44)。

https://whc.unesco.org/en/series/44/

UNESCO World Heritage Centre. 2016. *The Future of the World Heritage Convention for Marine Conservation. Celebrating 10 years of the World Heritage Marine Programme.* Paris, UNESCO World Heritage Centre (World Heritage Papers 45)

https://whc.unesco.org/en/series/45/

联合国教科文组织世界遗产中心。《海洋保护世界遗产公约的未来。庆祝世界海洋遗产计划十周年》。巴黎，联合国教科文组织世界遗产中心（世界遗产文件 45)。

https://whc.unesco.org/en/series/45/

GENERAL AND THEMATIC REFERENCES

一般研究及主题参考

Badman T., Bomhard B. and Dingwall P. 2008. *World Heritage Nominations for Natural Properties: A Resource Manual for Practitioners.*

Badman T.，Bomhard B. 和 Dingwall P，2008 年,《申报世界自然遗产：实践者资源手册》，瑞士 Gland，世界自然保护联盟

Gland, Switzerland, IUCN.

http://cmsdata.iucn.org/downloads/whmanagement.pdf

Batisse M., Bolla G. 2005. *The Invention of World Heritage*. Paris, UNESCO.

Cameron C. 2005. *Background Paper for the Special Expert Meeting of the World Heritage Convention: The Concept of Outstanding Universal Value*. Kazan, Republic of Tatarstan, Russian Federation.

https://whc.unesco.org/archive/2005/whc05-29com-inf09Ae.pdf

Cameron C., Rössler M. 2013. Many Voices, One Vision: The Early Years of the World Heritage Convention. Farnham, Ashgate.

Galla A. (ed.). 2012. *World Heritage – Benefits Beyond Borders*. Paris/Cambridge, UNESCO Publishing/Cambridge University Press.

Feilden B.M. and Jokilehto J. 1993. *Management Guidelines for World Cultural Heritage Sites*. (First edition). Rome, ICCROM.

Francioni F. (ed). 2008. The 1972 *World Heritage Convention: A Commentary*. Oxford Commentaries on International Law, UK.

ICOMOS. 1965. International Charter for the Conservation and Restoration of Monuments and Sites (The Venice Charter 1964). Paris, ICOMOS.
https://www.icomos.org/charters/venice_e.pdf

ICOMOS. 2004. ICOMOS Analysis of the World Heritage List and Tentative Lists and Follow-Up Action Plan. Paris, ICOMOS.

http://cmsdata.iucn.org/downloads/whmanagement.pdf

Batisse M., Bolla G. 2005 年,《世界遗产的发明》, 巴黎, 联合国教科文组织。

Cameron C.2005 年,《世界遗产公约特别专家会议背景文件: 突出普遍价值的概念》, 俄罗斯联邦鞑靼斯坦共和国喀山。

http://whc.unesco.org/archive/2005/whc05-29com-inf09Ae.pdf

Cameron C., Rössler M, 2013 年,《不同声音一个愿景: 早期的世界遗产公约》, 法纳姆, 阿什盖特。

Galla A.(编辑). 2012 年,《世界遗产 – 跨国界的优势》, 巴黎 / 剑桥, 联合国教科文组织出版社 / 剑桥大学出版社。

Feilden B.M. 和 Jokilehto J, 1993 年,《世界文化遗产地管理指南》(第一版), 罗马, 国际文物与修复保护研究中心。

Francioni F.(编辑), 2008 年《1972 年世界遗产公约: 评论》, 牛津国际法律评注, 英国。

国际古迹遗址理事会, 1965 年《国际古迹保护与修复宪章》(威尼斯宪章 1964 年), 巴黎, 国际古迹遗址理事会。
http://www.icomos.org/venice_charter.html

国际古迹遗址理事会, 2004 年,《国际古迹遗址理事会世界遗产名录、预备名录及后续行动规划分析》, 巴黎, 国际古迹遗址理事会。

ICOMOS. 2005. *The World Heritage List: Filling the Gaps – An Action Plan for the Future.* Paris, ICOMOS.

http://www.international.icomos.org/world_heritage/gaps.pdf

ICOMOS. 2005. *Xi'an Declaration on the Conservation of the Setting of Heritage Structures, Sites and Areas.*

http://www.international.icomos.org/charters/xian-declaration.pdf

ICOMOS. 2008. *Compendium on Standards for the Inscription of Cultural Properties to the World Heritage List.*

https://whc.unesco.org/en/sessions/32COM/documents/

ICOMOS. 2011. *Guidance on Heritage Impact Assessments for Cultural World Heritage Properties.* Paris, ICOMOS.

http://openarchive.icomos.org/266/1/ICOMOS_Heritage_Impact_Assessment_2010.pdf

ICOMOS technical and thematic studies
http://www.icomos.org/en/documentation-center

IUCN. 2006. *Enhancing the IUCN Evaluation Process of World Heritage Nominations: A Contribution to Achieving a Credible and Balanced World Heritage List.*

https://www.iucn.org/sites/dev/files/import/downloads/vilm2005.pdf

IUCN. 2006. *The World Heritage List: Guidance and Future Priorities for Identifying Natural Heritage of Potential Outstanding Universal Value.*

http://cmsdata.iucn.org/downloads/ouv2006_english.pdf

国际古迹遗址理事会，2005 年，《世界遗产名录：填补空白－未来行动规划》，巴黎，国际古迹遗址理事会。

http://www.international.icomos.org/world_heritage/gaps.pdf

国际古迹遗址理事会，2005 年，《西安宣言——关于古建筑、古遗址和历史地区的环境的保护》。

http://www.international.icomos.org/charters/ xian-declaration.pdf

国际古迹遗址理事会，2008 年，《文化遗产列入世界遗产名录标准纲要》。

http://whc.unesco.org/en/sessions/32COM/documents/

国际古迹遗址理事会，2011 年，《世界文化遗产影响评估指南》，巴黎，国际古迹遗址理事会。

http://openarchive.icomos.org/266/1/ICOMOS_Heritage_Impact_Assessment_2010.pdf

国际古迹遗址理事会技术及主题研究
http://www.icomos.org/en/documentation-center

世界自然保护联盟，2006 年，《强化世界自然保护联盟对申报世界遗产的评估程序：促进建立可信的、平衡的世界遗产名录》。

https://portals.iucn.org/library/efiles/documents/2006-059.pdf

世界自然保护联盟，2006，《世界遗产名录：指导和未来优先辨别潜在突出普遍价值》的自然遗产。

http://cmsdata.iucn.org/downloads/ouv2006_english.pdf

IUCN. 2008. *Outstanding Universal Value – Standards for Natural World Heritage, A Compendium on Standards for Inscriptions of Natural Properties on the World Heritage List.*

http://cmsdata.iucn.org/downloads/ouv_compendium_english.pdf

IUCN Technical and Thematic Studies:

https://www.iucn.org/theme/world-heritage/resources/publications

Pressouyre L. 1993. *The World Heritage Convention, twenty years later.* UNESCO, Paris.

https://whc.unesco.org/en/280/?id=564&

Stovel H. 1998. *Risk Preparedness: A Management Manual for World Cultural Heritage.* Rome, ICCROM.

https://www.iccrom.org/sites/default/files/ICCROM_17_RiskPreparedness_en.pdf

Swiss Federal Office of Culture, Martin O., Gendre S. (eds). 2010. *UNESCO World Heritage: serial properties and nominations.* Bern. Switzerland.

https://whc.unesco.org/document/124860

UNESCO World Heritage Centre. Education Kit. 2002. *World Heritage in Young Hands.* Paris, UNESCO World Heritage Centre.

https://whc.unesco.org/en/educationkit/

UNESCO World Heritage Centre. 2003. *World Heritage 2002 - Shared Legacy, Common Responsibility.* Paris, UNESCO World Heritage Centre.

https://whc.unesco.org/en/activities/563/

UNESCO World Heritage Centre. 2007. *World Heritage – Challenges for the Millenium.* Paris,

世界自然保护联盟，2008 年，《突出普遍价值 – 世界自然遗产标准，世界自然遗产列入世界遗产名录标准纲要》。

http://cmsdata.iucn.org/downloads/ouv_compendium_english.pdf

世界自然保护联盟技术及主题研究：

http://www.iucn.org/knowledge/publications_doc/

Pressouyre L. 1993 年，《世界遗产公约：二十年之后》，联合国教科文组织，巴黎。

http://whc.unesco.org/en/280/?id=564&

Stovel H. 1998 年，《风险准备：世界文化遗产管理手册》，罗马，国际文物与修复保护研究中心。

http://www.iccrom.org/pdf/ICCROM_17_RiskPreparedness_en.pdf

瑞士联邦文化办公室，Martin O., Gendre S.（主编）。2010.《联合国教科文组织世界遗产：系列遗产和申报》。伯尔尼，瑞士，

https://whc.unesco. org/document/124860

联合国教科文组织世界遗产中心，教育工具箱，2002 年，《世界遗产在年轻人手中》，巴黎，联合国教科文组织世界遗产中心。

http://whc.unesco.org/en/educationkit/

联合国教科文组织世界遗产中心，2003 年，《世界遗产 2002 年 – 共有遗产和共同责任》，巴黎，联合国教科文组织世界遗产中心。

http://whc.unesco.org/en/activities/563/

联合国教科文组织世界遗产中心，2007 年，《世界遗产 – 千年挑战》，巴黎，联合国教科文

UNESCO World Heritage Centre.
https://whc.unesco.org/en/challenges-for-the-Millennium/

UNESCO World Heritage Centre. 2007. *Case Studies on Climate Change and World Heritage.* Paris, UNESCO World Heritage Centre.
https://whc.unesco.org/en/activities/473/

UNESCO World Heritage Centre. 2012. *African World Heritage – A Remarkable Diversity.* Paris, UNESCO World Heritage Centre.

UNESCO World Heritage Centre. 2013. *Celebrating 40 years of the World Heritage Convention.* Paris, UNESCO World Heritage Centre.
https://whc.unesco.org/en/celebrating-40-years

UNESCO World Heritage Centre. 2013. *Report of the 40th Anniversary of the World Heritage Convention.* Paris, UNESCO World Heritage Centre.
https://whc.unesco.org/en/report-40th-Anniversary

UNESCO World Heritage Centre. *Patrimonito's World Heritage Adventures.* Paris, UNESCO World Heritage Centre.
https://whc.unesco.org/en/patrimonito/

von Droste B., Plachter H. and Rössler M. (eds.). 1995. *Cultural Landscapes of Universal Value: Components of a Global Strategy*, Jena (Germany), Fischer Verlag.

von Droste B., Rössler M. and Titchen, S. (eds.). 1999. *Linking Nature and Culture*, Report of the Global Strategy Natural and Cultural Heritage Expert Meeting, 25-29 March 1998, Amsterdam, The Netherlands, UNESCO/ Ministry for Foreign

组织世界遗产中心。
http://whc.unesco.org/en/challenges-for-the-Millennium/

联合国教科文组织世界遗产中心，2007 年，《气候变化与世界遗产案例研究》，巴黎，联合国教科文组织世界遗产中心。
http://whc.unesco.org/en/activities/473/

联合国教科文组织世界遗产中心，2012 年，《非洲世界遗产 – 显著多样性》，巴黎，联合国教科文组织世界遗产中心。

联合国教科文组织世界遗产中心，2013 年，《庆祝世界遗产公约 40 周年》，巴黎，联合国教科文组织世界遗产中心。
http://whc.unesco.org/en/celebrating-40-years

联合国教科文组织世界遗产中心，2013 年，《世界遗产公约 40 周年报告》，巴黎，联合国教科文组织世界遗产中心。
http://whc.unesco.org/en/report-40th-Anniversary

联合国教科文组织世界遗产中心，《世界遗产青年保护者世界遗产探险》，巴黎，联合国教科文组织世界遗产中心。
http://whc.unesco.org/en/patrimonito/

von Droste B., Plachter H. 和 Rössler M.（编辑.），1995 年，《文化景观的普遍价值：全球战略的组成部分》，耶拿（德国），菲舍尔出版社。

von Droste B., Rössler M. 和 Titchen S.（编辑.），1999 年，《连接自然与文化：世界自然遗产与文化遗产全球战略专家会议报告》，1998 年 3 月 25-29 日，荷兰阿姆斯特丹，联合国教科文组织，海牙外交部、教育、科学和文化部。

Affairs/Ministry for Education, Science, and Culture, The Hague.

https://whc.unesco.org/archive/amsterdam98.pdf

http://whc.unesco.org/archive/amsterdam98.pdf

World Commission on Protected Areas (WCPA) Best Practice Guidelines

https://www.iucn.org/theme/protected-areas/resources/best-practice-guidelines

世界保护区委员会（WCPA）最佳实践指南

https://www.iucn.org/about/union/commissions/wcpa/wcpa_puball/wcpa_bpg/

● *National System Planning for Protected Areas, 1998*

● *Economic Values of Protected Areas: Guidelines for Protected Area Managers, 1998*

● *Guidelines for Marine Protected Areas, 1999*

● *Indigenous and Traditional Peoples and Protected Areas, 2000*

● *Financing Protected Areas: Guidelines for Protected Area Managers, 2000*

● *Transboundary Protected Areas for Peace and Co-operation, 2001*

● *Sustainable Tourism in Protected Areas: Guidelines for Planning and Management, 2002*

● *Management Guidelines for IUCN Category V Protected Areas: Protected Landscapes/Seascapes, 2002*

● *Guidelines for Management Planning of Protected Areas, 2003*

● *Indigenous and Local Communities and Protected Areas: Towards Equity and Enhanced Conservation, 2004*

● *Forests and Protected Areas: Guidance on the use of the IUCN protected area management categories, 2006*

● *Sustainable Financing of Protected Areas: A global review of challenges and options, 2006*

● *Evaluating Effectiveness: A Framework for Assessing Management Effectiveness of Protected Areas, 2006*

●《国家保护区系统规划》，1998 年

●《保护区的经济价值：保护区管理者指南》，1998 年

●《海洋保护区指南》，1999 年

●《土著传统居民及保护区》，2000 年

●《为保护区融资：保护区管理人员指南》，2000 年

●《跨境保护区的和平及合作》，2001 年

●《保护区可持续旅游：规划及管理指南》，2002 年

●《世界自然保护联盟第五类保护区：受保护陆地和海洋景观》，2002 年

●《保护区管理规划指南》，2003 年

●《本土传统居民及保护区：实现均衡的、强化的保护》，2004 年

●《森林和保护区：世界自然保护联盟保护区管理分类应用指南》，2006 年

●《为保护区提供可持续融资：全球挑战及选择述评》，2006 年

●《有效性评估：保护区管理有效性评估框架》，2006 年

- *Identification and Gap Analysis of Key Biodiversity Areas, 2007*
- *Sacred Natural Sites: Guidelines for Protected Area Managers, 2008*

THEMATIC AND COMPARATIVE STUDIES BY THE ADVISORY BODIES

ICOMOS

Rock art in East Asia (2019)
http://openarchive.icomos.org/2086/2/Final-version_e-book_21052019-opt.pdf

Cultural Heritages of Water: The cultural heritages of water in the Middle East and Maghreb. Thematic study 2nd ed. (2017)
http://openarchive.icomos.org/1846/1/Copie%20Finaleopt.pdf

Heritage sites of astronomy an Archaeoa-stronomy in the context of the UNESCO World Heritage Convention. Thematic study No. 2. (2017)
http://openarchive.icomos.org/1856/1/Astronomy2%20Final%20low%20res.pdf

The Cultural Heritages of Water in the Middle-East and the Maghreb (2015)
https://www.icomos.org/images/DOCUMENTS/World_Heritage/CH%20of%20water_201507_opt.pdf

The Silk Roads: an ICOMOS Thematic Study (2014)
https://www.icomos.org/images/mediatheque/ICOMOS_WHThematicStudy_SilkRoads_final_lv_201406.pdf

Rock art in Central Asia: a thematic study (Nov 2011)

- 《主要生物多样化区域确认及差距分析》，2007 年
- 《自然圣境：保护区管理人员指南》，2008 年

咨询机构进行的专题和比较分析研究

国际古迹遗址理事会

《东亚岩石艺术》（2019）
http://openarchive.icomos.org/2086/2/Final-version_e-book_21052019-opt.pdf

《水文化遗产：中东和马格里布的水文化遗产》。专题研究第二版（2017）

http://openarchive.icomos.org/1846/1/Copie%20Finaleopt.pdf

《联合国教科文组织世界遗产公约范围内的天文学和天文学考古遗址》。专题研究二。(2017)

http://openarchive.icomos.org/1856/1/Astronomy2%20Final%20low%20res.pdf

《中东和马格里布的水文化遗产》(2015)

https://www.icomos.org/images/DOCUMENTS/World_Heritage/CH%20of%20water_201507_opt.pdf

《国际古迹遗址理事会丝绸之路专题研究》(2014)
https://www.icomos.org/images/mediatheque/ICOMOS_WHThematicStudy_SilkRoads_final_lv_201406.pdf

《中亚岩石艺术：专题研究》(2011 年 11 月）

Early Human Expansion and Innovation in the Pacific (Dec 2010)

《人类在太平洋的早期扩张和创新》(2010年12月)

Heritage Sites of Astronomy and Ar-chaeoa-stronomy in the context of the UNESCO World Heritage Convention (by ICOMOS and IAU) (2010)

http://openarchive.icomos.org/267/1/ICOMOS_IAU_Thematic_Study_Heritage_Sites_Astronomy_2010.pdf

《联合国教科文组织〈世界遗产公约〉范围内的天文学和考古天文学遗产地》(国际天文学理事会和国际天文学联合会)(2010年)

http://openarchive.icomos.org/267/1/ICOMOS_IAU_Thematic_Study_Heritage_Sites_Astronomy_2010.pdf

Cultural landscapes of the Pacific Islands (2007)

https://www.icomos.org/studies/cultural-land-scapes-pacific/cultural-landscapes-pacific.pdf

《太平洋岛屿文化景观》(2007)

https://www.icomos.org/studies/cultural–landscapes–pacific/cultural–landscapes–pacific.pdf

Rock Art of Sahara and North Africa (2007)

https://www.icomos.org/studies/rockart-sahara-northafrica/rockart-sahara-northafrica.pdf

《撒哈拉和北非的岩石艺术》(2007)

https://www.icomos.org/studies/rockart–sahara–northafrica/rockart–sahara–northafrica.pdf

Rock Art of Latin America and the Caribbean (2006)

https://www.icomos.org/studies/rockart-latina-merica/fulltext.pdf

《拉丁美洲和加勒比的岩石艺术》(2006)

https://www.icomos.org/studies/rockart–latinamerica/fulltext.pdf

Les paysages culturels viticoles (2004)

https://www.icomos.org/studies/paysages-viti-coles.pdf (in French only)

《葡萄酒文化景观》(2004)

https://www.icomos.org/studies/paysages–viticoles.pdf (仅限法国)

Les Monastères orthodoxes dans les Balkans (2003)

https://www.icomos.org/studies/balkan.pdf (in French only)

《巴尔干半岛的东正教修道院》(2003)

https://www.icomos.org/studies/balkan.pdf (仅限法国)

L'Art rupestre (2002)

https://www.icomos.org/studies/images/rupestre.pdf (in French only)

《岩石艺术》(2002)

https://www.icomos.org/studies/images/rupestre.pdf (仅限法国)

Evaluations of World Heritage Nominations

《评估世界遗产申报时涉及与最近冲突记

related to Sites Associated with Memories of Recent Conflicts. ICOMOS Discussion Paper (2018)

https://www.icomos.org/images/DOCU-MENTS/World_Heritage/ICOMOS_Discussion_paper_Sites_associa ted_with_Memories_of_Recent_Conflicts.pdf

Sites associated with memories of recent conflicts and the World Heritage Convention. Reflection on whether and how these might relate to the Purpose and Scope of the World Heritage Convention and its Operational Guidelines. ICOMOS Second Discussion Paper (2020)

https://www.icomos.org/en/home-wh/75087-sites-associated-with-memories-of-recent-conflicts-and-the- world-heritage-convention-icomos-second-discussion-paper

IUCN

Wells, 1996: Earth's Geological History - A Contextual Framework Assessment of World Heritage Fossil Site Nominations.

https://www.iucn.org/content/earths-geological-history-a-contextual-framework-assessment-world-heritage- fossil-site-nominations

Geological World Heritage: a global framework: a contribution to the global theme study of World Heritage Natural Sites (2005)

https://portals.iucn.org/library/node/12797

Outstanding universal value: standards for Natural World Heritage (2008)

https://portals.iucn.org/library/node/9265

World Heritage caves and karst: a thematic study (2008)

https://portals.iucn.org/library/node/9267

忆有关的遗址》。国际古迹遗址理事会讨论文件（2018）

https://www.icomos.org/images/DOCUM ENTS/World_Heritage/ICOMOS_Discussion_paper_Sites_associa ted_with_Memories_of_Recent_Conflicts.pdf

《与最近冲突记忆和《世界遗产公约》有关的遗址》。反思这些是否以及如何与《世界遗产公约》及其《操作指南》的宗旨和范围有关。国际古迹遗址理事会第二次讨论文件 (2020)

https://www.icomos.org/en/home−wh/75087−sites−associated−with−memories−of−recent−conflicts−and−the− world−heritage−convention−icomos−second−discussion−paper

世界自然保护联盟

韦尔斯，1996：《地球地质历史 – 申报化石类世界遗产的背景框架评估》

https://www.iucn.org/content/earths−geological−history−a−contextual−framework−assessment−world−heritage− fossil−site−nominations

《地质类世界遗产：全球框架：对世界自然遗产全球主题研究的贡献》(2005)

https://portals.iucn.org/library/node/12797

《突出普遍价值：世界自然遗产标准》(2008)

https://portals.iucn.org/library/node/9265

《洞穴和喀斯特类世界遗产：专题研究》(2008)

https://portals.iucn.org/library/node/9267

Nominations and management of serial natural World Heritage properties: present situation, challenges and opportunities (2009)

https://portals.iucn.org/library/node/12693

World Heritage desert landscapes: potential priorities for the recognition of desert landscapes and geomorphological sites on the World Heritage List (2011)

https://portals.iucn.org/library/node/9818

Marine natural heritage and the World Heritage List: interpretation of World Heritage criteria in marine systems, analysis of biogeographic representation of sites, and a roadmap for addressing gaps (2013)

https://portals.iucn.org/library/node/29196

Study on the application of criterion (vii): considering superlative natural phenomena and exceptional natural beauty within the World Heritage Convention (2013)

https://portals.iucn.org/library/node/10424

Terrestrial biodiversity and the World Heritage List: identifying broad gaps and potential candidate sites for inclusion in the natural World Heritage network (2013)

https://portals.iucn.org/library/node/10399

World heritage, wilderness, and large landscapes and seascapes (2017)

https://doi.org/10.2305/IUCN.CH.2017.06.en

Natural marine World Heritage in the Arctic Ocean: report of an expert workshop and review process (2017)

https://portals.iucn.org/library/node/46678

World Heritage volcanoes: classification, gap

《世界系列自然遗产的申报与管理：现状、挑战与机遇》(2009)

https://portals.iucn.org/library/node/12693

《沙漠景观类世界遗产：世界遗产名录上沙漠景观和地貌遗址的潜在优先事项》(2011 年)

https://portals.iucn.org/library/node/9818

《海洋自然遗产和世界遗产名录：解释海洋系统世界遗产标准、遗址的生物地理表征分析和解决差距的路线图》(2013 年)

https://portals.iucn.org/library/node/29196

《标准 (vii) 适用研究：考虑世界遗产公约中的顶级自然现象和非凡自然美》(2013 年)

https://portals.iucn.org/library/node/10424

《陆地生物多样性与世界遗产：确定世界自然遗产中的空白和潜在申报遗产》(2013 年)

https://portals.iucn.org/library/node/10399

《世界遗产中的荒野、大型陆地和海洋景观》(2017 年)

https://doi.org/10.2305/IUCN.CH.2017.06.en

《北冰洋的世界自然遗产：专家研讨会报告及评审过程》(2017 年)

https://portals.iucn.org/library/node/46678

《火山类世界遗产：分类、差距分析和对未

analysis, and recommendations for future listings (2019)

　　https://doi.org/10.2305/IUCN.CH.2019.07.en

《来名单的建议》(2019 年)

　　https://doi.org/10.2305/IUCN.CH.2019.07.en

Natural World Heritage in Africa: progress and prospects (2020)

　　https://portals.iucn.org/library/node/49029

《非洲的世界自然遗产 : 进展与展望》(2020 年)

　　https://portals.iucn.org/library/node/49029

World Heritage thematic study for Central Asia: priority sites for World Heritage nomination under criteria (ix) and (x) (2020)

　　https://doi.org/10.2305/IUCN.CH.2020.02.en

《中亚世界遗产专题研究 : 根据标准 (ix) 和 (x) 申报世界遗产的优先地点》(2020)

　　https://doi.org/10.2305/IUCN.CH.2020.02.en

Tabe'a: nature and world heritage in the Arab States: towards future IUCN priorities (2011)

　　https://portals.iucn.org/library/node/10060

《阿拉伯国家的世界自然遗产 : 未来世界自然保护联盟的优先事项》(2011 年)

　　https://portals.iucn.org/library/node/10060

TABE'A Ⅱ report: enhancing regional capacities for World Heritage (2015) https://doi.org/10.2305/IUCN.CH.2015.04.en

塔皮耶阿Ⅱ报告 : 加强世界遗产区域能力 (2015)https://doi.org/10.2305/IUCN.CH.2015.04.en

Tabe'a Ⅲ: Nature-Culture linkages, Conflict and Climate Change Impacts on Natural Heritage in the Arab Region (in press)

《塔皮耶阿Ⅲ: 自然 – 文化的联系 , 冲突和气候变化对阿拉伯地区自然遗产的影响》(正在出版)

WEB ADDRESSES

网址

UNESCO

http://www.unesco.org

联合国教科文组织

http://www.unesco.org

UNESCO World Heritage Centre

https://whc.unesco.org

联合国教科文组织世界遗产中心

http://whc.unesco.org

UNESCO World Heritage Centre publications

https://whc.unesco.org/en/publications/

联合国教科文组织世界遗产中心出版物

http://whc.unesco.org/en/publications/

UNESCO World Heritage Review

https://whc.unesco.org/en/review/

联合国教科文组织世界遗产评论

http://whc.unesco.org/en/review/

UNESCO World Heritage Map

联合国教科文组织世界遗产地图

https://whc.unesco.org/en/map/

ICCROM
http://www.iccrom.org

ICCROM publications
http://www.archivalplatform.org/resources/
entry/iccrom_publications/

ICOMOS
http://www.icomos.org

ICOMOS publications
http://www.icomos.org/en/documentation-center

IUCN
http://www.iucn.org

IUCN publications
https://www.iucn.org/resources/publications

World Commission on Protected Areas
(WCPA) Best Practice Guidelines
https://www.iucn.org/theme/protected-areas/
resources/best-practice-guidelines

http://whc.unesco.org/en/map/

国际文物与修复保护研究中心
http://www.iccrom.org

国际文物保护与修复研究中心出版物
http://www.archivalplatform.org/resources/entry/
iccrom_publications/

国际古迹遗址理事会
http://www.icomos.org

国际古迹遗址理事会出版物
http://www.icomos.org/en/documentation−center

世界自然保护联盟
http://www.iucn.org

世界自然保护联盟出版物
http://www.iucn.org/knowledge/publications_doc/

保护区世界委员会（WCPA）最佳实践指南
www.iucn.org/about/union/commissions/wcpa/
wcpa_puball/wcpa_bpg/

后　记
POSTSCRIPT

In 1972, UNESCO issued the *Convention concerning the Protection of the World Cultural and Natural Heritage*, which combines nature conservation and cultural protection together, and considers the protection of natural heritage and cultural heritage from an international perspective, so that they could jointly undergo the examination of Outstanding Universal Values. The Convention has become a programmatic document to protect the rich material and spiritual gifts left by the million-year history of the earth's evolution, and 8,000 years history of human civilization, passing on these unique heritages to future generations, continuing the diversity of global cultural and natural heritage, and promoting exchanges and mutual learning among different regions and peoples around the world, while providing valuable wisdom and experience for the development of future generations. The World Heritage List which is advocated by the Convention has also been strongly sought after by countries around the world. At present, 194 countries have been ratified the Convention, and 1,154 heritage sites in 167 countries have been inscribed on the World Heritage List.

On 17-18 November 2022, UNESCO, in cooperation with the Government of Greece, organized an international conference in Delphi to commemorate the 50th anniversary of the *Convention concerning the Protection of the World Cultural and Natural Heritage* (hereinafter referred to as the

1972 年联合国教科文组织发布了《保护世界文化与自然遗产公约》（以下简称《公约》），把自然保护和文化保护结合起来，从国际视角通盘考虑自然遗产和文化遗产的保护，共同接受突出普遍价值的检验。《公约》成为百万年地球演变史和八千多年人类文明史留下的丰厚的物质和精神馈赠，将这些独特遗产传递给子孙后代，延续全球文化和自然遗产的多样性，促进全球不同地区和民族的交流互鉴，为后世发展提供宝贵智慧和经验的纲领性文件。《公约》倡导的《世界遗产名录》也得到世界各国的大力追捧，目前已有 194 个国家批准了该《公约》，167 个国家的 1154 处遗产列入《世界遗产名录》。

2022 年 11 月 17 至 18 日，联合国教科文组织与希腊政府合作，在德尔斐举办国际会议，纪念《保护世界文化与自然遗产公约》发布五十周年。我们编辑此套《〈实施保护世界文化与自然遗产公约操作指南〉选编》的目的，一是为了纪念这一重要时刻，二是便于学者系统地梳

Convention) . The purpose of compiling this set of *Select Edit of "Operational Guidelines for the Implementation of the World Heritage Convention"* include: first, to commemorate this important event; second, to facilitate scholars to systematically sort out and review the emergence, development and evolution of the Convention, better understand the essence of the Convention, and grasp the development context of World Heritage.

As the principal responsible body for the implementation of the Convention, the World Heritage Committee adopted the *Operational Guidelines for the Implementation of the World Heritage Convention* (hereinafter referred to as the Guidelines) at its first meeting (Paris, 27 June - 1 July 1977) , which set out criteria for the inscription of properties on the World Heritage List and the use of the World Heritage Fund for international assistance. At the same time, the World Heritage Committee noted that the Guidelines would need to be adjusted, revised and/or supplemented in the future in order to reflect the Committee's latest decision. The Guidelines is essential because it set out the principles of the Committee's future work, and provid procedures and methodologies for each step of the nomination process as clearly and comprehensively as possible for State Parties, serve as a programmatic document that States Parties must comply with in their nomination procedure.

Over years, the World Heritage Committee has continually made adjustments, revisions and additions to the Operational Guidelines, which are directly reflected in the number of articles and annexes. In 1977, there were only 28 articles in the Operational Guidelines, which were expanded to 99 articles in 1984, 139 articles in 1997 and 290 articles in 2005, and maintained at 290 articles since then, but continued to be revised in the form of supplementary articles and annexes. Looking back on the history of the Operational Guidelines, it

理、回顾《公约》的产生、发展以及演变的历程，更好地了解《公约》的实质，把握世界遗产的发展脉络。

世界遗产委员会，作为负责执行《公约》的主要机构，在其第一次会议（1977 年 6 月 27 至 7 月 1 日，巴黎）上，通过了《实施〈世界文化与自然遗产公约〉操作指南》（以下简称《指南》），为将遗产列入《世界遗产名录》和利用世界遗产基金提供国际援助，制定了的标准。同时，世界遗产委员会指出，今后将不断地对该《指南》加以调整、修订或补充，以反映委员会最新的决定。该《指南》至关重要，因为它说明了委员会今后工作的各项原则，尽可能明确而全面地为申报国提供每一步工作的程序和方法，是各缔约国进行遗产申报工作时，必须遵守的纲领性文件。

历年来，世界遗产委员会一直在对《指南》进行调整、修订和补充，直观表现在条款和附件的数量上。1977 年《指南》只有 28 条，1984 年扩展为 99 条，1997 年增加到 139 条，2005 年发展到 290 条，此后维持在 290 条，但继续以补充条款、附件等形式加以修订。回顾《指南》的历史，可以看到世界遗产委员会对《指南》进行或大或小的修订，旨在不断丰富和发展世界遗产的概念，并利于实际执行。本书受篇幅限制，选择了 1997 年、2005 年、2015 年、2021 年版本，有些增订或修改可能早于这几个年份。

can be seen that the World Heritage Committee has made major or minor revisions to the Operational Guidelines continually in order to enrich and develop the concept of World Heritage and facilitate its practical implementation. Due to the space limitation of the book, we have chosen the 1997, 2005, 2015, and 2021 editions, although some additions or revisions may predate these years.

In the 1977 edition of the Operational Guidelines, only 28 articles were set out, listing six evaluation criteria for cultural heritage and four evaluation criteria for natural heritage, briefly explaining the concepts of Outstanding Universal Value, Authenticity and Integrity of World Heritage, and offering nomination forms, approval procedures, International Assistance and other basic requirements.

The 1984 Operational Guidelines, with nearly 100 articles, recommended that States Parties establish their Tentative List, explicitly required relevant advisory bodies to carry out Comparative Analysis, emphasized the function of Buffer Zones, recommended measures to be taken to maintain the balance of cultural and natural heritage in the process of implementing the Convention, and expressed initial requirements for the use of the World Heritage Emblem. States Parties were also requested to undertake activities at the national level to raise public awareness of the Convention.

The 1997 Operational Guidelines, revised articles of the concepts of Outstanding Universal Value, Authenticity and Integrity, necessary conservation laws for heritage nominations, Reports on State of World Heritage Conservation, needs of video documents and other materials, and priorities for international assistance etc., and proposed the concepts of Historical Towns and Cultural Landscapes. Noting the impact of Natural disasters and Climate Change on the heritage itself, it was also decided to apply the Periodic Reporting and Reactivity Monitoring Procedures for routine monitoring of the state

在 1977 年版本的《指南》中，仅用 28 个条款，提出了评估文化遗产的六条标准和自然遗产的四条标准，简单说明世界遗产的突出普遍价值（Outstanding Universal Value）、真实性（Authenticity）、完整性（Integrity）概念，提出申报格式、审批程序、国际援助（International Assistance）等基本要求。

1984 年的《指南》，条款增加至近百条，建议各缔约国建立《预备名录》（Tentative List），明确要求相关咨询机构进行比较分析（Comparative Analysis），强调缓冲区（Buffer Zone）的功能。在实施《公约》的进程中，保持文化和自然遗产的平衡（Balance），对使用世界遗产标识有初步要求，还要求缔约国在国家层面开展提高公众对《公约》认识的活动。

1997 年的《指南》，修订了突出普遍价值、真实性、完整性概念，强调遗产申报时必备的保护法律、世界遗产保护状况报告（Reports on State of Wold Heritage Conservation）、影像文件等材料、国际援助侧重点等条款，提出历史城镇（Historical Towns）和文化景观（Cultural Landscapes）的理念。注意到自然灾害（Natural Disaster）和气候变化（Climate Change）对遗产本体的影响，并决定采用定期报告（Periodic Reporting）和反应性监测程序（Reactivity Monitoring Process）对世界遗产保护状况进行常规监测。重视与文化和自然遗产保护相关的文

of World Heritage conservation. The synergies with other international conventions that relate to the protection of cultural and natural heritage were also emphasized.

In 2005, the number of articles in the Operational Guidelines reached 290 for the first time, and since then there has been no further increase, but only supplementation of the relevant articles and additions of necessary annexes to the relevant articles. 2005's Guidelines further elaborated the requirements on the Outstanding Universal Value as well as Integrity and Authenticity, and the ideas of Upstream Procedure, Mixed Cultural and Natural Heritage, Heritage Canals, Cultural Routes, etc. were introduced. Procedures for modifying the boundaries, inscription criteria or names of World Heritage Sites have been added. The Global Strategy for a Representative, Balanced and Credible World Heritage List was proposed. It was clearly required that there should be a corresponding conservation management plan when the heritage was inscribed on the national's Tentative List. Specific requirements were also put forward for the use of the World Heritage Emblem, with detailed tables listed in the annex to explain the authorizing authority, the right to use, the usage occasion etc.

In the 2015 Operational Guidelines, the originally relatively independent six cultural heritage criteria and four natural heritage criteria were integrated into ten World Heritage criteria, so that both natural and cultural heritage would be jointly subject to the test of Outstanding Universal Value, considering the protection of natural and cultural heritage from an international perspective at the same time. New requirements such as Preliminary Assessment, dispatch of reactivity monitoring working groups and advisory body working groups were appended, the application procedure, information required for submission of the nomination document, and the timetable

件及其他国际公约的协同作用。

2005 年,《指南》的条款首次达到 290 条,此后数目上没有再增加,仅在相关条款后加以补充,并增加相关条款所需的附件。2005 年进一步阐述了对突出普遍价值及完整性、真实性要求,引进了上游程序(Upstream Procedure)、混合遗产(Mixed Cultural and Natural Heritage)、运河遗产(Heritage Canals)、文化线路(Cultural Routes)等概念,并增加了修改世界遗产的边界、列入标准或名称的程序,提出了实施具有代表性、平衡性、可信性的世界遗产全球战略(The Global Strategy for a Representative, Balanced and Credible World Heritage List)。明确要求在把遗产列入《预备名录》时,就要有相应的保护管理规划。对使用世界遗产标识也提出了具体要求,并在附件中列出了详细的表格,对授权机构、使用权限、使用场合等加以说明。

2015 年的《指南》,把原来相对独立的 6 条文化遗产评选标准和 4 条自然遗产评选标准,整合为世界遗产的 10 条标准,共同接受突出普遍价值的检验,从国际视角同时考虑自然遗产和文化遗产的保护。增加了初步评估(Preliminary Assessment)、派遣反应性监测工作组、咨询机构工作组等要求,对申报程序、提交申遗文本时需要的资料、申遗时间表做了大幅修订,重视咨询机构的评估意见,实施了加强遗产地社区和原住民等利益相关方参与遗产保护的社区 5 "C" 战略(The "fifth C" for Communities)和世界遗产减少灾害风险战略(Strategy for Reducing Risks from Disasters at World Heritage Properties)等。在附件中提供了一些文件的格式,如未来申报

for inscription were significantly revised, and the assessment opinions of advisory bodies have been valued. The Guidelines also employed the "fifth C" for Communities strategy to strengthen the participation of all stakeholders including local communities and indigenous peoples in heritage conservation, as well as the World Heritage Disaster Risk Reduction Strategy. In the annex, some document formats were provided, such as the future nomination of transnational and transboundary heritage, the statement of outstanding universal value, factual errors submitted by advisory bodies, and other formatted documents, so as to facilitate users to file the online nomination while submitting paper documents.

The 2021 Operational Guidelines, the latest edition on the UNESCO World Heritage Centre's website before the publication of the book, placed greater emphasis on assisting at the earliest stages of nominations, emphasizing that the Secretariat would strengthen its assistance to States Parties throughout the nomination process, from the very beginning of their preparation and revision of the Tentative List, through Upstream Process and Preparatory Assistance. By encouraging the active participation of all stakeholders in the nomination process, States Parties would avoid wasting time and energy on nominations that are unlikely to be successful. The World Heritage Committee were required to revise and adopt the Monitoring Indicators and Analytical Framework for periodic reporting at appropriate intervals and, when necessary.

There have been also minor cuts to the Operational Guidelines over years. For example, in 2015, in accordance with Decision 39 COM 11 which explicitly required the management plan to be included in the nomination dissier, article "115. In some circumstances, a management plan or other management system may not be in place at the time when a property is nominated for the consideration of the World Heritage Committee. The State Party

跨国跨界遗产、突出普遍价值声明、咨询机构提交事实性错误等格式性文件，便于申报者在提交纸质文件同时进行网络申报。

2021 年的《指南》是本书出版前教科文组织世界遗产中心网站上最新的版本，更重视在遗产申报的最初阶段提供帮助，强调秘书处从缔约国准备和修订《预备名录》时，就通过上游程序（Upstream Process）、筹备性援助（assistance throughout the preparation of nominations），在整个申报过程中加强对缔约国的帮助，通过鼓励利益相关方积极参与申报过程，避免缔约国把时间和精力浪费在不可能成功的申报上。规定世界遗产委员会在适当的时限内，修订定期报告的监测指标（Monitoring Indicators）和分析框架（Analytical Framework），并予以通过。

历年来，《指南》也有少量删减，比如 2015 年根据第 39 COM 11 号决议，明确要求申报文件中必须有管理规划，因而删除了 "115. 在某些情况下，管理计划或其他管理体制在该遗产向世界遗产委员会提出申报时还没有到位。相关缔约国则需要说明管理计划或体制何时能到位、以及如何调动准备和实施新的管理计划或体制的所需资源。缔约国还需要提供其他文件（例如，运作计划），在管理计划确定之前指导遗产的管

concerned should then indicate when such a management plan or system would be put in place, and how it proposes to mobilize the resources required for the preparation and implementation of the new management plan or system. The State Party should also provide other document (s) (e.g. operational plans) which will guide the management of the site until such time when a management plan is finalized." was thus deleted. In 2019, in accordance with Decision 43 COM 11A, the relevant provisions of international assistance were amended, articles "248. All requests for international assistance for cultural heritage are evaluated by ICOMOS and ICCROM, except requests up to and including US$ 5,000. *Decision 13 COM XII.34 and Decision 31 COM 18B, 249.* All requests for international assistance for mixed heritage are evaluated by ICOMOS, ICCROM and IUCN, except requests up to and including US$ 5,000. *Decision 31 COM 18B, and 250.* All requests for international assistance for natural heritage are evaluated by IUCN, except requests up to and including US$ 5,000. *Decision 31 COM 18B*" were deleted thereafter.

Such a simple list is not enough to show the changes and revisions in the Operating Guidelines over the decades, but it still shows that the revisions are mainly detailed in procedures for easy implementation. In brief, after 2005, the Guidelines has been improved in a comprehensive and instructive way, providing a basis for nominations and offering explanations with as few objections as possible. In 2015, the Guidelines began to focus on the common attributes of natural and cultural heritage, focusing on transnational and transboundary heritage nominations. The 2021 Guidelines reviewed its nomination procedures, focusing on guidance and assistance to the nominating State Parties, while taking into account the experience of globalization, encouraging the active participation of countries in Asia, Africa and Latin America. Just as Mr. Jing

理"。又如，2019 年根据第 43 COM 11A 决议，修订了国际援助的相关条款，随后删除了"248. 所有关于文化遗产的国际援助申请，均由国际古迹遗址理事会和国际文物保护与修复研究中心评估，申请金额低于 5000 美元的除外。249. 所有关于混合遗产的国际援助申请均由国际古迹遗址理事会、国际文物保护和修复研究中心和世界自然保护联盟评估，申请金额低于 5000 美元的除外。250. 所有自然遗产国际援助的申请都将由世界自然保护联盟做出评估，申请金额低于 5000 美元的除外"等条款。

这样的简单罗列不足以表现《指南》几十年来的变化和修订，但仍然能表达出，修订主要是对具体程序的细化，更便于使用者执行。简而言之，2005 年的《指南》得到全面性、指导性的完善，为申报提供依据并做出少有异议的说明。2015 年的《指南》开始关注自然与文化遗产的共同属性，关注跨区域、跨国界的申报。2021 年的《指南》检视自身的申报程序，关注对申报国的辅导与帮助，同时结合全球化的经验，鼓励亚非拉国家的积极参与。正如景峰先生所言，"他山之石可以攻玉，世界遗产保护反映了人类对于自身所处的环境和历史、文化的认识，这种认识不仅基于资源角度的可持续保护，也基于文化多样性和哲学的思考。它对于保护对象，特别是文化遗产，无论在类型、保护观念和保护方法上，都在不断的变化和更新"。

Feng said, "The protection of World Heritage reflects humanity's understanding of its environment, history and culture, which is based not only on sustainable conservation from the perspective of resources, but also on cultural diversity and philosophical consideration. The objects of protection, especially cultural heritage, are constantly changing and updating in terms of types, protection concepts and protection methods."

On the celebration of the 50th anniversary of the UNESCO World Heritage Convention, Madam Audrey Azoulay, Director-General of UNESCO, announced a three-pronged action plan to make World Heritage more representative, accessible and sustainable over the coming decade. In fact, these also are challenges to the future of World Heritage. The awareness and participation of local communities and indigenous peoples in the protection of World Heritage sites needs to be increased. As direct stakeholders and direct beneficiaries, they should be fully involved in the heritage nomination process and the ongoing management of heritage sites. The main purpose of the Convention is to ensure that such properties are preserved and transmitted to future generations. However, due to economic and regional differences, many heritage sites are "raised in purdah" which are out of more protection, publicity and inheritance, and can not enjoy the dividends of World Heritage. In order to ensure all sites are truly accessible to everyone, and in particular to the younger, beyond full utilization of traditional methods, the international community will need to employ the new tool of digital technology to share and disseminate World Heritage in the coming years. Faced with multiple human pressures including climate change, urban development, exploitation of resources, pollution, over tourism, as well as the resurgence of conflicts, the sustainable protection and utilization of World Heritage has become a continuous, long-term and

在纪念《世界遗产公约》五十周年大会上，奥黛丽·阿祖莱总干事在致辞中宣布未来几十年世界遗产的三管齐下的发展计划：更具代表性、更具可抵达性、更具可持续性，其实也是世界遗产未来需要应对的挑战。遗产地居民和原住民对世界遗产保护意识和参与度还需要提高，他们作为直接利益相关者和直接受益者，应该全面参与遗产申报过程和遗产地的持续管理。《公约》的主要任务是，确保对全人类具有突出普遍价值遗产，得到保护并传承给后代。因经济和地域差异，很多遗产"养在深闺无人知"，未能得到更多的保护、宣传和传承，无法享受世界遗产的红利，为了确保所有人特别是年轻群体，能够真正接触到这些遗产，在充分利用传统方法同时，国际社会在未来数年需要用好数字技术这一新工具，分享和传播世界遗产。由于气候变化、城市发展、资源开发、环境污染、过度旅游以及冲突重现等诸多原因，使得世界遗产的可持续保护和利用，成为一项延续性的、长期的、艰苦的工作，是全人类的责任和挑战。作为各国申报世界遗产的系统性、指导性文件，《指南》始终重视实操性，不断完善程序和步骤，从细节处入手，力图通过申报世界遗产这项具体工作，从立法、规划、管理、保护和保存、防灾、提升民众的遗产保护意识、国际援助等各个方面，为所有类型的遗产，提供尽可能全面的保护。

hard work, and it is the responsibility and challenge of all humankind. As a systematic and guiding document for State Parties to nominate World Heritage sites, the Operational Guidelines always attach importance to practical operations, and constantly improve procedures and steps starting from the details. Through the specific work of World Heritage nomination, it strives to provide the most comprehensive protection for all types of heritage in the whole society from aspects of legislation, planning, management, protection and preservation, disaster prevention, raising public awareness of heritage protection, international assistance, etc.

ICOMOS International Conservation Center-Xi'an (IICC-X) , serving as the operational center of ICOMOS in the Asia-Pacific region, is committed to suppore international and regional cooperation in the protection of monuments, sites and surrounding environments in the Asia-Pacific region; it is also an international organization dedicated to protection, management and display of cultural heritage, technical personnel exchange and training, as well as research, development and consulting on cultural heritage protection and planning projects. Under the guidance and support of ICOMOS, the State Administration of Cultural Heritage of China, the Shaanxi Provincial Administration of Cultural Heritage and the Xi'an Municipal Administration of Cultural Heritage, after twice compiling the selection of international cultural heritage protection documents in 2007 and 2020, the *Select Edit of "Operational Guidelines for the Implementation of the World Heritage Convention"* is specially compiled. Through the phased inclusion of the revision process of the systematic document the Operational Guidelines, some basic data and materials are provided for the study and research of the development and changes, so that the academic community can fully grasp the dynamics and direction of the development of World Heritage,

国际古迹遗址理事会西安国际保护中心（IICC-X），作为国际古迹遗址理事会（ICOMOS）在亚太地区的业务中心，是致力于支持亚太地区的古迹、遗址及周边环境保护的国际和区域合作；致力于文化遗产保护、管理、展示、相关技术人员交流与培训；致力于文化遗产保护和规划项目的研究与开发；致力于提供文化遗产项目咨询的国际组织。在国际古迹遗址理事会、国家文物局、陕西省文物局、西安市文物局的指导和支持下，继 2007 年、2020 年连续两次编译国际文化遗产保护文件选编后，专题编译国际文化遗产保护文件《〈实施保护世界文化与自然遗产公约操作指南〉选编》。我们对《指南》的修订过程做阶段性收录，是为研究《指南》的发展变化提供一些基础性资料，以便学界更完整的掌握世界遗产发展的动态和方向，展望世界遗产的未来。此次我们依然采用汉英对照的排版方法，以便各位读者回归英文，深入理解，彼此修正，更好地了解世界遗产保护文件的发展变化的脉络。

and look forward to the future of World Heritage. Here, we still use the Chinese-English composition typesetting, so that readers can return to English, have an in-depth understanding, correct each other, and better understand the development and evolution of World Heritage protection documents.

Many thanks to the State Administration of Cultural Heritage for its long-term guidance, the Shaanxi Provincial Administration of Cultural Heritage for its continuous help, the Xi'an Municipal Administration of Cultural Heritage for its continuous support and leadership; thanks to the Xi'an Institute of Cultural Relics Protection and Archaeology for its financial support. Sincere gratitude to the UNESCO World Heritage Center, ICOMOS and ICOMOS China for offering English and Chinese text. Appreciation to Mr. Tong Mingkang, Mr. Shunyuki Kono, Mr. Xu Mingfei, Mr. Zhao Rong, Mr. Zheng Yulin, for their enthusiastic guidance, Special gratitude to Madam Zhou Jianhong and her team from North-west University for their hard work.

Your criticism and feedback are what keep us moving forward!

Feng jian
Depute Director
ICOMOS International Conservation Center - Xi'an
2023.07.03

感谢国家文物局长期的指导，感谢陕西省文物局持续的帮助，感谢西安市文物局一直的支持与领导，感谢联合国教科文组织世界遗产中心、国际古迹遗址理事会、中国古迹遗址保护协会提供中英文本，感谢西安市文物保护考古研究院的财政支持，感谢童明康先生、河野俊行先生、徐明非先生、赵荣先生、郑育林先生的悉心指导，感谢西北大学周剑虹老师及她团队的帮助，使本书得以顺利完稿。

您的指正，是我们继续前行的动力！

冯健
常务副主任
国际古迹遗址理事会西安国际保护中心
2023.07.03